Dedication

To my brothers Richard and Randy, with whom I shared my formative years.

And to the memory of members of my family who were kind to me many times in many different ways: my grandparents, Edna and Max, Jennie and Hy; my Aunt Anne, and my Uncle Eli.

RAB

And to my brother's four offspring

    My niece

        Rebecca Byrne McCurdy—Coarsegold, California

    My nephews

        Phil Byrne—Wareham, Massachusetts

        Deven Byrne—Fresno, California

        Mike Byrne—Cobb, California

DB

Brief Contents

1 The Field of Social Psychology: How We Think about and Interact with Others 2

2 Social Perception: Understanding Others 36

3 Social Cognition: Thinking about the Social World 78

4 Attitudes: Evaluating the Social World 116

5 Aspects of Social Identity: Self and Gender 156

6 Prejudice and Discrimination 208

7 Interpersonal Attraction: Initial Contact, Liking, Becoming Acquainted 252

8 Close Relationships: Family, Friends, Lovers, and Spouses 302

9 Social Influence: Changing Others' Behavior 354

10 Prosocial Behavior: Helping Others 392

11 Aggression: Its Nature, Causes, and Control 438

12 Groups and Individuals: The Consequences of Belonging 478

13 Social Psychology in Action: Legal, Medical, and Organizational Applications 522

Contents

Preface   *xvii*
About the Authors   *xxiii*
Acknowledgments   *xxv*

1 The Field of Social Psychology
How We Think about and Interact with Others   *2*

Social Psychology: A Working Definition   *6*
Social Psychology Is Scientific in Nature   *6*
Social Psychology Focuses on the Behavior of Individuals   *9*
Social Psychology Seeks to Understand the Causes of Social Behavior and
    Thought   *10*
Social Psychology: Summing Up   *13*

Social Psychology: Where It Is Now, and Where It Seems to Be Going   *14*
Influence of a Cognitive Perspective   *14*
Growing Emphasis on Application: Exporting Social Psychology   *15*
Adoption of a Multicultural Perspective: Taking Full Account of Social
    Diversity   *15*
Increasing Attention to the Potential Role of Biological Factors   *17*

**Answering Questions about Social Behavior and Social Thought: Research
    Methods in Social Psychology**   *19*
Systematic Observation: Describing the World around Us   *19*
Correlation: The Search for Relationships   *20*
The Experimental Method: Knowledge through Systematic
    Intervention   *23*
Interpreting Research Results: The Use of Statistics, and Social
    Psychologists as Perennial Skeptics   *27*
The Role of Theory in Social Psychology   *28*

**The Quest for Knowledge and Rights of Individuals: Seeking an Appropriate
    Balance**   *30*

Using This Book: A Road Map for Readers   *32*
IDEAS TO TAKE WITH YOU: Why Correlation Doesn't Equal Causation   *33*

Summary and Review of Key Points   *34*
Key Terms   *35*
For More Information   *35*

2 Social Perception
Understanding Others   *36*

Nonverbal Communication: The Unspoken Language   *39*
Nonverbal Communication: The Basic Channels   *40*
Facial Expressions and Social Thought: Why "Smile When You Say That, Partner" May Not Always Be Good Advice   *45*
BEYOND THE HEADLINES: AS SOCIAL PSYCHOLOGISTS SEE IT: Body Language in the Courtroom   *47*

Attribution: Understanding the Causes of Others' Behavior   *49*
Theories of Attribution: Frameworks for Understanding How We Attempt to Make Sense of the Social World   *50*
Attribution: Some Basic Sources of Error   *57*
SOCIAL DIVERSITY: A CRITICAL ANALYSIS: Cultural Differences in the Self-Serving Bias   *60*
Applications of Attribution Theory: Insights and Interventions   *62*

Impression Formation and Impression Management: How We Combine—and Use—Social Information   *64*
CORNERSTONES OF SOCIAL PSYCHOLOGY: Asch's Research on Central and Peripheral Traits   *65*
Impression Formation: The Modern Cognitive Approach   *66*
Impression Management: The Fine Art of Looking Good   *68*
The Accuracy of Social Perception: Evidence That It's Higher Than You Might Guess   *71*
CONNECTIONS: Integrating Social Psychology   *74*
IDEAS TO TAKE WITH YOU: Minimizing the Impact of Attributional Errors   *75*

Summary and Review of Key Points   *75*
Key Terms   *77*
For More Information   *77*

3 Social Cognition
Thinking about the Social World   *78*

Schemas: Mental Frameworks for Organizing—and Using—Social Information   *81*
Types of Schemas: Persons, Roles, and Events   *82*
The Impact of Schemas on Social Cognition: Attention, Encoding, Retrieval   *83*
CORNERSTONES OF SOCIAL PSYCHOLOGY: Evidence for the Self-Confirming Nature of Schemas: When and Why Beliefs Shape Reality   *84*

Heuristics: Mental Shortcuts in Social Cognition   *86*
Representativeness: Judging by Resemblance   *86*
Availability: "If I Can Think of It, It Must Be Important"   *86*

Potential Sources of Error in Social Cognition: Why Total Rationality Is Scarcer Than You Think   *89*
Rational versus Intuitive Processing: Going with Our Gut-Level Feelings Even When We Know Better   *90*

BEYOND THE HEADLINES: AS SOCIAL PSYCHOLOGISTS SEE IT: Do Safety Devices Save Lives? Don't Bet on It! *91*
  Dealing with Inconsistent Information: Paying Attention to What Doesn't Fit *93*
  The Planning Fallacy: Why We Often Think We Can Do More, Sooner, Than We Really Can *94*
  The Potential Costs of Thinking Too Much: Why, Sometimes, Our Tendency to Do As Little Cognitive Work As Possible May Be Justified *96*
  Counterfactual Thinking: The Effects of Considering "What Might Have Been" *97*
  Magical Thinking: Would You Eat a Chocolate Shaped Like a Spider? *100*
  Thought Suppression: Why Efforts to Avoid Thinking Certain Thoughts Sometimes Backfire *101*
  Social Cognition: A Word of Optimism *104*

Affect and Cognition: How Feelings Shape Thought and Thought Shapes Feelings *104*
  Connections between Affect and Cognition: Some Intriguing Effects *105*
  The Affect Infusion Model: How Affect Influences Cognition *109*
  SOCIAL DIVERSITY: A CRITICAL ANALYSIS: Culture and the Appraisal of Emotions *111*
  CONNECTIONS: Integrating Social Psychology *112*
  IDEAS TO TAKE WITH YOU: Common Errors in Social Cognition *113*

Summary and Review of Key Points *114*
Key Terms *115*
For More Information *115*

4 Attitudes
Evaluating the Social World   *116*

Attitude Formation: How We Come to Hold the Views We Do *120*
  Social Learning: Acquiring Attitudes from Others *120*
  Social Comparison and Attitude Formation *123*
  Genetic Factors: Some Surprising Recent Findings *124*

Do Attitudes Influence Behavior? And If So, *When* and *How*? *125*
  CORNERSTONES OF SOCIAL PSYCHOLOGY: Attitudes versus Actions: When Saying Is Definitely Not Doing *126*
  When Do Attitudes Influence Behavior? Specificity, Strength, Accessibility, and Other Factors *127*
  How Do Attitudes Influence Behavior? Intentions, Willingness, and Action *130*
  BEYOND THE HEADLINES: AS SOCIAL PSYCHOLOGISTS SEE IT: When Personal Health and Looking Sexy Collide, Guess Which Wins? *133*

The Fine Art of Persuasion: Using Messages to Change Attitudes *134*
  Persuasion: The Early Approach *135*
  The Cognitive Approach to Persuasion: Systematic versus Heuristic Processing *136*

Other Factors Affecting Persuasion: Attitude Function and the Role of
Nonverbal Cues   *138*

When Attitude Change Fails: Resistance to Persuasion   *140*
Reactance: Protecting Our Personal Freedom   *140*
Forewarning: Prior Knowledge of Persuasive Intent   *141*
Selective Avoidance   *141*
Biased Assimilation and Attitude Polarization: "If It's Contrary to What I
Believe, Then It Must Be Unreliable—or Worse!"   *141*

**Cognitive Dissonance: Why Our Behavior Can Sometimes Influence
Our Attitudes**   *143*
Cognitive Dissonance: What It Is and Various Ways (Direct and Indirect)
to Reduce It   *144*
Dissonance and Attitude Change: The Effects of Induced
Compliance   *146*
Dissonance As a Tool for Beneficial Changes in Behavior: When
Hypocrisy Can Be a Force for Good   *149*
SOCIAL DIVERSITY: A CRITICAL ANALYSIS: Is Dissonance Culture-Bound?
Evidence from a Cross-National Study   *151*
CONNECTIONS: Integrating Social Psychology   *153*
IDEAS TO TAKE WITH YOU: Resisting Persuasion: Some Useful Steps   *153*

Summary and Review of Key Points   *154*
Key Terms   *155*
For More Information   *155*

5 Aspects of Social Identity
Self and Gender   *156*

The Self: Components of One's Identity   *159*
Self-Concept: The All-Important Schema   *160*
SOCIAL DIVERSITY: A CRITICAL ANALYSIS: Cultural Influences on the Self: The
Effects of Individualism versus Collectivism   *165*
Self-Esteem: Attitudes about Oneself   *169*
CORNERSTONES OF SOCIAL PSYCHOLOGY: Rogers, Self-Theory, Self–Ideal
Discrepancy, and Personality Change   *174*

Other Aspects of Self-Functioning: Focusing, Monitoring, and Efficacy   *176*
Focusing on Oneself versus Focusing on the External World   *176*
Monitoring One's Behavior on the Basis of Internal versus External
Factors   *179*
Self-Efficacy: Having Confidence in Oneself   *182*

Gender: Maleness or Femaleness As a Crucial Aspect of Identity   *185*
Gender Identity and Gender Stereotypes   *186*
Gender-Role Behavior and Reactions to Gender-Role Behavior   *191*
BEYOND THE HEADLINES: AS SOCIAL PSYCHOLOGISTS SEE IT: Does Gender
Discrimination Still Occur in the Workplace?   *193*
When Men and Women Differ: Biology, Gender Roles, or Both?   *197*
CONNECTIONS: Integrating Social Psychology   *203*
IDEAS TO TAKE WITH YOU: Dealing with Negative Self-Perceptions   *204*

Summary and Review of Key Points   *205*
Key Terms   *206*
For More Information   *207*

6   Prejudice and Discrimination   *208*

Prejudice and Discrimination: Their Nature and Effects   *211*
Prejudice: Choosing Whom to Hate   *211*
Prejudice: Why It Persists   *213*
Discrimination: Prejudice in Action   *214*

The Origins of Prejudice: Contrasting Perspectives   *219*
Direct Intergroup Conflict: Competition As a Source of Prejudice   *219*
CORNERSTONES OF SOCIAL PSYCHOLOGY: The Economics of Racial Violence: Do
Bad Times Fan the Flames of Prejudice?   *221*
Early Experience: The Role of Social Learning   *222*
Social Categorization: The Us-versus-Them Effect and the "Ultimate"
Attribution Error   *223*
SOCIAL DIVERSITY: A CRITICAL ANALYSIS: Perceived Similarity to Out-groups:
Russians' Reactions to Ukrainians, Moldavians, and Georgians   *225*
Cognitive Sources of Prejudice: The Role of Stereotypes   *226*
Other Cognitive Mechanisms in Prejudice: Illusory Correlations and Out-
group Homogeneity   *230*

**Why Prejudice Is *Not* Inevitable: Techniques for Countering
Its Effects**   *233*
Breaking the Cycle of Prejudice: On Learning *Not* to Hate   *233*
Direct Intergroup Contact: The Potential Benefits of Acquaintance   *234*
Recategorization: Redrawing the Boundary between "Us" and
"Them"   *237*
Cognitive Interventions: When Stereotypes Shatter—or at Least Become
Less Compelling   *238*

Prejudice Based on Gender: Its Nature and Effects   *239*
Gender Stereotypes: The Cognitive Core of Sexism   *240*
Discrimination against Females: Subtle but Often Deadly   *241*
Sexual Harassment: When Discrimination Hits Rock Bottom   *244*
BEYOND THE HEADLINES: AS SOCIAL PSYCHOLOGISTS SEE IT: Can a Lecture Be
Sexually Harassing?   *247*
CONNECTIONS: Integrating Social Psychology   *248*
IDEAS TO TAKE WITH YOU: Techniques for Reducing Prejudice   *249*

Summary and Review of Key Points   *249*
Key Terms   *250*
For More Information   *251*

7   Interpersonal Attraction
Initial Contact, Liking, Becoming Acquainted   *252*

Recognizing and Evaluating Strangers: Proximity and Emotions   *255*
Attraction: An Overview   *255*
Repeated Unplanned Contacts Lead to Attraction   *257*
BEYOND THE HEADLINES: As Social Psychologists See It: Can Classroom Seating
Assignments Affect One's Life?   *260*
Affective State: Positive versus Negative Emotions As the Basis
for Attraction   *263*

Becoming Acquaintances: The Need to Affiliate and the Effect of Observable Characteristics   *270*

Affiliation Need: Dispositional and Situational Determinants of Interpersonal Associations   *270*

CORNERSTONES OF SOCIAL PSYCHOLOGY: Festinger's Social Comparison Theory   *274*

Responding to Observable Characteristics: Instant Cues to Attraction   *275*

Becoming Close Acquaintances and Moving toward Friendship: Similarity and Reciprocal Positive Evaluations   *288*

Opposites Don't Attract, but Birds of a Feather Really Do Flock Together   *288*

SOCIAL DIVERSITY: A CRITICAL ANALYSIS: Interracial Dating among Asian Americans   *293*

Reciprocal Positive Evaluations: If You Like Me, I Like You   *294*

CONNECTIONS: Integrating Social Psychology   *297*

IDEAS TO TAKE WITH YOU: How to Encourage Others to Like You   *298*

Summary and Review of Key Points   *299*

Key Terms   *300*

For More Information   *300*

8 Close Relationships
Family, Friends, Lovers, and Spouses   *302*

Interdependent Relationships with Family and Friends—or Loneliness   *305*

The First Relationships Are a Family Matter   *305*

SOCIAL DIVERSITY: A CRITICAL ANALYSIS: Felt Obligation toward Parents: Differences within Families and across Cultures   *309*

Relationships beyond the Family: Finding a Close Friend   *312*

Effects of Attachment Style on Adult Relationships   *316*

Loneliness: Failing to Establish Close Relationships   *320*

Romantic Relationships, Love, and Physical Intimacy   *323*

Romantic Relationships   *324*

BEYOND THE HEADLINES: As Social Psychologists See It: Romance in the Workplace   *325*

What Is This Thing Called Love?   *328*

Sexuality in Romantic Relationships   *334*

Marriage: Moving beyond Romance   *339*

Similarity and Marriage   *339*

CORNERSTONES OF SOCIAL PSYCHOLOGY: Terman's Study of Husband–Wife Similarity and Marital Success   *340*

Marital Sex, Love, Parenthood, and Other Influences on General Satisfaction   *340*

Troubled Relationships and the Effects of Marital Failure   *342*

CONNECTIONS: Integrating Social Psychology   *350*

IDEAS TO TAKE WITH YOU: All You Need Is Love?   *351*

Summary and Review of Key Points   *352*

Key Terms   *353*

For More Information   *353*

9 Social Influence
Changing Others' Behavior   *354*

Conformity: Group Influence in Action   *357*
    CORNERSTONES OF SOCIAL PSYCHOLOGY: Asch's Research on Conformity: Social Pressure—the Irresistible Force?   *358*
    Factors Affecting Conformity: Variables That Determine the Extent to Which We "Go Along"   *360*
    SOCIAL DIVERSITY: A CRITICAL ANALYSIS: The Persistence of Social Norms: Some Unsettling Effects of the "Culture of Honor"   *362*
    The Bases of Conformity: Why We Often Choose to "Go Along"   *364*
    The Need for Individuality and the Need for Personal Control: Why, Sometimes, We Choose *Not* to Go Along   *367*
    BEYOND THE HEADLINES: AS SOCIAL PSYCHOLOGISTS SEE IT: Dress Codes versus Personal Freedom: When Norms Collide   *368*
    Minority Influence: Does the Majority Always Rule?   *369*

Compliance: To Ask—Sometimes—Is to Receive   *372*
    Compliance: The Underlying Principles   *372*
    Tactics Based on Friendship or Liking: Ingratiation   *373*
    Tactics Based on Commitment or Consistency: The Foot in the Door and the Lowball   *373*
    Tactics Based on Reciprocity: The Door-in-the-Face and the "That's-Not-All" Approach   *374*
    Tactics Based on Scarcity: Playing Hard to Get and the Fast-Approaching-Deadline Technique   *376*
    Other Tactics for Gaining Compliance: Complaining and Putting Others in a Good Mood   *378*
    Individual Differences in the Use of Social Influence: Do Different Persons Prefer Different Tactics?   *380*

Obedience: Social Influence by Demand   *382*
    Destructive Obedience: Some Basic Findings   *383*
    Destructive Obedience: Its Social Psychological Basis   *385*
    Destructive Obedience: Resisting Its Effects   *386*
    CONNECTIONS: Integrating Social Psychology   *388*
    IDEAS TO TAKE WITH YOU: Tactics for Gaining Compliance   *388*

Summary and Review of Key Points   *389*
Key Terms   *390*
For More Information   *390*

10 Prosocial Behavior
Helping Others   *392*

Responding to an Emergency: Why Are Bystanders Sometimes Helpful, Sometimes Indifferent?   *395*
    CORNERSTONES OF SOCIAL PSYCHOLOGY: Darley and Latané: Why Bystanders Don't Respond   *397*
    Providing Help—Yes or No? Five Essential Steps in the Decision Process   *399*

SOCIAL DIVERSITY: A CRITICAL ANALYSIS: Big Cities versus Small Towns:
Does Prosocial Behavior Depend in Part on Where You Live?   *403*
Situational Factors That Enhance or Inhibit Helping: Attraction,
Attributions, and Prosocial Models   *406*

The Helpers and Those Who Receive Help   *412*
Helping As a Function of the Bystander's Emotional State   *413*
Dispositional Differences in Prosocial Responding   *414*
BEYOND THE HEADLINES: AS SOCIAL PSYCHOLOGISTS SEE IT: Ordinary People
Sometimes Do Extraordinary Things   *420*
Volunteering: Motivations for Long-Term Help   *421*
Who Receives Help, and How Do People React to Being Helped?   *423*

Explaining Prosocial Behavior: Why Do People Help?   *428*
Empathy–Altruism: It Feels Good to Help Those in Need   *430*
Negative-State Relief: It Reduces One's Negative Affect to Relieve a
Stressful Situation   *431*
Empathic Joy: Successful Helping As a Way to Arouse Positive
Affect   *431*
Genetic Determinism: Helping Maximizes the Survival of Genes Like
One's Own   *432*
CONNECTIONS: Integrating Social Psychology   *434*
IDEAS TO TAKE WITH YOU: Being a Responsive Bystander   *435*

Summary and Review of Key Points   *436*
Key Terms   *436*
For More Information   *437*

11 Aggression
Its Nature, Causes, and Control   438

**Theoretical Perspectives on Aggression: In Search of the Roots of
Violence**   *441*
Instinct Theories and the Role of Biological Factors: Are We Programmed
for Violence?   *441*
Drive Theories: The Motive to Harm Others   *443*
Modern Theories of Aggression: Taking Account of Learning, Cognitions,
Mood, and Arousal   *443*

Determinants of Human Aggression: Social, Personal, Situational   *445*
CORNERSTONES OF SOCIAL PSYCHOLOGY: The Buss Technique for Studying
Physical Aggression: "Would You Electrocute a Stranger?" Revisited   *446*
Social Determinants of Aggression: Frustration, Provocation, Media
Violence, and Heightened Arousal   *447*
Personal Causes of Aggression   *454*
BEYOND THE HEADLINES: AS SOCIAL PSYCHOLOGISTS SEE IT: Murder of the
Truly Defenseless: When Mothers Go Berserk   *457*
Situational Determinants of Aggression: The Effects of High Temperatures
and Alcohol Consumption   *458*

**Child Abuse and Workplace Violence: Aggression in Long-Term
Relationships**   *463*
Child Maltreatment: Harming the Innocent   *463*
Workplace Violence: Aggression on the Job   *465*

The Prevention and Control of Aggression: Some Useful Techniques   *468*
Punishment: An Effective Deterrent to Violence?   *468*

Catharsis: Does Getting It out of Your System Really Help?   *470*
Cognitive Interventions: Apologies and Overcoming Cognitive
    Deficits   *470*
Other Techniques for Reducing Aggression: Exposure to Nonaggressive
    Models, Training in Social Skills, and Incompatible Responses   *472*
SOCIAL DIVERSITY: A CRITICAL ANALYSIS: "Would You Murder Someone You
    Truly Hated If You Could Get Away with It?" Cultural and Gender
    Differences in Aggressive Intentions   *473*
CONNECTIONS: Integrating Social Psychology   *474*
IDEAS TO TAKE WITH YOU: Causes of Human Aggression: An Overview   *475*

Summary and Review of Key Points   *475*
Key Terms   *476*
For More Information   *476*

12 Groups and Individuals
The Consequences of Belonging   *478*

Groups: Their Nature and Function   *480*
Group Formation: Why Do People Join Groups?   *482*
How Groups Function: Roles, Status, Norms, and Cohesiveness   *482*

**How Groups Affect Individual Performance: Facilitation or Social
Loafing?**   *484*
Social Facilitation: Performance in the Presence of Others   *485*
CORNERSTONES OF SOCIAL PSYCHOLOGY: Performance in the Presence of
    Others: The Simplest Group Effect?   *486*
Social Loafing: Letting Others Do the Work When Part of a Group   *490*

Coordination in Groups: Cooperation or Conflict?   *494*
Cooperation: Working with Others to Achieve Shared Goals   *495*
Conflict: Its Nature, Causes, and Effects   *499*
BEYOND THE HEADLINES: AS SOCIAL PSYCHOLOGISTS SEE IT: How to Start a
    Conflict When There Is None   *501*
Resolving Conflicts: Some Useful Techniques   *502*
SOCIAL DIVERSITY: A CRITICAL ANALYSIS: Conflict across Ethnic and Cultural
    Boundaries   *506*

Perceived Fairness in Groups: Getting What We Deserve—or Else!   *507*
Judgments of Fairness: Outcomes, Procedures, and Courtesy   *507*
Reactions to Perceived Unfairness: Tactics for Dealing with
    Injustice   *510*

Decision Making by Groups: How It Occurs and the Pitfalls It Faces   *512*
The Decision-Making Process: How Groups Attain Consensus   *512*
The Nature of Group Decisions: Moderation or Polarization?   *514*
Potential Dangers of Group Decision Making: Groupthink and the
    Tendency of Group Members to Tell One Another What They
    Already Know   *516*
CONNECTIONS: Integrating Social Psychology   *518*
IDEAS TO TAKE WITH YOU: Maximizing Your Own Performance and Minimizing
    Social Loafing by Others   *518*

Summary and Review of Key Points   *519*
Key Terms   *520*
For More Information   *520*

13 Social Psychology in Action
Legal, Medical, and Organizational Applications   522

Applying Social Psychology to the Interpersonal Aspects of the Legal System   *525*
Before the Trial Begins: Effects of Police Interrogation and Pretrial Publicity   *526*
The Testimony of Eyewitnesses: Problems and Solutions   *533*
The Effects of Attorneys and Judges on Verdicts   *537*
Additional Influences on Verdicts: Defendant Characteristics and Juror Characteristics   *540*
SOCIAL DIVERSITY: A CRITICAL ANALYSIS: Race As a Crucial Factor in the Courtroom   *540*

Applying Social Psychology to Health-Related Behavior   *544*
Processing Health-Related Information   *544*
BEYOND THE HEADLINES: AS SOCIAL PSYCHOLOGISTS SEE IT: What Are the Effects of Vitamin C?   *546*
The Emotional and Physiological Effects of Stress   *548*
Coping with Stress   *552*

Applying Social Psychology to the World of Work: Job Satisfaction, Helping, and Leadership   *559*
Job Satisfaction: Attitudes about Work   *559*
Organizational Citizenship Behavior: Prosocial Behavior at Work   *563*
Leadership: Patterns of Influence within Groups   *566*
CORNERSTONES OF SOCIAL PSYCHOLOGY: What Style of Leadership Is Best? Some Early Insights   *568*
CONNECTIONS: Integrating Social Psychology   *574*
IDEAS TO TAKE WITH YOU: Don't Rush to Judgment   *575*

Summary and Review of Key Points   *576*
Key Terms   *577*
For More Information   *578*

References   *579*
Glossary   *632*
Name Index   *641*
Subject Index   *659*

Preface
A Note to Our Readers

WHY YOU SHOULD TAKE SOCIAL PSYCHOLOGY WITH YOU WHEN THE COURSE IS OVER

We (Robert Baron and Donn Byrne) grew up in different states, have very different family backgrounds, and took our first courses in social psychology in different decades. Yet we both had the same reaction to this experience: "Wow!" we remember thinking, "This field is not only interesting—it's *useful*—something we can use in the future."

Several decades have passed since we first had those thoughts, but we remain convinced that they are true. We continue to believe, perhaps more strongly than ever, that social psychology is much more than merely a set of interesting findings and ingenious research methods. In addition it also *offers a unique and valuable way of looking at the social world and a set of basic principles that* everyone *can—and probably should—use in their own lives.*

That idea forms a basic theme for this new edition. As in the past, we've tried to describe the findings of social psychology in as accurate and up-to-date a manner as possible. But, we have also tried to accomplish something else—to maximize the chances that you, our readers, will indeed take social psychology with you and use it in the years ahead. How have we tried to accomplish this goal? Primarily by building several new features into the book.

NEW FEATURES RELATING TO THE THEME OF "TAKING SOCIAL PSYCHOLOGY WITH YOU"

Here is a brief overview of the new features we just mentioned:

- *Beyond the Headlines: As Social Psychologists See It.* These special sections, which appear in every chapter, take an actual newspaper headline and examine it from the perspective of social psychology. They illustrate how social psychologists think, and how the principles of our field can be applied to virtually *any* aspect of human social behavior. The topics of these *Beyond the Headlines* sections:

  - Body Language in the Courtroom (Chapter 2)
  - Do Safety Devices Save Lives? Don't Bet on It! (Chapter 3)
  - When Personal Health and Looking Sexy Collide, Guess Which Wins? (Chapter 4)

- Does Gender Discrimination Still Occur in the Workplace? (Chapter 5)
- Can a Lecture Be Sexually Harassing? (Chapter 6)
- Can Classroom Seating Assignments Affect One's Life? (Chapter 7)
- Romance in the Workplace (Chapter 8)
- Dress Codes versus Personal Freedom: When Norms Collide (Chapter 9)
- Ordinary People Sometimes Do Extraordinary Things (Chapter 10)
- Murder of the Truly Defenseless: When Mothers Go Berserk (Chapter 11)
- How To Start a Conflict When There Is None (Chapter 12)
- What Are the Effects of Vitamin C? (Chapter 13)

- *Ideas to Take with You.* One of these special features occurs in each chapter; each is designed to highlight important concepts you should remember—and use—long after this course is over. In our view, you will definitely find these principles helpful in many contexts in the years ahead. They include:
  - Why Correlation Doesn't Equal Causation (Chapter 1)
  - Minimizing the Impact of Attributional Errors (Chapter 2)
  - Common Errors in Social Cognition (Chapter 3)
  - Resisting Persuasion: Some Useful Steps (Chapter 4)
  - Dealing with Negative Self-Perceptions (Chapter 5)
  - Techniques for Reducing Prejudice (Chapter 6)
  - How to Encourage Others to Like You (Chapter 7)
  - All You Need Is Love? (Chapter 8)
  - Tactics for Gaining Compliance (Chapter 9)
  - Being a Responsive Bystander (Chapter 10)
  - Causes of Human Aggression (Chapter 11)
  - Maximizing Your Own Performance and Minimizing Social Loafing by Others (Chapter 12)
  - Don't Rush to Judgment (Chapter 13)

ADDITIONAL SPECIAL FEATURES: REFLECTING RECENT TRENDS

Additional features of this book are designed to reflect important current trends in social psychology:

1. *Growing interest in cultural and ethnic diversity.* This current theme in the field is reflected in special sections titled *Social Diversity: A Critical Analysis.* These sections present information concerning differences between ethnic groups within a given society or differences across various cultures, and are designed to reflect a growing interest in such issues among social psychologists. The topics they cover include:
- Cultural Differences in the Self-Serving Bias (Chapter 2)
- Culture and the Appraisal of Emotions (Chapter 3)
- Is Dissonance Culture-Bound? Evidence from a Cross-National Study (Chapter 4)
- Cultural Influences on the Self: The Effects of Individualism versus Collectivism (Chapter 5)

- Perceived Similarity to Out-groups: Russians' Reactions to Ukrainians, Moldavians, and Georgians (Chapter 6)
- Interracial Dating among Asian Americans (Chapter 7)
- Felt Obligation toward Parents: Differences within Families and across Cultures (Chapter 8)
- The Persistence of Social Norms: Some Unsettling Effects of the "Culture of Honor" (Chapter 9)
- Big Cities versus Small Towns: Does Prosocial Behavior Depend in Part on Where You Live? (Chapter 10)
- "Would You Murder Someone You Truly Hated If You Could Get Away with It?" Cultural and Gender Differences in Aggressive Intentions (Chapter 11)
- Conflict across Ethnic and Cultural Boundaries (Chapter 12)
- Race As a Crucial Factor in the Courtroom (Chapter 13)

In addition, diversity-related discussions throughout the main text are marked by the symbol .

   2. *Growing integration within the field.* Boundaries between various lines of research and topics within our field have blurred in recent years, as growing sophistication has revealed processes that link them together. To help you understand how the various areas of social psychology are related to one another, we've included special *Connections* tables at the end of each chapter. These tables provide a kind of global review, reminding you of related topics discussed elsewhere in the book. In addition, they emphasize the fact that many aspects of social behavior and thought are closely linked: they do not occur in isolation from one another. These tables are followed by special critical thinking questions designed to give you practice in thinking about these connections.

   3. *Growing interest in a biological perspective.* Social psychologists have recently shown increased interest in the potential role of biological or genetic factors in social behavior. We discuss this perspective at numerous points in the text; to help you recognize such discussions, we have marked them with the symbol.

FEATURES DESIGNED TO MAKE THIS BOOK MORE USEFUL

Although it was many years ago, both of us can vividly recall struggling to understand the textbooks we used in our first courses in social psychology. Because we don't want *you* to experience the same difficulties, we have worked hard to make this book as easy to read and understand as possible. Here is an overview of the steps we've taken in this respect.

- Each chapter begins with an outline. Within the text itself, key terms are printed in **dark type** like this and are followed by a definition. These terms are also defined in a running glossary in the margins, as well as in a glossary at the end of the book; and they are listed alphabetically after each chapter-end summary.
- To help you understand and remember what you have read, we have included brief summaries of *Key Points* at regular intervals. All figures and

tables are clear and simple, and figures contain special labels and notes designed to help you understand them (see Figure 1.11 on page 4 for an example).

- Finally, each chapter ends with a *Summary and Review of Key Points*. Reviewing this section can be an important aid to your studying.

KEEPING UP TO DATE: CHANGES IN CONTENT

Social psychology is a rapidly changing field, so we have always felt that is crucial for this book to be very current. To attain this goal, we have reorganized several chapters to take account of recent trends and findings and have thoroughly updated every chapter. The result: *many of the references are from 1997, 1998, and 1999.* We haven't neglected the foundations of our field, however; special *Cornerstones of Social Psychology* sections describe truly classic studies in the field—ones that started major lines of research and thus exerted a lasting impact on social psychology.

Here is an overview of the changes we have made to keep this book truly on the cutting edge.

- *Reorganization of several chapters.* Chapter 12 has been reorganized to include discussion of coordination in groups—important topics such as cooperation, conflict, and conflict resolution. In addition, applied social psychology is now covered in a single chapter (Chapter 13), which focuses on key legal and medical applications of social psychology, and applications to business and work settings. (In the previous edition, these topics were covered in two chapters.)
- *Inclusion of dozens of new topics.* We have included literally dozens of new topics not present in the previous edition. A sample:
  - Cognitive tuning (Chapter 2)
  - Attribution and punishment (Chapter 2)
  - The "slime effect" (Chapter 2)
  - Accuracy of social perception (Chapter 2)
  - Role of amount of information in the availability heuristic (Chapter 3)
  - Role of motivation in the "planning fallacy" (Chapter 3)
  - Thought suppression and its effects (Chapter 3)
  - "Bracing for the Worst" Effect (Chapter 3)
  - Contrasting motives for processing of persuasive messages (Chapter 4)
  - Biased assimilation and attitude polarization in resistance to persuasion (Chapter 4)
  - The self as an adaptive product of evolution (Chapter 5)
  - Children's perceptions of a child whose play is gender appropriate or inappropriate (Chapter 5)
  - Hypermasculinity and hyperfeminity (Chapter 5)
  - Modern racism and its potential effects (Chapter 6)
  - Reverse discrimination in feedback to minorities (Chapter 6)
  - New information on how stereotypes exert their effects (Chapter 6)
  - Gender differences in perceptions of sexual harassment (Chapter 6)
  - Direct and indirect effects of emotional states on attraction (Chapter 7)
  - Cultural differences in the content of attractiveness stereotypes (Chapter 7)
  - Physical attractiveness and health (Chapter 7)
  - Effects of ingratiation on attraction, salary, and promotions (Chapter 7)

- Differences between conversations of male–male friends and female–female friends (Chapter 8)
- Costs and benefits of a romantic relationship (Chapter 8)
- Impact of adult attachment style on marital success, jealousy, and responses to unsatisfactory relationships (Chapter 8)
- Need for individuality and its role in conformity (Chapter 9)
- Role of current moods in compliance (Chapter 9)
- Individual differences in preferences for social influence tactics (Chapter 9)
- The role of "mindlessness" in the that's-not-all technique (Chapter 9)
- Population density and helping behavior (Chapter 10)
- Genetic and experiential components of empathy (Chapter 10)
- Links between generativity and prosocial behavior (Chapter 10)
- The general affective aggression model (Chapter 11)
- Effects of high temperatures and alcohol on aggression (Chapter 11)
- Narcissism, ego-threat, and aggression (Chapter 11)
- Nature and causes of workplace aggression (Chapter 11)
- Coordination in groups, including cooperation and conflict (Chapter 12)
- Interpersonal justice (Chapter 12)
- Why groups fail to share information (Chapter 12)
- Recovered memories of childhood abuse: accurate recollections, or fictions elicited by suggestion? (Chapter 13)
- Pessimistic beliefs and shortened life span (Chapter 13)
- Genetic and personal factors in job satisfaction (Chapter 13)
- Organizational citizenship behavior—helping at work (Chapter 13)

Supplementary Materials

All good texts should be supported by a complete package of supplementary materials, both for the student and for the instructor. This book provides ample aid for both. For the student, we offer a *Study Guide* written by Bem Allen and Gene Smith of Western Illinois University. It provides students with practice in taking many kinds of examination questions—short-answer, definitions, matching, multiple choice, and completion items.

We also invite students using this edition to visit our website at: *www.abacon.com/baronbyrne*. This website provides a wealth of information that we hope will enhance your experience using the text. The site includes: references to other interesting websites, multiple choice questions that allow you to "practice" taking test questions, and information about the fascinating field of social psychology.

For the instructor:

The ninth edition of Baron and Byrne offers more instructional support than ever before. A test bank, written by Tom Jackson of Fort Hayes State University, accompanies the book and is also available from your Allyn and Bacon sales representative in Windows, MacIntosh and DOS formats.

The Instructor's Resource Manual, written by George Schreer of Plymouth State College provides ideas for discussion topics, classroom activity ideas and demonstration handouts, and lists of web resources.

A new set of transparency acetates was designed to accompany this edition. Organized by topic, over 60 full-color acetates are useful for classroom presentation. Also for classroom presentation, a set of PowerPoint slides prepared by George Schreer of Plymouth State College are available for this edition. The PowerPoint slides are available from your Allyn and Bacon sales representative in Windows.

A new video, "The Allyn and Bacon Interactive Video for Social Psychology" accompanies the book. Short video segments from news sources explain and enhance topics related to the field of social psychology. A useful video guide explains the video clips and offers suggestions of how the video might be used in class.

Material for the instructor can also be found at the web site: *www.abacon.com/baronbyrne.*

Some Concluding Comments . . . and a Request for Help

Now, once again, it's time to ask for *your* help. As was true of past editions, we have spared no effort to make this new one the best ever. While human beings can imagine perfection, however, they always fall far short of it. So we realize that there is always room for improvement! In this respect, we sincerely request your comments. If there's something you feel can be improved, please let us know. Write, call, fax, or e-mail us at the addresses below. We'll be genuinely glad to receive your input and—even more important—*we will definitely listen*. Thanks in advance for your help.

Robert A. Baron
Pittsburgh Building
Rensselaer Polytechnic Institute
Troy, NY 12180-3590
Phone: 518/276-2864
Fax: 518/276-8661
E-mail: baronr@rpi.edu

Donn Byrne
Department of Psychology
University at Albany, SUNY
Albany, NY 12222
Phone: 518/442-4857
Fax: 518/442-4867
E-mail: vyaduckdb@aol.com

About the Authors

Robert A. Baron is Professor of Psychology and Professor of Management at Rensselaer Polytechnic Institute. Former Chair of the Department of Psychology, he received his Ph.D. from the University of Iowa in 1968. Professor Baron has held faculty appointments at Purdue University, the University of Minnesota, University of Texas, University of South Carolina, University of Washington, and Princeton University. In 1982 he was a Visiting Fellow at Oxford University. From 1979 to 1981 he served as a Program Director at the National Science Foundation (Washington, D.C.). He has been a Fellow of the American Psychological Association since 1978 and is a Charter Fellow of the American Psychological Society.

Professor Baron has published more than ninety-five articles in professional journals and twenty-six chapters in edited volumes. He is the author or co-author of thirty-eight books, including *Psychology* (4th ed.), *Behavior in Organizations* (7th ed.), *Social Psychology* (9th ed.), *Human Aggression* (2nd ed.), and *Understanding Human Relations* (3rd ed.).

Professor Baron served on the Board of Directors of the Albany Symphony Orchestra (1993–1996) and is President of Innovative Environmental Products, Inc., a company that applies the findings and principles of psychology to the development of new products designed to enhance the quality of everyday life. He holds three U.S. patents, two of which apply to the *P.P.S.*®—a desk-top device

Robert A. Baron (right) and Donn Byrne (left)

(Photograph by Professor Dean Falk)

that reduces distracting noise, increases privacy, and both filters and freshens the air. This device, and the basic psychological research behind it, were featured in the APA *Monitor* (March, 1995).

Professor Baron's hobbies include (1) music (he plays piano and wrote and copyrighted a song that was recorded and released in the 1960s); (2) fine woodworking (he makes everything from small wooden boxes to large pieces of furniture), and (3) coin collecting. Professor Baron has been a runner for more than twenty years, and—perhaps because he never gains weight!—has had a life-long interest in fine food and wine.

Professor Baron's research currently focuses primarily on the following topics: (1) workplace aggression, (2) impact of the physical environment (e.g., lighting, air quality, temperature) on social behavior and task performance, and (3) cognitive and social factors in entrepreneurship.

Donn Byrne (Ph.D., Stanford, 1958) holds the rank of Distinguished Professor of Psychology at the University at Albany, State University of New York. He previously held faculty positions at the California State University–San Francisco, the University of Texas, and Purdue University and the position of visiting professor at the University of Hawaii and Stanford University. At various times he has served as the Chair of Albany's Psychology Department, the Head of the Social-Personality Program at Purdue and at Albany, and a member of Surgeon General C. Everett Koop's Workshop on Pornography and Health. A past president of the Midwestern Psychological Association and of the Society for the Scientific Study of Sexuality, he is a Fellow of the Society for Personality and Social Psychology, and the Society for the Scientific Study of Sexuality. He is also a Charter Fellow of the American Psychological Society.

Professor Byrne has published more than one hundred and forty articles in professional journals and thirty-three chapters in edited volumes. He is the author or co-author of fourteen books including *Psychology: An Introduction to a Behavioral Science* (4th ed.), *Personality Change, An Introduction to Personality* (3rd ed.), *The Attraction Paradigm,* and *Adolescents, Sex, and Contraception.* His current research focuses on such core topics as (1) the effect of adult attachment patterns on interpersonal relationships, (2) dispositional predictors of coercive sexual behavior, and (3) the evolutionary significance of responsiveness to similarity and dissimilarity.

Professor Byrne's non-professional time is spent in being (1) a "professional father" in that his two youngest offspring are busily engaged in, respectively, elementary and high school, (2) a lifelong consumer of literature (primarily novels) that may progress into the authorship of a novel one of these days, and (3) an appreciative fan of theater in all its forms, including stage, screen, and television. The latter interest was fostered in childhood when his stage roles included a pajama-clad boy telling the story of "The Littlest Christmas Tree" and when he became the co-star of a weekly radio program in Austin, Texas—"Nana and Donn." As best he remembers, Nana read fairy tales while a preliterate Donn interrupted to ask stupid questions.

Acknowledgments

SOME WORDS OF THANKS

Each time we write this book, we gain a stronger appreciation of the following fact: We couldn't do it without the help of many talented, dedicated people. While we can't possibly thank all of them here, we do wish to express our appreciation to those whose help has been most valuable.

First, our sincere thanks to the colleagues listed below who read and commented on various portions of the manuscript:

Todd D. Nelson, California State University

Brian Gladue, University of Cincinnati

George Schreer, Plymouth State College

Grace Galliano, Kennesaw State University

Ann Weber, University of North Carolina, Asheville

Randy Fisher, University of Central Florida

David Bush, Utah State University

David A. Houston, University of Memphis

A. Sandra Willis, Stanford University

Stuart Oskamp, Claremont College

Second, we also wish to thank the colleagues who responded to the Baron/Byrne, 8th edition Survey:

Charles A. Alexander, Rock Valley College

Linda J. Allred, East Carolina University

Gordon Bear, Ramapo College

Lisa M. Bohon, California State University, Sacramento

Robert F. Bornstein, Gettysburg College

Nyla Branscombe, University of Kansas

David Bush, Utah State University

John Childers, East Carolina University

Winona Cochran, Bloomsburg University

Diana Cordova, Yale University

Lori Dawson, Worcester State College

William Delahoyde, Marist College

John F. Dovido, Colgate University

Karen Duffy, SUNY—Geneseo

Phil Finney, Southeast Missouri State University

Robin Franck, Southwestern College

Grace Galliano, Kennesaw State University

David A. Gershaw, Arizona Western College

Brian Gladue, University of Cincinnati

Drusilla Glascoe, Salt Lake
  Community College
Karen Harris, Western Illinois
  University
John Harvey, University of Iowa
Matthew Hogben, Centers for
  Disease Control and Prevention,
  Atlanta
Tony Johnson, Lagrange College
Jeffery Scott Mio, California State
  Polytechnic University—Pomona
Mitchell S. Nesler, Regents College
Robert Pellegrini, San Jose State
  University

Jackie Pope, Western Kentucky
  University
Jack Powell, University of Hartford
Brad Redburn, Johnson County
  Community College
Jay G. Riggs, Eastern Kentucky
  University
Delia S. Saenz, Arizona State
  University
Tom Smith, Iona College
Michael Strube, Washington
  University
Donna Webster, Winthrop
  University

Third, we wish to thank colleagues who kindly read and commented on draft chapters when it was in the proof stage; their comments were indeed invaluable to use in polishing the final product:

Paul Kwon, Washington State
  University
David F. Lopez, Bard College
Charles Martin-Stanley, Central
  State University

Betsy Morgan, University of
  Wisconsin—La Crosse
David Simpson, Carroll College
Charles Stangor, University of
  Maryland—College Park

Fourth, we also wish to offer our personal thanks to Carolyn Merrill and Sean Wakely, our two editors at Allyn and Bacon. Carolyn worked closely with us from the very start and helped to shape both the form and content of the book. And just as the first draft of the manuscript was completed, Carolyn paused to give birth to Caitlin O'Sullivan Merrill—certainly a very auspicious sign for the project! Sean, who joined the project later, provided invaluable support and guidance through key stages of the production process. Together, they have been immensely helpful. We view them not simply as editors but as good friends.

Fifth, our sincere thanks to our project manager, Mary Beth Finch. She oversaw many key aspects of production, and we were indeed fortunate to have her as part of the team.

Sixth, our thanks to Jay Howland for very careful and constructive copyediting. Her comments were insightful and thought-provoking and certainly helped to improve the writing measurably.

Seventh, our thanks to all of those others who contributed to various aspects of the production process: to Helane Manditch-Prottas for photo research, to Glenna Collett for design work, and to Linda Knowles for the cover design.

We also wish to offer our thanks to the many colleagues who provided reprints and preprints of their work. These individuals are too numerous to list here, but their help is gratefully acknowledged.

Finally, our sincere thanks to George Schreer for outstanding work on the Instructor's Resource Manual; to Tom Jackson for his work on the test bank; and to Bem Allen and Gene Smith for their help in preparing the Study Guide. To all these truly outstanding people, and to many others, too, our warmest personal regards and thanks.

Social Psychology

1

The Field of Social Psychology: How We Think about and Interact with Others

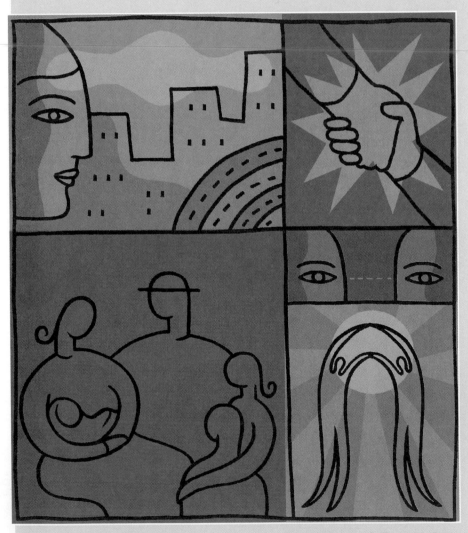

Chapter Outline

Social Psychology: A Working Definition
    Social Psychology Is Scientific in Nature
    Social Psychology Focuses on the Behavior of Individuals
    Social Psychology Seeks to Understand the Causes of Social Behavior
        and Thought
    Social Psychology: Summing Up

Social Psychology: Where It Is Now, and Where It Seems to Be Going
    Influence of a Cognitive Perspective
    Growing Emphasis on Application: Exporting Social Psychology
    Adoption of a Multicultural Perspective: Taking Full Account of
        Social Diversity
    Increasing Attention to the Potential Role of Biological Factors

**Answering Questions about Social Behavior and Social Thought:
Research Methods in Social Psychology**
    Systematic Observation: Describing the World around Us
    Correlation: The Search for Relationships
    The Experimental Method: Knowledge through
        Systematic Intervention
    Interpreting Research Results: The Use of Statistics, and Social
        Psychologists as Perennial Skeptics
    The Role of Theory in Social Psychology

**The Quest for Knowledge and Rights of Individuals: Seeking an
Appropriate Balance**

Using this Book: A Road Map for Readers
    IDEAS TO TAKE WITH YOU: Why Correlation Doesn't Equal Causation

Summary and Review of Key Points
Key Terms
For More Information

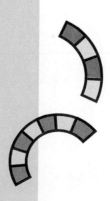

- *How can you tell when another person is lying?*
- *Do magazine ads or TV commercials really influence people's behavior—for instance, get them to start smoking if they don't already smoke?*
- *Why do people fall in—and out of—love?*
- *What makes people lose their tempers? And why do they sometimes attack others whom they love—spouses or even their own children?*
- *Do physically attractive people have an "edge" at work or on the job? And just what is beauty anyway?*
- *What makes some leaders charismatic—able to exert truly amazing control over their followers?*

If you've ever wondered about questions like these, welcome: you've come to the right place. These questions, and hundreds like them form the core of *social psychology*—the field you are about to study. Social psychology is a branch of psychology; and as its name suggests, it is concerned with the social side of life—how people interact with and think about others. This means that every form of social behavior or social thought you can imagine is included within its scope (see Figure 1.1). Because other people and our relations with them are such an important part of our lives, we believe that social psychology, too, is important. After all, isn't a field that investigates everything from love, cooperation, and helping on the one hand, through prejudice, conflict, and violence on the other, intrinsically valuable? We believe that it is, and also feel that once you have examined the range of topics currently being studied by social psychologists (see Table 1.1), you will agree with us.

At this point we'd very much like to plunge right in and describe the fascinating findings uncovered by social psychologists in their research. But before

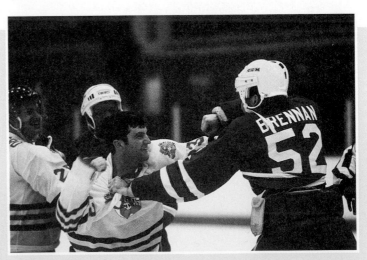

Figure 1.1
The Broad Scope of Social Psychology. All forms of social behavior and social thought are included within the scope of modern social psychology.

Table 1.1

Questions Currently Being Investigated by Social Psychologists. As shown here, social psychologists ask—and attempt to answer—many intriguing questions about the social side of life.

Question	Chapter in Which It Is Covered
How can we make favorable first impressions on other people?	Chapter 2
What happens when we imagine "what might have been" in various situations?	Chapter 3
Can our attitudes be changed by information we don't even notice?	Chapter 4
If we are confident that we can perform a task successfully, does this increase the chances that we really can?	Chapter 5
Do women and men really differ in their behavior? And if so, why?	Chapter 5
How can prejudice be reduced?	Chapter 6
Can we separate our liking or disliking for another person from our judgments about him or her?	Chapter 7
What is jealousy? What are its major causes?	Chapter 8
Does "playing hard to get" really work?	Chapter 9
Is there such a thing as "pure altruism"—helping others without expecting *anything* in return?	Chapter 10
Does alcohol really increase aggression?	Chapter 11
Do people accomplish more when working together with others or when working alone?	Chapter 12
Are jurors influenced by the appearance of defendants?	Chapter 13

we do so, it's important to provide you with some background information about the scope, nature, and methods of social psychology. Why is such information useful? Because research findings in psychology indicate that people have a much better chance of understanding, remembering, and using new information if they are first provided with a framework for organizing it. That's what this introductory chapter is all about: providing you with a framework for interpreting and understanding social psychology. Specifically, we'll use the remainder of this chapter for the following tasks.

First, we'll present a more formal *definition* of social psychology. Every field has basic assumptions, and it is important to recognize these at the start. Becoming familiar with them will help you understand why social psychologists have chosen certain topics for detailed study and why they have approached these topics in specific ways. Second, we'll take a look at some of the major characteristics of social psychology as it exists right now: where it is and where it seems to be going as a new millennium approaches. Third, we'll examine some of the methods used by social psychologists to answer questions about the social side of life. Knowledge of these *research methods* will help you understand later discussions of specific research projects, and it will also help you understand how the knowledge and conclusions presented throughout this text were actually obtained.

SOCIAL PSYCHOLOGY: A WORKING DEFINITION

Providing a formal definition of almost any field is a complex task. In the case of social psychology, this difficulty is increased by two factors: the field's broad scope and its rapid rate of change. As suggested by Table 1.1, social psychologists have a very wide range of interests. Yet despite this fact, most social psychologists focus mainly on the following task: understanding how and why individuals behave, think, and feel as they do in social situations—ones involving the actual or imagined presence of other persons. Reflecting this fact, we will define **social psychology** as *the scientific field that seeks to understand the nature and causes of individual behavior and thought in social situations.* In other words, social psychologists seek to understand how we think about and interact with others. We will now clarify several key aspects of this definition.

Social Psychology Is Scientific in Nature

What is *science?* Many people seem to believe that this term refers only to fields such as chemistry, physics, and biology—ones that use the kind of equipment shown in Figure 1.2. If you share that view, you may find our suggestion that

social psychology • The scientific field that seeks to understand the nature and causes of individual behavior and thought in social situations.

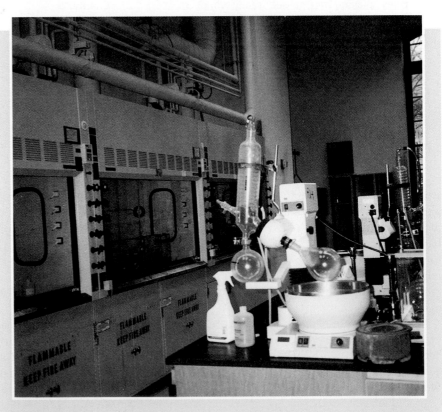

Figure 1.2
Does Fancy Equipment Equal Science? Many people seem to believe that only fields that use equipment like this can be described as "scientific." In fact, however, this is not really so.

social psychology is a scientific discipline somewhat puzzling. How can a field that seeks to study the nature of love, the causes of aggression, and everything in between be scientific in the same sense as astronomy, biochemistry, and computer science? The answer is surprisingly simple.

In reality, the term *science* does not refer to a special group of highly advanced fields. Rather, it refers to two things: (1) a set of values, and (2) several methods that can be used to study a wide range of topics. In deciding whether a given field is or is not scientific, therefore, the critical question is: *Does it adopt these values and methods?* To the extent that it does, it is scientific in nature. To the extent that it does not, it falls outside the realm of science. We'll examine the procedures used by social psychologists in their research in detail in a later section; here, we'll focus on the core values that all fields must adopt to be considered scientific in nature. Four of these are most important:

Accuracy: A commitment to gathering and evaluating information about the world (including social behavior and thought) in as careful, precise, and error-free a manner as possible.

Objectivity: A commitment to obtaining and evaluating such information in a manner that is as free from bias as humanly possible.

Skepticism: A commitment to accepting findings as accurate only to the extent that they have been verified over and over again.

Open-Mindedness: A commitment to changing one's views—even views that are strongly held—if existing evidence suggests that these views are inaccurate.

Social psychology, as a field, is deeply committed to these values and applies them in its efforts to understand the nature of social behavior and social thought. For this reason, it makes sense to describe our field as scientific in orientation. In contrast, fields that are *not* scientific make assertions about the world, and about people, that are not subjected to the careful testing and analysis required by the values listed above. In such fields—ones like astrology and aromatherapy—intuition, faith, and unobservable forces are considered to be sufficient (see Figure 1.3).

"But why adopt the scientific approach? Isn't social psychology just common sense?" Having taught for many years (more than seventy between us!), we can almost hear you asking this question. And we understand why you might feel this way; after all, each of us has spent our entire life interacting with other

Figure 1.3

Science versus Nonscience: Different Values, Different Methods. Fields such as aromatherapy are definitely *not* scientific, because they do not accept the core values of science (accuracy, objectivity, skepticism, open-mindedness) and do not use scientific methods to test specific hypotheses.

persons. As a result of such experience, we are all amateur social psychologists. So why not rely on our own experience—or even on folklore and "the wisdom of the ages"—in order to understand the social side of life? Our answer is straightforward: Because such sources provide inconsistent and unreliable guides to social behavior.

For instance, consider the following statement, suggested by common sense: "Absence makes the heart grow fonder." Do you agree? Is it true that when people are separated from those they love, they miss them and so experience increased longing for them? Many people would agree. They would answer "Yes, that's right. Let me tell you about the time I was separated from. . . ." But now consider the following statement: "Out of sight, out of mind." (Variation: "When I'm not near the girl/boy I love, I love the girl/boy I'm near.") How about this statement? Is it true? When people are separated from those they love, do they quickly find someone else on whom to focus their affections? As you can see, these two views—both suggested by common sense—are contradictory. The same is true for many other informal observations about human behavior (e.g., "Birds of a feather flock together"—similarity leads to attraction; "Opposites attract"—*dis*similarity attracts). We could go on to list others, but by now the main point is clear: Common sense often suggests a confusing and inconsistent picture of human behavior. This is one important reason why social psychologists put their faith in the scientific method: it yields much more conclusive evidence.

But this is not the only reason why we must be wary of common sense. Another one relates to the fact that unlike Mr. Spock of *Star Trek* fame, we are *not* perfect information-processing machines. On the contrary, as we'll note over and over again (e.g., in Chapters 2, 3, and 4), our thinking is subject to several forms of error that can lead us badly astray. Because of these errors in thinking, we cannot rely on informal observation, common sense, or intuition to provide us with accurate information about social behavior. Many such errors exist; here, let's take a brief look at three important ones. Others will be examined in Chapters 2 and 3.

The Confirmation Bias: The Temptation to Verify Our Own Views. Quick: Do you like it better when views you hold are confirmed or when they are refuted? The answer is obvious: We strongly prefer to have our views confirmed. Consider what this means when we attempt to use informal observation as a source of knowledge about social behavior. Because we prefer to have our views confirmed, we tend to notice and remember mainly information that lends support to these views—information that confirms what we already believe. This tendency is known as the **confirmation bias.** When it operates, it places us in a kind of closed cognitive system in which only evidence that confirms our existing views and beliefs gets inside; other information is sometimes noticed but is quickly rejected as false (e.g., Bardach & Park, 1996). Clearly, then, the confirmation bias can lead us into errors in our efforts to understand the social world.

The Availability Heuristic: Emphasizing What Comes to Mind First. Now answer this question: Are more people in the United States killed by fires or by drowning? Most people reply "fires," but in fact the opposite is true. What's responsible for this type of error? A mental shortcut known as the **availability heuristic.** This shortcut, which helps save us mental effort, suggests that the easier it is to bring something to mind, the more frequent or important it is. Fires are dramatic events, so they get more coverage in newspapers and on television. The result: We tend to overestimate the frequency of their occurrence. In general, the availability heuristic, like other mental shortcuts, makes sense; events or objects that are common *are* usually easier to think of than ones that are less common. But relying on this shortcut in making judgments can also lead to se-

confirmation bias • The tendency to notice and remember mainly information that lends support to our views.

availability heuristic • A mental shortcut that suggests that the easier it is to bring something to mind, the more frequent or important it is.

rious errors, as we just illustrated (e.g., Schwarz et al., 1991). That it can distort our social thought and judgments is also clear. For instance, suppose that in the future you hold a job in which you are in charge of several other people. You are asked to evaluate one of them for a promotion. When you think back over this person's performance, what events are likely to come to mind? The ones that are most unusual or dramatic. Because these come to mind readily, they may bias your judgment: you may give them too much weight in deciding whether this person should be promoted. We'll examine other examples of the availability heuristic in operation in Chapter 2.

Mood Effects: How We Feel Often Influences the Way We Think. One day, you wake up feeling absolutely great. Another day, you wake up feeling miserable. Will these contrasting *moods*—your current feelings—influence the way you think? Research on this topic leaves little room for doubt: Absolutely! When you are in a good mood, you will tend to think happy thoughts, remember happy events, and view everything around you in a positive light. In contrast, when you are in a bad mood, the opposite will be true: you will think unhappy thoughts, remember sad events, and see everything around you negatively (e.g., Forgas, 1995a). Can these *mood effects* influence your social thought and social behavior? Definitely. For instance, imagine that you meet someone for the first time while in a good mood; will you be more likely to form a favorable impression of that person than if you meet her while in a bad mood? Research findings suggest that you would (see Chapter 7). Similarly, if someone asks you for a favor, are you more likely to view it as a reasonable request and to agree when you are in a good mood or a bad one? Again, the findings of many studies indicate that your mood will indeed play a role (e.g. Cialdini et al., 1997).

We could continue, but by now the main point should be clear: Many potential sources of bias can influence our thinking about the social world and so lead us to false conclusions about it. This is one important reason why social psychologists, in their efforts to understand the social side of life, prefer to rely on the findings of carefully conducted research carried out in accordance with the methods of science rather than on common sense. And that approach, of course, is the one we'll adopt throughout this text.

Social Psychology Focuses on the Behavior of Individuals

Societies differ greatly in terms of their views concerning courtship and marriage; yet it is still individuals who fall in love. Similarly, societies vary greatly in terms of their overall levels of violence; yet it is still individuals who perform aggressive actions or refrain from doing so. The same argument applies to virtually all other aspects of social behavior, from prejudice to helping: the actions are performed by, and thoughts occur in the minds of, individuals. Because of this basic fact, the focus, in social psychology, is squarely on individuals. Social psychologists realize, of course, that individuals do not exist in isolation from social and cultural influences—far from it. But the field's major interest lies in understanding the factors that shape the actions and thoughts of individual humans in social settings. This contrasts sharply with the field of *sociology*, which you may have studied in other courses. Sociology studies some of the same topics as social psychology, but it is concerned not with the behavior and thoughts of individuals but with large groups of persons or with society as a whole. For instance, both social psychology and sociology study the topic of violent crime. While social psychologists focus on the factors that cause specific persons to engage in such behavior, however, sociologists are interested in comparing rates of violent crime in different segments of the society (e.g., high- and low-income groups), or in examining trends in the rate of violent crime over time.

Social Psychology Seeks to Understand the Causes of Social Behavior and Thought

In a key sense, the heading of this section states the most central aspect of our definition. What it means is that social psychologists are primarily interested in understanding the wide range of conditions that shape the social behavior and thought of individuals—their actions, feelings, beliefs, memories, and inferences—concerning other persons. Obviously, a huge number of factors play a role in this regard. It is also clear, though, that most of these factors fall into the five major categories described below.

The Actions and Characteristics of Other Persons.   Imagine the following events:

> *You are standing on line outside a movie theater; suddenly, another person walks up and cuts in line in front of you.*
>
> *The person you've been dating exclusively for six months suddenly says: "I think we should date other people."*
>
> *You are playing a computer game when two attractive strangers walk up and begin to watch your performance with great interest.*

Will these actions by other persons have any effect on your behavior and thoughts? Absolutely. So it's clear that often, we are strongly affected by the actions of other persons (see Figure 1.4).

Now be honest: Have you ever felt uneasy in the presence of a person with a physical disability? Do you ever behave differently toward highly attractive persons than toward less attractive ones? Toward elderly persons than toward young ones? Toward persons belonging to racial and ethnic groups different from your own? Your answer to some of these questions is probably *yes*, for we are often strongly influenced by the visible characteristics and appearance of others too. Such effects are dramatically illustrated by a recent study in which college students were told to imagine that they worked in a restaurant or bar and were then shown a photo of either an unattractive stranger or a very attractive stranger (McCall, 1997). After seeing the photo, they were asked how likely they would be to "card" this person (require proof of age before serving the person alcohol). Results were clear: Participants in the study were far less likely to card the attractive stranger than the unattractive one. So their behavior toward the person was strongly influenced by his or her appearance—a finding

Figure 1.4
Others' Behavior: An Important Factor in Our Social Behavior and Thought. As shown here, we are often strongly affected by the actions of other persons.

(*Source: The New Yorker*, 1996.)

"They're from David. He's been so much more considerate since I shot him."

that has been confirmed in literally hundreds of other studies. Indeed, even others' names can have strong effects on our reactions to them, and on their perceptions of themselves (e.g., Twenge & Manis, 1998).

Cognitive Processes. Suppose that you have arranged to meet a friend, and this person is late. In fact, after thirty minutes you begin to suspect that your friend will never arrive. Finally, the person does appear and says, "Sorry . . . I forgot all about meeting you until a few minutes ago." How will you react? Probably with considerable annoyance. Now imagine that instead, your friend says, "I'm so sorry to be late. . . . There was a big accident, and the traffic was tied up for miles." Now how will you react? Probably with less annoyance—but not necessarily. If your friend is often late and has used this excuse before, you may be suspicious about whether this explanation is true. In contrast, if this is the first time your friend has been late, or if your friend has never used such an excuse in the past, you may accept it as true. In other words, your reactions in this situation will depend strongly upon your *memories* of your friend's past behavior and your *inferences* about whether her or his explanation is really true. Situations like this one call attention to the fact that *cognitive processes* play a crucial role in social behavior and social thought. Social psychologists are well aware of the importance of such processes and realize that in order to understand people's behavior in social situations, we must understand their thinking about such situations—*construals,* as they are often termed (e.g., Killeya & Johnson, 1998; Swann & Gill, 1997).

Environmental Variables: Impact of the Physical World. Are people more prone to wild impulsive behavior during the full moon than at other times (Rotton & Kelley, 1985)? Do we become more irritable and aggressive when the weather is hot and steamy than when it is cool and comfortable (Anderson, Bushman, & Groom, 1997; Cohn & Rotton, 1997)? Does exposure to a pleasant smell in the air make people more helpful to others (Baron, 1997)? Research findings indicate that the physical environment does indeed influence our feelings, thoughts, and behavior; so ecological variables certainly fall within the realm of modern social psychology.

Cultural Context. Every year, as the holiday season approaches, I (Robert Baron) find small gifts from students in my mailbox. This was never true at other universities where I worked, so at first it puzzled me: was I really improving so much that students in my classes felt the urge to reward me with gifts? Actually, the explanation was much simpler than this; many of the students at the university where I teach are from Asian countries, and in these societies it is considered appropriate to give small gifts to professors at the end of the semester. This illustrates yet another important point about social behavior: it does not occur in a cultural vacuum. On the contrary, it is often strongly affected by cultural norms (social rules concerning how people should behave in specific situations; see Chapter 9), membership in various groups, and changing societal values. Whom should people marry? Is obesity attractive or unattractive (e.g., Hebl & Heatherton, 1998)? How many children should couples have? Should people keep their emotional reactions to themselves or demonstrate them openly? How close should people stand to others when talking to them? Is it appropriate to give gifts to professors or government officials? To business associates? These are only a small sampling of the aspects of social behavior that can be—and are—influenced by cultural factors. By *culture* we simply mean the organized system of shared meanings, perceptions, and beliefs held by persons belonging to any group (Smith & Bond, 1993).

As we'll note below, attention to the effects of cultural factors is an increasingly important trend in social psychology as our field attempts to take account of the growing cultural diversity in many different countries.

Biological Factors. Is social behavior influenced by biological processes and genetic factors? As recently as the mid-1980s, most social psychologists would have answered *no,* at least to the genetic part of this question. Now, however, many have come to believe that our preferences, behaviors, emotional reactions, and even attitudes are affected to some extent by our biological inheritance (Buss, 1999; Nisbett, 1990).

The view that genetic factors play an important role in social behavior is represented in social psychology by the **evolutionary** perspective (e.g., Buss, 1995; Buss & Shackelford, 1997a). This perspective suggests that natural selection can play a role in shaping various aspects of social behavior and social thought as well as physical characteristics. *Natural selection* is the process whereby biological features or patterns of behavior that help organisms reproduce—get their genes into the next generation—tend to spread throughout a species over time. In essence, if some characteristic that is genetically determined increases the chances that organisms will reproduce, it becomes increasingly common in succeeding generations.

Social psychologists who adopt the evolutionary perspective suggest that this process applies to at least some aspects of social behavior. For instance, consider the question of mate preference. Why, for instance, do we find people such as those in Figure 1.5 attractive? According to the evolutionary perspective, it is because the characteristics they show—symmetrical facial features, shapely and well-toned bodies (e.g., a relatively small waist-to-hip ratio in females; Tesser & Martin, 1996), clear skin, lustrous hair—are associated with youth and health, and thus with reproductive capacity. Therefore, a preference for these charac-

Figure 1.5

Mate Preference: Do Genetic Factors Play a Role? According to the evolutionary perspective, our preference for people with certain characteristics—symmetrical faces, clear skin, shiny hair—may be, in part, genetically determined. Because these characteristics are associated with reproductive capacity, a preference for them helped our ancestors get their genes into the next generation. As a result, we may be biologically "programmed" to find these characteristics attractive. (Recent findings, however, call this reasoning into question.)

evolutionary social psychology • An area of research that seeks to investigate the potential role of genetic factors in various aspects of social behavior.

teristics in mates among our ancestors increased the chances that they would reproduce successfully; this, in turn, contributed to our preference for these aspects of appearance. (Interestingly, reasonable as these suggestions seem to be, they have not been uniformly confirmed in recent research; e.g., Tassinary & Hansen, 1998.)

The evolutionary perspective has been applied to many aspects of social behavior. For instance, consider sexual jealousy. Which of the following would cause you to become more upset and experience stronger feelings of jealousy: (1) sexual infidelity (intimate sexual contact with another person) on the part of your spouse or lover, or (2) emotional infidelity (signs of falling in love with someone else) on the part of this person? The evolutionary perspective predicts that males and females may differ in their reactions. Because they can never know for sure that they are the father of a woman's children, men should be more upset by sexual infidelity. In contrast, because in the past (although less so today) females depended on males to help them support their children, females should be more upset by signs of emotional infidelity—indications that their mates are about to transfer their affections and support to another female and *her* children. The results of many studies agree with these predictions (e.g., Paul, Foss, & Galloway, 1993; Shackelford & Buss, 1997).

Because the evolutionary perspective makes many intriguing predictions about social behavior and thought, it has gained increasing recognition in social psychology. Thus, we'll have reason to refer to it at several points in this book.

Social Psychology: Summing Up

In sum, social psychology focuses mainly on understanding the causes of social behavior and social thought—on identifying factors that shape our feelings, behavior, and thought in social situations. It seeks to accomplish this goal through the use of scientific methods, and it takes careful note of the fact that social behavior and thought are influenced by a wide range of social, cognitive, environmental, cultural, and biological factors.

The remainder of this text is devoted to describing some of the key findings of social psychology. This information is truly fascinating, so we're certain that you will find it of interest. We're equally sure, however, that you will also find some of this information surprising, and that it will challenge many of your ideas about people and social relations. So please get ready for some new insights. We predict that after reading this book, you'll never think about social behavior in quite the same way as before.

Key Points

- *Social Psychology* is the scientific field that seeks to understand the nature and causes of individual behavior and thought in social situations.
- It is scientific in nature because it adopts the values and methods used in other fields of science.
- Social psychologists adopt the scientific method because "common sense" provides an unreliable guide to social behavior, and because our thought is influenced by many potential sources of bias.
- Social psychology focuses on the behavior of individuals and seeks to understand the causes of social behavior and thought.
- Important causes of social behavior and thought include the behavior and characteristics of other persons, cognitive processes, aspects of the physical environment, culture, and biological factors.

SOCIAL PSYCHOLOGY: WHERE IT IS NOW, AND WHERE IT SEEMS TO BE GOING

Earlier, we noted that the major purpose of this chapter is providing you with a framework for understanding the big picture—what social psychology is all about and how it "does its thing." Continuing with this theme, we'll now comment briefly on several major aspects of modern social psychology. These aspects play an important role in shaping the questions and topics social psychologists study and the methods they choose for their research. Thus, they have guided the work we'll describe in the rest of this book. Three issues seem especially worthy of our attention.

Influence of a Cognitive Perspective

Recall that we have defined social psychology as the field that studies both social behavior and social thought. This definition reflects the fact social psychologists have always been interested in how individuals think about other persons and about social situations. In recent decades, however, research on the cognitive side of social psychology has grown dramatically in scope and importance. At the present time, most social psychologists believe that how people act in various social situations is strongly determined by their thoughts about these situations. Thus, understanding social thought is, in a very real sense, a powerful key for unraveling the complex patterns of our social relations with other persons.

The cognitive perspective in social psychology is reflected in social psychological research in many ways, but two of these are perhaps most important. First, social psychologists have attempted to apply basic knowledge about *memory, reasoning,* and *decision making* to various aspects of social thought and behavior. For instance, within this context, researchers have recently sought to determine whether prejudice stems, at least in part, from our tendency to remember only information consistent with stereotypes of various groups, or from our tendency to process information about our own social group differently from information about other social groups (e.g., Forgas & Fiedler, 1996). Recent findings, for example, suggest that individuals tend to perceive people belonging to their own group much more favorably than persons belonging to other groups; indeed, the results of one study (Klar & Giladi, 1997) indicate that people tend to perceive everyone belonging to their own group as better than average!

Second, there has been growing interest in the question of how we process social information—in a quick-and-dirty manner designed to reduce effort (*heuristically*), or in a more careful, effortful manner (*systematically*; e.g., Eagly & Chaiken, 1998; Killeya & Johnson, 1998). As we'll see in several later chapters (Chapters 2, 3, 6, and 12), these differences in style of processing can strongly influence our inferences, conclusions, decisions, and judgments about others; so they are a key aspect of social cognition.

Third, social psychologists have sought to understand the role of *construals*—individuals' understanding and interpretation of social situations and events—as determinants of behavior in these situations. Results of such work suggest that our thoughts about other persons and social situations play a key role in virtually *all* forms of social behavior—from love and sexual attraction on the one hand through conflict and violence on the other. For instance, consider workplace violence, a topic that has been much in the news in recent years. Why do some individuals suddenly explode, launching deadly attacks against

Figure 1.6
Cognitive Factors: A Key Determinant of Social Behavior. Why do individuals sometimes suddenly explode and attack people with whom they have worked for years? One important cause of such behavior is such persons' belief that they have been treated unfairly. Thus, cognitive factors play a key role in workplace violence, just as they do in virtually all forms of social behavior.

coworkers or bosses (see Figure 1.6)? A growing body of evidence suggests that an important part of the answer involves beliefs on the part of these persons that they have been treated *unfairly:* they haven't received the rewards they deserve, and—more important—they have not been treated with respect and courtesy (e.g., Folger & Baron, 1996; Greenberg & Alge, 1997). In short, individuals' interpretations of past events and situations are powerful determinants of their behavior.

In sum, insights provided by a cognitive approach have added greatly to our understanding of many aspects of social behavior, and this approach is definitely a major theme of social psychology as we move toward the year 2000.

Growing Emphasis on Application: Exporting Social Psychology

A second major theme in social psychology today is growing concern with the *application* of social knowledge. An increasing number of social psychologists have turned their attention to questions concerning *personal health, the legal process, social behavior in work settings, environmental issues,* and a host of other topics. In other words, there has been growing interesting in attempting to apply the findings and principles of social psychology to the solution of practical problems. This theme is certainly not new in the field: Kurt Lewin, one of the founders of social psychology, once remarked, "There's nothing as practical as a good theory"—by which he meant that theories of social behavior and thought developed through systematic research often turn out to be extremely useful in solving practical problems. There seems little doubt, however, that interest in applying the knowledge of social psychology to practical issues has increased in recent years, with many beneficial results. We'll examine this work in Chapter 13.

Adoption of a Multicultural Perspective: Taking Full Account of Social Diversity

When I (Robert Baron) was in high school, my uncle gave me an interesting book—a guide for Europeans visiting the United States for the first time. A section describing the ethnic background of the people of the United States began

Figure 1.7

Growing Diversity: Definitely the Wave of the Future. As shown here, the size of various minority groups is projected to increase sharply in the United States in the years ahead. Similar trends are occurring in many other countries as well.

(*Source:* U.S. Department of Labor, 1995.)

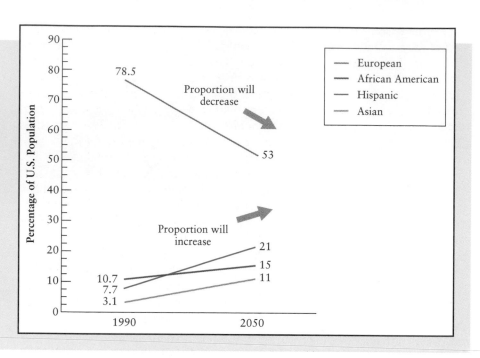

with the following statement: "The population of the United States is approximately 90 percent of European descent." How the United States—and the world!—has changed since then. Ethnic diversity has increased dramatically in many countries. Consider the following statistics:

> *In California, the most populous state in the United States, there is now no single majority group; rather, the population consists of many different groups, with persons of Hispanic and Asian descent showing the fastest growth in numbers.*

> *Current projections by the Census Bureau indicate that by the year 2050, 53 percent of people in the United States will be of European descent, 21 percent will be Americans of Hispanic descent, 15 percent will be African Americans, and 11 percent will be Asian Americans (see Figure 1.7).*

> *Ethnic diversity in U.S. colleges and universities has increased greatly. At present about 78 percent of students are of European descent, 9.2 percent African American, 5.5 percent of Hispanic descent, and 4 percent Asian (Chronicle of Higher Education, 1996). The proportion of females has increased; and at the graduate level, females now receive the majority of the advanced degrees awarded in many fields, including psychology.*

This growing diversity raises important questions for social psychology. At present, a majority of the world's social psychologists live and work in North America. As a result, a high proportion of all research in social psychology has been conducted in the United States and Canada. Can the findings of these studies be generalized to other cultures? As noted by Smith and Bond (1993), this is an open question. Most social psychologists have assumed that the findings of their research can be generalized across cultures and that the processes they study occur among human beings everywhere. At first glance, this seems reasonable. Why should love, conformity, persuasion, or prejudice operate differently on different continents?

On closer examination, however, it seems possible that even these basic processes may be strongly affected by cultural factors (Smith & Bond, 1993).

For example, some cultures do not seem to possess the notion of *romantic love* so prevalent in Western cultures. Do people in these cultures form long-term relationships in the same way as people in cultures where the idea of romantic love is popular? Perhaps; but perhaps they do not. Similarly, recent findings (e.g., Choi & Nisbett, 1998) indicate that people in different cultures may differ in their perceptions of other persons—for example, in their tendency to perceive others' behavior as stemming from internal causes such as their own traits or motives rather than from external causes. As we'll see in Chapter 2, we have a strong tendency to assume that others' actions stem from internal causes, but the strength of this tendency may vary from one culture to another (e.g., Choi and Nisbett, 1998). Further, persons living in different cultures may even differ in the ways they perceive various situations, describing them in different terms and interpreting them along different dimensions (Scherer, 1997). To the extent that such differences exist, they may limit the extent to which the findings of research conducted in one culture can be extended to other cultures.

Similarly, social psychologists have increasingly recognized the fact that findings obtained with one gender may not necessarily apply to the other gender. While differences between the behavior of females and males have often been exaggerated, and appear to be quite small in most instances, some differences in social behavior do exist (Feingold, 1994; Oliver & Hyde, 1993). For instance, males engage in acts of physical aggression much more often than females—especially in the absence of strong provocation. When strong provocation is present, however, the size of this difference decreases (Bettancourt & Miller, 1996). Further, females appear to engage in indirect forms of aggression (e.g., spreading rumors, ignoring people) more frequently than males (e.g., Bjorkqvist, Osterman, & Kaukiainen, 1992). Thus, studies that focus on only one gender may miss part of the total picture (see Chapter 5).

We should add that cultural differences are now recognized as an important topic of research in their own right and, as such, are receiving increased attention from social psychologists. In sum, modern social psychology has adopted an increasingly **multicultural perspective**—a perspective marked by recognition of the importance of cultural factors and human diversity. We will highlight this aspect of the field in special sections throughout the text entitled *Social Diversity: A Critical Analysis*. These sections describe research dealing with cultural diversity and its effects, and point out the relationship of such research to other topics in social psychology. Other special features of this text are described in a later section. In addition, other sections of this book that focus on social diversity are marked, in the margin, by the special symbol.

Increasing Attention to the Potential Role of Biological Factors

Finally, we should note once again the growing influence of a biological or evolutionary perspective in modern social psychology (e.g., Buss, 1998). While social psychologists certainly do *not* accept the view that the many complexities of social behavior and social thought can be fully understood in terms of biological processes, researchers have shown increasing interest, in recent years, in the potential role of biological and genetic factors. As we noted earlier, growing evidence suggests that biological and genetic factors play at least some role in many forms of social behavior—in everything from physical attraction and mate selection to aggression and helping behavior (see Chapters 7, 10, and 11). As an illustration of the breadth of this research, consider the following study by Dabbs, Alford, and Fielden (1998).

multicultural perspective • A focus on understanding the cultural and ethnic factors that influence social behavior.

Figure 1.8
Trial Attorneys: Is There a Biological Basis for Their Behavior?
Recent findings (e.g., Dabbs et al., 1998) suggest that trial attorneys have higher levels of testosterone than other kinds of attorneys. Moreover, this is true for female as well as male trial attorneys. These findings suggest that biological factors may play a role even in processes as complex as choice of occupation.

These researchers reasoned that trial attorneys—who must often act in a dominant, energetic, and confrontational manner—might have higher levels of testosterone (the principal male sex hormone) than other kinds of attorneys. To test this hypothesis, the researchers measured the level of testosterone shown by male and female trial attorneys and by attorneys working in other areas of law. Results offered strong support for the hypothesis: trial attorneys, whether they were females or males, showed higher levels of testosterone than did other kinds of attorneys (see Figure 1.8). Of course, this study leaves unanswered the important question of *why* these differences occurred. Were certain kinds of persons—persons with high levels of testosterone—attracted to becoming trial attorneys? Or did trial lawyers' testosterone increase as a function of the competitive, confrontational behavior they had to show in the courtroom? Only further research can answer this question, but the findings reported by Dabbs and his colleagues (1998) suggest that biological factors may play a role even in such complex processes as occupational choice.

Key Points

- One major theme in modern social psychology is the growing influence of a cognitive perspective. This perspective suggests that individuals' interpretations of social situations strongly shape their behavior.

- Another major theme of modern social psychology is interest in application—in applying the knowledge and findings of social psychology to many practical problems.

- Modern social psychology adopts a *multicultural perspective*. This perspective recognizes the importance of cultural factors in social behavior and social thought, and notes that research findings obtained in one culture do not necessarily generalize to other cultures.

- There is growing recognition, in modern social psychology, of the potential role of biological and genetic factors in social behavior and social thought.

ANSWERING QUESTIONS ABOUT SOCIAL BEHAVIOR AND SOCIAL THOUGHT: RESEARCH METHODS IN SOCIAL PSYCHOLOGY

Now that we've described social psychology, we can turn to the third major task mentioned at the start of this chapter: explaining how social psychologists attempt to answer questions about social behavior and social thought—how, in short, they conduct their research. To provide you with basic information about this important issue, we'll examine three related issues. First, we will describe several methods of research in social psychology. Next, we will consider the role of theory in such research. Finally, in the next section, we will touch on some of the complex ethical issues relating to social psychological research.

Systematic Observation: Describing the World around Us

One basic technique for studying social behavior is **systematic observation**—carefully observing behavior it as it occurs. Such observation is not the kind of informal observation we all practice from childhood on; rather, in a scientific field such as social psychology, it is observation accompanied by careful, accurate measurement. For example, suppose that a social psychologist wanted to find out how frequently people touch one another in different settings. The researcher could study this topic by going to shopping malls, airports, college campuses, and many other settings and observing, in those settings, who touches whom, how they touch, and with what frequency (see Figure 1.9). Such research (which has actually been conducted—see Chapter 2), would be employing what is known as

systematic observation • A method of research in which behavior is systematically observed and recorded.

Figure 1.9
Naturalistic Observation in Operation. How frequently do people touch one another in public places? Who touches whom, and how? One way to find out would be to perform research employing naturalistic observation.

naturalistic observation—observation of behavior in natural settings (Linden, 1992a). Note that in such observation, the researcher would simply notice what was happening in various contexts; she or he would make no attempt to change the behavior of the persons being observed. In fact, such observation requires that the researcher take great pains to *avoid* influencing the persons in any way. Thus, the researcher would try to be as inconspicuous as possible, and might even try to hide behind natural barriers such as telephone poles, walls, or even bushes. This is what I (Robert Baron) did more than twenty years ago in a study I conducted on the effects of temperature on motorists' horn honking (Baron, 1976). We arranged for an accomplice to drive up to a red light and then to remain motionless after the light turned green. An assistant hid behind some bushes and recorded the number of seconds that passed before drivers honked at our accomplice. We found that they did, in fact, honk sooner on hot days than on cooler ones (see Chapter 11 for more information).

Another technique that is often included under the heading of systematic observation is known as the **survey method.** Here, researchers ask large numbers of persons to respond to questions about their attitudes or behavior. Surveys are used for many purposes. Social psychologists sometimes use this method to measure attitudes concerning social issues—for instance, national health care or affirmative action programs. Scientists and practitioners in other fields use the survey method to measure voting preferences prior to elections and to assess consumer reactions to new products.

Surveys offer several advantages. Information can be gathered about thousands or even hundreds of thousands of persons with relative ease. Further, since surveys can be constructed quickly, public opinion on issues can be obtained rapidly—very soon after the issues arise. In order to be useful as a research tool, though, a survey must meet certain requirements. First, there is the question of *sampling*: the persons who participate must be *representative* of the larger population about which conclusions are to be drawn. If this condition is not met, serious errors can result. For instance, some years ago, one of our students brought us a magazine article with the following headline: "Ninety-two percent of wives cheat on their husbands." The article went on to report the results of a survey of several thousand married women, so the student assumed that the conclusion was correct—and this troubled her a great deal. But when we pointed out that the survey was conducted through the mail and involved only readers of a magazine aimed at a special market (women who viewed themselves as in the forefront of the sexual revolution), the student quickly realized that these results probably did *not* generalize to the entire U.S. population: they applied only to a very limited sample—persons who read this magazine and who decided to complete and return the survey.

Yet another issue that must be carefully addressed with respect to surveys is this: The way in which the items are worded can exert strong effects on the outcomes obtained. For example, when asked to indicate how satisfied they are with their current jobs, more than 85 percent of persons indicate that they are "satisfied" or "very satisfied." When asked whether they would choose the same job or career again, however, less than 50 percent indicate agreement. So, as experts in the survey method well know, it's often true that "the way you ask the question determines the answer you get."

In sum, the survey method can be a useful approach for studying some aspects of social behavior, but the results obtained are accurate only to the extent that issues relating to sampling and wording are carefully addressed.

Correlation: The Search for Relationships

At various times, you have probably noticed that some events appear to be related to each other: as one changes, the other appears to change, too. For ex-

survey method • A method of research in which a large number of persons answer questions about their attitudes or behavior.

ample, perhaps you've noticed that people who drive new, expensive cars tend to be older than people who drive old, inexpensive ones; or that when interest rates rise, the stock market often falls. When two events are related in this way, we say that they are *correlated* or that a correlation exists between them. The term *correlation* refers to a tendency for one aspect of the world to change as the other changes. Social psychologists refer to such changeable aspects of the world as *variables,* because they can take different values, so we'll use that term from now on.

From the point of view of science, the existence of a correlation between two variables can be very useful. This is so because when a correlation exists, it is possible to predict one variable from information about one or more other variables. The ability to make such *predictions* is one important goal of all branches of science, including social psychology. Being able to make accurate predictions can be very useful. For instance, imagine that a correlation was observed between certain attitudes on the part of individuals (one variable) and the likelihood that individuals would later commit serious crimes such as rape (another variable). This correlation could be very useful in identifying potentially dangerous persons so that they could receive treatment designed to prevent them from engaging in such harmful behavior. Similarly, suppose that a correlation was observed between certain patterns of behavior in married couples (e.g., the tendency to criticize each other harshly) and the likelihood that they would later divorce. Again, this information might be helpful in counseling the persons involved and perhaps, if this was what they desired, in saving their relationships. (See Chapter 8 for a discussion of why long-term relationships sometimes fail.)

How accurately can such predictions be made? The stronger the correlation between the variables in question, the more accurate the predictions. Correlations can range from 0 to −1.00 or +1.00; the greater the departure from 0, the stronger the correlation. Positive numbers mean that as one variable increases, the other increases too. Negative numbers indicate that as one variable increases, the other decreases. For instance, there is a negative correlation between age and the amount of hair on the heads of males: the older men grow, the less hair they have.

These basic facts underlie an important method of research sometimes used by social psychologists: the **correlational method.** In this approach, social psychologists attempt to determine whether, and to what extent, different variables are related to each other. This involves making careful observations of each variable, and then performing appropriate statistical tests to determine whether and to what degree the variables are correlated. Perhaps a concrete example will help illustrate the nature of this research method.

Imagine that a social psychologist has reason to believe that the higher the temperature, the more irritable people become, and hence the greater the likelihood that they will aggress against others. How could research on this **hypothesis**—an as yet unverified prediction—be conducted? While many possibilities exist, a very basic approach would go something like this. The researcher might obtain records of daily temperatures in many different cities (one variable) and records of the number of violent crimes such as assaults and murders in these locations (the other variable). If a positive correlation were obtained, the researcher would have some evidence for a relationship between temperature and violence.

Now for the most important point: Suppose that the researcher found such a correlation (e.g., a correlation of +.26 between temperature and violent crimes); what could she or he conclude? That high temperatures cause violence? Perhaps; but this conclusion, reasonable as it may seem, may be totally false. Here's why: *The fact that two variables are correlated, even highly correlated, does not guarantee that there is a causal link between them—that changes in*

correlational method • A method of research in which a scientist systematically observes two or more variables to determine whether changes in one are accompanied by changes in the other.

hypothesis • An as yet unverified prediction based on a theory.

Figure 1.10
An Illustration of the Fact that Correlation Does *Not* Equal Causation. When one event precedes another, it is sometimes tempting to assume that the first event caused the second. As you can see from this cartoon, however, such assumptions are often on shaky ground.

(*Source:* King Features syndicate, 1990.)

one cause *changes in the other*. The correlation between the variables may be due to chance or random factors, as shown in Figure 1.10. In many other cases, a correlation between variables simply reflects the fact that changes in both are related to a third variable. For example, it may well be the case that as temperatures rise, individuals drink more alcohol in an effort to reduce their discomfort. It may be this factor—consumption of alcohol—rather than high temperature that actually causes an increase in aggression. In other words, alcohol consumption is related both to high temperatures (it rises as temperatures go up) and to increased aggression, but there is in fact no direct link between temperatures and violence. (Research on this issue is described in Chapter 11; e.g., Anderson, Bushman, & Groom, 1997; Cohn & Rotton, 1997).

Here's another illustration of the same point: The greater the number of storks nesting on roofs in northern Europe in spring, the greater the number of babies born the next summer and fall. Does this mean that storks really do bring babies? Certainly not! Rather, both variables—the number of nesting storks and the number of births—are caused by a third factor: climate. The colder the winter, the more storks nest on roofs, where escaping heat keeps them warm. And the colder the weather, the more time people spend indoors, cuddling . . . with predictable results. (Additional illustrations of the fact that even a strong correlation between two variables does not necessarily mean that one causes the other are presented in the *Ideas to Take with You* feature on p. 33.)

Despite this major drawback, the correlational method of research is sometimes very useful to social psychologists. It can be used in natural settings, and it is often highly efficient: a large amount of information can be obtained in a relatively short period of time. However, the fact that it is generally not conclusive with respect to cause-and-effect relationships is a serious flaw—one that leads social psychologists to prefer a different method. It is to this approach that we turn next.

Key Points

- In *systematic observation*, behavior is carefully observed and recorded. Naturalistic observation involves observation conducted in the settings where the behavior naturally occurs.

- In the *survey method*, large numbers of persons respond to questions about their attitudes or behavior.

- In the *correlational method,* researchers measure two or more variables to determine if they are related to one another in any way.

- The existence of even strong correlations between variables does not indicate that they are causally related to each other.

The Experimental Method: Knowledge through Systematic Intervention

As we have just seen, the correlational method of research is very useful from the point of view of one important goal of science: the ability to make accurate predictions. It is less useful, though, from the point of view of reaching yet another goal: *explanation.* This is sometimes known as the "why" question, because scientists do not merely wish to describe the world and relationships between variables in it: they want to be able to *explain* these relationships, too. For instance, continuing with the heat-and-aggression example used above, if a link between high temperatures and crimes of violence exists, social psychologists would want to know *why* this is so. Do high temperatures make people irritable? Do they reduce restraints against harming others? Do they get more people out on the street so that there is a greater chance people will get into fights?

In order to attain the goal of explanation, social psychologists employ a method of research known as **experimentation** or the **experimental method.** As the heading of this section suggests, experimentation involves the following strategy: One variable is changed systematically, and the effects of these changes on one or more other variables are carefully measured. If systematic changes in one variable produce changes in another variable (and if two additional conditions we'll describe below are also met), it is possible to conclude with reasonable certainty that there is indeed a causal relationship between these variables: that changes in one do indeed *cause* changes in the other. Because the experimental method is so valuable in answering this kind of question, it is frequently the method of choice in social psychology. But please bear in mind that there is no single "best" method of research. Rather, social psychologists, like all other scientists, choose the method that is most appropriate for studying a particular topic.

Experimentation: Its Basic Nature. In its most basic form, the experimental method involves two key steps: (1) The presence or strength of some variable believed to affect an aspect of social behavior or thought is systematically altered, and (2) the effects of such alterations (if any) are carefully measured. The factor systematically varied by the researcher is termed the **independent variable,** while the aspect of behavior studied is termed the **dependent variable.** In a simple experiment, then, different groups of participants are exposed to contrasting levels of the independent variable (such as low, moderate, and high). The researcher then carefully measures the participants' behavior to determine whether it does in fact vary with these changes in the independent variable. If it does—and if two other conditions are also met—the researcher can tentatively conclude that the independent variable does indeed cause changes in the aspect of behavior being studied.

To illustrate the basic nature of experimentation in social psychology, let's return again to the heat-and-aggression example. How could a psychologist study this topic through experimentation? One possibility is as follows. The researcher would arrange for participants in the study to come to a laboratory where she or he can control the temperature (and perhaps other environmental

experimentation (experimental method) • A method of research in which an experimenter systematically changes one or more factors (the independent variables) to determine whether such variations affect one or more other factors (dependent variables).

independent variable • The variable that a researcher systematically alters in an experiment.

dependent variable • The variable that is measured in an experiment.

Figure 1.11
Experimentation: A Simple Example. In this experiment participants in three different conditions were exposed to contrasting temperatures: 70–72, 80–82, and 90–92 degrees Fahrenheit. They were annoyed by an assistant, then given an opportunity to aggress against this person. Results indicated that as temperatures rose, aggression increased. This finding provided evidence for the existence of a causal link between temperature and aggression.

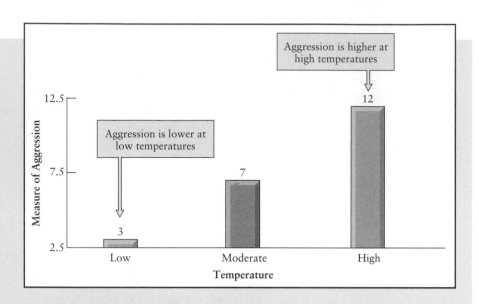

variables as well). Temperature would then be systematically varied so that, for example, some participants in the study are exposed to comfortable conditions (temperatures of 70 to 72 degrees Fahrenheit), others to moderately hot conditions (temperatures of 80 to 82 degrees Fahrenheit), and still others to very hot conditions (temperatures of 90 to 92 degrees Fahrenheit). At the same time, some measure of participants' irritability or tendency to aggress against others would also be obtained. For instance, the researcher could arrange for participants to be annoyed in some way by an assistant and then ask participants to rate this person's performance, explaining that low ratings would cause the assistant to lose her or his job. If results now looked like those in Figure 1.11, the researcher could conclude, at least tentatively, that high temperatures do indeed increase aggression. It's important to note that in experimentation, such knowledge is obtained through direct intervention: temperature—the independent variable—is systematically changed by the researcher. In the correlational method, in contrast, variables are *not* altered in this manner; rather, naturally occurring changes in them are simply observed and recorded.

Incidentally, experiments of the type we have just described have actually been conducted. In fact, they were among the very first research studies carried out by Professor Baron (e.g., Baron, 1972a) and started a line of investigation in social psychology that has continued up to the present time (e.g., Anderson et al., 1997).

Experimentation: Two Requirements for Its Success. Earlier we referred to two conditions that must be met before a researcher can conclude that changes in an independent variable have caused changes in a dependent variable. Let's consider these conditions now. The first involves what is termed **random assignment of participants to experimental conditions.** This requirement means that all participants in an experiment must have an equal chance of being exposed to each level of the independent variable. The reason for this rule is simple: If participants are *not* randomly assigned to each condition, it may later be impossible to determine if differences in their behavior stem from differences they brought with them to the study, from the impact of the independent variable, or from both. For instance, imagine that in the study just described, it is difficult to change the temperature in the laboratory very quickly, so the researcher decides to collect all data for each temperature condition on a different day. It just so happens that on the high-

random assignment of participants to experimental conditions • The requirement that participants in research experiments have an equal chance of being exposed to each level of the independent variable; a basic requirement for conducting valid experiments.

temperature day, all the participants in the study are members of a martial arts club: they are experts in judo, karate, and so on. In contrast, on the low-temperature day, many of the participants are members of a religious club that held its monthly meeting on that date. Results indicate that participants in the high-temperature condition are more aggressive than those in the low-temperature condition. Why? Because of the effects of temperature? Because of differences between the participants in these two conditions (martial arts club members versus religious club members)? Because of both factors? We can't tell. If, in contrast, members of these two clubs had been randomly distributed across the temperature conditions, differences between them would, presumably, have "canceled out." Then any differences between the low- and high-temperature conditions could still be attributed to this variable. As you can see, then, it is crucial that all participants have an equal chance of being assigned to all experimental conditions; if they do not, the potential value of an experiment may be seriously reduced.

The second condition essential for successful experimentation is as follows: Insofar as possible, all factors other than the independent variable that might also affect participants' behavior must be held constant. To see why this is so, consider what will happen if, in the study on heat and aggression, the assistant acts in a more annoying way in the high-temperature condition than in the low-temperature condition. Once again, those in the high-temperature condition are more aggressive. What is the cause of this result? The aggression-increasing effects of heat, the stronger annoyance produced by the assistant, or possibly both factors? Once again, we can't tell; and since we can't, the value of the experiment as a source of new information about human behavior is greatly reduced. In situations like this, the independent variable is said to be *confounded* with another variable—one that is *not* under systematic investigation in the study. When confounding occurs, the findings of an experiment may be largely meaningless (see Figure 1.12).

But why, you may be now be wondering, would a psychologist make such a muddle of a research project? Why would the researcher allow the assistant to be more annoying in the high-temperature condition than in the low-temperature condition? The answer is that the researcher certainly wouldn't do this on

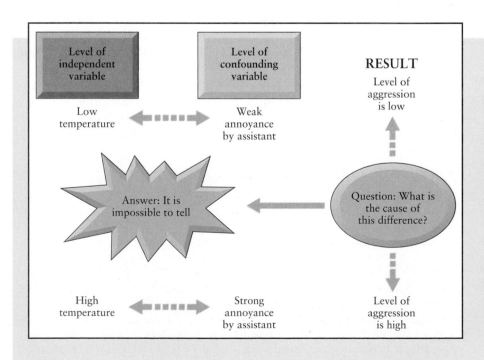

Figure 1.12
Confounding of Variables: A Fatal Flaw in Experimentation. In the experiment illustrated here, temperature—the independent variable—is confounded with another variable: degree of annoyance. The assistant annoys persons in the high-temperature condition more strongly than those in the low-temperature condition. As a result of this confounding, it is impossible to tell whether any differences between the behavior of participants in these two conditions stem from the independent variable, the confounding variable, or both.

purpose. But suppose that the assistant knows the hypothesis of the study—that high temperatures increase aggression. This knowledge might then lead the assistant to act differently in the high- and low-temperature conditions either consciously (she or he wants to "help" the results turn out right!) or unconsciously (the assistant changes her or his behavior without intending to do so). To avoid such **experimenter effects**—unintended effects on participants' behavior produced by researchers—social psychologists often use a *double-blind procedure*, in which the research assistants who have contact with participants do not know the hypothesis under investigation. Since they don't, the likelihood that they will influence results in subtle ways is reduced.

In sum, experimentation is, in several respects, the crown jewel among social psychology's methods. It certainly isn't perfect; for example, because it is often conducted in laboratory settings quite different from the locations in which social behavior actually occurs, the question of **external validity** often arises—to what extent can the findings of experiments be generalized to real-life social situations and perhaps to persons different from those who participated in the research? But when experimentation is used with skill and care, it can yield results that help us answer complex questions about social behavior and social thought. So why, you may be wondering, isn't it used all the time? The answer is that in some situations, experimentation simply cannot be used because of practical or ethical considerations. For example, imagine that a social psychologist formulates the following hypothesis: The more often politicians use certain techniques of persuasion in their speeches, the more likely they are to win elections. Could the psychologist convince two groups of politicians to vary their speeches so that one group used these techniques often and the other rarely? Probably not. So, although this research could, theoretically, be conducted, there are practical barriers that prevent it from actually taking place.

Second, ethical constraints may prevent a researcher from conducting a study that is in fact feasible. In other words, the study could be conducted, but doing so would violate ethical standards accepted by scientists or society. Suppose, for example, that a researcher has good reason to believe that certain kinds of cigarette ads increase teenagers' tendency to start smoking. Could the researcher ethically conduct an experiment on this topic, exposing some teenagers to lots of these ads and others to none and then comparing their rates of smoking? In principle, such research is possible; but no ethical social psychologist would perform it, because it might harm some of the participants in serious ways.

It is partly because of these and related problems that social psychologists often turn to systematic observation and the correlational method in their research. So, to repeat: All research methods offer a mixed bag of advantages and disadvantages, and social psychologists simply choose the method that seems best for studying a particular topic or question.

---

experimenter effects • Unintended effects on participants' behavior produced by researchers.

external validity • The extent to which findings of an experiment can be generalized to real-life social situations and perhaps to persons different from those who participated in the research.

Key Points

- *Experimentation* involves systematically altering one or more variables (independent variables) in order to determine whether these alterations affect some aspect of behavior (dependent variable).

- Successful use of the experimental method requires *random assignment of participants to experimental conditions;* it also requires that the experimenter hold constant all other factors that might also influence behavior so as to avoid confounding of variables.

- *Experimenter effects* occur when researchers unintentionally influence the behavior of participants. Such effects can be eliminated or minimized by double-blind procedures.

> • Although it is a very powerful research tool, the experimental method is not perfect—questions concerning its *external validity* often arise. Further, it cannot be used in some situations because of practical or ethical considerations.

Interpreting Research Results: The Use of Statistics, and Social Psychologists as Perennial Skeptics

Once a research project has been completed, social psychologists must turn their attention to another crucial task: interpreting the results. The key question is this: How much confidence can we place in the results? Are correlations between variables or observed differences between experimental conditions real ones we can accept with confidence as being accurate? In order to answer this question, social psychologists generally employ **inferential statistics**—a special form of mathematics that allows us to evaluate the likelihood that a given pattern of research results occurred by chance alone. To determine whether the findings of a study are indeed real—unlikely to be a chance event—psychologists perform appropriate statistical analyses on the data they collect. If these analyses suggest that the likelihood of obtaining the observed findings by chance is low (usually, fewer than 5 chances in 100), the results are described as *significant*. Only then are they interpreted as being of value in helping us understand some aspect of social behavior or social thought. All of the findings reported in this book have passed this basic test, so you can be confident that they refer to real (i.e., significant) results.

It's important to realize, however, that the likelihood that a given pattern of findings is a chance event is *never* zero. It can be very low—1 in 10,000, for instance—but it can never be zero. For this reason, a specific finding is always viewed as tentative until it is replicated—reported again by different researchers in different laboratories. Only when findings have passed this additional test are they viewed with confidence by social psychologists. But here is where a serious problem arises: only rarely do the results of social psychological research yield totally consistent findings. A more common pattern is for some studies to offer support for a given hypothesis while others fail to offer such support. For instance, some research on the effects of heat on aggression suggests that this relationship has limits: when it gets extremely hot, people become too exhausted or tired to engage in aggression, so such behavior actually decreases in frequency (e.g., Bell, 1992; Cohn & Rotton, 1997). In contrast, other research suggests that aggression continues to increase as temperatures rise, even at extreme levels of heat (e.g., Anderson et al., 1997). Why do such discrepancies arise? In part because different researchers may use different methods. For instance, in heat-and-aggression research, they may use somewhat different measures of aggression (e.g., murders versus less deadly assaults); or different researchers may conduct their research in regions with different climates. What is defined as "hot" by local residents, for instance, may be very different in Houston or Bombay than it is in Boston or London. Whatever the cause, contrasting results in different studies pose a serious issue that must be carefully addressed.

Interpreting Diverse Results: The Role of Meta-Analysis. So what do social psychologists do when confronted with contrasting results from different studies? One answer involves the use of a technique known as **meta-analysis** (e.g., Bond & Smith, 1996). This procedure allows us to combine the results of many different studies in order to estimate both the direction and the magnitude of the effects of independent variables. Meta-analytic procedures are mathematical in nature, so they eliminate potential sources of errors that might arise if we attempted to examine the findings of several studies in a more informal manner, such as through a simple count to see how many studies offered support for a

inferential statistics • A special form of mathematics that allows us to evaluate the likelihood that a given pattern of research results occurred by chance alone.

meta-analysis • A statistical technique for combining data from independent studies in order to determine whether specific variables (or interactions between variables) have significant effects across these studies.

hypothesis and how many did not. For example, meta-analysis helps eliminate the confirmation bias we described above—the tendency to seek confirmation of our views or preferences. Overall, therefore, meta-analysis is an important tool for interpreting the results of social psychological research, and we'll describe many studies that use this tool in later chapters.

The Role of Theory in Social Psychology

There is one more aspect of social psychological research we should consider before concluding this discussion. As we noted earlier, in their research social psychologists seek to do more than simply describe the world; they want to be able to *explain* it too. For instance, social psychologists don't want merely to state that racial prejudice is common in the United States; they want to be able to explain *why* some persons hold these negative views. In social psychology, as in all branches of science, explanation involves the construction of **theories**— frameworks for explaining various events or processes. The procedure involved in building a theory goes something like this:

1. On the basis of existing evidence, a theory that reflects this evidence is proposed.
2. This theory, which consists of basic concepts and statements about how these concepts are related, organizes existing information and makes predictions about observable events. For instance, the theory might predict the conditions under which individuals acquire racial prejudice.
3. These predictions, known as *hypotheses*, are then tested by actual research.
4. If results are consistent with the theory, confidence in its accuracy is increased. If they are not, the theory is modified and further tests are conducted.
5. Ultimately, the theory is either accepted as accurate or rejected as inaccurate. Even if it is accepted as accurate, however, the theory remains open to further refinement as improved methods of research are developed and additional evidence relevant to the theory's predictions is obtained.

This may sound a bit abstract, so let's turn to a concrete example. Suppose that one reason why people acquire racial prejudice is that they are exposed to negative information about minority groups in the mass media—newspapers, magazines, television. This leads some people to perceive racial minorities in negative terms; and because these people may have little contact with members of minority groups, their views are not refuted by experience. The result: Racial prejudice develops and strengthens over time.

This theory leads logically to various predictions such as these: (1) The greater people's exposure to negative depictions of racial minorities in the mass media, the stronger will be their prejudice against them; (2) the greater the frequency of contact with racial minorities, the *weaker* will be the prejudice against them, as this may serve to counter the impact of the media. Research designed to test these predictions can now be conducted. If findings are consistent with these predictions and with others derived from the theory, confidence in the theory will be increased. If findings are *not* consistent with the theory, it will be modified or perhaps rejected, as noted above. (See Chapter 6 for a discussion of the causes of racial prejudice.) This process—theory formulation, test, theory modification, retest, and so on—lies close to the core of the scientific method, so it is an important aspect of social psychological research (see Figure 1.13). This book will present many different theories relating to important aspects of social behavior and social thought.

Two final points: First, theories are never proven in any final, ultimate sense. Rather, they are always open to test and are accepted with more or less

theories • Frameworks constructed by scientists in any field in an effort to explain why certain events or processes occur as they do.

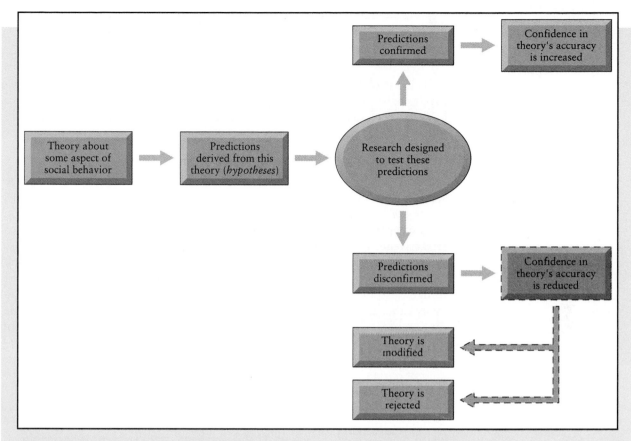

Figure 1.13

The Role of Theory in Social Psychological Research. Theories both organize existing knowledge and make predictions about how various events or processes will occur. Once a theory is formulated, *hypotheses* (predictions) derived logically from it are tested through careful research. If results agree with the predictions, confidence in the theory is increased. If results disagree with such predictions, the theory may be modified—or, ultimately, rejected as false.

confidence depending on the weight of available evidence. Second, research is *not* undertaken to prove or verify a theory; it is performed to gather evidence relevant to the theory. If a researcher sets out to "prove" her or his pet theory, this a serious violation of the principles of scientific skepticism, objectivity, and open-mindedness we described at the beginning of this chapter.

Key Points

- In order to determine whether the results of a research project are real or due to chance, social psychologists use *inferential statistics*.

- If the likelihood is small that research results occurred by chance (fewer than 5 chances in 100), results are described as significant.

- In order to assess the direction and magnitude of the effects of independent variables across different studies, social psychologists use a statistical technique known as *meta-analysis*.

- *Theories* are frameworks for explaining various events or processes. They play a key role in social psychological research.

THE QUEST FOR KNOWLEDGE AND RIGHTS OF INDIVIDUALS: SEEKING AN APPROPRIATE BALANCE

In their use of experimentation, correlation, and systematic observation, social psychologists do not differ from researchers in many other fields. One technique, however, does seem to be unique to research in social psychology: **deception.** This technique involves efforts by researchers to withhold or conceal from participants information about the purposes of a study. The reason for using deception is simple: Many social psychologists believe that if participants know the true purposes of a study, their behavior in it will be changed by that knowledge. Thus, the research will not yield valid information about social behavior or social thought.

Some kinds of research do seem to require the use of temporary deception. For example, imagine that in a study designed to examine the effects of physical attractiveness on first impressions, participants are informed of this purpose. Will they now react differently to a highly attractive stranger than they would have in the absence of this information? Perhaps they may lean over backwards to demonstrate that *they* are not affected by others' appearance. In this and many other cases, social psychologists feel compelled to employ temporary deception in their research (Suls & Rosnow, 1988). However, the use of deception raises important ethical issues that cannot be ignored.

First, there is the chance, however slim, that deception may result in some kind of harm to the persons exposed to it. Participants may be upset by the procedures used or by their own reactions to them. For example, in several studies concerned with helping in emergencies, participants were exposed to staged but seemingly real emergency situations. In one such study, for instance, they overheard what seemed to be a medical emergency—another person having an apparent seizure (e.g., Darley & Latané, 1968). Many participants were strongly upset by these staged events; others were disturbed by the fact that although they recognized the need to help, they failed to do so. Clearly, the fact that participants experienced emotional upset raises complex ethical issues about just how far researchers can go when studying even very important topics such as this one.

We should hasten to emphasize that such research represents an extreme use of deception; generally, deception takes much milder forms. For example, participants may receive a request for help from a stranger who is actually an accomplice of the researchers; or they may be informed that most other students in their university hold certain views when in fact they do not. Still, even in such cases, the potential for some kind of harmful effects to participants exists, and this is a potentially serious drawback to the use of deception.

Second, there is the possibility that participants will resent being "fooled" during a study and that as a result they will acquire negative attitudes toward social psychology and psychological research in general. For instance, they may become suspicious about information presented by researchers (Kelman, 1967). To the extent that such reactions occur—and recent findings indicate that they do, at least to a degree (Epley & Huff, 1998)—they have disturbing implications for the future of social psychology, which places so much emphasis on scientific research.

Because of such possibilities, the use of deception poses something of a dilemma to social psychologists. On the one hand, it often seems essential to their research. On the other, its use raises serious problems. How can this issue be resolved? While opinion remains somewhat divided, most social psychologists agree on the following points. First, deception should *never* be used to persuade people to take part in a study; withholding information or providing misleading information about what will happen in an experiment in order to induce people to take part in it is definitely *not* acceptable (Sigall, 1997). Second, most social psychologists agree that temporary deception is acceptable provided two basic

deception • A technique whereby researchers withhold information about the purposes or procedures of a study from persons participating in it.

safeguards are employed. One of these is **informed consent**—a procedure in which participants are given as much information as possible about the procedures to be followed before they make their decision to participate. In short, this is the opposite of withholding information in order to persuade people to participate. The second safeguard is careful **debriefing**—providing participants with a full description of the purposes of a study after they have participated in it (see Figure 1.14). Such information should also include an explanation of deception and of why it was necessary to employ it.

Fortunately, a growing body of evidence indicates that together, informed consent and thorough debriefing can substantially reduce the potential dangers of deception (Smith & Richardson, 1985). For example, most participants report that they view temporary deception as acceptable, provided that potential benefits outweigh potential costs and if there is no other means of obtaining the information sought (Rogers, 1980; Sharpe, Adair, & Roese, 1992). However, as we noted above, there is some indication that they do become somewhat more suspicious about what researchers tell them during an experiment; even worse, such increased suspiciousness seems to last several months (Epley & Huff, 1998). Further, persons who have participated in research employing deception report generally favorable attitudes about psychological research—attitudes just as favorable as those of persons who have not participated in such research (Sharpe et al., 1992).

In sum, existing evidence seems to indicate that most research participants do not react negatively to temporary deception as long as its purpose and necessity are clear. Indeed, they may be more upset by what happens during an experiment—for instance, receiving negative feedback on their work—than by the fact that such information was false and that they were deceived by the researcher. However, these findings do *not* mean that the safety or appropriateness of deception should be taken for granted (Rubin, 1985). On the contrary, the guiding principles for all researchers planning to use this procedure should be: (1) Use deception only when it is absolutely essential to do so—when no other means for conducting the research exists; (2) always proceed with caution; and (3) make certain that every possible precaution is taken to protect the rights, safety, and well-being of research participants.

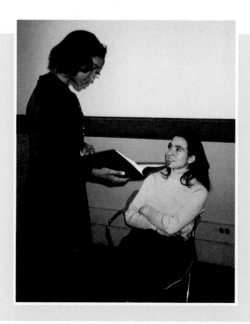

Figure 1.14
Careful Debriefing: A Requirement in Studies that Use Deception. After an experiment is completed, participants should be provided with *debriefing*—full information about the experiment's goals and the reasons why temporary deception was used.

informed consent • A procedure in which research participants are provided with as much information as possible about a research project before deciding whether to participate in it.

debriefing • Procedures at the conclusion of a research session in which participants are given full information about the nature of the research and the hypothesis or hypotheses under investigation.

> ### Key Points
>
> - *Deception* involves efforts by social psychologists to withhold or conceal information about the purposes of a study from participants.
> - Most social psychologists believe that temporary deception is often necessary in order to obtain valid research results.
> - However, they view deception as acceptable only when important safeguards are employed: *informed consent* and thorough *debriefing*.

USING THIS BOOK: A ROAD MAP FOR READERS

Although it was a long time ago, both of us can remember our own first course in social psychology—and can also recall struggling long and hard to understand many sections of the textbooks we used. Because we don't want you to experience the same difficulties, we have worked hard to make this book easy to read; we have also included special features designed to make the book more enjoyable—and useful. Here is an overview of the steps we've taken in this respect.

First, each chapter begins with an outline and ends with a summary. Within the text itself, key terms are printed in **dark type** like this and are followed by a definition. These terms are also defined in a running glossary in the margins, as well as in a glossary at the end of the book. To help you understand and remember what you have read, each major section is followed by a list of *Key Points*—a brief summary of major points. All figures and tables are clear and simple, and most contain special labels and notes designed to help you understand them (see Figure 1.11 on page 24 for an example). Finally, each chapter ends with a summary and review of the Key Points. Reviewing this section can be an important aid to your studying.

Second, this book has an underlying theme that can be stated as follows: Social psychology is much more than just a collection of interesting findings to be enjoyed for the moment, recalled on tests, and then quickly forgotten. On the contrary, we believe that it provides a new way of looking at the social world that everyone should take with them, and use, long after this course is over. To emphasize this theme of "taking social psychology with you," we've included several special features that appear in each chapter. One of these is labeled *Beyond the Headlines: As Social Psychologists See It*. These sections take an actual newspaper article and examine it from the perspective of social psychology. They illustrate how social psychologists think, and how the principles of our field can be applied to virtually *any* aspect of human social behavior.

Another feature relating to our theme is labeled *Ideas to Take with You*. One of these special sections occurs at the end of each chapter (see page 33 for an example), and each is designed to highlight important concepts you should remember—and use—long after this course is over. In our view you may well find these concepts useful in your own life in the years ahead.

Two additional features we think you'll find interesting and useful are special sections titled *Social Diversity: A Critical Analysis* and *Cornerstones of Social Psychology*. *Social Diversity* sections present information concerning differences between ethnic groups within a given society or differences across various cultures, and are designed to reflect the growing multicultural perspective in social psychology we described earlier. *Cornerstones of Social Psychology* sections describe truly classic studies in our field—studies that started major lines of research and thus exerted a lasting impact on the field. Because most of the studies described in this text are very recent (many are from 1997, 1998, and even 1999), we feel that it is important to emphasize the origins of this modern work and its links to what went before.

As we noted earlier, modern social psychology is distinguished by growing interest in social diversity and in the potential role of biological and genetic factors in human social behavior. Topics related to these important themes are discussed at numerous points throughout the text. To help you identify them, the special symbols  and appear in the margin next to these discussions.

Finally, to help you understand how research in each area of social psychology is related to research in other areas, we've included a special *Connections* table at the end of each chapter. These tables provide a kind of global review, reminding you of related topics discussed elsewhere in the book. In addition, they emphasize the fact that many aspects of social behavior and thought are closely linked: they do not occur in isolation from one another.

All of these features are designed to help you get the most out of your first encounter with social psychology. But, in a key sense, only *you* can transfer the information on the pages of this book into your own memory—and into your own life. So please do *use* this book. Read the summaries and chapter outlines, review the Key Points, and pay special attention to the Ideas to Take with You pages. Doing so, we believe, will improve your understanding of social psychology—and your grade, too! Finally, please do think of this book as a reference source—a practical guide to social behavior to which you can refer over and over again in the years ahead. In contrast to some other fields you will study, social psychology really is directly relevant to your daily life—to understanding others and to getting along better with them. So consider keeping this text as part of your permanent library; we're certain that you'll find it useful. Good luck—and may your first encounter with our field be one you'll enjoy and remember for many years to come.

Ideas to Take with You
Why Correlation Doesn't Equal Causation

The fact that two variables are correlated—even strongly correlated—does not necessarily mean that changes in one variable cause changes in the other. This is true because changes in both variables may actually be related to—or caused by—a third variable. Two examples:

OBSERVATION: As weight increases, income increases.

Possible interpretations:

1. Weight gain causes increased income.

Weight gain $\xrightarrow{\text{Causes}}$ Increased income

2. As people grow older, they tend to gain weight *and* also to earn higher incomes; both variables are actually related to *age*.

OBSERVATION: The more violent television and movies people watch, the more likely they are to engage in dangerous acts of aggression.

Possible Interpretations:

1. Exposure to media violence is one factor that increases aggression.

$$\text{Exposure to media violence} \xrightarrow{\text{Causes}} \text{Increased aggression}$$

2. People who prefer a high level of stimulation have little control over their impulses; thus, they choose to watch displays of violence and also act aggressively more often than other people. Both variables are related to a need for certain kinds of stimulation.

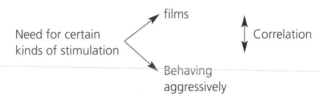

Watching violent TV programs, films

Need for certain kinds of stimulation

Behaving aggressively

Correlation

KEY CONCLUSION: EVEN IF TWO VARIABLES ARE STRONGLY CORRELATED, THIS DOES NOT NECESSARILY MEAN THAT CHANGES IN ONE CAUSE CHANGES IN THE OTHER.

SUMMARY AND REVIEW OF KEY POINTS

Social Psychology: A Working Definition

- *Social psychology* is the scientific field that seeks to understand the nature and causes of individual behavior and thought in social situations.
- It is scientific in nature because it adopts the values and methods used in other fields of science.
- Social psychologists adopt the scientific method because "common sense" provides an unreliable guide to social behavior, and because humans' thought is influenced by many potential sources of bias.
- Social psychology focuses on the behavior of individuals, and seeks to understand the causes of social behavior and thought.
- Important causes of social behavior and thought include the behavior and characteristics of other persons, cognitive processes, aspects of the physical environment, culture, and biological factors.

Social Psychology: Where It Is Now, and Where It Seems to Be Going

- One major theme in modern social psychology is the growing influence of a cognitive perspective. This perspective suggests that individuals' interpretations of social situations strongly shape their behavior.

- Another major theme of modern social psychology is interest in application—in applying the knowledge and findings of social psychology to many practical problems.
- Modern social psychology adopts a *multicultural perspective*. This perspective recognizes the importance of cultural factors in social behavior and social thought, and notes that research findings obtained in one culture do not necessarily generalize to other cultures.
- There is growing recognition, in modern social psychology, of the potential role of biological and genetic factors in social behavior and social thought.

Answering Questions about Social Behavior and Social Thought: Research Methods in Social Psychology

- In *systematic observation*, behavior is carefully observed and recorded. Naturalistic observation is observation conducted in the settings where the behavior naturally occurs.
- In the *survey method*, large numbers of persons respond to questions about their attitudes or behavior.
- In the *correlational method*, researchers measure two or more variables to determine if they are related to one another in any way.

- The existence of even strong correlations between variables does not indicate that they are causally related to each other.
- *Experimentation* involves systematically altering one or more variables (independent variables) in order to determine whether these alterations affect some aspect of behavior (dependent variable).
- Successful use of the experimental method requires *random assignment of participants to experimental conditions;* it also requires that the experimenter hold constant all other factors that might also influence behavior so as to avoid confounding of variables.
- *Experimenter effects* occur when researchers unintentionally influence the behavior of participants. Such effects can be eliminated or minimized by double-blind procedures.
- Although it is a very powerful research tool, the experimental method is not perfect—questions concerning its *external validity* often arise. Further, it cannot be used in some situations because of practical or ethical considerations.
- In order to determine whether the results of a research project are real or due to chance, social psychologists use *inferential statistics.*

- If the likelihood is small that research results occurred by chance (fewer than 5 chances in 100), results are described as significant.
- In order to assess the direction and magnitude of the effects of independent variables across different studies, social psychologists use a statistical technique known as *meta-analysis.*
- *Theories* are frameworks for explaining various events or processes. They play a key role in social psychological research.

The Quest for Knowledge and Rights of Individuals: Seeking an Appropriate Balance

- *Deception* involves efforts by social psychologists to withhold or conceal information about the purposes of a study from participants.
- Most social psychologists believe that temporary deception is often necessary in order to obtain valid research results.
- However, they view deception as acceptable only when important safeguards are employed: *informed consent* and thorough *debriefing.*

KEY TERMS

availability heuristic (p. 8)

confirmation bias (p. 8)

correlational method (p. 21)

debriefing (p. 31)

deception (p. 30)

dependent variable (p. 23)

evolutionary social psychology (p. 12)

experimentation (experimental method) (p. 23)

experimenter effects (p. 26)

external validity (p. 26)

hypothesis (p. 21)

independent variable (p. 23)

inferential statistics (p. 27)

informed consent (p. 31)

meta-analysis (p. 27)

multicultural perspective (p. 17)

random assignment of participants to experimental conditions (p. 24)

social psychology (p. 6)

survey method (p. 20)

systematic observation (p. 19)

theories (p. 28)

FOR MORE INFORMATION

Jackson, J. M. (1993). *Social psychology, past and present.* Hillsdale, NJ: Erlbaum.

A thoughtful overview of the roots and development of social psychology. Organized around major themes in social psychological research, the book emphasizes the multidisciplinary roots of social psychology. The chapter on current trends is especially valuable.

Semin, G., & Fiedler, K. (1996). *Applied social psychology.* Thousand Oaks, CA: Sage.

How are social psychologists applying their knowledge and skills to solving practical problems? This book presents a broad and thorough overview of such efforts. Topics covered include the application of social psychology to law, the media, health, language, decision making, and survey research. A good source to consult if you want to know more about the applied aspects of social psychology.

2 Social Perception: Understanding Others

Sun, Health, and Meridians. © José Ortega/Stock Illustration Source

Chapter Outline

Nonverbal Communication: The Unspoken Language
  Nonverbal Communication: The Basic Channels
  Facial Expressions and Social Thought: Why "Smile When You Say That, Partner" May Not Always Be Good Advice
  BEYOND THE HEADLINES: AS SOCIAL PSYCHOLOGISTS SEE IT: Body Language in the Courtroom

Attribution: Understanding the Causes of Others' Behavior
  Theories of Attribution: Frameworks for Understanding How We Attempt to Make Sense of the Social World
  Attribution: Some Basic Sources of Error
  SOCIAL DIVERSITY: A CRITICAL ANALYSIS: Cultural Differences in the Self-Serving Bias
  Applications of Attribution Theory: Insights and Interventions

Impression Formation and Impression Management: How We Combine—and Use—Social Information
  CORNERSTONES OF SOCIAL PSYCHOLOGY: Asch's Research on Central and Peripheral Traits
  Impression Formation: The Modern Cognitive Approach
  Impression Management: The Fine Art of Looking Good
  The Accuracy of Social Perception: Evidence That It's Higher Than You Might Guess
  CONNECTIONS: Integrating Social Psychology
  IDEAS TO TAKE WITH YOU: Minimizing the Impact of Attributional Errors

Summary and Review of Key Points
Key Terms
For More Information

I (Robert Baron) will always remember the interview that landed me my first job as a professor. It was at a large university in the southern United States, and I had never been to that part of the country before—at least not as an adult. (I spent the first eighteen months of my life in Florida and Mississippi, as my parents moved from military base to military base during World War II.) I wanted this job very much, so I tried to do everything I could to make a good first impression on the people who interviewed me. Everything seemed to be going well until, on the second day of my visit, I had a private meeting with the department head. He was about to retire, so the difference in our ages made me a little uncomfortable. The biggest problem, though, was the difference in our styles of speech. I grew up in New York, where people speak very quickly—far more quickly than in this southern state. In addition, the department head was an especially calm and slow-speaking person. The result? I found myself interrupting him repeatedly, because I thought, from the pauses in his speech, that he had finished and was waiting for me to reply! The interview lasted about an hour, but even today, I remember it as seeming endless. I left the interview with my hopes crushed, assuming that I had come across as a rude, brash Yankee and would never get the job. Fortunately for me, other members of the department saw through these differences in style and voted to hire me; in fact, the only person who voiced reservations about me was—you guessed it—the department head!

Why do I begin with this incident? Because it illustrates the central role of in our lives of **social perception**—the process (or, really, processes) through which we seek to understand other persons. The purpose of that job interview so many years ago (or of any other interview) was to provide my potential colleagues with the opportunity to figure out what kind of person I was and whether they would enjoy working with me. What traits did I possess? What were my major motives? Would I be a good teacher? Researcher? Colleague? These are some of the questions they certainly sought to answer during my two-day visit.

Of course, our efforts to understand other persons are not restricted to job interviews. On the contrary, we engage in social perception in many other contexts—probably, in every social situation we encounter. Despite all our efforts and experience in this task, however, other people often remain one of the true mysteries of life. They say and do things we don't expect, have motives we don't understand, and seem to see the world through eyes very different from our own. Yet, given the central role of other people in our lives, this is one mystery we can't afford to leave unsolved. The result: As suggested by the cartoon in Figure 2.1, we engage in efforts to form accurate social perceptions of others in many different contexts.

Because it plays such a crucial role in our daily lives, social perception has long been a topic of careful study in social psychology. To acquaint you with the key findings of this research, we'll focus on four important topics. First, we'll examine the process of *nonverbal communication*—communication between individuals involving an unspoken language of facial expressions, eye contact, body movements, and postures (e.g., Zebrowitz, 1997). As we'll soon see, information provided by such nonverbal cues can often tell us much about others' current moods or emotions. Next, we'll examine *attribution*, the complex process through which we attempt to understand the reasons behind others' behavior—*why* they have acted as they have in a given situation. Third, we'll examine the nature of *impression formation*—how we form first impressions of others—and *impression management (or self-presentation)*—our efforts to ensure that the impressions we make are favorable ones. As we'll soon see, first

social perception • The process through which we seek to know and understand other persons.

"*Jumpy and Jitter won't bother you unless you are selling something you ought __not__ to be selling. What are you selling?*"

Figure 2.1

Efforts to Understand Others: A Basic Part of Social Life. Because other persons play such an important role in our lives, we often try to understand them. As shown here, though, not everyone is highly successful at this task.

(*Source: The New Yorker.*)

impressions do indeed tend to exert lasting effects on social thought and social behavior, so our concern that they be favorable seems to be well justified, at least in this respect. Finally, we'll turn to the question of how *accurate*, in general, social perception really is. Recent findings suggest that although our perceptions of others are subject to many potential errors, we often *are* quite accurate in this respect; for this reason, we'll be able to end on a positive and optimistic note.

Nonverbal Communication: The Unspoken Language

Often, social behavior is strongly affected by temporary factors or causes. Changing moods, shifting emotions, fatigue, illness, drugs—all can influence the ways in which we think and behave. For example, most people are more willing to do favors for others when in a good mood than when in a bad mood (e.g., R. A. Baron, 1997a). Similarly, most people are more likely to lose their tempers and lash out at others in some manner when feeling irritable than when feeling pleasant (Anderson, 1997).

Because such temporary factors exert important effects on social behavior and thought, we are often interested in them: we try to find out how others are feeling right now. How do we go about this process? Sometimes, in a very straightforward way: we ask other persons directly. Unfortunately, this strategy often fails, because others are frequently unwilling to reveal their inner feelings to us. On the contrary, they may actively seek to conceal such information or may even lie to us about their current emotions (e.g., DePaulo et al., 1996; DePaulo & Kashy, 1998). For example, negotiators often hide their reactions to offers from their opponents; salespersons frequently show more liking and friendliness toward potential customers than they really feel.

In situations like these, we often fall back upon another, less direct method for gaining information about others' reactions: we pay careful attention to *nonverbal cues* provided by changes in facial expressions, eye contact, posture, body movements, and other expressive actions. As noted by DePaulo (1992), such behavior is relatively *irrepressible*—difficult to control—so that even when others try to conceal their inner feelings from us, these often leak out in many ways through nonverbal cues. In an important sense, then, nonverbal behaviors constitute a silent but eloquent language. The information they convey, and our efforts to interpret this input, are often described by the term **nonverbal communication.** In this section we'll first examine the basic channels through which nonverbal communication takes place. Then we'll turn to some interesting findings on the effects of such cues on social thought (e.g., Krull & Dill, 1998).

Nonverbal Communication: The Basic Channels

Think for a moment: Do you act differently when you are feeling happy than when you are feeling really sad? Most likely, you do. People tend to behave differently when experiencing different emotional states. But precisely how do differences in your inner states—your emotions, feelings, and moods—show up in your behavior? This question relates to the basic channels through which such nonverbal communication takes place. Research findings indicate that, in fact, information about our inner states is often revealed through five basic channels: *facial expressions, eye contact, body movements, posture,* and *touching.*

Unmasking the Face: Facial Expressions As Clues to Others' Emotions. More than two thousand years ago, the Roman orator Cicero stated: "The face is the image of the soul." By this he meant that human feelings and emotions are often reflected in the face and can be read there in specific expressions. Modern research suggests that Cicero—and many other observers of human behavior—were correct: it *is* possible to learn much about others' current moods and feelings from their facial expressions. In fact, it appears that six different basic emotions are represented clearly, and from a very early age, on the human face: anger, fear, happiness, sadness, surprise, and disgust (Izard, 1991; Rozin, Lowery, & Ebert, 1994). Additional findings suggest that another expression—contempt—may also be quite basic (e.g., Ekman & Heider, 1988, 1992). However, agreement on what specific facial expression represents this emotion is less consistent than that for the other six emotions just mentioned.

It's important to realize that these findings concerning a relatively small number of basic facial expressions in no way imply that human beings can show only a small number of facial expressions. On the contrary, emotions occur in many combinations (for example, joy tinged with sorrow, surprise combined with fear); and each of these reactions can vary greatly in strength. Thus, while there may be only a small number of basic themes in facial expression, the number of variations on these themes is immense (see Figure 2.2).

nonverbal communication • Communication between individuals that does not involve the content of spoken language, but relies instead on an unspoken language of facial expressions, eye contact, and body language.

Figure 2.2

Facial Expressions: The Range Is Immense. Although there is general agreement among researchers that only a small number of emotions are represented by distinct facial expressions, emotions can occur in many combinations, so people actually show an enormous number of different expressions.

Now for another important question: Are facial expressions universal? In other words, if you traveled to a remote part of the world and visited a group of people who had never before met an outsider, would their facial expressions in various situations resemble your own? Would they smile in reaction to events that made them happy, frown when exposed to conditions that made them angry, and so on? Further, would you be able to recognize these distinct expressions as readily as the ones shown by persons belonging to your own culture? Early research on this question seemed to suggest that facial expressions *are* universal in both respects (e.g., Ekman & Friesen, 1975). More recent findings, however, have called this conclusion into question (Russell, 1994). The results of these recent studies (e.g., Russell, 1994; Carroll & Russell, 1996) indicate that while facial expressions may indeed reveal much about others' emotions, our judgments in this respect are also affected by the context in which the facial expressions occur and various situational cues. For instance, if individuals view a photo of a face showing what would normally be judged as *fear* but also read a story suggesting that this person is actually showing *anger,* many describe the face as showing this emotion, not fear (see Figure 2.3; Carroll & Russell, 1996).

Figure 2.3

Interpreting Facial Expressions: The Role of Contextual Cues. If you saw only this facial expression, you would probably identify it as showing fear. However, suppose you also learned that this man showed this expression after seeing another person push in front of him in line. Now you might well interpret it as showing anger, or fear mixed with anger. This suggests that our interpretation of facial expressions can be strongly influenced by contextual information, and so may not be as universal in meaning as was once believed.

Findings such as these suggest that facial expressions may not be as universal in terms of providing clear signals about underlying emotions as was previously assumed. However, additional evidence (e.g., Rosenberg & Ekman, 1995) provides support for the view that when situational cues and facial expressions are *not* inconsistent, others' facial expressions do provide an accurate guide to their underlying emotions. Overall, then, it seems safest to conclude that while facial expressions are not totally universal around the world—cultural and contextual differences do exist with respect to their precise meaning—they generally need very little "translation" as compared to spoken languages.

Gazes and Stares: Eye Contact As a Nonverbal Cue. Have you ever had a conversation with someone wearing very dark or mirror-lensed glasses? If so, you realize that this can be an uncomfortable situation. Because you can't see the other person's eyes, you are uncertain about how she or he is reacting. Taking note of the importance of cues provided by others' eyes, ancient poets often described the eyes as "windows to the soul." In one important sense, they were correct: we do often learn much about others' feelings from their eyes. For example, we interpret a high level of gazing from another as a sign of liking or friendliness—"the look of love" (Kleinke, 1986). In contrast, if others avoid eye contact with us, we may conclude that they are unfriendly, don't like us, or are simply shy (Zimbardo, 1977).

While a high level of eye contact with others is usually interpreted as a sign of liking or positive feelings, there is one exception to this general rule. If another person gazes at us continuously and maintains such contact regardless of what we do, she or he can be said to be **staring**. A stare is often interpreted as a sign of anger or hostility—as in *cold stare*—and most people find this particular nonverbal cue disturbing (Ellsworth & Carlsmith, 1973). In fact, we may quickly terminate social interaction with someone who stares at us and may even leave the scene (Greenbaum & Rosenfield, 1978). This is one reason why experts on road rage—highly aggressive driving by motorists, sometimes followed by actual assaults—recommend that drivers avoid eye contact with people who are disobeying traffic laws and rules of the road (e.g., B. J. Bushman, personal communication, February 18, 1998). Apparently, such persons, who are already in a highly excitable state, interpret anything approaching a stare from another driver as an aggressive act and may react accordingly (see Figure 2.4).

Body Language: Gestures, Posture, and Movements. Try this simple demonstration for yourself:

First, remember some incident that made you angry—the angrier the better. Think about it for a minute.

Now try to remember another incident, one that made you feel sad—again, the sadder the better.

Compare your behavior in the two contexts. Did you change your posture or move your hands, arms, or legs as your thoughts shifted from the first event to the second? There is a good chance that you did, for our current moods or emotions are often reflected in the position, posture, and movement of our bodies. Together, such nonverbal behaviors are termed **body language,** and they too can provide us with useful information about others.

First, body language often reveals others' emotional states. Large numbers of movements—especially ones in which one part of the body does something to another part (touching, rubbing, scratching)—suggest emotional arousal. The greater the frequency of such behavior, the higher the level of arousal or nervousness.

staring • A form of eye contact in which one person continues to gaze steadily at another regardless of what the recipient does.

body language • Cues provided by the position, posture, and movement of others' bodies or body parts.

Figure 2.4
Staring and Road Rage.
If you encounter another driver who is showing signs of road rage—driving in a highly aggressive manner—*don't* stare at him or her to show your annoyance. If you do, you may cause the person to erupt in unpredictable and dangerous ways.

Larger patterns of movements, involving the whole body, can also be informative. Such phrases as "she adopted a *threatening posture*" and "he greeted her with *open arms*" suggest that different body orientations or postures indicate distinct emotional states. In fact, research by Aronoff, Woike, and Hyman (1992) confirms this possibility. These researchers first identified two groups of characters in classical ballet: ones who played a dangerous or threatening role (e.g., Macbeth, the Angel of Death, Lizzie Borden) and ones who played warm, sympathetic roles (Juliet, Romeo). Then they examined examples of dancing by these characters in actual ballets to see if they adopted different kinds of postures. Aronoff and his colleagues predicted that the dangerous, threatening characters would show more diagonal or angular postures, while the warm sympathetic characters would show more rounded postures; and results strongly confirmed this hypothesis. These and related findings indicate that large-scale body movements or postures can sometimes provide important information about others' emotions, and even about their apparent traits.

Further evidence for the conclusion that body posture and movements can be an important source of information about others is provided by research conducted by Lynn and Mynier (1993). These researchers arranged for waitpersons of both genders either to stand upright or to squat down next to customers when taking drink orders. Lynn and Mynier (1993) predicted that squatting down would be interpreted as a sign of friendliness, because in this position waitpersons would make more eye contact with customers and would be physically closer to them (Argyle, 1988). As a result, they expected servers to receive larger tips when they squatted down than when they did not. As you can see from Figure 2.5 on page 44, this is what happened. Regardless of servers' gender, they received larger tips when they bent down than when they did not. As shown in Figure 2.5, male servers received larger tips than female servers; but it is difficult to interpret this difference, because the males and females worked in different restaurants.

Finally, we should add that more specific information about others' feelings is often provided by gestures. Gestures fall into several categories, but perhaps

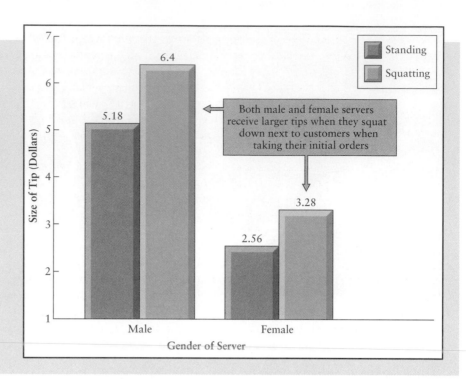

Figure 2.5

Body Position and Tipping. When male and female servers squatted down next to the customers when taking their drink orders, the servers received larger tips than when they remained standing.

(*Source:* Based on data from Lynn & Mynier, 1993.)

Both male and female servers receive larger tips when they squat down next to customers when taking their initial orders

the most important are *emblems*—body movements carrying specific meanings in a given culture. Do you recognize the gestures shown in Figure 2.6? In the United States and several other countries, these movements have clear and definite meanings. In other cultures, however, they may have no meaning, or even a different meaning. For this reason, it is wise to be careful about using gestures while traveling in cultures different from your own: you may offend the people around you without meaning to do so!

Touching: The Most Intimate Nonverbal Cue. Suppose that during a brief conversation with another person, she or he touched you briefly. How would you react? What information would this behavior convey? The answer to both question is, *it depends*. And what it depends upon is several factors relating to who

Figure 2.6

Gestures As a Nonverbal Cue. Do you recognize the gestures here? Can you tell what they mean? In the United States and other Western cultures, each of these gestures has a specific meaning. However, they may well have no meaning, or entirely different meanings, in other cultures.

does the touching (a friend or a stranger, a member of your own or the other gender); the nature of this physical contact (brief or prolonged, gentle or rough, what part of the body is touched); and the context in which the touching takes place (a business or social setting, a doctor's office). Depending on such factors, touch can suggest affection, sexual interest, dominance, caring, or even aggression. Despite such complexities, existing evidence indicates that *when touching is considered appropriate,* it often produces positive reactions in the person being touched (e.g., Alagna, Whitcher, & Fisher, 1979; Smith, Gier, & Willis, 1982). The potentially beneficial effects of touching are illustrated by yet another ingenious study performed in restaurants. The researchers (Crusco & Wetzel, 1984) arranged for waitresses working in two different restaurants to interact with customers in one of three different ways when giving them their change: the waitresses either refrained from touching customers in any manner, touched them briefly on the hand, or touched them for a somewhat longer period on the shoulder. The size of the tips left for the waitresses was, again, the dependent measure. Results indicated that both a brief touch on the hand (about 0.5 seconds) and a longer touch on the shoulder (1.0 to 1.5 seconds) significantly increased tipping over the no-touch control condition. So, consistent with other findings, being touched in an innocuous, nonthreatening way seemed to generate positive reactions among the persons being touched.

Needless to add, touching does not always produce such effects. If it is perceived as a status or power play, or if it is too prolonged or intimate, or if it occurs in a context where touching is *not* viewed as appropriate (e.g., a business setting), this form of nonverbal behavior may evoke powerful negative reactions on the part of the person being touched; it may even lead to charges of sexual harassment. So beware. Touching is a very powerful form of nonverbal communication, and should be reserved for persons we know well and for settings where this intimate form of behavior is considered appropriate.

Key Points

- *Social perception* involves the processes through which we seek to understand other persons. It plays a key role in social behavior and social thought.
- In order to understand others' emotional states, we often rely on *nonverbal communication*—an unspoken language of facial expressions, eye contact, and body movements and postures.
- While facial expressions may not be as universal as once believed, they do often provide useful information about others' emotional states. Useful information is also provided by eye contact, body language, and touching.

Facial Expressions and Social Thought: Why "Smile When You Say That, Partner" May Not Always Be Good Advice

When other people smile, we usually interpret this as a sign that they are happy; so it is not surprising that others' smiles often make *us* feel happy too. So far, so good. But what, in turn, are the effects of these positive feelings on our social thought—for instance, on our understanding of what a smiling person is saying? A growing body of evidence indicates that while positive emotions or feelings are certainly enjoyable, they may reduce our tendency to think carefully or systematically, unless we are specifically (and highly) motivated to do so (e.g., Bodenhausen, Kramer, & Susser, 1994; Mackie & Worth, 1989). Why do such effects occur? One explanation is provided by a theory known as the **cognitive tuning model** (Schwarz, 1990). This theory suggests that positive affective states, such as those induced by seeing another person smile, inform us that the current situation is safe and therefore doesn't require careful attention or processing of information. In contrast, negative affective states, such as those induced by seeing another person frown, signal us that the situation is potentially dangerous and that we had better pay careful attention to what's happening.

Applying this model to facial expressions leads to the following intriguing prediction: If another person smiles while presenting information to us (for example, while giving a speech), we may be less likely to think carefully and systematically about the content of the speech than if this person shows a neutral facial expression or frowns in anger. We'll return to these aspects of social thought in more detail in Chapter 3, where we discuss the differences between *heuristic processing*, a low-effort, quick-and-dirty kind of thinking that leads us to jump to conclusions (often wrong ones), and *systematic processing*, a higher-effort and more careful mode of thought. But here, we want to call your attention to the fact that facial expressions, an important form of nonverbal cue, not only provide information about others' feelings and influence our own feelings—they also influence the way we think (e.g., Krull & Dill, 1998).

Evidence for precisely such effects is provided by research conducted by Ottati, Terkildsen, and Hubbard (1997). In this study, the researchers had participants watch a videotape of a man described as a state senator. This man described his views on a number of important issues (e.g., AIDS, gun control, welfare, drugs, homelessness). Overall, he took a very conservative position, but his views did differ somewhat across specific topics. In three different experimental conditions, the speaker either smiled, showed a neutral face, or frowned in anger throughout the presentation. After watching the videotape, participants rated the speaker on a number of dimensions (e.g., personal warmth, decency, compassion, kindness, power hunger, fairness, prejudice, selfishness, arrogance); they also indicated how they felt while watching the tape, once again on several different dimensions (e.g., happy, interested, angry, proud, hopeful, fearful). Finally, they also completed an item designed to measure their motivation to clearly understand political messages (the extent to which they paid careful attention to such information).

The researchers predicted that when the speaker smiled, this would be a signal to participants that they did not need to pay careful attention to his remarks; thus, as compared to participants in the conditions in which he showed a neutral face or frowned a lot, they would be influenced by his overall position (his ideology) more than by his specific statements concerning each issue. (This would reflect a tendency to engage in heuristic processing instead of more effortful systematic processing; see Chapter 3 for more information.) However, Ottati and his colleagues also predicted that these effects would be stronger for persons who were *not* highly motivated to think carefully about political messages than for persons who *were* strongly motivated to think about such messages. Results offered strong support for these predictions. When participants reported that they were not strongly motivated to think carefully about political messages, the smiling candidate elicited more heuristic (ideology-based) processing than the candidate who showed neutral or angry facial expressions. When participants *were* strongly motivated to think carefully about such messages, however, these differences disappeared (see Figure 2.7).

These findings, and those of related studies (e.g., Krull & Dill, 1998), indicate that facial expressions do indeed do more than simply inform us about others' emotional states—they may also serve as cues about how much and what

cognitive tuning model • A theory suggesting that positive affective states, such as those induced by seeing another person smile, inform us that the current situation is safe and doesn't require careful attention or processing of information. In contrast, negative affective states, such as those induced by seeing another person frown, signal us that the situation is potentially dangerous and that careful processing is required.

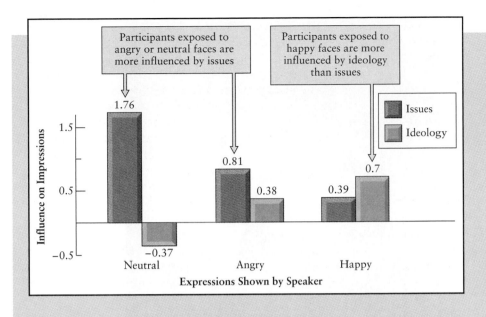

Figure 2.7
Facial Expressions and Social Cognition. When a speaker smiled during an interview, participants were more influenced by his overall position (ideology) than by his statements on each issue. This pattern was reversed when he showed a neutral expression or frowned in anger. These findings suggest that smiles serve as a cue that a situation does not require careful processing of information presented in it.

(*Source:* Based on data from Ottati, Terkildsen, & Hubbard, 1997.)

kind of social thought is required in a given situation. So, as you can see, there is much more to these nonverbal cues than you might at first expect. For information about the role of nonverbal cues in an important practical setting—courtrooms—please see the *Beyond the Headlines* section below.

Beyond the Headlines: As Social Psychologists See It
Body Language in the Courtroom

JUDGES TRY CURBING LAWYER'S BODY-LANGUAGE ANTICS

Albany Times Union, September 9, 1997. This summer, Thomas Pirtle, a Houston lawyer, engaged in some unspeakable acts during a big trial. The . . . lawyer headed a team suing Dow Chemical Co. in state court in Louisiana over allegedly defective silicon breast implants. During the

trial, he shook his head in disbelief, waved his arms disgustedly, and during crucial defense testimony looked directly at jurors and laughed. . . . State Judge Yada Magee then fined him and a partner $2,500 each, saying their actions amounted to misconduct under Louisiana law. . . .

What's going on here? Social psychologists would answer: An example of lawyers who are using nonverbal cues to sway juries. In fact, the actions by Mr. Pirtle seem mild when compared to those used by some other trial lawyers. For example, one famous attorney looks at his watch repeatedly to signal the jury that he finds cross-examinations being conducted by the opposing attorney boring. Another slips a paper clip onto his cigar to keep the ash from falling off, thus distracting the jury just as his opponent is trying to make a critical point.

Figure 2.8
Nonverbal Cues in the Courtroom. Many attorneys are aware of the powerful impact of nonverbal cues and try to use them to influence juries.

The fact that lawyers believe in the power of nonverbal cues to influence jurors' reactions is suggested by the growing number who hire consultants, including former actors, to train them in the use of eye contact, facial expressions, and gestures. As a result of such training, trial lawyers—long known for their flamboyant behavior in the courtroom—have recently become even more extreme in their displays of emotion (see Figure 2.8).

Not all judges or other legal experts believe that this is necessarily a bad thing. They believe that juries should be trusted to evaluate attorneys' behavior on their own. But a growing number of judges are ruling that attorneys cannot engage in behavior such as that shown by Mr. Pirtle, who laughs out loud, smirks, and snickers during trials, or by another lawyer who, in order to illustrate the pain and suffering of his client to a skeptical jury, spilled a large container of prescription painkillers on the floor. (The jury in that case got the message and found for the attorney's client.)

What would social psychologists say about such tactics? Since they know from their own research that nonverbal cues can exert powerful effects on people—and can even influence the extent to which people think carefully about information presented at the same time—many would probably share judges' concern about the use of nonverbal cues in the courtroom. Of course, many facial expressions and gestures are natural expressions of individuals' inner feelings, and eliminating these would be quite artificial—and probably virtually impossible. But when nonverbal cues are used in a cold and calculating way to tip the scales of justice, perhaps that is the time for judges to say "Enough is enough."

Key Points

- Facial expressions influence our affective states, and hence important aspects of social thought.

- The *cognitive tuning model* suggests that when others smile, we interpret this as a sign that we do not need to think carefully about what they are saying. When they frown, however, we sense that careful thought about their words *is* required.

- Lawyers often use nonverbal cues to influence juries. To minimize such effects, judges have sometimes imposed restrictions on the kind of nonverbal behavior lawyers can emit during trials.

ATTRIBUTION: UNDERSTANDING THE CAUSES OF OTHERS' BEHAVIOR

Accurate knowledge of others' current moods or feelings can be useful in many ways. Yet, where social perception is concerned, this knowledge is often only the first step. In addition, we usually want to know more—to understand others' lasting traits and to know the causes behind their behavior. Social psychologists believe that our interest in such questions stems in large measure from our basic desire to understand cause-and-effect relationships in the social world (Pittman, 1993; Van Overwalle, 1998). In other words, we don't simply want to know *how* others have acted; like the pet in Figure 2.9, we want to understand *why* they have done so, too. The process through which we seek such information is known as **attribution**. More formally, *attribution* refers to our efforts to understand the causes behind others' behavior and, on some occasions, the causes behind *our* behavior, too. Social psychologists have studied attribution

Figure 2.9

"Why?": A Basic Question in Social Perception. Like the dog shown in this cartoon, we often want to understand *why* other people behave as they do.

(*Source:* Universal Press Syndicate, 1990.)

attribution • The process through which we seek to identify the causes of others' behavior and so gain knowledge of their stable traits and dispositions.

for several decades, and their research has yielded many intriguing insights into this important process (e.g., Graham & Folkes, 1990; Heider, 1958; Read & Miller, 1998).

Theories of Attribution: Frameworks for Understanding How We Attempt to Make Sense of the Social World

Because attribution is complex, many theories have been proposed to explain its operation. Here, we will focus on two classic views that have been especially influential.

From Acts to Dispositions: Using Others' Behavior as a Guide to Their Lasting Traits. The first of these classic theories—Jones and Davis's (1965) theory of **correspondent inference**—asks how we use information about others' behavior as a basis for inferring that they possess various traits. In other words, the theory is concerned with how we decide, on the basis of others' overt actions, that they possess specific characteristics or dispositions that remain fairly stable over time.

At first glance, this might seem to be a simple task. Others' behavior provides us with a rich source on which to draw, so if we observe it carefully, we should be able to learn a lot about them. Up to a point, this is true. The task is complicated, however, by the following fact: Often, individuals act in certain ways not because doing so reflects their own preferences or traits but because external factors leave them little choice. For example, suppose you observe a woman rushing through an airport, pushing people out of the way in her haste. Does this mean that she is impatient and rude? Not necessarily; she may simply be responding to the fact that her plane is about to leave without her. This traveler may actually be quite shy and polite most of the time; her behavior now may be the exception, not the rule. Situations like this are very common, and in them using others' behavior as a guide to their lasting traits or motives can be very misleading.

How do we cope with such complications? According to Jones and Davis's theory (Jones & Davis, 1965; Jones & McGillis, 1976), we accomplish this task by focusing our attention on certain types of actions—those most likely to prove informative.

First, we consider only behavior that seems to have been freely chosen, while largely ignoring actions that were somehow forced on the person in question. Second, we pay careful attention to actions that involve what Jones and Davis term **noncommon effects**—effects that can be caused by one specific factor but not by others. (Don't confuse this word with *uncommon*, which simply means infrequent.) Why are actions that produce noncommon effects informative? Because they allow us to zero in on the causes of others' behavior. Perhaps a concrete example will help.

Imagine that one of your casual friends has just gotten engaged. Her future spouse is very handsome, has a great personality, is wildly in love with your friend, and is very rich. What can you learn about her from her decision to marry this man? Not much. There are so many good reasons that you can't choose among them. In contrast, imagine that your friend's fiancé is very handsome but that he treats her with indifference and is known to be extremely boring; also, he has no visible means of support and intends to live on your friend's salary. Does the fact that she is marrying him tell you anything about her personal characteristics? Definitely. You can probably conclude that she places more importance on physical attractiveness in a husband than on personality or wealth. As you can see from this example, we can usually learn more about

correspondent inference (theory of) • A theory describing how we use others' behavior as a basis for inferring their stable dispositions.

noncommon effects • Effects produced by a particular cause that could not be produced by any other apparent cause.

Figure 2.10
Behavior Low in Social Desirability: A Valuable Guide to Others' Traits. As shown here, the dean of my school often dresses informally. This is unusual behavior for a dean; so, according to Jones and Davis's theory of *correspondent inference,* it provides valuable information about the dean's traits.

others from actions on their part that show noncommon effects than from ones that do not.

Finally, Jones and Davis suggest that we also pay greater attention to actions by others that are low in *social desirability* than to actions that are high on this dimension. In other words, we learn more about others' traits from actions they perform that are somehow out of the ordinary than from actions that are very much like those performed by most other persons. For instance, the dean of my school almost never wears a tie; instead, he wears silk shirts with large, bright patterns (see Figure 2.10). Because this behavior is unusual for a college dean, it tells me much about our dean's personal traits: he is an independent free spirit who believes that people should be judged on their contributions rather than on their clothes. (Lucky us!)

In sum, according to the theory proposed by Jones and Davis, we are most likely to conclude that others' behavior reflects their stable traits (that is, we are likely to reach correspondent inferences about them) when that behavior (1) is freely chosen; (2) yields distinctive, noncommon effects; and (3) is low in social desirability.

Kelley's Theory of Causal Attributions: How We Answer the Question "Why?"
Consider the following events:

You receive a much lower grade on a term paper than you expect.

You leave several messages for a friend on her answering machine, but she never returns your calls.

You have applied for a job and feel that you are highly qualified for it, but you don't get it.

What question would arise your mind in each of these situations? The answer is clear: *Why?* You'd want to know *why* you received a lower grade on the paper than you expected, *why* your friend didn't return your calls, and *why* you didn't get the job. In many situations this is the central attributional task we face: we want to know why other people have acted as they have or why events have turned out in a specific way. Such knowledge is crucial, for only if we understand the causes behind others' actions or behind events that occur can we hope to make sense out of the social world—and perhaps do better in the future. Obviously, the number of specific causes behind others' behavior is very large. To make the task more manageable, therefore, we often begin with a preliminary question: Did others' behavior stem mainly from *internal* causes (their own traits, motives, intentions), mainly from *external* causes (some aspect of the social or physical world), or from a combination of the two? For example, you might wonder whether you received a lower grade than expected because you didn't spend enough time on the paper (an internal cause), because the professor was unfairly harsh in grading (an external cause), or perhaps because of both factors. How do we attempt to answer this question? A theory proposed by Kelley (Kelley, 1972; Kelley & Michela, 1980) provides important insights into this process.

According to Kelley, in our attempts to answer the question *why* about someone's behavior, we focus on information relating to three major sources of information. First, we consider **consensus**—the extent to which others react to some stimulus or event in the same manner as the person we are considering. The higher the proportion of other people who react in the same way, the higher the consensus. Second, we consider **consistency**—the extent to which the person in question reacts to the stimulus or event in the same way on other occasions; that is, over time. And third, we examine **distinctiveness**—the extent to which this person reacts in a different manner to other, different stimuli or events.

How do we use such information? According to Kelley's theory, we are most likely to attribute another's behavior to *internal* causes under conditions in which consensus and distinctiveness are low, but consistency is high. In contrast, we are most likely to attribute another's behavior to *external* causes when consensus, consistency, and distinctiveness are all high. Finally, we usually attribute another's behavior to a combination of internal and external factors when consensus is low, but consistency and distinctiveness are high. Perhaps a concrete example will help illustrate the very reasonable nature of these ideas.

Imagine that a student in one of your classes suddenly gets up, smiling, and says to the professor: "Professor _____, you are a wonderful human being, and it's a privilege to be in your class." Why does the student act this way? Because of internal causes or external causes? Is this student someone who reacts very favorably to all professors? Or is the student responding to some external cause—something the professor did or said? According to Kelley's theory, your decision (as an observer of this scene) will depend on information relating to the three factors mentioned above. First, assume that the following conditions prevail: (1) Many other students also stand up and heap praise on the professor (consensus is high); (2) you have seen this student praise the same professor on other occasions (consistency is high); and (3) you have not seen this student praise other professors (distinctiveness is high). Under these conditions—high consensus, consistency, and distinctiveness—you will probably attribute the student's behavior to external causes: this professor really *is* great.

Now, in contrast, assume these conditions exist: (1) No other students praise the professor (consensus is low); (2) you have seen this student praise the same professor on other occasions (consistency is high); and (3) you have seen this student praise many other professors, too (distinctiveness is low). In this case, Kelley's theory suggests that you will attribute the student's behavior to internal causes: this person loves all professors, no matter what they are like (see Figure 2.11).

The basic assumptions of Kelley's theory have been confirmed in a wide range of social situations, so the theory seems to provide important insights into

consensus • The extent to which other persons react to some stimulus or event in the same manner as the person under consideration.

consistency • The extent to which an individual responds to a given stimulus or situation in the same way on different occasions (i.e., across time).

distinctiveness • The extent to which an individual responds in a different manner to different stimuli or events.

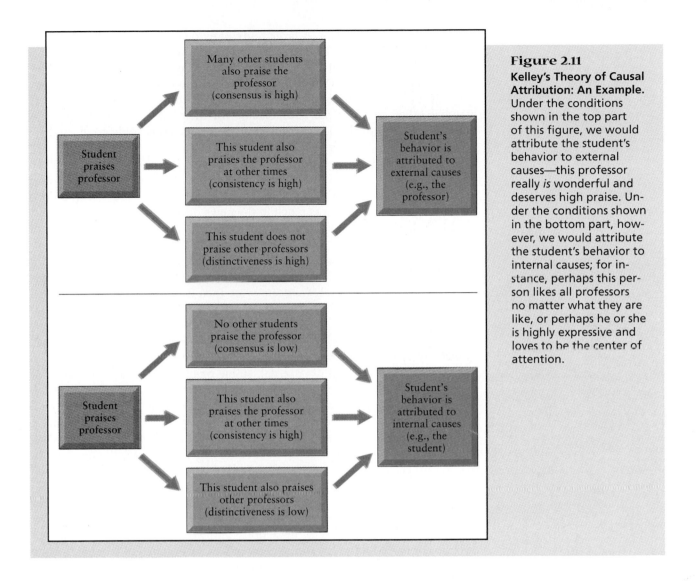

Figure 2.11
Kelley's Theory of Causal Attribution: An Example. Under the conditions shown in the top part of this figure, we would attribute the student's behavior to external causes—this professor really *is* wonderful and deserves high praise. Under the conditions shown in the bottom part, however, we would attribute the student's behavior to internal causes; for instance, perhaps this person likes all professors no matter what they are like, or perhaps he or she is highly expressive and loves to be the center of attention.

the nature of causal attributions. However, research on the theory also suggests the need for certain modifications or extensions, as described below.

Other Dimensions of Causal Attribution. While we are often very interested in knowing whether others' behavior stemmed mainly from internal or external causes, this is not the entire story. In addition, we are also concerned with two other questions: (1) Are the causal factors that influence someone's behavior likely to be *stable* over time or to change? And (2) are these factors *controllable*—can the individual change or influence them if she or he wishes to do so (Weiner, 1993, 1995)? These dimensions are independent of the internal–external dimension we have just considered. For instance, some internal causes of behavior, such as personality traits and temperament, tend to be quite stable over time (e.g., Miles & Carey, 1997). In contrast, other internal causes can and often do change greatly—for instance, motives, health, and fatigue. Similarly, some internal causes are controllable; individuals can, if they wish, learn to hold their tempers in check. Other internal causes, such as chronic illnesses or disabilities, are not. I (Robert Baron) am nearsighted, so no matter how hard I try, I can't see distant objects clearly without my glasses—this causal factor is not under my personal control. A large body of evidence indicates that in trying to understand the causes behind others' behavior, we do take note of all three of these dimensions—internal–external, stable–unstable, and controllable–uncontrollable (Weiner, 1985, 1995). Moreover, our thinking in this respect strongly influences our conclusions concerning important matters, such as whether others are *personally responsible* for their own actions. A very dramatic illustration of this fact is provided by an ingenious study conducted recently by Graham, Weiner, and Zucker (1997).

These researchers approached male and female passersby on a large urban college campus as well as in public places such as shopping malls, supermarkets, libraries, and parks. They asked these individuals a series of questions concerning an event that was much in the news during 1995: the alleged murder by O. J. Simpson of his wife and a male friend. (Simpson was acquitted of the murder in his criminal trial, but later lost a civil suit relating to the same alleged crimes.) Passersby were first asked to rate their views about O. J.'s guilt on a five-point scale ranging from "definitely yes" to "definitely no." People who felt O. J. was definitely innocent were then excluded from the study, because one of the major goals was to examine the role of attributions in recommended punishments.

Additional items on the questionnaire asked participants to list what they thought were the main causes of the murders and to rate the extent to which these causes were internal or external, stable or unstable, and controllable or uncontrollable. Participants also reported on the extent to which they felt O. J. was responsible for his actions (from "not responsible at all" to "entirely responsible") and on their degree of anger at and sympathy for O. J. Simpson. Finally, participants answered several questions relating to the punishment O. J. should receive—should it be designed to make him suffer, to rehabilitate him, or to deter others from performing similar violent acts? On the basis of attribution theory principles, the researchers predicted that to the extent participants believed that O. J. Simpson's behavior stemmed from controllable causes, they would experience high levels of anger and low levels of sympathy toward him; would hold him responsible for his actions; and would recommend punishment designed to make him suffer and to deter others, rather than to rehabilitate him (see Figure 2.12). Results strongly confirmed these predictions.

While the same general pattern of findings was obtained for all research participants, regardless of their race, some differences did emerge between whites and African Americans. For example, while both whites and African Americans listed O. J.'s extreme jealousy and his anger and rage as the most important causes of his behavior, African Americans rated his ex-wife's behavior (e.g., her affairs with other persons) as a significantly more important cause than did whites. Similarly, whites were more likely than African Americans to call for punishment that would cause O. J. to suffer, while African Americans were significantly more likely to recommend punishment designed to rehabilitate him. Overall, though, predictions derived from attribution theory were confirmed: to the extent that O. J.'s behavior was seen as stemming from factors under his control, he was held more responsible for the crimes, viewed less sympathetically by participants, and assigned harsher punishment.

These findings and those of many other studies (e.g., Schlenker et al., 1994) suggest that when trying to decide whether others should be held responsible for their actions, we do focus on more than just the locus of causality of such factors (whether they are internal or external in nature): we consider their stability and controllability, too. Thus, extending Kelley's theory to include these variables appears to be a very useful step.

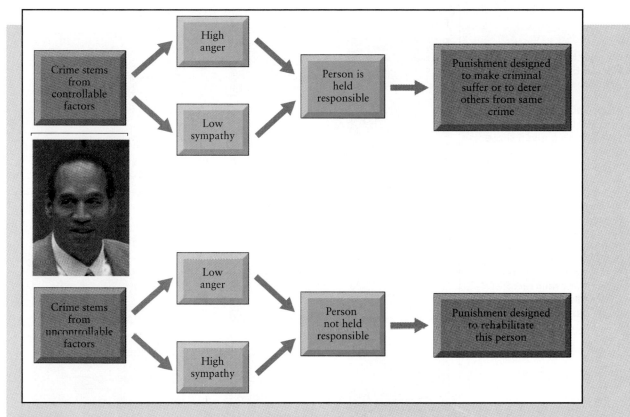

Figure 2.12

The Role of Attributions in Recommended Punishment. When individuals believe that a crime has stemmed from factors that could be controlled, they experience high levels of anger and low levels of sympathy for the criminal. They then hold the person responsible for the crime and recommend punishment designed to make this person suffer or to deter others from the same crime. In contrast, when they view the crime as stemming from *uncontrollable* factors, they report less anger and more sympathy toward the criminal, hold this person less responsible for the crime, and recommend punishment focused on rehabilitation.

(*Source:* Based on suggestions and findings by Graham, Weiner, & Zucker, 1997.)

Augmenting and Discounting: How We Handle Multiple Potential Causes. Suppose, as actually happened during 1997 and 1998, a woman accuses the president of the United States of sexual harassment—for example, of making unwanted sexual advances to her. Why has she done this? One possible cause is that she was very upset at the time and feels it is her duty to call this inappropriate (and illegal) behavior by the president to public attention. But now suppose that soon after she makes her claim, a reporter discovers that the woman had an affair with the president and was upset over being dumped by him. So another possible cause for her action is revenge: perhaps she wants to pay him back for what she views as mistreatment. After learning of this second potential cause, how do you view the first cause (her desire to do her duty and warn other women)? The chances are good that you will view it as a less likely or less important cause—that you will *discount* it as an explanation for her behavior, because now you know about another potential cause that may have led to her actions. Social psychologists refer to this tendency to downplay the importance

Figure 2.13
Augmenting and Discounting in Causal Attribution. According to the *discounting principle* (upper diagram), we attach less weight or importance to a given cause of some behavior when other potential causes of that behavior are also present. According to the *augmenting principle* (lower diagram), we attach greater weight to a potential cause of some behavior if the behavior occurs despite the presence of another factor that would tend to inhibit its occurrence.

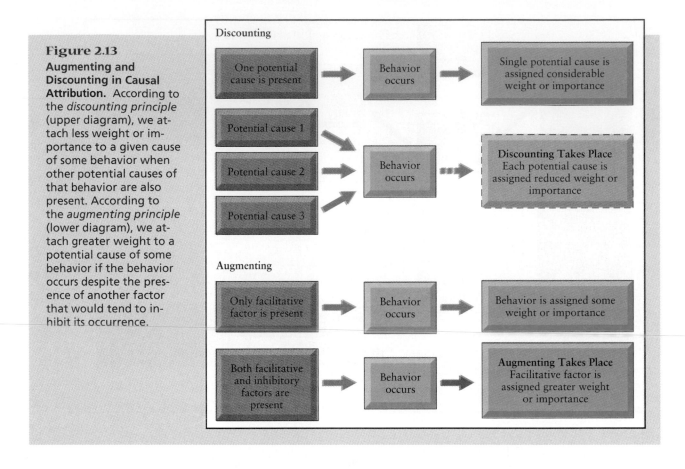

discounting principle •
The tendency to attach less importance to one potential cause of some behavior when other potential causes are also present.

augmenting principle •
The tendency to attach greater importance to a potential cause of behavior if the behavior occurs despite the presence of other, inhibitory causes.

of one potential cause of another person's behavior to the extent that other potential causes also exist as the **discounting principle** (or, sometimes, as the *subtraction* rule; see Figure 2.13), and many studies indicate that it can exert a strong impact upon our attributions (e.g., Gilbert & Malone, 1995; Morris & Larrick, 1995). While discounting seems to occur in many situations, however, very recent findings indicate that it is far from universal (McClure, 1998). Sometimes, when we learn about one cause first, this serves as an *anchor* for our later thinking, and so we don't discount it even though other potential causes (such as revenge, in the above example) are brought to our attention. Similarly, if a cause is judged to be necessary for a particular effect to occur, we may not discount it even if we learn about other potential causes (McClure, 1998). In many instances, however, two (or more) reasons may not necessarily be better than one reason from the point of view of understanding the causes of others' behavior; in fact, finding out about additional potential causes may make our task of figuring out *why* others behaved as they did harder, not easier.

Now, in contrast, imagine the same situation involving the president with one difference: The woman makes her claim of sexual harassment even though she strongly supported the president and worked vigorously for his election in the past. What will you conclude about her claim now? Probably that it is true, and that it is motivated by the woman's desire to warn the public about the president's behavior. This is so because she has made the claim despite the fact that another factor that might be expected to prevent her from doing so is present. This illustrates the **augmenting principle,** which states that when a factor that might facilitate a given behavior and a factor that might inhibit it are both present *and the behavior still occurs,* we assign added weight or importance to the facilitative factor. We do so because that factor has succeeded in producing the behavior even in the face of an important barrier (the inhibitory factor).

Key Points

- In order to obtain information about others' lasting traits, motives, and intentions, we often engage in *attribution*—efforts to understand *why* others have acted as they have.
- According to Jones and Davis's theory of *correspondent inference,* we attempt to infer others' traits from observing certain aspects of their behavior—especially behavior that is freely chosen, produces *noncommon effects,* and is low in social desirability.
- According to another theory, Kelley's theory of causal attribution, we are interested in the question of whether others' behavior stemmed from internal or external causes. To answer this question, we focus on information relating to consensus, consistency, and distinctiveness.
- When two or more potential causes of another person's behavior exist, we tend to downplay the importance of each—an effect known as the *discounting principle.* When a cause that facilitates a behavior and a cause that inhibits it both exist but the behavior still occurs, we assign added weight to the facilitative factor—the *augmenting principle.*

Attribution: Some Basic Sources of Error

Our discussion so far seems to imply that attribution is a highly rational process in which individuals seeking to identify the causes of others' behavior follow orderly cognitive steps. To a large extent, this is so. We should also note, however, that attribution is subject to several forms of error—tendencies that can lead us into serious errors concerning the causes of others' behavior. Several of these errors are described below.

The Correspondence Bias: Overestimating the Role of Dispositional Causes. Imagine that you witness the following scene. A man arrives at a meeting one hour late. On entering, he drops his notes on the floor. While he is trying to pick them up, his glasses fall off and break. Later, he spills coffee all over his tie. How would you explain these events? The chances are good that you would reach conclusions such as "This person is disorganized and clumsy." Are such attributions accurate? Perhaps; but it is also possible that the man was late because of unavoidable delays at the airport, dropped his notes because they were printed on slick paper, and spilled his coffee because the cup was too hot to hold. The fact that you would be less likely to consider such potential external causes illustrates what Jones (1979) labeled **correspondence bias**—the tendency to explain others' actions as stemming from (corresponding to) dispositions even in the presence of clear situational causes (e.g., Gilbert & Malone, 1995). This bias seems to be so general in scope that many social psychologists refer to it as the *fundamental attribution error.* In short, we tend to perceive others as acting as they do because they are "that kind of person," rather than because of the many external factors that may influence their behavior. We should add that while the fundamental attribution error does seem to be very widespread in occurrence, recent findings (e.g., Van Overwalle, 1997) indicate that the tendency to attribute others' actions to dispositional (internal) causes seems to be strongest in situations where both consensus and distinctiveness are low, as predicted by Kelley's theory.

correspondence bias (fundamental attribution error) • The tendency to explain others' actions as stemming from dispositions even in the presence of clear situational causes.

Social psychologists have conducted many studies in order to find out why the correspondence bias is so prevalent (e.g., Robins, Spranca, & Mendelsohn, 1996), but the issue is still somewhat in doubt. One possibility is that when we observe another person's behavior, we tend to focus on his or her actions; the context in which the person behaves, and hence potential situational causes of the behavior, often fade into the background. As a result, dispositional causes (internal causes) are more *salient*—easier to notice—than situational ones. In other words, from our perspective, the person we are observing is high in *perceptual salience* and is the focus of our attention, while situational factors that might also have influenced this person's behavior are less salient and so seem less important to us. Another explanation is that although we do notice such situational causes, we give them insufficient weight in our attributions. Still another explanation is that when we focus on others' behavior, we tend to begin by assuming that their actions reflect their underlying characteristics. Then we attempt to correct for any possible effects of the external world—the current situation—by taking these into account. This correction, however, is often insufficient—we don't make enough allowance for the impact of external factors. We don't give enough weight to the possibility of delays at the airport or slippery paper, when reaching our conclusions (Gilbert & Malone, 1995).

Is this tendency to emphasize dispositional causes truly universal? Or is it, like many other aspects of social behavior and thought, influenced by cultural factors? Research findings indicate that in fact culture does play a role. Specifically, the correspondence bias (fundamental attribution error) appears to be more common or stronger in cultures that emphasize individual freedom—*individualistic* cultures such as those in Western Europe or the United States and Canada—than in *collectivistic* cultures that emphasize group membership, conformity, and interdependence (e.g., Triandis, 1990). For example, in one study Miller (1984) asked people living in India and people living in the United States to think of behaviors on the part of their friends and also to explain why those behaviors occurred. Results indicated that American participants were more likely to use dispositional explanations than were Indians. In other words, they were more likely to say that their friends acted as they did because they were "that kind of person."

In a more recent study, Morris and Pang (1994) carefully analyzed newspaper articles about two mass murders in the United States—one committed by a Chinese graduate student and one committed by a Caucasian postal worker. The articles were published in English in the *New York Times* and in Chinese in the *World Journal*, a Chinese-language newspaper published in the United States. Results were clear: The articles in English attributed both murderers' actions to dispositional factors to a greater extent than did the articles written in Chinese.

Results confirming the fact that the correspondence bias is stronger in Western cultures than in Asian cultures has also been reported by Choi and Nisbett (1998). These researchers asked students in the United States and Korea to read essays written by another person. The essays were either in favor of or against capital punishment, and participants were led to believe either that the person who wrote the essay did so of his or her own free choice, or did so because he or she was told to write an essay favoring one point of view or the other. When asked questions about the writer's actual attitude toward capital punishment, U.S. students showed the correspondence bias quite strongly: they acted as if the essay reflected this person's true attitudes even if the writer had been *told* to write the essay they read. In contrast, Korean students showed this bias to a much lesser degree; indeed, in one condition, when it was made clear that the essay-writer had simply repeated arguments given to him by the researchers, they showed no correspondence bias at all! Clearly, then, cultural factors play a role even in this very basic aspect of attribution.

The Actor–Observer Effect: You Fell; I Was Pushed. Another and closely related type of attributional error involves our tendency to attribute our own behavior to situational (external) causes, but that of others to dispositional (internal) ones. Thus, when we see another person trip and fall, we tend to attribute this event to his or her clumsiness. If *we* trip, however, we are more likely to attribute this event to situational causes, such as ice on the sidewalk. This "tilt" in our attributions is known as the **actor–observer effect** (Jones & Nisbett, 1971) and has been observed in many different contexts.

Recent findings concerning this type of error suggest that differences between actors' and observers' attributions also occur with respect to the kinds of behaviors we try to explain (Malle & Knobe, 1997). For other persons, we tend to focus on behaviors that are intentional and observable. We realize that we can learn more from actions that a person intended to perform and that we can observe than from ones the person did not intend to perform or which we can't readily observe. With respect to our own behavior, however, we tend to focus, instead, on understanding the causes behind unintentional behaviors. When we find that we have done or said something without intending to do so, we wonder *why* this occurred, and we actively search for the causes of this behavior. So actors and observers differ in this respect, too.

Why does the actor–observer effect occur? In part, because we are quite aware of the many external factors affecting our own actions but are less aware of such factors when we turn our attention to the actions of other persons. Thus, we tend to perceive our own behavior as arising largely from situational causes, but that of others as deriving mainly from their traits or dispositions.

The Self-Serving Bias: I'm Good; You're Lucky. Suppose that you write a term paper—and when you get it back, you find the following comment on the first page: "An outstanding paper—one of the best I've seen in years. A+." To what will you attribute this success? Probably you will explain it in terms of internal causes: your high level of talent, the effort you invested in writing the paper, and so on.

Now, in contrast, imagine that when you get the paper back, *these* comments are written on it: "Horrible paper—one of the worst I've seen in years. D–." How will you interpret this outcome? The chances are good that you will be tempted to focus mainly on external (situational) factors—the difficulty of the task, your professor's unfairly harsh grading standards, the fact that you didn't have enough time to do a good job, and so on.

This tendency to attribute our own positive outcomes to internal causes but negative ones to external factors is known as the **self-serving bias,** and it appears to be both general in scope and powerful in its effects (Brown & Rogers, 1991; Miller & Ross, 1975).

Why does this tilt in our attributions occur? Several possibilities have been suggested, but most of these fall into two categories: cognitive and motivational explanations. The cognitive model suggests that the self-serving bias stems mainly from certain tendencies in the way we process social information (see Chapter 3; Ross, 1977). Specifically, it suggests that we attribute positive outcomes to internal causes but negative ones to external causes because we *expect* to succeed and because we have a tendency to attribute expected outcomes to internal causes more than to external causes. In contrast, the motivational explanation suggests that the self-serving bias stems from our need to protect and enhance our self-esteem or from the related desire to look good to others

actor–observer effect • The tendency to attribute our own behavior mainly to situational causes but the behavior of others mainly to internal (dispositional) causes.

self-serving bias • The tendency to attribute one's own positive outcomes to internal causes (e.g., one's own traits or characteristics) but negative outcomes or events to external causes (e.g., chance, task difficulty).

(Greenberg, Pyszczynsik, & Solomon, 1983). While both cognitive and motivational factors may well play a role in this kind of attributional error, research evidence seems to offer more support for the motivational view (e.g., Brown & Rogers, 1991).

Whatever the origins of the self-serving bias, it can be the cause of much interpersonal friction. It often leads persons who work with others on a joint task to perceive that *they,* not their partners, have made the major contributions. I see this effect in my own classes every semester when students rate their own contributions and those of the other members of their team in a term project that I require. The result? Most students take lots of credit for themselves when the project has gone well, but tend to blame (and downrate) their partners if it has not.

Before concluding this discussion, we should note that despite all the errors described here, plus others we'll consider later in this chapter (e.g., Swann & Gill, 1997), growing evidence suggests that social perception *can* be quite accurate: we do, in many cases, reach accurate conclusions about others' traits and motives from observing their behavior—or even, it seems, from their physical appearance (Zebrowitz & Collins, 1997)! We'll examine some of the evidence pointing to this latter conclusion as part of our discussion of the process of impression formation later in this chapter.

See the *Ideas to Take with You* feature on page 75 for some tips on how to avoid various attributional errors. Does the self-serving bias occur to the same extent all over the world? Or is it stronger in some cultures than in others? For information on this intriguing issue, please see the *Social Diversity* section below.

Social Diversity: A Critical Analysis
Cultural Differences in the Self-Serving Bias

At first glance, it might seem that the tendency to take credit for good outcomes while blaming bad ones on other persons or on external events beyond one's control would be a universal human tendency. After all, by showing this self-serving bias, we can maximize our pleasure at positive events and perhaps minimize the psychological pain of negative ones. Yet even a moment's reflection suggests that these tendencies may be tempered by cultural values. In Western societies, which emphasize individual accomplishments, football players leap into the air in joy when they score a goal, and movie stars who win an Oscar make little attempt to hide their glee at receiving this honor: they are all too willing to take credit for these positive outcomes. In other cultures, however, such as those in Asia, greater emphasis is placed on group outcomes and group harmony, and displays of joy at personal wins may be viewed as violating strong cultural beliefs about the importance of modesty. Do such differences influence the prevalence or strength of the self-serving bias? The results of several studies suggest that they do (e.g., Oettingen, 1995; Oettingen & Seligman, 1990). Perhaps the clearest illustration of cultural differences with respect to this particular tilt in attributions,

however, was provided in a study conducted by Lee and Seligman (1997).

These researchers asked three groups of participants—Americans of European descent, Americans of Chinese descent, and Chinese residents of the People's Republic of China—to complete a questionnaire relating to their attributions about positive and negative events. For each item (e.g., looking for a job unsuccessfully; going out on a date that turned out well) participants in the study indicated the extent to which the event stemmed from internal or external causes. In addition, they rated the extent to which the causes of these events were stable or unstable as well as specific or general in nature.

One basic prediction was that Americans of European descent would be more optimistic overall in their attributions than both Chinese Americans and mainland Chinese, and this was confirmed. Compared to the other two groups, Americans of European descent were more likely to attribute positive events to internal, stable, and global factors, but negative events to external, unstable, and specific factors.

A second prediction, and the one directly related to this discussion, was that Americans of European descent

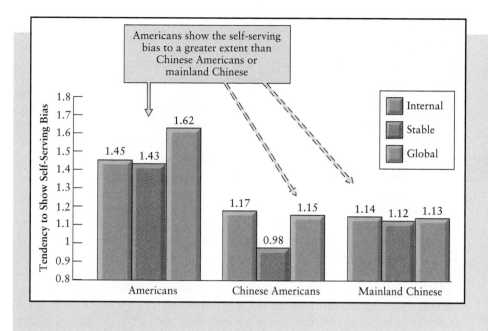

Figure 2.14
Cultural Differences in Susceptibility to the Self-Serving Bias. As shown here, Americans of European descent showed a stronger tendency to attribute good events to stable, global, and internal causes than did either Chinese Americans or mainland Chinese. These findings indicate that cultural factors can strongly influence the nature of attributions individuals make concerning the causes of events.

(*Source:* Based on data from Lee & Seligman, 1997.)

would show a stronger self-serving bias than either Chinese Americans or Chinese. In other words, they would show a greater tendency than the other two groups to attribute successes to themselves and failure to others and external events. As shown in Figure 2.14, this is precisely what happened. Interestingly, Chinese Americans and mainland Chinese did not differ in this respect: both groups showed smaller susceptibility to the self-serving bias than did white Americans. Apparently, certain values central to Chinese culture—modesty, self-effacement, group orientation—combine to temper our tendency to pat ourselves on the back for good

outcomes while blaming bad ones on factors outside our control.

The results obtained by Lee and Seligman (1997) and many other researchers (Lee, 1995) underscore a point we will make repeatedly throughout this text: While social behavior and social thought are highly similar throughout the world, cultural differences *do* matter, and can lead to important differences in the behavior of people from different societies. In short, a scientific field of social psychology is certainly possible, but cultural factors must be included in it if it is to provide a complete and accurate account of the topics it seeks to study.

Key Points

- Attribution is subject to many potential sources of error. One of the most important of these is the *correspondence bias*—the tendency to explain others' actions as stemming from internal dispositions even in the presence of situational causes. This tendency seems to be stronger in Western than in Asian cultures.

- Two other attributional errors are the *actor–observer effect*—the tendency to attribute our own behavior to external (situational) causes but that of others to internal causes—and the *self-serving bias*—the tendency to attribute our own positive outcomes to internal causes but negative ones to external causes.

- The strength of the self-serving bias differs across cultures, being stronger in Western societies such as the United States than in Asian cultures such as that of China.

Applications of Attribution Theory: Insights and Interventions

Kurt Lewin, one of the founders of modern social psychology, remarked that "There's nothing as practical as a good theory." By this he meant that once we obtain scientific understanding of some aspect of social behavior or social thought, we can, potentially, put this knowledge to practical use. Where attribution theory is concerned, this has definitely been the case. As basic knowledge about attribution has grown, so too has the range of practical problems to which such knowledge has been applied (Graham & Folkes, 1990). Here, we'll examine two important, and especially timely, applications of attribution theory.

Attribution and Depression. Depression is the most common psychological disorder. In fact, it has been estimated that almost half of all human beings experience this problem at some time during their lives (e.g., Blazer et al., 1994). Although many factors play a role in depression, one that has received increasing attention is what might be termed a *self-defeating* pattern of attributions. In contrast to most people, who show the self-serving bias described above, depressed individuals tend to adopt an opposite pattern. They attribute *negative* outcomes to lasting, internal causes such as their own traits or lack of ability, but attribute *positive* outcomes to temporary, external causes such as good luck or special favors from others (see Figure 2.15). As a result, such persons perceive that they have little or no control over what happens to them—they are mere chips in the winds of unpredictable fate. Little wonder that they become depressed and tend to give up on life.

Fortunately, several forms of therapy that focus on changing such attributions have been developed, and these appear to be quite successful (e.g., Bruder et al., 1997; Robinson, Berman, & Neimeyer, 1990). These new forms of therapy focus on getting depressed persons to change their attributions—to take personal credit for successful outcomes, to stop blaming themselves for negative outcomes (especially ones that can't be avoided), and to view at least some

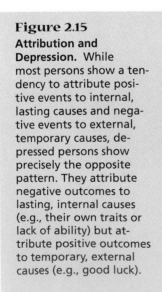

Figure 2.15
Attribution and Depression. While most persons show a tendency to attribute positive events to internal, lasting causes and negative events to external, temporary causes, depressed persons show precisely the opposite pattern. They attribute negative outcomes to lasting, internal causes (e.g., their own traits or lack of ability) but attribute positive outcomes to temporary, external causes (e.g., good luck).

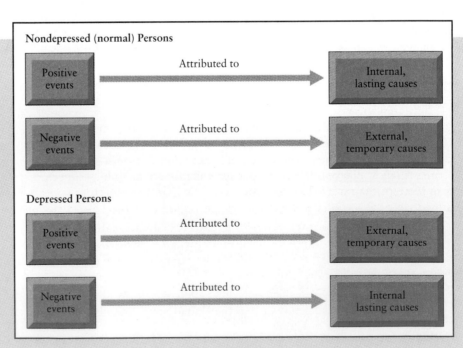

failures as the result of external factors beyond their control. These new forms of therapy do not explore repressed urges, inner conflicts, or traumatic events during childhood, but they *do* seem to help. Attribution theory provides the basis for these new forms of treatment, so it has certainly proved very useful in this respect.

Attribution and Rape: Blaming Innocent Victims. It has been estimated that in the United States a rape—forced sexual intercourse—occurs every eleven minutes (Baron & Richardson, 1994). Further, in a national survey approximately 15 percent of female college students reported that they had been raped—in most cases, by persons they knew (Koss et al., 1988). Clearly, these are frightening statistics. Perhaps even more unsettling, however, is the strong tendency of many persons to hold the victims of rape responsible for this crime (Fischer, 1986; Shotland & Goodstein, 1983). "She must have led him on." "What was she doing in a bar or on the street at that hour of the night?" "She was asking for trouble!" These are the kind of comments people sometimes make when they read or hear reports of vicious sexual assaults. From the perspective of attribution theory, in short, blame is often attributed to victims rather than to the perpetrator. Males are more likely to make such attributions than females (Cowan & Curtis, 1994); but women, too, often show some tendency to attribute responsibility for rape to its victims.

What accounts for this unsettling tendency? One possibility involves what has been termed *belief in a just world*—our desire to assume that the world is basically a fair place where good people experience good outcomes and bad people suffer (Lerner, 1980). According to this reasoning, if a woman is sexually assaulted, she "must" have done something to deserve it; thinking the opposite—that she is a completely blameless victim—violates our belief in a just world.

Indirect support for this view is provided by the findings of a study by Bell, Kuriloff, and Lottes (1994). These researchers asked male and female college students to read one of four descriptions of a rape. In two case descriptions, the woman was attacked by a stranger. In two others, the woman was raped by a date. After reading one of these accounts, participants were asked to rate the extent to which the victim was to blame for the crime. Results indicated that both males and females blamed the victim to a greater extent when she knew the rapist (someone she dated) than when this person was a stranger. In addition, while males attributed greater blame to the victim than females, both genders seemed to hold her responsible, to some degree, for the assault.

These findings and those of many other studies (e.g., Cowan & Curtis, 1994) have important implications with respect to rape prevention. First, they suggest that the victims of date rape—an alarmingly common event (Koss et al., 1988)—are especially likely to be blamed by other persons. Perhaps this is one reason why so many women who are assaulted by dates are reluctant to report the crime (Koss & Harvey, 1991). Second, the fact that men tend to blame rape victims to a greater extent than women is consistent with research findings indicating that men—especially those who engage in sexual violence—often misinterpret communications from females. Specifically, they mistrust women's statements about sexual interest (Malamuth & Brown, 1994); as a result, they don't take it seriously when a woman says no. To the extent that such misperceptions on the part of males contribute to date rape, it seems possible that the incidence of this odious crime can be reduced through programs designed to improve communication between males and females, especially with respect to sexual matters. The development of such programs is currently under way, and we can only hope that they will be effective in reducing the incidence of date rape and all other forms of rape as well.

Key Points

- Attribution theory has been applied to many practical problems, often with great success.
- Depressed persons often show a pattern of attributions opposite to that of the self-serving bias: they attribute positive events to external causes and negative ones to internal causes. Therapy designed to change this pattern has proved highly effective.
- The victims of rape are often held partly responsible for this crime—it is assumed that they somehow "asked for trouble." Such tendencies seem to stem partly from our strong desire to believe that the world is just and that "good" people don't suffer undeserved harm.

IMPRESSION FORMATION AND IMPRESSION MANAGEMENT: HOW WE COMBINE—AND USE—SOCIAL INFORMATION

First impressions, it is widely believed, are very important. Most of us assume that the initial impressions we make on others will shape the course of our future relations with them in crucial ways. Further, we believe that such impressions may be quite resistant to change once they are formed. It is for these reasons that most people prepare carefully for first dates, job interviews, and other situations in which they will meet others for the first time (see Figure 2.16). Are these assumptions about first impressions accurate? The answer provided by decades of research is a solid *yes*. First impressions *do* seem to exert a lasting impact on both social thought and social behavior (e.g., Sherman & Klein, 1994; Swann & Gill, 1997; Wyer et al., 1994).

But what, exactly, *are* first impressions? How are they formed? What steps can we take to make sure that we make good first impressions on others? And finally, how accurate are first impressions—and social perception generally? These are among the questions we'll now consider. Before turning to modern research on impression formation and impression management, however, we'll examine the origins of such research in what is without a doubt one of the *Cornerstones* of social psychology.

Figure 2.16
Trying to Make a Good First Impression. As suggested by this cartoon, most people try to make a good impression on others when meeting them for the first time—but these efforts do not always succeed!
(*Source:* NEA, 1987.)

Cornerstones of Social Psychology
Asch's Research on Central and Peripheral Traits

As we have already seen, some aspects of social perception, such as attribution, require lots of hard mental work: it's not always easy to draw inferences about others' motives or traits from their behavior. In contrast, forming first impressions seems to be relatively effortless. As Solomon Asch (1946) put it in a classic paper on this topic: "We look at a person and immediately a certain impression of his character forms itself in us. A glance, a few spoken words are sufficient to tell us a story about a highly complex matter . . ." (1946, p. 258). How do we manage this feat? How, in short, do we form unified impressions of others in the quick and seemingly effortless way that we often do? This is the question Asch set out to study.

At the time Asch conducted his research, social psychologists were heavily influenced by the work of *Gestalt psychologists,* specialists in the field of perception. A basic principle of Gestalt psychology was this: "The whole is often greater than the sum of its parts." This means that what we perceive is often more than the sum of individual sensations. To illustrate this point for yourself, simply look at any painting (except a very modern one!). What you see is *not* individual splotches of paint on the canvas; rather, you perceive an integrated whole—a portrait, a landscape, a bowl of fruit, whatever the artist intended. In other words, Gestalt psychologists suggested that each part of the world around us is interpreted, and understood, only in terms of its relationships to other parts or other stimuli.

Asch applied these ideas to understanding impression formation, suggesting that we do *not* form impressions simply by adding together all of the traits we observe in other persons. Rather, we perceive these traits *in relation to one another* so that the traits cease to exist individually and become, instead, part of an integrated, dynamic whole. How could these ideas be tested? Asch came up with an ingenious answer. He gave individuals lists of traits supposedly possessed by a stranger, then asked them to indicate their impressions of this person by putting check marks next to traits (on a much longer list) that they felt fit their overall impression of the stranger.

In one study, for example, participants read one of the following two lists:

intelligent—skillful—industrious—warm—determined—practical—cautious

intelligent—skillful—industrious—cold—determined—practical—cautious

As you can see, the lists differ only with respect to two words: *warm* and *cold.* Thus, if people form impressions merely by adding together individual traits, the impressions formed by persons exposed to these two lists shouldn't differ very much. However, this was not the case. Persons who read the list containing *warm* were much more likely to view the stranger as generous, happy, good-natured, sociable, popular, and altruistic than were people who read the list containing *cold.* The words *warm* and *cold,* Asch concluded, described *central traits*—ones that strongly shaped overall impressions of the stranger and colored the other adjectives in the lists. Asch obtained additional support for this view by substituting the words *polite* and *blunt* for *warm* and *cold.* When he did this, the two lists yielded highly similar impressions of the stranger. So it appeared that *polite* and *blunt* were *not* central traits that colored the entire impressions of the stranger.

In further studies Asch varied not the content but the *order* of the words on each list. For example, one group read the following list:

intelligent—industrious—impulsive—critical—stubborn—envious

Another group read:

envious—stubborn—critical—impulsive—industrious—intelligent

Here, the only difference was in the order of the words on the two lists. Yet, again, there were large differences in the impressions formed by participants. For example, while 32 percent of those who read the first list described the stranger as *happy,* only 5 percent of those who read the second list did so. Similarly, while 52 percent of those who read the first list described the person as humorous, only 21 percent of those who read the second list used this adjective.

On the basis of many studies such as these, Asch concluded that forming impressions of others involves more than simply adding together individual traits. As he put it: "There is an attempt to form an impression of the *entire* person. . . . As soon as two or more traits are understood to belong to one person they cease to exist as isolated traits, and come into immediate . . . interaction. . . . The subject perceives not this *and* that quality, but the two entering into a particular relation . . ." (1946, p. 284). While research on impression formation has become far more sophisticated since Asch's early work, both the methods he developed and many of his basic ideas about impression formation have stood the test of time. Clearly, then, his research is still worthy of careful attention and definitely qualifies as an important cornerstone of our field.

Impression Formation: The Modern Cognitive Approach

Creative as it was, Asch's research was only the beginning where the study of **impression formation**—the process through which we form impressions of others—is concerned. Social psychologists have investigated this topic from several different perspectives. Initially research focused on the question of how we combine so much diverse information about others into unified impressions. One answer, suggested by early studies, was as follows: We combine this information into a *weighted average,* in which each piece of information about another person is weighted in terms of its relative importance (Anderson, 1981). Research conducted from this perspective then focused on identifying the factors that influence this relative weighting. Among the most important factors identified were these: (1) Source of the input—information from sources we trust or admire is weighted more heavily than information from sources we distrust (Rosenbaum & Levin, 1969); (2) whether the information is positive or negative in nature—we tend to weight negative information about others more heavily than positive information (Mellers, Richards, & Birnbaum, 1992); (3) the extent to which the information describes behavior or traits that are unusual or extreme—the more unusual, the greater the weight placed on information; and finally, (4) the sequence of input—as Asch found, information received first is weighted more heavily than information received later (this is known as a *primacy effect*).

While this research certainly added to our knowledge of impression formation, recent investigations of first impressions have adopted a very different approach. Drawing on our growing knowledge of *social cognition*—the ways in which we interpret, analyze, remember, and use information about the social world (see Chapter 3)—recent research on impression formation has adopted a cognitive approach (e.g., Ruscher & Hammer, 1994; Wyer et al., 1994). This approach has provided many new insights into the nature of this important process. For example, it now seems clear that impressions of others involve two major components: concrete examples of behaviors they have performed that are consistent with a given trait—*exemplars* of this trait; and mental summaries that are abstracted from repeated observations of others' behavior—*abstractions,* as they are usually termed (e.g., Klein, Loftus, & Plog, 1992; Smith & Zarate, 1992). Some models of impression formation stress the role of behavioral exemplars. These models suggest that when we make judgments about

impression formation • The process through which we form impressions of others.

others, we recall examples of their behavior and base our judgments—and our impressions—on these. For example, we recall that during our first conversation with a new acquaintance, she smiled repeatedly, made flattering remarks about other people, and rushed to help someone who dropped a stack of papers on the floor. All these actions are exemplars of the trait of kindness, so we include this trait in our first impression of her.

In contrast, other models stress the role of abstractions. Such views suggest that when we make judgments about others, we simply bring our previously formed abstractions to mind and then use these as the basis for our impressions and our decisions. We recall that we have previously judged a person to be kind or unkind, friendly or hostile, optimistic or pessimistic, and then combine these traits into an impression of this individual.

A growing body of evidence suggests that both exemplars and mental abstractions play a role in impression formation (e.g., Budesheim & Bonnelle, 1998; Klein et al., 1992; Klein & Loftus, 1993). In fact, it appears that the nature of impressions may shift as we gain increasing experience with others. At first, our impression of someone we have just met consists largely of exemplars (concrete examples of behaviors they have performed). Later, as our experience with this person increases, our impression comes to consist mainly of mental abstractions derived from many observations of the person's behavior (Sherman & Klein, 1994; see Figure 2.17). In addition, while abstractions are generally used as the basis for causal judgments about others' behavior, behavioral exemplars are used if they are easily accessible and if individuals are highly motivated to engage in effortful processing (e.g., Budesheim & Bonnelle, 1998.)

In sum, the modern view of impression formation emphasizes the cognitive basis of our mental pictures of other persons. While we seem to form impressions of others in a rapid and seemingly effortless manner, recent research suggests that in fact, these impressions emerge out of the operation of many cognitive processes relating to the storage, recall, and integration of social information. In short, there appears to be a lot more going on beneath the surface than we might at first suspect.

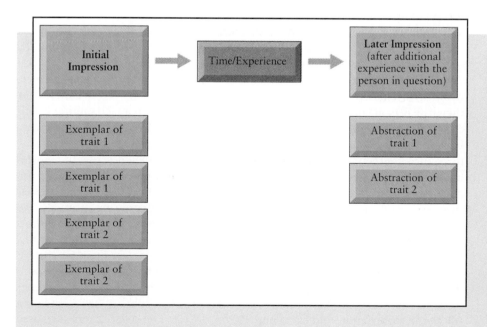

Figure 2.17

Impressions of Others: How They Develop. One model of impression formation suggests that initially our impressions of others consist mainly of examples of behaviors they show that are indicative of specific traits. After we have more experience with another person, however, our impressions shift toward consisting mainly of abstractions— mental summaries of the person's behavior on many occasions.

(*Source:* Based on suggestions by Sherman & Klein, 1994.)

Key Points

- Most people are concerned with making good first impressions on others, because they believe that these impressions will exert lasting effects.
- Research on *impression formation*—the process through which we form impressions of others—suggests that first impressions are indeed important. Asch's classic research on impression formation also indicates that our impressions of others involve more than simple summaries of their traits.
- Modern research, conducted from a cognitive perspective, has confirmed and extended this view, suggesting that impressions of others emerge out of the operation of many cognitive processes and consist of both examples of behavior relating to specific traits (exemplars) and mental abstractions based on observations of many instances of behavior.

Impression Management: The Fine Art of Looking Good

The desire to make a favorable impression on others is a strong one, so most of us do our best to look good to others when we meet them for the first time. Social psychologists use the term **impression management** (or *self-presentation*) to describe these efforts to make a good impression on others, and the results of research on such efforts suggest that they are worthwhile: persons who perform impression management successfully do often gain important advantages in many situations (e.g., Sharp & Getz, 1996; Wayne & Liden, 1995). What tactics do individuals use to create favorable impressions on others? Which work best? These are the issues we'll consider next.

Tactics of Impression Management and Their Relative Success. While individuals use many different techniques for boosting their image, most of these fall into two major categories: *self-enhancement,* or efforts to increase one's own appeal to others, and *other-enhancement,* or efforts to make the target person feel good in various ways.

With respect to self-enhancement, specific strategies include efforts to boost one's physical appearance through style of dress, personal grooming, and the use of various props (e.g., eyeglasses, which have been found to encourage impressions of intelligence; Terry & Krantz, 1993). Additional tactics of self-enhancement involve describing oneself in positive terms, explaining, for instance, how they (the person engaging in impression management) overcame daunting obstacles or rose to meet a challenge (Stevens and Kristof, 1995). Recent findings, (e.g., Rowatt, Cunningham, & Druen, 1998) indicate that many persons use this tactic to increase their appeal to potential dating partners; they describe themselves in very favorable terms (more favorable than they really deserve!) in order to impress persons they want to date. In short, they bend the truth to enhance their own appeal. A variation on this basic tactic involves expressing attitudes and preferences that are currently popular or in vogue (e.g., Sharp & Getz, 1996). At the present time, for instance, expressing knowledge of and appreciation for fine cigars would gain individuals points in at least some circles (see Figure 2.18).

Turning to *other-enhancement*, individuals use many different tactics to induce positive moods and reactions in others. A large body of research findings suggests that such reactions, in turn, play an important role in generating liking for the person responsible for them (Byrne, 1992). The most commonly used tactic of other-enhancement is *flattery*—making statements that praise the target person, his or her traits or accomplishments, or the organizations with which

---

impression management (self-presentation) • Efforts by individuals to produce favorable first impressions on others.

Figure 2.18
Self-Enhancement: A Basic Part of Impression Management. In order to make a good first impression on others, individuals often engage in self-enhancement—tactics designed to increase their appeal others. Such tactics include boosting their appearance through personal grooming and certain styles of dress, using various props, and expressing views that show how with-it they are. Smoking expensive cigars seems to accomplish several of these goals at once, at least among some groups.

the target person is associated (Kilduff & Day, 1994). Such tactics are often highly successful, provided they are not overdone. Additional tactics of other-enhancement involve expressing agreement with target persons' views, showing a high degree of interest in them as people, doing small favors for them, asking for their advice and feedback in some manner (Morrison & Bies, 1991), or expressing liking for them nonverbally (e.g., through high levels of eye contact, nodding in agreement, and smiling; Wayne & Ferris, 1990).

That individuals often employ such tactics is obvious: you can probably recall many instances in which you either used or were the target of such strategies. A key question, however, is this: Does impression management work? Do these tactics succeed in generating positive feelings and reactions on the part of the persons toward whom they are directed? The answer provided by a growing body of literature is clear: *Yes,* provided they are used with skill and care. For instance, consider a study by Wayne and Liden (1995).

These researchers arranged for persons recently hired for staff positions at two large universities to complete questionnaires in which they indicated how frequently they had used various impression management tactics during their first six weeks on the job. At the same time, the supervisors of these employees completed questionnaires in which they rated their liking for and degree of similarity to these newly hired subordinates. Six months later, supervisors rated the performance of the new employees. Results indicated that impression management did indeed pay off for this group of persons. The more the new employees engaged in self-enhancing tactics, the more their supervisors liked them. Further, the greater the extent to which the employees engaged in other-enhancing tactics, the more their supervisors viewed them as similar to themselves. Most important, increased liking and increased feelings of similarity translated into higher performance ratings: the more supervisors liked their subordinates and felt similar to them, the higher they rated their performance. These findings, and those of many related studies (e.g., Paulhus, Bruce, & Trapnell, 1995; Wayne & Kacmar, 1991), indicate that impression management tactics often do succeed in enhancing the appeal of persons who use them effectively.

We should hasten to add, however, that the use of these tactics involves potential pitfalls. If impression management is overused, or used ineffectively, it can backfire and produce negative rather than positive reactions from others. For instance, in ingenious recent research, Vonk (1998) found strong evidence for what he terms the "slime effect"—a tendency to form very negative impressions of persons who "lick upward but kick downward"; that is, persons in a work setting who play up to their superiors but treat subordinates with disdain and contempt. Specifically, Vonk (1998) asked students at a university in the Netherlands to read descriptions of an individual who showed one of several patterns of behavior: (1) *slimy behavior*—likable actions toward superiors (e.g., getting coffee for them) but dislikable actions toward subordinates (e.g., refusing to help them); (2) *nonslimy behavior*—dislikable behavior toward superiors but likable behavior toward subordinates; (3) *mixed behavior*—a mixed pattern of likable and dislikable behaviors toward both superiors and subordinates; (4) *negative behaviors*—only dislikable behaviors toward everyone; or (5) *positive behaviors*—only likable behaviors toward everyone. After reading these descriptions, participants rated this person in terms of how slimy he was and how likable he was. As you can see from Figure 2.19, results offered clear evidence for the dangers of too much impression management: the stranger was rated most negatively (least likable and most slimy) when he engaged in slimy behavior. Indeed, he was rated as slightly less likable in the slimy condition than in the negative condition, when he engaged in uniformly dislikable actions. The moral of these findings is clear: While tactics of impression management often succeed, this is not always the case; sometimes they can boomerang, adversely affecting reactions to the persons who use them.

Impression Management: Is It Always a Conscious Process? Before concluding this discussion, we should address one additional point: Are favorable first im-

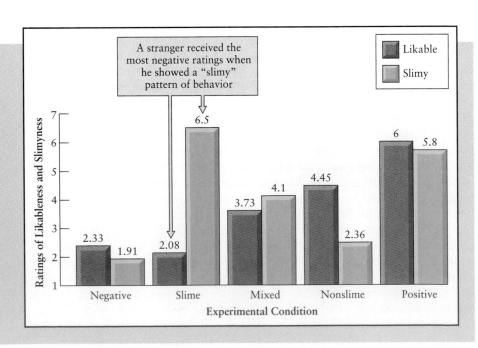

Figure 2.19
The "Slime Effect": When Impression Management Fails. An individual who showed a pattern of "licking upward but kicking downward" (directing likable behaviors toward superiors but dislikable behaviors toward subordinates) was perceived in very negative terms by research participants. In fact, they viewed him as even more negative than someone who showed only dislikable behaviors.

(*Source:* Based on data from Vonk, 1998.)

pressions always the result of conscious efforts at impression management? In other words, if you meet someone for the first time and find that you have formed a favorable first impression of this person, is this necessarily the result of deliberate attempts on his or her part to induce such liking through the tactics described above? As we saw earlier in this chapter, identifying others' motives or intentions is a tricky business; so this is a difficult question to answer. However, it is our view that existing evidence points to the following conclusion: Many of the factors that influence our impressions of others are *not* easily "managed" or controlled—so we can, and often do, form impressions of others quite independent of their efforts to look good (e.g., Berry, 1991; DePaulo, 1992). For example, certain aspects of individuals' appearance that can't readily be changed have been found to influence first impressions. "Baby-faced" persons—individuals with large eyes, full lips, small nose, high thin eyebrows, and a small chin—are perceived as being warmer and less dominant than those with more mature features (e.g., Kramer et al., 1995; Zebrowitz et al., 1993). Similarly, persons with high-pitched, childlike voices are perceived as warmer and less dominant than those with deeper and more mature voices (e.g., Berry, 1990). Such characteristics strongly influence our impressions of others, but can't readily be altered by them.

Further evidence pointing to the conclusion that impressions are influenced by factors individuals can't readily control, and of which they may not even be aware, has been provided by Berry and her colleagues (Berry et al., 1997). They found that the impressions individuals make on others are often strongly affected by such factors as facial appearance (e.g., the degree to which they are "baby-faced" or "mature-faced") and subtle aspects of their speech (e.g., their tendency to use negations such as "no" or "not" or a tendency to use present-tense verbs rather than past-tense verbs). These findings suggest that our impressions of people are not always the result of conscious efforts on their part to look good. Rather, they may represent direct reactions to their spontaneous behavior and personal characteristics.

Key Points

- In order to make a good impression on others, individuals often engage in *impression management*.
- Many techniques are used for this purpose, but most fall under two major headings: *self-enhancement*—efforts to boost one's appeal to others, and *other-enhancement*—efforts to induce positive moods or reactions in others. These tactics must be used with care, however, or they can backfire.
- While individuals use tactics of impression management consciously, impressions are also influenced by factors that are not under conscious control, such as aspects of physical appearance and even certain subtle aspects of speech.

The Accuracy of Social Perception: Evidence That It's Higher Than You Might Guess

Conflicting nonverbal cues, attributional errors, tactics of impression management—having read our discussions of these topics, you may now be feeling less than confident about your ability to form accurate perceptions of others; and in fact we are far from perfect at this task, even when we are confident that we are performing it accurately (Swann & Gill, 1997). But take heart: a growing body of evidence gathered by social psychologists suggests that there is actually considerable room for optimism on this score. Despite the complexity of this task and the many potential pitfalls that can lead us into error, we *do* seem capable of forming accurate perceptions and impressions of others (e.g., Berry, 1991; Gifford, 1994; Kenney et al., 1994). Moreover, this is not true only when we have had many opportunities to interact with them—for instance, teachers with their students (Madon et al., 1998). We can also form accurate perceptions of others from a very brief meeting with them; if we spend a few minutes speaking to them, see videotapes of their behavior, or even if we see photos of their faces. On the basis of such fragmentary information, we seem capable of forming accurate impressions of where other persons stand on several basic dimensions of personality—dimensions such as submissive–dominant, agreeable–quarrelsome, and responsible–irresponsible (e.g., Kenney et al., 1994). How do we know that these first impressions are accurate? Because they correlate quite highly with ratings of the same persons provided by people who know them very well—family members, spouses, best friends (e.g., Ambady & Rosenthal, 1992; Zebrowitz & Collins, 1997)—and also with the individuals' overt behavior (e.g., Moskowitz, 1990).

Such findings, of course, raise an intriguing question: How do we accomplish this task? How do we form accurate perceptions of other persons, even on the basis of a very brief meeting or by merely seeing their photos? Two social psychologists who have studied this question in detail, Zebrowitz and Collins (1997), provide an insightful answer. They suggest that there are several ways in which observable traits (e.g., physical characteristics) may actually come to be linked to psychological qualities.

One possible basis for such links is that certain physical characteristics and certain psychological traits are both produced by the same genetic or biological factors. For example, a recently discovered medical condition known as Bloom's syndrome (Saltus, 1995) involves increased susceptibility to cancer, several distinctive physical qualities (large, sun-sensitive markings on the face, short stature), *and* certain personality traits: high levels of optimism coupled with childlike trust in others and a pleasant, charming manner. In this case and in others, Zebrowitz and Collins (1997) suggest, genetic factors may influence both outward appearance *and* psychological traits.

Another way in which physical characteristics and psychological traits can be linked is that the psychological traits cause the physical characteristics to develop—something known as the *Dorian Gray* effect, after the famous novel by Oscar Wilde. In this novel, a man continues to look young and handsome despite the passing years because all his evil actions are reflected in the appearance of his portrait, rather than in his face. In real life, Zebrowitz and Collins (1997) suggest, our actions or traits may well come to be reflected in our faces, so we look like the kind of persons we really are (Zebrowitz, Collins, & Dutta, 1998). A third possibility is that physical characteristics cause psychological traits to develop. For example, highly attractive persons are treated in certain ways by other persons (e.g., they are invited to many social gatherings and are eagerly sought after in many contexts). As a result, they come to have more confidence, poise, and charm than less attractive persons. In sum, there appear to be several different mechanisms through which outward appearance can become linked to psychological traits. And to the extent that such links exist or develop, we can form accurate impressions of others even from brief first meetings: what we see on the outside *is* evidence of what goes on inside!

Going further, Zebrowitz and Collins (1997) also suggest that our perceptions of others may also be accurate because over time, these perceptions exert a self-fulfilling effect: people gradually come to possess the traits others *expect* them to have. For instance, the results of many studies indicate that people with a "baby face" not only look somewhat childlike, they also show traits associated with children. They are less dominant and warmer than those with more mature faces (e.g., Zebrowitz, Montepare, & Lee, 1993). Similarly, people whose facial features suggest certain emotions to others—anger or friendliness—may be treated in ways that cause them to fulfill these perceptions. For instance, people with low, dark, thick eyebrows are perceived as angrier and more dominant than persons with high, light, thin eyebrows and may thus be treated as potentially more dangerous by other persons. The result? They really do become more forceful or dominant. In sum, Zebrowitz and Collins (1997) suggest that we are often accurate in our perceptions of other persons because (1) several mechanisms may produce actual links between the way people look and their psychological qualities, and (2) the way people look leads us to *expect* them to have certain traits, and our expectations in turn cause them to actually develop these traits (see Figure 2.20). Whatever the precise mechanisms

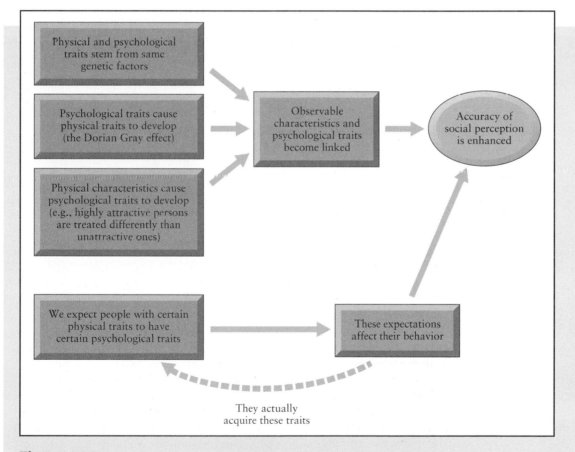

Figure 2.20
Why Social Perception Is Often Accurate. Despite many potential sources of error, our perceptions of other persons are often quite accurate. This seems to be the case for two major reasons: (1) Several mechanisms may operate to create actual links between physical appearance and psychological traits (upper diagram); and (2) our expectations exert a self-fulfilling effect—over time, other people gradually come to possess the traits we *expect* them to have (lower diagram).

(*Source:* Based on suggestions by Zebrowitz & Collins, 1997.)

involved, however, one fact seems clear: We are often quite successful in forming accurate perceptions of others. So in this respect the actress Lauren Bacall
was correct when she remarked (1988): "I think your whole life shows in your
face and you should be proud of that."

Key Points

- Growing evidence suggests that our social perceptions are actually
  quite accurate: we can form accurate perceptions of others from brief
  meetings with them or even from merely seeing their photos.

- This may be so because several mechanisms lead to actual links between the way people look (their physical characteristics) and their
  psychological traits.

- In addition, our social perceptions may exert a self-fulfilling effect,
  causing people to behave in ways that confirm our expectations.

Connections: Integrating Social Psychology

In this chapter, you read about . . .	*In other chapters, you will find related discussions of . . .*
basic channels of nonverbal communication	the role of nonverbal cues in interpersonal attraction (Chapter 7), persuasion (Chapter 4), prejudice (Chapter 6), and charismatic leadership (Chapter 12)
theories of attribution	the role of attribution in persuasion (Chapter 4), social iden-tity and self-perception (Chapter 5), prejudice (Chapter 6), long-term relationships (Chapter 8), prosocial behavior (Chapter 10), and aggression (Chapter 11)
first impressions and impression management	the role of first impressions in interpersonal attraction (Chapter 7); the role of impression management in job interviews (Chapter 13)

Thinking about Connections

1. As we'll point out in Chapters 4 (Attitudes) and 9 (Social Influence), influence is an important fact of social life: each day, we attempt to change others' attitudes or behavior and they attempt to change ours. Having read about attribution in this chapter, do you think that influence attempts that conceal their true goal will be more successful than ones that do not? If so, why? If not, why?

2. In Chapter 11 (Aggression), we'll see that some persons are involved in much more than their fair share of aggressive encounters. Such per-sons, it appears, are lacking in basic social skills, such as the ability to accurately read nonverbal cues. On the basis of the discussion of nonverbal cues in this chapter, can you explain how this lack

could contribute to these persons' problems with respect to aggression?

3. Suppose you were preparing for an impor-tant job interview (see Chapter 13). On the basis of information presented in this chapter, what steps could you take to improve your chances of actually getting the job?

4. Suppose you compared happy couples with ones that were unhappy and likely to break up. Do you think that the members of these different types of couples would differ in their attributions concerning their partners' behavior? For instance, would the happy couples attribute their partners' behavior to more positive causes than the un-happy couples?

Ideas to Take with You
Minimizing the Impact of Attributional Errors

Attribution is subject to many errors, and these can prove quite costly both to you and to the people with whom you interact. Thus, it's well worth the effort to avoid such pitfalls. Here are our suggestions for recognizing—and minimizing—several important attributional errors.

The Correspondence Bias: The fundamental attribution error.

We have a strong tendency to attribute others' behavior to internal (dispositional) causes even when strong external (situational) factors that might have influenced their behavior are present. To reduce this error, always try to put yourself in the shoes of the person whose behavior you are trying to explain. In other words, try to see the world through their eyes. If you do, you will often realize that from their perspective, there are many external factors that played a role in their behavior.

The Actor–Observer Effect: "I behave as I do because of situational causes; you behave as *you* do because you are that kind of person."

Consistent with the fundamental attribution error, we have a strong tendency to attribute our own behavior to external causes, but that of others to internal causes. This can lead us to false generalizations about other people and the traits they possess. To minimize this error, try to imagine yourself in the other person's place and ask yourself, "Why would *I* have acted in that way?" If you do, you'll quickly realize that external factors might have influenced your behavior. Similarly, ask yourself, "Did I behave that way because doing so reflected traits or motives of which I'm not very aware?" This may help you to appreciate the internal causes of your own behavior.

The Self-Serving Bias: "I'm good; you're lucky."

Perhaps the strongest attributional error we make is that of attributing our own positive outcomes to internal causes such as our own abilities or effort but our negative outcomes to external factors such as luck or forces beyond our control. This can lead us to overestimate our own contributions to group projects, thus producing unnecessary friction with others. It can also reduce the chances that we will learn something valuable from negative outcomes—for instance, how we might do better the next time. You can help minimize this error simply by being aware of it; once you know it exists, you may realize that not all your positive outcomes stem from internal causes, and that you may have played a role in producing negative ones. In addition, try to remember that other people are subject to the same bias; they, too, instinctively want to take credit for positive outcomes but to shift the blame for negative ones to external causes—such as you!

SUMMARY AND REVIEW OF KEY POINTS

Nonverbal Communication: The Unspoken Language

- *Social perception* involves the processes through which we seek to understand other persons. It plays a key role in social behavior and social thought.

- In order to understand others' emotional states, we often rely on *nonverbal communication*—an unspoken language of facial expressions, eye contact, and body movements and postures.

- While facial expressions may not be as universal as once believed, they do often provide useful information about others' emotional states. Useful information is also provided by eye contact, body language, and touching.

- Facial expressions influence our affective states, and hence important aspects of social thought.

- The *cognitive tuning model* suggests that when others smile, we interpret this as a sign that we do not need to think carefully about what they are saying. When they frown, however, we sense that careful thought about their words *is* required.

- Attorneys often use nonverbal cues to influence juries. To minimize such effects, judges have sometimes imposed restrictions on the kind of nonverbal behavior attorneys can emit during trials.

Attribution: Understanding the Causes of Others' Behavior

- In order to obtain information about others' lasting traits, motives, and intentions, we often engage in *attribution*—efforts to understand *why* others have acted as they have.

- According to Jones and Davis's theory of *correspondent inference,* we attempt to infer others' traits from observing certain aspects of their behavior—especially behavior that is freely chosen, produces *noncommon effects,* and is low in social desirability.

- According to another theory, Kelley's theory of causal attribution, we are interested in the question of whether others' behavior stemmed from internal or external causes. To answer this question, we focus on information relating to consensus, consistency, and distinctiveness.

- When two or more potential causes of another person's behavior exist, we tend to downplay the importance of each—an effect known as the *discounting principle.* When a cause that facilitates a behavior and a cause that inhibits it both exist but the behavior still occurs, we assign added weight to the facilitative factor—the *augmenting principle.*

- Attribution is subject to many potential sources of error. One of the most important of these is the *correspondence bias*—the tendency to explain others' actions as stemming from internal dispositions even in the presence of situational causes. This tendency seems to be stronger in Western than in Asian cultures.

- Two other attributional errors are the *actor–observer effect*—the tendency to attribute our own behavior to external (situational) causes but that of others to internal causes—and the *self-serving bias*—the tendency to attribute our own positive outcomes to internal causes but negative ones to external causes.

- The strength of the self-serving bias differs across cultures, being stronger in Western societies such as the United States than in Asian cultures such as that of China.

- Attribution theory has been applied to many practical problems, often with great success.

- Depressed persons often show a pattern of attributions opposite to that of the self-serving bias: they attribute positive events to external causes and negative ones to internal causes. Therapy designed to change this pattern has proved highly effective.

- The victims of rape are often held partly responsible for this crime—it is assumed that they somehow "asked for trouble." Such tendencies seem to stem partly from our strong desire to believe that the world is just and that "good" people don't suffer undeserved harm.

Impression Formation and Impression Management: How We Combine— and Use—Social Information

- Most people are concerned with making good first impressions on others, because they believe that these impressions will exert lasting effects.

- Research on *impression formation*—the process through which we form impressions of others—suggests that first impressions are indeed important. Asch's classic research on impression formation also indicated that our impressions of others involve more than simple summaries of their traits.

- Modern research, conducted from a cognitive perspective, has confirmed and extended this view, suggesting that impressions of others emerge out of the operation of many cognitive processes and consists of both examples of behavior relating to specific traits (exemplars) and mental abstractions based on observations of many instances of behavior.

- In order to make a good impression on others, individuals often engage in *impression management.*

- Many techniques are used for this purpose, but most fall under two major headings: *self-enhancement*—efforts to boost one's appeal to others, and *other-enhancement*—efforts to induce positive moods or reactions in others. These tactics must be used with care, however, or they can backfire.

- While individuals use tactics of impression management consciously, impressions are also influenced by factors that are not under conscious control, such as aspects of physical appearance and even certain subtle aspects of speech.

- Growing evidence suggests that our social perceptions are actually fairly reliable: we can form quite accurate perceptions of others from brief meetings with them or even from merely seeing their photos.

- This may be so because several mechanisms lead to actual links between the way people look (their physical characteristics) and their psychological traits.

- In addition, our social perceptions may exert a self-fulfilling effect, causing people to behave in ways that confirm our expectations.

KEY TERMS

actor–observer effect (p. 59)

attribution (p. 49)

augmenting principle (p. 56)

body language (p. 42)

cognitive tuning model (p. 46)

consensus (p. 52)

consistency (p. 52)

correspondence bias (fundamental attribution error) (p. 57)

correspondent inference (theory of) (p. 50)

discounting principle (p. 56)

distinctiveness (p. 52)

impression formation (p. 66)

impression management (self-presentation) (p. 68)

noncommon effects (p. 50)

nonverbal communication (p. 40)

self-serving bias (p. 59)

social perception (p. 38)

staring (p. 42)

FOR MORE INFORMATION

Kenny, D. A. (1994). *Interpersonal perception: A social relations analysis.* New York: Guilford.

This well-written and relatively brief book provides an excellent overview of what social psychologists have discovered about many different aspects of interpersonal perception. The book focuses on the key questions of how we see other people, how we see ourselves, and how we think we are seen by others. All in all, a very thoughtful and useful volume.

Malandro, L. A., Barker, L., & Barker, D. A. (1994). *Nonverbal communication* (3rd ed). New York: Random House.

A basic and very readable text that examines all aspects of nonverbal communication. Body movements and gestures, facial expression, eye contact, touching, smell, and voice characteristics are among the topics considered.

Zebrowitz, L. A. (1997). *Reading faces.* Boulder, CO: Westview Press.

A well-known researcher provides an overview of the influence of facial features and expressions on social perception. The discussions of the ways in which physical appearance can actually be linked to psychological traits are especially revealing.

3 Social Cognition: Thinking about the Social World

Four Human Figures. © José Ortega/Stock Illustration Source

Chapter Outline

Schemas: Mental Frameworks for Organizing—and Using—
Social Information
    Types of Schemas: Persons, Roles, and Events
    The Impact of Schemas on Social Cognition: Attention,
        Encoding, Retrieval
    CORNERSTONES OF SOCIAL PSYCHOLOGY: Evidence for the
        Self-Confirming Nature of Schemas: When and Why
        Beliefs Shape Reality

Heuristics: Mental Shortcuts in Social Cognition
    Representativeness: Judging by Resemblance
    Availability: "If I Can Think of It, It Must Be Important"

Potential Sources of Error in Social Cognition: Why Total Rationality Is
Scarcer Than You Think
    Rational versus Intuitive Processing: Going with Our Gut-Level
        Feelings Even When We Know Better
    BEYOND THE HEADLINES: AS SOCIAL PSYCHOLOGISTS SEE IT: Do Safety
        Devices Save Lives? Don't Bet on It!
    Dealing with Inconsistent Information: Paying Attention to What
        Doesn't Fit
    The Planning Fallacy: Why We Often Think We Can Do More,
        Sooner, Than We Really Can
    The Potential Costs of Thinking Too Much: Why, Sometimes, Our
        Tendency to Do As Little Cognitive Work As Possible May
        Be Justified
    Counterfactual Thinking: The Effects of Considering "What Might
        Have Been"
    Magical Thinking: Would You Eat a Chocolate Shaped Like a Spider?
    Thought Suppression: Why Efforts to Avoid Thinking Certain
        Thoughts Sometimes Backfire
    Social Cognition: A Word of Optimism

Affect and Cognition: How Feelings Shape Thought and Thought
Shapes Feelings
    Connections between Affect and Cognition: Some Intriguing Effects
    The Affect Infusion Model: How Affect Influences Cognition
    SOCIAL DIVERSITY: A CRITICAL ANALYSIS: Culture and the Appraisal
        of Emotions
    CONNECTIONS: Integrating Social Psychology
    IDEAS TO TAKE WITH YOU: Common Errors in Social Cognition

Summary and Review of Key Points
Key Terms
For More Information

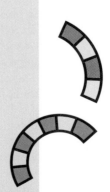

For several years I (Robert Baron) served as chair of my department. The job was a tough one, but it had its ups as well as its downs—for instance, through my efforts the department obtained a new research laboratory, and that pleased me very much. Looking back, the aspect of the job I disliked most was the yearly performance reviews I was required to conduct with all faculty members. Each spring I sat down with every member of the department to discuss their performance during the previous year. On the basis of these discussions, I formulated recommendations for each person's raise—recommendations I then discussed with the dean of the college.

Most of the meetings were friendly; I got along quite well with virtually everyone in the department. Yet I dreaded these discussions anyway. Why? Mainly for this reason: As a social psychologist I knew full well that no matter how hard I tried, my efforts to evaluate my colleagues as fairly as possible might still be subject to potential errors. Could I remember everything that had happened during the past year that was relevant to evaluating each person's teaching, research, and service? Probably not. Could I totally eliminate the potential effects of my personal reactions to each faculty member (my liking or disliking for them), or even the possible effects of my current mood at the time of each meeting, from my evaluations? Perhaps—but again, I knew from the findings of my own field (and even my own research) that doing so is extremely difficult. In short, I worried a lot about the possibility that try as I might, my evaluations could still be influenced by factors unrelated to each person's performance—sources of bias I could not totally eliminate.

As you'll soon see from the contents of this chapter, my concerns were well founded: research on **social cognition**—how we interpret, analyze, remember, and use information about the social world—suggests that we are far from perfect in our ability to think clearly about other persons and reach accurate decisions or judgments about them. On the contrary, our social thought is often subject to tilts or biases stemming from limitations of our own cognitive abilities (we simply can't process more than a limited amount of information at a given time), motives we have (for instance, our desire to reach certain decisions or conclusions about others), plus many other factors (see Figure 3.1). This does not mean that we generally do a poor job of making sense of the social world— far from it. We usually do amazingly well, given the complexity of the social world and the huge amount of information provided by the actions, words, and even appearance of others. But we do often make errors and jump to false conclusions, so it is important to recognize these potential pitfalls too.

Social cognition is a very important area of research in social psychology; in fact, as we noted in Chapter 1, it has become a guiding framework for *all* research in the field. To acquaint you with some of the truly fascinating aspects of social thought uncovered by social psychologists, we'll focus on the following topics. First, we'll examine a basic component of social thought—*schemas*. These are mental structures or frameworks that allow us to organize large amounts of information in an efficient manner. Once formed, however, schemas exert strong effects on social thought—effects that are not always beneficial from the point of view of accuracy. Second, we'll turn to *heuristics*: shortcuts and strategies we use in our efforts to make sense out of the social world. A basic finding of research on social cognition is that in general we try to accomplish this task with the least amount of effort possible—in part because we often find ourselves having to deal with more information than we can readily handle (e.g., Wyer & Srull, in press). Mental shortcuts and strategies allow us to cope with this state of affairs—known as *information overload*—in an efficient manner. Thus, such shortcuts often succeed; but only, as we'll soon see, at some potential cost to accuracy.

social cognition • The manner in which we interpret, analyze, remember, and use information about the social world.

Figure 3.1

Making Social Judgments: Harder Than It Seems. Research on *social cognition* suggests that we are far from perfect in our ability to make accurate social judgments.
(*Source:* Universal Press Syndicate, 1991.)

Third, we'll examine several specific tendencies or "tilts" in social thought—tendencies that can lead us to false conclusions and other kinds of errors in our efforts to understand the social world. Many of these exist, so here we'll focus on several that appear to exert strong effects on social thought; for example, our tendency to assume that we can accomplish more in a given period of time than we actually can—the *planning fallacy*—and our tendency to imagine "what might have been" in a given situation and the effects such *counterfactual thinking* can then have on our judgments, decisions, and emotions. Finally, we'll consider the complex interplay between *affect*—our current feelings or moods—and various aspects of social cognition. This relationship is indeed a two-way street: feelings influence cognition and cognition, in turn, influences affect (e.g., Forgas, 1995a).

Please note that we'll explore another important aspect of social cognition—our efforts to understand *ourselves*—in Chapter 5.

SCHEMAS: MENTAL FRAMEWORKS FOR ORGANIZING —AND USING—SOCIAL INFORMATION

Suppose that you are at a party and that you start talking to another person. As you do, you notice that she or he continues to look around the room and only half listens to what you are saying. Will it take you long to figure out what's going on? Probably not. You'll quickly realize that this person does not find you interesting or attractive and is looking for an excuse to make a quick exit.

How are you able to reach such conclusions so quickly and easily? Part of the answer involves the fact that you have been in many other situations like this one in the past; as a result of those experiences, you have built up a kind of mental framework for understanding such situations and others' behavior in them. Such frameworks are known as **schemas,** and they generally center on a particular topic or theme. For instance, in the situation we've described, the schema that is activated may be your "party schema": a mental framework, built up through experience at many previous parties, that helps you to make sense of the social information you are now encountering—the behavior of another person you have just met at a party (see Figure 3.2 on page 82).

Once they are formed, schemas exert powerful effects on several aspects of social cognition, and therefore on our social behavior. Let's take a closer look at these frameworks to better understand their nature and how they exert such effects.

schemas • Mental frameworks centering around a specific theme that help us to organize social information.

Figure 3.2

Schemas: Cognitive Frameworks for Interpreting the Social World. You probably already have a well-developed *schema* for the kind of situation shown here. Your schema is a mental framework for understanding what typically happens at parties and how people act in such settings.

Types of Schemas: Persons, Roles, and Events

Let's return to the party example. Suppose that the stranger you met who was so obviously bored with you had these characteristics: This person was not physically attractive, was dressed in last year's styles, wore thick glasses, and couldn't really hold a conversation with you. Would this pattern help you to interpret his or her behavior? It might, because you already have a well-established *person schema* for individuals like this one: a schema for *nerds*. Person schemas are mental frameworks suggesting that certain traits and behaviors go together and that individuals having them represent certain *types*. Once such a schema comes into operation, you don't have to think very long or hard about why this stranger is bored with you: you aren't a nerd yourself, know very little about high-tech topics, and usually have very little to say to such persons. So when the stranger walks off, you aren't very surprised; in fact, you are somewhat relieved—this is just what you'd expect from a nerd.

This isn't the only kind of schema we have however. In addition, we have schemas relating to specific social roles—*role schemas*. These schemas contain information about how persons playing specific roles generally act, and what they are like. For example, consider your schema for *professors*. You expect professors to stand in front of the room; to talk about the topic of the course; and to answer questions from students, prepare exams, and so on. You *don't* expect them to try to sell you a product or to do magic tricks; such actions are definitely not part of your role schema for *professor*.

In a sense, our party example above illustrated a third type of schema—*event schemas*, or *scripts*, as they are often known. Such schemas indicate what is expected to happen in a given setting—a party, a restaurant, a classroom, or almost any other situation you can imagine. In a restaurant, for instance, you expect someone to greet you and either lead you to a seat or put your name on a list. Then you expect a server to come to your table to offer drinks and to take your order. Next on the agenda is the appearance of the food—followed, eventually, by the bill. Think how surprised you'd be if, instead of following this expected sequence of events, the server sat down at your table and began a conversation; or if this person brought over the dessert tray before you ordered your main course. Once established, scripts save us a great deal of mental effort, because they tell us what to expect in a given situation: how other persons are likely to behave, and what will happen, and in what order. (We'll examine another important type of schema—*self-schemas*—in Chapter 5.)

In sum, all schemas, whether they relate to persons, roles, or events, help us to understand the complex social world around us. In a sense, they provide frameworks for organizing and interpreting new, incoming information; and in this way they save us considerable effort. Unfortunately, though, these gains in efficiency are not the entire story. While schemas are often very helpful, they can sometimes lead us seriously astray. Such effects can be very important, so we'll examine them carefully now.

The Impact of Schemas on Social Cognition: Attention, Encoding, Retrieval

How do schemas influence social thought? Research findings suggest that they exert strong effects on three basic processes: attention, encoding, and retrieval. *Attention* refers to what information we notice. *Encoding* refers to the processes through which information we notice gets stored in memory. Finally, *retrieval* refers to the processes through which we recover information from memory in order to use it in some manner—for example, in making judgments about other people, as I tried to do when, as department chair, I had the task of evaluating the performance of each faculty member.

Schemas have been found to influence all of these basic aspects of social cognition (Wyer & Srull, 1994). With respect to attention, schemas often act as a kind of filter: only information consistent with them "registers" and enters our consciousness. Information that does not fit with our schemas is often ignored (Fiske, 1993), unless it is so extreme that we can't help but notice it. And even then, it is often discounted as "the exception that proves the rule."

In the encoding process the effects of schemas are more complex. Existing evidence indicates that once schemas have been formed, information consistent with them is easier to remember than information that is inconsistent. Earlier in the process, however, when schemas are first being formed, information *inconsistent* with them may be more readily noticed and thus encoded (e.g., Stangor & Ruble, 1989).

Finally, schemas also influence what information is retrieved from memory. To the extent that schemas are activated when we are trying to recall some information, they determine precisely what information is actually brought to mind—in general, information that is part of these schemas or at least consistent with them (e.g., Conway & Ross, 1984).

Overall, then, schemas really *do* seem to operate as filters: once formed, they determine what social information we notice, what we enter into memory, and what we retrieve later from memory. As we noted earlier, such effects can enhance our efficiency in dealing with incoming social information: they make the task of sorting through a wealth of new information easier to perform. In addition, they make it easier for us to relate new experiences to past ones, and so provide a framework for interpreting new events or social encounters.

We should quickly add, however, that there is a serious downside to schemas too. By influencing what we notice, enter into memory, and later remember, schemas can produce distortions in our understanding of the social world. Here's an example from my own experience. I (Robert Baron) am a professor at a famous engineering university that, in the past, had very few psychologists on the faculty. When I first came to campus, I found that many engineers had a schema for psychologists that included the following ideas: Psychologists are not very smart, have no understanding of science or mathematics, study "sick" people, and are generally pretty weird. Time and time again, I found myself running up against this schema. The people with whom I interacted could not seem to remember that I was a social psychologist interested in such topics as workplace aggression and the effects of the physical environment on social behavior; they seemed genuinely amazed that I understood the basic principles of science and even knew some mathematics. As one of them put it, "Gee, you seem pretty normal for a psychologist!" Did I manage to change their schemas? Perhaps; but research findings indicate that schemas are often very resistant to change—they show a strong **perseverance effect,** remaining unchanged even in the face of contradictory information (e.g., Ross et al., 1975). But at least I did try!

For a discussion of an even more unsettling effect of schemas—the fact that they can often be *self-confirming*—please see the *Cornerstones of Social Psychology* section below.

Cornerstones of Social Psychology
Evidence for the Self-Confirming Nature of Schemas: When and Why Beliefs Shape Reality

Robert Rosenthal.
Rosenthal received his Ph.D. from UCLA in 1956 and has contributed to several areas of research in social psychology, especially social perception (e.g., gender differences in nonverbal communication). His research on the effects of the self-fulfilling prophecy—instances in which social perceptions, even ones that are false, strongly influence the behavior of persons who are the targets of such perceptions—has important implications for education and other applied fields.

During the depression of the 1930s, many banks faced the following situation: They were quite solvent, but rumors circulated indicating that they were not. As a result, so many depositors lined up to withdraw their funds that ultimately the banks really did fail; they didn't have enough money on hand to meet all their customers' demands (see Figure 3.3). In a sense, depositors in the banks actually caused their own worst fears to be confirmed.

Figure 3.3
The Self-Confirming Nature of Beliefs. During the depression of the 1930s, many people believed rumors indicating that their banks would fail. As a result, large numbers rushed to withdraw their deposits, and this actually caused perfectly sound banks to fail. The same kind of self-confirming effects are often produced by schemas concerning social groups (e.g., racial or ethnic minorities).

perseverance effect •
The tendency for beliefs and schemas to remain unchanged even in the face of contradictory information.

Interestingly, schemas, too, can produce such effects, which are sometimes described as **self-fulfilling prophecies**—predictions that, in a sense, make themselves come true. The first evidence for such effects was provided by Robert Rosenthal and Lenore Jacobson (1968) during the turbulent 1960s. During that period there was growing concern over the possibility that teachers' beliefs about minority students—their schemas for such youngsters—were causing them to treat such children differently (less favorably) than majority-group students, and that as a result the minority-group students were falling farther and farther behind. No, the teachers weren't overtly prejudiced; rather, their behavior was shaped by their expectations and beliefs—their schemas for different racial or ethnic groups.

To gather evidence on the possible occurrence of such effects, Rosenthal and Jacobson conducted an ingenious study that exerted a profound effect on subsequent research in social psychology. They went to an elementary school in San Francisco and administered an IQ test to all students. They then told the teachers that some of the students had scored very high and were about to bloom academically. In fact, this was not true: the researchers chose the names of these students randomly. But Rosenthal and Jacobson predicted that this information might change teachers' expectations (and schemas) about these children, and hence their behavior toward them. Teachers were not given such information about other students, who constituted a control group.

To check on their prediction, Rosenthal and Jacobson returned eight months later and tested both groups of children once again. Results were clear—and dramatic: Those who had been described as "bloomers" to their teachers showed significantly larger gains on the IQ test than those in the control group. In short, teachers' beliefs about the students had operated in a self-fulfilling manner: the students teachers believed would bloom academically actually did so.

How did such effects occur? In part, through the impact of schemas on the teachers' behavior. Further research (Rosenthal, 1994) indicated that teachers gave the bloomers more personal attention, more challenging tasks, more and better feedback, and more opportunities to respond in class. In short, the teachers acted in ways that benefited the students they expected to bloom, and as a result, these youngsters really did.

As a result of this early research, social psychologists began to search for other self-confirming effects of schemas in many settings—in education, therapy, and business, to name just a few. They soon uncovered much evidence that schemas do often shape behavior in ways that lead to their confirmation. For example, they soon found that teachers' lower expectancies for minority students or females often undermined the confidence of these groups and actually contributed to poorer performance by them (e.g., Sakder & Sakder, 1994). So the research conducted by Rosenthal and Jacobson has had far-reaching effects and can be viewed as one important cornerstone of research in our field.

Key Points

- Research on *social cognition* suggests that our thinking about other persons and social situations is subject to many sources of error.
- One source of such effects is *schemas*—mental frameworks centering around a specific theme that help us to organize social information.
- Schemas can relate to persons, events, or situations. Once formed, schemas exert powerful effects on what we notice (attention), enter into memory (encoding), and later remember (retrieval).
- While schemas help us to process information, they often persist in the face of disconfirming information. As a result, they can distort our understanding of the social world.
- Schemas can also exert self-confirming effects, causing us to behave in ways that confirm them.

self-fulfilling prophecies •
Predictions that, in a sense, make themselves come true.

Heuristics: Mental Shortcuts in Social Cognition

Have you ever tried to cook while watching the evening news on television? Drive while talking on a cellular phone? If so, you know from firsthand experience that it is easy for us to overload our capacity to process new information—to enter a state of **information overload**. Because we encounter situations like this quite often, we adopt various strategies designed to stretch our cognitive resources—to let us do more, with less effort, than we could otherwise manage. To be successful, such strategies must meet two requirements: They must provide a quick and simple way of dealing with large amounts of social information, and they must work—they must be reasonably accurate much of the time. Many potential shortcuts for reducing mental effort exist, but among these perhaps the most useful are **heuristics**—simple rules for making complex decisions or drawing inferences in a rapid and seemingly effortless manner.

Representativeness: Judging by Resemblance

Suppose that you have just met your next-door neighbor for the first time. While chatting with her, you notice that she is dressed in a conservative manner, is neat in her personal habits, has a very large library in her home, and seems to be very gentle and a little shy. Later you realize that she never mentioned what she does for a living. Is she a business manager, a physician, a waitress, an attorney, a dancer, or a librarian? One quick way of making a guess is to compare her with other members of each of these occupations. How well does she resemble persons you have met in each of these fields? If you proceed in this manner, you may quickly conclude that she is probably a librarian; her traits seem closer to those associated with this profession than they do to the traits associated with being a physician, dancer, or executive. If you made your judgment about your neighbor's occupation in this manner, you would be using the **representativeness heuristic.** In other words, you would make your judgment on the basis of a relatively simple rule: *The more similar an individual is to typical members of a given group, the more likely she or he is to belong to that group.*

Are such judgments accurate? Often they are, because belonging to certain groups does affect the behavior and style of persons in them, and because people with certain traits are attracted to particular groups in the first place. But sometimes judgments based on representativeness are wrong, mainly for the following reason: Decisions or judgments made on the basis of this rule tend to ignore *base rates*—the frequency with which given events or patterns (e.g., occupations) occur in the total population (Tversky & Kahneman, 1973; Koehler, 1993). In fact, there are many more business managers than librarians—perhaps fifty times as many. Thus, even though your neighbor seemed more similar to librarians than to managers in her personal traits, the chances are actually higher that she is in business than that she is a librarian. In this and related ways, the representativeness heuristic can lead to errors in our thinking about other persons.

Availability: "If I Can Think of It, It Must Be Important"

Which are more common: words that start with the letter *k* (e.g., king) or words with *k* as the third letter (e.g., awkward)? In English there are more than twice as many words with *k* in the third position as there are with *k* in the first posi-

---

information overload • Instances in which our ability to process information is exceeded.

heuristics • Simple rules for making complex decisions or drawing inferences in a rapid and seemingly effortless manner.

representativeness heuristic • A strategy for making judgments based on the extent to which current stimuli or events resemble other stimuli or categories.

tion. Yet despite this fact, when asked this question most people guess incorrectly (Tversky & Kahneman, 1982). Why? In part because of the operation of another heuristic—the *availability heuristic,* discussed in Chapter 1, which suggests that the easier it is to bring information to mind, the greater its importance or relevance to our judgments or decisions. This heuristic, too, makes good sense; after all, the fact that we can bring some piece of information to mind quite easily suggests that it must be important and *should* influence our judgments and decisions. But relying on availability in making social judgments can also lead to errors. For instance, suppose that when I was evaluating the teaching performance of each professor in my department, I had relied on this heuristic: the more readily I could recall instances in which students had praised a professor's teaching, the higher I set my rating. Would this have been a good way to proceed? Definitely not; perhaps I might have found it easier to recall praise of professors I liked than of ones I didn't like; or I might have found it easier to recall praise from *students* I liked or found attractive than from others. In such cases the availability heuristic can lead us into errors, because our subjective feeling that something is easy to bring to mind is not a reliable guide to its importance or accuracy.

Interestingly, research suggests that there is more to the availability heuristic than merely the subjective ease with which relevant information comes to mind. In addition, the *amount* of information we can bring to mind seems to matter (e.g., Schwarz et al., 1991b). The more information we can think of, the greater its impact on our judgments. Which of these two factors is more important? The answer appears to depend on the kind of judgment we are making. If it is one involving emotions or feelings, we tend to rely on the "ease" rule; if it is one involving facts or information, we tend to rely more on the "amount" rule. This pattern has been demonstrated clearly in studies by Rothman and Hardin (1997).

These researchers reasoned that in making judgments about our own group (the one to which we belong), we will tend to focus on facts or information; thus, the more information we can bring to mind, the stronger its impact on our judgments. In contrast, when making judgments about other groups (*out-groups,* as they are termed in social psychology), we will tend to focus more on emotions or feelings and so will rely more on the ease-with-which-it-comes-to-mind rule. To test this reasoning, Rothman and Hardin asked male and female students to recall either three or six impolite behaviors they had recently seen by members of their own gender (ingroup) or of the other gender (outgroup). Then, in a later task, participants rated both the women and men on several dimensions, including impoliteness.

Rothman and Hardin knew from past research that remembering three examples of impolite behavior was easier than remembering six examples, so thinking of three examples should have a stronger impact on participants' judgments if they followed the ease rule. In contrast, six examples of impolite behavior should have stronger impact if they used the amount-of-information rule. The overall prediction, then, was that participants would rate their own gender as more impolite when they had previously recalled six behaviors than after recalling three behaviors (they would rely on the amount-of-information rule), but that they would rate the other gender as more impolite when they recalled three behaviors (here, they would rely on the ease rule). As shown in Figure 3.4 on page 88, this is precisely what happened.

So the availability heuristic seems to include two different rules for judging the importance of information: how easily it comes to mind, and how much we can remember. And which of these rules we follow depends strongly on the kind of judgment we are making.

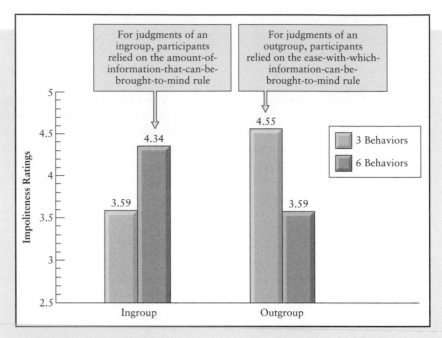

Figure 3.4

Two Bases for the Availability Heuristic. When making judgments about their own group, individuals relied primarily on the amount of information they could bring to mind; thus, they assigned higher impoliteness ratings when they thought of six examples of rude behavior than when they thought of only three examples. In contrast, when making judgments about an outgroup, individuals relied mainly on the ease with which information could be brought to mind. Because three examples of impolite behavior were easier to bring to mind than six, they assigned higher ratings when asked to think of only three examples.

(*Source:* Based on data from Rothman & Hardin, 1997.)

Priming: Some Effects of Increased Availability. The availability heuristic has been found to play a role in many aspects of social thought, including the self-serving bias (see Chapter 2) and several topics we'll examine in this and later chapters (e.g., stereotyping; see Chapter 6). Before concluding this discussion, therefore, let's take a look at the role of this heuristic in one other important process: **priming**—increased availability of information resulting from exposure to specific stimuli or events.

Here's a good example of such priming. During the first year of medical school, many students experience the "medical student syndrome": they begin to suspect that they or others have many serious illnesses. An ordinary headache may lead them to wonder if they have a brain tumor, while a mild sore throat may lead to anxiety over the possibility of some rare but fatal type of infection. What accounts for such effects? The explanation favored by social psychologists is as follows. The students are exposed to descriptions of diseases day after day in their classes and assigned readings. As a result, such information increases in availability. This, in turn, leads them to imagine the worst when confronted with mild symptoms.

Priming effects also occur in many other contexts—for example, our magnified fears after we watch a horror film, or our increased romantic feelings after we watch love scenes. Thus, they appear to be an important aspect of social

priming • Increased availability of information in memory or consciousness resulting from exposure to specific stimuli or events.

thought (e.g., Higgins & King, 1981; Higgins, Rohles, & Jones, 1977). In fact, research evidence indicates that priming may occur even when individuals are unaware of the priming stimuli—an effect known as *automatic priming* (e.g., Bargh & Pietromonaco, 1982). In other words, the availability of certain kinds of information can be increased by priming stimuli even though we are not aware of having been exposed to these stimuli. For instance, if you are sitting in the movies waiting for the film to start and are thinking about some important matter, you may not even notice that a message urging you to eat candy has appeared on the screen. Yet, a few minutes later, you may suddenly feel the urge to buy something to munch during the film. Such effects may well stem from automatic priming or related effects.

In sum, it appears that priming is a basic fact of social thought. External events and conditions—or even our own thoughts—can increase the availability of specific types of information. And increased availability, in turn, influences our judgments with respect to such information. "If I can think of it," we seem to reason, "then it must be important, frequent, or true"; and we often reach such conclusions even if they are not supported by social reality.

Key Points

- Because our capacity to process information is limited, we often experience *information overload*. To avoid this, we use *heuristics*—rules for making decisions in a quick and relatively effortless manner.

- One such heuristic is *representativeness,* which suggests that the more similar an individual is to typical members of a given group, the more likely she or he is to belong to that group.

- Another heuristic is *availability,* which suggests that the easier it is to bring information to mind, the greater its impact on subsequent decisions or judgments. In some cases, availability may also involve the amount of information we bring to mind.

- *Priming* refers to increased availability of information resulting from exposure to specific stimuli or events.

POTENTIAL SOURCES OF ERROR IN SOCIAL COGNITION: WHY TOTAL RATIONALITY IS SCARCER THAN YOU THINK

Human beings are definitely not computers. While we can *imagine* being able to reason in a perfectly logical way, we know from our own experience that we often fall short of this goal. This is definitely true with respect to many aspects of social thought. In our efforts to understand others and make sense out of the social world, we are subject to a wide range of tendencies that, together, can lead us into serious error. In this section we'll consider several of these "tilts" in social cognition. Before doing so, however, we should emphasize the following point: While these aspects of social thought do sometimes result in errors, they are also quite adaptive. In other words, they often help us focus on the kinds of information that are most informative, and they reduce the effort required for understanding the social world. So they are definitely something of a mixed bag, supplying us with tangible benefits as well as exacting important costs.

Rational versus Intuitive Processing: Going with Our Gut-Level Feelings Even When We Know Better

Imagine the following situation: You are shown two bowls containing red jelly beans and white jelly beans. One holds a single red bean and nine white ones; the other bowl holds ten reds and ninety whites. Further, imagine that you will win money each time you select (blindfolded) a red bean. From which bowl would you prefer to draw? Rationally, it makes no difference: the chances of winning are exactly 10 percent in both cases. But if you are like most people, you'd prefer the bowl with one hundred beans. In fact, in several studies, more than two-thirds of the participants given this choice preferred the bowl with the larger number of jelly beans—and, even more surprisingly, *they were willing to pay money to guarantee this choice* (Kirkpatrick & Epstein, 1992). In a sense, it's hard to imagine a clearer illustration of the fact that our thinking is far from perfectly rational in many situations.

What accounts for this and related findings? A model of cognition proposed by Epstein and his colleagues (e.g., Denes-Raj & Epstein, 1994; Epstein, 1994) offers one explanation. According to this model, known as **cognitive–experiential self-theory** (CEST for short), our efforts to understand the world around us proceed in two distinct ways. One of these is deliberate, rational thinking, which follows basic rules of logic. The other is a more *intuitive* system that operates in a more automatic, holistic manner—a kind of do-it-by-hunches-or-intuition kind of approach. CEST theory suggests that we tend to use these contrasting styles of thought in different kinds of situations. Rational thinking is used in situations involving analytical thought—for example, when we are solving mathematical problems. Intuitive thinking is used in many other situations, including most social ones. In other words, when we try to understand others' behavior, we often revert to intuitive, gut-level thinking. Will someone make a good roommate, partner, or spouse? We could try to answer such questions through totally rational thought; but, it appears, we usually try to do so in a far less systematic manner. If we "feel good" about someone, we predict that he or she will work out well; if we "have a bad feeling" about the person, we predict that he or she will fail, and we act accordingly.

So why do we choose the bowl with more jelly beans, even though the chances of winning are the same as for the smaller bowl with fewer beans? CEST theory suggests that in situations such as this, the intuitive system is dominant. We *know*, rationally, that the odds of winning are the same in both cases; but we *feel* that we have a better chance of winning when there are ten red jelly beans rather than only one. Perhaps this happens because we can visualize a solitary red jelly bean surrounded by nine white ones more easily than we can visualize ten red and ninety white ones—and because we can't visualize the latter situation as clearly, it seems to hold a greater chance of winning.

Does your state or country have a lottery? If so, you may have seen these effects in action. Some forms of the lottery sell a very large number of tickets for a relatively low price per ticket, while other forms sell a smaller number of tickets at a higher price. As you can probably guess, the lower-priced tickets sell very well—usually, much better than the higher-priced tickets. The odds of winning in both lotteries are precisely the same (the odds are usually fixed by law), so why do many people prefer the low-priced tickets? Because they feel that by purchasing several low-priced tickets, they have a better chance of winning. This may not be correct, because the number of low-priced tickets is so huge; but that doesn't matter—people are guided by intuitive thought, so the low-priced tickets literally fly across the counter (see Figure 3.5). For another and more serious illustration of the impact of intuitive thought on judgments and decisions, please see the following *Beyond the Headlines* section.

cognitive–experiential self-theory • A theory suggesting that our efforts to understand the world around us involve two distinct modes of thought: intuitive thought and deliberate, rational thought.

Figure 3.5
Intuitive Processing In Action. Sales of relatively low-priced lottery tickets usually far exceed sales of more expensive lottery tickets. Although the odds of winning are generally precisely the same in both cases, many people feel intuitively that they have a greater chance of winning if they buy several low-priced tickets rather than one higher-priced ticket. This is an example of intuition or hunch-based thought.

Beyond the Headlines:
As Social Psychologists See It
Do Safety Devices Save Lives? Don't Bet On It!

INSURANCE-CLAIMS DATA DON'T SHOW ADVANTAGE OF SOME AUTO DEVICES: AIR BAGS AND ANTILOCK BRAKES DON'T PAY OFF IN FEWER INJURIES, REPAIRS

Wall Street Journal, March 17, 1994—Detroit—In pursuit of a safer car, consumers will fork over an extra several hundred dollars for air bags and antilock brakes. Insurers egg them on by offering discounts. Auto companies . . . have poured billions into developing, making, and heavily promoting the new safety systems.

But so far, there's no demonstrable payoff in terms of fewer accidents and injuries and lower repair bills. The statistics aren't there, and no one is sure why. . . .

"What?!" we can almost hear you saying. "Air bags and antilock brakes *don't* reduce injuries and repair bills? How can that be?" The answer is complex and seems to involve many factors. For instance, as you may have heard on the news, air bags may actually injure smaller drivers and passengers—women and children in particular (see Figure 3.6 on page 92). Further, many drivers (perhaps most) don't use antilock brakes correctly. They try to pump such brakes, because that's what they've learned to do in the past with regular brakes. But that doesn't work with antilock brakes and may even totally defeat their value.

So there are clear reasons why these devices may not deliver all the benefits predicted for them. An even more intriguing question from the point of view of social psychology, however, is this: Why did so many people, from lawmakers and government officials to manufacturers and millions of consumers, put their faith in these devices? Why, in short, did almost everyone believe they would work—reduce injuries and costs—even though there was not sufficient evidence to validate such conclusions?

Figure 3.6
Adoption of Safety Devices: Another Example of Intuitive Processing?
Government regulations require the installation in automobiles of devices designed to save lives and reduce injuries. Growing evidence suggests, however, that these safety devices do not always work—that they don't produce the intended effects. It seems possible, then, that widespread public support for such devices stems more from intuitive thinking about what *should* work than from data indicating what actually *does* work.

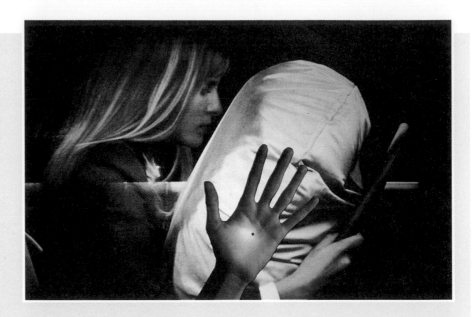

One answer, it appears, is through the operation of intuitive thought. As one expert in the insurance business put it: "It makes sense that air bags would generate lower losses and therefore . . . lower premiums, but there's little fact to back that intuition." In other words, these devices won so much support not because of strong evidence they would succeed, but rather because many people assumed—largely on the basis of hunches and intuition—that they would work. When they didn't, many experts were surprised.

Another possibility is that with the safety devices in place, drivers take bigger chances and drive more aggressively. "I found that risk-taking behavior completely offset the lifesaving effects of mandated safety equipment," commented one economist who conducted research on this possibility.

In sum, the strong public support that has carried many automobile safety devices from the planning stage to government regulations requiring their installation in millions of new vehicles may be unjustified. In some cases, at least, such support may have been based more on intuition and hunches about what "should be" or "ought to be" than on data about what actually is. Don't misunderstand. We are not against safety devices—quite the contrary! But as social psychologists, we view these events as one more illustration of the fact that beliefs are often more important than reality and that as human beings, we are definitely *not* perfect information-processing or decision-making devices.

Key Points

- In our efforts to understand the external world, we can use either rational processing, which follows basic rules of logic, or intuitive processing, which relies on intuition and hunches.

- Growing evidence suggests that we rely largely on intuitive processing when we think about other persons or social situations.

- A reliance on intuitive thought may be one reason why automobile safety devices (e.g., air bags) have been adopted on a large scale even in the absence of clear evidence for their potential value.

Dealing with Inconsistent Information: Paying Attention to What Doesn't Fit

Imagine the following situation: You are watching a talk show on television. One of the guests is Madonna. You only half listen as she makes several fairly extreme but, for her, not surprising comments about life, music, and sex. Then, in a quiet voice, she says something totally unexpected: Since becoming a parent, she has lost interest in money and material things and has decided to retire to grow flowers and spend time with her child. You sit up straight in disbelief. Can you believe your ears? Did she really say *that?*

This somewhat bizarre scenario illustrates an important fact about social cognition: In general, we tend to pay much more attention to information that is *unexpected* or somehow *inconsistent* with our expectations than to information that is expected or consistent. Thus, a statement by Madonna that she has lost interest in her lucrative career would literally leap out at you, demanding close and careful attention.

This tendency to pay greater attention to information inconsistent with our expectations than to information consistent with them is an important and basic aspect of social cognition. It is apparent in a wide range of contexts (e.g., Belmore & Hubbard, 1987; Hilton, Klein, & von Hippel, 1991), and seems to stem from the fact that because inconsistent information is unexpected and surprising, we work harder to understand it. And because the greater the amount of attention we pay to information, the better its chance of entering memory and influencing our later judgments (Fiske & Neuberg, 1990), this tendency to notice what's inconsistent has important implications.

One final point: While it is usually the case that information to which we pay particular attention exerts stronger effects on our social thought and judgments than other information, this is not always so. Sometimes, although we readily *notice* information that is inconsistent with our expectations, we tend to discount it or downplay it: it's simply too unexpected to accept. For example, you probably can't help noticing the weird headlines on the tabloid newspapers displayed near the checkout lines in supermarkets (see Figure 3.7). These head-

Figure 3.7

Noticing Surprising or Inconsistent Information Does *Not* Equal Being Influenced by It. Although you probably notice surprising headlines like these very readily, this does not necessarily mean that you will accept them or be influenced by them. In fact, information that is highly inconsistent with our knowledge, views, or expectations is often rejected as false.

lines make assertions that are unexpected and inconsistent with views you already hold. But the likelihood that they will influence you is slight, because they are *so* bizarre that you discount them. So the fact that we often pay careful attention to information inconsistent with our current views or thinking does not mean that such information is necessarily especially influential with respect to social thought.

The Planning Fallacy: Why We Often Think We Can Do More, Sooner, Than We Really Can

Several years ago, one of my neighbors decided to build an addition to his house. The builder he chose estimated that the job would take about nine months. It is now more than two years since the work began, and *it is still not done.* In fact, I can hear the hammering today, as I write these words. This is not a rare event: many projects seem to take longer, and cost more, than initially predicted.

Why is this the case? One possibility is as follows: In predicting how long a given task will take, people tend to be overly optimistic; they predict that they can get the job done much sooner than actually turns out to be the case. Or, turning this around somewhat, they expect to get more done in a given period of time than they really can. You can probably recognize this tendency in your own thinking. Try to remember the last time you worked on a major project (for instance, a term paper). Did it take more time or less time to complete than you originally estimated? Probably, your answer is "More time . . . of course!" So this tendency to make optimistic predictions about how long a given task will take—a tendency known as the **planning fallacy** (or *optimistic bias*)—is both powerful and widespread. What features of social thought account for this common error?

According to Buehler, Griffin, and Ross (1994), social psychologists who have studied this tendency in detail, several factors play a role. One is that when individuals make predictions about how long it will take them to complete a given task, they enter a *planning* or *narrative* mode of thought in which they focus primarily on the future: how they will perform the task. This, in turn, prevents them from looking backward in time and remembering how long similar tasks took them in the past. As a result, one important reality check that might help them avoid being overly optimistic is removed. In addition, when individuals do consider past experience in which tasks took longer than expected, they tend to attribute such outcomes to factors outside their control. The result: They tend to overlook important potential obstacles when predicting how long a task will take, and so fall prey to the planning fallacy. These predictions have been confirmed in several studies (e.g., Buehler et al., 1994), so they seem to provide important insights into the origins of the tendency to make optimistic predictions about task completion.

This is not the entire story, though. Research suggests that another factor, too, may play an important role in the planning fallacy: *motivation* to complete a task. When predicting what will happen, individuals often guess that what will happen is what they *want* to happen (e.g., Johnson & Sherman, 1990). In cases where people are strongly motivated to complete a task, therefore, they make overoptimistic predictions concerning when this desired state of affairs will occur.

To test the role of motivation in the planning fallacy, Buehler, Griffin, and MacDonald (1997) conducted a series of ingenious studies. In one of these, they phoned people chosen at random from the telephone directory of a large Canadian city and asked them whether they expected to receive an income tax re-

planning fallacy • The tendency to make optimistic predictions concerning how long a given task will take for completion; also known as the optimistic bias.

fund. Then they asked these individuals when, relative to the deadline, they expected to mail in their tax forms. Later, one week after the actual deadlines for submitting the forms, the researchers phoned the same persons again and asked them to indicate when their tax forms had actually been mailed.

Buehler and his colleagues reasoned that persons expecting a refund would have strong motivation to complete the task of filing their forms, and so would make overoptimistic predictions about when they would file them. As you can see from Figure 3.8, this is precisely what happened. While all persons surveyed showed the planning fallacy, those who expected a refund were much more optimistic in their predictions than those who did not: people expecting refunds estimated that they would submit their forms twenty-eight days before the deadline, whereas those not expecting refunds estimated that they would submit the forms about seventeen days before the deadline. Both groups actually submitted their forms later than they predicted—about fifteen days in advance for those expecting a refund and thirteen days in advance for those not expecting one.

These results and those of a follow-up laboratory study (Buehler et al., 1997) indicate that the planning fallacy stems, at least in part, from motivation to complete a task. In other words, individuals' estimates of when they will complete a task are influenced by their hopes and desires: they *want* to finish early, so they predict that they will do so. Sad to relate, however, this appears to be one of the many situations in life where wishing does not necessarily make it so.

Before concluding, we should note that the optimistic bias takes another important form, too: a tendency on the part of most persons to believe that they are *more* likely than others to experience positive events, and *less* likely

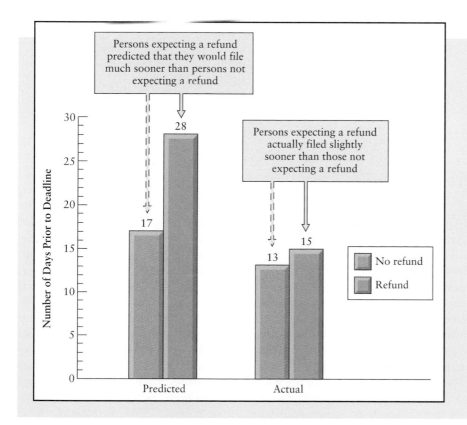

Figure 3.8

Motivation and the Planning Fallacy. As expected, individuals who expected a tax refund, and therefore had stronger motivation to file their forms, showed the planning fallacy to a greater extent than persons who were not expecting a refund.

(*Source:* Based on data from Buehler, Griffin, & MacDonald, 1997.)

to experience negative events (e.g., Shepperd, Ouellette, & Fernandez, 1996). This tendency is powerful and occurs in many contexts—for example, most people believe that they are more likely than others to get a good job, have a happy marriage, or live to a ripe old age, but less likely to experience negative outcomes such as being fired, getting seriously ill, or divorce (e.g., Schwarzer, 1994). However, there appears to be one exception to this strong tendency toward optimism: When individuals expect to receive feedback or information that may be negative in nature and has important consequences, they seem to brace for the worst and show a tendency to believe that they are *more* likely than others to experience negative outcomes (i.e., pessimism; e.g., Taylor & Shepperd, 1998). If you have ever had the following experience, you know about such effects from your own life: Before you take a test, you are quite confident that you will do better than average; later, seconds before you receive your grade, this optimism vanishes, and you become convinced that you probably did *worse* than average. By preparing for the worst, you allow yourself to be pleased if you did at least O.K. (e.g., average or even slightly below). So, are we optimistic? In general, yes. But there are situations in which we tend to be pessimistic because doing so helps us protect our self-esteem from being crushed!

Key Points

- In general, we notice information that is inconsistent with our expectations more readily than information that is consistent with them. As a result, inconsistent information may exert stronger effects on our later judgments or decisions although this is not always the case.

- Individuals tend to make overly optimistic predictions about how long it will take them to complete a given task, an effect known as the *planning fallacy.*

- The planning fallacy seems to stem from the tendency to focus on the future while ignoring related past events, and also from motivation to have tasks completed quickly.

- The optimistic bias also shows up in our tendency to assume that we are more likely than others to experience positive outcomes, but less likely than others to experience negative ones.

The Potential Costs of Thinking Too Much: Why, Sometimes, Our Tendency to Do As Little Cognitive Work As Possible May Be Justified

As we have already seen, there are many instances in which we adopt an intuitive approach to thinking about the social world. Yet there are other instances in which we do try to be as rational and systematic as possible in our thought, despite the extra effort this involves. At first glance, such deliberate, rational thought would seem to be uniformly beneficial: after all, it should be less prone to errors or bias. But on close examination, it appears that perhaps this is not always so. Have you ever had the experience of thinking about some problem or decision so long and so hard that ultimately you found yourself becoming more and more confused? If so, you are aware of the fact that even where rational thought is concerned, there can sometimes be too much of a good thing.

Surprising as this conclusion may be, it has been confirmed by many studies (e.g., Schooler & Engstler-Schooler, 1990; Wilson, 1990). Perhaps the most dramatic evidence for the potential downside of thinking too much is that provided by Wilson and Schooler (1991). These researchers asked college students to sample and rate several strawberry jams. Half of the participants were simply asked to taste the jams and rate them; the others were asked to analyze their reactions to the jams—to indicate why they felt the way they did about each product. Wilson and Schooler (1991) reasoned that when individuals engage in such careful introspection, the reasons they bring to mind may simply be the ones that are most prominent and accessible—the easiest to remember or put into words. However, these reasons may not really be the most important factors in their judgments. As a result, people may actually be misled by the reasons they themselves report, and this can cause them to make less accurate judgments.

To determine if this actually happens, Wilson and Schooler (1991) compared the judgments made by the participants who analyzed the reasons behind their ratings, and the judgments by those who did not, with ratings by a panel of experts—persons who make their living comparing various products. As expected, participants who simply rated the jams agreed much more closely with the experts than participants who tried to report the reasons behind their reactions to the various jams.

Similar findings have been obtained in several related studies, so there appear to be strong grounds for concluding that sometimes thinking too much can get us into serious cognitive trouble. Yes, trying to think systematically and rationally about important matters is important; such high-effort activities do often yield better decisions and more accurate judgments than shoot-from-the-hip modes of thought. But careful thought, like anything else, can be overdone; and when it is, the result may be increased confusion and frustration rather than better and more accurate decisions or conclusions.

Counterfactual Thinking: The Effects of Considering "What Might Have Been"

Suppose that you take an important exam; when you receive your score, it is a C–: much lower than you hoped. What thoughts will enter your mind as you consider your grade? If you are like most people, you may quickly begin to imagine "what might have been"—receiving a higher grade—along with reflecting on how you could have obtained that better outcome. "If only I had studied more, or come to class more often," you may think to yourself. Then, perhaps, you may begin to formulate plans for actually *doing* better on the next test.

Such thoughts about what might have been—known in social psychology as **counterfactual thinking**—occur in a wide range of situations, not just ones in which we experience disappointments. For instance, suppose you read an article in the newspaper about someone who was injured by bricks falling off the front of a large office building. Further, the article indicates that this person was a stranger in town who had never been on that street before. Would you feel sympathy toward this person? Probably you would; after all, you can readily imagine this person *not* being on that street and therefore *not* being injured. But now imagine that the article indicates, instead, that this person works in the building next door and passes this way several times a day. Would you feel as much sympathy? Perhaps, but perhaps not. It is somewhat harder to imagine the person *not* being injured, because he or she often passes this way; as a result, you may not feel quite as sympathetic toward the victim.

Many studies indicate that in fact we do tend to feel more sympathy for people who experience harm as a result of unusual actions on their part than as a result of more typical behavior. For instance, we may feel lots of sympathy

counterfactual thinking • The tendency to imagine outcomes in a situation other than those that actually occurred—to think about "What might have been."

toward a man who never picks up hitchhikers but one day, when it is raining very hard, *does* give a stranger a lift—only to be robbed by this person. In contrast, we may feel less sympathy toward another man who routinely picks up hitchhikers and is also robbed by one of them; after all, we reason, he was asking for trouble. Moreover, we can't imagine another outcome (not being robbed) as readily, because this driver puts himself at risk so often (e.g., Macrae, 1992; Miller & McFarland, 1986).

Counterfactual thinking is also closely related to the experience of regret. To see how, answer the following question: What are the three things you regret most in your entire life? If you are like most people, the events you named are things you *did not do*, rather than things you *did* do: missed educational opportunities, failures to "seize the moment," missed romantic opportunities, missed career opportunities (Gilovich & Medvec, 1994). Why is this the case? In part, because when we think about things we *did* do that turned out badly, we know what happened and can rationalize away any regret about our decisions or actions, finding good reasons for them. When we think about missed opportunities, however, the situation is very different. As time passes, we gradually downplay or lose sight of the factors that prevented us from acting at the time—these seem less and less important. Even worse, we tend to imagine in vivid detail the wonderful benefits that would have resulted if we *had* acted. The result: Our regrets intensify over time and can haunt us for an entire lifetime (Medvec, Madey, & Gilovich, 1995).

Interestingly, it appears that people who start their own businesses—entrepreneurs—are less likely to engage in counterfactual thinking, and less likely to experience regret over missed opportunities, than other persons (Baron, 1999). Apparently, such individuals believe that missed opportunities don't matter: there's always a new one around the corner. Accordingly, they don't waste their time thinking about what might have been: they are too busy thinking about what may yet be!

These are not the only effects of counterfactual thinking, however. As noted recently by Neal Roese (1997), a social psychologist who has conducted many studies on counterfactual thinking, engaging in such thought can yield a wide range of effects, some of which are beneficial and some of which are costly to the persons involved (e.g., Roese & Maniar, 1997). For instance, counterfactual thinking can, depending on its focus, yield either boosts to or reductions in our current moods. If individuals engage in *upward counterfactual thinking*, comparing their current outcomes with more favorable ones they can imagine, the result may be strong feelings of dissatisfaction or envy, especially if they do not feel capable of obtaining better outcomes in the future (Sanna, 1997). For instance, Olympic athletes who win a silver medal but imagine winning a gold one experience such reactions (e.g., Medvec, Madey, & Gilovich, 1995). Alternatively, if individuals engage in downward counterfactual thinking, comparing their current outcomes with less favorable ones, or if they contemplate various ways in which disappointing results could have been avoided and positive ones attained, they may experience positive feelings of satisfaction or hopefulness. Such reactions have been found among Olympic athletes who win bronze medals, and who therefore imagine what it would be like to have won no medal whatsoever (e.g., Gleicher et al., 1995). In sum, engaging in counterfactual thought can strongly influence affective states. A very clear illustration of such effects is provided by research conducted by Medvec and Savitsky (1997).

These researchers reasoned that in general, the better people do on a task, the more positive their reactions—the higher their satisfaction. An important exception to this rule, however, may occur as the result of counterfactual thinking. Imagine, for instance, that you take an exam and score right at the minimum cutoff point for a B. How will you feel? Probably very pleased, since you "just made it" into the B category. Your counterfactual thinking will tend to center on what would have happened if you had scored just one point lower! In contrast, imagine that you do better on the exam but fall one point *under* the cutoff for an A. Your score is higher, but will you feel happier? Almost certainly you will not; in this case, your counterfactual thinking will focus on what might have happened if you had scored just one little point higher.

To see if such effects actually occur, Medvec and Savitsky (1997) asked students to imagine that they had just missed a higher grade or that they had just made a higher grade by exceeding a cutoff. Then the students indicated how satisfied they would be with the grade they got. Results were exactly as predicted: those who had just made it into the higher grade category reported significantly higher satisfaction than those who had just missed a higher grade. Further, as expected, within a given grade category, those who scored lower and just made the grade were more satisfied than those who scored higher and had missed the next higher grade. In short, cutoff points and the kinds of counterfactual thinking they generated were more important in predicting students' satisfaction than were their actual scores on the exams.

Still another effect of counterfactual thinking—or in this case, of anticipating that we will engage in it—is known as *inaction inertia*. This occurs when an individual has decided *not* to take some action and so loses the opportunity to gain a positive outcome. As a result, he or she becomes less likely to take similar actions in the future, especially if these actions will yield smaller gains. For instance, imagine that you meant to buy a stereo when it was on sale at 50% off the regular price, but didn't get down to the store in time. Now the stereo is on sale at 25% off. Will you buy it? Research findings indicate that you may actually be less likely to do so than if you hadn't missed the original sale (e.g., Tykocinski, Pittman, & Tuttle, 1995). Why? Apparently, because we realize that if we buy the stereo now, we'll remind ourselves of the fact that we could have bought it for less; we want to avoid that, because such counterfactual thinking will result in unpleasant feelings of regret. Recent findings reported by Tykocinski and Pittman (1998) offer clear support for this reasoning. Individuals in these studies were most likely to show inaction inertia when such inertia could indeed protect them from thinking about past missed opportunities. When they couldn't avoid thinking about these missed opportunities (e.g., every day they had to walk past a very desirable apartment they had failed to rent) inaction inertia decreased. So, even the anticipation of counterfactual thinking can have strong effects on our behavior!

In addition to affecting emotional states, counterfactual thinking can provide individuals with increased understanding of the causal factors that contributed to the negative or disappointing outcomes they experienced—enhanced insight into *why* these outcomes occurred. Such information, in turn, can assist people in planning changes in behavior or new strategies that can improve their future performance (e.g., McMullen, Markman, & Gavanski, 1995; Roese, 1997). And recent findings indicate that the magnitude of such changes in behavior is closely linked to the magnitude of improvements in obtained outcomes that individuals desire. In other words, the greater the improvements desired, the larger the changes in behavior such persons imagine. For instance, if I receive a C in a course but would be happy with a B, I think about studying somewhat more for each exam. If, instead, I desire an A (a much larger improvement in obtained outcomes), I think about studying much more (Sim & Morris, 1998). Regardless of the specific thoughts involved, engaging in counterfactual

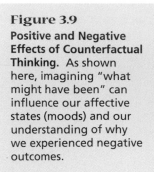

Figure 3.9
Positive and Negative Effects of Counterfactual Thinking. As shown here, imagining "what might have been" can influence our affective states (moods) and our understanding of why we experienced negative outcomes.

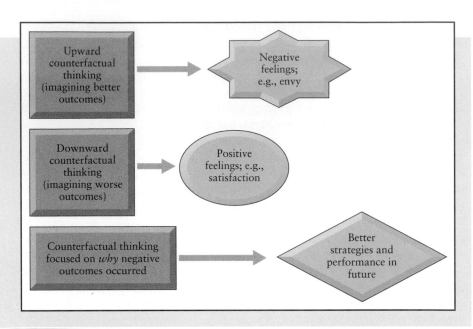

thinking may be one technique that assists individuals in learning from past experience and in profiting from their mistakes. (Figure 3.9 presents a summary of all these potential effects.)

In sum, imagining what might have been in a given situation can yield many effects, ranging from despair and intense regret on the one hand, through hopefulness and increased determination to do better on the other. Our tendency to think not only about what is but also about what *might* be, therefore, can have far-reaching effects on many aspects of our social thought and social behavior.

Key Points

- When individuals think too deeply about some topic, they may become confused about the factors that actually play a role their behavior, with the result that they make less accurate judgments or decisions.

- In many situations, individuals imagine "what might have been"—they engage in *counterfactual thinking*. Such thinking can affect our sympathy for persons who have experienced negative outcomes and can cause us to experience strong regret over missed opportunities.

- Counterfactual thinking can also strongly influence our affective states. And it may increase our understanding of *why* we experienced negative outcomes; in this way, such thought can help us to improve our performance in the future.

Magical Thinking: Would You Eat a Chocolate Shaped Like a Spider?

Answer truthfully:

Suppose someone with AIDS bought a sweater sealed in a plastic bag and put it away in a drawer for a year; would you wear it if they gave it to you?

Imagine that someone offered you a piece of chocolate shaped like a spider—would you eat it?

When you are in class and don't want the professor to call on you, if you think about her calling on you, does this increase the chances that she really will?

On the basis of purely rational considerations, you know what your answers should be to these questions: *Yes, yes,* and *no.* But are those the answers you actually gave? If you are like most persons, perhaps not. In fact, research findings indicate that as human beings, we are quite susceptible to what has been termed **magical thinking** (Rozin & Nemeroff, 1990). Such thinking makes assumptions that don't hold up to rational scrutiny but which are compelling nonetheless. One principle of such magical thinking is the *law of contagion:* it holds that when two objects touch, they pass properties to one another, and that the effects of contact may last well beyond the end of the contact between them (Zusne & Jones, 1989). Another is the *law of similarity,* which suggests that things that resemble one another share basic properties. Still a third assumes that one's thoughts can influence the physical world in a manner not governed by the laws of physics. Can you see how these assumptions relate to the questions above? The law of contagion is linked to the question about the sweater; the law of similarity has to do with the chocolate; and the third principle relates to the possibility that thinking about some event can make it happen.

Surprising as it may seem, our thinking about many situations—including social ones—is often influenced by such magical thinking. For example, in one study on this topic, Rozin, Markwith, and Nemeroff (1992) asked individuals to rate a sweater owned either by a person with AIDS or by a healthy person, which had been left in a sealed plastic bag and never touched by the owner. Consistent with the law of contagion, participants rated the sweater less favorably when it had been owned by the person with AIDs, even though they knew that there was no chance they could catch the disease from the sweater.

Additional evidence for the operation of magical thinking is provided by a study Keinan (1994) conducted with residents of Israel during the Gulf War of 1990. Participants lived either in cities that had been attacked by Iraqi missiles or in cities that were never attacked. Persons in both groups completed a questionnaire designed to measure magical thinking—for example, agreement with such items as "If during a missile attack I had a photo of Saddam Hussein with me, I would rip it to pieces," and "I have the feeling that the chances of being hit during a missile attack are greater if a person whose house is attacked is at home." It was predicted that magical thinking would be greater among those in the cities that had been attacked, and this was confirmed. Apparently the high stress resulting from the missile attacks increased individuals' tendencies to engage in magical thinking, a finding consistent with the general principle that we are more subject to errors and biases in social cognition when we confront conditions of information overload—circumstances often generated by high levels of stress.

So, the next time you are tempted to make fun of someone's superstitious belief (e.g., fear of the number thirteen or of black cats crossing one's path), think again: while you may not accept these superstitions yourself, this does not suggest that your own thinking is totally free from the kind of "magical" assumptions considered here.

Thought Suppression: Why Efforts to Avoid Thinking Certain Thoughts Sometimes Backfire

At one time or another, everyone has tried to suppress certain thoughts—to keep ideas and images from coming into consciousness. For example, a person on a diet may try to avoid thinking about delicious desserts, someone who is trying to quit smoking may try to avoid thoughts about the pleasures of lighting up, and someone who is nervous about giving a speech may try to avoid thinking about

magical thinking • Thinking involving assumptions that don't hold up to rational scrutiny—for example, the notion that things that resemble one another share fundamental properties.

Figure 3.10
Thought Suppression: Harder Than It Seems! As the cartoon character has discovered, when told *not* to think about something (e.g., some activity or object), many people find that this is precisely what they *do* think about.

(*Source:* Washington Post Writers Group, 1997.)

all the ways in which he or she risks looking foolish while speaking to a large audience. (See Figure 3.10 for another example.)

How do we accomplish such **thought suppression,** and what are the effects of this process? According to Daniel Wegner (1992b, 1994), a social psychologist who has studied thought suppression in detail, efforts to keep certain thoughts out of consciousness involve two components. First, there is an automatic *monitoring process,* which searches for evidence that unwanted thoughts are about to intrude. When such thoughts are detected by the monitoring component, a second process, which is more effortful and less automatic (i.e., more controlled), swings into operation. This *operating process* involves effortful, conscious attempts to distract oneself by finding something else to think about. In a sense, the monitoring process is an "early warning" system that tells the person unwanted thoughts are present, and the second process is an active prevention system that keeps such thoughts out of consciousness through distraction.

Under normal circumstances, the two processes do a good job of suppressing unwanted thoughts. When information overload occurs or when individuals are fatigued, however, the monitoring process continues to identify unwanted thoughts but the operating process no longer has the resources to keep them from entering consciousness. The result: The individual actually experiences a pronounced *rebound* effect in which the unwanted thoughts occur at an even higher rate than was true before efforts to suppress them began. As we'll soon see, this can have serious consequences for the person involved.

The operation of the two processes described by Wegner (1992a, 1994) has been confirmed in many different studies (e.g., Wegner & Zanakos, 1994) and with respect to thoughts ranging from strange or unusual images (e.g., a white elephant) to thoughts about old romantic flames (Wegner & Gold, 1995). So this model of thought suppression appears to be an accurate one.

Now for the second question we posed above: What are the effects of engaging in thought suppression—and of failing to accomplish this task? Generally, people engage in thought suppression as a means of influencing their own

thought suppression •
Efforts to prevent certain thoughts from entering consciousness.

feelings and behavior. For example, if you want to avoid feeling angry, it's best not to think about incidents that cause you to feel resentment against others. Similarly, if you want to avoid feeling depressed, it's useful to avoid thinking about events or experiences that make you feel sad. But sometimes people engage in thought suppression because they are told to do so by someone else— such as, a therapist who is trying to help them cope with a personal problem. For instance, imagine that someone is trying to suppress thoughts of alcohol in order to deal with a drinking problem. A therapist may tell this individual to avoid thinking about the pleasures of drinking. If the individual succeeds in suppressing such thoughts, this may be a plus for his or her treatment. But consider what happens if the individual fails in these efforts at thought suppression. This may lead the patient to think: "What a failure I am—I can't even control my thoughts!" As a result, the person's motivation to continue these efforts, or even to continue therapy, may drop—with predictable negative consequences (e.g., Kelly & Kahn, 1994).

Unfortunately, some people, because they possess certain personal characteristics, seem especially likely to experience such failures. Individuals high in *reactance*—ones who react very negatively to perceived threats to their personal freedom—may be especially at risk for such effects. Such persons often reject advice or suggestions from others because they want to do their own thing, so they may find instructions to suppress certain thoughts hard to follow. That this is actually so is indicated by research carried out by Kelly and Nauta (1997).

These researchers asked individuals previously found to be high or low in reactance to generate their own most frequently occurring unwanted intrusive thought and then either to suppress that thought or express it in writing. Later, participants were asked to rate the extent to which they felt out of control and distressed by their intrusive thoughts. Kelly and Nauta (1997) predicted that persons high in reactance would have more difficulty in following instructions to suppress intrusive thoughts and would later report being more disturbed by these thoughts when they occurred. As shown in Figure 3.11, that is precisely what happened. Persons high in reactance did not differ from those low in reactance when told to express their intrusive thoughts in writing; this was predicted, because reactance should *not* influence people's behavior under these conditions. When told to suppress intrusive thoughts, however, persons high in reactance reported a significantly higher incidence of the thoughts they were told to suppress.

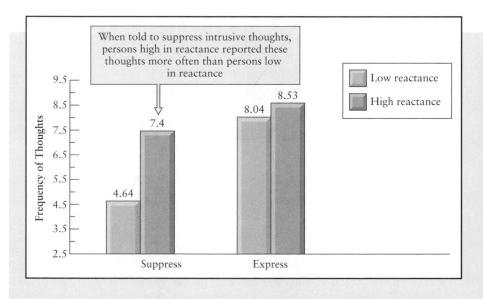

Figure 3.11

Reactance and Thought Suppression. When told to suppress intrusive thoughts, persons high in reactance reported more instances of such thoughts and greater disturbance over them than persons low in reactance. No differences between these groups occurred when they were told to express their intrusive thoughts in writing rather than suppress them.

(*Source:* Based on data from Kelly & Nauta, 1997.)

Apparently, they either acted in a manner opposite to the experimenters' instructions (this is what persons high in reactance often do!) or tried to suppress their thoughts more completely—with the result that they experienced a greater rebound effect. Whatever the precise explanation, it seems clear that personal characteristics can indeed play a role in thought suppression, and that persons high in reactance may not be very good candidates for forms of therapy that include suppressing unwanted thoughts as part of their procedures.

For an overview of the many sources of error that can influence social cognition, see the *Ideas to Take with You* feature on page 113.

Social Cognition: A Word of Optimism

The planning fallacy, the costs of thinking too much, counterfactual thinking, magical thinking, thought suppression—having considered these sources of error in social thought, you may be ready to despair: can we ever get it right? The answer, we believe, is *absolutely*. No, we're not perfect information-processing machines. We have limited cognitive capacities, and we can't increase these by buying pop-in memory chips. And yes, we are somewhat lazy: we generally do the least amount of cognitive work possible in any situation. Despite these limitations, though, we frequently do an impressive job in thinking about others. Despite being flooded by truly enormous amounts of social information, we manage to sort, store, remember, and use a large portion of this input in an intelligent and highly efficient manner. Our thinking is indeed subject to many potential sources of bias, and we do make errors. But by and large, we do a very good job of processing social information and making sense out of the social world in which we live. So, while we can imagine being even better at these tasks than we are, there's no reason to be discouraged. On the contrary, we can even take pride in the fact that we accomplish so much with the limited tools at our disposal.

Key Points

- We often engage in *magical thinking*—thinking based on assumptions that don't hold up to rational scrutiny. For instance, we may believe that if two objects are in contact, properties can pass from one to the other.

- Individuals often engage in *thought suppression*, trying to prevent themselves from thinking about certain topics (e.g., delicious desserts, alcohol, cigarettes).

- Although efforts at thought suppression are often successful, they sometimes result in a rebound effect, in which such thoughts actually increase in frequency. Persons high in reactance are more likely than those in low in reactance to experience such effects.

- While social cognition is subject to many sources of error, we generally do an excellent job of understanding the social world.

AFFECT AND COGNITION: HOW FEELINGS SHAPE THOUGHT AND THOUGHT SHAPES FEELINGS

Have you ever had an experience like the one shown in Figure 3.12? If you are like most people, you have: because you were in a very good mood, you tended to perceive everything around you more favorably—other people, films or television shows, groceries, even your professors. Experiences such as this call

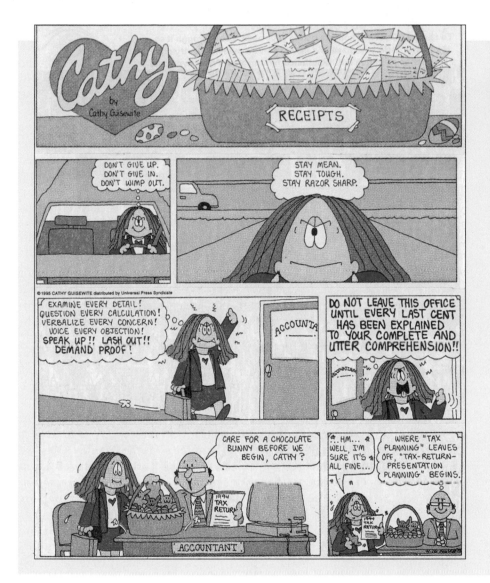

Figure 3.12
An Example of How Affect Influences Cognition. Like Cathy, most of us have had the experience of viewing everything—other people, various events, even tax forms!—in a positive light when we are in a good mood.

(*Source:* King Features Syndicate.)

attention to the fact that there is often a complex interplay between **affect**—our current moods, and *cognition*—the ways in which we process, store, remember, and use social information (Forgas, 1995a; Isen & Baron, 1991). We say *interplay* because research on this topic indicates that in fact the relationship is very much a two-way street: our feelings and moods strongly influence several aspects of cognition, and cognition, in turn, exerts strong effects on our feelings and moods (e.g., McDonald & Hirt, 1997; Seta, Hayes, & Seta, 1994). What are these effects like? Let's see what research findings indicate about this topic.

Connections between Affect and Cognition: Some Intriguing Effects

Because the relationship between affect and cognition seems to be reciprocal—it works both ways—research has focused on both of these links. Reflecting this fact, we'll consider these two kinds of connections separately. But please keep in mind they are really two sides of the same basic coin.

The Influence of Affect on Cognition. Suppose that you have just received some very good news—you did much better on an important exam than you expected.

affect • Our current feelings and moods.

As a result, you are feeling great. Now you run into one of your friends and she introduces you to someone you don't know. You chat with this person for a while and then leave for another class. Will your first impression of the stranger be influenced by the fact that you are feeling so good? The findings of many different studies suggest strongly that it will (Bower, 1991; Clore, Schwarz, & Conway, 1993; Mayer & Hanson, 1995). In other words, our current moods can strongly affect our reactions to new stimuli we encounter for the first time, whether these are people, foods, or even geographic locations where we've never been before. As an old song puts it, when we are in a good mood we tend to "see the world through rose-colored glasses"—everything takes on a positive glow.

Another way in which affect influences cognition is by its impact on the style of information processing we adopt. A growing body of research findings indicate that *positive* affect encourages us to adopt a flexible, creative style of thinking, while *negative* affect leads us to engage in more systematic and careful processing (e.g., Stroessner & Mackie, 1992). This can result in important effects. For instance, recent findings (Forgas, 1998c) indicate that people in a positive mood are more likely to show the fundamental attribution error (a tendency to overestimate the role of internal, dispositional factors as causes of others' behavior) than those who are in a negative mood. Why? Apparently because being in a good mood makes us more likely to focus on information that's readily available (e.g., what another person does), while being in a bad mood makes us more likely to focus on information that's not so readily accessible, such as the constraints that may have influenced this person's actions.

A third way in which affect influences cognition involves its impact on memory. Here, two different, but related, kinds of effects seem to occur. One is known as **mood-dependent memory.** This term refers to the fact that what we remember while in a given mood may be determined in part by what we learned when previously in that mood. For instance, if you stored some information into long-term memory when in a good mood, you are more likely to remember this information when in a similar mood. A second kind of effect is known as **mood congruence effect.** This refers to the fact that we are more likely to store or remember positive information when in a positive mood and negative information when in a negative mood; in other words, we are likely to notice or remember information that is congruent with our current moods (Blaney, 1986). A simple way to think about the difference between mood-dependent memory and mood congruence effects is this: In mood-dependent memory, the nature of the information doesn't matter—only your mood at the time you learned it and your mood when you try to recall it is relevant. In mood congruence effects, in contrast, the affective nature of the information—whether it is positive or negative—is crucial. When we are in an upbeat mood, we tend to remember cheerful information; when in a down mood, we tend to remember more depressing information (see Figure 3.13).

Research findings confirm the existence of mood-dependent memory (Eich, 1995) and also suggest that such effects may be quite important. For instance, mood-dependent memory helps explain why depressed persons have difficulty in remembering times when they felt better (Schachter & Kihlstrom, 1989): being in a very negative mood now, they tend to remember information they entered into memory when in the same mood—and this information relates to feeling depressed. This is important, because being able to remember what it felt like *not* to be depressed can play an important part in successful treatment of this problem. (We'll discuss other aspects of personal health in Chapter 13.)

Our current moods also influence another important aspect of cognition: creativity. The results of several studies suggest that being in a happy mood can

mood-dependent memory •
The fact that what we remember while in a given mood may be determined in part by what we learned when previously in that mood.

mood congruence effects •
Our tendency to store or remember positive information when in a positive mood and negative information when in a negative mood.

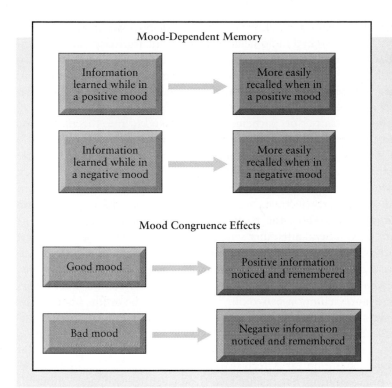

Figure 3.13
The Effects of Mood on Memory. Our moods can influence what we remember through two mechanisms: *mood dependent memory,* which refers to the fact that what we remember while in a given mood is determined, in part, by what we learned when previously in that mood; and *mood congruence effects,* which refer to the fact that we are more likely to store or remember positive information when in a good mood and negative information when in a bad mood.

increase creativity—perhaps because being in a happy mood activates a wider range of ideas and associations than being in a negative mood, and creativity consists in part of combining such associations into new patterns (e.g., Estrada, Isen, & Young, 1995).

A fourth way in which affect can influence cognition involves its impact on our plans and intentions in a wide range of social situations. For instance, recent findings reported by Forgas (1998) suggest that negotiators who are in a good mood adopt more cooperative strategies and expect better outcomes than ones who are in a bad mood.

Finally, and perhaps most dramatically, recent findings indicate that information that evokes affective reactions may be processed differently than other kinds of information and that, as a result, this information may be almost impossible to ignore or disregard (e.g., Edwards, Heindel, & Louis-Dreyfus, 1996; Wegner & Gold, 1995). Perhaps the most convincing evidence pointing to such conclusions has been reported by Edwards and Bryan (1997).

These researchers reasoned that emotion-stirring information may be a potent cause of **mental contamination**—a process in which our judgments, emotions, or behaviors are influenced by mental processing that is unconscious and uncontrollable (Wilson & Brekke, 1994). Specifically, Edwards and Bryan suggested that information that evokes emotional reactions may be especially likely to produce such effects because individuals often have little control over their emotional reactions, and because emotional reactions are diffuse in nature and foster integrative rather than analytic processing. The result: Once we are exposed to emotion-generating information, we can't ignore it, no matter how hard we try.

To test this reasoning, the researchers conducted an experiment in which participants played the role of jurors. They read a transcript of a murder trial that contained information about the defendant's previous criminal record. In one experimental condition this information was presented in an emotion-generating

mental contamination • A process in which our judgments, emotions, or behaviors are influenced by mental processing that is unconscious and uncontrollable.

manner (it described a vicious attack the man had made on a woman); in another condition it was presented in a more neutral manner (the transcript simply mentioned that he was accused of a prior assault). For half the participants the transcript indicated that this information about the defendant was admissible and should be considered; for the other half the transcript described the information as inadmissible and told the "jurors" to ignore it in reaching their verdict.

After reading the transcript, participants were asked to rate the guilt of the defendant and to recommend a sentence for him. Edwards and Bryan (1997) predicted that because of mental contamination, individuals would *not* be able to ignore the emotion-generating information. In fact, when told to do so, they might find themselves thinking about it more often than when *not* told to do this—the kind of rebound effect we described in connection with our discussion of thought suppression. Thus, the participants would view the defendant as more guilty and recommend a harsher sentence for him under these conditions; that is, when they were exposed to emotion-generating information and told to ignore it. As you can see from Figure 13.14, results confirmed these predictions. These findings have important implications for the legal system, where jurors are often told to ignore emotion-provoking information. The results obtained by Edwards and Bryan (1997) and other researchers suggest that this may be an impossible task. We'll return to this and related topics in Chapter 13.

The Influence of Cognition on Affect. Most research on the relationship between affect and cognition has focused on how feelings influence thought. However, there is also strong evidence for the reverse—the impact of cognition on affect. One aspect of this relationship is described in what is known as the two-factor theory of emotion (Schachter, 1964). That theory suggests that often, we don't know our own feelings or attitudes directly. Rather, since these internal reactions are often somewhat ambiguous, we infer their nature from the eternal world—from the kinds of situations in which we experience these reactions. For example, if we experience increased arousal in the presence of an

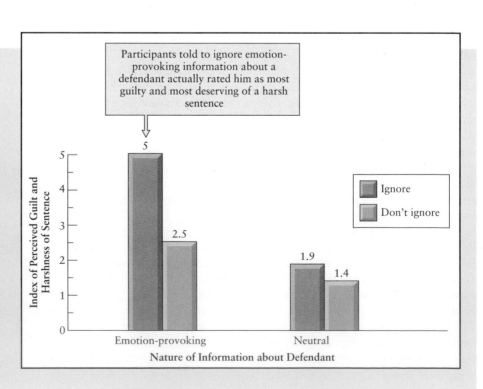

Figure 3.14

Evidence for Our Inability to Ignore Emotion-Provoking Information. Jurors instructed to ignore emotion-generating information about a defendant actually rated this person as more guilty than persons not told to ignore this information or persons who received the same information presented in a nonemotional form. These findings underscore the difficulty of ignoring emotion-provoking information, and have important implications for the legal system.

(*Source:* Based on data from Edwards & Bryan, 1997.)

Participants told to ignore emotion-provoking information about a defendant actually rated him as most guilty and most deserving of a harsh sentence attractive person, we may conclude that we are in love. In contrast, if we experience increased arousal after being cut off in traffic by another driver, we may conclude that what we feel is anger.

A second way in which cognition can influence emotions is through the activation of schemas containing a strong affective component. For example, if we label an individual as belonging to some group, the schema for this social category may suggest what traits he or she probably possesses. In addition, the schema may tell us how we *feel* about such persons. Thus, activation of a strong racial, ethnic, or religious schema or stereotype may exert powerful effects upon our current feelings or mood. (We'll return to this topic in Chapter 6.)

Third, our thoughts can often influence our reactions to emotion-provoking events. For example, as we'll see in our discussion of aggression in Chapter 11, anger can often be reduced if we receive apologies or reasonable explanations for why another person acted in a provocative manner (Ohbuchi, Kameda, & Agarie, 1989). Further, anger can often be reduced—or even prevented—by such techniques as thinking about events other than those that generate anger (Zillmann, 1993). In these instances the effects of cognition can have important social consequences.

The Affect Infusion Model: How Affect Influences Cognition

Before concluding, we should address one final issue: *How,* precisely, does affect influence cognition? Through what mechanisms do our feelings influence our thought? A theory proposed by Forgas (1995), known as the **affect infusion model** (or AIM), offers revealing answers. According to Forgas (1995a), affect influences social thought and, ultimately, social judgments through two major mechanisms. First, affect serves to *prime* (i.e., trigger) similar or related cognitive categories. When we are in a good mood, positive feelings serve to prime positive associations and memories; when we are in a bad mood, in contrast, negative feelings tend to prime mainly negative associations and memories (Bower, 1991; Erber, 1991).

Second, affect may influence cognition by acting as a *heuristic cue*—a quick way for us to infer our reactions to a specific person, event, or stimulus. According to this *affect-as-information* mechanism (Clore et al., 1993), when asked to make a judgment about something in the social world, we examine our feelings and then respond accordingly. If we are in a good mood, we conclude: "I like it" or "I'm favorable toward it." If we are in a bad mood, we conclude: "I don't like it" or "I'm against it." In other words, we ask ourselves: "How do I feel about it?" and use our current affective state to answer this question—*even if it is unrelated to the object, person, or event itself.* (For instance, several studies [e.g., Baron, 1995] indicate that interviewers' moods can influence their ratings of job applicants, even if the moods have nothing to do with these applicants.)

The findings of many different studies lend support to the view that affective states can influence judgments and decisions through both of these mechanisms (e.g., Clore et al., 1994; Forgas, 1993). The key remaining question, however, is this: Precisely *when* do such effects occur? When do our current moods strongly influence our thoughts, judgments, and decisions? The AIM model offers a surprising answer. It suggests that the likelihood of affect infusion is *higher* when individuals engage in careful, effortful thought about some issue or topic than when they engage in simpler and relatively "automatic" modes of thought. Relatively simple modes of thought occur in situations where individuals make judgments or decisions by recalling previous evaluations; for example, someone who has already formed the judgment "I don't like

affect infusion model • A theory explaining the mechanisms through which affect influences social thought and social judgments.

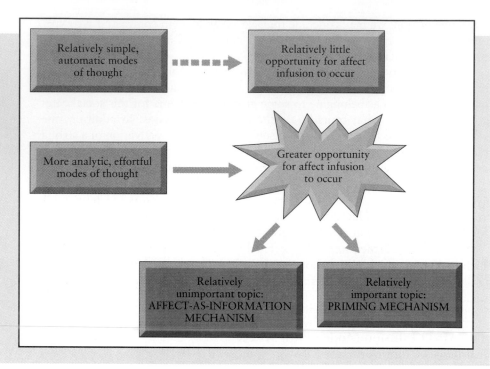

Figure 3.15

The Affect Infusion Model. The affect infusion model (AIM; Forgas, 1995a) makes a somewhat surprising prediction: It suggests that our affective states are more likely to influence our social judgments and decisions when we engage in careful analytic thought than when we engage in simpler and more automatic modes of thought.

cheesecake" can quickly eliminate it as a potential choice among an array of desserts simply by bringing this judgment to mind. Similarly, relatively simple or automatic modes of thought occur when individuals are strongly motivated to reach a particular conclusion; in such cases, they merely extract available information pointing to this decision or conclusion rather than engaging in a detailed analysis of all available information. According to the AIM model, current moods are unlikely to exert strong effects in these instances, because these kinds of thinking are so rapid and lacking in effort that there is little opportunity for current moods to enter the picture (see Figure 3.15).

Careful, reasoned thought, however, presents a markedly different picture. Here, individuals engage in active, effortful processing of information, often with the goal of transforming this information (the raw materials of cognition) into something new (Forgas, 1995a). According to the AIM model, when individuals engage in such thought, affect infusion has ample opportunity to occur. When such thought is relatively unimportant to the persons performing it and they do not feel compelled to seek maximum accuracy, affect infusion will occur primarily through the *affect-as-information* mechanism described above. In contrast, when such thought *is* important or personally relevant to the persons performing it and they do feel compelled to examine all pertinent information, affect infusion will occur primarily through the *priming* mechanism. In both cases, the main point—and the one that is certainly counterintuitive—remains the same: Current moods are more likely to influence judgments and decisions when individuals engage in active, effortful thought about issues; for example, when they are attempting to form an impression of another person or to evaluate him or her very carefully (Forgas, 1995a).

The results of many studies offer support for these suggestions (e.g., Forgas, 1998b; Forgas & Fiedler, 1996; Sedikides, 1995), so it appears that the AIM provides a useful framework for understanding how and when our affective states influence our thought and social judgments.

Do people all around the world interpret their affective states the same way? See the *Social Diversity* section for some interesting research on this question.

Social Diversity: A Critical Analysis
Culture and the Appraisal of Emotions

Emotional experiences are a common aspect of social life; over the course of days, weeks, or months, most persons encounter situations that cause them to experience such emotions as joy, anger, fear, sadness, and guilt. As we noted in Chapter 2, several emotions appear to be quite universal in nature: people all around the world experience them in certain kinds of situations, and show certain easily recognized facial expressions when they do (e.g., Rosenberg & Ekman, 1995). But a key question remains: Do cultural factors influence such reactions? In other words, do people living in different cultures experience basic emotions in the same way, or do they *appraise*—evaluate and interpret—such experiences differently? This is a complex question, but recent research by Scherer and his colleagues (Scherer, 1997; Scherer & Walbott, 1994) has begun to provide some intriguing answers.

In one very large-scale study, these researchers asked almost three thousand persons living in thirty-seven different countries to remember situations that caused them to experience seven emotions: joy, anger, fear, sadness, disgust, shame, and guilt. Then the researchers asked the participants several questions about how they appraised these situations, questions such as: (1) To what extent did you expect this situation to occur? (2) Did you find the event pleasant or unpleasant? (3) How important was the event for your goals or needs? (4) Was the situation or event that caused your emotion unjust or unfair? (5) Who do you think was responsible for the event in the first place? (6) If the event was caused by someone else's behavior, would

this behavior be judged as improper or immoral by your acquaintances?

On the basis of previous research, Scherer and his colleagues predicted that across all the cultures evaluated, there would be a high degree of similarity in participants' responses. That is, although they would answer the questions listed above differently for each emotion (for example, they would rate joy as much more pleasant than anger), the overall pattern would be much the same. This prediction was confirmed. However, Scherer (1997) also predicted that there might be some differences in answers to these questions for persons living in different cultures. To test this possibility, the researchers divided the thirty-seven countries into categories based on their geographic location: North/Central Europe, New World (North America), Africa, Mediterranean Basin, Latin America. When this was done, some interesting differences among the various groups of countries did emerge. For instance, for all emotions except joy, persons living in African cultures rated the situations that caused them to experience various emotions higher on the unfairness, external causation, and immorality dimensions. In contrast, those from Latin American countries appraised these situations as significantly lower on immorality.

What accounted for these differences? Additional findings indicated that *urbanism*—the extent to which people in each region lived in large cities—may have played a key role (see Figure 3.16). As noted by Scherer, urbanism is quite low in African countries but much higher in Latin American ones. Thus, differences with respect to the

Figure 3.16
Degree of Urbanization: One Factor That May Play a Role in Cultural Differences in Emotional Appraisal. Recent findings indicate that people living in different cultures appraise (interpret) emotion-provoking situations somewhat differently. One factor that may be responsible for such differences is the degree of urbanization in these cultures.

ratings of immorality may reflect the effects of living or not living in large cities. Similarly, some findings also suggested that *religion* played a role in generating cultural differences in emotional appraisal. While a large majority of persons in Latin America reported being Catholic, a much smaller proportion of persons living in African countries reported adherence to this religion or other forms of Christianity. Scherer (1997) speculates that this factor, too, may play a role in the cultural differences observed. However, other differences could also be involved, so these findings should be interpreted as only preliminary in nature.

Overall, the findings of this very large-scale study, plus those of other research (e.g., Mesquita, Frijda, & Scherer, 1997), point to the following conclusions: (1) Human beings all around the world and in many different cultures share many of the basic experiences of social life; but (2) their reactions to and interpretations of many events are colored and influenced by the specific cultures in which they live. So although we are all alike in many respects, cultural diversity is a real and potent force and should never be overlooked in our efforts to understand social thought and social behavior.

Key Points

- Affect influences cognition in several ways. Our current moods can cause us to react positively or negatively to new stimuli, including other persons, the extent to which we think systematically or in a more flexible, creative way, and can influence memory through *mood-dependent memory* and *mood congruence effects*.

- Affect can also influence creativity. Recent findings indicate, too, that emotion-provoking information can strongly influence judgments and decisions even if we try to ignore it.

- Cognition influences affect through the activation of schemas containing a strong affective component, and by shaping our reactions to emotion-provoking events.

- The *affect infusion model* (AIM) suggests that affect influences cognition through two mechanisms—through priming and by serving as a heuristic cue. The model also suggests that affect is more likely to influence judgments and decisions when individuals engage in analytic thought than when they engage in simpler and relatively automatic modes of thought.

- Cultural differences have subtle effects on people's appraisals of emotional experiences. Factors such as urbanism and religion may play a role in these differences.

Connections: Integrating Social Psychology

In this chapter, you read about . . .	*In other chapters, you will find related discussions of . . .*
schemas	the effects of schemas and prototypes on other aspects of social behavior such as attitudes (Chapter 4) and prejudice (Chapter 6)
potential sources of error in social cognition	the role of these errors in first impressions (Chapter 2), persuasion (Chapter 4), and the legal system (Chapter 13)
the interplay between affect and cognition	the role of these links in many forms of social behavior, including prejudice (Chapter 6), attraction (Chapter 7), helping (Chapter 10), aggression (Chapter 11), and behavior in work settings (Chapter 13)

Thinking about Connections

1. Schemas help us understand and interpret many social situations. Do you think they play a role in intimate relationships (see Chapter 8)? For instance, do you think we possess relatively clear schemas suggesting that relationships should change in various ways over time, and even suggesting *when* such changes should occur?

2. Have you ever tried to suppress certain thoughts in order to make a beneficial change in your own behavior—for instance, to lose weight or change a bad habit? If so, were you successful? Do you think that after reading the information in this chapter, you might be able to do a better job in this respect? Could you, for instance, do a better job of keeping your temper in check (see Chapter 11) or avoiding negative feelings toward members of various minority groups (Chapter 6)?

3. Suppose that something you did turned out very badly. Do you think that trying to imagine how it might have turned out better would be of any help to you in actually improving your performance in the future? Could this technique, based on counterfactual thinking, help you get along better with other people (Chapters 8 and 12)?

Ideas to Take with You
Common Errors in Social Cognition

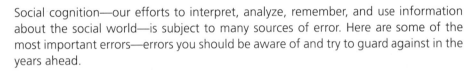

Social cognition—our efforts to interpret, analyze, remember, and use information about the social world—is subject to many sources of error. Here are some of the most important errors—errors you should be aware of and try to guard against in the years ahead.

The Self-Confirming Effects of Schemas

Once they are formed, *schemas*—mental frameworks for organizing and interpreting social information—tend to become self-confirming: they lead us to notice only information that is consistent with them, and they cause us to act in ways that confirm their validity.

The Planning Fallacy

Often, we underestimate the amount of time it will take us to complete a task. The stronger our motivation to be done with the task, the stronger this effect.

Counterfactual Thinking: Imagining What Might Have Been

When we imagine outcomes different from those that actually occurred, we are engaging in counterfactual thinking. Such thought can increase our satisfaction if we imagine worse outcomes than actually occurred; but it can lead to strong feelings of regret or envy if we imagine better outcomes than actually occurred.

Thought Suppression: Trying to Keep Certain Thoughts Out of Consciousness

In many situations we try to suppress thoughts that we believe will get us into trouble. For example, dieters try to suppress thoughts of delicious foods, and people trying to quit smoking try to avoid thinking about the pleasure of lighting up. Unfortunately, trying to suppress such thoughts often causes the thoughts to intrude *more* than they would otherwise do.

The Role of Affective States

When we are in a good mood, we evaluate almost everything more positively than would otherwise be the case. The opposite is true when we are in a bad mood. Unfortunately, such effects can lead to serious errors in our efforts to make judgments about other persons.

SUMMARY AND REVIEW OF KEY POINTS

Schemas: Mental Frameworks for Organizing— and Using—Social Information

- Research on *social cognition* suggests that our thinking about other persons and social situations is subject to many sources of error.

- One source of such effects is *schemas*—mental frameworks centering around a specific theme that help us to organize social information.

- Schemas can relate to persons, events, or situations. Once formed, schemas exert powerful effects on what we notice (attention), enter into memory (encoding), and later remember (retrieval).

- While schemas help us to process information, they often persist in the face of disconfirming information. As a result, they can distort our understanding of the social world.

- Schemas can also exert self-confirming effects, causing us to behave in ways that confirm them.

Heuristics: Mental Shortcuts in Social Cognition

- Because our capacity to process information is limited, we often experience *information overload*. To avoid this, we use *heuristics*—rules for making decisions in a quick and relatively effortless manner.

- One such heuristic is *representativeness*, which suggests that the more similar an individual is to typical members of a given group, the more likely she or he is to belong to that group.

- Another heuristic is *availability*, which suggests that the easier it is to bring information to mind, the greater its importance or relevance to our decisions or judgments. In some cases, availability may also involve the amount of information we bring to mind.

- *Priming* refers to increased availability of information resulting from exposure to specific stimuli or events.

Potential Sources of Error in Social Cognition: Why Total Rationality Is Scarcer Than You Think

- In our efforts to understand the external world, we can use either rational processing, which follows basic rules of logic, or intuitive processing, which relies on intuition and hunches.

- Growing evidence suggests that we rely largely on intuitive processing when we think about other persons or social situations.

- A reliance on intuitive thought may be one reason why automobile safety devices (e.g., air bags) have been adopted on a large scale even in the absence of clear evidence for their potential value.

- In general, we notice information that is inconsistent with our expectations more readily than information that is consistent with them. As a result, inconsistent information may exert stronger effects on our later judgments or decisions, although this is not always the case.

- Individuals tend to make overly optimistic predictions about how long it will take them to complete a given task, an effect known as the *planning fallacy*.

- The planning fallacy seems to stem from the tendency to focus on the future while ignoring related past events, and also from motivation to have tasks completed quickly.

- When individuals think too deeply about some topic, they may become confused about the factors that actually play a role in their behavior, with the result that they make less accurate judgments or decisions.

- In many situations, individuals imagine "what might have been"—they engage in *counterfactual thinking*. Such thinking can affect our sympathy for persons who have experienced negative outcomes and can cause us to experience strong regret over missed opportunities.

- Counterfactual thinking can also strongly influence our affective states. And it may increase our understanding of *why* we experienced negative outcomes; in this way, such thought can help us to improve our performance in the future.

- We often engage in *magical thinking*—thinking based on assumptions that don't hold up to rational scrutiny. For instance, we may believe that if two objects are in contact, properties can pass from one to the other.

- Individuals often engage in *thought suppression*, trying to prevent themselves from thinking about certain topics (e.g., delicious desserts, alcohol, cigarettes).

- Although efforts at thought suppression are often successful, sometimes they result in a rebound effect, in which such thoughts actually increase in frequency. Persons high in reactance are more likely than those in low in reactance to experience such effects.

- While social cognition is subject to many sources of error, we generally do an excellent job of understanding the social world.

Affect and Cognition: How Feelings Shape Thought and Thought Shapes Feelings

- Affect influences cognition in several ways. Our current moods can cause us to react positively or negatively to new stimuli, including other persons, the extent to which we think systematically or in a more flexible, creative way, and can influence memory through *mood-dependent memory* and *mood congruence effects*.

- Affect can also influence creativity. Recent findings indicate, too, that emotion-provoking information can strongly influence judgments and decisions even if we try to ignore it.

- Cognition influences affect through the activation of schemas containing a strong affective component, and by shaping our reactions to emotion-provoking events.

- The *affect infusion model* (AIM) suggests that affect influences cognition through two mechanisms—through priming and by serving as a heuristic cue. The model also suggests that affect is more likely to influence judgments and decisions when individuals engage in analytic thought than when they engage in simpler and relatively automatic modes of thought.

- Cultural differences have subtle effects on people's appraisals of emotional experiences. Factors such as urbanism and religion may play a role in these differences.

KEY TERMS

affect (p. 105)

affect infusion model (p. 109)

cognitive–experiential self-theory (p. 90)

counterfactual thinking (p. 97)

heuristics (p. 86)

information overload (p. 86)

magical thinking (p. 101)

mental contamination (p. 107)

mood congruence effects (p. 106)

mood-dependent memory (p. 106)

perseverance effect (p. 84)

planning fallacy (p. 94)

priming (p. 88)

representativeness heuristic (p. 86)

schemas (p. 81)

self-fulfilling prophecies (p. 85)

social cognition (p. 80)

thought suppression (p. 102)

FOR MORE INFORMATION

Forgas, J. P. (Ed.). (1991). *Emotion and social judgments.* Elmsford, NY: Pergamon Press.

Chapters in this volume deal with the complex interplay between affect and cognition. The many ways in which our feelings can influence our social judgments are carefully examined by experts in this field.

Wyer, R. S., Jr., & Bargh, J. A. (Eds.). (1997). *The automaticity of everyday life (Advances in social cognition,* Vol. 10). Mahwah, NJ: Erlbaum.

To what extent is our social thought and social behavior "automatic"—occurring without conscious thought? The papers in this excellent volume present data suggesting that in fact, our thought and behavior are often triggered in an automatic manner by external conditions. This book is on the very cutting edge of research on social cognition and is filled with ideas you are sure to find both surprising and interesting.

Roese, N. J., & Olson, J. M. (Eds.). (1997). *What might have been: The social psychology of counterfactual thinking.* Mahwah, NJ: Erlbaum.

This book focuses on counterfactual thinking in specific situations. The nature of such thought and its effects are examined from many different perspectives by social psychologists who have studied this fascinating topic.

4

Attitudes:
Evaluating the Social World

24 Human Figures. © José Ortega/Stock Illustration Source

Chapter Outline

Attitude Formation: How We Come to Hold the Views We Do
  Social Learning: Acquiring Attitudes from Others
  Social Comparison and Attitude Formation
  Genetic Factors: Some Surprising Recent Findings

Do Attitudes Influence Behavior? And If So, *When* and *How*?
  CORNERSTONES OF SOCIAL PSYCHOLOGY: Attitudes versus Actions:
      When Saying Is Definitely Not Doing
  When Do Attitudes Influence Behavior? Specificity, Strength,
      Accessibility, and Other Factors
  How Do Attitudes Influence Behavior? Intentions, Willingness,
      and Action
  BEYOND THE HEADLINES: AS SOCIAL PSYCHOLOGISTS SEE IT:
      When Personal Health and Looking Sexy Collide, Guess
      Which Wins?

The Fine Art of Persuasion: Using Messages to Change Attitudes
  Persuasion: The Early Approach
  The Cognitive Approach to Persuasion: Systematic versus
      Heuristic Processing
  Other Factors Affecting Persuasion: Attitude Function and the Role of
      Nonverbal Cues

When Attitude Change Fails: Resistance to Persuasion
  Reactance: Protecting Our Personal Freedom
  Forewarning: Prior Knowledge of Persuasive Intent
  Selective Avoidance
  Biased Assimilation and Attitude Polarization: "If It's Contrary to
      What I Believe, Then It Must Be Unreliable—or Worse!"

**Cognitive Dissonance: Why Our Behavior Can Sometimes Influence
  Our Attitudes**
  Cognitive Dissonance: What It Is and Various Ways (Direct and
      Indirect) to Reduce It
  Dissonance and Attitude Change: The Effects of Induced Compliance
  Dissonance As a Tool for Beneficial Changes in Behavior: When
      Hypocrisy Can Be a Force for Good
  SOCIAL DIVERSITY: A CRITICAL ANALYSIS: Is Dissonance Culture-Bound?
      Evidence from a Cross-National Study
  CONNECTIONS: Integrating Social Psychology
  IDEAS TO TAKE WITH YOU: Resisting Persuasion: Some Useful Steps

Summary and Review of Key Points
Key Terms
For More Information

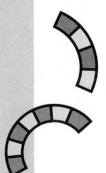

When it comes to having dinner with friends, I (Robert Baron) try to stick to the following rule: Never discuss politics. Yet recently I broke my rule, and did enter into a political discussion while eating a delicious meal in one of my favorite restaurants. Here's what happened. At one point during the evening, conversation turned to a major bill pending in our state's legislature. This bill, if passed, would increase state aid to school districts; in return, school districts receiving these funds would agree to limit the increase in their annual budgets to the rate of inflation. The goal is to strengthen schools while at the same time reducing local property taxes, which have been going up at three times the rate of inflation in our area in recent years. I'm strongly in favor of this bill, and said so—thereby breaking my "No politics" rule.

My comments brought an immediate reaction from Jan, one of the other people in our group. "What!" she exclaimed in surprise. "You favor the bill? Don't you realize it will limit school budgets? You're not against education, are you?" How could I resist answering? As a professor, of course I'm not against education. But in our area, I reminded Jan, local property taxes have gone up so fast that they have placed a tremendous burden on retired persons living on pensions. She was unmoved by these comments. "I don't care," she said heatedly. "We have to spend more on education; how else can schools improve?" At this point my blood pressure began to rise. I'm strongly in favor of education, but I'm just as strongly against waste; so I countered by pointing out that despite huge increases in spending, students' performance in our local schools had actually dropped—mainly because the increased taxes were being used to hire more administrators and to buy items I didn't view as essential, such as cellular phones for every school bus, not to improve what went on in the classroom. None of this made the slightest impact on Jan; she simply restated her original view that no matter how much we spent on education, it wasn't enough. At this point, my wife kicked me in the leg—a signal to cool it, fast. Fortunately, I did, and the conversation shifted to other, less controversial topics.

Why do I begin with this incident? Because, for me, it illustrates a key theme of recent research on *attitudes*, a central topic in social psychology and the focus of this chapter. **Attitudes** refer to our evaluations of virtually any aspect of the social world (e.g., Fazio & Roskos-Ewoldsen, 1994; Tesser & Martin, 1996)— the extent to which we have favorable or unfavorable reactions to issues, ideas, persons, social groups, objects—any and every element of the social world (see Figure 4.1). In the incident above, for instance, I was *for* the bill in question and had a favorable attitude about it, while my friend Jan was against the bill and had an unfavorable attitude about it.

So what point does this incident illustrate? The central fact that once attitudes are established, they are usually very difficult to change. Attitudes, once formed, often seem to operate as *schemas*, the kind of cognitive frameworks we discussed in Chapter 3; as such, they strongly color our perceptions and thought about the issues, persons, objects, or groups to which they refer. For instance, research findings indicate that we view information offering support for our attitudes as far more convincing and accurate than information that refutes them (e.g., Munro & Ditto, 1997). Similarly, we view sources that provide evidence contrary to our views as highly suspect—biased and unreliable (e.g., Giner-Sorolla & Chaiken, 1994, 1997). Given such reactions, attitudes, once formed, tend to persist, especially if they are strongly accepted and closely related to the interests or outcomes of the persons who hold them (e.g., Crano, 1997). Could I have succeeded in changing Jan's attitudes about the pending legislation?

attitudes • Evaluations of various aspects of the social world.

Figure 4.1
Attitudes: Evaluations of the Social World. Do you have any reactions—favorable or unfavorable—to the people and objects shown here? If so, you hold *attitudes* toward them.

Given her passionate and long-standing views on this topic and on education generally, I doubt it. No matter how much evidence I presented, she might still reject it and maintain her existing opinions. And the same holds for me, too: it's unlikely that Jan could have swayed *my* views on this issue. So my wife was probably right in kicking me in the leg; this was definitely not the right time or setting for a heated—and probably pointless—debate.

But if attitudes are so hard to change, you may now be wondering, why are they so important? Basically, for two reasons. First, as we have just noted, they strongly influence our social thought—the ways in which we think about and process many kinds of social information. In fact, growing evidence suggests that when defined as evaluations of the world around us, attitudes may represent a very basic aspect of all forms of thought. Indeed, the tendency to categorize stimuli as positive or negative appears to be the initial step in our information processing (e.g., Ito & Cacioppo, 1999). Recent evidence suggests, for instance, that negative stimuli (e.g., a photo of a mutilated face) produce larger event-related potentials in our brains (changes in electrical activity) than do positive stimuli (e.g., a photo of a sports car; Ito, Larsen, Smith, & Cacioppo, 1998). The effects of attitudes on the processing of social information have been a key theme of recent research on attitudes, and we will examine such research carefully here (e.g., Eagly & Chaiken, 1998).

Second, social psychologists have been interested in attitudes for several decades because, it has been widely assumed, attitudes strongly affect behavior. Do you believe that abortion is wrong and should be outlawed? Then you may join a demonstration against it. Do you hold a negative attitude toward the current president (or other leaders of your country)? Then you may not vote for these persons or their designated successors in the next election. If attitudes influence behavior, then knowing something about them can help us predict people's behavior in a wide range of contexts. As we'll see in Chapter 7, we also hold attitudes toward specific persons—for example, we like them or dislike them. Clearly, such attitudes can play a crucial role in our relations with these persons.

For these and other reasons, attitudes have been a central concept in social psychology since its earliest days (e.g., Allport & Hartman, 1924). In this chapter we'll provide you with an overview of what social psychologists have discovered

ROBOTMAN® by Jim Meddick

Figure 4.2
Changing Attitudes Is a Difficult Task! Contrary to what this cartoon suggests, changing
attitudes is a difficult and tricky business.
(*Source:* NEA Inc., 1991.)

about these evaluations of the social world and their effects. Beginning at what
is, logically, the beginning, we'll first consider the ways in which attitudes are
formed. Next, we'll consider a crucial question: Do attitudes really influence behavior, as social psychologists (and many other persons) generally assume? (To
get ahead of ourselves, they *do*, but this link is far more complex than you might
imagine.) Third, we'll turn to the question of how, sometimes, attitudes are
changed—the process of *persuasion*. Please emphasize the word *sometimes*; because, as we noted above, changing attitudes is a difficult business—far more difficult than advertisers, politicians, salespersons, and many other would-be
persuaders seem to assume (see Figure 4.2). Fourth, we'll examine some of the
reasons *why* attitudes are usually difficult to change—why people are often so resistant to persuasion. Finally, we'll consider the intriguing fact that on some occasions, our actions shape our attitudes rather than vice versa. The process that
underlies such effects is known as *cognitive dissonance*, and it has fascinating implications, not just for attitude change but for many aspects of social behavior.

ATTITUDE FORMATION: HOW WE COME TO HOLD THE VIEWS WE DO

What are your views about gun control? Affirmative action? Recent events in
Kosovo? Sexual harassment? The film *Titanic*? Pizza? Almost certainly, you
have views—attitudes—about all of these. But where, precisely, did these attitudes come from? Were you born with them? Or did you acquire them as a result
of various life experiences? Most people—and most social psychologists—
accept the view that attitudes are *learned*, and most of our discussion of this issue will focus on the processes through which attitudes are acquired. But please
take note: We would be remiss if we did not mention that a small but growing
body of evidence suggests that attitudes may be influenced by genetic factors,
too. We'll describe some of the evidence for this surprising idea below.

Social Learning: Acquiring Attitudes from Others

One important source of our attitudes is obvious: we acquire them from other
persons through the process of **social learning**. In other words, many of our

social learning • The
process through which we
acquire new information,
forms of behavior, or attitudes from other persons.

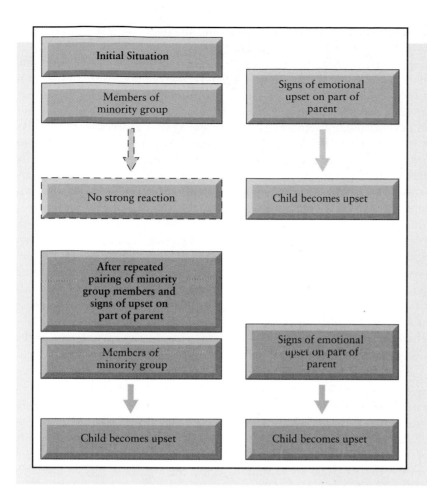

Figure 4.3
Classical Conditioning of Attitudes. Initially, a young child has little or no emotional reaction to the visible characteristics of members of some minority group. If she sees her mother showing signs of negative reactions when in the presence of these persons, however, she too may gradually acquire negative reactions to them, through the process of classical conditioning.

views are acquired in situations where we interact with others or merely observe their behavior. Social learning occurs through several processes.

Classical Conditioning: Learning Based on Association. It is a basic principle of psychology that when one stimulus regularly precedes another, the one that occurs first may soon become a signal for the one that occurs second. In other words, when the first stimulus occurs, individuals expect that the second will soon follow. As a result, they gradually acquire the same kind of reactions to the first stimulus as they show to the second stimulus, especially if the second is one that induces fairly strong and automatic reactions. For instance, consider a woman whose shower emits a low hum just before the hot water runs out and turns into an icy stream. At first, she may show little reaction to the hum. After the hum is followed by freezing water on several occasions, though, she may well experience strong emotional arousal (fear!) when it occurs. After all, it is a signal for what will soon follow—icy cold water.

What does this process, which is known as **classical conditioning,** have to do with attitude formation? Potentially, quite a lot. To see how this process might influence attitudes under real-life conditions, imagine the following scene. A young child sees her mother frown and show other signs of displeasure each time the mother encounters a member of a particular ethnic group. At first, the child is neutral toward members of this group and their visible characteristics (e.g., skin color, style of dress, accent). After these cues are paired with the mother's negative emotional reactions many times, however, classical conditioning occurs; the child comes to react negatively to these stimuli, and to members of this ethnic group (see Figure 4.3). The result: The child acquires a

classical conditioning • A basic form of learning in which one stimulus, initially neutral, acquires the capacity to evoke reactions through repeated pairing with another stimulus. In a sense, one stimulus becomes a signal for the presentation or occurrence of the other.

negative attitude toward such persons—an attitude that may form the core of a full-blown ethnic prejudice. (We'll examine prejudice in detail in Chapter 6.)

Interestingly, studies indicate that classical conditioning can occur below the level of conscious awareness—even when people are not aware of the stimuli that serve as the basis for this kind of conditioning. For instance, in one experiment on this topic (Krosnick et al., 1992), students saw photos of a stranger engaged in routine daily activities such as shopping in a grocery store or walking into her apartment. While these photos were shown, other photos known to induce either positive or negative feelings were presented very briefly—so briefly that participants were not aware of their presence. One group of research participants was exposed to photos that induced positive feelings (e.g., a bridal couple, people playing cards and laughing); another group was exposed to photos that induced negative feelings (e.g., open-heart surgery, a werewolf). Later, both groups expressed their attitudes toward the stranger. Results indicated that even though participants were unaware of the second group of photos (the ones presented very briefly), these stimuli significantly influenced their attitudes toward the stranger. Those exposed to the positive photos reported more favorable attitudes toward this person than those exposed to the negative photos. These findings suggest that attitudes can be influenced by **subliminal conditioning**—classical conditioning that occurs in the absence of conscious awareness of the stimuli involved.

Instrumental Conditioning: Learning to Hold The "Right" Views. Have you ever heard a three-year-old state, with great conviction, that she is a Republican or a Democrat? Or that Fords (or Hondas) are better than Chevrolets (or Toyotas)? Children of this age have little understanding of what these statements mean. Yet they make them all the same. Why? The answer is obvious: They have been praised or rewarded in various ways by their parents for stating such views. As we're sure you know, behaviors that are followed by positive outcomes are strengthened and tend to be repeated. In contrast, behaviors that are followed by negative outcomes are weakened, or at least suppressed. Thus, another way in which attitudes are acquired from others is through the process of **instrumental conditioning**. By rewarding children with smiles, approval, or hugs for stating the "right" views—the ones they themselves favor—parents and other adults play an active role in shaping youngsters' attitudes. It is for this reason that until they reach their teen years, most children express political, religious, and social views highly similar to those of their families. Given the powerful effect of reinforcement on behavior, it would be surprising if they did not.

Observational Learning: Learning by Example. A third process through which attitudes are formed can operate even when parents have no desire to transmit specific views to their children. This process is **observational learning,** and it occurs when individuals acquire new forms of behavior or thought simply by observing the actions of others. Where attitude formation is concerned, observational learning appears to play an important role. In many cases, children hear their parents say things not intended for their ears, or observe their parents engaging in actions the parents tell them not to perform. For example, parents who smoke often warn their children against this habit, even as they light up (see Figure 4.4). What message do children acquire from such instances? The evidence is clear: They often learn to do as their parents *do,* not as they *say.*

In addition, of course, both children and adults often acquire attitudes from exposure to the mass media—television, magazines, films, and so on. For

subliminal conditioning •
Classical conditioning that occurs through exposure to stimuli that are below individuals' threshhold of conscious awareness.

instrumental conditioning •
Basic form of learning in which responses that lead to positive outcomes or that permit avoidance of negative outcomes are strengthened; also known as *operant conditioning.*

observational learning •
Basic form of learning in which individuals acquire new forms of behavior or thought through observing others.

Figure 4.4
Observational Learning in Action. Children learn many things through observation, including attitudes their parents may not want the children to acquire, such as a positive view of smoking.

instance, the characters in most American films now make liberal use of four-letter words that in the past were considered unacceptable. The result: Persons under the age of thirty, who have grown up watching such films, don't find these words as objectionable as older persons like myself. In fact, my students sometimes use them while making presentations in class—something I find very unpleasant.

Social Comparison and Attitude Formation

While many attitudes are formed through social learning, this is not the only way in which they are acquired. Another mechanism involves **social comparison**—our tendency to compare ourselves with others in order to determine whether our view of social reality is or is not correct (Festinger, 1954). To the extent that our views agree with those of others, we conclude that our ideas and attitudes are accurate; after all, if others hold the same views, the views *must* be right. Because of this process, we often change our attitudes so as to hold views closer to those of others. On some occasions, moreover, the process of social comparison may contribute to the formation of new attitudes. For instance, imagine that you heard others you know, like, and respect expressing positive views about some product you've never tried. Do you think you'd acquire a positive attitude toward it and be more likely to try it yourself? The chances are good that you would. After all, you admire the people expressing these views, and want to be like them; and one of way of doing so is to share their attitudes.

The same processes may operate with respect to attitudes directed toward various social groups. For example, imagine that you heard persons you like and respect expressing negative views toward a group with whom you've had no contact. Would this influence your attitudes? It's tempting to say, "Of course not! I wouldn't form any views without meeting these people for myself!" Research findings indicate, however, that hearing others state negative views might actually lead you to adopt similar attitudes—without ever meeting a member of the group in question (e.g., Maio, Esses, & Bell, 1994; Shaver, 1993). In such cases, our attitudes are shaped by social information from others, coupled with our own desire to be similar to people we like or respect.

social comparison • The process through which we compare ourselves to others in order to determine whether our view of social reality is or is not correct.

Genetic Factors: Some Surprising Recent Findings

Can we inherit our attitudes, or at least a tendency to develop certain views about various topics or issues? Your first reply is likely to be "No way!" While we readily accept the fact that genetic factors can influence our height, eye color, and other physical traits, the idea that they might also play a role in our thinking seems strange, to say the least. Yet if we remember that thought occurs within the brain and that brain structure, like every other part of our bodies, is affected by genetic factors, the idea of genetic influences on attitudes becomes, perhaps, a little easier to imagine. In fact, a small but growing body of evidence indicates that genetic factors may actually play some role, although a small one, in attitudes (e.g., Arvey et al., 1989; Keller et al., 1992).

Most of this evidence involves comparisons between identical (monozygotic) and nonidentical (dizygotic) twins. Because identical twins share the same genetic inheritance while nonidentical twins do not, higher correlations between the attitudes of identical twins than between those of nonidentical twins would suggest that genetic factors play a role in shaping such attitudes. This is precisely what has been found: the attitudes of identical twins *do* correlate more highly than those of nonidentical twins (e.g, Waller et al., 1990). Moreover, this is the case even if the twins have been separated early in life and raised in sharply contrasting environments from then on (see Figure 4.5; Bouchard et al., 1992; Hershberger, Lichtenstein, & Knox, 1994). Under these conditions, greater similarity in the attitudes of identical twins than in the attitudes of other persons can't be attributed to similarity in environmental factors.

Additional results suggest, not surprisingly, that genetic factors play a stronger role in shaping some attitudes than others—in other words, that some attitudes are more *heritable* than others. While it is too early to reach definite conclusions, some findings seem to suggest that attitudes involving gut-level preferences (e.g., a preference for certain kinds of music) may be more strongly influenced by genetic factors than attitudes that are more "cognitive" in nature (e.g., attitudes about abstract principles or about situations and objects with which individuals have had little direct experience; Tesser, 1993). In addition, it appears that attitudes that are highly heritable may be more difficult to change than ones that are not, and that highly heritable attitudes may exert stronger effects on behavior (e.g., Crealia & Tesser, 1998). For instance, we seem to like

Figure 4.5

Evidence for the Role of Genetic Factors in Attitudes. The attitudes of identical twins separated very early in life correlate more highly than those of unrelated persons or even those of nonidentical twins. This finding provides evidence for the view that attitudes are influenced by genetic factors, at least to some extent.

strangers who express attitudes similar to ours more when these attitudes are highly heritable than when they are less heritable (Tesser, 1993). We'll return to these points in a later discussion of the effects of attitudes on behavior.

But how, we can almost hear you asking, can such effects occur—how can genetic factors influence attitudes? One possibility is that genetic factors influence more general dispositions, such as the tendency to experience mainly positive or negative affect—to be in a positive or negative mood most of the time (George, 1990). Such tendencies, in turn, could then influence evaluations of many aspects of the social world. For instance, an individual who tends to be in a positive mood much of the time may tend to express a high level of job satisfaction, no matter where he or she works; in contrast, someone who tends to be in a negative mood may tend to express more negative attitudes in virtually any work setting. Only time, and further research, will allow us to determine whether, and how, genetic factors influence attitudes. But given that such factors appear to influence many other aspects of social behavior and social thought, ranging from our choice of romantic partners through aggression (e.g., Buss, 1999), the idea that attitudes, too, may be subject to such influences is no longer viewed as weird or improbable by most social psychologists.

Key Points

- *Attitudes* are evaluations of any aspects of the social world.

- Attitudes are often acquired from other persons through *social learning*. Such learning can involve *classical conditioning, instrumental conditioning,* or *observational learning*.

- Attitudes are also formed on the basis of *social comparison*—our tendency to compare ourselves with others to determine whether our view of social reality is or is not correct. In order to be similar to others we like or admire, we often accept the attitudes they hold.

- Studies conducted with identical twins suggest that attitudes may also be influenced by genetic factors, although the strength of such effects varies greatly for different attitudes.

DO ATTITUDES INFLUENCE BEHAVIOR? AND IF SO, *WHEN* AND *HOW?*

Do our attitudes influence our behavior? Your first reaction is probably to say, "Of course!" Before you leap to this conclusion, though, let me (Robert Baron) tell you about one of my own experiences concerning this issue. A couple of years ago, my village had a paint-collection day. Everyone who had cans of old oil-based paint was supposed to bring the paint to a collection point on Saturday morning so that it could be safely destroyed without damaging the environment. I have had strong "protect the environment" attitudes for many years, so on the designated Saturday morning, my wife and I drove to the collection area. As we approached, we could see a line of cars stretching almost a mile. "There goes our Saturday!" I remarked, and I was right: we sat in line for more than two hours before getting a chance to give our four cans of paint to the people doing the collecting. So far, so good: my strong attitudes about protecting the environment did predict my behavior. But here's where things get tricky. Two weeks later, the village announced another paint-collection day, this time for latex-based paint. I had three cans of this kind of paint in my basement, so I put them aside with the intention of taking them to the collection point. But then I began to think about that long line and another ruined Saturday. . . . Guess what I did? Shame on me, but I left the cans where they were and conveniently "forgot" all about the collection day. So much for my proenvironmental attitudes.

While you may never have experienced events exactly like these, we're willing to bet that you too have had plenty of opportunities to observe sizable gaps between your attitudes and your behavior. To the extent that such gaps exist, social psychologists find themselves facing a disturbing question: Have they been wasting their time studying attitudes for so long? That a gap between attitudes and behavior is sometimes present is obvious. In fact, as described in the *Cornerstones* section below, this gap was brought to the attention of social psychologists in a dramatic way more than sixty years ago (LaPiere, 1934). It is equally clear, however, that our attitudes often *do* exert important effects on our behavior; after all, think of the many times when your reactions to people, ideas, or issues *do* shape your actions concerning these aspects of the social world. So our answer to the question above is: *No*, social psychologists have definitely *not* wasted their time by studying attitudes. The key question, however, is not "Do attitudes influence behavior?" but rather "*When* and *how* do they exert such effects?" These issues have been very central to modern research on the attitude–behavior link, so we'll focus on them in this discussion. Before turning to recent research on this topic, however, let's take a look at the first study that brought the attitude–behavior question sharply into focus.

Cornerstones of Social Psychology
Attitudes versus Actions: When Saying Is Definitely Not Doing

Richard T. LaPiere. *A social psychologist at Stanford University during the 1930s, LaPiere conducted unique research demonstrating that people's attitudes are not always reflected in their overt behavior. His study initiated research on the link between attitudes and behavior that continues up to the present time.*

It was 1930, and all over the world, the deepest depression in living memory had set in. But Richard LaPiere, a social psychologist at Stanford University, wasn't interested in economics: he was concerned, in his research, with the link between attitudes and behavior. At the time, social psychologists generally defined attitudes largely in terms of behavior—as tendencies or predispositions to behave in certain ways in social situations (Allport, 1924). Thus, they assumed that attitudes were usually reflected in overt behavior. LaPiere, however, was not so certain. He wondered whether persons holding various prejudices—negative attitudes toward the members of specific social groups (see Chapter 6)—would demonstrate these attitudes in their overt behaviors as well as in their verbal statements. To find out, he spent two years traveling around the United States with a young Chinese couple. During these travels they stopped at 184 restaurants and 66 hotels and "tourist camps" (predecessors of the modern motel). In the overwhelming majority of cases, the three of them were treated courteously. In fact, they were refused service only once; and in most cases, LaPiere reported, they received what he considered to be average to above-average service.

Now, however, the study gets really interesting. After the travels were complete, LaPiere wrote to all the businesses where he and the Chinese couple had stayed or dined, and asked whether they would offer service to Chinese visitors. The results were startling: Of the 128 businesses that responded, 92 percent of the restaurants and 91 percent of the hotels said no. In short, there was a tremendous gap between the attitudes expressed (generally by the owners or managers) and what these businesses had done when confronted with live, in-the-flesh Chinese customers (see Figure 4.6). Similar attitudes were expressed by hotels and restaurants LaPiere did not visit, so the sample appears to have been a representative one.

What accounts for these findings? LaPiere himself noted that the young couple with whom he traveled spoke English well and—as he put it—were "skillful smilers."

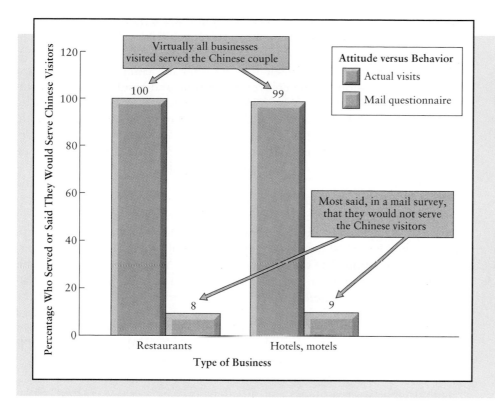

Figure 4.6

Evidence that Attitudes Don't Always Predict Behavior. Virtually all restaurants, hotels, and motels visited by LaPiere and a young Chinese couple offered courteous service. When asked by mail whether they would serve Chinese customers, however, more than 90 percent of these establishments said *no.* These findings suggests that a sizable gap between attitudes and behavior sometimes exists.

(*Source:* Based on data from LaPiere, 1934.)

In other words, they were friendly and socially skilled. Faced with such customers, the owners of businesses ignored their own prejudiced attitudes and welcomed the guests with courtesy. In fact, LaPiere reported that in the only "yes" letter he received from motels they had visited, the owner noted that she would be glad to accept Chinese guests, because she had enjoyed a pleasant visit from a Chinese couple the previous summer!

Putting such factors aside, LaPiere (1934) interpreted his results as indicating that there is often a sizable gap between attitudes and behavior—between what people say and what they actually do. This classic study, and related findings reported in later decades (e.g., Wicker, 1969), led social psychologists to focus a great deal of attention on the questions of *when* and *how* attitudes predict behavior. In this respect, LaPiere's study, conducted so long ago and with methods so different from the rigorous ones used in modern research, exerted a strong and lasting impact on our field.

When Do Attitudes Influence Behavior? Specificity, Strength, Accessibility, and Other Factors

Research on the question of *when* attitudes influence behavior has uncovered several different factors that serve as what social psychologists term *moderators*—factors that influence the extent to which attitudes affect behavior. We'll now consider two of the most important of these moderators: aspects of the situation and aspects of attitudes themselves.

Aspects of the Situation: Factors that Prevent Us from Expressing Our Attitudes. Have you ever been in the following situation? You are in a restaurant eating with a group of friends, and when the food arrives, there's something wrong—for instance, it's not what you ordered or it's cold. Yet when the waitperson asks, "How is everything?" you and your friends all answer: "Fine."

Why don't you express your true reactions? In other words, why doesn't your behavior in this situation reflect your underlying attitudes? Mainly because in the United States, most people are reluctant to complain about such matters, especially when dining with their friends. After all, complaining will put a damper on what should be an enjoyable situation; and besides, if you do complain, you may have to wait a long time for the kitchen to correct the mistake, and may end up sitting there watching your friends eat while you have no food. In this and many other contexts, *situational constraints* moderate the relationship between attitudes and behavior: they prevent attitudes from being expressed in overt behavior (e.g., Ajzen & Fishbein, 1980; Fazio & Roskos-Ewoldsen, 1994).

Situational factors can influence the link between attitudes and behavior in one additional way worth noting. Think for a moment: Whom are you likely to find at a rally against affirmative action? The answer is clear: Except perhaps for a few hecklers, most people present at such a rally will be fervent opponents of affirmative action. The same principle holds for many other situations, and this points to an important fact: In general, we tend to prefer situations that allow us to express our attitudes in our behavior. In other words, we often choose to enter and spend time in situations in which what we say and what we do can coincide (Snyder & Ickes, 1985). Indeed, because individuals tend to choose situations where they can engage in behaviors consistent with their attitudes, the attitudes themselves may be strengthened by this overt expression and so become even better predictors of behavior (DeBono & Snyder, 1995). In sum, the relationship between attitudes and situations may be a two-way street. Situational pressures shape the extent to which attitudes can be expressed in overt actions; but in addition, attitudes determine whether individuals enter various situations. In order to understand the link between attitudes and behavior, then, we must carefully consider both sets of factors.

Aspects of Attitudes Themselves.   Years ago, I witnessed a very dramatic scene. A large timber company had signed a contract with the government allowing the company to cut trees in a national forest. Some of the trees scheduled to become backyard fences were ancient giants, hundreds of feet tall. A group of conservationists objected strongly to cutting these magnificent trees, and they quickly moved to block this action. They joined hands and formed a human ring around each of the largest trees, thus preventing the loggers from cutting them down. The tactic worked: so much publicity occurred that the contract was revoked and the trees were saved—at least temporarily.

Why did these people take such drastic action? The answer is clear: They were passionately committed to saving the trees. In other words, they held powerful attitudes that strongly affected their behavior. Incidents like this one are far from rare. For example, residents of my neighborhood held a rally two years ago to prevent construction of a locomotive factory less than half a mile from our homes; tempers grew heated, and for a while I thought that pro-factory and anti-factory people would come to blows! Incidents like these call attention to the fact that the link between attitudes and behavior is strongly determined (moderated) by several aspects of attitudes themselves. Let's consider some of the most important of these aspects.

Attitude Origins.   One such factor has to do with how attitudes are formed in the first place. Considerable evidence indicates that attitudes formed on the basis of direct experience often exert stronger effects on behavior than ones formed indirectly, through hearsay. Apparently attitudes formed on the basis of direct experience are easier to bring to mind, and this increases their impact on behavior.

Attitude Strength. Another factor—clearly one of the most important—involves what is typically termed the *strength* of the attitudes in question. The stronger attitudes are, the greater their impact on behavior (Petkova, Ajzen, & Driver, 1995). The term *strength,* however, includes several components: the extremity or *intensity* of an attitude (how strong is the emotional reaction provoked by the attitude object); its *importance* (the extent to which an individual cares deeply about and is personally affected by the attitude); *knowledge* (how much an individual knows about the attitude object); and *accessibility* (how easily the attitude comes to mind in various situations). Research findings indicate that all these components play a role in attitude strength and that all are related (Krosnick et al., 1993). So important is attitude strength in determining the extent to which attitudes are related to overt behavior that it is worth taking a closer look at it (Kraus, 1995).

A major component of attitude strength is attitude *importance*—the extent to which an individual cares about the attitude (Krosnick, 1988). And one of the key determinants of such importance is what social psychologists term *vested interest*—the extent to which the attitude is personally relevant to the individual who holds it, in that the object or issue to which it refers has important consequences for this person. The results of many studies indicate that the greater such vested interest, the stronger the impact of the attitude on behavior (e.g., Crano, 1995; Crano & Prislin, 1995). For instance, in one famous study on this issue, Sivacek and Crano (1982) telephoned students at a large university and asked them if they would participate in a campaign against raising the legal age for drinking alcohol from eighteen to twenty-one. The researchers reasoned that students who would be affected by this new law—those younger than twenty-one—would have stronger vested interest in this issue than would those who would not be affected by the law (because they were already twenty-one or would reach this age before the law took effect). Thus, it was predicted that those in the first group would be much more likely to agree to join the rally than those in the second group. This is exactly what happened: more than 47 percent of the students with high vested interest agreed to take part in the campaign, whereas only 12 percent of those in the low-vested-interest group did so.

More recent research by Crano (1997) offers additional convincing support for the conclusion that vested interest does indeed strongly moderate the relationship between attitudes and behavior: that this link is much stronger when vested interest is high than when it is low. In this research Crano used information collected at the time of one presidential election in the United States—an election that pitted George McGovern, a strong advocate of busing children to achieve racial integration in the public schools, against Richard Nixon, a strong opponent of such busing. At the time of the election, large numbers of persons answered questionnaires designed to measure several things: their vested interest in this issue—the extent to which they would personally be affected by busing (e.g., Did they have children in school? Would busing occur in their neighborhood?); their attitudes toward African Americans; and their attitudes toward busing. To this information Crano (1997) added one additional measure: participants' intentions to vote for one or the other candidate. He reasoned that the higher participants' vested interest in the busing issue, the more accurately would their attitudes toward busing predict their choice of candidate. As you can see from Figure 4.7 on page 130, results confirmed these predictions. These findings are important because previous studies (e.g., Sears, 1997; Sears, Hensler, & Speer, 1979) had found that participants' attitudes toward busing were more strongly influenced by their racial attitudes (their attitudes toward African Americans) than by their vested interest—a finding that seemed to contradict other results emphasizing the importance of vested

Figure 4.7

Vested Interest and the Attitude–Behavior Link. Attitudes about busing were a better predictor of individuals' voting preferences when this issue was high in vested interest for them than when it was lower in vested interest. These findings suggest that vested interest is indeed a moderator of the link between attitudes and behavior.

(*Source:* Based on data from Crano, 1997.)

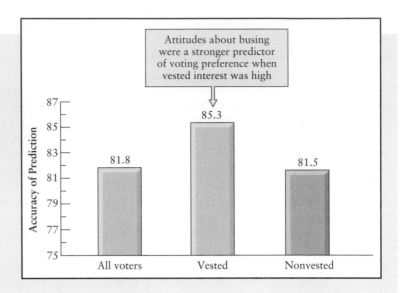

interest. Crano's (1997) research suggests that both strongly held attitudes *and* the extent to which individuals have vested interest in these views play an important role in determining behavior, and that in many cases vested interest moderates the strength of the attitude–behavior link.

Attitude Specificity. A third aspect of attitudes themselves that influences their relationship to behavior is *attitude specificity*—the extent to which attitudes are focused on specific objects or situations rather than on general ones. For example, you may have a general attitude toward religion (e.g., you believe that it is important for everyone to have religious convictions as opposed to not having them); in addition, you may have several specific attitudes about various aspects of religion—for instance, about the importance of attending services every week (this is important or unimportant) or about wearing a religious symbol (it's something I like to do—or don't like to do). Research findings indicate that the attitude–behavior link is stronger when attitudes and behaviors are measured at the same level of specificity. For instance, we'd probably be more accurate in predicting whether you'll go to services this week from your attitude about the importance of attending services than from your attitude about religion generally. On the other hand, we'd probably be more accurate in predicting your willingness to take action to protect religious freedoms from your general attitude toward religion than from your attitude about wearing religious jewelry (Fazio & Roskos-Ewoldsen, 1994). So attitude specificity, too, is an important moderator of the attitude–behavior link.

In sum, as we noted earlier, existing evidence suggests that attitudes really *do* affect behavior (e.g., Petty & Krosnick, 1995). However, the strength of this link is strongly determined by many different factors—situational constraints that permit or do not permit us to give overt expression to our attitudes, as well as several aspects of attitudes themselves (e.g., their origins, strength, and specificity, among others).

How Do Attitudes Influence Behavior? Intentions, Willingness, and Action

Understanding *when* attitudes influence behavior is an important topic. But, as we noted in Chapter 1, social psychologists are interested not only in the *when* of social thought and behavior but in the *why* and *how* as well. So it should come as no surprise that researchers have also tried to understand *how* attitudes influence behavior. Work on this issue points to the conclusion that in fact there are several basic mechanisms through which attitudes shape behavior.

Attitudes, Reasoned Thought, and Behavior. The first of these mechanisms operates in situations where we give careful, deliberate thought to our attitudes and their implications for our behavior. Insights into the nature of this process are provided by the *theory of reasoned action* (and a later version of this framework known as the **theory of planned behavior**), proposed by Ajzen and Fishbein (1980; Ajzen, 1991). This theory suggests that the decision to engage in a particular behavior is the result of a rational process that is goal-oriented and that follows a logical sequence. In this process we consider our behavioral options, evaluate the consequences or outcomes of each, and reach a decision to act or not to act. That decision is then reflected in our *behavioral intentions,* which, according to Fishbein, Ajzen, and many other researchers are often strong predictors of how we will act in a given situation (Ajzen, 1987). Perhaps a specific example will help illustrate the very reasonable nature of this idea.

Suppose a student is considering body piercing—for instance, wearing a nose ornament. Will she actually take this action? According to Ajzen and Fishbein, the answer depends on her intentions; and these, in turn, are strongly influenced by three key factors. The first factor is the person's attitudes toward the behavior in question. If the student really dislikes pain and the idea of someone sticking a needle through her nose, her intention to engage in such behavior may be weak. The second factor is the person's beliefs about how others will evaluate this action (this factor is known as *subjective norms*). If the student thinks that others will approve of body piercing, her intention to perform it may be strengthened. If she believes that others will disapprove of it, her intentions may be weakened. Finally, intentions are also influenced by *perceived behavioral control*—the extent to which a person perceives a behavior as hard or easy to accomplish. If it is viewed as difficult, intentions are weaker than if it is viewed as easy to perform. Together, these factors influence intentions; and intentions are the best single predictor of an individual's behavior.

Attitudes and Immediate Behavioral Reactions. The model described above seems to be quite accurate in situations where we have the time and opportunity to reflect carefully on various actions. But what about situations in which we have to act quickly—for example, when a panhandler approaches on a busy street? In such cases, attitudes seem to influence behavior in a more direct and seemingly automatic manner. According to one theory—Fazio's **attitude-to-behavior process model** (Fazio, 1989; Fazio & Roskos-Ewoldsen, 1994)—the process goes something like this. Some event activates an attitude; the attitude, once activated, influences our perceptions of the attitude object. At the same time, our knowledge about what's appropriate in a given situation (our knowledge of various *social norms*—rules governing behavior in a particular context) is also activated (see Chapter 9). Together, the attitude and this previously stored information about what's appropriate or expected shape our definition of the event. This definition, in turn, influences our behavior. Let's consider a concrete example.

Imagine that a panhandler approaches you on the street. What happens? This event triggers your attitude toward panhandlers and also your understanding of how people are expected to behave on public streets. Together, these factors influence your definition (perception) of the event, which might be "Oh no, another one of those worthless bums!" or "Gee, these homeless people have it rough!" Your definition of the event then shapes your behavior. Several

theory of planned behavior • A theory of how attitudes guide behavior suggesting that individuals consider the implications of their actions before deciding to perform various behaviors. An earlier version was known as the *theory of reasoned action.*

attitude-to-behavior process model • A model of how attitudes guide behavior that emphasizes the influence of both attitudes and stored knowledge of what is appropriate in a given situation on an individual's definition of the present situation. This definition, in turn, influences overt behavior.

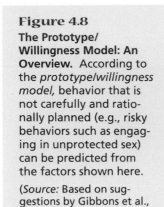

Figure 4.8

The Prototype/ Willingness Model: An Overview. According to the *prototype/willingness model,* behavior that is not carefully and rationally planned (e.g., risky behaviors such as engaging in unprotected sex) can be predicted from the factors shown here.

(*Source:* Based on suggestions by Gibbons et al., 1998.)

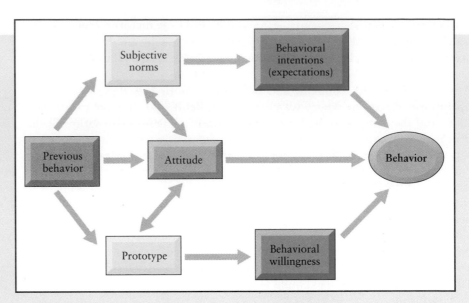

studies provide support for this model, so it seems to offer a useful explanation of how attitudes influence behavior in some situations.

In short, it appears that attitudes affect our behavior through at least two mechanisms, and that these operate under somewhat contrasting conditions. When we have time to engage in careful, reasoned thought, we can weigh all the alternatives and decide, quite deliberately, how to act. Under the hectic conditions of everyday life, however, we often don't have time for this kind of deliberate weighing of alternatives; in such cases, our attitudes seem to spontaneously shape our perceptions of various events and thus our immediate behavioral reactions to them (e.g., Bargh, 1997; Dovidio et al., 1996).

The Prototype/Willingness Model: Attitudes and Risky Behavior. Behavior, we have repeatedly noted, is not always rational. On the contrary, individuals often behave impulsively, without careful planning or consideration of the likely outcomes of their actions. Taking note of this fact, Gibbons and his colleagues (e.g., Gibbons et al., 1998) have suggested that in addition to attitudes and behavioral intentions, *willingness* to perform various actions is often a strong predictor of actually engaging in these behaviors. According to the theory proposed by these researchers—known as the **prototype/willingness model**—behavior is often influenced by several factors, including: attitudes toward the behavior in question, subjective norms (whether others engage in this behavior), behavioral intentions (what individuals plan to do in the future), willingness to engage in a specific form of behavior (the extent to which a person is willing to perform these actions under various circumstances), and *prototypes* (social images of what people who engage in certain forms of behavior are like) (see Figure 4.8).

The difference between behavioral intentions and willingness to engage in a specific form of behavior is readily illustrated. For instance, consider a risky behavior such as smoking. Behavioral intentions relate to whether an individual intends to smoke in the future (e.g., "Do you think that you will smoke cigarettes in the future?"). In contrast, we could measure *behavioral willingness* by asking individuals to indicate whether they would actually smoke in various situations. We might ask, for example, "Suppose you were with some friends and one of them offered you a cigarette. How likely is it that you would take it and try it, or that you would tell them no thanks or even leave the situation?"

prototype/willingness model • A theory suggesting that attitudes influence behavior through their impact on behavioral intentions and behavioral willingness (willingness to engage in specific actions).

A growing body of evidence suggests that all of the factors included in the prototype/willingness model are indeed predictors of actual behavior (e.g., Gibbons et al., 1995, 1998). Further, existing evidence suggests that attitudes influence both behavioral intentions and behavioral willingness. Thus, in answer to the question, "How do attitudes affect behavior?" the prototype/willingness model suggests: By influencing both *intentions* to behave in ways consistent with these attitudes, and the *willingness* to engage in such attitude-consistent behaviors.

While attitudes do often influence our behavior, this isn't always the case—even when the consequences of this gap are important. For a discussion of this issue, please see the *Beyond the Headlines* section.

Key Points

- Several factors serve as moderators of the link between attitudes and behavior, affecting the strength of this relationship

- Situational constraints may prevent us from expressing our attitudes overtly. In addition, we tend to prefer situations that allow us to express our attitudes, and this may further strengthen these views.

- Several aspects of attitudes themselves also moderate the attitude–behavior link. These include attitude origins (how attitudes were formed), attitude strength (which includes attitude accessibility and importance), and attitude specificity.

- Attitudes seem to influence behavior through several mechanisms. When we can give careful thought to our attitudes, intentions derived from our attitudes strongly predict behavior. In situations where we can't engage in such deliberate thought, attitudes influence behavior by shaping our perceptions of the situation. Willingness, subjective norms, and prototypes also affect the attitude–behavior link.

Beyond the Headlines:
As Social Psychologists See It
When Personal Health and Looking Sexy Collide, Guess Which Wins?

THIS SPRING BREAK, THE HOTTEST THING IS UNPROTECTED SKIN: SEARCHING FOR A DEEPER TAN, STUDENTS . . . FIND INTERESTING USES FOR CRISCO

Panama City Beach, Florida, March 16, 1996—In an age when everyone knows how harmful sun rays can be, Nichole Dornin is aiming for just the right skin tone. Call it crispy bacon.

Legions of college students arriving here . . . are right behind her, looking for the deep—and dangerous—dark tan of the 1970s. . . .

Young people know the evils of the sun. They've just stopped caring to the point of ignoring virtually every sunbathing precaution championed by modern science. Wrinkles? They're many years away. Skin cancer? The odds of getting it are low. Sunscreen? "We have it in the car. Does that count?"

Figure 4.9

A Potentially Dangerous Attitude–Behavior Gap. Despite the fact that most college students know all about the dangers of exposure to the sun, large numbers put themselves at risk for wrinkles and skin cancer. Actually, though, such behavior is consistent with other attitudes students hold relating to what makes people physically attractive.

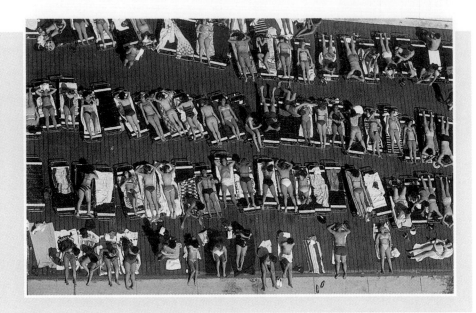

What's going on here? How can such a large gap between important health-related attitudes and overt behavior exist? Largely as a result of public health campaigns during the 1980s and 1990s, the students know all about the dangers of unprotected exposure to the sun. Yet they sunbathe anyway, holding contests for the best tan and awarding booby prizes to people who show up on the beach looking pale (see Figure 4.9).

Actually, from the point of social psychology, such seemingly self-destructive behavior is easy to understand. Basically, it derives from the fact that the sun-worshipping students *are* acting in ways that are consistent with their attitudes; it's just that the relevant attitudes—or at least the ones important to these young people—have more to do with "looking good" and "being sexy" than with personal health. As one student puts it, "tanned women are sexier, and tan lines are a turn-on." So in fact, students who lie in the sun covered with substances ranging from baby oil through lime juice, or who use products designed to "accelerate" the tanning process by magnifying the effects of the sun's rays, *are* acting on their attitudes—favorable reactions to a tanned appearance plus beliefs about the benefits of this look.

Moreover, while students do believe that getting a tan can be dangerous to their health, they view such results as far off in the distant future—so why worry about them now? In contrast, being physically attractive confers immediate benefits, and isn't that what really matters? Finally, students willing to trade off today's tanned appearance for tomorrow's wrinkles and potential skin cancers have countless ways to *rationalize* their behavior—to find reasonable explanations for it. As one female senior puts it: "You are going to die of something eventually, so you as might as well die tanned." In a sense, there's no arguing with logic like that!

THE FINE ART OF PERSUASION: USING MESSAGES TO CHANGE ATTITUDES

How many times during the past day has someone tried to change your attitudes? If you stop and think for a moment, you may be surprised at the answer, for it is clear that each day we are bombarded with numerous efforts of this type

Figure 4.10
Efforts at Persuasion: Part of Daily Life. Each day, we are bombarded with literally dozens of messages designed to change our attitudes.

(see Figure 4.10). Billboards, radio and television commercials, newspaper and magazine ads, political speeches, appeals from charities...the list seems almost endless. To what extent are such attempts at **persuasion**—efforts to change our attitudes through the use of various kinds of messages—successful? And what factors determine whether these attempts succeed or fail? Social psychologists have studied these issues for decades; and as we'll soon see, their efforts have recently yielded important new insights into the cognitive processes that play a role in persuasion (e.g., Eagly, Wood, & Chaiken, 1996; Lavine, Thomsen, & Gonzales, 1997; Munro & Ditto, 1997).

Persuasion: The Early Approach

In most cases, efforts at persuasion involve the following elements: Some *source* directs some type of *message* (the *communication*) to some person or group of persons (the *audience*). Taking note of this fact, early research on persuasion (e.g., Hovland, Janis, & Kelley, 1953) focused on these key elements, asking "*Who* says *what* to *whom* with what effect?" This approach yielded many interesting findings, among which the following were the most consistent:

- Communicators who are attractive in some way (e.g., physically) or who seem to have expertise in matters relating to their message are more persuasive than communicators who are low in attractiveness and expertise (Hovland & Weiss, 1951). This is why advertisements often include attractive models or white-coated "experts."
- Messages that do not appear to be designed to change our attitudes are often more successful in this respect than ones that are obviously intended to reach this goal (Walster & Festinger, 1962).
- People are sometimes more susceptible to persuasion when they are distracted by some extraneous event than when they are paying full attention to what is being said (Allyn & Festinger, 1961).
- When an audience holds attitudes contrary to those of a would-be persuader, it is often more effective for the communicator to adopt a *two-sided* approach, in which both sides of the argument are presented, than to take a *one-sided* approach.

persuasion • Efforts to change others' attitudes through the use of various kinds of messages.

- People who speak rapidly are often more persuasive than persons who speak more slowly (e.g., Miller et al., 1976).
- Persuasion can be enhanced by messages that arouse strong emotions in the audience. Messages evoking fear are especially effective, particularly when the communication provides specific recommendations about how to prevent or avoid the fear-producing events described (e.g., Leventhal, Singer, & Jones, 1965; Robberson & Rogers, 1988).

We're confident that you find all these points to be reasonable ones that probably fit with your own experience, so early research on persuasion certainly provided important insights into the factors that influence persuasion. What such work *didn't* do, however, was offer a comprehensive account of *how* persuasion occurs. Fortunately, this question has been the focus of more recent research, and it is to this highly sophisticated work that we turn next.

The Cognitive Approach to Persuasion: Systematic versus Heuristic Processing

What happens when you are exposed to a persuasive message—for instance, when you watch a television commercial or listen to a political speech? Your first answer may be something like "I think about what's happening or what's being said"; and, in a sense, that's correct. But, as we saw in Chapter 3, social psychologists know that in general we do the least amount of cognitive work we can in a given situation. So the central issue—the one that seems to provide the key to understanding the entire process of persuasion—is really a cognitive question: "How do we process (absorb, interpret, evaluate) the information contained in persuasive messages?" The answer that has emerged from hundreds of separate studies is that basically we process persuasive messages in two distinct ways.

The first of these is known as **systematic processing** or the **central route,** and it involves careful consideration of message content, the ideas it contains, and so on. Such processing is quite effortful and absorbs much of our information-processing capacity. The second approach, known as **heuristic processing** or the **peripheral route,** involves the use of simple rules of thumb or mental shortcuts—such as the belief that "experts' statements can be trusted" or the idea that "if it makes me feel good, I'm in favor of it." This kind of processing is much less effortful and allows us to react to persuasive messages in an automatic manner, like the character in the cartoon in Figure 4.11. It occurs in response to cues in the message or situation that evoke various mental shortcuts (e.g., beautiful models who evoke the "What's beautiful is good and worth listening to" heuristic).

When do we engage in each of these two distinct modes of thought? Modern theories of persuasion such as the **elaboration likelihood model** (ELM for short; e.g., Petty & Cacioppo, 1986; Petty et al., 1994) and the heuristic–systematic model (e.g., Chaiken, Liberman, & Eagly, 1989; Eagly & Chaiken, 1998) provide the following answers. Briefly, we engage in the effortful type of processing (systematic processing) when our capacity to process information relating to the persuasive message is high (e.g., when we have lots of knowledge about the subject or lots of time to engage in such thought) or when we are *motivated* to do so—when the issue is important to us, when we believe it is important to form an accurate view, and so on (e.g., Maheswaran & Chaiken, 1991; Petty & Cacioppo, 1990). In contrast, we engage in the less effortful type of processing (heuristic processing) when we lack the ability or capacity to process more carefully (we must make up our minds very quickly, we have little knowledge about the issue, and so on) or when our motivation to perform such cognitive work is low (the issue is unimportant to us or has little potential effect

systematic processing • Processing of information in a persuasive message that involves careful consideration of message content and ideas.

central route (to persuasion) • Attitude change resulting from systematic processing of information presented in persuasive messages.

heuristic processing • Processing of information in a persuasive message that involves the use of simple rules of thumb or mental shortcuts.

peripheral route (to persuasion) • Attitude change that occurs in response to persuasion cues—information concerning the expertise or status of would-be persuaders.

elaboration likelihood model (of persuasion) • A theory suggesting that persuasion can occur in either of two distinct ways, which differ in the amount of cognitive effort or elaboration they require.

Figure 4.11
Heuristic Processing: An Everyday Example. Like the character in this cartoon, we often process persuasive messages in terms of *heuristics*—mental shortcuts that require very little effort.

(*Source:* King Features Syndicate, 1992.)

on us, and so on). Advertisers, politicians, salespersons, and others wishing to change our attitudes prefer to push us into the heuristic mode of processing because, for reasons we'll describe below, it is often easier to change our attitudes when we think in this mode than when we engage in more careful and systematic processing.

Earlier, we noted that the discovery of these two contrasting modes of processing provided an important key to understanding the process of persuasion. The existence of these two modes of thought has helped us solve many intriguing puzzles. For instance, it has been found that when persuasive messages are not interesting or relevant to individuals, the amount of persuasion they produce is *not* strongly influenced by the strength of the arguments they contain. But when such messages are highly relevant to individuals, they are much more successful in inducing persuasion if the arguments they contain are strong and convincing. Can you see why this so? According to modern theories such as the ELM and the heuristic–systematic model, when relevance is low, individuals tend to process messages through the heuristic mode, by means of cognitive shortcuts. Thus, argument strength has little impact on them. In contrast, when relevance is high, they process persuasive messages through the systematic (central) route, and in this mode, argument strength *is* important (e.g., Petty & Cacioppo, 1990).

Similarly, the systematic-versus-heuristic distinction helps explain why people are more easily persuaded when they are somehow distracted—in a sense, asked to do two things at once—than when they are not. Under these conditions, the capacity to process the information in a persuasive message is limited, so people adopt the heuristic mode of thought. If the message contains the "right" cues (e.g., communicators who are attractive or seemingly expert), persuasion may occur because distracted people respond to these cues and not to the arguments being presented. In sum, this modern cognitive approach really does seem to provide a crucial key to understanding many aspects of persuasion.

Contrasting Motives and Message Processing. In our discussion of systematic versus heuristic processing, we noted that people tend to engage in effortful, systematic processing when motivated to do so. This raises an intriguing question: What motives, precisely, play a role in this choice? According to Chaiken and her colleagues (e.g., Chaiken et al., 1996), three distinct motives can be influential. The first of these is *accuracy motivation*—the desire to form an accurate view of the world (e.g., Johnson, 1994; Killeya & Johnson, 1998). As you can readily guess, such motivation is higher for issues we view as important than for ones we view as unimportant or irrelevant. The second motive, known as *defensive motivation,* involves the desire to hold views that are consistent with our own interests or with other attitudes we view as central to our self-concept, the kind of person we are, and so on. Finally, we may be motivated to engage in systematic processing because we want our attitudes to put us in a favorable light—to make a good impression on others; this is known as *impression motivation* (Chen, Schechter, & Chaiken, 1996). All of these motives have been found to play a role in whether we process persuasive messages systematically or in a relatively automatic manner (i.e., heuristically). For instance, recent findings (Lundgren & Prislin, 1998) suggest that to the extent individuals have any of these motives, they exert more effort in examining information relevant to their attitudes—for instance, they spend more time reading arguments relating to these attitudes. However, defensive motivation is in some ways the most interesting. This is because defensive motivation has especially important implications for *biased assimilation*—for viewing information that contradicts our current views as unreliable (e.g., Giner-Sorolla & Chaiken, 1997). We'll return to such effects and and their role in resistance to persuasion in a later section.

Other Factors Affecting Persuasion: Attitude Function and the Role of Nonverbal Cues

As we're sure you appreciate by now, the distinction between systematic and heuristic processing has been a guiding principle of recent research on persuasion. However, we do not want to leave you with the impression that where the study of persuasion is concerned, that's all there is. On the contrary, persuasion is a central topic of research in social psychology, so it has been studied from several other perspectives as well. In this section we'll examine some of this interesting work.

Attitude Functions. Attitudes can, and often do, serve several different functions for the persons who hold them. Sometimes they help the attitude holders to organize and interpret diverse sets of information (a *knowledge function*). Sometimes they permit individuals to express their central values or beliefs (a *self-expression* or *self-identity function*). And in other instances attitudes help the persons who hold them maintain or enhance their self-esteem (a *self-esteem function*) by, for example, allowing them to compare themselves favorably with others.

The functions served by attitudes are important from the point of view of persuasion. Persuasive messages containing information relevant to specific attitudes and to the functions served by those attitudes will be processed differently (perhaps more carefully) than persuasive messages that do not contain such information. For example, if an attitude helps one boost one's self-esteem, then efforts to change this attitude should focus on the benefits this change will confer on one's image. Similarly, if an attitude helps someone express his or her central values, then persuasive appeals should focus on how the recommended change will assist the target person in attaining *this* goal. The results of several studies offer support for this reasoning (e.g., Shavitt, 1989, 1990), so it appears that where persuasion is concerned, the functions served by attitudes are important to consider. Messages that draw a bead on the functions served by a given attitude (for the person who holds it) may have greater impact than those that do not—perhaps, in part, because the individuals engage in closer scrutiny of message content that matches the functional basis of their attitudes than of message content that does not match these functions (e.g, Petty & Wegener, 1998).

Nonverbal Cues and Persuasion: Delivery Style Matters, but Only Sometimes. Suppose you listen to two speakers favoring contrasting views. One speaks in a confident and friendly manner (e.g., she smiles a lot and speaks fluently); the other comes across as nervous and unfriendly (e.g., she frowns a lot, pauses often, and so on). Which speaker will have a better chance of changing your attitudes? Common sense suggests that the first will do better; but here, once again, is where the cognitive perspective offers added insights. Modern theories of persuasion suggest that if the two speakers are talking about an issue you find to be relatively unimportant or uninteresting, you may well be influenced by the speakers' style—their nonverbal cues. This is because you will process the speech via the heuristic mode. But if the issue is one you judge to be of great importance, you will tend to listen carefully to and be influenced more by the speakers' arguments than by their nonverbal behavior (see Figure 4.12; Burgoon & Hale, 1988; Petty & Cacioppo, 1986).

This reasoning has been confirmed in a study carried out by Marsh, Hart-O'Rourke, and Julka (1997). These researchers had students watch a videotape of a speaker who emitted either neutral or negative nonverbal cues while talking. The speaker offered either weak or strong arguments in favor of permitting sororities and fraternities on campus (they were not currently allowed). After hearing the speech, participants rated the speaker's performance. In addition, they reported their attitudes toward the sorority–fraternity issue and listed all the arguments made by the speaker that they could remember. As Marsh and her colleagues predicted (1997), the speaker was downrated by participants when she emitted negative nonverbal cues relative to neutral nonverbal cues. However, this did not necessarily lead to her being less persuasive. Even in the

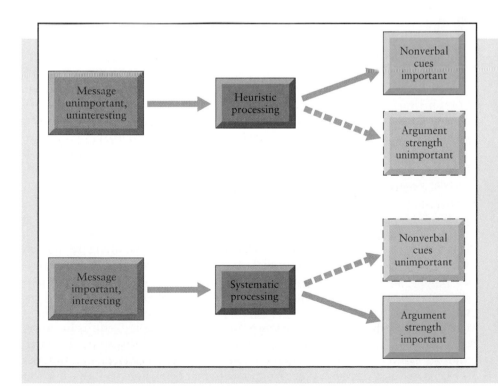

Figure 4.12
Speakers' Style: When Does It Matter? According to modern theories of persuasion, we are most likely to be influenced by a speaker's style—for instance, her or his nonverbal cues—if we find a message unimportant or uninteresting and process it heuristically. In contrast, we are more likely to be influenced by the arguments the speaker makes if we find the message important or interesting and process it systematically.

negative nonverbal cue condition, she produced more attitude change when she presented strong arguments in favor of the new policy than when she presented weak arguments. This latter finding provides further evidence for the view that we *will* engage in careful, systematic processing when we feel it is important to do so; and that when we do, we tend to pay more attention to what a would-be persuader says (the strength of his or her arguments) than to the personal style or appearance of this person.

> ### *Key Points*
>
> - Early research on *persuasion*—efforts to change attitudes through the use of messages—focused primarily on characteristics of the communicator (e.g., expertise, attractiveness), the message (e.g., one-sidedness versus two-sidedness), and the audience.
> - More recent research has focused on the cognitive processes that play a role in persuasion. Such research suggests that we process persuasive messages in two distinct ways: through *systematic processing*, which involves careful attention to message content, or through *heuristic processing*, which involves the use of mental shortcuts (e.g., "experts are usually right").
> - Which of these two modes of thought we choose depends on our motivation, our capacity to process information, and our knowledge about the issue in question. Several motives exist for engaging in systematic processing (accuracy motivation, defensive motivation, impression motivation).
> - Other factors that influence persuasion include attitude function and the communicator's style (e.g., use of nonverbal cues).

WHEN ATTITUDE CHANGE FAILS: RESISTANCE TO PERSUASION

In view of the frequency with which we are exposed to persuasive messages, one point is clear: We are highly resistant to them. If we were not, our attitudes on a wide range of issues would be in a constant state of change. So no surefire technique for producing persuasion exists or is ever likely to exist. Why are we such a tough sell where efforts to change our attitudes are concerned? As we'll now see, several factors play a role in our ability to resist even highly skilled efforts at persuasion.

Reactance: Protecting Our Personal Freedom

Have you ever had an experience like this? Someone exerts mounting pressure on you to get you to change your attitudes. As they do, you experience growing levels of annoyance and resentment. The final outcome: Not only do you resist persuasion; you may actually lean over backwards to adopt views *opposite* to those the would-be persuader wants you to adopt. Such behavior is an example of what social psychologists call **reactance**—a negative reaction to efforts by others to reduce our freedom by getting us to do what they want us to do. Research findings indicate that in such situations, we often really do change our attitudes (or behavior) in a direction exactly opposite to that being urged on us—an effect known as *negative attitude change* (Brehm, 1966; Rhodewalt & Davison, 1983).

reactance • Negative reaction to threats to one's personal freedom; often increases resistance to persuasion.

The existence of reactance is one reason why hard-sell attempts at persuasion often fail. When individuals perceive such appeals as direct threats to their personal freedom (or to their self-image as an independent person), they are strongly motivated to resist. Such resistance, in turn, virtually ensures that would-be persuaders will fail.

Forewarning: Prior Knowledge of Persuasive Intent

When we watch television, we expect commercials to interrupt most programs (except on public television). We know full well that these messages are designed to change our views—to get us to buy various products. Similarly, we know, when we listen to a political speech, that the person delivering it has an ulterior motive: she or he wants our vote. Does the fact that we know in advance about the persuasive intent behind such messages help us to resist them? Research on the effects of such advance knowledge—known as **forewarning**—indicates that it does (e.g., Cialdini & Petty, 1979; Johnson, 1994). When we know that a speech, taped message, or written appeal is designed to alter our views, we are often less likely to be affected by it than when we do not possess such knowledge. Why is this the case? Because forewarning influences several cognitive processes that play a role in persuasion.

First, forewarning provides us with more opportunity to formulate *counterarguments* that can lessen the message's impact. In addition, forewarning also provides us with more time in which to recall relevant facts and information that may prove useful in refuting a persuasive message (Wood, 1982). The benefits of forewarning are more likely to occur with respect to attitudes we consider important (Krosnick, 1989), but they seem to occur to a smaller degree even for attitudes we view as fairly trivial. In many cases, then, it appears that to be forewarned is indeed to be forearmed where persuasion is concerned.

Selective Avoidance

Still another way in which we resist attempts at persuasion is through **selective avoidance,** a tendency to direct our attention away from information that challenges our existing attitudes. Selective avoidance is one of the ways in which schemas guide the processing of social information (as explained in Chapter 3), and attitudes often operate as schemas. A clear illustration of the effects of selective avoidance is provided by television viewing. People do not simply sit in front of the tube passively absorbing whatever the media decide to dish out. Instead, they channel surf, mute the commercials, or simply cognitively tune out when confronted with information contrary to their views. The opposite effect occurs as well. When we encounter information that *supports* our views, we tend to give it our full attention. These tendencies to ignore or avoid information that contradicts our attitudes while actively seeking information consistent with them constitute two sides of what social psychologists term *selective exposure,* and such selectivity in what we make the focus of our attention helps ensure that our attitudes remain largely intact for long periods of time.

Biased Assimilation and Attitude Polarization: "If It's Contrary to What I Believe, Then It Must Be Unreliable—or Worse!"

Selective avoidance is not, however, the only way in which we protect our attitudes from efforts to change them. In addition, as we noted in our earlier discussion of defensive motivation and information processing, we often engage in **biased assimilation**—evaluating information that disconfirms our existing

forewarning • Advance knowledge that one is about to become the target of an attempt at persuasion; often increases resistance to the persuasion that follows.

selective avoidance • Tendency to direct attention away from information that challenges existing attitudes; increases resistance to persuasion.

biased assimilation • The tendency to evaluate information that disconfirms our existing views as less convincing or reliable than information that confirms these views.

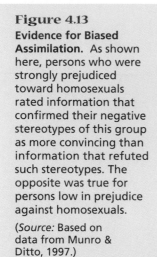

Figure 4.13
Evidence for Biased Assimilation. As shown here, persons who were strongly prejudiced toward homosexuals rated information that confirmed their negative stereotypes of this group as more convincing than information that refuted such stereotypes. The opposite was true for persons low in prejudice against homosexuals.

(*Source:* Based on data from Munro & Ditto, 1997.)

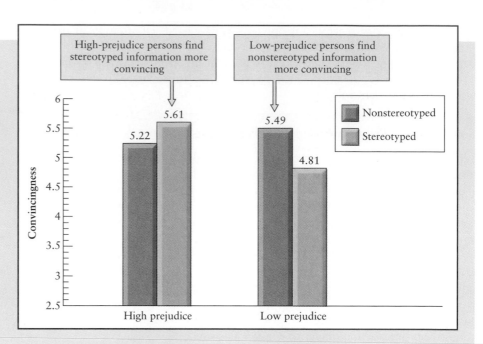

views as less convincing and less reliable than information that confirms our existing views (e.g., Lord, Ross, & Lepper, 1979; Miller et al., 1993). And to put the icing on the cake, we also show an effect known as **attitude polarization**—a tendency to evaluate mixed evidence or information in such a way that it strengthens our initial views and makes them more extreme (e.g., Pomeranz et al., 1995). As a result of these two tendencies, our attitudes really *do* seem to be beyond the reach of many efforts to change them; and, as we've noted at several other points in this chapter, they tend to persist even when we are confronted with new information that strongly challenges them.

Evidence for the powerful nature of biased assimilation and attitude polarization is provided by many studies, but one of the clearest of these was conducted by Munro and Ditto (1997). These researchers first selected two groups of participants—one group strongly prejudiced toward homosexuals and another group low in prejudice toward homosexuals. Then they exposed both groups to the results of two scientific studies, one that supported common negative stereotypes of homosexuals (e.g., that they suffer from more psychological disorders than heterosexuals) and one that refuted such views. As participants received this mixed information, they rated the quality of each of the scientific studies and indicated how convincing they found it to be. In addition, they reported on how each study made them feel (its impact on their current affective state) and on their general attitudes about homosexuals. Munro and Ditto (1997) predicted that participants would rate information that contradicted their current views about homosexuals as being less reliable or convincing than information that confirmed their current views; and, as you can see from Figure 14.13, this is precisely what happened. Highly prejudiced persons rated the study that confirmed the negative stereotype of homosexuals (and thus their own attitudes) as more convincing than the study that refuted the negative stereotype, and the opposite was true for persons low in prejudice against homosexuals. In addition, participants reported more negative feelings when confronted with information inconsistent with their current views than when confronted with information consistent with their current views. Moreover, such affective reactions seemed to play a key role in biased assimilation; when

attitude polarization • The tendency to evaluate mixed evidence or information in such a way that it strengthens our initial views and makes them more extreme.

the effects of such changes in current mood were removed statistically, biased assimilation, too, was eliminated.

Some evidence for attitude polarization was also obtained. Although participants' attitudes did not become more extreme after they read the mixed evidence presented in the two studies, they perceived that their views had shifted in this manner. In other words, highly prejudiced persons believed that the studies caused them to become more prejudiced, while less prejudiced persons believed that the studies caused them to become less prejudiced.

The findings reported by Munro and Ditto (1997) and other researchers (e.g., Giner-Sorolla & Chaiken, 1997; Miller et al, 1993) point to another reason why efforts at persuasion often fail. When individuals receive information that disagrees with their current views, they tend to react with annoyance and contempt, and they quickly discount such input as biased. In addition, other research (e.g., Duck, Terry, & Hogg, 1998; Vallone, Ross, & Lepper, 1985) indicates that people may also tend to perceive the *source* of such information, not just the information itself, as biased—an effect known as the *hostile media bias,* as in "Media coverage that disagrees with *my* views is biased!" (e.g., Duck, Terry, & Hogg, 1997). To the extent that such effects occur, even strong arguments are rejected, and there is little chance that attitude change will occur.

Please see *Ideas to Take with You* feature on page 153 for our advice on how to resist persuasion.

Key Points

- Our attitudes tend to remain quite stable despite many efforts to change them. Several factors contribute to such resistance to persuasion.

- One such factor is *reactance*—negative reactions to efforts by others to reduce or limit our personal freedom. When we interpret efforts at persuasion as producing such effects, we reject them and may even adopt views *opposite* to these being urged upon us.

- Resistance to persuasion is often increased by *forewarning*—the knowledge that someone is trying to change our attitudes and by *selective avoidance*—the tendency to avoid exposure to information that contradicts our views.

- Two additional processes, *biased assimilation* and *attitude polarization,* also play a role in resistance to persuasion. Biased assimilation is our tendency to evaluate information that contradicts our attitudes as less reliable or convincing than information that confirms our current views. Attitude polarization is the tendency to interpret mixed evidence in ways that strengthen our existing views and make them more extreme.

COGNITIVE DISSONANCE: WHY OUR BEHAVIOR CAN SOMETIMES INFLUENCE OUR ATTITUDES

Do you remember my experience with the paint-collection days in my village? I went to the first one, because doing so was consistent with my strong proenvironmental attitudes. But after having to wait several hours to get rid of a few cans at the first session, I didn't go to the second one. Instead, I just left my old paint in the basement and tried to "forget" about it. Doing so caused me some discomfort, and to this day, when I see the cans down there, I feel a twinge of guilt. Why? Because in this situation my behavior was *not* consistent with my attitudes. Social psychologists term the kind of discomfort I experienced **cognitive dissonance**—an unpleasant state that occurs when we notice that various attitudes we hold, or our attitudes and our behavior, are somehow inconsistent.

As you probably know from your own experience, cognitive dissonance is a frequent occurrence in everyday life. Any time you say things you don't really believe (e.g., praise something you don't actually like just to be polite), make a difficult decision that requires you to reject an alternative you find attractive, or discover that something you've invested effort or money to obtain is not as good as you expected, you may well experience dissonance. In all these situations, there is a gap between your attitudes and your actions, and such gaps tend to make us quite uncomfortable. Most important from the present perspective, cognitive dissonance can sometimes lead us to change our attitudes—to shift them so that they *are* consistent with other attitudes we hold or with our overt behavior. Put another way, because of cognitive dissonance and its effects, *we sometimes change our own attitudes,* even in the absence of any strong external pressure to do so. Let's take a closer look at cognitive dissonance and its intriguing implications for attitude change.

Cognitive Dissonance: What It Is and Various Ways (Direct and Indirect) to Reduce It

Dissonance theory, we've already noted, begins with a very reasonable idea: People don't like inconsistency and are uncomfortable when it occurs. In other words, when we notice inconsistencies between our attitudes and our behavior, we are motivated to do something about this situation—to reduce the dissonance. How can we accomplish this goal?

In its early forms (e.g., Aronson, 1968; Festinger, 1957), dissonance theory focused on three basic mechanisms. First, we can change our attitude or our behavior so that these are more consistent with each other. For instance, consider someone who is on a diet but gives in to temptation and orders a huge, rich dessert. This person can reduce the dissonance he experiences as a result of this inconsistency by changing his attitude toward dieting; "Diets don't really work," he might reason, "so why bother?" Second, we can acquire new information that supports our attitude or our behavior. Many persons who smoke, for instance, search for evidence suggesting that the harmful effects of this habit are minimal or occur only for very heavy smokers—people who smoke much more than they do! Finally, we can decide that the inconsistency actually doesn't matter; in other words, we can engage in **trivialization**—concluding that the attitudes or behaviors in question are not important so that any consistency between them is insignificant (Simon, Greenberg, & Brehm, 1995).

All of these strategies can be viewed as *direct* approaches to dissonance reduction: they focus on the attitudes–behavior discrepancies that are causing the dissonance. Research by Steele and his colleagues (e.g., Steele, 1988; Steele & Lui, 1983), however, indicates that dissonance can also be reduced through *indirect* tactics—ones that leave the basic discrepancy between attitudes and behavior intact but reduce the unpleasant negative feelings generated

cognitive dissonance • An unpleasant internal state that results when individuals notice inconsistency between two or more of their attitudes or between their attitudes and their behavior.

trivialization • A technique for reducing dissonance by mentally minimalizing the importance of attitudes or behavior that are inconsistent with each other.

by dissonance. According to Steele (1988), adoption of such indirect routes to dissonance reduction is most likely to occur when an attitude–behavior discrepancy involves important attitudes or self-beliefs. Under these conditions, Steele suggests (e.g., Steele, Spencer, & Lynch, 1993), individuals experiencing dissonance may focus not so much on reducing the gap between their attitudes and their behavior as on *self-affirmation*—restoring positive self-evaluations that are threatened by the dissonance (e.g., Elliot & Devine, 1994; Tesser, Martin, & Cornell, 1996). How can they accomplish this goal? By focusing on their positive self-attributes—good things about themselves (e.g., Steele, 1988). For instance, when I experienced dissonance as a result of not taking my paint cans to the collection center, I could have reminded myself that I had recently made a large donation to a charity, served as a volunteer for our local public television station, and so on. Contemplating these positive actions would have helped reduce the discomfort produced by my failure to act in a way consistent with my proenvironmental attitudes.

Other research suggests, however, that engaging in self-affirmation may not be necessary for dissonance reduction via the indirect route. In fact, almost anything we do that reduces the discomfort and negative affect generated by dissonance can sometimes succeed in this respect—everything from consuming alcohol (e.g., Steele, Southwick, & Critchlow, 1981) to engaging in distracting activities that take one's mind off the dissonance (e.g., Zanna & Aziza, 1976) to simple expressions of positive affect (see Figure 4.14) (Cooper, Fazio, & Rhodewalt, 1978).

In sum, dissonance can be reduced in many different ways—through indirect tactics as well as through direct ones focused on reducing the attitude–behavior discrepancy. And as we'll soon see, the choice among these various alternatives may be a function of what's available and the specific context in which dissonance occurs (e.g., Fried & Aronson, 1995).

Is Dissonance Really Unpleasant?   In our comments so far, we've suggested that dissonance is an unpleasant state. This idea certainly fits with our everyday ex-

Figure 4.14
Reducing Dissonance: The Indirect Route. The results of many studies indicate that it is not necessary to reduce a discrepancy between attitudes and behavior to reduce dissonance. Other indirect routes exist; these range from self-affirmation through engaging in enjoyable or distracting activities such as those shown here.

perience: when we say or do things contrary to our true beliefs, we often *do* feel uncomfortable as a result of doing so. Until recently, however, there was little direct scientific evidence relating to this issue.

That dissonance is arousing in a physiological sense had been well documented (e.g., Elkin & Leippe, 1986; Losch & Cacioppo, 1990). For instance, consider an ingenious study conducted some years ago by Steele, Southwick, and Critchlow (1981).

These researchers arranged for college students to engage in attitude-discrepant behavior designed to induce strong feelings of dissonance: the students provided arguments in *favor* of a large tuition increase. Then the students expressed their own attitudes about this issue. Before doing so, however, some of the participants were asked to taste and rate a vodka-laced cocktail while others tasted and rated distilled water or coffee. It was reasoned that if dissonance is physiologically arousing, drinking alcohol (a depressant) might counter this biological state, whereas drinking water or coffee would not. Thus, when later asked to express their views about the tuition hike, those who drank alcohol would be less favorable toward the tuition hike than those who drank water or coffee. Why? Because in these two latter groups, dissonance (and the arousal it produces) would still be present and so would produce attitude change in the direction of the pro–tuition hike arguments provided by the students. Results offered strong support for these predictions, and hence indirect support for the view that dissonance is physiologically arousing.

In contrast to clear evidence for the suggestion that dissonance is arousing, however, there was until recently little direct evidence that dissonance is also unpleasant—a central assumption of dissonance theory. (After all, it is this unpleasantness, supposedly, that motivates efforts to reduce dissonance when it occurs.) Fortunately, this gap in our knowledge has been closed by research by Elliot and Devine (1994). These researchers found that students who wrote an essay arguing against their own views (an essay in favor of a large tuition increase) reported high levels of emotional discomfort immediately after completing this task. In contrast, those who wrote the same kind of essay, then reported on their attitudes toward the tuition hike, and only *then* rated their feelings, reported lower levels of discomfort. This is what dissonance theory would predict; because students in this later condition would have an opportunity to reduce dissonance by changing their attitudes (making them more favorable to the tuition hike), and this change would reduce the discomfort they experienced. These and other findings reported by Elliot and Devine (1994) suggest that dissonance really is an unpleasant state, one that often motivates attitude changes designed to reduce it.

Dissonance and Attitude Change: The Effects of Induced Compliance

induced compliance • Situations in which individuals are somehow induced to say or do things inconsistent with their true attitudes; also known as *forced compliance*.

There are many occasions in everyday life when we must say or do things inconsistent with our real attitudes. For example, suppose your friend buys a sport utility vehicle and proudly asks you how you like it (see Figure 14.15). You have just read an article indicating that SUV's are gas-guzzlers that pollute the environment and that they get into more accidents than other types of vehicles. But what do you say? Probably something like "Great; I really like it." After all, you don't want to hurt your friend's feelings, or worse. Social psychologists refer to such situations as ones involving **induced compliance** (or *forced compliance*)—situations in which we feel compelled to say or do something

Figure 4.15
Induced Compliance as a Source of Dissonance. Many situations in life induce us to say things we don't believe—to act in ways inconsistent with our true attitudes. If a friend asks you how you like something she has just bought, you may say "Great!" even if you actually dislike it. As a result, you may experience dissonance.

contrary to our real views. And by now you can probably guess what social psychologists predict will happen in such situations: dissonance will be aroused, and we may feel pressure to change our attitudes so that they are more consistent with our words or other actions. Moreover, we are especially likely to make such changes when other techniques for reducing dissonance are unavailable or require greater effort. This is a general rule about various techniques for reducing dissonance: All other things being equal, we prefer the technique that requires the least effort.

Dissonance and the Less-Leads-to-More Effect. So far, so good. Predictions derived from dissonance theory seem to make good sense. But now consider this question: Will the reasons why you engaged in behavior inconsistent with your attitudes matter? Obviously, we can engage in attitude-discrepant behavior for many reasons, and some of these are stronger or more compelling than others. For instance, if you expect your friend with the new SUV to give you a lift to a party that evening, you have strong reasons for concealing your real views about the vehicle. But if your friend is about to move to another town and you don't expect to see her very often, your reasons for saying that you like it when you don't are weaker. Now for the key question: When will dissonance be stronger—when we have many good reasons for engaging in attitude-discrepant behavior or when we have few such reasons? Dissonance theory offers an unexpected answer: Dissonance will be stronger, it suggests, when we have *few* reasons for engaging in attitude-discrepant behavior. This is so because under these conditions, we can't explain away our behavior to ourselves; we performed our actions even though there was no strong reason for doing so. The result: Dissonance is quite intense.

In other words, as shown in Figure 4.16 on page 148, dissonance theory predicts that it may be easier to change individuals' attitudes by offering them

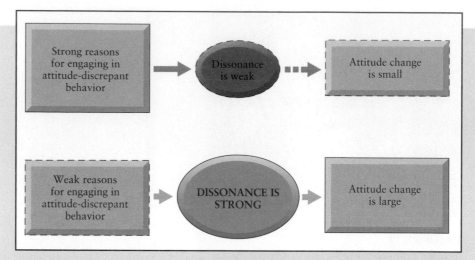

Figure 4.16
Why Less (Smaller Inducements) Often Leads to More (Greater Attitude Change) after Attitude–Discrepant Behavior. When individuals have strong reasons for engaging in attitude–discrepant behavior, they experience relatively weak dissonance and weak pressure to change their attitudes. When they have weak reasons for engaging in attitude–discrepant behavior, in contrast, they experience stronger dissonance and stronger pressure to change their attitudes. The result: less leads to more.

just barely enough inducement to get them to engage in attitude-discrepant behavior. Additional reasons or rewards beyond this level will reduce dissonance—and subsequent attitude change. Social psychologists sometimes refer to this surprising prediction as the **less-leads-to-more effect**—less reason or smaller reward lead to more attitude change—and it has been confirmed in many studies (e.g., Riess & Schlenker, 1977). For example, in the first and most famous of these experiments (Festinger & Carlsmith, 1959), participants were offered either a small rewards ($1) or a large one ($20) for telling another person that some dull tasks they had just performed were very interesting. One of these tasks involved placing spools on a tray, dumping them out, and repeating the process over and over again. After engaging in the attitude–discrepant behavior—telling another person the dull tasks were interesting—participants were asked to indicate their own liking for these tasks. As predicted by the less-leads-to-more effect, those given the small reward for misleading a stranger actually reported liking the tasks more than those given the large reward.

While the less-leads-to-more effect has been confirmed many times, we should note that it does not occur under all conditions. Rather, it seems to happen only when several conditions exist (Cooper & Scher, 1994). First, this effect occurs only in situations in which people believe that they have a choice as to whether or not to perform the attitude-discrepant behavior. Second, small rewards lead to greater attitude change only when people believe that they were personally responsible for both the chosen course of action and any negative effects it produced. And third, the less-leads-to-more effect occurs only when people view the reward they receive as a well-deserved payment for services rendered, not as a bribe. Since these conditions do often exist, however, the strategy of offering others just barely enough to induce them to say or do things

less-leads-to-more effect •
The fact that offering individuals small rewards for engaging in counterattitudinal behavior often produces more dissonance, and so more attitude change, than offering them larger rewards.

Figure 4.17
Health-Related Attitudes and Health-Related Behavior: The Gap Is Often Large. Almost everyone wants to avoid the risks inherent in failing to wear safety belts, smoking, being much overweight, and engaging in unprotected sex. Yet these attitudes often fail to influence behavior. Techniques based on dissonance theory may be effective in closing this important kind of gap.

contrary to their true attitudes can often be an effective technique for inducing attitude change.

Dissonance As a Tool for Beneficial Changes in Behavior: When Hypocrisy Can Be a Force for Good

People who don't wear safety belts are much more likely to die in accidents than those who do. People who smoke heavily are much more likely to suffer from lung cancer and heart disease than those who don't. People who are extremely overweight are much more likely to suffer from diabetes, heart attacks, and many other health problems than persons of normal weight. And people who engage in unprotected sex are much more likely than those who engage in safe sex to contract dangerous venereal diseases, including AIDS.

As we move into the twenty-first century, most people know these statements are true (e.g., Carey, Morrison-Beedy, & Johnson, 1997); so most people have generally favorable attitudes toward using seat belts, quitting smoking, losing weight, and engaging in safe sex. Yet, as you well know, these attitudes are often *not* translated into overt actions: people continue to drive without seat belts, to smoke, and so on (see Figure 4.17). What's needed, in other words, is not so much changes in attitudes as shifts in overt behavior. Can dissonance be useful in promoting such beneficial changes? A growing body of evidence suggests that it can (e.g., Gibbons, Eggleston, & Benthin, 1997; Stone et al., 1994b), especially when it is used to generate feelings of **hypocrisy**—awareness that one is publicly advocating some attitude or behavior but then acting in a way that is inconsistent with these attitudes or behavior. Under these conditions, several researchers have reasoned (e.g., Aronson, Fried, & Stone, 1991), an individual should experience strong feeling of dissonance. Moreover, these feelings should be so intense that adopting indirect modes of dissonance reduction (e.g., distracting oneself or bolstering one's ego by thinking about or engaging in

hypocrisy • Publicly advocating some attitude or behavior and then acting in a way that is inconsistent with this espoused attitude or behavior.

other positively evaluated behaviors) would not do the trick: only actions that reduce dissonance directly, removing the discrepancy between one's words and deeds, would be effective.

These predictions have been tested in several studies. For instance, Stone and his colleagues (1994b) had students in one condition—the hypocrisy group—prepare a videotape urging others to engage in safe sex. Then they asked the students to recall situations in which they had failed to behave this way themselves. It was expected that as a result, the participants would experience strong feelings of hypocrisy; after all, they had urged others to do something they themselves did not always do. Other groups of participants in the study engaged in only one of these two activities—they prepared the tape *or* remembered situations in which they had failed to engage in safe sex. Later, all participants were given an opportunity to buy condoms at a discounted price. Results indicated that those in the hypocrisy group were much more likely to purchase the condoms: 83 percent bought them, versus an average of only 38 percent in the other two groups. Thus, exposing individuals to strong dissonance by calling their attention to their own hypocrisy seemed to be a highly effective means of changing their behavior.

But is behavior change really likely to occur in such situations? Couldn't persons aware of their own hypocrisy also reduce their dissonance through indirect tactics—any actions that allow them to feel good about themselves, or simply to feel good? Stone and his colleagues (1997) argue that such indirect tactics of dissonance reduction are unlikely to succeed in situations involving hypocrisy, because the discrepancy between attitudes and behavior is so clear and public that adopting the behavior one has advocated is the most effective—and in some respects the least effortful—way to proceed.

To test these predictions, Stone and his colleagues (1997) conducted research in which individuals were asked to prepare a videotape advocating the use of condoms (safe sex) to prevent transmission of HIV. Then they were asked to think about reasons why they themselves hadn't used condoms in the past (personal reasons) or about reasons why people in general sometimes fail to use condoms (normative reasons that didn't center on their own behavior). It was reasoned that in the personal reasons condition, hypocrisy would be be maximized. Finally, all participants were given a choice between a direct means of reducing dissonance (purchasing condoms at a reduced price) and an indirect means of reducing dissonance (making a donation to a program designed to aid homeless persons).

Results indicated that when participants were asked to focus on the reasons why they hadn't engaged in safe sex in the past, an overwhelming majority chose to purchase condoms—the direct route to dissonance reduction. In contrast, when asked to think about reasons why people in general didn't engage in safe sex, more participants actually chose the indirect route to dissonance reduction—a donation to the aid-the-homeless project (see Figure 4.18).

These findings suggest that using dissonance to generate awareness of hypocrisy can indeed be a powerful tool for changing people's behavior in desirable ways—ones that protect their health and safety. To be maximally effective, however, such procedures must involve several elements: The persons in question must publicly advocate the desired behaviors (e.g., using condoms, wearing safety belts), must be induced to think about their own failures to show these behaviors in the past, and must be given access to direct means for reducing their dissonance. When these conditions are met, beneficial changes in behavior can definitely follow. Do people all around the world experience dissonance? Or is the experience of dissonance—and its effects—influenced by cultural factors? For information on this issue, please see the *Social Diversity* section that follows.

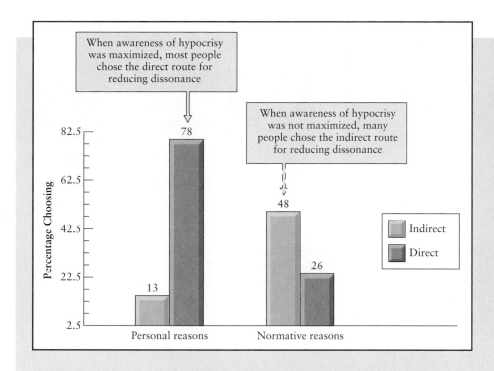

Figure 4.18
Using Hypocrisy to Change Behavior. When individuals were made to confront their own hypocrisy—by being asked to list reasons why they hadn't engaged in safe sex in the past—most chose to reduce such dissonance through direct means (by purchasing condoms). In contrast, when individuals were asked to think about reasons why people in general didn't engage in safe sex, many chose to reduce dissonance via an indirect route (making a donation to an aid-the-homeless project).

(*Source:* Based on data from Stone et al., 1997.)

Social Diversity: A Critical Analysis
Is Dissonance Culture-Bound? Evidence from a Cross-National Study

Human beings, dissonance theory contends, dislike inconsistency. They feel uncomfortable when they perceive inconsistency in their attitudes or behavior, and this often leads them to engage in active efforts to reduce it. As we have already seen, a large body of evidence offers support for these ideas, so dissonance theory has long been seen as providing important insights into several aspects of social thought. There is one major fly in this ointment, however: the vast majority of studies on dissonance have been conducted in North America and Western Europe. Does cognitive dissonance exist and operate in the same manner in other countries? A few studies have examined this question (e.g., Takata & Hashimoto, 1973; Yoshida, 1977), but the findings of this work have been inconsistent; some studies have suggested that dissonance operates in the same way everywhere, while others have called this generality into question.

Fortunately, important new insights into the effects of cultural factors on dissonance have recently been provided by Heine and Lehman (1997). Drawing on past research suggesting that dissonance often springs from inconsistencies in attitudes and behavior that threaten individuals' positive view of themselves (self-affirmation theory), Heine and Lehman (1997) reasoned that dissonance might actually be less likely to occur and to influence attitudes in some cultures than in others. Specifically, these researchers suggested that after making a choice between

closely ranked alternatives, persons from cultures such as those in the United States and Canada would be more likely to experience dissonance than persons from cultures such as those in Japan and other Asian countries. Why? Because in Western cultures the self is linked to individual actions, such as making correct decisions. Thus, after making a choice, individuals in Western cultures often experience considerable dissonance because of the potential threat to the self posed by the possibility of having made a wrong decision. In many Asian cultures, in contrast, the self is not as closely linked to individual actions or choices. Rather, it is more strongly tied to roles and status—to an individual's place in society and the obligations this involves (see Figure 4.19 on page 152). Thus, persons in Asian cultures should be less likely to perceive the possibility of making an incorrect decision as a threat to their self, and so also less likely to experience dissonance.

To test this reasoning, Heine and Lehman (1997) had both Canadian students and Japanese students temporarily living in Canada choose from a group of forty CDs the ten CDs that they would most like to own. The participants also evaluated how much they would like each of these ten CDs. At this point, participants were told that they could actually have *either* the CD they ranked fifth or the one they ranked sixth. After making their choices, participants rated the two CDs once again. Previous research suggests

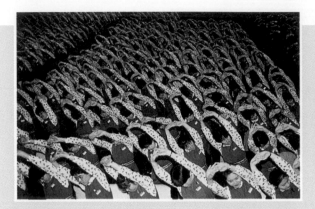

Figure 4.19
Cultural Factors in the Occurrence of Dissonance. In Western cultures, the self is linked closely to individual actions or choices. In many Asian cultures, however, the self is more strongly tied to roles and status—to an individual's place in society and the obligations this involves. For these reasons, postdecision dissonance may be stronger for persons from Western cultures than for persons from several Asian cultures. This prediction has recently been confirmed (Heine & Lehman, 1997).

that in order to reduce dissonance, individuals who make such decisions often downrate the item they didn't choose while raising their ratings of the item they did choose—an effect known as *spreading of alternatives* (e.g., Steele et al., 1993). The researchers predicted that such effects would be stronger for Canadians than for Japanese participants, and this is precisely what happened. The Canadian students showed the spreading of alternatives effect which results from dissonance reduction to a significant degree; the Japanese students did not.

These findings suggest that cultural factors do indeed influence the operation of dissonance. While all human beings are made somewhat uneasy by inconsistencies between their attitudes or inconsistencies between their attitudes and their behavior, the intensity of such reactions, the precise conditions under which they occur, and the strategies used to reduce them may all be influenced by cultural factors. Even with respect to very basic aspects of social thought, then, it is essential to take careful account of cultural diversity.

Key Points

- *Cognitive dissonance* is an unpleasant state that occurs when we notice discrepancies between our attitudes or between our attitudes and behavior.

- Dissonance often occurs in situations involving *induced compliance*—ones in which we are induced by external factors to say or do things that are inconsistent with our true attitudes.

- In such situations, attitude change is maximum when we have reasons that are barely sufficient to get us to engage in attitude-discrepant behavior. Stronger reasons (or larger rewards) produce less attitude change—the *less-leads-to-more effect*.

- Inducing individuals to advocate certain attitudes or behaviors and then reminding them of their hypocrisy—the fact that they haven't always behaved in ways consistent with these views—can be a powerful tool for inducing dissonance and thus promoting beneficial changes in behavior.

- Dissonance appears to be a universal aspect of social thought, but the conditions under which it occurs and the tactics individuals choose to reduce it appear to be influenced by cultural factors.

Connections: Integrating Social Psychology

In this chapter, you read about . . .	*In other chapters, you will find related discussions of . . .*
the role of social learning in attitude formation	the role of social learning in several forms of social behavior—attraction (Chapter 7), helping (Chapter 10), and aggression (Chapter 11)
persuasion and resistance to persuasion	other techniques for changing attitudes and behavior and why they are effective or ineffective (Chapter 9); the use of persuasive techniques in health-related messages (Chapter 13)
cognitive dissonance	the role of cognitive dissonance in various attitudes and forms of social behavior; for example, job satisfaction (Chapter 13)

Thinking about Connections

1. Suppose you wanted to launch a campaign to persuade adults of all ages to engage in safe sex (e.g., use condoms). What specific features would you include in this program in order to maximize its effectiveness and so improve the health of large numbers of persons (see Chapter 13)?

2. Suppose you are part of a group that has to make a choice between two alternative courses of action (see Chapter 12). You don't agree with the final decision; but you have to go along with it, because in this group the majority rules. Will you

experience dissonance as a result of the decision? If so, how can you reduce it?

3. If attitudes are learned, it is reasonable to suggest that the mass media (television, films, magazines) are an important factor in attitude formation. What do you think these media are currently teaching children about key aspects of social behavior—love and sexual relations (Chapters 7 and 8), aggression (Chapter 11), honesty and integrity (Chapters 5 and 12)? Would you change any of this if you could?

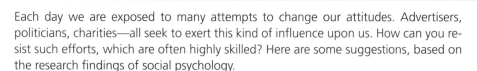

Ideas to Take with You
Resisting Persuasion: Some Useful Steps

Each day we are exposed to many attempts to change our attitudes. Advertisers, politicians, charities—all seek to exert this kind of influence upon us. How can you resist such efforts, which are often highly skilled? Here are some suggestions, based on the research findings of social psychology.

View Attempts at Persuasion As Assaults on Your Personal Freedom.

No one likes being told what to do; but in a sense, this is precisely what would-be persuaders are trying to do when they attempt to change your attitudes. So when you are on the receiving end of such appeals, remind yourself that *you* are in charge of your own life and that there's no reason to listen to or accept what advertisers, politicians, and the like tell you.

Recognize Attempts at Persuasion When You See Them.

Knowing that someone is trying to persuade you—being forewarned—is often useful from the point of view of resisting efforts at persuasion. So whenever you encounter someone or some organization that seeks to influence your views, remind yourself that no matter how charming or friendly they are, *persuasion* is their goal. This will help you resist.

Remind Yourself of Your Own Views and of How These Differ from the Ones Being Urged upon You.

While biased assimilation—the tendency to perceive views different from our own as unconvincing and unreliable—can prevent us from absorbing potentially useful information, it is also a useful means for resisting persuasion. When others present views different from your own as part of a persuasive appeal, focus on how different these ideas are from those you hold. The rest will often take care of itself!

SUMMARY AND REVIEW OF KEY POINTS

Attitude Formation: How We Come to Hold the Views We Do

- *Attitudes* are evaluations of aspects of the social world.

- Attitudes are often acquired from other persons through *social learning*. Such learning can involve *classical conditioning, instrumental conditioning,* or *observational learning.*

- Attitudes are also formed on the basis of *social comparison*—our tendency to compare ourselves with others to determine whether our view of social reality is or is not correct. In order to be similar to others we like or admire, we often accept the attitudes that they hold.

- Studies conducted with identical twins suggest that attitudes may also be influenced by genetic factors, although the strength of such effects varies greatly across different attitudes.

Do Attitudes Influence Behavior? And If So, *When* and *How?*

- Several factors serve as moderators of the link between attitudes and behavior, affecting the strength of this relationship.

- Situational constraints may prevent us from expressing our attitudes overtly. In addition, we tend to prefer situations that allow us to express our attitudes, and this may further strengthen these views.

- Several aspects of attitudes themselves also moderate the attitude–behavior link. These include attitude origins (how attitudes were formed), attitude strength (which includes attitude accessibility and importance), and *attitude specificity.*

- Attitudes seem to influence behavior through several mechanisms. When we can give careful thought to our attitudes, intentions derived from our attitudes strongly predict behavior. In situations where we can't engage in such deliberate thought, attitudes influence behavior by shaping our perceptions of the situation. Willingness to engage in attitude-consistent behavior and social prototypes also play roles in the attitude–behavior interaction.

The Fine Art of Persuasion: Using Messages to Change Attitudes

- Early research on *persuasion*—efforts to change attitudes through the use of messages—focused primarily on characteristics of the communicator (e.g., expertise, attractiveness), the message (e.g., one-sidedness versus two-sidedness), and the audience.

- More recent research has focused on the cognitive processes that play a role in persuasion. Such research suggests that we process persuasive messages in two distinct ways: through *systematic processing,* which involves careful attention to message content, or through *heuristic processing,* which involves the use of mental shortcuts (e.g., "experts are usually right").

- Which of these two modes of thought we choose depends on our motivation, our capacity to process information, and our knowledge about the issue in question. Several motives exist for engaging in systematic processing (accuracy motivation, defensive motivation, impression motivation).

- Other factors that influence persuasion include attitude function and the communicator's style (e.g., use of nonverbal cues).

When Attitude Change Fails: Resistance to Persuasion

- Our attitudes tend to remain quite stable despite many efforts to change them. Several factors contribute to such resistance to persuasion.

- One such factor is *reactance*—negative reactions to efforts by others to reduce or limit our personal freedom. When we interpret efforts at persuasion as producing such effects, we reject them and may even adopt views opposite to these being urged upon us.

- Resistance to persuasion is often increased by *forewarning*—the knowledge that someone is trying to change our attitudes—and by *selective avoidance*—the tendency to avoid exposure to information that contradicts our views.

- Two additional processes, *biased assimilation* and *attitude polarization,* also play a role in resistance to persuasion. Biased assimilation is our tendency to evaluate information that contradicts our attitudes as less reliable and convincing than information that confirms our current views. Attitude polarization is the tendency to interpret mixed evidence in ways that strengthen our existing views and make them more extreme.

Cognitive Dissonance: Why Our Behavior Can Sometimes Influence Our Attitudes

- *Cognitive dissonance* is an unpleasant state that occurs when we notice discrepancies between our attitudes or between our attitudes and behavior.
- Dissonance often occurs in situations involving *induced compliance*—ones in which we are induced by external factors to say or do things that are inconsistent with our true attitudes.

- In such situations, attitude change is maximum when we have reasons that are barely sufficient to get us to engage in attitude-discrepant behavior. Stronger reasons (or larger rewards) produce less attitude change—the *less-leads-to-more effect.*
- Inducing individuals to advocate certain attitudes or behaviors and then reminding them of their *hypocrisy*—the fact that they haven't always behaved in ways consistent with their espoused views—can be a powerful tool for inducing dissonance and thus promoting beneficial changes in behavior.
- Dissonance appears to be a universal aspect of social thought, but the conditions under which it occurs and the tactics individuals choose to reduce it appear to be influenced by cultural factors.

KEY TERMS

attitude polarization (p. 142)

attitudes (p. 118)

attitude-to-behavior process model (p. 131)

biased assimilation (p. 141)

central route (to persuasion) (p. 136)

classical conditioning (p. 121)

cognitive dissonance (p. 144)

elaboration likelihood model
  (of persuasion) (p. 136)

forewarning (p. 141)

heuristic processing (p. 136)

hypocrisy (p. 149)

induced compliance (p. 146)

instrumental conditioning (p. 122)

less-leads-to-more effect (p. 148)

observational learning (p. 122)

peripheral route
  (to persuasion) (p. 136)

persuasion (p. 135)

prototype/willingness model (p. 132)

reactance (p. 140)

selective avoidance (p. 141)

social comparison (p. 123)

social learning (p. 120)

subliminal conditioning (p. 122)

systematic processing (p. 136)

theory of planned behavior (p. 131)

trivialization (p. 144)

FOR MORE INFORMATION

Eagly, A. H., Wood, W., & Chaiken, S. (1996). Principles of persuasion. In E. T. Higgins & A. W. Kruglanski (Eds.), *Social psychology: Handbook of basic principles* (pp. 702–742). New York: Guilford Press.

Two experts on the process of persuasion provide an insightful overview of the findings of recent research on this important topic.

Gollwitzer, P. M., & Barth, J. A. (1996). *The psychology of action: Linking motivation and cognition in behavior.* New York: Guilford Press.

A collection of insightful chapters focused on recent efforts by social psychologists to understand one of the essential puzzles of life: why other people behave the way they do.

Shavitt, S., & Brock, T. C. (1994). *Persuasion: Psychological insights and perspectives.* Boston: Allyn and Bacon.

Explores all aspects of persuasion. The chapters on when and how attitudes influence behavior, on cognitive dissonance, and on the cognitive perspective on persuasion are all excellent.

5

Aspects of Social Identity: Self and Gender

Man and Woman Sharing Vision. © José Ortega/Stock Illustration Source

Chapter Outline

The Self: Components of One's Identity
    Self-Concept: The All-Important Schema
    SOCIAL DIVERSITY: A CRITICAL ANALYSIS: Cultural Influences on the Self:
        The Effects of Individualism versus Collectivism
    Self-Esteem: Attitudes about Oneself
    CORNERSTONES OF SOCIAL PSYCHOLOGY: Rogers, Self-Theory, Self–Ideal
        Discrepancy, and Personality Change

Other Aspects of Self-Functioning: Focusing, Monitoring, and Efficacy
    Focusing on Oneself versus Focusing on the External World
    Monitoring One's Behavior on the Basis of Internal versus
        External Factors
    Self-Efficacy: Having Confidence in Oneself

Gender: Maleness or Femaleness As a Crucial Aspect of Identity
    Gender Identity and Gender Stereotypes
    Gender-Role Behavior and Reactions to Gender-Role Behavior
    BEYOND THE HEADLINES: AS SOCIAL PSYCHOLOGISTS SEE IT: Does Gender
        Discrimination Still Occur in the Workplace?
    When Men and Women Differ: Biology, Gender Roles, or Both?
    CONNECTIONS: Integrating Social Psychology
    IDEAS TO TAKE WITH YOU: Dealing with Negative Self-Perceptions

Summary and Review of Key Points
Key Terms
For More Information

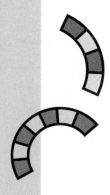

When I (Donn Byrne) was about eight or nine years old, my parents gave me an Erector set for Christmas. I can still remember my joy in opening the heavy box and seeing the array of metal pieces and the little packages of nuts and bolts. Even better was the booklet that had pictures of the many remarkable things that you could make—from a simple wagon with a handle to a very complex Ferris wheel that could be made to revolve when attached to a tiny electric motor. There were even little passenger seats that hung loosely from the wheel itself so that they always remained upright, just like the real ones.

As grand as all of this appeared, there was a major problem that soon dawned on me. I would have to look at the pictures and somehow figure out how to create these wonderful objects. How in the world could I know which metal pieces to use and how to put them together? To construct something myself, having only the pictures to guide me, was totally different from anything I had ever done. Undertaking such a task was not at all a part of who I was, and the necessary skills were sadly lacking. Clearly, I couldn't do it.

Why couldn't I? The best explanation is that I had no experience with using tools to build anything and no role models whose behavior I could imitate. My mother (a housewife) couldn't even imagine herself engaging in something involving nuts and bolts. For my father (a cotton broker), physical activity was limited to driving the car and playing golf. My grandfather (a bank teller) lived with us and was an avid reader and a great storyteller, but he was not one who built or repaired things. To the best of my recollection, I had never seen any of these individuals holding a hammer, saw, or screwdriver. I later joked that had my brother and I not been born, the adults would have had to hire someone to change light bulbs. That was not quite true, but almost.

In any event, I was stuck with a truly wonderful gift that was of no use to me. Finally, for reasons unknown, I decided that maybe I could build one or two of the simpler items. I quickly learned that looking at the finished product didn't help; you had to start with the basic elements and deal with one small detail at a time. Much later, I decided that most tasks are like that. For example, you can't write a book, but you can write a word, then a sentence, then a paragraph, then a page, and so forth until all the pieces eventually come together as the finished product. In just that way, the metallic pieces eventually came together for one surprised little boy, and there before me was a Ferris wheel!

Following that unexpected accomplishment, I became convinced that I must actually possess the skill to follow almost any set of instructions and reach a goal. Over the years, that skill became an important part of who I was and what I could do in undertaking tasks as diverse as learning algebra, delivering mail, conducting research, giving a classroom lecture, assembling toys for my children, operating a computer, and programming a VCR.

In a familiar childhood story, a little locomotive was called upon to haul a train full of Christmas toys over a steep mountain and into the valley beyond where children were anxiously waiting. Struggling uphill, the engine said to itself over and over, "I think I can, I think I can . . . ," and eventually it succeeded. The "little engine that could" remains an important role model for all of us.

After many years had passed, I learned to think of that experience as representing one of many that altered my views about just who I was (my self-concept) and my expectancies about what I could accomplish (my feelings of self-efficacy). We will return to those psychological concepts shortly.

Very early in life, each person begins acquiring a view of who he is or who she is, and even of whether to be identified as "he" or "she." That is, we each develop a **social identity,** a self-definition that indicates just how we conceptualize and evaluate ourselves (Deaux, 1993a; Ellemers, Wilke, & van Knippenberg, 1993). Our social identity includes unique characteristics such as our name and *self-concept* along with many other characteristics that we share with others (Sherman, 1994). Among the latter are our gender and relationship to others (woman, man, daughter, son, spouse, parent, etc.); our vocation or avocation (student, musician, psychologist, surfer, jock, bird-watcher, etc.); political or ideological affiliation (feminist, environmentalist, Democrat, Republican, vegetarian, etc.); specific attributes that may cause us to be the targets of prejudice (homosexual, drug user, disabled, idle rich); and ethnicity or religious affiliation (Catholic, Southerner, Hispanic, Jewish, African American, Muslim, atheist, etc.) (Deaux et al., 1995).

Despite the obvious fact that we have to acquire many aspects of our self-concepts from other people, there are additional aspects of the self that are strongly determined by genetics. Hur, McGue, and Iacono (1998) compared several hundred pairs of identical and nonidentical twin girls (aged eleven and twelve) with respect to the similarity of their self-concepts. To simplify somewhat, greater similarity between identical twins than between nonidentical twins suggests the operation of inherited rather than environmental factors. These investigators discovered that about a third of the variation in the girls' self-concepts was attributable to genetic differences. Specifically, genetic factors had the greatest effect on self-perceived popularity and physical appearance, a moderate effect on behavior problems and anxiety, and a smaller effect on happiness and academic competence. Clearly, part of who we are and how we perceive ourselves is a matter of heredity.

These many categories that make up social identity are tied to our interpersonal worlds, and they indicate precisely how each of us is like and also unlike other individuals. When a person's social context changes, social identity can be a source of stress that requires a coping response. For example, when Hispanic students in the United States leave a subculture in which they are the majority and enter a primarily Anglo subculture such as a university or workplace, the resulting stress often leads to one of two common reactions. One alternative is to become increasingly *more* identified with and involved in Hispanic activities, Spanish-speaking groups, Hispanic music and clothing styles, and so forth, thus strengthening and affirming an identification with the ethnic aspect of social identity. The opposite reaction is to become *less* identified with Hispanic matters, perhaps even adopting an Anglo version of one's name, learning to speak accent-free English, and generally becoming *assimilated* and indistinguishable from others in the majority culture (Ethier & Deaux, 1994).

In this chapter, we will concentrate on just two of the major components of social identity. First, we describe several of the crucial elements that make up the *self,* including self-concept, self-esteem, self-focusing, self-monitoring, and self-efficacy. Second, we examine *gender,* especially the social determinants of gender identity, gender roles, and the way behavior is influenced by these attributes.

THE SELF: COMPONENTS OF ONE'S IDENTITY

Thinking about oneself is an unavoidable human activity—most people are literally self-centered. That is, the self is the center of each person's social universe. One's self-identity, or self-concept, is acquired through interactions with other

social identity • A person's definition of who he or she is, including personal attributes (self-concept) and attributes shared with others such as gender and race.

people—beginning with immediate family members and then broadening to interactions with those beyond the family. Our beliefs about self are even affected by the supposed characteristics associated with astrological signs. For example, if you are a Leo, you are likely to accept what you read about the personality characteristics of Leos (but not the characteristics of Libras) as an accurate description of yourself (Hamilton, 1995).

The **self-concept** is an organized collection of beliefs and self-perceptions about oneself. In other words, it operates as a very important schema that functions like any other schema, as discussed in Chapter 3. The self is a framework that determines how we process information about ourselves, including our motives, emotional states, self-evaluations, abilities, and much else besides (Klein, Loftus, & Burton, 1989; Van Hook & Higgins, 1988).   *in humans*

Sedikides and Skowronski (1997) propose that the self evolved as an adaptive characteristic. The first aspect to emerge was **subjective self-awareness;** this involves the ability of the organism to differentiate itself to some degree from its physical and social environment. Most animals share this characteristic, which makes it possible to survive (Damasio, 1994; Lewis, 1992). Over time, **objective self-awareness** developed among primates; this term refers to the organism's capacity to be the object of its own attention (Gallup, 1994), to be aware of its own state of mind (Cheney & Seyfarth, 1992), and "to know it knows, to remember it remembers" (Lewis, 1992, p. 124). Only humans seem to have developed the third level of self-functioning—**symbolic self-awareness**—which permits adults of our species to form an abstract cognitive representation of self through language. This representation, in turn, makes it possible for us to communicate, form relationships, set goals, evaluate outcomes, develop self-related attitudes, and defend ourselves against threatening communications. Throughout each person's life, interactions with others in multiple contexts continue to influence and to modify the specific contents of that person's self-identity.

self-concept • One's self-identity, a schema consisting of an organized collection of beliefs and feelings about oneself.

subjective self-awareness • The ability of an organism to differentiate itself, however crudely, from its physical and social environment.

objective self-awareness • An organism's capacity to be the object of its own attention, to be aware of its own state of mind, and to know that it knows and remember that it remembers.

symbolic self-awareness • An organism's ability to form an abstract concept of self through language; this ability enables the organism to communicate, form relationships, set goals, evaluate outcomes, develop self-related attitudes, and defend itself against threatening communications.

Self-Concept: The All-Important Schema

Who are you? Before you read further, try to give twenty different answers to that question.

The Content of a Person's Self Concept. Questions such as "Who are you?" and "Who am I?" have been asked for more than a hundred years as psychologists, beginning with William James (1890), have endeavored to determine the specific content of the individual self-concept (Ziller, 1990).

Rentsch and Heffner (1994) utilized this technique when they asked more than two hundred college students to give repeated answers to the question "Who are you?" The investigators analyzed the responses statistically in order to determine the basic categories of self as perceived by the research participants. The study rested on the assumption that each person possesses a unique self-concept with *specific content,* but that the *overall structure* of the self-concept is the same for all individuals. As shown in Figure 5.1, these students described themselves on the basis of eight categories (or factors). Some of these categories refer to some aspects of social identity (described earlier), whereas others refer to personal attributes. One goal for social psychologists is to establish a clear picture or blueprint of the self-structure. If you answered the question about yourself, which of these factors did you utilize? Did you refer to other categories, different from those listed in the figure?

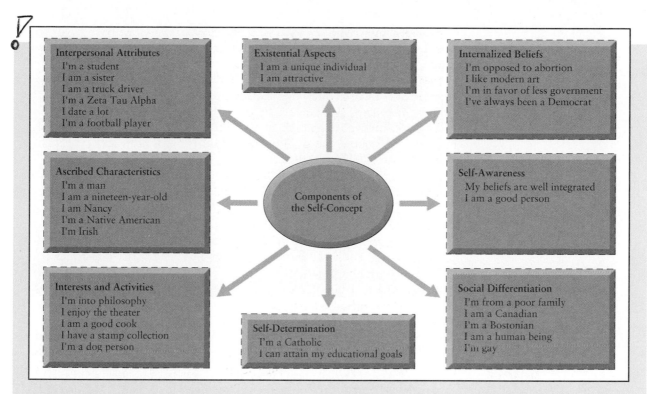

Figure 5.1

Who Am I? Eight Components of Self-Concept. More than two hundred college students were asked to respond to the question "Who am I?" twenty times in a row, giving a different answer each time. Statistical analysis of their responses indicated eight distinct categories. The investigators suggested the category headings that are shown in the figure. Though different people tend to use the same eight categories in describing themselves, the specific content of each category varies from person to person

(*Source:* Based on data from Rentsch & Heffner, 1994.)

The Cognitive Effects of a Person's Self-Schema. Self-schemas are probably much more complex and detailed than can be determined by questions about who you are. Consider the possibilities. Beyond an overall framework, such a schema would include your meaningful past experiences, your detailed knowledge about what you are like at present, and your expectancies about changes that will characterize your future self. In other words, a self-schema is the sum of everything a person remembers, knows, and can imagine about herself or himself. One's self-schema can also play a role in guiding behavior (Kendzierski & Whitaker, 1997). For example, the intention to lose weight is quite common, but the ability to link that intention to mildly unpleasant behaviors (dieting, engaging in exercise) requires a strong guiding force. Without a strong and consistent conceptualization of who you are now and who you want to be in the future, it is much easier simply to eat what you want and avoid working up a sweat.

Because the self is the center of each person's social world and because self-schemas are very well developed, it follows that we are able to do a better job of processing self-relevant information than any other kind of information—a phenomenon known as the **self-reference effect**. For example, because my last name is Byrne, I notice and am able to store and retrieve certain bits of information that would be more difficult for a non-Byrne than for me

self-reference effect • The fact that cognitive processing of information relevant to the self is more efficient than the processing of other types of information.

Figure 5.2

The Self-Reference Effect: Who Played the Musketeers in *The Man in the Iron Mask*? The *self-reference effect* specifies that information relevant to oneself is processed more effectively than information about other topics. Playing an informal game of trivial pursuit while driving, my daughter and I attempted to name the four actors who were the musketeers in the movie *The Man in the Iron Mask.* For both of us, the first and most rapid response was that Gabriel Byrne played one of the four—a simple demonstration of the self-reference effect. If, however, you had been with us and your last name happened to be Irons, Malkovich, or Depardieu, you very probably would have responded with the name that matched yours. If your name is none of the above, you may remember only that Leonardo DiCaprio played the king (and his brother)—the Leo effect.

(see Figure 5.2). That is, I am well aware of Gabriel Byrne, the Irish actor; Jane Byrne, the former mayor of Chicago; Brendan Byrne, the former governor of New Jersey; and Barbara Byrne, whose work on social self-concept is discussed later in this chapter—even though I've never met or even seen any of these individuals in person.

In a similar way, imagine you participate in an experiment in which you are shown a series of words and asked about each one, "Does this word describe you?" Now imagine you are in an experiment and are shown the same words and asked to think about the question "Is this word printed in big letters?" In which condition do you think you would remember more words afterward? You, of course, would do best when asked whether each word describes you. Any self-relevant information is most likely to catch your attention, to be retained in memory, and to be recalled easily (Higgins & Bargh, 1987).

Some investigators have pursued the question of just *how* self-relevant information is processed more efficiently. Klein and Loftus (1988) reasoned that that recall could be facilitated in one of two ways. First, you are likely to spend more time thinking about words or events that are relevant to yourself than about any other words or events. By doing so, you are engaging in *elaborative processing,* which connects new material to existing information that is already stored in memory. It is easier to process anything associated with something you know well (current Top 40 songs, for example) than anything associated with something about which you are relatively uninformed (tunes popular during World War II, for example). Second, self-relevant material is likely to be well organized in your memory; as a result, new self-relevant information can easily be placed in categories that are already present—a phenomenon known as *categorical processing*. That is analogous to having a filing system already set up and ready for new material to be inserted in the appropriate folders. In a test of the effects of these two types of processing, Klein and Loftus (1988) encouraged research participants to engage in elaborative processing of words ("think of a definition of each") or to engage in categorical processing of the words ("think about a personal experience related to each"). By comparing how well the participants remembered the words afterward, the investigators were able to show that we deal with self-relevant material very efficiently because it is based on *both* elaborative and categorical processing. In sum, we think more about whatever is relevant to ourselves, and we also categorize such material effectively. As a result, we are able to recall self-relevant information much better than information unrelated to ourselves.

How Is the Self-Concept Structured? It is correct to say that each of us possesses a self-concept, but the structure of this all-important schema involves multiple aspects.

For example, self-conceptions can be relatively *central* or relatively *peripheral* (Sedikides, 1995). Central self-conceptions are more extreme (positive or negative) than peripheral self-conceptions. For example, perhaps you think of yourself as extremely trustworthy and extremely hot-tempered (central) and also as moderately predictable and moderately proud (peripheral). When research participants are induced to feel sad, neutral, or happy, peripheral self-conceptions are influenced by current mood, but central self-conceptions are not. In the example just given, induced sadness might make you describe yourself as less predictable and less proud, but your perception of yourself as trustworthy and hot-tempered would very likely remain unaffected. In general, it is more difficult to bring about change in central self-perceptions than in peripheral ones because central self-conceptions are elaborated in greater detail, more strongly consolidated, and held with greater certainty.

Another structural aspect of the self-concept is *clarity*—the extent to which beliefs about oneself are clearly defined, consistent with one another, and stable across situations and over time (Campbell et al., 1996). The higher an individual's clarity, the higher the self-esteem and the more agreeable he or she tends to be. Thus, it seems to be beneficial to "know oneself."

Self-concepts can also be *interrelated* in that they are defined in part by the characteristics of other people (better than, worse than; like, unlike; etc.); or they may be *isolated,* in that their content does not depend on any other individual (Niedenthal & Beike, 1997). In addition, a given person's self-concept may be relatively complex or relatively simple (Davies, 1996).

Each person's self concept can also be divided into specific *content areas*. For example, Andersen and Cyranowski (1994) have investigated **sexual self-schema,** one's cognitive representations of the sexual aspects of oneself. These psychologists identified three distinct types of such schema among women; and the women's sexual attitudes, emotional reactions, and behavior tended to be based on these three schemas. Thus, the research participants described themselves as passionate and romantic (warm, loving, sympathetic), open and direct (frank, outspoken, uninhibited), or embarrassed and conservative (cautious, self-conscious, timid). More recently, Andersen and Cyranowski (1998) have categorized the romantic/passionate and open/direct schemas as

sexual self-schema • Cognitive representations of the sexual aspects of oneself.

positive and the embarrassed/conservative schema as negative. As expected, women with relatively positive sexual self-schemas are more sexually active, engage in more varied sexual activity, and have more sexual partners than women with negative self-schemas. In addition, some women (*aschematics*) are low on both positive and negative dimensions; these women report low levels of sexual desire, little anxiety about sex, and weak romantic attachments. Other women (*co-schematics*) are high on both positive and negative dimensions, and they report conflicting responses to both sex and romance. These latter individuals have high levels of sexual desire and preoccupation with sex along with anxiety about sex; similarly, they report strong feelings of passionate love but fear being unloved by their partners and abandoned. (See Chapter 8 for a discussion of both passionate love and conflicts about close relationships.)

Another content area—social self-concept—can be further subdivided. For example, Byrne and Shavelson (1996) categorize young people's social interactions into those involving school and those involving family, as outlined in Figure 5.3.

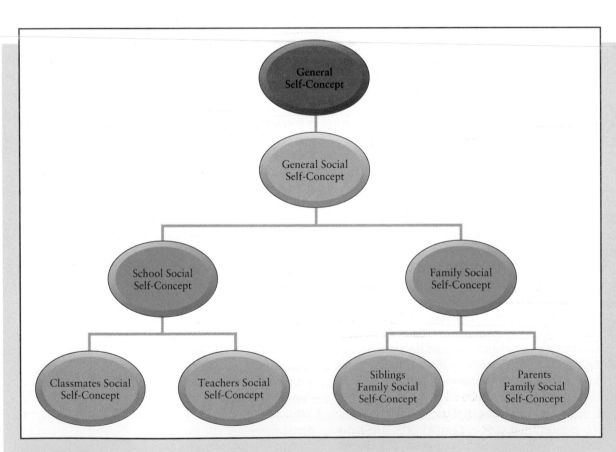

Figure 5.3

Social Self-Concept: One of the Many Aspects of One's General Self-Concept. Each person's overall self-concept is composed of many distinct components that provide schemas for specific aspects of one's life. One such component, social interaction, is shown here. For young people this social self-concept can be further divided into more specific categories such as social interactions at school and social interactions with family. Any attempt to depict all of the elements of anyone's self-concept would clearly be a major undertaking.

(*Source:* Based on information in Byrne & Shavelson, 1996.)

These investigators studied three age groups (preadolescents, early adolescents, and late adolescents) and found that the social self-concept becomes increasingly differentiated and better defined with age.

To what extent do the self-concepts of people who belong to a specific ethnic or cultural group tend to be similar to one another and different from those of people who belong to other groups? We will examine this question in the following *Social Diversity* section.

social self • A collective identity that includes interpersonal relationships plus aspects of identity derived from membership in larger, less personal groups based on race, ethnicity, and culture.

Social Diversity: A Critical Analysis
Cultural Influences on the Self: The Effects of Individualism versus Collectivism

Though it is commonly assumed that one's self-concept is formed in the context of social interactions, the implications of this proposal are difficult to appreciate within a single culture. When we look across cultures or subcultures, however, aspects of the self that are based on social factors become much more obvious.

Brewer and Gardner (1996) observe that psychological theories of the self have emphasized the individual and the importance of a unique identity for each person. Cross-cultural research, in contrast, makes it clear that there are also social aspects of the self that are shared with others. In part, we each define ourselves in terms of these social aspects. It is not simply that we form associations, for example, with a given ethnic group, but that the self is actually different in different groups. Part of who we are and how we think of ourselves is determined by a *collective identity* that is sometimes labeled the **social self** (as opposed to the *personal self*). The social self, in turn, involves two somewhat different components: (1) that derived from *interpersonal relationships* and (2) that derived from belonging to larger, less personal *collective groupings* such as race, ethnicity, or culture. Such relationships and categories become part of the self (Smith & Henry, 1996). Remember that in Figure 5.1, responses to the question "Who am I?" frequently included various relationships and groups. Baumeister and Leary (1995) argue that the social self is based on a fundamental "need to belong" that is an inborn characteristic of humans. (In Chapter 7 we'll describe relevant work on the biological basis of this need for affiliation.)

One of the many implications of these various formulations is that people in different cultures would be expected to develop self-concepts that differ in specific ways. As one example, Kitayama and his colleagues (1997) proposed that people raised in Western, individualistic cultures learn that everyday life presents repeated opportunities for self-enhancement. In contrast, for those in Eastern, collectivist cultures, everyday life is believed to present opportunities for self-criticism and thus self-improvement. These investigators described an American who spent some of his undergraduate years at a Japanese university where he observed that the same event felt quite different in the two countries. Playing volleyball in the United States was a loud, relaxed, enjoyable activity. In Japan, volleyball was a serious matter with the goal of winning, and the players were expected to expend effort and do their best throughout the game. This difference made the same game a very different experience in the two countries. Presumably, many seemingly parallel events in different cultures do not "feel" the same.

In comparing the behavior of college students in Japan and the United States, the investigators found the expected differences between self-enhancing Americans and self-criticizing Japanese. In addition, students in the two countries differ when they indicate the types of situations that raise their self-esteem (success) or lower it (failure). As shown in Figure 5.4 on page 166, Americans tend to emphasize the individual and Japanese the group as most relevant.

One way to characterize such differences is in terms of self-serving tendencies in Western but not in Eastern cultures. Across many studies, North Americans are found to express unrealistically optimistic self-evaluations (Regan, Snyder, & Kassin, 1995) and to show self-serving attributional biases (see Chapter 2), while Japanese do neither. In a similar way, Chinese college students in Hong Kong are much less self-enhancing than comparable students in North America (Yik, Bond, & Paulhus, 1998). Heine and Lehman (1997b) raised the possibility that in Asian cultures, self-enhancement might be replaced by group enhancement. A comparison of Canadian and Japanese students revealed, however, that the latter not only engage in self-criticism but in group criticism as well. For example, Japanese participants evaluated their family members and their universities less positively than Canadians did. In effect, in individualistic cultures there is the assumption that "We're number one!" whereas in collectivist cultures the assumption is that "We could do better if we made sufficient effort."

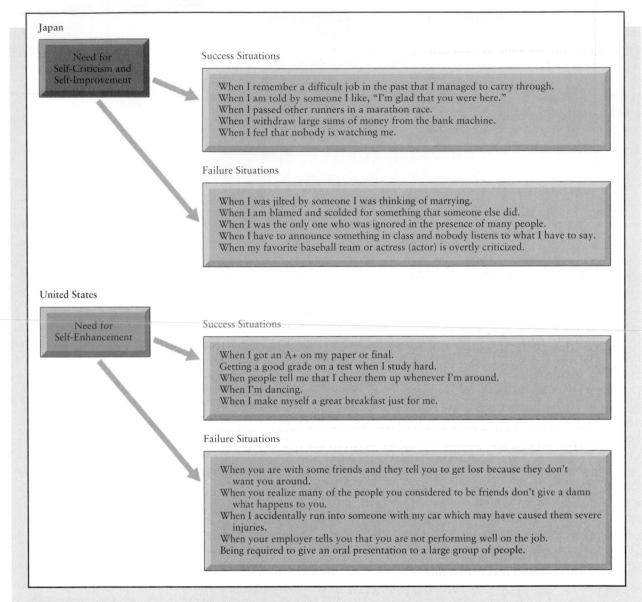

Figure 5.4

Success and Failure in Collectivist and Individualist Cultures. Cultural differences result in differences in self-concept. In a collectivist culture such as Japan, self-criticism is the norm, while in an individualist culture such as the United States, self-enhancement is the norm. This difference leads to different interpretations of what constitutes success and failure and to different behavior.

(*Source:* Based on information in Kitayama et al., 1997.)

It is worth noting, however, that even within an individualistic culture, self-enhancement and more critical self-assessment each occur under specific circumstances. For example, students in the Western world want favorable feedback about unchangeable aspects of themselves, but they are willing to receive accurate, unfavorable feedback about a characteristic that can be improved (Dunning, 1995). Analogously, self-enhancement occurs even within a collectivist culture, but only in a modest and nonobvious way. For example, Japanese students prefer the letters in their own names and the numbers corresponding to the month and day of their birth over other letters and other numbers (Kitayama & Karasawa, 1997).

One Self-Concept or Many? We usually speak of ourselves as though the self always remained the same, but we are aware that we can and do change over time. You are not the same person you were ten years ago, and you are not likely to be the same person ten years from now that you are today. In more specific terms, you may imagine what your life will be like after college—beginning a career, getting married, having children, earning more money, moving elsewhere. In effect, not only do you have a self-concept, but you are also aware of other **possible selves** that you may become.

Markus and Nurius (1986) suggest that one's self-concept at any given time is actually just a *working self-concept,* something open to change in response to new experiences, new feedback, and new self-relevant information. The existence of alternative possible selves affects us in several ways. The image of a future self may influence *motivation;* you are likely to find it easier to study more or to give up cigarettes if you imagine a new and improved you that will emerge as a consequence of these behavioral changes. Optimistic individuals have more confidence than pessimistic individuals that they will be able to achieve a positive possible self (Carver, Reynolds, & Scheier, 1994). Lore Segal, a professor of English, describes the same process in terms of hope:

> Hope pities our dowdiness. It promises that we will find the treasure,
> marry the prince, and inherit the kingdom. Hope says that it is our birth-
> right to win the lottery and write a classic novel. If we are American it
> will be a bestseller. We will make the NBA, be a rock star, become president
> (Segal, 1996).

Though you may have a clear image of your future self, others tend to perceive only your present self, and the difference between the two can cause misunderstandings. Even more upsetting is a discrepancy between the person you are and the person you would rather be (Higgins, 1990).

People differ with respect to the number of possible selves they can imagine. Those who can envision only a relatively limited number of alternatives tend to be especially vulnerable to discouraging feedback (Niedenthal, Setterlund, & Wherry, 1992). For example, a person who is considering twenty different possible careers is not overwhelmed by discovering that he lacks the necessary ability to succeed in one of them; after all, there are nineteen other possibilities. If a person has a single career goal, however, discovering an obstacle is devastating. Similarly, an athletic injury is more upsetting to someone who identifies strongly with the role of athlete than to someone for whom athletics is one of several alternatives (Brewer, 1993). More broadly, it appears that those who can envision many different selves adjust better to many kinds of setbacks (Morgan & Janoff-Bulman, 1994).

Altogether, having a complex view of one's possible selves (so long as the possibilities are realistic) is emotionally beneficial. Interestingly, research indicates that among white students, strategies designed to attain achievement-related possible selves are predicted by adherence to individualism and the Protestant work ethic, and also by the awareness of positive selves that can be adopted and of negative selves to avoid. For black students, effective strategies are predicted by adherence to collectivism and by emphasis on ethnic identity (Oyserman, Gant, & Ager, 1995). The importance of ethnic identity rests in part on the fact that self-esteem and self-enhancement actually benefit from group discrimination (Rubin & Hewstone, 1998). Though it seems a bit odd, some personal benefits can result from discriminating and being discriminated

possible selves • Mental representations of what we might become, or should become, in the future.

against. Nevertheless, this positive outcome in no way excuses discrimination, nor does it make it generally desirable.

In the context of education, it is important for young people to be encouraged to make connections between alternative possible selves and whatever they are currently doing in school. For example, most children can't imagine any connection between learning how to multiply and the kind of lives they might have when they grow up. Day and her colleagues (1994) worked with Mexican American children in the third, fourth, and fifth grades. The youngsters were asked to consider many possible future careers, and the emphasis was on the relevance of the work they were given in school to their future selves. To take a simple example, owning a house and driving a fancy car require having an adequate income; the income requires working at a job; and the highest-paying jobs require the skills learned in school. Children who were given special educational enrichment pointing out such connections subsequently showed greater interest (compared with those not in the program) in the possibility of entering occupations such as medicine or law rather than limited, stereotyped occupations. Exposure to multiple role possibilities and information about what is required for attainment of specific future goals helped these children develop a larger number of possible selves.

Changing the Self-Concept. We have already indicated that as we age, the self-concept changes slowly over time. Specific events, however, can alter our beliefs about who we are in a very short period of time. For example, change is very likely to occur when one receives feedback that is inconsistent with his or her existing self-schema (Bober & Grolnick, 1995) or when one moves from one community to another (Kling, Ryff, & Essex, 1997).

A more dramatic example of change is the negative effect on a person's self-concept when he or she loses a job and suddenly has a new social identity—for example, when "an accountant" becomes "an unemployed person" (Sheeran & Abraham, 1994). The experience of entering a new occupation also brings about changes in self-concept (see Figure 5.5). For example, new

Figure 5.5
New Employment Status Equals Changed Self-Concept. Among the many factors that bring about changes in self-concept are those associated with one's job. For example, our self-perception undergoes change if we enter a new occupation.

police officers develop new and different perceptions of themselves (Stradling, Crowe, & Tuohy, 1993); to understand this, visualize a late adolescent working as a mechanic who becomes an officer of the law complete with a uniform, weapons, and new responsibilities. Even greater changes occur when an individual joins the armed forces and is thrust into combat. Most of us have had no experience in situations that involve a high probability of killing or being killed. As a consequence, it is possible to become confused about whether you are simply a civilian wearing a uniform or a real military person and about why you feel old even though you are still young. Military experience sometimes results in the development of a totally new, and often negative, self-identity (Silverstein, 1994).

Less impactful events can also bring about changes in self-concept. For example, just thinking about a significant other leads research participants to shift their self-descriptions to reflect the way they are when they're with this other person (Hinkley & Andersen, 1996). McNulty and Swann (1994) examined changes in the self-concept that occur during interpersonal interactions. They investigated the self-perceptions and interpersonal perceptions of same-sex college roommates over several weeks. The participants rated themselves and the roommate on characteristics such as social skills, attractiveness, and agreeableness. The findings indicate a reciprocal process in which self-perceptions influence the other person's perceptions, and those perceptions in turn have an effect on self-perceptions. The investigators propose that the self acts as an "architect" in shaping and determining the reactions of others, but that then the self is also altered by how others react. Given the fact that mutual influences occur in pairs of roommates, it seems very likely that this process is even stronger in close relationships such as friendship and marriage.

Rather than the self's undergoing change in a social context, a different interpretation is possible. That is, it may be that each person has a central *core self* plus many different *social selves* that are activated by different people in different social interactions. Roberts and Donahue (1994) pursued this question with a sample of middle-aged women by assessing several of their *role-specific self-concepts* as well as their *general self-concepts*. The role-specific concepts for each individual were worker, wife, friend, and daughter (see Figure 5.6 on page 170). The women were asked to describe themselves in these different roles with respect to positive affect, competence, and dependability. As hypothesized, self-conceptions differed across roles, but there was also a high degree of consistency for individuals as they shifted from role to role. For example, two women might each describe themselves as having more positive affect in the role of friend than in the role of daughter, thus indicating role-specific self-concepts. Nevertheless, the same two women might also differ from each other in that one expressed more positive affect in both roles than the other. This consistent difference across roles reflects the operation of a general self-concept.

Self-Esteem: Attitudes about Oneself

Probably the most important attitude that any of us form is the attitude about self, an evaluation that is known as **self-esteem** (James, 1890). If you were asked right now to evaluate yourself on a scale of 1 to 10 (with 1 indicating an extremely negative evaluation and 10 an extremely positive one), what number do you think would best describe your attitude toward yourself? Keep your answer in mind as you read the following section.

self-esteem • The self-evaluation made by each individual; one's attitude toward oneself along a positive–negative dimension.

Figure 5.6

General Self-Concept and Role-Specific Self-Concepts. When Roberts and Donahue (1994) asked women to describe themselves with respect to several characteristics, the women produced different self-descriptions to fit different roles in their lives. Role-specific self-concepts emerged when they considered themselves as worker, wife, friend, or daughter. Thus, the self-concept differs somewhat in different interpersonal situations. The women nevertheless showed some consistency from role to role, indicating the presence of a general self-concept as well.

Sedikides (1993) proposes three possible motives for self-evaluation: *self-assessment* (seeking accurate self-knowledge), *self-enhancement* (seeking positive self-knowledge), and *self-verification* (seeking self-knowledge that confirms what is already known). Which of these motives is activated is a function of cultural differences, personality differences, and the specific situation that is encountered (Taylor, Neter, & Wayment, 1995). As we have discussed, self-enhancement is common in Western societies; but Swann (1997) also points out the importance of self-verification for individuals with negative self-views. In order to avoid having to change their self-assessments, these individuals seek partners who view them negatively, behave so as to elicit negative evaluations from their partners, and perceive the reactions of others as more negative than is actually the case.

Self-Evaluations. Having high self-esteem means that an individual likes himself or herself. Such evaluations are based in part on the opinions of others and in part on specific experiences. As we will see in Chapter 8, these attitudes about self may begin with the earliest interactions between an infant and a caregiver. Cultural differences also influence what is important to one's self-esteem. For example, harmony in interpersonal relationships is an essential element in collectivist cultures, whereas self-worth is all-important in individualistic cultures (Kwan, Bond, & Singelis, 1997).

Relatively negative (as opposed to positive) self-perceptions result in more predictable behavior. The reason seems to be that negative self-schemas are more tightly organized than positive ones (Malle & Horowitz, 1995). As a result, a person with low self-esteem typically overgeneralizes (interprets too broadly) the implications of failure (Brown & Dutton, 1995) and rejection (Nezlek et al., 1997). In the world of Pooh, Eeyore has a negative self-view and interprets everything that happens from this perspective. In contrast, Tigger's self-esteem is high, and he has multiple explanations for his ups and downs.

Different levels of self-esteem can be associated with specific aspects of ourselves. What if you are great in dealing with people, only so-so in math, and terrible as a dancer? Global self-esteem is based on a multitude of such specific self-evaluations (Marsh, 1995; Pelham, 1995a, 1995b). Beyond that, however, specific self-evaluations predict *cognitive* reactions to success and failure whereas global self-esteem predicts *emotional* reactions to such outcomes (Dutton & Brown, 1997).

Rather than treating attitudes about self as a simple rating, some researchers have taken a different approach: comparing individuals' self-concept with their conception of an ideal self. The greater the discrepancy between the two, the lower the self-esteem; and this discrepancy tends to remain stable over time, even though the specific content may change (Strauman, 1996). The gentleman in Figure 5.7 on page 172 describes himself in terms that most of us would find negative, but he seems quite satisfied with his characteristics. As a result, his self–ideal discrepancy is low, and hence his self-esteem is high. He is what he wants to be. It's a positive experience to receive feedback indicating that some aspects of our ideal self are functioning well, and a negative one to receive evidence that we are not living up to our ideal (Eisenstadt & Leppe, 1994).

It also matters whether one's "good" and "bad" qualities are very common or quite unusual. If a person perceives his or her most positive characteristics to be commonplace and the most negative characteristics to be rare, self-esteem suffers as a result. My teenage daughter, Lindsey, is one of the most talented writers I've ever encountered, but she is average in algebra; she mistakenly believes that almost everyone can write well but that she is one of a tiny minority who have trouble with math.

Self-Esteem and Social Comparison. As we will explain in Chapter 7, people tend to make self-evaluations by comparing themselves to other people (Brown, 1992), and this is especially true of individuals who are low in self-esteem (Wayment & Taylor, 1995). Depending on your comparison group, specific successes and failures may contribute to high or low self-evaluations—or may be completely irrelevant. For example, Osborne (1995) points out that despite better academic performance among whites than among African Americans in U.S. schools, global self-esteem is significantly higher for the latter group. Why? In the earliest grades, students of both races base self-evaluation in part on academic success and failure. By the tenth grade, however, this rela-

Figure 5.7

Self-Concept: Perceptions of Oneself Need Not Please Everyone. The gentleman here who describes himself in socially unacceptable terms may be offering an accurate self-portrait, although not necessarily a likable one. The point is that our thoughts, emotions, and actions are driven by such self-schemas, regardless of whether they are "good" or "bad."

(*Source: The New Yorker,* September 30, 1996, p. 65.)

"I was a ruthless, driven, unfeeling son of a bitch—and it worked out extremely well."

tionship drops dramatically for African American students, especially males (Steele, 1992). For them, the comparison groups that determine self-esteem are no longer classmates engaged in schoolwork but nonclassmates engaged in other activities.

Although such social comparisons are relatively complex, the general underlying principle is that any experience that creates a positive mood raises self-esteem, whereas a negative mood lowers self-esteem (Esses, 1989). Consider three possible comparison groups: strangers, ingroup peers, and people who are very close to you. The effect of discovering someone worse off than yourself (a "downward comparison") can help or hurt your self-esteem depending on the comparison group. That is, when you compare yourself to strangers, your affect is positive and your self-esteem tends to rise when you perceive some inadequacy in any of them (Crocker, 1993): "She's fatter than I am, so I feel better about myself." In this instance, a *contrast effect* leads to a positive outcome (Reis, Gerrard, & Gibbons, 1993). An inadequacy in members of your ingroup is also positive as a contrast effect: "I can draw better than any of them." This is the kind of boost to self-esteem experienced by a big frog in a little pond (McFarland & Buehler, 1995). But when someone *very close to you* exhibits inferior qualities, this has a negative effect on your self-esteem; because this kind of downward comparison means that you are associated with the inadequacy—an *assimilation effect.* "My best friend is emotionally disturbed (so maybe I'm a little off myself)." Analogous differences occur when you observe others better off than yourself. An "upward comparison" can be a matter of indifference if the comparison is with strangers: "I could never play chess as well as the Russian champion, but who cares?" If, however, the upward comparison is with your usual comparison ingroup (classmates, for example), their superiority makes you feel depressed and lowers your self-esteem (Major, Sciacchitano, & Crocker, 1993). The contrast here is a negative one: "I'm the worst tennis player in the tenth grade." Finally, social comparison with someone with qualities superior to your own can enhance your self-esteem, *if* that person is someone to whom you feel close—again, an assimilation effect (Pelham & Wachsmuth, 1995): "My brother won the tennis tournament, and that makes me look good."

The Effects of Having High versus Low Self-Esteem. Research consistently indicates that high self-esteem has beneficial consequences while low self-esteem has the opposite effect (Leary, Schreindorfer, & Haupt, 1995). For example, negative self-evaluation is associated with less adequate social skills (Olmstead et al., 1991), loneliness (McWhirter, 1997), depression (Jex, Cvetanovski, & Allen, 1994), and decreased effort on a task following a failure experience (Tafarodi & Vu, 1997).

For some individuals, competence and self-esteem do not match, and *paradoxical self-esteem* refers to unrealistically high or unrealistically low self-esteem (Tafarodi, 1998). There is some indication that *unrealistically positive* self-esteem can temporarily benefit one's mental health (Taylor & Brown, 1988); more generally, however, research indicates that accurate self-evaluation is preferable in the long run (Colvin, Block, & Funder, 1995).

As will be discussed in Chapter 13, low self-esteem is one of the psychological factors that can weaken the body's immune system, while high self-esteem helps ward off infections and illness (Strauman, Lemieux, & Coe, 1993). There is even some evidence that as self-esteem goes up, *serotonin* levels in the blood increase, and that the result is decreased likelihood of impulsivity and aggressiveness (Wright, 1995).

Short-term increases in self-esteem can be brought about fairly easily. In the laboratory, when participants are given false feedback about how well they did on a personality test, self-esteem goes up (Greenberg et al., 1992). Similarly, interpersonal feedback indicating acceptance or rejection by others can raise or lower one's self-evaluation (Leary et al., 1998). A familiar, but important, effect is based on clothing: self-esteem increases when people like the clothes they are wearing (Kwon, 1994). It is even possible to bring about such changes by directing your thoughts toward positive or negative content. For example, simply thinking about desirable versus undesirable aspects of oneself can, respectively, raise or lower self-esteem (McGuire & McGuire, 1996).

Despite the fact that self-esteem can be changed, we are generally motivated to maintain a relatively stable level of self-esteem, as shown in research involving favorable and unfavorable feedback. Those with high self-esteem recall the favorable material more accurately; similarly, low-self-esteem individuals recall the unfavorable material more accurately (Story, 1998). Following a failure experience, those with low self-esteem focus on their weaknesses, while those with high self-esteem focus on their strengths and suppress thoughts of their weaknesses (Dodgson & Wood, 1998).

Given the generally negative behavioral and emotional effects of low self-esteem (or of high self–ideal discrepancy), interventions aimed at bringing about lasting increases in self-esteem or decreases in discrepancy are potentially of great importance. One of the earliest therapeutic attempts to do just that is described in the following *Cornerstones* section.

Cornerstones of Social Psychology
Rogers, Self-Theory, Self–Ideal Discrepancy, and Personality Change

Carl Rogers. *Rogers was born in 1902 in Illinois and died in 1987 in California. His distinguished career was somewhat unusual in that he worked in clinical settings for the first decade after receiving the Ph.D. degree and then entered academia with the rank of full professor. At Ohio State, Chicago, Wisconsin, and the Western Behavioral Sciences Institute in La Jolla, he developed a theory of personality based on the self, devised a new method of psychotherapy, and established a rigorous research program to evaluate both his theoretical constructs and his therapeutic procedures. Late in his career, I (Donn Byrne) had the privilege of spending an afternoon in informal conversation with him and one of his former students. Carl Rogers was as impressive in person as in his written work; he struck me as the kind of man anyone would be pleased to have as a favorite uncle.*

Though Carl Rogers was a clinical psychologist, his theorizing about the self became an integral part of the field of personality psychology, and his research on the origins of the self-concept and on changing self-perceptions is directly relevant to the current interests of many social psychologists.

Rogers (1951) emphasized that the self is the most important aspect of each person's world. He believed that, in addition to maintaining and enhancing the self, people are inherently motivated to seek "positive regard." That is, from infancy on, we need love and affection, and parents are most often the primary source of such emotional comfort. Because each person strongly needs love, and a child's self-concept and self-esteem are in large part dependent on the amount of dependable affection provided by parents and others. The discussion of attachment style in Chapter 8 is based on this same general conceptualization about the role of adults who are responsible for the care of infants and small children. In Rogers's formulation, problems are created (1) when the child is not given the necessary positive regard and/or (2) when there is a discrepancy between what the child actually feels and what the child is taught he or she ought to feel. In the first instance, the result is low self-esteem and general mistrust of others. In the second, the result is the tendency to distort one's actual perceptions and emotional responses in an effort to maintain a stable self-view.

Rogers came to believe that it is possible to raise unrealistically low self-esteem and to correct a maladaptive self-concept through what he described as "client-centered" or "nondirective" therapy. In this procedure the therapist acts as an interested, accepting, and nonjudgmental parent figure who does not impose his or her external viewpoint but lets the client experience total acceptance along with the freedom to explore his or her true emotions and perceptions. The result is the opportunity for the client to reexperience the emotional learning of infancy and childhood in a positive, nonevaluative atmosphere and, as a result, to undergo change.

Pursuing this formulation of self-theory as well as his innovative therapeutic methods, Rogers initiated a great deal of research designed to test the validity of both theory and practice. Among the investigations conducted by his research group were studies that focused on the difference between a person's *self* and *ideal self* (self–ideal discrepancy) as an indicator of maladjustment. The higher the discrepancy (and hence the lower the person's self-esteem), the less well adjusted, the more unhappy, and the more defensive the individual. Note that more than one kind of self-change is able to reduce the discrepancy. For example, a client can become convinced that the self and the ideal self are really much closer than he or she originally perceived them to be (a change in self-perception). Or the self can become more like the ideal (a change in self-concept). Or unreasonably high standards for the ideal self can be lowered (a change in ideal self). Also, more than one type of change can occur simultaneously.

In an influential book, Rogers and Dymond (1954) described research that provided evidence relevant to these propositions. For example, one relatively basic study compared measures of self–ideal discrepancy for clients before and after they took part in therapy. The control group consisted of volunteers who were not seeking therapeutic help. Measures of self and ideal self were taken at the beginning of the project and again six to twelve months after the clients had completed therapy.

As shown in Figure 5.8, the clients who were judged most improved—and even those who were judged as less improved—revealed a significant decrease in self–ideal

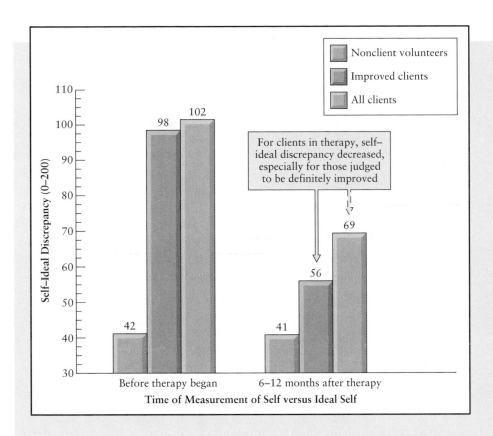

Figure 5.8
The Effect of Client-Centered Therapy on Self–Ideal Discrepancy. In a landmark study of the effects of therapy on self-esteem, Carl Rogers and his colleagues were able to document a decrease in self–ideal discrepancy by comparing measures made before therapy and six to twelve months after therapy. The decrease was greatest for those clients who showed definite improvement. Participants who were not in therapy or seeking it had less self–ideal discrepancy than the therapy clients and showed no change over the time period of the study.

(*Source:* Based on data from Butler & Haigh, 1954.)

discrepancy, with the greatest drop among the most-improved clients. As would be expected, at both time periods the participants in the control group had less self–ideal discrepancy than did the clients, and self–ideal discrepancy did not change among these individuals.

Rogers championed the developmental roots of maladaptive self-perceptions, client-centered therapy as a way to raise self-esteem and correct misperceptions, and the importance of conducting research to validate one's formulations and procedures. His approach remains an invaluable and influential guide for anyone interested in the application of psychology (Shechtman, 1993).

Variable Self-Esteem. We pointed out earlier that depression is associated with low self-esteem, but negative emotions are associated even more strongly with *variable self-esteem*. That is, people whose self-evaluations fluctuate up and down in response to changes in the situation are the ones most likely to become depressed (Butler, Hokanson, & Flynn, 1994).

The reason seems to be that anyone whose self-esteem is strongly affected by minor occurrences has a less stable base of self-worth than people whose self-esteem remains relatively constant (Kernis et al., 1998). High, stable self-esteem acts as a buffer when negative events occur (Wiener, Muczyk, & Martin, 1992). Besides depression, other characteristics are also related to variable self-esteem. For example, self-centered, narcissistic individuals are especially affected by negative interpersonal experiences (Rhodewalt, Madrian, & Cheney, 1998).

> ## *Key Points*
>
> - One's identity, or *self-concept,* consists of self-beliefs and self-perceptions organized as a cognitive schema.
> - Because the self is the center of each person's social world and because self-schemas are well developed, we can process information about ourselves more efficiently than other types of information—the *self-reference effect.* The processing is both elaborative and categorical.
> - The complex structure of the self-concept involves such structural elements as central versus peripheral self-conceptions, varying degrees of clarity in one's beliefs, and a large number of specific content areas.
> - In addition to the personal self, the *social self* includes interpersonal relationships and a collective identity derived from membership in groups based on such factors as race, religion, ethnicity, and so forth.
> - In addition to our current self-concept, there are many possible different and better selves that we can envision in the future.
> - Self-concepts change with age, but also in response to feedback, changes in one's environment or occupational status, and interactions with others.
> - *Self-esteem* consists of self-evaluation or the attitudes we hold about ourselves in general and in specific domains. It is based in part on social comparison processes.
> - Rogerian therapy is often aimed at raising self-esteem or at decreasing the gap between one's self and one's ideal self.
> - There are many positive benefits associated with high as opposed to low self-esteem, but variable self-esteem has even more negative consequences than low self-esteem.

OTHER ASPECTS OF SELF-FUNCTIONING: FOCUSING, MONITORING, AND EFFICACY

Though the self-concept and self-esteem are of considerable importance in self-theory, several other aspects of self-functioning are also of interest. We will examine three of these: *self-focusing, self-monitoring,* and *self-efficacy.*

Focusing on Oneself versus Focusing on the External World

At any given moment, a person's attention may be directed inward toward the self or outward toward the external world (Fiske & Taylor, 1991). **Self-focusing** is defined as the extent to which attention is directed toward oneself.

Cognitive and Affective Aspects of Focusing on Self. Situational factors have a strong effect on self-focusing, and even simple instructions can determine where one focuses. For example, right now, please think about the ceiling in your room. If you did so, your focus was away from yourself. Now, please think about the most positive aspects of yourself. If you did, you just engaged in self-

self-focusing • The act of directing attention inward toward oneself as opposed to outward toward one's surroundings.

focusing. Self-focusing also occurs when such environmental cues as a mirror or a video camera are present (Fenigstein & Abrams, 1993).

Recalling relevant past events and processing relevant current information are required for self-focusing to occur (Dixon & Baumeister, 1991; Klein, Loftus, & Burton, 1989). A question such as "Where were you born?" directs you to retrieve factual information about yourself. A question such as "How would you describe your relationship with your parents?" can elicit relatively simple or relatively complex judgments about yourself. The tendency to focus on oneself increases between childhood and adolescence (Ullman, 1987), and some adults consistently self-focus more than others (Dana, Lalwani, & Duvall, 1997).

A brief period of self-focusing can improve insight. After deliberately spending a few minutes thinking about themselves, research participants show increased accuracy in judging social feedback (Hixon & Swann, 1993). This ability to change one's focus is part of the more general process of *self-regulation* of one's thoughts (Macrae, Bodenhausen, & Milne, 1998). Darwin (1871) recognized the importance of such mental activity when he said that "the highest possible stage in moral culture is when we recognize that we ought to control our thoughts" (p. 123). So the key is not simply to self-focus but to control and regulate the content of the thought processes. On a long-term basis, for example, continued self-focusing can simply involve replaying the same thoughts over and over rather than making progress toward self-awareness (Conway et al., 1993).

And sometimes focusing away from oneself is the best thing to do. For example, external focusing is helpful in improving the affective state of someone who is depressed (Lyubomirsky & Nolen-Hoeksema, 1995). If you are not depressed, however, the direction of focus has no effect on your feelings (Nix et al., 1995).

The ability to self-focus can be part of a very useful coping strategy (see Chapter 13) in which a person responds to stressful situations by managing his or her affective state and thinking about ways to solve problems (Taylor et al., 1998). In effect, people who cope this way are able to envision possibilities for the future and develop plans to bring about those possibilities. Evidence suggests that a positive mood greatly facilitates the processing of goal-relevant information (Aspinwall, 1998).

Because a person's self-concept is complex and contains many discrete elements, it is possible to focus on only a small fraction of oneself at any given time—much like pointing a flashlight at various objects in a large, dark room. Where the focus is directed within the self depends in part on how the question is framed (Kunda et al., 1993). For example, if your knowledge about your social life contains both positive and negative elements, you might focus on and retrieve positive material if you ask yourself, "What is the best thing about my social life?" On the other hand, your focus and the material retrieved might be quite different in response to the question, "What is the worst thing about my social life?"

Storing Positive and Negative Information about Self in Memory. Research indicates that some people tend to file positive and negative aspects of their experiences separately in memory—to engage in *compartmentalized self-organization* (Showers, 1992a; Showers & Kling, 1996). For these people, mood can be influenced by whether the focus is on positive or negative elements. If you think only about the negative aspects of yourself, you can easily become unhappy (such connections between affect and cognition were discussed in Chapter 3). Not only does self-focusing influence mood (Sedikides, 1992), but mood also affects self-focusing (Salovey, 1992). Think of a situation in which you have

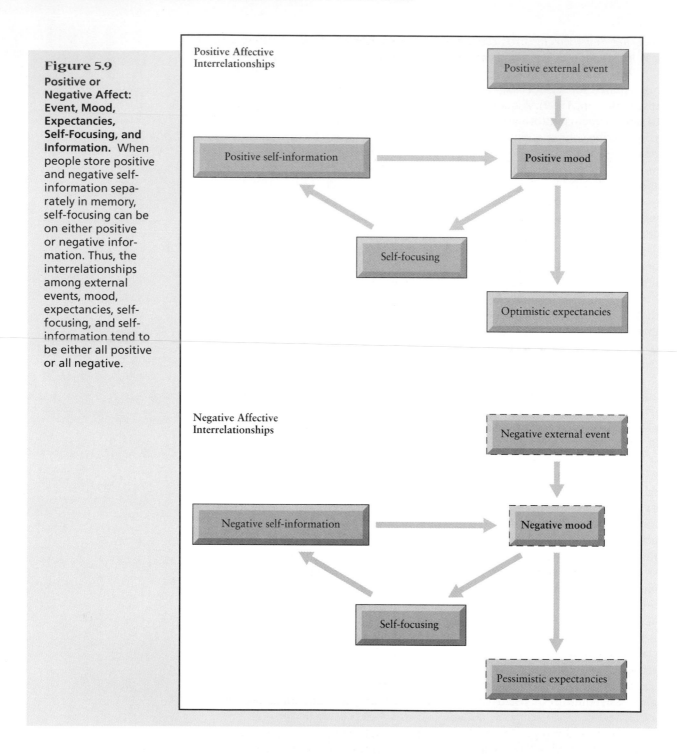

Figure 5.9
Positive or Negative Affect: Event, Mood, Expectancies, Self-Focusing, and Information. When people store positive and negative self-information separately in memory, self-focusing can be on either positive or negative information. Thus, the interrelationships among external events, mood, expectancies, self-focusing, and self-information tend to be either all positive or all negative.

been unhappy following a disagreement with a friend; feeling sad leads you to focus on and recall negative things about yourself and to feel pessimistic about the future. These interconnections are outlined in Figure 5.9.

Showers (1992b) has also found that *some* people store positive and negative self-knowledge together in the same mental "files"—a pattern called *evaluatively integrated self-organization*. When this occurs, self-focusing can never involve purely negative elements, because positive elements are also present.

The overall effect is the experience of less negative affect and higher self-esteem. That sounds good, but there are also some drawbacks. If things are going badly and you experience a lot of stress, it is very helpful to be able to think about some purely positive self-material. The presence of separate, important, positive elements of the self to fall back on acts as a protection against depression (Showers & Ryff, 1996).

Monitoring One's Behavior on the Basis of Internal versus External Factors

One person I (Donn Byrne) know fairly well behaves in exactly the same friendly and outgoing way in every setting in which I've ever observed him— with employees, colleagues, wife, close friends, and strangers. At the opposite extreme, I also know someone who behaves like a Nazi general with employees, a serious and concerned equal among colleagues, a slightly hostile tease with her husband, and a totally unresponsive mystery woman with strangers. The first individual is solidly predictable no matter what the situation, while the second is a "social chameleon."

Monitoring as a Dispositional Factor. The term **self-monitoring** refers to the relative tendency of individuals to regulate their behavior on the basis of external events such as the reactions of other people (high self-monitoring) or on the basis of internal factors such as their own beliefs, attitudes, and interests (low self-monitoring). Obviously, low self-monitors are consistent across situations, whereas high self-monitors change in response to situational changes (Koestner, Bernieri, & Zuckerman, 1992).

Self-monitoring was first conceptualized by Snyder (1974) and his colleagues (Gangestad & Snyder, 1985; Snyder & Ickes, 1985). Note that both self-monitoring and self-focusing involve attending to internal versus external cues; but work on self-focusing has emphasized the affective and cognitive consequences of differential focusing, while research on self-monitoring has emphasized the regulation of one's own behavior on the basis of focusing.

One way to think about self-monitoring is in terms of differences in responding to social situations (Hoyle & Sowards, 1993). A high self-monitor analyzes a social situation by assessing the relationship between his or her public self and what is socially appropriate in the setting, then strives to alter the public self to match the situation. In contrast, a low self-monitor analyzes a social situation by assessing the relationship between his or her private self and personal standards of behavior, then strives to alter the situation to match the private self.

Snyder proposed that high self-monitors must engage in role-playing, because they want to be positively evaluated by others. To gain acceptance, they mold their behavior to fit the audience—a useful characteristic for politicians, salespeople, and actors. You might think about that the next time you watch a candidate in action, interact with a successful salesperson, or observe a stage actor (see Figure 5.10 on page 180).

Psychologists measure self-monitoring by a true–false scale (Snyder, 1974) in which some of the items reflect high self-monitoring ("In different situations and with different people, I often act like very different persons"). Other items reflect low self-monitoring ("My behavior is usually an expression of my true inner feelings, attitudes, and beliefs"). High and low scorers on this scale behave quite differently in social interactions (Lippa & Donaldson, 1990). In one study, the diaries of high self-monitors over a ten-day period indicated that

self-monitoring • Regulation of one's behavior on the basis of the external situation and reactions of others (high self-monitoring) or on the basis of internal factors such as beliefs, attitudes, and values (low self-monitoring).

Figure 5.10

High and Low Self-Monitoring: Attending to Self or to One's Audience. In interpersonal situations, a person who is a high self-monitor compares his or her public self to social demands, then attempts to alter the public self to match the situation. A low self-monitor, in contrast, compares his or her private self to personal standards of behavior, then attempts to alter the situation to match the private self. High self-monitoring tends to be associated with success in politics, acting, and sales.

they tailored their behavior to specific situations and specific audiences. Low self-monitors reported behaving in the same way regardless of the situation.

Other Behaviors Associated with Differences in Self-Monitoring. Guided by the general idea that self-monitoring is related to focusing either on the external audience or on internal values, social psychologists have examined a variety of behavioral differences among those high and low on this dispositional variable. For example, high self-monitors tend to speak in the third person (he, she, his, her, their, etc.), but low self-monitors use the first person (I, me, my, mine, etc.) (Ickes, Reidhead, & Patterson, 1986). DeBono and Packer (1991) found that highs respond best to advertising that is image-based ("Heineken—you're moving up") and lows to quality-based ads ("Heineken—you can taste the difference"), as depicted in Figure 5.11.

In interpersonal behavior as well, high self-monitors choose companions on the basis of external qualities (how well they play tennis, for example), whereas low self-monitors make choices on the basis of how much they like the other person (Snyder, Gangestad, & Simpson, 1983). Even in romantic relationships, low self-monitors are more committed to the other individual (and so have fewer and longer-lasting relationships), while high self-monitors are attuned to the situation, thus engaging in more and relatively briefer relationships (Snyder & Simpson, 1984). When dating, low self-monitors do so for intrinsic reasons, such as having similar interests, while high self-monitors report extrinsic reasons, such as the other person's having the right connections (Jones, 1993).

A less negative characterization of high self-monitors has been offered by Howells (1993). He found that high self-monitors have more positive personality characteristics than lows, in that they are more sociable, affectionate, energetic, sensitive, open, and intellectually curious. This finding suggests that the interpersonal differences between highs and lows could be based on the fact that low self-monitors lack the necessary social skills and confidence to be able to deal with people successfully. High self-monitors are also high in self-esteem, and their monitoring behavior may simply be a way to maintain good feelings about themselves, to make themselves likable (Leary et al., 1995), and

People will

Could you really blame them? The aggressive styling and rambunctious

stare for all the

curves of the stylish Celica will make more than a few heads turn

right reasons.

in your direction. Oh, the center of attention is a nice place to be.

Celica

TOYOTA | *everyday*

Figure 5.11
Image versus Quality in Advertising. Advertising that stresses the image of the product is most appealing to high self-monitors, because they are attuned to externals such as other people's attitudes. Advertising that stresses the quality of the product is most appealing to low self-monitors, because they are attuned to internals such as values and beliefs.

to regulate their own emotional state (Graziano & Bryant, 1998). Interestingly, either extremely high or extremely low self-monitors are more neurotic and less well adjusted than those falling in the middle of this dimension (Miller & Thayer, 1989).

What are the origins of these different behaviors? Only a limited amount of research has dealt with this question, but Gangestad and Simpson (1993) provide evidence indicating genetic differences between high and low monitors. Among questionnaire items answered in a more similar way by identical than by nonidentical twins are those involving having an ability to imitate others, trying to impress or entertain people, playing charades, and being able to lie. All four of these behaviors are more likely for high than low self-monitors, and all are more similar in identical twins than in fraternal twins.

Self-Efficacy: Having Confidence in Oneself

Self-efficacy is a person's evaluation of his or her ability or competency to perform a task, reach a goal, or overcome an obstacle (Bandura, 1977). Do you think you could do well in a calculus course, skiing, or changing a tire? Your answer may differ across tasks, because self-efficacy varies across different kinds of activity. This kind of specificity was shown by college students in California who had recently experienced a severe earthquake. They expressed low self-efficacy with respect to being able to cope with natural disasters; but with quite different activities (doing well in school, for example), their self-efficacy was unaffected by the quake (Burger & Palmer, 1992). The fact that perceived self-efficacy involves specifics does not necessarily mean that there is *no* consistency across situations, however. Cervone (1997) provides evidence that individuals have general patterns of high or low self-efficacy that are evident across sets of quite different specific situations.

Performance as a Function of Self-Efficacy. Performance in both physical and academic tasks is enhanced by feelings of self-efficacy. For example, those high in athletic self-efficacy can continue longer at a physical endurance task than those low in this kind of self-efficacy (Gould & Weiss, 1981). One reason for such physical effects is that feelings of efficacy stimulate the body to produce *endogenous opioids* that function as natural painkillers (Bandura et al., 1988). Also, high self-efficacy about one's physical skills leads to perceived success at athletic tasks and to attributions of personal control (Courneya & McAuley, 1993).

In academics, self-efficacy is equally beneficial. Students high in self-efficacy for school-related activities expect to do well, actually perform better than they expect, and evaluate themselves positively (Sanna & Pusecker, 1994; Tuckman & Sexton, 1990). College professors in research fields also are more successful if they are high in feelings of efficacy (Taylor et al., 1984). Such individuals engage in many projects simultaneously, set goals for completing articles and books, publish a great deal, and achieve recognition by other researchers. As a result of such activity, they are likely to become tenured and obtain salary increases.

In medicine, physicians differ in effectiveness, and ineffective practices lead to increased medical costs. For example, physicians who lack confidence in themselves are more likely to order redundant or unnecessary tests and procedures and thus to increase the costs. Huang (1998) proposed that medical practices vary as a function of doctors' self-efficacy and self-esteem. He tested this proposal among resident physicians at a large teaching hospital in southern Taiwan. As shown in Figure 5.12, the greater the physicians' feelings of self-efficacy, the less stress they experienced when they were uncertain about reaching a diagnosis or prescribing a specific treatment. And the less stress they felt, the more effective and efficient were their medical practices. In addition, the higher the self-esteem of these doctors, the better their medical practices. The investigator proposed that medical education should include an emphasis on developing self-esteem, self-efficacy, and effective ways to cope with the stress of uncertainty.

self-efficacy • A person's evaluation of his or her ability or competency to perform a task, reach a goal, or overcome an obstacle.

The Effect of Self-Efficacy on Interpersonal Behavior. Low social self-efficacy is often based on the lack of social skills, and a common response is anxiety and the desire to avoid interpersonal interactions (Morris, 1985). For example, Alden (1986) investigated the effect of efficacy on attributions. When an interpersonal situation results in negative feedback, high-efficacy individuals per-

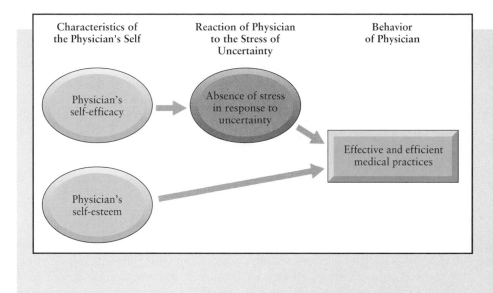

Figure 5.12
Medical Practice: Effects of the Physician's Self-Efficacy and Self-Esteem. The greater the self-efficacy felt by resident physicians, the less stress they feel when they experience uncertainty in reaching a diagnosis and prescribing treatment; and more efficient and effective medical practices are the result. In addition, physicians with high self-esteem also engage in better medical practices.

(*Source:* Based on data in Huang, 1998.)

ceive the cause as external ("this was an unpleasant group of people"), but low-efficacy individuals make internal attributions ("I'm not a very likable guy").

A measure of social self-efficacy was constructed by Fan and Mak (1998), who worked with undergraduates from Australia and overseas, some with English-speaking and some with non-English-speaking parents. The resulting scale indicates four aspects (or factors) of social efficacy: *absence of social difficulties* (e.g., "I do not find it difficult to hold a conversation with most people"), *social confidence* (e.g., "I feel confident in asking questions in class"), *sharing interests* (e.g., "I have common topics for conversation with local people"), and *friendship initiatives* (e.g., "If I see someone I would like to meet, I go to that person instead of waiting for him or her to come to me"). Fan and Mak found students who scored relatively high on this scale to be low in social avoidance, to be high in internal locus of control (the belief that good and bad outcomes depend on one's own actions), and to have English-speaking parents. Future research is planned in which training in social skills is expected to be reflected in higher scores.

Feelings of self-efficacy are consistently predictive of sexual assertiveness among women (Morokoff et al., 1997). When women find themselves involved in a potential sexual interaction, they benefit from being assertive in two ways. First, if they wish to avoid sex, they can be assertive about refusing. Second, if they agree to engage in sex, they can be assertive about the necessity to prevent pregnancy and/or sexually transmissible diseases.

Increases in Feelings of Efficacy. Self-efficacy is by no means fixed or unchanging. For example, as suggested earlier, many psychologists believe that it should be possible to increase feelings of professional self-efficacy among physicians and social self-efficacy among students. Also, you may remember my experience with the Erector set at the beginning of this chapter: positive information about one's skills leads to a rise in self-efficacy (Bandura, 1986a).

In the first of a series of related experiments, Bandura and Adams (1977) were able to show that a phobia based on a strong fear of snakes can be viewed as a reaction involving low self-efficacy—a lack of confidence in one's ability to cope with a snake. Using behavioral therapy, the investigators provided snake-phobic individuals with a series of *desensitizing* sessions, teaching the clients to relax while viewing a snake photograph, then a toy snake, then a small snake in a glass cage, and so on. Eventually, these formerly phobic individuals could deal comfortably with a large snake, actually holding it in their hands or letting it crawl on their shoulders. As the phobia decreased, physiological arousal in response to snakes decreased, and feelings of self-efficacy increased. Psychologists have used analogous procedures to decrease fears concerning spiders, dogs, and open spaces (Bandura, Adams, & Hardy, 1980).

In a frightening situation, self-efficacy and external cues can interact to determine the strength of one's negative emotional response. In studying the fear of tarantulas, Riskind and Maddux (1993) manipulated feelings of self-efficacy by asking research participants to imagine one of two situations. Some of these undergraduates were asked to imagine a large spider that they could either smash with a magazine or escape by leaving the room—thus inducing feelings of high efficacy. The remaining students were asked to imagine themselves helpless, strapped to a chair in a locked soundproofed room with a large spider—inducing feelings of low efficacy. To vary external cues, the researchers showed participants a video of a tarantula moving toward the camera, moving away from the camera, or not moving. As shown in Figure 5.13, both the approaching spi-

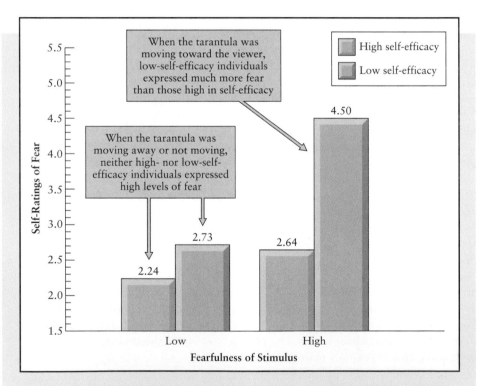

Figure 5.13

How Frightening? Fearfulness of Stimulus and Self-Efficacy. The more fearful a stimulus and the lower one's feelings of self-efficacy, the more fear one experiences. Feelings of high or low self-efficacy in dealing with spiders were induced in research participants, who were then shown a video of a tarantula that was relatively low in fearfulness (moving away or standing still) or high in fearfulness (moving toward the viewer). Little fear was aroused in the low-fearfulness condition, and self-efficacy had little effect. Much more fear was aroused in the high-fearfulness condition, especially among participants who felt low self-efficacy.

(*Source:* Based on data from Riskind & Maddux, 1993.)

der and feelings of low efficacy resulted in increased fear. The still or retreating tarantula was not very frightening, regardless of efficacy. The approaching tarantula was more frightening, but only for those low in self-efficacy.

> ## Key Points
>
> - *Self-focusing* refers to the extent to which an individual is directing attention toward self or toward the external world.
> - How one stores positive and negative material in memory (together or separately) is an important determinant of mood regulation and one's ability to cope with stressful events.
> - *Self-monitoring* refers to a dispositional tendency to regulate behavior on the basis of external factors (high self-monitoring) or on the basis of internal beliefs and values (low self-monitoring).
> - Differences in self-monitoring tendencies influence speech patterns, response to advertising content, and interpersonal behavior. Individual levels of self-monitoring are based in part on genetic factors.
> - *Self-efficacy* refers to an individual's evaluation of his or her ability to perform a task, reach a goal, or overcome an obstacle.
> - High self-efficacy is associated with better performance (physical and intellectual), more socially skilled behavior, the ability to overcome phobias, and skill in coping with fearful events.

GENDER: MALENESS OR FEMALENESS AS A CRUCIAL ASPECT OF IDENTITY

It seems that the most pervasive element of personal identity is that aspect of social identity in which we categorize ourselves as either female or male. That is, you may or may not pay much attention to your ethnic identity or your social class or whatever, but it would be extremely rare to find someone who was unaware and unconcerned about being a male versus being a female. In hundreds and hundreds of ways, we are reminded each day of our gender by how we dress, how we act, and how others respond to us.

The terms *sex* and *gender* are often used interchangeably, but we will adopt the terminology of those in the field (e.g., Beckwith, 1994) who distinguish them in the following way. **Sex** is defined in biological terms as the anatomical and physiological differences between males and females that are genetically determined. **Gender** refers to everything else associated with an individual's sex, including the roles, behaviors, preferences, and other attributes that define what it means to be a male or a female in a given culture. (Please see Figure 5.14 on page 186.) Note, however, that these definitions are not universally accepted by those whose research focuses on sex and gender (see Deaux, 1993b; Gentile, 1993; Unger & Crawford, 1993).

The origin of gender differences is sometimes a matter of dispute, but we are willing to assume that many gender attributes are probably based entirely on what one learns (such as an association between long hair and femininity), while other attributes may very well be based entirely on biological determinants (such as the presence of facial hair) or on both learning and biology (such as a preference for football versus figure skating) (Aube, Norcliffe, & Koestner, 1995).

sex • Maleness or femaleness as determined by genetic factors present at conception that result in anatomical and physiological differences.

gender • The attributes, behaviors, personality characteristics, and expectancies associated with a person's biological sex in a given culture. Gender differences can be based on biology, learning, or a combination of the two.

Figure 5.14

Sex Differences and Gender Differences. Though terminology varies, psychologists most often speak of *sex* when they are referring to anatomical and physiological differences between males and females that are genetically determined. *Gender* refers to other attributes and behaviors associated with being a male or a female in a given culture. Gender differences are assumed to be acquired from one's culture or to rest on a combination of biological and cultural factors.

Bem (1995, p. 334) borrows an analogy from anthropologist Kathryn March to make a more general point: "Sex is to gender as light is to color." That is, sex and light are physical phenomena, whereas gender and color are culturally based categories that arbitrarily divide sex and light into designated groups. With color, some cultures have only two categories, others three, while in the United States there are Crayola boxes with 256 different hues, each with its own assigned name. With respect to gender, the reverse is true. We emphasize only two genders, whereas other cultures have a Crayola box of possibilities ranging from bisexuality to an array of heterosexual and homosexual roles and lifestyles.

Gender Identity and Gender Stereotypes

Each of us has a **gender identity** in that a key part of our self-concept is the label of "male" or "female." For the vast majority of people, biological sex and gender identity correspond, though there is a relatively small proportion of the population in which gender identity differs from sex.

The Development of Gender Identity. The first thing most adults ask about a baby (theirs or anyone else's) is whether it's a boy or a girl. The birth announcement begins with that information, an appropriate name is selected, pink or blue clothing is bought, the baby's room is decorated in either a feminine or a masculine style, and "gender-appropriate" toys and clothing are provided. Though the role of learning may seem obvious in this instance, a great many people believe that boys and girls are predisposed to enjoy different kinds of toys and different kinds of play. (See Figure 5.15.)

Despite this pervasive emphasis on gender differentiation, infants and even toddlers are usually unaware of either sex or gender until they are about two years of age. Then they learn to identify themselves as a "girl" or a "boy"—though with some confusion about what those words mean. Gradually, gender identity is acquired as the child develops a sense of self that includes maleness or femaleness (Grieve, 1980).

Between ages four and seven, children begin to comprehend **gender consistency.** That is, they accept the principle that gender is a basic attribute of each person—and of pets and cartoon characters as well. Once these cognitions are

gender identity • That part of the self-concept involving a person's identification as a male or a female. Consciousness of gender identity usually develops at about the age of two.

gender consistency • The concept that gender is a basic, enduring attribute of each individual. A grasp of gender consistency usually develops between the ages of four and seven.

Figure 5.15

Gender and Toys: Are the Preferences Built-In or Acquired? It is obvious that boys and girls play with different toys in different ways. While these gender differences could be based on physiological differences, it seems more likely that cultural influences from advertising to peer modeling are responsible. Whatever the explanation, parents such as the father depicted here find it extremely difficult to avoid playthings that "reinforce preconceived gender roles."

Copyright© 1997 art spiegelman. Reprinted by permission.

firmly in place, our perceptions are strongly affected by what we have learned about gender.

Imagine that you are a participant in an experiment watching videotapes of nine-month-old infants named Mary, Karen, Stephen, and Matthew. Do you believe that these names will affect your judgments of the infants' size, attractiveness, and other attributes? Of course not—right? Vogel and colleagues (1991) conducted just such an experiment with those names assigned to different babies (of both sexes) for different participants. Children and adolescents both agreed that "Mary" and "Karen" were smaller, more beautiful, nicer, and softer than "Stephen" and "Matthew," regardless of which infant was supposed to have which name. It seems clear that the stereotypes associated with each gender determine our perceptions of them even when they are still infants.

What Is the Basis of Gender Identity? Though all differences between men and women were once assumed to be based on biological factors, it now seems very likely that many "typical" masculine and feminine characteristics are in fact acquired (Bem, 1984). Bem's (1981, 1983) *gender schema theory* proposes that children have a "generalized readiness" to organize information about the self on the basis of cultural definitions of appropriate male and female attributes. Once a young child learns to apply the appropriate sex label to himself or herself, the stage is set for the child to learn the "appropriate" roles that accompany the labels.

As childhood progresses, **sex typing** occurs when children have learned the stereotypes associated with maleness and femaleness in their culture. A great deal of what children learn about gender is based on their observing their parents and trying to be like them. Generally, children are rewarded for engaging in gender-appropriate behavior and discouraged (often with ridicule) when their behavior is gender-inappropriate. Consider, for example, how parents are likely to respond to a little girl who wants a doll for Christmas versus the response to a little boy who makes the same request. And do you suppose that parents respond differently to a little boy who wants boxing gloves and a punching bag for his birthday versus a little girl who expresses a similar desire? Based on how those around them respond, little girls gradually learn to ask for dolls and little boys for boxing gloves. I once had neighbors who rejected the stereotypes and tried to teach their children to be less bound by them; but the children were nevertheless strongly influenced by other factors, such as advertising and whatever "gender-appropriate" toys their friends owned. These parents finally gave up their ideals and bought their daughter a Barbie doll and their son a GI Joe action figure.

Do other children care whether a youngster's play is gender-appropriate? The answer seems to be *yes*. In Israel, fifth- and sixth-grade boys were shown a videotape of a boy their age playing a masculine (soccer), feminine (jump-rope), or neutral (cards) game with boys or girls (Lobel, 1994). The viewers attributed stereotypic feminine traits to the boy who played a feminine game with girls, and they judged him to be low in popularity. The boy who played a masculine game with other boys was perceived as the most masculine and most popular.

Though it is tempting to ridicule politically correct language, research indicates that words actually do influence our perceptions. For example, an individual is perceived as masculine if his or her job title is Chairman, least masculine if the title is Chairperson, and in between with the title Chair (McConnell & Fazio, 1996).

After observing parents, peers, advertising, and all the other role models, a child gradually acquires the gender stereotypes of his or her culture. It is OK for girls to cry and for boys to fight. Boys can wrestle, and girls can play cat's cradle. Clothes and hairstyles and chores around the home tend to be gender-specific. As the years pass, the lessons are well learned, and by the time U.S. children reach the sixth grade, they understand the prevailing stereotypes (Carter & McCloskey, 1984). In adolescence, teen magazines provide gender-appropriate scripts (Carpenter, 1988). Even people who disagree with the stereotypes know what they are. Figure 5.16 summarizes this developmental process.

Psychological Androgyny as an Alternative to Masculinity and Femininity. More than two decades ago, Sandra Bem (1974, 1975) produced a new theoretical formulation and a measuring device that revolutionized how gender is conceptualized and studied. At the time she began this work, most people (including psychologists) assumed that masculinity and femininity represented the opposite ends of a single dimension. Thus, each person was relatively masculine and therefore not feminine or relatively feminine and therefore not masculine.

sex typing • Comprehension of the stereotypes associated with being a male or a female in one's culture.

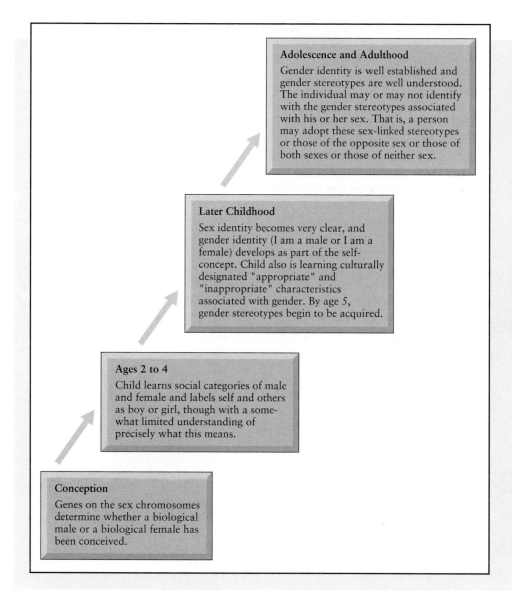

Adolescence and Adulthood

Gender identity is well established and gender stereotypes are well understood. The individual may or may not identify with the gender stereotypes associated with his or her sex. That is, a person may adopt these sex-linked stereotypes or those of the opposite sex or those of both sexes or those of neither sex.

Later Childhood

Sex identity becomes very clear, and gender identity (I am a male or I am a female) develops as part of the self-concept. Child also is learning culturally designated "appropriate" and "inappropriate" characteristics associated with gender. By age 5, gender stereotypes begin to be acquired.

Ages 2 to 4

Child learns social categories of male and female and labels self and others as boy or girl, though with a somewhat limited understanding of precisely what this means.

Conception

Genes on the sex chromosomes determine whether a biological male or a biological female has been conceived.

Figure 5.16
From Sex Differences to Gender Identity. Beginning with the genetic determination of sex at conception, each of us progresses through a series of developmental stages in which we learn to label self and others as either male or female, internalize gender identity as part of our self-concept, acquire the specific details of our culture's gender stereotypes, and eventually adopt a gender role that may or may not match these stereotypes.

Of course, many people actually do fit into just one of these two categories (Kagan, 1964; Kohlberg, 1966). And a person who fits a masculine or feminine stereotype is motivated to behave in ways consistent with the gender role he or she has learned: small children are not the only ones encouraged to conform to stereotypes, and "inappropriate" gender behavior is strongly discouraged. Sissy adolescent boys and aggressive adolescent girls are much too threatening to be tolerated.

Bem rejected the idea of a single dimension and suggested that various personal characteristics associated with masculinity and femininity lie on two separate dimensions: one ranging from low to high masculinity and the other ranging from low to high femininity. In this conceptualization, many individuals may actually be high on characteristics associated with both genders. For example a person could be competitive (supposedly masculine) and also sensitive to the needs of others (supposedly feminine). A person who combines traditional masculine characteristics with traditional feminine ones is considered to be **androgynous.**

androgynous • Characterized by possessing both traditional masculine characteristics and traditional feminine ones.

To identify masculine, feminine, and androgynous individuals, the **Bem Sex-Role Inventory (BSRI)** was developed. Note that in the terminology used in this chapter, this measure would be labeled the "Bem Gender-Role Inventory." Research participants identified more than four hundred positive characteristics as being socially desirable for men and/or for women. The final measure contains twenty items desirable for males but not for females, twenty items desirable for females but not desirable for males, and twenty that are equally desirable for males and females. The male and female items are shown in Table 5.1. Note that additional studies have indicated very little change in these gender stereotypes over time (Martin, 1987; Raty & Snellman, 1992).

A person taking the BSRI indicates, for all sixty items, how accurate each one is as a description of herself or himself. On the basis of the items that are selected as self-descriptive, the individual is classified as a particular sex-typed (gender-typed) individual. The possibilities are a sex-typed masculine male or feminine female, a reverse-typed individual (a masculine female or feminine male), an androgynous individual of either gender, or an undifferentiated type who has few characteristics of either gender. Research indicates that about a third of males fit the masculine gender type, and about the same proportion of females fit the feminine gender type. About one out of three males is androgynous, as are a third of females. The undifferentiated and cross-gender categories make up the rest. This classification indicates **gender-role identification,**

Bem Sex-Role Inventory (BSRI) • Bem's measure of the extent to which an individual's self-description is characterized by traditional masculine characteristics, traditional feminine characteristics, both (androgyny) or neither (undifferentiated).

gender-role identification • The extent to which an individual identifies with the gender stereotypes of his or her culture.

Table 5.1

Gender Stereotypes: Self-Descriptions on the Bem Sex-Role Inventory. On the BSRI, each person rates himself or herself on each of a series of characteristics as to how self-descriptive each is. These items represent those that research participants judged to be the most characteristic of males or of females.

Characteristics of the Male Stereotype	Characteristics of the Female Stereotype
Acts as a leader	Affectionate
Aggressive	Cheerful
Ambitious	Childlike
Analytical	Compassionate
Assertive	Does not use harsh language
Athletic	Eager to soothe hurt feelings
Competitive	Feminine
Defends own beliefs	Flatterable
Dominant	Gentle
Forceful	Gullible
Has leadership abilities	Loves children
Independent	Loyal
Individualistic	Sensitive to the needs of others
Makes decisions easily	Shy
Masculine	Soft-spoken
Self-reliant	Sympathetic
Self-sufficient	Tender
Strong personality	Understanding
Willing to take a stand	Warm
Willing to take risks	Yielding

(*Source:* Based on information in Bem, 1974.)

or the extent to which an individual does or does not identify with the culture's gender stereotypes.

We realize that the various terms used by those studying sex and gender can become confusing. As a reminder, *sex* refers to biological maleness or femaleness; *gender* refers to one's social categorization as a female or male; *gender identity* refers to a person's self-perception as a male or female; and *gender-role identification* refers to an individual's self-reported androgyny, femininity, or masculinity.

Gender-Role Behavior and Reactions to Gender-Role Behavior

Once people develop a specific pattern of gender-relevant characteristics, they tend to behave in ways consistent with their assumptions about such characteristics (Chatterjee & McCarrey, 1991). That is, they behave in ways that are identified as masculine, feminine, androgynous, or none of the above.

Androgynous versus Gender-Typed Behavior. To the extent that social norms remain gender-typed, many people believe that men should be powerful, dominant, and self-assertive, while women should be caring, intimate with others, and emotionally expressive. For those who accept these norms, experiences that conform to them create positive feelings as well as less self–ideal discrepancy (Wood et al., 1997).

Much of the research on gender and gender roles has focused on androgyny, however, and a common underlying theme is that an androgynous role is preferable to either male or female gender-typed roles. Rather than argue about whether androgyny represents the ideal, it might be useful simply to think of gender roles as falling along a continuum from androgyny to traditional masculinity and femininity—and beyond, to *extreme* gender-role adherence (which will be discussed shortly).

Much research does in fact suggest that "androgyny is good." For example, compared to gender-typed individuals, androgynous men and women are found to be better liked (Major, Carnevale, & Deaux, 1981), better adjusted (Williams & D'Alessandro, 1994), better able to adapt to situational demands (Prager & Bailey, 1985), more flexible in coping with stress (McCall & Struthers, 1994), less likely to develop eating disorders (Thornton, Leo, & Alberg, 1991), more comfortable with their sexuality (Garcia, 1982), and more satisfied with their interpersonal relationships (Rosenzweig & Daley, 1989). In a sample of elderly people, androgynous individuals were more satisfied with their lives (Dean-Church & Gilroy, 1993); and happier marriages are reported by couples with two androgynous partners than by any other combination of roles (Zammichieli, Gilroy, & Sherman, 1988). Further, sexual satisfaction is greater if at least one of the partners is androgynous than if both are gender-typed (Safir et al., 1982).

In some cultural contexts, masculinity can be as advantageous as androgyny. Abdalla (1995) examined the self-efficacy of Arab students in Qatar and Kuwait in making decisions about their careers. In this instance, masculine and androgynous roles were each superior to feminine and undifferentiated ones.

Adherence to traditional gender roles is associated with right-wing political views (Duncan, Peterson, & Winter, 1997). Traditional masculinity seems to create numerous interpersonal problems. For example, men who identify strongly with the masculine role behave more violently and aggressively than men whose identification is moderate (Finn, 1986). Among adolescent males, high masculinity is associated with having multiple sex partners, the view that men and women are adversaries, and the belief that impregnating a partner is a positive indication of one's masculinity (Pleck, Sonenstein, & Ku, 1993).

Feminine role identification also has pitfalls. Those of either gender who indicate high femininity tend to be lower in self-esteem than either masculine or androgynous individuals (Lau, 1989). High femininity is associated with depression, especially by the time a woman is middle-aged (Bromerger & Matthews, 1996). Note that throughout the world, females are about twice as likely as males to experience depression (Culbertson, 1997).

The extremes of gender-role identification are represented by **hypermasculinity** and **hyperfemininity,** perhaps the least desirable gender types. Hypermasculinity is characterized by the endorsement of a constellation of attitudes and beliefs associated with an exaggerated version of the traditional male role (Mosher, 1991; Mosher & Tomkins, 1988). The hypermasculine (or macho) man expresses callous sexual attitudes toward women, believes that violence is manly, and enjoys danger as a source of excitement. Such men report a high rate of sexually coercive behavior (Mosher & Sirkin, 1984), express little discomfort when asked to imagine scenes of rape (Mosher & Anderson, 1986), and indicate their willingness to commit rape if they could be assured of not getting caught (Smeaton & Byrne, 1987).

Analogously, the hyperfeminine woman endorses attitudes and beliefs associated with an exaggerated version of the traditional female role (Murnen & Byrne, 1991). The hyperfeminine woman believes that relationships with men are of central importance in her life, agrees that it is acceptable to use attractiveness and sexual interactions to "get a man and keep him," and admits that she "sometimes says no but means yes." Compared to women low on this dimension, those high in hyperfemininity are more likely to report having been the target of sexual coercion (Murnen, Perot, & Byrne, 1989) and feeling attracted to hypermasculine men (Smith, Byrne, & Fielding, 1995). Hyperfemininity is also associated with endorsement of many legal forms of aggression, ranging from spanking children to the death penalty (Hogben, Byrne, & Hamburger, 1999).

Hamburger and his colleagues (1996) have developed a Hypergender Ideology Scale that combines the basic elements of exaggerated gender roles with test items that are equally applicable to men and women.

Effects of Gender Roles on Behavior. We will describe in Chapter 6 just how gender stereotypes can lead to prejudice and discrimination. Despite remarkable changes in Western cultures over the past few decades, traditional gender roles still influence what men and women do within the home (Major, 1993). Even when both partners are employed in demanding and high-paying jobs, work around the house is most often divided along gender lines, as we will discuss in Chapter 8. That is, men usually take out the garbage, make repairs, and do yard work. Women, in turn, clean the house, cook, and care for children. Interestingly, one's occupation also has an effect. In Israel, both men and women in male-typed occupations (such as university professors) spend less time on family and domestic duties than men and women in female-typed occupations (such as high school teachers) (Moore, 1995). Altogether, though, women spend more time doing housework than men, regardless of their gender-role identification (Gunter & Gunter, 1991). When it comes time to clean the bathroom or paint the garage, the culturally prescribed gender roles still exert more influence than a person's self-description on the BSRI.

In the workplace, gender and gender roles also remain of central importance. For example, when women are chosen to do a task and then informed that gender constituted the primary reason for their selection, they evaluate their own performance as less adequate than do women told that the assignment was based on merit (Turner, Pratkanis, & Hardaway, 1991). It is possible that men would react in a similar way, but research has not been conducted to find out how men react to being chosen on the basis of gender. Women in non-

hypermasculinity • An extreme gender-role identification with an exaggerated version of the traditional male role; includes callous sexual attitudes toward women, the belief that violence is manly, and the enjoyment of danger as a source of excitement.

hyperfemininity • An extreme gender-role identification with an exaggerated version of the traditional female role; includes the belief that relationships with men are of central importance in one's life, that attractiveness and sexuality should be used to get a man and keep him, and that it is reasonable to sometimes say *no* but mean *yes.*

traditional female occupations (such as steelworkers) are not as likely to be viewed as the victims of harassment as women in traditional female occupations (such as secretaries), even when the other aspects of the alleged harassment situation are identical (Burgess & Borgida, 1997). In a nationwide survey of U.S. physicians, more than a third of the female doctors reported experiences of sexual harassment during medical school, during later training, and/or while practicing medicine (Coleman, 1998).

Gender also affects expectancies and motivation. Despite equal performance by males and females on intelligence tests and superior performance by women in school, males estimate their own IQ as higher than that of females; and both genders rate their fathers as smarter than their mothers and their grandfathers as smarter than their grandmothers (Furnham & Rawles, 1995). Also, when confronted by a novel task, women underestimate and men overestimate their expected performance (Beyer & Bowden, 1997).

Compared to women, men have higher expectations of occupational success and place more stress on salary (Subich et al., 1986). In general, men respond more to extrinsic motives such as money and success; women are more concerned about obtaining personal satisfaction from the job. When those in charge try to influence the behavior of employees by making threats and demands, this dominant approach is often ineffective—but such strategies generate especially negative responses in women (Copeland, Driskell, & Salas, 1995).

The U.S. Bureau of the Census expects about 63 percent of American women to be employed outside the home by the year 2000 (Heilman, 1995). Despite this vast increase in the percentage of women in the workforce and federal laws that forbid gender discrimination, gender bias still seems to operate in the labor market. For an example of the problems faced by women, see the *Beyond the Headlines* section (based on an article by Koch, 1998).

Beyond the Headlines:
As Social Psychologists See It
Does Gender Discrimination Still Occur in the Workplace?

STATE DEPARTMENT LAGS IN PROMOTING WOMEN

Washington, DC, January 11, 1998—Madeleine Albright, America's first female secretary of state, often refers to her gender.

She has joked that one advantage to being female is the use of makeup. "If a 60-year-old male secretary of state has had a bad day, he has two choices—to look like a tired old man—or look like a tired old man with makeup."

On a more serious level, she has addressed issues affecting women around the world with respect to domestic violence, child prostitution, and women's rights. In her own department, however, problems of discrimination remain common. Most State Department employees are men. Especially when there are openings in top positions, women are much less likely than men to be nominated. In dozens of lawsuits over the past two decades, women have accused the department of discrimination in hiring, making assignments, promotions, evaluations, and awards.

Changes are under way, however, and at the present time, 40 percent of those entering the foreign service are women. Altogether, the situation is slowly improving, but problems remain.

Figure 5.17
Madeleine Albright, the First Female to Become U.S. Secretary of State. Despite her status and her concern with women's issues around the world, Secretary Albright presides over a department that has historically favored male over female employees.

What sorts of problems do you suppose arise when women are treated equally with respect to hiring, promotions, salary, and all the rest? A common response is anger. Despite the successes of a few prominent women such as Madeleine Albright (Figure 5.17), many occupational groups (such as airline pilots, surgeons, and dentists) have traditionally been viewed as male turf, and the presence of women in these fields as a threat. For example, men feel that increased opportunities for women mean less opportunity for themselves and less money to support their families. There is also the question of quotas, and men fear that they will be passed over in favor of a less able individual simply on the basis of gender. There is the feeling that in organizations' efforts to help women (as well as minorities), white men are being placed at a disadvantage.

Across occupations in the United States, women earn about seventy-six cents for every dollar earned by men (Johnston, 1998). Why? Is it possible that men and women inherently have different skills and work habits, so that differences in hiring, promotions, and salaries simply reflect the realistic consequences of gender differences? Is it possible that as we learn different gender roles, men and women learn to have different occupational and income expectancies—which, in turn, lead to differential success in the workplace? Or could it be that most of the male–female occupational differences that have been documented can be explained on the basis of active discrimination against women by the men who have historically dominated various fields? Depending on how you answered these questions, what can (or should) be done about the situation?

In academia, women remain at a disadvantage compared to men with respect to doctoral degrees granted, salaries, and professorships (Callaci, 1993). One reason is that a woman is more likely than a man to believe that she *deserves* a lower salary (Janoff-Bulman & Wade, 1996). Even in carrying out a laboratory task, women suggest lower pay for themselves than men do (Desmarais & Curtis, 1997). One possible explanation is that men are taught to evaluate themselves in a more egotistical way. Students even evaluate professors differently on the basis of gender (Burns-Glover & Veith, 1995): it is desirable for a male professor to be enterprising, self-confident, stable, and steady, whereas a female professor should be jolly and talkative.

Though sexism and gender stereotypes may well play a major role in differential male–female success, Tannen (1994) stresses the additional importance of gender differences in communication styles. For example, women are not as likely as men to brag about their accomplishments; as a result, they often fail to receive the appropriate credit when their work is exceptionally good (Tannen, 1995). Women are expected to express positive emotions about the successes of others but not about their own achievements (Stoppard & Gruchy, 1993). This traditional social role encourages females to be modest about their achievements (Rudman, 1998), but this may be fading. When explicitly reminded of such expectations, American women express strong resistance and engage in role reversal (Cialdini et al., 1998).

Historically, men have held a disproportionate share of occupational roles that enhance gender inequality. Pratto and her colleagues (1997) provide evidence that three factors underlie this difference: gender differences in self-selection that tend to reinforce inequality, hiring biases that favor matching applicants' values to the values held by the organization, and hiring biases based on gender stereotypes. The result is the perpetuation of a system that promotes male dominance.

What happens when women catch up to men in a given occupation? A common male reaction is "There goes the neighborhood." That is, when barriers are overcome in a specific occupation, more and more women enter that field, and as a consequence the job loses its value. Psychology is a field that has shifted from being predominantly male to being predominantly female. Women now account for 72 percent of those graduating as psychology majors and 67 percent of the graduate students. For those obtaining Ph.D. degrees, 24.7 percent were women in 1971, but 62 percent are women today (Pion et al., 1996). Although this shift has not resulted in a loss of prestige for psychology, Pion and her colleagues do report salary declines between 1973 and 1991 (adjusted for inflation) for both males and females employed as psychologists. There is no direct evidence, however, that this decline is necessarily attributable to the change in gender composition.

Why Are Traditional Gender Roles Still Powerful? There is a long history of belief in male–female differences associated with male superiority. In the Judeo-Christian tradition, men were originally designated as the owners of their families (Wolf, 1992). In the Talmud, Jews were taught that categories of property included cattle, women, and slaves. In the New Testament, Ephesians (5:22–24) instructs Christian wives to "be subject to your husbands as you are to the Lord. For the husband is the head of the wife just as Christ is the head of the Church."

Many centuries have passed since those sentiments were first written, but gender differences still have strong cultural support. For example, in 1998 the U.S. Southern Baptist Convention (the nation's largest Protestant denomination) agreed on a declaration that a woman should "submit herself graciously" to her husband's leadership and that a man should "provide for, protect, and lead his family" (Niebuhr, 1998). At a less formal level, children's books and stories have until fairly recently presented mostly traditional stereotypes of boys and girls and of men and women (McArthur & Eisen, 1976; Weitzman et al., 1972). Such fiction presented men and boys as engaged in active, initiating roles while women and girls either tagged along as followers or needed to be rescued when they found themselves in danger. As the artificiality of these stereotypes became increasingly obvious in the 1970s, a few quite different books came along. In *He Bear, She Bear* (1974) the Berenstains instructed their readers that fatherhood is reserved for boy bears and motherhood for girl bears but that activities and occupations are otherwise independent of gender—"There's *nothing* that we cannot try. We can do all these things you see, whether we are he *or* she."

Despite this new consciousness, traditional childhood stories still remain popular. Lurie (1993) points out that our familiar fairy tales were deliberately designed to teach children moral and behavioral lessons. A common story line involves a child being informed of a rule; the child then breaks the rule and must suffer the consequences. An example is Little Red Riding Hood, who failed to follow her mother's advice about the best path to take to Grandma's house. The hungry wolf then became the instrument of a terrible punishment for her reckless independence. Once that lesson sunk in, the woodsman could wield his ax to save Red Riding Hood and her grandmother too.

In countless old children's stories and the modern movies that are based on them, heroines such as Snow White, Sleeping Beauty, Cinderella, the Little Mermaid, and all the rest get into serious trouble. According to these familiar presentations, the only hope for a female is to be sufficiently attractive that a handsome prince will kiss her and/or fight the evil witch and/or stepmother so that the couple can marry and live happily ever after (see Figure 5.18). Older, kindly females tend to be relatively powerless (a queen whose husband has all the power) or somewhat inept (good witches who are amusing because they make multiple mistakes). When the hero is the leading character (as in *Bambi, The Lion King, The Jungle Book, Dumbo,* etc.), the usual female role is simply to be a mother who gives birth to the hero or to be sexually attractive so she can mate with the hero and bear his offspring. Studies of prime-time television, daytime soap operas, advertising, and even PBS's *Sesame Street* reveal that such traditional gender roles are still being portrayed (Helman & Bookspan, 1992).

Figure 5.18

Helpless Females and Helpful Males: Role Models for Gender Differences. In countless stories, movies, and children's television programs, gender stereotypes have been perpetuated for all of us. Youthful females are beautiful but are helpless in overcoming their problems until rescued from danger by a strong, handsome male they barely know. The only assertive women are elderly stepmothers or witches who are clever and evil. It seems likely that some of the stereotypes we hold are influenced at least in part by these role models.

Leaving aside books, television, and the movies for the moment—what about the technology of computers with their state-of-the-art games and learning devices? The story of gender differentiation has remained much the same. Most students in the sixth, seventh, and eighth grades react with stress to computer software that is not designed to fit their own gender stereotypes (Cooper, Hall, & Huff, 1990). Possibly because most educational software is based on male stereotypes, boys greatly outnumber girls in computer courses, use of computer labs, enrollment in computer camps, and expressed interest in the field of computer science.

Encouraging Signs of Progress beyond Gender Stereotypes. There is evidence that we are very gradually moving away from gender stereotypes in U.S. culture. Despite the fact that most individuals are well aware of the traditional assumptions about gender differences, research indicates that American college students today often think of people in ways that ignore these stereotypes and that students now tend to downplay gender differences (Swim, 1994).

Another sign of change is that more stories are now being written in which brave and intelligent heroines fight when necessary, rescue male victims, and otherwise engage in nontraditional feminine behavior (Phelps, 1981). In many movies and television programs, women such as Pocahontas, Demi Moore (in *G.I. June*), Melissa Joan Hart (as *Sabrina the Teenage Witch*), and Ellen DeGeneres (as *Ellen*) represent a new tradition quite different from that of *Snow White* and from the housewife–mother figures of *Ozzie and Harriet, Leave It to Beaver,* and *The Brady Bunch* (Bellafante, 1997). In Disney's *Mulan,* for example, a strong woman battles to save her country.

In her syndicated newspaper column, Ellen Goodman (1998) pointed out that the heroines of three successful movies were presented as smart women making smart choices or avoiding bad ones. In *Titanic* Kate Winslet passes up a wealthy, abusive fiancé in favor of a poor but steroid-free artist. In *The Object of My Affection* Jennifer Aniston is a social worker who advises teenage girls that "Keeping your boyfriend happy is not your full-time job." Also, she likes a gay man who knows how to listen—in contrast to her boyfriend, who is a "bulldozer." In *City of Angels* Meg Ryan is a cardiovascular surgeon whose unemotional surgeon boyfriend proposes by saying, "I'm not very good at matters of the heart . . . please be my wife." She prefers an angel who gives up heaven in order to be with her. Columnist Goodman suggests that young boys are exposed primarily to images of heroes who hurl balls, crash cars, and wave Uzis at their enemies, while the females on the screen are beginning to show a preference for sensitive men.

As shown in Figure 5.19 on page 198, even advertising has begun to present men and women in nontraditional ways. You may wonder whether these various kinds of role models have any effect. They do. For example, experimental evidence makes clear that when small children are exposed to stories in which the traditional male and female roles are reversed, both boys and girls indicate higher expectancies about the possibility of female accomplishment (Scott & Feldman-Summers, 1979).

When Men and Women Differ: Biology, Gender Roles, or Both?

Some argue that sex differences in social behavior are explained better by evolutionary factors than by cultural ones (Archer, 1996). To others, it is clear that social factors determine the ways in which maleness and femaleness are defined; for example, cross-cultural research provides convincing evidence that the characteristics associated with each gender differ when cultural influences differ

Figure 5.19
Advertising: Nontraditional Gender Roles. Ads have been one of the many places where traditional gender stereotypes have been regularly featured. An increasing proportion of advertising has begun to present reversed male and female roles. This is one of many small steps that can serve to break down arbitrary roles based on gender.

(Mischel, 1967). The fact that we all learn culturally based gender roles does not, however, rule out the possibility that at least *some* gender differences are based on sex-linked genetic differences (Diamond, 1993; Wright, 1994). The question is not whether *all* male–female differences are learned or inherited, but whether any specific difference is based on biology, learning, or some combination of the two (Eagly & Steffen, 1986). Though such questions often lead to arguments that are more political than scientific (Eagly, 1995; Hyde & Plant, 1995), most undergraduate men and women now agree that both social and biological factors are involved in determining gender differences. They also believe that what we learn is more important than what we inherit (Martin & Parker, 1995).

To illustrate the broader issues, we will describe differences in *interpersonal behavior*, which seem to be based on both biological and experiential factors, and differences in *self-perception,* which seem to be associated more strongly with culturally acquired factors.

Differences in the Interpersonal Behavior of Males and Females. A good deal of the research on sex differences has centered on the role of the male hormone **testosterone.** This biochemical secretion has only a limited effect on human sexual behavior, but it is consistently associated with the tendency to dominate and control others. Presumably, those males in our prehistoric (and even prehuman) past whose bodies produced the most testosterone were the ones who were most combative and dominant, thus being the individuals best able to subdue rival males and obtain mates. As a consequence, these same individuals were most successful at reproducing and thus passing on their genes, including those that controlled high testosterone production in their male descendants. Modern males have higher testosterone levels than women, and they behave in more aggressive and dominant ways (Berman, Gladue, & Taylor, 1993), especially when interacting with male strangers (Moskowitz, 1993). Young men are also more likely than young women to engage in risky behavior in pursuit of short-term gains (Wilson et al., 1996).

What are some of the consequences of testosterone differences? Males with the highest testosterone levels tend to choose dominant and controlling occupations such as those of trial lawyer, actor, politician, or criminal (Dabbs, 1992). As we mentioned in Chapter 1, even *female* trial lawyers have higher testosterone levels than other female lawyers. The male preference for competitive sports could be based in part on the fact that before a competitive game such as basketball begins, both the team members and their male fans show a rise in testosterone level; if a person's own team wins, the level goes even higher (Dabbs, 1993). Men are consistently found to be more likely to initiate sexual contact (in or out of marriage), but this may have little or nothing to do with differential sexual motives; rather, it may result from the male need to dominate (Anderson & Aymami, 1993).

Given these investigations of how testosterone affects behavior, you might wonder about the behavioral effects of the female hormone **estrogen.** Strangely enough, research on estrogen effects has tended to concentrate on physical matters such as skin tone, vaginal lubrication, and the risk of cancer rather than on interpersonal behavior.

Perhaps the reason that women are more likely than men to share rewards (Major & Deaux, 1982) or to deprive themselves in order to help someone else (Leventhal & Anderson, 1970) is based on biochemistry rather than culture. It is also possible to make the argument that learned gender roles underlie such differences (Major & Adams, 1983). That is, many women spend their lives experiencing social pressure to accept second place in assertive and aggressive situations, and that acquired difference could well explain why they deal with people in a more cooperative way than men do (Nadkarni, Lundgren, & Burlew, 1991). Similarly, it is possible that women have better social skills than men (Margalit & Eysenck, 1990) because they *have* to. Women are more concerned with relationships and more willing to indicate that they are powerless, while men are oriented toward control and power in their interactions (Timmers, Fischer, & Manstead, 1998).

Interpersonal behavior is also influenced by differences in experience, and men and women are found to use and interpret many words in quite different ways. Bader and Brazell (1998) have collected humorous examples of how different meanings are attached to words as a function of one's gender. If you look beyond the humor in Table 5.2 on page 200, you may think of incidents in

testosterone • The male "sex hormone."

estrogen • The female "sex hormone."

Table 5.2

What Does He Mean? What Does She Mean? It has been observed that men and women have different communication styles and that they often use the same words but with different meanings. The examples here are based on those in the 1998 book *He Meant, She Meant: The Definitive Male/Female Dictionary,* by Jenny Lyn Bader and Bill Brazell.

Word	Used by a Man, This Means	Used by a Woman, This Means
Babe	a compliment, but women don't seem to like it	an insulting and degrading nickname for women
Exotic	a type of dancer	a type of vacation
Love affair	a strong affection for a basketball, football, or baseball team	a relationship so good that it combines the wonder of love and the excitement of an affair
Outfit	a military group	an effective combination of clothing
Weekend	a time to do as little as possible	a time when love becomes more important than ever

which your own interactions have run into difficulty because of male–female differences in the use of language.

Differences in the Self-Perceptions of Males and Females. Though girls in the United States today are performing better in school and avoiding unwanted sexual activity more than was true a decade ago, they are significantly more depressed than boys (Mathis, 1998). Among the many factors linked to their unhappiness is a pervasive worry about how they look.

Compared to men, women are much more likely to be concerned about body image (Pliner, Chaiken, & Flett, 1990), to express dissatisfaction about their bodies (Heinberg & Thompson, 1992) and about physical appearance in general (Hagborg, 1993), and to develop eating disorders (Stice, Shaw, & Nemeroff, 1998; Walsh & Devlin, 1998). Furthermore, the male–female differences in satisfaction with body image has shown an increase between the pre-1970s era and the 1990s (Feingold & Mazzella, 1998).

Columnist Dave Barry (1998) describes the gender differences as follows: Men think of themselves as average looking, and average is fine; women, in contrast, evaluate their appearance as "not good enough." A television commercial for Special K cereal depicts a series of men expressing comments about their appearance; these female-typical words coming from men are so incongruous as to be amusing. A common theme on daytime talk shows is the male assertion that "After we were married a couple of years, my wife started getting fat; I lost interest in making love, and it's all her fault." In real life, sadly enough, when males unfairly blame females for being overweight, many women actually accept the responsibility (Crocker, Cornwell, & Major, 1993). Both men and women might gain a better perspective of some of the issues involved by considering the *Ideas to Take with You* section on page 204.

Women are more reluctant than men to reveal their age, presumably because growing older is a handicap for females, though not for males. As they grow older, women are perceived as being less and less feminine, though men are not viewed as less masculine with increased age (Deutsch, Zalenski, & Clark, 1986).

For women, weight is a special issue. My daughter Lindsey is a very attractive girl who was a little overweight for a brief period. As a result, her self-image became quite negative. She incorrectly perceived herself as "fat and ugly" and produced a drawing containing multiple words (portly, chubby, stocky, bovine, etc.) that are applied to individuals who "weigh too much." Some of the negativity remained even after the excess weight disappeared. The ease with which such concerns spread among young females is amazing. Her younger sister, Rebecka, was nine at the time; and after listening to Lindsey's preoccupation with weight for several months, she asked for her own scale so that she could weigh herself daily and began posting her daily food intake (complete with calorie count) on the refrigerator. As can be seen in Figure 5.20, Rebecka had no realistic basis for thinking of herself as obese.

Overweight women attribute rejection in the workplace to unfair bias; they tend to perceive romantic rejection on the basis of weight, however, as justified (Crocker & Major, 1993). In contrast, men worry less about how they look, and a man's weight seems to be irrelevant on the job and in relationships unless it is truly extreme. When women are at the correct weight according to height–weight charts, they still want to lose additional pounds, whereas men at the correct weight want to gain (Raudenbush & Zellner, 1997). Altogether, young men express very little dissatisfaction with their bodies, though there is a mild disappointment at not measuring up to the body-builder male ideal (Davis, Brewer, & Weinstein, 1993).

Self-objectification refers to the tendency to adopt the perspective of others when focusing on one's physical attributes (Fredrickson & Roberts, 1997). These psychologists propose that women, but not men, are socialized to self-objectify in the American culture. To test this hypothesis, Fredrickson and her

Figure 5.20

A Problem among Western Females: Dissatisfaction with One's Body. Women more than men express dissatisfaction about their bodies, with weight as a common focus of unhappiness. My nine-year-old, Rebecka, after hearing her teenage sister's complaints about weight and seeing her preoccupation with dieting, decided that she too must do something to lose weight. With both daughters, I discovered that weight charts and the opinions of parents and other adults are totally irrelevant to their perceptions and concerns about weight.

colleagues (1998) manipulated self-objectification by asking undergraduates to try on a swimsuit or think about how it feels to wear a particular item of clothing. For women, such tasks led to feeling ashamed of their bodies, restraining their food intake, and performing less well on a math test. Among men, the self-objectification manipulation led to none of these effects.

Why is appearance a major problem for women? One explanation is that from infancy on, other people place more emphasis on the appearance of females than of males. College women report a high frequency of childhood experiences in which they were teased by peers and siblings about how they looked and how much they weighed (Cash, 1995). Even parents discriminate against overweight daughters (but not overweight sons) by being less willing to give them financial support for college (Crandall, 1995). Presumably, the assumption—perhaps unconscious—is that an overweight female won't do well at either finding a husband or getting a job, so why waste the money?

The cultural basis of this dramatic difference in self-perceptions between men and women is strongly suggested by the fact that such problems are much more common in Western industrialized nations than in developing countries. Even within the United States, Canada, and the United Kingdom, women of Asian and African descent have fewer eating disorders than Caucasian women. Caucasian females are also more likely to view themselves as overweight and to evaluate their bodies negatively. White women denigrate overweight women much more than black women do (Hebl & Heatherton, 1998). One possible explanation is that men of Asian and African descent are less concerned about the weight of their romantic partners. Whatever the reason, white women have more weight concerns than their nonwhite counterparts. Comparing white and Asian female students aged fourteen to twenty-two in London schools, Wardle and colleagues (1993) found that both groups had the same ideals about appearance (thin is good). Nevertheless, white females differed from Asian females in wanting to lose weight, being actively involved in trying to lose weight, and weighing themselves more frequently—even when their current size and weight did not differ from those of their Asian classmates. Among the thinnest participants, more white than Asian females said that they felt "fat." See Chapter 7, too, for research on the effects of exposure to images of ultrathin models on the feelings and self-evaluations of women.

At this time, no one can come to a defensible grand conclusion about the reason men and women differ in various behaviors and emotional concerns. For example, perhaps women respond with greater emotional intensity (Grossman & Wood, 1993) because they have learned to do so, because differential treatment has made them more sensitive, because men and women use different areas of the brain in thinking and responding to emotional cues (Shaywitz et al., 1995), or because of a combination of such influences.

We realize that such uncertainty about the cause of gender differences is probably frustrating to you. It's frustrating to us as well, but it reflects the reality of current scientific research. Certainly it is easier if one just relies on opinions instead of objective data. Some people undoubtedly still agree with something Queen Victoria said in 1881: she opined that "God created men and women different" and that any attempt to change things and speak of women's rights was a "mad, wicked folly." We are pleased to note that more than a hundred years have passed since such views were common. Today, many of us are convinced that the Berenstain bears were closer to the truth than was Queen Victoria; the bears proposed that men and women differ primarily because they have learned to differ. The final answer to questions about the origin of gender differences will almost certainly lie in the specifics concerning which differences are biologically based, which are acquired, and which reflect both kinds of influence.

Key Points

- *Sex* refers to the anatomical and physiological differences between males and females that are genetically determined at conception. *Gender* refers to everything else associated with a person's sex.

- Children attain a grasp of *gender identity* (the awareness of being a boy or a girl) at about age two. Between ages four and seven, children become aware that gender is a basic attribute of each person.

- As childhood progresses, children learn the stereotypes associated with being a male or a female in their culture, and gender-appropriate behavior is strongly encouraged.

- Bem's conception of masculinity and femininity as two separate dimensions led to her formulation indicating that each individual's *gender-role identification* can be masculine, feminine, both (*androgynous*), or neither (undifferentiated).

- Much of the research on gender-role identification supports the assumption that androgynous people have many advantages over those who are sex-typed. Also, masculinity tends to be associated with more positive outcomes than femininity. Extreme gender-role identification for either males or females seems to be relatively maladaptive.

- Gender roles affect the behavior of men and women in the home and on the job.

- Traditional gender roles receive powerful support throughout the culture from family, peers, and every aspect of the media. Nevertheless, there is evidence that the content of movies, television programs, and advertising is shifting away from traditional portrayals and that young people are becoming less bound by the traditional stereotypes.

- When males and females exhibit different behavior or different attitudes, the explanation may in part be biological (e.g., hormonal differences), in part cultural (e.g., the emphasis on female attractiveness), and in part perhaps a combination of the two.

Connections: Integrating Social Psychology

In this chapter, you read about . . .	In other chapters, you will find related discussions of . . .
self-schemas	schemas and information processing (Chapter 3); attitudes as schemas (Chapter 4); and stereotypes as schemas (Chapter 6)
self-esteem	effects of self-esteem in persuasion (Chapter 4); self-esteem after receiving help (Chapter 10)
self-monitoring	effects of self-monitoring in persuasion (Chapter 4)
self-efficacy	effects of self-efficacy on health (Chapter 13)
gender stereotypes	prejudice and stereotypes (Chapter 6)
concern with appearance	the role of attractiveness, weight, and other aspects of appearance in interpersonal attraction (Chapter 7)
male–female interactions	gender differences in romantic and marital relationships (Chapter 8)

(continued)

Thinking about Connections

1. Try to think of a famous or well-known person who has the same last name or first name as yourself. Now try to think of a famous or well-known person who has the same last name or first name as your psychology instructor. Which task was easier? Were you able to think of more names matching your own or those of your instructor? If there was a difference, why? What cognitive processes described in Chapter 3 were involved in your search for names?

2. Recall situations in which your feelings of self-esteem had an effect on your behavior or situations in which your self-esteem was affected by what happened. You might consider incidents in which someone tried to influence your behavior—or vice versa (Chapter 4); in which you met someone for the first time (Chapter 7); in which you were in a relationship that ended (Chapter 8); in which you asked for help (Chapter 10); or when you became ill (Chapter 13).

3. What do you believe are the most common stereotypes about men and women? Do you personally (or some of your friends) hold these stereotypes? Are these stereotypes at all related to the kind of stereotypes that lead to prejudice and discrimination (Chapter 6)? Do you think that these stereotypes have any effect on interpersonal attraction (Chapter 7) or on romantic relationships (Chapter 8)? How accurate are these stereotypes, and where do they come from? Can you think of any situations in which your interpersonal behavior was affected by what you believe about typical male or female characteristics?

4. Are you satisfied with your appearance? Why or why not? Do you believe that the way you look has any effect on how much other people like you (Chapter 7) or on your chances of establishing a lasting relationship (Chapter 8)? Do you plan to do something to change your looks? If so, what kind of difference would the change make in your life? What relationship is there between your appearance and your self-concept, self-esteem, self-focusing, and self-efficacy? Try to explain the relationship using any of the concepts you read about in this book.

Ideas to Take with You
Dealing with Negative Self-Perceptions

A very consistent and pervasive difference between men and women in Western societies involves the way they perceive and evaluate their appearance. Beginning in adolescence, women are much more concerned about body image than men. Can anything be done to make this less of a problem?

Be Realistic about the Importance of Appearance.

"Be realistic" is obviously easier to say than to accept; but, as you will discover in Chapter 7, the adage that "you can't judge a book by its cover" is true. The most attractive individuals in the world do not differ from the rest of us in intelligence, creativity, character, kindness, or anything else that matters—except in the fact that they are liked on the basis of their looks. Think of the most unkind, dishonest, and totally detestable human being you know. Would you find that person more acceptable if he or she suddenly acquired a very attractive face and body? If you meet an attractive person for the first time, try to remember that appearance gives you no information at all about this individual.

Ask Yourself How Important Your Weight Is to Others.

Women in the United States and other Western nations are often obsessed with their weight. Do you know how much you should weigh on the basis of height–weight charts? If you fit within those norms, are you satisfied? Or do you want to weigh less? Why? Do other people perceive you as underweight, average, or overweight? How much do you think you would have to lose or to gain for anyone to notice? Some of us know that you can work hard to lose ten pounds or so, only to find that no one has a clue unless you tell them. You may think about your weight a lot and about fatness/thinness as you observe others, but other people are *not* obsessed with *your* weight! They don't care nearly as much as you do.

Consider Whether Men Are Aware of Every Detail of a Woman's Appearance.

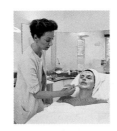

Humorist Dave Barry (1998) sums up the situation nicely: "Men don't even notice 97 percent of the beauty efforts you make anyway. Take fingernails. The average woman spends 5,000 hours per year worrying about her fingernails; I have never once, in more than 40 years of listening to men talk about women, heard a man say, 'She has a nice set of fingernails!' Many men would not notice if a woman had upward of four hands." Also remember that cross-cultural studies indicate that Hispanic and African American men are concerned even less than other groups about such things as how much a woman weighs. It would help if both men and women could relax and pay much more attention to what people are like and much less attention to how they look.

Compare Yourself with Others like Yourself, Not with Models and Stars.

When you look through magazines showing page after page of ultrathin models and movie stars, you can easily assume that because you don't measure up to these unrealistic standards, you must be inadequate. You're not. For whatever reason, most men do not feel depressed that they are not as tall as the average NBA star and don't run as fast as the average NFL halfback and are not as cute as the average young male movie star. By definition, most of us lie outside of the top one-tenth of one percent of the population who are represented in professional sports, modeling, movie stardom, or anything else. If you decide you are imperfect because you are not in such a category, you will spend many unhappy hours brooding about not reaching an impossible goal. Should the young swan have been depressed because he was not a duckling?

SUMMARY AND REVIEW OF KEY POINTS

The Self: Components of One's Identity

- One's identity, or *self-concept*, consists of self-beliefs and self-perceptions organized as a cognitive schema.

- Because the self is the center of each person's social world and because self-schemas are well developed, we can process information about ourselves more efficiently than other types of information—the *self-reference effect*. The processing is both elaborative and categorical.

- The complex structure of the self-concept involves such structural elements as central versus peripheral self-conceptions, varying degrees of clarity in one's beliefs, and a large number of specific content areas.

- In addition to the personal self, the *social self* includes interpersonal relationships and a collective identity derived from membership in groups based on such factors as race, religion, ethnicity, and so forth.

- In addition to our current self-concept, there are many possible different and better selves that we can envision in the future.

- Self-concepts change with age, but also in response to feedback, changes in one's environment or occupational status, and interactions with others.

- *Self-esteem* consists of self-evaluation, or the attitudes we hold about ourselves in general and in specific domains. It is based in part on social comparison processes.

- Rogerian therapy is, in part, aimed at raising self-esteem or at decreasing the gap between one's self and one's ideal self.

- There are many positive benefits associated with high as opposed to low self-esteem, but variable self-esteem has even more negative consequences than low self-esteem.

Other Aspects of Self-Functioning: Focusing, Monitoring, and Efficacy

- *Self-focusing* refers to the extent to which an individual is directing attention toward self or toward the external world.

- How one stores positive and negative material in memory (together or separately) is an important determinant of mood regulation and ability to cope with stressful events.

- *Self-monitoring* refers to a dispositional tendency to regulate behavior on the basis of external factors (high self-monitoring) or on the basis of internal beliefs and values (low self-monitoring).

- Differences in self-monitoring tendencies influence speech patterns, response to advertising content, and interpersonal behavior. Individual levels of self-monitoring are based in part on genetic factors.

- *Self-efficacy* refers to an individual's evaluation of his or her ability to perform a task, reach a goal, or overcome an obstacle.

- High self-efficacy is associated with better performance (physical and intellectual), more socially skilled behavior, the ability to overcome phobias, and skill in coping with fearful events.

Gender: Maleness or Femaleness As a Crucial Aspect of Identity

- *Sex* refers to the anatomical and physiological differences between males and females that are genetically deter-

mined at conception. *Gender* refers to everything else associated with a person's sex.

- Children attain a grasp of *gender identity* (the awareness of being a boy or a girl) at about age two. Between ages four and seven, children become aware that gender is a basic attribute of each person.

- As childhood progresses, children learn the stereotypes associated with being a male or a female in their culture, and gender-appropriate behavior is strongly encouraged.

- Bem's conception of masculinity and femininity as two separate dimensions led to her formulation indicating that each individual's *gender-role identification* can be masculine, feminine, both (*androgynous*), or neither (undifferentiated).

- Much of the research on gender-role identification supports the assumption that androgynous people have many advantages over those who are sex-typed. Also, masculinity tends to be associated with more positive outcomes than femininity. Extreme gender-role identification for either males or females seems to be relatively maladaptive.

- Gender roles affect the behavior of men and women in the home and on the job.

- Traditional gender roles receive powerful support throughout the culture from family, peers, and every aspect of the media. Nevertheless, there is evidence that the content of movies, television programs, and advertising is shifting away from traditional portrayals and that young people are becoming less bound by the traditional stereotypes.

- When males and females exhibit different behavior or different attitudes, the explanation may in part be biological (e.g., hormonal differences), in part cultural (e.g., the emphasis on female attractiveness), and in part perhaps a combination of the two.

KEY TERMS

androgynous (p. 189)

Bem Sex-Role Inventory (BSRI) (p. 190)

estrogen (p. 199)

gender (p. 185)

gender consistency (p. 186)

gender identity (p. 186)

gender-role identification (p. 190)

hyperfemininity (p. 192)

hypermasculinity (p. 192)

objective self-awareness (p. 160)

possible selves (p. 167)

self-concept (p. 160)

self-efficacy (p. 182)

self-esteem (p. 169)

self-focusing (p. 176)

self-monitoring (p. 179)

self-reference effect (p. 161)

sex (p. 185)

sex typing (p. 188)

sexual self-schema (p. 163)

social identity (p. 159)

social self (p. 165)

subjective self-awareness (p. 160)

symbolic self-awareness (p. 160)

testosterone (p. 199)

FOR MORE INFORMATION

Baumeister, R. F. (Ed.). (1993). *Self-esteem: The puzzle of low self-regard.* New York: Plenum.

Active investigators provide a comprehensive view of research and theory involving self-esteem. Among the many topics covered are the origins of low self-esteem, fluctuations in self-esteem, and how self-esteem is defended in response to threat.

Geary, D. C. (1998). *Male, female: The evolution of human sex differences.* Washington, DC: American Psychological Association.

A comprehensive and readable introduction that offers an evolutionary explanation of why men and women differ.

Hattie, J. (1992). *Self-concept.* Hillsdale, NJ: Erlbaum.

This book presents a model of the self-concept based on empirical research. The author emphasizes the development of the self-concept and intervention procedures such as psychotherapy that are designed to enhance the self-concept.

Oskamp, S., & Costanzo, M. (Eds.). (1993). *Gender issues in social psychology.* Newbury Park, CA: Sage.

Leading psychologists in the field examine research and theory on gender and gender differences. Included are such topics as a feminist perspective on research methodology, gender-role development in childhood and adolescence, masculine ideology, gender differences in marital conflict, gender stereotypes, and job issues ranging from salary discrepancies to sexual harassment.

I (Robert Baron) had my first experiences with both love (puppy love, that is) and prejudice when I was six years old. I was in the first grade, and for some reason I became the object of intense affection from one of the girls in my class. Her name was Nadia, and she certainly wasn't shy: she held my hand when we went out to recess, sat next to me when we had our milk and cookies in the afternoon, and soon began giving me a kiss on the cheek at the end of the each day. Nadia was also generous and brought me many little presents: cookies her mother had baked, candies, crayon drawings. Then one day she told me that she was going to bring me something special. She did; it was a small gold-colored metal pencil. Nadia assured me that it was really gold, so I was very excited when I showed it to my mother that afternoon. Her reaction surprised me. "Who is this little girl?" she asked. "What's her last name?" And when I told her, she seemed to become upset. I assured her that Nadia was very nice, but it didn't seem to matter. She told me that I would have to return Nadia's gift. When I asked why, my mother looked embarrassed but explained that Nadia's family was "different" from ours, and that it wouldn't be good to get too friendly with her. Needless to say, I couldn't make any sense out of this answer. I liked Nadia: she had pretty black hair and smelled good! But my mother meant what she said; the next day, when she came to pick me up, she approached Nadia's mother and returned the pencil. I don't know what else she said, but after that Nadia did not hold my hand, bring me presents, or kiss me good-bye.

Looking back, I now realize that what I witnessed so many years ago was an instance of ethnic prejudice in action. My family was mainly from Austria; Nadia's family, I suspect, was from Poland or perhaps Russia. In 1949, when these events took place, people from different European countries simply didn't mix. They usually lived in separate neighborhoods and attended different schools. Even if the children of these families did go to the same school, they didn't socialize after class. Moreover, as I learned in later years, each group typically held negative attitudes about the others, perceiving them as lazy, dirty, immoral, dangerous, or worse.

Why do I begin with this incident? Mainly to call your attention to the following point: *At some time or other, virtually everyone comes face to face with prejudice.* It may not be the truly evil form that leads to atrocities such as Nazi death camps or "ethnic cleansing" in Europe or Africa (see Figure 6.1); and it may focus on age, occupation, or even simply bodyweight (e.g., Brown, 1998) rather than on race, religion, gender, or ethnic background. Regardless of its form or focus, however, prejudice is both real and damaging. I sometimes find myself imagining how Nadia must have felt when her mother told her to avoid me. It truly makes me sad even now, almost fifty years later.

As you can probably guess, social psychologists have long recognized the importance of prejudice in human behavior and human societies. Thus, they have studied this topic for several decades. What have they discovered? To provide you with an overview of their major conclusions, we'll proceed as follows. First, we'll examine the nature of *prejudice* and *discrimination*—two words that are often used as synonyms but which in fact refer to very different concepts. Second, we'll consider the causes of prejudice and discrimination—why they occur and what makes them so intense and persistent. Third, we'll explore various strategies for reducing prejudice and discrimination. Finally, because it has been the subject of an especially large amount of research and because it influences the lives of more than half of all human beings, we will focus on *sexism*—prejudice based on gender.

Figure 6.1
The Evil Face of Prejudice.
At one time or another, every one of us comes face to face with prejudice. We can only pray that our experience with it will not be as devastating as it has been for the people shown here.

PREJUDICE AND DISCRIMINATION: THEIR NATURE AND EFFECTS

In everyday speech, the terms *prejudice* and *discrimination* are often used interchangeably. Social psychologists, however, draw a clear distinction between them. *Prejudice* refers to a special type of *attitude*—generally, a negative one—toward the members of some social group. In contrast, *discrimination* refers to negative *actions* toward those individuals—attitudes translated into behavior.

Prejudice: Choosing Whom to Hate

We'll begin with a more precise definition. **Prejudice** is *an attitude (usually negative) toward the members of some group, based solely on their membership in that group.* In other words, a person who is prejudiced toward some social group tends to evaluate its members in a specific manner (usually negatively) merely because they belong to that group. Their individual traits or behaviors play little role; they are disliked (or, in a few cases, liked) simply because of their membership in the group.

When prejudice is defined as a special type of attitude, two important implications follow. First, as we saw in Chapters 3 and 4, attitudes often function as *schemas*—cognitive frameworks for organizing, interpreting, and recalling information (e.g., Wyer & Srull, 1994). Thus, individuals who are prejudiced toward particular groups tend to process information about these groups differently from the way they process information about other groups. For example, information relating to the prejudice is often given more attention, or processed more carefully, than information not relating to it. One example: Racially prejudiced persons take significantly longer than persons who are not racially prejudiced to decide whether strangers whose racial identity is ambiguous belong to one racial category or another (Blascovich et al., 1997). Similarly, information that is consistent with individuals' prejudiced views often receives closer attention and so is remembered more accurately than information that is not consistent with these views (e.g., Fiske & Neuberg, 1990; Judd, Ryan, &

prejudice • Negative attitudes toward the members of specific social groups.

Parke, 1991). As a result of such effects, prejudice becomes a kind of closed cognitive loop and tends to increase in strength over time.

Second, if prejudice is a special kind of attitude, then it may involve more than negative evaluations of the groups toward whom it is directed; it may also include negative feelings or emotions on the part of prejudiced persons when they are in the presence of, or merely think about, members of the groups they dislike (Bodenhausen, Kramer, & Susser, 1994b). These emotional reactions are shown very clearly in research conducted by Vanman and his colleagues (Vanman et al., 1997). In this investigation, white participants of both genders were asked to imagine working on several cooperative tasks (e.g., a team running race, a debate team competition, a team research project, or team participation on a game show) with a partner who was either white or black. They were further told to imagine either that their rewards in each situation would be determined by their joint efforts or by their own individual performance. While participants were imagining these situations, the researchers made recordings of electrical activity in their facial muscles—muscles related to smiling and to frowning.

The researchers predicted that although participants would not *report* more negative attitudes toward black than white partners, their facial muscles would show more activity indicative of negative emotional reactions when their imagined partner was black than when this person was white. Moreover, they reasoned that that this would occur under both the independent and joint reward conditions. As you can see from Figure 6.2, results offered clear support for the predictions concerning facial muscles; in addition, other findings indicated that these reactions occurred despite the fact that participants actually reported more *positive* attitudes toward their partners when these persons were supposedly black than when they were supposedly white. Additional evidence suggesting that these negative emotional reactions to a black partner were indeed related to prejudice was provided by a follow-up study in which white participants known to be high or low in racial prejudice were shown photos of white and black strangers. Activity from their facial muscles indicated that for the low-prejudiced persons, there was no difference in muscle activity for white and

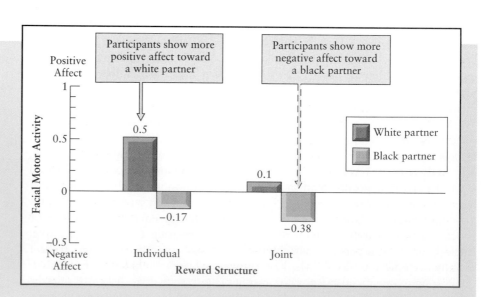

Figure 6.2

A More Subtle Face of Prejudice. Because it is a negative attitude, prejudice can influence our affective reactions to people belonging to groups other than our own. As shown here, this is precisely what was found in one recent study. White participants who expressed positive feelings about a black partner on a questionnaire showed facial muscle activity indicative of negative reactions to this person.

(*Source:* Based on data from Vanman et al., 1997).

black strangers. For highly prejudiced persons, however, activity patterns indicative of less positive and more negative feelings occurred. So, to repeat: Prejudice can strongly influence affective reactions toward other persons.

In addition, prejudice often involves beliefs and expectations about members of various groups—for instance, beliefs that all members of these groups show certain traits. We'll discuss such beliefs, known as *stereotypes,* later in this chapter (e.g., Jussim, 1991). Finally, prejudice may involve tendencies to act in negative ways toward those who are the object of prejudice; we'll turn shortly to several of the many ways in which prejudice is expressed in overt behavior. First, however, we should address one additional question: Why, specifically, do people hold prejudiced views?

Prejudice: Why It Persists

Research findings point to two explanations for the persistence of prejudice. First, individuals hold prejudiced views because doing so allows them to bolster their own self-image (e.g., Steele, Spencer, & Lynch, 1993). When prejudiced individuals put down a group toward whom they hold negative views, this allows them to affirm their own self-worth—to feel superior in various ways. In other words, prejudice may play an important role in protecting or enhancing the self-concept of some persons (see Chapter 5) (Higgins, 1996).

Convincing evidence that this actually is so is provided by an ingenious study conducted by Fein and Spencer (1997). These researchers asked male and female students to evaluate the personality and job qualifications of a job candidate. Information and a photo attached to the application indicated that she was either Jewish or Italian. (The same person was shown in each case, but subtle changes were made to bolster the suggestion that she belonged to one ethnic group or the other; for instance, she wore a Star of David when described as being Jewish but a cross when describe as Italian.) Before making their evaluations, participants received feedback from a bogus IQ test indicating that they had scored either very high (93rd percentile) or very poorly (47th percentile). Fein and Spencer (1997) predicted that after receiving positive feedback, participants would have little reason to derogate either job applicant. After the negative feedback, however, their self-concept would be threatened, so they would tend to derogate (downrate) the job applicant when she was described as being Jewish. This latter prediction was based on the fact that a negative stereotype for Jewish females ("Jewish American princesses" or JAPs) existed at the college where the research was conducted. Results strongly confirmed these predictions.

But did putting down the Jewish job applicant actually enhance participants' self-esteem? To see if this was so, Fein and Spencer had the students complete a measure of self-esteem twice: at the start of the study, and again after evaluating the job applicant. Results were clear: Those who had received negative feedback and downrated the Jewish applicant did in fact show the largest gain in self-esteem. Together, these results offer strong support for the view that when their self-esteem is threatened, some people tend to disparage groups toward whom they are prejudiced, and that this in turn boosts their self-esteem (see Figure 6.3 on page 214).

A second basis for holding prejudiced views is that doing so can save us considerable cognitive effort. As noted in Chapters 3 and 4, human beings are "cognitive misers"—they invest the least possible amount of cognitive effort in most situations. *Stereotypes,* in particular, seem to serve the function of saving us mental effort. Once stereotypes are formed, we don't have to bother engaging in careful, systematic processing; after all, since we "know" what members of a given group are like, we can rely on quicker, heuristic-driven processing and

Figure 6.3

One Reason Why Prejudice Persists. Recent findings indicate that when their self-esteem is threatened, prejudiced individuals derogate groups they dislike. This helps to boost or restore their self-esteem.

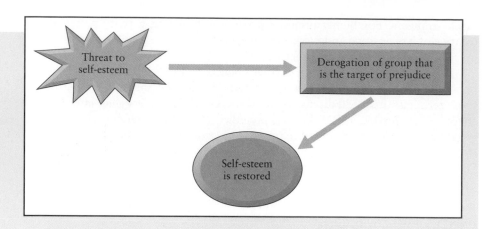

preconceived beliefs. The results of several studies offer support for this view (e.g., Bodenhausen, 1993; Macrae, Milne, & Bodenhausen, 1994), so our strong tendency to save mental effort seems to be another reason why prejudices are formed and persist.

Key Points

- *Prejudice* is an attitude (usually negative) toward members of some social group based solely on their membership in that group.
- Prejudice, like other attitudes, influences our processing of social information. In addition, prejudice influences our beliefs about persons belonging to various groups, and our feelings about them.
- Prejudice persists because disparaging groups we dislike can boost our self-esteem, and because stereotypes save us cognitive effort.

Discrimination: Prejudice in Action

Attitudes, we noted in Chapter 4, are not always reflected in overt actions; and prejudice is definitely no exception to this rule. In many cases, persons holding negative attitudes toward the members of various groups cannot express these views directly. Laws, social pressure, fear of retaliation—all serve to deter people from putting their prejudiced views into open practice. For this reason, blatant forms of **discrimination**—negative actions toward the objects of racial, ethnic, or religious prejudice—have decreased in recent years in the United States and in many other countries (e.g., Swim et al., 1995). Such actions as restricting members of various groups to certain seats on buses or in movie theaters or barring them from restaurants, schools, or neighborhoods—all common practices in the past (see Figure 6.4)—have now largely vanished in many countries. Of course, they have not disappeared completely: anyone who watches the evening news well knows that open expressions of prejudice, and violent confrontations stemming from them, still occur throughout the world with disturbing frequency. For the most part, though, the expressions of prejudice in social behavior has become increasingly subtle in recent decades. What are these *subtle* or *disguised* forms of discrimination like? Research by social psychologists points to several interesting conclusions.

discrimination • Negative behaviors directed toward members of social groups who are the object of prejudice.

The "New" Racism: More Subtle, but Just As Deadly. At one time many people felt no qualms about expressing openly racist beliefs. They would state that they were against school desegregation, that they viewed members of

Figure 6.4
Blatant Discrimination: Mainly, a Thing of the Past. In the past, racial and ethnic prejudices were expressed openly in the United States, in forms such as those shown here. Now, however, they are more often expressed in more subtle ways.

minority groups as inferior in various ways, and that they would consider moving away if persons belonging to these groups took up residence in their neighborhoods (Sears, 1988). Now, of course, very few persons would openly state such views. Does this mean that racism, a particularly virulent form of prejudice, has disappeared, or at least decreased? Some social psychologists would argue that this is so (e.g., Martin & Parker, 1995). Others believe that in fact all that has happened is that "old-fashioned" (read "blatant") racism has been replaced by more subtle forms, which they term *modern racism*. What is such racism like? There is growing agreement that it focuses on three major components (e.g., Swim et al., 1995): (1) denial that there is continuing discrimination against minorities (e.g., "Discrimination against African Americans is no longer a problem in the United States"); (2) antagonism to the demands of minorities for equal treatment (e.g., "African Americans are getting too demanding in their push for equal rights"); and (3) resentment about special favors for minority groups (e.g., "Over the past few years, the government and news media have shown more respect to African Americans than they deserve"). This last point is often linked to popular, widely held beliefs, such as the general principle that merit should be a criterion in the division of rewards and opportunities. Although no one would argue with that principle, there appear to be instances in which it is used as camouflage for more sinister beliefs or motives, such as the desire to exclude members of various minority groups from schools, jobs, loans, or other potential benefits (see Figure 6.5 on page 216).

As you can readily see, modern racism is certainly different from old-fashioned racism in several respects, but it can still be very damaging to the victims of lingering discrimination. For example, as noted by Swim and her colleagues (1995), subtle prejudice may influence the likelihood of voting for a minority candidate to an even greater extent than old-fashioned racist attitudes. So—and we want to emphasize this point—despite the fact that blatant forms of racial discrimination have all but vanished from public life in the United States and many other countries, this repulsive and damaging expression of prejudice is still very much alive and represents a very serious problem in many societies.

Tokenism: Small Benefits, High Costs. Imagine that you are hired for a job you really want and at a higher starting salary than you expected. At first you are

Figure 6.5
Modern Racism or Sincere Conviction? Are persons such as these expressing their sincere commitment to long-held values in their society, or are they showing disguised forms of prejudice social psychologists term "modern racism"? Even they may not know for sure.

tokenism • The performance of trivial or small-scale positive actions for people who are the targets of prejudice. Prejudiced groups often use tokenistic behaviors as an excuse for refusing more meaningful beneficial actions.

reverse discrimination • The tendency to evaluate or treat persons belonging to groups that are the object of prejudice more favorably than members of the dominant group.

happy about your good fortune. But now assume that one day you learn that you got the job mainly because you belong to a specific group—one whose members the company must hire in order to avoid charges of discrimination. How will you react? And how will other employees at your company, who know that you were hired for this reason, perceive you? With respect to the first of these questions, research findings indicate that many persons find this kind of situation quite disturbing. They are upset to realize that they have been hired or promoted solely because of their ethnic background, gender, or some other aspect of their personal identity (e.g., Chacko, 1982). Further, they may object to being hired as a token member of their racial, ethnic, or religious group.

Turning to the second question raised above, growing evidence indicates that persons who are hired as token representatives of their groups are perceived quite negatively by fellow employees (Summers, 1991). For example, Heilman, Block, and Lucas (1992) found that job applicants who were identified as "affirmative action hirees" were perceived as less competent by persons who reviewed their files than applicants who were not identified in this manner.

Hiring persons as token members of their groups is just one form of **tokenism;** it occurs in other contexts as well. In its most general form, tokenism involves performing trivial positive actions for the targets of prejudice and then using these as an excuse or justification for later forms of discrimination. "Don't bother me," prejudiced persons who have engaged in tokenism seem to say; "I've done enough for those people already!" (Dutton & Lake, 1973; Rosenfield et al., 1982). Whenever it occurs, tokenism seems to have at least two negative effects. First, it lets prejudiced people off the hook; they can point to tokenistic actions as public proof that they aren't really bigoted. Second, it can be damaging to the self-esteem and confidence of the targets of prejudice, including those few persons who are selected as tokens or who receive minimal aid. Clearly, then, tokenism is one subtle form of discrimination worth preventing.

Reverse Discrimination: Giving with One Hand, Taking with the Other. A second type of subtle discrimination occurs in situations in which persons holding at least some degree of prejudice toward the members of a group lean over backward to treat members of that group favorably—more favorably than they treat other people. At first glance, such **reverse discrimination,** as it is sometimes termed, might appear to be beneficial for persons it affects (Chidester, 1986). On one level, this is certainly true: people exposed to reverse discrimination do receive praise, promotions, and other benefits. On another level, however, this kind of favorable treatment may prove harmful, especially in the long run. For example, consider what may happen if well-intentioned teachers "lean over backward" and assign inflated grades or ratings to minority children (Fajardo, 1985). To the extent that they do, they run the risk of setting these youngsters up for severe later disappointment. After all, at some point, a clash between false expectations and reality may occur. But please don't misunderstand; we are *not* suggesting that this is always the case. On the contrary, there is considerable evidence suggesting that on many occasions, such actions—extra help for persons who have previously been the target of strong discrimination—may benefit them in several important ways (i.e., by enhancing their self-esteem, giving them opportunities to demonstrate their motivation and potential which they would otherwise never have). The belief that such benefits will result from giving minority groups extra help is, of course, one important basis for affirmative action programs—programs that encourage businesses, universities, and many other organizations to make special efforts to hire, promote, or admit persons belonging to minority groups. Although such programs are somewhat controversial, they do assist minority groups by enabling them to obtain jobs, training, and other opportunities they would otherwise have been denied.

Despite these obvious benefits, the overall picture is somewhat clouded by evidence suggesting that sometimes, leaning over backwards to assist such persons can indeed set them up for later disappointments. For instance, consider the results of a study by Harber (1998). He asked white students at Stanford University to evaluate essays supposedly written either by white students or by black students. The essays were, in fact, generated by the experimenter, and they were quite poor in quality. Participants evaluated the essays both in terms of their content (ideas and style) and their mechanics (e.g., length, spelling, grammar). Harber (1998) predicted that the tendency to provide positive feedback to a black author would be stronger for essay content than for essay mechanics; and, as shown in Figure 6.6 on page 218, this is just what was found. In other words, the white participants leaned over backward to provide lenient, positive evaluations to an essay's author when they thought this person was black. As noted earlier, this tendency—kind and well-intentioned as it may seem—can have the unintended effect of giving minority persons false expectations about the level of their accomplishments and the standards they must meet to reach their ultimate goals. Thus, it can ultimately have harmful effects.

Quite apart from such findings, critics of affirmative action programs have objected to them on other grounds, noting that such programs—especially ones that reserve a fixed percentage of jobs or college admissions for minority groups—necessarily prevent persons not in these groups from obtaining benefits they deserve. Such objections are especially strong in cases where businesses hire, or universities admit, minority applicants whose qualifications appear to

Figure 6.6
"Leaning Over Backward" in Providing Feedback to Minorities. As shown here, white participants in one recent study seemed to "lean over backward" when evaluating the work of a black fellow student. They rated the same essay more favorably when it was supposedly written by a black student than by a white student.

(*Source:* Based on data from Harber, 1998.)

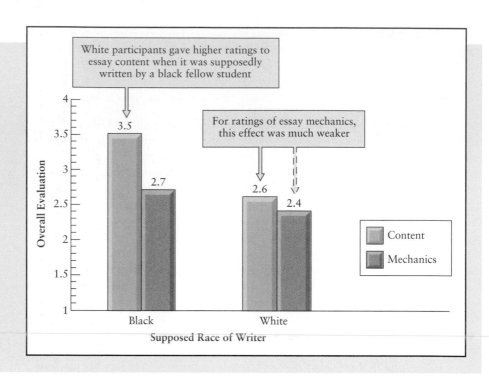

be lower than those of majority group members and are rejected. For instance, at the University of Michigan, Jennifer Gratz brought suit against the university after it failed to admit her, despite her 3.76 high school GPA and good scores on the ACT (a widely used college entrance test), but *did* admit minority students with lower qualifications in this respect (Sharf & Wolf, 1998). If Gratz's suit succeeds, the university will have to stop using race as one criterion in its admission policies. Even if Gratz loses in a lower court, however, her case is viewed as being so important that it may ultimately go the Supreme Court, where a decision in her favor would affect the admission policies of all colleges and universities in the United States. Clearly, then, the issues involved are complex; for instance, since college entrance tests may be unfairly biased against minority groups, and the schools they attend are often substandard in several ways, (see Figure 6.7) perhaps it is unfair to compare their scores or grades with those of persons from more advantaged backgrounds. Clearly then, the complex issues raised by affirmative actions programs will only be resolved through a long and searching legal process.

Key Points

- *Discrimination* involves negative actions, based on prejudice, toward members of various social groups.
- While blatant discrimination has clearly decreased in Western societies, more subtle forms such as modern racism, *tokenism,* and *reverse discrimination* persist.
- Recent findings indicate that white persons in the United States often "lean over backward" to provide positive feedback to members of minority groups.
- Critics of affirmative action programs contend that they are a form of reverse discrimination that actually harms other groups.

Figure 6.7
Unequal Opportunities: One Rationale for Affirmative Action. Persons in favor of affirmative action programs at universities note that the high schools minority students attend are often inferior to those attended by more advantaged students. As a result, such students need special assistance in order to gain admission to the universities of their choice.

THE ORIGINS OF PREJUDICE: CONTRASTING PERSPECTIVES

As we have already seen, holding the seemingly irrational negative views that constitute the core of prejudice can produce important benefits for the persons involved. Thus, the existence of prejudice itself is far from mysterious. But precisely how do such negative attitudes take shape? What are the social origins of prejudice—the social conditions from which it derives? Research by social psychologists provides many insights into this important question.

Direct Intergroup Conflict: Competition As a Source of Prejudice

It is sad but true that the things people want and value most—good jobs, nice homes, high status—are always in short supply. This fact serves as the foundation for what is perhaps the oldest explanation of prejudice—**realistic conflict theory** (e.g., Bobo, 1983). According to this view, prejudice stems from competition among social groups over valued commodities or opportunities. In short, prejudice develops out of the struggle over jobs, adequate housing, good schools, and other desirable outcomes. The theory further suggests that as such competition continues, the members of the groups involved come to view each other in increasingly negative terms (White, 1977). They label each other as "enemies," view their own group as morally superior, and draw the boundaries between themselves and their opponents more and more firmly. The result is that what starts out as simple competition relatively free from hatred gradually develops into full scale, emotion-laden prejudice.

Evidence from several different studies confirms the occurrence of this process. As competition persists, individuals come to perceive one another in increasingly negative ways. Even worse, such competition often leads to direct, and sometimes violent, conflict. A very dramatic demonstration of this principle in operation is provided by a well-known field study conducted by Sherif and his colleagues (Sherif et al., 1961).

realistic conflict theory • The view that prejudice sometimes stems from direct competition between social groups over scarce and valued resources.

For this innovative study, the researchers sent eleven-year-old boys to a special summer camp in a remote area where, free from external influences, the nature of conflict and its role in prejudice could be carefully studied. When the boys arrived at the camp (named "The Robber's Cave" in honor of a nearby cave that was once, supposedly, used by robbers), they were divided into two separate groups and assigned to cabins located quite far apart. For one week, the campers in each group lived and played together, engaging in such enjoyable activities as hiking, swimming, and other sports. During this initial phase the boys quickly developed strong attachments to their own groups. They chose names for their teams (*Rattlers* and *Eagles*), stenciled them onto their shirts, and made up flags with their groups' symbols on them.

At this point the second phase of the study began. The boys in both groups were told that they would now engage in a series of competitions. The winning team would receive a trophy, and its members would earn prizes (pocket knives and medals). Because these were prizes the boys strongly desired, the stage was set for intense competition. Would such conflict generate prejudice? The answer was quick in coming. As the boys competed, the tension between the groups rose. At first it was limited to verbal taunts and name-calling, but soon it escalated into more direct acts—for example, the Eagles burned the Rattlers' flag. The next day the Rattlers struck back by attacking the rival group's cabin, overturning beds, tearing out mosquito netting, and seizing personal property. Such actions continued until the researchers intervened to prevent serious trouble. At the same time, the two groups voiced increasingly negative views of each other. They labeled their opponents as "bums" and "cowards," while heaping praise on their own group at every turn. In short, after only two weeks of conflict, the groups showed all the key components of strong prejudice toward each other.

Fortunately, the story had a happy ending. In the study's final phase, Sherif and his colleagues attempted to reduce the negative reactions described above. Merely increasing the amount of contact between the groups failed to accomplish this goal; indeed, it seemed to fan the flames of anger. But when conditions were altered so that the groups found it necessary to work together to reach *superordinate goals*—ones they both desired—dramatic changes occurred. After the boys worked together to restore their water supply (previously sabotaged by the researchers), combined their funds to rent a movie, and jointly repaired a broken-down truck, tensions between the groups largely vanished and many cross-group friendships were established.

There are, of course, major limitations to this research. The study took place over a relatively short period of time; the camp setting was a special one; all participants were boys; and, perhaps most important, the boys were quite homogeneous in background—they did not belong to different racial, ethnic, or social groups. Despite these restrictions, however, the findings reported by Sherif and his colleagues are compelling. They offer a chilling picture of how direct competition over scarce resources can quickly escalate into full-scale conflict, which then in turn fosters the accompanying negative attitudes toward opponents that form the core of prejudice.

The research reported by Sherif and his colleagues is viewed as a "classic" in the study of prejudice. Yet it was not the first or the most dramatic study of the relationship between conflict and prejudice conducted by social psychologists. That honor goes to a much earlier, and much more disturbing, investigation conducted by Hovland and Sears (1940)—a study described in detail in the following *Cornerstones* section.

Cornerstones of Social Psychology
The Economics of Racial Violence: Do Bad Times Fan the Flames of Prejudice?

In 1939, several psychologists published an influential book entitled *Frustration and Aggression* (Dollard et al., 1939). In this book they suggested that aggression often stems from *frustration*—interference with goal-directed behavior. In other words, aggression often occurs in situations where people are prevented from getting what they want. As we'll see in Chapter 11, this hypothesis is only partially correct. Frustration *can* sometimes lead to aggression, but it is definitely not the only, or the most important, cause of such behavior.

In any case, the frustration–aggression hypothesis stimulated a great deal of research in psychology, and some of this work was concerned with prejudice. The basic reasoning was as follows: When groups are competing for scarce resources, they come to view one another as potential or actual sources of frustration. After all, if "they" get the jobs, the housing, and other benefits, then "we" don't. The result, it was reasoned, is not simply negative attitudes toward opposing groups; in addition, strong tendencies to aggress against them may also be generated.

Although this possible link between conflict, prejudice, and aggression was studied in several different ways, the most chilling findings were reported by Carl I Hovland and Robert R. Sears (1940)—two psychologists who made important contributions to social psychology in several different areas (e.g., in the study of attitudes and persuasion; see Chapter 4). These researchers hypothesized that economic conditions provide a measure of frustration, with "bad times" being high in frustration for many people and "good times" somewhat lower. They reasoned that if this is so, then racially motivated acts of violence such as lynchings should be higher when economic conditions are poor than when they are good. To test this unsettling hypothesis, Hovland and Sears obtained data on the number of lynchings in the United States in each year between 1882 and 1930. Most of these lynchings (a total of 4,761) occurred in fourteen Southern states, and most (though not all) of the victims were African Americans. Next, Hovland and Sears (1940) related the number of lynchings in each year to two economic indexes: the farm value of cotton (the total value of cotton produced that year) and the per-acre value of cotton. Because cotton played a major role in the economies of the states where most lynchings occurred, Hovland and Sears assumed that these measures would provide a good overview of economic conditions in those states.

As you can see from Figure 6.8 on page 222, results were both clear and dramatic: The number of lynchings rose when economic conditions declined, and fell when economic conditions improved. Hovland and Sears (1940, p. 307) interpreted these findings as reflecting *displaced aggression:* since farmers could not aggress against the factors that were causing their frustration (e.g., a lack of rainfall), they aggressed against African Americans—a group they disliked and that was, at that time, relatively defenseless. Today most social psychologists prefer a somewhat different interpretation—one suggesting that competition for scarce economic resources increases when times are bad, and that this increased competition intensifies racial prejudice. Lynchings and other violence then result from increased prejudice rather than from displaced aggression.

Regardless of the precise mechanisms involved, however, Hovland and Sears's study was important for several reasons. First, it demonstrated an important link between economic conditions and racial violence—a finding that has been confirmed with more sophisticated modern research methods (Hepworth & West, 1988). Clearly, this relationship is relevant to government programs designed to improve economic conditions for disadvantaged persons, many of whom are the victims of racial or

Carl Hovland and Robert Sears. *Hovland and Sears conducted many important studies during the 1940s and 1950s. Their research on prejudice, based in part on the famous frustration–aggression hypothesis, had a major effect on subsequent research in this area. In addition, both psychologists made important contributions to the study of attitudes and persuasion.*

Figure 6.8

Racial Violence and Economic Conditions. As shown here, the number of lynchings in the United States—primarily of African Americans, and mainly in Southern states—varied with economic conditions. Lynchings increased when times were bad, but decreased when economic conditions improved. These findings provide indirect support for the direct conflict model of prejudice.

(*Source:* Based on data from Hovland & Sears, 1940.)

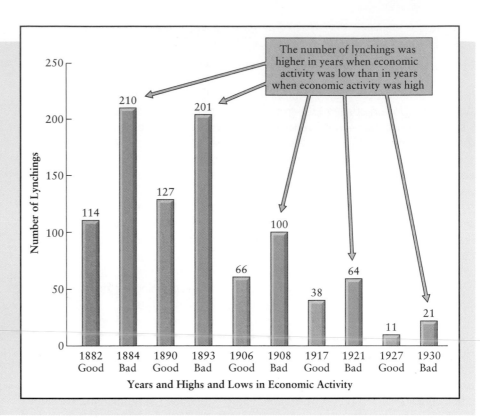

ethnic prejudice. Second, this research provided a dramatic illustration of the value of applying psychological theory to important real-life events. Finally, it showed how important social problems can be investigated by means of *archival data*—existing records of social and economic events. In these and other ways, Hovland and Sears's research paved the way for further and more sophisticated investigations of the roots of prejudice—research that has continued without interruption ever since.

Early Experience: The Role of Social Learning

A second explanation for the origins of prejudice is straightforward: it suggests that prejudice is *learned* and that it develops through social learning—in much the same manner, and through the same basic mechanisms, as other attitudes (refer to our discussion in Chapter 4). According to this *social learning view*, children acquire negative attitudes toward various social groups because they hear such views expressed by parents, friends, teachers, and others, and because they are directly rewarded (with love, praise, and approval) for adopting these views. In addition to direct observation of others, *social norms*—rules within a given group suggesting what actions or attitudes are appropriate—are also important (Pettigrew, 1969). As we will see in Chapter 9, most persons choose to conform to most social norms of groups to which they belong. The development and expression of prejudice toward others often stems from this tendency. "If the members of my group dislike them," many children seem to reason, "then I should too!" (As we'll soon see, evidence that the members of one's group *like* persons belonging to another group that is the target of strong prejudice can also serve to weaken such negative reactions; e.g. Pettigrew, 1997; Wright et al., 1997).

The mass media also play a role in the development of prejudice. Until recently, members of various racial and ethnic minorities were shown infrequently

Figure 6.9
How the Mass Media Currently Represent People of Color.
The mass media in the United States represent African
Americans and other minority groups in a much more
favorable light today than was true in the past.

in movies or on television. And when they did appear, they were often cast in
low-status or comic roles. Fortunately, this situation has changed greatly in recent years in the United States and elsewhere. Members of various racial and
ethnic minorities are now shown in a considerably more favorable manner than
was true in the past—as heroes or heroines (see Figure 6.9) and as persons holding high-status positions, such as those of physician, scientist, attorney, general,
or president. So, while the mass media were certainly a source of prejudice in the
past, it seems reasonable to suggest that they are much less likely to play this
role at the present time.

Social Categorization: The Us-versus-Them Effect and the "Ultimate" Attribution Error

A third perspective on the origins of prejudice begins with a basic fact: People
generally divide the social world into two distinct categories—*us* and *them*. In
other words, they view other persons as belonging either to the **in-group** (their

in-group • The social group
to which an individual perceives herself or himself as
belonging ("us").

own group) or to an **out-group** (another group). Such **social categorization** takes place on many dimensions, including race, religion, sex, age, ethnic background, occupation, and income, to name just a few.

If the process of dividing the social world into "us" and "them" stopped there, it would have little bearing on prejudice. Unfortunately, however, it does not. Sharply contrasting feelings and beliefs are usually attached to members of one's in-group and members of various out-groups. Persons in the former (us) category are viewed in favorable terms, while those in the latter (them) category are perceived more negatively. Out-group members are assumed to possess more undesirable traits, are perceived as being more alike (more homogeneous) than members of the in-group, and are often disliked (Judd, Ryan, & Park, 1991; Lambert, 1995; Linville & Fischer, 1993). The in-group/out-group distinction also affects *attribution*—the ways in which we explain the actions of persons belonging to these two categories. We tend to attribute desirable behaviors by members of our in-group to stable, internal causes (e.g., their admirable traits), but to attribute desirable behaviors by members of out-groups to transitory factors or to external causes (Hewstone, Bond, & Wan, 1983). This tendency to make more favorable and flattering attributions about members of one's own group than about members of other groups is sometimes described as the **ultimate attribution error,** for it carries the self-serving bias we described in Chapter 2 into the area of intergroup relations—with potentially devastating effects.

That strong tendencies to divide the social world into "us" and "them" exist and color our perceptions of these groups has been demonstrated in many studies (e.g., Stephan, 1985; Tajfel, 1982). In one recent experiment (Harasty, 1997), for example, pairs of same-sex students discussed their own gender group or the other. Ratings of their discussion comments indicated that the students made more stereotypical and negative comments about the out-group (the other gender) than about their own group. Moreover, when they made negative comments about the out-group, these tended to be global in nature—"All men/women are like that!" These findings provide clear evidence for the negative effects that can follow when we divide the world into "us" and "them."

But how, precisely, does social categorization lead to prejudice? An intriguing answer has been provided by Tajfel and his colleagues (e.g, Tajfel & Turner, 1986; Vanbeselaere, 1991). These researchers suggest that individuals seek to enhance their self-esteem by identifying with specific social groups. This tactic can succeed, however, only to the extent that the persons involved perceive these groups as somehow superior to other, competing groups. Because all individuals are subject to the same tendencies, the final result is inevitable: Each group seeks to view itself as not only different from but better than its rivals, and prejudice arises out of this clash of social perceptions. Recent findings indicate that balanced against these tendencies is our desire to be fair-minded, and this may somewhat moderate our propensity to boost our own group and put other groups down (Singh, Choo, & Poh, 1998). However, existing evidence suggests that in general, the strong need to enhance our self-esteem wins out, and we see other groups as inferior to our own (e.g., Meindl & Lerner, 1985). In short, our tendency to divide the social world into two opposing camps often plays a role in the development of prejudice.

Do persons from all cultures tend to emphasize the differences between their in-group and various out-groups? And what happens if we discover that an out-group is similar in certain respects to our in-group? For information on these issues, see the *Social Diversity* section below.

out-group • Any group other than the one to which individuals perceive themselves as belonging.

social categorization • The tendency to divide the social world into two separate categories: one's in-group ("us") and various out-groups ("them").

ultimate attribution error • The tendency to make more favorable and flattering attributions about members of one's own group than about members of other groups.

Social Diversity: A Critical Analysis
Perceived Similarity to Out-groups: Russians' Reactions to Ukrainians, Moldavians, and Georgians

As we will see in Chapter 7, similarity often leads to liking: the more similar we perceive others as being to ourselves, the more we tend to like them. Does this apply to the distinction between in-groups and out-groups? At first glance it might seem that this would be the case. But, as we noted in our discussion of direct intergroup contact, social identity theory points to another possibility: Learning that out-group members are similar to us in various ways could threaten our self-esteem and cause us to evaluate these persons even *more* negatively (e.g., Tajfel, 1982).

Another possibility exists, however: Perhaps the relationship between degree of in-group/out-group similarity and prejudice is strongly determined by the extent to which an out-group is perceived as a *threat* to our own group. According to this theory, if an out-group is seen as a strong threat, then its similarity to us will induce negative reactions and cause us to like this group less. But if the out-group is not seen as a threat, then perhaps the similarity-leads-to-attraction effect will dominate, and perceived similarity to members of an out-group will cause us to evaluate that group more favorably (i.e., to show less in-group favoritism).

Several countries that emerged when the former Soviet Union collapsed offer a unique location in which to test these effects, because before 1991 they were all part of the same nation. Thus, in a sense, they were part of a single in-group. Since that date, however, these countries have been independent and, as such, have become out-groups for each other (see Figure 6.10). To test the hypothesis that evaluations of out-group members would vary as a function of both their degree of perceived similarity and the level of threat they posed to the in-group, Henderson-King and his colleagues (1997) asked several hundred students at a large Russian university to rate the traits of three out-groups: Ukrainians, Moldavians, and Georgians. Ratings were made on such dimensions as hostility, friendliness, intelligence, and greed. In addition, participants rated the extent to which each of these groups was similar to their own in-group (Russians). Finally, participants also rated the extent to which these three out-groups posed a threat to Russia, either externally or internally (as contributors to violence within Russia's borders).

Figure 6.10
When In-groups Become Out-groups. Before 1991 Russians, Moldavians, Ukrainians, and Georgians were all part of one country—the Soviet Union. Since that time, they have become independent countries and so, to an extent, are now out-groups for one another.

It was predicted that for out-groups that posed little or no threat to Russia, the greater their perceived similarity to Russians, the more favorably they would be rated (i.e., the less in-group bias participants would show). For out-groups that posed a threat, however, perceived similarity would result in less favorable evaluations. Results confirmed these predictions. For Ukrainians and Moldavians—groups that were *not* seen as a threat to Russia—higher perceived similarity led to less in-group bias. But for Georgians, a group that *was* seen as a threat to Russia, the opposite was true: Russians who felt threatened by this group showed increasing in-group bias as perceived similarity increased.

So, in sum, it appears that our reactions to out-groups are a function of both their degree of perceived similarity to us and the threat they seem to pose. As noted by Henderson-King and his colleagues (1997), these findings have implications not only for social groups within a given culture but, perhaps, for international relations as well.

Key Points

- Prejudice stems from several different sources. One of these is direct intergroup conflict—situations in which social groups compete for the same scarce resources.

- A second basis for prejudice is early experience, which often trains children to hate various groups.

- Prejudice also stems from our tendencies to divide the world into "us" and "them" and to view our own group much more favorably than various out-groups.

- Recent findings indicate that perceived similarity to an out-group can reduce prejudice toward its members unless the group is viewed as a threat.

Cognitive Sources of Prejudice: The Role of Stereotypes

Next, we come to potential sources of prejudice that are, in some respects, the most unsettling of all. These involve the possibility that prejudice stems, at least in part, from basic aspects of *social cognition*—the ways in which we think about other persons, store and integrate information about them, and later use this information to draw inferences about them or make social judgments. Because the influence of such factors has been at the very center of recent research on the origins of prejudice, we'll divide our discussion of this topic into two parts. First we'll examine the nature and operation of *stereotypes*—a key cognitive component in prejudice. Then we'll examine other cognitive mechanisms that also play a role in the occurrence of prejudice.

Stereotypes: What They Are and How They Operate. Consider the following groups: Korean Americans, homosexuals, Jews, Cuban Americans, African Americans, homeless people. Suppose you were asked to list the traits most characteristic of each. Would you find this to be a difficult task? Probably not. You would probably be able to construct a list for each group; and, moreover, you could probably do so *even for groups with whom you have had limited or no personal contact.* Why? The reason involves the existence and operation of **stereotypes**—cognitive frameworks consisting of knowledge and beliefs about specific social groups and the typical or "modal" traits supposedly possessed by persons belonging to these groups (Judd, Ryan, & Parke, 1991). Stereotypes suggest, in other words, that all persons belonging to social groups possess certain traits, at least to a degree. Once a stereotype is activated, these traits come readily to mind, and it is this fact that explains the ease with which you can probably construct lists like the ones mentioned above. You may not have had much direct experience with Korean Americans, Cuban Americans, Jews, or homeless people, but you *do* have stereotypes for them, so you can readily bring these to mind.

I (Robert Baron) encounter this aspect of stereotypes myself at virtually every party I attend. As soon as I tell a new acquaintance that I'm a psycholo-

stereotypes • Beliefs to the effect that all members of specific social groups share certain traits or characteristics. Stereotypes are cognitive frameworks that strongly influence the processing of incoming social information.

gist, I can almost see reflections in their eyes of their stereotypes about my field. "Hmm . . . I'd better watch what I say; he's probably analyzing everything. And I'd better not look him in the eye too much . . . he might read my mind or even hypnotize me!" That's the kind of thoughts many people seem to have.

Like other cognitive frameworks we have considered, stereotypes exert strong effects on how we process social information. Information relevant to an activated stereotype is often processed more quickly than information unrelated to it (e.g., Dovidio, Evans, & Tyler, 1986; Macrae et al., 1997). Similarly, stereotypes lead persons holding them to pay attention to specific types of information—usually, information consistent with the stereotypes. And when information *inconsistent* with stereotypes does manage to enter consciousness, it may be actively refuted or changed in subtle ways that make it seem *consistent* with the stereotype (Kunda & Oleson, 1995; O'Sullivan & Durso, 1984). For instance, research findings indicate that when we encounter information about someone who belongs to a group about which we have a stereotype and this information is inconsistent with the stereotype, we draw *tacit inferences* (conclusions and ideas not contained in the information) that change the meaning of this information to *make* it consistent with the stereotype (e.g., Kunda & Sherman-Williams, 1993). Clear evidence for such effects is provided by a thought-provoking series of studies conducted by Dunning and Sherman (1997).

These researchers presented college students with sentences describing fictitious people—sentences that, Dunning and Sherman reasoned, would be likely to generate tacit inferences (conclusions and ideas *not* contained in the sentences). Two versions of each sentence existed, each designed to activate a different stereotype. Here's a pair of examples: "The nun was unhappy about the amount of liquor being served at the party." "The rock musician was unhappy about the amount of liquor being served at the party." Presumably, upon seeing these sentences, participants would make tacit inferences concerning the amount of liquor in question—for instance, that the nun was unhappy because *too much* liquor was being served, while the rock musician was unhappy because *too little* liquor was being served.

After seeing these sentences, participants (who were simply told to try to form impressions of the persons described), were then shown additional sentences prompting inferences that were either consistent or inconsistent with the stereotypes activated. "The nun was unhappy about the large amount of liquor being served at the party" prompts an inference *consistent* with the stereotype for nuns, whereas "The rock musician was unhappy about the large amount of liquor being served at the party" prompts an inference *inconsistent* with the relevant stereotype. Participants' task concerning these new sentences was simple: to indicate whether they had or had not seen each sentence before. It was predicted that they would falsely report having seen more sentences generating stereotype-*consistent* inferences than sentences generating stereotype *inconsistent* inferences, and this is precisely what was found: they falsely recalled 35 percent of the former but only 15 percent of the latter. Additional studies indicated that such effects could occur for a wide range of stereotypes—for instance, ones relating to gender—and also that tacit inferences are made at the time that information relating to a stereotype is first encountered. Together, these findings led Dunning and Sherman (1997, p. 459), to describe stereotypes as *"inferential prisons"*: once they are formed, stereotypes shape our perceptions of other persons so that we interpret new information about these persons as confirming our stereotypes even if this not the case (see Figure 6.11 on page 228).

Unfortunately, additional findings from other research suggest that these inferential prisons are often largely of our own making. That is, we don't need

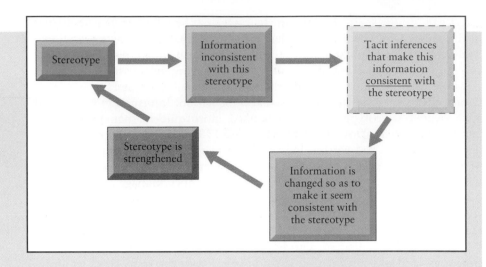

Figure 6.11
Stereotypes: Inferential Prisons? Once stereotypes exist, they strongly influence the way we process information relating to them. When we encounter information inconsistent with a stereotype, for instance, we formulate tacit inferences that make the information seem to fit with the stereotype.

external cues to activate our stereotypes—we switch them on ourselves (e.g., Macrae et al., 1992). In one recent study, for example, Whaley and Link (1998) asked more than fifteen hundred people living in large cities in the United States to estimate the percentages of homeless people who were African American, Hispanic, or simply male. Then they asked the same people to rate the extent to which homeless people were dangerous and lazy. The researchers predicted that the higher the participants' estimates of the proportion of homeless people who were black, the more strongly would a negative racial stereotype be activated, and thus the lazier and more dangerous homeless people would be perceived to be. Results confirmed these predictions, thus suggesting that merely estimating the frequency with which a stereotyped group is represented in a given population is sufficient to activate a negative stereotype about that group.

Two more points about stereotypes are worth noting. First, while you might assume that stereotypes exert stronger effects on the thinking of people who are "cognitively lazy" than on ones who actually enjoy thinking deeply and carefully, recent findings suggest that this is not so (Crawford & Skowronski, 1998). On the contrary, "deep-thinkers"—people high in what social psychologists term *need for cognition*—seem to remember *more* information consistent with their stereotypes than persons who don't enjoy effortful cognitive activity (persons low in need for cognition). Second, stereotypes can sometimes be activated spontaneously, without conscious effort or intention (e.g., Bargh, 1997). When we encounter persons belonging to a group for which we possess a stereotype, the stereotype may be activated and influence our thinking even if we don't want this to happen and are unaware that it *has* occurred. Such effects are often reduced if we are busy thinking about other things, because stereotypes require cognitive resources and if these are not available, the stereotypes can't come into play (e.g., Wittenbrink, Judd, & Park, 1997). However, recent findings indicate that after experiencing some threat to our self-esteem, stereotypes may be activated spontaneously even if we are cognitively busy because, as we noted earlier in this chapter, putting others down helps us to bolster our self-esteem (Spencer et al., 1998).

In addition to influencing the social thought of people who hold them, stereotypes can also influence the overt behavior of the persons toward whom they are directed. One of the most potentially damaging effects of this type is known as **stereotype threat**—the threat, perceived by persons who are the tar-

stereotype threat • The threat perceived by persons who are the target of stereotypes, that they will be evaluated in terms of these stereotypes.

get of stereotypes, that they will be evaluated in terms of these stereotypes (Steele, 1997). Concerns about stereotype threat may disrupt task performance in many contexts. For example, in one recent study on this possibility, Croizet and Claire (1998) had persons from high or low socioeconomic backgrounds work on a test that was described either as a measure of their intellectual ability or as a measure of the role of attention in memory. The researchers predicted that when the test was described as one of intellectual ability, this would induce anxiety about stereotype threat among persons from low socioeconomic background, who would fear that they would be evaluated in terms of a negative stereotype. Thus, individuals from low socioeconomic background would actually perform worse on the test than those from high socioeconomic background. When the test was described as a measure of attention, however, such differences would not occur. Results offered clear support for these predictions. Findings such as these suggest that the existence of stereotypes can indeed have harmful effects on the persons to whom they apply—effects that are quite distinct from those generated by discrimination against such persons.

Stereotypes and Prejudice.   That stereotypes exist and exert strong effects on social thought is clear. But are they closely related to prejudice? Surprisingly, until recently, evidence for the existence of this link was not as strong or clear as you might guess (e.g., Dovidio et al., 1996). Recent research using sophisticated techniques for measuring both stereotypes and prejudice, however, has yielded stronger results. For instance, consider a study by Kawakami and her colleagues (Kawakami et al., 1998).

These researchers exposed students at a large Canadian university to words designed to prime (activate) either racial stereotypes or no stereotypes: "Black," "White," and the letters CCC. These words were presented either for 0.3 seconds, a period too short to allow for controlled (i.e., careful) processing, or for 2.0 seconds, a period long enough for such processing to occur. Shortly after each of these words appeared on a computer screen, a second word that was related to a positive or negative racial stereotype for blacks appeared. Examples of words related to positive stereotypes included *athlete, musical, hip, funny, cool*; examples of words related to negative stereotypes included *aggressive, angry, poverty, criminal, welfare*. Participants were asked to say this second word out loud as quickly as possible. It was reasoned that the faster they said the stereotype-related words, the stronger the activation of racial stereotypes.

Kawakami and her colleagues (1998) predicted that if stereotypes are related to prejudice, then high- and low-prejudiced persons would differ in their responses to the stereotype-related words. Specifically, highly prejudiced persons would respond more quickly to stereotype-related words following the prime "Black" but more quickly to non-stereotype-related words following the prime "White." In contrast, no differences of this type would occur among low-prejudiced persons. To test this reasoning, the researchers obtained a measure of participants' racial prejudice. As shown in Figure 6.12 on page 230, their hypothesis was confirmed.

These results, and those of other studies (Lepore & Brown, 1997), suggest that stereotypes are indeed linked to prejudice. In other words, negative attitudes we hold toward various social groups can serve to activate negative stereotypes about them. Because these stereotypes then tilt our processing of new information about such groups toward confirming the stereotypes, an especially vicious circle in which prejudice activates stereotypes and stereotypes strengthen prejudice can occur—with dire consequences for the targets of

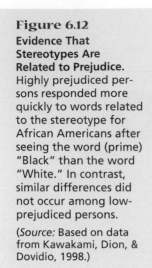

Figure 6.12

Evidence That Stereotypes Are Related to Prejudice. Highly prejudiced persons responded more quickly to words related to the stereotype for African Americans after seeing the word (prime) "Black" than the word "White." In contrast, similar differences did not occur among low-prejudiced persons.

(*Source:* Based on data from Kawakami, Dion, & Dovidio, 1998.)

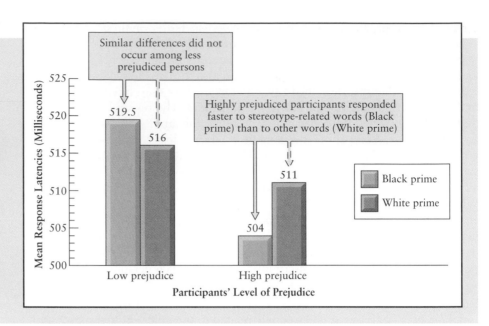

prejudice. As we noted at the start of this section, cognitive sources of prejudice are indeed, in some ways, the most disturbing of all.

Other Cognitive Mechanisms in Prejudice: Illusory Correlations and Out-group Homogeneity

Consider the following set of information: (1) There are 1,000 members of Group A but only 100 members of Group B; (2) 100 members of Group A were arrested by the police last year, and 10 members of Group B were arrested. Suppose you were asked to evaluate the criminal tendencies of these two groups. Would your ratings of them differ? Your first answer is probably "Of course not—why should they? The rate of criminal behavior is 10 percent in both groups, so why rate them differently?" Surprisingly, though, a large body of evidence suggests that you might actually assign a less favorable rating to Group B (Johnson & Mullen, 1994; McConnell, Sherman, & Hamilton, 1994). Social psychologists refer to these kinds of overestimations of the rate of negative behaviors in relatively small groups as **illusory correlations.** This term makes a great deal of sense, because such effects involve perceptions of links between variables that aren't really there—in this case, links between being a member of a Group B and the tendency to engage in criminal behavior.

As you can readily see, illusory correlations, to the extent they occur, have important implications for prejudice. In particular, they help explain why negative behaviors and tendencies are often attributed by majority group members to the members of various minority groups. For example, some social psychologists have suggested that illusory correlation effects help explain why many white persons in the United States overestimate crime rates among African American males (Hamilton & Sherman, 1989). For many complex reasons, young African American men are, in fact, arrested for various crimes at higher rates than young white men or men of Asian descent (United States Department of Justice, 1994). But white Americans tend to *overestimate* the size of this difference, and this can be interpreted as an illusory correlation.

Why do such effects occur? One explanation is based on the *distinctiveness* of infrequent events or stimuli. According to this view, infrequent events are dis-

illusory correlations • Perceived associations between variables that are stronger than actually exist; occur when each variable is distinctive so that the the co-occurrence of the variables is readily entered into and retrieved from memory.

tinctive—readily noticed. As such, they are encoded more extensively than other items when they are encountered, and so become more accessible in memory. When we make judgments about the groups involved at later times, therefore, the distinctive events come readily to mind, and this leads us to overinterpret their importance. Consider how this explanation applies to the tendency of white Americans to overestimate crime rates among African Americans. African Americans are a minority group (they constitute about 12 percent of the total population); thus, they are high in distinctiveness. Many criminal behaviors, too, are highly distinctive (relatively rare), despite the fact that their incidence has increased greatly in recent decades. When news reports show African Americans being arrested for crimes, therefore, this information is processed extensively and becomes highly accessible in memory. Thus, it is readily available at later times and may lead to the tendency to overestimate crime rates among minority groups—an instance of illusory correlation.

A large number of studies offer support for this *distinctiveness-based interpretation* of illusory correlations (Hamilton et al., 1989; Stroessner, Hamilton, & Mackie, 1992). However, other research findings indicate that this interpretation should be modified in at least one important respect. Apparently, it is not crucial that information be distinctive when it is first encountered; rather, information can *become* distinctive at later times and produce illusory correlations when this occurs (McConnell, Sherman, & Hamilton, 1994). It seems that we review and reconsider social information again and again, in the light of new input. As a result of this process, information that was not highly distinctive when it was first encountered may become distinctive at a later time. And if it does, it may then exert unduly strong effects on judgments relating to it; in other words, it may serve as a source of illusory correlation. In practical terms, this means that even if individuals don't extensively encode negative information about minority group members when they first receive it, they may go back and do so in the light of new and perhaps even more attention-getting news coverage of negative events. Then such information may produce illusory correlations: the tendency to overestimate the rate of negative behaviors among minority groups.

Interestingly, recent evidence (e.g., McConnell, Leibold, & Sherman, 1997) indicates that illusory correlations can exist not only for specific social groups and their supposed behaviors but also for specific contexts or settings in which behaviors take place. For instance, in a classic study conducted almost fifty years ago, Minard (1952) found that white coal miners held positive attitudes toward their black coworkers when in the mine, but negative attitudes about them when they encountered the same people in town. How could this be? One explanation is the operation of illusory correlations: white miners rarely encountered black miners in town (because of segregation), and they also rarely encountered undesirable behavior by other people. Thus, when they *did* encounter a black coworker showing such behavior (e.g., being drunk), an illusory correlation between race and these behaviors emerged. Research by McConnell, Leibold, and Sherman (1997) offers support for this reasoning, so it appears that the potential negative effects of illusory correlations may be even more general than was previously believed.

Out-group Homogeneity, In-group Differentiation: "They're All the Same"—or Are They? Persons who hold strong prejudice toward some social group often make remarks like these: "You know what they're like; they're all the same." What such comments imply is that the members of an out-group are much more similar to one another (more homogeneous) than the members of one's own group. This tendency to perceive persons belonging to groups other than one's own as all alike is known as the **illusion of out-group homogeneity** (Linville et

illusion of out-group homogeneity • The tendency to perceive members of out-groups as more similar to one another (less variable) than the members of one's own in-group.

al., 1989). The mirror image of this is **in-group differentiation**—the tendency to perceive members of our own group as showing much larger differences from one another (as being more heterogeneous) than those of other groups.

Existence of the illusion of out-group homogeneity has been demonstrated in many different contexts. For example, individuals tend to perceive persons older or younger than themselves as more similar to one another in terms of personal traits than persons in their own age group—an intriguing type of generation gap (Linville et al., 1989). Students even perceive students from another university as more homogeneous than those at their own university—especially when these persons appear to be biased against *them* (Rothgerber, 1997). Perhaps the most disturbing example of the illusion of out-group homogeneity, however, appears in the context of *cross-racial facial identification*—the tendency for persons belonging to one racial group to be more accurate in recognizing the faces of strangers from their own group than those of strangers from another racial group (e.g., Bothwell, Brigham, & Malpass, 1989). In the United States, this tendency has been observed among both African Americans and whites, although it appears to be somewhat stronger among whites (Anthony, Cooper, & Mullen, 1992).

What accounts for our tendency to perceive members of other groups as more homogeneous than members of our own group? One explanation may be that we have a great deal of experience with members of our own group, and so are exposed to a wider range of individual variation within that group. In contrast, we generally have much less experience with members of other groups, and hence less exposure to their individual variations (e.g., Linville et al., 1989). Whatever the precise basis for its existence (see, e.g., Lee & Ottati, 1993), the tendency to perceive other groups as more homogeneous than our own can play an important role in prejudice and in the persistence of negative stereotypes. Once we conclude that members of some disliked group are "all alike," there is little reason to seek contact with them—we expect to learn nothing from such encounters, and we also expect them to be unpleasant. So the illusion of out-group homogeneity provides yet another basis for both the development and the persistence of prejudice.

in-group differentiation •
The tendency to perceive members of one's own group as showing much larger differences from one another (as being more heterogeneous) than those of other groups.

Key Points

- Prejudice sometimes stems from basic aspects of social cognition—the ways in which we process social information.

- *Stereotypes* are cognitive frameworks suggesting that all persons belonging to a social group show similar characteristics. Stereotypes strongly influence social thought. For instance, when activated, they lead us to draw tacit inferences about others that then make information inconsistent with stereotypes seem to be consistent with them.

- Recent findings indicate that stereotypes are closely linked to prejudice; for example, highly prejudiced persons respond more quickly to stereotype-related words than less prejudiced persons.

- Other cognitive sources of prejudice include *illusory correlations*—overestimations of the strength of relationships between social categories and negative behaviors, and the *illusion of out-group homogeneity*—the tendency to perceive out-groups as more homogeneous than our own in-group.

WHY PREJUDICE IS *NOT* INEVITABLE: TECHNIQUES FOR COUNTERING ITS EFFECTS

Sad to relate, prejudice appears to be an all-too-common aspect of life in most, if not all, societies. Does this mean that it is inevitable? Or can prejudice, and the repulsive effects it produces, be eliminated—or at least reduced? Social psychologists are by nature an optimistic group, so they have generally approached this question from the following perspective: "Yes, prejudice *can* be reduced, and it is our job to find out how." Let's now take a look at several promising techniques for reducing prejudice.

Breaking the Cycle of Prejudice: On Learning *Not* to Hate

Few persons would suggest that children are born with prejudices firmly in place. Rather, most would contend that bigots are made, not born. Social psychologists share this view: they believe that children acquire prejudice from their parents, other adults, their peers, and—as we noted earlier—the mass media. Given this fact, one useful technique for reducing prejudice follows logically: somehow, we must discourage parents and other adults from training children in bigotry.

Having stated this principle, we must now admit that putting it into practice is far from simple. How can we induce parents who are themselves highly prejudiced to encourage unbiased views among their children (see Figure 6.13)? One possibility involves calling parents' attention to their own prejudiced views. Few persons are willing to describe themselves as prejudiced; instead, they view their own negative attitudes toward various groups as entirely justified. A key initial step, therefore, would be to convince parents that the problem exists. Once people come face to face with their own prejudices, many do seem willing to modify their words and behavior so as to encourage lower levels of prejudice among their children. True, some extreme fanatics actually *want* to

Figure 6.13
Breaking the Cycle of Hate. Can parents who are themselves highly prejudiced be encouraged to raise children who do not share their bigotry? This is a difficult task, but progress may be made if such parents realize that holding prejudiced views can adversely affect their children's future prospects at a time when many societies are becoming more culturally and ethnically diverse.

turn their children into hate-filled copies of themselves. Most people, however, recognize that we live in a world of increasing diversity and that this environment calls for a higher degree of tolerance than ever before.

Another argument that can be used to shift parents in the direction of teaching their children tolerance rather than prejudice lies in the fact that prejudice harms not only those who are its victims but those who hold such views as well (Dovidio & Gaertner, 1993; Jussim, 1991). Persons who are prejudiced, it appears, live in a world filled with needless fears, anxieties, and anger. They fear attack from presumably dangerous social groups; they worry about the health risks stemming from contact with such groups; and they experience anger and emotional turmoil over what they view as unjustified incursions by these groups into *their* neighborhoods, schools, or offices. In other words, their enjoyment of everyday activities and life itself is reduced by their own prejudice (Harris et al., 1992). Of course, offsetting such costs is the boost in self-esteem prejudiced persons sometimes feel when they derogate or scapegoat out-group members (see our earlier discussion of this topic) (Branscombe & Wann, 1994; Fein & Spenser, 1997). Overall, though, it is clear that persons holding intense racial and ethnic prejudices suffer many harmful effects from these views. Most parents want to do everything in their power to further their children's well-being, so calling these costs to parents' attention may help discourage them from transmitting prejudiced views to their offspring.

Direct Intergroup Contact: The Potential Benefits of Acquaintance

Many U.S. cities today resemble a social donut: a disintegrating and crime-ridden core inhabited primarily by minority groups, surrounded by a ring of relatively affluent suburbs inhabited mainly by whites and minority group members who have "made it" economically. Needless to say, contact between the people living in these different areas is minimal.

This state of affairs raises an intriguing question: Can we reduce prejudice by somehow increasing the degree of contact between different groups? The idea that we can is known as the **contact hypothesis,** and there are several good reasons for predicting that such a strategy might prove effective (Pettigrew, 1981, 1997). First, increased contact between persons from different groups can lead to a growing recognition of similarities between them. As we will see in Chapter 7, perceived similarity can generate enhanced mutual attraction. Second, while stereotypes are resistant to change, they *can* be altered when sufficient information inconsistent with them is encountered, or when individuals meet a sufficient number of "exceptions" to their stereotypes (Kunda & Oleson, 1995). Third, increased contact may help counter the illusion of out-group homogeneity described earlier. For these reasons, it seems possible that direct intergroup contact may be one effective means of combating prejudice. Is it? Existing evidence suggests that it is, but only when certain conditions are met. The groups interacting must be roughly equal in social status; the contact between them must involve cooperation and interdependence; the contact must permit them to get to know one another as individuals; norms favoring group equality must exist; and the persons involved must view one another as typical of their respective groups.

When contact between initially hostile groups occurs under these conditions, prejudice between them does seem to decrease (e.g., (Aronson, Bridgeman, & Geffner, 1978; Schwarzwald, Amir, & Crain, 1992). As you can readily see, however, such conditions are rare. Moreover, contact with persons from out-groups, especially when these groups are the target of strong prejudice,

contact hypothesis • The view that increased contact between members of various social groups can be effective in reducing prejudice between them; seems to be valid only when contact takes place under certain favorable conditions.

can generate negative emotions such as anxiety, discomfort, and fear of appearing to be prejudiced (Bodenhausen, 1993; Wilder, 1993). Such reactions can work against the potential benefits of contact. In view of such considerations, many social psychologists have voiced pessimism concerning the effectiveness of intergroup contact as a means of reducing prejudice. Recently, however, a modified version of the contact hypothesis, known as the extended contact hypothesis, has helped to reverse these gloomy conclusions.

The **extended contact hypothesis** suggests that direct contact between persons from different groups is not essential for reducing prejudice between them. In fact, such beneficial effects can be produced if the persons in question merely *know* that persons in their own group have formed close friendship with persons from the other group (e.g., Pettigrew, 1997; Wright et al., 1997). How can knowledge of such cross-group friendship help to reduce prejudice? In several different ways. For instance, knowledge of such friendship can indicate that contact with out-group members is acceptable—that the norms of one's own group are not so anti-out-group as one might initially have believed. Similarly, knowing that members of one's own group enjoy close friendships with members of an out-group can help to reduce anxiety about interacting with them: if someone we know enjoys such contact, why shouldn't we? Third, the existence of such cross-group friendships suggests that members of an out-group don't necessarily dislike members of our own in-group. Finally, such friendships can indirectly generate increased empathy and understanding between groups; in other words, we don't necessarily have to experience personal contact with persons from an out-group to feel more positively toward them—learning that members of our own in-group have had such experiences can be sufficient.

A growing body of research evidence provides support for the accuracy of this reasoning, and for the extended contact hypothesis. For instance, in one investigation of this hypothesis (Pettigrew, 1997), almost four thousand people living in several European countries completed a questionnaire that measured the extent to which these people had friendships with others outside their own cultural group, their level of prejudice toward out-groups generally, their beliefs about immigration, and their feelings toward a very wide range of ethnic and cultural groups (e.g., people from various European countries, North Africans, Turks, black Africans, Asians, West Indians, Jews). Results offered striking support for the benefits of intergroup friendships. The greater the number of cross-group friendships participants reported, the lower their prejudice toward various out-groups and the more favorable their beliefs about immigration into their country. In addition, the greater their experience with intergroup friendships, the more positive their feelings toward many other groups—including ones with which they had experienced little or no contact. This latter finding is very important, for it suggests that reductions in prejudice produced by friendships with persons from one out-group may generalize to other out-groups as well, and then provide some support for the extended contact hypothesis.

Additional support for the value of intergroup friendships is provided by laboratory as well as survey research. For example, in one ingenious study, Wright and his colleagues (1997) arranged for students to participate in a study that was similar in certain respects to the famous "Robber's Cave" experiment described earlier in this chapter. Briefly, the researchers divided the students into teams, which, after an initial period designed to create within-team solidarity, competed against each other on several tasks. After these competitions, one person from each team took part in an exercise designed to generate strong feelings of friendship with a person from the opposing team (e.g., the two contact persons engaged in mutual self-disclosure and other relationship-building

extended contact hypothesis • A view suggesting that simply knowing that members of one's own group have formed close friendships with members of an out-group can reduce prejudice against this group.

activities). The other team members worked on filler tasks unrelated to the study during this time. Afterwards, the contact persons reported back to their own teams and described their experiences to the other members. Finally, the teams competed against each other once again.

During the experiment (which lasted all day), participants completed measures of their reactions to the other team on several occasions—after the initial team-building phase, after the first set of competitions, and again after the two team members who formed a friendship returned to the team. It was predicted that the comments these persons made to their teammates about their new intergroup friendship would reduce prejudice toward the opposing team, and this is what happened. For example, one of the measures of prejudice involved each team's dividing an imaginary $500 prize between themselves and the opposing team. The tendency to take most of the money for one's own team dropped sharply after the teams learned about the intergroup friendship formed by one of their members (see Figure 6.14). Similar results occurred for ratings of the quality of the interactions between the groups and for ratings of the other team with respect to several traits (e.g., friendliness, warmth).

In sum, it appears that contact between persons belong to different groups can be a highly effective means for reducing prejudice between them, especially if these contacts develop into friendships. Moreover, the beneficial effects of such friendships can readily spread to other persons who have not themselves experienced such contacts: simply knowing about them can be enough. In other words, merely learning that some people in one's own group get along well with persons belonging to other groups can be a highly effective way to reduce the hateful effects of prejudice. So in this respect, at least, English essayist Joseph Addison appears to have been correct when he stated, more than two centuries ago (1794), that "The greatest sweetener of human life is friendship."

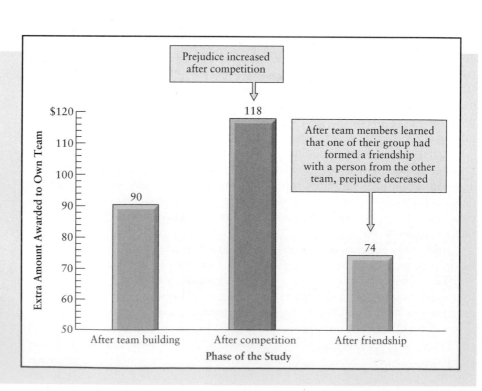

Figure 6.14
Evidence for the Extended Contact Effect. When members of opposing teams learned that a person on their own team had formed a friendship with a person from the other team, their prejudice toward the opposing group decreased. For example, as shown here, they showed less tendency to take more than their fair share of a financial prize.

(*Source:* Based on data from Wright et al., 1997.)

> ### Key Points
>
> - Social psychologists believe that prejudice is not inevitable; it can be reduced by several techniques.
> - One approach involves changing children's early experiences so that they are not taught bigotry by their parents and other adults.
> - Another technique involves direct contact between persons from different groups. When this occurs under certain conditions, prejudice can be reduced.
> - Recent findings indicate that simply knowing that members of one's own group have formed friendships with members of an out-group may be sufficient to reduce prejudice; this is known as the *extended contact hypothesis*.

Recategorization: Redrawing the Boundary between "Us" and "Them"

Think back to your high school days. Imagine that your school's basketball team was playing an important game against a rival school from a nearby town or neighborhood. In this case, you would certainly view your own school as "us" and the other school as "them." But now imagine that the other school's team won, and went on to play against a team from another state or province in a national tournament. *Now* how would you view them? The chances are good that under these conditions, you would view the other school's team as "us"; after all, it represents your state or province. And of course, if a team from a state or province other than your own was playing against teams from other countries, you might now view it as "us" relative to those "foreigners."

Situations like this, in which we shift the boundary between "us" and "them," are quite common in everyday life, and they raise an interesting question: Can such shifts—or **recategorizations,** as they are termed by social psychologists—be used to reduce prejudice? A theory proposed by Gaertner and his colleagues (1989, 1993b) suggests that it can. This theory, known as the **common in-group identity model,** suggests that when individuals belonging to different social groups come to view themselves as members of a *single social entity,* their attitudes toward one another become more positive. These favorable attitudes then promote increased positive contacts between members of the previously separate groups, and this in turn reduces intergroup bias still further. In short, weakening or eliminating initial us–them boundaries starts a process that carries the persons involved toward major reductions in prejudice and hostility (see Figure 6.15 on page 238)

How can this process be launched? In other words, how can we induce people belonging to different groups to perceive one another as members of a single group? Gaertner and his colleagues (1990) suggest that one crucial factor is the experience of working together cooperatively. When individuals belonging to initially distinct groups work together toward shared goals, they come to perceive themselves as a single social entity. Then feelings of bias or hostility toward the former out-group—toward "them"—seem to fade away, taking prejudice with them. Such effects have been demonstrated in several studies, both in the laboratory and the field (e.g., Brewer et al., 1987; Gaertner et al., 1989, 1990, 1993b), so it appears that recategorization can be another useful technique for reducing many kinds of prejudice.

recategorization • Shifts in the boundary between an individual's in-group ("us") and some out-group ("them"), causing persons formerly viewed as out-group members now to be viewed as belonging to the in-group.

common in-group identity model • Theory suggesting that to the extent that individuals in different groups view themselves as members of a single social entity, positive contacts between them will increase and intergroup bias will be reduced.

Figure 6.15
When "Them" Becomes "Us," Prejudice Decreases. When individuals shift the boundary between "us" and "them" so as to include people previously excluded, processes that lead to major reductions in prejudice may be set in motion.

Cognitive Interventions: When Stereotypes Shatter—or at Least Become Less Compelling

Throughout this chapter, we have noted that stereotypes play an important role in prejudice. The tendency to think about others in terms of their membership in various groups or categories (a tendency known as *category-driven processing*) appears to be a key factor in the occurrence and persistence of several forms of prejudice. If this is so, then interventions designed to reduce the impact of stereotypes may prove highly effective in reducing prejudice and discrimination. How can this goal be attained? Several techniques seem to be useful.

First, the impact of stereotypes can be reduced if individuals are encouraged to think carefully about others—to pay attention to their unique characteristics rather than to their membership in various groups. Research findings indicate that such *attribute-driven processing* can be encouraged even by such simple procedures as informing individuals that their own outcomes or rewards in a situation will be affected by another's performance, or telling them that it is very important to be accurate in forming an impression of another person. Under these conditions, individuals are motivated to be accurate, and this reduces their tendency to rely on stereotypes (Neuberg, 1989).

Second, the impact of stereotypes can sometimes be reduced by techniques based on principles of attribution (see Chapter 2) (Mackie et al., 1992). How do such procedures work? Several are based on the fact that often, we make inferences about others on the basis of their outcomes, while ignoring factors that might have produced these outcomes (Allison, Worth, & King, 1990). For example, suppose you learn that a stranger scored 70 on an exam and that 65 was passing. Thus, the outcome is "Passed." In contrast, suppose you learn that 75 was passing and that the person scored 70; here, the outcome is "Failed." If you were asked to rate this person's intelligence or motivation, the chances are good that you would assign higher ratings in the first instance than in the second, despite the fact that in both cases the stranger's performance was *identical*. This illustrates our strong tendency to base inferences about others on their outcomes.

Now let's apply this to prejudice, and to the task of countering stereotypes. Suppose you learn that a woman was promoted to a high-level managerial job in a large company. The outcome is clear: she was promoted. Will this outcome influence your estimations of her talent or motivation? Again, the chances are good that it will and—crucially—that this would be the case *even if you learned that her company has a strong affirmative action program and actively seeks to promote women and minorities.* In cases such as this, our tendency to base our inferences about others on their outcomes can lead us to conclusions that are *counterstereotypic* in nature; and the result may be a weakening of the stereotypes involved. Effects of this type have been reported in several different studies (e.g., Mackie et al., 1992), and they suggest a complex but effective means of weakening various stereotypes.

This effect has important implications for efforts to reduce prejudice through *affirmative action programs*. These programs are designed to improve the outcomes of people in various groups who were previously the victims of discrimination by increasing the chances that they will obtain such benefits as jobs and promotions. To the extent that such outcomes improve, perceptions of the characteristics of these groups, too, may improve. In other words, our tendency to base inferences about others on the outcomes they receive may lead us to perceive members of these groups as higher in talent, motivation, and intelligence than was the case before they experienced these outcomes. In a sense, this is a case of "fighting fire with fire"—using a basic tilt in our attributions to reduce the impact of harmful social stereotypes.

For an overview of techniques useful in combating prejudice, please see the *Ideas to Take with You* feature on page 249.

Key Points

- Prejudice can sometimes be reduced through *recategorization*—shifting the boundary between "us" and "them" so as to include former out-groups in the "us" category.
- Cognitive techniques for reducing prejudice are also effective. These focus on reducing the impact of stereotypes on social thought.
- Inducing individuals to focus on others' specific traits and outcomes rather than on their group membership helps reduce stereotypes' impact on social thought.

PREJUDICE BASED ON GENDER: ITS NATURE AND EFFECTS

More than half of the world's population is female. Yet despite this fact, in many cultures females have been treated like a minority group. They have been excluded from economic and political power; they have been the subject of strong negative stereotypes; and they have faced overt discrimination in many areas of life—work settings, higher education, government (Fisher, 1992; Heilman, Block, & Lucas, 1992). In the late 1990s, this situation is changing in at least some countries and to some degree. Overt discriminatory practices have been banned by laws in many nations, and there has been at least some weakening of negative gender-based stereotypes. Yet such progress has been spotty at best, and **sexism**—prejudice based on gender—continues to exert harmful effects upon females in many countries (e.g., Kanekar, Kolswalla, & Nazareth, 1988). Because prejudice based on gender affects more individuals than any other single kind (more than half the human race) and produces negative outcomes for males as well as females, we will consider it here in detail.

sexism • Prejudice based on gender.

Gender Stereotypes: The Cognitive Core of Sexism

Females have often been the object of strong, persistent stereotypes, as we saw in Chapter 5. To an extent, so have males: they too are perceived as being "all alike" with respect to certain traits—and in many cultures, woe to the male who fails to live up to these stereotypes (Aube & Koestner, 1993). But stereotypes about females are, by and large, more negative in content than those about males. For example, in many cultures males are assumed to possess such desirable traits as *decisiveness, forcefulness, confidence, ambition,* and *rationality.* In contrast, the corresponding assumptions about females include less desirable traits such as *passivity, submissiveness, indecisiveness, emotionality,* and *dependence* (Deaux, 1993b; Unger, 1994).

Are such **gender stereotypes** accurate? Do men and women really differ in the ways these stereotypes suggest? This question is complex, for such differences between the sexes, even if observed, may be more a reflection of the impact of stereotypes and their self-confirming nature than of basic differences between females and males. Existing evidence, however, points to the following conclusion: *There are indeed some differences between males and females with respect to various aspects of behavior, but in general the magnitude of such differences is much smaller than prevailing gender stereotypes suggest* (e.g., Bettancourt & Miller, 1996; Voyer, Voyer, & Bryden, 1995) (see Figure 6.16).

"An excellent defense. Let's give her the doctorate."

Figure 6.16

Gender Stereotypes: Often Inaccurate. Gender stereotypes suggest that females are passive and males are active and aggressive. As suggested by this cartoon, such stereotypes are often inaccurate and falsely exaggerate differences between females and males.

(Source: The New Yorker.)

gender stereotypes •
Stereotypes concerning the traits supposedly possessed by females and males, which distinguish the two genders from each other.

The fact that gender stereotypes are inaccurate to a large degree, however, does not prevent them from exerting harmful effects—for example, from preventing females from obtaining some jobs (Van Vianen & Willemsen, 1992), some promotions (Stroh, Brett, & Riley, 1992), and equal pay for the jobs they do obtain (Lander, 1992). How do gender stereotypes exert these negative effects? This is the question to which we turn next.

Key Points

- *Sexism*—prejudice based on gender—affects more than half the human race.
- At the core of sexism are *gender stereotypes*—cognitive frameworks suggesting that males and females possess sharply different patterns of traits and behavior
- Existing evidence suggests that while males and females do differ in some respects, gender stereotypes greatly exaggerate these differences.

Discrimination against Females: Subtle but Often Deadly

In the late 1990s, overt discrimination on the basis of gender is illegal in many countries. As a result, businesses, schools, and social organizations no longer reject applicants for jobs or admission simply because they are female (or male). Despite this fact, females continue to occupy a relatively disadvantaged position in many societies in certain respects. They are concentrated in low-paying, low-status jobs (A. B. Fisher, 1992); and their average salary remains lower than that for males, even in the same occupations. Why is this the case? One possibility is that sufficient time has not passed for women to realize the full benefits of the changes that occurred during the 1970s and 1980s. Another possibility—one supported by a large body of research evidence—is that while overt barriers to female advancement have largely disappeared, other, more subtle forces continue to operate against women in many contexts. We'll now review several of these.

The Role of Expectations. One factor impeding the progress of females involves their own expectations. In general, women seem to hold lower expectations about their careers than men. They expect to receive lower starting and peak salaries (Jackson, Gardner, & Sullivan, 1992; Major & Konar, 1984). And they view lower salaries for females as being somehow fair (Jackson & Grabski, 1988). Why do females hold these lower expectations? Research findings (e.g., Jackson et al., 1992) indicate that several factors play a role.

First, females expect to take more time out from work (for example, to spend with their children); this tends to lower their expectations for peak career salaries. Second, women realize that females do generally earn less than males. Thus, their lower expectations may simply reflect their recognition of current reality and its likely impact on their own salaries. Third, as we noted earlier, women tend to perceive relatively low levels of pay as more fair than males do. (Jackson et al., 1992). Finally, and perhaps most important, women tend to compare themselves with other women; and because women earn less than men in many instances, this leads them to conclude that they aren't doing too badly after all (Major, 1989). Whatever the specific basis for women's lower salary expectations, it is a fact of life that in general people tend to get what they expect or what they request. Thus, females' lower expectations with respect to such outcomes may be one important factor operating against them in many contexts.

The Role of Confidence and Self-Perceptions. Confidence, it is often said, is the single best predictor of success. People who expect to succeed often do; those who expect to fail find *that* prediction confirmed. Unfortunately, women tend to express lower self-confidence than men in many achievement-related situations. This may be one reason why almost 10 percent of the executives who responded to one survey reported believing that females are not as aggressive or as determined to succeed as males (Lander, 1992). In short, women are less self-confident than men in at least some situations, and other persons notice these differences. This, in turn, may contribute to the fact that they have not yet attained full equality with men in many work settings.

We should quickly add that such effects do not occur in all contexts. Recent findings reported by Beyer and Bowden (1997), for instance, indicate that females do tend to underestimate their own abilities and performance with respect to masculine tasks—ones in which they expect men to have an edge (e.g., answering questions relating to sports). However, they do *not* show such effects with respect to tasks in which females are expected to excel (e.g., answering questions about TV shows or movies) or tasks that are gender-neutral (e.g., tests of common knowledge, such as "In what U.S. city is the United Nations located?"). So, while relatively low self-confidence or inaccurately negative self-perceptions may adversely affect females in some contexts, the potential impact of this factor should not be overemphasized.

Negative Reactions to Female Leaders. In the late 1990s, most people agree that females can definitely be effective leaders. Women have been elected to major offices (prime minister, senator), have been appointed as senior judges (e.g., to the Supreme Court of the United States), hold high ranks in the military, and—in a few cases—head major companies and organizations. But how do people react to female leaders? Do they hold them in equally high regard and evaluate them as favorably as men? The answer to both questions appears to be no. First, although subordinates often *say* much the same things to female and male leaders, they may actually demonstrate more negative *nonverbal behaviors* toward female leaders (Butler & Geis, 1990). Moreover, such differences occur even when individuals strongly deny any bias against females.

Perhaps even more disturbing than this is the fact that when females serve as leaders, they tend to receive lower evaluations from subordinates than males do (Butler & Geis, 1990; Eagly, Makhijani, & Klonsky, 1992). This is especially true for female leaders who adopt a style of leadership viewed as stereotypically masculine (autocratic, directive), in fields where most leaders are males, and when the persons who evaluate the leaders are males. These findings suggest that females continue to face subtle disadvantages even when they do obtain positions of leadership and authority (Kent & Moss, 1994). (We'll return to the topic of *leadership* in Chapter 13.)

The Glass Ceiling—and Above: Why Women Don't Rise to the Top. Between the 1970s and the 1990s, the proportion of managers who are female rose from 16 percent to more than 42 percent (U.S. Department of Labor, 1992). Yet the proportion of *top* managers who are women increased only from 3 percent to 5 percent (Glass Ceiling Commission, 1995; Woody & Weiss, 1994). These facts have led many authors to suggest the existence of a **glass ceiling**—a final barrier that prevents females, as a group, from reaching the top positions in many organizations. More formally, the U.S. Department of Labor has defined the glass ceiling as "those artificial barriers based on attitudinal or organizational bias that prevent qualified individuals from advancing upward in their organization" (U.S. Department of Labor, 1991).

glass ceiling • Barriers based on attitudinal or organizational bias that prevent qualified females from advancing to top-level positions.

Is the glass ceiling real? And if so, why does it occur? Existing evidence on these issues presents something of a mixed picture. On the one hand, as we noted in Chapter 5, several studies suggest that women do experience less favorable outcomes in their careers than men because of their gender (e.g., Heilman, 1995; Morrison, 1992). On the other hand, however, additional findings point to two more encouraging conclusions.

First, if the glass ceiling exists, it does not appear to be the result of conscious efforts on the part of male executives to keep women out of their domain (Powell & Butterfield, 1994). Rather, more subtle factors seem to produce this effect. For example, females may receive fewer opportunities to develop their skills and competency than males—opportunities that prepare them for top-level jobs (Ohlott, Ruderman, & McCauley, 1994). For instance, females report fewer chances than males to take part in projects that increase their visibility or widen the scope of their responsibilities. In short, they are not given the kind of work assignments that teach them new skills and, at the same time, permit them to demonstrate their competence. In addition, females report encountering more obstacles in their jobs: they note that it is harder to find personal support, that they are often left out of important networks, and that they have to fight hard to be recognized for excellent work (Ohlott et al., 1994).

Second, some recent findings can be viewed as suggesting that the glass ceiling has been, if not shattered, at least dented. The clearest evidence in this respect has been reported by Lyness and Thompson (1997). These researchers compared the outcomes and experiences of female and male executives in a large company. Executives of both genders provided information on their salaries and bonuses, the number of people they supervised, their past developmental opportunities, obstacles they had encountered, and previous career interruptions. While it was predicted that female and male executives would differ in all these respects, very few differences between the two groups actually emerged. Females did supervise fewer subordinates, had more career interruptions, and reported more obstacles (e.g., difficulty trying to influence other people without the needed authority to back up such attempts). But they did *not* differ from their male colleagues in terms of salary, bonuses, developmental opportunities, or ability to fit into the male-dominated organizational culture (see Figure 6.17 on page 244).

Why did this large-scale study fail to uncover evidence for the kind of glass ceiling seen in previous research (e.g., Glass Ceiling Commission, 1995)? Lyness and Thompson (1997) suggest that in part this result may have been due to the fact that they closely matched the female and male samples in their study. In past research, the male and female employees studied may have differed in various ways, such as in holding different jobs or working in different organizations. In contrast, all the participants in this study worked in a single large company, and the researchers made vigorous efforts to match the females and males as closely as possible in all respects—except, of course, gender. In addition, Lyness and Thompson (1997) note that the female executives in their study were all ones who were very high in competence; their median salary, after all, was close to $170,000! So perhaps these were women who had already passed through the glass ceiling by virtue of exceptional competence. This barrier may still exist for other, less exceptional females, however.

In addition, it's important to note that some of the differences this study did uncover are quite disturbing. For instance, the female executives supervised fewer persons than did their male counterparts—a sign that they had less power or authority. Similarly, they reported having encountered more obstacles on their way to the top than did males. Finally, when asked to estimate their future career opportunities, the females responded less optimistically than the males. Given that the two groups were so closely matched in many respects other than

Figure 6.17
Female Executives: Have They Made It through the Glass Ceiling? Recent findings suggest that highly competent females do sometimes manage to break thorugh the "glass celing" and obtain high-level positions in at least some companies.

gender, these differences suggest that while the glass ceiling may have been breached, a second, higher ceiling may still exist and operate against even exceptionally competent females. Only further research can resolve this question, but one point seems clear: Major change has occurred in many work settings in recent years, and at least some of these changes appear to be ones that have lessened, if not eliminated, barriers to females' success.

Sexual Harassment: When Discrimination Hits Rock Bottom

During 1997 and 1998, citizens of the United States were exposed to a sad spectacle: several women came forward to accuse President Clinton of having engaged in **sexual harassment** against them (see Figure 6.18). They claimed that the president had engaged in actions that met the legal definition of this term: unwelcome sexual advances, requests for sexual favors, and other verbal or physical conduct of a sexual nature under conditions where:

1. Submission to such conduct is made either explicitly or implicitly a term or condition of employment;

2. Submission to or rejection of such conduct by an individual is used as a basis for employment decisions affecting that individual; and/or

3. Such conduct has the purpose or effect of unreasonably interfering with an individual's work performance or creating an intimidating, hostile, or offensive working environment.

These charges, with which newspapers, magazines, and television had a field day, served to underscore the fact that sexual harassment is an all-too-common occurrence. In fact, more than 30 percent of employed women responding to

sexual harassment • Unwelcome sexual advances, requests for sexual favors, and other verbal or physical conduct of a sexual nature.

Figure 6.18

Sexual Harassment: Present Even in the White House? In 1997 and 1998 several women claimed that President Clinton had sexually harassed them. Debate over whether these charges were accurate still continues.

one poll indicated that they had been the object of such harassment on at least one occasion (BNA's *Employee Relations Weekly*, 1994). In contrast, only 7 percent of male respondents to the same survey indicated that they had been the victim of such actions. It's important to note, by the way, that sexual harassment is not restricted to extreme actions such as physically assaulting a coworker or threatening an employee with firing if she or he doesn't grant sexual favors. On the contrary, in the United States sexual harassment can involve any actions of a sexual nature that create a hostile work environment for employees—posting offensive pinups, staring at portions of a coworkers' anatomy, making repeated remarks about someone's appearance. In short, a boss or fellow employee doesn't have to request sexual favors or make these a condition of employment to commit sexual harassment: many other forms of behavior meet the legal definition.

Fortunately, recognition of sexual harassment as a problem has increased greatly in recent years, with the result that many organizations have established clear policies against such behavior and have taken other steps to lessen its occurrence. Several of these steps are summarized in Table 6.1 on page 246 (Bohren, 1993). Growing evidence suggests that together, such steps can be quite effective in reducing the incidence of this detestable form of discrimination and so in protecting the psychological and physical welfare of tens of millions of employees—men as well as women.

Just what constitutes sexual harassment in a given setting? Aside from the legal definition, this is partly a matter of social perception: actions are sexually harassing when they are perceived as such. But what factors determine the extent to which a given action is perceived as sexual harassment? A theory known as **sex-role spillover theory** makes some interesting predictions (e.g., Fitzgerald, 1993; Gutek, 1985). According to this framework, women working in certain environments—ones in which most of the employees are males—will be more likely to experience sexual harassment than ones working in more traditional environments for females. And yet people will tend to view such harassment, when it occurs, as less threatening or coercive than it would be in traditional

sex-role spillover theory • A theory suggesting that females working in nontraditional jobs will be seen as "role deviates" and so as more appropriate targets for sexual harassment.

Table 6.1

Steps for Reducing Sexual Harassment at Work. There is general agreement that the steps shown here can be useful in reducing the frequency of sexual harassment in many work settings.

Step or Policy	Description
Develop a clear policy prohibiting sexual harassment.	This policy should describe in detail what is meant by sexual harassment; it should also note that the company will not tolerate such behavior.
Train all employees to understand what sexual harassment is and how to avoid it.	Employees should receive training that will help them become sensitive to the possible ways in which they may be offending others without meaning to do so.
Set up clear grievance procedures.	The persons to whom complaints should be made should be clearly identified and readily available.
Specify in advance how the company will treat offenders and *strictly* enforce this policy.	The consequences of engaging in sexual harassment should be stated clearly and enforced *vigorously*.

(*Source:* Based on suggestions by Bohren, 1993.)

environments. Why? Because women working in nontraditional settings where most employees are male will be perceived as *role deviates*—people who depart from traditional roles. Exposure to sexual harassment may then be seen by males as part of the price women must pay for access to such fields.

Burgess and Borgida (1997) tested these predictions in a study in which men and women read descriptions of incidents of sexual harassment against women occurring in traditional (secretarial) or nontraditional (steelworking) occupations for females. The sexual harassment took several forms: unwanted sexual attention (a male employee tells a female employee how "hot" she is), gender harassment (a male employee puts an obscene centerfold on a female's desk), or sexual coercion (a male employee indicates that if a female doesn't go out with him, she will regret it). In addition, each form of harassment did or did not involve physical actions (e.g., touching, grabbing, fondling).

After reading these descriptions, participants rated the extent to which the incidents involved sexual harassment, indicated how they felt the female employee's supervisor should handle the situation, and indicated what the female should do about it. As expected, males and females differed in their perceptions of the incidents. For instance, females rated all the incidents as more harassing than did males, and rated all three types as harassing. Males, in contrast, rated sexual coercion as significantly more harassing than the other forms. The most interesting findings, however, involved reactions to these incidents as a function of the victim's occupation. As expected, both males and females perceived sexual coercion as less threatening and less coercive when the female target worked in a nontraditional occupation than in a traditional one. So, as noted above, judgments about what is and what is not sexually harassing are influenced by several factors and are, at least to some extent, in the eye of the beholder. For further discussion of the complex issues related to sexual harassment, see the following *Beyond the Headlines* section.

Beyond the Headlines:
As Social Psychologists See It
Can a Lecture Be Sexually Harrassing?

WAS PROF'S LECTURE ACADEMIC FREEDOM OR
SEX HARASSMENT? A MALE STUDENT IRKED BY
"MALE-BASHING" ASSERTS IT WAS THE LATTER

Sacramento, California, March 7, 1995—Craig Rogers and scores of other students walked into a Psychology 100 class . . . expecting a guest lecture on issues like TV violence. Instead, Joanne Marrow, a tenured professor and lesbian activist, launched into a lecture on one of her life's goals: to empower women to masturbate so they can overcome the "hardship" of sex with men.

Mr. Rogers, 33 years old, cringed . . . as the professor's lecture presented personal sex tales, how-to tips, and close-up slides of women's genitals. . . . She went on to describe how she bought autoerotic sex devices for her sisters for Christmas, and invited students to ask her after class for copies of a sex-toys catalog. . . . At one point, Prof. Marrow showed slides of a mother's genitals, followed by slides of the woman's two young daughters. . . . Jean Finley, a 45-year-old mother in the class, says she steamed as Ms. Marrow pointed at photos of a woman's genitals before and after pregnancy, to show how giving birth "mutilates" women's bodies. "It's like she wants to take the pleasure away from male and female partners. She has an almost hatred for men," remarked Ms. Finley.

Was Professor Marrow's lecture sexual harassment or just the exercise of academic freedom? Opinions differ strongly. Craig Rogers has filed a $2.5 million sexual-harassment claim. His attorney, Kathleen Smith, suggests that Professor Marrow went too far; she adds that a male professor who delivered a lecture demeaning to women would certainly be punished. In contrast, Professor Marrow's attorney, John Poswall, suggests that Rogers wants to "put sexuality back in the closet."

Who's correct? Because Rogers and his classmates were required to attend the lecture (five questions on it were included on the final exam) and felt that it created a very hostile environment for the male students, Professor Marrow's lecture does seem to meet the legal definition of sexual harassment: it created an intimidating, hostile, or offensive work environment. On the other hand, Professor Marrow's remarks were not directed against Rogers specifically, and she was only a guest lecturer in the class—not the regular professor. As far as we know, the case has not yet been decided by the courts; but if nothing else, it does seem to illustrate the many complexities involved in decisions about what is and what is not sexual harassment. Legal codes and definitions aside, such behavior ultimately relates to human relationships. And where these are concerned, as we've noted repeatedly, simple, concrete answers are often very difficult to obtain.

Key Points

- Although blatant forms of discrimination based on gender have decreased, females continue to be adversely affected by more subtle forms.

- Gender-based obstacles include lower expectations by females, inaccurately low self-confidence and self-perceptions, negative reactions to female leaders, and the glass ceiling.

- *Sexual harassment* constitutes one very disturbing form of discrimination against females. Recent findings indicate that males and females differ somewhat in their perceptions of what constitutes sexual harassment. Research also indicates that women working in nontraditional fields for females are at greater risk of experiencing such treatment.

Connections: Integrating Social Psychology

In this chapter, you read about . . .	*In other chapters, you will find related discussions of . . .*
stereotypes as mental shortcuts—one means of saving cognitive effort	heuristics and other mental shortcuts (Chapters 3, 4)
the role of frustration (economic hard times) in prejudice and racial violence	the role of frustration in aggression and conflict (Chapter 11)
the tendency to divide the social world into "us" and "them" and its effects	other effects of group membership (Chapter 12)
the effects of perceived similarity on prejudice	the effects of perceived similarity on attraction (Chapter 7)
evaluations of female leaders	other aspects of leadership (Chapter 13)
sexual harassment in work settings	other aspects of social behavior in work settings (Chapter 13)

Thinking about Connections

1. Some observers suggest that as open forms of discrimination have decreased, more subtle forms have increased. In other words, they believe that the attitudes underlying discrimination remain unchanged (see Chapter 4), and that only overt behavior relating to these attitudes has changed. What do you think? If there *has* been a drop in overt discrimination, is it related to real changes in intergroup attitudes?

2. Some evidence indicates that prejudice persists because it produces benefits for the people who hold it (e.g., it boosts their self-concept; see Chapter 5). But prejudice harms the people who hold it, too (e.g., they experience ungrounded fear of harm from out-group members; see Chapter 11). Which do you think is dominant where prejudice is concerned—its benefits or its costs?

3. In your view, why do we show such a strong tendency to divide the social world into two categories—"us" and "them"? Do you think this tendency could stem, in part, from our biological heritage—for instance, the conditions under which our species evolved (see Chapter 1)? Or is it mainly the result of our tendency to save cognitive effort and other cognitive factors (see Chapter 3)?

4. Some evidence suggests that the "glass ceiling" has finally shattered. However, beyond it, some contend, may lie a second ceiling that prevents women from reaching the very top positions in organizations. Do you think that such a barrier exists? And if so, what are its roots—gender stereotypes (see Chapter 5), the desire by males to hold onto an unfair share of available rewards (see Chapter 12)?

Ideas to Take with You
Techniques for Reducing Prejudice

Prejudice is an all-too-common part of social life, but most social psychologists believe that it *can* be reduced—it is not inevitable. Here are some techniques that seem to work.

Teaching Children Tolerance instead of Bigotry

If children are taught from an early age to respect all groups —including ones very different from their own—prejudice can be nipped in the bud, so to speak.

Increased Intergroup Contact—or Merely Knowledge That It Occurs

Recent findings indicate that if people merely know that friendly contacts occur between members of their own group and members of various out-groups, their prejudice toward these groups can be sharply reduced.

Recategorization

Once individuals mentally include people they once excluded from their in-group *within* it, prejudice toward them may disappear. Reminding people that they are part of larger groups—for instance, that they are all Americans, Canadians, and so on—can help accomplish this kind of recategorization.

Undermining Stereotypes

Stereotypes suggest that all persons belonging to specific social groups are alike—that they share the same characteristics. Such beliefs can be weakened if people are encouraged to think about others as *individuals,* not simply as members of social groups. Also, some evidence suggests that affirmative action programs may actually encourage positive perceptions of the persons who benefit from them, and so serve to counter prejudice by undermining stereotypes.

SUMMARY AND REVIEW OF KEY POINTS

Prejudice and Discrimination: Their Nature and Effects

- *Prejudice* is an attitude (usually negative) toward members of some social group based solely on their membership in that group.
- Prejudice, like other attitudes, influences our processing of social information. In addition, prejudice influences our beliefs about persons belonging to various groups, and our feelings about them.
- Prejudice persists because disparaging groups we dislike can boost our self-esteem, and because stereotypes save us cognitive effort.
- *Discrimination* involves negative actions, based on prejudice, toward members of various social groups.

- While blatant discrimination has clearly decreased in Western societies, more subtle forms such as modern racism, *tokenism,* and *reverse discrimination* persist.
- Recent findings indicate that white persons in the United States often "lean over backward" to provide positive feedback to members of minority groups.
- Critics of affirmative action programs contend that they are a form of reverse discrimination that actually harms other groups.

The Origins of Prejudice: Contrasting Perspectives

- Prejudice stems from several different sources. One of these is direct intergroup conflict—situations in which social groups compete for the same scarce resources.

- A second basis for prejudice is early experience, which often trains children to hate various groups.
- Prejudice also stems from our tendencies to divide the world into "us" and "them" and to view our own group much more favorably than various out-groups.
- Recent findings indicate that perceived similarity to an out-group can reduce prejudice toward its members unless the group is viewed as a threat.
- Prejudice sometimes stems from basic aspects of social cognition—the ways in which we process social information.
- *Stereotypes* are cognitive frameworks suggesting that all persons belonging to a social group show similar characteristics. Stereotypes strongly influence social thought. For instance, when activated, they lead us to draw *tacit inferences* about others that then make information which is inconsistent with stereotypes seem to be consistent with them.
- Recent findings indicate that stereotypes are closely linked to prejudice; for example, highly prejudiced persons respond more quickly to stereotype-related words than less prejudiced persons.
- Other cognitive sources of prejudice include *illusory correlations*—overestimations of the strength of relationships between social categories and negative behaviors, and the *illusion of out-group homogeneity*—the tendency to perceive out-groups as more homogeneous than our own in-group.

Why Prejudice Is *Not* Inevitable: Techniques for Countering Its Effects

- Social psychologists believe that prejudice is not inevitable; it can be reduced by several techniques.
- One approach involves changing children's early experiences so that they are not taught bigotry by their parents and other adults.
- Another technique involves direct contact between persons from different groups. When this occurs under certain conditions, prejudice can be reduced.

- Recent findings indicate that simply knowing that members of one's own group have formed friendships with members of an out-group may be sufficient to reduce prejudice; this is known as the *extended contact hypothesis*.
- Prejudice can sometimes be reduced through *recategorization*—shifting the boundary between "us" and "them" so as to include former out-groups in the "us" category.
- Cognitive techniques for reducing prejudice are also effective. These focus on reducing the impact of stereotypes on social thought.
- Inducing individuals to focus on others' specific traits and outcomes rather than on their group membership helps reduce stereotypes' impact on social thought.

Prejudice Based on Gender: Its Nature and Effects

- *Sexism*—prejudice based on gender—affects more than half the human race.
- At the core of sexism are *gender stereotypes*—cognitive frameworks suggesting that males and females possess sharply different patterns of traits and behavior.
- Existing evidence suggests that while males and females do differ in some respects, gender stereotypes greatly exaggerate these differences.
- Although blatant forms of discrimination based on gender have decreased, females continue to be adversely affected by more subtle forms.
- Gender-based obstacles include lower expectations by females, inaccurately low self-confidence and self-perceptions, negative reactions to female leaders, and the glass ceiling.
- *Sexual harassment* constitutes one very disturbing form of discrimination against females. Recent findings indicate that males and females differ somewhat in their perceptions of what constitutes sexual harassment. Research also indicates that women working in nontraditional fields for females are at greater risk of experiencing such treatment.

KEY TERMS

common in-group identity model (p. 237)
contact hypothesis (p. 234)
discrimination (p. 214)
extended contact hypothesis (p. 235)
gender stereotypes (p. 240)
glass ceiling (p. 242)
illusion of out-group homogeneity (p. 231)
illusory correlations (p. 230)
in-group (p. 223)
in-group differentiation (p. 232)
out-group (p. 224)
prejudice (p. 211)

realistic conflict theory (p. 219)
recategorization (p. 237)
reverse discrimination (p. 216)
sexism (p. 239)
sex-role spillover theory (p. 245)
sexual harassment (p. 244)
social categorization (p. 224)
stereotype threat (p. 228)
stereotypes (p. 226)
tokenism (p. 216)
ultimate attribution error (p. 224)

FOR MORE INFORMATION

Oskamp, S., & Costanzo, M. (Eds.). (1993). *Gender issues in contemporary society.* Newbury Park, CA: Sage.

Leading experts on all aspects of gender contribute chapters to this book. The discussions of gender stereotyping and discrimination are closely related to topics covered in this chapter.

Winstead, B. A., Derlega, V. J., & Rose, S. (1997). *Gender and close relationships.* Thousand Oaks, CA: Sage.

This interesting book examines the nature of gender—including gender stereotypes and gender-role development—and considers the role of gender in close relationships as well as in a wide range of social behavior (e.g., conflict, violence, friendship).

Zanna, M. P., & Olson, J. M. (1994). *The psychology of prejudice: The Ontario Symposium on Personality and Social Psychology* (Vol. 7). Mahwah, NJ: Erlbaum.

Thought-provoking chapters by experts in the fields of stereotypes, intergroup conflict, and attitudes. Together, the authors present a very comprehensive view of what social psychologists have discovered about the origins and effects of prejudice.

7 Interpersonal Attraction:
Initial Contact, Liking, Becoming Acquainted

Three Figures with Arms Up. © José Ortega/Stock Illustration Source

Chapter Outline

Recognizing and Evaluating Strangers: Proximity and Emotions
Attraction: An Overview
Repeated Unplanned Contacts Lead to Attraction
BEYOND THE HEADLINES: As Social Psychologists See It: Can Classroom
Seating Assignments Affect One's Life?
Affective State: Positive versus Negative Emotions As the Basis
for Attraction

**Becoming Acquaintances: The Need to Affiliate and the Effect of
Observable Characteristics**
Affiliation Need: Dispositional and Situational Determinants of
Interpersonal Associations
CORNERSTONES OF SOCIAL PSYCHOLOGY: Festinger's Social
Comparison Theory
Responding to Observable Characteristics: Instant Cues to Attraction

**Becoming Close Acquaintances and Moving toward Friendship:
Similarity and Reciprocal Positive Evaluations**
Opposites Don't Attract, but Birds of a Feather Really Do
Flock Together
SOCIAL DIVERSITY: A CRITICAL ANALYSIS: Interracial Dating among
Asian Americans
Reciprocal Positive Evaluations: If You Like Me, I Like You
CONNECTIONS: Integrating Social Psychology
IDEAS TO TAKE WITH YOU: How to Encourage Others to Like You

Summary and Review of Key Points
Key Terms
For More Information

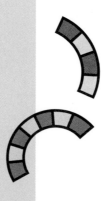

When I (Donn Byrne) was ten, my family moved from Austin, Texas, to Bakersfield, California, a month or two after the Japanese attack on Pearl Harbor. I suddenly found myself in a new neighborhood, new town, new state, and new school. Among the many challenges associated with such major changes in one's life are those that involve interacting with strangers, becoming acquainted with some of them, and deciding who you like and dislike.

My first contact was with a fellow fourth-grader whose seat was next to mine in our classroom. He was Chinese American, and in our initial brief conversation we exchanged names—Donn and Terry. During the first few days of school, he was the only one I talked to in class, at recess, during lunch, and when we had air raid drills and crawled under our desks as protection against any bombs dropped by enemy planes that might attack California. We discovered that we had many interests and attitudes in common—including marbles and model airplanes. As the months went by, Terry and I often got together in the afternoon and on weekends.

Though I didn't really understand what was involved at the time, I now know that the two of us were enacting various aspects of the attraction process. Looking back, I can not only ask, but sometimes actually answer, questions about what took place. Why was Terry my first friend in this new location? Could race have had anything to do with it? That seems unlikely, because (as strange as it may sound today) I had never before even seen anyone of Asian descent in real life—only in the movies. And on film such individuals were usually someone not really Asian (a Caucasian with makeup playing Charlie Chan), someone funny (Inspector Chan's Number 1 son), or someone evil (untrustworthy Japanese spies). Terry fit none of these categories.

So why did he become my friend? Eventually I discovered the answer. When I entered graduate school, one of the first requirements was to generate a testable idea, design an empirical research project, gather and analyze the necessary data, and write up the whole project in the form of an article that was potentially publishable. After considering several possible ideas, I more or less stumbled on a plan to investigate whether college freshmen tend to become acquainted in classrooms simply because of their seating assignments. I was not consciously aware of putting together a study based on what had taken place in my fourth-grade class, but it seems obvious now that this was exactly what I was doing. When I first began the project, I was also unaware of the small but consistent body of sociological and psychological literature dating back to the 1930s that dealt with the effects of proximity on interpersonal relationships. In my simple study, I found that pairs of students who were assigned seats side by side were much more likely to become acquainted during the semester than any other pairs of students, and my description of this work became my first publication as a psychologist-to-be (Byrne & Buehler, 1955). Jack Buehler was the professor who supervised my work.

As time passed, I carried out many more experimental and correlational projects that dealt with the factors influencing our interpersonal likes and dislikes. Such research is known as the study of interpersonal attraction, and some of the major findings about attraction will be described in this chapter.

Let's quickly preview the subject matter of this chapter. We will first describe the initial factors involved in becoming acquainted. Attraction begins when two people come into contact with one another. Most such contacts are made accidentally, depending on factors such as seats in a classroom, room assignments in a dormitory, or the physical arrangements of a workplace. On the basis of where we live, sit, or work, the details of our physical surroundings increase the odds that we will come into repeated contact with some people and decrease the odds that such contact will occur with others. As a result, although this may seem surprising, *physical proximity* very often constitutes the first step in our becoming aware of and attracted to another person—as Terry and I unwittingly demonstrated several decades ago. Another important factor that influences whether or not you like those you happen to encounter is your *affective state* at the time. It is simple, but true, that we tend to like others on the basis of positive and negative emotions, no matter who or what caused the emotions. Your affective state may be based on something the other person has said or done (for example, something that amuses you versus something that you interpret as an insult)—or on something totally unrelated to the other person (for example, a good or a bad course grade you receive shortly before you encounter that individual).

Next, after you become aware of and evaluate the other person, the attraction process continues or fails to do so on the basis of each person's interpersonal motivation and his or her responses to what can be observed about the other. As will be discussed, even after multiple contacts with another person and even if your emotions are positive, you may be only mildly attracted and thus fail to interact unless your *affiliation motivation* is sufficiently strong. That is, at least one of you (and preferably both) must desire to form a relationship. Also, attraction depends in part on one's reactions to various possible *observable characteristics*. For example, people may react positively (or negatively) to a stranger's physical attractiveness, skin color, age, or any other factor that can activate stereotypes (as described in Chapter 6).

If all goes well and two people *do* begin to interact, they enter the third stage of the attraction process. We will describe how liking versus disliking is strongly determined by the extent to which the two individuals are *similar* (rather than dissimilar) in their attitudes, beliefs, values, and other characteristics. While similarity almost always has a positive effect on attraction, an even more powerful determinant is the expression of mutual liking in the form of *positive evaluations* of one another, as indicated both in what is said and in what is done.

RECOGNIZING AND EVALUATING STRANGERS: PROXIMITY AND EMOTIONS

Before we pursue the details of the factors that influence attraction, let's pause to consider just what we mean by this term.

Attraction: An Overview

Attraction involves the attitudes we form about other people, and affect plays a key role in forming such attitudes.

Attitudes about a Person. In Chapter 4 we discussed the very human tendency to evaluate just about everything and everyone we encounter. In effect, we form attitudes about people, objects, and events. At school, at work, and where we live, we come in contact with other people and develop attitudes about them.

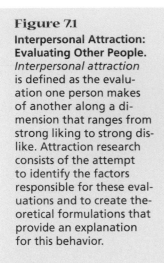

Figure 7.1

Interpersonal Attraction: Evaluating Other People. *Interpersonal attraction* is defined as the evaluation one person makes of another along a dimension that ranges from strong liking to strong dislike. Attraction research consists of the attempt to identify the factors responsible for these evaluations and to create theoretical formulations that provide an explanation for this behavior.

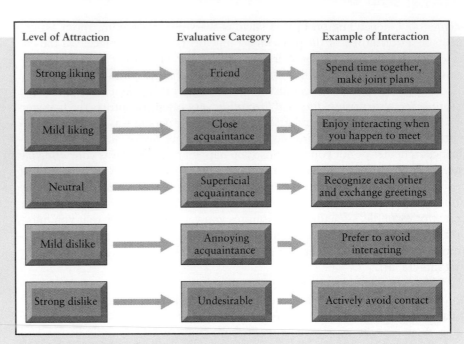

The term **interpersonal attraction** refers to these interpersonal evaluations, which fall along a dimension ranging from like to dislike (Figure 7.1).

You might find it helpful to consider an example. Any given person (including you) is liked by some people, disliked by some, and a matter of indifference to many others. Why? To some extent, differences in attraction are based on the characteristics and actions of the individual himself or herself. To a degree, attraction depends on the person who is making the evaluation. Attraction also depends in part on the similarities and differences between the evaluator and the person being evaluated. Finally, attraction is also influenced by the situational context in which they are interacting.

To illustrate these determinants, let's take a specific individual, one who won't get his feelings hurt or institute a law suit: Benjamin Franklin. Do you like old Ben or dislike him? In his day, he was well liked by many of those who knew him. There is no one now alive who knew him personally, but we have all seen his picture and know of his inventions and his sayings in *Poor Richard's Almanac;* and we may have seen him portrayed as a wise and amusing character in the play and movie *1776.* We have read of his accomplishments as one of the founding fathers of the United States and as a diplomat who represented his country in Europe. Probably most people today would evaluate Ben Franklin positively, based on these various bits of knowledge we have about him. He seems to have been a genial, intelligent, witty, and successful individual. What's not to like?

Historian Robert Middlekauff (1996) provides evidence that some of those who knew him actually disliked Franklin (Figure 7.2) intensely. As an example, one Pennsylvanian who was a political rival wrote that Franklin had a wicked spirit and a foul mouth; he described him as a very bad man who bore "the most unpopular and odious name in the province" (Breen, 1996, p. 37). John Adams and Benjamin Franklin worked together quite well in Philadelphia in 1776 when engaged in deciding the future of the thirteen British colonies, agreeing that independence was worth the risk. But in a quite different situation, when they were in Europe working on peace negotiations with England, John Adams observed Franklin's very successful political and social interactions and ex-

interpersonal attraction • One person's evaluation of someone else along a dimension that ranges from strong liking to strong dislike.

Figure 7.2

Benjamin Franklin: Liked by Some, Disliked by Others. In the course of interacting with other people, everyone (including you, me, and Ben Franklin) is evaluated positively by some and negatively by others. What determines such evaluations? Some of the factors involve aspects of the person being evaluated (e.g., Franklin's wit and charm), some on aspects of the evaluator (e.g., an observer's interpretation of Franklin's "charm" as dishonesty), some on differences between the evaluator and the one being evaluated (e.g., differences in political beliefs), and some on the situation (e.g., working with Franklin on the Declaration of Independence versus being with him in a social setting where he flirted with every attractive woman).

pressed a strongly negative evaluation of Franklin, saying he "could not bear" to "go near him" (Breen, 1996, p. 37). In general, Franklin was disliked by those who interpreted his behavior as manipulative and deceitful rather than charming, those who disagreed with his political views, and those who envied his social skills and his success with women. Keep in mind that there is no "correct" evaluation of another person; each of us is almost certain to be liked by some and disliked by others.

Affect As the Basic Factor Underlying Attraction. The purpose of research on interpersonal attraction is to identify in detail the factors responsible for one person's evaluation of another. As you read about the research dealing with the effects of each factor, it is easy to lose sight of the forest, because we must first focus on individual trees. It may be helpful for you to keep in mind a very simple but all-important concept. Some social psychologists propose that we make positive evaluations whenever we are experiencing positive feelings and negative evaluations whenever we are experiencing negative feelings. Simply put, our interpersonal likes and dislikes are determined by emotions. Therefore, any factor that has an effect on a person's emotional state also has an effect on attraction. As you read this chapter, the reasoning behind that general proposal will become increasingly clear. You should also note that interpersonal behavior is sometimes more complex than simply the effect of positive and negative emotions on liking and disliking. For example, our evaluations can become quite complicated and quite extreme, as you will see when you read about love in Chapter 8 and hate in Chapter 11.

Repeated Unplanned Contacts Lead to Attraction

There are at least six billion people on our planet, and several thousand of them could conceivably become your friends. That is exceedingly unlikely to happen, however; any one of us is likely to become aware of, interact with, and get to know only a tiny percentage of these individuals. Of those in this relatively small subgroup, only a few will become acquaintances, fewer still will become friends, while most will remain strangers. What determines awareness, interaction, and differential attraction? Let's begin with our physical surroundings. Seemingly unimportant environmental details constitute an important and

Figure 7.3

Surrounded by Strangers in a New Situation. When you find yourself in a new setting on your first day at a new school or at a new job, you are surrounded by strangers. As time passes and you encounter some of these individuals more than once, such repeated exposure leads to recognition, a positive evaluation, and the increased likelihood that you will become acquainted with them.

proximity • In attraction research, the closeness between two individuals' residences, classroom seats, work areas, and so on. The closer the physical distance, the greater the probability of the individuals' coming into regular contact and thus experiencing repeated exposure.

repeated exposure • Frequent contact with a stimulus. According to Zajonc's theory, repeated exposure to any mildly negative, neutral, or positive stimulus results in an increasingly positive evaluation of that stimulus.

often overlooked initial determinant of those we are likely to meet. Simply stated, two people tend to become acquainted if they are brought into regular contact. Such contact is primarily based on physical **proximity** (or closeness), and proximity is most often a function of the location and design of such ordinary aspects of the environment as dormitory rooms and hallways, classroom seats, sidewalks, and our workplaces.

Think of yourself on the first day of college, coming in contact with many individuals who are strangers to you. In the beginning, you find yourself surrounded by a confusing blur of people you don't know (see Figure 7.3). In a relatively brief time, however, as you walk down your dormitory corridor and sit in your classrooms, some faces begin to stand out because you pass by or sit beside some of the same individuals more than once. These casual and unplanned contacts soon lead to mutual recognition. You probably don't yet know who the people are, but you recognize their faces, and they recognize yours. Next, you may well exchange a brief greeting ("Hi") when you see one another, and maybe a word or two about the weather or the course you're taking or whatever.

Oddly enough, as a stranger's face becomes a familiar face through repeated contacts, the sight of this person arouses positive feelings in you and possibly even makes you smile. Beginning in infancy, humans tend to smile at a photograph of someone they have seen before, but not at a photograph of someone they are seeing for the first time (Brooks-Gunn & Lewis, 1981). This general tendency to like a familiar face also applies to most anything—music, products in ads, and abstract art. Something familiar is preferable to something new and strange. As an even less obvious example, faculty and staff on a college campus not only correctly identify but prefer buildings close to the one in which they work, compared to more distant buildings (Johnson & Byrne, 1996). Apparently, the more often one sees a building, the better one likes that building.

How can these reactions to people and buildings and other aspects of our surroundings be explained? Why do we like something or someone better after repeated exposure? Zajonc (1968) proposed that **repeated exposure** to a new stimulus (that is to say, frequent contact with that stimulus) will under most circumstances result in an increasingly positive evaluation. The more frequent the exposure, the more positive the response (Moreland & Zajonc, 1982). The general idea is that we ordinarily respond with at least mild discomfort when we encounter anyone or anything unfamiliar. For our ancient ancestors, it was probably beneficial to distrust strangers, unfamiliar animals, and unknown food. If the people, animals, and food are encountered over and over, however, the new stimulus gradually becomes a familiar stimulus. The word "familiar" is related to the word "family," and in a way repeated exposure to strangers expands our zone of comfort and safety to include new individuals and new objects in our expanded "family." Note that strangers who simply reside somewhere in the same dormitory or sit somewhere in the same classroom do not tend to become friendly unless the living and seating arrangements actually cause them to come into repeated contact.

To provide evidence of just how this process operates, Moreland and Beach (1992) asked a female research assistant to attend a college class fifteen times during one semester, another assistant to attend the class ten times, another five times, and one not to attend at all. At the end of the semester, all four assistants entered the class, and the experimenters asked the students to fill out rating scales indicating how much they liked each of these four people. The assistants were fairly similar in appearance, and none had interacted with any members of the class at any time during the semester. Nevertheless, the more times a particular assistant had been in class, the more she was liked, as shown in Figure 7.4. In this and many other experimental tests of the proposition, repeated exposure is found to have a positive effect on attraction.

Repeated exposure seems to be even more powerful when it occurs beyond our awareness. As you might expect from the discussion of subliminal

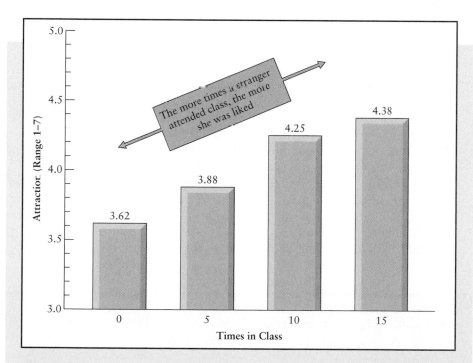

Figure 7.4

Frequency of Exposure and Liking in the Classroom. In a test of the repeated exposure effect in a college classroom, four female research assistants pretended to be fellow students. One of them did not attend the class all semester, another attended the class five times, a third attended ten times, and the fourth came to class fifteen times. At the end of the semester, all four assistants appeared, and the students were asked to indicate how much they liked each of them. The more times an assistant had attended class, the more she was liked.

(*Source:* Based on data from Moreland & Beach, 1992.)

conditioning in Chapter 4, repeated exposure to a stimulus influences our evaluation of that stimulus even when we are unaware that exposure has taken place. And in fact, the effect is stronger under these conditions. Bornstein and D'Agostino (1992) presented stimuli to some research participants at a normal speed and to others at a sufficiently rapid speed that they afterward were not aware of having seen anything. The repeated exposure effect was found in both conditions, but it was greater when a stimulus was presented subliminally than when it was presented at a normal speed. Possibly this is why, in our everyday lives, we often encounter people who seem familiar and likable, although we are not aware of where or when we might have previously seen them. In other words, we were exposed to them, but didn't know it.

There are exceptions to the repeated exposure effect. The most important exception is that if one's initial reaction to a person or to anything else is extremely negative, repeated exposure does not increase liking and sometimes even leads to greater dislike (Swap, 1977). For example, as a college freshman I was assigned a roommate who seemed unpleasant and condescending from the first day we met. He was richer than I was, he owned a car, and his parents were both professors. Repeated exposure to this individual only made me like him less, not more. Quite probably, his reaction to me was also an initially negative one—as astonishing as that may be for me to imagine. Over time, greater exposure to each other made us like each other less and less. In most interpersonal situations, however, the initial reaction to other people is only mildly negative, neutral, or even mildly positive. As a result, repeated exposure ordinarily results in increasingly positive, friendly reactions. Is there any evidence that such effects occur in everyday life and have an effect on which individuals become our acquaintances? As you will soon discover, the answer is a definite yes.

Effects of Proximity: Acquaintances, Friends, Spouses. Numerous investigations over the years have shown consistently that repeated exposure frequently occurs as the result of proximity and that such exposure is related to people's responding to one another in a positive way and getting to know one another. This is true in other countries as well as in the United States, as demonstrated by Maisonneuve, Palmade, and Fourment (1952) in France.

We've already noted that most students seated side by side in a classroom become acquainted. You may not find that to be a very surprising or a very important occurrence in anyone's life. So what if you meet someone in the next seat? Sometimes it means a great deal, however. For an example of a genuinely far-reaching influence, consider the *Beyond the Headlines* section.

Beyond the Headlines:
As Social Psychologists See It
Can Classroom Seating Assignments Affect One's Life?

COUPLE REPAYS UNIVERSITY FOR BRINGING THEM TOGETHER

University Update, Albany, October 29, 1997—In 1934, two undergraduates (Edward George and Frances Gildea) sat next to each other in a classroom because the course instructor assigned seats on an alphabetical basis. As a result, these two young students became acquainted, began dating, fell in love, and were married.

Another important event occurred before they graduated in 1938. Mr. George was told by a friend that it might be worth his while to buy shares (at 12 cents each) of a promising oil stock, and he borrowed $200 from the Credit Union to give it a try. By 1945, he was able to sell his shares for $4,000, and he used the profits to begin a program of regular investment in the stock market. Both Mr. and Mrs. George worked, but their salaries were modest. Nevertheless, they lived simply and invested well. By the 1970s, they were able to retire, divide their time between Florida and New York (depending on the season), and still have enough money remaining to be able to donate one million dollars to the University at Albany.

Mrs. George said that the university gave them their start in life, ". . . and it gave us each other." Her husband added that "We really believe in the power of education." The million dollars was given with no strings attached as their way of expressing their gratitude.

The university responded by renaming the building that houses the School of Public Health as the Edward and Frances Gildea George Education Center. The couple agreed that a university building would be a more lasting and more satisfying way to spend money than to use it on "swimming pools and Rolls-Royces."

The story of Mr. and Mrs. George (Figure 7.5) is not unique; the fact that classroom seating leads people to become acquainted with one another and to form friendships is well documented (Segal, 1974). As an experiment, an instructor who taught three sections of the same course manipulated classroom seating differently in each section to determine the effect on attraction among the students. One section was randomly assigned places that remained unchanged during the semester. In the other two sections, seating assignments were randomly rearranged once (at midsemester) for one and twice during the semester for the other. The number of side-by-side seating contacts for each student was lowest in the class that did not change seats and highest in the class in which seating was rearranged twice (Byrne, 1961a). And the greater the number of side-by-side seating contacts during the semester, the greater the average number of fellow students known by each individual by the end of the semester.

Figure 7.5

Proximity and Attraction: A Real-Life Example. Because they both had last names beginning with the letter G, two undergraduates were assigned seats next to each other and became acquainted in a classroom. They eventually dated, fell in love, and were married. More than sixty years later, they returned to the university that had brought them together to express their appreciation by making a donation of $1,000,000.

(*Source:* Albany *Times Union,* November 7, 1997. Photo by Steve Jacobs.)

Among the participants in this field experiment, the group whose seats were re-arranged twice reported the highest rate of meeting outside of class, having dates, joining a classmate's fraternity or sorority, and so on, on the basis of becoming acquainted in class. It may seem odd, but the seating assignments in these three course sections clearly influenced the interpersonal behavior of many of the students whose seat assignments were randomly manipulated.

Over the years, have you personally ever become friends with anyone you met just because of where you and the other person sat in a classroom? Beyond that, can you think of people you have known simply because they lived close to you, worked where you did, or took the same bus as you? For most of us, proximity factors have played an important role in determining many of the people we know and like.

Beyond the classroom, residential proximity in dwelling places such as dormitories, apartments, and neighborhoods also affects interpersonal interactions, dating, and marriage. Two of the oldest studies reporting a relationship between proximity and attraction were conducted in the 1930s. Bossard (1932) examined the first 500 marriages performed in Philadelphia in 1931 and then determined where the bride and groom lived before their wedding. About a third of the couples resided within five blocks of one another before they married, and more than half lived within a twenty-block radius. A similar study was conducted in New Haven based on 1,000 marriages there, and almost identical results were obtained (Davie & Reeves, 1939). The closer the residential proximity of a man and a woman, the more likely they are to come into accidental contact, to meet and like one another, and even to marry. When movies depict romance with the boy or girl next door, it's not simply fiction.

Rather than proximity's leading to attraction, such research findings could of course indicate something quite different. That is, it is possible that attraction encourages people to live near one another; if so, attraction may lead to proximity. It is even possible that the selection of a dwelling could be based on some other factor (such as one's ethnic group) and that this third factor (ethnicity) could, in turn, influence attraction. In Chapter 1 we cautioned that a correlation between two variables does not necessarily indicate a causal relationship. To eliminate these competing explanations, most of the investigations that followed the very first ones have utilized situations in which people were assigned randomly to a dwelling place. In each instance, the findings clearly indicate that attraction does indeed result from proximity rather than vice versa or as a function of some third factor.

In one study of residential proximity, for example, when couples were allotted apartments in married student housing on a first-come, first-served basis, proximity was once again found to determine attraction (Festinger, Schachter, & Back, 1950). Couples whose apartments were located within twenty-two feet of one another were quite likely to become acquainted; in contrast, if the apartments are more than eighty-eight feet apart, such relationships were quite unlikely.

So whenever you are free to choose your own classroom seat or place to live, you may want to apply what you have just learned about proximity effects. In housing, take a look at your new neighbors as well as at the new apartment or home. In a classroom, if you want to make new friends, you should select a seat between two likely prospects, not a seat on the end of a row or by an empty desk. Also, whenever you don't especially like your seat neighbors, you can move to another location (assuming that is permitted). In contrast, if you don't want new friends because you want to maintain your privacy (Larson & Bell, 1988), select a dwelling place or a classroom seat that is as isolated as possible from other people—a house next to a busy street or a seat on the aisle in the back of the room, for example (Pedersen, 1994).

Affective State: Positive versus Negative Emotions As the Basis for Attraction

We experience and express emotions throughout our daily lives, and our emotional state at any given moment influences perception, cognition, motivation, decision making, *and* interpersonal judgments (Berry & Hansen, 1996; Erber, 1991; Forgas, 1995; Zajonc & McIntosh, 1992). As you may remember from Chapter 3, psychologists often use the term *affect* when referring to emotions or feelings. The two most important characteristics of affect are of *intensity* (the strength of the emotion) and *direction* (whether the emotion is positive or negative). Positive emotions such as excitement were once thought to fall at one end of a single continuum, with negative emotions such as anxiety falling on the opposite end. Research indicates, however, that positive and negative emotions represent two separate and independent dimensions that are reflected in people's self-ratings of their feelings (Byrne & Smeaton, 1998) and in the different brain structures that are activated by positive and negative emotions (George et al., 1995). This means that you can experience a mixture of positive and negative feelings, and that one sort of emotion can increase without the other necessarily decreasing (Barrett & Russell, 1998; Goldstein & Strube, 1994).

Experiments consistently indicate that positive feelings lead to positive evaluations of others—liking—while negative feelings lead to negative evaluations—disliking (Dovidio et al., 1995). Affect can influence attraction in two different ways. A *direct effect* occurs when another person says or does something that makes you feel good or bad; the obvious result is that you like an individual who makes you feel good and dislike one who makes you feel bad (Downey & Damhave, 1991; Shapiro, Baumeister, Kessler, 1991). It is not very surprising that you prefer a person who brightens your day with a compliment and dislike one who brings you down with an insulting remark. An *associated effect* is much less obvious; it occurs when another person is simply present when your feelings happen to be positive or negative (for some reason unrelated to that person), but you still tend to evaluate him or her on the basis of your own affective state. For example, if you meet someone on your way to visit your dentist, you are less inclined to like him or her than if you met the person on your way to a long-anticipated new movie. We will now take a look at research dealing with both direct and associated effects of affective states.

Direct Effects of Affective State: Attraction toward a Person Who Arouses Your Positive or Negative Feelings.

We have already seen that affect aroused by repeated exposure can determine how much a person is liked, and we will later describe how attraction can be based on affective reactions to a person's appearance, attitudes, and other attributes. The more direct effects of affect on attraction are almost too obvious to require extensive research. For example, it's probably safe to bet that people almost always prefer someone who rewards them to someone who punishes them.

Less clear-cut are other kinds of behavior that can also arouse affect—often not the kind of affect that is intended. When someone meets a stranger and attempts to initiate a conversation, what influence do you think "opening lines" might have?

In settings in which individuals are on the look-out for potential dates, Kleinke, Meeker, and Staneski (1986) investigated the remarks people report making when they first interact with someone they don't know. Many individuals, especially men, attempt to be amusing by saying something cute or flippant. The goal is to arouse positive affect (with laughter as the evidence of success) and thus to be liked. Research indicates, however, that cute or flippant remarks such as "Hi. I'm easy, are you?" or "Bet I can out drink you" usually arouse negative rather than the intended positive affect and will thus be likely to cause rejection rather than acceptance. Positive affective responses, on the other hand, are much more likely when the opening line is either innocuous ("Where are you from?") or simple and direct ("Would you like to dance?"). Because opening lines differ in their affective consequences, the researchers hypothesized that they would be a determinant of initial attraction toward the person saying them.

That hypothesis was tested in a laboratory experiment conducted by Kleinke and Dean (1990). As shown in Figure 7.6, attraction was most positive toward a person who said something simple and direct and most negative toward a person whose opening line was cute or flippant. Other investigators tested these effects by sending research assistants to cruise singles bars and try out the different kinds of statements on strangers (Cunningham, 1989). The same results were obtained in bars as in the laboratory—those who try to be too cute actually annoy rather than amuse strangers and thus invite rejection. It might be helpful for males to know the nonverbal indications of such annoyance. Women demonstrate their rejection by, among other things, yawning, frowning, attending to their nails, and staring at the ceiling. These and other "silent brushoffs" were identified in a field study of singles bars in St. Louis by psychologist Monica Moore (O'Neil, 1998). Cute and flippant lines lead to such brushoffs whereas simple and innocuous lines lead to further interaction.

Indirect Effects of Affective States: Attraction toward a Person on the Basis of Independently Aroused Feelings. Often, our positive or negative feelings have nothing directly to do with the person with whom we are interacting (Johnston & Short, 1993). How you feel at any given moment can be influenced by some

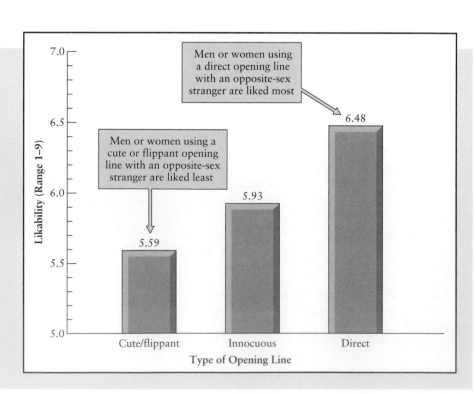

Figure 7.6

Opening Lines: Cute or Direct? Students watched videotapes in which a man or woman approached an opposite-sex stranger and began a conversation using an opening line that was one of three types. Consistent with other research, those using cute or flippant opening lines were liked least by the viewers; those taking a straightforward, direct approach were liked best.

(*Source:* Based on data from Kleinke & Dean, 1990.)

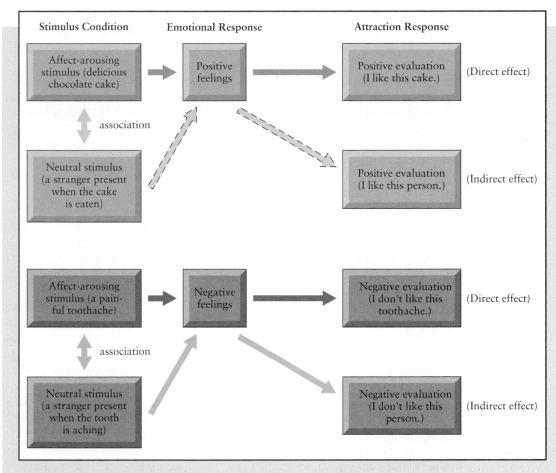

Figure 7.7

Attraction: Direct and Indirect Effects of Feelings. When any stimulus (including another person) arouses positive affect, that stimulus is liked. If it arouses negative affect, it is disliked. In both instances, affect has a direct effect on attraction. When any neutral stimulus (including another person) is present at the same time that something *else* arouses positive or negative affect, the neutral stimulus becomes associated with the positive or negative affect and is subsequently either *liked* or *disliked.* In this instance, affect has an indirect effect on attraction. Indirect effects represent a type of classical conditioning.

(*Source:* Based on material in Byrne & Clore, 1970.)

recent experience, what you happen to be thinking about, your physical state, and many other factors. As proposed about three decades ago (Byrne & Clore, 1970), if another person just happens to be there when your feelings are positive, you tend to like that individual; but if the person is present when your feelings are negative, your reaction tends to be one of dislike. The general idea is based on classical conditioning, as shown in Figure 7.7. In direct tests of the conditioning model, after a neutral stimulus is paired with an emotion-arousing one, participants tend to evaluate the previously neutral stimulus on the basis of the associated affect. For example, when experimenters pair a stranger's photograph with pleasant pictures presented subliminally, that stranger is liked; when paired with unpleasant subliminal pictures, the stranger is disliked (Krosnick et al., 1992). In analogous experiments, emotions have been aroused by such manipulations as pleasant versus unpleasant background music (May & Hamilton, 1980), good versus bad news on the radio (Kaplan, 1981), and pleasant versus unpleasant room lighting (Baron, Rea, & Daniels, 1992). In these and numerous other experiments, positive affect resulted in positive evaluations (liking) by participants experiencing positive emotions and negative evaluations (disliking) by participants experiencing negative emotions.

It is also true that the affect aroused by an individual can become associated with something else. Have you ever disliked someone a great deal and then found yourself disliking the town where that person lives? In an experimental test of this kind of conditioning, Rozin, Millman, and Nemeroff (1986) found that a laundered shirt that had been worn by a disliked person was rated as less desirable than a laundered shirt that had been worn by a liked person. Though the shirts did not actually differ, one elicited a positive response and the other a negative response on the basis of learned associations.

Taking this model a step further, the affect aroused by one person can become associated with a second person. Because we have already described how attitudes in general can be acquired through conditioning (see Chapter 4), it should not be surprising that evaluations of people can be acquired in the same way. Evaluation by association occurs when we have an emotional reaction to person A, observe person A interacting with person B, and then transfer our negative feelings about A to B. For example, if I very much dislike John and see him talking to Bill—someone I barely know—I will tend to dislike Bill. This transfer of negative emotions and negative evaluations is often observed with respect to a **stigma.** This term refers to a characteristic of a person that is perceived negatively by some individuals. Stigmas can include race, age, a foreign accent, a physical disability or disease, unattractiveness, obesity, sexual orientation, or whatever (Frable, 1993; Neuberg et al., 1994; Rodin & Price, 1995). As with any other type of prejudice (see Chapter 6), stigmatization is most often based on irrational assumptions, but the emotions that are aroused can nevertheless be quite strong.

Affect is reflected not only in ratings of others but also in interpersonal behavior. For example, Cunningham (1988) exposed male research participants to movies and to false feedback about themselves in order to induce feelings of happiness or sadness. Afterward, each participant entered a waiting room where a female assistant was seated. The males who felt happy communicated more with the assistant and disclosed more about themselves than did those who felt sad.

In addition to looking at temporary affective states, research has also focused on the characteristic moods expressed by different individuals. That is, some people are generally positive and others generally negative. On self-report scales, positive people indicate that they usually feel enthusiastic, proud, and so on. Negative people say that they usually feel hostile, nervous, and the like. In a laboratory study, such characteristic differences in mood were found to be associated with the quality of students' social interactions as rated by the participants themselves as well as by observers who viewed videotapes (Berry & Hansen, 1996). In a follow-up study, other participants kept diaries of their everyday social interactions for a week. Students who described themselves as usually positive reported more pleasant interactions over the seven days than did students who described themselves as usually negative.

What If There Are Multiple Sources of Affect? And What If We Are Not Aware of Why We Feel As We Do? We have already described how repeated exposure results in increased positive affect, which in turn results in liking. We have also described how associated affect, especially if aroused by subliminal stimuli that prime (see Chapter 3) positive and negative feelings, also determines liking. Murphy, Monahan, and Zajonc (1995) investigated just what happens when these two independent sources of affect occur simultaneously.

Instead of having participants evaluate people, the investigators chose Chinese words or phrases as stimuli—material that was totally unfamiliar to the

stigma • A personal characteristic that at least some other individuals perceive negatively.

undergraduates who took part in the experiments. Each Chinese character was rated for liking after being presented either three times, once, or not at all. Across a series of experiments, the students liked these stimuli more as the number of showings increased. Once more, then, repeated exposure resulted in greater liking. In order to introduce another source of affect besides repeated exposure, the Chinese characters were also shown along with male or female faces that expressed either happiness or anger. The faces were presented either subliminally (for 4 milliseconds) or at a speed that made viewing easy (1,000 milliseconds). Results indicated that the emotional priming had an effect only when it was subliminal. Rapid exposure to the happy face increased liking for the Chinese figures, but such exposure to the angry face decreased liking. Under these conditions, the two independent sources of affect (repeated exposure and subliminal priming) combined to yield evaluations that represented their net value.

Why should "nonconscious affect" that results from subliminal presentation be more influential than equally strong affect based on clearly presented stimulus material? One possible explanation is that people resent having their judgments controlled in obvious ways and somehow manage to resist. In effect, no one likes to admit liking something because of being shown an unrelated happy face or disliking something because of being shown an angry face. If, however, we are unaware of the source of our emotions, our judgments are easily influenced. Murphy and her colleagues (1995) suggest that in everyday life we are often unaware of the sources of our feelings—we just know that we are sometimes cheerful and sometimes depressed. As a result, our likes and dislikes can easily be determined by our moods.

Just How Vulnerable Are We to Affective Manipulations? It is no secret that people trying to sell products or services attempt to manipulate attraction on our part by creating ads designed to arouse positive feelings and by offering free samples, discounts, and compliments to potential customers. In a similar way, political strategists have learned to use feel-good campaign techniques and to offer uplifting phrases in order to associate positive affect with a given candidate and thus entice voters to support him or her (see Figure 7.8). At the same time, negative political ads are designed to associate unpleasant affect with one's opponent.

Figure 7.8
Positive Affect and Politics. In advertising and in politics, there is an obvious attempt to associate positive affect with a product, a service, or a candidate. This practice represents a widespread application of the indirect effects of emotional states on attraction.

Is that an effective strategy? Research suggests that it is. Pentony (1995) presented undergraduates with information about two politicians running for office. One candidate was described with only positive information, the other with equally positive information plus one negative allegation about an extramarital affair or about obtaining tax breaks for friends. That single negative allegation (either sexual or financial) resulted in less positive evaluations of the candidate. More importantly, it affected voting behavior. Even when the negatively described candidate refuted the charge, the positively described candidate "won" the mock election.

In addition to positive and negative affective manipulations, the affect expressed personally by a candidate (happiness, anger, sadness, etc.) can also influence how voters evaluate that individual. When, for example, someone in a position of power smiles (especially a man), we are likely to assume that a genuine emotion is being expressed; a smile from a low-power person, in contrast, is interpreted as something he or she feels obligated to do (Hecht & LaFrance, 1998). A powerful political candidate's affective expressions are assumed to reveal basic personality characteristics of that individual (Glaser & Salovey, 1998). These inferences about personality, in turn, influence how much the individual is liked, and liking influences voting.

Are we helpless in the face of such manipulations of positive and negative affect designed to influence our level of attraction and hence our decision making? Ottati and Isbell (1996) argue that the effects of mood on evaluations are greatest when the person being manipulated is relatively uninformed. These researchers identified students who were either well informed or uninformed politically on the basis of the students' responses to a series of questions about political figures (e.g., "identify Pat Shroeder") and about political organizations ("what is the Federal Reserve Board?"). The 25 percent who were the most knowledgeable and the 25 percent who were the least knowledgeable were then selected to participate in the study. In a series of experiments, the investigators manipulated mood by asking some participants to write about a recent experience that made them happy and others to write about a recent experience that made them sad. Following that, they presented information about a political candidate's views on twelve issues such as the death penalty and the use of federal funds for abortion. The participants then evaluated the candidate. The results are presented in Figure 7.9. You can see that the participants who were the least informed about politics were most vulnerable to the mood manipulation. For them, a positive mood led to greater liking for the candidate, and a negative mood led to a relatively negative evaluation. In contrast, those who were best informed not only resisted the manipulation of affect; they actually reacted in the opposite way. That is, they were more positive about the candidate in the negative mood condition and more negative in the positive mood condition.

Why should there be a direct effect of emotions on attraction for the least informed and a reverse effect for those best informed? It seems to be generally true that people are most likely to base their evaluations on affect when they know the least about the target being evaluated. We learned earlier that affect is most influential when its source is unknown. Thus, the most helpless and easily manipulated individuals are those who aren't aware of why they feel as they do and who know very little about whatever or whoever is being evaluated. Knowledge is clearly helpful, therefore. When you know the source of your affective state, such manipulations may have little or no effect on the attraction you feel. And when you know a lot about products or candidates or whatever, you may even react in a way opposite from that intended by the manipulator because you feel insulted about being the target of such influence tactics. You may find it helpful to keep these studies in mind the next time you are exposed to an affect-arousing commercial or political ad.

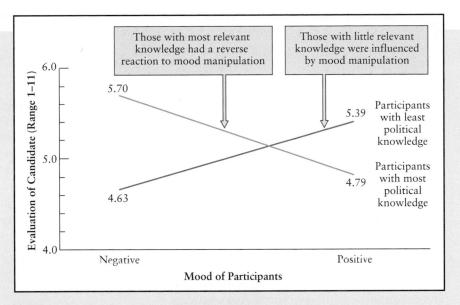

Figure 7.9

Affective Association: The Least Informed Are Influenced Most. Students who were either well or poorly informed about political issues were told about the views of a political candidate while in a happy or sad mood. When asked to evaluate the candidate later, the students who knew the least about politics were influenced in the expected way by the mood manipulation. That is, they evaluated the candidate more positively in the happy condition than in the sad condition. Students who were best informed about politics actually showed a reverse effect—they evaluated the candidate more positively in the sad condition than in the happy condition.

(*Source:* Based on data in Ottati & Isbell, 1996.)

Key Points

- The term *interpersonal attraction* refers to the attitudes we form about other people, expressed along a dimension ranging from like to dislike, based on feelings ranging from extremely positive to extremely negative.

- One's initial contact with others is very often based on *proximity* resulting from such physical aspects of the environment as classroom seating assignments, the location of residences, and how a workplace is arranged.

- Proximity leads to *repeated exposure* to some individuals in one's environment; repeated exposure tends to result in positive affect; and positive affect results in attraction.

- Positive and negative affective states can influence attraction either through direct effects (when the other person is responsible for the positive or negative emotion) or through indirect effects (when the emotion is created by a different source, but the other person happens to be associated with it).

- Affect from more than one source is additive, and we are most influenced by associated affect if we are unaware of its source and if we are relatively uninformed about the person or object we are evaluating.

BECOMING ACQUAINTANCES: THE NEED TO AFFILIATE AND THE EFFECT OF OBSERVABLE CHARACTERISTICS

Once two people come into contact and experience relatively positive affect, they are at a transition point. They may simply remain *superficial acquaintances,* who exchange friendly greetings whenever they happen to encounter one another but never interact otherwise. A second possibility is that they may begin to talk, learn each other's names, and exchange bits and pieces of information; if so, they may be described as *close acquaintances.* Which of these two outcomes occurs depends on (1) the extent to which each person is motivated by *affiliation need* and (2) the way each person reacts to the *observable characteristics* of the other.

Affiliation Need: Dispositional and Situational Determinants of Interpersonal Associations

Most people spend a large part of their free time interacting with other people. Recent research indicates that the tendency to affiliate has a neurobiological basis (Rowe, 1996), possibly derived from the fact that our prehistoric ancestors who formed interpersonal relationships thereby improved their chances for survival and thus for passing on their genes to us (Wright, 1984). People differ, of course, in the strength of this **need for affiliation,** and such differences constitute a relatively stable *trait* (or *disposition*). People whose need to affiliate is weak usually prefer spending time alone, while those with strong affiliation needs choose to interact with other people whenever possible. People seem to seek the amount of social contact that is optimal for them, preferring to be alone part of the time and in social situations part of the time (O'Connor & Rosenblood, 1996). In addition to individual differences in affiliation motivation, however, specific situations also can bring about relatively temporary affiliative states. Let's look at the effects of both types of affiliation need on behavior.

Individual Differences in the Need to Affiliate. Beginning with the early work of Murray (1938), psychologists have investigated behavioral differences in those high and low in the need to affiliate. Some of these findings are summarized in Table 7.1.

The trait aspects of the need for affiliation have been measured in two quite different ways. Self-report measures simply ask direct questions about affiliation-relevant desires and activities (*explicit motivation*). Projective measures, in contrast, seek to tap less conscious needs (*implicit motivation*) by asking respondents to tell brief stories based on a series of somewhat ambiguous pictures. Research suggests that explicit and implicit affiliation motivation can lead to somewhat different kinds of affiliative behavior. Craig, Koestner, and Zuroff (1994) found that college students scoring high on an explicit measure were very sociable and interacted with many people; those scoring high on an implicit measure were more likely to interact in two-person situations involving close relationships. That is, high affiliation need on the explicit measure seems to represent the desire to be with other people in a social context, whereas high affiliation need on the implicit seems to represent to desire to be with another person who is a very close friend.

need for affiliation • Tendency to establish interpersonal relationships.

Table 7.1

Need for Affiliation and Social Responsiveness. Over the years, investigators have found differences in interpersonal behavior that are associated with measures of affiliation need. Consistent with Murray's (1938) original definition of this disposition, an individual's need for affiliation is related to the tendency to form friendships and to socialize, to interact closely with others, to cooperate and communicate with others in a friendly way, and to fall in love.

Individuals Who Are Comparatively High in the Need for Affiliation

Write more letters and make more local telephone calls (Lansing & Heyns, 1959).

Laugh more and remain physically close to others (McAdams, 1979).

Avoid making negative comments to fellow workers (Exline, 1962).

Desire more dates per week and are more likely to be emotionally involved in a relationship (Morrison, 1954).

Are more likely to express a desire to marry right after college (Bickman, 1975).

Engage in fewer antisocial or negative acts with fellow workers Spend less time alone (Constantian, 1981).

Are more likely to be described by other people as likable, natural, and enthusiastic (McAdams, 1979).

More generally, it is found that different people have different reasons for affiliating. Hill (1987) has proposed four basic motives. Two of these seem to reflect the explicit and implicit differences just described; that is, the *need for positive stimulation* leads to social interactions that involve interesting, lively interactions, and the *need for social support* leads to close, companionate interactions. Hill also includes the *need for attention*, which underlies affiliative behaviors designed to elicit the praise and approval of others. The fourth type of motivation is the *need for social comparison;* this results in interactions aimed at reducing uncomfortable feelings of uncertainty.

Situational Determinants of the Need to Affiliate. Newspaper stories quite often describe situations in which strangers are brought together by out-of-the-ordinary experiences, including natural disasters such as floods or forest fires or special public events such as Mardi Gras in New Orleans or Woodstock in upstate New York (Byrne, 1991). Humphriss (1989) provided an account of a California earthquake in which a dreadful natural disaster that destroyed many homes led neighbors to unite in an unusually friendly atmosphere. In a similar way, in 1998 a crippling ice storm hit parts of Canada and northern New England and New York; fallen trees blocked roads and downed power lines, leaving residents without electricity for an extended period (Benjamin, 1998). People in the affected area gathered in Red Cross shelters and other facilities in a surprisingly cheerful atmosphere of shared companionship. (Some even appreciated the beauty of the icy surroundings, making comments about "a crystal palace" that was "kind of incredible when the sun glints off the ice.") In addition, people who suffered less damage volunteered to deliver food, baby formula, bottled water, pasta, bread, peanut butter, generators, and other supplies to those in need.

The underlying reason for responding to a stressful situation with friendliness and affiliative behavior was first identified by Schachter (1959). He designed experiments indicating that fear led people to want to be with other people. In one investigation, for example, some participants were told they would receive painful electric shocks, while others expected to receive only mild, tickling electrical stimulation. As they waited for this (nonexistent) procedure to begin, the participants were asked to indicate whether they preferred to remain alone or to spend the time with others. Many of those expecting pain preferred to wait with other participants, while those not expecting pain wanted to wait alone or expressed no preference. And Schachter (1959, p. 24) also found that "misery doesn't love just any kind of company, it loves only miserable company."

Why should real-life events as well as laboratory manipulation arouse the need to affiliate? Why should frightened, anxious people want to be with other frightened, anxious people? The proposed explanation is the need for social comparison: the tendency to seek out other people—even strangers—in order to communicate about what is going on, to compare perceptions, and to make decisions about what to do. People also want to compare their emotional reactions to the reactions of others. Research clearly suggests that people facing threat want to interact with others in order to increase "cognitive clarity"—that is, they want to understand what exactly is going on (Kulik, Mahler, & Earnest, 1994). They also want to increase "emotional clarity"—to understand what they are feeling (Gump & Kulik, 1997). What are the effects of seeking increased clarity? Does it occur in stressful situations in the real world? And if so, does it help?

Evidence for the positive effects of such affiliation is provided by a study of patients before and after coronary bypass surgery (Kulik, Mahler, & Moore, 1996). The research participants were males undergoing nonemergency coronary surgery for the first time. Each participant was assigned to a hospital room with a male roommate who was also hospitalized for surgery that was either similar (cardiac surgery) or dissimilar (noncardiac surgery). Also, the roommate's situation was either similar (preoperative) or dissimilar (postoperative) with respect to when the operation took place.

The extent to which the patients responded to stress with affiliative behavior was indicated by the amount of time they spent talking to their roommates. Those with a fellow cardiac patient spent significantly more time talking to him and seeking cognitive clarity than did those with a roommate not having cardiac surgery. The patients also spent more time talking to a postoperative roommate than to a preoperative one; that is, someone who had already undergone the surgery could provide the most information about the procedure. Further, there were more emotion-focused conversations with a fellow cardiac patient than with a noncardiac roommate. Thus, in this very real stressful situation, affiliative behavior occurred, and the participants clearly sought cognitive and emotional clarity.

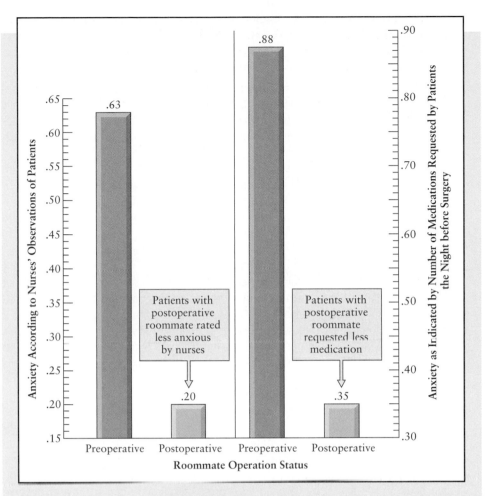

Figure 7.10

The Beneficial Effects of Affiliation. When surgical patients are given the opportunity to interact with another patient who can provide both emotional and cognitive clarity about the operation and its effects, they experience less anxiety before the operation and are able to leave the hospital more quickly after the operation.

(*Source:* Based on data in Kulik, Mahler, & Moore, 1996.)

In addition, patients having the opportunity to obtain such clarity experienced beneficial effects. As shown in Figure 7.10, preoperative anxiety (as indicated by the nurses' notes and by the amount of medication requested) was less among those patients who had a postoperative roommate. Altogether, the "best" roommate was a fellow cardiac patient who had already undergone the operation, and the "worst" roommate was a noncardiac patient who had not yet undergone surgery. Most impressive was the fact that patients were able to leave the hospital in a significantly shorter period of time if their roommate was in the "best" rather than "worst" category.

The general explanation for the effect of stress on affiliation, then, rests on our use of *social comparison* processes (Van der Zee et al., 1998). Remember that "social comparison" was the name applied to one of the four types of affiliation motives. The origin of the concept of social comparison and a description of it is outlined in the following *Cornerstones* section.

Cornerstones of Social Psychology
Festinger's Social Comparison Theory

Leon Festinger. *The late Leon Festinger (1919–1989) was born in New York City. His distinguished career as a social psychologist included work on friendship patterns based on proximity, the response of cult members when the predicted end of the world failed to occur, social comparison processes, cognitive dissonance, and perception. In informal interactions at Stanford and Texas, I (Donn Byrne) perceived him as creative, challenging, and amusing. Though Festinger spent much of his life elsewhere, he remained a New Yorker in spirit. During one of his visits to the University of Texas, at the end of the day, he remarked that he would return to his hotel by going out on the street and hailing a taxi. He found it quaint when we informed him that, unlike the custom in midtown Manhattan, cabs did not ordinarily cruise the streets of Austin.*

Leon Festinger is probably best known for proposing the theory of cognitive dissonance (discussed in Chapters 1 and 4); but his **social comparison theory** was equally creative, and probably even more influential in terms of the amount of research influenced by his idea. We will summarize some of the main concepts involved in this formulation and point out their relevance to interpersonal attraction.

In an early version of the social comparison concept, Festinger (1950) dealt with how group members alter their opinions when they are exposed to the opinions of fellow group members. Festinger's more general theory of social comparison (Festinger, 1954) expanded his original emphasis on opinions by including abilities along with some additional theoretical implications.

Festinger hypothesized, first, that human beings are motivated to evaluate their opinions and abilities. Each of us has cognitions about specific situations as they arise and about our capacity to deal with them. These cognitions include judgments about ourselves and about the external world. If we are incorrect and arrive at false conclusions, the result can be unpleasant or even fatal. For example, if you decide that it would be reasonable to drink several bottles of beer in order to feel more relaxed during a job interview, you are unlikely to be hired. If you overestimate your ability to handle an automobile at high speed, you may be badly injured—or worse. It seems quite clear that we need to be as accurate as possible in evaluating both ourselves and our surroundings in order to avoid negative outcomes.

The problem is *how* to distinguish accurate evaluations from inaccurate ones. Festinger suggested that whenever possible people will turn to objective criteria. If, for example, you believe that a meter is longer than a yard (or vice versa), you can look in a table that shows metric and English equivalents; or you can place a yard-stick next to a meter stick and observe their relative lengths directly. If you believe you can take off like a bird by flapping your arms rapidly, you can try it and observe whether or not you remain on the ground.

Such direct tests are not always available, however. What can you do in the many instances in which an objective approach isn't possible? Take a simple example, as illustrated in Figure 7.11. Are you short or tall? That sounds objective enough, but the answer really depends on the height of other people. That is, your shortness or tallness is not an absolute matter but a relative one that depends on comparing yourself to others.

In a similar way, Festinger's second hypothesis suggests that we ordinarily have to evaluate our opinions and abilities by comparing them to the opinions and abilities of others. For example, do you believe that abortions should be outlawed because they constitute murder or that they should be legal because they represent a woman's freedom to make decisions about her own body? However strongly you may feel about an issue such as this, there is no objective, physical test to determine whether one or the other of those opposing views is "correct." The best any of us can do in the absence of objective criteria is to compare ourselves with others. That is, we make *social comparisons*.

Festinger's third hypothesis states that we prefer to make comparisons with other people who are similar to ourselves—unlike Ziggy in Figure 7.11. You cannot evaluate yourself accurately if you compare yourself with someone who is very different from you. For example, if you slightly favor applying the death penalty in specific circumstances, you won't be inclined to evaluate the validity of your position by discussing the matter with members of extreme groups who believe that defendants convicted of any kind of felony should be executed or with members of other groups who believe that no one should ever be executed for any crime.

Figure 7.11
Relying on Social Comparisons to Evaluate One's Perceptions. Like Ziggy, we engage in social comparison processes to evaluate what we think and do because there is no objective way to make such evaluations. According to Festinger, we compare such aspects of ourselves as opinions, abilities, actions, and much else besides with those of other people as a way to validate what we perceive and believe. Unlike Ziggy, most people tend to make such comparisons with people who are fairly similar to themselves.

(*Source:* Universal Press Syndicate, February 4, 1998.)

These three hypotheses, as well as additional ones in the theory, have been extremely important in the study of interpersonal attraction. In investigations of situational determinants of affiliation, as we have seen, people are found to communicate with similar others in order to obtain a clearer understanding of what is going on and of their feelings. (More generally, people prefer the company of similar others, whether as friends, coworkers, or spouses—as will be discussed later in this chapter and also in Chapter 8.) In addition, this cornerstone theory has been applied to many social psychological concerns, including the study of conformity, opinion change, and prejudice.

In recent research, for example, Blanton and his colleagues (1999) examined the effect of social comparisons on academic performance. Extending Festinger's original proposal, various investigators have found that we sometimes make social comparisons with those worse off than ourselves (in order to enhance feelings of self-worth and self-esteem) and sometimes with those who are better off (in order to motivate self-improvement or to learn how to deal with threats) (Buunk & Ybema, 1997; Wood, 1996). Blanton and his colleagues extended these findings to the academic performance of ninth-grade students in the Netherlands. They predicted that for any given student a high comparison level (self-comparison with those who earned good grades) and a high evaluation of the student's own ability (self-evaluation as more capable than other classmates) would each result in improved academic performance over the school year. And the prediction was accurate: both a high comparison level and a high evaluation level correlated with higher grades. In this situation, many students compared themselves with others who differed from themselves in scholastic success, but it is also interesting that more than 94 percent chose comparison others of the same gender as themselves. Altogether, the criteria for choice of comparison others seem to represent a blend of general similarity to self and very specific dissimilarities from self.

Responding to Observable Characteristics: Instant Cues to Attraction

When we like—or dislike—someone at first sight, it is an indication that we have observed something about that person that appears to provide information about him or her. For example, if a stranger reminds you of someone you know

social comparison theory • Festinger's very influential theory dealing with our tendency to evaluate our opinions and abilities by comparing them with the opinions and abilities of others, including our preference for making such comparisons with those who are relatively similar to ourselves.

and like, your positive response to the person you already know is extended by association to a person you don't know at all (Andersen & Baum, 1994). You tend to like the stranger simply on the basis of a superficial resemblance to someone else. In other instances, the cue may not be related to a specific person in your past but to a subgroup of people to whom you respond positively—the stranger has a southern accent, for example, and you have a fondness for southerners. In a similar way, resemblance to a specific person you know and hate or to a subgroup of people you dislike may cause you instantly to dislike a stranger. As discussed in Chapter 6, stereotypes are poor predictors of behavior, but we nevertheless find ourselves reacting to other people on the basis of associated affect and incorrect assumptions based on superficial characteristics. Among the numerous examples of this tendency to be guided by affect and stereotypes is one's reaction to appearance, so we will first examine the pervasive effects of **physical attractiveness**—the facial and bodily characteristics that people in a given culture regard as visually appealing (or unappealing).

Physical Attractiveness: Judging People As Well As Books by Their Covers. Despite the wisdom expressed in familiar sayings such as "beauty is only skin deep," most people do in fact respond positively to those who are very attractive and negatively to those who are very unattractive (Collins & Zebrowitz, 1995; Hatfield & Sprecher, 1986). Physical attractiveness influences many types of interpersonal evaluations (such as judgments of a defendant's guilt in court, as described in Chapter 13), but appearance is especially crucial with respect to attraction to members of the opposite sex (Sprecher & Duck, 1994). When romance is a possibility, attractiveness often outweighs all other considerations. For example, consider an experiment in which undergraduate men interacted with an attractive or an unattractive female research assistant. These males were sufficiently eager to be liked by an attractive woman that they tried to ingratiate themselves by lying about their attitudes on several issues in order to agree with her so that she would respond positively. With an unattractive woman, in contrast, they did the opposite and actually expressed false disagreements in order *not* to be liked (Plesser-Storr, 1995). Though both genders are responsive to the attractiveness of potential romantic partners, female attractiveness is more important to men than is male attractiveness to women (Feingold, 1990; Pierce, 1992).

Why should physical appearance lead to attraction? For one thing, attractive individuals arouse positive affect (Johnston & Oliver-Rodriguez, 1997; Kenrick et al., 1993), and we have described how positive affect results in attraction. But, going back a step, why does physical attractiveness arouse positive affect? The reason that female beauty appeals to men can be explained according to evolutionary theory. When men are attracted to women whose appearance suggests youth and health and hence fertility, reproductive success becomes more likely (Johnston & Franklin, 1993). Thus, over hundreds of thousands of years, attraction to female appearance proved to be a crucial male preference that increased the odds of the man's genes being passed on to the next generation. This explanation seems quite logical, and there are various bits of indirect supporting evidence. For example, Singh (1993) has found that men are sensitive to a woman's waist-to-hip ratio. The smaller a woman's waist relative to her hips, Singh found, the more she is preferred by men and rated by them as attractive, healthy, and well built to bear children—though Tassinary and Hansen (1998) provide evidence indicating many exceptions to that generalization. In addition, Singh (1995) has argued that waist-to-hip ratio is also important in the attractiveness of men; perhaps this is because it indicates the distribution of body fat, and obesity is associated with a greater risk of many diseases as well as a short

physical attractiveness •
The combination of facial and bodily characteristics that are evaluated as beautiful or handsome at the most attractive extreme of the dimension and unattractive at the other extreme of the dimension.

life span. Whatever the reason, women of quite varied ages, educational backgrounds, and income levels rated line drawings of men most favorably when they were in the normal range rather than being underweight or overweight.

The idea that beauty equals youth and good health is an appealing one, and research shows that attractive strangers are rated as being healthier than unattractive ones. Nevertheless, there is actually *no* relationship between the attractiveness of male and female adolescents and their health—either during either adolescence or adulthood (Kalick et al., 1998). A related question that has not yet been investigated is whether attractiveness is related to fertility or to the health of offspring. A quite different assumption about attractiveness and health has been discovered recently (Smeaton, 1998). Undergraduate women were found to perceive attractive males as posing a greater risk of sexually transmitted disease than unattractive ones. Presumably, women assume that attractive men have had more sexual partners than those who are unattractive.

Considerations involving attractiveness and fertility differ for men and women, because women have a relatively limited age span in which reproduction is possible, whereas males ordinarily can reproduce from puberty into old age. From a female perspective, male youthfulness is not a prerequisite for successful reproduction. Instead, it is in the woman's best interest to choose a male who has the ability (and the inclination) to provide resources and protection for his mate and their children (Kenrick et al., 1994).

An interesting way to investigate such gender differences is to examine personal ads placed by males and females who are seeking a romantic partner. It is generally found that women stress their appearance and men stress their material resources (Deaux & Hanna, 1984; Harrison & Saeed, 1977). It could be, of course, that those who write such ads are simply echoing widespread cultural beliefs about what people assume is most appealing to the opposite sex. Baize and Schroeder (1995) went a step farther by looking at ad content in relation to the number of replies each ad received. In other words, do some factors in the ads attract more potential mates than others? Several interesting gender differences were found, and they are consistent with predictions based on evolutionary considerations. For women, age as stated in their ads was negatively related to the number of replies—that is, the older a woman was, the fewer replies. For men, the opposite was true—the older a man was, the more replies. Also, the higher men's stated income and educational level, the more replies. For women, in contrast, these factors were unrelated to how many responses the ad generated. Thus, a personal ad placed by a man was most effective if it indicated a mature, rich, educated individual. In ads placed by a woman, the only relevant ad content related to its effectiveness was age—the younger the better.

Interestingly, ads placed by gay men indicate a preference for younger male partners, just as such ads placed by heterosexual men indicate a preference for younger female partners (Kenrick et al., 1995). Reproductive fitness is obviously not directly involved in this instance, but it may be that preferences that originally evolved among heterosexual men operate just as strongly for homosexual men despite their irrelevance for genetic survival. In an analogous way, heterosexual and homosexual men and women engage in body-building exercises designed to exaggerate maleness and femaleness, regardless of sexual orientation (Mealey, 1997). Again, it is suggested that these male and female tendencies originally developed because they enhanced reproductive fitness, but they continue to function as gender characteristics regardless of one's sexual orientation.

Whatever the reason, for both genders and for both heterosexuals and homosexuals, appealing physical appearance is a positive characteristic that influences attraction, and numerous stereotypes are consistently associated with

Figure 7.12

Can You Guess What These Individuals Are Like? For each of these two individuals, make a list of the characteristics that you believe would best describe them. For example, what would you guess about each person's sociability, adjustment, intelligence, masculinity/femininity, kindness, laziness, and other qualities? When you are finished, return to the text to find out whether your answers correspond to those of the many research participants who have been asked to make similar judgments.

appearance (Calvert, 1988). It would not be surprising if you have acquired some of these stereotypes yourself. Before you continue reading this paragraph, please take a look at Figure 7.12. People generally believe that attractive men and women are more poised, interesting, sociable, independent, dominant, exciting, sexy, well adjusted, socially skilled, and successful than unattractive men and women (Dion & Dion, 1987; Moore, Graziano, & Miller, 1987). Handsome men seem more masculine and beautiful women more feminine than those who are not handsome or beautiful (Gillen, 1981). Although cross-cultural research suggests that the existence of positive stereotypes about attractiveness is universal, however, the specific content of the stereotypes depends on the culture (Dion, Pak, & Dion, 1990). For example, in a collectivist culture such as Korea, attractiveness is assumed to be associated with integrity and concern for others; these attributes do not appear among the traits stereotypically associated with attractiveness among individualistic North Americans (Wheeler & Kim, 1997). Even so, there is agreement across cultures that attractiveness indicates social competence, adjustment, intelligence, and sexual warmth.

Such stereotypes influence various interpersonal judgments. For example, essays supposedly written by attractive students receive higher ratings than identical essays supposedly written by unattractive ones (Cash & Trimer, 1984). Even among people identified as HIV-positive, attractiveness matters. The best-looking individuals are assumed to have contracted the infection in a heterosexual relationship, but unattractive ones are assumed to have acquired the virus from a homosexual partner or through sharing a needle with another drug user (Agnew & Thompson, 1994). Altogether, as social psychologists discovered almost three decades ago, most people assume that "what is beautiful is good" (Dion, Berscheid, & Hatfield, 1972).

Despite these widespread beliefs, most of the stereotypes based on appearance are *incorrect* (Feingold, 1992b; Kenealy et al., 1991). For example, the serial killer Ted Bundy was considered quite good looking, and Golda Meir was a highly successful prime minister of Israel but not generally considered a beauty queen. The stereotypes are valid only when applied to a very few characteristics. For example, attractive individuals are believed to be more popular (they are) and to have better interpersonal skills and feel better about themselves (they do) then unattractive ones (Diener, Wolsic, & Fujita, 1995; Johnstone, Frame, & Bouman, 1992; O'Grady, 1989). Also, in interacting with an opposite-sex stranger, attractive men and women disclose more about themselves than unattractive individuals, and such disclosure facilitates the establishment of a relationship (Stiles et al., 1996). It is reasonable to suppose that positive characteristics associated with appearance occur primarily because very attractive people have lifelong experiences of being liked and treated nicely by others (Zebrowitz, Collins, & Dutta, 1998).

And appearance is not only important for adolescents and young adults. The personality traits of attractive senior citizens are assumed to be more positive than those of unattractive ones (Johnson & Pittenger, 1984), and people respond more positively to attractive infants than to unattractive ones (Karraker & Stern, 1990).

You may not find it surprising that adults respond well to pretty babies, but would you guess that infants respond differently to attractive versus unattractive adults? Langlois, Roggman, and Rieser-Danner (1990) set up a situation in which twelve-month-olds interacted briefly with a female assistant who was made to look either attractive or unattractive by means of a theatrical mask. To guard against the possibility that the assistant might behave differently when wearing the two different masks, the experimenters did not tell her which one was being applied to her face for each experimental session with an infant, and there were no mirrors in the room. Thus, she had no cues to her own attractiveness. Each infant was in the experimental room with its mother, and the assistant entered the room, talked briefly to the mother, and then picked up the child and played with some nearby toys. These one-year-olds behaved quite differently with the attractive stranger than with the unattractive one, as summarized in Figure 7.13. The experimenters observed that the infants expressed more positive affect and became more involved in their play activity when the woman wore the attractive mask than when she wore the unattractive one.

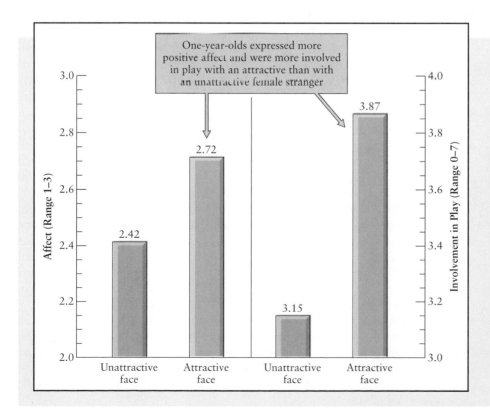

Figure 7.13

Infants Respond to Adult Attractiveness. One-year-olds reacted differently to an attractive female stranger than to an unattractive one, even though the stranger was the same research assistant wearing either an attractive or an unattractive theatrical mask. Infants expressed more positive affect and became more involved in playing with her when she wore the attractive mask. Clearly, differential responsiveness based on physical attractiveness begins at a very early age.

(*Source:* Based on data from Langlois, Roggman, & Rieser-Danner, 1990.)

Later research discovered that infants prefer attractive to unattractive adults regardless of the adults' gender, race, or age (Langlois et al., 1991). Children also spend more time with attractive than with unattractive dolls.

Despite the pervasive effects of attractiveness, people are not very accurate in estimating how attractive they themselves appear to others. Men, unlike women, overestimate how others rate them (Gabriel, Critelli, & Ee, 1994). Women worry more than men about how attractive they are, and they fear being judged negatively by others. Undue concern about one's looks is known as **appearance anxiety.** Dion, Dion, and Keelan (1990) designed a measure of appearance anxiety using items such as "I enjoy looking at myself in the mirror" (answered false by those with the greatest anxiety) and "I feel that most of my friends are more physically attractive than myself" (answered true). Though women score higher on this test than men, the higher the score for both genders, the greater the person's social anxiety, the fewer dates she or he has, and the more uncomfortable the individual feels in social interactions (K. L. Dion, personal communication, March 1993).

Finally, it should be noted that a few *negative* attributes are associated with good looks. For example, beautiful women are often perceived as vain and materialistic (Cash & Duncan, 1984). Also, though attractive male politicians receive more votes than unattractive ones, beauty does not benefit females who run for office (Sigelman et al., 1986), possibly because an elected official who is "too feminine" is assumed to be somehow ineffective.

What, Exactly, Do We Mean by "Attractive"? We have seen that judgments of one's own attractiveness do not match very well the judgments of other people, but people do agree surprisingly well with one another when they are rating a third person. Agreement as to who is or is not attractive is quite good, even when the person being judged represents a different racial or ethnic group from that of the rater (Cunningham et al., 1995). Despite this pervasive consensus about attractiveness, it is not easy for any of us to verbalize the precise cues that combine to create an attractive or an unattractive person. It is as if we have no difficulty in identifying a forest, but are unclear about the specific trees.

Investigators have sought in two primary ways to identify the detailed components of physical attractiveness. One approach is to identify a group of attractive individuals on which raters agree and then to determine what exactly they have in common. Cunningham (1986) used this method with male undergraduates who rated the attractiveness of a series of young women shown in photographs. Those women who were rated as most attractive fell into two distinct groups. The first group consisted of women who had "childlike features" with large, widely spaced eyes and a small nose and chin—women stereotyped as "cute" (McKelvie, 1993a). Other research has also identified this type of female beauty as a combination of wide eyes and full lips (Johnston & Oliver-Rodriguez, 1997). Meg Ryan can be identified as "cute." The second beautiful group had "mature" features with prominent cheekbones, high eyebrows, large pupils, and a big smile. Julia Roberts fits this category of beauty. These same two general facial types are found among white, African American, and Asian women, and they are even represented among the dimensions of attractiveness identified in ratings of female fashion models (Ashmore, Solomon, & Longo, 1996). Analogous research on male attractiveness has not yet been reported.

A second and quite different approach to the essence of attractiveness was taken by Langlois and Roggman (1990). They began with facial photographs, then combined several faces into one by means of computer digitizing. As shown in Figure 7.14, the image in each photo is divided into microscopic squares, and each square is translated into a number that represents a specific

appearance anxiety • Apprehension or worry about whether one's physical appearance is adequate and about the way one's appearance is evaluated by other people.

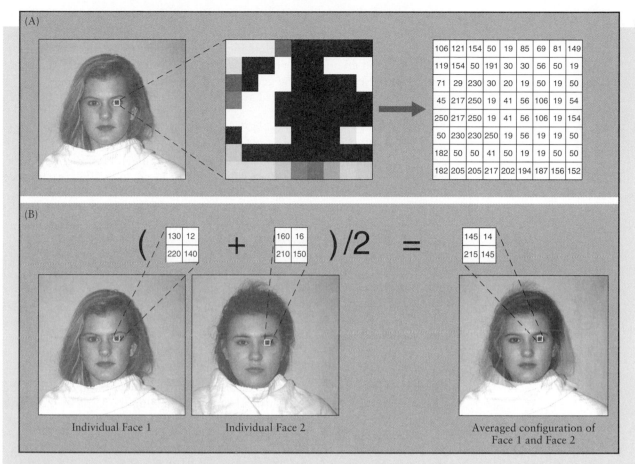

Figure 7.14

An Average Face Equals an Attractive Face. In order to create a picture of an average face, a black-and-white photograph is translated into a series of numbers that represent shades of gray, a process known as digitizing, as shown in A. These numerical values from several different faces are then averaged, and the resulting numbers are transformed back into a photograph, as shown in B. An averaged face is rated as more attractive than the individual faces that were combined to create it. And the more faces that are combined to make the average one, the more attractive is the resulting face.

(*Source:* Langlois, Roggman, & Musselman, 1994.)

shade of gray. Then the numbers are averaged across a group of pictures, and the result is translated back into a composite image.

You might reasonably think that a face created by averaging would receive an average attractiveness rating, but the actual results were quite different. For both men and women, a composite face was rated as being *more* attractive than most of the individual faces on which it was based. Even more surprising, the more faces that were combined to make the composite, the more attractive the result. These investigators concluded that, for most people, an attractive face is simply one whose components represent the average of the details of many faces (Langlois, Roggman, & Musselman, 1994). Sometimes, however, deviations from the average are attractive; for example, if you start with fifteen *very* attractive faces, their composite is preferred to a composite of sixty ordinary faces (Perrett, May, & Yoshikawa, 1994). Somewhat surprisingly, both men and women prefer a computerized image that has feminine rather than masculine features (Angier, 1998). Males who appear to be extremely macho (big jaw, square face, heavy brow) such as Gaston in "Beauty and the Beast" are perceived as less warm and honest than men with a slender nose, cupid's lips, lightened brow, and an adorable chin—Brad Pitt and Matt Damon were suggested as examples. Nevertheless, the general finding is that a face that represents the average of many faces is perceived as more attractive than most individual faces (Rhodes & Tremewan, 1996).

Why? The explanation takes us back to the earlier discussion of the effects of repeated exposure. An average of the faces of multiple strangers is perceived as more *familiar* than the specific face of any one stranger. Presumably, the average face is representative of the total sample of faces. In real life, we are not likely ever to see a truly average face (or an average cat or an average anything). Nevertheless, we define what we mean by "face" or "cat" or whatever by using an informal averaging process. We construct a mental prototype from our many experiences with specific representatives of each object. Cognitively, we have a schema for face, a schema for cat, and so forth. Such schemas make it possible for us to process and recognize a given face (or a given cat) very rapidly and efficiently. Thus, a computer-averaged face produced in the experiment is believed to be more like each participant's own cognitive schema for face than is any specific face. As a result, the averaged face is familiar, evokes a positive response, and is rated as being attractive.

Situational Influences on Perceived Attractiveness. Judgments of attractiveness are influenced by aspects of the situation as well as by the physical details of the person being judged. What if, instead of simply judging the attractiveness of a stranger, the research participant is first shown pictures of several extremely attractive individuals? Kenrick and his colleagues (1993) found that when this is done, the stranger is rated as being less attractive than when it is not done. The difference between the attractive individuals and the stranger creates what is known as a "contrast effect." That same effect alters our perception of people we know. Men who are shown photographs of very attractive women are found to rate their own romantic partners less positively afterward (Kenrick & Gutierres, 1980). It seems reasonable to surmise, then, that when members of a movie audience are exposed to attractive male and female stars, they may feel less satisfied with their own partners—at least for the moment.

In addition to influencing how we perceive others, do you think the contrast effect might influence your own self-perception? Thornton and Moore (1993) found just such an effect for both men and women. Students were seated facing a poster board containing twenty-four color photographs of very attractive same-sex models or (in the control condition) no poster board and no photographs. Each research participant was asked to fill out several self-ratings. As can be seen in Figure 7.15, exposure to the attractive same-sex models led to more negative ratings of participant's own physical attractiveness and lower social self-esteem and to higher scores on a measure of social anxiety. Similarly, after women are shown photographs of very thin models, they express lower self-esteem, more self-consciousness, and more anxiety and dissatisfaction about their own bodies (Thornton & Maurice, 1998). In related research, women who were already disturbed about their appearance became more deeply depressed after watching television commercials depicting culturally ideal images of attractiveness and thinness (Heinberg & Thompson, 1995).

A different sort of situational effect was suggested by Mickey Gilley's song about the search for romance in bars where "the girls all get prettier at closing time." Social psychological research has confirmed just such an effect; as the evening progresses, both "girls" and "boys" in the bar are perceived as more attractive (Nida & Koon, 1983; Pennebaker et al., 1979). In one field study con-

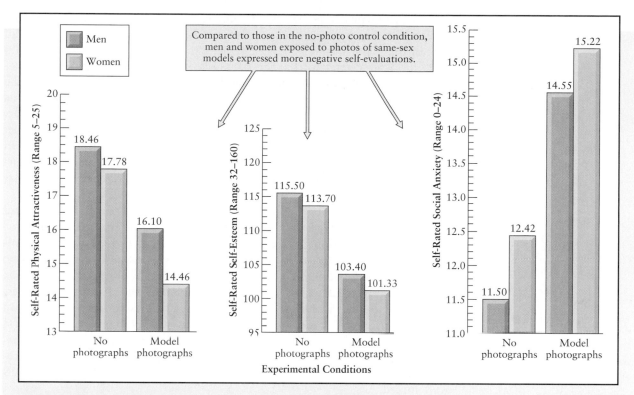

Figure 7.15

Comparisons of Self to Very Attractive Others: Negative Consequences. When male and female undergraduates filled out self-ratings on several characteristics, those in the experimental group sat facing a display of photos of very attractive same-sex models; those in the control group did not face such a display. Compared to the control group, both men and women seated in front of the attractive photographs rated themselves as less physically attractive, expressed lower self-esteem, and indicated higher social anxiety.

(*Source:* Based on data from Thornton & Moore, 1993.)

ducted in a college bar at night, Gladue and Delaney (1990) asked the customers to rate same- and opposite-sex fellow drinkers at 9:00, 10:30, and midnight. As closing time approached, opposite-sex strangers were judged to be increasingly attractive. Because the ratings of same-sex strangers did not change over the course of the evening, the results don't appear to be based on a warm alcoholic glow. Instead, the effect is believed to occur because the number of unattached potential partners decreases as the evening progresses. The resulting scarcity results in more positive evaluations of those who remain available.

Influence of Physique and Weight on Perceived Attractiveness. When we meet someone for the first time, we usually react to a variety of factors in addition to attractiveness. Any observable cue, no matter how superficial, may act as the trigger that evokes a stereotype, and the resulting emotional reactions lead to instant likes and dislikes.

Physique is one example. Both men and women stereotype those they meet on the basis of bodily characteristics. A once-popular theory proposed that one's *somatotype*—the shape of one's body—provides information about personality traits. Sheldon, Stevens, and Tucker (1940) developed a system that classified the human physique into three primary somatotypes: *endomorphs,* who are round and fat; *mesomorphs,* who are hard and muscular; and *ectomorphs,* who are thin and angular. Each of these subtypes was supposedly associated with specific personality traits. Despite decades of disappointing research attempting to link physique and personality, these inaccurate assumptions remain a solid part of the popular culture. For example, Ryckman and his colleagues (1989) asked undergraduates to describe strangers on the basis of information provided by somatotypes. The students agreed fairly well in their reactions to the strangers and in their assumptions about them. Endomorphs were perceived as ugly, sloppy, sad, dirty, and slow. Mesomorphs were described as not very smart or kind, but as popular, healthy, brave, and attractive. Ectomorphs were believed to be fearful, intelligent, and neat. Such stereotypes about physique seem to develop in childhood, perhaps partly on the basis of how characters are portrayed in stories, books, and on film. Brylinski and Moore (1994) found that negative reactions to a chubby body build first appear between the first and second grade. You might take a look at a few children's TV shows or movies, and note what is being suggested about obese children and adults.

Examining physique stereotypes in greater detail, Ryckman and his colleagues (1997) were able to identify more specific stereotypes and characteristic reactions to them within each somatotype. For example, although endomorphs in general are viewed negatively, people like endomorphic clowns, housewives, and mothers—and Santa Claus. Women who are mesomorphic athletes are liked, but men in the same category (along with jocks, bodybuilders, and studs) get mixed ratings. Some mesomorphic males are perceived as steroid users, bullies, and showoffs—and such individuals are disliked. Among ectomorphs, reactions to male scholars were positive, while reactions to female fashion models were mixed.

Whenever you read about somatotype research, or when you find yourself applying these stereotypes in your own life, please keep in mind that they are incorrect guides to other people. Body type does *not* inform you about intelligence, kindness, bravery, or anything else.

One research team produced an interesting demonstration of how the same person can be judged differently on the basis of differences in body type by altering the photographs of several men and women, using computer simulation to modify each individual's apparent somatotype (Gardner & Tockerman, 1994), as depicted in Figure 7.16. The people in the photographs were all

Figure 7.16
The Same Individual with Three Different Somatotypes. Investigators presented research participants with one of three different images of the same individual by using a picture of the actual person plus distorted narrow and wide versions of that person. Participants attributed more negative personality characteristics to the person when the wide image was shown than for either the normal or the narrow image.

(*Source:* Gardner & Tockerman, 1994).

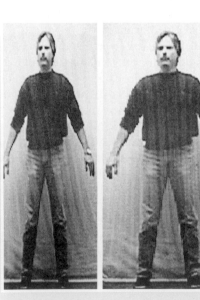

Table 7.2

Antifat Prejudice. A negative evaluation of overweight individuals is very much like racial prejudice—a negative attitude and negative attributions based on stereotypes. Crandall used a questionnaire to measure three aspects of antifat attitudes, emotional reactions, and beliefs: dislike of those who are fat, fear of becoming fat, and the belief that people become fat because they lack willpower.

Type of Antifat Attitude	Sample Questionnaire Item
Dislike	I really don't like fat people much.
	If I were an employer looking to hire, I might avoid hiring a fat person.
Fear of fat	I feel disgusted with myself when I gain weight.
	I worry about becoming fat.
Willpower	People who weigh too much could lose some of their weight through a little exercise.
	Fat people tend to be fat pretty much through their own fault.

(*Source:* Based on information in Crandall, 1994.)

of normal weight, of average physical attractiveness, and in their mid-twenties. College students were asked to rate the people in the photographs with respect to several personality traits. Most striking was the reaction to the endomorphic simulation compared to the other two. The apparently overweight stranger was perceived to be less sincere, honest, intelligent, friendly, humorous, pleasant, ambitious, talented, and neat (as well as more aggressive, lonely, envious, obnoxious, and cruel) than the same person when shown either normally or as an ectomorph.

In this as in many other investigations, the least-liked physique is the one characterized by excess fat (Harris, Harris, & Bochner, 1982; Lundberg & Sheehan, 1994), and those who are overweight all too often experience social rejection. Crandall (1994) compared prejudice against obesity to racial prejudice and developed a measure of antifat attitudes (see Table 7.2). This prejudice and the ideology of personal responsibility that underlies it are particularly widespread among those living in the United States. Despite the prevailing U.S. prejudice against fatness, however, the percentage of Americans who *are* fat continues to increase. In Mexico there is much less concern about one's weight and much less prejudice against people who are overweight (Crandall & Martinez, 1996).

When overweight individuals are rejected on the basis of antifat prejudice, the result is often social anxiety and low self-esteem. These reactions, in turn, might be expected to make it more difficult for obese people to learn how to deal successfully with social situations. Miller and her colleagues (1990) tested this possibility by having obese and nonobese college women engage in telephone conversations with undergraduate research participants who knew nothing about the woman's appearance or weight. Presumably because of differences in past social experiences, the obese strangers were judged—sight unseen—as less likable, less socially skilled, and less attractive than those whose weight was average. Follow-up research indicates, however, that overweight women are often able to overcome antifat prejudice and develop strong social skills (Miller,

Rothblum, Brand et al., 1995; Miller, Rothblum, Felicio et al., 1995). Further, a comparison of obese and nonobese women indicated no difference in social anxiety or competence, and no difference in the number of people with whom they interacted.

Other Aspects of Appearance and Behavior That Influence Attraction. Several other observable characteristics also serve as instant cues to attraction. For example, adults who look or sound very young are judged to be weak, naïve, incompetent, warm, and honest (Berry & Brownlow, 1989; Berry & Zebrowitz-McArthur, 1988). "Mature"-sounding adults are perceived as dominant and attractive, but not as warm or agreeable (Zuckerman, Miyake, & Elkin, 1995). In their daily interactions with women, baby-faced men reported less control and influence than did men with mature faces, but for women, being baby-faced was unrelated to what went on in their social interactions (Berry & Landry, 1997). (See Chapter 2 for other research on reactions to those who are baby-faced.)

Stereotypes and assumptions have also been found to be associated with clothing (Cahoon & Edmonds, 1989; Cheverton & Byrne, 1998), grooming (Mack & Rainey, 1990), height (Pierce, 1996), disabilities (Fichten & Amsel, 1986), age (McKelvie, 1993b; Perdue & Gurtman, 1990), eyeglasses (Hasart & Hutchinson, 1993; Lundberg & Sheehan, 1994), and many other observable details as well.

Behavioral differences are as important in interpersonal judgments as are differences in appearance. As one example, to the extent that a person behaves in ways suggesting that he or she is happy, others tend to respond more positively to that person than they do to someone indicating unhappiness. People respond negatively to narcissistic, self-centered, egotistical individuals (Carroll et al., 1998). Krull and Dill (1998) found that someone who smiles leads others to make multiple inferences about that person's positive disposition and about possible positive situational factors that made him or her happy. In contrast, people tend to make only limited inferences about a frowning stranger. A person with a youthful walking style elicits a more positive response than one who walks like an elderly individual, regardless of gender or actual age (Montepare & Zebrowitz-McArthur, 1988). There are additional behavioral stereotypes that lead us to make assumptions about others, and these assumptions lead to emotional reactions that influence liking. When two people engage in a discussion, observers believe an individual whose behavior is expressive (active, animated, and exaggerated) is more sympathetic than a nonexpressive individual (Bernieri et al., 1996). In a similar way, a student who is talkative during class discussions is perceived as more creative, friendly, dynamic, and less shy than a relatively quiet student (Bell, 1995).

When there is not much information available, men who behave in ways suggesting a dominant, authoritative, competitive personality (one that fits a traditional masculine image) are preferred to submissive, noncompetitive, less masculine males (Friedman, Riggio, & Casella, 1988; Sadalla, Kenrick, & Vershure, 1987). When there is additional information, however, the preference shifts to men who exhibit prosocial tendencies and behave with sensitivity (Jensen-Campbell, West, & Graziano, 1995; Morey & Gerber, 1995). In this instance, nice guys finish first.

People sometimes perceive behavior that is inconsistent with other information about a person as being especially meaningful. How would you evaluate an individual whose religious beliefs seem incompatible with his or her sexual conduct? Bailey and Vietor (1996) presented research participants with information about a female student who was described in various conditions as going to church frequently, occasionally, or never. As expected, participants rated the woman who attended church frequently as more moral than the one who never went to church. Later, the participants were given additional information about the woman they had previously rated: she was reported to have engaged in casual sex with someone she barely knew. On the basis of these new facts, the participants judged the frequent churchgoer to be *less* moral than the one who never attended church. This reversal of judgment suggests that casual sex is perceived to be worse for someone who is religious than for someone who is not. Or, people may simply react negatively to hypocrisy.

Interpersonal judgments are also influenced by what a person eats (Stein & Nemeroff, 1995). With weight, height, physical fitness, and other background factors held constant, the eating preferences of a stranger were communicated to research participants. A man or a woman who supposedly ate "good food" (e.g., oranges, salad, whole-wheat bread, and chicken) was judged to be more attractive and more likable than, and even morally superior to, one who ate "bad food" (e.g., steak, hamburgers, French fries, doughnuts, and double-fudge sundaes). Good food was also associated with femininity and bad food with masculinity. It may not be true that "you are what you eat," but you may well be judged on that basis by others.

One final, and perhaps most surprising, aspect of a stranger to which we apply positive and negative stereotypes is that person's first name. Mehrabian and Piercy (1993a) found that a man who calls himself by a nickname such as Bill (as opposed to the more formal William) is perceived to be more cheerful and popular, though less successful and moral. Leaving aside American presidential politics, this may be true in part because longer male names in general lead to less positive reactions than shorter ones. In further research, these same investigators also determined that various male and female names are associated with specific positive and negative stereotypes (Mehrabian & Piercy, 1993b); some of their findings are summarized in Table 7.3. Name length again played a role in determining reactions to men, but not to women.

Table 7.3

Personal Attributions Based on First Names. Initial impressions are sometimes based on a person's name. Once again, interpersonal attraction can be influenced by inaccurate stereotypes.

Male Names	Female Names	Attributions about the Individual
Alexander	Elizabeth	*Successful*
Otis	Mildred	*Unsuccessful*
Joshua	Mary	*Moral*
Roscoe	Tracy	*Immoral*
Mark	Jessica	*Popular*
Norbert	Harriet	*Unpopular*
Henry	Ann	*Warm*
Ogden	Freida	*Cold*
Scott	Brittany	*Cheerful*
Willard	Agatha	*Not cheerful*
Taylor	Rosalyn	*Masculine*
Eugene	Isabella	*Feminine*

(*Source:* Based on information in Mehrabian & Piercy, 1993b.)

Key Points

- Individuals high, as opposed to low, in *need for affiliation* are more likely to engage in establishing and maintaining interpersonal relationships and are more interpersonally skilled.

- People can be differentiated with respect to their reasons for wanting to affiliate, and these reasons lead to different types of affiliative behavior oriented toward different goals. When unusual circumstances, such as natural disasters, arise, people are likely to affiliate with others. They are motivated to engage in social comparison in order to clarify the situation and to clarify their own emotional reactions to it. Such clarification results in reduced anxiety.

- Interpersonal attraction and interpersonal judgments based on stereotypes are strongly influenced by various observable characteristics of those we meet, including *physical attractiveness*. Across a variety of cultures, people are found to like and to make positive attributions about attractive men and women of all ages, despite the fact that assumptions based on appearance are usually inaccurate.

- In addition to physical attractiveness, many other observable factors influence initial interpersonal evaluations; these include physique, weight, youthfulness, behavior, clothing, eyeglasses, food preferences, first names, and many other superficial characteristics.

BECOMING CLOSE ACQUAINTANCES AND MOVING TOWARD FRIENDSHIP: SIMILARITY AND RECIPROCAL POSITIVE EVALUATIONS

What have we learned about attraction so far? Briefly, we know that once two people are brought together by physical proximity (or some other means), the odds of a positive relationship increase if each is in a positive emotional state, is motivated by affiliation needs, and evaluates the observable characteristics of the other in a positive way. The next two steps toward interpersonal intimacy involve communication. Two crucial aspects of this communication are the degree to which the interacting individuals discover areas of *similarity* and the extent to which they feel and express *positive evaluations* of one another.

Opposites Don't Attract, but Birds of a Feather Really Do Flock Together

More than two thousand years ago, Aristotle wrote about friendship. He proposed that people who agree with one another become friends, while those who disagree do not. Throughout the twentieth century, sociological and social psychological research has consistently indicated that Aristotle was right. A friendly relationship is very often based on the discovery of **attitude similarity.** Note that this phrase is usually taken to mean similarity of beliefs, values, and interests as well as of attitudes. As you will soon discover, the importance of similarity to attraction also extends to many other factors. Shock jock Howard Stern takes the general proposition even farther when he proclaims, "If you're not like me, I hate you" (Zoglin, 1993). With respect to how most people react to dissimilarity, Mr. Stern is not exaggerating very much.

attitude similarity • The extent to which two individuals share the same attitudes about a range of topics; in practice, often includes similarity of beliefs, values, and interests.

Attitude Similarity As a Determinant of Attraction. Data confirming the association between attitude similarity and attraction was first provided by correlational studies in the early 1900s. For example, Schuster and Elderton (1906) studied more than four hundred families and reported significant agreement between husbands and wives about such topics as politics and religion. Many similar investigations were carried out during this period; and, in addition to married couples, friends were also found to be more similar than could have occurred by chance with respect to their attitudes, beliefs, and so on. But again note, as was pointed out in Chapter 1, that a correlation between two variables does not indicate that one necessarily causes the other. Such findings could mean that similarity leads to attraction; or that people like each other for other reasons and that liking leads to similarity; or that some other, unknown factor (e.g., having approximately the same socioeconomic status) causes people to like one another and also to hold similar attitudes.

To eliminate the liking-leads-to-similarity idea, the late social psychologist Theodore Newcomb (1956) studied friendship formation in a controlled field setting with a longitudinal design. Working at the University of Michigan, Newcomb measured the attitudes of a group of male transfer students before they ever met one another, assessed the development of friendship patterns in a housing unit over the students' first semester, and then determined whether similarity of prior attitudes predicted who would become friends. Because that is what he found, Newcomb reached the tentative conclusion that attitude similarity actually led to attraction rather than vice versa. Other determinants of attraction, such as proximity (in this instance, where their rooms were located in the housing unit) were the first determinants of who became acquainted. Attitude similarity was unrelated to these initial expressions of interpersonal attraction, because the students could not know one another's attitudes until they interacted over time. As the weeks passed, however, attitude similarity began to exert an increasing influence on attraction. The more similar they were before they met, the more the students came to like one another.

Findings such as those of Newcomb were not consistent with the hypothesis that attraction causes people to change their attitudes toward greater similarity, but it was still possible that some other factor determined both attitude similarity and attraction. To rule out that possibility, experimental investigations were needed. Similarity could be manipulated as an independent variable and attraction assessed as a dependent variable while other factors were held constant. Such experiments *were* conducted, and it became clear that similarity does indeed lead to attraction (Byrne, 1961b; Smith, 1957).

When two people interact, attitudes on many topics arise as the individuals discuss school, work, music, television, politics, or whatever, because we humans seem to enjoy expressing our likes and dislikes. Such communication makes it possible for each person to learn the attitudes of the other (Hatfield & Rapson, 1992). And, whether the topic is something of vital importance or something relatively trivial, people respond positively to those with similar views and want to be with them, while responding negatively to those with dissimilar views—preferring to avoid them, as illustrated in Figure 7.17 on page 290.

Is Attraction Influenced by Similarity, Dissimilarity, or Both? Our response to the views of others is surprisingly precise. It is almost as if we classify a person's position on each topic as similar to or different from our own, then add up the number of times the person agrees with us and divide that number by the total number of topics discussed. On the basis of this information, our evaluation of the person depends on the **proportion of similar attitudes** he or she has

proportion of similar attitudes • The number of topics on which two individuals hold the same views divided by the total number of topics on which they compare their views; can be expressed as a percentage (or ratio).

Figure 7.17

People Usually Like Similar Others and Dislike Dissimilar Others. Most people most of the time respond to similar people with positive affect, attraction, and the desire to associate with them; dissimilar people generally evoke the opposite responses. Fortunately, these reactions do not ordinarily extend to segregating lifeboats on the basis of relative preferences for cats versus dogs.

(*Source: The New Yorker,* April 15, 1996, p. 72.)

"*Sorry, we're all cat people. The dog people are in that boat over there.*"

repulsion hypothesis • Rosenbaum's provocative but inaccurate proposal that attraction is not enhanced by similar attitudes but only decreased by dissimilar attitudes.

expressed. And it doesn't matter whether the total number of topics is 4 or 400 (Byrne & Nelson, 1965): the higher the percentage of similar attitudes, the greater the liking. This relationship results in a straight-line function that can be expressed in simple mathematical terms.

The wide-ranging generality of the similarity–attraction relationship holds for college students and high school dropouts; for children and senior citizens; and for students representing a variety of cultures, including India, Japan, and Mexico as well as the United States (Byrne et al., 1971). Even on the Internet, people using e-mail exchange lists are likely to seek out others who share their views and to exclude those with dissimilar views (Schwartz, 1994). There is only limited evidence indicating that individual differences in personality can modify how we respond to attitude similarity. The best example involves need for affiliation. Individuals differing in this need respond about the same to a dissimilar stranger, but those high in affiliation need are more positive toward a similar stranger than are individuals low in affiliation need, as shown in studies in the United States and Singapore (Kwan, 1998).

Though the effect of similarity on attraction is extremely well established (Cappella & Palmer, 1990), critics often rise to the challenge by seeking to disprove it in one way or another (Sunnafrank, 1992)—but without lasting success (Byrne, 1992). Perhaps the best-known, most cogent, and most testable proposal has come from Rosenbaum (1986), who offered the **repulsion hypothesis.** Because most research on attitude similarity and attraction has asked participants to respond to another person on the basis of his or her similar *and* dissimilar attitudes, the assumption has been that similarity increases attraction while dissimilarity decreases it. Rosenbaum suggested that similar attitudes are irrelevant and that we like a person about whom we know nothing just as well as we like someone who agrees with us. In Rosenbaum's formulation, only *dissimilar* attitudes have an effect on attraction: we are repulsed by those who disagree with us. But the hypothesis that similar attitudes have no effect was shown to be incorrect in an experiment in which, in three different conditions, a stranger expressed the same number of dissimilar attitudes but three different numbers of similar attitudes (Smeaton, Byrne, & Murnen, 1989). The repulsion hypothesis would have predicted no differences in attraction across the conditions, because the conditions differed only in the number of similar attitudes. The proportion hypothesis, in contrast, predicted attraction differences across the three conditions because of the differences in proportion of similar attitudes across conditions. The repulsion hypothesis as originally stated was found to be incorrect, while the proportion hypothesis was confirmed.

Rosenbaum's interesting proposal was of value, however, in leading to additional research that produced new findings about similar and dissimilar attitudes. Specifically, though both types of attitude information influence attraction, dissimilar views do have a greater effect than similar ones (Chapman, 1992). In part, this reflects a general tendency for negative information to influence evaluations more strongly than positive information (Ito et al., 1998). With respect to attitudinal information, if someone agrees with you about who should be the next president, you think "that's nice," and you tend to evaluate the individual positively. If, however, someone disagrees with you on the same topic, your negative response to this disagreement is much stronger than your positive response to the agreement (Singh & Tan, 1992).

Why should this be so? It is well established that most people believe that those they encounter hold attitudes similar to their own (Krueger & Clement, 1994), a belief that is sometimes labeled the *false consensus effect* (Alicke & Largo, 1995). The false belief that "most everyone agrees with me" is found among children (Tan & Singh, 1995) and among people in the general population (Fabrigar & Krosnick, 1995) as well as among college students. The false consensus effect is relevant to the different effects of similar versus dissimilar information, because agreement is expected—"of course this person agrees with me; everyone does"—while disagreement comes as a surprise (Tan & Singh, 1995). Disagreement therefore has a greater effect on attraction, because this negative information "stands out."

As Duck and Barnes (1992) have pointed out, the proposed causal relationship between proportion of similar attitudes and attraction resembles the history of the *Titanic* in reverse: many are sure it will sink, but it remains afloat despite the icebergs.

Why Do Similar and Dissimilar Attitudes Influence Attraction? The basic explanation for the effect of attitudes on attraction is a simple one: Similar attitudes arouse positive affect and dissimilar attitudes arouse negative affect—and, as we have already shown, affect influences attraction. Though this affective link is accurate, we still must ask *why* the attitudes of another person cause us emotional pleasure or pain.

The oldest explanation, proposed independently by Newcomb and by Heider as well as others, is **balance theory** (Hummert, Crockett, & Kemper, 1990). This formulation states that people naturally organize their likes and dislikes (including interpersonal attraction and attitudes about most anything) in a symmetrical way. When two people like each other and agree about some topic, this represents *balance*, which produces a pleasant emotional state (Newcomb, 1961). When two people like each other but disagree about something, the result is *imbalance*, and an unpleasant state is aroused (Orive, 1988). In response to imbalance, each person is motivated to restore balance. How? By changing his or her attitudes so as to replace disagreement with agreement, by convincing the other person to change attitudes to reach agreement, by getting rid of the disagreement by misperceiving it, or by deciding simply to dislike the other person (Monsour, Betty, & Kurzweil, 1993). When two people dislike each other, they are in a state of *nonbalance;* this is neither pleasant nor unpleasant, because each feels indifferent about the attitudes of the other person.

balance theory • Theory that specifies the relationships among (1) an individual's liking for another person, (2) his or her attitude about a give topic, and (3) the other person's perceived attitude about the same topic.

Though the balance concept appears to be accurate, and though it leads to many interesting predictions about how two interacting people will respond to imbalance, it still doesn't really explain why attitudinal information matters in the first place. Why should you care if somebody agrees with you about Marilyn Manson or disagrees with you about Puffy Combs? A convincing answer is provided by Festinger's (1954) social comparison theory, which we discussed earlier. In effect, you compare your attitudes with those of other people because that is the only way to evaluate what you believe to be true. You turn to others to obtain **consensual validation;** that is, their agreement is the only source of "evidence" that you are right. It is pleasing to discover that you have sound judgment, are bright, remain in contact with reality, and so forth. Disagreement, however, suggests the reverse—and it is quite uncomfortable when someone else's attitudes raise the possibility that you have bad judgment, are stupid, have lost reality contact, and so forth. As we discussed in Chapter 5 (with respect to seeking information about one's self-concept), this analysis suggests that we are interested in the views of other people not because we are seeking objective evidence, but only because we want to verify what we already believe.

In a broader sense, however, the positive response to similarity of all kinds is a very general one and may be based on a useful biological tendency to respond most positively to those who are genetically similar to ourselves and most negatively to those who are genetically different (Rushton, 1989, 1990). In this way, we act so as to maximize the survival of our own genes as well as the survival of the genes of whoever is most like us. We will explore some of the consequences of the positive response to similarity in the following section.

The Matching Hypothesis: Liking Those Who Are Most Like You. Whether or not the evolutionary explanation for the similarity effect is entirely accurate, it *is* true that attraction is affected by interpersonal similarity with respect to many factors. Though it is commonly believed that "opposites attract," research overwhelmingly indicates that the reverse is true: similarity is the general rule in attraction.

Sir Francis Galton first determined that "like marries like" in 1870, but the **matching hypothesis** was first formulated by social psychologists engaged in research on physical attractiveness (Berscheid et al., 1971). That is, researchers have found that romantic partners tend to pair off on the basis of being similar in attractiveness. This is true for those who are dating, but it is equally true for married couples (Zajonc et al., 1987). Interestingly, observers often react negatively when they encounter couples who are "mismatched" with respect to looks; and they rate the partners in such relationships as having less ability, being less likable, and having a less satisfactory relationship than those in "typical" (matched) relationships (Forgas, 1993). Cognitively, it requires longer and more elaborate processing for us to deal with the fact that a couple is "atypical"—mismatched for physical appearance (Forgas, 1995b).

Although it is perhaps more surprising, matching for attractiveness also occurs in same-sex friendships, for men as well as women (Cash & Derlega, 1978; McKillip & Reidel, 1983). Even college roommates who are dissimilar in attractiveness are less satisfied than if they are similar (Carli, Ganley, & Pierce-Otay, 1991).

Beyond attitude and appearance similarity, numerous studies have reported that attraction is enhanced by similarity with respect to a wide variety of factors (Hogg, Cooper-Shaw, & Holzworth, 1993). Included are similarity in sociability (Joiner, 1994); emotional expressiveness (Alliger & Williams, 1991); marijuana smoking (Eisenman, 1985); religious affiliation (Kandel, 1978); self-concepts (LaPrelle et al., 1990); smoking, drinking, and engaging in premarital

consensual validation • The perceived validation of one's views that is provided when someone else expresses identical views.

matching hypothesis • The proposal that individuals are attracted to one another as friends, romantic partners, or spouses on the basis of similar attributes—physical attractiveness; age; race; personality characteristics; or social assets such as wealth, education, or power.

sex (Rodgers, Billy, & Udry, 1984); adhering to traditional gender roles (Smith, Byrne, & Fielding, 1995); defining oneself as a "morning person" or an "evening person" (Watts, 1982); and laughing at the same jokes (Cann, Calhoun, & Banks, 1995). Further, attitude similarity affects many interpersonal evaluations in addition to attraction. Examples range from assessments of intelligence, morality, and adjustment (Byrne, 1971) to evaluations of the quality of an athletic team (Lancaster, Royal, & Whiteside, 1995).

Given the importance of many types of similarity in influencing interpersonal evaluations, what would you predict about the effect of racial or ethnic similarity on friendships, dating, and marriage? Even among children aged eight to ten in racially mixed schools in the United Kingdom, both Asians and whites expressed greater liking for members of their own race than for those of the other race (Boulton & Smith, 1996). In the following *Social Diversity* section, we examine other aspects of interracial attraction.

Social Diversity: A Critical Analysis
Interracial Dating among Asian Americans

One of the more obvious ways that our behavior is influenced by similarity is shown in the effects of race and ethnicity on interpersonal choices for dates and marriage partners. Around the world, racial and ethnic similarity is much more likely in romantic relationships than is dissimilarity. Even in the United States, where the "melting pot" analogy has long been held to be the ideal, dating and marriage have tended to be confined to one's own group—however that group may be defined.

But the times they are a-changin'. For one thing, by the year 2050, if present trends continue, whites will no longer represent a majority of the U.S. population (White, 1997). One implication of this demographic shift for these individuals is that among potential romantic partners, most will not be white. Other groupings will face change as well. Though the number and proportion of black Americans will continue to grow, African Americans will nevertheless lose their place as the largest minority group because of the more rapid increases among Hispanics as well as among Asians and Pacific Islanders. Accompanying these societal shifts has been a rapid increase in interracial marriages: from fewer than 500,000 in 1970 to 1,500,000 in 1990. Since 1970 the number of multiracial children in the United States has quadrupled to more than 2,000,000, according to the Bureau of the Census. The vague promise of the melting pot is rapidly becoming a biological reality.

For many racial and ethnic groups, this merging is viewed as a threat (Fujino, 1997). For example, the group with the highest intermarriage rate in the nation consists of Asian Americans, with 23 percent choosing partners from other groups. Also, Asian American women are marrying white partners at higher rates than are Asian American men (Lee & Yamanaka, 1990), as shown in Figure 7.18 on page 294. This gender difference has been observed since the 1940s, and it holds for each Asian subgroup (Japanese, Chinese, Koreans, etc.) as well as for the total Asian population (Kitano et al., 1998). As Fujino (1997) points out, the worry among groups of Americans of Asian ancestry, as among other minority groups, is that they will cease to exist as distinct entities in a few generations. The disappearance of racial–ethnic distinctions can be viewed as a threat to one aspect of social identity (see Chapter 5)—or as a unique opportunity to end racial prejudice for all times, as various groups merge in the "browning of America."

Regardless of one's position on such issues, the question for social psychologists is "Why?" What are the factors leading to this change? Fujino (1997) proposed that we can best determine the causes of the phenomenon by examining how males and females of different races become friends and begin dating. She hypothesized that dating patterns should closely resemble marriage patterns and, more crucially, that "outdating" would occur for the same reasons that relationships are formed *within* racial groups; that is, on the basis of factors in attraction such as proximity, physical attractiveness, and attitude similarity.

To assess the factors leading to interracial attraction, Fujino administered a questionnaire to a sample of almost six hundred Asian and white college students at UCLA. The participants provided demographic information, their dating history, and information on their attitudes. The data from these unmarried students closely paralleled the figures for marriage, although there were two differences: Asian American men and women were equally involved in outdating, and dating those of another race occurred more frequently than outmarriage. That is, 69 to 87 percent of Chinese and Japanese male and female students

Figure 7.18
Interracial Marriages: Increasingly Frequent in the United States. Over the past several decades, interracial dating and marriages have increased steadily in the United States. This trend is criticized by those who fear the loss of racial identity but welcomed by those who see racial blending as a way to end prejudice. For the individual men and women directly involved, the determining factors seem to be the same ones that determine interpersonal attraction of all kinds—proximity, physical attractiveness, attitude similarity, and so forth.

reported outdating, but the comparable figures for interracial marriages in Los Angeles County for the same groups range from 27 to 55 percent.

It had been expected that the more acculturated an Asian student (that is, the more the individual had adopted aspects of the American culture), the more likely he or she would be to date someone of another race; but in fact acculturation did not predict interracial dating. Instead, the strongest predictor was proximity, followed by physical attractiveness. Such findings suggest that if students are brought together in the classroom and other campus settings and they find one another physically attractive, the effects on interpersonal attraction are the same regardless of their racial backgrounds.

Reciprocal Positive Evaluations: If You Like Me, I Like You

Once two people discover that they are sufficiently similar that it makes sense to move toward establishing a friendship, one additional step is crucial. Each individual must somehow communicate liking and positive evaluation to the other (Condon & Crano, 1988). Each of us is almost always pleased to receive positive feedback and displeased to receive negative evaluations (Gordon, 1996). Even "helpful" information that is negative (see Figure 7.19) is not usually well received. There is one exception to the unpleasant response to negative information. When a person's self-concept is relatively negative (see Chapter 5), he or she may respond well to an accurate negative evaluation (Swann, Stein-Serossi, & Giesler, 1992) because the unflattering evaluation is consistent with his or her self-schema.

In the opposite instance, even a positive evaluation that is inaccurate (Swann et al., 1987) or an attempt at flattery (Drachman, DeCarufel, & Insko, 1978) is *very* welcome. To an observer such flattery may seem transparently insincere, but to the person being flattered it is more likely to appear honest and accurate (Gordon, 1996). Verbal flattery is even more effective than actions such as doing someone a favor. When an employee is especially nice to a superior in an organization but not nice to subordinates, he or she is seen as especially dislikable and slimy—the *slime effect* (Vonk, 1998). This pattern of "licking upward but kicking downward" is greatly disliked by the ones being "kicked" and even by those who are not involved; but as you can guess, the pos-

"Do you mind if I say something helpful about your personality?"

Figure 7.19

Positive Evaluations: If You Can't Say Something Positive, Keep Quiet. In interpersonal interactions, we very much like to receive positive evaluations of any kind and very much dislike receiving negative evaluations of any kind. Such evaluations are more powerful determinants of attraction than similarity–dissimilarity or anything else. Except in rare circumstances, even "something helpful" is likely to be resented if it implies criticism.

(*Source: The New Yorker,* August 4, 1997, p. 61.)

itive behavior toward a superior is nevertheless often an effective interpersonal strategy. When Alexis de Tocqueville came from France in 1831 to study the United States, he observed that Americans, despite their crude clothing and customs, had a special talent for ingratiating themselves with anybody and everybody who could do something for them (Lapham, 1996).

Ingratiation through flattery is a skill that salespeople, politicians, and most everyone else as well are apt to find useful. When you use ingratiation tactics, you are not necessarily perceived as more competent, but you *are* better liked (Gordon, 1996). In a study of almost 150 managers employed in public and private organizations, those who used ingratiation techniques on the job reported the greatest salary increases and the most promotions over a five-year period (Orpen, 1996). In the same investigation, the use of self-promotion tactics (praising oneself and making assertions about one's good qualities) had *no* effect on raises and promotions. In the workplace, it seems that flattery is much more successful than bragging.

Note, however, that most people don't like to criticize others; many times people make positive interpersonal statements in order to be polite and to avoid hurting someone's feelings rather than simply to get something in return.

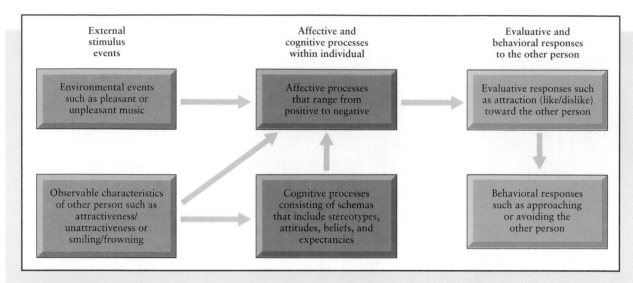

Figure 7.20

The Affect-Centered Model of Attraction. Essentially, attraction to a given person is based on affective responses that are aroused by various events (e.g., pleasant versus unpleasant music), by relatively stable characteristics of the person (e.g., physical appearance), and by changeable characteristics of the person (e.g., smiling versus frowning). Some of the person's characteristics have a relatively direct effect on one's emotional responses (e.g., flattering comments or hostile insults); other characteristics must be processed cognitively in ways that activate schemas involving stereotypes, attitudes, beliefs, and expectancies (e.g., attractiveness, race, similarities and differences, etc.). The net affective state leads to an evaluative response along a dimension ranging from liking to dislike and to approach or avoidant behavior consistent with the evaluation.

(*Source:* Based on material in Byrne, 1992.)

affect-centered model of attraction • A conceptual framework in which attraction is assumed to be based on positive and negative emotions. These emotions can be aroused directly by another person, simply associated with that person, and/or mediated by cognitive processes.

DePaulo and Bell (1996) asked research participants to discuss student paintings, some of which the participants liked and some of which they disliked. When the artist was present, the participants did not give totally honest feedback and attempted to make positive statements of one kind or another, including some outright lies. Sadly enough, this tendency toward politeness and kindness is more apt to disappear when we know the other person well (as within a family or a long-term relationship) than with strangers, as we shall see in Chapter 8.

Though mutual liking is ordinarily expressed in words, the first signs of attraction may be nonverbal cues (discussed in Chapter 2). For example, when a woman maintains eye contact while conversing with a man and leans toward him, the man tends to interpret these acts (sometimes incorrectly) to mean that she likes him. Such positive signs, in turn, often lead him to like her (Gold, Ryckman, & Mosley, 1984).

It seems very clear that we like those who like us or who we believe like us. You may find it useful to consider several techniques that should lead people to like you, as outlined in the *Ideas to Take with You* feature on page 298.

Attraction: The Bigger Picture. Throughout this chapter, we have stressed the proposal that attraction is based on affective responses. This general concept is known as the **affect-centered model of attraction.** The emphasis on affect does not mean, however, that cognitive processes are irrelevant. As shown in Figure 7.20, person A's affective state (whether directly aroused by person B or simply associated with him or her) is believed to play a major role in determining the evaluation A makes of B. This evaluation, in turn, influences A's interpersonal interactions (both verbal and nonverbal) with B. It is also necessary for A to engage in cognitive processing of all available information about B. Because this information (including stereotypes, beliefs, and factual knowledge) can be affectively arousing, it contributes to A's evaluation of B. At the same time A is reacting and processing information about B, B is of course doing the same thing with respect to A. One possible end result is a positive relationship between A and B.

Key Points

- One of the factors determining attraction is similarity of attitudes, beliefs, values, and interests.

- Though dissimilarity has a greater impact on attraction than similarity, we respond to both. The higher the *proportion of similar attitudes* (as well as beliefs, opinions, values, etc.), the greater the attraction.

- The positive response to similarity seems to rest on the positive affect that is aroused. Though various theories have been offered to account for that affective response, a social comparison explanation seems most convincing. We like people who agree with us because agreement provides *consensual validation* that we are "correct."

- On a wide variety of factors, people are most attracted to others who resemble them in every respect. That is, we like, become friends with, date, and marry those who are similar to us.

- We also like other people who indicate positive evaluations of us, either in what they say or in what they do; and we tend to dislike others who evaluate us negatively. In a wide variety of situations, flattery will get you everywhere.

- An overall summary of the major determinants of attraction is provided by the *affect-centered model of attraction,* which specifies that attraction is determined by direct and associated sources of affect, often mediated by cognitive processes.

Connections: Integrating Social Psychology

In this chapter, you read about . . .	*In other chapters, you will find related discussions of . . .*
attitudes about people	attitudes in general (Chapter 4)
conditioning of attraction	conditioning of attitudes (Chapter 4)
affect and attraction	affect and cognition (Chapter 3)
correlational versus experimental findings in similarity–attraction research	types of research (Chapter 1)
similarity and attraction	similarity and friendship, love, and marriage (Chapter 8)
effects of physical attractiveness	attractiveness and love (Chapter 8); effects of attractiveness in the courtroom (Chapter 13)
appearance and stereotypes	prejudice and stereotypes (Chapter 6)
preferring positive information about self	seeking positive information about self (Chapter 5)

(continued)

Thinking about Connections

1. Pick one person you know (or once knew) very well. Can you remember exactly how you met? When did you decide you liked that individual, and why? If the relationship no longer exists, what happened to end it? Are there any connections between your personal experience with this person and the factors involved in attraction, as discussed in this chapter?

2. Consider some issues about which you have strong feelings. Do you ever discuss these issues with your acquaintances, friends, or family? How do you react when others agree with you? What happens when they disagree with you? Have disagreements ever caused you to stop interacting with someone you once liked? Think about your reactions and about why agreement and disagreements might matter to you.

3. Think about the physical appearance of someone you see in class, in your dormitory, or at work, but don't know very well. On the basis of the person's physique, accent, clothing, behavior, or whatever, what do you think you know about him or her? Have you ever talked to this person? Why or why not? Do you see any connections between prejudice and your evaluation of this individual?

4. Do you ever compliment other people, tell them you like them, or comment favorably on something they have done? If so, how did they respond? Describe what you believe is going on in this kind of interaction. Consider the opposite situation, in which you have criticized another person, indicated dislike, or given a negative evaluation. What happens in this kind of interaction?

Ideas to Take with You
How to Encourage Others to Like You

Most of us would much rather be liked than disliked, and yet many of us have trouble getting to know other people and establishing friendly relationships. The suggestions outlined here are based on social psychological research, and you may find them helpful. If, of course, you don't want to be liked and prefer to be left alone, just do the opposite.

Control Proximity Factors.

Whenever possible, play an active role in arranging the ordinarily *accidental* contacts that control who becomes acquainted with whom. In the classroom, for example, sit beside others and avoid seats on the end of rows or in the corners. After a while, if you haven't become acquainted with those sitting near you, move to a new location and start over.

Provide Positive Affect.

In situations where you hope to make friends, do whatever you can to create a pleasant mood. Depending on the situation, this could involve setting a comfortable temperature, playing pleasant music, finding upbeat conversational topics, providing something good to eat and drink, and so forth.

Affiliate When Unusual Situations Arise.

From time to time we find ourselves in unexpected situations, including natural disasters (floods, hurricanes, etc.) and disruptions of our ordinary lives (power outages, accidents, the odd behavior of a stranger, etc.). In such situations most people very much want to interact with others (including total strangers) in order to clarify what is going on and what emotional reactions are appropriate. You can initiate conversations, provide new information, and disclose your own reactions. Instant interpersonal contact is uniquely possible when we encounter an unusual situation, even a very stressful one.

Make the Most of Your Appearance and Look Beyond Appearances.

Because observable characteristics play an important role in how others react to you, anything you can do to improve your physical appearance and outward manner can be helpful. Without becoming obsessed about it, there are multiple ways to improve how you look and (much more easily) to improve whatever you say or do that pleases or offends others. On the other hand, try very hard to overcome inaccurate stereotypes based on superficial characteristics that may influence your response to others.

Stress Similarities and Minimize Differences.

Remember that people respond well to agreement and similarity. You don't need to deceive anyone about your own views or beliefs or interests, but there is absolutely no need to emphasize and dwell on areas of dissimilarity when you can find areas of similarity instead. No one likes to have their beliefs and values continually challenged (and potentially threatened), so approach disagreements in an open-minded and nondogmatic way. At the same time, try to make sense of the views of others without becoming threatened and defensive yourself. Keep in mind that agreement need not mean you are correct, and disagreement need not mean you are wrong.

Be Nice.

It's as easy to be nice as to be obnoxious, and "nice" includes saying sincerely positive things to others. Compliments, praise, congratulations, and positive evaluations are almost always guaranteed to please; insults, criticisms, derogatory remarks, and negative evaluations are almost always guaranteed to cause discomfort.

SUMMARY AND REVIEW OF KEY POINTS

Recognizing and Evaluating Strangers: Proximity and Emotions

- The term *interpersonal attraction* refers to the attitudes we form about other people, expressed along a dimension ranging from like to dislike, based on feelings ranging from extremely positive to extremely negative.
- One's initial contact with others is very often based on *proximity* resulting from such physical aspects of the environment as classroom seating assignments, the location of residences, and how a workplace is arranged.
- Proximity leads to *repeated exposure* to some individuals in one's environment; repeated exposure tends to result in positive affect, and positive affect results in attraction.
- Positive and negative affective states can influence attraction either through direct effects (when the other person

is responsible for the positive or negative emotion) or through indirect effects (when the emotion is created by a different source, but the other person happens to be associated with it.

- Affect from more than one source is additive, and we are most influenced by associated affect if we are unaware of its source and if we are relatively uninformed about the person or object we are evaluating.

Becoming Acquaintances: The Need to Affiliate and the Effect of Observable Characteristics

- Individuals high, as opposed to low, in *need for affiliation* are more likely to engage in establishing and maintaining interpersonal relationships and are more interpersonally skilled.

- People can be differentiated with respect to their reasons for wanting to affiliate, and these reasons lead to different types of affiliative behavior oriented toward different goals. When unusual circumstances, such as natural disasters, arise, people are likely to affiliate with others. They are motivated to engage in social comparison in order to clarify the situation and to clarify their own emotional reactions to it. Such clarification results in reduced anxiety.

- Interpersonal attraction and interpersonal judgments are strongly influenced by various observable characteristics of those we meet, including *physical attractiveness*. Across a variety of cultures, people are found to like and to make positive attributions about attractive men and women of all ages, despite the fact that assumptions based on appearance are usually inaccurate.

- In addition to physical attractiveness, many other observable factors influence initial interpersonal evaluations; these include physique, weight, youthfulness, behavior, clothing, eyeglasses, food preferences, first names, and many other superficial characteristics.

Becoming Close Acquaintances and Moving toward Friendship: Similarity and Reciprocal Positive Evaluations

- One of the factors determining attraction is similarity of attitudes, beliefs, values, and interests.

- Though dissimilarity has a greater impact on attraction than similarity, we respond to both. The higher the *proportion of similar attitudes* (including beliefs, beliefs, values, etc.) the greater the attraction.

- The positive response to similarity seems to rest on the positive affect that is aroused. Though various theories have been offered to account for that affective response, a social comparison explanation seems most convincing. We like people who agree with us because agreement provides *consensual validation* that we are "correct."

- On a wide variety of factors, people are most attracted to others who resemble them in every respect. That is, we like, become friends with, date, and marry those who are similar to us.

- We also like other people who indicate positive evaluations of us, either in what they say or in what they do; and we tend to dislike others who evaluate us negatively. In a great many situations, flattery will get you everywhere.

- An overall summary of the major determinants of attraction is provided by the *affect-centered model of attraction*, which specifies that attraction is determined by direct and associated sources of affect, only mediated by cognitive processes.

KEY TERMS

affect-centered model of attraction (p. 296)

appearance anxiety (p. 280)

attitude similarity (p. 288)

balance theory (p. 291)

consensual validation (p. 292)

interpersonal attraction (p. 256)

matching hypothesis (p. 292)

need for affiliation (p. 270)

physical attractiveness (p. 276)

proportion of similar attitudes (p. 289)

proximity (p. 258)

repeated exposure (p. 258)

repulsion hypothesis (p. 290)

social comparison theory (p. 275)

stigma (p. 266)

FOR MORE INFORMATION

Byrne, D. (1997). An overview (and underview) of research and theory within the attraction paradigm. *Journal of Social and Personal Relationships, 14,* 417–431.
A personal account describing how and why one social psychologist became involved in research on interper-

sonal attraction and how that research expanded from a simple experimental confirmation of one of the factors that determines attraction to an exploration of a complex array of such factors and the theoretical explanation that ties them together.

Hatfield, E., & Sprecher, S. (1986). *Mirror, mirror . . . : The importance of looks in everyday life.* Albany, NY: SUNY Press.

A well-written and extremely interesting summary of research dealing with the effects of physical attractiveness on interpersonal relationships. The scientific literature is well covered, and the findings are illustrated throughout with anecdotes, photographs, and drawings that consistently enliven the presentation.

Newcomb, T. M. (1961). *The acquaintance process.* New York: Holt, Rinehart and Winston.

This slim volume by the late Ted Newcomb contains a description of balance theory and presents the landmark study that investigated how strangers living in a university housing unit became acquainted with one another over the course of a semester.

Close Relationships: Family, Friends, Lovers, and Spouses

Little Family. © José Ortega/Stock Illustration Source

Chapter Outline

Interdependent Relationships with Family and Friends—or Loneliness
The First Relationships Are a Family Matter
SOCIAL DIVERSITY: A CRITICAL ANALYSIS: Felt Obligation toward
   Parents: Differences within Families and across Cultures
Relationships beyond the Family: Finding a Close Friend
Effects of Attachment Style on Adult Relationships
Loneliness: Failing to Establish Close Relationships

Romantic Relationships, Love, and Physical Intimacy
Romantic Relationships
BEYOND THE HEADLINES: As Social Psychologists See It: Romance in
   the Workplace
What Is This Thing Called Love?
Sexuality in Romantic Relationships

Marriage: Moving beyond Romance
Similarity and Marriage
CORNERSTONES OF SOCIAL PSYCHOLOGY: Terman's Study of
   Husband–Wife Similarity and Marital Success
Marital Sex, Love, Parenthood, and Other Influences on
   General Satisfaction
Troubled Relationships and the Effects of Marital Failure
CONNECTIONS: Integrating Social Psychology
IDEAS TO TAKE WITH YOU: All You Need Is Love?

Summary and Review of Key Points
Key Terms
For More Information

There was an eight-year gap between me (Donn Byrne) and my brother, Bill, and this age difference made it difficult for the two of us to feel especially close. For example, an eight-year-old-boy is not likely to find great joy in dealing with an infant, a four-year-old and a twelve-year-old are not likely to enjoy hanging out together, and so forth. When Bill was in high school—dating, taking part in interschool debates, and acting in plays (Charlie's Aunt was the one I remember best)—I was playing cowboys and Indians. Then I was asked to be on a local radio show for children (Nanna and Donn), and Bill and I finally had something in common. One evening, the two of us went to the radio studio with small roles in the same drama. I played the little boy who grew up and went overseas to help the British fight the Germans, and Bill was the Western Union boy who brought the telegram announcing that I had been killed.

Shortly after that program, on a Sunday morning in 1941, I was in the living room with our parents, reading the funnies, when Bill came in to ask where Pearl Harbor was. My dad told him that it was a naval base in Hawaii and wondered why he wanted to know. That's the moment we learned that a distant part of America had been attacked by Japan. In effect, World War II began that morning for the United States, though it was not official until the next day. Bill was eager to sign up for the Army Air Corps and left Austin High School halfway through his senior year to do so. By Christmas he was in basic training in San Antonio.

Age had kept us apart up until that time, but now we were physically separated as well. We exchanged letters throughout the war, however, and probably communicated more and in more detail than we would have if Bill had continued to live at home. I remember being thrilled to receive censored mail from the Aleutian Islands. Less exotic letters came from Miami when Bill was selected for Officers Candidate School. We were living in Galveston, Texas, when he returned on leave as a second lieutenant, and I will always remember the pride I felt walking around downtown with him as he was saluted by enlisted men in various branches of the military. In my eyes he was at least the equivalent of President Roosevelt or General Eisenhower, and I was very happy to bask in his reflected glory.

After the war, Bill returned home (Bakersfield, California, by that time) with a wife. Soon afterward, the first of their four children was born. So now I was the kid in high school—and he was a veteran with a wife, child, home, and job. We were still far apart in our interests and concerns.

But by the time I was in graduate school with a wife of my own, the age difference between my brother and me began to shrink in significance. In the years after that, we became equals and actually had some things in common beyond early memories of living in the same family setting and being on the radio. Not to be outdone, I also became the father of four children. (Sibling rivalry takes many forms.) The last time Bill and I spent several days together was when he traveled from California to Indiana in order to spend time with our mother in the last months of her life. She had leukemia but was in remission at the time, and it was fun to have our original family group temporarily restored and to have a brother around.

Because of differences in age, geography, and occupations, Bill and I would have been unlikely even to have known each other had we not been brothers. Nonetheless, the ties of genetics, early family experiences, and sporadic meetings over the years made us a part of each other's life. When he died unexpectedly of a heart attack a few years ago, I realized more clearly than ever before that each member of one's family is irreplaceable and that we would be wise to enjoy and appreciate each one of them before it is too late.

The study of *interpersonal attraction* (Chapter 7) has been a major focus of social psychological research for most of the twentieth century, but work on *interpersonal relationships* has tended to lag behind. One possible reason for the difference is that an ongoing relationship between A and B is more complex and more difficult to study than the relatively simple question of how much A and B like one another at a given moment. In recent years, however, social psychologists have made up for lost time by becoming extremely active in the study of love and intimacy (Hatfield & Rapson, 1993b), marriage (Sternberg & Hojjat, 1997), relationships within families (Boon & Brussoni, 1998), and the cognitive representation of social relationships (Haslam, 1994). A great deal of research in social psychology is now concentrating on relationships—including friendships in childhood, adulthood (Adams & Blieszner, 1994), and old age (Matthews, 1986); cross-gender friendships (Gaines, 1994); and the role of friendship in the lives of gays and lesbians (Nardi & Sherrod, 1994). Given the importance of family, friendship, love, and marriage to most people, knowledge about the factors underlying success and failure in relationships are likely to be of widespread interest to all of us (Canary, Cupach, & Messman, 1995).

In this chapter, we will first describe what is known about two important kinds of *interdependent relationships*—those within the family and those involving close friendships—along with the inability of some individuals to establish lasting interdependent relationships and the resultant prospect of *loneliness*. We next examine *intimate relationships* and the factors involved in romance, love, and sexual intimacy. The final topic, *marital relationships*, focuses on the factors associated with successful and unsuccessful marriages and the often painful effects of dissolving a relationship.

INTERDEPENDENT RELATIONSHIPS WITH FAMILY AND FRIENDS—OR LONELINESS

The common element of all close relationships is **interdependence,** an interpersonal association in which two people consistently influence each other's lives, focus their thoughts and emotions on one another, and regularly engage in joint activities whenever possible. Such interdependence occurs across age groups and among individuals representing a variety of quite different relationships.

According to the college students surveyed by Berscheid, Snyder, and Omoto (1989), the one person in the world to whom they feel the greatest degree of closeness is a romantic partner (almost half of the respondents), a friend (about a third), or a family member (a little over 10 percent). We will consider all three categories of relationship, turning first to the family.

The First Relationships Are a Family Matter

Most parent–child interactions have later implications, because the family is the setting in which each of us learns how to deal with other people. Even the way in which parents play with their children provides youngsters with information about how to interact with others, thus enabling them to engage in cooperative play later on with their peers (Lindsey, Mize, & Pettit, 1997). Because of the lasting effects of early experience on later interpersonal behavior, the study of family relationships extends beyond the usual boundaries of social psychology.

interdependence • The characteristic common to all close relationships—an interpersonal association in which two people influence each other's lives and engage in many joint activities.

For that reason, in the present chapter we will be describing research on infants, children, and adolescents that could easily be labeled "developmental psychology" rather than "social psychology." By the time you finish reading this chapter, however, it should be clear that early interpersonal experiences and early relationships are crucial determinants of how we deal with relatives, friends, and romantic partners throughout our lives.

We pointed out in Chapter 5 that the basic aspects of the self-concept and social self-concept develop through the social interactions within a family. Who we are, what we think of ourselves, and how we respond to others are based in large part on our interactions with our closest relatives and on what they say, do, and believe. Let's look more closely at these extremely important interpersonal determinants of the self.

Attachment Style: Learning Self-Esteem and Trust. In research on newborns, Bowlby (1982) proposed that during the interactions between an infant and its primary caregiver (usually the mother), the child develops cognitions centering on two crucial "working models." One working model is that aspect of the self-schema that we described in Chapter 5 as *self-esteem*. That is, the actions and attitudes of the caregiver teach the infant that he or she is a valued, important, loved individual or that he or she is relatively valueless, unimportant, and unloved. We have already discussed the fact that self-esteem is an influential factor in our lives.

The second working model that develops during this all-important period of one's life is an aspect of the social self that involves one's beliefs and expectancies about other people—**interpersonal trust.** The general idea is that the infant experiences the caregiver as being trustworthy, dependable, and reliable or as being relatively untrustworthy, undependable, and unreliable. Either the caregiver is dedicated to taking care of the infant's needs or, for whatever reasons, he or she is not. As the infant grows and interacts with other people within and outside of the family, this basic cognitive and emotional representation of the caregiver generalizes to them. It is as if, long before we have acquired language skills, we have the capacity to acquire basic schemas involving self and others, schemas that guide our interpersonal behavior throughout our lives.

Based on his conceptualizations about these early interactions and the resulting schemas, Bowlby proposed that infants develop one of three types of **attachment style** (see Figure 8.1) as a function of their early experiences. These attachment styles were identified as *secure, insecure-avoidant,* or *insecure ambivalent*. These three patterns can also be observed in a controlled laboratory interaction between children and their mothers: on two occasions the mother exits the room, leaving the child briefly, and then returns (Ainsworth et al., 1978). In this situation, secure children are mildly upset by the mother's absence but are quickly soothed by her return. Avoidant children tend to reject the mother and show emotional control and restraint when they are with her. Those who are ambivalent give evidence of conflict—they cry when separated from the mother but continue crying and expressing anger when she returns. Very similar reactions are displayed among adults in an airport when couples are facing separation because one of the individuals is departing while the other is not (Fraley & Shaver, 1998).

Studies of later childhood suggest that these behavior patterns continue to influence how each individual responds in various contexts. Secure attachment is associated with such later characteristics as a positive affective state (see Chapter 7), empathy (see Chapter 10), high self-esteem (see Chapter 5), and positive interactions with peers and adults. Insecure avoidant attachment is as-

interpersonal trust • A dimension involving one's belief that other people are trustworthy, dependable, and reliable or that they are untrustworthy, undependable, and unreliable.

attachment style • Degree of security in interpersonal relationships; develops in infancy and appears to affect interpersonal behavior throughout life.

Figure 8.1
The Basic Interpersonal Relationship. The interaction between a mother and her infant appears to be a critical determinant of the infant's *attachment style*—secure, avoidant, or ambivalent. The offspring's attachment style, in turn, is reflected in later interpersonal relationships throughout life.

sociated with hostile and distant interpersonal relationships and a tendency to resist seeking adult help to solve problems. Insecure ambivalent attachment seems to result in dependency on adults accompanied by anger as well as behavior that is noncompliant, unenthusiastic, and unsociable.

In effect, the child can learn to trust and to love the most important person in his or her early life, to mistrust and avoid that person, or a mixture of the two reactions. Although this division into three attachment styles is widely used, some investigators have found it useful to conceptualize four attachment styles, as we shall describe shortly. The basic and most important concept to remember, however, is that a person's original interpersonal experiences shape his or her basic beliefs about self and others, and that these beliefs influence interpersonal relationships from childhood to adulthood. Cross-cultural research in the Netherlands (Gerlsma, Buunk, & Mutsaers, 1996) provides evidence of the universality of the attachment phenomenon.

What specific behaviors characterize mothers who make their infants feel secure or insecure? Becker and Becker (1994) investigated emotional bonding between mothers and infants as a function of how the mothers interacted with their offspring. They observed many such interactions and recorded the mothers' physical contact, visual contact, verbal contact, and awareness of and reactions to the infant's needs. Some of the details of the variations in maternal behaviors are provided in Table 8.1 on page 308. The ultimate goal of such research is to be able to predict infant attachment style on the basis of the mother's behavior.

We will return to the topic of attachment when we discuss interpersonal relationships in childhood, adolescence, and adulthood.

The Importance of Other Interactions between Parents and Their Offspring.
Beyond mother–infant interactions, both mother and father (and other adults in the family as well) interact in various ways with toddlers, young children, and adolescents. All such interactions have some effect on children's development and on what children learn about relationships (O'Leary, 1995).

Table 8.1

Interacting with One's Baby. Observations of mothers interacting with their babies suggest major differences that may contribute to differences in attachment style. Mothers differ in the security they provide when touching, looking at, and talking to their infants—and in their awareness of and responsiveness to the infant's needs.

Mother's Behavior	Levels of Security	Examples
How does mother touch her infant?	*Low security*	Touches infant only with her fingertips
	Medium security	Holds infant in arms away from her chest
	High security	Presses infant closely to her chest
How does mother look at her infant?	*Low security*	Avoids looking at infant
	Medium security	Looks at infant briefly, without comment
	High security	Seeks face-to-face contact and maintains it
How does mother talk to infant?	*Low security*	Few or no verbalizations to or about infant
	Medium security	Positive and negative verbalizations to or about infant
	High security	Mostly positive verbalizations to or about infant *plus* statements about the infant's care and well-being
How aware and responsive is mother to infant's needs?	*Low security*	Appears to be unaware of infant's needs
	Medium security	Aware of infant's needs but responds inappropriately
	High security	Is aware of and responds promptly and appropriately to infant's needs

(*Source:* Based on material in Becker & Becker, 1994.)

Parents often dread the transition of their offspring from childhood to adolescence, because they expect to be rejected by a rebellious teenager. To some extent these fears and expectations are justified. Flannery and his colleagues (1993) observed girls and boys in grades 5 to 9 as they held two conversations with each parent. One conversation was about a pleasant, enjoyable event and the other about a topic of disagreement or conflict. The older and more physically mature the youngster, the less positive and more negative the affect expressed during the interactions and the greater the degree of conflict. Russell and Searcy (1997) studied the way Australian teenagers responded to mildly controlling parental behavior. Some responded negatively to parental control (especially when a stepparent was involved), whereas others responded in a positive way (especially when a birth parent was involved). Not surprisingly, the adolescents responded best to parental behavior that was perceived as warm and affectionate.

In general, the belief that parent–offspring relations become less pleasant as puberty arrives appears to be an accurate one. Despite this general truth, however, most adolescents express very positive feelings about their parents, even though they are less close to and less dependent on them than in childhood (Galambos, 1992)—see Figure 8.2. Jeffries (1993) finds that adolescents love their parents to the extent that they *like* them and to the extent that the adolescent is *virtuous* (a good person who behaves in a moral and ethical way). Thus, a teenager who is genuinely attracted to his or her parents and who is a "good" person not only loves but feels loved in return, is happy and satisfied with the relationship, exhibits empathy, has high self-esteem, and trusts other people. You might note that this description overlaps with what we described as a secure attachment style.

Figure 8.2
Adolescence: Not Necessarily a Time of Rebellion. During the teenage years the parent–offspring relationship is often strained by the adolescent's increasing sense of independence in the transition to adulthood. Nevertheless, the relationship can be a positive and loving one rather than a time of rebellion and anger.

As life expectancy increases, a growing number of adults find themselves facing a new kind of relationship with one or both parents. That is, after being cared for as children and adolescents and later being independent as adults, they must now consider the transition to becoming a caregiver for their mother and/or father. People differ in their willingness to undertake this new role, and cross-cultural studies of family structure and effects on subsequent feelings about one's parents provide some clues as why these differences occur. The following *Social Diversity* section suggests some interesting possibilities.

Social Diversity: A Critical Analysis
Felt Obligation toward Parents: Differences within Families and across Cultures

A special problem arises when elderly parents are in need of care and siblings fail to respond equally. In the majority of cases, only one of the siblings accepts responsibility for parental care (Merrill, 1996). For example, throughout my (Donn Byrne's) childhood, my grandfather lived with us. For me, it was a wonderful experience to have someone who seemed to have unlimited time to read to me, tell me stories, play checkers, take me for walks, go to the movies, play catch, and so forth. It never occurred to me to ask why my grandfather lived with this particular son and daughter-in-law rather than with one of his other sons or daughters, or to wonder how any of them felt about the arrangement. Later in my life, when my parents needed help, they lived with my family, and once again I observed children benefiting from the presence of grandparents in the home. Why me and my family and not my brother and his family? I now know that siblings seldom respond in the same way to this situation, though the reasons are not entirely clear.

While most U.S. families do not emphasize a belief system that includes an obligation to take care of one's parents, such beliefs are quite common in other cultures. For example, a study of Chinese people aged sixteen to seventy-eight in Hong Kong revealed that they commonly develop feelings of empathy and assumed responsibility for the well-being of their parents (Cheung, Lee, & Chan, 1994). A possible explanation lies in collectivist versus individualistic values. The typical individualistic society stresses self-interest, autonomy, privacy, and independence; the typical collectivist society stresses loyalty to the family, emotional dependence on one another, less personal privacy, and interdependence (Dion & Dion, 1993).

A direct comparison of such cultural differences provides valuable information. Freeberg and Stein (1996) undertook just such a comparison by examining Mexican American and Anglo-American families. The research participants were one hundred young adults (aged eighteen to twenty-five) who came from intact families and who

Figure 8.3
Family Attitudes and Interactions in Hispanic Families. When adults face the prospect of helping their fathers and/or mothers as they grow old, individuals differ in the degree to which they feel obligated to provide help. Comparisons of families with different cultural backgrounds suggest that the beliefs and behaviors of Mexican Americans lead to a stronger feeling of obligation than the beliefs and behaviors of Anglo-Americans.

lived in a midwestern U.S. city. Half were male and half were female. Half identified themselves as "white" or "Caucasian" and half as "Chicano," "Mexican," or "Mexican American" with both parents of Mexican descent.

The first question was whether these representatives of two American subcultures would describe their families in different ways. And indeed, there were striking differences: the Mexican Americans expressed attitudes and described family interactions that were unlike those of Anglo-Americans in several respects (see Figure 8.3). That is, compared to Anglo-Americans, Mexican Americans were *more* likely to stress collectivism—the importance of family support and family membership—and were more likely to assist parents in various daily tasks. They were also

less likely to emphasize the importance of interacting with others outside of the home. Clearly associated with these differences were differences in their feelings of obligation toward their parents. Mexican Americans felt more strongly than Anglo-Americans that it was important to avoid conflict with their parents, to help their mothers and fathers, and to strive for self-sufficiency rather than depending on parents to continue helping them.

This and related investigations indicate the importance of cultural and ethnic values in defining how a family functions and in later interactions among family members when the children have become adults. You might consider the way in which you and your family would be characterized in such a comparison.

Relationships between and among Siblings. Most children (about 80 percent) grow up in a household with at least one sibling, and sibling interactions provide one important way to learn and practice interpersonal skills (Dunn, 1992). Brothers and sisters very often experience a mixture of feelings about one another. Among both American and Dutch children aged five to twelve, for example, researchers have described sibling relationships as a mixture of affection, hostility, and rivalry (Boer et al., 1997).

A familiar refrain for siblings is some version of "Mom always liked you best," and that complaint strikes a meaningful chord in most of us. As a child I remember being convinced that my brother was the favored one; he was older and more accomplished and his well being was a source of concern when he was stationed overseas. I later learned that he was convinced that I was the favored one who was spoiled and always got what he wanted. Now, my two youngest children (ages ten and sixteen) are forever asking me which one I like best, which one is more attractive, and so forth. When I say that I love them both equally and that

Figure 8.4
Sibling Rivalry: Mom Always Disliked You Less.
Competition for parental approval is a common theme in sibling relationships. In this cartoon the mother puts a new twist on the idea of "Mom always liked you best."

(*Source: The New Yorker,* July 13, 1998, p. 54.)

both are very attractive, they are simply convinced that I am lying. (The mother in Figure 8.4 expresses the concept of equal affection in a more unusual way.)

Manke and Plomin (1997) found that siblings often resemble one another in certain personal tendencies (e.g., initiating conflict and self-disclosing positive information) on the basis of genetic factors. Similarity on other tendencies is based on shared experiences rather than on genetics (e.g., warmth and self-disclosing negative information).

An affectionate relationship between siblings is most likely if each sibling has a warm relationship with each parent (Stocker & McHale, 1992). Though both positive and negative feelings toward one's siblings are common, sometimes the hostility outweighs the warm feelings. In such instances, not only do both the children and their parents perceive the sibling–sibling and parent–child relationships as negative; the parents also rate their marriage in more negative terms (McGuire, McHale, & Updegraff, 1996). Sibling relationships are important because the affect aroused in response to siblings is also aroused over and over again throughout one's life in other relationships. That is, friendships, love affairs, and marriages tend to bring out the kinds of reactions originally associated with one's brothers and sisters (Klagsbrun, 1992). As one example, an English study of middle school children found that schoolyard bullies were children who also had bad relationships with other members of their families, especially their siblings (Bowers, Smith, & Binney, 1994). One interesting, and hopeful, investigation found that women who reported negative childhood sibling relationships were especially concerned as adults about preventing conflicts and promoting positive interactions among their own children (Kramer & Baron, 1995).

Of course, siblings can be quite close. Floyd (1996) found that brothers are most likely to feel close if they engage in shared conversations (e.g., about women, sports, or school), express a feeling of solidarity (e.g., standing up for one another), experience companionship (e.g., in sports, fishing, or constructing a house), share perceptions and memories (e.g., about something they did together in childhood or adolescence), and have experienced some adversity or helped one another cope with it (e.g., the illness and death of a family member). This kind of closeness to a brother was expressed by Canin (1991):

> Who can fathom the relations of brothers? To this day I consider my life as tied to yours as to anyone else's in the world, to my wife's or to my son's, to our sister's or to our mother's. You are more a part of me than any of them.

Even when siblings are very close in childhood, they tend to grow apart in adolescence and young adulthood (Rosenthal, 1992). By the time they reach middle age, however, the vast majority of them once again establish positive relationships. These relationships have been characterized as one of four types: caretaker (the older one functions as a semiparent), buddy (the two perceive themselves as allies in responding to their parents), casual (in which friends are more important than siblings), or loyal (the sibling relationship represents a responsibility rather than a personal bond) (Stewart, Verbrugge, & Beilfuss, 1998). Also, not all adult siblings are equally close. Older adults differentiate quite sharply between siblings to whom they feel close and other siblings who are emotionally distant. Of the 20 percent of siblings who are never again able to reestablish any degree of closeness, about half are indifferent to their siblings, and half actively dislike their brothers and sisters (Folwell et al., 1997).

Relationships beyond the Family: Finding a Close Friend

Beginning in childhood, most of us establish casual friendships with peers of our own age with whom we share common interests (see Chapter 7). We are also likely to establish a close friendship, usually with just one person. The transition from simply being acquainted with another person to being that person's friend is a gradual process that depends on a series of incidents or signs of mutual liking—making a nice gesture, reciprocating a favor, sharing moments of closeness, and so on. (Lydon, Jamieson, & Holmes, 1997). Interestingly, people tend to engage in self-enhancing behavior such as bragging with nonfriends but shift toward an emphasis on modesty with a friend (Tice et al., 1995). In a similar way, those in a close relationship are less likely to lie to each other—unless the lie is specifically intended to make the other person feel better (DePaulo & Kashy, 1998). Once established, a **close friendship,** compared to a casual relationship, results in the two individuals spending more time together, interacting in more varied situations, excluding others from the relationship, and providing mutual emotional support (Kenney & Kashy, 1994). Closeness in a relationship means self-disclosure, support, and shared interests (Laurenceau, Barrett, & Pietromonaco, 1998; Parks & Floyd, 1996); and people are most satisfied with their best friends if they are approachable, open-minded, active, industrious, and emotionally balanced (Cole & Bradac, 1996). A casual friend is someone who is "fun to be with," while a close friend is valued for generosity, sensitivity, and honesty (Urbanski, 1992).

Childhood Friends. The basic motivation underlying friendship among children is the desire to engage in mutually enjoyable activities (Enright & Rawlinson, 1993). This kind of social interaction can begin as early as age one or two, and such relationships often remain stable over time (Whaley & Rubenstein, 1994). My daughter Lindsey met Chanda when both were still in diapers. Chanda lived with her grandparents in the house across the street, and physical proximity led to chance encounters when the two babies were taken out in their strollers. They began playing together when they could barely walk and have continued as friends ever since; see Figure 8.5. Now both girls are in high school, much of their conversation is about dieting and boys, and they tie up our respective telephone lines when they chat on e-mail.

That friendship between two little girls began (and continued) much as you might expect, in light of what you have learned about attraction; and other chil-

close friendship • A relationship in which two people spend a great deal of time together, interact in a variety of situations, exclude others from the relationship, and provide emotional support to each other.

Figure 8.5

A Lasting Childhood Friendship. Children are often brought together by proximity: they may live in the same neighborhood, attend the same day-care facility, and so forth. If they enjoy engaging in the same activities, they are likely to form friendships, even long-lasting friendships. Lindsey and Chanda live across the street from one another; they first interacted when they were very young and have remained friends from the time they were toddlers to today, when they are high school students.

(*Source:* Photograph supplied by the author.)

dren become friends for the same reasons. That is, as described in Chapter 7, children like one another and become acquainted when they are in close *proximity;* when their interaction results in *positive affect;* and if they are *similar* in interests, abilities, age, attitudes, and behavior (Boivin, Dodge, & Coie, 1995; Kupersmidt, DeRosier, & Patterson, 1995; Schneider, Wiener, & Murphy, 1994). Lindsey and Chanda responded in ways consistent with almost all of these findings, with the exception of racial similarity. Even today, neither one seems to notice that one is black and the other white.

What do childhood friends do? Much like adolescents and adults, they help one another, engage in self-disclosure, and express mutual trust (Bernath & Feshbach, 1995). There are some changes with age, as you might expect. Children gradually acquire appropriate social norms, for example, third-grade friends divide rewards more equally than do first-grade friends (Pataki, Shapiro, & Clark, 1994).

Attachment style influences how children interact and, as a result, has an effect on childhood relationships. For example, preschoolers with secure attachment to their mothers and fathers tend to interact positively with their peers and to be involved in interactive play (Kerns & Barth, 1995). In a similar way, friends who are four and five years old interact more positively if they are both secure than if one is secure and the other is not (Kerns, 1994). We noted earlier that insecure avoidant children tend to be hostile and aggressive; and as you might expect, highly aggressive children are likely to be rejected by their peers (Coie & Cillessen, 1993).

As children move into preadolescence, attachment style continues to be associated with their interpersonal behavior. Over a four-week period at each of two summer day camps, Shulman, Elicker, and Sroufe (1994) carefully observed friendship formation among boys and girls whose average age was ten. The children's attachment styles had been assessed when they were infants. Among other findings of this study, *close friendships* (relationships with what the children called a "special friend") were more common among the secure children than among those with insecure attachment styles. Nevertheless, most of the insecure children believed that they too had special friends. The psychologists who observed the campers developed a three-stage model of preadolescent friendship development. As shown in Figure 8.6, secure, avoidant, and ambivalent children differed from one another across the three stages. Once again, it was clear that individuals with a secure attachment history have better social skills than those whose experiences have led to insecure attachment.

Figure 8.6

Attachment and Friendship Formation in Preadolescence. Preadolescents at a summer day camp were observed as they formed friendships. Behavior prior to friendship formation, during the formation of friendship pairs, and after the establishment of relationships was influenced by each child's attachment style.

(*Source:* Based on information from Shulman, Elicker, & Sroufe, 1994.)

The Development of Close Friendships in Adolescence and Adulthood. With increased age, friendships tend to become more intimate than in childhood, and women report having more close friends than men do (Fredrickson, 1995). To return to a common theme, adolescents with a secure attachment style are the best adjusted (Cooper, Shaver, & Collins, 1998) and best able to establish and maintain friendships. There are benefits to having close friends. For example, adults who have such a friend at work are more satisfied with their jobs (Winstead et al., 1995). The downside is that it is painful to lose or to be separated from a highly valued friend. For example, when a close friendship is interrupted by college graduation, the two individuals must adapt to the separation because it constitutes an emotional threat (Fredrickson, 1995). As a result, graduating seniors report more intense emotional involvement in interacting with close friends than is true for students not facing graduation.

How do close friends interact? Friends of the same or opposite gender feel free to engage in self-disclosing behavior, express their feelings, provide and receive emotional support, experience trust, make physical contact, and generally relax in each other's company (Monsour, 1992; Planalp & Benson, 1992).

Do the conversations of male–male friends differ from those of female–female friends? Martin (1997) identified several gender-specific aspects of what friends talk about. Topics common in a male–male conversation are women, sports, fighting, being trapped in a relationship, and alcohol consumption. Topics often associated with female–female conversations are relationships, men, clothes, problems with roommates, and giving or receiving presents.

Key Points

- Close relationships are characterized by *interdependence*, in which two people influence each other's lives, focus their thoughts and emotions on each other, and engage in joint activities.

- One's first relationships are within the family. On the basis of interactions with the mother (or other caregiver), the infant develops an *attachment style* that is secure, insecure avoidant, or insecure ambivalent. These styles are believed to generalize to other interpersonal relationships throughout the individual's life.

- As adolescence approaches, teenagers begin to draw away from parents, but only some can be described as "rebellious." Many express love and affection for their mother and father.

- As their parents grow older, adults often find themselves reversing roles and being obligated to care for one or both of them.

- Sibling relationships frequently involve a mixture of affection, hostility, and rivalry. Siblings of both genders can be very close in childhood, drift apart in adolescence and young adulthood, but then become close once again as they grow older.

- Friendships outside of the family begin in childhood and are based on most of the same factors that are responsible for attraction between adults. Many people are able to form a *close friendship* that involves spending time together, interacting in various situations, excluding others from the relationship, providing mutual support, and engaging in self-disclosure.

- At whatever age, attachment style seems to exert a major influence on the ease with which people make friends, on the way they interact, and on their success in maintaining relationships.

Effects of Attachment Style on Adult Relationships

Students of college age are in the process of transferring attachment functions from their parents to their peers; that is, either to a best friend or to a romantic partner (Fraley & Davis, 1997). Just as with an infant and its caregiver, young adults experience attachment with a friend or a lover, attachment that involves trust and intimate contact. A representative sample of U.S. citizens revealed that most (59 percent) are secure, while about one out of four is insecure avoidant, and only about 11 percent are insecure ambivalent (Mickelson, Kessler, & Shaver, 1997).

Two Working Models and Four Attachment Styles.   You may remember our description of Bowlby's two "working models" (children's views of self and others): self-esteem and interpersonal trust. Bartholomew and her associates (Bartholomew, 1990; Bartholomew & Horowitz, 1991) proposed that these two basic dimensions underlie adult interactions, as well, and research verifies that they are independent (McGowan, Daniels, & Byrne, 1999a). That is, interpersonal behavior is influenced by the extent to which a person's self-evaluation is positive or negative *and* by the extent to which the person's evaluation of others is positive or negative (Griffin & Bartholomew, 1994a, 1994b).

Consider for a moment some of the implications of these two positive-to-negative dimensions and how they relate to the original concept of attachment style. With respect to the self-esteem dimension, a person with a positive self-image tends to assume that others will respond positively, because he or she expects to be liked and accepted. On this basis, such a person should make friends easily. A negative self-image is associated with the expectation that others will respond negatively; the expected dislike and rejection would presumably lead to fear and anxiety in response to interpersonal interactions and to difficulty in making friends. At the same time, on the trust dimension, a positive image of other people leads to expectations of support, and so close relationships should be a desired goal. A negative image of others, however, leads to expectations of nonsupport and betrayal; so there should be strong motivation to avoid close relationships. Bartholomew's conceptualization goes farther and indicates that when the dimensions of self-worth and interpersonal trust are considered simultaneously, individuals can fall on the positive or the negative half of each dimension. As shown in Figure 8.7, the resulting grid yields *four attachment styles* rather than the original three.

What are these four adult attachment styles? Two of the patterns are very clear. The person characterized by a **secure attachment style** is positive about self and about other people, so he or she seeks interpersonal closeness and feels comfortable in relationships. For example, secure individuals express trust in their partners (Mikulincer, 1998b) and are able to engage in collaborative problem solving with their partners (Lopez et al., 1997). It has been argued that a secure attachment style is roughly equivalent to the concept of *androgyny* that was described in Chapter 5—an ideal combination of masculine and feminine characteristics (Shaver et al., 1996). A person with a secure style tends not only to have a warm relationship with parents (Bringle & Bagby, 1992) but (in adulthood) to describe both his or her original and his or her new family in positive and nonpunitive terms (Diehl et al., 1998; Levy, Blatt, & Shaver, 1998) and to provide warmth and security for his or her own offspring (Scher & Mayseless, 1994). Compared to the people with other attachment styles, secure individuals are less prone to becoming angry, attribute less hostile intent to others, and expect more positive and constructive outcomes when an angry interaction occurs (Mikulincer, 1998a). Only people who are secure seem to be able to form long-

secure attachment style •
In Bartholomew's model, a style characterized by high self-esteem and also high interpersonal trust; usually described as the ideal and most successful attachment style.

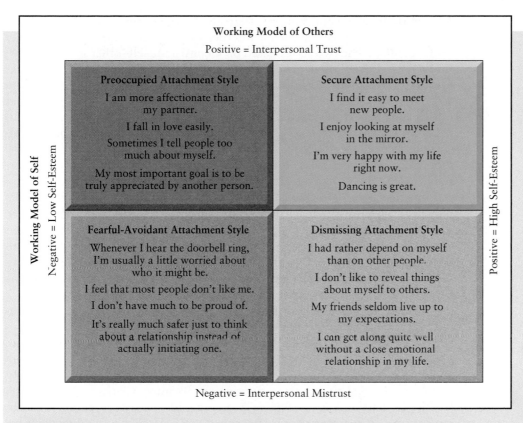

Figure 8.7

Four Attachment Styles Based on Two "Working Models" of Self and Others.
Bartholomew extended Bowlby's work on attachment styles in infancy by identifying four adult attachment styles. The two underlying dimensions are based on "working models" (conceptions) of one's self (ranging from positive to negative) and of other people (ranging from positive to negative). Depending on an individual's views of self and others, four possible attachment patterns exist: *secure, dismissing, fearful–avoidant,* or *preoccupied.* Sample statements shown as characterizing each attachment pattern are taken from the *Albany Measure of Attachment Style (AMAS).*

(*Source:* Based on information from Griffin & Bartholomew, 1994a, 1994b and from McGowan, Daniels, & Byrne, 1999b.)

lasting, committed, satisfying relationships (Shaver & Brennan, 1992). Altogether, such individuals get along well with people, feel close to their parents, and express positive feelings about relationships (McGowan et al., 1999b). Compared to people with other attachment styles, secure individuals have a more balanced, complex, and coherent self-concept (Mikulincer, 1995).

Those with a **fearful–avoidant attachment style** are negative both about self and about other people, so they avoid rejection by minimizing interpersonal closeness. Thus, they can regulate the possible threat of a close relationship by simply staying away from such situations. College students who are fearful–avoidant describe their parents as punitive and malicious (Levy et al., 1998). Among the characteristics of these individuals is a high level of hostility and a failure to realize when they are becoming angry (Mikulincer, 1998a). Also, fearful–avoidant individuals report less intimacy and enjoyment in interacting with the opposite sex (Tidwell, Reis, & Shaver, 1996). Those who are fearful–avoidant also report not getting along with others, experiencing jealousy, and using alcohol to reduce anxiety in social situations (McGowan et al., 1999b).

fearful–avoidant attachment style • In Bartholomew's model, a style characterized by low self-esteem and also low interpersonal trust; usually described as an insecure and quite maladaptive style of attachment.

For those whose attachment pattern involves an inconsistency between self-image and the image of others, interpersonal relationships pose an emotional conflict. The two styles based on inconsistent self–other images in Bartholomew's formulation probably represent separate aspects of what was previously labeled an *insecure ambivalent style*. The person with a **preoccupied attachment style** has a negative view of self along with the expectation that other people will be loving and accepting. As a result, the preoccupied individual seeks closeness in relationships (sometimes excessive closeness) but experiences anxiety about not being "worthy" of the other person and distress at the thought of being rejected. Peroccupied persons, along with those who are fearful–avoidant, are prone to feelings of shame (Lopez et al., 1997).

The **dismissing attachment style** is characterized by a positive (sometimes unrealistically positive) image of self as being worthwhile and independent. Dismissing individuals feel that they "deserve" to have a close relationship; but they avoid genuine closeness, because they expect the worst from others. Both dismissing and fearful–avoidant individuals evaluate relationships in negative terms, avoid face-to-face interactions in favor of impersonal contacts such as e-mail, and tend to drink alone (McGowan et al., 1999b).

Identifying individuals' attachment styles has primarily involved conducting intensive interviews focusing on family and peer relationships and asking research participants to read paragraphs that describe each style and then to rate how well each one describes themselves (Bartholomew & Horowitz, 1991). In addition, investigators have attempted to improve on these methods by creating a multi-item scale based on these descriptions (Brennan, Clark, & Shaver, 1998; Griffin & Bartholomew, 1994b). More recently, social psychologists constructed the *Albany Measure of Attachment Style (AMAS)* by creating items believed to tap some of the specific elements of each of the four styles (McGowan, Daniels, & Byrne, 1999b).

preoccupied attachment style • In Bartholomew's model, a style characterized by low self-esteem and high interpersonal trust; usually described as a conflicted and somewhat insecure style in which the individual strongly desires a close relationship but feels that he or she is unworthy of the partner and thus vulnerable to being rejected.

dismissing attachment style • In Bartholomew's model, a style characterized by high self-esteem and low interpersonal trust; usually described as a conflicted and somewhat insecure style in which the individual feels that he or she "deserves" a close relationship but mistrusts potential partners and is thus likely to reject the other person in order to avoid being the one who is rejected.

Attachment and Behavior in Adulthood. How is attachment related to specific adult behavior? It is generally true that attachment style is most likely to influence social interactions to the extent that such interactions are relevant to interpersonal concerns (Pietromonaco & Barrett, 1997). Thus, an interaction with a mail carrier should have little to do with attachment, but interaction with a date is likely to be closely related to attachment style. Canadian undergraduates reported attachment relationships with an average of about five individuals, including family members, romantic partners, and friends (Trinke & Bartholomew, 1997). Hazan and Shaver (1990) hypothesize that when an adult enters a relationship, the attachment style the person formed in infancy determines the nature of that relationship.

In what ways do secure, fearful–avoidant, preoccupied, and dismissing individuals differ in how they respond to other people? As Collins (1996) suggests, adults who differ in attachment style are predisposed to think, feel, and behave in different ways in their relationships. In part, attachment style affects interpersonal relationships because of differences in social perception (see Chapters 2 and 3). And differences in social perception lead to differences in emotional reactions and in interpersonal behavior. For example, in responding to events in a relationship, preoccupied individuals interpret what is going on in more negative ways than do secure individuals, report more emotional distress, and expect more conflict (Collins, 1996). Fearful–avoidant people also explain these events in a negative way but without the emotional distress. As an additional example, compared with those who are insecure, secure individuals process information about social situations in ways that involve curiosity, less need for closure, and the tendency to rely on new information in making social judgments (Mikulincer, 1997).

As you might guess from the descriptions of the four attachment styles, people prefer a secure romantic partner over any of the other three, regardless of their own attachment style (Chappell & Davis, 1998; Latty-Mann & Davis, 1996). As with blood transfusions—in which everyone can accept Type O blood—everyone anticipates compatibility with a secure partner.

Among college students, researchers actually found that the perceived parental support experienced by secure individuals predicted higher grade point average when academic ability was held constant (Cutrona et al., 1994). A possible explanation for an association between security and good grades is that college students who report secure childhood attachment are able to establish secure relationships with their professors (Lopez, 1997).

Though the idea may seem farfetched at first, Kirkpatrick (in press) hypothesized that religious belief is in part a function of attachment style. It is possible to think of God as the ultimate attachment figure. If so, how does an individual's own pattern of attachment affect his or her response to a Supreme Being and to religion in general? In seeking an answer to these questions, Kirkpatrick (1998) asked undergraduates about their image of and perceived relationship to God at two points in time. In the first session, the most positive response to God was expressed by the secure attachment individuals, next by the fearful avoidant individuals, then by the dismissing individuals, and least positive by those who were preoccupied. Four months later, secure students remained high and dismissing students remained low in how positively they evaluated God. In effect, secure individuals consistently responded positively and dismissing individuals consistently responded negatively to a Supreme Being in much the same ways both groups respond to people in their lives. The greatest change in religious attitudes occurred among preoccupied and fearful avoidant students who responded more positively after four months had passed. The investigator suggested that the change took place because God can serve as a substitute attachment figure for those whose self-esteem makes it difficult for them to establish firm attachments in their interpersonal relationships.

We will return to the subject of attachment style from time to time, because these concepts are being applied to many aspects of interpersonal behavior. Be cautious, however, in making the easy (and appealing) assumption that the "working models" or expectancies developed in infancy are perfect predictors of attachment patterns in childhood, adolescence, and adulthood. There is a good deal of consistency (Klohnen & Bera, 1998), but our images of self and of others and hence our attachment styles can be changed by our experiences in relationships—for the better or for the worse (Brennan & Bosson, 1998; Fagot, Gauvain, & Kavanagh, 1996; Shaver & Hazan, 1994). Some investigators go farther and propose that later experiences are the all-important determinants of later attachment style. For example, a recent longitudinal study found *no* correlation between babies' attachment styles measured at age one and the adjustment of these same individuals when they were seniors in high school (Blakeslee, 1998; Lewis, 1998). One interpretation is that people differ in the extent to which their attachment styles fluctuate or remain the same (Davila, Burge, & Hammen, 1997). So, although infant attachment style may be very important, this does not mean that each person's interpersonal future is etched in stone during the first few months of life.

The most accurate conclusion at this point is that a general tendency toward positive versus negative self-evaluations and positive versus negative evaluations of others act as major determinants of interpersonal behavior at all ages.

Loneliness: Failing to Establish Close Relationships

Most of us place a high value on establishing relationships, but many individuals find it difficult to achieve such a goal. A familiar outcome is the experience of **loneliness**—an emotional and cognitive reaction to having fewer and less satisfying relationships than one desires (Archibald, Bartholomew, & Marx, 1995; Peplau & Perlman, 1982). Loneliness occurs when there is a discrepancy between what a person wants and the reality of his or her interpersonal life; those who prefer to be alone and actively seek solitude are usually not lonely at all (Burger, 1995). It is also possible to have a best friend and still be lonely. An investigation using Dutch students found that lack of reciprocity in a relationship was associated with loneliness, especially among those who perceived themselves as giving more than they were receiving (Buunk & Prins, 1998). You might expect loneliness to be high among people who move to a new location. Actually, studies of North American college students studying in Israel find that any feeling of loneliness is temporary because it only takes a few weeks for new relationships to be established (Wiseman, 1997).

What Are the Consequences of Loneliness? Much of the research on loneliness has used the *UCLA Loneliness Scale* to assess the extent to which a person feels lonely (Russell, Peplau, & Cutrona, 1980). This measure asks respondents to indicate how frequently (from "never" to "often") they experience specific emotions or engage in specific behaviors. The items include such statements as "I feel left out" and "I have a lot in common with the people around me." The lonely individual, for example, tends to feel left out and doesn't believe he or she has much in common with others. We pointed out in Chapter 7 that there is a general tendency for people to believe that others share their attitudes and beliefs, but this false consensus effect is *not* characteristic among those who are lonely (Bell, 1993).

As you might expect, people who feel lonely tend to spend their leisure time in solitary activity, to have very few dates, and to have only casual friends or acquaintances as opposed to a close friend (R. A. Bell, 1991; Berg & McQuinn, 1989). Loneliness is accompanied by various negative emotions such as depression, anxiety, unhappiness, dissatisfaction, self-blame (Anderson et al., 1994), and shyness (Jones, Carpenter, & Quintana, 1985; Neto, 1992). Lonely individuals are perceived as maladjusted by those who know them (Lau & Gruen, 1992; Rotenberg & Kmill, 1992).

How Does Loneliness Develop? Several explanations concerning the origins of loneliness have been offered. Culture affects explanations for loneliness; for example, North Americans place the most blame on unfulfilling intimate relationships, but South Asians are more apt to attribute loneliness to personal inadequacies such as shortcomings in character (Rokach, 1998). Duggan and Brennan (1994) trace the problem to attachment style, noting that both dismissing and fearful–avoidant individuals are hesitant to become involved in relationships. This explanation is consistent with the finding that loneliness is associated with a lack of trust in other people (Rotenberg, 1994) and with a fear of intimacy with either a dating partner or a close same-sex friend (Sherman & Thelan, 1996).

loneliness • The unhappy emotional and cognitive state that results from desiring close relationships but being unable to attain them.

Other investigators propose that the problem of loneliness begins in childhood with a failure to develop the social skills needed for successful interaction with peers (Braza et al., 1993); see Figure 8.8. For example, a child who is either aggressive or inappropriately withdrawn is very likely to be rejected as a playmate (Johnson, Poteat, & Ironsmith, 1991; Ray et al., 1997). Unless there is

Figure 8.8
Loneliness: Wanting Friends, But Not Having Them. From childhood through adulthood, many people are lonely: they desire to establish close interpersonal relationships but are unable to do so. Loneliness is an emotional and cognitive reaction to having fewer and less satisfying relationships than one desires. Major causes seem to be the failure to acquire appropriate social skills as well as maladaptive cognitions about interpersonal interactions.

some form of intervention to alter such self-defeating social behavior, interpersonal difficulties typically continue throughout childhood and adolescence and into adulthood—they don't simply go away (Asendorpf, 1992).

What is it like to be a lonely youngster who later becomes a lonely adult? An important characteristic of those who have interpersonal difficulties is *personal negativity:* a general tendency to be unhappy and dissatisfied with oneself. The greater the personal negativity of an individual, the more maladaptive are his or her social interactions, the more negatively other people respond, and the more negative the person's social reputation becomes (Furr & Funder, 1998). Lonely individuals do not perceive themselves in a positive way and believe that others view them the same way—even when they do not (Christensen & Kashy, 1998).

Many of the specific details of good and bad social skills have been identified in research (Segrin & Kinney, 1995). For example, a socially skilled adolescent is friendly, possesses high self-esteem, seldom responds angrily, and finds it easy to make conversation (Reisman, 1984). Those who are socially unskilled are likely to be shy, have low self-esteem, and feel self-conscious when interacting with a stranger (Bruch, Hamer, & Heimberg, 1995).

Observations of college students interacting with a peer reveal other behavioral differences associated with social skills. For example, teasing behavior can be friendly and complimentary or critical and humiliating. People who are generally disagreeable tend to tease in bullying, unpleasant ways that make their targets feel hurt and unhappy (Keltner et al., 1998). An unskilled individual is generally uninterested in and insensitive to the other person. Instead, he or she refers to himself or herself, fails to ask questions or to follow up on what the other person says, and misinterprets the other's sexual intentions (Kowalski, 1993). Lonely individuals react negatively to the intimate disclosures of others (Rotenberg, 1997), and the socially unskilled may disclose very little about themselves—or may go to the opposite extreme and make inappropriately intimate disclosures (B. Bell, 1991), thus driving potential friends away (Meleshko & Alden, 1993). Repeated interpersonal rejections confirm a person's negative expectations about being successful in attracting friends and being in control of his or her life, thus adding to feelings of depression and pessimism (Davis et al., 1992; Johnson, Johnson, & Petzel, 1992). Further compounding the problem is that negative emotions and a pessimistic outlook tend to turn off potential friends (Carver, Kus, & Scheier, 1994).

Because peer relationships assume very great importance in adolescence as the young person grows away from parents and family, this is the time when a social phobia is most likely to develop (Herbert, 1995). A **social phobia** is a debilitating anxiety disorder in which interpersonal situations become sufficiently frightening that a person avoids them as much as possible in order to guard against experiences of embarrassment and humiliation. When a teenager is sufficiently lonely and fearful, there is a sense of complete *hopelessness,* and the resulting despair can sometimes lead to suicide (Page, 1991).

People who experience social fears and lack social skills are usually very much aware of how badly they function in interpersonal situations (Duck, Pond, & Leatham, 1994), but they don't know what to do about the problem. What *can* be done?

One approach is *cognitive therapy.* Langston and Cantor (1989) studied socially successful and unsuccessful college students and found striking differences in how people think about social situations. Individuals who are socially unskilled appraise social situations negatively and react with anxiety. This perception and the resulting emotional reaction lead to a restrained and conservative strategy designed to avoid rejection. This strategy of holding back and "playing it safe" does not have the desired effect, however, because it creates a negative impression. Similar effects are found among college students in Finland (Salmela-Aro & Nurmi, 1996). The lonely, unskilled individual has a negative self-schema (see Chapter 5) and tends to seek information that simply confirms his or her negative self-image (Frankel & Prentice-Dunn, 1990). Therapy can help a person break this pattern and develop different ways of thinking about and responding to social situations.

A major goal of cognitive therapy is to encourage cognitions resembling those of socially skilled individuals—perceptions of new social situations as interesting challenges and as opportunities to make new friends—thus promoting a more positive self-image. These altered perceptions and emotional reactions can lead to an interpersonal strategy in which the person is open to experience

social phobia • A debilitating anxiety disorder in which an individual perceives interpersonal situations as frightening and thus avoids them in order to guard against embarrassment and humiliation.

and to information about self, and this behavior in turn often elicits a positive response from others.

It is often useful to combine *social skills training* with cognitive therapy to bring about the most lasting behavioral changes (Hope, Holt, & Heimberg, 1995). How can social skills be taught? One approach is to provide a lonely and unskilled individual with the chance to observe interpersonally successful role models on videotape. He or she can then practice these behaviors in a non-threatening context and view the results afterward. Sometimes it is necessary to provide direct instruction about such specifics as how to initiate a conversation, how to talk to another person in an animated way, and how to give compliments. Again, practice and rehearsal can take place before the individual plunges into an actual social situation.

The effects of such training can be remarkable, even in a short period of time. Once a lonely person learns to think about social situations in a new way, learns precisely how to interact with people, and alters his or her interpersonal strategies, the result is greater social success, decreased loneliness, and a more positive self-concept. Note that a socially skilled individual is able to interact effectively with others in a variety of situations that extend well beyond simple social interactions—for example, in employment interviews, in the context of the legal system, and in the process of becoming a successful entrepreneur (Baron & Markman, 1998). In each of these realms, the key social skills include impression management (Chapter 2), accurate social perception (Chapter 2), and emotional intelligence. It would seem to be at least as important to teach people these vital social skills as to teach them the multiplication tables or how to drive a car.

Key Points

- Adult attachment style can be characterized as the combination of a person's level of self-esteem and degree of interpersonal trust. This conceptualization yields four resulting behavioral patterns: *secure, dismissing, fearful–avoidant,* and *preoccupied attachment styles.* Those who are secure are best able to form long-lasting, committed, satisfying relationships.

- *Loneliness* occurs when a person has fewer and less satisfying relationships than he or she desires. The result is depression, anxiety, unhappiness, dissatisfaction, and self-blame.

- The causes of loneliness may include an individual's attachment style, a failure to develop adequate social skills, and inappropriate cognitions about interpersonal interactions. Cognitive therapy and social skills training are very helpful in bringing about change.

ROMANTIC RELATIONSHIPS, LOVE, AND PHYSICAL INTIMACY

Moving from close friendships to romantic relationships, social psychological research in recent years has provided considerable information about what is involved in romance, love, and sexual intimacy. Note that as a relationship develops, each of these three components may or may not be involved; and they may take place simultaneously or in any sequence. Also, it is generally true that people who are successful in making friends and establishing close friendships are likely to be successful in forming romantic relationships (Connolly & Johnson, 1996).

Romantic Relationships

Some degree of physical intimacy is one of the defining characteristics of romantic relationships, as suggested in Figure 8.9. The specific behaviors that constitute physical intimacy vary among individuals and across cultures. Intimacy may involve simply kissing, holding hands, or embracing, but it can also involve sexual interactions ranging from petting to intercourse. Rapid cultural changes in the United States over the last part of the twentieth century make it difficult to know just what people mean by terms such as "hanging out together," "dating," "going steady," "having a significant other," "living together," and "being engaged." Nevertheless, each term suggests romantic attraction, feelings of love, the strong likelihood of sexual interest, and the possibility of eventual marriage.

Most of the following discussion will be based on heterosexual relationships, because most of the psychological research deals with such relationships. Relationships in gay and lesbian couples *probably* resemble those of heterosexual

Figure 8.9
Romantic Relationships Equal Physical Intimacy. Romantic relationships almost always include some degree of physical intimacy; this differentiates them from close friendships, in which verbal intimacy is more common. Cultural influences determine what degree of physical contact is acceptable.

couples in many ways (Schreurs & Buunk, 1995), but we will avoid leaping to that assumption except in instances in which specific data are available. Sometimes, obviously, there are differences based on sexual orientation. For example, unlike their heterosexual counterparts, gay men prefer partners who are masculine and lesbian women prefer partners who are feminine (Bailey et al., 1997).

Similarities and Differences between Close Friendships and Romantic Relationships. In some respects romantic attraction between a male and a female is much like other relationships. For example, those with secure attachment styles are most likely to be satisfied with the relationship and to trust their partners (Keelan, Dion, & Dion, 1994), and there is some evidence that similarity in attachment style leads to attraction (Brennan & Shaver, 1995; Frazier et al., 1996).

More generally, as you would expect from the discussion in Chapter 7, men and women are first attracted to one another on the basis of physical proximity, appearance, similarities of various kinds, and so forth (Shaffer & Bazzini, 1997; Whitbeck & Hoyt, 1994). An example of just how such factors operate is illustrated in the following *Beyond the Headlines* section.

Beyond the Headlines: As Social Psychologists See It
Romance in the Workplace

TRAFFIC SAFETY DIVISION JOBS
BECOME A TICKET TO ROMANCE

Albany *Times Union*, May 28, 1998 —Albany, N.Y.—It was a match made in on-street parking. The boot guy and the meter maid met and fell in love among the cars on the streets of Albany.

Earlier this month, two city employees were married. After a brief honeymoon, they were back on the job in the Traffic Safety Division of the Police Department. The bride tickets illegally parked vehicles. If the computer search shows unpaid fines of $150, she calls her husband, who slaps a "boot" on the wheel, making it impossible for the offender to drive away.

The bride said that they met in

their sergeant's office during her second day on the job with the police department. The groom disagreed, saying they met on the steps of City Hall. Actually, they were both correct. They first spotted each other in the office, and later that day he introduced himself to her on the City Hall steps because he thought she was cute. Each worked the 8 a.m. to 4 p.m. shift, and a few weeks later, their paths crossed in the course of the workday on the street. He said the chance meeting helped him get his "nerve up" to ask her for a date. They went out several times, became engaged four months later, and were married a month after that.

Many versions of this same story (DeMare, 1998) are enacted each day at every type of workplace in which men and women are employed, from academia to the military. As one observer of the business world has put it, "Corporate romance is as inevitable as earthquakes in California" (Westhoff, 1985, p. 21).

Figure 8.10
Workplace Romance: Some of the Contributing Factors. Romance in the workplace is a common occurrence, and the factors that facilitate it are many of the same factors that lead to interpersonal attraction and love in any setting.

(*Source:* Adapted from information in Pierce, Byrne, & Aguinis, 1996.)

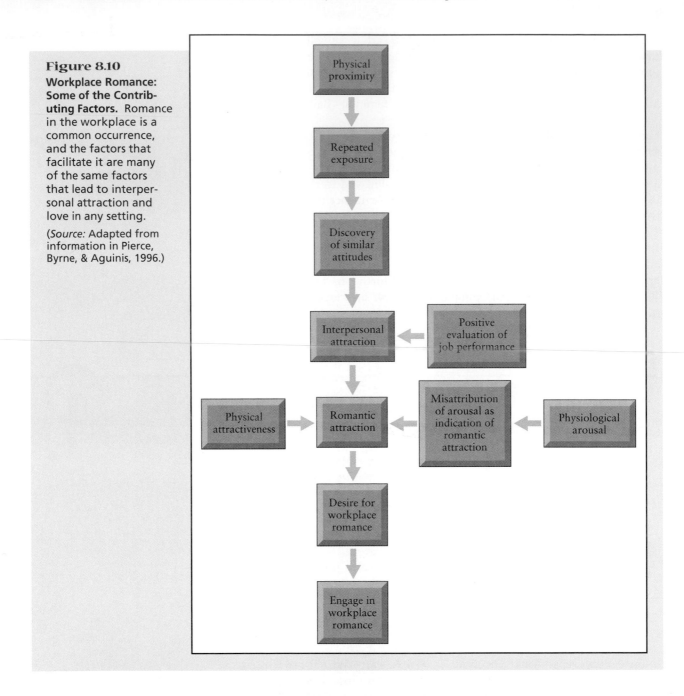

Why should that be? Actually, it is possible to view romantic relationships on the job as being no different from such interpersonal behavior at school, in one's neighborhood, or anywhere else. That is, people are brought together by proximity, respond to each other's appearance, converse, discover areas of similarity and dissimilarity, and—sometimes—experience sexual attraction and the desire for an intimate relationship (Seal, 1997). The effects of such factors have been conceptualized by Pierce, Byrne, and Aguinis (1996) as shown in Figure 8.10. From this perspective, stories such as the one involving the two police department employees really *would* seem to be as inevitable as California earthquakes. In a poll of 1,400 employees (Workers unite, 1994), 40 percent indicated making a hiring decision based in part on sexual attraction, 50 percent reported an unwelcome pass from another employee, and 68 percent reported having sex with a coworker (including 56 percent who did so at the place of business),

Though we don't know whether the romance in the traffic division had any effect on job performance, research suggests that productivity, morale, motivation, managerial decisions, job satisfaction, and job involvement (see Chapter 13) can be affected by romantic interactions between people at work (Pierce et al., 1996). The nature of the effect depends on such matters as the relative status of the two individuals in the organization, the organizational rules about relationships, the question of whether either or both individuals are already married to other partners, and the motive for and obviousness of the romance (Pierce, 1998). Among the many potential problems are the possibility that romantic interest on one person's part can lead to sexual harassment (Pierce & Aguinis, 1997) and the various job-related difficulties that can arise when a romance ends (Pierce, Aguinis, & Adams, 1999).

One big difference between a friendship and a romantic relationship is the special problem of how to initiate a romance. College undergraduates say that they hesitate to "make the first move" because they fear rejection, but at the same time they interpret a partner's hesitation as indicating a lack of interest. And certain other aspects of romantic relationships also differentiate them from friendships (Snell, 1998). For example, Swann, De La Ronde, and Hixon (1994) report that among friends, college roommates, and even married couples, most people prefer a partner who provides accurate feedback concerning his or her self-concept, someone who can provide verification for one's self-view (De La Ronde & Swann, 1998). That is, it is good to be with someone who knows us well enough to understand our best and worst characteristics. A romantic relationship, however, is different. At least at the beginning, two people are not looking for accuracy. Instead, they are looking for acceptance—wanting to like and to be liked as demonstrated by compliments and praise. People go out to have a good time, and they are on their best behavior (see Figure 8.11). Judgments are very often unrealistic, because each individual is searching for uncomplicated, totally positive feedback from the partner (Simpson, Ickes, & Blackstone, 1995).

A disconcerting aspect of the dating process is that many people who badly want acceptance tend to use deception in order to appear as desirable as possi-

"You certainly know how to show a girl a good time."

Figure 8.11
Dating Behavior: Having Fun and Acting Nice. When two people are falling in love, they tend to engage in enjoyable activities, seek only compliments and positive evaluations from each other, experience positive illusions about each other and about the relationship, and behave as nicely as possible. This somewhat unrealistic context can nevertheless lead to a lasting relationship that is actually enhanced by the romantic fantasies.

(*Source: The New Yorker,* January 18, 1988, p. 37.)

ble to the other person. In one investigation, 90 percent of the participants admitted being willing to tell at least one lie (about their personality, interests, hobbies, competence, status, etc.) in order to get a date (Rowatt, Cunningham, & Druen, 1998). Men and women are equally likely to be deceptive, but those who are high self-monitors (see Chapter 5) are the ones most likely to lie about themselves.

Another way to describe romance, then, is to say that such relationships are built in part on fantasy and positive illusions and that such illusions actually help to create better relationships (Martz et al., 1998; Murray & Holmes, 1997; Murray, Holmes, & Griffin, 1996). Perceptions of one's partner tend to be biased; the other person is perceived as being more like one's ideal self (see Chapter 5) than is actually the case (Klohnen & Mendelsohn, 1998). Actually, it is not as important to be accurate about a romantic partner as to be *confident* that one is accurate (Swann & Gill, 1997). One consequence of these tendencies is that, in both the United States and the Netherlands, for example, couples judge their own relationships to be more positive than the relationships other people have (Van Lange & Rusbult, 1995). As other investigators note, the feeling is that "most relationships are good, but ours is best" (Buunk & van der Eijnden, 1997). Another sort of illusion is *belief in romantic destiny*—the conviction that two people are either meant for each other (or that they are not). If a relationship begins positively, it is likely to be maintained for a longer period of time among those who hold this belief (Knee, 1998). That is, if two people care for each other, and believe they were meant to be together, such beliefs can help hold the relationship together.

The hidden, or sometimes not so hidden, agenda of one or both partners in romance is sexual motivation. In addition to sexuality, dating often involves another type of interaction that is rare in friendships: one of the partners (usually the male) may physically abuse the other. Sugarman and Hotaling (1989) report that 40 percent of U.S. women experience violence from the person they are dating. As with spouse abuse, many abused women continue their romance with a violent male long after the violence begins. The target of abuse stops dating her abuser only when she realizes that his behavior will not change. She then decides to take control of her own life, often after having an experience that is the "last straw" (Rosen & Stith, 1995).

One other characteristic of romances is the use of *baby talk*, as shown in Table 8.2. The term refers to a relatively high-pitched and melodious way of speaking that adults often use in talking to infants and young children, pets, and older adults in need of care. Bombar and Littig (1996) propose that the use of baby talk by adults in a romantic relationship facilitates an intimate psychological connection, and it is found to be more common among those who are most secure and least avoidant in attachment style. Research indicates that this form of communication indicates intimacy, attachment, affection, and a playful way to make a personal connection with a partner.

What Is This Thing Called Love?

love • A combination of emotions, cognitions, and behaviors that can be involved in intimate relationships.

Love is one of the most common themes in songs, movies, and our everyday lives. Most people in our culture perceive love as a very common experience, and in a 1993 poll almost three out of four American adults said they were currently "in love." Love is described as an emotion that is as basic as anger, sadness, happiness, and fear (Shaver, Morgan, & Wu, 1996). It is even possible that love is good for you. Aron, Paris, and Aron (1995) find that falling in love leads to an increase in self-efficacy and self-esteem (see Chapter 5). What is meant by this word *love?* The specific details of what love means vary from culture to cul-

Table 8.2
How Do I Wuv Thee, Babykins? Baby talk (a high-pitched, melodious way of speaking) is often used by adults talking to the very young, to pets, to elderly adults—and to a romantic partner. In the latter instance, baby talk facilitates an intimate psychological connection. It is most common among individuals who are most secure and least avoidant in attachment style.

Examples of Romantic Baby Talk
"Hewwo! I wuv you, Jellybean."
"Oh, Punkin, are you okay?"
"How are you, my wittle wuv bunny?"
"Give me a hug, my little sweetie."
"You're such a guppie!"
"I'm sorryyy. Please forgive meee. I looove you."
"Awww, is my lil' Jerr-Bear not feeling well?"
"You're sooo sweet!"
"I miss you; come home now!"
"I wuv you very very very very much."
"You're the best thing in the whole world."
"Honeyeee, would you please, please tell me?"
"I love you lots and lots, bunches and bunches!"
"Kins, can I have a backrub, pweeze?"
"Oh poor baby! I feel so sorry for you. I love you though! Yes! I do."
"Of course I love you. How could I not love someone as cutsey-wutsey as you?"
"Okay, see you later. Wuv you."

ture (Beall & Sternberg, 1995), but there is evidence that the general phenomenon is a universal one (Hatfield & Rapson, 1993a). About three decades of social psychological research provides evidence that love is often something more than a simple friendship that progresses to romance and sexual interest.

Passionate Love Is Very Different from a Close Friendship. Aron and his colleagues (1989) point out that many people fall in love, but no one ever says that they have "fallen in friendship." Unlike simple attraction or friendship, **passionate love** involves an intense and often unrealistic emotional reaction to a potential romantic partner. It often occurs suddenly, and it depends on (among other things) specific aspects of the other person and what one has been taught about love (Duran & Prusank, 1997).

How would you differentiate liking someone, loving someone, and being in love with someone? Do these words and phrases mean different things? German university students identified the most distinctive characteristic of *liking* as the desire to interact with the other person. With respect to *love*, the distinctive characteristic was perceived as trusting the other person. *Being in love* meant being aroused by the other person (Lamm & Wiesmann, 1997). Further research using this student population also identified the key elements in the decline of each of these three types of relationship. The primary reason for a decrease in liking was negative behavior by the other person. Love was most frequently destroyed when the other person abused the trust that had existed. And people fell

passionate love • An intense and often unrealistic emotional response to another person. The person experiencing this emotion usually interprets it as "true love," whereas those who simply observe it are likely to use the term "infatuation."

out of love when they became disillusioned with the other person (Lamm, Wiesmann, & Keller, 1998). The better two people know each other, the more possible it is for one to hurt the feelings of the other; the one who is hurt feels rejected, and the relationship often does not survive (Leary et al., 1998).

It is even possible to love someone who does not love you. This one-way flow of affection is known as *unrequited love*. In one large survey about 60 percent of respondents said that they had had such an experience within the past two years (Bringle & Winnick, 1992). Men in late adolescence and early adulthood report more instances of unrequited love than women do, and more instances of unrequited than of mutual love (Hill, Blakemore, & Drumm, 1997). The incidence of love that is not reciprocated is greatest among those whose attachment style is insecure–ambivalent (Aron, Aron, & Allen, 1998). When unrequited love develops, the one who loves in vain feels rejected and loses self-esteem, while the one who fails to respond to the other's love feels guilty (Baumeister, Wotman, & Stillwell, 1993).

We now turn to a more common experience—two people falling in love with each other.

Falling in Love. When people describe themselves as being in love, they usually mean passionate love (Hatfield, 1988); but love can take a variety of forms, as we shall discuss shortly. Passionate love usually begins as an instant, overwhelming, surging, all-consuming positive reaction to another person—a reaction that feels as if it's beyond your control, an unpredictable accident. The experience has been described as "falling head over heels in love." Age and knowledge seem to have no effect on this condition. I (Donn Byrne) first had such an experience in the fourth grade, reexperienced the feeling from time to time over the years, and once again had such an experience within the past year. A person in love is preoccupied with the loved one and can think of little else. The emotion is so intense that merely thinking about a past experience of falling in love creates a positive mood (Clark & Collins, 1993).

Meyers and Berscheid (1997) note that sexual attraction is a necessary but not sufficient condition for being in love with another person. That is, you can be sexually attracted but not in love, but you aren't likely to be in love in the absence of sexual attraction. College students of both genders agree that sexual desire is an important component of romantic love, and its absence in one or both partners is likely to doom the relationship (Regan, 1998). There is even scattered evidence that humans may respond to chemical signals from the opposite sex that elicit sexual attraction (Azar, 1998).

Passionate love seems to be a mixture of sexual attraction, physiological arousal, the desire to be physically close, an intense need to be loved as much as you love, and a recurring fear that something may happen to end the relationship. Separation, as in long-distance romance, is experienced as frustrating and unsatisfactory; nevertheless, long-distance relationships are as likely to last as those involving close geographic proximity (Van Horn et al., 1997). Hatfield and Sprecher (1986) developed the *Passionate Love Scale* to measure this emotion with items such as "I would feel deep despair if _____ left me" and "For me, _____ is the perfect romantic partner."

You might think it would happen only in the movies, but most people report having had the experience of falling in love with a stranger (Averill & Boothroyd, 1977). Even in a laboratory situation, something like this can occur. When two opposite-sex strangers are asked to gaze into each other's eyes for two minutes, they report feelings of affection (Kellerman, Lewis, & Laird, 1989). The positive effects of such physical acts as gazing and holding hands are most likely to occur for individuals who strongly believe in romantic ideals such as love at first sight and the notion that "love conquers all" (Williams & Kleinke, 1993). In a similar way, when strangers are asked to engage in such relationship-building activities as self-disclosure in a laboratory interaction, they later express greater feelings of closeness (Aron et al., 1997).

Three circumstances seem to facilitate falling in love (Hatfield & Walster, 1981). First, it helps to be exposed throughout one's life to romantic images such as those in fairy tales, love songs, and love stories. We eventually react to these influences by telling ourselves stories about love and then seeking to experience romance in our own lives (Sternberg, 1996). Second, an appropriate love object must turn up. "Appropriate" may be defined as physically attractive, of the opposite sex, and youthful (for females) or able and willing to protect and provide for a family (for males) (Buss, 1988; Greer & Buss, 1994). The third circumstance involves Schachter's (1964) two-factor theory of emotion. That is, an aroused state of any kind can be attributed to love if an individual believes in love and if an appropriate love object is present (Foster et al., 1998). Thus, the arousal elicited by fear (Dutton & Aron, 1974), frustration and anger (Driscoll, Davis, & Lipetz, 1972), having a secret relationship (Wegner, Lane, & Dimitri, 1994), or sexual excitement (Istvan, Griffitt, & Weidner, 1983) can be interpreted as a love experience.

Why Love? Why should human beings experience love? One possibility involves attachment theory, in that romantic love may constitute a reenactment of the intense love for the mother felt most strongly by individuals with secure and preoccupied attachment styles.

A completely different explanation of passionate love's worldwide occurrence is based on evolutionary theory (Buss & Schmidtt, 1993; Fisher, 1992). About four or five million years ago, our ancestors began to walk in an upright position and forage for whatever food could be carried back to a safe shelter. The survival of our species depended on reproductive success (Buss, 1994). That is, men and women had to be sexually attracted and also willing to invest time and effort in feeding and protecting their offspring. These two equally important characteristics (lust and commitment) were most likely to occur among humans whose physiology led them to seek and enjoy not only sexual satisfaction but also bonding between men and women and between parent and offspring (Rensberger, 1993). With emotional attachment, early human male–female pairs were more than simply sex partners; they also liked and trusted one another and divided up tasks such as hunting, gathering food, and caring for children. Thus, according to this scenario, love enhances reproductive success. As a consequence, today's humans are genetically primed to seek sex, fall in love, and care for their children. Brain chemistry may underlie monogamy (Insel & Carter, 1995), and most young married adults expect their relationship to be a monogamous one (Wiederman & Allgeier, 1996).

Keep in mind that even if this evolutionary explanation is accurate, cultural influences can still overcome people's tendencies to fall in love; guide these tendencies into quite specific and varied forms; and even add new elements based on stories, religious practices, and the laws societies enact (Allgeier & Wiederman, 1994).

The Many Forms of Love. Passionate love may be a common experience, but it is too intense to be maintained indefinitely. Love that is totally based on emotion is sufficiently fragile that simply being asked to think about a relationship and answer questions about it can interfere with one's feelings of love (Wilson & Kraft, 1993). Passionate love seems to thrive best when our fantasies are not interrupted by detailed, rational examination.

> ## Key Points
>
> - One defining characteristic of romantic relationships is some degree of physical intimacy, ranging from holding hands to sexual interactions.
> - As in attraction and friendship, romantic relationships are influenced by factors such as physical proximity, appearance, and similarity. Added factors in romance are sexual attraction, the desire for total acceptance from the other individual, and a touch of fantasy based on positive illusions. Romantic relationships are very likely to start wherever people spend time—in their neighborhoods, at school, or on the job.
> - Several varieties of love have been identified. In *passionate love* there is a sudden, overwhelming emotional reaction. *Companionate love* is based on close friendship, caring, mutual liking, and respect. Various love styles have also been categorized.
> - Sternberg's *triangular model of love* describes love as a blend of three possible components: intimacy, passion, and decision/commitment.

Sexuality in Romantic Relationships

Despite a long history of religious and legal sanctions against premarital sex in many parts of the world, dramatic changes in sexuality occurred during the twentieth century. Over this time period, sexual interactions became a common and widely accepted component of romantic relationships in most of the industrialized nations.

Changes in Sexual Attitudes and Behavior. Surveys taken before and after World War II provide evidence of the shift toward more permissive sexual expression, especially in the United States, Europe, Australia, and Canada. In the late 1940s, even the tables of statistics produced by surveys such as those conducted by Alfred Kinsey and his colleagues were denounced as an attack on the moral code that held society together (Jones, 1997). Twenty years later, changes in the general perception of sexuality were sufficiently dramatic and sufficiently pervasive that they were said to constitute a "sexual revolution." As just one example of these changes, in the first half of the century, oral sex was considered both a psychosexual perversion and a criminal act. By the 1990s, most American men and women reported that they enjoyed and frequently engaged in this kind of sexual activity (Michael et al., 1994).

Such changes were not universal. For example, in the People's Republic of China, a similar shift in sexual attitudes and practices did not begin until about 1988. The government's response was to ban all written, audio, and visual material dealing with sexuality, to arrest the producers of such material, and to execute the merchants who sold it (Pan, 1993). Cultural norms have a strong influence on how people think and on what they do, as shown by studies of Chinese American students. Their attitudes and behaviors are much more permissive than is true for their counterparts in China, and the more they have adapted to the general cultural values of the U.S., the more their sexuality resembles that of other American students (Huang & Uba, 1992).

There is, of course, not perfect uniformity within any culture, and people differ a great deal in their sexual beliefs and practices. Simpson and Gangestad (1991, 1992) find strong differences in individuals' primary motives for seeking a romantic partner. The basic driving force can be simply the sex itself or a desire for closeness. Along a dispositional dimension known as **sociosexuality,**

sociosexuality • A dispositional characteristic that ranges from an unrestricted orientation (willingness to engage in casual sexual interactions) to a restricted orientation (willingness to engage in sex only with emotional closeness and commitment).

some people express an *unrestricted sociosexual orientation* in which purely sexual interactions are sought without the necessity for closeness, commitment, or emotional bonding. Others reveal a *restricted sociosexual orientation* in which a sexual relationship is acceptable only when accompanied by affection and tenderness. Individuals with a secure attachment style are most likely to favor restricted sociosexuality (Brennan & Shaver, 1995). Males tend to be more unrestricted than females, especially when seeking a short-term versus a long-term partner (Schmitt & Buss, 1996). The probable biological underpinnings of such behavioral differences is supported by other research, which also finds that age of first intercourse is in part genetically determined (Dunne et al., 1997).

The choice of sexual partners is much like the choice of other interpersonal partners. For example, 90 percent of all sexual relationships involve partners of the same ethnic group, and 84 percent involve partners with the same educational background (McDonald, 1995).

Gender differences are reflected not only in sociosexuality but in various other aspects of sexuality. In the Western world, before about 1950 a typical finding in sex surveys was that most men were sexually active prior to marriage but that most women were not (Kinsey, Pomeroy, & Martin, 1948; Kinsey et al., 1953). Though movies and sitcoms usually portray the 1950s as the last decade of sexual innocence (see Figure 8.13), during that time period premarital sex became an increasingly common experience among couples involved in a close relationship (Coontz, 1992). By the 1980s, a study of college couples in the United States revealed that only 17 percent reported not having had intercourse (Christopher & Cate, 1985). Among young adults in the United States, only 5 percent of women and 2 percent of men have intercourse for the first time on their wedding night (Laumann et al., 1994; Michael et al., 1994). A necessary implication of such findings is that the changes in sexuality have been even greater for women than for men. By the early 1980s, with a few exceptions (such as Northern Ireland; Sneddon & Kremer, 1992), women in the Western world were as likely as men to report engaging in premarital intercourse (Breakwell & Fife-Schaw, 1992; Clement, Schmidt, & Kruse, 1984; McCabe, 1987; Weinberg, Lottes, & Shaver, 1995). Nevertheless, men still play a traditional role as the one who initiates sexual activity (O'Sullivan & Byers, 1992). Both

Figure 8.13
On The Eve of the Sexual Revolution? The very real changes in sexual attitudes and behaviors about sexuality that characterized much of the western world in the twentieth century began roughly in the late 1940s. Change was well under way in the 1950s, and that decade is still perceived by many as the end of a period of sexual innocence.

male and female undergraduates say they offer token resistance when sexual activity is suggested by the partner. The reasons given by both genders include maintaining their image, teasing and game playing, trying to gain control, and wanting to slow things down (O'Sullivan & Allgeier, 1994).

Beyond initiation, other gender differences are also found. Men still say that they want (and actually have) more sexual partners than is true for women (Buss & Schmitt, 1993). College men and women also differ in how long they believe one must know the other person before it is acceptable to engage in intercourse. As shown in Figure 8.14, men are more likely than women to endorse having sex with someone they've known for a day or less, while women prefer knowing a person for a longer period of time before becoming sexually intimate (Buss & Schmitt, 1993). Once they are involved in an ongoing relationship, women want their partners to express more love and feelings of intimacy, while men want more exciting and more varied sexual activity (Hatfield et al., 1989). It is possible that such findings simply reflect gender differences in sociosexuality.

Is the Sexual Revolution Over? Though the "flower children" of the 1960s and 1970s had high hopes that the world would become a better place where people "made love, not war," by the end of that era warning signs began to raise doubts about the new values. It seemed that permissive sexuality was not an all-purpose solution to the problems of love and relationships.

For one thing, it soon became fairly obvious that engaging in sex was not necessarily a personal decision, freely made. Rather than enjoying sex as an expression of freedom, many engaged in sex in response to social pressures to conform. Sometimes sexual activity took place only because of a partner's insistence

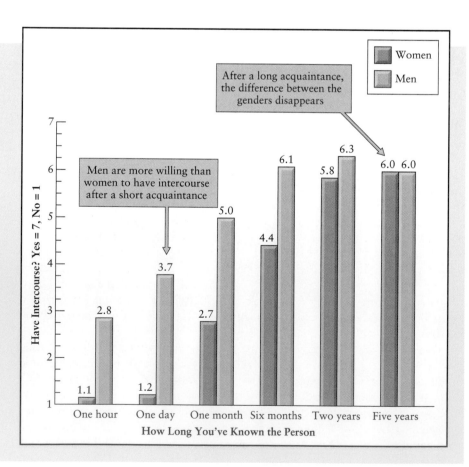

Figure 8.14

Gender Differences in Views on Appropriate Length of Presex Relationship. College students were asked, "If the conditions were right, would you consider having sexual intercourse with someone you viewed as desirable if you had known that person for one hour? One day? (And so on, up to five years.) The students answered on a seven-point scale ranging from "definitely not" to "definitely yes." While both men and women were more likely to say *yes* as the time period increased, men more than women say *yes* to sex at every acquaintance level up through two years. At the five-year point, gender differences disappear.

(*Source:* Based on data from Buss & Schmitt, 1993.)

Figure 8.15
Negative Consequences of the Sexual Revolution. Increased sexual permissiveness led to greater sexual freedom and fewer restrictions on behavior. The idealistic aspects of the "make love, not war" model and the Age of Aquarius began to waver in response to the reality of unwanted pregnancies as well as incurable sexually transmitted diseases.

or in response to the assumption that anyone who abstained was necessarily uptight, repressed, and out of it (DeLamater, 1981). When surveyed about this topic, many women said they felt vulnerable, guilty, and exploited (Townsend, 1995; Weis, 1983).

In addition to these subjective concerns, the 1980s and 1990s brought heightened awareness of two different but equally serious consequences of physical intimacy that became too obvious to ignore. That is, casual sex could result in *unwanted pregnancies* and *sexually transmitted diseases* or *STDs*. See Figure 8.15.

Unintended, unwanted, and unwise pregnancies sounded the first alarm. A surprisingly large proportion of sexually active teenagers and young adults failed to use effective contraceptives or used them inconsistently. This was especially true for those who felt sufficiently "liberated" to engage in sexual acts but at the same time felt too much guilt and negative affect to deal with the embarrassment of contraception (Byrne, Kelley, & Fisher, 1993; Gerrard & Luus, 1995). Alcohol played a role, because drinking leads to a lowering of risk estimates and the tendency to act on one's erotic desires (Murphy, Monahan, & Miller, 1998). As a result, by the late 1970s more than a million teenage pregnancies were occurring each year in the United States, and similar data were reported in other countries as well. Most of these pregnancies ended in abortion, and both "pro-life" and "pro-choice" advocates were in agreement that the situation had become unacceptable (Ambuel, 1995). This *teenage pregnancy epidemic* became a continuing source of distress for the individuals involved and for society at large.

Disease was the second negative aspect of the new sexual freedom. At first, people had to deal only with curable infections such as syphilis, gonorrhea, and chlamydia. These were soon followed by two viral diseases for which no cure is yet available—genital herpes and HIV (human immunodeficiency virus) infection, which develops into AIDS, the acquired immune deficiency syndrome (Barringer, 1993). The United States has the highest rate of STDs of any developed country: about 12 million new cases each year, about 3 million of which are among teenagers.

Individuals infected with *genital herpes* experience periodic outbreaks of painful blisters on the genitals and elsewhere. About 31 million Americans are infected, with approximately 200,000 to 500,000 new cases reported each year. The greater threat, of course, is the fatal disease first identified in 1981, *AIDS.* As of 1994 a quarter of a million Americans had died of this disease and a million more had become infected (Clinton and AIDS, 1994). The rate is now about 74,000 new cases each year in the United States, although the number is dropping slightly (New AIDS cases down, 1996). Worldwide, more than half a million people had died of AIDS by the early 1990s (Living memorial, 1992) and that number rose rapidly to 14 million by the late 1990s, according to the World Health Organization, Centers for Disease Control (The Global Epidemic, 1998). An important footnote is that in the United States, for whatever reasons, AIDS hits hardest among minorities. In Miami and Fort Lauderdale (each having large Hispanic populations), AIDS is the leading cause of death among women aged twenty-five to forty-four (Bardach, 1995). In the mid-1990s three out of five new AIDS cases in the United States were among African Americans (Rosin, 1995). More than half of those infected with HIV live in Africa (Altman, 1998).

Unwanted teenage pregnancies and incurable diseases might be expected to cause a decrease in premarital sexual activity, and some decline has been reported. In the mid-1990s, the U.S. Centers for Disease Control and Prevention announced that the number of sexually active teenagers had leveled off at about 53 percent, and that more than half of these individuals regularly used condoms. One result has been a 6 percent decrease in the teenage birth rate, a 21 percent decrease in the rate of second births to teenage mothers, and a decline in the incidence of gonorrhea (Births to teen girls, 1995; Edwards, 1998; Number of, 1995; Vobejda, 1998).

Often, young people do not view the threat of sexually transmissible diseases as personally relevant. They tend to express the belief that they are invulnerable to various kinds of diseases and accidents—"That may happen to others, but not to me." For example, research found little concern about HIV/AIDS among Australian undergraduates, and little behavioral change (Rosenthal & Shepherd, 1993). Among unemployed adolescents in that country, the level of sexual activity is high and the rate of condom use low (Buzwell & Rosenthal, 1995).

The difficulty in inducing behavioral change is not confined to teenagers. Adults, too, may acquire relevant knowledge but resist changing what they do. For example, a campaign designed to prevent the spread of AIDS was effective in changing attitudes and beliefs in St. Lucia, St. Vincent, and the Grenadines, but there was little effect on behavior (Middlestadt et al., 1995). The greatest behavioral changes (safer sexual practices and fewer partners) have been confined to gays and prostitutes—groups at high risk for HIV infection (Ehrhardt, Yingling, & Warne, 1991). In general, health messages about condoms that emphasize the negative social consequences of unprotected sex are more effective than messages that emphasize the positive social consequences of protected sex.

One disturbing finding involves possible problems with the validity of self-reported behavior. When asked personal questions on a pencil-and-paper survey, male teenagers are much less apt to admit engaging in dangerous practices than they are when responding to the same questions on a computer (Computer survey reveals, 1998). As an example, significantly higher rates of homosexual contact and sex with prostitutes were reported in computer surveys than in standard ones. Presumably, the anonymity of the computer leads to greater honesty in responding.

What Is the Effect of Premarital Sexual Experience on Later Marriages? Cohabitation has become increasingly common. According to the Census Bureau, the number of unmarried U.S. couples living together in 1960 was less than half a million, but in 1997 more than four million couples were cohabiting (More Americans, 1998).

Despite the hopes of those who view premarital sex as a realistic way to prepare for marriage and the fears of those who believe that such immorality will destroy family life as we know it, research indicates little effect of premarital sex on subsequent relationships. That is, couples who engage in premarital intercourse, including those who live together, are as likely to marry as those who remain virgins, and marital success is unrelated to the sexual histories of the two partners (Markman, 1981). A study of Australian couples who did or did not cohabit before their marriage found them to differ in only two ways: Those who had lived together had more sexual experience and a less stereotyped division of household chores than did those who had not lived together (Cunningham & Antill, 1994).

Key Points

- Based in part on changes in sexual attitudes and sexual practices (the "sexual revolution"), premarital sexual interactions have become increasingly the norm among couples in close relationships.

- The most permissive aspects of the new sexual attitudes have become less attractive in the wake of negative subjective feelings involving pressures to conform to the new sexual norms and the negative objective consequences of unwanted pregnancies and incurable diseases such as genital herpes and AIDS.

- Despite the increased likelihood of premarital intercourse and cohabitation, there is no consistent evidence indicating either a positive or a negative effect of such experiences on subsequent marital satisfaction or stability.

MARRIAGE: MOVING BEYOND ROMANCE

As you might expect from our discussion so far concerning the factors that lead to attraction (in Chapter 7) and to friendship, romance, love, and sex (in this chapter), those same factors also influence who marries whom. Similarity is one example.

Similarity and Marriage

Not surprisingly, almost a century of research consistently indicates that spouses are similar in their attitudes, values, interests, and other attributes (e.g., Pearson & Lee, 1903; Schuster & Elderton, 1906; Smith et al., 1993). Interestingly, a longitudinal study of couples from the time they were engaged through twenty years of marriage indicated very little change in the degree of similarity over the entire period (Caspi, Herbener, & Ozer, 1992). In other words, similar people marry, and the similarity neither increases nor decreases over time.

Similarity is very important, but there are two problems that are often overlooked: (1) It is easy enough to find a potential mate who is similar to oneself in many respects, but practically impossible to find one who is *exactly* similar. As a result, there are always areas of dissimilarity, so the two individuals must learn to accept various differences and adjust to them. And (2) because many factors other than similarity influence the choice of a partner, it is common at the beginning of a relationship to overlook or minimize some important areas of dissimilarity because of the other person's physical attractiveness, sexual enthusiasm, wealth, or whatever. The dissimilarities may seem trivial at the beginning of a marriage; but over time attractiveness may decline, sex may become a matter of less importance, and wealth may be taken for granted. At that point the various differences may unexpectedly become extremely important and a source of dissatisfaction in the marriage.

One of the first detailed investigations of such questions is described in the following *Cornerstones* section.

Cornerstones of Social Psychology
Terman's Study of Husband–Wife Similarity and Marital Success

Lewis M. Terman.
Lewis Terman was born in 1877 in Indiana. Much of his professional career (beginning with his doctoral dissertation) dealt with the study of intelligence, and he created the Stanford–Binet Intelligence Test. Though Terman had already retired by the time I (Donn Byrne) entered graduate school at Stanford, I caught glimpses of him in the hallway once or twice before his death in 1956. His many accomplishments included the longitudinal study of the intellectually gifted, the development of the first group intelligence test for use by the military in the First World War, and the investigation of some of the factors contributing to marital satisfaction. It is the latter work that constitutes his major contribution to social psychology.

Though Lewis M. Terman's major contributions to psychology center on his lifelong work on human intelligence, Terman was also interested in identifying the factors that underlie marital compatibility. In the 1930s, based on what was already known about similarity and attraction, he and a colleague examined the differences between happy and unhappy married couples (Terman & Buttenwieser, 1935a, 1935b).

These two psychologists proposed that because similarity appeared to result in mutual attraction, highly similar spouses should be more satisfied in their marriage than less similar spouses. These psychologists administered a measure of marital happiness to hundreds of couples and identified three couple categories (the 100 most happy, the 100 least happy, and 100 who had divorced). The three groups were matched for factors such as age, education, and occupational status. Then the investigators gave these 600 individuals psychological inventories with hundreds of items, on which each respondent independently indicated whether he or she felt positively or negatively about various activities, occupations, kinds of people, and famous individuals.

One finding was that, across all couples, people who marry are more similar than could be expected by chance. Once again, similarity was found to be associated with attraction. For the purposes of this investigation, however, a more crucial finding was that the relative similarity/dissimilarity of the couples was associated with the happiness of the marriage. A small sample of Terman's findings is presented in Table 8.4. Note that—as in attraction research—the role of similar attitudes is just as strong for issues that seem to be irrelevant to the couple (such as attitudes about Thomas Edison) as for seemingly central concerns within the marriage (such as attitudes about avoiding arguments).

You might think about a list of such issues that could matter to you and your spouse or future spouse. For example, would you care how the other person felt about the social security system, global warming, music, movies, TV, e-mail, the U.S. president, dogs versus cats, pornography, or forcing children to eat their vegetables? For these or any of hundreds of other issues that might matter, how similar do you suppose you are to someone to whom you are attracted?

Though we cannot draw firm conclusions about the role of any specific areas of similarity on the basis of a study such as this, the general finding that marital success is greater among similar than among dissimilar pairs has been confirmed repeatedly over the years. Terman's cornerstone study was the initial step that has led to decades of continuing research on the factors that influence marital relationships.

Marital Sex, Love, Parenthood, and Other Influences on General Satisfaction

A common question for married couples and for those studying married couples is the degree to which the partners are content with their relationship. Do people ever live happily ever after? Or are they often disappointed by the realities

Table 8.4

Similarity-Dissimilarity and Marital Success. In an early study of marital compatibility, Terman and his colleague found a general tendency for happily married couples to be more similar than either unhappily married or divorced couples in their attitudes about a wide variety of topics.

Attitude Topics on Which Happily Married Couples Were More Similar Than Unhappy or Divorced Couples	
Attitudes about oneself	Avoiding arguments
	Earning a definite salary versus a commission
	Getting attention from acquaintances when ill
	Contributing to charity
	Looking at a collection of antique furniture
	Having a pet canary
	Being alone at times of emotional stress
Attitudes about other people	Life insurance salesmen
	Dentists
	Men who use perfume
	Energetic people
	General Pershing
	Thomas Edison
	Ranchers
	Conservative people

(*Source:* Based on data from Terman & Buttenwieser, 1935a, 1935b.)

of spending a lifetime with a given spouse? Let's look at a few of the factors that influence marital satisfaction.

Marital Sex, Love, and Parenthood. Surveys of married couples indicate that sexual interactions become less frequent over time, the most rapid decline occurring during the first four years of marriage (Udry, 1980). Nevertheless, 41 percent of all married couples have sex twice a week or more often, whereas only 23 percent of single individuals have sex that frequently. Cohabiting couples are the most sexually active category, however, in that 56 percent have sex at least twice a week (Laumann et al., 1994; Michael et al., 1994). One reason, of course, is that unmarried couples who live together are usually within the early years of their sexual relationship.

Though it is common for passionate love to decrease within a marriage as the years pass (Tucker & Aron, 1993), women who continue to feel such love toward their husbands feel more satisfied with their marriages than women who do not (Aron & Henkemeyer, 1995). Male marital satisfaction is apparently unrelated to whether or not passionate love remains. For both men and women, satisfaction is related to behavior that suggests companionate love—sharing activities, exchanging ideas, laughing together, and working together on projects. So companionate love seems to be the key ingredient in a happy marriage, but women are even happier if they also continue to feel the sparks of passionate love.

Parenthood can interfere with marital sexuality and also create other new problems in the relationship (Alexander & Higgins, 1993; Hackel & Ruble,

1992). Nevertheless, both men and women who have children say that they enjoy being parents (Feldman & Nash, 1984). With multiple children, women report less and men report more marital satisfaction (Grote, Frieze, & Stone, 1996). Presumably, this gender difference occurs because mothers ordinarily have the major responsibility for the difficult day-to-day job of caring for the physical and psychological needs of offspring. It may be somewhat simplistic and not at all true for some marriages, but in general it is accurate to say that many fathers are spared some of the drudgery of parenthood while mothers do the dirty work.

Married versus Single. Compared to single individuals, those who are married consistently report being happier and healthier (Steinhauer, 1995). The differences between married and single individuals are not as great as they used to be, however, because unmarried men are happier now than in the past whereas married women are less happy (Glenn & Weaver, 1988). A possible explanation for these changes may lie in the greater availability of sexual relationships for unmarried men (Reed & Weinberg, 1984) and the conflicts women face between motherhood and a career (Batista & Berte, 1992).

Perhaps in response to such changes, Americans are living alone to a greater extent than ever before (one in four citizens over the age of 18) and waiting longer before marrying—until age 26.7 for men and 24.5 for women (More delay marriage, 1996). Nevertheless, those who are single say they want to marry, especially if they have never been married (Frazier et al., 1996). A slightly more complicated picture is provided by a study of married and single individuals in Norway. Those who are married have a greater sense of well-being and a lower suicide rate up until their late 30s, but after that the advantages of being married decline rapidly (Mastekaasa, 1995). It seems that young adults benefit psychologically from the security of a close marital relationship and are harmed psychologically by the absence of such a relationship.

Two-Career Families. A major task for both spouses is to discover how best to adjust to the demands of a two-career family (Gilbert, 1993). For one thing, as discussed in Chapter 5, even when women have an active career, they still do 75 percent of the cooking and 70 percent of the cleaning (Yu, 1996). (They do, however, leave 71 percent of the household repairs to their husbands.) In fact, compared to heterosexual and gay couples, only lesbian pairs seem to be able to share household labor in a fair and equitable manner (Kurdek, 1993).

Key Points

- Married couples are more similar in attitudes, values, interests, and other attributes than would be expected by chance, and the greater the similarity the more satisfying the marriage.

- The frequency of sex decreases during the first four years of marriage; but the frequency of marital sex is is higher than that of single individuals, although lower than that of cohabiting couples.

- Compared to people who are single, married couples are happier and healthier. Coping with the demands of a two-career family is a major challenge for couples.

Troubled Relationships and the Effects of Marital Failure

People usually enter marriage with high hopes; but, as Figure 8.16 suggests, people can change after they marry, and many people seem to be nicer as roman-

"It's as though everything nice about you had been just some kind of introductory offer."

Figure 8.16
Relationship Problems. One of the many potential problems in a long-term relationship is that one or both individuals may eventually begin to behave less nicely than they did early in the relationship. If each person could continue over time to be as nice and as considerate in interacting with a partner as was true on their first date, many problems could be avoided.

(*Source: The New Yorker,* June 10, 1991, p. 89.)

tic partners than they are as spouses. Maintaining a relationship is a never-ending job (Harvey & Omarzu, 1997), and success is not guaranteed. Each year, about 2.4 million American couples marry and another 1.2 million get divorced. Marriages that fail usually do so in the first two to six years (Glick, 1983). Many children around the world have had to go through the painful experience of their family's breaking up—in the United States this is true of about one child in three (Bumpass, 1984). Even without a divorce, an unhappy marriage can create problems for children. Those who are exposed to high levels of conflict between their parents become more aware of and apprehensive about aggression, and there are other changes in the way these children process information as well (O'Brien & Chin, 1998). A chain of events seems to occur in which aggressive marital conflict is associated with the mother's angry behavior with her children; this negative mother-child interaction, in turn, is associated with behavior problems in school (O'Brien & Bahadur, 1998). Among the consequences of divorce for children are negative long-term effects on their health and well-being (Friedman et al., 1995a; Vobejda, 1997), though various factors can moderate the severity of such effects (Hetherington, Bridges, & Insabella, 1998). Children from divorced families show a higher risk for mortality throughout their lives, in part because males whose parents were divorced are more likely to have less education and women from divorced families tend to smoke more. For both genders, a parental divorce increases the likelihood that the offspring, too, will divorce (Tucker et al., 1997). Such findings have led to a growing movement to make it more difficult for couples to divorce, especially when children are involved (Kirn, 1997).

Problems and Solutions. What happens to transform a loving romantic relationship into one characterized by unhappiness, dissatisfaction, and—often—hate? Some observers have suggested that the growing trend for married women to keep their surnames—either as a substitute for or hyphenated with the surname of their husbands—may be one of the causes of marital failure. That is, in the past, women more or less automatically adopted their husband's last names, and divorce was rare. One again, note that correlation does not necessarily indicate causation. In this instance, for example, there is *no effect* on marital satisfaction, commitment, or love associated with the wife's changing her name to that of her husband, keeping her maiden name, or using both names with a hyphen in between (Kline, Stafford, & Miklosovic, 1996).

Beyond name changes or non-changes, what happens in a relationship to destroy the initial positive feelings and create the subsequent negative feelings? Some marital problems are universal, because being in any kind of close relationship involves some degree of compromise. For example, one person living alone can do as he or she wishes, but two people living together must decide together what to eat for dinner and what time to serve it, whether to turn on the TV and which program to watch, and at what temperature to set the thermostat—along with hundreds of other major and minor decisions. Neither individual can always do exactly what he or she wants, and there is an inevitable conflict between the desire for independence and the need for closeness (Baxter, 1990). Only 1.2 percent of married couples say that they *never* have any disagreements, and most report that conflicts arise monthly or more often (McGonagle, Kessler, & Schilling, 1992). We will describe some of the common difficulties that arise in marriage and the painful effects of relationship failure.

Because no partner (including oneself) is perfect, spouses who once believed that they were ideally suited for each other almost inevitably come to realize that there are negative as well as positive elements in the relationship. Spouses greatly overestimate how much they are in agreement about most matters (Byrne & Blaylock, 1963), and they are then disappointed when they discover that their views actually differ (Sillars et al., 1994). People find it difficult (and perhaps impossible) to sustain unrealistic fantasies about love and totally positive illusions about each other indefinitely. Even personal characteristics that once seemed to be especially positive attributes of the future spouse can become a primary reason for disliking him or her as time passes (Felmlee, 1995; Pines, 1997). For example, dissimilarity from oneself may seem interesting and intriguing in a romantic partner, but this can eventually become a source of distress and dislike. Early in the relationship, some things the other person says or does may seem cute. Later on, what was once cute becomes annoying. Felmlee's (1998) research suggests that if you are drawn to someone because that person is very different from yourself or even unique, chances are good that disenchantment will set in over time.

Some of the interactions in a marriage can be conceptualized in terms of costs and benefits. Presumably, the greater the number of benefits relative to the number of costs, the higher the quality of the relationship. Clark and Grote (1998) have identified various kinds of costs and benefits; they further subdivide costs and benefits between those that are intentionally negative or positive and those that are unintentional but happen to be associated with the relationship. In addition, Clark and Grote suggest that other costs have to do with voluntary decisions to engage in difficult or undesired behavior in order to meet the needs of one's partner. This is characterized as *communal behavior*—a "cost" that actually benefits the relationship rather than detracts from it. Examples of the various types and costs and benefits are shown in Figure 8.17.

Differences in ways of handling conflict can create problems. Some of these are gender differences; for example, men more than women believe that one legitimate way to deal with a conflict is simply to avoid the issue (Oggins, Veroff, & Leber, 1993). In attempting to retain their mates, men tend to stress their resources, whereas women attempt to enhance their appearance (Buss & Shackleford, 1997). That is, men tend to believe that stressing such factors as their income and the things it can buy should reawaken their mate's commitment to the relationship. Women believe that improvements in appearance—such as a new hair color or weight loss—will rekindle love and desire in their mates.

One very common and very maladaptive tendency is for disagreeing partners to express negative words or engage in negative acts that then provoke further

Marriage: Moving beyond Romance   **345**

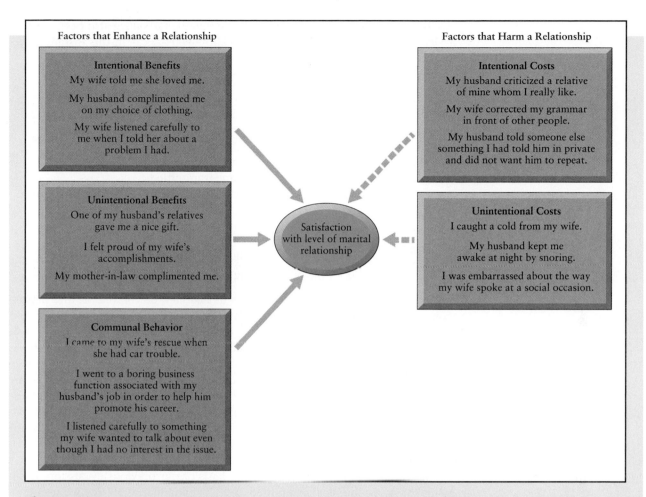

Figure 8.17

Costs and Benefits of a Marital Relationship. One approach to understanding relationship success and failure is to examine the relative costs and benefits. Clark and Grote (1998) developed a measure to assess intentional and unintentional costs and benefits in a marital relationship. In addition, they added a fifth category of "costs" (communal behavior) that actually function as benefits. Marital satisfaction is believed to depend on the relative number of costs and benefits spouses experience in the marriage. Samples of some of the test items are shown here.

(*Source:* Based on information in Clark & Grote, 1998.)

negative and destructive responses. When people take the time to consider the long-term consequences for the relationship, a constructive response is more likely to follow (Yovetich & Rusbult, 1994). For example, when one partner makes the effort to apologize for something that was said or done and the other makes the effort to indicate forgiveness, they have engaged in constructive behavior (Azar, 1997; McCullough, Worthington, & Rachal, 1997). Less obviously, those who learn simply to give in are more likely to have happy, stable marriages (Maugh, 1998). Marital disagreement is not a sport in which you need to score points or win every time. Couples interact in a more favorable way if each individual responds to the other person's need to maintain a positive self-evaluation (Mendolia, Beach, & Tesser, 1996) and works to understand the partner's perspective when problems arise (Arriaga & Rusbult, 1998). The most general characteristic of people who deal well with interpersonal conflict is *agreeableness* (Graziano, Jensen-Campbell, & Hair, 1996). As indicated in many sections of this book, the ability to get along with other people is an all-important skill.

In a more informal way, some of these same points have also been made in a Dear Abby column as "Rules for a Happy Marriage." In this instance, folk wisdom is entirely consistent with the research literature (Van Buren, 1996):

1. Never both be angry at the same time.
2. Never yell at each other unless the house is on fire.
3. If one of you has to win an argument, let it be your mate.
4. If you must criticize, do it lovingly.
5. Never bring up mistakes of the past.
6. Neglect the whole world rather than each other.
7. Never go to sleep with an argument unsettled.
8. At least once every day say a kind or complimentary word to your life partner.
9. When you have done something wrong, admit it and ask for forgiveness.
10. It takes two to make a quarrel, and the one in the wrong usually is the one who does the most talking.

People differ in characteristics such as hostility, defensiveness, and depression, and such differences are important determinants of how two people interact in dealing with disagreements (Newton et al., 1995; Thompson, Whiffen, & Blain, 1995). Rejection sensitivity presents special difficulties in a relationship. A person who enters a relationship expecting rejection readily perceives it in what his or her partner says or does (Downey & Feldman, 1996). Men who are sensitive to rejection become jealous; rejection-sensitive women become hostile and less supportive. Given both the importance of personality factors in influencing how people interact and the importance of genes in determining some personality factors, it follows that one's risk of divorce is in part genetically determined (Jockin, McGue, & Lykken, 1996).

As you probably could guess on the basis of our previous discussions of attachment styles, the most committed and satisfying marriages involve secure individuals (Radecki-Bush, Farrell, & Bush, 1993). The more secure the individual, the more likely he or she is to engage in caregiving activity with a partner. It is especially difficult for a fearful–avoidant individual to support a partner who is trying to cope with stress (Carnelley, Pietromonaco, & Jaffe, 1996). Partners who are different in the way they cope with stress are less satisfied with their relationship than those who use similar coping strategies (Ptacek & Dodge, 1995).

Buss (1989) has proposed that many difficulties arise because of built-in differences between men and women. For reasons based on evolutionary pressures, women seek a mate who will be loving and protective, and women become especially upset by any indication that a partner is not affectionate or not eager to provide protection. Men primarily seek a young, healthy partner who is able to reproduce, and they become especially upset by sexual rejection. Consequently, although jealousy is a common problem in relationships (Buunk, 1995; Sharpsteen, 1995), the reason for jealousy differs as a function of gender. A man becomes most jealous when his partner is sexually unfaithful, but a woman becomes most jealous when her partner becomes emotionally committed to someone else (Buss et al., 1992). (Also see Chapter 11.) A rival's potential is also based on these gender differences. Males are most troubled by a male rival who is dominant and powerful while females are most threatened by a female rival who is young and physically attractive (Dijkstra & Buunk, 1998). The evolutionary explanation of these differences is strengthened by the finding that the same gender differences are found cross-culturally in the Netherlands, Germany, and the United States (Buunk, 1995).

Jealousy has also been studied from the perspective of attachment effects (Sharpsteen & Kirkpatrick, 1997). Securely attached individuals tend to express anger toward the partner but to maintain the relationship. Those with a fearful–avoidant style tend to express anger and blame toward the outsider rather than the partner, while insecure, ambivalent individuals resist expressing any anger based on jealousy. In response to feeling jealous, preoccupied individuals express the most negative affect, whereas dismissing individuals report the least fear and unhappiness (Guerrero, 1998).

Other conflicts arise because partners slowly discover (or at least begin to attend to the fact) that they are dissimilar in various ways (Byrne & Murnen, 1988). If, for example, two people who are dating never discuss how they feel about saving money versus spending it, they may be in for a shock at some point when they discover that he wants to buy an expensive car and she wants to buy treasury bonds. Other dissimilarities can arise later in the relationship if one partner changes and the other does not. I knew two people who were both very active in left-wing politics during the Vietnam War; after several years of marriage, he became increasingly conservative, but she did not. They argued frequently about political issues and eventually divorced. Secure individuals are most accurate in perceiving how similar they are to another individual, while those who are fearful avoidant underestimate and insecure ambivalent overestimate similarity (Mikulincer, Orbach, & Iavnieli, 1998).

Still other sources of conflict may be irrelevant while two people are dating but create a major problem later on. A young couple may never even think about or discuss what to do if his father or her mother should become disabled in the future, but may find themselves in disagreement about how best to provide care when the time comes.

For some, a long-term relationship begins to be uncomfortable simply because it has become *boring*. Married couples are very likely to develop unchanging routines in their daily interactions (sexual and otherwise) and then gradually perceive themselves to be in a rut. Also, if one person wants variety and excitement while the other prefers regularity and predictability, these dissimilar goals create stress, and each spouse blames the difficulty on the other (Fincham & Bradbury, 1992, 1993).

Considering the importance of affect in relationships (see Chapter 7), it is not surprising that sexual satisfaction is closely associated with the perception of marital well-being for both women and men (Henderson-King & Veroff, 1994). Beyond good and bad sexual experiences, other sources of pleasure and displeasure easily spill over into the marriage and affect how it is evaluated. For example, negative emotions aroused in the course of one's job can affect one's home life (Chan & Margolin, 1994; Geller & Hobfoll, 1994). An important gender difference for couples with children is that mothers experience more positive feelings when they are away from home (including time at work), whereas fathers are happier at home than elsewhere (Larson, Richards, & Perry-Jenkins, 1994). As we noted earlier, home often means work for mothers and relaxation for fathers.

The most devastating effect on a marriage can result from the negative affect created by conflicts and disagreements (Margolin, John, & O'Brien, 1989). Instead of trying to solve a given problem, unhappy partners may simply express their mutually negative evaluations as they blame one another and express their anger (Davila, Bradbury, & Fincham, 1998; Kubany et al., 1995). Calling one another names ("You bitch!") or delivering global negative evaluations ("You're a total mess!") cannot resolve a conflict. This kind of verbal abuse simply creates more negativity. Miller (1991, p. 63) observes that some of the "most hateful, caustic, and abusive interactions take place with those we say we love."

Videotaped interactions of satisfied and dissatisfied partners reveal much more negative verbal and nonverbal behavior in the latter pairs than in the former (Halford & Sanders, 1990). Unhappy couples express less positive affect

Figure 8.18
Successful Marriages: A Glass Half Full. Though it is often stressed that half of all marriages end in divorce, this also means that half of all marriages do not. Many people do succeed in establishing successful lifelong relationships. Among the key ingredients are an emphasis on friendship, commitment, similarity, and the creation of positive affect.

and more negative affect than those who are satisfied with their relationship (Levenson, Carstensen, & Gottman, 1994). All expressions of positive affect—including nicknames such as "sweet pea" and "pussycat"—are more common in satisfying than in unhappy marriages (Bruess & Pearson, 1993). Avoiding communication and withdrawal from interaction with a partner also lead to relationship dissatisfaction (Bodenmann et al., 1998). Decreases in positive affect and increases in negative affect are responsible for deteriorating relationships and the resulting distress in gay and lesbian couples as well as in heterosexual couples (Kurdek, 1996, 1997).

Though a lot of marital research focuses on problems, it should be remembered that as many marriages succeed as fail, as in Figure 8.18. A successful marriage seems to involve an emphasis on friendship, commitment, similarity, and efforts to create positive affect (Adams & Jones, 1997; Lauer & Lauer, 1985). Older couples who remain married express more positive affect than younger and middle-aged couples (Levenson, Cartensen, & Gottman, 1994), perhaps because people get smarter and mellower about relationships as they grow older (Locke, 1995).

Relationship Failure: When Dissatisfaction Leads to Dissolution. Though it is possible for two friends simply to drift apart, the partners in an intimate relationship are more likely to feel intense distress and anger when the relationship fails (Fischman, 1986). In part, lovers and spouses have greater difficulty in separating because they have usually invested a great deal of time in one another, exchanged powerful rewards, and expressed a lasting commitment to the relationship (Simpson, 1987).

Men and women differ in how they cope with a failed relationship. Women confide in their friends, whereas men tend to start a new relationship as quickly as possible (Sorenson et al., 1993). Divorce is, of course, a stressful experience for almost anyone; but, compared to persons with insecure attachment styles, an individual with a secure style experiences less distress and has a greater ability to cope (Birnbaum et al., 1997).

Rusbult and Zembrodt (1983) have pointed out that people respond either actively or passively to an unhappy partnership. To summarize the alternatives they suggest, an active response can involve ending the relationship (*exit*—"Here's the name of my lawyer; I'm filing for divorce") or working to improve it (*voice*—"I believe we should give marital counseling a try"). Passively, one can simply wait for improvement (*loyalty*—"I'll stand by my partner until things get better") or wait for the inevitable breakup (*neglect*—"I just won't do anything until the situation gets totally impossible"). These alternatives are diagrammed in Figure 8.19. If the goal is to maintain a relationship, *exit* and *neglect* are clearly the least constructive and *voice* the most constructive choice. Compared to secure individuals, those who are insecure are more likely to react with exit and neglect and less likely to react with voice. *Loyalty* tends to go unnoticed or to be misinterpreted: often, when people say that they have responded with loyalty, their partners perceive them as being uninterested or unaware (Drigotas, Whitney, & Rusbult, 1995).

Among quite divergent types of couples (college students, older spouses, gays, and lesbians), men and women with high self-esteem (see Chapter 5) tend to respond to relationship failure by exiting, while low self-esteem is often associated with passive neglect (Rusbult, Morrow, & Johnson, 1990). Although it is very difficult to reverse a deteriorating relationship, problems can sometimes be solved. The couple can reconcile if (1) the partnership satisfies the needs of each individual, (2) each remains committed to staying together, and (3) alternative lovers are not available (Rusbult, Martz, & Agnew, 1998). The more dependent a person is on the relationship, the less he or she is motivated to dissolve it (Drigotas & Rusbult, 1992), even in response to physical abuse (Rusbult & Martz, 1995).

Despite the shattered hopes of living happily ever after and the pain of a marital breakup, it is interesting to note that most divorced individuals remarry,

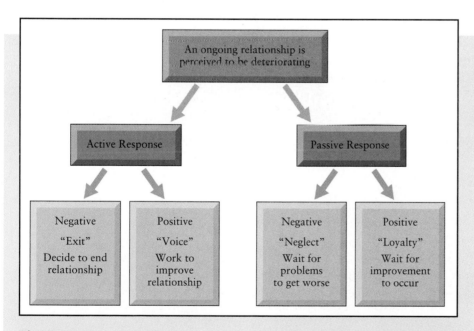

Figure 8.19
Responding to a Troubled Relationship. When a relationship is beginning to fail, the partners can respond in either an active or a passive way. Within each of these two alternatives, the response can be either positive or negative. Rusbult and Zembrodt label the active–negative decision (to end the relationship) as "exit," and the active–positive decision (to attempt to improve the relationship) as "voice." A passive–negative response, simply waiting for the problems to get worse, is labeled "neglect"; and a passive-positive response, simply waiting for improvement, is known as "loyalty."

(*Source:* Based on information from Rusbult & Zembrodt, 1983.)

especially men. In fact, nearly half of all U.S. marriages are remarriages for one or both partners (Koch, 1996). The desire for future love and happiness in a relationship seems to have a greater influence on behavior than negative past experiences. Or, as Samuel Johnson put it, "Remarriage, sir, represents the triumph of hope over experience."

Key Points

- In the United States, about 50 percent of marriages end in divorce, and the consequences are especially devastating for children.

- Most married couples have some degree of conflict and disagreement, and whether such difficulties are resolved constructively or simply result in destructive interactions becomes a major factor in the success of the relationship.

- Among the factors that lead to conflicts and affect the way they are handled are the need to compromise, the relative number of costs and benefits in the relationship, coping styles, the agreeableness of each individual, personality differences including rejection sensitivity and attachment style, jealousy, dissimilarity, boredom, and the presence of positive versus negative affect.

- When marital dissatisfaction becomes great, the individuals involved generally can respond either actively or passively in moving toward restoring or ending the relationship.

- Most people who divorce decide to remarry (especially men), and nearly half of all marriages performed in the United States involve remarriages for one or both partners.

Connections: Integrating Social Psychology

In this chapter, you read about . . .	In other chapters, you will find related discussions of . . .
the association between self-esteem and attachment style and the effect of falling in love on self-esteem	self-esteem (Chapter 5)
the role of similarity in determining friendships, romantic relationships, and marital partners	similarity and attraction (Chapter 7)
social skills and cognitive processes	cognitive processes (Chapters 2 and 3)
love as emotional misattribution	misattribution and emotions (Chapter 3)
affect and relationships	affect and attraction (Chapter 7)
responses to conflicts on the part of spouses	response to conflicts in organizations (Chapter 13)

Thinking about Connections

1. Do you believe that your relationship with your parents has anything to do with how you react to other people? Did your mother and father make you feel good about yourself? Do you still feel the same way about yourself? In your childhood, were the adults around you dependable? Did they keep their promises? Did you think of them as kind? How do you feel about most of the people you meet? Do you believe they are more or less trustworthy?

2. Think of someone who is (or was) your closest friend. What was it about that person that first attracted you? Did proximity, similarity, positive affect, or appearance play a role in your getting to know one another? What do (or did) you do when together? Are there any parallels between your childhood friendships and your current friendships?

3. Think about yourself in a close romantic relationship—either in the past, in the present, or in an imaginary romance. How did you meet? What attracted you? Did you gradually develop positive feelings, or was it love at first sight? Is there any match between your own experience and such research questions as the role of misattributed emotions, evolutionary reproductive strategies, or expectancies based on stories about love to which you have been exposed since childhood?

4. When you find yourself in a disagreement with a romantic partner, a friend, or anyone else, what do you do? Is the interaction constructive, or do you just get mad and exchange insults? Have you ever broken up with someone to whom you felt very close? Why did it happen? Who initiated the breakup, and how was it done? Could either of you have done a better job?

Ideas to Take with You
All You Need Is Love?

There are few (if any) words that appear more often in songs, stories, movies, fairy tales, and in our everyday lives than "love." Nevertheless, a question people frequently ask themselves (and Ann Landers) is "How do I know if I'm really in love?" The columnist answers that question with "If you have to ask, you're not." There is some wisdom in that response, but don't count on being accurate just because you're so sure of yourself that you don't have to ask. You might find it more helpful to consider what has been learned about this topic in social psychological research.

Emotional Arousal Is Not Necessarily Love.

When you encounter someone who appeals to you, it is easy to mistake a variety of arousal states as indicating love. As Elaine Hatfield has said, we often fall in lust and interpret it as love. More generally, research on emotional misattribution indicates that the physiological arousal associated with excitement, fear, happiness, anxiety, and even anger can be mislabeled. Think of various things that may occur on a date (from kissing to watching a horror film to riding a roller coaster) that can potentially elicit arousal and lead to misattribution. If you find yourself surging with emotion and decide that you must be madly in love, pause and think about pinpointing alternative explanations for what you may be feeling.

What Do You Know about This Person?

None of us has an acceptable and effective way to go about getting to know someone else in depth. That is, we don't prepare detailed questionnaires for potential dates, lovers, or spouses to fill out. A simple but reasonable alternative is for two people to learn as much as they can about each other by talking, writing, chatting on line, or whatever else they find comfortable. And each person should be aware of issues that are of special personal importance. For example, "Dr. Laura" Schlessinger recently received a call from a man who had become emotionally involved with a woman only to find out late in the relationship that the two of them were of different religions. He was heartbroken. The commonsense advice was that in the future he should ask about religion when he first became attracted to a woman, because for him marrying within his faith was a central concern. The same advice should hold for anything and everything you believe is critical—from politics to sex to parenthood. Ask. That may seem awkward, but it's better to be awkward than to be surprised.

What Is Your Love Style?

Look over the definitions of the six love styles discussed in this chapter along with the Chinese concept of love as a matter of fate and predestination. Which one fits you best? That is, do you conceive of love as a friendship, a fun game, a logical arrangement, or what? Then consider the style of your partner or potential partner. If the two of you match, you will encounter fewer romantic problems than if your concepts of love are not at all alike.

Is Consummate Love a Possibility?

In Sternberg's triangular model of love, the ideal or "consummate" match is between two individuals in whom intimacy, passion, and commitment are all present in equal strength. Is that possible? Well, few relationships are perfect; but consummate love is surely an ideal worth striving for. At the very least, two people who are at all serious about each other should know where each individual fits on the triangle.

Summary and Review of Key Points

Interdependent Relationships with Family and Friends—or Loneliness

- Close relationships are characterized by *interdependence*, in which two people influence each other's lives, focus their thoughts and emotions on each other, and engage in joint activities.
- One's first relationships are within the family. On the basis of interactions with the mother (or other caregiver), the infant develops an *attachment style* that is secure, insecure avoidant, or insecure ambivalent. These styles are believed to generalize to other interpersonal relationships throughout the individual's life.
- As adolescence approaches, teenagers begin to draw away from parents, but only some can be described as "rebellious." Many express love and affection for their mother and father.
- As their parents grow older, adults often find themselves reversing roles and being obligated to care for one or both of them.
- Sibling relationships frequently involve a mixture of affection, hostility, and rivalry. Siblings of both genders can be very close in childhood, drift apart in adolescence and young adulthood, but then become close once again as they grow older.
- Friendships outside of the family begin in childhood and are based on most of the same factors that are responsible for attraction between adults. Many people are able to form a *close friendship* that involves spending time together, interacting in various situations, excluding others from the relationship, providing mutual emotional support, and engaging in self-disclosure.
- At whatever age, attachment style seems to exert a major influence on the ease with which people make friends, on the way they interact, and on their success in maintaining relationships.
- Adult attachment style can be characterized as the combination of a person's level of self-esteem and degree of

interpersonal trust. This conceptualization yields four resulting styles that are labeled: *secure, dismissing, fearful–avoidant,* and *preoccupied attachment* styles. Those who are secure are best able to form long-lasting, committed, satisfying relationships.

- *Loneliness* occurs when a person has fewer and less satisfying relationships than he or she desires. The result is depression, anxiety, unhappiness, dissatisfaction, and self-blame. The causes of loneliness may include an individual's attachment style, a failure to develop adequate social skills, and inappropriate cognitions about interpersonal interactions. Cognitive therapy and social skills training are very helpful in bringing about change.

Romantic Relationships, Love, and Physical Intimacy

- One defining characteristic of romantic relationships is some degree of physical intimacy, ranging from holding hands to sexual interactions.
- As in attraction and friendship, romantic relationships are influenced by factors such as physical proximity, appearance, and similarity. Added factors in romance are sexual attraction, the desire for total acceptance from the other individual, and a touch of fantasy based on positive illusions. Romantic relationships are very likely to start wherever people spend time—in their neighborhoods, at school, or on the job.
- Several varieties of love have been identified. In *passionate love* there is a sudden, overwhelming emotional reaction. *Companionate love* is based on close friendship, caring, mutual liking, and respect. Various other love styles have also been categorized.
- Sternberg's *triangular model of love* describes love as a blend of three possible components: intimacy, passion, and decision/commitment.
- Based in part on changes in sexual attitudes and sexual practices (the "sexual revolution"), premarital sexual

interactions have become increasingly the norm among couples in close relationships.

- The most permissive aspects of the new sexual attitudes have become less attractive in the wake of negative subjective feelings involving pressures to conform to the new sexual norms and the negative objective consequences of unwanted pregnancies and incurable diseases such as genital herpes and AIDS.
- Despite the increased likelihood of premarital intercourse and cohabitation, there is no consistent evidence indicating either a positive or a negative effect of such experiences on subsequent marital satisfaction or stability.

Marriage: Moving beyond Romance

- Married couples are more similar in attitudes, values, interests, and other attributes than would be expected by chance, and the greater the similarity the more satisfying the marriage.
- The frequency of marital sex decreases during the first four years of marriage; but the frequency of marital sex is higher than that of single individuals, although lower than that of cohabiting couples.

- Compared to those who are single, married couples are happier and healthier. Coping with the demands of a two-career family is a major challenge for couples.
- In the United States, about 50 percent of marriages end in divorce, and the consequences are especially devastating for children.
- Most married couples have some degree of conflict and disagreement, and whether such difficulties are resolved constructively or simply result in destructive interactions becomes a major factor in the success of the relationship.
- Among the factors that lead to conflicts and affect the way they are handled are the need to compromise, the relative numbers of costs and benefits in the relationship, coping styles, the agreeableness of each individual, personality differences including rejection sensitivity and attachment style, jealousy, dissimilarity, boredom, and the presence of positive versus negative affect.
- When marital dissatisfaction becomes great, the individuals involved generally respond either actively or passively in moving toward restoring or ending the relationship.
- Most people who divorce decide to remarry (especially men), and nearly half of all marriages performed in the U.S. involve remarriages for one or both partners.

KEY TERMS

attachment style (p. 306)

close friendship (p. 312)

companionate love (p. 332)

decision/commitment (p. 333)

dismissing attachment style (p. 318)

fearful–avoidant attachment style (p. 317)

interdependence (p. 305)

interpersonal trust (p. 306)

intimacy (p. 333)

loneliness (p. 320)

love (p. 328)

passion (p. 333)

passionate love (p. 329)

preoccupied attachment style (p. 318)

secure attachment style (p. 316)

social phobia (p. 322)

sociosexuality (p. 334)

triangular model of love (p. 332)

FOR MORE INFORMATION

Duck, S. (1994). *Meaningful relationships: Talking, sense, and relating*. Thousand Oaks, CA: Sage.

A leading investigator and theorist in the field of interpersonal behavior, Professor Duck describes how relationships are a continual challenge because of the need to think about and to respond to what the other person says and does. Relationships are never a "done deal." They require constant effort in order to be maintained.

Gurdin, J. B. (1996). *Amitie/friendship: An investigation into cross-cultural styles in Canada and the United States*. Bethesda, MD: Austin & Winefield.

This book has been described as a landmark contemporary comparative study of friendship. Using data from surveys, participant observations, and small group research, the au-

thor describes how friendships are affected by ethnicity, gender, class, marital status, and age.

Simpson, J. A., & Rholes, W. S. (Eds.). (1998). *Attachment theory and close relationships*. New York: Guilford.

An up-to-date collection of chapters by psychologists directly involved in research on attachment theory. This book provides an invaluable summary of progress in this active field of research.

Weber, A. L., & Harvey, J. H. (Eds.). (1994). *Perspectives on close relationships*. Boston: Allyn and Bacon.

Several active investigators describe research and theory relevant to most of the topics in this chapter. Included are close relationships, attachment, love, commitment, sexuality, jealousy, and the need to cope with relationship dissolution.

9 Social Influence: Changing Others' Behavior

Flame in the Heart. © José Ortega/Stock Illustration Source

Chapter Outline

Conformity: Group Influence in Action

    CORNERSTONES OF SOCIAL PSYCHOLOGY: Asch's Research on
        Conformity: Social Pressure—the Irresistible Force?

    Factors Affecting Conformity: Variables That Determine the Extent to
        Which We "Go Along"

    SOCIAL DIVERSITY: A CRITICAL ANALYSIS: The Persistence of Social
        Norms: Some Unsettling Effects of the "Culture of Honor"

    The Bases of Conformity: Why We Often Choose to "Go Along"

    The Need for Individuality and the Need for Personal Control: Why,
        Sometimes, We Choose *Not* to Go Along

    BEYOND THE HEADLINES: AS SOCIAL PSYCHOLOGISTS SEE IT:
        Dress Codes versus Personal Freedom: When Norms Collide

    Minority Influence: Does the Majority Always Rule?

Compliance: To Ask—Sometimes—Is to Receive

    Compliance: The Underlying Principles

    Tactics Based on Friendship or Liking: Ingratiation

    Tactics Based on Commitment or Consistency: The Foot-in-the-Door
        and the Lowball

    Tactics Based on Reciprocity: The Door-in-the-Face and the "That's-
        Not-All" Approach

    Tactics Based on Scarcity: Playing Hard to Get and the Fast-
        Approaching-Deadline Technique

    Other Tactics for Gaining Compliance: Complaining and Putting
        Others in a Good Mood

    Individual Differences in the Use of Social Influence: Do Different
        Persons Prefer Different Tactics?

Obedience: Social Influence by Demand

    Destructive Obedience: Some Basic Findings

    Destructive Obedience: Its Social Psychological Basis

    Destructive Obedience: Resisting Its Effects

    CONNECTIONS: Integrating Social Psychology

    IDEAS TO TAKE WITH YOU: Tactics for Gaining Compliance

Summary and Review of Key Points

Key Terms

For More Information

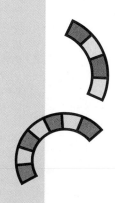

Figure 9.1

Social Influence: What the Future Has in Store?
While efforts to change our attitudes and behavior haven't yet reached this stage, they are becoming increasingly sophisticated—and perhaps effective.

(*Source: The New Yorker*)

"*Sometimes I wish they'd never perfected setless television.*"

I don't know about you, but I (Robert Baron) almost never answer my phone anymore. Instead, I let my answering machine take the call, and only pick up the receiver if it's someone I know or with whom I wish to speak. Why do I do this? Not because I'm unfriendly; almost everyone who knows me would say that just the opposite is true. Rather, I have adopted this strategy to protect myself from literally dozens of calls each day from people trying to sell me something or to get me to make a donation to some cause or vote for their candidate. In short, I screen my calls so that I can avoid many attempts at **social influence**—*efforts by others to change my attitudes, beliefs, perceptions, or behavior (Cialdini, 1994). Unfortunately, such efforts at social influence are an extremely common fact of life in today's world; and while they haven't yet reached the level shown in Figure 9.1, they do seem to be increasingly frequent and intrusive.*

Where social influence is concerned, however, we dish it out as well as receive it. How many times each day do you try to influence others— friends, roommates, family members, romantic partners? If you are like most people, you practice many forms of social influence each day. Consider my own daily life. I have no trouble getting up in the morning, but my wife does; so my day often starts with gentle efforts on my part to coax her out of bed. As the hours pass, I find myself using social influence in many other contexts. I ask one of my colleagues if she'll take over my class while I am at away at a conference; I ask the waitperson at lunch to toast the bread on my sandwich and to hold the mayonnaise; I drop my car off for servicing and ask if I can have it back by 4:00 p.m.; I plead with my daughter to drive carefully when she goes to visit her boyfriend . . . and so it goes, all day long.

social influence • Efforts by one or more individuals to change the attitudes, beliefs, perceptions, or behaviors of one or more others.

conformity • A type of social influence in which individuals change their attitudes or behavior in order to adhere to existing social norms.

Because of its importance in our daily lives, social influence has long been a central topic of research in social psychology. We have already considered some of this work in Chapter 4, where we examined the process of *persuasion*. Here, we'll expand on that earlier discussion by examining many other aspects of social influence. First, we'll focus on the topic of **conformity**—changing one's attitudes or behavior in order to go along with the crowd, to act the same as other

Figure 9.2
Social Norms: Regulators of Everyday Life. Social norms tell us what we should do (or not do) in a given situation. They are often stated explicitly in signs like these.

persons in one's group or society. As we'll soon see, pressures toward conformity can be amazingly strong and hard to resist. Next, we'll turn to **compliance**—efforts to get others to say yes to various requests. Finally, we'll examine **obedience**—a form of social influence in which one person simply orders one or more others to do what they want.

CONFORMITY: GROUP INFLUENCE IN ACTION

Have you ever found yourself in a situation in which you felt that you stuck out like the proverbial sore thumb? If so, you have already had direct experience with pressures toward *conformity*. In such situations, you probably experienced a strong desire to "get back into line"—to fit in with the other people around you. Such pressures toward conformity stem from the fact that in many contexts there are explicit or unspoken rules indicating how we *should* or *ought to* behave. These rules are known as **social norms,** and they often exert powerful effects on our behavior. In some instances, social norms are both detailed and precise. For instance, governments generally function through constitutions and written laws, and athletic contests are usually regulated by written rules. Signs in many public places (e.g., along highways, in parks, at airports) describe expected behavior in considerable detail, as in SPEED LIMIT 55, NO SWIMMING, NO PARKING, and KEEP OFF THE GRASS; see Figure 9.2.

In contrast, other norms are unspoken or implicit. Most of us obey such unwritten rules as "Don't stand too close to strangers on elevators if you can help it" and "Don't arrive at parties exactly on time." Similarly, we are often influenced by current and rapidly changing standards of dress, speech, and grooming. Regardless of whether social norms are explicit or implicit, though, one fact is clear: *Most people obey them most of the time.* For instance, few persons visit restaurants without leaving a tip for the server; and virtually everyone, regardless of personal political beliefs, stands when the national anthem of their country is played at sports events or other public gatherings.

At first glance, this strong tendency toward conformity—toward going along with our society's or our group's expectations about how we should behave in various situations—may strike you as objectionable. After all, it does place restrictions on personal freedom. Actually, though, there is a strong basis for so much conformity: without it, we would quickly find ourselves facing so-

compliance • A form of social influence involving direct requests from one person to another.

obedience • A form of social influence in which one person simply orders one or more others to perform some action(s).

social norms • Rules indicating how individuals are expected to behave in specific situations.

cial chaos. Imagine what would happen outside movie theaters, at stadiums, or at supermarket checkout counters if people did *not* obey the norm "Form a line and wait your turn." And consider the danger to both drivers and pedestrians if there were *not* clear and widely followed traffic regulations. In many situations conformity serves a useful function. In other situations, though, norms governing individual behavior appear to have little if any practical value; they simply exist. For example, in some settings, especially in the business world, many companies (although a decreasing number) still require that their male employees wear neckties and that their female employees wear skirts or dresses, at least part of the time. But wearing such clothing is unrelated to the performance of many jobs and can cause considerable discomfort (e.g., wearing a tie on a sweltering day), so such norms may well have outlived their usefulness.

Given that strong pressures toward conformity exist in many social settings, it is surprising to learn that conformity, as a social process, received relatively little attention in social psychology until the 1950s. At that time, Solomon Asch (1951), whose research on impression formation we considered in Chapter 2, carried out a series of experiments that yielded dramatic results. In fact, the results obtained by Asch were so strong and so surprising that they quickly captured the attention of both social psychologists and the general public. This research is described in the *Cornerstones* section below.

Cornerstones of Social Psychology
Asch's Research on Conformity: Social Pressure— the Irresistible Force?

Solomon Asch. *Asch was one of the founders of modern social psychology; his research on several important topics—including impression formation and conformity—started new lines of work, and played an important role in shaping the nature of the field. I (Robert Baron) met him in the late 1970s, and we soon struck up a friendship. I found Professor Asch to be as kind and considerate as he was intelligent and insightful.*

Suppose that just before an important math exam, you discover that your answer to a homework problem—a problem of the type that will be on the test—is different from that obtained by one of your friends. How do you react? Probably with mild concern. Now imagine that you learn that a second person's answer, too, is different from yours. To make matters worse, it agrees with the answer reported by the first person. How do you feel *now*? The chances are good that your anxiety will be considerable. Next, you discover that a third person agrees with the other two. At this point, you know that you are in big trouble. Which answer should you accept? Yours or the one obtained by your three friends? The exam is about to start, so you have to decide quickly.

Life is filled with such dilemmas—instances in which we discover that our own judgments, actions, or conclusions are different from those reached by other persons. What do we do in such situations? Important insight into our behavior was provided by studies conducted by Solomon Asch (1951, 1955), studies that are viewed as true classics in social psychology.

In his research, Asch asked participants to respond to a series of simple perceptual problems such as the one in Figure 9.3. On each problem each participant indicated which of three comparison lines matched a standard line in length. Several other persons (usually six to eight) were also present during the session; but, unknown to the real participant, all were assistants of the experimenter. On certain occasions known as *critical trials* (twelve out of the eighteen problems), the accomplices offered answers that were clearly wrong: they unanimously chose the wrong line as a match for the standard line. Moreover, they stated their answers *before* the participants responded. Thus, on these critical trials, the participants faced the type of dilemma described above. Should they go along with the other persons present or stick to their own judgments? Results were clear: A large majority of the persons in Asch's research chose conformity. Across several different studies, fully 76 percent of those tested went along with the group's false answers at least once; overall, they voiced agreement with these errors 37 percent of the time. In contrast, only 5 percent

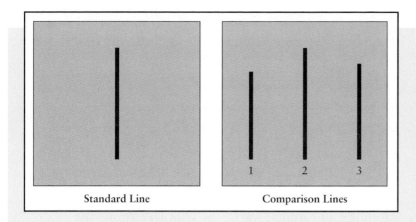

Figure 9.3
Asch's Line Judgment Task:
An Example. Participants in Asch's research were asked to report their judgments on problems such as this one. Their task was to indicate which of the comparison lines (1, 2, or 3) best matched the standard line in length. To study conformity, Asch had participants make these judgments only after hearing the answers of several other people—all of whom were his assistants.

of the participants in a control group, who responded to the same problems alone, made such errors.

Of course, there were large individual differences in conformity. Almost 25 percent of the participants *never* yielded to the group pressure. At the other extreme, some persons went along with the majority nearly all the time. When Asch questioned them, some of these persons said, "I am wrong, they are right"; they had little confidence in their own judgments. Others said they felt that the other persons present were the victims of some sort of optical illusion or were merely sheep following the responses of the first person. Yet when it was their turn to speak, these people, too, went along with the group.

In further studies, Asch (1951, 1956) investigated the effects of shattering the group's unanimity by having one of the accomplices break with the others. In one study, this person gave the correct answer, becoming an "ally" of the real participant; in another group, he chose an answer in between the one given by the group and the correct one; and in a third, he chose the answer that was even more incorrect than that chosen by the majority. In the latter two conditions, in other words, he broke from the group but still disagreed with the real participant. Results indicated that conformity was reduced under all three conditions. Somewhat surprisingly, however, this reduction was greatest when the dissenting assistant expressed views even more extreme (and wrong) than the majority. Together, these findings suggest that it is the unanimity of the group that is crucial; once that unanimity is broken, no matter how, resisting group pressure becomes much easier.

There's one more aspect of Asch's research that is important to mention. In later studies, he repeated his basic procedure, but with one important change: Instead of stating their answers out loud, participants wrote them down on a piece of paper. As you might guess, conformity dropped sharply. This finding points to the importance of distinguishing between *public conformity*—doing or saying what others around us say or do—and *private acceptance*—actually coming to feel or think as others do. Often, it appears, we follow social norms overtly but don't actually change our private views (Maas & Clark, 1984). This distinction between public conformity and private acceptance is an important one, and we'll refer to it at several points in this book.

Asch's research was the catalyst for a flurry of activity in social psychology, as many other researchers rushed to investigate the nature of conformity, to identify factors that influence it, and to establish its limits (e.g., Crutchfield, 1955; Deutsch & Gerard, 1955). Indeed, such research is continuing today and is still adding to our understanding of this crucial form of social influence (e.g., R. S. Baron, Vandello, & Brunsman, 1996; Bond & Smith, 1996; Buehler & Griffin, 1994). Clearly, then, Asch's early studies of conformity exerted a lasting impact as one of the basic cornerstones of social psychology.

Factors Affecting Conformity: Variables That Determine the Extent to Which We "Go Along"

Asch's research demonstrated the existence of powerful pressures toward conformity, but even a moment's reflection suggests that conformity does not occur to the same degree in all settings. For instance, body piercing and tattoos are really in right now, with the result that many teenagers and some young adults experience strong pressures to adorn themselves in these ways. Yet despite this fact, many are *not* tattooed or pierced. Why? In other words, what factors determine the extent to which individuals yield to conformity pressure or resist it? Systematic research on this issue suggests that many factors play a role; here, we'll examine the ones that appear to be most important.

Cohesiveness and Conformity: Accepting Influence from Those We Like. Let's return to the craze for body piercing I mentioned above. Recently I read an article indicating that this fashion has moved into a new phase; not content to wear simple rings or jewels, some young people are having much larger items attached to their bodies, including artificial horns—which presumably give them that "devil-may-care" look they've always wanted (Leonard, 1998)! Suppose that this fashion suddenly appeared in your own neighborhood. Further, imagine that the people who adopted it were the most popular and admired in the entire area. Would their adoption of this new style lead to its rapid spread? Perhaps; in any case, the fact that they adopted it would tempt many persons to do the same. But now suppose that instead, the only ones who adopted the new fad were the losers in your neighborhood—people who were viewed as weird and unpopular. Would their adoption of the new fashion lead to its rapid expansion? Probably not; after all, who would want to be like them?

This example illustrates one factor that plays an important role where conformity is concerned: **cohesiveness,** which can be defined as the degree of attraction felt by individuals toward some group. When cohesiveness is high—when we like and admire some group of persons—pressures toward conformity are magnified. After all, we know that one way of gaining the acceptance of such persons is to be like them in various ways, even if this involves alterations in our own anatomy. When cohesiveness is low, on the other hand, pressures toward conformity are also low; why should we change our behavior to be like other people we don't especially like or admire? Research findings indicate that cohesiveness exerts strong effects on conformity (Crandall, 1988; Latané & L'Herrou, 1996), so it is definitely one important determinant of the extent to which we yield to this type of social pressure.

Conformity and Group Size: Why More Is Better with Respect to Social Pressure. A second factor that exerts important effects on the tendency to conform

cohesiveness • With respect to conformity, the degree of attraction felt by an individual toward an influencing group.

is the size of the influencing group. Asch (1956) and other early researchers (e.g., Gerard, Wilhelmy, & Conolley, 1968) found that conformity increased with group size, but only up to about three members; beyond that point, it appeared to level off or even decrease. More recent research, however, has failed to confirm these early findings (e.g., Bond & Smith, 1996). Instead, these later studies have found that conformity tends to increase with group size up to eight group members and beyond. So it appears that the larger the group, the greater our tendency to go along with it, even if this means behaving in ways different from the ones we'd really prefer.

Type of Social Norm in Operation: What We *Should* Do versus What We *Actually* Do. Social norms, we have already seen, can be formal or informal in nature—as different as rules printed on large signs and informal guidelines such as "Don't leave your shopping cart in the middle of a parking spot outside a supermarket." This is not the only way in which norms differ, however. Another important distinction is that between **descriptive norms** and **injunctive norms** (e.g., Cialdini, Kallgren, & Reno, 1991; Reno, Cialdini, & Kallgren, 1993). Descriptive norms are ones simply indicating what most people do in a given situation. They influence behavior by informing us about what is generally seen as effective or adaptive behavior in that situation. In contrast, injunctive norms specify what *ought* to be done—what is approved or disapproved behavior in a given situation. Both kinds of norms can exert strong effects upon behavior; for instance, teenagers' beliefs about the extent to which their friends drive while under the influence of alcohol are strongly related to their own tendency to engage in this risky and illegal behavior (S. L. Brown, 1998). However, Cialdini and his colleagues believe that in certain situations—especially ones in which antisocial behavior (behavior not approved of by a given group or society) is likely to occur—injunctive norms may exert somewhat stronger effects. This is true for two reasons. First, such norms tend to shift attention away from how people *are* acting in a particular situation (e.g., littering) to how they *should be* behaving (e.g., putting trash into containers). Second, such norms may activate the social motive to do what's right in a given situation regardless of what others have done.

Cialdini and his colleagues have tested this prediction in several studies, and have obtained evidence that confirms it. For example, in one of these studies (Reno, Cialdini, & Kallgren, 1993), individuals crossing a parking lot encountered an accomplice walking toward them. In one condition, this person carried a bag from a fast-food restaurant and dropped it on the ground. In another, this person was not carrying anything but actually stopped to *pick up* a fast-food bag dropped by someone else. The researchers reasoned that seeing someone drop a bag would activate a *descriptive* norm—information about what other people did in this situation. In contrast, seeing another person actually pick litter up from the ground would remind participants of society's disapproval of littering, and so would activate an *injunctive* norm against littering. Another variable in the study was whether the environment was already littered with trash or newly cleaned by the researchers. To test the effects of these norms on behavior, Reno and his colleagues (1993) observed what participants did with a handbill that had been placed on the windshield of their car. The researchers predicted that the descriptive norm would reduce people's tendency to litter when the environment was clean (because it would indicate the bag-dropper was out of line) but not when it was dirty, but that the injunctive norm would reduce littering in both conditions. As you can see from Figure 9.4 on page 362, this is exactly what happened.

These findings, and those of other studies, suggest that both descriptive and injunctive social norms do exist, and that the two types may influence our

descriptive norms • Norms that simply indicate what most people do in a given situation.

injunctive norms • Norms specifying what ought to be done—what is approved or disapproved behavior in a given situation.

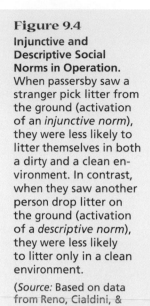

Figure 9.4

Injunctive and Descriptive Social Norms in Operation. When passersby saw a stranger pick litter from the ground (activation of an *injunctive norm*), they were less likely to litter themselves in both a dirty and a clean environment. In contrast, when they saw another person drop litter on the ground (activation of a *descriptive norm*), they were less likely to litter only in a clean environment.

(*Source:* Based on data from Reno, Cialdini, & Kallgren, 1993.)

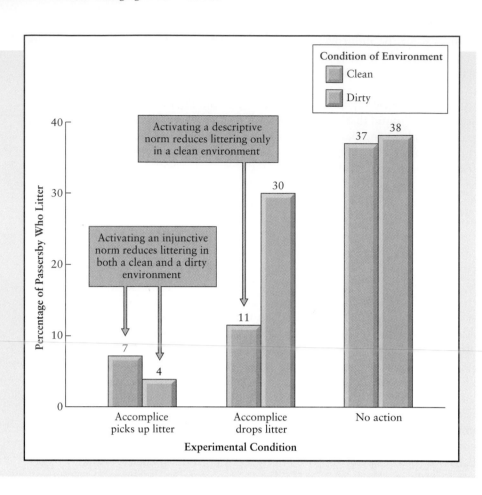

behavior through somewhat different mechanisms. A practical implication of this finding is that efforts to change people's behavior should focus on activating the type of norm most likely to succeed. In situations in which most people already behave in a prosocial manner, calling their attention to this fact—activating a descriptive norm—may further strengthen this tendency. But in situations in which many people do not behave in a prosocial manner, activating an injunctive norm, and so reminding people of how they *should* behave, may be more effective.

For information on another type of social norm and its effects on important forms of social behavior, please see the *Social Diversity* section below.

cultures of honor • Cultures in which strong social norms condone violence as a means of answering an affront to one's honor.

Social Diversity: A Critical Analysis
The Persistence of Social Norms: Some Unsettling Effects of the "Culture of Honor"

When I (Robert Baron) was a boy, I loved Westerns—films starring John Wayne, Jimmy Stewart, and other actors I viewed as heroes. One theme that emerged in these films over and over again was that of protecting or restoring one's honor. In literally dozens of films, I saw scenes in which characters felt compelled to duel another person because their honor had somehow been sullied (see Figure 9.5). The only way to restore one's honor, the films

suggested, was through violence. Since the "good guys" always won, I always left the theater feeling happy and satisfied. At the tender age of eight or nine, I didn't realize that these movies actually illustrated strong social norms condoning violence as a means of answering an affront to one's honor. Anthropologists describe cultures that strongly endorse such norms as **cultures of honor,** and social psychologists have recently noted that cultures

Figure 9.5
The Culture of Honor: How Hollywood Once Saw It. In many old Westerns, an affront to someone's honor often led to duels such as this one. Research suggests that norms requiring such behavior are still active in certain regions of the United States.

of honor appear to be alive and well in two sections of the United States: the West and the South. Why is this so? Cohen and Nisbett (1994, 1997), two social psychologists who have studied the culture of honor in detail, suggest that this may be the case because in these areas of the country, much wealth was once in cattle—an asset that could be readily stolen. Thus, it became important for individuals to demonstrate that they would not tolerate such theft—or any other affront to their honor. The result? Social norms condoning violence in response to insults to one's honor emerged and were widely accepted.

The development of such norms in frontier locations is far from surprising. More unexpected, however, is the fact that they may persist even today (Cohen & Nisbett, 1994, 1996). Nisbett and Cohen (1997) point to such facts as these: The West and South, in comparison to other sections of the United States, have looser gun controls and more laws allowing people to use violence in defense of self; in addition, murders stemming from brawls, arguments, and conflicts occur at higher rates in the West and South.

How powerful are these norms at the present time? Research findings (e.g., Cohen, 1998; Cohen & Nisbett, 1997) point to the following answer: stronger than you might guess! For instance, consider a study by Cohen & Nisbett (1997). In this research, a fictitious job applicant wrote letters to almost one thousand organizations throughout the United States, requesting an application form and other information. In half the letters, the individual indicated that he had killed a man in a fight brought on by strong insults to his honor (the victim had claimed to be having an affair with the job applicant's fiancée and had called both the fiancée and the ap-

plicant's mother "slut"). In the other letters, the individual indicated that he had performed a different crime—car theft.

Cohen and Nisbett (1997) reasoned that if the "culture of honor" was still operating in the West and South, the job applicant would receive greater compliance with his requests for information and friendlier letters from these sections of the country than from other sections. In fact, this is what happened. As you can see from Figure 9.6 on page 364, there were no differences in compliance or tone of response between the North and the South and West in responses to the letter that mentioned car theft. However, significant differences *did* emerge in responses to the letter that mentioned the crime of honor: in both compliance and friendliness, responses from companies in the South and West were more favorable.

These findings, and those of additional research (e.g., Cohen, 1998; Ellison, 1991), illustrate the power of social norms and their tendency to persist even in the face of sharply changing social conditions. The South and West of the United States stopped being frontier regions many years ago; yet it appears that visible traces of the norms that developed in those regions to cope with frontier conditions still exist today, when traffic jams on the interstate are far more likely to influence most people's lives than theft of their cattle! Apparently, social norms can be and often are passed down from generation to generation, in the same manner as attitudes and various forms of prejudice (see Chapters 4 and 6). So, although the Western heroes I watched as a boy have all ridden off into the sunset, they definitely did *not* take the code of honor they represented with them. On the contrary, it seems to be very much with us even today.

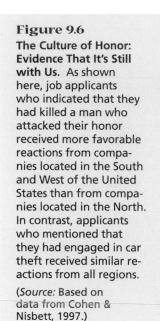

Figure 9.6

The Culture of Honor: Evidence That It's Still with Us. As shown here, job applicants who indicated that they had killed a man who attacked their honor received more favorable reactions from companies located in the South and West of the United States than from companies located in the North. In contrast, applicants who mentioned that they had engaged in car theft received similar reactions from all regions.

(*Source:* Based on data from Cohen & Nisbett, 1997.)

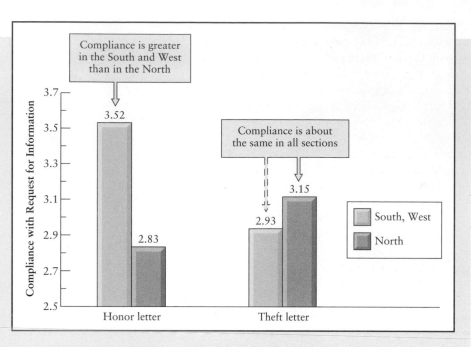

The Bases of Conformity: Why We Often Choose to "Go Along"

As we have just seen, factors such as group cohesiveness and different types of social norms often determine whether and to what extent conformity occurs. Yet this does not alter the essential point: Conformity is a basic fact of social life. Most people conform to the norms of their groups or societies much, if not most, of the time. Why is this so? Why do people often choose to go along with these social rules or expectations instead of resisting them? The answer seems to involve two powerful motives possessed by all human beings—the desire to be liked or accepted by others and the desire to be right, to have accurate understanding of the social world (Deutsch & Gerard, 1955; Insko, 1985)—plus cognitive processes that lead us to view conformity as fully justified after it has occurred (e.g., Buehler & Griffin, 1994).

The Desire To Be Liked: Normative Social Influence.   How can we get others to like us? This is one of the eternal puzzles of social life. As we saw in Chapter 7, many tactics can prove effective in this regard. One of the most successful of these is to appear to be as similar to others as possible. From our earliest days, we learn that agreeing with the persons around us, and behaving as they do, causes them to like us. Parents, teachers, friends, and others often heap praise and approval on us for showing such similarity (see our discussion of attitude formation in Chapter 4). One important reason we conform, therefore, is this: We have learned that doing so can help us win the approval and acceptance we crave. This source of conformity is known as **normative social influence,** because it leads us to alter our behavior to meet others' expectations.

Such influence can be powerful indeed; for instance, if individuals learn that others they admire or with whom they identify hold views different from their own, they don't simply change what they say in order to "fit in." In addition, they often *reinterpret* the views expressed by these other persons so that they can find these views more acceptable (e.g., Pool, Wood, & Leck, 1998). In other words, they do considerable cognitive work in order to be able to accept these views privately as well as to endorse them publicly.

normative social influence
• Social influence based on individuals' desire to be liked or accepted by other persons.

The Desire To Be Right: Informational Social Influence. If you want to know your weight, you can step onto a scale. If you want to know the dimensions of a room, you can measure them directly. But how can you establish the accuracy of your political or social views or decide what hairstyle suits you best? There are no simple physical tests or measuring devices for answering these questions. Yet we want to be correct about these matters, too. The solution to this dilemma is obvious: to answer such questions, we refer to other people. We use *their* opinions and actions as guides for our own. Our reliance on others, in turn, is often a powerful source of the tendency to conform. Other people's actions and opinions define social reality for us, and we use these as a guide for our own actions and opinions. This basis for conformity is known as **informational social influence,** because it draws its power from our tendency to depend on others as a source of information about many aspects of the social world.

Recent evidence suggests that because our motivation to be correct or accurate is very strong, informational social influence is a very powerful source of conformity. However, as you might expect, this is more likely to be true in situations in which we care about the outcome yet are highly uncertain about what is "correct" or "accurate" than in situations in which we have more confidence in our own ability to make the right decision. That this is so is clearly illustrated by the results of a study conducted by Robert S. Baron, Vandello, and Brunsman (1996). (Robert S. Baron is *not* the Robert Baron who is a coauthor of this text.) In this investigation the researchers used an ingenious modification of the Asch line-judging task. They showed participants a drawing of a person and then asked them to identify this person from among several other drawings in a kind of simulated eyewitness lineup. In one condition, the drawing was shown for only 0.5 seconds; this made the identification task quite difficult to perform. In another condition, it was shown for 5.0 seconds, and the task was much easier. Another key aspect of the study involved the importance of making an accurate decision. Half the participants were told that the study was only preliminary in nature, so results were not very important. The others were told that the results were very important to the researchers.

To measure conformity, the researchers exposed participants to the judgments of two assistants, who identified the *wrong* person before the participants made their own choice in the simulated lineup. The overall prediction was that when the study was described as being very important, participants would be more likely to conform when the task was difficult (when they saw the drawing for only 0.5 seconds) than when the task was easy (they saw the drawing for 5.0 seconds). This would be so because under these conditions, participants would be uncertain of their own decisions and would rely on the judgments of the assistants. When the study was described as being relatively unimportant, however, task difficulty wouldn't matter: conformity would be the same in both conditions. As you can see from Figure 9.7 on page 366, results offered clear support for these predictions. These findings suggest that our desire to be correct or accurate can be a strong source of conformity, but primarily when we feel that accuracy is important yet are uncertain about what is correct.

Justifying Conformity: The Cognitive Consequences of Going Along with the Group. Asch (1951, 1955) reported that some people who conform do so without any reservations: they conclude that they are wrong and the others are right. For these people, conforming poses only a very temporary dilemma at most. But for many other persons, the decision to yield to group pressure and do as others do is more complex. Such persons feel that their own judgment is correct, but at the same time they don't want to be different; so they behave in ways that are inconsistent with their private beliefs. What are the effects of conformity on such persons? Research findings (e.g., Buehler & Griffin, 1994; Griffin

informational social influence • Social influence based on individuals' desire to be correct—to possess accurate perceptions of the social world.

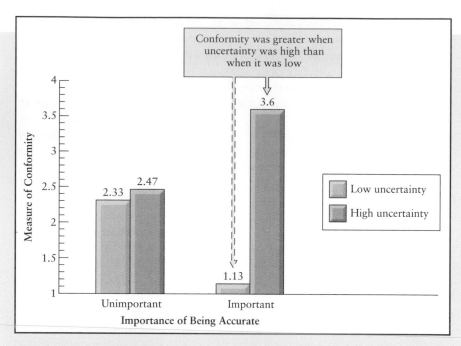

Figure 9.7

Evidence for the Operation of Informational Social Influence. When the motivation to be accurate was high (the task was described as important), research participants showed a greater tendency to conform to the judgments of others when they were uncertain about the correct answer (the task was difficult) than when they had greater confidence in their own judgments (the task was easy). When motivation to be accurate was low (the task was described as unimportant), no such differences occurred. These findings suggest that our susceptibility to informational social influence varies with several factors.

(*Source:* Based on data from R. S. Baron, Vandello, & Brunsman, 1996.)

& Buehler, 1993) suggest that one effect may involve a tendency for people to alter their perceptions of the situation so that conformity appears, in fact, to be justified. As John Kenneth Galbraith stated, "Faced with the choice between changing one's mind and proving that there is no need to do so, almost everyone gets busy on the proof!" (cited in Buehler & Griffin, 1994, p. 993).

Given these results, an interesting question arises: Will this same pattern occur in all cultures? In cultures that value individuals' individual choice backed by rational analysis of available information (e.g., the United States and many Western countries), such effects would be expected to occur: people feel a strong need to explain why they conformed. In cultures that place greater value on group judgments and on avoiding disagreements with others, however, the pressures toward such cognitive self-justification may be weaker (Bond & Smith, 1996). As noted by Buehler and Griffin (1994), this is an intriguing issue well deserving of further study.

Key Points

- Many factors determine whether, and to what extent, conformity occurs. These include *cohesiveness,* or the degree of attraction felt by an individual toward some group; group size; and type of social norms operating in that situation—*descriptive* or *injunctive social norms.*

- Because of frontier conditions and other factors, norms condoning violence in response to affronts to one's honor developed in the South and West of the United States. Recent evidence suggests that such norms are still present and continue to influence behavior in these regions.

- Two important motives seem to underlie our tendency to conform: the desire to be liked by people whom we like or respect and the desire to be right or accurate. These two motives are reflected in two distinct types of social influence, *normative* and *informational social influence*.

- Once we show conformity in a given situation, we tend to view our conforming as justified, even if it has required us to behave in ways contrary to our true beliefs.

The Need for Individuality and the Need for Personal Control: Why, Sometimes, We Choose *Not* to Go Along

Having read our discussion of normative and informational social influence, you may now have the distinct impression that pressures toward conformity are so strong that they are all but impossible to resist. If so, take heart. In many cases, individuals—or groups of individuals—*do* resist. This was certainly true in Asch's research: as you may recall, most of the participants yielded to social pressure, *but only part of the time*. On many occasions they stuck to their guns, even in the face of a unanimous majority that disagreed with them. What accounts for this ability to resist even powerful pressures toward conformity? Many factors appear to play a role (e.g., Burger, 1992), but two seem to be most important: the need to maintain our individuality, and the need to maintain control over our own lives.

The need to maintain our individuality, in particular, appears to be a powerful one. Yes, we want to be like others—but not, it seems, to the extent that we lose our personal identity. In other words, along with the needs to be right and to be liked, most of us possess a desire for **individuation**—for being distinguishable from others in some respects (e.g., Maslach, Santee, & Wade, 1987). In general, we want to be like others, especially others we like or respect; but we don't want to be *exactly* like these persons, because that would involve giving up our individuality (e.g., Snyder & Fromkin, 1979).

If this is so, then an interesting prediction relating to cultural diversity follows: The tendency to conform will be lower in cultures that emphasize individuality (individualistic cultures) than in ones that emphasize being part of the group (collectivistic cultures). A large-scale study by Bond and Smith (1996) examined this hypothesis by comparing conformity in seventeen different countries. They examined the results of 133 past studies that used the Asch line-judging task to measure conformity. Among these studies, they identified ones conducted in countries with collectivistic cultures (e.g., countries in Africa and Asia) and in ones with individualistic cultures (e.g., in North America and western Europe). Then they compared the amount of conformity shown in these two groups of countries. Results were clear: More conformity did indeed occur in the countries with collectivistic cultures, where the motive to maintain one's individuality was expected to be lower; and this was true regardless of the size of the influencing group (see Figure 9.8 on page 368). Similar results were obtained in other studies (e.g., Hamilton & Sanders, 1995). So it does appear that the need for individuation varies greatly across different cultures—and that these differences, in turn, influence the tendency to conform.

Another reason why individuals often choose to resist group pressure involves their desire to maintain control over the events in their lives (e.g., Burger, 1992; Daubman, 1993). Most persons want to believe that they can determine

individuation • The need to be distinguishable from others in some respects.

Figure 9.8
Culture and Conformity.
A recent review of existing evidence suggests that conformity is higher in collectivistic cultures (ones that emphasize being part of the group) than in individualistic cultures (ones that emphasize individuality). This appears to be true regardless of whether the influencing groups are small or large.

(*Source:* Based on data from Bond & Smith, 1996.)

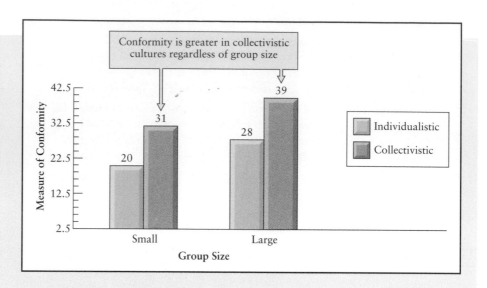

what happens to them, and yielding to social pressure sometimes runs counter to this desire. After all, going along with a group implies behaving in ways one might not ordinarily choose; and this, in turn, can be viewed as a restriction of personal freedom and control. The results of many studies suggest that the stronger an individual's need for personal control, the less likely he or she is to yield to social pressure; so this factor, too, appears to be an important one where resisting conformity is concerned.

In sum, two motives—the desire to retain our individuality and the desire to keep control over our own lives—serve to counter the motives that tend to increase conformity—our desires to be liked and to be accurate. Whether we conform in a given situation, then, depends on the relative strength of these various motives and the interplay between them. Once again, therefore, we come face to face with the fact that trying to understand the roots of social behavior is often as complex as it is fascinating. For more information on what happens when pressures for conformity clash with desires for individuality and personal freedom, please see the following *Beyond the Headlines* section.

Beyond the Headlines:
As Social Psychologists See It
Dress Codes versus Personal Freedom: When Norms Collide

AT ST. PETER'S YOU MAY BARE
YOUR SOUL, BUT NOT MUCH SKIN

Associated Press, October 9, 1997—Vatican City, Italy—When his knee-length shorts didn't past muster, Berend Ike, a 17-year-old from the Netherlands, thought he had solved the problem. He borrowed a green cloth from a friend and tied it around his waist. Now covered to the ankles, he approached the door, hoping for mercy. But mercy, here at the entrance of St. Peter's Basilica, isn't the object. Mr. Ike was stopped by an elegantly dressed guard who held up a hand and stopped him in his tracks. While he had obeyed the letter of the law, the guard explained, he was not obeying its spirit, and so could not enter. . . .

Figure 9.9
When Norms Collide.
Tourists, seeing other persons dressed in any style they wish, accept the *descriptive norm* that "anything goes" where dress is concerned. But some famous landmarks (e.g., the Vatican) seek to impose clear dress codes—strong *injunctive norms*. When these two types of norms clash, the results can be embarrassing—or worse—for the people involved.

In many places around the world, strict dress codes have disappeared, or at least been modified. But at the Vatican they are very much alive. In this holy place the code is simple: Men must wear long pants and shirts that cover their shoulders; women must cover shoulders, midriffs, and cleavage, and wear skirts no higher than four fingers above the knee. Yet, simple as these rules seem to be, thousands of tourists visiting the Vatican try to ignore them every year. The result: They are turned away at the door by the guards, known as "God's Bouncers," who are specially chosen to be large, strong, and imposing. Over the years these guards have rejected women in see-through blouses, men and women in short shorts, teenagers in baseball caps, and people in a host of other outfits judged to be too revealing or racy (see Figure 9.9).

Why does this situation occur over and over again? Social psychologists would put it this way: There is a clash over norms. The tourists are following a *descriptive norm,* which tells them that almost any style of dress is appropriate for tourists; after all, they see other tourists dressed in a wide range of outfits. In contrast, the Vatican is following the dictates of strong *injunctive norms*—rules indicating what is and is not an appropriate style of dress. This clash of norms leads to the kind of scenes at the doorway described in the news item above.

But this is not the only clash between norms that occurs in this setting. In the past, the Vatican guards could deter tourists with a simple shake of the head or an up-raised palm. In recent years, however, tourists have begun refusing to take such gentle *no's* seriously and have resorted to violence. In one recent summer, for instance, a guard was kicked and punched by a male tourist in shorts who was refused entry, and other guards have been slapped and cursed by men and women turned back at the door. It appears that for many persons, norms requiring politeness in such situations have now been replaced by ones indicating that force is appropriate.

In short, when norms collide—when different groups of people hold contrasting ideas about what kind of behavior is appropriate in a given situation—the results can be unsettling. And if neither side is willing to budge—to change or adjust its ideas about what is and is not permitted—watch out. Sparks are almost certain to fly.

Minority Influence: Does the Majority Always Rule?

As we have noted, individuals can, and often do, resist group pressure. Lone dissenters or small minorities can dig in their heels and refuse to go along. Yet there is more to the story than this; in addition, there are instances in which such persons—*minorities* within their groups—can turn the tables on the majority and exert rather than merely receive social influence. History provides many examples of such events. Giants of science, such as Galileo, Pasteur, and Freud, faced virtually unanimous majorities that initially rejected their views. Yet, over time, these famous persons overcame this resistance, and won widespread acceptance for their theories. More recent examples of minorities' influencing majorities are provided by the successes of environmentalists. Initially such persons were viewed as wild-eyed radicals with strange ideas. Over time, however, they succeeded in changing the attitudes of the majority. Today, many of their views are widely accepted: strong legislation has been enacted to reduce air and water pollution, nearly everyone recycles their trash, and so on.

But when, precisely, do minorities succeed in influencing majorities? Research findings suggest that they are most likely to succeed under certain conditions (Moscovici, 1985). First, the members of such groups must be *consistent* in their opposition to majority opinions. If they waver or seem to be divided, their impact is reduced. Second, members of the minority must avoid appearing to be rigid and dogmatic (Mugny, 1975). A minority that merely repeats the same position over and over again is less persuasive than one that demonstrates a degree of flexibility. Third, the general social context in which a minority operates is important. If a minority argues for a position that is consistent with current social trends (e.g., a conservative view at a time of growing conservatism), its chances of influencing the majority are greater than if it argues for a position out of step with wider trends.

Of course, even when these conditions are met, minorities face a tough uphill fight. The power of majorities is great, especially in ambiguous or complex social situations; in such situations majorities are viewed as more reliable sources of information about what is true than are minorities. In other words, majorities function as an important source of both informational and normative social influence (Wood et al., 1996). Why then, are minorities sometimes able to get their message across?

One possibility is that when people are confronted with a minority stating views that they don't initially accept, they are puzzled and exert cognitive effort to understand why these people hold their views and why they are willing to take a strong stand against the majority (Nemeth, 1995; Vonk & van Knippenberg, 1995). In other words, vocal and deeply committed minorities can induce members of the majority to engage in *systematic processing* with respect to the messages and information they provide (e.g., Smith, Tindale, & Dugoni, 1996; Wood et al., 1996). Another, and related, possibility is that when people believe they are part of a minority, they themselves engage in more careful (systematic) thought about their views. As a result, they generate stronger arguments; and this contributes to their success in influencing the majority.

Evidence for precisely these kinds of effects is provided by an experiment conducted by Zdaniuk and Levine (1996). These researchers led participants in their study to believe that they were members of either a majority or a minority faction in a group that had the task of discussing and reaching a consensus on a controversial issue: whether their university should require graduating seniors to pass a comprehensive examination in their major field. After participants gave their initial opinions about this proposal (most were strongly opposed), Zdaniuk and Levine (1996) gave each participant information about the views of the five other persons with whom they would discuss this issue. Some individuals were told that four of the five agreed with their view; in other words, they were led to believe that they were part of a strong majority. Other participants were told that three of the five, two of the five, or only one of the five agreed with them. In this last case, then, they found themselves part of a minority. The researchers then asked participants to rate how much pressure they believed they would face in the group discussion and how likely they thought it was that the proposal would be adopted. Finally, the participants were also asked to write down their initial thoughts about the comprehensive examination proposal. This provided information on the extent to which they engaged in systematic processing about the issue.

Zdaniuk and Levine (1996) predicted that when participants in the study believed they were part of a minority, they would anticipate strong group pressure against them; as a result, they would think more systematically about the issue (and generate more thoughts). As you can see from Figure 9.10, this is precisely what happened. Participants who were led to believe that they were part of a minority perceived that they would face greater social pressure and generated more initial thoughts about the examination issue than participants who thought they were part of a majority.

If minorities do the cognitive work necessary to generate strong and persuasive arguments for their views, it seems possible that during actual group debates (which didn't take place in the 1996 study by Zdaniuk and Levine, but which do occur frequently in everyday life) minorities may lead members of the majority to consider ideas they would otherwise have ignored. For instance, would large numbers of people have paid any attention to the hole in the ozone layer or the

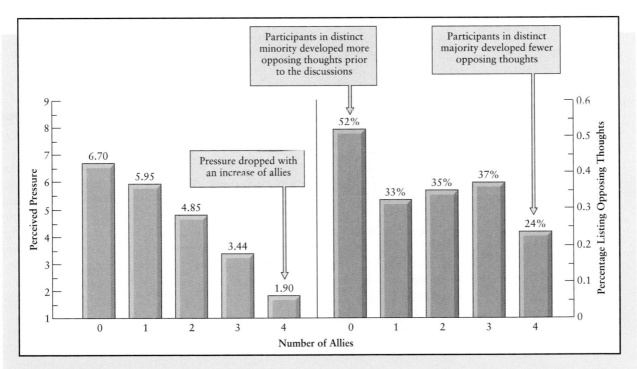

Figure 9.10

Systematic Thought: One Reason Why Minorities Sometimes Prevail. When research participants were told that they were part of a minority, they anticipated stronger social pressure to change their views (left-hand graph). In addition, they generated more thoughts about their position and so, presumably, were better prepared to defend it (right-hand graph). These findings suggest that minorities often engage in more systematic thought about their views than the majority, and this may give them an important edge when they confront the majority.

(*Source:* Based on data from Zdaniuk & Levine, 1996).

possibility of the greenhouse effect during the 1980s and 1990s if vocal minorities had not called these problems vigorously to their attention? It seems unlikely. In sum, even if minorities fail to sway majorities initially, they may initiate processes, such as more careful consideration of opposing ideas, that lead to eventual social change (e.g, Alvaro & Crano, 1996). In this sense, as well as in several others, there is much truth to Franklin D. Roosevelt's remark that "No democracy can long survive which does not accept as fundamental to its very existence the recognition of the rights of minorities" (June 5, 1938).

Key Points

- Although pressures toward conformity are strong, many persons resist them, at least part of the time. This resistance seems to stem from two strong motives: the desire to retain one's individuality, and the desire to exert control over one's own life.

- When groups holding contrasting norms interact, the result can be annoyance, misunderstandings, and even open conflict. This is precisely what seems to happen at the Vatican when tourists are turned away at the door for violating the strictly enforced dress code.

- Under some conditions, minorities can induce even large majorities to change their attitudes or behavior. Evidence suggests that this may occur, in part, because minorities induce majorities to think more systematically about the issues they raise, and also because minorities themselves engage in such systematic processing; as a result, they formulate strong and persuasive arguments for their views.

COMPLIANCE: TO ASK—SOMETIMES—IS TO RECEIVE

Suppose that you wanted someone to do something for you, how would you go about getting them to do it? If you think about this question for a moment, you'll quickly realize that you have quite a few tricks up your sleeve for gaining *compliance*—for getting others to say yes to your requests. What are these techniques like? Which ones work best? These are among the questions studied by social psychologists in their efforts to understand this, the most frequent form of social influence. In the discussion that follows, we'll examine many tactics for gaining compliance. Before turning to these however, we'll introduce a basic framework for understanding the nature of all of these procedures and why they often work.

Compliance: The Underlying Principles

Some years ago, the well-known social psychologist Robert Cialdini decided that the best way to find out about compliance was to study what he termed *compliance professionals*—people whose success (financial or otherwise) depends on their ability to get others to say yes. Who are such persons? They include salespeople, advertisers, political lobbyists, fund-raisers, politicians, con artists, professional negotiators, and many others. Cialdini's technique for learning from these people was simple: he temporarily concealed his true identity and took jobs in various settings where gaining compliance is a way of life. In other words, he worked in advertising, direct (door-to-door) sales, fund-raising, and other compliance-focused fields. On the basis of these firsthand experiences, he concluded that although techniques for gaining take many different forms, they all rest to some degree on six basic principles (Cialdini, 1994):

- *Friendship/liking:* In general, we are more willing to comply with requests from friends or from people we like than with requests from strangers or people we don't like.
- *Commitment/consistency:* Once we have committed ourselves to a position or action, we are more willing to comply with requests for behaviors that are consistent with this position or action than to accede to requests that are inconsistent with it.
- *Scarcity:* In general, we value, and try to secure, outcomes or objects that are scarce or decreasing in their availability. As a result, we are more likely to comply with requests that focus on scarcity than with ones that make no reference to this issue.
- *Reciprocity:* We are generally more willing to comply with a request from someone who has previously provided a favor or concession to us than to oblige someone who has not. In other words, we feel impelled to pay people back in some way for what they have done for us.
- *Social validation:* We are generally more willing to comply with a request for some action if this action is consistent with what we believe persons similar to ourselves are doing (or thinking). We want to be correct, and one way to do so is to act and think like others.
- *Authority:* In general, we are more willing to comply with requests from someone who holds legitimate authority—or who simply appears to do so.

According to Cialdini (1994), these six basic principles underlie many techniques that professionals—and we ourselves—use for gaining compliance from others. We'll now examine specific techniques based on these principles, plus a few others as well.

Tactics Based on Friendship or Liking: Ingratiation

We've already considered several techniques for increasing compliance through liking in our discussion of *impression management* (Chapter 2). As you may recall, impression management involves various procedures for making a good impression on others. While this can be an end in itself, impression management techniques are often used for purposes of **ingratiation**—for getting others to like us so that they will be more willing to agree to our requests (Jones, 1964; Liden & Mitchell, 1988).

What ingratiation techniques work best? A review of existing studies on this topic (Gordon, 1996) suggests that *flattery*—praising others in some manner, is one of the best. Complimenting others on their appearance, accomplishments, intelligence, or other attributes can be a powerful means for winning their goodwill—and their compliance with our wishes (e.g., DeBono & Krim, 1997). Other techniques that seem to work are improving one's own appearance, emitting many positive nonverbal cues, and doing small favors for the target persons (Gordon, 1996; Wayne & Liden, 1995). We described many of these tactics in detail in Chapter 2, so we won't repeat that information here. Suffice it to say that many of the tactics used for purposes of impression management are also successful from the point of view of increasing compliance.

Tactics Based on Commitment or Consistency: The Foot in the Door and the Lowball

Every time my wife and I (Robert Baron) visit the food court of our local shopping mall, we are approached by one or more persons who offer us free samples

ingratiation • A technique for gaining compliance in which requesters first induce target persons to like them, then attempt to change their behavior in some desired manner.

of various foods. The reason behind these actions is obvious: The persons offering the free samples hope that once we have accepted these gifts, we'll like the taste of the food and will be more willing to buy our lunch at their business. This is the basic idea behind an approach for gaining compliance known as the **foot-in-the-door technique.** In operation, this tactic involves inducing target persons to agree to a small initial request ("Accept this free sample") and then hitting them with a larger request—the one desired all along. The results of many studies indicate that this tactic works: it succeeds in inducing increased compliance (e.g., Beaman et al., 1983; Freedman & Fraser, 1966). Why is this the case? Because the foot-in-the-door technique rests on the principle of *consistency:* once we have said yes to the small request, we are more likely to say yes to subsequent and larger ones, too, because refusing these would be inconsistent with our previous behavior. For example, imagine that you wanted to borrow lecture notes for several weeks' classes from one of your friends. You might begin by asking for the notes from one lecture. After copying these, you might come back with a larger request: the notes for all the other classes. If your friend complied, it might well be because refusing would be inconsistent with his or her initial yes (e.g., DeJong & Musilli, 1982).

The foot-in-the-door technique is not the only tactic based on the consistency/commitment principle, however. Another is the **lowball procedure.** In this technique, which is often used by automobile salespersons, a very good deal is offered to a customer. After the customer accepts, however, something happens that makes it necessary for the salesperson to change the deal and make it less advantageous for the customer—for example, the sales manager rejects the deal. The totally rational reaction for customers, of course, would be to walk away. Yet often, they agree to the changes and accept the less desirable arrangement.

These informal observations have been confirmed by careful research. In one investigation of the lowball procedure, for example, students first agreed to participate in a psychology experiment. Only after making this commitment did they learn that it started at 7:00 a.m. (Cialdini et al., 1978). Despite the inconvenience of this early hour, however, almost all students in this lowball condition appeared for their appointments. In contrast, a much smaller proportion of students who learned about the 7:00 a.m. starting time *before* deciding whether to participate agreed to take part in the study. In instances such as this, an initial commitment seems to make it more difficult for individuals to say no, even though the conditions under which they said yes are now changed.

Tactics Based on Reciprocity: The Door-in-the-Face and the "That's-Not-All" Approach

Reciprocity is a basic rule of social life: we usually do unto others as they have done unto us. If they have done a favor for us, therefore, we feel that we should be willing to do one for them in return. While this convention is viewed by most persons as being fair and just, the principle of reciprocity also serves as the basis for several techniques for gaining compliance. One of these is, on the face of it, the opposite of the foot-in-the-door technique. Instead of beginning with a small request and then escalating to a larger one, persons seeking compliance sometimes start with a very large request and then, after this is rejected, shift to a smaller request—the one they wanted all along. This tactic is known as the **door-in-the-face technique** (because the first refusal seems to slam the door in the face of the requester), and several studies indicate that it can be quite effective. For example, in one well-known experiment, Cialdini and his colleagues

foot-in-the-door technique • A procedure for gaining compliance in which requesters begin with a small request and then, when this is granted, escalate to a larger one (the one they actually desired all along).

lowball procedure • A technique for gaining compliance in which an offer or deal is changed (made less attractive) after the target person has accepted it.

door-in-the-face technique • A procedure for gaining compliance in which requesters begin with a large request and then, when this is refused, retreat to a smaller one (the one they actually desired all along).

"How much would you pay for all the secrets of the universe? Wait, don't answer yet. You also get this six-quart covered combination spaghetti pot and clam steamer. <u>Now</u> how much would you pay?"

Figure 9.11
The "That's-Not-All"
Technique. Would you
be influenced by this type
of commercial? Research
evidence indicates that
throwing in some small
extra before people make
up their minds about a
request or a product can
often tip the balance in
favor of a yes.

(*Source: The New Yorker.*)

(1975) stopped college students on the street and presented a huge request: Would the students serve as unpaid counselors for juvenile delinquents two hours a week for the next *two years?* As you can guess, none agreed. When the experimenters then scaled down their request to a much smaller one—would the same students take a group of delinquents on a two-hour trip to the zoo—fully 50 percent agreed. In contrast, fewer than 17 percent of those in a control group agreed to this smaller request when it was presented cold rather than after the larger request.

The same tactic is often used by negotiators, who may begin with a position that is extremely advantageous to themselves but then retreat to a position much closer to the one they really hope to obtain. Similarly, sellers often begin with a price they know buyers will reject, then lower the price to a more reasonable one—but one that is still quite favorable to themselves, and close to what they wanted all along.

A related procedure for gaining compliance is known as the **"that's-not-all" technique.** Here, an initial request is followed, *before the target person can say yes or no,* by something that sweetens the deal—a small extra incentive from the persons using this tactic (e.g., a reduction in price, "throwing in" something additional for the same price). For example, as suggested by Figure 9.11, television commercials for various products frequently offer something extra to induce viewers to pick up the phone and place an order. Several studies confirm informal observations suggesting that the *"that's-not-all"* technique really works (Burger, 1986). In addition, these studies suggest that the tactic succeeds because it is based on the principle of reciprocity: persons on the receiving end of this technique view the "extra" thrown in by the other side as an added concession, and so feel obligated to make a concession themselves. The result: The probability that they will say yes is increased.

Another possibility is that creating the appearance of a bargain by reducing the price of an item or offering to add something extra causes individuals

"that's-not-all" technique •
A technique for gaining compliance in which a requester offers target persons additional benefits before they have decided whether to comply with or reject specific requests.

Other Tactics for Gaining Compliance: Complaining and Putting Others in a Good Mood

While many techniques for inducing compliance seem to rest on the basic principles described by Cialdini (1994), others appear to involve other mechanisms. One of the most interesting of these involves an action in which most of us engage every day: **complaining**. Complaining involves expressions of discontent or dissatisfaction with oneself or some aspect of the external world. In many cases, such statements are simple expressions of personal states ("I feel lousy today!") or comments on the external world ("Wow, is it hot!"). Sometimes, however, complaining is used as a tactic of social influence: "Why do we always see the movie you want?" "I wish you wouldn't snore at night!" or the classic "You don't love me anymore!" Comments such as these are directed toward the goal of getting the recipient to change his or her attitudes or behavior in some manner, and research conducted by Alicke and his colleagues (1992) indicates that complaints are often successful in this respect.

These researchers asked college students to keep diaries in which they recorded their daily complaints over a three-day period. Each time they complained, participants indicated when and where they made the complaint, the reason for it, and the response of the other person or persons involved. Results indicated that most complaints fell into several distinct categories. These included (1) global statements expressing attitudes or feelings about a person, object, or event ("This course is one of the worst I've ever taken"); (2) specific complaints about others' behavior ("You forgot to take out the garbage again"); (3) complaints about one's physical state ("I've got a pounding headache"); and (4) complaints about obligations ("I wish I didn't have to do a term paper for this course").

The reasons for complaining, too, varied widely, with the desire to vent or express frustration being by far the most common (50.0 percent). However, participants indicated that they also complained to get advice (9.6 percent), sympathy (6.1 percent), or information (3.8 percent). Most important to the present discussion, some complaints (7.5 percent) involved direct efforts to change others' attitudes or behaviors, and such efforts often worked: the targets of complaints agreed with the complainer or tried to resolve the complaints more than 25 percent of the time. So complaining to others did seem to be least a moderately effective technique for gaining compliance in some situations. An additional finding relating to gender is worthy of note (Klotz & Alicke, 1993). Overall, females reacted more supportively to others' complaints than did males. Females often responded to complaints with suggestions for dealing with the problem or with expressions of sympathy, whereas males were more likely to change the subject, say nothing, or to be overtly *nonsupportive* ("Who cares—that's your problem"). So if you feel like complaining, it appears, don't expect much help from your male friends.

Another tactic for gaining compliance is one with which we're sure you are already familiar: putting others in a good mood before making your request. Flattery and other tactics of ingratiation, as we noted earlier, are often used for this purpose and can be quite successful if not overdone (Gordon, 1996). But many other techniques can—and apparently do—accomplish the same end (e.g., Rind, 1996).

Consider, for example, an ingenious study by Rind and Bordia (1996). These researchers asked waitpersons of both genders either to draw a smiling face on the back of the checks they gave to customers or to leave this artwork off the checks. On the basis of previous studies, the researchers predicted that customers would interpret the smiling face as a sign of friendliness on the part

complaining • Expressing discontent, dissatisfaction, resentment, or regret; may be used as a means of exerting social influence on others.

of female waitpersons and that this, in turn, would put customers in a slightly better mood. As a result, they would leave larger tips than would customers who did not see the smiling face. However, such effects would not occur for male waitpersons, because drawing the smiling face would be seen as less gender appropriate for them. Results confirmed these predictions: The female waitpersons' tips rose almost 19% when they drew the smiling face, but similar effects were *not* observed for male waitpersons. These results, and those of many other studies conducted both in the lab and in the field (e.g., Baron, 1997; Rind, 1996), suggest that almost *anything* that puts people in a better mood (i.e., that induces positive affect) can increase their tendency to say yes to various requests.

But why, precisely, does being in a good mood increase our tendency to comply? One interesting possibility is suggested by the affect infusion model (AIM) that we discussed in Chapter 3. As you may recall, this model is designed to explain the effects of our current moods (affective states) on our judgments and decisions. This model suggests that our current moods can influence our thought in several ways, and one of these involves the *priming* of associations and memories related to our current mood. When we are in a good mood, our thoughts may run along pleasant lines—we bring happy memories to mind, think about positive future outcomes, interpret the current situation or events in a favorable manner, and so on. When we are in a bad mood, the opposite occurs. According to this model, then, putting people into a good mood may increase their willingness to say yes to a request by causing them to think about the request and its potential effects in positive ways: "That's a reasonable thing to ask" or "If I agree, good things will follow." These are the kind of thoughts people in a good mood may have, and such thoughts may increase their tendency to comply.

But when, precisely, will such effects occur? As we noted in Chapter 3, the AIM suggests that such effects are most likely to occur when we engage in careful, systematic thought. Thus, by extension, being in a good mood should also increase our tendency to say yes to requests when something about these requests induces us to think carefully (systematically) about them. To test this interesting prediction, Forgas (1998a) conducted a field study in which students visiting a university library were first exposed to materials designed to influence their current mood; they found a sheet of paper on the desk containing either humorous materials, a sad description of a death from cancer, or neutral information about the library. These materials were designed to induce a happy, neutral, or sad mood. A few minutes later an assistant approached each student and made either a polite request ("Excuse me, I need some paper to finish an assignment; could I please get a sheet if you have any to spare?"), an impolite request ("Give me a sheet of paper"), or an intermediate request ("Sorry, would you have a sheet of paper?").

Forgas (1998a) reasoned that the impolite request, because it was so unexpected, would trigger more careful thought about it than the polite request; the intermediate request would fall somewhere in between. If this was the case, he further predicted, then participants' mood (happy, sad, neutral) would exert a larger impact on their responses to the impolite request than on their responses to the polite one. As shown in Figure 9.13 on page 380, results confirmed these predictions. Participants' current mood exerted strong effects on their willingness to comply with the impolite request but somewhat weaker effects on their willingness to comply with the polite one. As predicted, the intermediate request fell in between. (Because only students who had paper with them could comply, compliance was measured in terms of their ratings of how much they complied—from "as little as possible" to "as much as possible.") One additional

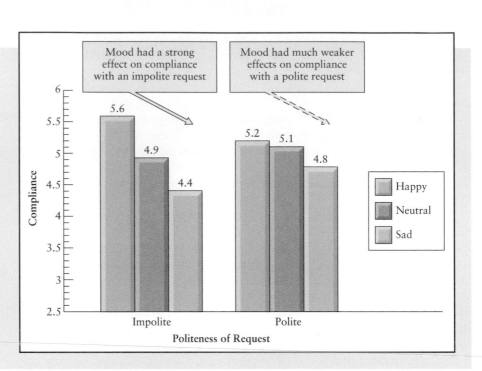

Figure 9.13

Mood and Compliance. As shown here, individuals' current moods exerted strong effects on their willingness to comply with an impolite request; the impoliteness, because it was unusual, caused them to engage in systematic processing. Participants' moods exerted weaker effects on their willingness to comply with a polite request, which elicited such systematic processing to a smaller extent.

(*Source:* Based on data from Forgas, 1998a).

feature of the study obtained evidence on the suggestion that impolite requests induce deeper, more systematic thought. Participants were also asked to recall the exact request. It was expected that those exposed to the impolite request would do better at this task, and this was in fact what happened. Greater recall of the impolite request suggests that individuals did think more carefully about it than about the polite or intermediate request.

In sum, the findings reported by Forgas (1994a) and other researchers (e.g., Baron, 1997; Sedikides, 1995) help explain why putting others in a good mood is often a useful first step to attaining their compliance. Apparently, when we are in a good mood, we tend to interpret events—including requests—in a more favorable light; and this, along with other factors, can increase our tendency to say yes.

For an overview of various tactics for gaining compliance, please see the *Ideas to Take with You* feature on page 388.)

Individual Differences in the Use of Social Influence: Do Different Persons Prefer Different Tactics?

Group pressure, the foot in the door, the door in the face, playing hard to get, flattery—the list of tactics people use to influence one another seems almost endless. We're sure you have encountered most, if not all, of these approaches in your own life, and we're also certain you have used some of them yourself. But which do *you* prefer? A direct approach in which you try to persuade other people to accept your views or do what you want through rational arguments and information? More subtle tactics such as putting people in a good mood before asking for a favor? Or do you prefer what have been described as *pressure tactics*—making demands instead of requests, blowing up in anger to frighten others into compliance, and so on (e.g., Yukl & Tracey, 1992)? Part of the answer to this question, it appears, may involve your own personality. In other words, different persons, possessing different patterns of traits, may well prefer certain tactics over others. Evidence for just such differences has recently been reported by Caldwell and Burger (1997).

These researchers reasoned that several of the important "Big Five" Dimensions of personality (Costa & McCrae, 1992), as well as degree of self-monitoring (Lennox & Wolfe, 1984) and level of desire for personal control (Burger & Cooper, 1979), would be related to preferences for various tactics of social influence. (These aspects of personality are described in Table 9.1.) To test this general hypothesis, Caldwell and Burger asked several hundred business students to complete a survey indicating the extent to which they used a wide range of influence tactics: rational argument and persuasion, pressure tactics, ingratiation, inspirational appeals designed to engage others' enthusiasm, and reciprocity—offering them something in return. Measures of various aspects of the students' personality were also obtained. Then the researchers analyzed these two sets of data (preferences for social influence tactics and aspects of personality) to see if any links between them existed.

In fact, as shown in Table 9.1, such links did exist. For instance, individuals high in agreeableness (the tendency to trust others and deal with them cooperatively) and conscientiousness (the tendency to be neat, orderly, organized, and responsible) were associated with a strong preference for rational persuasion and inspirational appeals and a *low* preference for pressure tactics. Similarly, persons high in extraversion and high in self-monitoring showed a preference for all tactics of influence *except* rational persuasion. Finally, persons high in the desire for control strongly preferred rational persuasion and pressure tactics over more subtle tactics such as ingratiation.

So it appears that depending on their own personality traits, different individuals do tend to prefer different tactics for influencing others. In other words, we all want to get our way and have others do what we would like them to do; but, depending on our own traits, we tend to choose different paths to this goal.

Table 9.1

Personality and Tactics of Social Influence. As shown here, individuals with contrasting personality profiles tend to prefer different techniques for exerting social influence. In other words, the specific tactics we choose seem to reflect our own traits and characteristics.

Aspects of Personality	Preferred Tactics of Influence	Nonpreferred Tactics of Influence
High agreeableness (trust, cooperativeness) High conscientiousness (neatness, orderliness, responsibleness)	Rational persuasion Inspirational appeals	Pressure tactics
High extraversion (friendliness, sociability) High self-monitoring (sensitivity to reactions of others; willingness to change behavior across situations)	Almost all tactics	Rational persuasion
High desire for control (control over events in one's life)	Rational persuasion Pressure tactics	Ingratiation

(*Source:* Based on data from Caldwell & Burger, 1997.)

One final point: Not only do individuals differ in their preferences for various tactics for exerting social influence; they also differ in terms of how successful they are in this respect. For example, individuals high in the *need for cognition*—motivation for and enjoyment of effortful cognitive activities (e.g., Shestowsky, Wegener, & Fabrigar, 1998)—are often more successful in changing others' views than persons lower in this characteristic. Why? Perhaps because they offer stronger arguments and engage in more active and vigorous attempts to influence others. Whatever the precise reasons for such differences, however, it is clear that where influence is concerned, large individual differences in effectiveness exist.

Key Points

- Individuals often engage in *complaining*—expressing discontent or dissatisfaction with oneself or some aspect of the external world. Complaints are sometimes used as a tactic for changing others' behavior (gaining compliance), and growing evidence suggests that they are often successful in this respect.

- However, additional findings indicate that females are more likely to respond in a helpful, sympathetic way to complaints than are males.

- Another tactic for gaining compliance involves putting others in a good mood before making a request. Recent evidence indicates that this tactic is especially likely to succeed if something about the request induces target persons to think systematically about it.

- While everyone engages in efforts to exert social influence on others, research findings indicate that the specific tactics individuals choose are related to their own traits and characteristics.

OBEDIENCE: SOCIAL INFLUENCE BY DEMAND

Have you ever seen a military officer shout commands at troops who then carry out these orders instantly? Have you ever watched a sports coach deliver a lecture to a player who towers over him but who listens meekly and quickly obeys the coach's commands? If so, you are aware of another form of social influence: *obedience*—instances in which someone in a position of authority simply tells or orders one or more other persons to do something—and they do it! Obedience is less frequent than conformity or compliance, because even persons who possess authority and could use it often prefer to exert influence through the *velvet glove*—through requests rather than direct orders (e.g., Yukl & Falbe, 1991). Still, obedience is far from rare; as noted above, it occurs in many settings, ranging from schools (wouldn't you obey an order from your principal when you were in high school?) through military bases. Obedience to the commands of persons who possess authority is far from surprising, because such persons usually have effective means for enforcing their orders. More surprising is the fact that often persons lacking power can also induce high levels of submission from others. The clearest and most dramatic evidence for such effects was reported by Stanley Milgram in a series of famous—and controversial—studies (Milgram, 1963, 1965a, 1974).

Destructive Obedience: Some Basic Findings

In his research, Milgram wished to learn whether individuals would obey commands from a relatively powerless stranger requiring them to inflict what seemed to be considerable pain on another person—a totally innocent stranger. Milgram's interest in this topic derived from tragic events in which seemingly normal, law-abiding persons actually obeyed such directives. For example, during World War II, troops in the German army frequently obeyed commands to torture and murder unarmed civilians—millions of them. In fact, the Nazis established horrible but highly efficient death camps designed to eradicate Jews, Gypsies, and other groups they felt were inferior or a threat to their own racial purity. These events are described in vivid detail in the National Holocaust Museum in Washington, D.C., and we strongly recommend that you visit this museum if you ever get the chance to do so (see Figure 9.14).

In an effort to gain insights into the nature of such events, Milgram designed an ingenious, if unsettling, laboratory simulation. The experimenter informed participants in the study (all males) that they were taking part in an investigation of the effects of punishment on learning. One person in each pair of participants would serve as a "learner" and would try to perform a simple task involving memory (supplying the second word in previously memorized pairs of words after hearing only the first word). The other participant, the "teacher," would read these words to the learner and would punish errors by the learner (failures to provide the second word in each pair) through electric shock. These shocks would be delivered by means of the equipment shown in Figure 9.15 on page 384. As you can see from the photo, this device contained thirty numbered switches; labels on the switches indicated voltage ranging from "15 volts" (the first) through "450 volts" (the thirtieth). The two persons present—a real participant and an assistant—drew slips of paper from a hat to determine who would play each role; as you can guess, the drawing was rigged so that the real participant always became the teacher. The teacher was then told to deliver a shock to the learner each time he made an error on the task. Moreover—and this is crucial—teachers were told that they had to *increase the strength of the shock each time the learner made an error.* This meant that if the

Figure 9.14
Destructive Obedience: Its Ultimate Costs. The National Holocaust Museum in Washington, D.C., presents dramatic evidence of the tragic results that may occur when destructive obedience is carried to extreme levels.

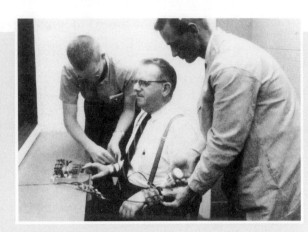

Figure 9.15
Studying Obedience in the Laboratory. The left-hand photo shows the apparatus Stanley Milgram used in his famous experiments on destructive obedience. The right photo shows the experimenter (right front) and a participant (rear) attaching electrodes to the learner's (accomplice's) wrist.

(*Source:* From the film *Obedience,* distributed by the New York University Film Library, Copyright 1965 by Stanley Milgram. Reprinted by permission of the copyright holder.)

learner made many errors, he would soon be receiving strong jolts of electricity. It's important to note that this information was false: in reality, the assistant (the learner) *never received any shocks during the experiment.* The only real shock ever used was a mild pulse from button number 3 to convince participants that the equipment was real.

During the session, the learner (following prearranged instructions) made many errors. Thus, participants soon found themselves facing a dilemma: Should they continue punishing this person with what seemed to be increasingly painful shocks? Or should they refuse to go on? If they hesitated, the experimenter pressured them to continue with a graded series of "prods": "Please continue"; "The experiment requires that you continue"; "It is absolutely essential that you continue"; "You have no other choice; you *must* go on."

Since participants were all volunteers and were paid *in advance,* you might predict that most would quickly refuse to follow the experimenter's orders. In reality, though, *fully 65 percent showed total obedience*—they proceeded through the entire series to the final 450-volt level. Many participants, of course, protested and asked that the session be ended. When ordered to proceed, however, a majority yielded to the experimenter's influence and continued to obey. Indeed, they continued doing so when the victim pounded on the wall as if in protest over the painful shocks (at the 300-volt level), and even when he *no longer responded,* as if he had passed out. The experimenter told participants to treat failures to answer as errors; so from this point on, many participants believed that they were delivering dangerous shocks to someone who might already be unconscious!

In further experiments Milgram (1965b, 1974) found that similar results could be obtained even under conditions that might be expected to reduce such obedience. When the study was moved from its original location on the campus of Yale University to a run-down office building in a nearby city, participants' level of obedience remained virtually unchanged. Similarly, a large proportion continued to obey even when the accomplice complained about the painfulness of the shocks and begged to be released. Most surprising of all, many (about 30 percent) obeyed even when they were required to grasp the victim's hand and force it down upon a metal shock plate! That these chilling results are not restricted to a single culture is indicated by the fact that similar findings were soon reported in studies conducted in several different countries (e.g., Jordan, Germany, Australia) and with children as well as with adults (e.g., Kilham & Mann, 1974; Shanab & Yahya, 1977). Thus, Milgram's findings seemed to be alarmingly general in scope.

I (Robert Baron) went to high school with Milgram's niece, and I can remember the disbelief with which students in my class reacted when she told us about her uncle's findings, several years before they were published. I was dismayed again when, as a college student, I read the actual report of his study. Psychologists, too, found Milgram's results highly disturbing. On the one hand, many wondered whether it was appropriate to conduct such research; many participants experienced extreme stress when faced with the dilemma of either harming an innocent stranger or disobeying a white-coated authority figure. Milgram conducted a complete and thorough debriefing after each session (see Chapter 1); but still, important ethical issues remained and could not be readily dismissed. On the other hand, psychologists were shaken by the results: Milgram's studies seemed to suggest that ordinary people are willing, even though with some reluctance, to harm an innocent stranger if ordered to do so by someone in authority. This led to an important question: What factors lie behind this tendency to obey, even when obedience results in potential harm to others?

Destructive Obedience: Its Social Psychological Basis

As we noted earlier, one reason why Milgram's results are so disturbing is that they seem to parallel many real-life events involving atrocities against innocent victims. Why does such *destructive obedience* occur? Why were participants in these experiments—and why are many persons in tragic situations outside the laboratory—so willing to yield to this powerful form of social influence? Social psychologists have identified several factors that seem to play a role.

First, in many situations, the persons in authority relieve those who obey of the responsibility for their own actions. "I was only carrying out orders" is the defense many offer after obeying harsh or cruel commands. In life situations, this transfer of responsibility may be implicit; the person in charge (e.g., a military or police officer) is assumed to have the responsibility for what happens. In Milgram's experiments, the transfer of responsibility was explicit. Participants were told at the start that the experimenter (the authority figure), not they, would be responsible for the learner's well-being. In view of this fact, it is not surprising that many obeyed; after all, they were completely off the hook.

Second, persons in authority often possess visible badges or signs of their status. They wear special uniforms or insignia, have special titles, and so on (see Figure 9.16 on page 386). Faced with such obvious reminders of who's in charge, most people find it difficult to disobey (e.g., Bushman, 1988; Darley, 1995).

A third reason for obedience in many situations where the targets of such influence might otherwise resist involves the gradual escalation of the authority figure's orders. Initial commands may call for relatively mild actions, such as merely arresting people. Only later do orders require behavior that is dangerous or objectionable. For example, police or military personnel may at first be

Figure 9.16

Symbols of Authority: Often, They Are Hard to Resist. Few of us would choose to ignore someone in an official uniform. Uniforms are outward signs of authority that are designed, in many cases, to tell us who is in charge; we disobey people who wear them at our own risk.

ordered only to question or threaten potential victims. Gradually, demands escalate to the point where these personnel are commanded to beat, torture, or even murder unarmed civilians. In a similar manner, participants in Milgram's research were first required to deliver only mild and harmless shocks to the victim. Only as the sessions continued did the intensity of these "punishments" rise to potentially harmful levels.

Finally, in many situations involving destructive obedience, events move very quickly: demonstrations quite suddenly turn into riots, arrests into mass beatings or mass murder. The fast pace of such events gives participants little time for reflection or systematic processing: people are ordered to obey and—almost automatically—they do so. Such conditions prevailed in Milgram's research; within a few minutes of entering the laboratory, participants found themselves faced with commands to deliver strong electric shocks to the learner. This fast pace, too, may tend to increase obedience.

In sum, the high levels of obedience generated in Milgram's laboratory studies are not as mysterious as they may seem. A social psychological analysis of the conditions existing both in the lab and in many real-life contexts identifies several factors that, together, may make it very difficult for individuals to resist the commands they receive. The consequences, of course, can be truly tragic for innocent and often defenseless victims.

Destructive Obedience: Resisting Its Effects

Now that we have considered some of the factors responsible for blind obedience to destructive commands from sources of authority, we will turn to a related question: How can this type of social influence be resisted? Several strategies may be helpful in this respect.

First, individuals exposed to commands from authority figures can be reminded that they, not the authorities, are responsible for any harm produced. Under these conditions, sharp reductions in the tendency to obey have been observed (e.g., Hamilton, 1978; Kilham & Mann, 1974).

Second, individuals can be provided with a clear indication that beyond some point, total submission to destructive commands is inappropriate. One procedure that is highly effective in this regard involves exposing individuals to the actions of *disobedient models*—persons who refuse to obey an authority figure's commands. Research findings indicate that such models can greatly reduce unquestioning obedience (e.g., Rochat & Modigliani, 1995).

Third, individuals may find it easier to resist influence from authority figures if they question the expertise and motives of these figures. Are those in authority really in a better position to judge what is appropriate and what is not? What motives lie behind their commands—socially beneficial goals or selfish gains? Dictators always claim that their brutal orders reflect their undying love for their fellow citizens and are in the people's best interest; but if large numbers of persons question these motives, the power of such dictators can be eroded and perhaps, ultimately, be swept away.

Finally, simply knowing about the power of authority figures to command blind obedience may be helpful in itself. Some research findings (e.g., Sherman, 1980) suggest that when individuals learn about the results of social psychological research, they sometimes change their behavior in light of this new knowledge. With respect to destructive obedience, there is some hope that knowing about this process can enhance individuals' resolve to resist. To the extent that this is so, then even exposure to findings as disturbing as those reported by Milgram can have positive social value.

To conclude: The power of authority figures to command obedience is certainly great, but it is *not* irresistible. Under appropriate conditions, it can be countered or reduced. As in many other areas of life, there *is* a choice. Deciding to resist the commands of persons in authority can, of course, be highly dangerous. For example, dictators usually control most of the weapons, the army, and the police. Yet, as events in Russia, Eastern Europe, and elsewhere in the late 1980s and early 1990s indicate, the outcome is by no means certain when committed groups of citizens choose to resist. Ultimately, victory may go to those on the side of freedom and decency rather than to those who wish to exert ruthless and total control over their fellow citizens.

Key Points

- *Obedience* is a form of social influence in which one or more persons are ordered to do something, and they do it. It is, in a sense, the most direct form of social influence.

- Research by Stanley Milgram indicates that many persons readily obey commands from a relatively powerless source of authority, even if these commands require them to harm an innocent stranger.

- Such destructive obedience, which plays a role in many real-life atrocities, stems from several factors. These include shifting of responsibility to the authority figure, outward signs of authority on the part of this person, a gradual escalation of the scope of the commands given, and the rapid pace with which such situations proceed.

- Several strategies can help reduce the occurrence of destructive obedience. These include reminding individuals that they share in the responsibility for any harm produced, reminding them that beyond some point obedience is inappropriate, calling into question the motives of authority figures, and informing people of the findings of social psychological research on this topic.

Connections: Integrating Social Psychology

In this chapter, you read about . . .	*In other chapters, you will find related discussions of . . .*
the role of social norms in conformity	the role of social norms in attraction (Chapter 7), helping (Chapter 10), aggression (Chapter 11), and group decision making (Chapter 12)
the basic principles underlying many different techniques for gaining compliance	the role of these principles in other aspects of social behavior: . . . the role of reciprocity in attraction (Chapter 7), aggression (Chapter 11), and cooperation (Chapter 12) . . . the role of the desire to be consistent in attitude change (Chapter 4), the self-concept (Chapter 5), and helping (Chapter 10) . . . the role of liking or friendship in social perception (Chapter 2), social relationships (Chapter 8), leadership (Chapter 12), and the legal process (Chapter 13)
the role of mood in compliance	the effects of mood on social cognition (Chapter 3), attitudes (Chapter 4), and helping (Chapter 10)
obedience to the commands of authority figures	the role of power and conflict in racial prejudice (Chapter 6) and in leadership (Chapter 13)

Thinking About Connections

1. As we'll see in Chapter 11, a large body of evidence suggests that exposure to scenes of violence on television and in the movies can lead to increased aggression by persons who watch such scenes. Despite these findings, the level of violence in television shows and in movies has actually *increased* in recent years. Do you think that this could reflect changing norms concerning aggression—that norms now define aggression more appropriate or acceptable than was true in the past? If so, why have such changes occurred?

2. As we'll describe in Chapter 13, charismatic leaders are often viewed as masters of social influence: they seem to possess an amazing ability to bend others to their will. Do you think they use the principles and tactics for gaining compliance described in this chapter? And which of these do you feel might be most important to such leaders in their efforts to influence their followers?

3. It has sometimes been argued that social influence is the most basic and important aspect of social behavior. Do you agree? Can you think of any forms of social behavior (e.g., aggression, Chapter 11; Helping, Chapter 10) in which influence does *not* play a role? What about attraction and love (Chapters 7 and 8); are these aspects of social behavior affected by social influence?

Ideas to Take with You
Tactics for Gaining Compliance

How can we get other persons to say yes to our requests? This is an eternal puzzle of social life. Research by social psychologists indicates that all of the techniques described here can be useful—and that they are widely used. So, whether or not you use these approaches yourself, you are likely to be on the receiving end of many of them during your lifetime. Here are tactics that are especially common.

Ingratiation: Getting others to like us so that they will be more willing to agree to our requests. We can ingratiate ourselves through flattery, by making ourselves attractive, and by showing liking for and interest in the target person.

The Foot-in-the-Door Technique: Starting with a small request and, after it is accepted, escalating to a larger one.

The Door-in-the-Face Technique: Starting with a large request and then, when this is refused, backing down to a smaller one.

Playing Hard to Get: Making it appear as though we are much in demand, thereby making it more likely that others will value us and agree to our requests—implicit or explicit.

Complaining: Expressing discontent or dissatisfaction with oneself or with the world—or with another person.

Putting Others in a Good Mood: Using any of countless tactics to make other people feel more cheerful—and thus more likely to say yes to our requests.

SUMMARY AND REVIEW OF KEY POINTS

Conformity: Group Influence in Action

- *Social influence*—efforts by one or more persons to change the attitudes or behavior of one or more others—is a common part of life.

- Most people behave in accordance with *social norms* most of the time; in other words, they show strong tendencies toward *conformity*.

- Conformity was first systematically studied by Solomon Asch, whose classic research indicated that many persons will yield to social pressure from a unanimous group.

- Many factors determine whether, and to what extent, conformity occurs. These include *cohesiveness*, or the degree of attraction felt by an individual toward some group; group size; and type of social norm operating in that situation—*descriptive* or *injunctive social norms*.

- Because of frontier conditions and other factors, norms condoning violence in response to affronts to one's honor developed in the South and West of the United States. Recent evidence suggests that such norms are still present and continue to influence behavior in these regions.

- Two important motives seem to underlie our tendency to conform: the desire to be liked by people whom we like or respect and the desire to be right or accurate. These two motives are reflected in two distinct types of social influence, *normative* and *informational social influence*.

- Once we show conformity in a given situation, we tend to view our conforming as justified, even if it has required us to behave in ways contrary to our true beliefs.

- Although pressures toward conformity are strong, many persons resist them, at least part of the time. This resistance seems to stem from two strong motives: the desire to retain one's individuality, and the desire to exert control over one's own life.

- When groups holding contrasting norms interact, the result can be annoyance, misunderstandings, and even open conflict. This is precisely what seems to happen at the Vatican when tourists are turned away at the door for violating the strictly enforced dress code.

- Under some conditions, minorities can induce even large majorities to change their attitudes or behavior. Recent evidence suggests that this may occur, in part, because minorities induce majorities to think more systematically about the issues they raise, and also because minorities themselves engage in such systematic processing; as a result, they formulate strong and persuasive arguments for their views.

Compliance: To Ask—Sometimes—Is to Receive

- Individuals use many different tactics for gaining *compliance*—getting others to say yes to various requests. Many of these tactics rest on basic principles well known to social psychologists.

- Two widely used tactics, the *foot-in-the-door technique* and the *lowball procedure,* rest on the principle of commitment/consistency. In contrast, the *door-in-the-face technique* and the *"that's-not-all"* technique rest on the principle of reciprocity.

- *Playing hard to get* and the *deadline technique* are based on the principle of scarcity—the idea that what is scarce or hard to obtain is valuable.

- Individuals often engage in *complaining*—expressing discontent or dissatisfaction with oneself or some aspect of the external world. Complaints are sometimes used as a tactic for changing others' behavior (gaining compliance), and growing evidence suggests that they are often successful in this respect.

- However, additional findings indicate that females are more likely to respond in a helpful, sympathetic way to complaints than are males.

- Another tactic for gaining compliance involves putting others in a good mood before making a request. Recent evidence indicates that this tactic is especially likely to succeed if something about the request induces target persons to think systematically about it.

- While everyone engages in efforts to exert social influence on others, research findings indicate that the specific tactics individuals choose are related to their own traits and characteristics.

Obedience: Social Influence by Demand

- *Obedience* is a form of social influence in which one or more persons are ordered to do something, and they do it. It is, in a sense, the most direct form of social influence.

- Research by Stanley Milgram indicates that many persons readily obey commands from a relatively powerless source of authority, even if these commands require them to harm an innocent stranger.

- Such destructive obedience, which plays a role in many real-life atrocities, stems from several factors. These include shifting of responsibility to the authority figure, outward signs of authority on the part of this person, a gradual escalation of the scope of the commands given, and the rapid pace with which such situations proceed.

- Several strategies can help reduce the occurrence of destructive obedience. These include reminding individuals that they share in the responsibility for any harm produced, reminding them that beyond some point obedience is inappropriate, calling into question the motives of authority figures, and informing people of the findings of social psychological research on this topic.

KEY TERMS

cohesiveness (p. 360)

complaining (p. 378)

compliance (p. 357)

conformity (p. 356)

cultures of honor (p. 362)

deadline technique (p. 376)

descriptive norms (p. 361)

door-in-the-face technique (p. 374)

foot-in-the-door technique (p. 374)

individuation (p. 367)

injunctive norms (p. 361)

informational social influence (p. 365)

ingratiation (p. 373)

lowball procedure (p. 374)

normative social influence (p. 364)

obedience (p. 357)

playing hard to get (p. 376)

social influence (p. 356)

social norms (p. 357)

"that's-not-all" technique (p. 375)

FOR MORE INFORMATION

Cialdini, R. B. (1993). *Influence: Science and practice* (3rd ed.). New York: HarperCollins.

An insightful and very readable account of the major techniques people use to influence others. The book draws both on the findings of systematic research and on informal observations made by the author in a wide range of practical settings (e.g., sales, public relations, fund-raising).

Milgram, S. (1974). *Obedience to authority.* New York: Harper & Row.

More than twenty-five years after it was written, this book remains the definitive work on obedience as a social psychological process. The untimely death of its author only adds to its value as a lasting contribution to our field.

Shavitt, S., & Brock, T. C. (1994). *Persuasion: Psychological insights and perspectives*. Boston: Allyn and Bacon.

In this excellent book, experts on persuasion and other aspects of social influence summarize existing knowledge about many fascinating topics. Among the chapters you are sure to find of interest are ones on how our actions affect our attitudes, cognitive processes in persuasion, many forms of interpersonal influence, and subliminal persuasion.

10 Prosocial Behavior: Helping Others

Man Flying Kite with Key. © José Ortega/Stock Illustration Source

Chapter Outline

Responding to an Emergency: Why Are Bystanders Sometimes Helpful, Sometimes Indifferent?

CORNERSTONES OF SOCIAL PSYCHOLOGY: Darley and Latané: Why Bystanders Don't Respond

Providing Help—Yes or No? Five Essential Steps in the Decision Process

SOCIAL DIVERSITY: A CRITICAL ANALYSIS: Big Cities versus Small Towns: Does Prosocial Behavior Depend in Part on Where You Live?

Situational Factors That Enhance or Inhibit Helping: Attraction, Attributions, and Prosocial Models

The Helpers and Those Who Receive Help

Helping As a Function of the Bystander's Emotional State

Dispositional Differences in Prosocial Responding

BEYOND THE HEADLINES: AS SOCIAL PSYCHOLOGISTS SEE IT: Ordinary People Sometimes Do Extraordinary Things

Volunteering: Motivations for Long Term Help

Who Receives Help, and How Do People React to Being Helped?

Explaining Prosocial Behavior: Why Do People Help?

Empathy–Altruism: It Feels Good to Help Those in Need

Negative-State Relief: It Reduces One's Negative Affect to Relieve a Stressful Situation

Empathic Joy: Successful Helping As a Way to Arouse Positive Affect

Genetic Determinism: Helping Maximizes the Survival of Genes Like One's Own

CONNECTIONS: Integrating Social Psychology

IDEAS TO TAKE WITH YOU: Being a Responsive Bystander

Summary and Review of Key Points

Key Terms

For More Information

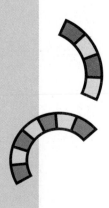

One very cold January morning, I (Donn Byrne) took a slightly different route than usual for the drive from my home to the university. The new route included a fairly steep downhill section as I left the Helderberg Mountains. After leaving the garage, I noticed that the roads were still icy from an overnight freezing rain. With four-wheel drive, this did not seem to be anything to worry about; even so, I drove slowly.

When I reached the downhill portion of my journey, I slowed the car even more. Then, about a third of the way down, the road curved to the left, but the car didn't. It had not been obvious to me, but a thin coat of ice covered the road surface, and the car simply slid in a straight line, no matter whether I turned the steering wheel left or right. Because a straight line meant heading off the road, I remember thinking that being compulsive about fastening my seat belt turned out to be a good kind of compulsion. It appeared that the car and I were going to plunge several yards down an embankment. Luckily, there was a patch of small but sturdy sumac trees in my path, just where the descent began. Rather than continuing downhill, the car came to a stop as it encountered the sumacs, but only after tilting over and coming to rest on its right side.

My new problem at that point was to climb slowly up through the door, which was now above my head, so as to get free of the car without rocking it loose and allowing it to continue on its original downward course. This acrobatic act was successful, but once back on the road, I found myself in a somewhat deserted area on a really cold day with no help in sight. At that moment, an elderly gentleman walked around the curve and beckoned for me to join him. I was very happy to do so, and we then walked up a winding driveway to his home, which was located on a flat patch of land high above the road.

Inside his house was a blazing wood fire that almost felt too hot in contrast to the winter wonderland outside, but that was OK with me. The man offered a chair and provided a cup of steaming coffee. He then asked for my auto club card, called for a tow truck to come rescue my car, and suggested that I just relax until it arrived.

As we talked, he said that he had been sitting by his window enjoying the view when he saw my car start to slide and guessed there would be trouble. He said with a wink, "You're the third one today."

Waiting for the tow truck in that warm, comfortable room, I couldn't avoid thinking about research on prosocial behavior. In this instance, I was the stranger in distress, and the man was a bystander who had come to my assistance. Without his intervention I would have had to take a long, painful walk in the frigid air to search for a phone. Instead, someone who didn't know me had responded helpfully to my predicament. Though I felt very appreciative of what he did, it was also obvious that he was quite pleased to have the opportunity to provide help to me—and no doubt to others who had trouble making it down that hill.

Even the most dangerous prosocial acts seem to involve a mixture of making a personal sacrifice in order to help someone and obtaining personal satisfaction from having done so. In social psychological research on acts of helpfulness, the primary goal has been to determine why people sometimes provide help to strangers and sometimes stand back and do nothing. As we describe some of this research in the following pages, remember this man who walked out of his house on a winter morning to offer assistance to a stranger. Keep in mind the question, "Why would he have done that when he could much more easily have remained inside, sitting by his window?"

When you read about the presence or absence of prosocial tendencies, also consider what you would have done. It is not at all unusual to find yourself as an unexpected bystander to a major or minor emergency in which a stranger is in need of assistance. In all probability, you have helped on some occasions and failed to help on others. In some instances the emergency is a sudden unexpected event—for example, you see someone fall down and then have trouble getting back up. Do you try to help? In other situations, there is a long-standing problem for which extended help is needed over a long period of time—for example, you become aware of children in your community who need someone to act as a "big brother" or "big sister." Do you volunteer your time? For more than three decades now, social psychologists have worked to identify the many factors that determine who is most likely to provide help under what circumstances.

That is, we want to understand and to predict **prosocial behavior.** A prosocial act is one that benefits another person but has no obvious benefits for the person who carries it out. Other terms, such as *helping behavior, charitable behavior, altruism,* and *volunteerism* are also used to describe the "good" things that people do to assist others.

Prosocial behavior first became a topic of major interest in social psychology in the 1960s. As you will soon learn, a widely publicized news story of an actual crime provided the original impetus for various investigators to offer theories in an effort to explain why bystanders sometimes help and sometimes fail to help in response to an emergency. Simultaneously, social psychologists began designing experiments to test the accuracy of these explanations. We will describe some of the formulations and some of the findings of subsequent research, which have expanded our knowledge far beyond these initial concerns with helpful and unhelpful bystanders.

First, we will describe the basic factors that influence the likelihood of a given individual's *responding to an emergency,* including crucial elements in the situation itself that enhance or inhibit prosocial behavior. Next, we will examine the *helpers and those who receive help,* including emotional and dispositional variables that influence helping both in emergencies and in long-term problem situations. In addition, we will describe the affective and motivational effects on those who receive help. And, as the last topic, we will outline some of the major theoretical *explanations of prosocial motivation,* ranging from theories based on selfish versus unselfish motives to the possible role of genetic determinants in the helping process.

RESPONDING TO AN EMERGENCY: WHY ARE BYSTANDERS SOMETIMES HELPFUL, SOMETIMES INDIFFERENT?

At a minimum, providing help requires that you stop whatever you are doing and spend some amount of time dealing with the needs of others, as in Figure 10.1 on page 396. Even when the problem is only one of stupidity or ignorance, the need is real. And the factors that determine bystanders'

prosocial behavior • Helpful actions that benefit others but have no obvious benefits for the person who carries out the action and sometimes even involve risk for the one who helps.

Figure 10.1

Some People Need a Lot of Help. *Prosocial behavior* takes many forms—from risking one's life in order to save the life of a stranger to providing information to tourists who can't read a map. However different prosocial acts may be, they each require some amount of time and effort and have an outcome that is beneficial to the one who receives help but of no obvious benefit to the one who helps.

(*Source: New Yorker,* February 23 and March 2, 1998, p. 145.)

"O.K., this is the West Coast, O.K.? What you want is the East Coast, so turn around and go back twenty-four, twenty-five hundred miles, and that's the East Coast. You can't miss it."

readiness to help remain the same, whether bystander behavior involves providing information to map-challenged tourists, bringing a stranger into your warm home after an automobile accident, driving angrily past an injured woman lying on a busy interstate highway (Drivers indifferent, 1998), walking away and taking no action after discovering that your teenage friend is molesting and murdering a seven-year-old child (Booth, 1998), returning a bag containing $70,000 to its owner (Hurewitz, 1998), or risking death by diving 150 feet off of a bridge in order to save a woman intent on suicide (Fitzgerald, 1996).

In addition to requiring that you spend time and effort and sometimes face physical risk, helping can entail interpersonal risks as well. It is possible for a dishonest person to pretend to be in need of help as a way of taking advantage of you. According to Scruton (1998), two men armed with a handgun robbed a store in Ballston Spa, New York, of $14,000. It was early evening, and they ran with their loot to a nearby house, telling the man who lived there that they urgently needed a ride to nearby Saratoga Springs. They appeared to be "clean-cut, polite young men," and the homeowner asked his son to take them in his Jeep. After the three of them departed, the father took his dog for a walk and noticed a police car driving up and down the street. It suddenly occurred to him that the law officers might be looking for the men who were in the Jeep with his son. They were. The son called soon afterward and told of being forced from his car at gunpoint. The thieves drove away and later abandoned the car and set it on fire. Although the outcome could have been far worse, this is the kind of incident that has given rise to the cynical phrase "No good deed goes unpunished." In any event, a man and his son responded to strangers in a prosocial way, but with unpleasant consequences for themselves.

Back in 1964, another actual emergency took place. Help was badly needed, many bystanders were present, but not one of them responded. As a result, a young woman was murdered. This instance of seemingly indifferent bystanders motivated two social psychologists to try to understand why no one had helped, as described in the following *Cornerstones* section.

Cornerstones of Social Psychology
Darley and Latané: Why Bystanders Don't Respond

The event involving the absence of prosocial behavior became a matter of widespread concern. It took place in the early morning hours of March 13, 1964. In New York City, Catherine (Kitty) Genovese was returning home from her job as manager of a bar. As she crossed the street from her car to the apartment building where she lived, a man armed with a knife approached her. She began running in an effort to avoid him, but he ran in pursuit, caught up to Ms. Genovese, and then stabbed her. She screamed for help, and numerous people apparently heard her, because lights quickly came on in several of the apartment windows that overlooked the street. The attacker retreated briefly, but when no one came to help his bleeding victim, he returned to finish the job. She screamed again, but he stabbed her repeatedly until she lay dead. It was later determined that this horrifying forty-five-minute interaction was seen and heard by thirty-eight witnesses, but no one took direct action or even bothered to call the police (Rosenthal, 1964).

On the basis of the many news stories about this incident, the general response was one of shock and disappointment about the failure of the bystanders to come to the victim's aid. Why didn't they help? Possibly people in general had become apathetic, cold, and indifferent to the problems of others. Perhaps living in a big city made people callous. Perhaps violence on TV and in the movies had desensitized viewers to the horror of real violence and real suffering. Maybe modern American society, which had recently experienced the assassination of a president, was no longer able to empathize with the plight of a stranger in need of help.

As we now know, there are psychological explanations for the failure of those bystanders to respond—explanations that do not involve apathy, indifference, callousness, or a general absence of empathy. A novel idea began to take shape shortly after the murder as Professors John Darley and Bibb Latané ate lunch and discussed what had happened in their city. They believed that the problem was not that the bystanders didn't care about the crime victim, but that something about the situation must have made them hesitate to act. As these psychologists speculated, they began to outline proposed experiments on their tablecloth (Krupat, 1975).

The first hypothesis to be tested was that bystanders fail to respond if there is **diffusion of responsibility.** In other words, the more bystanders there are, the less responsibility to do something any one of them assumes. From this it follows that in situations with only one bystander, help is very likely to be given to someone in need. For example, the man who saw my car sliding off the road was alone, and he was the only witness to my problem. So the responsibility was unmistakably his, and he acted. With multiple witnesses, as in the attack on Kitty Genovese, any one of thirty-eight people looking out their windows *could* have acted, but each had only one thirty-eighth of the total responsibility. That was apparently not enough to motivate any one of them to act. The general prediction, then, was: As the number of bystanders to an emergency increases, the likelihood of a prosocial response decreases.

To test this hypothesis in a controlled experiment, Darley and Latané needed to create an "emergency" in a laboratory, arrange for different numbers of bystanders to be present, and then observe possible differences in prosocial responsiveness. These social psychologists devised a realistic yet safe procedure that permitted them to determine the accuracy of their proposal that bystander helpfulness is inhibited by diffusion of responsibility.

Male students took part in what was supposedly a study of student life. After this bogus study was underway, the participants were suddenly confronted by an emergency—what seemed to be a severe medical problem experienced by a fellow

John Darley. *John Darley (1938–   ) obtained the Ph.D. degree at Harvard University in 1965, and he has spent most of his academic life at Princeton University. His recent research interests have included, in addition to prosocial behavior, community attitudes about the deaths of terminally ill patients, strategies used in apologizing, judgments about attempted crimes, and an analysis of the research participants who took part in Milgram's obedience experiments.*

diffusion of responsibility • Decreased tendency of any individual bystander in an emergency to assume personal responsibility for providing help as the result of the presence of multiple bystanders. The greater the number of bystanders, the less the individual's sense of responsibility to act.

student. Varying the number of bystanders was a matter of deception. Each participant was led to believe that he was the only one aware of the medical problem—or that he was one of two bystanders, or one of five. The "other bystanders" were in fact tape recordings. The crucial question, of course, was whether a helpful response to the emergency was most likely to occur with only one bystander, and less likely to occur as the number of bystanders increased.

To set up this elaborate deception, the investigators met each participant individually as he arrived at the laboratory and told him that the study required students to discuss some of the problems they had encountered in attending college in a high-pressure urban setting. Each participant was to sit alone in a small room, communicating with others by means of an intercom. In order "to avoid embarrassment," the experimenters said they would not be able to hear the students as they talked to one another. This false information was necessary to ensure that the only ones who could possibly be aware of the "emergency" were the research participants.

In each session, there was only one actual research participant. Either he was alone with the student who was to have an "emergency," or there was one additional bystander, or there were four additional bystanders. The tape of the student "victim-to-be" began with his saying that he was ashamed to admit it, but he sometimes had seizures when he was in a stressful situation. Then the genuine participant spoke, followed by (in the multiple-bystander conditions) the other taped participant or participants. Then it was again the "victim's" turn to speak.

> I er I think er if if could er er somebody er er help because I er I'm er h-h-having a a a real problem er right now and and and I er if somebody could help me out it would er er s-s-sure be good . . . because er there er er a thing's coming on and and I could really er use some help so if somebody here er help er uh uh uh (choking sounds) . . . I'm gonna die er er I'm gonna die er help er er seizure (chokes, then is quiet). (Darley & Latané, 1968, p. 379)

If you had been a research participant listening to that emergency message, what do you think you would have done? Because of the way the situation had been arranged, the only way to help was to leave the experimental room and search the nearby rooms in an effort to locate the person having the seizure. Would you have done that? Would you hesitate, not knowing exactly how best to respond? Would you do nothing at all? In fact, some of the original participants helped immediately, some hesitated, and some did nothing. Was diffusion of responsibility the reason for these differences?

In this cornerstone experiment, bystander responsiveness was assessed in two ways: (1) the percentage of participants in each condition who tried to help; and (2) if they did make an effort, how long they waited before doing something. As shown in Figure 10.2, Darley and Latané were correct: the more bystanders present when an emergency occurs, the less responsiveness. As the number of bystanders increased, fewer tried to help, and more time passed before a response occurred.

It is well worth noting that the student bystanders who hesitated or failed to respond were *not* apathetic or uncaring. Compared to the 85 percent of lone bystanders who helped in the first sixty seconds, far fewer participants tried to help in the conditions in which fellow bystanders were believed to be present; but even the totally unhelpful individuals appeared to be concerned, upset, and confused.

The conclusion is that the prosocial tendencies of a single witness to an emergency are inhibited by the presence of additional witnesses, a phenomenon that became known as the **bystander effect.** Darley (1991) has indicated that neither he nor his colleague could have foreseen the flood of research that their experiment initiated. As you will see in the remainder of this chapter, however, this one experiment was just the first of a great many investigations that have made prosocial behavior much more understandable and predictable. The initial insight about diffusion of responsibility was only the beginning.

bystander effect • The fact that the likelihood of a prosocial response to an emergency is affected by the number of bystanders who are present: as the number of bystanders increases, the probability that any one bystander will help decreases and the amount of time that passes before help occurs increases.

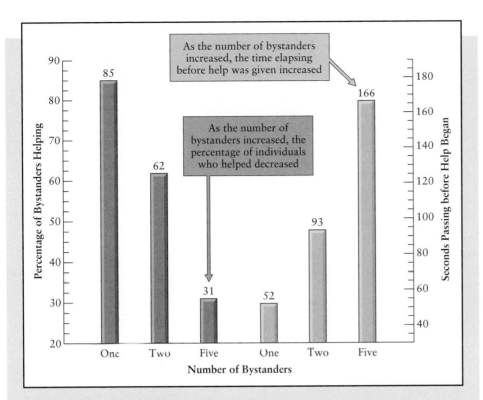

Figure 10.2

Less Help from More Bystanders. In the initial experiment designed to explore the *bystander effect,* students heard what seemed to be a fellow student experiencing a seizure and calling out for help. Each research participant believed himself to be either the only bystander aware of this emergency, one of two bystanders, or one of five. As the number of bystanders increased, the percentage of individuals who tried to help the "victim" decreased. In addition, among those who did help, the more bystanders present, the more time it took for helping behavior to begin. The proposed explanation for the inhibiting effect of additional bystanders was the *diffusion of responsibility* among those who could potentially provide help.

(*Source:* Based on data from Darley & Latané, 1968.)

Providing Help—Yes or No? Five Essential Steps in the Decision Process

If you are sitting in a comfortable chair while reading this book's description of real and staged emergencies, you are surely having no problem in figuring out what bystanders should do. That is, the witnesses to Kitty Genovese's murder should have shouted at the attacker, called the police, and perhaps even have come to the rescue as an angry group. The participants in the seizure experiment should have rushed out immediately to help a fellow student.

When you are face to face with such emergencies, however, the situation is not the same. There are a great many reasons why people fail to do the right thing. As their research progressed, Latané and Darley (1970) conceptualized the individual's response to an emergency as a series of five essential steps: five choice points that can either lead toward a prosocial act or toward doing nothing. These steps and the necessary decisions are summarized in Figure 10.3 on page 400. At each step, the simplest choice is the path of least resistance—the easiest thing to do is nothing. By failing to help a victim in distress, you avoid a lot of potential problems for yourself. In fact, though, most of us would not deliberately choose to be heartless and unhelpful.

Figure 10.3

From an Emergency to a Prosocial Response: Five Essential Steps. Latané and Darley conceptualized prosocial behavior as the end point of a series of five steps: five choice points that lead the individual toward or away from making a helpful response. At each step in the process, the yes/no choices (whether conscious or unconscious, rapid or slow) result in either (1) no—so help will not occur; or (2) yes—so there is progress to the following step and toward a prosocial response.

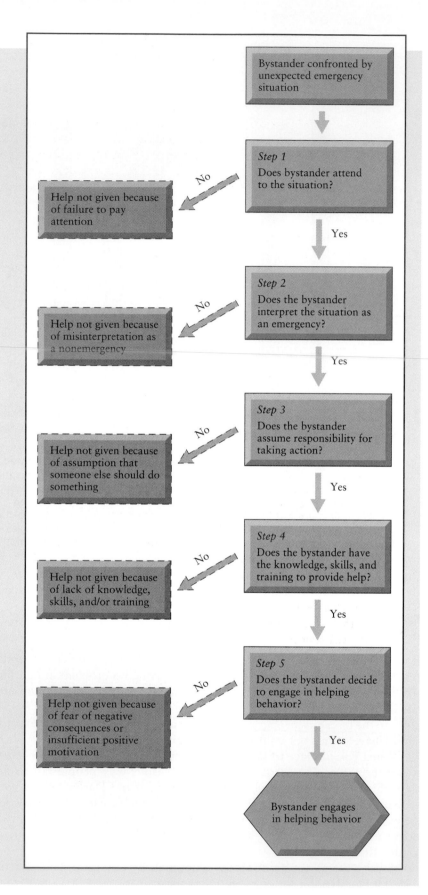

Moral attitudes do not predict moral behavior, in part because it is apparently quite easy to convince oneself that a given course of action is morally acceptable (Bersoff, 1999). We often , therefore, choose not to help for various seemingly valid reasons.

Step 1: Noticing the Emergency Event. By definition, emergencies aren't announced in advance and don't occur on schedule, so there is no way to anticipate when or where one will occur. As a result, we usually are doing something else and thinking about other matters when we are suddenly confronted by an unexpected event. If you are too busy or preoccupied to direct your attention to the unexpected event, you are unaware of the need for engaging in prosocial behavior. For example, if some of the neighbors of Kitty Genovese were deeply absorbed in a television program or engaged in a family argument, they may not even have noticed her screams for help. Clearly, if you don't notice a problem, it simply doesn't exist for you. In our everyday lives, we ignore or screen out many sights and sounds because they are personally irrelevant. If we did not, we would be swamped by an overload of information. Generally, it is to our benefit not to pay attention to much of what goes on around us, and so it is surprisingly easy to overlook something important when it happens.

An interesting verification of the importance of this first step was provided in a field study. Darley and Batson (1973) proposed that when a person is preoccupied by special concerns, prosocial behavior is less likely to occur. The research was conducted with seminary students, individuals who would be expected to be especially likely to help someone in need. To make helpfulness as salient as possible, the experimenters asked some of the participants to walk to a nearby building on campus to talk to a group about Luke's parable of the good Samaritan. Other participants were asked to go to the nearby building to talk about jobs. In order to vary the degree of preoccupation, the investigators gave different participants different information about the amount of time they had to reach their destination. Some of the seminarians were told they were ahead of schedule and had plenty of extra time to reach the other building, some were told they were right on schedule, and still others were told that they were late for the speaking engagement. Presumably, as they walked to the building, the first group would be the least preoccupied and the third group would be the most preoccupied. The primary research question was whether prosocial behavior would decrease as amount of preoccupation increased.

Along the route to the building where the talk was to be given, a simulated emergency was staged. Each participant encountered a stranger (in fact, a research assistant) who was slumped in a doorway, coughing and groaning. Would the participants notice this apparently ill or injured individual and try to help? Though the topic of the upcoming talk (the good Samaritan versus jobs) had *no* effect on prosocial responding, preoccupation based on time pressure had a major effect. As you can see in Figure 10.4 on page 402, 63 percent of the participants who had time to spare provided help. Among those who were neither early nor late, 45 percent helped. In the most preoccupied group (those supposedly late for their appointment), only 10 percent provided aid. Many of the preoccupied seminarians seemed to pay little or no attention to the victim; they simply stepped over him in their hurry to reach their destination. It seems to be true that if you are too busy to pay attention to your surroundings, you won't notice there is a problem and you won't help.

Step 2: Interpreting an Emergency as an Emergency. Even when we pay attention to what is going on around us, we have only limited and incomplete

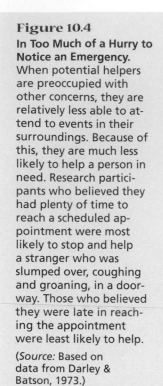

Figure 10.4

In Too Much of a Hurry to Notice an Emergency. When potential helpers are preoccupied with other concerns, they are relatively less able to attend to events in their surroundings. Because of this, they are much less likely to help a person in need. Research participants who believed they had plenty of time to reach a scheduled appointment were most likely to stop and help a stranger who was slumped over, coughing and groaning, in a doorway. Those who believed they were late in reaching the appointment were least likely to help.

(*Source:* Based on data from Darley & Batson, 1973.)

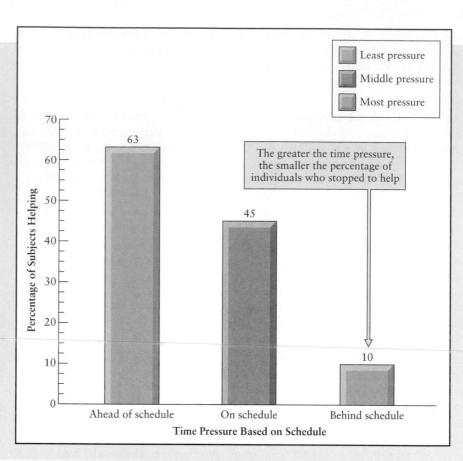

information about what strangers are doing. Most of the time it doesn't matter and it's none of our business. If you don't know why a man is running through a park, it is easier (and usually more accurate) to assume a routine, everyday explanation than a highly unusual and unlikely one (Macrae & Milne, 1992). As a result, we are more likely to believe that the man is jogging or rushing to catch a bus than to believe that he is a thief making a getaway or an undercover agent chasing a terrorist. And usually we are right. If there really is an emergency, however, the inclination to misperceive it as a nonemergency inhibits any tendency to make a prosocial response.

Whenever potential helpers are not completely sure about what is going on, they tend to hold back and wait for further information. It's quite possible that the neighbors of Kitty Genovese could not see the murder scene very clearly that evening. Besides, the screams might have been part of a loud argument between a girlfriend and boyfriend. Or perhaps a man and woman had been drinking and were just pretending to be an attacker and a victim as a joke. What are the odds, after all, that you would look out your window and see a murder taking place? If information is not absolutely clear-cut as to whether there is a serious problem or something inconsequential, most people are inclined to accept the comforting and nonstressful interpretation that nothing needs to be done (Wilson & Petruska, 1984).

All of this suggests that multiple witnesses may inhibit helping not only because of the diffusion of responsibility but also because it would be embarrassing to misinterpret a situation. Making such a serious mistake in front of others might lead them to evaluate your actions as dumb or as a silly overreaction. As discussed in Chapter 7, when we want evidence about the correctness of our opinions, we utilize social comparison (see also Chapters 4 and 9). If others do not seem excited about what is going on and if others don't react as though there is an emergency, we don't either. No one wants to look foolish, and it's bad to lose your cool.

The tendency of people in a group to hesitate and do nothing is based on what is known as **pluralistic ignorance.** That is, because none of the bystanders knows for sure what is going on, each depends on the others to provide accurate cues; as a result, no one responds. Latané and Darley (1968) provided a dramatic demonstration of just how far people will go to avoid making an "inappropriate" response to what may or may not be an emergency. The investigators placed research participants in a room alone or with two other participants as they filled out questionnaires. After several minutes had passed, the experimenters pumped smoke into the research room through a vent. When individuals were alone, most (75 percent) stopped what they doing when the smoke appeared and went out to report the problem. When three people were in the room, however, only 38 percent reacted to the smoke, while 62 percent did nothing—even after the smoke became so thick that it became difficult to see. Being with other people who fail to respond seems to be a powerful inhibitor. It is as if risking death by fire would be preferable to risk making a fool of yourself.

This fear of making a blunder and misinterpreting the situation is reduced under certain conditions, however. For example, social inhibitions are much weaker when the other bystanders are friends rather than strangers, because friends tend to communicate with one another about what is happening and about what to do. With such communication, the bystander effect is much less strong (Rutkowski, Gruder, & Romer, 1983). In addition, alcohol consumption reduces anxiety about the opinions of others and increases the tendency to help (Steele, Critchlow, & Liu, 1985). It seems very likely that three friends drinking beer would not sit quietly as smoke poured into the room.

One's place of residence can also affect the extent to which one is likely to pay attention to surrounding events and interact with strangers. The likelihood of people's taking the first two decision steps (attending to their surroundings and interpreting an emergency correctly) might be expected to be greater in a small community than in a large metropolitan area. If this were the case, the frequency of prosocial acts would also differ on the basis of population size. In the following *Social Diversity* section, we describe differences in prosocial behavior that occur as a function of residence in small versus large communities.

pluralistic ignorance • The tendency of bystanders in an emergency to rely on what other bystanders do and say even though no one is sure about what is happening or what to do about it; very often, all of the bystanders hold back and behave as if there is no problem, and all use this "information" to justify their failure to act.

Social Diversity: A Critical Analysis
Big Cities versus Small Towns: Does Prosocial Behavior Depend in Part on Where You Live?

Although social diversity is most often studied with respect to racial, ethnic, or national differences, place of residence can also be an important determinant of human behavior. If you have ever spent much time in a large city and/or in a small town, do you believe that interpersonal interactions and interpersonal behavior may be affected by such settings?

In fact, the answer is yes. The residents of big cities have often been described by novelists (Wolfe, 1940), college students (Schneider & Mockus, 1974), and sociologists

(Simmel, 1950) as being less considerate of others and less helpful than people who live in less populous communities. Why? Milgram (1970) suggested that the external demands of an urban environment involve stimulus overload for city dwellers. For example, crowded cities are noisier than small towns—filled with the sounds of traffic, sirens, and squealing brakes both day and night (Cooke, 1992). And, by definition, people in a city come into contact with more people (including more strangers) each day than people in a less crowded community. The best way to survive in such an environment is to screen out nonessential stimuli and go on about one's own business. For example, as population increases, the environment becomes more fast-paced (Sadalla, Sheets, & McCreath, 1990). The larger the city, the faster pedestrians walk (Walmsley & Lewis, 1989)—much like the seminary students rushing between campus buildings. Even those who commute from suburbia to city behave differently in the two locations. When they are in an urban train station, commuters make less eye contact with strangers than when they are in a suburban train station (McCauley, Coleman, & DeFusco, 1977)—much like the research participants who continued to work on their questionnaires rather than interact with the other participants as the room filled with smoke; they just don't communicate.

An expected consequence of stimulus overload, fast pace, and concentrating on oneself is a general disregard for others, especially strangers. As a result, as Levine and colleagues (1994) predicted, helpfulness should decrease. These researchers obtained relevant data on prosocial behavior in thirty-six small, medium, and large cities across the United States. They measured several different forms of helping, which included informing a stranger that he or she had dropped a pen, assisting a person in a leg brace pick up magazines when they slipped to the sidewalk, making change for a quarter, helping a blind person cross the street, picking up and mailing a stamped letter that apparently had been lost, and per capita charitable contributions to the United Way. A strong negative relationship was found between these combined indicators of prosocial acts and population density (Levine et al., 1994). That is, the greater the number of people living in a given locality, the less helpful the residents.

Earlier research also supported the generalization that city dwellers are less friendly and less helpful to strangers than are small-town residents (Korte, 1980, 1981; Krupat & Guild, 1980). And the relationship between population and helpfulness is not simply an American phenomenon. In a study of fifty-five cities and towns in Australia, Amato (1983) found that as community size increased, prosocial responsivity decreased.

Clearly, our surroundings can influence the decisions that are essential to prosocial actions.

Step 3: Assuming That Helpfulness Is Your Responsibility. Once an individual pays attention to some external event and interprets it correctly as an emergency, a prosocial act will follow only if the person takes responsibility for providing help. In many instances the responsibility is clear. Firefighters are the ones to do something about a burning house; police officers are the ones to do something about a crime; medical personnel deal with injuries and illnesses. When responsibility is not as clear as in those examples, people tend to assume that anyone in a leadership role must be responsible (Baumeister et al., 1988). For example, professors should be responsible for dealing with classroom emergencies and bus drivers for emergencies involving their vehicles. When there is one adult and several children, the adult is expected to take charge.

One of the reasons that a lone bystander is more likely to act than a bystander in a group is that there is no one else present who *could* take responsibility. With a group, as we have discussed, the responsibility is diffuse and much less clear.

Step 4: Knowing What to Do. Even if a bystander reaches the point of assumed responsibility, nothing useful can be done unless that person knows *how* to be helpful. Some emergencies are sufficiently simple that almost everyone has the necessary skills. If you see someone slip on an icy sidewalk, you help that person up. If you see two suspicious strangers trying to break into a parked car, you

Figure 10.5

Even Snoopy Can't Provide Help When He Lacks the Necessary Knowledge. Among bystanders who are aware of a problem, who correctly interpret the situation as an emergency, and who assume responsibility to take action, prosocial behavior may nevertheless be inhibited because of the absence of necessary skills.

(*Source:* United Feature Syndicate, Inc., March 8, 1998.)

find a phone and dial 911. Even in the latter instance, though, a child or a recent immigrant might not possess the necessary information. In Figure 10.5, for example, Snoopy is quite willing to act, but he can't because he doesn't know how to identify the number 9.

Some emergencies require special knowledge and skills that are not possessed by most bystanders. For example, you can help someone who is drowning only if you know how to swim and how to handle a drowning person. With bystanders at an accident, a registered nurse is more likely to assume responsibility and more likely to help than someone not employed in a medical profession (Cramer et al., 1988).

Step 5: Deciding to Help. Even if a bystander's response at each of the first four steps is yes, help will not occur unless he or she makes the final decision to act. Helping at this point can be inhibited by fears (often realistic) about potential negative consequences. For example, if you try to help a person who slipped on the ice, you might fall yourself. If your help leads to additional problems, you may be sued. A sick person who has collapsed in a doorway may throw up on your shoes when you try to provide assistance. The person who seems to be in need may be a crook who is only pretending—remember the two thieves who "needed a ride" to a nearby town?

An especially unpleasant consequence may arise when an individual is being threatened or harmed by someone in his or her own family. The well-meaning outsider often arouses only anger. For this reason, bystanders rarely offer help when they believe that a woman is being attacked by her husband or boyfriend (Shotland & Strau, 1976) or that a child is being physically abused by a parent (Christy & Voigt, 1994). And police have learned that even when they have been called to an angry domestic scene by someone involved in the situation, intervention in this kind of family violence is more dangerous than interference in a hostile interaction between two strangers.

For some very good reasons, then, bystanders may decide to hold back and avoid the risks that are sometimes associated with performing prosocial acts.

While the five steps are still fresh in your mind, you might want to review them by taking a close look at the *Ideas to Take with You* section on page 435.

Situational Factors That Enhance or Inhibit Helping: Attraction, Attributions, and Prosocial Models

Beyond the five decision-making steps that influence prosocial behavior, additional factors also have an effect on whether or not a bystander is likely to provide help. The most important of these include feelings of *attraction* toward the person needing help, the *attributions* that the bystander makes about the victim's responsibility for his or her plight, and the bystander's exposure to *prosocial models* either in the situation itself or in the past.

Helping Those You Like. In most of the examples of actual emergencies reported in the newspapers and of bogus emergencies devised by psychologists, the person in need is usually a total stranger. What if, instead of a stranger, the person being stabbed or the student having a seizure were a close friend of yours? Would that make you more inclined to go to their aid? The answer is obviously yes. An extreme example of the risks one will take for a loved one is provided by the case of a husband found guilty of manslaughter because he assisted in the suicide of his wife of thirty-three years. She had a form of Lou Gehrig's disease and repeatedly begged him to set her free from total paralysis and the mental deterioration and death that were certain to follow. The husband finally did as she wished, despite having to face up to fifteen years in prison as a consequence (Thompson, 1998).

Consider a less obvious situation, in which the victim is a stranger but some aspect of that person (similarity to yourself, physical appearance, and/or other factors discussed in Chapter 7) causes you to feel attraction. Would such characteristics have any effect on your prosocial tendencies? Again, the answer is yes. Whatever increases a bystander's attraction toward an individual increases the probability of a prosocial response if that individual needs help (Clark et al., 1987). Appearance provides a simple example: a physically attractive victim receives more help than an unattractive one (Benson, Karabenick, & Lerner, 1976). Also, because similarity almost always has a positive influence on attraction (see Chapter 7), you will not be surprised to learn that bystanders are more likely to help a similar victim than a dissimilar one (Dovidio & Morris, 1975; Hayden, Jackson, & Guydish, 1984).

We also noted in Chapter 7 that homosexuality is stigmatized by many people. On this basis, Shaw, Borough, and Fink (1994) predicted that a homosexual stranger in need would receive less help than a comparable heterosexual stranger. Using the "wrong number technique," a male research assistant, "Mike," dialed random telephone numbers from a pay phone, pretending to have a flat tire. He supposedly had used his last quarter to make this important call; so when he found that he had dialed a "wrong number," he could not tell his friend that he would arrive late. Because Mike had no more money for a phone call, he asked the person who answered please to make the call for him. He asked the stranger to call either his girlfriend ("Lisa") or his boyfriend

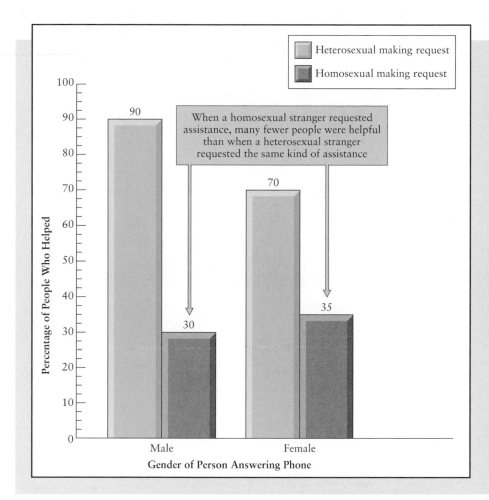

Figure 10.6

Do You Receive Help? It Depends on Your Sexual Orientation. When a male research assistant asked strangers to help him by making a telephone call to his girlfriend or to his boyfriend to say he would be late for their anniversary celebration, the odds of his receiving assistance depended on his perceived sexual orientation. He received twice as much help from women and three times as much help from men when he asked them to call his girlfriend as when he asked them to call his boyfriend. Apparently, a negative attitude about the person who needs help can inhibit prosocial behavior.

(*Source:* Based on data from Shaw, Borough, & Fink, 1994.)

("Rick") to say that Mike would be late for the celebration of their first anniversary together. The phone number provided by Mike was actually that of another research assistant, so the experimenters would know if the requested call was actually made. As shown in Figure 10.6, 70 percent of the women and 90 percent of the men who were called by Mike responded helpfully by telephoning his girlfriend, but only 35 percent of the women and 30 percent of the men called Mike's boyfriend. Clearly, random citizens were much more willing to assist a heterosexual stranger than a homosexual one.

Attributions of Victim Responsibility. If you were taking a walk and came across a man lying unconscious by the curb, your tendency to help or not help would be influenced by all of the factors we have discussed earlier—from the presence of other bystanders to interpersonal attraction. But let's add another element to this situation. Would you be more willing to help the man if his clothes were stained and torn and he clutched a wine bottle in his hand, or if his clothes were neat and clean and he had a bruise on his forehead? (See Figure 10.7 on page 408.) The odds are that you would be less strongly motivated to help the badly dressed man with the wine. Why? Despite the fact that both of these strangers seem to need assistance, you would be more likely to act if you did not make the attribution that the man was personally responsible for his difficulty. In general, if the victim is perceived to be the cause of the emergency, people are less motivated to help; in fact, they are likely to respond with disgust

Figure 10.7
Would You Help This Stranger? Why Not? One possible explanation is that you are making negative attributions as to the reason for his lying unconscious beside the curb. Do you believe that this man might be responsible for his difficulty?

and an unwillingness to help, because, after all, "the victim is to blame" (Weiner, 1980). Help is much more likely if the problem is believed to be caused by circumstances beyond the victim's control. Attributing blame to the victim is not always totally objective, however. For example, your reactions to the sleeping man will depend partly on your view of alcoholism. If you believe that alcoholism is a disease completely beyond the person's control, you will regard the man with a wine bottle as no different from a man who might appear to be injured.

Though you might assume that prosocial acts would be especially characteristic of religious individuals (Campbell, 1975), even religious individuals often refrain from helping because of attributions of victim responsibility. The crucial factor seems to be whether the victim poses a threat to the values of one's religion (Jackson & Esses, 1997). If an individual threatens your values, there is a strong tendency to make attributions of personal responsibility for his or her problems. If it's the victim's fault, there is no reason to provide help. The victim should engage in self-help or seek solutions elsewhere. To test these ideas, Jackson and Esses (1997) studied religious fundamentalists in Canada, individuals who believe in the absolute and literal truth of the teachings of a specific religion. The investigators found that the values of those high in religious fundamentalism were threatened by homosexuals and by single mothers. When gay men and unwed mothers were described as having problems with unemployment, the fundamentalists believed that such individuals were responsible for their own difficulties. They recommended that the unemployed persons change their lifestyles rather than relying on other people to provide help. But when fundamentalists were given unemployment information about individuals who did not threaten their values (e.g., Native Canadians and students), these victims were not perceived to be responsible for their predicament, and were seen as deserving help. The religious fundamentalists assumed these victims to be much more similar to themselves than were homosexuals or single mothers.

Is there a general tendency to attribute more personal responsibility to those different from ourselves than to those similar to ourselves? It seems so. Consider the crime of rape. Most sexual assaults are committed by men against women. As a result of this gender difference in perpetrators and victims, women are more likely than men to perceive themselves as similar to a woman who is attacked, while men are more likely than women to perceive themselves as similar to the male rapist (Bell, Kuriloff, & Lottes, 1994). Further, the more similar a woman feels to the female victim, the *less* she blames the victim for the attack. In contrast, the more similar a man feels to the male accused of rape, the *more* he blames the victim for what happened. Because of these differing attributions, women more than men are motivated to help those perceived as innocent rape victims, while men more than women are motivated to help those perceived to be falsely accused of the crime.

Despite the power of similarity demonstrated in such investigations, there are times when a victim who is very much like yourself can pose a threat. How could that be? The reason is that something bad happening to someone who matches you with respect to gender, age, race, and so forth, raises the unpleasant possibility that you too could become a victim. This is why it can be strangely comforting to discover that the victims of a plane crash or an earthquake or some other misfortune differ from you in race or ethnicity, age, nationality, economic status, or any other characteristic. It's a relief to find that this terrible thing happened to "them" and not to "us." Even if the victims *are* similar to you, your discomfort can be reduced if you misperceive them as being dissimilar to you in some way (Drout & Gaertner, 1994) or attribute their misfortune to something they did that you surely wouldn't be foolish enough to do. Blaming the victim is one way to restore your own sense of perceived control over events (Murrell & Jones, 1993), and this kind of defensive behavior can relieve your feelings of anxiety.

Thornton (1992) proposed that any encounter with a victim is threatening, because it reminds us that we too could be injured, robbed, or whatever. Two common and quite different cognitive mechanisms to defend against this threat are *repression* (avoiding or denying the problem) and *sensitization* (focusing on the problem and trying to control it) (Byrne, 1964). Thornton predicted that sensitizers would be more likely to blame the victim than repressors. His reasoning was that repressors can simply deny the seriousness of the threat, forget about it, or suppress any feelings of anxiety. In contrast, sensitizers are unable to block out the threat, so they make themselves feel better by blaming the victim and attributing the cause to that person's behavior (see the discussion of attributions in Chapter 2). In effect, the repressing individual denies and suppresses feelings of anxiety, while the sensitizing individual assumes that the victim is unlike himself or herself—"I would have avoided the terrible situation by being smarter or more careful."

To test his hypothesis about defense mechanisms and victim blame, Thornton first separated undergraduate women into repressors and sensitizers on the basis of a personality test. Then he asked the research participants to read an account of a young, unmarried female student at their university (in other words, someone like themselves). This student supposedly went to the campus library and talked to a young man she didn't know. He later intercepted her as she was returning to her dorm and forced her to have sexual intercourse. When asked about the victim's responsibility for the rape, the sensitizing women, as predicted, assigned more responsibility to the woman than did the repressing

Figure 10.8

Why Some May Be Inclined to Blame a Rape Victim. Undergraduate women were asked to read about a fellow student who had been raped. The threat of learning about an attack on a stranger similar to themselves was handled differently by participants who used repressing as opposed to sensitizing defense mechanisms. Repressors tended to handle the threat by denying and forgetting the incident. Sensitizers tended to handle the threat by blaming the victim and assuming that they themselves would behave in a safer and more intelligent fashion.

(*Source:* Based on data from Thornton, 1992.)

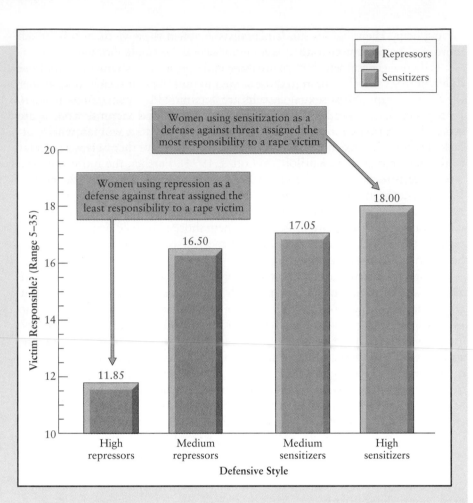

women, as shown in Figure 10.8. The sensitizers were more likely to say that she should not have talked to a stranger, shouldn't have walked alone at night, and so on. Four weeks later, the participants were asked to recall the scenario they had read. The repressors remembered fewer details of the rape story than was true for the sensitizers. When faced by a threat, repressors deal with their fears by forgetting, while sensitizers deal with their fears by distancing themselves from and blaming the victim.

Models for Prosocial Behavior: The Power of Positive Examples. If you are out shopping and notice someone collecting money for the homeless or for needy children, do you reach into your pocket or purse and make a contribution? Assume that you notice the person collecting money, agree that it is a worthy cause, believe that you are as responsible as anyone else for doing something to help, and have a couple of quarters that could be deposited in the bucket. Do you take that final step and contribute? Do you help? An important factor at this final step is whether you observe someone else make a donation. If others give money, you are more likely to do so (Macauley, 1970). Even the presence of coins and bills that were apparently contributed earlier in the day encourages you to make a charitable response. The various compliance techniques described in Chapter 9 are directly relevant to this type of helping behavior. In other words, collecting money for charity involves some of the same psychological processes as are involved in panhandling or selling a product or service.

In an emergency situation, we have said that the presence of fellow bystanders who fail to respond inhibits helpfulness. It is equally true, however, that the presence of a helpful bystander provides a strong *social model,* and the result is an increase in helping behavior among the remaining bystanders. An example of such modeling is provided by a field experiment in which a young woman (a research assistant) was parked just off of a road with a flat tire. Male motorists were much more inclined to stop and help this woman if they had earlier driven past a staged scene in which another woman with car trouble could be observed receiving assistance (Bryan & Test, 1967).

In addition to prosocial models in the real world, helpful models in the media also contribute to the creation of a social norm that encourages prosocial behavior. For example, the prosocial responsiveness of six-year-olds can be influenced by what they watch on TV (Sprafkin, Liebert, & Poulos, 1975). In a demonstration of the power of television, some youngsters were shown an episode of *Lassie* in which there was a rescue scene. Others saw a *Lassie* episode that did not have such a scene. A third group watched a humorous episode of *The Brady Bunch.* After watching one of these shows, the children played a game in which the winner could receive a prize. During the game they encountered a group of whining, unhappy puppies. Each child was faced with the choice between stopping the game in order to help the puppies (and thus losing the chance of getting the prize) or continuing the game in order to win (and thus ignoring the poor puppies). The children who had viewed the *Lassie* rescue episode spent much more time trying to comfort the little animals than did the children who watched either of the other two television programs.

Additional experiments have confirmed the influence of positive TV models on children (see Figure 10.9). For example, preschool children who watch prosocial programs such as *Mister Rogers' Neighborhood, Sesame Street,* or *Barney and Friends,* are much more apt to respond in a prosocial way than are children who do not watch such shows (Forge & Phemister, 1987). Altogether, it can be seen that appropriate models exert a very positive influence on prosocial behavior. But what about the effects of a very different type of role model

Figure 10.9

Prosocial Models for Children: Which Do You Prefer? Research consistently indicates that children are more likely to respond in a prosocial fashion after exposure to prosocial models in the media. If you were the victim in an emergency situation, would you prefer bystanders and potential helpers to model their attitudes and behavior on those of Big Bird or on those of Bart Simpson?

that is increasingly popular among children—the nonhelpful model? Examples of models that are not prosocial are contained in the television program *The Simpsons* and in the movie, *Beavis and Butt-head Do America*. These models, as amusing as they may be, demonstrate behavior quite different from that of Big Bird and Captain Kangaroo. Is it possible that the level of prosocial behavior among children is being negatively affected as a consequence? Could you design research that would test such a possibility?

Typically, the models represented by our parents are more powerful influences on our helping behavior than anything we see in the media. Psychiatrist Robert Coles (1997) emphasizes the importance of parents in shaping such behavior in his book *The Moral Intelligence of Children*. Coles suggests that the key is to teach children to be "good" or "kind" and to think about other people rather than just about themselves. Good children who are not self-centered are very likely to take the time and trouble to help others. Such moral intelligence isn't based on memorizing rules and regulations or learning abstract definitions. Instead, children learn by observing what their parents do and say in numerous situations. While experiences at any age are important, Cole believes that the elementary school years represent the critical time during which a child develops or fails to develop a conscience. Without appropriate models and appropriate experiences, children can easily grow into selfish and rude adolescents and then into equally unpleasant adults. You may even have known some people like that. Coles quotes novelist Henry James, whose nephew asked what he ought to do in his life. James replied, "Three things in human life are important. The first is to be kind. The second is to be kind. And the third is to be kind." Coles suggests that "being kind" reflects a strong commitment to help others rather than to hurt them. Not surprisingly, the end result of helpful behavior can benefit oneself as well as others.

Key Points

- In part because of *diffusion of responsibility,* the more bystanders present as witnesses to an emergency, the less likely is help to be given and the greater the delay before the help occurs.

- When faced with an emergency, a bystander must go through five crucial steps involving decisions that either inhibit or enhance the likelihood of a prosocial response. He or she must notice the emergency, correctly interpret what is occurring, assume responsibility for providing help, have the necessary skills and knowledge to help, and then actually decide to provide assistance.

- Prosocial acts occur most often when the bystander feels attraction toward the person in need and attributes the problem to circumstances beyond the victim's control.

- Exposure to prosocial models in real life and in the media has a positive effect on prosocial acts.

THE HELPERS AND THOSE WHO RECEIVE HELP

Up to this point, we have stressed the importance of the situation (for example, the number of bystanders) and of specific cognitive interpretations on the part of bystanders (for example, attributions of victim responsibility) in influencing prosocial behavior in emergencies. We now turn to other behavioral determinants. Some people are much more likely to help than others, and we will first examine the way in which affect and personality influence helping behavior. That is, variations in *emotional state* (mood and the affective changes that accompany good and bad events) have somewhat complex effects on prosocial responding. In addition, the likelihood of engaging in a prosocial act is influenced by *dispositional differences* (traits or personality characteristics). Next, we examine prosocial responses to ongoing problems that are not acute emergencies. Though emergencies were the focus of the initial research on prosocial behavior, people are often in need of long-term help that requires *volunteerism* and continued commitment to providing help. Then, we turn to the other major participants in prosocial interactions as we look at the *effects of helping on those who receive help*.

Helping As a Function of the Bystander's Emotional State

Offhand, it might seem that being in a good mood would make people more likely to help, while a bad mood would interfere with helping; and there is some evidence that supports such assumptions (Forgas, 1998a). Nevertheless, research indicates that the effects of emotional state on helping are someone more complicated than one might guess, because several additional factors must be taken into account (Salovey, Mayer, & Rosenhan, 1991). We will discuss these complications and then present a visual summary of the circumstances under which positive and negative emotions have the expected (or sometimes, unexpected) effects on prosocial behavior.

Positive Emotions and Their Effect on Prosocial Behavior. Children sometimes wait for the magic moment when their parents are in a good mood before they make a special request (see Figure 10.10). From a very early age, boys and girls assume that a happy parent is more likely to do something nice for them than is an unhappy parent. This is an accurate theory, at least under the right circumstances. For example, experimenters have put research participants in a positive mood by playing a comedy album (Wilson, 1981), arranging for them to find money in the coin return slot of a public phone (Isen & Levin, 1972), or asking them to spend time outdoors on a pleasant sunny day (Cunningham, 1979). In each instance, the resulting positive feelings led to prosocial behavior toward a stranger.

Figure 10.10

Ask for a Favor When the Mood Is Right. Children (and adults, too) believe that a request is more likely to be granted by someone in a good mood than by someone in a bad mood. Research supports this relationship between positive affect and a positive response to requests for help, but there are some specific factors that can complicate and alter this effect.

Our emotions are also influenced by what we smell, and billions of dollars are spent each year on products such as perfume, aftershave lotion, and air fresheners designed to make our lives more pleasant (Foderaro, 1988). If pleasant fragrances make us feel better, it follows that our behavior should also be affected (Baron, 1990c). In a study of prosocial influences, Baron and Thomley (1994) exposed participants to one of two pleasant odors (a lemon or a floral fragrance); the result was improved performance on a work task and increased willingness to volunteer time in response to a request for help. Another source of pleasant odors is less obvious—but have you ever been shopping in a mall and encountered enticing smells as you passed a bakery or a coffee shop? Baron (1997) found that such pleasant odors in our everyday environment not only result in pleasant affect but increase helpful behavior such as picking up a stranger's dropped pen or making change for a dollar. You can see that many quite different investigations consistently indicate the positive effect of positive emotions on prosocial behavior.

Additional factors complicate the relationship, however. Consider a somewhat different situation. What if a bystander is in a very positive mood when he or she encounters an ambiguous emergency situation? In unclear situations, a common reaction seems to be: Why spoil your happy feelings by assuming that someone needs help when you can just as easily assume that no real emergency exists? In effect, failure to interpret the event as a problem allows you to remain in a good mood. Further, what if the emergency is unmistakable, but helping would require you to do something unpleasant or even dangerous (Rosenhan, Salovey, & Hargis, 1981)? Research evidence indicates that you would prefer simply to say no and walk away from the problem. The fact that you feel good actually gives you a sense of power, including the power to refuse to be helpful. The general point is that whenever being helpful might spoil a person's good mood, a positive emotional state actually tends to result in *less* helpfulness (Isen, 1984).

In summary, if the need for help is very clear and does not involve negative consequences for the helper, positive emotions increase the probability of a prosocial response. If, however, the need for help is ambiguous or possible negative consequences are involved, positive emotions decrease the probability of a prosocial response.

Negative Emotions and Their Effects on Prosocial Behavior. Again, a common belief is that someone in a negative mood is less likely to be helpful; and again this effect has been confirmed by empirical research. When your affective state is negative through no fault of your own and you are focusing your attention on yourself and on how bad things are, you are unlikely to be helpful to someone in need (Amato, 1986; Rogers et al., 1982; Thompson, Cowan, & Rosenhan, 1980).

As you may have guessed, however, negative emotions can also have the opposite effect under specific conditions. For example, if the act of helping is something that seems likely to make you feel better, negative emotions tend to increase the occurrence of prosocial acts (Cialdini, Kenrick, & Bauman, 1982). This positive effect of negative emotions is most likely to occur *if your negative emotions are not extremely intense, if the emergency is clear, and if the act of helping is interesting and satisfying rather than difficult and unpleasant* (Berkowitz, 1987; Cunningham et al., 1990).

These mixed effects for positive and negative emotional states are summarized in Figure 10.11.

Dispositional Differences in Prosocial Responding

One question arises over and over again in research on prosocial behavior: Is any prosocial act truly unselfish? That is, does anyone ever provide help purely on the basis of **altruism** (an unselfish concern for the welfare of others), or is the

altruism • An unselfish concern for the welfare of others.

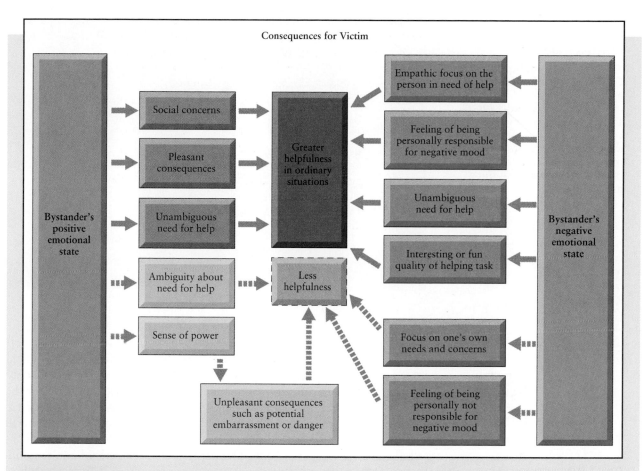

Consequences for Victim

Figure 10.11

Positive and Negative Emotions: Sometimes Enhancing, Sometimes Hindering Prosocial Behavior. Depending on several specific factors, a positive emotional state can either increase or decrease the likelihood of a prosocial response—and the same is true of a negative emotional state. This diagram summarizes the factors that influence these quite different effects based on emotions.

motivation always based at least in part on **egoism** (an exclusive concern with one's own personal welfare)? There is no way to provide a conclusive answer to that question, but you might want to consider how you would answer it.

Empathy: A Basic Requirement. Much of the interest in individual differences in helpfulness has concentrated on what appear to be the altruistic motives of bystanders based on **empathy** (Clary & Orenstein, 1991; Grusec, 1991). Empathy has been defined in several different ways, but two aspects are common to most definitions. There is an *affective* component: an empathetic person feels what another person is feeling (Darley, 1993). And there is a *cognitive* component: an empathetic person understands what another person is feeling and why (Azar, 1997). Thus, empathy means, to paraphrase President Clinton, that "I *feel* your pain and I *understand* your pain."

The affective component seems to be the essential component of empathy, and children as young as twelve months react in ways that indicate their tendency to feel distress in response to the distress of others (Brothers, 1990). This same characteristic is also observed in monkeys and apes (Ungerer et al., 1990) and perhaps among dogs and dolphins as well (Azar, 1997a), as suggested in

egoism • An exclusive concern with one's own personal needs and welfare rather than with the needs and welfare of others.

empathy • A complex affective and cognitive response to another's emotional distress; includes being able to feel the other person's distress, feeling sympathetic and attempting to solve the problem, and taking the other's perspective. One can be empathetic toward fictional characters as well as toward real-life victims.

Figure 10.12
The Biological Roots of Empathy. The affective aspects of empathy (responding with distress to the distress of others and indicating concern) can be observed in human infants, other primates, and perhaps in a few other mammals such as dogs and dolphins.

Figure 10.12. Evolutionary psychologists interpret such findings as indications of the biological underpinnings of prosocial behavior, probably stemming from its utility in the survival of various species. A second aspect of the affective component of empathy is *feeling sympathetic*—not only feeling another's pain but also expressing concern and attempting to do something to relieve the pain.

While the affective component of empathy is characteristic of adult and infant humans and a few other mammals, the cognitive component seems to be a uniquely human quality that develops only as we progress beyond infancy. One aspect of this cognitive component is the ability to consider the viewpoint of another person, sometimes referred to as *perspective taking*—being able "to put oneself in someone else's shoes" or, in a Native American expression, "walking a mile in my moccasins." To further expand the picture, social psychologists have identified three different types of perspective taking (Batson, Early, & Salvarani, 1997; Stotland, 1969). (1) You can imagine how the other person perceives an event and how he or she feels as a result; this is known as taking an "imagine other" perspective. (2) You can imagine how *you* would feel as a result; this is taking an "imagine self" perspective. Each of these two perspectives results in an increased emotional response to the person in need compared to the objective viewpoint of an uninvolved observer. The emotions are not the same for the two perspectives, however. Those who take the "imagine other" perspective experience relatively pure empathy that motivates altruistic behavior. The "imagine self" perspective also produces empathy, but it is accompanied by feelings of distress that arouse egoistic motives that can actually interfere with altruism. (3) A third type of perspective taking involves *fantasy*. This kind of perspective taking takes the form of empathy for a fictional character, as when someone reacts emotionally to the joys and sorrows of an imaginary person or animal. For example, it is not unusual to see children cry when Bambi discovers that his mother has died, or to see people of various ages cry when Jack, a fictional character played by Leonardo di Caprio, freezes to death in the North Atlantic beside the woman he loves after the *Titanic* has sunk beneath the waves.

How Does Empathy Develop, and Why Do People Differ in Empathy? Despite its biological roots, humans differ greatly in their ability to experience empathy,

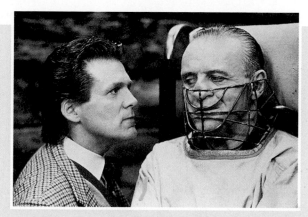

Figure 10.13

Empathic Ability: A Wide Range of Differences. The capacity for empathy plays a crucial role in differentiating those who engage in prosocial behavior from those who do not. Based on genetic differences and differences in their early experiences, humans demonstrate remarkable variability in this characteristic, as shown in the contrast between Princess Di and "Hannibal the Cannibal."

as illustrated in Figure 10.13. The range extends from highly empathetic individuals who consistently feel distress whenever someone else (real or fictional) is distressed to sociopaths who are indifferent to and unaffected by anyone's emotional state but their own.

Why do people differ so widely? Genetic differences in empathy were investigated by Davis, Luce, and Kraus (1994). They examined more than 800 sets of identical and nonidentical twins and found that inherited factors underlie the two affective aspects of empathy (personal distress and sympathetic concern). Genes account for about a third of the differences among people in affective empathy. Presumably, learning accounts for the remaining affective differences as well as for differences in the cognitive aspects of empathy, and children as young as two begin to show observable differences in empathy. A Canadian psychologist, Janet Strayer (quoted in Azar, 1997), suggests that we are all born with the biological and cognitive capacity for empathy. Depending on our experiences, this capacity can become a vital part of our self, or its development can be totally blocked.

What kind of experiences might be involved? Research has provided a few answers. The ability to feel empathy is enhanced by a mother's warmth and by clear and forceful messages from parents indicating how others are affected by hurtful behavior. It is beneficial to feel guilt about the harm that we cause, but not to feel guilt about bad events for which we are not to blame. Such distinctions must be learned. When parents are able to discuss emotions, their children's ability to empathize is enhanced (Azar, 1997a). A major inhibitor of empathic development is the parents' use of anger as the primary way to control their children.

Either because of genetic differences or because of different socialization experiences, women generally react with higher levels of empathy than men (Trobst, Collins, & Embree, 1994). Consistent with this finding are studies of non-Jewish Germans who helped rescue Jews from the Nazis in World War II. Gender differences in helping were common among these brave individuals, with a two-to-one ratio of female to male rescuers (Anderson, 1993).

Similarity to self also seems to play a part in empathy. To take an obvious example, humans are much more likely to respond empathetically to problems encountered by cuddly fellow mammals such as puppies, kittens, and baby seals than to similar problems encountered by noncuddly reptiles, fish, and insects. Even among fellow humans, we seem to respond most strongly to those like ourselves.

A special instance of empathy that has been investigated is the response of individuals to catastrophes experienced by total strangers (e.g., an earthquake, a terrorist attack, a long-lasting drought). Most people tend to respond with sympathy and, somewhat less often, with material assistance. Response to international disasters is determined in part by some of the same factors that influence response to individuals in need of help. Sympathy and assistance are more likely if the cause of the problem was something external and beyond the victims' control than if the victims have some responsibility for what happened (Russell & Mentzel, 1990). Also, the greater the emotional distress expressed by the victims, the greater the assistance (Sattler, Adams, & Watts, 1995). Similarity to self is also involved. For example, when freak tornadoes damaged homes in upstate New York, there was an outpouring of help in the form of money, supplies, and volunteers from nearby communities; but much worse natural disasters halfway around the world generated little interest. Also, people express greater empathy if they themselves have faced a similar source of stress (Batson et al., 1997). For example, those who have experienced hurricanes in the past are especially responsive to hurricane victims (Sattler et al., 1995); those who have experienced floods (e.g., in the Netherlands) are more responsive to flood victims (e.g., in Bangladesh) than those who have not (den Ouden & Russell, 1997).

Beyond Empathy: Additional Personality Factors in Prosocial Behavior. Among other dispositional factors, *need for approval* is an important aspect of helping behavior. Individuals high in this need respond best to rewards such as praise and similar signs of appreciation, and such reinforcement results in increased helpfulness on subsequent occasions (Deutsch & Lamberti, 1986). Also, people who are high in *interpersonal trust* engage in more prosocial acts than people who tend to distrust others (Cadenhead & Richman, 1996). Among children aged two to eight in child-care centers, the most empathetic and altruistic were also characterized as being *emotionally positive* and *sociable* (Miller & Jansen-op-de-Haar, 1997). Among schoolchildren, prosocial behavior is positively associated with *friendliness* and negatively associated with *aggression* and *emotional instability* (Menesini, 1997). A child is most likely to help others if he or she has developed a prosocial self-schema and if a connection is made between this aspect of the self and the specific situation in which help is needed (Froming, Nasby, & McManus, 1998).

Despite these and other positive findings, Knight and his colleagues (1994) point out that any single dispositional variable is only a weak predictor of actual behavior. One reason for this is that prosocial acts are determined by multiple factors and are thus likely to occur only when several different variables operate at the same time. Knight and his colleagues investigated the willingness of children aged six to eight to contribute money (out of $5.00 they were paid to be participants in the study) to a girl who had been badly burned. Substantial contributions were made only by those children who were high in sympathy (feelings of concern for the girl), high in comprehension of the feelings conveyed by facial expressions, and high in factual knowledge about money (e.g., the number of quarters in a dollar).

The importance of multiple variables has led some investigators to suggest that a combination of relevant factors constitutes what has been designated as an *altruistic personality* (Bierhoff, Klein, & Kramp, 1991). In order to specify the components of an altruistic personality, these investigators selected several personality variables that had previously been found to predict prosocial behavior and then tested their predictive power by comparing people who helped with people who failed to help in actual real-life emergencies. The participants were matched for gender, age, and social class, but they differed in their prosocial responsiveness. All had been at the scene of an accident, but some had administered first aid before an ambulance arrived on the scene (the altruistic group) and some had not provided any help (the nonaltruistic group). These two groups of bystanders were found to differ on five personality characteristics; and, interestingly enough, the same five personality characteristics were found among people throughout Europe who were active in the 1940s in rescuing Jews from Nazi persecution (Oliner & Oliner, 1988). The investigators identified the five key variables of the **altruistic personality** as follows.

1. *Empathy*, as you might expect, is higher in those who helped than in those who did not. The most altruistic participants also described themselves as responsible, socialized, conforming, tolerant, self-controlled, and wanting to make a good impression.

2. *Belief in a just world* was also characteristic. That is, helpful people perceive the world as a fair and predictable place in which good behavior is rewarded and bad behavior punished. This belief leads to the conclusion that not only is helping those in need the right thing to do, but the person who helps will actually benefit from doing so.

3. *Social responsibility* was high among those who offered assistance. They expressed the belief that each person is responsible for doing his or her best to help those in need.

4. *Internal locus of control* was another important variable. This is an individual's belief that he or she can choose to behave in ways that maximize good outcomes and minimize bad ones, and helpers tend to be high on this dimension. In contrast, individuals with an external locus of control believe that what they do is irrelevant because they are at the mercy of luck, fate, the people who run things, and other uncontrollable factors.

5. *Low egocentrism* was the fifth component of the altruistic personality. People who failed to help were relatively egocentric and tended to be self-absorbed and competitive.

Given not only these five but the many additional personality characteristics that have been found to influence prosocial behavior, it is probably reasonable to conceptualize the altruistic personality as consisting of many dispositional variables. No investigation to date has included all of these characteristics in a single study, but presumably charting such a combination of determinants would enhance our ability to predict who would and would not come to the aid of a stranger in distress.

Before leaving the topic of response to emergencies, let's look at a newspaper story about an actual emergency in which a victim was badly in need of help (Brown, 1995). As you read this *Beyond the Headlines* section, imagine yourself in the bystander's place and try to identify some of the factors that may have been operating to influence what this man did. Consider the five steps in the decision-making process, the geographic setting, situational factors, the emotional state of the bystander, and what dispositional variables might have been involved.

altruistic personality • A combination of dispositional variables that influences prosocial behavior. Among the many components are empathy, belief in a just world, acceptance of social responsibility, the assumption of an internal locus of control, and several others.

Beyond the Headlines:
As Social Psychologists See It
Ordinary People Sometimes Do Extraordinary Things

CLAVERACK GIRL'S SAVIOR SAYS
GOD MADE HIM A HERO

Albany *Times Union*, September 6, 1995—Chatham, N.Y.—A 39-year-old man was enjoying a Labor Day picnic at his parents' home when he heard the sounds of a car skidding and then what seemed to be a metallic crash.

This man immediately jumped up from the peaceful picnic with his family and soon discovered that the noise had been made by a car wreck. He saw that the automobile was in flames, but he rushed to the aid of a 7-year-old girl who was unable to get out of her seat. The car's driver was her 50-year-old grandmother, who died in the accident.

"I ran down the driveway. As soon as I could see the car it was upside down. It was burning pretty good at that point," the hero said Tuesday. "My first instinct was to go the other way. The little girl was standing next to the car. She couldn't get away from it, because the seat belt was around her and still attached to the car. I heard someone in the distance yelling for her to get away from the burning auto, but she wasn't able to do that.

"I went over and kind of put one arm around her, grabbed the seat belt and gave it a good yank. By the grace of God, it broke free. I just took the little girl over by the driveway and ended up carrying her down the road to the police. She was crying and calling for her mommy and grammy. I figured the Lord had me there for a reason, and there wasn't much more I could do but go to help her."

The hero has four children of his own. He burned his hand and the paramedics told him that his injuries were worse than the little girl's. Both were treated in the Columbia-Greene Medical Center and released.

Why did this man engage in an act of heroism to save a little girl he didn't know? Remember that he said his first instinct was "to go the other way." Instead, he did something that took a great deal of courage, as shown in Figure 10.14. Why did he feel that "there wasn't much more I could do but go to help her"?

As you may have noticed, newspaper stories about how people react to emergencies tend to represent one of two extremes. When bystanders fail to act, the emphasis is on the lack of concern among uncaring and indifferent people in today's society. When a bystander does act, the emphasis is on the way in which any ordinary citizen can suddenly become a hero. Rather than puzzling about the mystery of apathy versus heroism, social psychologists attempt to identify what it is about the situation and (to some extent) what it is about some individuals that accounts for these quite different behavioral extremes.

On the basis of the information provided in this chapter, can you suggest why the apartment dwellers did not do anything to help Kitty Genovese when she was under attack, whereas the man at the family picnic rushed to save a child trapped next to a burning car? Keep these factors in mind in the future when you encounter emergency situations or read about such events.

Figure 10.14
Providing Help Can Be Dangerous. Responding to some emergencies is a high-risk activity. A man saved a little girl who was trapped next to the burning wreckage of her grandmother's car. This heroic prosocial act carried the risk of injury and even death to the person who provided help.

Volunteering: Motivations for Long-Term Help

Helping in response to either personal emergencies or international disasters tends to be a one-time event that occurs within a brief time period. Quite different helping behavior is required when someone (whether a relative, friend, or stranger) has a chronic, continuing problem that requires help (Williamson & Schulz, 1995). Anyone who volunteers to provide assistance must commit his or her time, special skills, and/or money over an extended period of time. In the United States alone, almost one hundred million adults volunteer 20.5 billion hours each year, averaging 4.2 hours of prosocial activity each week (Moore, 1993). It is reasonable to assume that, around the world, a very large number of people are voluntarily spending an enormous amount of time engaging in prosocial activity.

The five steps to a prosocial response to an acute emergency also apply to volunteering one's time and effort. In order to help the homeless, for example, you must become aware of the problem (usually through the news media), interpret the situation accurately (they need food, shelter, and medical supplies), assume responsibility to provide help, decide on a course of action that is possible for you (volunteering your time or donating money), and then actually respond. Let's consider some of the factors that determine that crucial last step.

Volunteering on the Basis of a Variety of Motives. An example of a continuing problem that requires a time-consuming commitment to help is the epidemic of HIV infections that are the first step toward the development of AIDS. In 1981 the Centers for Disease Control first issued reports on that then unknown disease (see Chapter 8). Despite great progress, there is still no effective way to immunize against HIV infections or to cure the disease. As a result, a large number of people throughout the world continue to develop AIDS, and they require assistance as they await death. Volunteers can provide emotional support, and they can help with household chores and transportation. In addition, they can staff hot lines and become political activists in the cause of prevention and/or research funding, and so on.

Table 10.1

Why Volunteer? People who volunteer to help in the AIDS epidemic do so for different reasons. The same prosocial act can satisfy a variety of motives. These motives not only influence the initial decision to volunteer, but help determine who will remain active in this work over the long term. Those who continue (versus those who drop out) are more likely to be motivated by "self-centered" needs such as the desire to increase understanding, to enhance self-esteem, and to further their personal development.

Specific Motivation for Volunteering to Help in AIDS Epidemic	Example of Reason Given by Volunteer
Desire to increase one's understanding	"Because I want to learn how people cope with AIDS."
Enhancement of one's self-esteem	"I want to feel better about myself."
Personal development	"I want to challenge myself and test my skills."
Community concern	"Because of my concern and worry about the gay community."
Personal values	"Because of my humanitarian obligation to help others."

(*Source:* Based on data from Omoto & Snyder, 1995; Snyder & Omoto, 1992a.)

There are many reasons not to help, of course. As we discussed earlier, there is little sympathy or assistance when the victim is perceived to be responsible for his or her difficulty—"They have only themselves to blame." Such reasoning is very often applied to the sexual practices or the intravenous drug use that put people at risk for HIV infection in the first place. As Pullium (1993) found, there is much less empathy for and willingness to help an AIDS patient who is homosexual or who shares needles when injecting drugs than someone who contracted the disease from a blood transfusion and is thus an "innocent victim." Even if potential volunteers don't react by pointing the finger of blame, they nevertheless may feel that the costs of working with such patients are too high. Not only is AIDS frightening to many people, but there are those who worry about acquiring a stigma by association (see Chapter 7) if they interact with AIDS patients.

So, given the various negatives, a person must be strongly motivated to volunteer help with this particular problem. Snyder and Omoto (1992a, 1992b) have identified five basic motives that lead volunteers to work with AIDS patients. As summarized in Table 10.1, the decision to volunteer can be based on personal values, the need to understand the phenomenon, concern about the community, the desire for personal development, and/or a need to enhance one's self-esteem. In other words, volunteers may work side by side doing exactly the same job, but for quite different reasons.

A practical implication of identifying these motivational differences is that those who recruit volunteers will be most successful when they stress multiple reasons to become involved instead of just a single reason. Alternatively, the persuasive appeal of messages can be enhanced if the recruitment message is matched to the recipient's motivation (Clary et al., 1998).

Note also that recruitment is not the only issue in volunteer work; retention is actually a more difficult problem (Omoto & Snyder, 1995). About half of those who volunteer quit within twelve months. Why? Once again, motivational differences are crucial. People who continue working as volunteers for at least two and a half years tend to be motivated by the need to gain self-understanding, enhance self-esteem, and help their own personal development. These seemingly "selfish" needs are more important motivators of continuation as a volunteer than the seemingly "selfless" needs centering on community concern and the value of helping others.

Volunteering As a Matter of Having an Altruistic Personality. As you might expect from the previous discussion of other types of prosocial behavior, volunteerism of various kinds also is influenced by dispositional differences. For example, volunteer behavior is related to individual differences in empathy (Penner & Finkelstein, 1998) and in locus of control (Guagnano, 1995).

A somewhat different approach to understanding individual differences in volunteering is offered by McAdams and his colleagues (1997). They define **generativity** as an adult's interest in and commitment to the well-being of future generations. People high in generativity can show their concern by becoming parents, by teaching others, or by engaging in acts that will have positive effects beyond their own lifetimes.

Men and women in modern societies are able to find some semblance of unity and purpose in their lives by constructing stories about themselves. Each of us can describe a personal past, present, and future that constitutes a meaningful (even if inaccurate) self-portrait. Highly generative adults are the ones most likely to construct *commitment stories* that make up an important part of their self-concepts (see Chapter 5). The typical commitment story of a generative person depicts a life history in which the individual remembers an enjoyable early family experience, but is also exposed to suffering at an early age; is guided through life by a clear and stable personal ideology; succeeds in transforming bad events into good outcomes; and attempts to set prosocial goals that benefit society.

Generative adults construct commitment stories about their lives, and they believe that people need to care for others. They possess enduring moral values that give purpose and meaning to their lives, perceive bad events as opportunities to create good outcomes, and make an effort to contribute to the progressive development of a better society. Figure 10.15 on page 424 lists traits or dispositions—including generativity—that characterize altruistic individuals.

Who Receives Help, and How Do People React to Being Helped?

Most prosocial research has been focused on those individuals who provide or fail to provide help. We will now turn briefly to what is known about those who are in need of assistance. Specifically, we will discuss the effect of *gender* on the likelihood of receiving help, the relevance of *asking for help,* and *how people react to receiving help.*

Gender As a Factor in Who Receives Help. Though it sounds like a sexist stereotype, research has consistently shown that men are very likely to provide help to women (Latané & Dabbs, 1975; Piliavin & Unger, 1985). How can such findings be explained? Helpful men are puzzling, because adult women are higher in empathy than men, and the same is true for young girls versus young boys (Shigetomi, Hartmann, & Gelfand, 1981).

One possibility lies in Step 4 of the decision-making model. Many emergency situations require certain skills and knowledge (for example, changing a flat tire or determining what is wrong with an automobile engine) or a level of strength and special training (for example, overpowering an attacker or ripping a seat belt out of a car) that have traditionally been associated with men rather than women. Perhaps it is for this reason that a female motorist in distress by

generativity • An adult's concern for and commitment to the well-being of future generations.

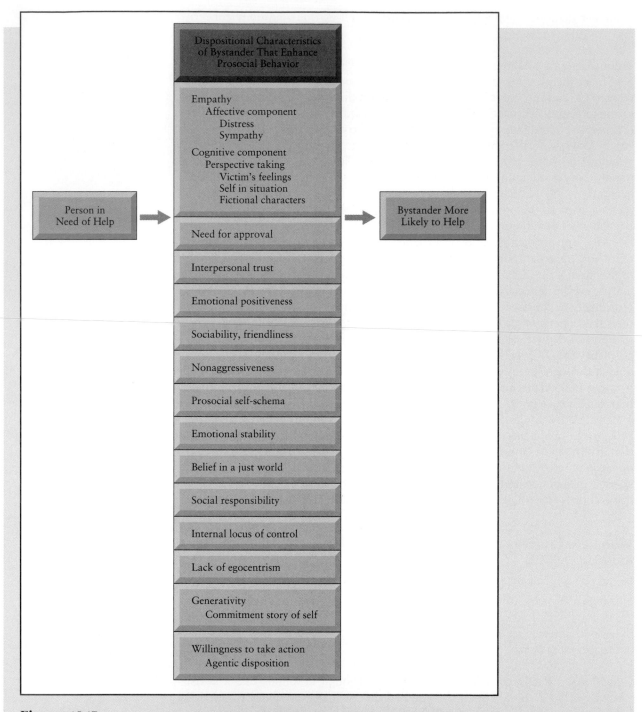

Figure 10.15

The Altruistic Personality: A Combination of Characteristics. People obviously differ in their prosocial tendencies, and investigators have identified numerous personality differences between those who help and those who don't. Shown here are several of the relevant traits (or dispositions) that enhance or inhibit prosocial responsiveness.

the side of the road (see Figure 10.16) receives more offers of assistance than a male or a male–female couple in the same predicament (Pomazal & Clore, 1973; Snyder, Grether, & Keller, 1974). Also, the motorists who stop to provide help are most often young males who are driving alone.

Figure 10.16
Helping a Lady in Distress: What Motivates Helpful Males? In many situations, women are more likely to receive help than either men or couples, and men are more likely to provide help than women. Because attractive women receive more help than unattractive ones, and because men exposed to erotic stimuli are more helpful to women than men not exposed to such stimuli, it seems reasonable to suggest that the motivation for male helpfulness in these instances is sometimes based on sexual attraction rather than on altruism.

The motivation for providing such help may not be entirely prosocial or altruistic, however. For one thing, men stop to help an attractive woman more frequently than to help an unattractive one (West & Brown, 1975). It seems possible, then, that the motivation is primarily romantic or sexual. To test this hypothesis, Przybyla (1985) conducted a laboratory experiment in which undergraduate men were shown either an arousing erotic videotape or a tape that was nonarousing and nonerotic. The men who had just seen the erotic tape were more helpful than men in the control group when a female research assistant "accidentally" knocked over a stack of papers. The helpful males also spent more time (six minutes) helping this female stranger than other males spent helping a male assistant who had the same problem with dropped papers (thirty seconds). Altogether, the most help was provided by sexually aroused males in response to a female stranger. Note also that viewing or not viewing an erotic tape had no effect on the helping behavior of women in response to representatives of either gender. These various findings strongly suggest the possibility that males may assist females, at least in part, on the basis of sexual motivation.

Asking for Help. We have pointed out that uncertainty about what is happening in an emergency and about what to do can inhibit the helpfulness of bystanders. Such ambiguity results in the tendency to do nothing until there is clarification. The most direct and most effective way for the victim to reduce ambiguity is to *ask for help* in very clear terms. If possible, the person in need would do well to make a specific request such as "Call the police" or "Help me get back on my feet." But even just saying "Help" is more effective than saying nothing.

It may sound obvious (and easy) to ask for help, but those in need often fail to do so for a variety of reasons. For example, shy men and women are reluctant to seek help from a member of the other gender (DePaulo et al., 1989). Several demographic factors are also associated with differences in requesting assistance. Asking for help is more characteristic of women than of men, of young adults than of the elderly, and of those whose socioeconomic status is high than of those whose status is low (Nadler, 1991). The decision to seek help is also influenced by stereotypes associated with potential helpers (see Chapter 6). If you needed help with a mathematical problem, would you be more likely to turn to a stranger whose last name was Riley or whose name was Nakamura? White college students holding positive stereotypes about the quantitative skills of Asians were found to request help on a math test from an Asian American student more frequently than from a fellow white student (Bogart, 1998).

Bystanders are not the only ones worried about doing the wrong thing and being evaluated negatively as a consequence. The victim has the same worries. In a crisis you may need help, but you don't want to "overreact." Victims often sense that if they react emotionally to an emergency, this response may be perceived as inappropriate and indicative of character faults (Yates, 1992). With some kinds of problems, many people choose the anonymity of a call-in radio program with millions of listeners in preference to discussing the same problem face to face (Raviv, 1993). People very much want to avoid making fools of themselves when others can see them and know who they are. When you tune in to a televised talk show and see people scream and fight and threaten to bash each other with chairs, you can assume that they are motivated by money and a few minutes of "fame" rather than by a desire to deal honestly with such problems as "my mother stole my boyfriend."

In a more general sense, people fear that they will be perceived as incompetent if they need to request aid (DePaulo & Fisher, 1980). Being dependent on others for anything can be stigmatizing, especially in Western cultures (Nadler, 1993). As one example, when a seemingly prosocial individual provides *too much* help to someone who is having difficulty with something, the result can be negative. Often without meaning to, the overeager helper makes it appear that the person receiving the help is less bright or less skilled (Gilbert & Silvera, 1996). You may have observed a child respond angrily to a too-helpful adult—"Let me do it myself!" You may even have reacted the same way yourself.

How Does It Feel to Receive Help? You're in need of help, and someone comes along to provide assistance. You react with totally positive emotions, and you are overflowing with gratitude, right? No. In fact, that is very often not the reaction at all. Instead, not only may the person who is helped experience negative emotions; there is also the tendency to resent the one who helped. As suggested above, a person who needs help is likely to feel uncomfortable, dependent, and incompetent. Being helped can lower self-esteem (see Chapter 5), especially if the helper is a friend or someone similar to you in age, education, and so on. (DePaulo et al., 1981; Nadler, Fisher, & Itzhak, 1983). When self-esteem is threatened, the resulting negative affect creates feelings of dislike toward the good Samaritan (see Chapter 7). An equally negative response tends to occur when a member of a stigmatized group (for example, a black student) receives unsolicited help from a member of a nonstigmatized group (for example, a white student). Such help is often perceived as an insult—a putdown (Schneider et al., 1996).

Help from a sibling can be especially unpleasant, and help from a younger brother is much worse than help from an older sister (Searcy & Eisenberg, 1992). Help from a nonsibling or a dissimilar stranger is relatively nonthreatening, however, so the affective response is much more positive (Cook & Pelfry, 1985). In the automobile incident on the icy road (described at the beginning of this chapter), I felt a purely positive reaction to the elderly stranger who helped me. If, however, assistance had been given by a fellow social psychologist successfully driving down the hill in a four-wheel-drive vehicle, I might well have been upset and embarrassed about my comparative lack of driving skill.

Whenever a person responds negatively to having received help, there is also a positive aspect that is not obvious. When being helped is sufficiently unpleasant that the person wants to avoid appearing incompetent again, he or she is motivated to engage in self-help in the future (Fisher, Nadler, & Whitcher-Alagna, 1982; Lehman et al., 1995). Among other benefits, this motivation can reduce feeling dependent on helpers (Daubman, 1995). In contrast, help that arouses positive feelings fails to motivate future self-help. The various reactions are summarized in Figure 10.17.

Among the implications of such motivational effects is that help for major problems (e.g., financial difficulties) that comes from friends family, and neighbors can result in feelings of inadequacy and resentment but can also motivate the individual to avoid future problems. If, in contrast, the help comes from strangers such as employees in a government agency, the person in need retains a positive self-image ("I was entitled to that check") and feels appreciative of the help—but remains totally unmotivated to avoid future crises of the same type.

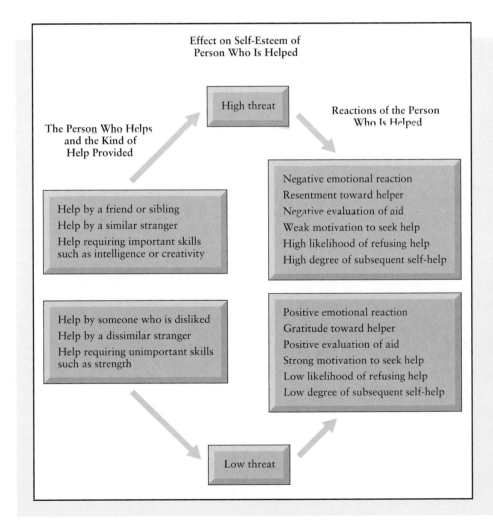

Figure 10.17
Reactions to Receiving Help: It Depends. A person who receives help sometimes responds negatively and sometimes positively. It is threatening to be helped by a friend or by a stranger similar to oneself, especially when the help involves important skills. The effect on the person receiving assistance is lowered self-esteem and negative affect—but a stronger motivation to attempt self-help in the future. Receiving help from a stranger who is dissimilar to oneself, especially when the help involves unimportant skills, is not threatening, does not lower self-esteem, and arouses positive affect—but leads to less self-help in the future.

(*Source:* Based on information in Fisher, Nadler, & Whitcher-Alagna, 1982.)

> ### *Key Points*
>
> - Positive and negative emotional states can either enhance or inhibit *prosocial behavior*, depending on specific factors in the situation, in the individual, and in the nature of the required assistance.
> - Individual differences in altruistic behavior are based in large part on *empathy*, a complex response that includes both affective and cognitive components. The extent to which a person is able to respond with empathy depends on both genetic and environmental factors.
> - The *altruistic personality* consists of empathy plus other relevant dispositional variables. Combined, such multiple determinants affect prosocial behavior more than does any one of them in isolation.
> - People volunteer to provide help on a long-term basis on the basis of several quite different motives, dispositional variables, and levels of generativity.
> - Help is given by men to women more often than vice versa.
> - Asking for help reduces ambiguity and increases the probability of receiving help.
> - With high helper–victim similarity, the person who is helped tends to react negatively and to feel incompetent, to experience decreased self-esteem, and to resent the helper, but such negative feelings also tend to motivate self-help in the future.

EXPLAINING PROSOCIAL BEHAVIOR: WHY DO PEOPLE HELP?

Based on the discussion so far, it is obvious that many factors influence whether prosocial behavior will or will not occur: aspects of the situation, what other people do and say, dispositional differences among potential helpers, and characteristics of the person in need of help. We now turn to a different sort of question about prosocial responses—not who will help under what circumstances, but rather why anyone would ever engage in such behavior. In other words, what motivates a prosocial act? Many theories have been formulated, but most rest on the familiar assumption that people attempt to maximize rewards and minimize punishments.

Existing theories tend to stress either relatively selfish or relatively unselfish motives for behaving in a prosocial manner (Campbell & Specht, 1985). As you might guess, people tend to attribute their own helpful behavior to unselfish motives, usually suggesting basic moral values—"It was the right thing to do"; "That was the way my parents raised me"; "The Lord had me there for a reason." When, however, the help is provided by someone else, an observer is equally likely to attribute either unselfish motives or selfish ones—"She was hoping for a reward" or "He wanted the glory of being a hero" (Doherty, Weigold, & Schlenker, 1990). Even those who spend their lives trying to solve such problems as global warming are often viewed as acting in terms of their own long-run self-interest (J. Baron, 1997). The ultimate example of such attributions is to say that the person who spends his or her life doing good deeds is doing so only because of the prospect of being rewarded by going to heaven.

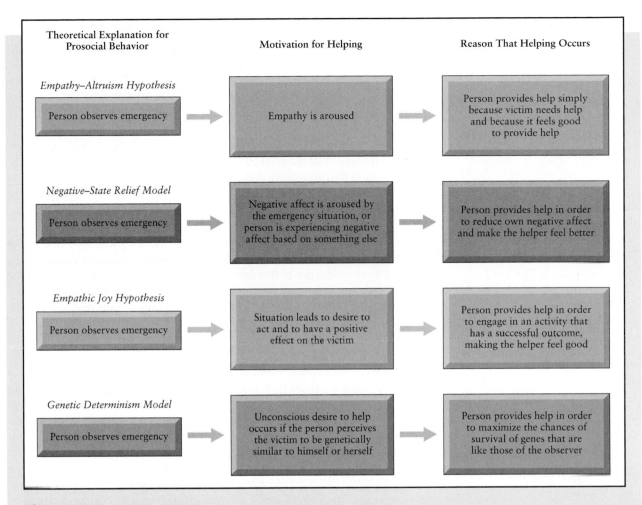

Figure 10.18

What Motivates Helping Behavior? Four major explanations of the motivation underlying prosocial behavior are shown here. The *empathy–altruism hypothesis* proposes that people experience feelings of empathy when they encounter someone who needs help, and they provide the necessary assistance because such behavior is satisfying. The *negative–state relief model* suggests that people experience unpleasant feelings when they encounter someone in need, and they provide assistance because doing so relieves their own negative affective state. The *empathic joy hypothesis* indicates that people help in order to achieve success by solving someone else's problem, and that this accomplishment is rewarding. The *genetic determinism model* is based on the proposition that prosocial behavioral tendencies occur because they have maximized reproductive success over the millennia and thus made it possible to pass on prosocial genes to future generations. In this model, similarity between victim and bystander increases the probability that help will be given because similarity between two individuals is assumed to be associated with genetic overlap.

It's possible, then, to interpret all prosocial behavior as selfish and self-centered. We prefer to take the position that prosocial behavior is often based in part on selfish and in part on unselfish motives.

We now turn to the four major theories dealing with prosocial motivation. These formulations are summarized in Figure 10.18, and you might find it helpful to take a good look at that summary information before you read the following discussion.

Empathy–Altruism: It Feels Good to Help Those in Need

Perhaps the least selfish explanation of prosocial behavior is that empathetic people help others because "it feels good to do good." On this underlying assumption, Batson and his colleagues (1981) proposed the **empathy–altruism hypothesis.** They suggest that at least some prosocial behavior is motivated solely by the unselfish desire to help someone in need (Batson & Oleson, 1991). This motivation to help can be sufficiently strong that the individual who provides help is willing to engage in unpleasant, dangerous, and even life-threatening activity (Batson, Batson, et al., 1995). The feelings of compassion may be sufficiently strong that they outweigh all other considerations (Batson, Klein, et al., 1995). The powerful feeling of empathy provides validating evidence to the individual that he or she must *truly value* the other person's welfare (Batson, Turk, et al., 1995).

To test this altruistic view of helping behavior, Batson and his colleagues devised an experimental procedure in which they aroused a bystander's empathy by describing a victim and the bystander as being either similar or dissimilar (see Chapter 7). The bystander was then presented with an opportunity to be helpful (Batson et al., 1983; Toi & Batson, 1982). Each undergraduate research participant was given the role of "observer" who watched a "fellow student" on a TV monitor as she performed a task while (supposedly) receiving random electric shocks. The student who appeared to be getting shocked was in fact a research assistant recorded on videotape. After the task was under way, the assistant said that she was in pain and confided that as a child she had had a traumatic experience with electricity. She agreed to continue if necessary, but the experimenter asked whether the observer would be willing to trade places with her or whether they should simply discontinue the experiment. When empathy was low (dissimilar victim and participant), the participants preferred to end the experiment rather than engage in a painful prosocial act. When empathy was high (similar victim and participant), the participants agreed to take the victim's place and receive the shocks. It appears that this altruistic act was motivated solely by empathic concern for the victim. Further, other research indicates that when empathy-based helping is unsuccessful, the helper's mood becomes more negative (Batson & Weeks, 1996). In other words, high empathy not only leads to prosocial behavior because it feels good, but an unsuccessful attempt to provide help feels bad.

Arguing against this unselfish view of prosocial behavior, Cialdini and his colleagues (1997) agreed that empathy leads to altruistic behavior but argued that this depends on the participant's perceiving an overlap between self and other. If another person is perceived as overlapping with oneself—in effect, forms part of one's own self-concept—then a helpful participant is simply helping himself or herself. These investigators presented evidence that without this feeling of oneness, empathic concern does *not* increase helping. Batson and his colleagues (1997) responded with additional evidence indicating that the perception of overlapping is *not* necessary—empathy leads to helping even in the absence of oneness.

Despite these conceptual disagreements, there is clearly evidence that feelings of empathy lead to altruistic behavior.

Do you suppose that most people *like* to have their empathy aroused? Given a choice, would people want to receive information that aroused their empathy level? Apparently, such information is aversive (people seek to avoid it) if it means becoming motivated to engage in something difficult. Shaw, Batson, and Todd (1994) asked college students to take part in a new program to help a homeless man. The cost of helping was either low (spending an hour preparing letters that requested donations) or high (interacting with the homeless man

empathy–altruism hypothesis • The proposal that prosocial behavior is motivated solely by the desire to help someone in need.

himself for more than an hour on three separate occasions). After learning about the task (low cost or high cost), the students could choose between receiving factual information about the man or receiving an emotional, empathy-arousing message about the difficulties he was having. When the cost of helping was low, most students wanted to hear the emotional message. When the cost of helping was high, however, most wanted to hear the informational message. In other words, they seemed to engage in *empathy avoidance* in order not to become motivated to provide high-cost helping.

Empathy plays still another role in helping behavior. A major problem that arises when resources are limited is whether to allocate aid equally to all members of a group in need or only to specific individuals in the group. In the interest of the common good, it seems reasonable to distribute resources equally. In fact, Batson and his colleagues (1999) provide evidence that the group as a whole is neglected if the helper is motivated either by egoism (first you "take care of number one") or by empathy directed toward one individual in the group ("selective altruism" for the one who engages your emotions). Under certain circumstances, then, either egoism or altruism can function as threats to the common good. Though the effect of egoism is not surprising, that of selective altruism is. This finding brings to mind the advertisements seeking financial sponsorship for a specific child in need. This approch seems to be based on a realization that it is more difficult to generate helpfulness for thousands of hungry children than to do so for a specific child whose name and photograph you will receive. Further, when one's decision to help is made public, rather than kept private, the effect of egoism is inhibited, but not the effect of selective altruism.

Negative-State Relief: It Reduces One's Negative Affect to Relieve a Stressful Situation

Another theoretical possibility is that people sometimes help primarily because they are in a bad mood and want to make themselves feel better, a formulation known as the **negative-state relief model** (Cialdini, Baumann, & Kenrick, 1981). Prosocial behavior is thus viewed as a kind of self-help project to reduce one's negative affect.

Note that it doesn't matter whether the observer's negative emotions have been aroused before the emergency occurred or are aroused by the emergency itself. Whether you are upset about a bad grade or about seeing an injured stranger, you may engage in a prosocial act simply to make yourself feel better (Fultz, Schaller, & Cialdini, 1988).

In a test of this proposed model, Cialdini and his colleagues (1987) exposed research participants to a victim, and the participants reported feeling both empathy for the victim and sadness about the situation. When the experimenters separated these two emotions, sadness alone led to increased helping, but empathy alone did not. Such research suggests that, in some situations at least, the desire to relieve one's own negative feelings is the primary reason for providing assistance to someone else. In such instances, empathy is not a crucial component of prosocial behavior.

Empathic Joy: Successful Helping As a Way to Arouse Positive Affect

In general terms, it feels good to have a positive impact on other people (see Figure 10.19 on page 432). Smith, Keating, and Stotland (1989) offered the **empathic joy hypothesis** as yet another explanation of helping behavior.

negative-state relief model
• The proposal that prosocial behavior is motivated by the bystander's desire to reduce his or her own uncomfortable negative emotions.

empathic joy hypothesis •
The proposal that prosocial behavior is motivated by the positive emotion a helper anticipates experiencing as a result of having a beneficial impact on the life of someone in need.

Figure 10.19

It Feels Good to Make Someone Else Feel Good. The *empathic joy hypothesis* rests on the general truth that it is pleasant to have a positive impact on other people. Such an accomplishment can be attained by means of a gift (as in this advertisement), a compliment, or a prosocial act.

genetic determinism model
• The proposal that prosocial behavior is driven by genetic attributes that evolved because they enhanced reproductive success and thus the probability that individuals would be able to transmit their genes to subsequent generations.

Basically, the helper responds because he or she anticipates feeling good about accomplishing something.

One implication of this hypothesis is that it is crucial for the person who helps to know that his or her actions have a positive impact on the victim. That is, if helping were based purely on empathy, feedback about success would be irrelevant. Smith, Keating, and Stotland designed an experiment in which the research participants watched a videotape of a female student who expressed feelings of isolation and stress. In the tape, the student indicated that she might be withdrawing from college. After watching this tape, the viewers were given the opportunity to offer advice. Some were told they would receive feedback about the effectiveness of their advice, and others were told that they would receive no further information about what this women decided to do. The experiments aroused empathy in some participants by stressing their similarity to the woman on the tape; for other participants, lack of empathy was created by dissimilarity information. Under these conditions, empathy alone was not enough to produce prosocial behavior; knowledge of one's impact was also required.

In each of these three theoretical models, affect is all-important. That is, prosocial behavior occurs on the basis of an increase in positive affect or a decrease in negative affect. All three hypotheses rest on the assumption that people engage in helpful behavior because it makes them feel better. The positive emotion that accompanies prosocial acts is sometimes labeled *helper's high*—a feeling of calmness, self-worth, and warmth (Luks, 1988). In fact, it feels so good to be helpful that if a victim refuses help when it is offered, the frustrated prosocial individual sometimes becomes angry at the victim (Cheuk & Rosen, 1992).

Genetic Determinism: Helping Maximizes the Survival of Genes Like One's Own

The **genetic determinism model** is based not on emotions but rather on a more general theory of human behavior (Pinker, 1998). Rushton (1989) and other evolutionary psychologists stress that we are not conscious of responding to genetic influences but that we simply do so because we are built that way. In effect, humans are programmed to help just as they are programmed with respect to prejudice (Chapter 6), attraction (Chapter 7), mate selection (Chapter 8), and aggression (Chapter 11).

Archer (1991) describes how sociobiological theories are based on the concept of natural selection. As is well established for physical attributes, many behaviors are also assumed to be genetically based—selected through evolution on the basis of their relevance to reproductive success. The individual's only "goal" is the unconscious need to pass on his or her genes to the next generation. Any genetically based behavior that furthers this goal is more likely to be represented in future generations than are other behaviors that either are irrelevant to that goal, or, even more so, interfere with it.

In this chapter we have frequently noted the importance of similarity in influencing both empathy and actual helping. Studies on nonhuman animal species also indicate that the greater the genetic similarity between two individual organisms, the more likely it is that one will help the other when such help is needed (Ridley & Dawkins, 1981). Such behavior has been described as the result of the "selfish gene." That is, the more similar individual A is to individual B, the more genes they presumably have in common, and if A helps B, A's genes will be represented in future generations even if A dies in the process (Rushton, Russell, & Walls, 1984). Thus, the genetic "fitness" of each individual organism requires that it live long enough to reproduce *or* to enhance the reproductive odds of another individual whose genetic makeup is similar to his or her own (Browne, 1992).

Much the same conclusion was reached by Burnstein, Crandall, and Kitayama (1994), but with a slightly different approach. These researchers assumed that it was not in the best interest of prehistoric humans to help one another, and that natural selection would favor nonhelping. For example, any primitive human who rushed forward to help someone else who was drowning, being attacked by predators, or otherwise in serious trouble would be taking a serious risk and thus decreasing the odds of surviving and reproducing. The only exception to this rule would occur when the person in need of help was a close relative. In this instance, natural selection would favor those who help others who specifically *are most closely related to themselves* and even more specifically *are young enough to be able to reproduce*. Burnstein and colleagues conducted a series of studies based on hypothetical decisions to help. As predicted, research participants were more likely to help someone closely related than to help either a distant relative or someone totally unrelated. The importance of reproductive ability was indicated by the fact that more help was offered to young relatives than to old ones, and that more help was offered to women young enough to bear children than to women past menopause.

In a review of the altruism literature, Buck and Ginsburg (1991) concluded that, at least as yet, there is no evidence of a gene that determines prosocial behavior. Among humans, and among other animals as well (de Waal, 1996), there *are* genetically based capacities to communicate emotions and to form social bonds. Such inherited behaviors make it likely that we will help one another when problems arise. In effect, people are inherently sociable and capable of empathy. When they interact in social relationships, "they are always prosocial, usually helpful, and often altruistic" (Fiske, 1991, p. 209).

You would probably find it more satisfying if we used this final paragraph to announce which of these competing explanations of helping behavior is the correct one. Instead, it seems quite possible that prosocial behavior is based on a variety of motives, and that different individuals in different situations may well be helpful for quite different reasons. Regardless of the underlying reason for a prosocial response, it can be agreed that one very positive aspect of human behavior is that we frequently are willing to help those in need.

Key Points

- The *empathy–altruism hypothesis* proposes that, because of empathy, we help those in need because it feels good to do so.

- The *negative-state relief model* proposes that people help other people in order to relieve and make less negative their own unpleasant emotional state.

- The *empathic joy hypothesis* bases helping on the positive feelings of accomplishment that arise when the helper is able to have a beneficial impact on the person in need.

- The *genetic determinism model* traces prosocial behavior to the general effects of natural selection, which favors any attribute that increases the odds that one's genes will be transmitted to future generations.

Connections: Integrating Social Psychology

In this chapter, you read about . . .	*In other chapters, you will find related discussions of . . .*
bystanders' response to the nonverbal cues of other bystanders	interpretation of nonverbal cues (Chapter 2)
social comparison processes among the witnesses to an emergency	the importance of social comparison in the study of attitudes (Chapter 4), affiliation (Chapter 7), and social influence (Chapter 9)
attributions as to the cause of a victim's problem	attribution theory (Chapter 2)
self-concept as a determinant of helping behavior and the effect of receiving help on self-esteem	research and theory on self-concept and self-esteem (Chapter 5)
locus of control as one element of the altruistic personality	locus of control and health-related behavior (Chapter 13)
similarity of victim and bystander as a determinant of helping	similarity and attraction (Chapters 7 and 8)
genetics and helping	genetics as a factor in prejudice (Chapter 6), attraction (Chapter 7), mate selection (Chapter 8), and aggression (Chapter 11)
affective state and helping	affect as a factor in attitudes (Chapter 4), prejudice (Chapter 6), attraction (Chapter 7), relationships (Chapter 8), and aggression (Chapter 11)

Thinking about Connections

1. As you are walking out of the building after your social psych class, you see an elderly man lying face down on the sidewalk. Three students are standing nearby, not speaking but looking at the man. In trying to understand the situation, what might you observe in the facial expressions and bodily gestures of the three other bystanders (Chapter 2)? As you take a closer look at the man lying on the sidewalk, you may make some guesses as to why he is there. Many different attributions as to the reason or reasons for his being there are possible (Chapter 2). Suggest some of the possibilities that occur to you.

2. Your car won't start, and you are in a hurry. You know you have plenty of gas, and the battery is almost new. You open the hood but don't see anything obviously wrong. A fellow student comes along and offers to help. She looks under the hood, taps something or other, and says, "Try it now." You turn the key, and the car starts easily. How do you feel? Do you like the student who helped you (Chapter 7)? Is your self-esteem more

positive or more negative right now (Chapter 5)? Do you think you might be motivated to learn more about automobiles so this won't happen again (Chapter 10)?

3. On the evening news, you learn about a devastating earthquake in southern California that has destroyed a great many homes, leaving a large number of people without shelter or food. There is a request for contributions of money and food, and volunteers are asked to sign up in order to help with the cleanup. Do you ignore this situation, or do you respond in some way? What factors with respect to the disaster itself, where it occurred, and your own experiences with natural disasters influence your decision? If you volunteer your time, why do you do so? List the kinds of social psychological processes that may be operating.

4. Your cruise ship has collided with an iceberg and is sinking. You are in a crowded lifeboat that has room to pick up only one additional survivor. In the water you see your teenage cousin and his mother, your middle-aged aunt. Do you give up your place in the boat in order to save them both? If not, which one do you choose to save? On what basis do you make such decisions? Think about what you have read in this chapter about genetic influences as well as in other chapters about such factors as self-concept (Chapter 5), attraction (Chapter 7), and relationships (Chapter 8).

Ideas to Take with You
Being a Responsive Bystander

Throughout this chapter you have read examples of real and staged emergencies. In your own life you undoubtedly have in the past and will in the future come across numerous unexpected situations in which your help is badly needed. How you decide to respond is obviously up to you, but at least consider the following suggestions that might be useful in assisting you to make an informed decision.

Pay Attention to What Is Going On Around You.

In our everyday lives we often think more about ourselves (our plans, worries, expectancies, etc.) than about our surroundings. For many reasons, we would do well not only to stop and smell the roses, but also to stop and pay attention. Remember the seminary students who were behind schedule and in such a hurry that they ignored a man who appeared to have collapsed in a doorway? There are often other things worth thinking about and observing beyond yourself.

If You See Something Unusual, Consider More Than One Alternative.

The crying child might be unhappy about not getting a second piece of candy, but she also might be the target of abuse. The man who is running down the street might be a jogger, but he might also be a thief. The smoke you smell might be burnt toast, but it might indicate that the building is on fire. The idea is not to panic or jump to conclusions, but rather to consider various possibilities. Seek additional evidence. Is someone hitting the child? Is the running man carrying a large bag? Is there smoke coming out of the basement? Most unexpected events of this sort are probably easily explained and of little importance, but you need to be alert to the possibility that in rare instances there may really be an emergency.

Consider Yourself to Be as Responsible as Anyone Else for Responding.

No, it's not really your special responsibility, but think of it as everyone's responsibility. I (Donn Byrne) was once in a multiplex movie theater in a mall, and when it was time for the film to begin, nothing happened. A roomful of people sat in their seats and stared at a blank screen. This seemed ridiculous to me, so I left my seat, went to the refreshment counter, and asked the person selling the popcorn to inform someone that the movie had not begun on screen 12. She told the manager, someone pushed the right button, and the movie began. This was a very mild emergency, and I didn't expect a medal; but the same general principle applies to serious situations as well as to trivial ones. If you let the unresponsiveness of others be your guide, you are acting as foolishly as they are.

Be Willing to Act.

It is not reasonable simply to react to what others do and never to act on your own. If you are afraid of what other people might think of you and of being evaluated negatively, just remember that others are as uncertain and confused as you may be. It may feel cool to stand back and do nothing, but it often is actually the stupid choice. What if the worst possible thing occurs—that is, what if you make an honest mistake and look foolish? It's not the end of the world, and you will probably never see these people again anyway. Do what you think is the right thing to do. As Dr. Laura says, "Go take on the day."

SUMMARY AND REVIEW OF KEY POINTS

Responding to an Emergency: Why Are Bystanders Sometimes Helpful, Sometimes Indifferent?

- In part because of *diffusion of responsibility,* the more bystanders present as witnesses to an emergency, the less likely is help to be given and the greater the delay before the help occurs.

- When faced with an emergency, a bystander must go through five crucial steps involving decisions that either inhibit or enhance the likelihood of a prosocial response. He or she must notice the emergency, correctly interpret what is occurring, assume responsibility for providing help, have the necessary skills and knowledge to help, and then actually decide to provide assistance.

- Prosocial acts occur most often when the bystander feels attraction toward the person in need and attributes the problem to circumstances beyond the victim's control.

- Exposure to prosocial models in real life and in the media has a positive effect on prosocial acts.

The Helpers and Those Who Receive Help

- Positive and negative emotional states can either enhance or inhibit *prosocial behavior,* depending on specific factors in the situation, in the individual, and in the nature of the required assistance.

- Individual differences in altruistic behavior are based in large part on *empathy,* a complex response that includes both affective and cognitive components. The extent to which a person is able to respond with empathy depends on both genetic and environmental factors.

- The *altruistic personality* consists of empathy plus other relevant dispositional variables. Combined, such multiple determinants affect prosocial behavior more than does any one of them in isolation.

- People volunteer to provide help on a long-term basis on the basis of several quite different motives, dispositional variables, and levels of *generativity.*

- Help is given by men to women more often than vice versa.

- Asking for help reduces ambiguity and increases the probability of receiving help.

- With high helper–victim similarity, the person who is helped tends to react negatively and to feel incompetent, to experience decreased self-esteem, and to resent the helper; but such negative feelings also tend to motivate self-help in the future.

Explaining Prosocial Behavior: Why Do People Help?

- The *empathy–altruism hypothesis* proposes that, because of empathy, we help those in need because it feels good to do so.

- The *negative-state relief model* proposes that people help other people in order to relieve and make less negative their own unpleasant emotional state.

- The *empathic joy hypothesis* bases helping on the positive feelings of accomplishment that arise when the helper is able to have a beneficial impact on the person in need.

- The *genetic determinism model* traces prosocial behavior to the general effects of natural selection, which favors any attribute that increases the odds that one's genes will be transmitted to future generations.

KEY TERMS

altruism (p. 414)

altruistic personality (p. 419)

bystander effect (p. 398)

diffusion of responsibility (p. 397)

egoism (p. 415)

empathic joy hypothesis (p. 431)

empathy (p. 415)
empathy–altruism hypothesis (p. 430)
generativity (p. 423)
genetic determinism model (p. 432)

negative-state relief model (p. 431)
pluralistic ignorance (p. 403)
prosocial behavior (p. 395)

FOR MORE INFORMATION

Clark, M. S. (Ed.). (1991). *Prosocial behavior.* Newbury Park, CA: Sage

A general review of current research on prosocial behavior, consisting of chapters written by investigators who are actively involved in prosocial research. Included are such topics as empathy, volunteerism, mood, and help-seeking.

Coles, R. (1997). *The moral intelligence of children.* New York: Random House.

A thought-provoking discussion by psychiatrist Robert Coles, who is a Harvard professor and winner of the Pulitzer Prize for a previous book. Coles describes the various ways that parents and others shape the behavior of their children and direct or fail to direct them toward the development of a conscience, concern for others, kindness, and willingness to help.

Schroeder, D. A., Penner, L. A., Dovidio, J. F., & Piliavin, J. A. (1995). *The social psychology of helping and altruism: Problems and puzzles.* New York: McGraw-Hill.

The first text devoted entirely to the topic of prosocial behavior. The authors cover much of the material discussed in Chapter 10, plus such topics as the developmental aspects of helping, cooperation, and collective helping. They also present an integrative conceptual framework based on affect and cognition, as well as making suggestions for future research.

Wright, R. (1994). *The moral animal: The new science of evolutionary psychology.* New York: Pantheon.

A readable and creative explanation of how evolutionary factors affect human genetics and how genes, in turn, affect behavior. Wright's discussion includes prosocial behavior and feelings of compassion, but it also deals with many other aspects of human social behavior.

11

Aggression:
Its Nature, Causes, and Control

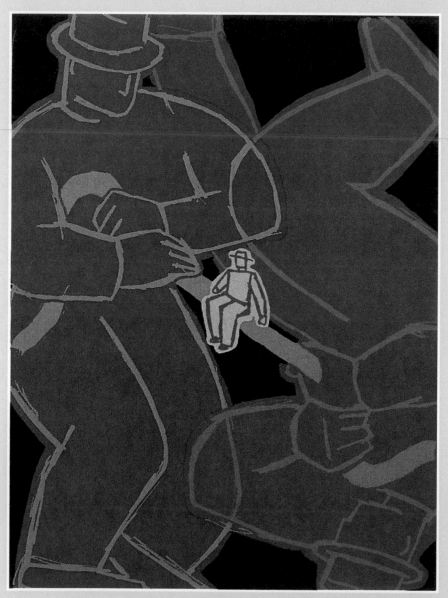

Tug of War. © José Ortega/Stock Illustration Source

Chapter Outline

Theoretical Perspectives on Aggression: In Search of the Roots of Violence
Instinct Theories and the Role of Biological Factors: Are We Programmed for Violence?
Drive Theories: The Motive to Harm Others
Modern Theories of Aggression: Taking Account of Learning, Cognitions, Mood, and Arousal

Determinants of Human Aggression: Social, Personal, Situational
CORNERSTONES OF SOCIAL PSYCHOLOGY: The Buss Technique for Studying Physical Aggression: "Would You Electrocute a Stranger?" Revisited
Social Determinants of Aggression: Frustration, Provocation, Media Violence, and Heightened Arousal
Personal Causes of Aggression
BEYOND THE HEADLINES: AS SOCIAL PSYCHOLOGISTS SEE IT: Murder of the Truly Defenseless: When Mothers Go Berserk
Situational Determinants of Aggression: The Effects of High Temperatures and Alcohol Consumption

Child Abuse and Workplace Violence: Aggression in Long-Term Relationships
Child Maltreatment: Harming the Innocent
Workplace Violence: Aggression on the Job

The Prevention and Control of Aggression: Some Useful Techniques
Punishment: An Effective Deterrent to Violence?
Catharsis: Does Getting It out of Your System Really Help?
Cognitive Interventions: Apologies and Overcoming Cognitive Deficits
Other Techniques for Reducing Aggression: Exposure to Nonaggressive Models, Training in Social Skills, and Incompatible Responses
SOCIAL DIVERSITY: A CRITICAL ANALYSIS: "Would You Murder Someone You Truly Hated If You Could Get Away with It?" Cultural and Gender Differences in Aggressive Intentions
CONNECTIONS: Integrating Social Psychology
IDEAS TO TAKE WITH YOU: Causes of Human Aggression: An Overview

Summary and Review of Key Points
Key Terms
For More Information

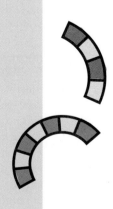

I (Robert Baron) have had a career-long interest in human aggression, and this puzzles many people. First, this was not the topic I studied in graduate school; yet I started to conduct research on aggression as soon as I received my Ph.D. Second, I'm quite cheerful and upbeat, so many people find it surprising that I've focused so much of my attention on the destructive side of human nature. Looking back, though, I think I can spot the origins of this interest. It all started when I was a college student working at a summer job in New York City. One of the full-time people in my office was a fellow named Luis, and we soon struck up a friendship. He was a recent immigrant from the Dominican Republic, and I was fascinated by his stories of life back home. Suddenly, though, Luis stopped being friendly: he refused to have lunch with me and soon stopped talking to me altogether unless it was absolutely necessary. When I asked him what was wrong, he simply said: "You know!" Gradually, it became clear to me that Luis thought I was "out to get him." He told other workers in the office he "knew" I was spreading lies about him. And he accused me of trying to steal his girlfriend. In fact, Maria was not his girlfriend and didn't like him; but besides, I had a girlfriend and had no interest in starting another relationship. The situation worsened. Often, I could see Luis looking angrily at me and muttering under his breath. Things came to a head when, one day, he followed me home on the subway. He kept fingering something in his pocket, so I was sure that it was a gun. When I got off the train, I turned to face him, hoping that the crowd would prevent him from doing anything violent. But he never left the subway car—perhaps because a police officer happened to be on the platform. Later that night, Luis was arrested for assaulting his neighbor, and he never came back to work.

In the years after the incident, I often wondered *why* this chain of events occurred. Was it something I said or did? Was it the record heat that summer, coupled with the repeated failure of our air conditioning? Was Luis jealous, not only over Maria but also because I was going back to college in the fall? Or was he simply mentally ill? I'll never know for sure; but I think I can trace my interest in human aggression back to the events of that hot, steamy summer.

As you can probably guess, I'm far from alone with respect to this interest. In fact, **aggression**—the intentional infliction of some form of harm on others—has long been a topic of concern to many social psychologists. Aggression is, after all, alarmingly frequent and shockingly devastating in its consequences (see Figure 11.1). Thus, it has been the subject of systematic research by social psychologists for several decades (e.g., Baron & Richardson, 1994; Geen & Donnerstein, 1998). To provide you with an overview of key findings of this work, we'll proceed as follows.

First, we'll describe several *theoretical perspectives* on aggression, contrasting views about its nature and origin. Next, we'll examine several important determinants of human aggression. These include *social factors* involving the words or deeds of other persons; *personal factors,* or traits that predispose specific persons toward aggressive outbursts; and *situational factors*—aspects of the external world such as high temperatures and alcohol. Third, we'll consider two especially disturbing forms of aggression: *child maltreatment* (Peterson & Brown, 1994) and *workplace aggression.* These forms of aggression are especially disturbing because they occur within the context of long-term relationships that should, instead, involve love, helping, and cooperation. Finally, to conclude on an optimistic note, we'll examine various techniques for the *prevention and control* of aggression.

aggression • Behavior directed toward the goal of harming another living being who is motivated to avoid such treatment.

Figure 11.1
Human Aggression:
A Devastating Problem.
As this scene from Kosovo
suggests, the costs of aggression in terms of human life
and suffering are staggering.

T HEORETICAL PERSPECTIVES ON AGGRESSION: IN SEARCH OF THE ROOTS OF VIOLENCE

Why do human beings aggress against others? What makes them turn, with bru-
tality unmatched by even the fiercest predators, against their fellow human beings? Thoughtful persons have pondered these questions for centuries and have
proposed many contrasting explanations for the paradox of human violence.
We'll examine several that have been especially influential, concluding with the
modern answer provided by social psychologists.

Instinct Theories and the Role of Biological Factors: Are We Programmed for Violence?

The oldest and probably best known explanation for human aggression is the
view that human beings are somehow "programmed" for violence by their basic nature. Such **instinct theories** suggest that human violence stems from built-
in (i.e., inherited) tendencies to aggress against others. The most famous
supporter of this theory was Sigmund Freud, who held that aggression stems
mainly from a powerful *death wish* (thanatos) possessed by all persons. According to Freud, this instinct is initially aimed at self-destruction but is soon
redirected outward, toward others.

A related view was proposed by Konrad Lorenz, a Nobel Prize–winning scientist. Lorenz (1966, 1974) suggested that aggression springs mainly from an inherited *fighting instinct* that human beings share with many other species.
Presumably, this instinct developed during the course of evolution because it
helped ensure that only the strongest and most vigorous individuals would pass
their genes on to the next generation. If you have ever seen nature programs
showing scenes in which males fight for dominance—and for the right to mate
with females (Figure 11.2 on page 442)—you can see why this view has been so
popular: it does seem to fit with what we observe in the natural world around us.

instinct theories • Views
suggesting that aggression
stems from innate tenden-
cies that are universal among
members of a given species.

Figure 11.2

Aggression: Is It Really Innate? While competition for mates and territory appears to be a built-in tendency underlying aggression in many species, most social psychologists question the role of such factors in human aggression.

Is there any scientific basis for the suggestion that human aggression stems from innate tendencies? Most social psychologists reject, or at least seriously question, this idea. They do so for the following reasons. First, as we'll see in later sections of this chapter, human aggression stems from a very large number of different factors; thus, emphasizing innate tendencies as a primary cause of such behavior seems inappropriate. Second, in most animal species, the kind of fighting behavior described by Lorenz does *not* lead to serious injury or death of the combatants. In contrast, human aggression is far more deadly: each year, millions of persons are killed and tens of millions seriously injured in assaults by other human beings. Innate tendencies to engage in such lethal behavior make little sense from an evolutionary perspective. Third, human aggression takes a tremendous range of forms—from ignoring another person or spreading false rumors about her to destroying the target's property or attacking this person directly, either verbally or physically. It is hard to imagine how all these forms of behavior could be the result of innate urges or tendencies. Finally, the frequency of instances of dangerous physical aggression, in which individuals are seriously hurt or even killed, varies tremendously across different cultures—perhaps by a factor of fifty or more (e.g., Fry, 1998). Moreover, the rate of violence within a given culture can change drastically over time as social conditions change (e.g., Robarchek & Robarchek, 1997). Clearly, such facts are inconsistent with the idea that human beings are genetically programmed for aggression.

While social psychologists generally reject the view that human aggression stems largely from innate factors, however, they do accept the possibility that genetic factors play *some* role in human aggression. In addition, they recognize the potentially important role of *biological factors* in such behavior. Indeed, research findings point to the conclusion that the inability to restrain aggressive urges may stem, at least in part, from disturbances in the nervous system—for instance, from low levels of certain neurotransmitters such as *serotonin* (Marazzitti et al., 1993). Similarly, there is growing evidence that certain sex hormones may also play a role in aggression (e.g., Van Goozen, Frijda, & de Poll, 1994). In one recent study on this topic, for example, participants completed questionnaires designed to measure both their tendencies to behave aggressively and their tendencies to behave in a helpful, nurturant manner in a wide range of situations (Harris et al., 1996). Here are two examples of the items used to measure aggression: "I have trouble controlling my temper"; "If somebody hits me, I hit back." Two examples of items used to assess prosocial behavior or nurturance: "I often take people under my wing"; "I like helping other people." The researchers also obtained two measures of participants' level of testosterone, an important male sex hormone. Results indicated that for both genders, the higher the testosterone levels, the higher the tendency to engage in aggression and the lower the tendency to engage in helpful, nurturant behaviors as reported by participants. Although these findings were based on correlations, further analyses indicated that the relationship between testosterone and aggression was a direct one: increments in testosterone appeared to cause increased tendencies to aggress.

While these results are far from conclusive—they are based on self-reports of aggression and helping rather than on actual observations of these behaviors—they agree with the results of other studies (e.g., Patrick, Bradley, & Lang, 1993) in suggesting that biological factors do indeed play a role in aggressive behavior. For this reason, it is important that biological aspects be included in our overall picture of the nature of human aggression.

Drive Theories: The Motive to Harm Others

When social psychologists rejected the instinct views of aggression proposed by Freud and Lorenz, they countered with an alternative of their own: the view that aggression stems mainly from an externally elicited *drive* to harm others. This approach is reflected in several different **drive theories** of aggression (e.g., Berkowitz, 1989; Feshbach, 1984). These theories propose that external conditions—especially *frustration*, or any interference with goal-directed behavior—can arouse a strong motive to harm others. This aggressive drive, in turn, leads to overt acts of aggression.

By far the most famous of the drive theories is the well-known *frustration–aggression hypothesis* (Dollard et al., 1939). According to this view, frustration leads to the arousal of a drive whose basic goal is that of harming some person or object—primarily the perceived cause of the frustration (Berkowitz, 1989). As we'll see below, the central role assigned to frustration by the frustration–aggression hypothesis has turned out to be largely false: frustration is only one of many different causes of aggression, and a fairly weak one at that. However, while social psychologists have largely rejected this theory as false, it still enjoys widespread acceptance outside our field. Thus, we felt it was important to call it to your attention here.

Modern Theories of Aggression: Taking Account of Learning, Cognitions, Mood, and Arousal

Unlike earlier views, modern theories of aggression (e.g., Anderson, 1997; Berkowitz, 1993; Zillmann, 1994) do not focus on a single factor as the primary cause of aggression. Rather, they draw on advances in many fields of psychology in order to gain added insight into such behavior. While no single theory includes all the elements that social psychologists now view as important, one approach—the **general affective aggression model,** proposed by Anderson (Anderson, 1997; Anderson et al., 1996)—provides a good illustration of the breadth and sophistication of these new perspectives.

According this theory, known as the *GAAM* for short, aggression is triggered or elicited by a wide range of *input variables*—aspects of the current situation and/or tendencies individuals bring with them to a given situation.

drive theories (of aggression) • Theories suggesting that aggression stems from external conditions that arouse the motive to harm or injure others; the most famous of these is the frustration–aggression hypothesis.

general affective aggression model • A modern theory of aggression suggesting that aggression is triggered by a wide range of input variables; these influence arousal, affective stages, and cognitions.

research that, in a sense, made much of the work described in this chapter possible. Buss's ingenious research is described in the *Cornerstones* section below.

Cornerstones of Social Psychology
The Buss Technique for Studying Physical Aggression: "Would You Electrocute a Stranger?" Revisited

Arnold Buss. *Arnold Buss devised a technique for studying physical aggression under safe laboratory conditions. He formulated this technique at almost precisely the same time that Stanley Milgram was developing his procedures for studying obedience to authority. I (Robert Baron) first met Arnie when I was a visiting professor at the University of Texas, and I have remained friends with him ever since. His book* The Psychology of Aggression, *published in 1961, is a true classic in the field and stimulated many social psychologists—including myself!—to conduct systematic research on human aggression. Arnie's son, David Buss, is also a well-known social psychologist and has made many important contributions to the rapidly growing field of evolutionary psychology.*

aggression machine • Apparatus used to measure physical aggression under safe laboratory conditions.

Creative minds, it seems, often run in the same directions. Do you remember our description of Stanley Milgram's research on obedience in Chapter 9? If so, you may recall that procedures he devised involved ordering research participants to deliver stronger and stronger electric shocks to an innocent victim. The key question was: Would participants obey? As you probably recall, they did—to an alarming extent. At the same time that Milgram was developing these procedures, Arnold Buss was working on a different but related question—the one we posed above. *How could researchers wishing to study human aggression do so in a way that would eliminate the risk of actual harm to participants?* The solution Buss formulated seems, on the surface, to be quite similar to the technique developed by Milgram. However, I (Robert Baron) knew both Stanley Milgram and Arnold Buss (I say "knew" because Milgram passed away several years ago); and they both confirmed what I suspected all along: they developed their similar research techniques simultaneously, but in a totally independent manner.

How do the procedures developed by Buss differ from those devised by Milgram? Let's take a closer look to see. In the approach designed by Buss, research participants are told that they are taking part, along with another person, in a study of the effects of punishment on learning. One of the two persons present serves as a *teacher* and the other as a *learner.* The teacher (always the real participant) presents various materials to the learner, who is actually an accomplice. This person attempts to learn these materials, and each time he or she makes a correct response, the teacher rewards the learner with a signal indicating "Correct." Each time the learner makes an error, however, the teacher delivers an electric shock to this person, using an apparatus like that shown in Figure 11.4.

So far, this sounds very much like the procedures we described in Chapter 9. But here is where they differ: *The teachers in Buss's study were given free choice as to how strong the shocks should be.* In fact, they were told that they could choose any button on the apparatus and hold it down for as long as they wished. The higher the number on the button, the stronger, supposedly, was the shock to the learner; and as in Milgram's procedures, teachers (real participants) were given several sample shocks to convince them that the equipment actually worked.

During each session, the learner (accomplice) made many errors, thus providing participants with lots of opportunities to deliver painful shocks. Buss reasoned that because participants were free to choose any shock they wished, these procedures would in fact measure participants' desire to hurt the accomplice; after all, if they wished, they could stick to the mildest shock (from button 1), which was described as being so mild that the learner would probably not even feel it.

Social psychologists interested in studying human aggression quickly seized on Buss's apparatus, sometimes known as the **aggression machine,** as a valuable new research tool. Before its appearance, researchers studying aggression were largely limited to asking individuals how they would respond in various imaginary situations or to measuring their *verbal* reactions to provocations or frustrations from others (usually, from accomplices). Here, it seemed, was a means of studying not what people guessed they would do in response to provocation but what they actually *would* do. Thus, the Buss technique, and related procedures such as one devised by Stuart Taylor (1967), were soon being used in a large number of studies designed to examine many

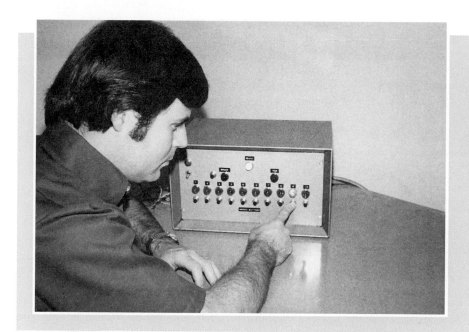

Figure 11.4
An Aggression Machine Similar to the One Developed by Arnold Buss. The apparatus shown here is used to study physical aggression without risk of harm to research participants. Participants are told that they can deliver shocks of varying strength to another person by pushing buttons on this machine; the higher the number of the button, the stronger the shock.

aspects of aggression (see, e.g., Baron & Richardson, 1994). But questions concerning the external validity of Buss's technique were quickly raised. Did pushing buttons on an aggression machine really provide a valid measure of individuals' willingness to harm another person? Or were social psychologists simply fooling themselves by putting faith in such procedures?

Although this question has never been totally resolved, several lines of evidence suggest that Buss's procedures do indeed provide a useful measure of human aggression. First, many studies found that people with a prior history of real aggressive behavior—for instance, violent criminals—chose stronger shocks than persons without such a history (e.g., Cherek et al., 1996; Gully & Dengerink, 1983; Wolfe & Baron, 1971). Second, and perhaps even more convincing, variables that influence aggression in real-life settings have also been shown to influence aggression in laboratory studies as measured through the procedures devised by Buss and others (e.g., Taylor, 1967). For instance, as reported by Anderson and Bushman (1997), aggression in laboratory studies is strongly increased by such factors as direct provocation, exposure to media violence, high temperatures, and the consumption of alcohol—variables that have also been found to influence aggression outside the laboratory.

On the basis of such evidence, many researchers have concluded that Buss's procedures do indeed provide at least a rough index of the central concept we wish to measure in research on aggression: people's willingness to inflict harm—physical or otherwise—on another human being. However, even the strongest supporters of these methods admit that they are far from perfect. So the most reasonable conclusion may be something like this: By all means, use these procedures if they seem appropriate; but always do so with great caution, and never, ever take their external validity for granted.

Social Determinants of Aggression: Frustration, Provocation, Media Violence, and Heightened Arousal

Now let's return to the major task we started above: describing some of the key social, personal, and situational causes of aggression—the factors referred to as *input variables* in the general affective aggression model described earlier.

Figure 11.5
An Illustration of the Fact That Frustration Does *Not* Always Lead to Aggression. As shown here, individuals often respond to frustration in ways other than aggression.

(*Source:* King Features Syndicate, 1990.)

Frustration: Why Not Getting What You Want (or What You'd Expect) Can Sometimes Lead to Aggression. Suppose that you asked twenty people you know to name the single most important cause of aggression. What would they say? The chances are good that most would reply *frustration*. And if you asked them to define frustration, many would say, "The way I feel when something— or someone—prevents me from getting what I want or expect to get in some situation." This widespread belief in the importance of frustration as a cause of aggression stems, at least in part, from the famous **frustration–aggression hypothesis** mentioned in our discussion of drive theories of aggression (Dollard et al., 1939). In its original form, this hypothesis made two sweeping assertions: (1) Frustration *always* leads to some form of aggression, and (2) aggression *always* stems from frustration. In short, the theory held that frustrated persons always engage in some type of aggression and that all acts of aggression, in turn, result from frustration. Bold statements like these are appealing, but this doesn't necessarily mean that they are accurate. In fact, existing evidence suggests that both portions of the original frustration–aggression hypothesis assigned far too much importance to frustration as a determinant of human aggression.

Look at Figure 11.5. It illustrates the important point that when frustrated, individuals do not always respond with aggression. On the contrary, they show many different reactions, ranging from sadness, despair, and depression on the one hand (like the character in the cartoon), to direct attempts to overcome the source of their frustration on the other. Aggression is definitely *not* an automatic response to frustration.

Second, it is equally clear that not all aggression stems from frustration. People aggress for many different reasons and in response to many different factors. For example, professional boxers hit their opponents because they wish to win valued prizes—not because of frustration. Similarly, during wars, air force pilots report that flying their planes is a source of pleasure, and they bomb enemy targets while feeling elated or excited—not frustrated. In these and many other cases, aggression stems from factors other than frustration. We'll consider many of these other causes of aggression below.

In view of these facts, few social psychologists now accept the idea that frustration is the only, or even the most important, cause of aggression. Instead, most believe that it is simply one of many factors that can potentially lead to aggression. Along these lines, Berkowitz (1989, 1993) has proposed a revised version of the frustration–aggression hypothesis that seems consistent with a large amount of evidence about the effects of frustration. According to this view, frus-

frustration–aggression hypothesis • The suggestion that frustration is a very powerful determinant of aggression.

tration is an unpleasant experience, and it may lead to aggression largely because of this fact. In other words, frustration sometimes produces aggression because of a basic link between negative affect (unpleasant feelings) and aggressive behavior—a relationship that has been confirmed in many studies (e.g., da Gloria, et al., 1994).

We should add that frustration *can* serve as a powerful determinant of aggression under certain conditions—especially when its cause is viewed as illegitimate or unjustified (e.g., Folger & Baron, 1996). For instance, if an individual believes that she deserves a large raise and then receives a much smaller one with no explanation, she may conclude that she has been treated very unfairly—that her legitimate needs have been thwarted. The result: She may have hostile thoughts, experience intense anger, and seek revenge against the perceived source of such frustration—her boss or her company. As we'll note in a later section, such reactions may play a key role in *workplace aggression* and in the aggressive reactions of some employees who lose their jobs through downsizing (e.g., Catalano, Novaco, & McConnell, 1997; Greenberg & Alge, 1997).

Direct Provocation: When Aggression Breeds Aggression. Suppose that one day, another shopper in a supermarket bumped you with her cart. Suppose she then remarked: "Out of my way, stupid!" How would you react? Probably with anger, and perhaps with some kind of retaliation. You might make a biting remark such as "What's wrong with you—are you nuts?" Alternatively, you might, if you were angry enough, push *your* cart into hers, or even into her!

This incident illustrates an important point about aggression: Often, it is the result of physical or verbal **provocation** from others. When we are on the receiving end of some form of aggression from others, we rarely turn the other cheek. Instead, we tend to reciprocate, returning as much aggression as we have received—or perhaps even slightly more, especially if we are certain that the other person *meant* to harm us (Dengerink, Schnedler, & Covey, 1978; Ohbuchi & Kambara, 1985). Such effects are demonstrated very clearly by a study conducted by Chermack, Berman, and Taylor (1997).

In this study, participants competed with an opponent on a competitive reaction-time task devised by Stuart Taylor. On each trial, the participant and his opponent (who was not really there) set a level of shock the loser—the person slower to respond—would receive after that trial. The shocks were set by means of ten buttons on the equipment and could range in intensity from ones that could not be felt to ones that participants found painful. Prior to each reaction-time trial, participants learned what level of shock had been set for them by their opponent. In one condition (low provocation), the opponent chose button 2 on all occasions. In another condition (high provocation), he gradually raised the level of shocks he set for the participant from 2 to 9. (Needless to say, participants were warned about the possibility of receiving actual shocks during the informed consent procedures.)

As you can see from Figure 11.6 on page 450, participants' aggression was strongly influenced by the level of provocation they received. In the low-provocation condition, they set relatively low shocks for their opponent and did not increase these over time. In the high-provocation condition, they set higher shocks (except in the first block of trials), and they raised these dramatically over time. The findings also illustrate the "and then some" effect mentioned above: even in the low-provocation condition, participants set a slightly higher level of shocks for their opponent than they received.

Exposure to Media Violence: The Effects of Witnessing Aggression. List several films you have seen in recent months. Now answer the following question: How

provocation • Actions by others that tend to trigger aggression in the recipient, often because they are perceived as stemming from malicious intent.

Figure 11.6

Effects of Provocation on Aggression. Research participants who were strongly provoked by another person directed much more aggression against this person than did participants who were not strongly provoked and also increased their aggression over time. Those who were weakly provoked did *not* increase aggression in this way.

(*Source:* Based on data from Berman, Chermack, & Taylor, 1997.)

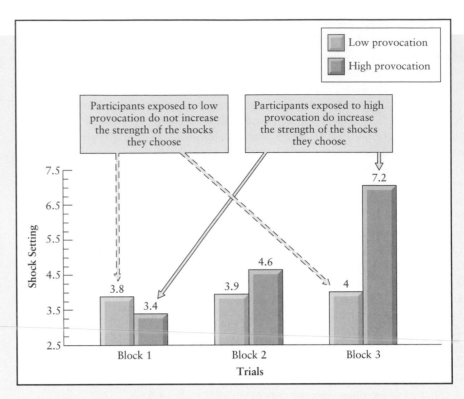

Low provocation

High provocation

Participants exposed to low provocation do not increase the strength of the shocks they choose

Participants exposed to high provocation do increase the strength of the shocks they choose

much aggression or violence did each movie contain? How often did the characters hit, shoot at, or otherwise attempt to harm others (see Figure 11.7)? Unless you chose very carefully, many of the films probably contained a great deal of violence—much more than you are ever likely to see in real life (Reiss & Roth, 1993; Waters et al., 1993).

This fact raises an important question that social psychologists have studied for decades: Does exposure to such materials increase aggression among children and/or adults? Literally hundreds of studies have been performed to

Figure 11.7

Media Violence: All Too Common. Many films and television shows currently contain large amounts of violence. Does exposure to such materials increase aggression among viewers? A large body of research evidence suggests that it does.

test this possibility, and the results seem clear: *Exposure to media violence may indeed be one factor contributing to high levels of violence in countries where such materials are viewed by large numbers of persons* (e.g., Anderson, 1997; Berkowitz, 1993; Paik & Comstock, 1994; Wood et al., 1991).

Many kinds of evidence lend support to this conclusion. For example, in *short-term laboratory experiments,* children or adults have viewed either violent films and television programs or nonviolent ones; then the participants' tendency to aggress against others has been measured. In general, the results of such experiments have revealed higher levels of aggression among participants who viewed the violent films or programs (e.g., Bandura, Ross, & Ross, 1963; Geen, 1991b).

Other and perhaps even more convincing research has employed *longitudinal* procedures, in which the same participants are studied for many years (e.g, Huesmann & Eron, 1984, 1986). Results of such research, too, are clear: The more violent films or television programs participants watch as children, the higher their levels of aggression as teenagers or adults; for instance, the higher the likelihood that they will be arrested for violent crimes. Such findings have been replicated in many different countries—Australia, Finland, Israel, Poland, and South Africa (Botha, 1990). Thus, they appear to hold across different cultures.

While these longitudinal studies have been carefully conducted, it's important to remember that they are still only correlational in nature. As we noted in Chapter 1, the fact that two variables are correlated does *not* imply that one necessarily causes the other. However, when the results of these studies are combined with the findings of short-term laboratory experiments, a strong case does seem to emerge for the suggestion that exposure to media violence is one potential cause of human aggression.

But why, you may be wondering, do these media effects occur? Several possibilities exist. First, individuals may simply learn new ways of aggressing from watching television programs and films—ways they would not have imagined before. "Copycat crimes," in which a real or fictional violent crime depicted in the media is then copied by different persons in distant locations, suggest that such effects are real. For instance, some years ago, a movie showed two armed men forcing three people to drink liquid Drano (a caustic drain cleaner). This killed them in a very painful way. A few months later, several actual murders were perpetrated by the same method (cited in Anderson, 1997).

Another effect of watching media violence involves what are known as *densensitization effects.* After viewing many vivid scenes of violence, individuals become hardened to the pain and suffering of other persons; they experience less emotional reaction to such cues than they did before (e.g., Baron, 1974a). This may lessen their own restraints against engaging in aggression.

Recent research indicates that a third effect may occur as well: watching scenes of violence may serve to "prime" hostile thoughts, so that these come to mind more readily—they become more accessible to conscious thought. This, in turn, can increase the likelihood that a person will engage in overt aggression (Anderson, 1997). Because repeated exposure to media violence may strengthen such priming effects over time, the impact of watching violence may be cumulative—and even more important than was previously assumed.

Since exposure to media violence may have harmful effects on society, why, you may be wondering, is there so much of it on television and in films? One answer is that the advertisers who pay for these programs believe that "violence sells"—it is one way to increase audience size. While this may be true, findings reported by Bushman (1998) suggest that media violence may actually backfire from the point of view of increasing the sales of products advertised on such shows. He found that audiences who watch violent programs are significantly *less* likely to remember the content of commercials shown during these programs than audiences who watch nonviolent programs. Apparently, violent images on the television screen trigger memories of other violent scenes, and such thoughts distract viewers from paying attention to commercials. These findings suggest that sponsoring violent television programs is not just questionable from a moral point of view; it may also make little economic sense for sponsors!

Heightened Arousal: Emotion, Cognition, and Aggression. Suppose that you are driving to the airport to meet a friend. On the way there, another driver cuts you off and you almost have an accident. Your heart pounds wildly and your blood pressure shoots through the roof; but, fortunately, no accident occurs. Now you arrive at the airport. You park and rush inside. When you get to the security check, an elderly man in front of you sets off the buzzer. He becomes confused and can't seem to understand that the security guard wants him to empty his pockets. You are irritated by this delay. In fact, you begin to lose your temper and mutter—not too softly—"What's wrong with him? Can't he get it?"

Now for the key question: Do you think that your recent near miss in traffic may have played any role in your sudden surge of anger? Could the emotional arousal from that incident have somehow transferred to the scene inside the airport? Growing evidence suggests that it could (Zillmann, 1988, 1994). Under some conditions, heightened arousal—whatever its source—can enhance aggression in response to provocation, frustration, or other factors. In fact, in various experiments, arousal stemming from such varied sources as participation in competitive games (Christy, Gelfand, & Hartmann, 1971), vigorous exercise (Zillmann, 1979), and even some types of music (Rogers & Ketcher, 1979) has been found to increase subsequent aggression. Why is this the case? A compelling explanation is offered by **excitation transfer theory** (Zillmann, 1983, 1988).

This theory suggests that because physiological arousal tends to dissipate slowly over time, a portion of such arousal may persist as a person moves from one situation to another. In the example above, some portion of the arousal you experienced because of the near miss in traffic may still be present as you approach the security gate in the airport. When you encounter minor annoyance at the gate, that arousal intensifies your emotional reactions to the annoyance. The result: You become enraged rather than just mildly irritated. Excitation transfer theory further suggests that such effects are most likely to occur when the persons involved are relatively unaware of the presence of residual arousal—a common occurrence, as small elevations in arousal are difficult to notice (Zillmann, 1994). Excitation transfer theory also suggests that such effects are likely to occur when the persons involved recognize their residual arousal but attribute it to events occurring in the present situation (Taylor et al., 1991). In the airport incident, for instance, your anger would be intensified if you recognized your feelings of arousal but attributed them to the elderly man's actions (see Figure 11.8.)

Sexual Arousal and Aggression: Are Love and Hate Really Two Sides of the Same Behavioral Coin? Love and hate, it is often contended, are closely linked. Consider the following quotation: *"The more one loves a mistress, the more one is ready to hate her"* (de La Rochefoucauld, 1678). Are such observations accurate? If *love* is taken to mean primarily sexual arousal or excitement, research by social psychologists offers some support for this age-old idea.

First, it appears that relatively mild levels of sexual arousal can reduce overt aggression. In several studies, the following procedures were followed: Participants were first annoyed by a stranger. Then they examined stimuli that were either mildly sexually arousing (e.g., pictures of attractive nudes) or neutral (e.g., pictures of scenery, abstract art). Finally, they had an opportunity to retaliate against their provoker (e.g., Baron, 1974b, 1979; Ramirez, Bryant, & Zillmann,

excitation transfer theory • A theory suggesting that arousal produced in one situation can persist and intensify emotional reactions occurring in later situations.

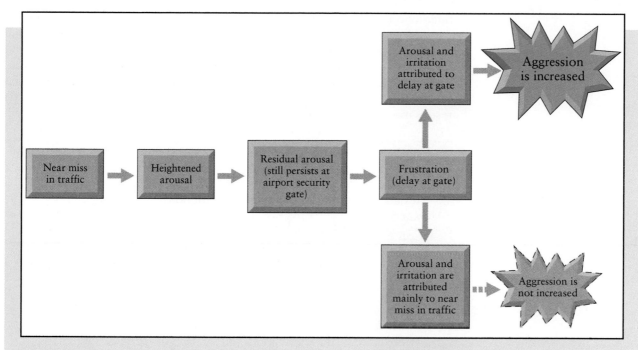

Figure 11.8

Excitation Transfer Theory. *Excitation transfer theory* suggests that arousal occurring in one situation can persist and intensify emotional reactions in later, unrelated situations. Thus, the arousal produced by a near miss in traffic can intensify feelings of annoyance stemming from delays at an airport security gate.

(*Source:* Based on suggestions by Zillmann, 1988, 1994.)

1983). Results indicated that people exposed to mildly arousing sexual materials showed lower levels of aggression than those exposed to the neutral stimuli.

The word *mild* should be emphasized, however. In subsequent studies in which participants were exposed to more arousing sexual materials, higher levels of arousal were found to *increase* rather than reduce aggression (e.g., Jaffe et al., 1974; Zillmann, 1984). Together, these findings suggest that the relationship between sexual arousal and aggression is *curvilinear* in nature. Mild sexual arousal reduces aggression to a level below that shown in the absence of such arousal, while higher levels of arousal actually increase aggression above this level. Why is this so? One explanation is provided by the following *two-component model* (Zillmann, 1984).

According to this theory, exposure to erotic stimuli produces two effects: It increases arousal and it influences current *affective states*—negative or positive moods or feelings. Whether sexual arousal will increase or reduce aggression, then, depends on the overall pattern of such effects. Mild erotic materials generate weak levels of arousal but high levels of positive affect—most people enjoy looking at them. As a result, aggression is reduced. In contrast, explicit sexual materials generate stronger levels of arousal, but also higher levels of negative affect—many people find some of the acts shown to be unpleasant or even repulsive. As a result, such materials may increase aggression. The findings of several studies support this two-factor theory (e.g., Ramirez, Bryant, & Zillmann, 1983), so it appears to provide a useful explanation for the curvilinear relationship between sexual arousal and aggression.

One important topic to which these findings seem relevant is *crimes of passion*—instances in which one lover or spouse attacks or even kills another. Do intense feelings of sexual arousal play a role in such events? No direct evidence currently exists on this issue. However, research findings indicate that *sexual jealousy*, another emotion often associated with such crimes, evokes powerful feelings of anger and strong desires to aggress against the source of such reactions (e.g., de Weerth & Kalma, 1993; Paul et al., 1993). It seems possible that when these powerful emotions combine with high levels of sexual arousal, the results may be truly explosive—with dire consequences for the persons involved.

Key Points

- In order to study aggression, social psychologists often use procedures devised by Arnold Buss and an apparatus known as the *aggression machine*.

- Contrary to the famous *frustration–aggression hypothesis*, not all aggression stems from frustration, and frustration does not always lead to aggression. Frustration is a strong elicitor of aggression only under certain limited conditions.

- In contrast, *provocation* from others is a powerful elicitor of aggression. We rarely turn the other cheek; rather, we match—or slightly exceed—the level of aggression we receive from others.

- Exposure to media violence has been found to increase aggression among viewers. This occurs because of several factors, such as the priming of aggressive thoughts and a weakening of restraints against aggression.

- Heightened arousal can increase aggression if it persists beyond the situation in which it was induced and is falsely interpreted as anger.

- Mild levels of sexual arousal reduce aggression, while higher levels increase such behavior.

Personal Causes of Aggression

Are some persons "primed" for aggression by their personal characteristics? Informal observation suggests that this is so. Some individuals rarely lose their tempers or engage in aggressive actions; but others seem to be forever losing it, with potentially serious consequences. In this section we will consider several personal traits or characteristics that seem to play an important role in aggression.

The Type A Behavior Pattern: Why the *A* in Type A Could Stand for *Aggression*. Do you know anyone you could describe as (1) extremely competitive, (2) always in a hurry, and (3) especially irritable and aggressive? If so, this person shows the characteristics of what psychologists term the **Type A behavior pattern** (Glass, 1977; Strube, 1989). At the opposite end of the continuum are persons who do not show these characteristics—individuals who are *not* highly competitive, who are *not* always fighting the clock, and who do *not* readily lose their temper; such persons are described as showing the **Type B behavior pattern**.

Given the characteristics mentioned above, it seems only reasonable to expect that Type A's would tend to be more aggressive than Type B's in many situations. And in fact, the results of several experiments indicate that this is actually the case (Baron, Russell, & Arms, 1985; Carver & Glass, 1978). For example, consider a study by Berman, Gladue, and Taylor (1993). These researchers exposed young men known to be Type A or Type B to increasing provocation from a stranger by means of the Taylor competitive reaction-time task described earlier. Another feature of the study involved measurement of

type A behavior pattern • A pattern consisting primarily of high levels of competitiveness, time urgency, and hostility.

type B behavior pattern • A pattern consisting of the absence of characteristics associated with the Type A behavior pattern.

participants' testosterone level; as we pointed out before, testosterone is an important sex hormone, found in much higher levels in males than in females. Results indicated that during the competitive task, Type A's who also had a high level of testosterone set the highest level of shocks for their opponent. In addition, Type A's with high testosterone levels were much more likely than other participants to use the highest shock setting available. These findings indicate that two different personal characteristics—the Type A behavior pattern and testosterone level—both play a role in determining aggressive behavior.

Additional findings indicate that Type A's are truly hostile people: they don't merely aggress against others because this is a useful means for reaching other goals, such as winning athletic contests or furthering their own careers. Rather, they are more likely than Type B's to engage in what is known as **hostile aggression**—aggression in which the prime objective is inflicting harm on the victim (Strube et al., 1984). In view of this fact, it is not surprising to learn that Type A's are more likely than Type B's to engage in such actions as child abuse or spouse abuse (Strube et al., 1984), topics we'll soon examine in more detail. In contrast, Type A's are *not* more likely to engage in **instrumental aggression**—aggression performed primarily to attain other goals aside from harming the victim, goals such as control of valued resources or praise from others for behaving in a "tough" manner.

Perceiving Evil Intent in Others: Hostile Attributional Bias. Remember the shopping cart example presented earlier? In that instance, it was clear that the person who rammed you with her cart meant to do so: her action stemmed from *hostile intentions*. But what if after hitting you she had said, "Oh, I'm sorry. Please excuse me." If she appeared to be genuinely sorry, the chances are good that you would not become angry and would not seek to retaliate against her. This would be the case because our *attributions* concerning the causes of others' behavior play an important role in aggression, just as they do in many other forms of social behavior (see our discussion of this topic in Chapter 2). But what if the woman muttered "Oh, sorry," but at the same time grinned at you in a malicious way; how would you react? The answer would depend strongly on your attributions concerning her behavior. If you attributed her hitting you with her cart to hostile intentions, you would still become angry; if you decided to believe her ambiguous apology, you might simply walk away instead.

The fact that attributions play an important role in our reactions to others' behavior—and especially to apparent provocations—is the starting point for another important personal characteristic that influences aggression—the **hostile attributional bias** (e.g., Dodge et al., 1986). This term refers to the tendency to perceive hostile intentions or motives in others' actions when these actions are ambiguous. In other words, persons high in hostile attributional bias rarely give others the benefit of the doubt: they simply *assume* that any provocative actions by others are intentional, and they react accordingly—often with strong anger and overt aggression.

The results of many studies offer support for the potential impact of this factor (e.g., Dodge & Coie, 1987). In one study on this topic, Dodge and his colleagues (1990) examined the relationship between hostile attributional bias and aggression among a group of male adolescents confined to a maximum security prison for juvenile offenders. These young men had been convicted of a wide range of violent crimes, including murder, sexual assault, kidnapping, and armed robbery. The researchers hypothesized that hostile attributional bias among these youths would be related to the number of violent crimes they had committed, as well as to trained observers' ratings of the prisoners' tendencies to engage in aggression in response to provocation from others. Results offered support for both predictions. In sum, it appears that the tendency to perceive

hostile aggression • Aggression in which the prime objective is to harm the victim, as opposed to aggression whose prime objective is some other purpose.

instrumental aggression • Aggression in which the primary objective is not harm to the victim but attainment of some other goal, such as access to valued resources.

hostile attributional bias • The tendency to perceive hostile intentions or motives in others' actions when these actions are ambiguous.

malice in the actions of others, even when it doesn't really exist, is one characteristic closely related to high levels of aggression against others.

Narcissism, Ego-Threat, and Aggression: On the Dangers of Wanting to Be Superior. Do you know the story of Narcissus? He was a character in Greek mythology who fell in love with his own reflection in the water and drowned trying to reach it. His name has now become a synonym for excessive self-love; for holding an over-inflated view of one's own virtues or accomplishments. Research findings indicate that this trait may be linked to aggression in important ways. Specifically, studies by Bushman and Baumeister (1998) suggest that persons high in narcissism (ones who agree with such items as "If I ruled the world it would be a much better place." and "I am more capable than other people.") react with exceptionally high levels of aggression to slights from others—feedback that threatens their inflated self-image. Why? Because such persons have nagging doubts about the accuracy of their inflated egos and so react with intense anger toward anyone who threatens to undermine them.

These findings have important implications because at the present time, many schools in the United States focus on building high self-esteem within their students. Up to a point, this may indeed be beneficial. But if such esteem-building tactics are carried too far and produce children whose opinions of themselves are unrealistically high (i.e., narcissistic), the result may actually be an increased potential for violence. Clearly, this is a possibility worthy of further, careful study.

Gender Differences in Aggression: Do They Exist? Are males more aggressive than females? Folklore suggests that they are, and research findings suggest that in this case, such informal observation is correct: when asked whether they have ever engaged in any of a wide range of aggressive actions, males report a higher incidence of many aggressive behaviors than do females (Harris, 1994, 1997). On close examination, however, the picture regarding gender differences in aggression becomes more complex. On the one hand, males are generally more likely than females both to perform aggressive actions and to be the targets of such behavior (Bogard, 1990; Harris, 1992, 1994). Further, this difference seems to persist throughout the lifespan, occurring even among people in their 70s and 80s (Walker, Richardson, & Green, 1999). On the other hand, however, the magnitude of these gender differences appears to vary greatly across situations.

First, gender differences in aggression are much larger in the absence of provocation than in its presence. In other words, males are significantly more likely than females to aggress against others when these persons have not provoked them in any manner (Bettencourt & Miller, 1996). But in situations where provocation *is* present, and especially when it is intense, females may be just as aggressive as males.

Second, the size—and even the direction—of gender differences in aggression seem to vary greatly with the *type* of aggression in question. Research findings indicate that males are more likely than females to engage in various forms of *direct* aggression—actions that are aimed directly at the target and which clearly stem from the aggressor (e.g., physical assaults, pushing, shoving, throwing something at another person, shouting, making insulting remarks) (Bjorkqvist et al., 1994). However, females are more likely to engage in various forms of *indirect* aggression—actions that allow the aggressor to conceal his or her identity from the victim and which, in some cases, even make it difficult for victims to know that they have been the target of intentional harm-doing. Such actions include spreading vicious rumors about the target person, gossiping behind this person's back, telling others not to associate with the intended victim, making up stories to get the victim in trouble, and so on. Research findings indicate that females' greater tendencies to engage in indirect aggression are present among children as young as eight and increase through age fifteen (Bjorkqvist et al., 1992; Osterman et al., 1998), and they seem to persist into adulthood as well (Bjorkqvist, Osterman, & Hjelt-Back, 1994; Green, Richardson, & Lago, 1996). Further, these tendencies have been observed in several different countries—Finland, Sweden, Poland, and Italy (Osterman et al., 1998)—and so appear to be quite general in scope. In sum, gender differences with respect to aggression exist, but they are smaller and more complex in nature than common sense might suggest.

Do personal factors play a role in the performance of extreme acts of aggression? Please see the *Beyond the Headlines* section for a discussion of this issue.

Key Points

- Persons showing the *Type A behavior pattern* are more irritable and more aggressive than persons with the *Type B behavior pattern*.

- Individuals high in *hostile attributional bias* tend to attribute others' actions to hostile intent even when this is not so. As a result, they are more aggressive than persons low in this characteristic.

- Males are more aggressive overall than females, but this difference tends to disappear in the face of strong provocation. Males are more likely to use direct forms of aggression, but females are more likely to use indirect forms of aggression.

Beyond the Headlines:
As Social Psychologists See It
Murder of the Truly Defenseless: When Mothers Go Berserk

WOMAN GIVES BIRTH, KILLS BABY ON PLANE, COPS SAY

Associated Press, November 27, 1997—Rio De Janeiro, Brazil—A woman gave birth in an airplane bathroom during a flight over Brazil, and then killed the baby by stuffing toilet paper in its mouth and flushing it down the toilet, police said. . . . Carla Dato, 24, gave birth alone Tuesday in the lavatory of Nordeste Airlines flight 242 from Sao Paulo to Salvador. . . .

"No one had any idea she was pregnant—no one in her family, no one on the plane. She didn't want the child, so she got rid of it," police Chief Katia Alvès said by telephone. . . ."A flight attendant noticed Dato spent an abnormally long time in the bathroom and then left with blood on her jeans. She told the attendant she had a heavier than usual menstruation," Alves said.

After Dato left the plane . . . the flight crew noticed the toilet she had been using was jammed . . . maintenance workers found the body of a baby boy. An autopsy determined the baby died of asphyxiation.

Crimes like this one are truly shocking. How could a new mother murder her own child? Are there no limits to the depths of human violence? One interpretation of such actions is that the persons who perform them are suffering from serious psychological disorders; their behavior seems so abnormal that we are tempted to label them as abnormal, too. Their aggression, we reason, must stem from deep-seated mental illness—a total lack of conscience, unfounded and excessive fears, or some other psychological disorder.

While mental problems may indeed play a role in tragic cases such as this one, social psychologists also realize that violence toward infants may stem from other causes, too. Consider the young woman described in the news item. Here are some of the social factors that may have contributed to her horrendous behavior: She was single and may well have come from a deeply religious family. As a result, she may have felt intense guilt over her pregnancy and believed that her family would be greatly shamed by the birth of an illegitimate baby. This would cause them to reject her, and leave her facing a situation in which she would be unable to support herself or her new baby. Such thoughts may have been intensified by her realization that public assistance for single mothers was lacking or difficult to obtain in her native country. Faced with these conditions, she felt truly desperate: she was having a baby she didn't want and would not be able to support. What should she do? Being far from home and in a setting where she was completely anonymous, she decided on a violent and shocking course of action: she would get rid of the baby and so escape these problems.

Although this mother's actions were truly monstrous and cannot in any way be excused, a social psychological perspective helps us to understand *why* she acted as she did—what factors may have combined to produce this shocking act. Of course, it is still possible that she *is* a mentally ill person—for instance, one without any trace of a conscience. But it is also possible that she is a basically decent person driven to extreme actions by a devastating set of circumstances. Recall our discussion of Milgram's research on destructive obedience in Chapter 9, where we noted that under the right conditions, most persons seem capable of seriously harming a stranger who has done them no harm.

How should Ms. Dato be treated by her society? This is a legal issue, largely outside the realm of science. But at the very least, social psychologists' research on the nature and causes of human aggression provides us with important insights into the factors that may underlie such seemingly incomprehensible events.

Situational Determinants of Aggression: The Effects of High Temperatures and Alcohol Consumption

While aggression is often strongly influenced by social factors and personal characteristics, it is also affected by factors relating to the situation or context in which it occurs—including the extent to which aggression is viewed as acceptable by a given culture (e.g., Cohen et al., 1996). Here, we'll examine two of the many *situational factors* that can influence aggression: high temperatures and alcohol.

High Temperatures and Aggression: Does Being Hot Really Make Us Boil? *In the heat of anger. Boiling mad. Hot-tempered.* Phrases like these suggest that there may well be a link between temperature and human aggression. And in fact, many people report that they often feel especially irritable and short-tempered on hot and steamy days (see Figure 11.9). Is there really a link between climate and human aggression? Social psychologists have been studying this question for three decades, and the answer provided by their research is *yes, but only up to a point.*

Actually, I (Robert Baron) started this line of research in the early 1970s (Baron, 1972a; Baron & Lawton, 1972). Two factors led me to conduct studies on the "heat and aggression" question at that time. First, I was a professor at the University of South Carolina. Being from the North, I had never experienced

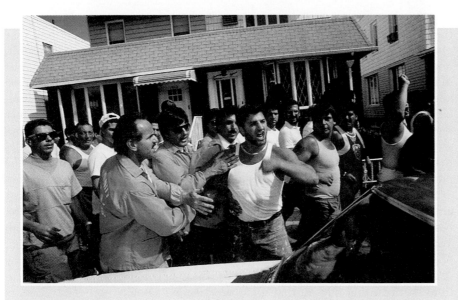

Figure 11.9
Do High Temperatures Lead to Aggression?
Research findings indicate that scenes like this one are more likely to occur when temperatures are high than when they are more moderate.

such unrelenting heat before, and I began to wonder whether it was affecting my social behavior, making me irritable and short-tempered. Second, a series of frightening riots had occurred recently in cities throughout the United States. Most of these, I noticed, took place during the summer months. Did high temperatures play a role in such events, I wondered?

These speculations led me to conduct a series of laboratory studies in which participants took part in a modified version of the teacher–learner procedures devised by Arnold Buss. In our studies we first provoked participants (by insults from an accomplice) or did not provoke them, then provided them with an opportunity to aggress against this accomplice by means of the aggression machine. In addition, we varied the temperatures in the experimental rooms. In one condition the air conditioning was on, so the rooms were comfortably cool (about 70 to 72 degrees Fahrenheit). In the other condition we shut off the air conditioning and opened the windows; this raised the temperatures to the mid- to upper 90s, the typical outdoor temperatures from May through September in Columbia, South Carolina. Results were both clear and surprising: High temperature *reduced* aggression for both provoked and unprovoked persons.

This unexpected pattern of results led me to consider the possibility that perhaps heat increases aggression, but only up to a point. Beyond some level, people become so uncomfortable that they lack the energy for engaging in aggression or any other kind of vigorous activity. To test this hypothesis—known as the *negative-affect escape model*—Paul Bell and I conducted a series of studies in which we varied temperature over a wider range (Baron & Bell, 1975; Bell & Baron, 1976). The results: Aggression did increase as temperatures rose into the mid 80s Fahrenheit, but it then dropped off at higher levels. So it appeared that, in the laboratory at least, heat does increase aggression; but that beyond a certain temperature aggression declines.

Of course, these were laboratory studies conducted under artificial and restricted conditions. Would a link between heat and aggression be found in the real world as well? Ingenious studies have been conducted to answer this question (e.g., Anderson, 1989a; Anderson & Anderson, 1996; Bell, 1992), and in general they have supported the existence of a heat–aggression link. For instance, consider a recent study by Anderson, Bushman, and Groom (1997).

These researchers collected average annual temperatures for fifty cities in the United States over a forty-five-year period (1950–1995). In addition, they obtained information on the rate of both violent crimes (aggravated assault, homicide) and property crimes (burglary, car theft), as well as on another crime that has often been viewed as primarily aggressive in nature: rape. Anderson and his colleagues then performed analyses to determine if temperature was related to these crimes. Results indicated that hotter years did indeed produce higher rates of violent crimes, but that they did *not* produce increases in property crimes or rape. This was true even when the effect of many other variables that might also influence aggressive crimes (e.g., poverty, age distribution of the population) were eliminated. In a follow-up study, Anderson and his colleagues examined the hypothesis that hot summers would lead to higher rates of violent crimes than cooler summers. Again, this relationship was obtained, but no link between heat and rape or heat and robbery or other property crime was noted. Together, these findings and those of related studies (e.g., Anderson, Anderson, & Deuser, 1996) suggest that heat is indeed linked to aggression. As noted by Anderson, Bushman, and Groom (1997), these findings have serious implications, because they suggest that if global warming actually occurs in the years ahead, this may lead to increased violence—something our species can clearly do without. One key question remains, however: does this heat–aggression relationship have any limits? In other words, does aggression increase with heat up to some point but then decrease as temperatures exceed this level, as was found in laboratory studies?

Evidence on this possibility is mixed. Several studies found no drop in aggression even at very high temperatures (e.g., Anderson & DeNeve, 1992), while others *did* report such a drop (Bell, 1992). A recent study by Cohn and Rotton (1997) helps to resolve this issue. These researchers reasoned that if the negative-affect escape model is accurate, the relationship between heat and aggression should be stronger in the evening hours, when temperatures are past their peak, than at midday. This would also be true because during the day most people are at work, and are therefore less likely to be exposed to very high temperatures. To test this hypothesis, Cohn and Rotton obtained records of physical assaults in one large city in the United States over a two-year period; they also obtained records of temperatures during each three-hour period of every day. Results indicated that the relationship between heat and aggression was indeed stronger during the evening hours than earlier in the day. In fact, most assaults occurred in the late evening or early morning hours—times when temperatures had clearly dropped from their peaks. More importantly, the overall relationship between heat and assaults was curvilinear, as shown in Figure 11.10.

So it appears that a finer-grained analysis in which several temperature readings are obtained for each day does offer support for the view that aggression increases with heat, but only up to a point. This finding is also consistent with basic biological facts; at very high temperatures, people experience physiological changes that make them feel tired. And at even higher temperatures, they may suffer effects that actually cause them to lose consciousness. Clearly, then, there *must* be limits to the heat–aggression relationship. The key question, however, is just *when* the downturn occurs. In all likelihood, this depends on many factors, such as steps people take to cope with heat, whether they work and live in air-conditioned or un-air-conditioned places, and the prevailing climate. What is "hot," subjectively, is probably very different in Houston, where temperatures are often in the 90s, than in Seattle, where such conditions are very rare. In any case, research on heat and aggression provides one clear illustration of the fact that situational factors, as well as social and personal ones, can strongly influence aggression.

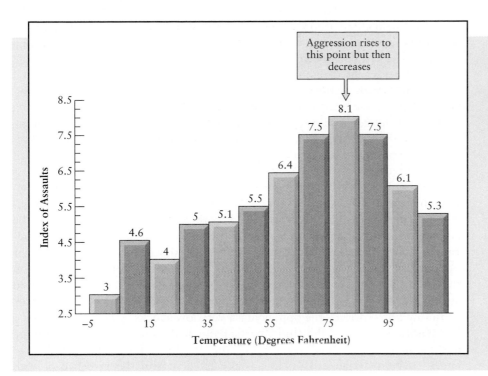

Aggression rises to this point but then decreases

Figure 11.10

Evidence That There Are Limits to the Heat-Leads-To-Aggression Relationship. As shown here, violent assaults in one city increased as temperatures rose—but only up to a point. Beyond this level, the incidence of such events actually decreased. These findings agree with the *negative-affect escape* model (Bell & Baron, 1976).

(*Source:* Based on data from Cohn & Rotton, 1997.)

Alcohol and Aggression: A Potentially Dangerous Mix. It is widely believed that some persons, at least, become more aggressive when they consume alcohol. This belief is supported by the fact that bars and nightclubs are frequently the scene of violence (see Figure 11.11). However, although alcohol is certainly consumed in these settings, other factors might be responsible for the fights—or worse—that often erupt: competition for desirable partners, crowding (which leads people to jostle one another), and even cigarette smoke, which irritates some people (Zillmann, Baron, & Tamborini, 1981). What does systematic

Figure 11.11

Alcohol and Aggression: A Volatile Mix. High levels of aggression occur in bars and other places where individuals consume alcohol. Is this pattern due to the alcohol or to other factors present in such locations? Research findings suggest that alcohol does play a role.

research reveal about a possible link between alcohol and aggression? Interestingly, it tends to confirm the existence of an alcohol–aggression link. In several experiments, participants who consumed substantial doses of alcohol—enough to make them legally drunk—have been found to behave more aggressively, and to respond to provocations more strongly, than those who did not consume alcohol (e.g., Bushman & Cooper, 1990; Gustafson, 1990). (Needless to state, participants in such research are always warned in advance that they may be receiving alcoholic beverages, and only those who consent to such procedures actually take part.) A recent study by Pihl, Lau, and Assaad (1997) illustrates such effects very clearly.

These researchers had young male volunteers consume drinks containing either substantial doses of alcohol (1 ml per kilogram of body weight) or no alcohol. Then the volunteers competed with a fictitious opponent in the competitive reaction-time task described earlier in this chapter. As you may recall, in this task, participants can set the level of shock to be received by their opponent on each trial if this person "loses" (responds slower than they do) on that trial. During the reaction-time task, participants were exposed either to strong provocation—their opponent set increasing shocks for them to receive, or to low provocation—the opponent set very low shocks.

Before the start of the study, participants had completed a questionnaire and an interview designed to reveal whether they were low or high in the tendency to behave aggressively. It was predicted that in the presence of high provocation, those high in aggressive tendencies (high aggressors) would be more aggressive regardless of whether they consumed alcohol. As shown in Figure 11.12, however, this was *not* the case. While high aggressors were more aggressive than low aggressors when both groups were sober, this difference disappeared after both groups consumed alcohol. High aggressors became slightly *less* aggressive when intoxicated, while low aggressors became significantly *more* aggressive. These findings, and those of many other studies (e.g., Gantner & Taylor, 1992), suggest that alcohol may indeed be one situational factor contributing to the occurrence of aggression, and that such effects may be especially strong for persons who do not normally engage in aggression. In view of these findings, perhaps a new phrase should be added to the warning label

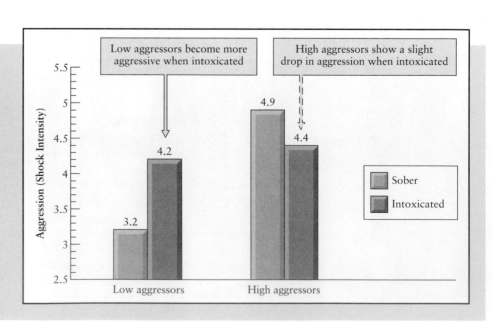

Figure 11.12
The Effects of Alcohol on Aggression: Empirical Evidence. Individuals with relatively weak tendencies to aggress (low aggressors) became more aggressive when intoxicated. In contrast, individuals with strong aggressive tendencies became slightly *less* aggressive when intoxicated.

(*Source:* Based on data from Pihl, Lau, & Assad, 1997.)

placed on all alcoholic beverages in the United States. The label currently mentions potential dangers relating to pregnancy and to driving a car or operating machinery. Perhaps it should add: "*(3) Consumption of alcohol may increase dangerous instances of aggression.*"

For an overview of the many factors that play a role in human aggression, please see the *Ideas to Take with You* section on page 475.

Key Points

- High temperatures tend to increase aggression, but only up to a point. Beyond some level, aggression declines as temperatures rise.

- Consuming alcohol can increase aggression—especially, it appears, in individuals who normally show low levels of aggression.

CHILD ABUSE AND WORKPLACE VIOLENCE: AGGRESSION IN LONG-TERM RELATIONSHIPS

Reports of instances in which persons are attacked by total strangers are disturbing. Even more unsettling, however, are situations in which individuals are harmed by persons they know or with whom they have long-term relationships. While such aggression takes many different forms, we'll focus here on two important topics: *child abuse* (or *maltreatment*) (Peterson & Brown, 1994) and *workplace violence* (Baron & Neuman, 1996).

Child Maltreatment: Harming the Innocent

Children, most adults would strongly agree, are to be cherished, protected, and loved. Yet a total of 2.7 million cases of **child maltreatment**—actions that harm children either physically or psychologically—occur each year in the United States alone (Children's Defense Fund, 1992). Such maltreatment takes many different forms, but most cases involve: (1) physical abuse (attacks that produce physical injuries); (2) sexual abuse (fondling, intercourse, and other forced sexual contacts); (3) physical neglect (living conditions in which children do not receive sufficient food, clothing, medical attention, or supervision); (4) emotional neglect (failure of parents or other adults to meet children's need for affection and emotional support); and/or (5) psychological abuse (actions that damage children emotionally, such as rejection and verbal abuse).

Who are the persons who commit such acts? You might assume that they would be some kind of monsters—seriously deranged persons who, perhaps, were abused themselves as children; but research findings paint a different picture. Although some persons who abuse children were indeed mistreated themselves, most were not. In fact, many persons who mistreat children appear to be quite normal psychologically (e.g., Emery, 1989). So there does not appear to be a single "abuse personality type" against which we must be carefully on guard.

What, then, are the roots of this disturbing problem? One model that helps clarify this issue has been proposed by Peterson and Brown (1994). As shown in Figure 11.13 on page 464, this model assumes that instances of child maltreatment involve *sociocultural variables*—factors such as poverty, crowded living conditions, frequent moves, and isolation from others—as well as *caregiver-based variables*—factors relating to caregivers such as having been abused themselves

child maltreatment •
Actions that harm children either physically or psychologically.

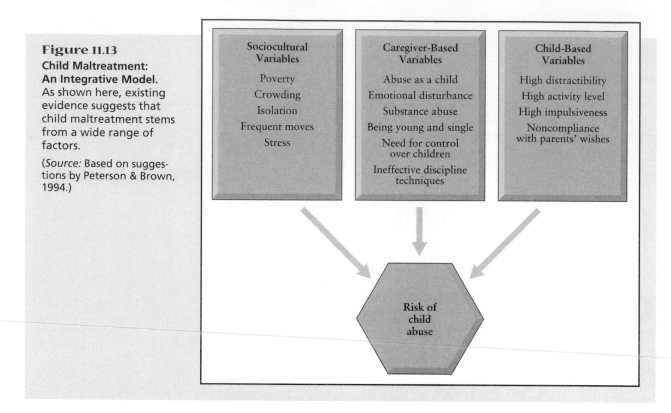

Figure 11.13
Child Maltreatment: An Integrative Model. As shown here, existing evidence suggests that child maltreatment stems from a wide range of factors.

(*Source:* Based on suggestions by Peterson & Brown, 1994.)

as youngsters, emotional disturbances, substance abuse, being young and single, and intense needs for exerting control over children. Finally, the model calls attention to the importance of *child-based variables*—characteristics of children that are related to maltreatment. These include being highly distractible, showing a high activity level, being impulsive, and being resistant to parental control and discipline. In short, this model, which is based on the results of many different studies, suggests that child maltreatment arises out of a complex interplay among many different variables. The overall portrait that emerges is one in which parents living in disadvantaged backgrounds must cope with overactive, resistant children and must do so under the burdens of their own emotional problems, youth, inexperience, and (often) drugs. This is not a pretty picture, but it does help explain why some parents and other caregivers harm rather than nurture children.

Familicide: Extreme Violence within Families. Tragic though maltreatment of children is, there are instances in which such behavior takes even more extreme forms. In these cases, parents actually murder their own children; we examined one instance of infanticide in the *Beyond the Headlines* section earlier in this chapter. Unfortunately, such actions are far from rare. In fact, they are often part of a larger pattern known as **familicide**—instances in which an individual kills his or her spouse and one or more of his or her children. We say "his or her," but the vast majority of these actions are carried out by males. A study that examined all cases of familicide in several countries during a sixteen-year period (Wilson et al., 1995) found that between 93 percent and 97 percent of these crimes were committed by men.

What factors lead men to perform such ghastly actions? Research suggests that two patterns are common. In the first, the killer expresses great anger at his wife, especially with respect to real or imagined sexual infidelities or the wife's

familicide • Instances in which an individual kills his or her spouse and one or more of his or her children.

intention to leave the marriage. "If I can't have her, no one else will!" is how many of these murderers put it.

The second pattern involves suicide by the man who has murdered his spouse and children, and it seems to stem from deep depression. Such persons often leave suicide notes stating that "this is the only way out." They seem to commit murder and then suicide when their lives become too painful to bear—for example, when illegal business activities are about to surface, or when they have experienced major failures. Whatever the precise reasons behind familicide, it is a truly frightening instance of aggression in the context of intimate long-term relationships.

Workplace Violence: Aggression on the Job

City of Industry, California—A postal worker walked up to his boss, pulled a gun from a paper bag and shot him dead, the latest incident in an alarming increase in workplace violence. Los Angeles Times, July 18, 1995.)

Portland, Oregon—A man accused of shooting two people and taking four others hostage in an office tower appeared in court Friday. . . . Police initially said Rancor intended to shoot female office workers for having him fired from his job . . . but investigators said Friday that Rancor had problems with authority in general. (Associated Press, 1996.)

Reports of incidents such as these have appeared with alarming frequency in recent years, and appear to reflect a rising tide of violence in workplaces. In fact, more than eight hundred people are murdered at work each year in the United States alone (National Institute for Occupational Safety and Health, 1993). These statistics might seem to suggest that workplaces are becoming truly dangerous locations where disgruntled employees frequently attack or even shoot one another, but two facts should be carefully noted: (1) A large majority of violence occurring in work settings is performed by outsiders—people who do not work there but who enter a workplace to commit robbery or other crimes (see Figure 11.14). And (2) careful surveys indicate that threats of physical harm or actual harm in work settings are quite rare. In fact, the chances of being killed at work—by outsiders or coworkers combined—are something like 1 in 450,000 overall (although this is considerably higher in some high-risk occupations such as taxi driving or police work) (Sloboda, 1996).

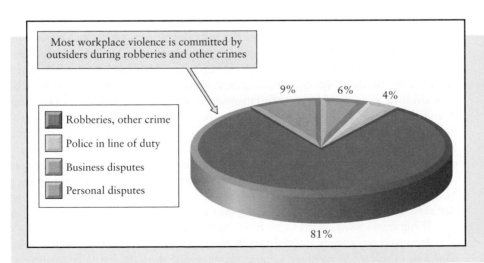

Figure 11.14
Workplace Violence: A Closer Look. As shown here, most instances of workplace violence are performed by outsiders during robberies and other crimes. Very few instances involve attacks by one employee upon another.

(*Source:* Adapted from Baron & Neuman, 1996.)

In sum, growing evidence suggests that workplace *violence,* although certainly an important topic worthy of careful study, is relatively rare and is actually only the dramatic tip of the much larger problem of **workplace aggression**—all forms of behavior through which individuals seek to harm others in their workplace (Baron & Neuman, 1996; Neuman & Baron, 1998). What is workplace aggression like? Research evidence indicates that it is largely *covert* rather than *overt* in nature. That is, like *indirect aggression,* which we discussed earlier, covert aggression is relatively subtle and allows aggressors to harm other persons while simultaneously preventing the targets from identifying them as the source of the harm. This type of aggression is strongly preferred in workplaces for the following reason: Aggressors in such settings expect to interact with their intended victims frequently in the future. Using covert forms of aggression reduces the likelihood that the victims will retaliate against them.

What specific forms of aggression do individuals actually use in workplaces? A recent study by Baron, Neuman, and Geddes (1999) provides information on this issue. These researchers asked almost five hundred employed persons to rate the frequency with which they had personally experienced a wide range of aggressive behaviors at work. Careful analysis of their responses indicated that most aggression occurring in workplaces falls into three major categories:

- *Expressions of hostility:* Behaviors that are primarily verbal or symbolic in nature (e.g., belittling others' opinions, talking behind their backs).
- *Obstructionism:* Behaviors designed to obstruct or impede the target's performance (e.g., failure to return phone calls or respond to memos, failure to transmit needed information, interference with activities important to the target).
- *Overt aggression:* Behaviors that have typically been included under the heading "workplace violence" (e.g., physical assault, theft or destruction of property, threats of physical violence).

Additional findings indicated that, as you might expect, expressions of hostility and instances of obstructionism are much more frequent than instances of overt aggression. Thus, covert forms of aggression do seem to be strongly preferred by most persons in most work settings.

What are the causes of such behavior? Again, as is true of aggression in any context, many factors seem to play a role. However, one that emerged again and again in research on this topic is *perceived unfairness* (e.g., Greenberg & Alge, 1997; Skarlicki & Folger, 1997; Neuman & Baron, 1997). When individuals feel that they have been treated unfairly by others in their organization—or by their organization itself—they experience intense feelings of anger and resentment and often seek to even the score by harming the people they hold responsible in some manner. As we'll see in Chapter 12, they may attempt to accomplish this goal through many different actions, ranging from subtle obstructionism to petty theft or vandalism to direct physical assaults. Have you heard the phrase "going postal"? This expression, meaning "going violently berserk," arose because in recent years several employees of the United States Postal Service have engaged in violence such as that in the incident at the start of this section. Recent research suggests that one important cause of these attacks is intense feelings of unfairness. The persons involved believe that they have been fired, passed over for promotion, or mistreated in some other way *unfairly,* and this belief plays an important role in their subsequent aggression (Folger et al., 1998).

Perceived unfairness is only part of the total story, however; other factors, too, play a role in workplace aggression. Some of these relate to changes that

workplace aggression • All forms of behavior through which individuals seek to harm others in their workplace.

Figure 11.15

Changes in Workplaces: One Important Cause of Workplace Aggression. In recent years millions of employees have lost their jobs because of layoffs, downsizing, and/or increased use of part-time help. These events generate negative feelings among persons who remain on the job, and so may increase the likelihood of workplace aggression.

have occurred recently in many workplaces: downsizing, layoffs, increased use of temporary and part-time employees, to name a few (see Figure 11.15). Several recent studies indicate that the greater the extent to which these changes have occurred, the greater the aggression occurring in such workplaces (e.g., Baron & Neuman, 1996; Neuman & Baron, 1998). Although these findings are only correlational in nature, it is known that downsizing, layoffs, and other changes produce negative feelings among employees (e.g., increased anxiety and feelings of resentment). So it seems possible that these changes may well contribute, through such reactions, to increased aggression. Because downsizing and other changes have occurred with increasing frequency in recent years, it seems possible that the incidence of workplace aggression, too, may be increasing for this reason.

In sum, media attention to dramatic instances of workplace violence may be somewhat misleading; while such actions do indeed occur, they are far less frequent than more subtle but still harmful instances of workplace aggression. And such behavior, in turn, appears to be influenced by many of the same factors that influence aggression in other contexts. Our conclusion: Workplace aggression is not a new or unique form of behavior; rather, it is simply aggression occurring in one kind of setting. Thus, efforts to understand it—and to reduce it—should be linked as closely as possible to the large body of research on human aggression summarized in this chapter and in other sources.

Key Points

- *Child maltreatment* stems from many factors, including sociocultural variables as well as characteristics of the persons who engage in such behavior and characteristics of the children they harm.

- *Familicide,* murder of members of one's own family, is performed almost entirely by males. It appears to stem most often from sexual jealousy or from the belief that this is the only way out of a hopeless situation.

- *Workplace aggression* takes many different forms but is usually covert in nature. A wide range of factors influence workplace aggression, including perceptions of unfairness and many disturbing changes that have occurred in workplaces in recent years.

THE PREVENTION AND CONTROL OF AGGRESSION: SOME USEFUL TECHNIQUES

If there is one idea in this chapter we hope you'll remember in the years ahead, it is this: Aggression is *not* an inevitable or unchangeable form of behavior. On the contrary, because it stems from a complex interplay of external events, cognitions, and personal characteristics, it *can* be prevented or reduced. In this final section we'll consider several procedures that, when used appropriately, can be effective in this regard.

Punishment: An Effective Deterrent to Violence?

In New York state, where we both live, a key issue in one recent election for governor was *capital punishment*—the death penalty. One of the candidates was strongly against capital punishment; the other favored it. Although the two candidates had many reasons for these opposing views, the one that was emphasized throughout the election campaign was the potential value of capital punishment as a *deterrent* to crimes of violence. One of the candidates felt that capital punishment would *not* deter criminals from engaging in aggressive acts, while the other felt that it would. As we'll explain below, this is a complex issue, and evidence relating to it is mixed. Thus, we can't resolve it here. What we *can* do, however, is point out a few pertinent facts about the use of **punishment**— delivery of aversive consequences in order to decrease some behavior—as a technique for reducing aggression.

First, we should note that existing evidence suggests that punishment *can* succeed in deterring individuals from engaging in many forms of behavior. However, such effects are neither automatic nor certain. Unless punishment is administered in accordance with basic principles, it can be totally *ineffective* in

punishment • Delivery of aversive consequences to individuals in order to decrease some behavior.

this respect. What conditions must be met for punishment to succeed? Four are most important: (1) It must be *prompt*—it must follow aggressive actions as quickly as possible. (2) It must be *certain*—the probability that it will follow aggression must be very high. (3) It must be *strong*—strong enough to be highly unpleasant to potential recipients. And (4) it must be perceived by recipients as *justified* or deserved.

Unfortunately, as you can readily see, these conditions are often *not* present in the criminal justice systems of many nations. In many societies the delivery of punishment for aggressive actions is delayed for months or even years; in the United States, for example, convicted murderers often spend more than a decade on death row, awaiting execution. Similarly, many criminals avoid arrest and conviction, so the certainty of punishment is low. The magnitude of punishment itself varies from one city, state, or even courtroom to another. For example, in one famous and controversial case, a young woman from the United Kingdom was convicted of causing the death of a child in her care. The judge then sentenced her to the amount of time she had already served in jail while waiting for her trial! This decision caused a public outcry against a legal system that could deliver such mild punishment for such a serious crime (see Figure 11.16). In view of all these inadequacies in the implementation of punishment, it is hardly surprising that most recipients of punishment view it as undeserved: after all, they are being punished while others are going totally free.

Would punishment prove valuable as a deterrent to violence if it were used more effectively? We can't say for sure, but existing evidence suggests that it could, potentially, exert such effects *if* it were used in accordance with the principles described above.

Before concluding, let's return briefly to the issue of capital punishment. Putting aside the complex ethical and religious issues it raises, we can ask: Is the death penalty an effective deterrent to crimes of violence? As currently used, we doubt it. So few people are ever executed that everyone, criminals included, realizes that the probability of experiencing this fate is close to nonexistent.

Figure 11.16
Punishment: Why It Often Fails to Deter Aggression. The young woman shown here was convicted by a jury of causing the death of a child in her care. Yet the judge in this case sentenced her only to a few months in prison— time she had already served waiting for the trial. When punishment is so mild and so uncertain, it is unlikely to deter aggressive crimes.

Under these conditions, it is difficult to see how capital punishment can be expected to exert any measurable deterrent effects. But there may be another justification for such punishment—one that is rarely mentioned in debates on this issue. While capital punishment may not deter others from performing aggressive acts, it does indeed make it impossible for those who receive it to harm additional defenseless victims. This may be an important consideration because, sad to relate, many crimes of violence are performed by repeat offenders—persons who were previously convicted of violent crimes but are now back on the street. We should hasten to add that all forms of punishment, and capital punishment especially, raise important ethical issues that neither we nor any other psychologists can resolve. However, given the high incidence of crimes of violence in many countries, it does seem important to examine carefully every available means for protecting innocent victims.

Catharsis: Does Getting It out of Your System Really Help?

When I (Robert Baron) was a little boy, my grandmother used to greet my temper tantrums by saying: "That's right, get it out . . . don't keep it bottled up inside—that will hurt you." She truly believed in the **catharsis hypothesis**—the view that if individuals give vent to their anger and hostility in relatively nonharmful ways, their tendencies to engage in more dangerous types of aggression will be reduced (Dollard et al., 1939).

Is this hypothesis valid? Contrary to what the cartoon in Figure 11.17 suggests, existing evidence offers a mixed picture (Feshbach, 1984; Geen, 1991b). On the one hand, participation in various activities that are not harmful to others (e.g., vigorous physical activity, shouting obscenities into an empty room) can reduce emotional arousal stemming from frustration or provocation (Zillmann, 1979). On the other hand, such effects appear to be temporary. Arousal stemming from provocation may reappear as soon as individuals remember the incidents that made them angry (Caprara et al., 1994).

What about the idea that performing "safe" aggressive actions reduces the likelihood of more harmful forms of aggression? The results of research on this issue are even less encouraging. Overt physical aggression, it appears, is not reduced by (1) watching scenes of media violence (Geen, 1978), (2) attacking inanimate objects (Bushman, Baumeister, & Stack, 1999; Mallick & McCandless, 1966), or (3) aggressing verbally against others. Indeed, some findings suggest that aggression may actually be *increased* by these activities. For instance, Bushman, Baumeister, and Stack (1999) recently found that hitting a punching bag increased rather than reduced aggression.

In short, contrary to popular belief, catharsis does not appear to be a very effective means for reducing aggression. Participating in "safe" forms of aggression or merely in vigorous, energy-draining activities may produce temporary reductions in arousal; but feelings of anger may quickly return when individuals meet, or merely think about, the persons who previously annoyed them. For this reason, catharsis may be less effective in producing lasting reductions in aggression than is widely believed.

Cognitive Interventions: Apologies and Overcoming Cognitive Deficits

Suppose that you are standing at the counter in a store, waiting your turn. Suddenly, another customer walks up and starts to place an order. You are beginning to get angry when this person turns toward you, notices you, and quickly apologizes. "I'm so sorry," he says. "I didn't see you. You were here first." How do you react? Probably, your anger will dissipate; you may even smile at this person in appreciation for his courtesy. This incident suggests that **apologies**—admissions

catharsis hypothesis • The view that opportunities to express anger and hostility in relatively safe ways will reduce a person's likelihood of engaging in more harmful forms of aggression.

apologies • Admissions of wrongdoing that include requests for forgiveness.

Figure 11.17

Catharsis: Is It Really Effective? Contrary to what this cartoon suggests, there is little evidence that releasing one's anger or hostility can reduce subsequent aggression.

(*Source:* Chicago Tribune News Syndicate, 1980.)

of wrongdoing that include expressions of regret and requests for forgiveness—often go a long way toward defusing aggression (see Figure 11.18). Research findings support this conclusion: apologies (e.g., Ohbuchi, Kameda, & Agarie, 1989), and excuses that make reference to factors beyond the excuse-giver's control, are quite effective in reducing aggression by persons who have been provoked in some manner (e.g., Baron, 1989b; Weiner et al., 1987). So if you feel that you are making another person angry, apologize without delay. The trouble you will save makes it quite worthwhile to say "I'm sorry."

Other cognitive mechanisms for reducing aggression relate to the fact that when we are very angry, our ability to think clearly—for instance, to evaluate the consequences of our own actions—may be sharply reduced. As a result, the effectiveness of restraints that normally serve to hold aggression in check (e.g., fear of retaliation) may be reduced. In addition, as noted recently by Lieberman and Greenberg (1999), we may adopt modes of thought in which we process information in a quick and impetuous manner, thus increasing the chances that we will "lash out against" someone else—including other persons who are *not* the

Figure 11.18

Apologies: One Effective Technique for Reducing Aggression. Research findings indicate that *apologies*—admissions of wrongdoing accompanied by pleas for forgiveness—are highly effective in reducing anger and subsequent aggression.

cause of our annoyance or irritation. (This phenomenon is known as *displaced aggression*—aggression is directed against innocent victims rather than the persons who provoked us or caused our discomfort (Lieberman & Greenberg, 1999; Tedeschi & Norman, 1985). Any procedures that serve to overcome such *cognitive deficits,* therefore, may help reduce overt aggression (Zillmann, 1993). One such technique involves *preattribution*—attributing annoying actions by others to *unintentional* causes before the provocation actually occurs. For example, before meeting with someone you know can be irritating, you could remind yourself that she or he doesn't mean to make you angry—it's just the result of an unfortunate personal style. Another technique involves preventing yourself (or others) from dwelling on real or imagined wrongs. You can accomplish this by distracting yourself in some way—for instance, by watching an absorbing movie or television program or working on complex puzzles. Such activities allow for a cooling-off period during which anger can dissipate. They also help to reestablish cognitive controls over behavior—controls that help to hold aggression in check.

Other Techniques for Reducing Aggression: Exposure to Nonaggressive Models, Training in Social Skills, and Incompatible Responses

Many other techniques for reducing overt aggression have been developed and tested. Here, briefly, are three more that appear to be quite effective.

Exposure To Nonaggressive Models: The Contagion of Restraint. If exposure to aggressive actions by others in the media or in person can increase aggression, it seems possible that exposure to *non*aggressive behavior might produce opposite effects. In fact, the results of several studies indicate that this is so (e.g., Baron, 1972b; Donnerstein & Donnerstein, 1976). When individuals who have been provoked are exposed to others who either demonstrate or urge restraint, the tendency of potential aggressors to lash out is reduced. These findings suggest that it may be useful to place restrained, nonaggressive models in tense and potentially dangerous situations. Their presence may well tip the balance against overt violence.

Training in Social Skills: Learning to Get Along with Others. One reason many persons become involved in aggressive encounters is that they are sorely lacking in basic social skills. They don't know how to respond to provocations from others in a way that will soothe these persons rather than annoy them. They don't know how to make requests, or how to say no to requests from others, without making people angry. Persons lacking in basic social skills seem to account for a high proportion of violence in many societies (Toch, 1985), so equipping such persons with improved social skills may go a long way toward reducing aggression.

Fortunately, procedures for teaching individuals such skills exist and are not very complex. For example, both adults and children can rapidly acquire improved social skills by watching other persons (social models) demonstrate both effective and ineffective behaviors (Schneider, 1991). Such gains can be obtained through just a few hours of treatment (Bienert & Schneider, 1993), so this approach is practical and cost-effective as well as successful.

incompatible response technique • A technique for reducing aggression in which individuals are exposed to events or stimuli that cause them to experience affective states incompatible with anger or aggression.

Incompatible Responses: People Who Feel Good Don't Aggress. Suppose you were in a situation where you felt yourself growing angry and then someone told a joke that made you laugh. Would you remain angry? Probably not. Why? Because laughter and the positive affect it generates are incompatible with feeling angry and actually aggressing. This is the basis for another approach to reducing aggression known as the **incompatible response technique** (e.g., Baron,

1993b). This technique attempts to defuse potential hostilities by exposing individuals to events or stimuli that cause them to experience affective states incompatible with anger or aggression.

What stimuli or experiences produce such incompatible affective states? Research findings indicate that humor, mild sexual arousal, and feelings of empathy toward the victim are all effective in this respect (e.g., Baron, 1983, 1993; Richardson et al., 1994). Of course, this technique can readily be overdone: trying to make someone laugh when they are already extremely angry can backfire and make them even angrier. But if used early in the process—before individuals have become enraged—efforts to replace negative internal states such as annoyance with positive ones can be quite effective.

Social Diversity: A Critical Analysis
"Would You Murder Someone You Truly Hated If You Could Get Away with It?" Cultural and Gender Differences in Aggressive Intentions

Throughout this chapter, we've tried to be upbeat—to emphasize the positive whenever we could. But aggression is a disturbing topic, and to cover the literature in this field accurately, we've touched on many unsettling issues—child maltreatment, workplace violence, and the "long hot summer" effect, to name just a few. Our discussions of these topics may have left you with the following thought: Virtually *anyone* is capable of engaging in serious forms of aggression under certain circumstances. While we generally agree with this conclusion, we wish to temper it with a note of optimism. At least one recent study suggests that in the battle between factors that lead to aggression and forces that restrain such activities—for instance, cultural and religious values against harming others—the restraining forces almost always win.

Evidence pointing to this conclusion is provided by a study conducted by Russell and Baenninger (1997). In this research students at two universities, one in a small town in Canada and one in a large city in the United States, were asked to respond to a series of unusual—one might say outrageous—questions. For example: "Would you be willing to help out a beginning knife-thrower by volunteering to be his/her practice target?" "Would you agree to be carried across Niagara Falls on the shoulders of an expert tightrope walker?" Included among the questions was the following item: *"If it were arranged that you could never be identified or arrested and there was no possibility of retaliation, would you personally kill someone you knew and thoroughly hated?"*

What would *you* answer to this question—yes or no? And what do you think the participants in this study said? Results were, from our point of view, quite encouraging: in both universities, a relatively small percentage of the students indicated that they would engage in such behav-

ior. As you might guess, males said yes significantly more often than females (more than 14.11 percent versus about 5.49 percent), and a slightly higher percentage of U.S. students than Canadian students answered yes (10.7 percent versus 8.9 percent). But overall, very similar results were obtained in both locations, despite the fact that the students at these two schools differed sharply in many ways (e.g., racial and ethnic background). In both cases, the number saying they would kill someone they hated was quite low.

Additional findings indicated that persons who described themselves as highly irritable were more likely to answer yes than those who reported being less irritable; also, persons who were religious answered yes less often than those who did not. These two findings make good sense and suggest that participants were in fact providing their true views when answering this outrageous question.

Of course, answers to any questionnaire are only that—marks on paper. As we noted in Chapter 4, they do not necessarily provide accurate predictors of actual behavior. But this suggests, of course, that the proportion who would actually engage in such aggression is even lower—perhaps considerably lower—than the numbers reported. For this reason, we prefer to interpret these results as somewhat encouraging: even under what could be described as ideal conditions for murder—a hated enemy at one's total mercy—large majorities of the persons questioned reported that they could not take advantage of the situation. The balance, it appears, is strongly in favor of restraint rather than violence. Can we tip the balance even farther in this direction? We aren't certain; but, given the massive weapons of destruction human beings have at their disposal, we don't see any choice but to try.

Key Points

- *Punishment* can be effective in reducing aggression, but only when it is delivered in accordance with specific principles.

- The *catharsis hypothesis* appears to be mainly false. Engaging in vigorous activities may produce reductions in arousal, but these are only temporary. Similarly, engaging in apparently "safe" forms of aggression does not reduce aggressive tendencies.

- Aggression can be reduced by *apologies*—admissions of wrongdoing that include requests for forgiveness—and by engaging in activities that distract attention away from causes of anger.

- Aggression can also be reduced by exposure to nonaggressive models, training in social skills, and the induction of affective states incompatible with aggression.

- Very few persons indicate that they would murder a hated enemy even if they were certain they could get away with this crime. This suggests the existence of strong values against violence in many cultures.

Connections: Integrating Social Psychology

In this chapter, you read about . . .	In other chapters, you will find related discussions of . . .
the role of cognitive and affective variables in aggression	the role of these variables in attitude change (Chapter 4), prejudice (Chapter 6), and helping (Chapter 10)
social factors that play a role in aggression	the effects of these factors on attributions (Chapter 2), arousal (Chapter 7), and prosocial behavior (Chapter 10)
personal characteristics that influence aggression	the role of these characteristics in impression formation (Chapter 2), attraction and relationships (Chapters 7 and 8), compliance (Chapter 9), and prosocial behavior (Chapter 10)

Thinking about Connections

1. Attorneys sometimes defend individuals who have commited violent acts—including murder—by suggesting that these persons were "overwhelmed" by emotions beyond their control. In view of our discussions in other chapters (e.g., Chapter 3, Chapter 10) of the effects of emotions on social thought and social behavior, what are your reactions to such defenses?

2. As we noted in Chapter 8, intimate relationships are complex. What aspects of such relationships do you think might determine how the persons in them would react to sexual jealousy? In other words, what facets of intimate relationships

might determine whether jealousy would lead to overt aggression?

3. Violence and other forms of aggression appear to be increasing in many workplaces. Do you think it would be possible to screen potential employees so as to reject those who have a high propensity for engaging in such behavior? If so, what aspects of their self-concept (Chapter 5), attitudes (see Chapter 4), or past behavior (e.g., the kind of relationships they have had with others, see Chapter 8), might be useful predictors of the likelihood that they would engage in workplace aggression if hired?

Ideas to Take with You
Causes of Human Aggression: An Overview

Research findings indicate that aggression stems from a wide range of variables—social factors, personal characteristics, and situational factors. Here is an overview of the most important factors identified by systematic research.

Social Determinants of Aggression

Frustration ⟶

Direct provocation ⟶   Aggression

Exposure to media violence ⟶

Heightened arousal ⟶

Personal Determinants of Aggression

Type A behavior pattern ⟶

Hostile attributional bias ⟶   Aggression

Gender ⟶

Situational Determinants of Aggression

High temperatures ⟶

Alcohol ⟶   Aggression

Cultural beliefs, values ⟶

SUMMARY AND REVIEW OF KEY POINTS

Theoretical Perspectives on Aggression: In Search of the Roots of Violence

- *Aggression* is the intentional infliction of harm on others.

- *Instinct theories* suggest that aggression stems largely from innate urges or tendencies. Social psychologists reject this idea, but they do recognize the potential role of biological factors in human aggression.

- *Drive theories* suggest that aggression stems from externally elicited drives to harm or injure others. The frustration–aggression hypothesis is the most famous example of such theories.

- Modern theories of aggression such as the *general affective aggression model* (GAAM) recognize the importance in aggression of learning, various eliciting input variables, cognitions, individual tendencies, and affective states.

Determinants of Human Aggression: Social, Personal, Situational

- In order to study aggression, social psychologists often use procedures devised by Arnold Buss and an apparatus known as the *aggression machine.*

- Contrary to the famous *frustration–aggression hypothesis,* not all aggression stems from frustration, and frustration does not always lead to aggression. Frustration is a strong elicitor of aggression only under certain limited conditions.

- In contrast, *provocation* from others is a powerful elicitor of aggression. We rarely turn the other cheek; rather, we match—or slightly exceed—the level of aggression we receive from others.

- Exposure to media violence has been found to increase aggression among viewers. This occurs because of several factors, such as the priming of aggressive thoughts and a weakening of restraints against aggression.

- Heightened arousal can increase aggression if it persists beyond the situation in which it was induced and is falsely interpreted as anger.

- Mild levels of sexual arousal reduce aggression, while higher levels increase such behavior.

- Persons showing the *Type A behavior pattern* are more irritable and more aggressive than persons with the *Type B behavior pattern.*

- Individuals high in *hostile attributional bias* tend to attribute others' actions to hostile intent even when this is not so. As a result, they are more aggressive than persons low in this characteristic.

- Persons high in *narcissism* (ones who hold an overinflated view of their own worth) react with exceptionally high levels of aggression to feedback from others that poses a threat to their egos.

- Males are more aggressive overall than females, but this difference tends to disappear in the face of strong provocation. Males are more likely to use direct forms of aggression, but females are more likely to use indirect forms of aggression.
- High temperatures tend to increase aggression, but only up to a point. Beyond some level, aggression declines as temperatures rise.
- Consuming alcohol can increase aggression—especially, it appears, in individuals who normally show low levels of aggression.

Child Abuse and Workplace Violence: Aggression in Long-Term Relationships

- *Child maltreatment* stems from many factors, including sociocultural variables as well as characteristics of the persons who engage in such behavior and characteristics of the children they harm.
- *Familicide,* murder of members of one's own family, is performed almost entirely by males. It appears to stem most often from sexual jealousy or from the belief that this is the only way out of a hopeless situation.
- *Workplace aggression* takes many different forms but is usually covert in nature. A wide range of factors influence

workplace aggression, including perceptions of unfairness and many disturbing changes that have occurred in workplaces in recent years.

The Prevention and Control of Aggression: Some Useful Techniques

- *Punishment* can be effective in reducing aggression, but only when it is delivered in accordance with specific principles.
- The *catharsis hypothesis* appears to be mainly false. Engaging in vigorous activities may produce reductions in arousal, but these are only temporary. Similarly, engaging in apparently "safe" forms of aggression does not reduce aggressive tendencies.
- Aggression can be reduced by *apologies*—admissions of wrongdoing that include requests for forgiveness—and by engaging in activities that distract attention away from causes of anger.
- Aggression can also be reduced by exposure to nonaggressive models, training in social skills, and the induction of affective states incompatible with aggression.
- Very few persons indicate that they would murder a hated enemy even if they were certain they could get away with this crime. This suggests the existence of strong values against violence in many cultures.

KEY TERMS

aggression (p. 440)
aggression machine (p. 446)
apologies (p. 470)
catharsis hypothesis (p. 470)
child maltreatment (p. 463)
drive theories (of aggression) (p. 443)
excitation transfer theory (p. 452)
familicide (p. 464)
frustration–aggression hypothesis (p. 448)
general affective aggression model (p. 443)

hostile aggression (p. 455)
hostile attributional bias (p. 455)
incompatible response technique (p. 472)
instinct theories (p. 441)
instrumental aggression (p. 455)
provocation (p. 449)
punishment (p. 468)
type A behavior pattern (p. 454)
type B behavior pattern (p. 454)
workplace aggression (p. 466)

FOR MORE INFORMATION

Baron, R. A., & Richardson, D. R. (1994). *Human aggression* (2nd ed.). New York: Plenum.

This book provides a broad overview of current knowledge about human aggression. Separate chapters focus on the biological, social, environmental, and personal determinants of aggression. Additional chapters examine the development of aggression, the prevention and control of such behavior, and its occurrence in many natural contexts.

Geen, R., & Donnerstein, E. (Eds.). (1998). *Human aggression: Theories, research and implications for policy.* Pacific Grove, CA: Brooks/Cole.

Leading experts examine recent research on the nature and causes of human aggression. Topics covered include the role of environmental factors in aggression (e.g., the effects of high temperatures), the effects of exposure to media violence, and the effects of exposure to violent pornography.

Van den Bos, G. R., & Bulato, E. Q. (Eds.). (1996). *Violence on the job: Identifying risks and developing solutions.* Washington, DC: American Psychological Association.

What are the causes of workplace violence? How can such behavior be reduced or prevented? These are the central questions addressed in this book, which reviews recent research on the ways in which people who work together seek to harm one another. A very good place to start if you want to know more about this timely and important topic.

12

Groups and Individuals: The Consequences of Belonging

Global Community. © José Ortega/Stock Illustration Source

Chapter Outline

Groups: Their Nature and Function
    Group Formation: Why Do People Join Groups?
    How Groups Function: Roles, Status, Norms, and Cohesiveness

How Groups Affect Individual Performance: Facilitation or Social Loafing?
    Social Facilitation: Performance in the Presence of Others
    CORNERSTONES OF SOCIAL PSYCHOLOGY: Performance in the Presence of Others: The Simplest Group Effect?
    Social Loafing: Letting Others Do the Work When Part of a Group

Coordination in Groups: Cooperation or Conflict?
    Cooperation: Working with Others to Achieve Shared Goals
    Conflict: Its Nature, Causes, and Effects
    BEYOND THE HEADLINES: AS SOCIAL PSYCHOLOGISTS SEE IT: How to Start a Conflict When There Is None
    Resolving Conflicts: Some Useful Techniques
    SOCIAL DIVERSITY: A CRITICAL ANALYSIS: Conflict across Ethnic and Cultural Boundaries

Perceived Fairness in Groups: Getting What We Deserve—or Else!
    Judgments of Fairness: Outcomes, Procedures, and Courtesy
    Reactions to Perceived Unfairness: Tactics for Dealing with Injustice

Decision Making by Groups: How It Occurs and the Pitfalls It Faces
    The Decision-Making Process: How Groups Attain Consensus
    The Nature of Group Decisions: Moderation or Polarization?
    Potential Dangers of Group Decision Making: Groupthink and the Tendency of Group Members to Tell One Another What They Already Know
    CONNECTIONS: Integrating Social Psychology
    IDEAS TO TAKE WITH YOU: Maximizing Your Own Performance and Minimizing Social Loafing by Others

Summary and Review of Key Points
Key Terms
For More Information

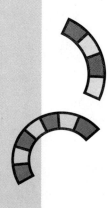

I'm not really a joiner, but when I (Robert Baron) was about ten years old, there was one group to which I desperately wanted to belong. It was a baseball team formed by other boys in my neighborhood—a team that would compete against other teams in a summer baseball league organized through our local schools. I was at the height of my enthusiasm for baseball, and this team included some of the best players in my school. Besides, if you became a member, you got to wear a special jacket and a baseball cap with the team's letter on it (RA for "Royal Aces"—not very original, but remember, this was 1953). The result? I wanted in so much I could almost taste it. I knew I was a pretty good player—I was a fast runner and a good hitter—so I was confident that I'd be accepted at once. But that wasn't what happened; when I asked to join, the answer was "We'll think about it; come back tomorrow." And that message was repeated several times. I didn't understand what was going on, but I dimly realized that the people who had organized the team—the true insiders— were selecting new members on the basis of factors other than how well they played. I wasn't sure what to do, but I reasoned that it wouldn't hurt to be friendly. So I always brought candy, ice cream, or cookies to the practice sessions and shared generously. Also, I began walking home from school with some of the team's members, even though this took me out of my way. These tactics paid off: I was accepted on the team and soon had my new jacket and cap. But then a funny thing happened: once I became a member, I found that I too wanted to make it hard to join. In fact, much to my surprise, I went along with the group's decision to reject my good friend Stan, who had counted on me for support. And when I wore my jacket and cap, I felt really special and—I admit it—better than other boys in the neighborhood. I mean, after all, I was now a Royal Ace!

Looking back, I realize that this was my first experience with what social psychologists term *group influence*—the effects of being part of a social group on how individuals think and behave. All of us belong to many different groups, and, as we'll soon see, the effects of such membership can be profound. To provide you with an overview of the scope and magnitude of group effects on individual behavior, we'll focus on five topics. First, we'll consider the basic nature of groups: what they are and how they influence their members. Second, we'll examine the impact of groups on *task performance*—how our performance on various tasks can be affected by our working with others or, in some cases, merely by others' presence on the scene. Third, we'll turn to the question of what might be termed *coordination* within groups—the extent to which individuals pool their efforts and work together toward goals (i.e., cooperate with one another) or, instead, choose to work against one another in what is known as *conflict*. Fourth, we'll examine the question of *fairness* in groups—the extent to which individuals believe that they are being treated fairly or unfairly, and the impact of such beliefs on their behavior. Finally, we'll consider *decision making* in groups, focusing on the potential benefits and costs of this process. Another important topic closely related to group functioning, *leadership*, is discussed in Chapter 13.

GROUPS: THEIR NATURE AND FUNCTION

group • Two or more persons who interact with one another, share common goals, are somehow interdependent, and recognize that they belong to a group.

Look at the photos in Figure 12.1. Which shows a social group? Probably you will identify the one on the left as a group but the one on the right as showing a mere collection of persons. Why? Because you already implicitly accept a definition of the term **group** close to the one adopted by social psychologists: *A group consists of two or more interacting persons who share common goals,*

Figure 12.1

What Makes a Social Group? The photo on the left shows a true social group: the people in this group interact with one another, have shared goals, and are interdependent. The photo on the right shows a mere collection of people who happen to be in the same location at the same time but do not constitute a true social group.

have a stable (i.e., lasting) relationship, are somehow interdependent, and perceive that they are in fact part of a group (Paulus, 1989). Let's examine this definition more closely.

First, the definition suggests that to be part of a group, individuals must *interact* with one another, either directly or indirectly. In the age of the internet, of course, such interaction does not necessarily involve face-to-face contact; tens of millions of persons around the world now belong to "virtual groups"—such as newsgroups—with which they often strongly identify (e.g., McKenna & Bargh, 1998). Second, the individuals involved must share at least some goals that they all seek to attain. Third, their relationship must be relatively stable—it must persist over appreciable periods of time (days, weeks, months, or even years). Fourth, they must be *interdependent* in some manner—what happens to one must affect what happens to the others. Finally, the persons involved must recognize that they are part of a group.

Are all of these conditions necessary before we can describe several persons as belonging to a group? While all are important, it's crucial to note that there are varying degrees of "groupness." At the high end are groups consisting of persons who have worked together for long periods of time. Clearly, such groups meet all the requirements of the definition. At the low end are persons who have only a fleeting relationship with one another—for example, the passengers on an airplane. They are interdependent to a degree: if one blocks the aisle, others can't pass and the plane can't take off. They share basic goals, such as getting safely to their destination. But they don't expect to interact in the future and usually don't perceive themselves as part of a group—unless there is an emergency in flight, which can change this picture radically. In between these high and low extremes are many social entities that we might be more or less inclined to describe as groups. My childhood baseball team was certainly a group, but we all knew that it would last only for one summer. The same is true for many other groups: they have some, but perhaps not all, of the features listed above. Whether several persons who interact constitute a true group, then, is a complex matter—one of degree rather than a simple yes/no decision. If there is a key issue, it is simply whether the persons involved perceive themselves as being part of a group. Only to the extent that they do does it make sense to describe them as constituting a social group (Moreland, 1987; Witte & Davis, 1996).

Figure 12.2

A Feeling of Belonging: One Benefit of Group Membership. When people belong to social groups—especially ones that are highly selective—they experience a feeling of belonging that can boost their self-image. This is one important benefit of belonging to such groups.

Group Formation: Why Do People Join Groups?

Think of all the groups you have ever joined: clubs, student associations, religious groups, informal groups consisting of people with whom you hang out. Why did you join them in the first place? The answer seems to involve several different reasons (Paulus, 1989). First, groups help us to satisfy important psychological or social needs, such as those for giving and receiving attention and affection or for a sense of belonging (see Figure 12.2). Second, groups help us achieve goals that we could not attain alone. By working with others, we can often perform tasks we could not accomplish ourselves. Third, group members often provide us with knowledge and information that we could not otherwise attain, or could gain only with difficulty. Fourth, groups help meet our needs for security; in many cases there *is* safety in numbers, especially if we happen to live in a dangerous urban environment.

Finally, group membership also contributes to a positive *social identity*—it becomes part of our self-concept (see Chapter 5). Recent findings, for instance, indicate that people who belong to "marginalized" groups—ones considered to be outside the mainstream (e.g., people with unusual sexual practices, people who belong to extreme political groups)—come to identify more strongly with their group, and also to experience boosts in self-acceptance and the desire to "come out" (i.e., reveal their hidden identity), as a result of participation in internet newsgroups (McKenna & Bargh, 1998). Not surprisingly, the greater the prestige of the groups to which we belong, the more our self-concept is boosted. Groucho Marx, a famous comedian of the 1930s, '40s, and '50s, once remarked: "I wouldn't want to belong to any club that would accept me!" He was well aware of the value of joining prestigious groups—ones that would not accept *him* as a member.

How Groups Function: Roles, Status, Norms, and Cohesiveness

That groups often exert powerful effects upon their members is obvious and will be a basic theme of this chapter. Before turning to group influence, however, we should address a basic issue: How, precisely, do groups affect their members? A complete answer to this question involves many processes we have already examined in this book, including conformity, persuasion, and attraction. In addition, four aspects of groups themselves play a key role in this regard: *roles, status, norms,* and *cohesiveness.*

Figure 12.3

The Outward Signs of Status. As you can readily tell, the woman who occupies the office on the right probably has much higher *status* in her organization (group) than the woman who occupies the office on the left.

Roles: Differentiation of Functions within Groups. Think of a group to which you belong or have belonged—anything from the Scouts to a professional association. Now consider this question: Did everyone in the group act in the same way or perform the same functions? Your answer is probably *no*. Different persons performed different tasks and were expected to accomplish different things for the group. In short, they played different **roles.** Sometimes roles are assigned; for instance, a group may select different individuals to serve as its leader, treasurer, or bouncer. In other cases individuals gradually acquire certain roles without being formally assigned to them. Regardless of how roles are acquired, people often *internalize* them; they link their roles to key aspects of their self-perceptions and self-concept (see Chapters 2 and 5). When this happens, a role may exert profound effects on a person's behavior, even when she or he is not in the group. For instance, a professor, used to lecturing to students, may lecture his or her family when at home—something I've been accused of doing myself!

Roles help to clarify the responsibilities and obligations of group members, so in this respect they are very useful. They do have a downside, though. Group members sometimes experience *role conflict*—stress stemming from the fact that roles they play within different groups are somehow at odds with each other. For instance, the parents of young children often experience conflict between their role as *parent* and their role as *student* or *employee,* and this can be highly stressful for them (Williams et al., 1991).

Status: The Prestige of Various Roles. Compare the two offices shown in Figure 12.3. Do they tell you anything about the people who occupy them? Clearly, the one on the right belongs to someone who has high standing or status, while the one on the left probably belongs to someone who is lower on this dimension. **Status** refers to social standing or rank within a group; and even today, a time when there is a strong tendency to downplay such differences in many settings, status distinctions continue to exist and to influence individual behavior. Different roles or positions in a group are often associated with different levels of status, and people are often extremely sensitive to this fact. Why? Because status is linked to a wide range of desirable outcomes—everything from salary and "perks" to first choice among potential romantic partners (Buss, 1993). For this reason, groups often use status as a means of influencing the behavior of their members: only "good" members—ones who follow the group's rules—receive high status.

roles • Sets of behaviors that individuals occupying specific positions within a group are expected to perform.

status • Social standing or rank within a group.

Norms: The Rules of the Game. We just alluded to a third factor responsible for the powerful impact of groups on their members: rules, or **norms,** established by groups to tell their members how they are supposed to behave. We discussed social norms in detail in Chapter 9; here, we simply want to note again that norms often exert powerful effects on behavior. Moreover, as mentioned above, adherence to norms is often a necessary condition for gaining status and other rewards controlled by groups.

Cohesiveness: The Force That Binds. Consider two groups. In the first, members like one another very much, strongly desire the goals their group is seeking, and feel that they could not possibly find another group that would better satisfy their needs. In the second, the opposite is true: members don't like one another very much, don't share common goals, and are actively seeking other groups that might offer them a better deal. Which group will exert stronger effects on the behavior of its members? The answer is obvious: the first. The reason for this difference involves what social psychologists describe as **cohesiveness**—all the forces that cause members to remain in the group, including factors such as liking for the other members and the desire to maintain or increase one's status by belonging to the "right" groups (Festinger et al., 1950). At first glance, it might seem that cohesiveness would involve primarily liking between individual group members. However, recent evidence suggests that it involves *depersonalized attraction*—liking for other group members stemming from the fact that they belong to the group and embody or represent its key features, quite apart from their traits as individuals (Hogg & Haines, 1996).

Several factors influence cohesiveness, including (1) status within the group (Cota et al., 1995)—cohesiveness is often higher for high- than for low-status members; (2) the effort required to gain entry into the group—the greater these costs, the higher the cohesiveness (see our discussion of dissonance theory in Chapter 4); (3) the existence of external threats or severe competition—such threats increase members' attraction and commitment to the group; and (4) size—small groups tend to be more cohesive than large ones.

In sum, several aspects of groups—roles, status, norms, and cohesiveness—determine the extent to which the groups can, and do, influence their members' behavior. We'll have reason to refer to these factors at later points in this chapter, as we discuss specific ways in which groups influence their members.

> ## Key Points
>
> - A *group* consists of two or more interacting persons who share common goals, have a stable (i.e., lasting) relationship, are somehow interdependent, and perceive that they are in fact part of a group.
> - People join groups to satisfy important needs, reach goals they can't achieve alone, boost their self-identity, and/or gain safety.
> - Groups influence their members in many ways, but such effects are often produced through *roles, status, norms,* and *cohesiveness.*

norms • Rules within a group indicating how its members should or should not behave.

cohesiveness • With respect to groups, all the forces that cause members to remain in the group, including factors such as attraction and desire for status.

How Groups Affect Individual Performance: Facilitation or Social Loafing?

Sometimes, when we perform a task, we work totally alone; for instance, you might study alone in your room or I might work in my shop with no one else around. In many other cases, even if we are working on a task by ourselves, other people are present—for instance, you might study in a crowded library, or in your room while your roommate sleeps or also studies. In still other cases, we work on tasks together with other persons, as part of a task-performing group. What are the effects of other persons on our performance in these various settings? The answer seems vary as a function of our relationship with these other persons. If others are simply present but not working with us, one set of effects occurs. If, instead, they are working with us as part of a group or team, another set occurs. Let's take a closer look at both situations.

Social Facilitation: Performance in the Presence of Others

Imagine that you are a young athlete—an ice-skater, for example—and that you are preparing for your first important competition. You practice your routines alone for several hours each day, month after month. Finally, the big day arrives and you skate out onto the ice in a huge arena filled with the biggest crowd you've ever seen (see Figure 12.4). How will you do? Better or worse than when

Figure 12.4
Presence of an Audience: Does It Improve or Impair Performance? Athletes such as the one shown here usually practice alone, but then often perform in front of a large audience. Will the watching crowds improve or impair an athlete's performance? Social psychologists have made interesting discoveries about this issue.

you practiced alone? This was one of the first topics ever studied in social psychology, so before we turn to modern findings concerning this issue, let's consider some very early research on it by Floyd Allport (1920), whose early and influential work is described in the *Cornerstones* section below.

Cornerstones of Social Psychology
Performance in the Presence of Others:
The Simplest Group Effect?

Floyd H. Allport. *In many ways Floyd H. Allport was the first truly modern social psychologist. He wrote the first textbook that defined social psychology as a scientific field, and his own research on social facilitation and attitudes shaped later research on these topics in important ways. In these respects, he was certainly one of the founders of our field.*

Social psychology was literally struggling for its existence as an independent field when Floyd Allport decided to study what, in his opinion, was a very basic question: What are the effects of working on a task in the presence of other persons who are working on the same, or even a different, task—persons who are not competing with each other? Allport felt that this was an important question and—more to the point—one that would allow the new field to replace speculation with scientific data. To study the effects of the presence of others on task performance, he used several different, but related, methods.

In one study, for example, he asked participants to write down as many associations as they could think of for words printed at the top of an otherwise blank sheet of paper (e.g., "building," "laboratory"). The participants were allowed to work for three one-minute periods, and they performed this task both alone and in the presence of two other persons. (In other words, Allport used what social psychologists describe as a *within-subjects* design: the same persons worked under both experimental conditions.) Results were clear: Ninety-three percent of the participants produced more associations when working in the presence of others than when working alone.

Allport was encouraged by these findings but realized that in many cases, participants could think of more words than they could actually list. This, he reasoned, might be affecting the results. To eliminate this problem, he asked participants to write down every third or every fourth word they thought of—not all of them. Again results indicated that performance was increased in the presence of others. But still Allport was not satisfied: he wondered whether the same effect would be found with a more complex task—one requiring high levels of thought. To find out, he asked participants to read short passages from ancient Roman authors, then to write down all the arguments they could think of that would tend to *disprove* the points made in these passages. Again, they performed this task while alone and while in the presence of several other persons; and once more, results indicated that performance was increased when individuals worked in groups. Not only did participants come up with more arguments—the quality of these ideas was better, too (see Figure 12.5).

While results generally supported a facilitation of performance in the presence of others, Allport was careful to note that this was *not* true for all individuals: some actually did worse in the presence of others than when alone. In other words, there were large individual differences even with respect to this very basic form of group influence. Although he lacked the sophisticated methodology available to modern social psychologists, Allport also concluded that the presence of others shifts individuals' thought processes toward what he described as a more "expansive" style. If you recall our discussion of the relationship between affect and cognition in Chapter 3, you will note that this is one of the effects of positive affect uncovered in modern research on this issue. In this and many other ways, Allport demonstrated that he was a keen observer of social behavior, and far ahead of his time in some of his insights about the cognitive processes that underlie such behavior.

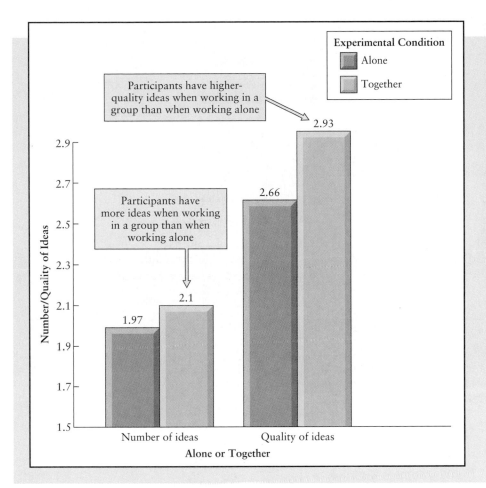

Participants have higher-quality ideas when working in a group than when working alone

Participants have more ideas when working in a group than when working alone

Experimental Condition
Alone
Together

Number/Quality of Ideas

2.93
2.66
2.1
1.97

Number of ideas   Quality of ideas
Alone or Together

Figure 12.5
Effects of Coactors on Cognitive Performance. Not only did participants in Allport's (1920) research think of more arguments when they worked in the presence of others; the quality of these arguments was better, too. On the basis of such findings, social psychologists concluded—in error, as it turned out—that the presence of other persons usually facilitates task performance.

(*Source:* Based on data from Allport, 1920.)

Allport's research paved the way for the study of what soon came to be known in social psychology as **social facilitation.** Early researchers defined this term as improvements in performance produced by the mere presence of others, either as audience or as coactors—persons performing the same task but independently (for example, students taking an exam in the same room). As we'll now see, the concept of social facilitation turned out to be premature: the presence of others does *not* always enhance performance, and social psychologists now understand why this is so. There can be little doubt, however, that although some of his conclusions were later shown to be false, Allport's early studies were, in many ways, a model for the young field of social psychology—a model still reflected in its scientific orientation today.

The Presence of Others: Is It Always Facilitating? Allport's research and that conducted by other early social psychologists (e.g., Triplett, 1989) seemed to indicate that the presence of others is a definite plus—it improves performance on many different tasks. As the volume of research on this topic increased, however, puzzling findings began to appear: sometimes the presence of others facilitated performance, but sometimes it produced the opposite effect (Pessin, 1933). So social facilitation did not always facilitate. Why? Why did the presence of others sometimes enhance but sometimes reduce performance? This question remained largely unanswered until the mid-1960s,

social facilitation • Effects upon performance resulting from the presence of others.

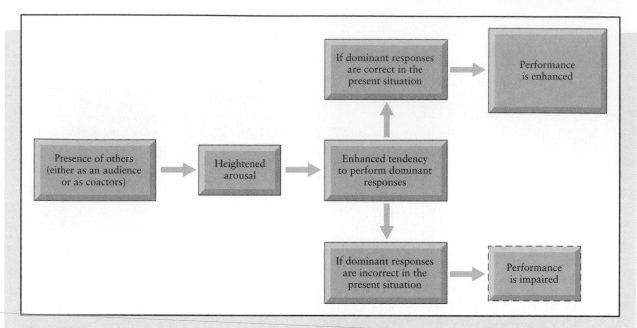

Figure 12.6
The Drive Theory of Social Facilitation. According to the *drive theory of social facilitation* (Zajonc, 1965), the presence of others increases arousal, and this in turn increases the tendency to perform dominant responses. If dominant responses are correct, performance is enhanced; if they are incorrect, performance is impaired.

when a famous researcher, Robert Zajonc, offered an insightful answer. Let's take a look at his ideas.

The Drive Theory of Social Facilitation: Other Persons As a Source of Arousal. Imagine that you are performing some task alone. Then several other people arrive on the scene and begin to watch you intently. Will your pulse beat quicker because of this audience? Informal experience suggests that it may—that the presence of other persons in the form of an interested audience can increase our activation or arousal. Zajonc suggested that this fact might provide the solution to the social facilitation puzzle. Here's why.

When arousal increases, our tendency to perform *dominant responses*—the ones we are most likely to perform in a given situation—also rises. Such dominant responses, in turn, can be correct or incorrect for that situation. If this is so, then it follows logically that if the presence of an audience increases arousal, this factor will *improve* performance when our dominant responses are correct ones, but may *impair* performance when such responses are incorrect (please see Figure 12.6).

Another implication of Zajonc's reasoning, which is known as the **drive theory of social facilitation** because it focuses on arousal or drive, is this: The presence of others will improve individuals' performance when they are highly skilled at the task in question (because in this case their dominant responses will tend to be correct) but will interfere with individuals' performance when they are not highly skilled—for instance, when they are learning to perform a task. (Under these conditions, their dominant responses will probably *not* be correct.)

drive theory of social facilitation • A theory suggesting that the mere presence of others is arousing and thus increases the tendency to perform dominant responses.

Many studies soon provided support for Zajonc's theory. Individuals were more likely to perform dominant responses in the presence of others than when alone, and their performance on various tasks was either enhanced or impaired depending on whether these responses were correct or incorrect in each situation (e.g., Geen, 1989; Zajonc & Sales, 1966).

Additional research raised an important question, however: Does social facilitation stem from the *mere physical presence of others?* Or do other factors, such as concern over others' evaluations of us, also play a role? Support for the latter conclusion was provided by the findings of several ingenious studies indicating that social facilitation effects occurred only when individuals believed that their performance could be observed and evaluated by others (e.g., Bond, 1982). For instance, such effects did *not* occur if the audience was blindfolded or showed no interest in watching (Cottrell et al., 1968). Such findings led some researchers to suggest that social facilitation actually stems either from **evaluation apprehension**—concern over being judged by others (which is often arousing)—or from concerns over *self-presentation*—making a good impression on others, a topic we discussed in Chapter 2.

Reasonable as these suggestions seem, they don't apply in all cases. For example, animals—even cockroaches!—perform simple tasks such as running through a maze better when in the presence of an audience than when alone (Zajonc, Heingartner, & Herman, 1969). It would seem weird to suggest that insects are concerned about the impressions they make on others, so these findings are not compatible with the suggestion that social facilitation stems solely from evaluation apprehension or self-presentation concerns. What's the final answer? Read on for one possibility.

Distraction–Conflict Theory: A Possible Resolution. The apparent answer is provided by a theory known as **distraction–conflict theory,** proposed by Robert S. Baron and his colleagues (yes, a different Robert Baron from the one who is writing these words). This theory, like Zajonc's view, assumes that audiences and coactors both increase arousal. It also suggests, however, that such arousal stems from conflict between two competing tendencies: (1) the tendency to pay attention to the task being performed, and (2) the tendency to direct attention to the audience or coactors. Such conflict is arousing; and this, in turn, increases the tendency to perform dominant responses (see Figure 12.7 on page 490). If these responses are correct, performance is enhanced; if they are incorrect, performance is impaired (e.g., Baron, 1986; Sanders, 1983).

Several findings offer support for this view. For example, audiences produce social facilitation effects only when directing attention to them conflicts in some way with task demands (Groff, Baron, & Moore, 1983). When paying attention to an audience does not conflict with task performance, social facilitation fails to occur. Similarly, individuals experience greater distraction when they perform various tasks in front of an audience than when they perform them alone (Baron, Moore, & Sanders, 1978). Finally, when individuals have little reason to pay attention to others present on the scene—for instance, when these persons are performing a different task—social facilitation fails to occur; but when they have strong reasons for paying attention to others, social facilitation occurs (Sanders, 1983).

One major advantage of distraction–conflict theory is that it can explain why animals, as well as people, are affected by the presence of an audience. Because animals, too, can experience conflicting tendencies to work on a task *and* pay attention to an audience, they should also be susceptible to social facilitation.

evaluation apprehension • Concern over being evaluated by others. Such concern can increase arousal and so contribute to social facilitation.

distraction–conflict theory • A theory suggesting that social facilitation stems from the conflict produced when individuals attempt to pay attention simultaneously to other persons and to the task being performed.

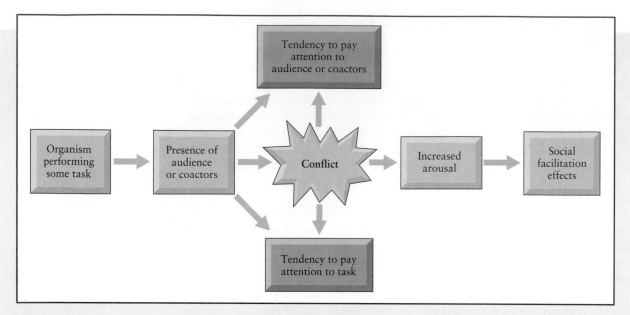

Figure 12.7
The Distraction–Conflict Theory. According to this theory, the presence of an audience or coactors increases arousal by inducing conflicting tendencies to (1) pay attention to the audience and (2) pay attention to the task being performed. This arousal, in turn, increases the tendency to perform dominant responses. This theory helps explain why animals as well as human beings show social facilitation effects.

A theory that can explain similar patterns of behavior among organisms ranging from cockroaches through human beings is powerful indeed, and worthy of very careful attention. So distraction–conflict theory, although it may not provide a complete or final answer to the question "Why does social facilitation occur?," clearly represents a major step toward this goal and remains social psychology's best answer to the persistent puzzle of social facilitation.

> ## Key Points
>
> - The mere presence of other persons either as an audience or as coactors can influence our performance on many tasks. Such effects are known as *social facilitation.*
> - The *drive theory of social facilitation* suggests that the presence of others is arousing and can either increase or reduce performance, depending on whether dominant responses in a given situation are correct or incorrect.
> - The *distraction–conflict theory* suggests that the presence of others is arousing because it induces conflicting tendencies to focus on the task being performed and on an audience or coactors. This theory helps explain why social facilitation occurs for animals as well as people.

Social Loafing: Letting Others Do the Work When Part of a Group

Suppose that you and several other people are helping a friend to move. In order to lift the heaviest pieces of furniture, you all pitch in. Will all of the people helping exert equal effort? Probably not. Some will take as much of the load as they can, while others will simply hang on, perhaps grunting loudly in order to pretend that they are helping more than they are.

This pattern is quite common in situations where groups perform what are known as **additive tasks**—tasks in which the contributions of all members are combined into a single group output. On such tasks, some persons work hard while others goof off, doing less than their share and less than they might do if working alone. Social psychologists refer to these effects as **social loafing**—reductions in motivation and effort that occur when people work collectively in a group compared to when they work individually as independent coactors (Karau & Williams, 1993).

That social loafing occurs has been demonstrated in many experiments. In one of the first, for example, Latané, Williams, and Harkins (1979) asked groups of male students to clap or cheer as loudly as possible at specific times, supposedly so that the experimenter could determine how much noise people make in social settings. They performed these tasks in groups of two, four, or six persons. Results were clear: Although the total amount of noise rose as group size increased, the amount produced *by each participant* dropped. In other words, each person put out less and less effort as group size increased. Such effects are not restricted to simple and seemingly meaningless situations like this; on the contrary, they appear to be quite general in scope and occur with respect to many different tasks—cognitive ones as well as ones involving physical effort (Weldon & Mustari, 1988; Williams & Karau, 1991). Moreover, social loafing appears among both genders, and among children as well as adults. The only exception to the generality of such effects seems to be a cultural one: social loafing effects don't seem to occur in *collectivistic* cultures, such as those in many Asian countries—cultures where the collective good is more highly valued than individual accomplishment or achievement (Earley, 1993). In such cultures, in fact, people seem to work *harder* when in groups than they do when alone. So, as we've noted repeatedly, cultural factors sometimes play a very important role in social behavior.

Aside from this important exception, however, social loafing appears to be a pervasive fact of social life. If this is indeed true, then two important questions arise: *Why* do such effects occur? And what steps can be taken to reduce their occurrence?

The Collective Effort Model: An Expectancy Theory of Social Loafing. Many different explanations for the occurrence of social loafing have been proposed. For example, one view—*social impact theory*—related social loafing to a topic we examined in Chapter 10, *diffusion of responsibility* (Latané, 1981). According to social impact theory, as group size increases, each member feels less and less responsible for the task being performed. The result: Each person exerts decreasing effort on it. In contrast, other theories have focused on the fact that in groups, members' motivation decreases because they realize that their contributions can't be evaluated individually—so why work hard? (Harkins & Szymanski, 1989). Perhaps the most comprehensive explanation of social loafing offered to date, however, is the **collective effort model** (CEM for short) proposed by Karau and Williams (1993).

These researchers suggest that we can understand social loafing by extending a basic theory of individual motivation—*expectancy–valence theory*—to situations involving group performance. Expectancy–valence theory suggests that individuals will work hard on a given task only to the extent that the following conditions exist: (1) They believe that working hard will lead to better performance (*expectancy*); (2) they believe that better performance will be recognized

additive tasks • Tasks for which the group product is the sum or combination of the efforts of individual members.

social loafing • Reductions in motivation and effort when people work collectively in a group compared to when they work individually or as independent coactors.

collective effort model • An explanation of social loafing suggesting that perceived links between individuals' effort and their outcomes are weaker when they work together with others in a group; this, in turn, produces tendencies toward social loafing.

and rewarded (*instrumentality*); and (3) the rewards available are ones they value and desire (*valence*). In other words, individuals working alone will exert effort only to the extent that they perceive direct links between hard work and the outcomes they want.

According to Karau and Williams (1993), these links often appear weaker when individuals work together in groups than when they work alone. First, consider *expectancy*—the belief that increased effort will lead to better performance. This may be high when individuals work alone, but lower when they work together in groups, because people realize that other factors aside from their own effort will determine the group's performance; for instance, the amount of effort exerted by other members. Similarly, *instrumentality*—the belief that good performance will be recognized and rewarded—may also be weaker when people work together in groups. They realize that valued outcomes are divided among all group members, and that as a result they may not get their fair share given their level of effort. Because there is more uncertainty about the links between how hard people work and the rewards they receive, social loafing occurs; and within the framework of the collective effort model, this is not surprising. After all, when individuals work together with others, the relationship between their own performance and rewards is more uncertain than when working alone.

Is the collective effort model accurate? To find out, Karau and Williams performed a meta-analysis of dozens of studies of social loafing. The CEM makes several predictions concerning the conditions under which social loafing should be most and least likely to occur. For example, it predicts that social loafing will be weakest (1) when individuals work in small rather than large groups; (2) when they work on tasks that are intrinsically interesting or important to them; (3) when they work with respected others (friends, teammates, etc.); (4) when they perceive that their contributions to the group product are unique or important; (5) when they expect their coworkers to perform poorly; and (6) when they come from cultures that emphasize group effort and outcomes rather than individual outcomes (Asian cultures versus Western ones, for instance). The results of the meta-analysis offered support for all these predictions. In other words, social loafing was weakest (and strongest) under conditions predicted by the theory (see Figure 12.8). In addition, it was found that social loafing was a very reliable and pervasive effect: it occurred across many different studies conducted with many different kinds of participants and many different kinds of tasks.

On the basis of these findings, Karau and Williams (1993) concluded that the CEM provides a useful framework for understanding social loafing. Moreover, they also noted that the results of their meta-analysis indicate that social loafing is a potentially serious problem: it is most likely to occur under conditions in which individuals' contributions can't be evaluated, when people work on tasks they find boring or uninspiring, and when they work with others they don't greatly respect or don't know very well. Unfortunately, precisely these conditions exist in many settings where groups of persons work together—for instance, in many manufacturing plants and government offices. If social loafing poses a threat to performance in many settings, the next question is obvious: What steps can be taken to reduce it? It is to this important issue that we turn next.

Reducing Social Loafing: Some Useful Techniques. Social loafing can exert disruptive effects on groups, because if it occurs, some members, at least, will feel that they are being taken advantage of by others. What steps can be taken to prevent this problem? Research findings offer some useful suggestions.

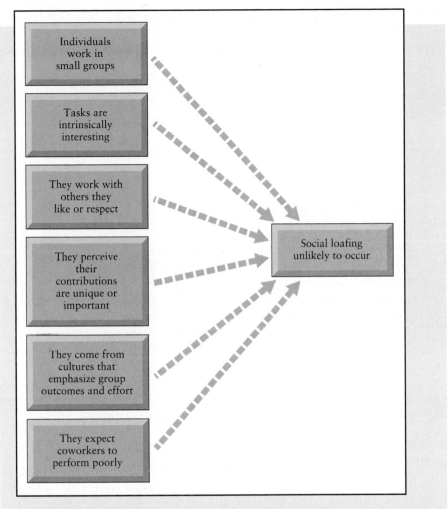

Figure 12.8
Social Loafing: When It Is Least Likely to Occur. Research findings indicate that the social loafing effect is weakest under the conditions shown here.

First, and most obvious, groups can devise ways to make the output or effort of each participant readily identifiable (e.g., Williams, Harkins, & Latané, 1981). Under these conditions, people can't sit back and let others do their work, so social loafing is in fact reduced. Second, groups can reduce social loafing by increasing members' commitment to successful task performance (Brickner et al., 1986). Pressures toward working hard will then serve to offset temptations to engage in social loafing. Third, groups can diminish social loafing by increasing the apparent importance or value of a task (Karau & Williams, 1993). Fourth, social loafing declines when individuals view their contributions to the task as unique rather than merely duplicating those of others (Weldon & Mustari, 1988). And finally, social loafing can be reduced through the strengthening of group cohesiveness—a factor we discussed earlier.

Together, these steps can sharply reduce the magnitude of social loafing in many situations. Social loafing, it appears, *can* be reduced if appropriate safeguards are built into the situation. When they are, individuals will perceive strong links between their effort, the group's performance, and their own outcomes. Then the tendency to goof off at the expense of others may be greatly reduced.

See the *Ideas to Take with You* feature on page 518 for some practical suggestions on how you can both benefit from social facilitation and protect yourself against social loafing by others.

Key Points

- When individuals work together on a task, *social loafing*—reduced output by each group member—sometimes occurs.
- According to the *collective effort model,* such effects occur because when working together with others as compared to working alone, individuals experience weaker links between their effort and outcomes.
- Groups can reduce social loafing in several ways: by making outputs individually identifiable, by increasing commitment to the task and sense of task importance, and by building group cohesiveness.

COORDINATION IN GROUPS: COOPERATION OR CONFLICT?

In Chapter 10 we explored the subject of *prosocial behavior*—actions that benefit others but have no obvious or immediate benefits for the persons who perform them. Although prosocial behavior is far from rare, another pattern—one in which helping is mutual and both sides benefit—is even more common. This pattern is known as **cooperation** and involves situations in which group members work together to attain shared goals. Cooperation can be highly beneficial; indeed, through this process, groups can attain goals that their individual members could never hope to reach by themselves. Surprisingly, though, cooperation does *not* always develop. Frequently, persons belonging to a group try to coordinate their efforts but somehow fail in this attempt (see Figure 12.9).

Even worse, group members may perceive their respective personal interests as incompatible, with the result that instead of working together and coordinating their efforts, they work *against* each other—often producing negative results for both sides. This state of affairs, known as **conflict,** can be defined as a process in which individuals or groups perceive that others have taken or will soon take actions incompatible with their own interests. Conflict is indeed a process; for, as you probably know from your own experience, it has a nasty way of escalating—starting, perhaps, with simple mistrust, and quickly moving through a spiral of anger, resentment, and actions designed to harm the other side. When conflict is carried to extremes, the ultimate effects can be very harmful to both sides.

In one sense, cooperation and conflict can be viewed as falling on opposite ends of a continuum relating to *coordination*—the extent to which individuals in groups work together or against one another. We'll now take a closer look at the nature of both of these processes as well as at some of the factors that influence their occurrence.

cooperation • Behavior in which group members work together to attain shared goals.

conflict • A process in which individuals or groups perceive that others have taken or will soon take actions incompatible with their own interests.

Figure 12.9

Cooperation: Why It Sometimes Fails. Even when individuals attempt to cooperate—to coordinate their efforts in order to reach a shared goal—they may fail to do so.

(*Source:* King Features Syndicate, 1986.)

Cooperation: Working with Others to Achieve Shared Goals

That cooperation can be highly beneficial is obvious. So why, you may be wondering, don't group members always coordinate their activities so that all can benefit? One answer is straightforward: Some goals that people seek simply can't be shared. Several people seeking the same job, promotion, or romantic partner can't combine forces to attain their goals: the desired outcome is available to only one person in each case, so cooperation is not possible. In such cases conflict may quickly develop, as each person attempts to optimize his or her own outcomes (Tjosvold, 1993).

In many other situations, however, cooperation *could* develop but does not. Why? The answer seems to involve a number of different factors that together serve to tip the balance either toward or away from the kind of coordination that cooperation requires.

The Nature of Cooperation: Dealing with Social Dilemmas. Many situations in which cooperation could potentially develop but does not can be described as ones involving **social dilemmas;** they are situations in which each person can increase his or her individual gains by acting in a certain way, but if all (or most) persons act that same way, the outcomes experienced by all are reduced (Komorita & Parks, 1994). As a result, the persons in such situations must deal with *mixed motives:* there are reasons to cooperate (to avoid negative outcomes for all), but also reasons to *defect*—to do what is best for oneself. After all, if only one or a few persons engage in such behavior, they will benefit while the others will not. Many situations in everyday life qualify as social dilemmas (e.g., Baron, Kerr, & Miller, 1992). For instance, my village has a strict recycling policy that requires me to separate glass, plastic, tin cans, and paper in my trash. From a purely selfish point of view, the easiest thing for me to do would be to ignore the rule and mix all my trash together. If everyone did this, however, we would all lose: our landfill would become full very quickly, and we would have to pay much higher taxes to ship our trash somewhere else. So yes, if I were the only one to "defect" and violate the rule, I'd gain, at least in the short run. But if all my neighbors also pursued their selfish self-interest in this

social dilemmas • Situations in which each person can increase his or her individual gains by acting in a certain way, but if all (or most) persons act that same way, the outcomes experienced by all are reduced.

Figure 12.10

The Nature of Social Dilemmas. In *social dilemmas,* each person can enhance her or his outcomes by acting in a selfish manner. However, when many of the persons involved behave this way, outcomes for all are reduced. In the situation shown here, the person driving the small, fuel-efficient car is behaving in a cooperative manner: such vehicles conserve natural resources and pollute the atmosphere to a relatively small degree. The person driving the large, gas-guzzling sport utility vehicle can be viewed as acting in a more selfish manner: such vehicles waste fuel and pollute to a much greater extent.

way, we would all lose (see Figure 12.10). The same principles apply to many other aspects of life—for instance, to traffic regulations, which may inconvenience each driver but which benefit the entire community by maintaining order on the roads.

In such situations, the key question becomes one of *trust* versus *defection.* Will everyone do what's good for the group, or will each person pursue his or her selfish interests? What factors tip the balance one way or the other? That question has been the subject of much research by social psychologists.

Factors Influencing Cooperation: Reciprocity, Personal Orientations, and Communication. Among the many different factors that determine whether individuals will choose to cooperate with others in situations involving the mixed motives generated by social dilemmas, three appear to be most important: tendencies toward *reciprocity, personal orientations* concerning cooperation, and *communication.*

Reciprocity is probably the most obvious of these factors. Throughout life, we are urged to follow the Golden Rule and to do unto others as we would like them to do unto us. Despite such appeals, however, we usually behave in a different manner. Most people tend to react to others not as they would prefer to be treated themselves, but rather as they have *actually* been treated by these people in the past. In short, people generally follow the principle of **reciprocity** much of the time: they return the kind of treatment they have previously received from others (e.g., Pruitt & Carnevale, 1993). The choice between

reciprocity • A basic rule of social life suggesting that individuals tend to treat others as these persons have treated them.

cooperation and competition is no exception to this powerful rule. When others cooperate with us and put their selfish interests aside, we usually respond in kind. In contrast, if they defect and pursue their own interests, we generally do the same (Kerr & Kaufman-Gilliland, 1994).

Now let's consider the role of *personal orientation* in cooperation. Think about the many people you have known during your life. Can you remember ones who strongly preferred cooperation—people who could be counted on to try to work together with other group members in almost every situation? In contrast, can you remember others who usually preferred to pursue their own selfish interests and could *not* be relied on to cooperate? You probably have little difficulty in bringing examples of both types to mind, for large individual differences in tendencies to cooperate exist. Such differences, in turn, seem to reflect contrasting perspectives toward working with others—perspectives that individuals carry with them from situation to situation, even over relatively long periods of time (e.g., Knight & Dubro, 1984). Clear evidence for the existence and impact of such differences in personal orientation or social motivation is provided by research carried out by DeDreu and McCusker (1997).

On the basis of previous research, DeDreu and McCusker (1997) reasoned that individuals can actually possess three distinct orientations toward situations involving social dilemmas: (1) a *cooperative* orientation, in which they prefer to maximize the joint outcomes received by all the persons involved; (2) an *individualistic* orientation, in which they focus primarily on maximizing their own outcomes; or (3) a *competitive* orientation, in which they focus primarily on defeating others—on obtaining better outcomes than other persons do (Van Lange & Kuhlman, 1994). Further, DeDreu and McCusker reasoned that the effects of these orientations on behavior in a situation in which people could choose to cooperate or defect would be maximized by a *negative frame*—by information that caused individuals to think about the situation in terms of potential losses rather than potential gains. Why? Because thinking about outcomes as losses increases the apparent difference in utility or value for these two strategies. Thus, negative framing would increase the tendency for persons with a competitive or individualistic orientation to defect, but would increase the tendency for persons with a cooperative orientation to cooperate.

To test these predictions, DeDreu and McCusker had students at a university in the Netherlands play a game in which they could choose either to cooperate with another person, thus maximizing joint gains, or defect, thus maximizing their own gains while reducing the outcomes of the other person. Before participants played the game, the researchers had them complete a measure that revealed their personal orientation—cooperative, individualistic, or competitive. (For instance, if individuals indicated that they preferred equal outcomes for all members of a group, they were classified as being cooperative in orientation; if they indicated that they preferred to maximize their own outcomes and reduce those of others, they were identified as being competitive.) To vary the presence of a negative frame, the researchers gave participants information at the start designed to make them think about the game they would play in terms of either gains (a positive frame) or losses (a negative frame). To induce a positive frame, they told them they would start with 0 points but could win points by making certain decisions; to induce a negative frame, they told them they would start with 22 points but would lose points if they made certain decisions. It was predicted that the negative frame would increase the tendency of persons with a cooperative orientation to make cooperative choices, but would increase the tendency of persons with an individualistic or competitive

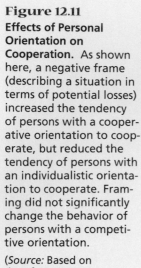

Figure 12.11

Effects of Personal Orientation on Cooperation. As shown here, a negative frame (describing a situation in terms of potential losses) increased the tendency of persons with a cooperative orientation to cooperate, but reduced the tendency of persons with an individualistic orientation to cooperate. Framing did not significantly change the behavior of persons with a competitive orientation.

(*Source:* Based on data from DeDreu & McCusker, 1997.)

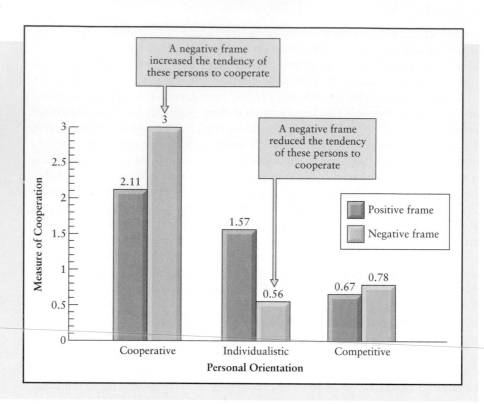

orientation to defect. As you can see from Figure 12.11, these predictions were confirmed for the cooperative and inividualistic orientations. However, persons with a competitive orientation cooperated less regardless of the frame they received. This latter finding was confirmed in another study; so it appears that persons with a competitive orientation have a strong tendency to defect and pursue their own interests—and even getting them to think about a situation in terms of losses can't alter this tendency. They compete no matter what! So personal orientations do play an important role in determining whether individuals will choose to cooperate with others.

Finally, let's consider the role of communication in the development of cooperation. Common sense suggests that if individuals can discuss a situation with others, they may soon conclude that the best option is for everyone to cooperate; after all, this will result in gains for all. Surprisingly, though, early research on this commonsense assumption produced mixed results. In many situations the opportunity for group members to communicate with one another about what they should do did *not* increase cooperation. On the contrary, group members seemed to use this opportunity primarily to *threaten* one another, with the result that cooperation did not occur (e.g., Deutsch & Kraus, 1960). Is this always the case? Fortunately, recent findings point to more optimistic conclusions: apparently, communication between group members *can* lead to increased cooperation, provided certain conditions are met (e.g., Kerr & Kaufman-Gilliland, 1994; Sally, 1998). Specifically, beneficial effects can and do occur if group members make personal commitments to cooperate with one another and if these commitments are backed up by a strong sense of obligation to honor them. For instance, consider a revealing study by Kerr and his colleagues (1997).

These researchers arranged for individuals to participate in a game in which if most group members made cooperative choices, all would benefit. If several members defected and pursued their own interests, however, these gains would *not* be obtained. Before playing this social dilemma game, participants in two conditions were given five minutes to meet and discuss the group's strategy face to face. Both groups were told that their later choices in the game would be known both to the experimenter and the other group members. However, in one condition later events made the participants aware that the experimenter could not know what went on in the group discussions: these discussions were video-taped, and in one condition (the discussion-anonymous group), the tape appeared to malfunction, so that the experimenter could *not* know what had been said by group members. In the other condition (the discussion-nonanonymous group), the tape worked perfectly, so the experimenter could know whether group members had made commitments to cooperate. Finally, in a third condition, the group was *not* given an opportunity to communicate before playing the game.

It was predicted that if communication among group members increases cooperation because individuals choose to adhere to their personal commitments, then cooperation would be higher in both conditions in which group members were given an opportunity to communicate; whether the experimenter had knowledge about what group members had decided would make no difference. If, instead, increased cooperation following communication stemmed from adherence to a group norm (see Chapter 9) rather than from personal commitments, cooperation would be higher only in the nonanonymous group. Results indicated that in fact, cooperation was higher in both discussion conditions. These findings, and those of related studies (e.g., Braver, 1995; Kerr & Kaufman-Gilliland, 1994) suggest that communication can strongly enhance cooperation if group members feel honor bound to hold to their commitments to behave this way. In short, cooperation based on communication in social dilemma situations appear to depend more on the effects of personal conscience than on public or group norms.

In sum, several factors, including tendencies toward reciprocity, personal orientations toward cooperation, and communication coupled with personal conscience and commitments, strongly determine what individuals do in situations where they can choose between cooperation and defection. The choice, in short, is neither simple nor automatic; rather, it is the result of a complex interaction between social and personal factors.

Key Points

- *Cooperation*—working together with others to obtain shared goals—is a common aspect of social life.

- However, cooperation does not develop in many situations in which it is possible. One reason is that such situations often involve *social dilemmas*, in which overall joint gains can be increased by cooperation but individuals can increase their own gains by defection.

- Several factors influence whether cooperation occurs in social dilemma situations. These include individuals' tendencies toward *reciprocity*, personal orientation toward cooperation, and communication.

Conflict: Its Nature, Causes, and Effects

If prosocial behavior and cooperation constitute one end of the coordination dimension—a dimension describing how individuals and groups work together—then *conflict* lies at or near the other end. As we noted earlier, conflict is a process in which one individual or group perceives that others have taken or will soon take actions incompatible with that individual's or group's own interests. The key elements in conflict, then, seem to include (1) opposing interests between individuals or groups, (2) recognition of such opposition, (3) the belief by each side that the other will act to interfere with its interests, and (4) actions that in fact produce such interference.

Conflict is, unfortunately, an all-too-common part of social life, and it can be extremely costly to both sides. What factors cause individuals and groups to enter into this seemingly irrational process? And, perhaps even more important, what can be done to reduce such behavior? These are the questions that social psychologists have addressed in their research.

Major Causes of Conflict. Our definition of conflict emphasizes the existence—and recognition—of incompatible interests. And indeed, incompatible interests constitute the defining feature of conflicts. Interestingly, though, conflicts sometimes fail to develop even though both sides have incompatible interests; and in other cases, conflicts occur even though the two sides don't really have opposing interests—they may simply *believe* that these exist (e.g., DeDreu & Van Lang, 1995; Tjosvold & DeDreu, 1997). Clearly, then, conflict involves much more than opposing interests. In fact, a growing body of evidence suggests that *social* factors may play a role as strong as or even stronger than incompatible interests in initiating conflicts.

One social factor that plays a role in this respect consists of what have been termed *faulty attributions*—errors concerning the causes behind others' behavior (e.g., Baron, 1989b). When individuals find that their interests have been thwarted, they generally try to determine *why* this occurred. Was it bad luck? A lack of planning on their part? A lack of needed resources? Or was it due to intentional interference by another person or group? If they conclude that the latter is true, then the seeds for an intense conflict may be planted—*even if other persons actually had nothing to do with the situation.* In other words, erroneous attributions concerning the causes of negative outcomes can and often do play an important role in conflicts, and sometimes cause conflicts to occur when they could readily have been avoided. (See Chapter 11 for a related discussion of the effects of the hostile attributional bias.)

Another social factor that seems to play an important role in conflict is what might be termed *faulty communication*—the fact that individuals sometimes communicate with others in a way that angers or annoys them, even though it is not their intention to do so. Have you ever been on the receiving end of harsh criticism—criticism you felt was unfair, insensitive, and not in the least helpful? The results of several studies indicate that feedback of this type, known as *destructive criticism,* can leave the recipient hungry for revenge—and so set the stage for conflicts that, again, do not necessarily stem from incompatible interests (e.g., Baron, 1990a; Cropanzano, 1993).

A third social cause of conflict involves our tendency to perceive our own views as objective and as reflecting reality, but to see those of others as biased by their ideology (e.g., Robinson et al., 1995). As a result of this tendency, which is known as *naïve realism,* we may tend to magnify differences between our views and those of others, and so also exaggerate conflicts of interest between us. Interestingly, recent findings indicate that this tendency may be stronger for groups or individuals who currently hold dominant or powerful positions: such persons tend to exaggerate differences between their own positions and those of potential opponents to an even greater degree than is true for individuals or groups who do not hold dominant positions (Keltner & Robinson, 1997).

Finally, personal traits or characteristics, too, seem to play a role in conflict. For example, *Type A* individuals—ones who are highly competitive, always in a hurry, and relatively irritable—tend to become involved in conflicts more often than calmer and less irritable Type B persons (Baron, 1989a).

So where does all this leave us? With the conclusion that conflict does *not* stem solely from opposing interests. On the contrary, it often derives from social factors—long-standing grudges or resentment, the desire for revenge, inaccurate social perceptions, poor communication, and similar factors. In short, conflict, like cooperation, has many different roots. While the most central of these may indeed be incompatible interests, this is far from the entire story, and the social and cognitive causes of this process should definitely not be overlooked. For a dramatic example of the role of such factors, please see the *Beyond the Headlines* section that follows.

Beyond the Headlines:
As Social Psychologists See It
How to Start a Conflict When There Is None

"SO BE IT"—WHY DELTA BOARD TOLD
THE BOSS IT WAS TIME TO TAKE OFF

Associated Press—Atlanta, May 30, 1997—In an era of hard-nosed business executives, Delta Air Lines chairman Ronald W. Allen seems to have been too hard-nosed for his own good. Last spring, with morale diving and customer complaints soaring, he acknowledged in an interview that his drastic cost-cutting campaign launched in 1994 had upset employees, "But so be it," he said. To Delta employees, those were fighting words and suddenly "So Be It" buttons appeared on the chests of pilots, flight attendants, and me-

chanics as a sign of protest. Mr. Allen did succeed in pulling . . . Delta out of a financial tailspin . . . but to Delta's Board, the cost was too much. They saw Delta's reputation for superb customer service getting trashed. They saw a parade of senior managers heading for the exits. Ultimately, they blamed Mr. Allen for the drop in morale. . . . In April, the board declined to renew his contract . . . stating "an accumulation of abrasions over time" had undermined confidence in Mr. Allen's leadership.

Talk about putting your foot in your own mouth! By uttering this one short phrase—"so be it"—a top executive who had actually done much good for his company lost his job. And most people—including many social psychologists—would say that he deserved to lose it. After all, think what these words imply. They seem to suggest a total lack of concern with the well-being of employees, some of whom had worked for Delta Air Lines for many years and felt a real commitment to the company. But here was the head of the company saying, essentially, "You people are totally expendable, and your feelings are irrelevant. If we have to get rid of you, we will." In a sense, there was no conflict of interest between Mr. Allen and employees: both sides wanted to save Delta from what looked like financial disaster. But through his words Mr. Allen

Figure 12.12
The Social Causes of Conflict in Operation. When told that his drastic cost-cutting steps had upset Delta employees, the head of the company, Ronald W. Allen, remarked: "So be it." This seemingly insensitive remark angered employees, who quickly began to wear buttons containing this phrase. The ultimate result? Mr. Allen was fired from his job by the Board of Directors of the company.

stirred up strong resentment and anger; he drove a wedge between himself and his employees that had not previously existed (see Figure 12.12).

A few months ago I (Robert Baron) found myself on a Delta flight. As the flight attendant passed, handing out peanuts, I mentioned the phrase "so be it." She stopped dead in her tracks, wheeled around, and looked straight at me. I then explained that I had read about this phrase and the situation it reflected, and I asked what she thought about it. Her reply: "He got what he deserved!" And several times during the flight she stopped by to chat with me about Mr. Allen and his lack of sensitivity to employees' feelings.

So, to repeat the main point: Conflicts, like hornets' nests, can be stirred up in situations in which everyone really shares the same ultimate goals and conflicts do not have to exist, simply because one or both sides forget that other people have feelings and expect to be treated decently. Like Mr. Allen, forget that guiding principle and you do so at your own peril.

Resolving Conflicts: Some Useful Techniques

Because conflicts are often very costly, the persons involved usually want to resolve them as quickly as possible. What steps are most useful for reaching this goal? While many strategies may succeed, two seem especially useful—*bargaining* and *superordinate goals.*

Bargaining: The Universal Process. By far the most common strategy for resolving conflicts is **bargaining** or negotiation (e.g., Pruitt & Carnevale, 1993). In this process, opposing sides exchange offers, counteroffers, and concessions, either directly or though representatives. If the bargaining process is successful, a solution acceptable to both sides is attained and the conflict is resolved. If, instead, bargaining is unsuccessful, costly deadlock may result and the conflict may intensify. What factors determine which of these outcomes occurs? As you can probably guess, many play a role.

First, and perhaps most obviously, the outcome of bargaining is determined, in part, by the specific *tactics* adopted by the bargainers. Many of these are

bargaining • A negotiating process in which opposing sides exchange offers, counteroffers, and concessions, either directly or though representatives.

designed to accomplish a key goal: to reduce the opponent's aspirations so that this person or group becomes convinced that it cannot get what it wants and should, instead, settle for something more favorable to the other side. Tactics for reducing opponents' aspirations include (1) beginning with an extreme initial offer—one that is very favorable to the side proposing it; (2) the "big lie" technique—convincing the other side that one's break-even point is much higher than it is so that they offer more than would otherwise be the case; for example, a used car salesperson may claim that she will lose money on the deal if she lowers the price, when in fact this is false; and (3) convincing the other side that you have an "out"—that if they won't make a deal with you, you can go elsewhere and get even better terms (Thompson, 1998). Perhaps even more unsettling than these tactics, however, is one involving misrepresentation concerning what are known as *common-value issues*.

Common-value issues are ones on which the opposing sides actually want the same thing, although one or both sides may not realize it. If one side is unaware of a common-value issue, this leaves lots of room for the other side to misrepresent its real position and so gain a key advantage. For instance, imagine a case of divorce in which there are two major issues: custody of the couple's children and alimony for the wife. Suppose that in fact, both husband and wife want the wife to have custody of the children. The husband quickly realizes this, but the wife continues to believe that he wants custody of them. As a result, the husband can suggest that he'll make a concession on *this* issue, allowing his wife to keep the children, but that in return he expects to pay lower alimony. If she accepts, the husband has used misrepresentation of his real position on the common-value issue—an issue on which the two sides actually agreed—to wring a concession from his wife on another issue. Evidence suggesting that this tactic is actually widely used is provided by a study conducted by O'Connor and Carnevale (1997).

These researchers had students play the role of union and management representatives, who then bargained on five contract issues: salary, vacation, start date of the contract, annual raises, and medical benefits. The two sides actually agreed on the start-date issue (this was the common-value issue); but in one condition (the asymmetric-information condition), one side knew this was so whereas the other did not. In two other conditions, either both sides (complete information) or neither side (incomplete information) had such knowledge. Another aspect of the study involved the motivation given to the bargainers before they started. Half were told to be cooperative—to focus on maximizing joint gains; the others were told to be individualistic—to focus on maximizing their own gains.

O'Connor and Carnevale (1997) predicted that misrepresentation with respect to the common-value issue would occur, and that this would be especially likely in the asymmetric-information condition. As shown in Figure 12.13 on page 504, these predictions were confirmed. The researchers also predicted that individuals who used this tactic would obtain better outcomes in the bargaining; findings supported this hypothesis too. What kind of misrepresentation did the bargainers who knew about the common-value issue use? There both *commissions* involved overt efforts to mislead the other side (e.g., "Okay . . . I'll go along with that; but since we're missing a couple of weeks, you should grant us a larger raise")—and *omissions*—simple failure to mention the fact that the two sides agreed on one issue. In sum, bargainers use many different tactics to lower the hopes of their opponents; and if used with skill, these tactics can succeed very well.

A second, and very important, determinant of the outcome of bargaining involves the bargainers' overall *orientations* toward the process (Pruitt

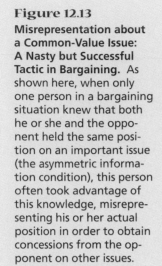

Figure 12.13
Misrepresentation about a Common-Value Issue: A Nasty but Successful Tactic in Bargaining. As shown here, when only one person in a bargaining situation knew that both he or she and the opponent held the same position on an important issue (the asymmetric information condition), this person often took advantage of this knowledge, misrepresenting his or her actual position in order to obtain concessions from the opponent on other issues.

(*Source:* Based on data from O'Connor & Carnevale, 1997.)

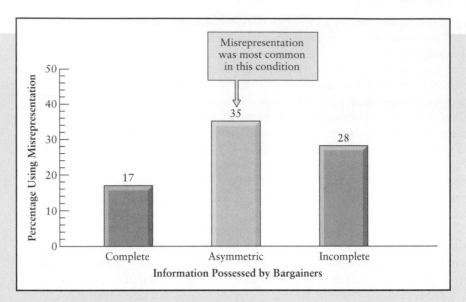

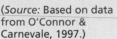

incompatibility error • The tendency for both sides in a negotiation to assume that their interests are entirely incompatible.

fixed-sum error • The tendency for bargainers to assume that each side places the same importance or priority as the other on every issue.

& Carnevale, 1993). People taking part in negotiations can approach such discussions from either of two distinct perspectives. They can view the negotiations as "win–lose" situations, in which gains by one side are necessarily linked with losses for the other. Or they can approach negotiations as potential "win–win" situations, in which the interests of the two sides are not necessarily incompatible and in which the potential gains of both sides can be maximized.

Not all situations offer the potential for win–win agreements; but, as our discussion of common-value issues suggests, many conflicts that at first glance seem to involve head-on clashes do in fact provide such possibilities. If participants are willing to explore all options carefully, they can sometimes attain what are known as *integrative agreements*—ones that offer greater joint benefits than simple compromise (in which all differences are split down the middle). An example: Suppose that two cooks are preparing recipes that call for an entire orange, and they have only one orange between them. What should they do? One possibility is to divide the orange in half. That leaves both with less than they need. Suppose, however, that one cook needs all the juice and the other needs all the peel. Here, a much better solution is possible: they can share the orange, each using the part she or he needs. Many techniques for attaining such integrative solutions exist; a few of these are summarized in Table 12.1.

Finally, the outcomes of bargaining are strongly influenced by the *perceptions* of the two sides—especially by errors in perception bargainers may make. One such error is known as the **incompatibility error**—the tendency for both sides to assume that their interests are entirely incompatible. This error overlooks the fact that the sides agree, or at least are largely in agreement, on some issues (e.g., Thompson & Hastie, 1990). Another error is known as the **fixed-sum error**—the tendency to assume that each side places the same importance or priority as the other on every issue (e.g., Thompson, 1998). Again, this assumption may be wrong. For instance, suppose three friends are discussing what apartment to rent for the coming year. They disagree on this overall issue,

Table 12.1

Tactics for Reaching Integrative Agreements. Many different strategies can be useful in attaining integrative agreements—ones that offer better outcomes than simple compromise. A few of these are summarized here.

Tactic	Description
Broadening the pie	Available resources are increased so that both sides can obtain their major goals.
Nonspecific compensation	One side gets what it wants; the other is compensated on an unrelated issue.
Logrolling	Each party makes concessions on low-priority issues in exchange for concessions on issues it values more highly.
Bridging	Neither party gets its initial demands, but a new option that satisfies the major interests of both sides is developed.
Cost cutting	One party gets what it desires, and the costs to the other party are reduced in some manner.

but it turns out that they place different weights on (1) rent, (2) location, and (3) number of bathrooms. For one friend, rent is the most important factor; for another, location is key; and for the third, number of bathrooms is most important. The friends may be able to find an apartment on which they all agree by juggling these different priorities so that all get what they want, or close to it, on their top issue. Finally, recent findings indicate that bargainers often suffer from another error known as *transparency overestimation*—the belief that their goals and motives are more clearly recognized by their opponents than is actually true (Vorauer & Claude, 1998). This overestimation can lead to serious problems. For instance, bargainer A may believe that she has clearly signaled to the other side her intention to compromise, but her opponent, bargainer B, may continue to act in a "tough" manner. In fact, bargainer B may have failed to notice A's compromise signal, but bargainer A may become angry with her opponent for not responding nonetheless.

Many other factors too, determine the outcome of bargaining, but the ones we've discussed are among the most important. Thus, all are worth considering the next time *you* must bargain with others over one or more issues.

Superordinate Goals: "We're All in This Together." As we saw in Chapter 6, individuals often divide the world into two opposing camps—"us" and "them." They perceive members of their own group (us) as quite different from, and usually better than, people belonging to other groups (them). These tendencies to magnify differences between one's own group and others and to disparage outsiders are very powerful and often play a role in the occurrence and persistence of conflicts. Fortunately, they can be countered through the induction of **superordinate goals**—goals that both sides seek and that tie their interests together rather than driving them apart (e.g., Sherif et al., 1961; Tjosvold, 1993).

I experienced a very powerful example of this at my own university recently. Opposition to our president's administrative policies had been growing for some time; but, as usual, different schools within the university were

superordinate goals • Goals that both sides to a conflict seek and that tie their interests together rather than driving them apart.

divided by what they perceived to be opposing interests—for example, a budget increase for one school would lead to a budget reduction for another, and so forth. Finally, however, the president took an action that reminded the faculties of all the schools that they shared important interests: he fired a dean and was about to replace him without any faculty input and without a formal search for the best person. A petition was started in one school (Engineering) and soon circulated throughout the university. More and more professors signed it every day, because they came to realize that if the president could do this to one school, he could do it to the others too. The result: The pressure became so intense that the president resigned! In cases like this, even long-standing conflicts can be put aside as all sides pursue common, overarching goals.

Should different tactics be used for resolving conflicts depending on whether they occur within or across cultural boundaries? Please see the *Social Diversity* section below for information on this topic.

Social Diversity: A Critical Analysis
Conflict across Ethnic and Cultural Boundaries

When individuals engage in conflict, the *outcomes* they receive are important to them. But, as noted by Tyler and Lind (1992) and other social psychologists (e.g., Ohbuchi, Chiba, & Fukushima, 1994), this is far from the entire story. In addition, because conflicts often involve individuals who know each other well—for instance, people who work together—the persons involved are often also interested in the *quality* of their relationships. Have they been treated with respect and dignity? Does the other side behave in a way suggesting that it can be trusted? According to a perspective known as the *relational model,* these are the kinds of questions individuals consider (e.g., Huo et al., 1996).

At this point another interesting issue arises. In recent decades the world's economy has become increasingly globalized. In addition, immigration has risen to unprecedented heights. This means that ever increasing numbers of people from different cultural and ethnic backgrounds now come into contact with one another and, inevitably, experience conflict. Will relational concerns be stronger or weaker in these cross-cultural contexts? Interestingly, the relational model suggests that they may be weaker, for two important reasons. First, the way we are treated by members of our own group may tell us more about how they view us than the way we are treated by people outside our own group. Second, we are less confident of our ability to "read" people from other cultures accurately, so we may be less likely to rely on their treatment of us as a source of useful information. Thus, when interacting with people from other groups, we may focus more on the outcomes we experience than on relational concerns.

Support for this reasoning has been reported in recent research by Tyler and his colleagues (1998). In the first of these studies, employees of a large university were asked to describe recent conflicts with their supervisor and to rate both the *outcomes* they received (e.g., "How favorable was the outcome to you?") and their *treatment* by this person (e.g., "How politely were you treated?" "How much concern was shown for your rights?"). In addition, participants also rated their willingness to accept the supervisor's decision in this dispute. Because participants and their supervisors varied in ethnic background, it was possible to compare employees' concern with how they were treated with their concern over outcomes in cases where these individuals were of the same ethnic background as their supervisor and in cases where they were of different backgrounds. Results were clear: For within-group conflicts, relational factors were more important in determining acceptance of the supervisor's decision; in between-group conflicts, outcomes were more important.

These findings were replicated in another study, which was conducted in Japan and examined disputes between Japanese and Western teachers of English. Again, participants rated the kind of treatment they received from a third party who mediated such disputes, the outcomes they received, and the extent to which they accepted these decisions. Results again indicated that relational concerns were more important for disputes between persons belonging to the same culture, while outcomes were more important for disputes involving persons from the two cultures.

These findings have important implications for efforts to resolve conflicts. In many conflicts, one or even both sides to a dispute may find the outcomes they receive disappointing. Yet individuals may still accept such results if they feel that they were treated with dignity and respect (e.g., Tyler & Smith, 1997). Unfortunately, however, such "relational adjustments" seem less likely to occur in conflicts between persons from different cultures—because in such situations, each sides focuses primarily on the outcomes it receives. In short, relational factors may combine with stereotyping, the "us" versus "them" division, and several other factors to make cross-cultural conflicts especially difficult to resolve. In a world where such conflicts seem likely to be increasingly common, this finding suggests the need for vigorous steps to develop new strategies for resolving them effectively.

Key Points

- *Conflict* is a process that begins when individuals or groups perceive that others' interests are incompatible with their own.
- Conflict can also stem from social factors such as faulty attributions, poor communication, the tendency to perceive our own views as objective, and personal traits.
- Conflict can be reduced in many ways, but *bargaining* and the induction of *superordinate goals* seem to be most effective.
- When individuals experience conflicts with members of their own cultural or ethnic group, they often focus on relational concerns. In conflicts with persons from other groups, however, they tend to focus on outcome concerns.

PERCEIVED FAIRNESS IN GROUPS: GETTING WHAT WE DESERVE—OR ELSE!

Group membership, as we've already seen, is definitely a two-way street. Groups demand—and generally receive—contributions from their members: adherence to the group's norms, effort on group tasks, support of the group and its goals. In return, individuals expect to get something back: information, boosts to their self-esteem, progress toward goals they want to attain. In addition, group members usually want something else, too: *fair treatment.* How important is this desire for fairness? If you've ever been in a situation in which you felt that you were getting less than you deserved, you already know the answer: very strong indeed. When we feel that we are being treated unfairly, we often experience, anger, resentment, and feelings of injustice (e.g., Cropanzano, 1993; Scher, 1997). Such feelings, in turn, often exert strong effects on our behavior. In effect, unfair treatment calls for action—efforts to reduce or eliminate it.

Social psychologists have long been aware of the important role of perceived fairness in the functioning of groups (Adams, 1965) and have investigated this topic from several different perspectives. Here, we'll focus on two important issues: the factors that lead individuals to conclude they have been treated fairly or unfairly, and the ways in which they attempt to deal with perceived unfairness when it occurs.

Judgments of Fairness: Outcomes, Procedures, and Courtesy

The summer before I (Robert Baron) entered college, I worked in the finance office of a large labor union. I was a summer fill-in, so the work was totally *boring.* My hours were long, and I had to punch a time clock when I arrived and

Figure 12.14

Distributive Justice: A Specific Example. In deciding whether we have been treated fairly, we often focus on *distributive justice*—the degree to which available rewards are divided in accordance with each person's contributions (the more each contributes, the larger the rewards they receive). In a summer job I held long ago, my contributions were larger but my outcomes were smaller than those of another student. The result: I experienced strong feelings of unfairness (*inequity*).

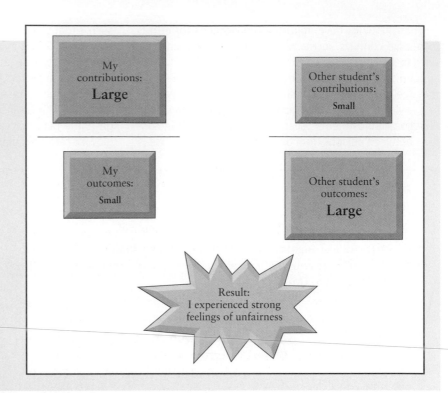

when I left. I had only forty-five minutes for lunch and one fifteen-minute break in the morning. I needed the money for college, so I would gladly have put up with all of this—except for one thing: another student also working there was treated much better. Tom, who was a year older than I was, arrived late every morning and often left early. He disappeared for long periods during the day, and he often took two-hour lunches. Worst of all, he was given the most interesting jobs to do. The final blow came when, by mistake, I received Tom's paycheck one week. It was 50 percent higher than mine! My head nearly exploded over the unfairness of it all. "Who the heck is this guy to get such special treatment?" I wondered. I soon found out: he was the nephew of the president of the union. End of mystery—but not of my feelings of being treated unfairly.

Distributive Justice: Why Outcomes Matter. My summer job experience provides a clear illustration of one set of conditions that leads individuals to conclude that they are being treated unfairly—an imbalance between the *contributions* they make to a group and the *outcomes* (rewards) they receive, *relative to those of other persons* (Adams, 1965). In general, we expect this ratio of contributions and rewards to be about the same for everyone in the group: the more each person contributes, the larger the rewards he or she receives. In other words, we seek **distributive justice**—the division of available rewards among group members according to what each has contributed to the group (or to any social relationship) (e.g., Brockner & Wiesenfeld, 1996; Greenberg, 1993a). It was the absence of this kind of fairness that upset me in that summer job: my contributions were actually *larger* than those of the other student, yet his rewards were greater than mine (see Figure 12.14).

Two more points are worth carefully noting. First, judgments about distributive justice are very much in the eye of the beholder; *we* do the comparing and *we* decide whether our share of available rewards is fair relative to that of other group members (Greenberg, 1990). Second, we are much more sensitive about receiving *less* than we feel we deserve than about receiving *more* than we

distributive justice • The division of available rewards among group members according to what each has contributed to the group (or to any social relationship).

Figure 12.15
The Self-Serving Bias: Its Role in Perceived Fairness. Research findings indicate that we are extremely sensitive to receiving less than we feel we deserve. As shown here, even very small departures from our perceived fair share can cause us to experience strong emotional reactions. In other words, the self-serving bias seems to play a role in our judgments of fairness.
(*Source:* King Features Syndicate, 1996.)

feel we deserve. In other words, the *self-serving bias* we described in Chapter 2 operates strongly in this context (Greenberg, 1996).

This is especially likely to occur when individuals consider the division of available rewards between themselves and others; in such cases, they tend to view "splits" favoring themselves as fair even if these would appear unfair or unjustified to an outside observer (e.g., Diekman et al., 1997). Why are most of us subject to this kind of bias? Perhaps because we feel it is appropriate to try to maximize our own outcomes, so a tendency to favor ourselves when evaluating the division of rewards seems excusable. In addition, most people believe that they are fair and impartial and may be quite unaware of the impact of self-interest on their judgments. Whatever the precise reason, it is clear that most of us have a strong tendency to believe that we deserve more available rewards than we have received, and this can be an important source of friction in many groups (see Figure 12.15).

Procedural and Interpersonal Justice: Why Procedures and Courtesy Matter Too. Although distributive justice plays a key role in shaping perceptions of fairness, it is not the entire story. In addition to concern over how much we receive relative to others, we are also interested in other issues: (1) the *procedures* followed in allocations of available rewards—**procedural justice,** and (2) the *considerateness and courtesy* shown to us by the reward allocators—**interpersonal justice** (e.g., Folger & Baron, 1996). In other words, in reaching conclusions about whether we have been treated fairly, we do not focus solely on our actual outcomes: we also care about how the decisions to distribute rewards in a specific way were reached (the fairness of the procedures followed) and about how we were treated throughout the process (interpersonal fairness).

What factors influence judgments concerning *procedural justice*? Ones such as these: (1) the consistency of procedures—the extent to which they are applied in the same manner to all persons; (2) accuracy—the extent to which procedures are based on accurate information about the relative contributions of all group members; and (3) opportunity for corrections—the extent to which any errors in distributions can be adjusted (e.g., Brockner et al., 1994; Leventhal, Karuza, & Fry, 1980).

Turning to *interpersonal justice,* two factors seem to play a key role in our judgments about how we have been treated: the extent to which we are given

procedural justice • The fairness of the procedures used to allocate available rewards among group members.

interpersonal justice • Considerateness and courtesy shown to group members by those responsible for distributing available rewards; an important factor in perceived fairness.

clear and rational reasons for why rewards were divided as they were (Bies, Shapiro, & Cummings, 1988a), and the courtesy and sensitivity with which we are informed about these divisions (e.g., Greenberg, 1993b). Here's an illustration of how these factors work. Suppose you receive a term paper back from one of your professors. On the top is the grade "C–." You expected at least a B, so you are quite disappointed. Reading on, though, you see a detailed explanation of why you received the grade you did; and after reading it, you have to admit that the explanation is clear and reasonable. Also, the professor adds the following comment: "I know you'll be disappointed with this grade, but I feel you are capable of much better work and would be glad to work with you to help you improve your results." How do you react? Probably by concluding that the grade is low but that the professor has treated you fairly. In contrast, imagine how you'd react if there were no explanation for the grade and the professor wrote the following comment: "Very poor work; you simply haven't met my standards. And don't bother to try to see me. I never change grades." Wow—talk about a good way to generate feelings of unfairness—and resentment!

In sum, we seem to judge fairness in several different ways—in terms of the rewards we have received (distributive justice), the procedures used to allocate these rewards (procedural justice), and the style in which we are informed about these allocations (interpersonal justice). Are any of these types of justice more important than the others? Although you might guess that we would pay more attention to the rewards we receive (i.e., distributive justice) than to procedures or courtesy, a growing body of evidence suggests that this is not necessarily so— we also care quite strongly about both procedures and courtesy (e.g., Brockner & Wiesenfeld, 1996; Greenberg & Alge, 1997). In addition, we seem to be most strongly influenced by the information we receive first. In other words, if we learn first about the *outcomes* we will receive and only later about *procedures,* our judgments of fairness are more strongly influenced by outcome information. If, instead, we learn first about procedures and only then about outcomes, our judgments are more strongly affected by procedure-related information (Van den Bos, Vermunt, & Wilke, 1997). Why is this the case? Apparently because the information we receive first plays a key role in shaping what are known as *fairness heuristics*—rules we use for evaluating the overall fairness of a situation (e.g., Lind, 1994). As we saw in Chapter 3, we often rely on heuristics in making judgments about other persons and social situations, and fairness is no exception to this general rule.

Reactions to Perceived Unfairness: Tactics for Dealing with Injustice

What do people do when they feel they have been treated unfairly? As you probably know from your own experience, many different things. First, if perceived unfairness has to do primarily with rewards (distributive justice), people may focus on changing the balance between their contributions and their outcomes. For example, they may reduce contributions or demand larger rewards. If this does not work, they may take more drastic actions, such as leaving the group altogether. All these reactions are readily visible in workplaces—settings where judgments concerning fairness play a key role. Employees who feel that they are being underpaid may come in late, leave early, do less on the job. And/or they may request more benefits—higher pay, more vacation, and so on. If these tactics fail, they may protest; join a union and go out on strike; or, ultimately, quit and look for another job.

If, in contrast, unfairness relates primarily to procedures (procedural justice) or a lack of courtesy on the part of the persons who announce or deliver reward divisions (interpersonal justice), individuals may adopt different tactics. Procedures are often harder to change than specific outcomes, because they frequently go on behind closed doors and may depart from announced policies in many ways. Similarly, changing the negative attitudes or personality traits that lie behind inconsiderate treatment by bosses, professors, or other reward allocators is a difficult if not impossible task. The result? Individuals who feel that they have been treated unfairly in these ways often turn to more covert (hidden) techniques for evening the score. For instance, a growing body of evidence suggests that feelings of procedural or interpersonal unfairness lie behind many instances of employee theft and sabotage (e.g., Greenberg & Scott, 1996). And, as we noted in Chapter 11, feelings of unfairness also play a major role in many forms of workplace aggression—especially in subtle, hidden actions individuals perform to get even with others who they believe have treated them unfairly.

Finally, individuals who feel that they have been treated unfairly but conclude that there is little they can do about it may cope with the situation simply by changing their perceptions. They may conclude, in short, that they *are* being treated fairly—because, for instance, other persons who receive larger rewards somehow *deserve* this special treatment by virtue of possessing something "special": extra talent, greater experience, a bigger reputation, or some other special qualities (see Figure 12.16). In such cases, individuals who feel that they cannot

Figure 12.16
Perceptual Distortion: One Technique for Coping with Unfairness. Individuals sometimes perceive that others who receive larger shares of available rewards or special privileges than they do somehow deserve these rewards. The result: They experience weaker feelings of unfairness.

eliminate unfairness can at least cope with it and reduce the discomfort it produces, even though they may continue to be treated unfairly by others.

Key Points

- Individuals wish to be treated fairly by the groups to which they belong. Fairness can be judged in terms of outcomes (*distributive justice*), in terms of procedures (*procedural justice*), or in terms of courteous treatment (*interpersonal justice*).

- When individuals feel that they have been treated unfairly, they often take steps to restore fairness.

- These steps include reducing their contributions, demanding greater rewards, protesting, engaging in covert actions such as employee theft or sabotage, and/or changing their own perceptions about fairness.

DECISION MAKING BY GROUPS: HOW IT OCCURS AND THE PITFALLS IT FACES

Groups are called upon to perform many tasks—everything from conducting surgical operations through harvesting the world's crops. One of the most important activities they perform, however, is **decision making**—combining and integrating available information in order to choose one out of several possible courses of action. Governments, large corporations, military units, sports teams—virtually all social entities entrust key decisions to groups. Why? While many factors play a role, the most important seems to be this: Most people believe that groups usually reach better decisions than individuals. After all, it is reasoned, they can pool the expertise of their members and avoid extreme courses of action.

Are such beliefs accurate? Do groups really make better or more accurate decisions than individuals? In their efforts to answer this question, social psychologists have focused on three major topics: (1) How do groups actually make decisions and reach consensus? (2) Do decisions reached by groups differ from those reached by individuals? (3) What accounts for the fact that groups sometimes make truly disastrous decisions—ones so bad it is hard to believe they were actually reached?

The Decision-Making Process: How Groups Attain Consensus

When groups first begin to discuss any issue, their members rarely voice unanimous agreement. Rather, the members come to the decision-making task with different information and so support a wide range of views (e.g., Larson, Foster-Fishman, & Franz, 1998; Gigone & Hastie, 1997). After some period of discussion, however, groups usually reach a decision. This does not always happen—juries become "hung," and other decision-making groups, too, sometimes deadlock. But in general some decision is reached. How is

decision making • The process of combining and integrating available information in order to choose one out of several possible courses of action.

this accomplished, and can the final outcome be predicted from the views initially held by a group's members? Here are the answers provided by recent research.

Social Decision Schemes: Blueprints for Decisions. Let's begin with the question of whether a group's decisions can be predicted from the views held by its members at the start. Here, the answer itself is quite straightforward, even though the processes involved are more complex: Yes. The final decisions reached by groups can often be predicted quite accurately by relatively simple rules known as **social decision schemes.** These rules relate the initial distribution of members' views or preferences to the group's final decisions. For example, one scheme—the *majority-wins rule*—suggests that in many cases the group will opt for whatever position is initially supported by the majority of its members. According to this rule, discussion serves mainly to confirm or strengthen the most popular initial view; that view is generally accepted no matter how passionately the minority argues for a different position. A second decision scheme is the *truth-wins rule*. This rule indicates that the correct solution or decision will ultimately be accepted as its correctness is recognized by more and more members. A third social decision scheme is known as the *first-shift rule*. It states that groups tend to adopt a decision consistent with the direction of the first shift in opinion shown by any member.

Surprising as it may seem, the results of many studies indicate that these simple rules are quite successful in predicting even complex group decisions. Indeed, they have been found to be accurate up to 80 percent of the time (e.g., Stasser, Taylor, & Hanna, 1989). Thus, they seem to provide important insights into how groups move toward consensus: apparently, it seems, in accordance with straightforward decision rules that can predict the final outcome with surprising accuracy.

Normative and Informational Influence in Groups: How Group Members Influence One Another's Views. Do you recall the distinction between *normative social influence* and *informational social influence* that we made in Chapter 9? If so, you remember that the former refers to influence attempts that focus on our desire to be liked or accepted, while the latter focuses on our desire to be right—to have accurate information about various issues or topics. It seems reasonable that group members may attempt to influence each through these distinct kinds of social influence; and, in fact, existing evidence suggests that they do (e.g., Kaplan, 1989). It also seems possible, though, that people may tend to prefer one or the other of these two kinds of influence under different conditions. Specifically, when a decision involves reaching a factually correct solution—what social psychologists term an *intellective task*—group members may tend to rely more on informational influence. In contrast, when a decision does not have any single "right" answer, members may tend to rely more heavily on normative influence. *Time pressures,* too, may make a difference. If a group is in a hurry and must make a decision quickly, there is little time to rely on information; under these conditions, most influence may be normative in nature. In contrast, when the group has more time for its discussions, influence may be primarily informational in nature. Evidence for the accuracy of these predictions has been reported recently by Kelly and her colleagues (1997).

In this study, groups of three college students worked on tasks requiring them to rank order various topics. One task involved rank-ordering the topics

social decision schemes •
Rules relating the initial distribution of group members' views to final group decisions.

people dream about most frequently; the other involved rank-ordering the leading causes of death. Both tasks had a "right" answer; but, as you can probably guess, the one concerning causes of death seemed more factual (intellective) than the one concerning dreams. Half of the groups worked under high time pressure: they were told that their performance would depend on the speed with which they completed the task. The other half worked under low time pressure: they were told to take as much time as they wished. Kelly and her colleagues (1997) predicted that group members would tend to utilize informational influence for the causes-of-death task and under low time pressure, but would employ normative influence for the dream task and when time pressure was high. This is precisely what was found.

These findings underscore an important point about how groups reach decisions. During group discussions, members try to influence one another in various ways, and whether these attempts are mainly normative or mainly informational depends on several factors. In other words, groups reach agreement through a complex process of reciprocal influence among members, but the specifics of this process vary with the task faced by the group.

The Nature of Group Decisions: Moderation or Polarization?

Truly important decisions are rarely left to individuals. Instead, they are usually assigned to groups—and highly qualified groups at that. Even total dictators usually consult with groups of skilled advisers before taking major actions. As we noted earlier, the major reason behind this strategy is the belief that groups are far less likely than individuals to make serious errors—to rush blindly over the edge. Is this really true?

Research on this issue has yielded surprising findings. Contrary to popular belief, a large body of evidence indicates that groups are actually *more* likely to adopt extreme positions than individuals making decisions alone. In fact, across many different kinds of decisions and in many different contexts, groups show a pronounced tendency to shift toward views more extreme than the ones with which they initially began (Burnstein, 1983; Lamm & Myers, 1978). This phenomenon is known as **group polarization,** and its major effects can be summarized as follows: Whatever the initial leaning or preference of a group prior to its discussions, it is strengthened during the group's deliberations. The result: Not only does the *group* shift toward more extreme views—individual members, too, often show such a shift. (The term *group polarization* does not refer to a tendency of groups to split apart into two opposing camps or poles; on the contrary, it refers to a strengthening of the group's initial preferences.)

Why does this effect occur? Research findings have helped provide an answer. Apparently, two major factors are involved. First, it appears that *social comparison,* a process we examined in Chapter 4, plays an important role. Everyone, it seems, wants to be "above average." Where opinions are concerned, this implies holding views that are "better" than those of most other persons—and, especially, better than those of other members of one's group. What does "better" mean? This depends on the specific group: Among a group of liberals, "better" would mean "more liberal." Among a group of conservatives, it would mean "more conservative." Among a group of racists, it would mean "even more bigoted." In any case, during group discussions, at least some members discover—to their shock!—that their

group polarization • The tendency of group members, as a result of group discussion, to shift toward more extreme positions than those they initially held.

views are *not* "better" than those of most other members. The result: After comparing themselves with these persons, they shift to even more extreme views, and the group polarization effect is off and running (Goethals & Zanna, 1979).

A second factor involves the fact that during group discussion, most arguments presented are ones favoring the group's initial leaning or preference. As a result of hearing such arguments, persuasion occurs (presumably through the *central route* described in Chapter 4), and members shift increasingly toward the majority view. This, of course, increases the proportion of arguments favoring this view, and ultimately members convince themselves that this is the "right" view and shift toward it with increasing strength. The result: Group polarization occurs (Vinokur & Burnstein, 1974).

While both of these factors seem to play a role in group polarization, research evidence (Zuber, Crott, & Werner, 1992) suggests that social comparison may be somewhat more important, at least in some contexts, or that group polarization can best be understood in terms of a social decision scheme comparable to the ones we described earlier. Specifically, it appears that the view supported by the typical group member is often the best predictor of the final group decision.

Regardless of the precise mechanisms of group polarization, this process definitely has important implications. The occurrence of polarization may lead many decision-making groups to adopt positions that are increasingly extreme, and therefore increasingly dangerous. In this context, it is chilling to speculate about the potential role of such shifts in disastrous decisions that have actually been made by political, military, and business groups that should, by all accounts, have known better—for example, the decision by the hard-liners in the now vanished Soviet Union to stage a coup to restore firm Communist rule (see Figure 12.17); or the decision by Apple computer not to license its software to other manufacturers, a decision that ultimately cost Apple most of its market. Did group polarization influence these and other disastrous decisions? It is impossible to say for sure, but research findings suggest that this is a real possibility.

Figure 12.17

Group Polarization and Disastrous Decisions. Did group polarization play a role in the decision of Communist hard-liners in the former Soviet Union to stage a coup in 1991—a decision that ultimately led to their total loss of power? We can't tell for sure, but it seems very possible that this and other disastrous group decisions were influenced by this important process.

Potential Dangers of Group Decision Making: Groupthink and the Tendency of Group Members to Tell One Another What They Already Know

Unfortunately, polarization is not the only process that can interfere with groups' ability to make accurate decisions. Several others, too, seem to emerge out of group discussions and can lead groups to make costly, even disastrous, decisions (Hinsz, 1995). Among the most important of these are (1) *groupthink,* and (2) groups' seeming inability to share and use information held by some but not all of their members.

Groupthink: When Too Much Cohesiveness Is a Dangerous Thing. Earlier, we suggested that tendencies toward group polarization may be one reason why decision-making groups sometimes go off the deep end, with catastrophic re-sults. However, another and even more disturbing factor may also contribute to such outcomes. This is a process known as **groupthink**—a strong tendency for decision-making groups to close ranks, cognitively, around a decision: to as-sume that the group *can't* be wrong, that all members must support the deci-sion strongly, and that any information contrary to it should be rejected (Janis, 1982). Once this collective state of mind develops, it appears, groups become unwilling—even, perhaps, *unable*—to change their course of action, even if ex-ternal events suggest very strongly that their original decision was a poor one. In fact, according to Janis (1982), the social psychologist who originated the concept of *groupthink,* norms soon emerge in the group that actively prevent its members from considering alternative courses of action. The group is viewed as being incapable of making an error, and anyone with lingering doubts is quickly silenced, both by group pressure and by his or her own desire to conform.

Why does groupthink occur? Research findings (e.g., Kameda & Sugimori, 1993; Tetlock et al., 1992) suggest that two factors may be crucial. The first is a very high level of *cohesiveness* among group members who are similar in background, interests, and values and so tend to like each other very much. The second is the kind of *emergent group norms* mentioned above—norms suggest-ing that the group is both infallible and morally superior, and that because of these factors, there should be no further discussion of the issue at hand; the de-cision has been made, and the only task now is to support it as strongly as pos-sible. Once groupthink takes hold in a decision-making group, Janis (1982) argues, pressure toward maintaining high levels of group consensus—*concur-rence seeking* is his term for it—overrides the motivation to evaluate all poten-tial courses of action as accurately as possible. The result: Such groups shift from focusing on making the best decision possible to focusing on maintaining a high level of consensus, with truly disastrous effects.

Why Groups Often Fail to Share Information Available to Some but Not All of Their Members. One reason why many key decisions are entrusted to groups is the belief that members will pool their resources—share information and ideas that are unique to each individual. This way, it is reasoned, the decisions groups reach will be better than those that would be reached by individuals working in isolation. Is this actually the case? Do groups really take full ad-vantage of the knowledge and expertise brought to them by their individual members? Research on this issue (Gigone & Hastie, 1993, 1997; Stasser, 1992) suggests that in fact, such pooling of resources may occur less often than com-mon sense would predict. When groups discuss a given issue and try to reach a

groupthink • The tendency of the members of highly co-hesive groups to assume that their decision can't be wrong, that all members must sup-port the group's decision strongly, and that informa-tion contrary to it should be ignored.

decision about it, they tend to discuss information shared by most, if not all, members, rather than information that is known to only one or a few. The result: The decisions they make tend to reflect the shared information (e.g., Gigone & Hastie, 1993). This is not a problem if such information points to the best decision. But consider what happens when information pointing to the best decision is *not* shared by most members. In such cases, the tendency of group members to discuss mainly the information they all already have at their disposal may prevent them from reaching the best decision. Such situations are said to possess a *hidden profile,* because information pointing to the best choice is present but is hidden from the group's view because it is held by only a few members and is not discussed.

Why do the decisions reached by groups tend to favor information most members share at the beginning? Two possibilities exist: (1) Group decisions simply reflect the views members hold before group discussion begins—members start with certain views, and these are further strengthened during the discussion; (2) group decisions reflect the information exchanged during the discussion, and because most of this is shared information, it is such information that shapes the decision. If this latter view is correct, then to the extent that groups *do* manage to bring to the surface unshared information, their decisions, too, may change. The results of several recent studies (e.g., Larson et al., 1998; Winquist & Larson, 1998) offer support for this idea. In these studies, the greater the tendency of groups to discuss information known to only some of the members—information pointing to the correct decision—the more accurate were the groups' final choices. This was true even in such important contexts as medical diagnosis; despite the potentially life-and-death nature of this activity, teams of interns and medical students were found to pool more shared than unshared information during group discussions. However, the more they pooled *unshared* information (information known, initially, to only some members), the more accurate were the groups' diagnoses.

In short, hidden profiles may be discovered and improved decisions made. The trick, of course, is to encourage groups to discover and discuss such information. What strategies can produce this result? One is to convince groups that there *is* a correct solution or decision and that their task is to find it (Stasser & Stewart, 1992). Another is to allow group members ample opportunity to work together: as they do, they may come to recognize what information most members share and what information is unique. Then the likelihood of a pooling-of-resources effect may tend to increase (Stasser & Hinkle, 1994). Taken as a whole, however, existing evidence indicates that decision-making groups do *not* automatically benefit from their members' unique knowledge and skills; often, they don't realize that these assets exist and so can't profit from them.

Key Points

- It is widely believed that groups make better decisions than individuals. However, research findings indicate that groups are often subject to *group polarization* effects, which lead them to make more extreme decisions than individuals.

- In addition, groups often suffer from *groupthink*—a tendency to assume that they can't be wrong and that information contrary to the group's view should be rejected.

• Groups often fail to pool information known to only some members. As a result, their decisions tend to reflect only the information most members already share.

Connections: Integrating Social Psychology

In this chapter, you read about . . .	*In other chapters, you will find related discussions of . . .*
the role of norms in the functioning of groups	the nature of norms and their role in social influence (Chapter 9)
the nature of cooperation and conflict and factors that affect their occurrence	other forms of behavior that either assist or harm others: discrimination (Chapter 6), helping behavior (Chapter 10), and aggression (Chapter 11)
individuals' concern with others' evaluations of their performance	the effects of others' evaluations on our self-concept (Chapter 5) and on our liking for others (Chapter 7)
perceived fairness	the effects of perceived fairness on many other forms of social behavior, such as helping (Chapter 10) and aggression (Chapter 11), and its role in close relationships (Chapter 8)
the role of persuasion and other forms of social influence in group decision making	the nature of persuasion (Chapter 4); various forms of social influence (Chapter 9)

Thinking about Connections

1. Suppose that despite high wages and excellent working conditions, a work group is performing very poorly. Do you think that the kind of social norms we discussed in Chapter 9 might play a role in these disappointing results? If so, how?

2. As we noted in Chapter 11, perceived unfairness is an important cause of workplace aggression. Suppose that at some point in the future, you find it necessary to tell someone who works under your supervision that you are *not* satisfied with his or her performance and that you won't

be recommending this person for a promotion. What can you do to avoid having this person conclude that you are being unfair? Would putting this person in a good mood first (see Chapter 3) be helpful—or would it merely "fan the flames" of anger?

3. Decision making by groups is a complex process. Drawing on previous discussions of gender throughout this book (Chapters 6, 7, 10, 11), do you think that decision making would be different in groups consisting of females than in groups consisting of males? If so, in what ways?

Ideas to Take with You
Maximizing Your Own Performance and Minimizing Social Loafing by Others

Social facilitation effects seem to occur because the presence of others is arousing. Arousal increases our tendency to perform dominant responses. If these are correct for the situation, our performance is improved; if they are incorrect, our performance is impaired. This analysis leads to several practical suggestions:

Study alone, but take tests in the presence of others.

If you study alone, you'll avoid the distraction caused by other persons and so will learn new material more efficiently. If you have studied hard, your dominant responses will probably be correct ones; so when you take a test, the increased arousal generated by other persons will improve your performance.

Work on simple tasks (e.g., ones requiring pure physical effort) in front of an audience.

The presence of an audience will increase your arousal and thus enhance your ability to exert physical effort on such tasks.

Social loafing occurs when persons working together put out less effort than they would if they were working alone. This can be costly to you if *you* work hard but others goof off. Here's how you can avoid such outcomes:

Make sure that the contribution of each member of the group can be assessed individually—don't let social loafers hide!

Try to work only with people who are committed to the group's goals.

Make sure that each person's contribution is unique—not identical to those of others.

In that way, each person can be personally responsible for what he or she produces.

Summary and Review of Key Points

Groups: Their Nature and Function

- A *group* consists of two or more interacting persons who share common goals, have a stable (i.e., lasting) relationship, are somehow interdependent, and perceive that they are in fact part of a group.
- People join groups to satisfy important needs, reach goals they can't achieve alone, boost their self-identity, and/or gain safety.
- Groups influence their members in many ways, but such effects are often produced through *roles, status, norms,* and *cohesiveness.*

How Groups Affect Individual Performance: Facilitation or Social Loafing?

- The mere presence of other persons either as an audience or as coactors can influence our performance on many tasks. Such effects are known as *social facilitation.*
- The *drive theory of social facilitation* suggests that the presence of others is arousing and can either increase or reduce performance, depending on whether dominant responses in a given situation are correct or incorrect.
- The *distraction–conflict theory* suggests that the presence of others is arousing because it induces conflicting ten-

dencies to focus on the task being performed and on an audience or coactors. This theory helps explain why social facilitation occurs for animals as well as people.

- When individuals work together on a task, *social loafing*—reduced output by each group member—sometimes occurs.
- According to the *collective effort model,* such effects occur because when working together with others as compared to working alone, individuals experience weaker links between their effort and outcomes.
- Groups can reduce social loafing in several ways: by making outputs individually identifiable, by increasing commitment to the task and sense of task importance, and by building group cohesiveness.

Coordination in Groups: Cooperation or Conflict?

- *Cooperation*—working together with others to obtain shared goals—is a common aspect of social life.
- However, cooperation does not develop in many situations in which it is possible. One reason is that such situations often involve *social dilemmas,* in which overall joint gains can be increased by cooperation but individuals can increase their own gains by defection.

- Several factors influence whether cooperation occurs in social dilemma situations. These include individuals' tendencies toward *reciprocity,* personal orientation toward cooperation, and communication.

- *Conflict* is a process that begins when individuals or groups perceive that others' interests are incompatible with their own.

- Conflict can also stem from social factors such as faulty attributions, poor communication, the tendency to perceive our own views as objective, and personal traits.

- Conflict can be reduced in many ways, but *bargaining* and the induction of *superordinate goals* seem to be most effective.

- When individuals experience conflicts with members of their own cultural or ethnic groups, they often focus on relational concerns. In conflicts with persons from other groups, however, they tend to focus on outcome concerns.

Perceived Fairness in Groups: Getting What We Deserve—or Else!

- Individuals wish to be treated fairly by the groups to which they belong. Fairness can be judged in terms of outcomes (*distributive justice*), in terms of procedures

(*procedural justice*), or in terms of courteous treatment (*interpersonal justice*).

- When individuals feel that they have been treated unfairly, they often take steps to restore fairness.

- These steps include their contributions, demanding greater rewards, protesting, engaging in covert actions such as employee theft or sabotage, and/or changing their own perceptions about fairness.

Decision Making by Groups: How It Occurs and the Pitfalls It Faces

- It is widely believed that groups make better decisions than individuals. However, research findings indicate that groups are often subject to *group polarization* effects, which lead them to make more extreme decisions than individuals.

- In addition, groups often suffer from *groupthink*—a tendency to assume that they can't be wrong and that information contrary to the group's view should be rejected.

- Groups often fail to pool information known only to some members. As a result, their decisions tend to reflect only the information most members already share.

KEY TERMS

additive tasks (p. 491)

bargaining (p. 502)

cohesiveness (p. 484)

collective effort model (p. 491)

conflict (p. 494)

cooperation (p. 494)

decision making (p. 512)

distraction–conflict theory (p. 489)

distributive justice (p. 508)

drive theory of social facilitation (p. 488)

evaluation apprehension (p. 489)

fixed-sum error (p. 504)

group (p. 480)

group polarization (p. 514)

groupthink (p. 516)

incompatibility error (p. 504)

interpersonal justice (p. 509)

norms (p. 484)

procedural justice (p. 509)

reciprocity (p. 496)

roles (p. 483)

social decision schemes (p. 513)

social dilemmas (p. 495)

social facilitation (p. 487)

social loafing (p. 491)

status (p. 483)

superordinate goals (p. 505)

FOR MORE INFORMATION

Baron, R. S., Kerr, N. L., & Miller, N. (1992). *Group process, group decision, group action.* Pacific Grove, CA: Brooks/Cole.

This book covers many of the topics examined in this chapter, including effects of groups on task performance, social facilitation, and decision making. Written in a clear and straightforward style, it provides an excellent overview of research on these important topics.

Thompson, L. (1998). *The mind and heart of the negotiator.* Upper Saddle River, NJ: Prentice Hall.

In this well-written and relatively brief book, a noted researcher describes the nature of negotiation from the perspective of modern social psychology. The roles of various cognitive processes and biases, perceived fairness, past experience, and group processes are all described. An excellent source to consult if you'd like to know more about bargaining.

Witte, E., & Davis, J. H. (Eds.). (1996). *Understanding group behavior: Consensual action by small groups.* Hillsdale, NJ: Erlbaum.

Noted experts summarize existing knowledge about many aspects of group behavior. The sections on decision making are especially interesting, and expand greatly upon the information on this topic presented in this chapter.

13

Social Psychology in Action:
Legal, Medical, and Organizational Applications

Building a Business. © José Ortega/Stock Illustration Source

Chapter Outline

Applying Social Psychology to the Interpersonal Aspects of the Legal System

Before the Trial Begins: Effects of Police Interrogation and Pretrial Publicity

The Testimony of Eyewitnesses: Problems and Solutions

The Effects of Attorneys and Judges on Verdicts

Additional Influences on Verdicts: Defendant Characteristics and Juror Characteristics

SOCIAL DIVERSITY: A CRITICAL ANALYSIS: Race As a Crucial Factor in the Courtroom

Applying Social Psychology to Health-Related Behavior

Processing Health-Related Information

BEYOND THE HEADLINES: AS SOCIAL PSYCHOLOGISTS SEE IT: What Are the Effects of Vitamin C?

The Emotional and Physiological Effects of Stress

Coping with Stress

Applying Social Psychology to the World of Work: Job Satisfaction, Helping, and Leadership

Job Satisfaction: Attitudes about Work

Organizational Citizenship Behavior: Prosocial Behavior at Work

Leadership: Patterns of Influence within Groups

CORNERSTONES OF SOCIAL PSYCHOLOGY: What Style of Leadership Is Best? Some Early Insights

CONNECTIONS: Integrating Social Psychology

IDEAS TO TAKE WITH YOU: Don't Rush to Judgment

Summary and Review of Key Points

Key Terms

For More Information

Being in a courtroom as a defendant is not a sought-after goal for most of us, and I (Donn Byrne) have had only one such experience. It happened when I was a new Ph.D. and an untenured assistant professor at the University of Texas. A colleague came to my house one evening and asked if I would cosign a note so that he could borrow money from the Credit Union for an upcoming temporary move. (He had been asked to spend a year as a visiting professor at a university in another state.) In my ignorance and innocence, I had only a vague idea about what was meant by "cosigning a note"—perhaps it was something like giving him a letter of reference. Besides, he was a full professor in my department, and it did not seem prudent to say no to his request. So I signed my name and thought nothing further about it, for a while at least.

In time I learned that several other young people in the department had also been asked to be cosigners. All of us had agreed to do so, none of us knew what we were doing, and none of us even asked how much money was being borrowed. Then one day, we all received legal documents indicating that our former colleague had failed to repay his loan and that the seven of us were obligated to pay the Credit Union a considerable sum of money immediately. Not being eager or even able to come up with the necessary funds, we hired a lawyer and went to court to fight for our economic survival.

The "Austin Seven" had no coordinated plan except to tell the truth to the judge and jury. The first thing in our favor was that we genuinely were ignorant about financial matters. I remember, for example, testifying about my misconceptions as to the meaning of cosigning. The Credit Union's lawyer immediately launched an attack designed to discredit me as a liar and a scoundrel. He sarcastically questioned me about my own experiences with borrowing money and getting someone to cosign, but I had actually never done so. My fellow defendants were similarly inexperienced, and we learned later that the jurors felt genuinely sorry for "these poor boys" who had been tricked by an unscrupulous colleague and then unfairly asked by this rich and evil organization (which even employed a mean lawyer) to pay that person's debt.

Our attorney must have picked up these vibrations early, because he suddenly transformed himself into a good old boy who was doing his best to save these pitiful absent-minded academics from their own stupidity. He pointed out that we had been pressured to sign a complicated document by the man who borrowed the money and that the Credit Union had made no effort to go out of state to seek repayment from the real culprit. Instead, they took the easy road and picked on us.

We learned later that although the jury loved us at this point, the legal defense apparently was weak. By chance, however, I noticed a discrepancy between the date of the note and the date of the signatures. The Credit Union had evidently approved the loan with the contingency that the borrower seek several suckers who would cosign and thus be liable for his debt. This, it seems, was an inappropriate procedure. Our attorney's last act in the drama was a masterpiece: he softly asked the Credit Union representative about the details of the organization's standard procedures in such matters. She testified that they always asked the applicant to obtain cosigners first; only then did the loan officer make a decision about loan approval. The dated document indicating a failure to follow this procedure was then produced with a flourish, and the jury needed very little time to rule in our favor. Afterward, most of the jurors actually came up to us in the hallway outside of the courtroom to offer congratulations and to give us motherly and fatherly advice. The general message was to stick to our books and classrooms and stay away from the real world.

Some years were to pass before I became familiar with social psychological research that dealt with the interpersonal aspects of courtroom procedures. It then became clear to me that each aspect of our trial had components directly relevant to the relationship between social psychology and the law. It is equally true that social psychology provides research and theory that is very much relevant to the field of health care and to the world of work in organizations.

In the first section of this chapter, we will describe applications to the *legal system,* including what is known about police interrogations, pretrial publicity in the media, eyewitness testimony, and the way a jury's decisions are affected by the interpersonal impact of attorneys, judges, and defendants and by characteristics of jurors themselves. Next, we will turn to applied research relevant to *health issues,* including the psychological factors involved in dealing with health-related information, how stress affects health and how people cope with stress, how they vary in responding to health problems, and the difficulties involved in coping with medical care. We will then turn to social psychological applications to *organizations,* focusing on several areas of research that rest directly on basic principles of our field: job satisfaction (individuals' attitudes toward their jobs), organizational citizenship behavior (prosocial behavior in the workplace), and leadership.

Applying Social Psychology to the Interpersonal Aspects of the Legal System

If the real world matched our ideals, the judicial process would provide an elaborate and totally fair set of procedures that ensured objective, unbiased, and consistent decisions about violations of criminal and civil laws. At the opposite extreme, our worst nightmares about injustice would be realized if the judicial system functioned in the way described by the judge in Figure 13.1 on page 526. In fact, the legal system is neither as perfect as it could ideally be nor as imperfect as the judge in the cartoon suggests. Instead, research indicates that those involved in the legal process—including the police, the opposing attorneys, the judge, the defendant, and the jurors—usually try their best to do what they believe to be right. As we have shown repeatedly in the previous chapters, however, the perceptions, cognitions, emotions, and judgments of human beings are influenced by many factors other than objectivity and the unbiased search for truth and justice. As a result, **forensic psychology** (the psychological study of legal issues) deals with the effects of psychological factors on legal processes (Davis, 1989). Among the many consequences of human fallibility in the courtroom are biased judgments, reliance on stereotypes, faulty memories, and incorrect or unfair decisions. The same influences operate in court as in the psychological laboratory, and the consequence is a less-than-perfect legal system. Increasingly, psychologists serve as expert—and sometimes controversial—witnesses on issues involving behavioral science (Nietzel, Hasemann, & McCarthy, 1998; Sleek, 1998).

forensic psychology • Psychological research and theory that deals with the effects of cognitive, affective, and behavioral factors on legal proceedings and the law.

Figure 13.1
What if Judicial Decisions Were Based Entirely on Chance? The judicial process suggested in this cartoon would be a frightening prospect. Though such factors as chance, misperception, and emotions are important in the courtroom, we are fortunate that the outcome rests much more heavily on factual evidence, reason, and legal precedents.

(*Source: Playboy,* 1984.)

"That's the law for you; you never know what the outcome of a trial is going to be. In this case, it's tails, and you're guilty."

Before the Trial Begins: Effects of Police Interrogation and Pretrial Publicity

Long before a case reaches a courtroom, two major factors influence the testimony that will eventually be presented as well as the pretrial attitudes of the jurors: (1) the way the police question witnesses and suspects, and (2) the information about the case as it is presented in the media.

The Widespread Effects of Police Procedures. Why do people generally obey the law? Why do people generally accept judicial decisions? Many legal authorities assume that people are basically motivated by self-interest (Misconceptions, 1997). Social psychological research indicates, however, that most people are very likely to obey the law and to accept the outcomes of legal procedures so long as they believe that the laws and the procedures are fair and just (Miller & Ratner, 1996; Tyler et al., 1997). Each individual's beliefs are based in part on personal experiences with the legal system, and such experiences begin with the police.

In both the United Kingdom and the United States, most citizens agree that police investigators should stress an *inquisitorial approach*—a search for the truth—rather than an *adversarial approach*—an attempt to prove guilt (Williamson, 1993). In the United Kingdom legislation was passed to provide training for police officers in an effort to persuade them to conduct interviews in a cooperative way—simply investigating the facts. One reason for such legislation is that court rulings in Britain and in the United States consistently agree that confessions obtained by means of coercive confrontation are unreliable and inadmissible (Gudjonsson, 1993).

Does police behavior actually conform to the guidelines preferred by the public and mandated by the courts? To some extent, but not entirely. In a Scotland Yard study designed to determine what detectives actually do, Williamson (1993) found that many officers had in fact adopted the desired investigative approach. Nevertheless, about half remained oriented toward obtaining a confession. The questioning of suspects can be viewed as falling along two dimensions. One dimension involves the goal of the interrogation: getting the suspect to confess (adversarial) versus gathering evidence to determine the truth (inquisitorial). The other dimension deals with the way the interrogator seeks to achieve either goal: a friendly, cooperative style versus an angry, confrontational style.

When both dimensions are considered simultaneously, there are four possible styles of interrogation, as shown in Figure 13.2. Of the British detectives who were studied, 40 percent were classified as *collusive;* that is, they used a helpful, ingratiating, and fatherly approach as a way to obtain a confession. Think of Peter Falk as Columbo almost out the door but adding in an offhand way, "there's just one more thing that's puzzling me." A *counseling* style was used by 30 percent; they made a friendly, unemotional, and nonjudgmental effort to obtain accurate evidence. This is the "good cop" in many fictional presentations, including Agatha Christie's Miss Marple. The *businesslike* style was characteristic of 21 percent of the detectives; like *Dragnet*'s Sergeant Friday ("Just the facts, Ma'am"), they were brusque, factual, and formal in the attempt to gather evidence. Only 9 percent were classified as *dominant*—behaving impatiently and emotionally as a way to get the suspect to confess. This style can be seen in many film noir offerings, often with members of the Los Angeles Police Department cast as the "bad cops."

Even though about half of the British detectives were observed seeking evidence rather than a confession, Moston and Stephenson (1993) raise doubts as to whether police in general are genuinely behaving in this fashion. They suggest that many officers still seek confessions but have learned to limit accusatory, persuasive questioning to times when outside observers and recording equip-

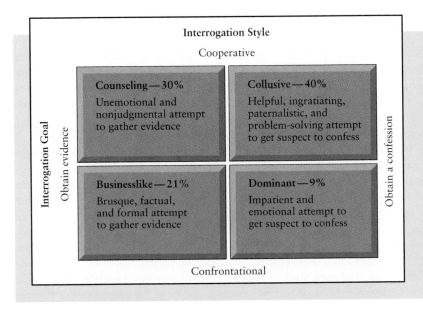

Figure 13.2
Evidence versus a Confession, Cooperation versus Confrontation. Police interrogations can be classified according to the goal of the questioning (to obtain evidence or to obtain a confession) and the style of the person asking the questions (cooperative or confrontational). About half of the detectives in a British study remained oriented toward obtaining a confession, despite official policy that stresses the importance of evidence.

(*Source:* Based on data from Williamson, 1993).

ment are absent. Suspects, witnesses, or even victims may be especially vulnerable; for example, they may be mentally ill, extremely anxious, or highly suggestible. Given these vulnerabilities, dominant interrogators can and do take unfair advantage (Pearse, 1995).

Whatever the style of interrogation, its impact on the person being questioned is increased by the physical setting of the questioning (Schooler & Loftus, 1986). For this reason, investigators much prefer to conduct a formal investigation in an intimidating location such as police headquarters rather than in nonthreatening surroundings such as the suspect's home or place of work. Both the setting and the authority of the questioner (a government representative) reinforce the ordinary citizen's belief that whoever is asking the questions is an expert possessing detailed knowledge of the case (Gudjonsson & Clark, 1986). The officer is in charge of what happens during the interview, and the person being questioned is not supposed to interrupt or argue about what is said. In effect, the individual finds himself or herself as the target of social influence procedures designed to obtain compliance or even obedience, as described in Chapter 9.

Under these circumstances, three factors operate to encourage compliant and obedient responding. The witness usually feels (1) some *uncertainty* about the "right" answers, (2) some degree of *trust* in the officer asking the questions, and (3) an unspoken *expectation* that he or she is supposed to know the answer. As a result, rather than saying "I don't know" or "I don't remember" or "I'm not sure," most people tend to provide answers, at least tentative ones. Once a person provides an answer, however, he or she is inclined to accept its accuracy, especially if the interrogator provides immediate reinforcement with a nod or by saying "good," or the like. One result is that the person being questioned can honestly believe and even "remember" the details of something that never happened. Let's look more closely at how this works.

Eliciting False Confessions from the Innocent. In seeking a confession, interrogators need not resort to heavy-handed methods, because more subtle approaches can be equally or even more effective (Kassin & McNall, 1991). For example, in interacting with a suspect, an interrogator can minimize the strength of the evidence and the seriousness of the charge, perhaps seeming to blame the victim for what happened. When a questioner deemphasizes the crime and seems supportive of the suspect, there is an implicit promise that any punishment is likely to be relatively mild. Not only is this pleasant and ingratiating approach very effective; it avoids the legal problems associated with threatening a suspect. Jurors tend to discount a confession obtained by threats of punishment, but the minimization approach is judged to be acceptable. Kassin and McNall (1991) point out, however, that although this soft-sell technique may seem to be noncoercive, it is simply a less obvious way to elicit compliance. In effect, the suspect confesses after being lulled into a false sense of security.

The use of social influence techniques to elicit confessions sometimes goes a step beyond the soft sell. Kassin and Kiechel (1996) point out that police can present the suspect with bogus polygraph results, fake fingerprint data, inaccurate eyewitness identifications, and false information about the alleged confession of a fellow suspect. To test the power of this deceitful approach, these investigators designed an experiment in which they attempted to obtain false confessions from nonguilty college students. The students (all male) were led to believe that they were simply engaged in a laboratory experiment involving reaction time, an "accident" occurred, and each student was accused of causing the problem.

In the experimental sessions, a research participant interacted with a female student who was actually a research accomplice. The two individuals were given a task in which the accomplice read a list of letters and the participant responded by typing each letter on a keyboard. There was a special warning *not* to press the ALT key because this would cause the program to crash and the data to be lost. No one actually did hit that key, but the question was whether each individual would admit some degree of nonexistent guilt. After the experiment was under way, the computer suddenly ceased functioning, and the apparently upset experimenter rushed in and accused the participant of pressing the forbidden key despite the warning not to do so. "Did you hit the ALT key?" How do you think the innocent participants might respond? The innocent student could (1) *comply* by signing a false confession, (2) *internalize* the false confession by telling another student privately that he pressed the key, or (3) *confabulate* by later recalling false details about his supposed transgression.

The possible effects of two situational factors were investigated. To manipulate vulnerability, the accomplice set the pace to be either *fast* so that the participant would be less able to remember exactly what occurred (high vulnerability) or *slow* so that the participant's memory would be more accurate (low vulnerability). To manipulate the effect of false evidence, the accomplice either said that she had seen the student hit the key or that she had not seen what happened.

Altogether, 69 percent of the participants signed the false confession; 28 percent internalized their guilt, as shown by their private confessions to another student; and 9 percent produced confabulated information, making up false details about what they had supposedly done. These percentages were strongly affected by vulnerability to confusion about what occurred (because of a fast pace) and the presence of false evidence provided by a witness. As shown in Figure 13.3 on page 530, both manipulations exerted an influence on the likelihood of a false confession. In the condition that included a fast pace *and* a false witness, *every participant confessed, most internalized their guilt,* and *more than a third falsely remembered details of their "crime"!*

The investigators stress the importance of these laboratory findings for actual cases in which false evidence may be presented to suspects. Not only do such techniques produce confessions, but they can actually convince the innocent person who confessed that he or she really is guilty and is able to remember false details about committing the crime. Kassin (1997) concludes that the criminal justice system currently does not provide adequate protection to the innocent person who becomes a suspect and that confessions obtained by means of manipulative procedures should not be considered credible.

Effects of the Media on Our Perceptions of Crime. Daily, in newspapers and on television and radio, we are provided with a great deal of information about crimes and criminals. Why do the media overemphasize such news? There is no reason to suspect the media of evil intentions. The explanation is that the general public finds such topics interesting (Henry, 1991). One result of the public interest and media overemphasis is that information about lawbreakers is so pervasive that we easily develop the distorted belief that illegal activity is more widespread and more of a threat to each of us than is actually the case (Ostrow, 1995). Surveys indicate that U.S. citizens believe that criminal activity has reached epidemic proportions and that crime is one of the greatest problems facing society (Jackson, 1996). In a Time/CNN poll, 89 percent of those asked about crime believed the crime problem in the United States to be getting progressively worse (Hull, 1995). Fear of crime is not based on having been a victim of crime but on cognitive factors (Winkel, 1998). Whenever we make assumptions about the crime rate and its dangers, we use what we have learned from the media—the availability heuristic, as discussed in Chapters 1 and 3. For example, because we have a lot more exposure to information about criminal behavior than to information about prosocial behavior (see Chapter 10), we are very likely to overestimate the frequency of illegal activity and underestimate acts of altruism.

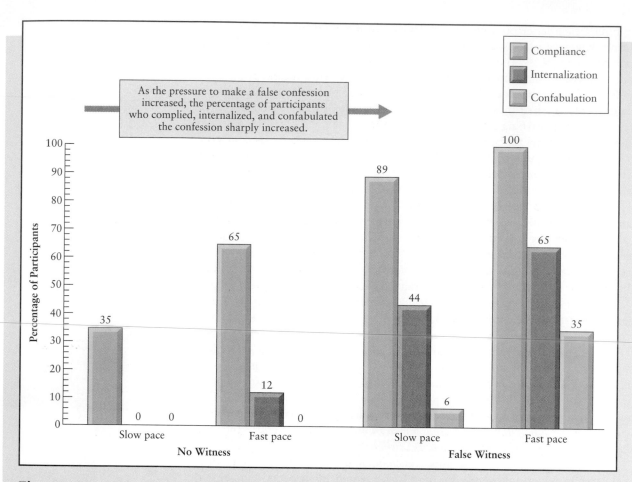

Figure 13.3

Influencing a Falsely Accused Person to Confess and Even to Believe the Confession.
Under the right circumstances, it is possible to persuade an innocent individual not only
to confess guilt for an unacceptable accident but to internalize the guilt (actually believe
that the act was committed) and to confabulate ("remember" details of events surrounding the act). In a lab study false confessions increased when a witness provided false evidence and a fast pace made the accused more vulnerable to error. With neither a false
witness nor a fast pace, about a third of the participants "confessed" but none internalized or confabulated. With both influences present, all participants "confessed," about
two thirds internalized the guilt, and more than a third confabulated.

(*Source:* Based on data from Kassin & Kiechel, 1996.)

In fact, violent crime in the United States, including murder and burglary,
set record highs in the early 1980s and has been dropping ever since (Butterfield, 1997; Hedges, 1996; Miller, 1998; Montgomery, 1996). The homicide
rate is now at its lowest point in 30 years (Easterbrook, 1999). One explanation
for the decrease in violent crime is the fact that more acts of violence are committed by young males than by any other group—and the baby boomer generation, including violent male boomers, is reaching middle age. But the bad news,
and one reason that we perceive more rather than less violence, is that the rate
of murders by teenage boys with guns is rapidly increasing (Lacayo, 1997;
Traub, 1996). In fact, the number of juvenile murderers has tripled over the last
decade (Number of young, 1996). Who are these young people shooting? Other
young people. The U.S. Bureau of Justice Statistics indicates that youngsters
aged twelve to fifteen now have a 1 in 8 chance of being a crime victim, whereas
the chance is only 1 in 179 for those sixty-five and older (Teens top, 1995). Al-

together, the facts about crime are potentially confusing. That is, violent crime is decreasing while teenage crime (especially against other teenagers) is increasing. Because we tend to simplify complex messages by leaving out the details, we find it easier simply to assume that violent crime is worse than ever.

In addition to the extensive coverage of crime news, we are especially aware of crime because negative information has a greater cognitive impact than positive information (Skowronski & Carlston, 1989). To take a simple example, if we learn that a public figure is doing a good job and is devoted to his family, we yawn and quickly forget about it. If we hear that the same man is accused of having ties to organized crime and is engaged in an extramarital affair with an exotic dancer, the impact is much greater and we remember it much longer.

A puzzling and less obvious determinant of what we want the media to provide and of what we remember is the fact that, as mentioned earlier, bad news is almost always more interesting than good news. As Pooley (1997) points out, the good news in the United States about reduced crime, a healthy economy, a longer life span, a budget surplus, and the absence of civil disturbances and international wars leaves a gap in our "desire for bad news." People seem to derive a perverse comfort from feeling pessimistic about the future. It's mildly pleasant, but hardly exciting, to learn that New York City has become a much safer place (Gladwell, 1996); it's much more interesting to think of Manhattan as frightening and dangerous. Perhaps we tend to satisfy a need for dramatic negative events by crowding into movies that entertain us with stories involving dangers from outer space, natural disasters, and a sinking ship.

Effects of Media Coverage on Perceptions of Those Suspected of Wrongdoing.
If extensive media coverage leads to distortions in our minds about the general incidence of crime, what effect does publicity have on the coverage of a specific crime and on our perceptions of a specific individual who is suspected of committing that crime? When a suspect is arrested for a serious crime, we quickly learn a great deal about that person, and are exposed to photos and videotapes of the accused wearing handcuffs and surrounded by officers of the law, as in Figure 13.4 on page 532. Because the public is not provided with any evidence indicating innocence, there is a strong tendency to form a negative impression of the suspect based on the primacy effect (see Chapter 2). Besides, people tend to believe assertions made in the media (Gilbert, Tafarodi, & Malone, 1993). Also, the crime is often a terrible one, and we would prefer a speedy conviction of whoever did it. So anyone who is arrested is very likely to be perceived as guilty: "Why else would the police have arrested and handcuffed him?" Surveys indicate that that is precisely how people responded to the accused assassin of President John F. Kennedy, the accused murderer of Nicole Brown Simpson and Ron Goldman, the man accused of bombing the federal building in Oklahoma City, and on and on. The point is that people leap to assumptions of guilt long *before* any evidence indicating either guilt or innocence has been presented in court.

Because of these effects on public opinion (including the views of the people who will eventually serve as jurors), pretrial publicity tends to help the prosecution and harm the defense. Moran and Cutler (1991) have documented that pretrial coverage does in fact lead to the assumption of guilt among potential jurors in actual cases. This assumption, in turn, affects the outcome of the case in court. Thus, the greater the amount of publicity about a crime, the greater the tendency of jurors to convict whoever is accused of committing it (Linz & Penrod, 1992). According to G. Moran (personal communication, February 23, 1993), government officials take advantage of these effects by providing as much crime information as possible to newspapers and television stations. Their goal is for the public and potential jurors to form a negative impression of the defendant and thus support the government's case.

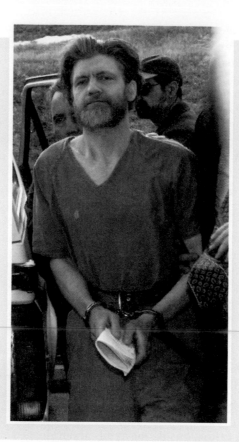

Figure 13.4
Guilty or Innocent? When a person suspected of a crime is arrested, the general public (including those who will become members of the jury) are exposed to a great deal of media coverage concerning the crime and the person suspected of committing it. Research indicates that such coverage usually leads to assumptions of guilt by the general public and by future jurors. For this reason, pretrial publicity strengthens the case against the suspect and weakens the case for the defense.

Research clearly indicates that media presentations affect the final verdict in spite of efforts to screen out jurors who have been exposed to news about the crime and to remind jurors of the importance of maintaining an open mind and an impartial attitude until they hear all of the evidence (Dexter, Cutler, & Moran, 1992). According to O'Connell (1988), asking those who are called for jury duty whether they can be fair and impartial is "as useless as asking an alcoholic if he can control drinking." In either instance, a yes response means very little.

One solution would be to change the law. For example, the United States allows publicity before and during trials, whereas Canada restricts such coverage in order to avoid "polluting" the jury. It has been said, only half jokingly, that the United States sequesters a jury after the trial begins, but Canada "sequesters" the public beforehand (Farnsworth, 1995). A simpler solution to the media problem has been suggested by the findings of Fein, McCloskey, and Tomlinson (1997). The biasing effect of pretrial publicity is greatly weakened if jurors are provided with reason to be suspicious about *why* incriminating evidence might have been given to the media. That is, this tactic shifts attention away from the content of the leaked evidence to the underlying *motivation* of those who leaked the evidence. For ways to avoid the kind of juror errors we have described here, please see the *Ideas to Take with You* feature on page 575.

Key Points

- People obey the law and accept legal decisions so long as they perceive the procedures to be fair and just.
- Most people would prefer police to search for the truth rather than attempt to prove guilt, but both interrogation approaches are common.

- For a variety of reasons, it is not uncommon for an innocent person to confess to a crime and even to believe himself or herself to be guilty.

- Extensive media coverage of crime leads to misperceptions about its frequency, but the coverage occurs because people find it interesting. Media concentration on a person accused of a crime leads to widespread assumptions of guilt, and thus prosecutors tend to provide the media with as much information as possible.

The Testimony of Eyewitnesses: Problems and Solutions

Anyone who witnesses a crime or who has observed something relevant to the case may be asked to testify about what was seen or heard. Each year witnesses in U.S. courtrooms provide crucial positive or negative evidence involving 75,000 suspects (Goldstein, Chance, & Schneller, 1989). Eyewitness testimony has a major impact on the conclusions reached by juries (Wolf & Bugaj, 1990), especially if witnesses seem sure of themselves, if they volunteer many details, and if they do not appear to be nervous (Bell & Loftus, 1988; Bothwell & Jalil, 1992). Obviously, the accuracy of those who testify as witnesses is crucial.

When Witnesses Are Wrong. In fact, however, witnesses very often make mistakes, in part because intense emotions tend to interfere with information processing (see Chapters 3 and 11). Emotional interference is clearly a problem when the witness is the victim of a crime. Loftus (1992a) described a case in which a rape victim identified the wrong man as the rapist; this man, though innocent, was convicted, imprisoned, and eventually released only when the actual rapist confessed. Mistaken identity is not a rare event; beginning with the applied research of Munsterberg (1907) at the beginning of the twentieth century, numerous experiments have consistently indicated that even the most honest, intelligent, and well-meaning witness to an event can make mistakes. Inaccurate eyewitnesses constitute the single most important factor in the wrongful conviction of innocent defendants (Wells, 1993; Wells, Luus, & Windschitl, 1994).

Loftus (1992b) has pointed out that a major obstacle to accuracy is the passage of time between when one witnesses an event and when one testifies about it. During that interval, the witness is almost always exposed to *misleading postevent information* from police questions, news stories, and the statements made by others. Such information becomes incorporated into what the witness remembers—it all blends together as part of what *seems* to be remembered. Inaccuracy occurs because it becomes very difficult to distinguish between what one actually remembers and what one has learned subsequently. As an analogous example, most of us have childhood memories that are a blend of memory, what our parents and others have told us, and the depictions in photograph albums and home videos to which we were later exposed. Note that when an individual remembers something from childhood or when a witness testifies, the person genuinely believes that his or her memory is accurate (Lindsay, 1993). Consider two examples. For many years, my son Keven "remembered" flying in the air over our backyard, and Robert Baron "remembered" seeing the uniform his great-grandfather wore in the kaiser's army in the First World War. For the record, my son cannot fly, and the German uniform was destroyed before my coauthor was born. Keven's memory was probably based on the content of a dream, while Professor Baron's recollection was probably based on scenes in Hollywood movies.

Other variables also have an adverse influence on testimony. Inaccuracy is more likely if the event involved a suspect with a weapon (Tooley et al., 1987),

Figure 13.5
Out of the Mouths of Babes? When children serve as witnesses in a trial, questions of credibility are inevitably raised. With the proper safeguards, however, even the very young can provide accurate and valuable evidence.

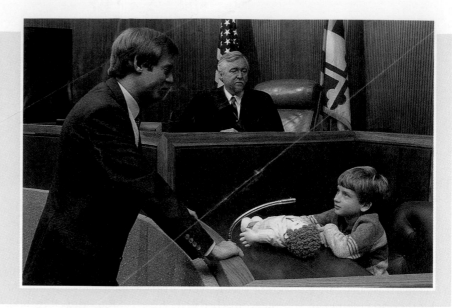

if the suspect and the witness belong to different racial or ethnic groups (Platz & Hosch, 1988), and if misleading suggestions have been offered to the witness (Ryan & Geiselman, 1991). Sometimes, too, an investigator is able to influence a witness in fairly subtle ways by manipulating that individual's confidence (Luus & Wells, 1994). For example, if a witness makes an identification of a specific person in a lineup, positive feedback ("Another witness identified the same suspect you did") helps to strengthen the witness's confidence in the choice—even when he or she has picked out the wrong person.

A special problem arises when a minor is asked to testify as a witness (see Figure 13.5); for example, in cases involving charges of child abuse (Lamb, 1998). Understandably, the testimony of children is less likely to be believed than that of adults (Leippe & Romanczyk, 1987). To protect children from the potential trauma of a courtroom, such testimony is often obtained in a less frightening setting and later presented to the judge and jury by an attorney. When, however, observers are able to view children testifying in their own words, a child seems more credible than in secondhand accounts (Luus, Wells, & Turtle, 1995). Research suggests that jurors believe a child witness to a greater extent if he or she is younger rather than older, if other witnesses support the child's story, if the defendant's character is questionable, and if the jurors are women rather than men (Bottoms & Goodman, 1994). Nevertheless, if suggestions can influence the testimony of adults, it is not surprising that questionable interviewing techniques can have even greater effects on children (Bruck & Ceci, 1997; Bruck, Ceci, & Hembrooke, 1998). As discussed in the next section, the problems of verifying the accuracy of children's testimony about abuse and even adult testimony about childhood experiences have become a major concern among psychologists and legal experts.

Recovering Forgotten Memories of Past Events. You may have heard of "recovered memories": instances in which an adult, often during therapy, suddenly remembers a traumatic past event, most often centering on having been the victim of sexual abuse. More women than men report such memories, possibly because more young girls than young boys are sexually abused in childhood. Several recent celebrity autobiographies contain such accounts. As evidence that many of these memories are false, however, Humphreys (1998) cites "memories" of sexual abuse by aliens from another planet, abuse during a previous lifetime, experiences in the womb, and abuse by Satan-worshipping cult members.

As one might expect, the concept of recovered memories—a topic that includes both gender differences and allegations of sexual misconduct—quickly generated polarized opinions and strong emotions (Dineen, 1998; Pope, 1996). Arrigo and Pezdek (1997) suggest a way to study these phenomena that should avoid political controversies. That is, it is possible to investigate other types of psychogenic amnesia (psychologically based forgetting) that do not involve either gender or sexuality. Many traumatic experiences result in memory loss: automobile accidents, natural disasters, combat, attempted suicide, criminal acts, and the death of a parent are some examples. When memories of such events are gradually recovered, independent evidence indicates that they are sometimes quite accurate and sometimes quite false. These findings suggest that recovered memories of childhood sexual abuse are also sometimes true and sometimes not, and that it would be extremely useful to develop ways to differentiate accurate memories from inaccurate ones (Poole & Lindsay, 1998).

At present, however, debate over **repressed memory** (totally forgetting a traumatic incident or incidents) involves a conflict between (1) those who believe that victims accurately recall previously forgotten traumatic events, and that these often involve child molesters who deserve punishment (Brown, 1997); and (2) those who believe that false recovered memories are subtly encouraged by well-meaning therapists and others, thereby posing a threat that innocent individuals will be unjustly accused of sex crimes (Loftus, 1998). Note that those who believe that recovered memories are often inaccurate do not suggest that therapists are evil. Rather, they propose that therapists may inadvertently engage in "memory-recovery" practices that accidentally plant suggestions, leading clients to remember events that did not actually occur (Frank, 1996; Lindsay, 1998).

Considering how easy it is to encourage false confessions and false memories about a very recent event, false memories of events in the distant past should be at least as easy to create and perhaps more so. This hypothesis was tested by Loftus and her colleagues (Loftus, Coan, & Pickrell, 1996; Loftus & Pickrell, 1995). Participants ranging in age from eighteen to fifty-three read material containing stories involving their early childhoods—three true accounts supplied by relatives and one false account of something that did not happen. The false event involved the participant supposedly being lost for an extended time in a public place at age five, crying, being helped by an elderly woman, and eventually being reunited with his or her family. After reading the four accounts, one out of four participants suddenly "remembered" the false episode of being lost. Similarly, Pezdek, Finger, and Hodge (1997) were able to create false childhood memories among graduate students and senior honors students about their having been lost in a shopping mall; 15 percent "remembered" this imaginary incident. Instead of simply being exposed to a story of their childhood, some research participants have been encouraged to remember nonevents by means of such techniques as "guided memory exercises" and hypnosis. Under these conditions, 60 percent of participants are able to "remember" events that occurred on the day they were born, and 25 percent "remember" an untrue kindergarten event (DuBreuil, Garry, & Loftus, 1998; Loftus, 1997). As Loftus concludes, "Planting memories is not a particularly difficult thing to do" (1997, p. 64).

Increasing Eyewitness Accuracy. Despite the possibility for errors, you should not conclude that eyewitnesses are *always* wrong; often they are extremely accurate (Yuille & Cutshall, 1986). In addition, many attempts have been made to increase the accuracy of all witnesses. In Munsterberg's (1907) early research,

repressed memory • A form of psychogenic amnesia: forgetting the details of a traumatic event as a way of protecting oneself from having to deal with the anxiety and fear associated with that event.

Table 13.1

Lineups and Experiments: How to Obtain Reliable and Objective Information. There are many parallels between police lineups and social psychological experiments, according to Wells and Luus (1990). Based on this analogy, it follows that police officers can improve the accuracy of lineups by following well-established experimental procedures that provide safeguards against contaminated data. In lineups as well as in experiments, it is crucial to avoid biasing the data, demand characteristics, and so forth.

Recommended Procedures for Police Lineups and Photo Lineups	Analogous Procedures in Psychological Experiments
Witnesses should be separated and not permitted to interact.	Participants cannot communicate with one another before responding; otherwise, their data are not independent.
A witness should not be told or led to believe that the actual perpetrator is in the lineup.	Experimental instructions should be worded so as not to create demands that the participants respond in a given way.
The officer conducting the lineup should not know the identity of the suspected perpetrator.	The experimental assistants who interact with the participants should be kept "blind" as to both the hypothesis and the experimental condition to which the participant is assigned.
If there is more than one witness, the position of the suspect in the lineup should be different for each witness.	The order in which stimuli are presented should be randomized or counterbalanced across participants.
Not until the lineup procedure is totally concluded should cues of any kind be given to a witness with respect to whether or not the person he or she identified is actually the suspect in the case.	Not until the experiment is concluded and all dependent measures collected should a participant be debriefed and told the experimenter's hypothesis.

he turned to hypnosis as a possible solution, but gave it up when he discovered the ease with which false memories can be suggested.

One target for improvement has been the police lineup in which witnesses examine several individuals (the suspect plus several nonsuspects) and try to identify the one who is guilty. Wells and Luus (1990) suggest that a lineup is analogous to a social psychological experiment. The officer conducting the lineup is the *experimenter,* the eyewitnesses are the *research participants,* the suspect is the primary *stimulus,* a witness's positive identification constitutes the *behavioral data,* and the presence of nonsuspects and the arrangement of the lineup constitute the *research design.* Also, the police have a *hypothesis* that the suspect is guilty. Finally, for either experiments or testimony, the data are stated in terms of *probability,* because neither experiments nor lineups can provide absolute certainty.

In Chapter 1 you read about factors that can interfere with obtaining accurate experimental results—for example, demand characteristics, experimenter bias, and the absence of a control group. The same factors can interfere with witness accuracy in police lineups. Based on this analogy, police can improve the accuracy of lineups by using common experimental procedures such a *control group.* For example, with a **blank-lineup control** procedure, a witness is first shown a lineup containing only innocent nonsuspects (Wells, 1984). If the witness fails to identify any of them, there is increased confidence in his or her accuracy. If an innocent person *is* identified, the witness is informed and then cautioned about the danger of making a false identification; this improves witness accuracy when actual lineups are presented. Table 13.1 summarizes paral-

blank-lineup control • A procedure in which a witness is shown a police lineup that does not include a suspect; this helps police to determine the accuracy of the witness and to emphasize the importance of being cautious in making a positive identification.

Figure 13.6
The Lawyer's Role in the Courtroom: More Than Just Presenting Evidence. In addition to dealing with legal issues, an attorney for the prosecution or for the defense has two primary messages to convey. First, he or she must be perceived by the jury as knowledgeable, honest, and likable. Second, he or she must weave a convincing and believable story that makes the defendant appear either guilty or not guilty. In many respects, then, the ideal trial lawyer is both a legal expert and a skilled actor.

lels between lineups and experiments and indicates possible ways to improve the accuracy of eyewitnesses.

Other procedures that improve accuracy include presenting pictures of the crime scene and of the victim to the witness before an identification is made (Cutler, Penrod, & Martens, 1987), showing the lineup one member at a time rather than as a group (Leary, 1988), and encouraging witnesses to give their first impressions (Dunning & Stern, 1994).

The Effects of Attorneys and Judges on Verdicts

Research indicates that the outcome of a trial is based not simply on objective evidence and logic but also on some seemingly irrelevant aspects of what is said and done by the opposing attorneys and by the judge. We will describe some of these effects.

Attorneys: An Adversarial Battle to Convince the Jurors. Lawyers play a major role in the courtroom, but their effect is not limited to matters of evidence and legal technicalities. As in the trial described at the beginning of this chapter, attorneys consciously attempt to portray the defendant as bad (the prosecution) or good (the defense) and to behave in such a way as to make themselves liked and trusted by the members of the jury; see Figure 13.6. Remember the "good old boy" role adopted by the attorney defending the Austin Seven against the Credit Union.

An important phase of an upcoming trial is jury selection through **voir dire,** a procedure in which attorneys for each side can "see and speak with" potential jurors to determine who is acceptable and who is not. The stated goal is to choose the most competent citizens to serve, but in fact the attorneys try very hard to select individuals who seem likely to favor their own side and to reject individuals who seem likely to favor the opposing side. Abramson (1994) suggests that jury trials have become a game in which each side attempts to load the jury with those showing the desired bias. Despite these elaborate attempts to

voir dire • A French term ("to see and to speak") used in law to mean the examination of prospective jurors to determine their competence to serve; both the judge and the opposing attorneys may dismiss prospective jurors for specific reasons or, within limits, for no stated reason.

stack the deck, however, research shows that experienced lawyers and untrained college students make almost identical decisions about prospective jurors. Further, both groups are more often wrong than right in guessing about how individual jurors will actually react to the opposing arguments.

During the trial itself, attorneys are not permitted to ask **leading questions** (questions designed to elicit specific answers) when examining witnesses for their side. For example, a leading question to one's own witness might ask, "How much blood did you see on Mr. Gardner's coat?" as opposed to the unbiased question "Could you describe Mr. Gardner's appearance when you saw him on the night of the murder?" In cross-examination of the other side's witnesses, however, leading questions are permitted; and, not surprisingly, responses are often influenced by how the questions are asked (Smith & Ellsworth, 1987). Despite the frequent use of this technique, it is interesting to note that jurors perceive witnesses as less competent and credible when they are responding to leading questions than when they respond to unbiased ones (McGaughey & Stiles, 1983).

The Judge's Role: Enforcing Rules and Controlling Bias. Though judges are expected to be entirely objective and fair, they are human beings who can make mistakes or hold biases. The consequences of judicial mistakes can affect the trial's outcome, as when a judge allows the jury to hear evidence that is later ruled inadmissible (Cox & Tanford, 1989) or when a judge attacks the credibility of a witness (Cavoukian & Doob, 1980). Many of the cognitive processes we described in Chapter 3 (such as priming) obviously apply to the way in which a judge's statements can influence the jurors.

Juries are instructed to base their verdicts entirely on facts that are formally admitted into evidence. Sometimes they are exposed to evidence that is challenged by the other side and then ruled inadmissible by the judge—"The jury will disregard the witness's last statement." Can jurors actually disregard what they have seen or heard? Kassin and Sommers (1997) proposed that a crucial factor would be the *reason* offered by the judge to explain the inadmissibility of a piece of evidence. Mock jurors were given the summary of a murder trial that included (for the control group) no mention of wiretap evidence or (in the experimental groups) wiretap evidence that was then ruled either admissible or inadmissible by the judge. The wiretap came from a taped telephone conversation in which the defendant told a friend, "I killed Marylou and some bastard she was with. God, I don't . . . yeah, I ditched the blade." The defense attorney objected, and the judge then ruled the evidence either admissible, inadmissible because the police recorded the conversation without first obtaining a proper warrant (lack of due process), or inadmissible because the tape was barely audible and difficult to understand (unreliable). All of the mock jurors were asked to give a verdict afterward. Those jurors who learned that the wiretap evidence was admissible were much more likely to decide that the defendant was guilty than were those in the no-wiretap control condition. Though inadmissibility because of due process slightly reduced the percentage of guilty verdicts, it was clear that many jurors ignored the judge's ruling. In contrast, however, jurors *did* follow the instructions to disregard when the reason was the unreliability of the tape recording. It seems that jurors are quite able to disregard inadmissible evidence, but whether or not they do so depends not on a legal ruling, but on the particular *reason* given for that ruling. In a similar way, a judge who simply prohibits jurors from considering evidence is more likely to be ignored than a judge who provides information as to *why* the evidence should be ignored (Shaw & Skolnick, 1995).

Additional research indicates that when inadmissible evidence is extremely emotional (e.g., graphic testimony that the defendant has hacked up a woman),

leading questions •
Questions designed to elicit specific answers.

jurors ignore the judge's instructions. In fact, as we noted in Chapter 3, they are actually *more* likely to vote guilty when such information is ruled inadmissible than when it is ruled admissible (Edwards & Bryan, 1997).

Though neither the judge nor the jury is supposed to make a final decision about guilt versus innocence until the end of the trial (Hastie, 1993), such suspension of judgment is difficult or impossible for most people. The judge, for example, often forms a private opinion and even speculates about what the verdict will be. To test the possible effects of such unstated opinions on jurors, Hart (1995) showed research participants videotapes of one trial followed by tapes of judges (actually judges from different trials) reading standard jury instructions. Then the mock jurors were asked to reach a verdict. The judge on each tape had confided to the experimenter whether he or she was expecting a guilty or not guilty verdict, and the question was whether these private opinions would influence the jurors' verdicts. Remember that the judges' beliefs dealt with a different trial with a different defendant from the one viewed by the research participants. As shown in Figure 13.7, when a judge believed a defendant

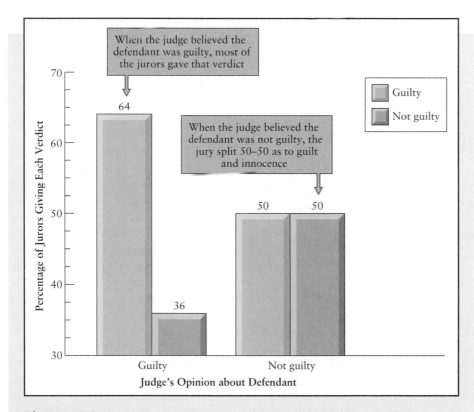

Figure 13.7

Unintentional Influence on the Jury by the Judge. Mock jurors drawn from an actual jury pool were shown videotapes of an actual trial and of judges in other trials giving their standard instructions to the jury. The experimenters knew whether the videotaped judge in each case privately believed in the guilt or in the innocence of the defendant. When the judge believed that the defendant was guilty, the "jurors" overwhelmingly returned a guilty verdict. When the judge believed that the defendant was not guilty, the jurors split 50–50 in their verdict. Apparently through inadvertent nonverbal cues, the judge communicated his or her opinion; and this opinion had an effect on the jurors' decisions.

(*Source:* Based on data from Hart, 1995.)

was guilty, most of these mock jurors in fact gave that verdict. When a judge believed a defendant was not guilty, the jury split 50–50 on the verdict. The judges' beliefs most likely were communicated by their nonverbal behavior, such as facial expressions and gestures (see Chapter 2), and this in turn influenced the jurors' decisions.

Additional Influences on Verdicts: Defendant Characteristics and Juror Characteristics

If you think of a defendant as a stranger at a party and a juror as someone who encounters and evaluates this stranger, you should be able to think of many social psychological factors that might determine how the juror would react to the defendant. Especially important are nonverbal communication, attribution, impression formation, and impression management (Chapter 2); prejudice and discrimination (Chapter 6), and interpersonal attraction (Chapter 7). Such matters as first impressions, stereotypes, and liking should, of course, be irrelevant when we judge the guilt or innocence of someone accused of committing a crime; but they nevertheless *do* influence the outcomes of both real and simulated trials (Dane, 1992).

Before summarizing some of these effects, let's turn first to the following *Social Diversity* section, which illustrates the importance of race with respect to the defendant and to members of the jury.

Social Diversity: A Critical Analysis
Race As a Crucial Factor in the Courtroom

In the United States, African American defendants have generally been found to be at a disadvantage. For example, they are more likely than whites to be convicted of murder, to receive the death penalty, and to be proportionally overrepresented on death row (Sniffen, 1991). The most obvious—but not necessarily correct—hypothesis is that white judges and juries tend to be racially biased. It is also possible that blacks are more likely than whites to be raised in a subculture of poverty, unemployment, and the glorification of antisocial role models. Also, if whites as a group have an economic advantage, that also means that they are better able to afford more skillful attorneys. But what happens in an instance in which the defendant is a wealthy African American who faces two trials (one criminal and one civil) for the same crime but with a predominantly black jury in one trial and a predominantly white jury in the other? As you may have guessed, the two trials of former football star O. J. Simpson, who also became well known as a movie and television personality, provide some evidence as to the relative importance of poverty, attorneys, and race in influencing judicial outcomes.

In June 1994, Simpson's former wife, Nicole Brown Simpson, and a male acquaintance (both white) were brutally murdered. Shortly afterward, Simpson was charged with the crime, and his celebrity status resulted in exten-

sive media coverage. Every detail of the case before, during, and after the criminal trial (in which he was found not guilty of committing murder) and the civil trial (in which he was found liable for the deaths of the two victims) was available on radio and television and in newspapers and magazines. Given the same crimes and the same defendant, why were the verdicts dramatically different? One of Simpson's lawyers, F. Lee Bailey, asserts that his client was smeared by the press, which assumed guilt from the beginning and continued to propagate that message despite the not-guilty verdict in the criminal trial (O. J., Sam, 1998). A different possibility is that a black defendant was judged to be not guilty of murder because he faced a predominantly black jury (drawn from downtown Los Angeles) in the first trial, but to be financially liable for the deaths because he faced a predominantly white jury (drawn from Santa Monica) in the second trial (Darden, 1997). Is it possible, as some have suggested, that most trials are actually over once the jury has been selected (Goleman, 1994a)?

Before either trial began and before any evidence was available to the public, surveys consistently indicated that most African Americans believed Simpson to be innocent but most white Americans believed him to be guilty (Toobin, 1995b). Even in the first week after the arrest, African Americans more than whites believed that the

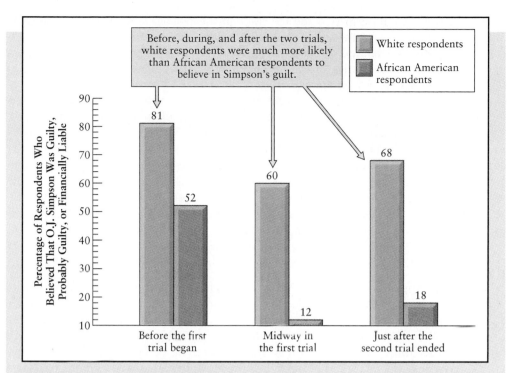

Figure 13.8

Did the Evidence Matter? Racial Differences in Judging O. J. Simpson. Opinion polls taken at various times between 1994, when O. J. Simpson was first accused of the murder of his former wife and her friend, and 1997, when the second (civil) trial ended, consistently indicated racial differences in evaluations of Simpson. Whether the question dealt with his guilt, his probable guilt, or financial liability to the families of the victims, white respondents overwhelmingly made more negative judgments than black respondents. These same racial differences were reflected in the positive decisions of the primarily black jury in the first (criminal) trial and the negative decisions of the primarily white jury in the second (civil) trial.

(*Source:* Based on data from Graham, Weiner, & Zucker, 1997; Lafferty, 1997; Toobin, 1995b.)

murder was caused by such factors as Nicole Brown Simpson's behavior. Also, whites stressed the need for severe punishment to make the accused suffer and to deter further crime, whereas, blacks stressed the need for rehabilitation (Graham, Weiner, & Zucker, 1997).

Racial differences in assumptions about Simpson's guilt continued through both trials and both verdicts, as indicated in Figure 13.8. Not only did blacks and whites differ in beliefs about Simpson's guilt; blacks also had more negative attitudes than whites about the criminal justice system, the prosecution, and the prosecution's witnesses and evidence (Mixon, Foley, & Orme, 1995). Further, the amount of knowledge any individual had about the case had no effect on that person's beliefs about guilt and innocence (Page & Gropp, 1995). Despite weeks and weeks of testimony about DNA evidence, thumps in the night, a glove that didn't fit, shoeprints at the crime scene, and on and on, the best predictor of either trial outcome was simply the racial composition of each jury.

The perceived importance of juror race was blatantly stated in a videotape made by Philadelphia's assistant district attorney several years *before* the murders of which O. J. Simpson was accused (Jury rigging, 1997). Despite the fact that the U.S. Supreme Court had ruled that lawyers were not permitted to eliminate potential jurors on the basis of race, the city's prosecutors were instructed:

Let's face it, the blacks from low-income areas are less likely to convict. There's a resentment toward law enforcement. There's a resentment toward authority. You don't want those people on your jury. It may appear as if you're being racist, but you're just being realistic. . . .

. . . sometimes I've had good luck with teachers who teach in the public school system. They may be so fed up with the garbage in their school that they may say, "I know this kind of kid. He's a pain in the ass." If you get a white teacher teaching in a black school who's sick of these guys, that may be the one you accept. (pp. 21, 24)

However unconstitutional and racist such remarks may be, they seem to provide an accurate guide to jury selection for prosecutors in a case involving race. The same perceptions could also guide jury selection in reverse for the defense. Lind (1995) argues that the jury system as practiced in the English-speaking common-law world is and has always been more unjust than the European civil-law tradition practiced by the other Western democracies. The difference is between a jury of ordinary citizens and a jury of professional and nonprofessional judges. Lind points out that, historically, a "jury of one's peers" in the United States has often meant a white jury deciding to lynch ("legally") Indians, blacks, and Asians while acquitting whites who murdered minority-group members. Follow-ing the civil rights revolution, urban black juries became possible, and they are equally able to put race above justice. These historical realities suggest an extremely negative view of the way race operates in our legal system. Do you agree?

Adler (1994) also argues that the U.S. jury system is failing because jurors are often incompetent, prejudiced, and too easily influenced by the attorneys' emotional manipulations. He proposes eliminating the right to challenge certain jurors and ensuring that well-educated members of society such as physicians, professors, and the clergy be required to perform jury duty. Would that increase fairness? Do *you* have any suggestions for improving the system?

The Appearance, Gender, Status, and Behavior of Defendants. As unfair as the effects of race are the effects of many other characteristics about which we hold stereotypes. For example, those accused of most major crimes are *less* likely to be found guilty if they are physically attractive, female, and of high rather than low socioeconomic status (Mazzella & Feingold, 1994). Attractiveness as a factor has been studied the most. In real as well as mock trials, attractive defendants have the advantage over unattractive ones with respect to being acquitted, receiving a light sentence, and gaining the sympathy of the jurors (Downs & Lyons, 1991; Quigley, Johnson, & Byrne, 1995; Wuensch, Castellow, & Moore, 1991). Some investigators conclude that attractiveness has such effects because of the stereotype that "what is beautiful is good." If this stereotype is operative, judicial decisions may be based primarily on inferences about character that are based on appearance (Egbert et al., 1992; Moore et al., 1994).

Beyond the influences of these various characteristics, the defendant's behavior also affects the decisions of jurors. For example, although smiling does not influence judgments of guilt, a smiling defendant is more likely to be recommended for leniency than a nonsmiling one (LaFrance & Hecht, 1995). The fact that a defendant denies guilt has no effect on the jury—but if the defendant goes on to deny accusations that were not actually made, he or she is perceived as untrustworthy, nervous, and responsible for the crime, *and* is more likely to be found guilty (Holtgraves & Grayer, 1994).

Juror Characteristics: Gender, Beliefs, Attitudes, and Values. We have already discussed some of the problems involved in jury selection and the effect of juror race on the outcome of trials. Gender also plays a role (Valliant & Loring, 1998). One of the consistent differences between male and female jurors is in their reactions to cases involving sexual assault. For example, in judging what occurred in cases of rape, men are more likely than women to conclude that the sexual interaction was consensual (Harris & Weiss, 1995). Schutte and Hosch (1997) analyzed the results of thirty-six studies of simulated cases of rape and child abuse and found that for both these crimes women were more likely than men to vote for conviction.

Research indicates that individuals differ in the way they process information, and these differences lead to incompetent decisions. For example, about a third of those sitting on juries have already made up their minds about the trial outcome by the time the opening arguments have been made. Once a juror makes such a decision, a schema is in place, and all of the evidence and testimony that follows is either interpreted so as to fit the schema or ignored if it doesn't fit (Kuhn, Weinstock, & Flaton, 1994). Such jurors tend to be very certain about their beliefs; to give extreme verdicts; and to be responsible for hung juries, because they resist changing their opinions. The most competent jurors, in contrast, process trial information by constructing alternate schemas so that each bit of evidence can be fit into one or another schema. In addition, as you might guess, the more complex and technical the evidence, the greater difficulty jurors have in processing whatever information they receive (Bourgeois, Horowitz, & Lee, 1993).

Jurors are also likely to hold various attitudes that have an effect on their decisions. One example is their attitude as to whether the blame for criminal acts should generally be placed primarily on society or on the accused. Thus, those with a **leniency bias** (the assumption that the defendant is also a victim) are least likely to vote guilty (MacCoun & Kerr, 1988). At the opposite extreme, jurors high in **legal authoritarianism** (the tendency to assume that the defendant is responsible for the crime) are most likely to vote guilty (Narby, Cutler, & Moran, 1993). In Australia as well as in the United States, relatively authoritarian jurors (that is, jurors who tend to see the world in "black and white" terms and to favor harsh punishment) tend to react to all offenses as relatively serious and hence as deserving punishment (Feather, 1996).

In states with a death penalty, potential jurors who oppose executions are routinely eliminated. Dismissals for this reason create a bias against the defendant, because individuals who are against the death penalty are also more likely to vote not guilty than are those who support the death penalty (Bersoff, 1987). In addition, attitudes about the death penalty are associated with a variety of other personal characteristics. Jurors who favor capital punishment are more likely to be white, male, married, Republican, conservative, authoritarian, and relatively better off financially than are those who are against the death penalty (Moran & Comfort, 1986).

Several very specific attitudes also are found to affect juror's views about what testimony to believe and hence how to vote. For example, positive versus negative attitudes about psychiatry can be crucial in a juror's accepting or rejecting testimony about a defendant's mental state (Cutler, Moran, & Narby, 1992). The insanity defense tends to be rejected by jurors who favor the death penalty, who reject expert psychological testimony about the defendant's mental state, and who believe that rehabilitation is impossible (Poulson, Braithwaite et al., 1997; Poulson, Wuensch et al., 1997).

As we have seen, jurors also bring various unstated rules to bear on the judgments they make. For example, we described how they apply different rules to inadmissible evidence depending on the reason for the inadmissibility, even though this differentiation does not rest on legal grounds. In a similar way, jurors making decisions in a rape trial often ignore the legalities. For example, a juror may simply make a decision than an act of intercourse was consensual sex rather than rape because of a personal belief that rape must involve physical injuries and a rapid complaint to the police (Harris & Weiss, 1995). Further, jurors who believe that traits are fixed and unchangeable are more likely to rely on indications of character and to generalize from information such as a defendant's clothing than are jurors who believe that traits are malleable (Gervey et al., 1999).

Altogether, research on the legal system provides evidence that judicial fairness and objectivity often fail because of quite common human reactions. The

leniency bias • A general tendency to make favorable assumptions about a person accused of a crime and to favor a verdict of not guilty.

legal authoritarianism • A general tendency to assume the worst about a person accused of a crime and to favor a verdict of guilty.

elimination of all biases in the courtroom is a laudable goal, but it may not be a reachable one.

Key Points

- Eyewitnesses to a crime often make mistakes, but a variety of procedures have been developed to help ensure greater accuracy.

- A serious and controversial legal problem is the recovery of *repressed memories* of past criminal events that turn out to be false memories.

- Attorneys act as adversaries who attempt to select juries biased toward their side and to convince the chosen jurors that their version of the truth is the accurate one.

- The words and even the unspoken beliefs of judges can influence the final verdict.

- Jurors' evaluation of a defendant is based in part on first impressions, stereotypes, and liking. For this reason, factors such as gender, race, and attractiveness play an unfair role in judicial decisions.

- The racial similarity or dissimilarity of defendants and jurors can have a major impact on the final verdict in a trial.

- Jurors differ in cognitive processing skills, attitudes, and personality dispositions, and these characteristics play an important role in the decision process.

APPLYING SOCIAL PSYCHOLOGY TO HEALTH-RELATED BEHAVIOR

Until the second half of the nineteenth century, illness was assumed to be a matter of inherited weaknesses, an immoral lifestyle, unhealthful surroundings (for example, bad air), or witchcraft. Many physicians initially rejected the concept of "invisible" microbes and the need for cleanliness and sterilization in doctors' offices and hospitals. Now, of course, we are quite willing to accept the reality of bacteria and viruses (Tomes, 1998). But the tiny organisms that bring on illness are not the total story. In recent decades it has become increasingly clear that psychological factors also affect all aspects of our physical well-being (Rodin & Salovey, 1989). As a result, investigators interested in **health psychology** focus on the psychological processes that affect the development, prevention, and treatment of physical illness (Glass, 1989). You may be puzzled as to how psychological and physiological processes can be interconnected, but the next few pages should help resolve any doubts you may have.

health psychology • The study of the effects of psychological factors in the origins, prevention, and treatment of physical illness.

Processing Health-Related Information

If headlines were our main source of knowledge, we would live in constant fear of AIDS, Lyme disease, mad cow disease, flesh-eating bacteria, and new viruses from African monkeys that turn our insides into spaghetti. In contrast to the headlines, the U.S. Centers for Disease Control and Prevention report data indicating that people are living longer than ever (the U.S. average is now seventy-six years) and that U.S. death rates from heart disease, cancer, stroke, lung disease, and pneumonia–influenza are all dropping (Latest figures, 1994). Improvements relevant to health include the first-ever decline in the incidence of cancer as well as decreased use of drugs and cigarettes; even the accidental death rate is declining (Easterbrook, 1999). But just as we generally overestimate the seriousness of the crime problem, we also overestimate the threat of disease on the basis of the availability heuristic (discussed in Chapters 1 and 3). How can we make sensible use of information on health and disease?

Using Health Information. The first step in attempting to maintain good health and prevent illness is the requirement that we process the very large amount of health information that bombards us daily (Thompson, 1992). We are told about which foods to eat and which to avoid, which vitamins and minerals are especially important, the vital importance of exercise, the effects of a multitude of supplements from St. John's Wort to grapefruit seed extract, and on and on (Greenwald, 1998). Then, as suggested in Figure 13.9, later on we may very well be told that new research findings indicate something different. One of the more pleasant examples of health-related news is one recent finding that people who eat candy regularly live about one year longer than those who completely avoid candy (Bowman, 1998). While waiting for scientific research to sort out inconsistencies, we must continue to make decisions about drinking alcohol, adding beta carotene supplements to our diets, avoiding specific kinds of fat, smoking cigars, adding shark cartilage to our orange juice, and so forth. And confusion about new information is not confined to the comic strips, as shown by the *Beyond the Headlines* section on page 546.

Figure 13.9

When Health Information Is Inconsistent, Do What You Want? Though it is frustrating to try to take account of health-related information that changes on the basis of new data, Sarge's solution is probably not the wisest alternative.

(*Source:* King Features Syndicate, Inc., 1995.)

Beyond the Headlines:
As Social Psychologists See It
What Are the Effects of Vitamin C?

STUDY CASTS SHADOW ON TAKING VITAMIN C

New York Times, April 9, 1998—A team of British investigators has found that taking 500 milligrams of vitamin C as a daily supplement can cause gene damage.

Many Americans take this much vitamin C (and often more) in the hope that its antioxidant effects will prevent cell damage caused by free radicals and thus help to fight off the common cold and to protect against heart disease, cancer, and other chronic problems.

The British scientists studied 30 healthy men and women who were given 500 milligrams of vitamin C each day for six weeks. The experimenters found that the vitamin had pro-oxidant effects as well as antioxidant effects, thus promoting genetic damage.

How, exactly, do you deal with that kind of new information after decades of being told that vitamin C is a valuable addition to your diet—a supplement that is routinely added to orange juice, children's vitamins, baby foods, and other products (Figure 13.10) to promote good health?

Before giving up on vitamin C, note that the story is based on one investigation of thirty people in one laboratory in Great Britain. That is not in any way a criticism of the study; but, as Dr. Charles Hennekens of Harvard Medical School cautions, "People shouldn't change their habits on the basis of one study" (Brody, 1995, p. A18).

Not only does the experiment need to be repeated on larger samples and in other locations; medical scientists—and we—need to know a lot more. For example,

Figure 13.10

Is Vitamin C Good for Us or a Danger to Our Genes? By its very nature, individual research findings relevant to health can be contradictory until all of the factors have been identified and all of the findings replicated. In the meantime, we in the general public often find ourselves trying to evaluate conflicting and inconsistent information about a variety of health-related issues. Recent research that indicates a possible negative effect of Vitamin C might can raise questions, but it is probably a bad idea to change your diet or your behavior based on the findings of a single study.

research at the Mount Sinai School of Medicine indicates that vitamin C occurring naturally in foods does *not* have this oxidizing effect. Also, you might wonder about the extent of the genetic damage. After all, genes are damaged by many factors, but the damage is essentially irrelevant to ourselves or our offspring. You might also ask about the effects of the supplement when vitamin C is taken over a longer period of time. Perhaps all of the damage occurs in the first six weeks. Another question is whether lower dosages of vitamin C have the same effects. If not, do the lower dosages give us the benefits of vitamin C without the risks? Also, we need information about how this particular vitamin interacts with other vitamins (or other foods) in our diet. Perhaps, for example, large doses of vitamin C *are* beneficial for persons who eat a lot of fast food, but are less so for people who eat a lot of leafy green vegetables. In short, the findings of possible negative effects of vitamin C, interesting as they are, are very incomplete and don't really allow us to reach firm conclusions concerning the contents of an ideal daily diet.

In the meantime, what should you personally do about taking vitamin C? The answer is that no one knows for sure until more research has been conducted and evaluated. Unsettling as it may be to many of us, much health information remains uncertain; but it is precisely such uncertainty that is often ignored in newspaper articles like the one reproduced here. After reading it, you might conclude that we "know" the answer and what to do. But as we've tried to explain, this is far from the case!

Accepting, Rejecting, and Acting on Health Information. When health information is unclear, people tend to accept some of the findings and reject others. Even when the information is very clear, some people change their behavior radically but others are reluctant to modify what they do. That is, some quit tobacco cold turkey and others continue to inhale; some concentrate on fitness and others find numerous reasons to stay on the couch and avoid strenuous exercise. What do we know about why people react in such divergent ways?

One factor is the affective nature of health warnings. Experts often present data about disease prevention in an emotion-arousing manner in the hope that fear will motivate us to do the right thing. One difficulty with this approach is that people often reject as "untrue" a health message that arouses anxiety. The rejection acts to reduce our anxiety and thus makes it unnecessary for us to change our behavior (Liberman & Chaiken, 1992). Information about something as frightening as breast cancer, for example, can activate defense mechanisms that interfere with women's attending to, remembering, and/or acting on relevant information about the importance of early detection (Millar, 1997).

One common way to deal with threatening information actually increases the odds that the person will engage in behavior involving health risks. Consider a situation in which unmarried individuals are contemplating sexual intercourse. Among many factors to consider are the threat of disease and the threat of unwanted pregnancy. Such considerations create anxiety. One "remedy" for anxiety is alcohol. Whenever people drink alcohol, anxiety is decreased—but so is cognitive capacity. The resulting *alcohol myopia* (Steele & Josephs, 1990) causes people to focus on the perceived benefits of having intercourse rather than on the potential negative consequences of failure to use condoms (MacDonald, Zanna, & Fong, 1996). Thus, drinking can lead to unsafe sex, and too much alcohol can also lead to unsafe driving and unsafe dining.

Altogether, the findings concerning the effects of health-related messages involving fear and threat are complex. Rothman and his colleagues (1993) were able to show, however, that a *positively framed* message is best for motivating *preventive* behavior ("Eat high-fiber food to promote good health and prevent disease"), whereas a *negatively framed* message is best for motivating *detection* behavior ("Get a Pap smear annually to avoid the pain and suffering associated with uterine cancer").

What factors predispose individuals toward behaviors that put their health at risk? Caspi and his colleagues (1997) found that personality characteristics assessed at age three and at age eighteen predict health risk behaviors at age twenty-one. Specifically, adults who drink, commit violent acts, engage in unsafe sex, and drive dangerously are found in adolescence and in childhood to be high on *aggression* (hurting, frightening, and otherwise discomforting their peers) but low on such traits as *traditionalism* (having high moral standards), *harm avoidance* (avoiding excitement and danger; preferring safe activities), and *control* (tending to be reflective, cautious, careful, rational, planful).

Additional individual characteristics have been related to health risk behaviors and to attempts to change such behaviors. Gibbons and Gerrard (1995) point out that people who are thinking about joining a group compare themselves with the *prototype* individual they perceive as associated with that group. The closer the match between self and prototype, the greater the interest in joining the group. In a large sample of entering college freshmen, the investigators assessed each student's prototype of the typical freshman who smokes cigarettes (or drinks alcohol, or drives recklessly, etc.). For example, is such a person smart, confused, popular, immature, cool, independent, careless, unattractive, or dull? One finding was that a student's perception of a typical smoker as being like himself or herself predicted smoking behavior, and changes in behavior led to changes in prototype perceptions. The underlying mechanism seems to be social comparison (see Chapter 7). Those who most often engage in social comparison show the strongest link between their perceptions of typical freshmen and changes in their own behavior.

Among people who engage in any kind of risky behavior, there is frequently a sense of *unrealistic optimism*. A bungee jumper, for example, is likely to feel that, compared to other bungee jumpers, he or she has a below-average chance of something bad happening and an above-average chance of having something good happen (Middleton, Harris, & Surman, 1996). "Bad consequences are unlikely to happen to me, so I'll do it." In a similar way, unrealistic optimism can lead the individual to drive while intoxicated or to consume large amounts of saturated fats.

The Emotional and Physiological Effects of Stress

During World War II, psychologists became especially interested in **stress** and its impacts on thoughts, actions, and physical well-being (Lazarus, 1993). At first, interest centered primarily on the physical effects of stress (Selye, 1956), but attention soon broadened to include psychological aspects (Lazarus, 1966). The term now is defined as any physical or psychological event perceived as being able to cause us harm or emotional distress. Many real and imagined dangers pose such threats, and individuals engage in **coping** behavior in an attempt to deal with stressful situations and their emotional reactions to them (Taylor, Buunk, & Aspinwall, 1990). Of special importance is the effect of stress on physical illness.

Illness As a Consequence of Stress. It is consistently found that as stress increases, depression and illness increase. We will look first at some of the many forms of stress.

Work-related stress is common across most occupations. Stressors at work include negative interpersonal relationships (Buunk et al., 1993); confusion

stress • Any physical or psychological event perceived as being able to cause harm or emotional distress.

coping • Responding to stress in a way that reduces the threat and its effects; includes what a person does, feels, or thinks in order to master, tolerate, or decrease the negative effects of a stressful situation.

about one's role on the job (Revicki et al., 1993); lack of control in the work environment (Schaefer & Moos, 1993); work overload (Marshall & Barnett, 1993); and—the worst such stress of all—unemployment (Schwarzer, Jerusalem, & Hahn, 1994).

College students encounter their own array of stressful events, such as low grades, problems revolving around romance and sexuality, and parental divorce. As stress mounts, physical illness is a common outcome. For each of us, everyday hassles such as arguing with a loved one (Chapman, Hobfoll, & Ritter, 1997), living under crowded conditions (Evans, Lepore, & Schroeder, 1996), commuting in heavy traffic (Weinberger, Hiner, & Tierney, 1987), and dealing with environmental noise (Evans, Bullinger, & Hygge, 1998; Staples, 1996) can increase the probability of catching a cold or coming down with the flu. Gender differences occur in response to stress in that women are more likely than men to react initially with anxiety, depression, physical symptoms, and eating problems, whereas men more than women respond by drinking alcohol to excess (Oliver, Reed, & Smith, 1998).

As more and more negative events occur, the stress tends to be cumulative, and the consequent risk of illness increases (Cohen, Tyrrell, & Smith, 1993). In Western cultures females report experiencing more hassles and more stressful hassles than males (Wagner & Compas, 1990), but only among Asian adolescents does the same gender difference also extend to physical symptoms (Lai, Hamid, & Chow, 1996). Also, a single extremely serious stressful event, such as the death of a loved one (Schleifer et al., 1983) or serving in the military in Vietnam (King et al., 1998) also raises the odds against being able to stay well (Schleifer et al., 1983).

There is increasing evidence that social interactions involve considerable stress. Among monkeys as well as among humans, individuals whose status is lower than those with whom they interact are more susceptible to disease (Shively, 1998). In human society, the effect involves a great deal more than simply socioeconomic status. Regardless of one's income or standard of living, the key factor appears to be whether individuals are in a subordinate social role or in a dominant role and in control. For example, coronary heart disease occurs more frequently among individuals with relatively low interpersonal status, and it is the leading cause of death among women in the United States. See Chapter 5 for evidence involving gender differences in interpersonal status.

How, exactly, could stress result in illness? In general, those who are stressed report a negative affective state, aches and pains, and more physical symptoms of illness (Affleck et al., 1994; Brown & Moskowitz, 1997); but the effects of stress go beyond that. As outlined in Figure 13.11 on page 550, Baum (1994) proposes both direct and indirect effects of stress. There are indirect effects when the emotional turmoil (depression and worry) caused by stress interferes with health-related behaviors such as seeking medical care or eating a balanced diet (Whisman & Kwon, 1993; Wiebe & McCallum, 1986). There are also direct physiological effects in that stress delays the healing process in wounds, has adverse effects on the endocrine system, and causes the body's immune system to function less well (Kiecolt-Glaser et al., 1998; Stone et al., 1987).

Focusing on one of the direct effects of stress, *psychoneuroimmunology* is the research field that explores the relationships among stress, emotional and behavioral reactions, and the immune system (Ader & Cohen, 1993). To consider one example, college students often show an increase in upper respiratory infections as exam time approaches (Dorian et al., 1982). In research on the origins of these infections, Jemmott and Magloire (1988) obtained samples of students' saliva over several weeks in order to assess the presence of *secretory*

Figure 13.11

Stress and Illness: Direct and Indirect Effects. It has long been known that as stress increases, the likelihood of illness also increases. The mechanisms underlying this relationship are gradually beginning to be understood. It appears that stress has indirect effects (it leads to behavioral changes) as well as direct physiological effects.

(*Source:* Based on material in Baum, 1994.)

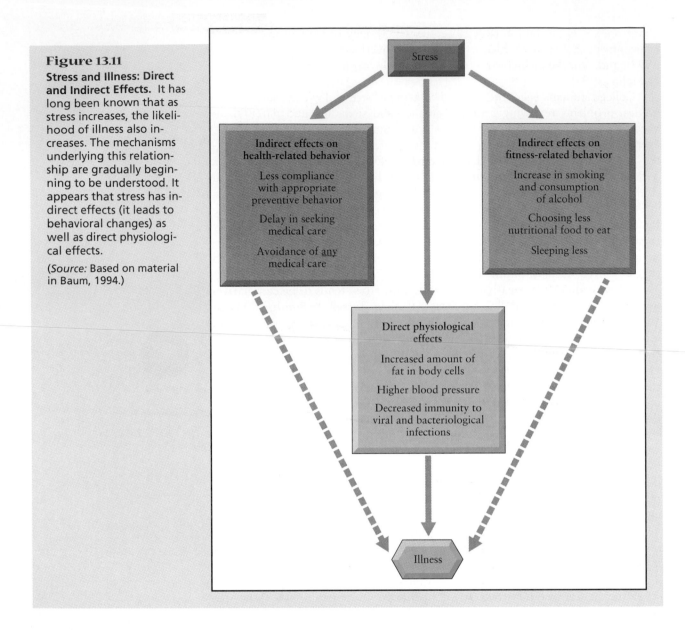

immunoglobulin A, the body's primary defense against infections. These investigators found that the level of this substance dropped during final exams and then returned to normal levels when the exams were over. It seems clear that the psychological stress of finals brought about a change in body chemistry and that this change, in turn, made the students more susceptible to disease. Cohen (1996) argues that we need to know even more about how the negative emotional effects of stress bring about neural, behavioral, and hormonal changes that impair the functioning of the immune system. For example, Uchino and his colleagues (1995) were able to identify distinct physiological pathways that are activated in response to acute psychological stress.

Death is obviously the ultimate harmful health effect of stress. A few studies have dealt with stressors that decrease life expectancy. A longitudinal study (covering several decades of the participants' lives) revealed a relationship between how people explain negative events in their lives and the probability of an early death (Peterson et al., 1998). The tendency to engage in **catastrophizing** (envisioning impending disaster and expecting bad events to occur repeatedly) was associated with untimely deaths—especially among males, and especially with death by accident or violence. The investigators suggest that those who hold a pessimistic belief about the frequency of bad events also have poor problem-solving skills, lack close interpersonal relationships, and engage in risky decision making. The latter characteristic, in particular, leads to life-threatening behaviors.

Another intriguing, but less easily explained, predictor of early death was reported by Christenfeld (1998). He found that people whose initials spell out a positive, neutral, or meaningless word (for example, ACE, GOD, JOY, WOW, JAY, WLW) live longer and are less likely to die in an accident or commit suicide than those whose initials spell out negative words (for example, APE, DUD, RAT, PIG, BUM, UGH). One possible explanation is that parents who would name a newborn son, Bradley Ulysses Morton are either too hostile or too lacking in awareness to raise their offspring properly, compared with parents who go to the trouble to name their newborn daughter Jane Olivia Young. Another possibility is that someone who grows up with the initials BUM is the target of more teasing and social rejection than someone whose initials spell out JOY. You might want to suggest alternative reasons for a relationship between initials and life span.

Oddly enough, positive events can be as stressful and sometimes cause as many physical problems as negative events. Why? For one thing, no matter how positive the idea of such joyful occasions as a vacation, a wedding, or the purchase of a fine new house, the planning can be complicated and a source of negative affect; things sometimes go wrong, and, if not, there is worry that things *might* go wrong. Langston (1994) finds that positive affect can be enhanced if the individual focuses on the positive aspects of what is happening (rather than on the possibly disastrous aspects) and works hard to remain in control of events. The concept of "control" often comes up in connection with stress, and we will have more to say in a later section about its importance.

Individual Differences in the Effects of Stress.   Given the same objectively stressful conditions, some people experience more negative emotional reactions than others and are thus more likely to get sick. Genetic factors explain some of the differences in the effects of stress (Kessler et al., 1992). There is, however, a growing body of evidence that each of us can be placed somewhere on a dispositional spectrum that ranges from the **disease-prone personality** to the **self-healing personality** (Friedman, Hawley, & Tucker, 1994).Those who are disease-prone respond to stressful situations with negative emotions and unhealthy behavior patterns, and the result is illness and a shorter life span. Self-healing individuals are at the opposite extreme—tending to be enthusiastic about life, emotionally balanced, alert, responsive to others, energetic, curious, secure, and constructive. Self-healing people can be described as people one likes to be around. Similarly, research on *subjective well-being* and *optimism* indicates the many emotional and physical benefits of interpreting one's daily life in positive terms, being fully engaged in work and in leisure activities, feeling a sense of purpose, and expecting positive future outcomes (Myers & Diener, 1995; Segerstrom et al., 1998).

Do self-healing people sound familiar? Similar characteristics were described in relation to those with a secure attachment style (Chapter 8) and those described as having an altruistic personality (Chapter 10). There apparently are a set of interconnected characteristics that promote positive behavior of various

catastrophizing • Interpreting negative life events in pessimistic, global terms. People (especially men) who consistently explain bad events as catastrophes are found to have a shortened life span.

disease-prone personality • Personality characterized by negative emotional reactions to stress, ineffective coping strategies, and unhealthy behavior patterns; often associated with illness and a shortened life span.

self-healing personality • Personality characterized by effective coping with stress; self-healing individuals are balanced, energetic, responsive to others, and positive about life.

Table 13.2

Personality Differences of Those Most and Least Vulnerable to Stress. In general, stress often leads to illness, but some individuals are far more vulnerable than others. The difference in vulnerability is associated with a variety of personality differences.

	Self-Healing Personality	Disease-Prone Personality
Behavioral tendencies	nonperfectionist	perfectionist
	extraverted	introverted
	completes school assignments on time	procrastinates
Expectancies and beliefs	internal locus of control	external locus of control
	believes in a just world	does not believe in a just world
	high self-efficacy	low self-efficacy
	optimistic	pessimistic
	approaches goals focusing on positive outcomes toward which to strive	avoidance goals focusing on negative outcomes from which to stay away
Personal characteristics	not neurotic	neurotic
	well adjusted	maladjusted
	high self-esteem	low self-esteem
	accessible attitudes: knows own likes and dislikes	inaccessible attitudes: unsure of own likes and dislikes
	independent	dependent

(*Sources, in order of listing in the table:* Joiner & Schmidt, 1995; Amirkhan, Risinger, & Swickert, 1995; Tice & Baumeister, 1997; Birkimer, Lucas, & Birkimer, 1991; Tomaka & Blascovich, 1994; Bandura, 1993; Dykema, Bergbower, & Peterson, 1995; Elliot & Sheldon, 1998; Booth-Kewley & Vickers, 1994; Bernard & Belinsky, 1993; Campbell, Chew, & Scratchley, 1991; Fazio & Powell, 1997; Bornstein, 1995.)

kinds and that serve as a protection against the negative physical effects of stress. Table 13.2 provides an overview of many of the personality differences between those who are disease-prone and those who are self-healing.

Given this kind of evidence about individual differences, we can examine just *how* such personality differences operate to influence health. Bolger and Zuckerman (1995) requested neurotic and nonneurotic college students to keep daily diaries for a two-week period, and these two groups reported three types of relevant behavioral differences. Those high in neuroticism exposed themselves to more situations involving conflict, reacted more negatively to these stressful situations, and chose less effective ways to cope with the resulting stress.

A specific personality characteristic that is associated with a specific health problem was introduced in Chapter 11. The *Type A* behavior pattern, described as a personal determinant of aggression, is also associated with an increased risk of heart disease. Type A individuals, compared to the more placid Type B individuals, are more hostile, have higher blood pressure (Contrada, 1989), produce less HDL—the "good cholesterol" (Type A's lack, 1992), and are twice as likely to develop heart disease (Weidner, Istvan, & McKnight, 1989). Anger seems to be the critical component that leads to coronary disease (Smith & Pope, 1990).

Coping with Stress

Because stress is essentially inevitable in our lives and because not everyone is fortunate enough to have a self-healing personality, we need strategies for dealing with stress. What strategies are helpful? A sensible first step is to be in the best possible physical condition.

Increasing Physical Fitness to Ward Off the Effects of Stress. A healthful pattern of eating nutritious foods, getting enough sleep, and engaging in regular physical exercise results in increased *fitness* (being in good physical condition as indicated by one's endurance and strength). Even fifteen to twenty minutes of aerobic exercise (jogging, biking, swimming, dancing, etc.) daily or every other day is an effective way to increase fitness, a sense of well-being, and feelings of self-efficacy as well as to decrease feelings of distress (Jessor, Turbin, & Costa, 1998; Lox & Rudolph, 1994; Mihalko, McAuley, & Bane, 1996). In a study of Korean undergraduates, Rudolph and Kim (1996) found positive emotional effects from aerobic activities as diverse as dancing and soccer, but not from less aerobic activities such as tennis and bowling. While some bodily exertion is better than none, the most beneficial exercise program is one that involves high intensity (Winett, 1998). High intensity means that an individual must train at a high percentage of his or her maximum heart rate with maximum oxygen uptake. Thus, the phrase "no pain, no gain" applies to disease prevention as basically as to other exercise goals.

Numerous investigations provide convincing evidence of the long-term beneficial effects of exercise. For example, Brown (1991) conducted a study of more than a hundred undergraduates to determine whether fitness moderates the link between stress and illness. He found that those students who experienced very little stress had very few illnesses, regardless of their degree of physical fitness. Among those whose level of stress was high, however, the low-fitness students visited the health center significantly more often than the high-fitness students. Keep in mind that dispositional variables are of equal importance: the combination of physical fitness *and* self-healing personality characteristics leads to the lowest level of illness in response to stress (Roth et al., 1989).

Though the positive effects of fitness are clear, the biggest barrier to becoming fit is the fact that changing from a sedentary lifestyle to one that includes regular exercise requires strong motivation, continuing commitment, and the ability to regulate one's own behavior (Mullan & Markland, 1997).

Coping Strategies. Compas and his colleagues (1991) proposed that **coping,** or responding effectively to stress, involves a two-level process. As outlined in Figure 13.12 on page 554, at the first level, emotional distress is ordinarily the initial response to a threatening event, and *emotion-focused coping* occurs as a way to deal with one's feelings by reducing the negative arousal. People most often reduce negative feelings by trying to increase positive affect or by seeking social support. If, for example, you received a very low grade in your social psych midterm exam, you might attempt to relieve your depression by watching a funny television show or by attending an enjoyable social event. At the second level, *problem-focused coping* represents an attempt to deal with the threat and gain control of the situation. Ideally, this leads not only to reduced negative emotions but also to reduced threat. Though less research has dealt with this second type of coping, presumably it involves the kinds of behaviors characteristic of those with self-healing personalities. With your imaginary low course grade, for example, you might study harder, hire a tutor, or find out what questions you missed on the exam so that you could try to figure out why.

A term that is applied to successful coping is **regulatory control**—the processes that enable an individual to guide his or her goal-directed activities over time and across situations. That is, some people are able to exert control over what they think, how they feel, what they do, and where they direct their

regulatory control • Successful coping by means of processes that enable one to exert control over what one thinks, how one feels, and where one directs his or her attention.

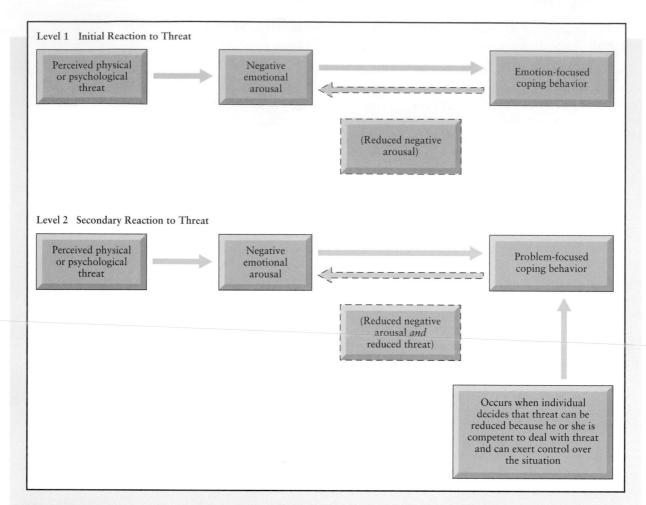

Figure 13.12

Responding to Threat: Focus on Emotions, Then Focus on Problem. We respond to threat in two ways. The initial reaction is an emotional one (level 1), and we must cope with our feelings of distress—emotion-focused coping. If the threat cannot be reduced in any way, emotional coping is all that can be done. If the threat can be modified or removed, however, it is possible to cope with the problem itself (level 2)—problem-focused coping.

(*Source:* Based on information in Compas et al., 1991.)

attention (Karoly, 1993). Holding positive beliefs and having positive experiences are helpful in making it possible for a person to maintain self-regulation (Reed & Aspinwall, 1998). Those who have learned to engage in regulatory control experience less negative affect when confronting stressful conditions, and they engage in constructive coping behavior (Fabes & Eisenberg, 1997). Underlying a person's ability to regulate his or her feelings is the following set of beliefs (Mayer & Salovey, 1995):

1. People can have the most pleasure if they give up short-term pleasures in order to gain long-term satisfactions.
2. People should strive to experience emotions that are pro-individual and prosocial.
3. The best emotions to feel are those that are appropriate to the situation, including painful ones.

Creating Positive Affect to Counteract the Negative Emotions Aroused by Stress. A useful emotion-focused strategy for coping with stress is to discover how to create positive affect for oneself. People who are able to regulate their emotions seek ways to experience positive, happy feelings and an optimistic outlook despite negative events (Chang, 1998; Mayer & Salovey, 1995). For example, when President Lincoln was asked how he could make jokes during the worst days of the Civil War, he replied, "I laugh because I must not cry." Laughter seems to provide a buffer against stressful events. As stress increases, those who seldom laugh respond with increasingly negative affect, but those who laugh the most do not (Kuiper & Martin, 1998).

Stress creates negative affect, and negative affect interferes with the immune system; but some people make matters worse by engaging in *counterfactual thinking* (see Chapter 3)—dwelling on alternative things they might have done to prevent the stressful event. Such thoughts only add to the person's negative feelings of distress (Davis et al., 1995). Equally ineffective is *avoidant coping,* in which the person attempts to deny or avoid thinking about the stressful events (Smith, 1996).

Still another unsatisfactory response to stress is to attempt to reduce the negative affect by turning to alcohol or other drugs (Cooper et al., 1995; Watten, 1995). The result is usually short-term emotional relief that does nothing to relieve the original source of stress and often simply adds a new problem. Among other findings, African Americans are more likely than Caucasians to engage in daily drinking in response to stress (Sample, Li, & Moore, 1997). Similarly, smoking among black teenagers increased 80 percent over six years in the 1990s, three times the rate of increase for young whites (Black smokers', 1998). For whatever reason, the smoking data are reversed among college students. In this specific population, whites smoke more than either blacks or Asians (Bad news on smoking, 1998).

The more adaptive alternative is to engage in activities that generate positive affect. Stone and his colleagues (1994) reported that positive events (such as a family gathering or spending time with friends) actually enhance the immune system for a longer time period than negative events (such as getting a low grade or being the target of criticism) weaken it. Further, a *decrease* in positive events has a negative effect on health similar to that of an *increase* in negative events (Goleman, 1994b).

Other effective aids to positive feelings range from enjoyable work (Csikszentmihalyi, 1993) to humor (Lefcourt et al., 1995) to pleasant fragrances (Baron & Bronfen, 1994). Any activity that helps improve one's mood seems able to counteract the negative effects of stress.

Seeking Social Support to Cope with Stressful Events. A very important coping strategy is to seek **social support**—the physical and psychological comfort provided by other people (Sarason, Sarason, & Pierce, 1994). In part, just being with those you like seems helpful. Monkeys show an increase in affiliative behavior in response to stressful situations (Cohen et al., 1992), and you may remember the discussion of a similar pattern of human affiliation in Chapter 7. As you might also guess on the basis of attraction research, people who desire social support tend to turn to others who are similar to themselves (Morgan, Carder, & Neal, 1997).

People are better able to avoid illness in response to threat (and to recover from any illness that develops) if they interact with others rather than remaining isolated (Roy, Steptoe, & Kirschbaum, 1998). The negative effects of workplace stress can be lessened when an employee is given support by coworkers or

social support • The physical and psychological comfort provided by a person's friends and family members.

are known as *organizational commitment* (e.g., Brown, 1996; Keller, 1997). Since job satisfaction is linked more directly to basic social psychological research on attitudes, we'll focus on this topic here.

Factors Affecting Job Satisfaction. Despite the fact that many jobs are repetitive and boring in nature, surveys involving literally hundreds of thousands of employees conducted over the course of several decades point to a surprising finding: Most people indicate that they are quite satisfied with their jobs (e.g., Page & Wiseman, 1993). In part, this may reflect the operation of *cognitive dissonance* (see Chapter 4). Because most persons know that they have to continue working and that there is often considerable effort—and risk—involved in changing jobs, stating that they are *not* satisfied with their current job tends to generate dissonance. To avoid or reduce such reactions, then, many persons find it easier to report high levels of job satisfaction—and may actually come to accept their own ratings as a true reflection of their views.

A wide range of job satisfaction levels do exist, though, so a key question remains: What factors influence such attitudes? Research on this issue indicates that two major groups of factors are important: *organizational factors* related to a company's practices or the working conditions provided, and *personal factors* related to the traits of individual employees.

The organizational factors that influence job satisfaction contain few surprises: people report higher satisfaction when they feel that the reward systems in their companies are fair (when raises, promotions, and other rewards are distributed fairly—see Chapter 12); when they like and respect their bosses and believe these persons have their best interests at heart (see Figure 13.14); when they can participate in the decisions that affect them; when the work they perform is interesting rather than boring and repetitive; and when they are neither *overloaded* with too much to do in a given amount of time nor *underloaded* with too little to do (e.g., Callan, 1993; Melamed et al., 1993; Miceli & Lane, 1991). Physical working conditions also play a role: when they are comfortable, employees report higher job satisfaction than when they are uncomfortable (e.g., too hot, too noisy, too crowded) (Baron, 1994).

Figure 13.14

Job Satisfaction: How to Destroy It. When employees believe that their bosses do not care about them—do not have their best interests at heart—job satisfaction can drop to dismal levels.

(*Source:* United Feature Syndicate, Inc., 1998.)

Turning to personal factors, some findings are, perhaps, more unexpected. First, and probably least surprising, job satisfaction is positively related to both seniority and status: the longer people have been in a given job and the higher their status, the greater their satisfaction (Zeitz, 1990). Similarly, the greater the extent to which jobs are closely matched to individuals' personal interests, the greater their satisfaction (Fricko & Beehr, 1992). A bit more surprising, perhaps, is the finding that certain personal traits are closely related to job satisfaction. For instance, Type A persons tend to be *more* satisfied than Type B's, despite their greater overall irritability (see Chapter 11). Perhaps this is so because jobs allow people to stay busy, and Type A's, of course, *like* to be busy all the time!

Now get ready for the really surprising findings: some results of recent research indicate that job satisfaction may actually have an important genetic component—and that as a result, individuals have a tendency to express either relatively high or relatively low levels of job satisfaction *no matter where they work*. The first research pointing to such conclusions was conducted by Arvey and his colleagues (1989) more than ten years ago. These researchers measured current job satisfaction in thirty-four pairs of identical (monozygotic) twins who had been separated at an early age and then raised apart. Because such twins have identical genetic inheritance but have had different life experiences (being raised in different homes), the extent to which they report similar levels of job satisfaction provides information on the potential role of genetic factors in such attitudes. Results obtained by Arvey and his colleagues (1989) indicated that the level of job satisfaction reported by these pairs of twins correlated significantly, and that these correlations were higher than was true for unrelated pairs of individuals—who, of course, do not share the same genes. Further, additional findings indicated that as much as 30 percent of variation in job satisfaction from one person to another may stem from genetic factors! While these findings remain somewhat controversial (e.g., Cropanzano & James, 1990), they have been replicated in other studies (e.g., Keller et al., 1992). Thus, it appears that job satisfaction may stem, at least in part, from genetic factors.

Even if genetic factors do not play the important role suggested by these results, additional studies indicate that attitudes toward work are highly stable over time, even when individuals change jobs. Persons who express high levels of satisfaction in one job at a given time are likely to express high levels of satisfaction in a different job at a later time, and so on. Clear evidence for such effects has been reported recently by Steel and Rentsch (1997). These researchers obtained measures of job satisfaction and job involvement (the extent to which individuals feel personally involved in their jobs) from almost two hundred persons who worked in a large government agency; these measures were obtained at two different times, ten years apart. In addition, Steel and Rentsch (1997) also obtained information on the extent to which the persons in the study were performing the same or a very different job the second time they were surveyed. Steel and Rentsch (1997) predicted that job satisfaction and job involvement at the two times would be related (i.e., would correlate), despite the passage of ten years. Further, they predicted that this would be true even for individuals who were now performing a different job. As you can see from Figure 13.15 on page 562, these predictions were confirmed. Job satisfaction and job involvement showed considerable stability over a ten-year period, both for individuals who reported performing much the same job and for those who reported performing different work. As expected, however, stability was greater for those performing the same job.

Figure 13.15

Job Satisfaction: Evidence That It Is Stable. As shown here, the job satisfaction expressed by a group of employees at one point in time correlated significantly with job satisfaction expressed by the same group of persons ten years later. This was true even if the participants' jobs had changed significantly during this period.

(*Source:* Based on data from Steel & Rentsch, 1997.)

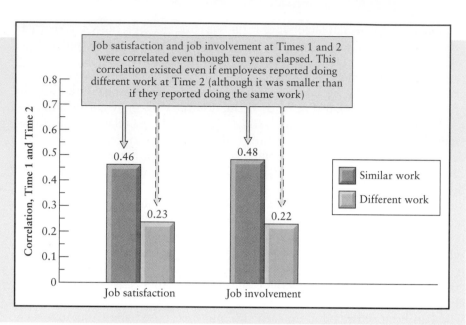

Job satisfaction and job involvement at Times 1 and 2 were correlated even though ten years elapsed. This correlation existed even if employees reported doing different work at Time 2 (although it was smaller than if they reported doing the same work)

These findings, and those of related research (e.g., Gerhart, 1987), suggest that personal factors—genetic or otherwise—play an important role in job satisfaction. While working conditions, the nature of the jobs people perform, and many organizational factors combine to shape job satisfaction (Steel and Rentsch also found evidence for the importance of such factors in their study), job satisfaction is also, to an important degree, very much in the eye of the beholder. Some persons express a high level of satisfaction no matter where they work, while others express a low level no matter where *they* work. It is clear that most of us would usually prefer to work with people who fall into the first category than with the kind of chronic complainers who fall into the second.

The Effects of Job Satisfaction on Task Performance: Weaker Than You Might Guess. Are happy workers—people who like their jobs—productive workers? Common sense seems to suggest that they would be, but it's important to remember that job satisfaction is a kind of attitude. And, as we noted in Chapter 4, attitudes are not always strong predictors of overt behavior. Thus, you should not be surprised to learn that although job satisfaction is related to performance in many jobs, this relationship is relatively weak—correlations in the range of .15 to .20 (e.g., Judge, 1993; Tett & Meyer, 1993).

Why isn't this relationship stronger? Because several factors may tend to weaken or moderate the impact of job satisfaction on performance. One of the most important of these is this: Many jobs leave little room for variations in performance. Think about production-line employees, for example. If they don't perform at a minimum level, they get behind "the line" and can't hold the job. But they can't *exceed* this minimum by much either: they'd just be standing around waiting for the next item on which to work (see Figure 13.16). Because of these limits in the range of possible performance, job satisfaction cannot exert a strong influence on performance in jobs of this type.

Another reason for the relatively weak link between job satisfaction and task performance is that many other factors also determine performance: working conditions, the availability of required materials and tools, the extent to which the task is structured, and so on. In many cases, the effects of these factors may be more important than job satisfaction in determining performance. For instance, even employees who love their jobs can't do their best work if the

Figure 13.16
No Room for Variations in Performance: One Reason Why Job Satisfaction Isn't Strongly Linked to Job Performance. Many jobs, such as the ones shown here, permit very little variation in performance: employees can't work slower, or faster, than the norm or standard. Under these conditions, employees' job satisfaction cannot strongly influence their performance.

environment in which they work is too hot, too cold, or too noisy. Similarly, they can't show excellent performance if they are working with broken or out-of-date equipment.

Still another reason why job satisfaction is not strongly related to task performance involves the possibility that positive attitudes toward one's job—or toward coworkers or the entire organization—may be reflected primarily in forms of behavior unrelated to performance (e.g., Keller, 1997). In other words, individuals who hold positive attitudes toward their jobs may express these attitudes through actions that are consistent with such views but are not directly linked to task performance—for instance, through praising their company to people outside it, conserving its resources, or helping other coworkers. Such actions can have very beneficial effects on an organization, so let's take a closer look at them now.

Organizational Citizenship Behavior: Prosocial Behavior at Work

In Chapter 10, we examined many aspects of *prosocial behavior*—helpful actions that benefit others but have no obvious benefits for the persons who perform them. As we saw in that chapter, prosocial behavior stems from many different factors and can yield a wide range of effects. Do such actions also occur in work settings, between persons who work together in an organization? And if so, what forms do they take, and what effects do they produce? These are the questions that have been investigated recently by industrial/organizational psychologists and others, and as you can see, they are directly related to basic research in the field of social psychology. Let's take a brief look at what research on these issues has revealed.

The Nature of Prosocial Behavior at Work: Some Basic Forms. While various terms have been used to describe prosocial behavior in work settings (e.g., Van Dyne & LePine, 1998), most researchers refer to such behavior as **organizational citizenship behavior** (*OCB* for short)—defined as prosocial behavior occurring within an organization that may or may not be rewarded by the organization (e.g., Organ, 1997). The fact that such behavior is not automati-

organizational citizenship behavior (OCB) • Prosocial behavior occurring within an organization that may or may not be rewarded by the organization.

cally or necessarily rewarded (e.g., through a bonus or a raise in pay) is important, because it suggests that OCB is performed voluntarily, often without any thought of external reward for doing so. Thus, it does indeed qualify as prosocial behavior according to the definition noted above. How do individuals working in an organization seek to help one another? Research findings suggest that they do so in many different ways. However, most helpful actions at work appear to take one of five different forms:

- *Altruism:* Helping others to perform their jobs. (Note that social psychologists do *not* use the term *altruism* in this way.)
- *Conscientiousness:* Going beyond the minimum requirements of a job, doing more than is required. For instance, an employee who prides himself on never missing a day of work or on taking short breaks is showing conscientiousness.
- *Civic virtue:* Participating in and showing concern for the "life" of the organization. One example: attending voluntary meetings. Another example: reading memos rather than throwing them in the trash!
- *Sportsmanship:* Showing willingness to tolerate unfavorable conditions without complaining. If an employee decides to grin and bear it rather than complain, she or he is showing this form of OCB.
- *Courtesy:* Making efforts to prevent interpersonal problems with others. Examples include "turning the other cheek" when annoyed by another person at work or behaving courteously toward others even when they are rude.

The results of several studies (e.g., Podsakoff & MacKenzie, 1994) suggest that a large proportion of prosocial behavior at work falls into one or more of these categories, so they seem to provide a useful framework for studying helpful actions in organizations (see Figure 13.17).

OCB: Its Causes and Effects. What factors lead individuals to engage in various forms of organizational citizenship behavior? Recent findings indicate that several different factors play a role. One of the most important of these appears to be *trust*—employees' belief that they will be treated fairly by their organizations and, more specifically, by their immediate bosses. The more that employees believe their bosses will treat them fairly (see Chapter 12), the greater their trust in these persons and thus the greater their willingness to engage in prosocial behavior (e.g., Konovsky & Pugh, 1994).

While trust seems to play a key role, other factors, too, are important. One of these involves employees' perceptions of the breadth of their jobs—what behaviors are required and which are voluntary. The more broadly employees define their jobs, the more likely they are to engage in instances of OCB (Morrison, 1994; Van Dyne & LePine, 1998). For example, if a professor believes that helping other professors by taking over their classes when they have to be out of town is part of her job—that this is simply the right thing to do—she may be much more willing to engage in such behavior than if she believes that this is definitely *not* part of her job and *not* her responsibility.

Finally, the frequency of OCB seems to be influenced by employees' attitudes about their organizations—attitudes generally known as *organizational commitment* (Randall, Fedor, & Longenecker, 1990). The more positive these attitudes, the higher the frequency of OCB. In sum, as is true of prosocial behavior in other settings, individuals' tendency to engage in such actions at work is influenced by several different factors.

Figure 13.17
Organizational Citizenship in Action: Prosocial Behavior at Work. *Organizational citizenship behavior* (OCB) takes many different forms, but most of these involve one or more of what have been termed altruism, conscientiousness, civic virtue, sportsmanship, and courtesy.

Now let's consider the effects of OCB. By definition, such prosocial behavior would be expected to produce beneficial effects; after all, it involves one person helping one or more others in some way. Unfortunately, though, it is difficult to demonstrate such effects in work settings. The reason: OCB is often not part of formal reward systems, so formal records of its occurrence are usually not kept. However, recent studies do indicate that the greater the incidence of OCB in an organization, the higher the level of performance (Podsakoff, Ahearne, & MacKenzie, 1997). In addition, it appears that individuals who engage in prosocial behavior are often recognized, both formally and informally. A recent study by Allen and Rush (1998) indicates that they are liked by their bosses and other coworkers and that they receive higher performance evaluations as a result of frequently behaving in a helpful, prosocial way. So overall, OCB does seem to produce the beneficial effects we would expect.

Leadership: Patterns of Influence within Groups

Try this simple demonstration with your friends. Ask them to rate themselves, on a seven-point scale ranging from 1 (very low) to 7 (very high) on *leadership potential*. Unless your friends are a very unusual group, here's what you'll find: most will rate themselves as *average* or *above* on this dimension. This suggests that they view leadership very favorably. But what *is* **leadership**? To a degree, it's like love: easy to recognize, but hard to define (see Chapter 8). However, psychologists generally use this term to mean *the process through which one member of a group (its leader) influences other group members toward attainment of shared group goals* (Yukl, 1994). In other words, being a leader involves *influence*—a **leader** is the group member who exerts most influence within the group.

Research on leadership has long been part of social psychology, but it is also an applied topic studied by other fields as well (e.g., Bass, 1998). We could easily devote an entire chapter to this topic, so to hold the length of this discussion within bounds, we'll focus on the following topics: (1) why some individuals, but not others, become leaders; (2) contrasting *styles* of leadership; and (3) the nature of *charismatic* and *transformational* leadership.

Who Becomes a Leader? The Role of Traits and Situations. Are some people born to lead? Common sense suggests that this is so. Famous leaders such as Alexander the Great, Queen Elizabeth I, and Abraham Lincoln seem to differ from ordinary people in several respects. Such observations led early researchers to formulate the **great person theory** of leadership—the view that great leaders possess certain traits that set them apart from most human beings, traits that are possessed by all such leaders, no matter when or where they lived (see Figure 13.18).

This is an intriguing theory, but until about 1980 research designed to test it generally failed to yield positive findings. Try as they might, researchers could not come up with a short list of key traits shared by all great leaders (Yukl, 1994). In recent years, however, this situation has changed greatly. More sophisticated research methods, coupled with a better understanding of the basic dimensions of human personality, have led many researchers to conclude that leaders do indeed differ from other persons in several important ways (Kirkpatrick & Locke, 1991). What special traits do leaders possess? Research findings point to the conclusion that leaders rate higher than most people on the following traits: *drive*—the desire for achievement coupled with high energy and resolution; *self-confidence*; *creativity*; and *leadership motivation*—the desire to be in charge and exercise authority over others. Perhaps the most important single characteristic of leaders, however, is a high level of *flexibility*—the ability to recognize what actions or approaches are required in a given situation and then to act accordingly (Zaccaro, Foti, & Kenny, 1991).

While certain traits do seem to be related to leadership, however, it is also clear that leaders do not operate in a social vacuum. On the contrary, different groups, facing different tasks and problems, seem to require different types of leaders—or at least leaders who demonstrate different styles (House & Podsakoff, 1994; Locke, 1991). So yes, traits do matter where leadership is concerned, but they are definitely only part of the total picture. With this thought in mind, let's take a closer look at precisely *how* leaders lead—the contrasting styles they can adopt.

leadership • The process through which one member of a group (its leader) influences other group members toward attainment of shared group goals.

leader • The group member who exerts the greatest influence within the group.

great person theory • A view of leadership suggesting that great leaders possess certain traits that set them apart from most human beings, traits that are possessed by all such leaders no matter when or where they lived.

Figure 13.18
The Great Person Theory of Leadership. According to the *great person theory*, all great leaders share certain traits that set them apart from other persons, and they possess these traits no matter where or when they lived. Research findings offer little support for this view, but research *does* suggest that leaders differ from other persons with respect to some traits.

How Leaders Operate: Contrasting Styles and Approaches. All leaders are definitely not alike. They may share certain traits to a degree, but they differ greatly in terms of personal *style* or approach to leadership (e.g., George, 1995; Peterson, 1997). While there are probably as many different styles of leadership as there are leaders, research on leader behavior or style suggests that in fact, most leaders can be placed along a small number of dimensions relating to their overall approach to leadership. This fact was recognized many years ago by social psychologists and provided the focus for some of the first research on leadership ever performed. Because this work has had a lasting impact on social psychology as well as on other fields, it is described in the following *Cornerstones* section.

Cornerstones of Social Psychology
What Style of Leadership is Best? Some Early Insights

Kurt Lewin. *Lewin was one of many European social psychologists who came to the United States to escape from Nazi persecution. He conducted important early studies on several major topics in social psychology, including leadership, and trained many students who went on to become famous social psychologists themselves.*

It is easy to illustrate for yourself the importance of leaders' style. Just answer the following question: Have you ever been part of a group in which the leader's style grated on your nerves or seemed to interfere with the group's success? Similarly, have you ever been part of a group in which the opposite was true—the leader's style seemed to facilitate everything the group did or tried to accomplish? I (Robert Baron) had experience of both types when I was in fourth and fifth grades. In the fourth grade I had a teacher who truly ran the show. She took firm control of all class activities and left no doubt as to who was in charge. She made all the decisions. She never asked for our input. She even posted a long list of rules in front of the room, telling us what to do or not to do in a wide range of situations.

My fifth-grade teacher offered a sharp contrast to this approach. She seemed to enjoy sharing her authority with us and let the class vote on many decisions. And although she too had rules, they were much more flexible and were never posted in a formal list. Which teacher did I prefer? As you can probably guess, the second one. But did I also do better work, and learn more, with this teacher than with the more directive one? In other words, was one of these contrasting styles of leadership superior to the other in terms of encouraging excellent performance?

This complex issue was the focus of a famous investigation on leader style conducted by Lewin, Lippitt, and White (1939). These researchers arranged for ten- and eleven-year-old boys to meet in five-member groups after school, to engage in hobbies such as woodworking and painting. To investigate the possible effects of leaders' style on the boys' behavior, each group was led by an adult who assumed one of three contrasting styles of leadership: *autocratic, laissez-faire,* or *democratic.*

The autocratic leader was very much like my fourth-grade teacher. He gave many orders and made all the decisions himself. He determined what activities the group would perform, and in what order, and simply assigned each boy a work partner without considering their personal preferences. This autocratic leader remained aloof from the group, never participating in its activities. In contrast, the *democratic* leader was much more like my fifth-grade teacher. When playing this role, the leader allowed the boys to participate in reaching decisions and often sought their input. He rarely gave orders or commands, allowed the boys to choose their own work partners, and permitted them to approach their work in whatever way they wished. The democratic leader also participated in the group's activities—he did not remain aloof as did the autocratic leader—but did not try to dominate these activities in any way. Finally, the *laissez-faire* leader adopted a hands-off approach (the French words *laissez faire* mean "let people do what they choose"). He avoided participating in group activities and did not intervene in them in any way. Rather, his role was primarily that of an interested observer who was there to provide technical information about the activities if requested to do so by the boys.

Trained observers watched the groups as they worked and rated several aspects of their behavior—for example, the amount of time the boys spent working while the leader was present, the amount of time they spent working when he left the room, aggressive activities such as hostility among group members, demands for attention, destructiveness, and *scapegoating*—a tendency to single out one group member as the target of continuous verbal abuse.

When the behavior of the boys in the three conditions was compared, some interesting differences emerged. For example, boys in the authoritarian and democratic groups spent about equal amounts of time working when the leader was present; those in laissez-faire groups worked less. When the leader left the room, however, work dropped off sharply in the authoritarian groups but remained unchanged in the democratic groups; it actually increased slightly in the laissez-faire groups. In addition, boys in the autocratic conditions seemed more at a loss when the leader left the room: they appeared to be heavily dependent on the leader for direction and did not know how to proceed without his commands and guidance. With respect to the measures of aggressiveness, it appeared that there were more signs of such behavior in the authoritarian groups than in the democratic or laissez-faire ones. For example, boys in the authoritarian groups expressed more discontent and made more aggressive demands for attention. Those in the democratic groups tended to be friendlier. Consistent with my own experiences in school, the boys tended to prefer the democratic leaders to the other two types.

What do these findings mean? Lewin and his colleagues interpreted them as suggesting that overall, a democratic style of leadership may be best. It encourages a high level of productivity, which persists even when the leader is absent. Further, it fosters positive and cooperative relations among group members. In contrast, an autocratic style of leadership produces high productivity only when the leader is present, and it seems to increase both dependence on the leader and higher levels of aggression. Lewin, Lippitt, and White (1939) conducted their research at a time when the world was poised on the brink of World War II—a war that would soon pit the democracies of France, England, and the United States against the autocratic regimes of Nazi Germany and Imperial Japan. As a result, these researchers' conclusions about leadership style were, and remain, somewhat comforting. However, recent research (e.g., Peterson, 1997), suggests that although a democratic style of leadership may indeed be preferred by group members, it is not always best from the point of group performance or even member satisfaction. Despite such refinements, however, the research conducted by Lewin, Lippitt, and White (1939) certainly qualifies as a cornerstone of social psychology: it added to our understanding of important topics and strongly shaped both the focus and the methods of much subsequent research on leadership and related group processes.

Now, back to our discussion of modern research on leader style. Such research has helped to clarify and refine the results obtained by Lewin and his colleagues (e.g., Muczyk & Reimann, 1987). One important point that has emerged from recent work is this: In their research, Lewin and his colleagues (1939) did indeed create sharply different styles of leadership; but in doing so, they actually combined several distinct dimensions of leader style. For instance, not only did their autocratic leader make all the decisions, he also closely directed group members' behavior after the decision were announced. Similarly, not only did the democratic leader give group members a chance to participate in group decisions, he also stood back and let them proceed in any way they wished. Modern research suggests that these actually represent two different and largely independent aspects of leadership style—the extent to which leaders make all the decisions themselves or allow participation by group members, and the extent to which leaders try to run the show by closely directing the activities of all group members, a *directive–permissive* dimension (Muczyk & Reimann, 1987). Further, recent findings suggest that this latter dimension itself can be divided into two separate components that exert sharply contrasting effects on a group's success.

The clearest evidence pointing to such conclusions is provided by an ingenious series of studies conducted by Peterson (1997). He reasoned that leaders of decision-making groups could show a directive style in two different ways. First, they could direct the group's discussion in such a way as to insist that all possible views and perspectives be heard; that is, the leader could show a high level of *process directiveness*. Second, leaders could state their own position and try to ram it down the throats of their group—a high level of *outcome directiveness*. Peterson (1997) further reasoned that these different approaches to being directive would have contrasting effects on group performance. Process directiveness, he suggested, would have mostly positive effects: it would improve the process through which the group made decisions, improve the quality or accuracy of decisions, and improve members' satisfaction with the group. In contrast, outcome directiveness would provide none of these benefits and might actually prove counterproductive.

To test these predictions, Peterson (1997) arranged for groups of students to play the role of an elite decision-making group facing an international crisis. To solve the crisis, the groups had to make a series of decisions. The leaders of the groups were appointed by the researchers and played various roles relating to process and outcome directiveness. To produce high process directiveness, the leaders were told to insist that all possible views be discussed and to encourage each member to participate. To produce low process directiveness, in contrast, the leaders were told simply to sit back and let the discussion proceed without trying to direct it. To generate high outcome directiveness, the leaders were instructed to state their own view and advocate it strongly during the discussion. To produce low outcome directiveness, the leaders were told to state their view but not to advocate it during the discussion.

Several different measures of group performance were collected: the quality of the group process, the extent to which groups made the correct decisions (the same decisions recommended by experts in international affairs), and member satisfaction with the group and the leader. On all these measures, results indicated that high *process* directiveness was beneficial. In contrast, high *outcome* directiveness was not (see Figure 13.19). In short, when leaders played a directive role by insisting that all views be discussed and that all members have a chance to participate, the groups' effectiveness was enhanced.

These findings suggest that leader directiveness is not, in and of itself, necessarily a bad thing. On the contrary, it can be seen as a neutral force that can produce positive or negative effects. If a leader adopts a take-charge directive style in order to insist that all views be considered and all members get a chance to participate, beneficial outcomes can result. However, if a leader adopts a directive style in order to force his or her own views on a group or to insist that the group act in specific ways, the opposite may be true. So, as decades of research have shown, no single style of leadership is always best; rather, which style succeeds best depends on the specific circumstances in which a group operates.

Charismatic Leaders: Leaders Who Change the World. Have you ever seen films of John F. Kennedy? Franklin Roosevelt? Martin Luther King, Jr.? Winston Churchill? If so, you may have noticed that there seemed to be something special about these leaders. As you listened to their speeches, you may have found yourself being moved by their words and stirred by the vigor of their presentations. You are definitely not alone in such reactions: these leaders exerted powerful effects on many millions of persons and, by doing so, changed their societies. Leaders who accomplish such feats are termed **charismatic leaders** (or, sometimes, *transformational* leaders) (House & Howell, 1992; Kohl, Steers, & Terborg, 1995).

charismatic leaders • Leaders who exert exceptionally powerful effects on large numbers of followers or on entire societies; also known as transformational leaders.

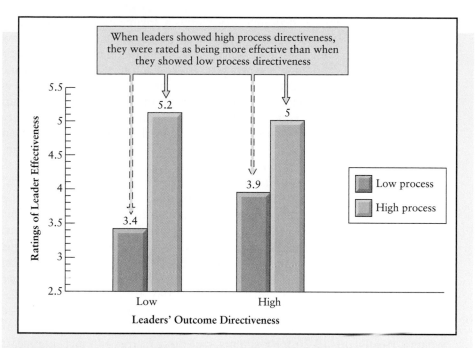

Figure 13.19

Leaders' Directiveness: Some of the Effects Are Positive. When an appointed leader showed a high level of *process directiveness,* insisting that all views be discussed and that all group members be given a chance to participate, many beneficial effects were obtained. One of these effects—high ratings of the leaders' effectiveness by group members—is shown here. In contrast a high level of *outcome directiveness* did not produce similar benefits.

(*Source:* Based on data from Peterson, 1997.)

What characteristics make certain leaders charismatic? And how do these leaders exert such dramatic influence on their followers? At first glance, it is tempting to assume that charismatic leaders are special because they possess certain traits. However, there is a growing consensus among researchers who have studied this topic that it makes more sense to try to understand such leadership in terms of a special type of *relationship* between leaders and their followers (House, 1977) and in terms of the actions taken by these leaders that seem to magnify their impact on followers (Pillai et al., 1997).

With respect to their relationship with followers, charismatic leaders seem to generate (1) high levels of devotion and loyalty, (2) high levels of enthusiasm for the leader and her or his ideas, (3) willingness by followers to sacrifice their own interests for the sake of the group's goals, and (4) levels of performance beyond those that would normally be expected. As one expert in this area puts it, charismatic leaders somehow "make ordinary people do extraordinary things" (Conger, 1991).

But what, precisely, do charismatic leaders do to produce such effects? Research findings emphasize the importance of the following factors. First, such leaders usually propose a *vision* (Howell & Frost, 1989). They describe in vivid, emotion-provoking terms an image of what their nation or group can—and should—become. To the extent that followers accept this vision, their level of commitment to the leader and the leader's goals can become intense.

Second, charismatic leaders go beyond stating a dream or vision: they also offer a route for reaching it. They tell their followers, in straightforward terms, how to get from here to there. This too seems crucial, for a vision that appears to be out of reach is unlikely to motivate people to work to attain it. Third, charismatic leaders engage in *framing* (Conger, 1991): they define the goals for their group in a way that gives extra meaning and purpose both to the goals and to the actions needed to attain them. A clear illustration of such framing is provided by the story of two stonecutters working on a cathedral in the Middle Ages. When asked what they were doing, one replied: "Cutting this stone, of course." The other answered: "Building the world's most beautiful temple to the glory of God." Which person would be likely to work harder and, perhaps, to do "extraordinary" things? The answer is obvious, and it is also clear that any leader who can induce such thinking in her or his followers can also have profound effects upon them.

Other facets of charismatic leadership include a high level of self-confidence, a high degree of concern for followers' needs, an excellent communication style, and a stirring personal style (House, Spangler, & Woycke, 1991). Finally, transformational leaders are often masters of *impression management,* a process we described in Chapter 2. When this skill is added to the various traits and behaviors, the vision, and the gift for framing described above, the ability of charismatic leaders to influence large numbers of followers loses some of its mystery. (See Figure 13.20 for a summary of these factors.) In fact, it appears

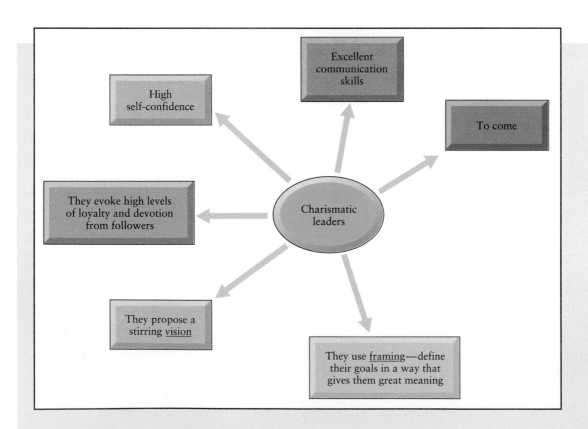

Figure 13.20
Charismatic Leaders: How They Exert Their Effects. Research findings indicate that charismatic leaders exert their powerful effects on followers because of the factors shown here.

that charisma rests firmly on principles and processes well understood by social psychologists.

Key Points

- People spend more time at work than in any other single activity. Because people often work with others, the findings and principles of social psychology help to explain behavior in work settings.

- *Job satisfaction* is an individual's attitude toward her or his job. Job satisfaction is influenced by organizational factors such as working conditions and the fairness of reward systems, and by personal factors such as seniority, status, and specific personality traits. Recent findings suggest that job satisfaction is often highly stable over time for many persons, and that it may be influenced by genetic factors.

- The relationship between job satisfaction and task performance is relatively weak, partly because many factors other than work-related attitudes influence performance.

- Individuals often engage in prosocial behavior at work. This is known as *organizational citizenship behavior* (OCB), and can take many different forms.

- OCB is influenced by several factors, including employees' trust in their boss and the organization, the extent to which employees define their job responsibilities broadly, and organizational commitment—their attitudes toward their organization.

- *Leadership* refers to the process through which one member of a group (its *leader*) influences other group members toward the attainment of shared group goals.

- Although the *great person theory* of leadership has been shown to be false, research findings suggest that leaders do indeed differ from other persons with respect to several traits.

- In addition, leaders vary with respect to their behavior or style. Classic research in social psychology suggested that a democratic style of leadership was far superior to an autocratic style, but more recent findings suggest that these styles are actually composed of several underlying dimensions, such as directiveness–permissiveness.

- Leaders high in process directiveness direct the group process so as to ensure that all views are heard and all members participate; this has a beneficial effect on group process and member satisfaction. Leaders high in outcome directiveness, in contrast, try to induce the group to accept their views; this often has harmful effects.

- *Charismatic leaders* exert profound effects on their followers and often change their societies. Research suggests that such leadership stems from certain behaviors by leaders such as stating a clear vision, framing the group's goals in ways that magnify their importance, and a stirring personal style. Charismatic leaders develop a special relationship with their followers; this permits the leaders to exert great influence.

Connections: Integrating Social Psychology

In this chapter, you read about . . .	In other chapters, you will find related discussions of . . .
forming attitudes about a suspect based on pretrial publicity	first impressions (Chapter 2); attitude formation (Chapter 4)
accuracy of eyewitness testimony	information processing and information retrieval (Chapter 3)
the similarity between police lineups and social psychological experiments	designing experiments to maximize the odds of obtaining objective and reliable results (Chapter 1)
nonverbal communication from judge to jury	basic channels of nonverbal communication (Chapter 2)
attraction toward and evaluation of defendants	factors influencing interpersonal attraction (Chapter 7)
stereotypes and prejudice in juries' evaluation of defendants	stereotypes and prejudice based on race and gender (Chapter 6)
processing health-related information	use of the availability heuristic and the resulting distortions (Chapters 1 and 3); and persuasive appeals (Chapter 4)
self-efficacy in responding to stress	the general effects of self-efficacy (Chapter 5)
the self-healing personality	secure attachment style (Chapter 8); the altruistic personality (Chapter 10)
hostile Type A behavior as a health risk	Type A behavior and aggression (Chapter 11)
seeking social support as a coping strategy	the importance of affiliation (Chapter 7); relationships versus loneliness (Chapter 8)
attachment style as a determinant of social support behavior	attachment style in interpersonal relationships (Chapter 8)
job satisfaction	the basic nature of attitudes (Chapter 4)
organizational citizenship behavior	prosocial behavior (Chapter 10)
leadership	other aspects of influence (Chapter 9); other group processes (Chapter 12)

Thinking about Connections

1. A theft has taken place where you work, and all of the employees are being questioned by the police about what they know. You are asked to remember where you were on Friday of the previous week, what your fellow employees did that day, and precisely what you may have seen. Think about what it is that you actually remember (Chapter 3) and what you only seem to remember (Chapter 13). Is it possible that the person interrogating you has already made up his mind and simply wants you to provide confirmation? Do the questions suggest certain answers that are expected? Are you comfortable in honestly saying such things as "I don't know" and "I can't remem-

ber," or do you feel you *should* come up with tentative guesses?

2. In the past year you have probably experienced at least one or two (and maybe many more) stressful situations. How did you respond? Were you physically fit at the time, or had you skipped exercise, stayed up late and missed sleep, and dined primarily on junk food? Did you find yourself feeling depressed? Did you think of options that might help solve the problem or at least deal with it? Did you seek the support of other people? How closely do you feel that you resemble the self-healing personality versus the disease-prone personality? Finally, did you get sick? If so, does it appear that your illness was related to the stress and your response to it?

3. Social psychologists have developed many techniques for changing attitudes (see Chapter 4). Do you think that these techniques might be useful in increasing employees' job satisfaction? If so, which techniques might prove most helpful in this respect?

4. It has been contended that effective leadership requires skill with respect to many important aspects of social behavior: effective use of nonverbal cues (Chapter 2), a high degree of persuasiveness (Chapters 4 and 9), skill at impression management (Chapter 2), and so on. Do you agree? And if you do, does this mean that we could train potential leaders to be more effective?

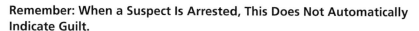

Ideas to Take with You
Don't Rush to Judgment

Whether as a potential juror or as an official member of a jury, you will be exposed to a great deal of information, many arguments, and diverse facts about any given crime and about the suspected criminal. Even if you are simply a member of the general public with no formal role to play, it is still important that you keep in mind some of the issues involved in reaching valid conclusions about legal matters. If you are actually a member of the jury, your open-mindedness can literally be a matter of life and death.

Remember: When a Suspect Is Arrested, This Does Not Automatically Indicate Guilt.

When you hear the details of a brutal crime and then learn on TV or in the newspapers that a suspect has been arrested, don't assume that the crime is necessarily solved or that the arrested individual had been found guilty. Before guilt or innocence is determined, there must be an indictment, a trial, the presentation of evidence for and against the defendant, a consideration of precise legal issues, and an attempt by the jury to reach consensus. The most reasonable position to take is that *either* the prosecution or the defense might be correct, so you would be wise to construct two alternative schemas for yourself—one in which you store all of the information indicating guilt and one in which you store all of the information indicating innocence. Wait until all the facts are in before deciding which schema makes more sense.

Separate Attraction from Judgments Based on Evidence.

It is probably not possible to enter any situation with a totally objective, open mind. Remember, research findings suggest that we automatically respond to stimuli with relatively positive or relatively negative attitudes. The best we can do is to separate how much we *like* the defendant from what we *know* on the basis of testimony and physical evidence. No matter how you feel about the individual's appearance, eth-nic background, political views, sexual orientation, or whatever else, the question is not how much you like him or her but whether or not the bulk of the evidence indicates guilt beyond a reasonable doubt. In everyday life, we often blur the distinction between attraction toward someone and factual knowledge about that person. In the courtroom, it is crucial that such distinctions be made.

Don't Let Your Opinion Be Swayed by Emotional Appeals.

We all know that the prosecutor and the defense attorney have very specific and quite different scenarios to "sell." Each side wants to convince the onlookers that there is only one version of the truth; and each side will try to appeal to your feelings, your prejudices, your patriotism, or whatever else might be effective in convincing you. Again, your task is not to deny the disgust you may feel about a brutal crime or the sympathy you may feel toward an innocent citizen who has been dragged into court and accused unfairly of committing a criminal act. Both feelings are reasonable. The question, however, is once again a matter of what is indicated by the evidence and what is prescribed as legally relevant. The courtroom is clearly a place where it is important to separate emotional processes from cognitive ones.

Don't Let the Judge Persuade You to Agree with His or Her Opinion.

It is your job to provide a verdict, and it is the judge's job to maintain orderly proceedings that are consistent with the rules. Like you, the judge may be tempted to jump to conclusions or be swayed by emotions. At times he or she may be unable to conceal a positive or negative opinion. Your task, however, is to avoid responding to irrelevant factors, and the judge's belief about guilt or innocence *is* irrelevant.

Summary and Review of Key Points

Applying Social Psychology to the Interpersonal Aspects of the Legal System

- People obey the law and accept legal decisions so long as they perceive the procedures to be fair and just.

- Most people would prefer police to search for the truth rather than attempt to prove guilt, but both interrogation approaches are common.

- For a variety of reasons, it is not uncommon for an innocent person to confess to a crime and even to believe himself or herself to be guilty.

- Extensive media coverage of crime leads to misperceptions about its frequency, but the coverage occurs because people find it interesting. Media concentration on a person accused of a crime leads to widespread assumptions of guilt, and thus prosecutors tend to provide the media with as much information as possible.

- Eyewitnesses to a crime often make mistakes, but a variety of procedures have been developed to help ensure greater accuracy.

- A serious and controversial legal problem is the recovery of *repressed memories* of past criminal events that turn out to be false memories.

- Attorneys act as adversaries who attempt to select juries biased toward their side and to convince the chosen jurors that their version of the truth is the accurate one.

- The words and even the unspoken beliefs of judges can influence the final verdict.

- Jurors' evaluation of a defendant is based in part on first impressions, stereotypes, and liking. For this reason, factors such as gender, race, and attractiveness play an unfair role in judicial decisions.

- The racial similarity or dissimilarity of defendants and jurors can have a major impact on the final verdict in a trial.

- Jurors differ in cognitive processing skills, attitudes, and personality dispositions, and these characteristics play an important role in the decision process.

Applying Social Psychology to Health-Related Behavior

- Health-related information comes to us daily, and new research findings often modify or reverse earlier findings. Consumers of health information need to remain informed, open-minded, and cautious.

- *Stress* is defined as any event that is perceived as a potential source of physical or emotional harm, and it is well established that stress can lead to physical illness both indirectly, by affecting health-related behavior, and directly, through its effect on physiological functioning.

- A wide variety of dispositional differences are associated with the ability to resist the negative effects of stress (the *self-healing personality*) as opposed to the tendency to be badly affected by stress (the *disease-prone personality*).

- Effective strategies for *coping* with stress include increasing one's physical fitness; taking control of one's feelings, thoughts, and activities through self-regulation; engaging in activities that arouse positive affect in order to counteract stress-induced negative emotions; and establishing networks of *social support*.

- Coping with the stress of illness and medical treatment requires all of these same coping strategies as well as (1) acquiring as much knowledge as possible about each aspect of one's condition and the treatment procedures and (2) gaining as much control as possible of every step of the process.

Applying Social Psychology to the World of Work: Job Satisfaction, Helping, and Leadership

- People spend more time at work than in any other single activity. Because people often work with others, the findings and principles of social psychology help to explain behavior in work settings.

- *Job satisfaction* is an individual's attitude toward her or his job. Job satisfaction is influenced by organizational factors such as working conditions and the fairness of reward systems, and by personal factors such as seniority, status, and specific personality traits. Recent findings suggest that job satisfaction is often highly stable over time for many persons, and that it may be influenced by genetic factors.

- The relationship between job satisfaction and task performance is relatively weak, partly because many factors other than work-related attitudes influence performance.

- Individuals often engage in prosocial behavior at work. This is known as *organizational citizenship behavior* (OCB), and can take many different forms.

- OCB is influenced by several factors, including employees' trust in their boss and the organization, the extent to which employees define their job responsibilities broadly, and organizational commitment—their attitudes toward their organization.

- *Leadership* refers to the process through which one member of a group (its *leader*) influences other group members toward the attainment of shared group goals.

- Although the *great person theory* of leadership has been shown to be false, research findings suggest that leaders do indeed differ from other persons with respect to several traits.

- In addition, leaders vary with respect to their behavior or style. Classic research in social psychology suggested that a democratic style of leadership was far superior to an autocratic style, but more recent findings suggest that these styles are actually composed of several underlying dimensions, such as directiveness–permissiveness.

- Leaders high in process directiveness direct the group process so as to ensure that all views are heard and all members participate; this has a beneficial effect on group process and member satisfaction. Leaders high in outcome directiveness, in contrast, try to induce the group to accept their views; This often has harmful effects.

- *Charismatic leaders* exert profound effects on their followers and often change their societies. Research suggests that such leadership stems from certain behaviors by leaders such as stating a clear vision, framing the group's goals in ways that magnify their importance, and a stirring personal style. Charismatic leaders develop a special relationship with their followers; this permits the leaders to exert great influence.

KEY TERMS

blank-lineup control (p. 536)

catastrophizing (p. 551)

charismatic leaders (p. 570)

coping (p. 548)

disease-prone personality (p. 551)

forensic psychology (p. 525)

great person theory (p. 566)

health psychology (p. 544)

industrial/organizational psychologists (p. 559)

job satisfaction (p. 559)

leader (p. 566)

leadership (p. 566)

leading questions (p. 538)

legal authoritarianism (p. 543)

leniency bias (p. 543)

organizational citizenship behavior (OCB) (p. 563)

regulatory control (p. 553)

repressed memory (p. 535)

self-healing personality (p. 551)

social support (p. 555)

stress (p. 548)

voir dire (p. 537)

FOR MORE INFORMATION

Bass, B. M. (1998). *Transformational leadership: Industrial, military, and educational impact.* Mahwah, NJ: Erlbaum.

An expert researcher who has studied leadership for several decades reviews existing evidence concerning the nature and effects of transformational leadership. The author compares transformational leadership with other types and styles of leadership and describes ways in which the principles of transformational leadership can be applied in many different settings. A stimulating, thought-provoking book.

Loftus, E. F. (1992). *Witness for the defense.* New York: St. Martin's Press.

A comprehensive summary of research in the area of forensic psychology by one of the leading investigators in this field.

Pope, K. S., & Brown, L. S. (1996). *Recovered memories of abuse: Assessment, therapy, forensics.* Washington, DC: American Psychological Association.

This guide presents an overview of the problem of recovered memories, dealing with both legal and psychological issues. The authors cover such issues as the study of memory, the effects of trauma, the ways in which people are questioned, and the issues that face therapists and expert witnesses.

Radley, A. (1994). *Making sense of illness: The social psychology of health and disease.* Thousand Oaks, CA: Sage.

The author cuts across the fields of health psychology, sociology, and medicine to clarify the importance of psychological factors in health issues. The book discusses responding to stress, coping with acute and chronic health problems, and behaving in ways that promote good health and prevent disease.

References

Abdalla, I. A. (1995). Sex, sex-role self-concepts and career decision-making self-efficacy among Arab students. *Social Behavior and Personality, 23,* 389–402.

Abramson, J. (1994). *We, the jury.* New York: Basic Books.

Adams, J. M., & Jones, W. H. (1997). The conceptualization of marital commitment: An integrative analysis. *Journal of Personality and Social Psychology, 72,* 1177–1196.

Adams, J. S. (1965). Inequity in social exchange. In L. Berkowitz (Ed.), *Advances in experimental social psychology* (Vol. 2, pp. 267–299). New York: Academic Press.

Adams, R. G., & Blieszner, R. (1994). An integrative conceptual framework for friendship research. *Journal of Social and Personal Relationships, 11,* 163–184.

Ader, R., & Cohen, N. (1993). Psychoneuroimmunology: Conditioning and stress. *Annual Review of Psychology, 44,* 53–85.

Adler, S. J. (1994). *The jury.* New York: Times Books.

Affleck, G., Tennen, H., Urrows, S., & Higgins, P. (1994). Person and contextual features of daily stress reactivity: Individual differences in relations of undesirable daily events with mood disturbance and chronic pain intensity. *Journal of Personality and Social Psychology, 66,* 329–340.

Agnew, C. R., & Thompson, V. D. (1994). Causal inferences and responsibility attributions concerning an HIV-positive target: The double-edged sword of physical attractiveness. *Journal of Social Behavior and Personality, 9,* 181–190.

Ainsworth, M. D. S., Blehar, M. C., Waters, E., & Wall, S. (1978). *Patterns of attachment.* Hillsdale, NJ: Erlbaum.

Ajzen, I. (1987). Attitudes, traits, and actions: Dispositional prediction of behavior in personality and social psychology. In L. Berkowitz (Ed.), *Advances in experimental social psychology* (Vol. 20). San Diego, CA: Academic Press.

Ajzen, I. (1991). The theory of planned behavior: Special issue: Theories of cognitive self-regulation. *Organizational Behavior and Human Decision Processes, 50,* 179–211.

Ajzen, I., & Fishbein, M. (1980). *Understanding attitudes and predicting social behavior.* Englewood Cliffs, NJ: Prentice-Hall.

Alagna, F. J., Whitcher, S. J., & Fisher, J. D. (1979). Evaluative reactions to interpersonal touch in a counseling interview. *Journal of Counseling Psychology, 26,* 465–472.

Alden, L. (1986). Self-efficacy and causal attributions for social feedback. *Journal of Research in Personality, 20,* 460–473.

Alexander, M. J., & Higgins, E. T. (1993). Emotional trade-offs of becoming a parent: How social roles influence self-discrepancy effects. *Journal of Personality and Social Psychology, 65,* 1259–1269.

Alicke, M. D., & Largo, E. (1995). The role of the self in the false consensus effect. *Journal of Experimental Social Psychology, 31,* 28–47.

Alicke, M. D., Braun, J. C., Glor, J. E., Klotz, M. L., Magee, J., Sederhold, H., & Siegel, R. (1992). Complaining behavior in social interaction. *Personality and Social Psychology Bulletin, 18,* 286–295.

Allen, T. D., & Rush, M. C. (1998). The effects of organizational citizenship behavior on performance judgments: A field study and a laboratory experiment. *Journal of Applied Psychology, 83,* 247–260.

Allgeier, E. R., & Wiederman, M. W. (1994). How useful is evolutionary psychology for understanding contemporary human sexual behavior? *Annual Review of Sex Research, 5,* 218–256.

Alliger, G. M., & Williams, K. J. (1991). Affective congruence and the employment interview. *Advances in Information Processing in Organizations, 4,* 31–43.

Allison, S. T., Worth, L. T., & King, M. C. (1990). Group decisions as social inference heuristics. *Journal of Personality and Social Psychology, 58,* 801–811.

Allport, F. H. (1920). The influence of the group upon association and thought. *Journal of Experimental Psychology, 3,* 159–182.

Allport, F. H. (1924). *Social psychology.* Boston: Houghton Mifflin.

Alvaro, E. M., & Crano, W. D. (1996). Cognitive responses to minority- or majority-based communications: Factors that underlie minority influence. *British Journal of Social Psychology, 34,* 105–121.

Allyn, J., & Festinger, L. (1961). The effectiveness of unanticipated persuasive communications. *Journal of Abnormal and Social Psychology, 62,* 35–40.

Altman, L. K. (1998, June 24). Report: AIDS an epic scourge. *New York Times.*

Amato, P. R. (1983). Helping behavior in urban and rural environments: Field studies based on a taxonomic organization of helping episodes. *Journal of Personality and Social Psychology, 45,* 571–586.

Amato, P. R. (1986). Emotional arousal and helping behavior in a real-life emergency. *Journal of Applied Social Psychology, 16,* 633–641.

Ambady, N., & Rosenthal, R. (1992). Thin slices of expressive behavior as predictors of interpersonal consequences: A meta-analysis. *Psychological Bulletin, 111,* 256–274.

Ambuel, B. (1995). Adolescents, unintended pregnancy, and abortion: The struggle for a compassionate social policy. *Current Directions in Psychological Science, 4,* 1–5.

Amirkhan, J. H., Risinger, R. T., & Swickert, R. J. (1995). Extraversion: A "hidden" personality factor in coping? *Journal of Personality, 63,* 189–212.

Andersen, B. L., & Cyranowski, J. M. (1994). Women's sexual self-schema. *Journal of Personality and Social Psychology, 67,* 1079–1100.

Andersen, S. M., & Baum, A. (1994). Transference in interpersonal relations: Inferences and affect based on significant-other representations. *Journal of Personality, 62,* 459–497.

Anderson, C. A. (1989a). Temperature and aggression: Effects on quarterly, yearly, and city rates of violent and nonviolent crime. *Journal of Personality and Social Psychology, 52,* 1161–1173.

Anderson, C. A. (1989b). Temperature and aggression: The ubiquitous effects of heat on the occurrence of human violence. *Psychological Bulletin, 106,* 74–96.

Anderson, C. A. (1997). Effects of violent movies and trait hostility on hostile feelings and aggressive thoughts. *Aggressive Behavior, 23,* 161–178.

Anderson, C. A., & Anderson, K. B. (1996). Violent crime rate studies in philosophical context: A destructive testing approach to heat and Southern culture of violence effects. *Journal of Personality and Social Psychology, 70,* 740–756.

Anderson, C. A., & Bushman, B. J. (1997). External validity of "trivial" experiments: The case of laboratory aggression. *Review of General Psychology, 1,* 19–41.

Anderson, C. A., & DeNeve, K. M. (1992). Temperature, aggression, and the negative affect escape model. *Psychological Bulletin, 111,* 347–351.

Anderson, C. A., Anderson, K. B., & Deuser, W. E. (1995). Hot temperatures, hostile affect, hostile cognition, and arousal: Test of a general model of affective aggression. *Personality and Social Psychology Bulletin, 21,* 434–448.

Anderson, C. A., Anderson, K. B., & Deuser, W. E. (1996). Examining an affective aggression framework: Weapon and temperature effects on aggressive thoughts, affect, and attitudes. *Personality and Social Psychology Bulletin, 22,* 366–376.

Anderson, C. A., Anderson, K. B., & Deuser, W. E. (1996). A general framework for the study of affective aggression: Tests of effects of extreme temperatures and of viewing weapons on hostility. *Personality and Social Psychology Bulletin, 22* 366–376.

Anderson, C. A., Bushman, B. J., & Groom, R. W. (1997). Hot years and serious and deadly assault: Empirical tests of the heat hypothesis. *Journal of Personality and Social Psychology, 73,* 1213–1223.

Anderson, C. A., Miller, R. S., Riger, A. L., Dill, J. C., & Sedikides, C. (1994). Behavioral and characterological attributional styles as predictors of depression and loneliness: Review, refinement, and test. *Journal of Personality and Social Psychology, 66,* 549–558.

Anderson, N. H. (1981). *Foundations of information integration theory.* New York: Academic Press.

Anderson, P. B., & Aymami, R. (1993). Reports of female initiation of sexual contact: Male and female differences. *Archives of Sexual Behavior, 22,* 335–343.

Anderson, V. L. (1993). Gender differences in altruism among holocaust rescuers. *Journal of Social Behavior and Personality, 8,* 43–58.

Angier, N. (1998, September 1). Nothing becomes a man more than a woman's face. *New York Times,* p. F3.

Anthony, T., Cooper, C., & Mullen, B. (1992). Cross-racial identification: A social cognitive integration. *Personality and Social Psychology Bulletin, 18,* 296–301.

Archer, J. (1991). Human sociobiology: Basic concepts and limitations. *Journal of Social Issues, 47*(3), 11–26.

Archer, J. (1996). Sex differences in social behavior: Are the social role and evolutionary explanations compatible? *American Psychologist, 51,* 909–917.

Archibald, F. S., Bartholomew, K., & Marx, R. (1995). Loneliness in early adolescence: A test of the cognitive discrepancy model of loneliness. *Personality and Social Psychology Bulletin, 21,* 296–301.

Argyle, M. (1988). *Bodily communication.* New York: Methuen.

Aron, A., & Henkemeyer, L. (1995). Marital satisfaction and passionate love. *Journal of Social and Personal Relationships, 12,* 139–146.

Aron, A., & Westbay, L. (1996). Dimensions of the prototype of love. *Journal of Personality and Social Psychology, 70,* 535–551.

Aron, A., Aron, E. N., & Allen, J. (1998). Motivations for unreciprocated love. *Personality and Social Psychology Bulletin, 24,* 787–796.

Aron, A., Paris, M., & Aron, E. N. (1995). Falling in love: Prospective studies of self-concept change. *Journal of Personality and Social Psychology, 69,* 1102–1112.

Aron, A., Dutton, D. G., Aron, E. N., & Iverson, A. (1989). Experiences of falling in love. *Journal of Social and Personal Relationships, 6,* 243–257.

Aron, A., Melinat, E., Aron, E. N., Vallone, R. D., & Bator, R. J. (1997). The experimental generation of interpersonal closeness: A procedure and some preliminary findings. *Personality and Social Psychology Bulletin, 23,* 363–377.

Aronoff, J., Woike, B. A., & Hyman, L. M. (1992). Which are the stimuli in facial displays of anger and happiness? Configurational bases of emotion recognition. *Journal of Personality and Social Psychology, 62,* 1050–1066.

Aronson, E. (1968). Dissonance theory: Progress and problems. In R. Abelson, E. Aronson, W. McGuire, T. Newcomb, M. Rosenberg, & P. Tannenbaum (Eds.), *The cognitive consistency theories: A source book* (pp. 5–27). Chicago: Rand McNally.

Aronson, E., Bridgeman, D. L., & Geffner, R. (1978). Interdependent interactions and prosocial behavior. *Journal of Research and Development in Education, 12,* 16–27.

Aronson, E., Fried, C., & Stone, J. (1991). Overcoming denial: Increasing the intention to use condoms through the induction of hypocrisy. *American Journal of Public Health, 18,* 1636–1640.

Arriaga, X. B., & Rusbult, C. E. (1998). Standing in my partner's shoes: Partner perspective taking and reactions to accommodative dilemmas. *Personality and Social Psychology Bulletin, 24,* 927–948.

Arrigo, J. M., & Pezdek, K. (1997). Lessons from the study of psychogenic amnesia. *Current Directions in Psychological Science, 6,* 148–152.

Arvey, R. D., Bouchard, T. J. Jr., Segal, N. L., & Abraham, L. M. (1989). Job satisfaction: Genetic and environmental components. *Journal of Applied Psychology, 74,* 187–192.

Asch, S. (1946). Forming impressions of personality. *Journal of Abnormal and Social Psychology, 41,* 258–290.

Asch, S. E. (1951). Effects of group pressure upon the modification and distortion of judgment. In H. Guetzkow (Ed.), *Groups, leadership, and men.* Pittsburgh: Carnegie.

Asch, S. E. (1955). Opinions and social pressure. *Scientific American, 193*(5), 31–35.

Asch, S. E. (1956). Studies of independence and conformity: A minority of one against unanimous majority. *Psychological Monographs, 70* (Whole No. 416).

Asendorpf, J. B. (1992). A Brunswickean approach to trait continuity: Application to shyness. *Journal of Personality, 60,* 55–77.

Ashmore, R. D., Solomon, M. R., & Longo, L. C. (1996). Thinking about fashion models' looks: A multidimensional approach to the structure of perceived physical attractiveness. *Personality and Social Psychology Bulletin, 22,* 1083–1104.

Aspinwall, L. G. (1998). Rethinking the role of positive affect in self-regulation. *Motivation and Emotion, 22,* 1–32.

Aube, J., & Koestner, R. (1993). Gender characteristics and adjustment: A longitudinal study. *Journal of Personality and Social Psychology, 63,* 485–493.

Aube, J., Norcliffe, H., Craig, J.-A., & Koestner, R. (1995). Gender characteristics and adjustment-related outcomes: Questioning the masculinity model. *Personality and Social Psychology Bulletin, 21,* 284–295.

Averill, J. R., & Boothroyd, P. (1977). On falling in love: Conformance with romantic ideal. *Motivation and Emotion, 1,* 235–247.

Azar, B. (1997a, November). Defining the trait that makes us human. *APA Monitor, 1,* 15.

Azar, B. (1997b, November). Forgiveness helps keep relationships steadfast. *APA Monitor,* 14.

Azar, B. (1998, January). Communicating through pheromones: What kinds of signals are our bodily chemicals really giving? *APA Monitor, 1,* 12.

BNA's *Employee Relations Weekly.* (1994, April 6). Survey finds 31 percent of women report having been harrassed at work. pp. 111–112.

Bader, J. L., & Brazell, B. (1998). *He meant, she meant: The definitive male/female dictionary.* New York: Warner Books.

Bad news on smoking. (1998, November 30). *Time,* p. 132.

Bailey, J. M., Kim, P. Y., Hills, A., & Linsenmeier, J. A. W. (1997). Butch, femme, or straight acting? Partner preferences of gay men and lesbians. *Journal of Personality and Social Psychology, 73,* 960–973.

Bailey, R. C., & Vietor, N. A. (1996). A religious female who engages in casual sex: Evidence of a boomerang effect. *Social Behavior and Personality, 24,* 215–220.

Baize, H. R., Jr., & Schroeder, J. E. (1995). Personality and mate selection in personal ads: Evolutionary preferences in a public mate selection process. *Journal of Social Behavior and Personality, 10,* 517–536.

Bandura, A. (1977). Self-efficacy: Toward a unifying theory of behavior change. *Psychological Review, 84,* 191–215.

Bandura, A. (1986a). The explanatory and predictive scope of self-efficacy theory. *Journal of Social and Clinical Psychology, 4,* 359–373.

Bandura, A. (1986b). *Social foundations of thought and action: A social cognitive view.* Englewood Cliffs, NJ: Prentice-Hall.

Bandura, A. (1993). Self-efficacy mechanisms in psychobiological functioning. *Stanford University Psychologist, 1,* 5–6.

Bandura, A., & Adams, N. E. (1977). Analysis of self-efficacy theory of behavioral change. *Cognitive Therapy and Research, 1,* 287–310.

Bandura, A., Adams, N. E., & Hardy, A. B. (1980). Tests of the generality of self-efficacy theory. *Cognitive Therapy and Research, 4,* 39–66.

Bandura, A., Ross, D., & Ross, S. (1963). Imitation of film-mediated aggressive models. *Journal of Abnormal and Social Psychology, 66,* 3–11.

Bandura, A., Cioffi, D., Taylor, C. B., & Brouillard, M. E. (1988). Perceived self-efficacy in coping with cognitive stressors and opioid activation. *Journal of Personality and Social Psychology, 55,* 479–488.

Barbee, A. P., Cunningham, M. R., Winstead, B. A., Derlega, V. J., Gulley, M. R., Yankeelov, P. A., & Druen, P. B. (1993). Effects of gender role expectations on the social support process. *Journal of Social Issues, 49,* 175–190.

Bardach, A. L. (1995, June 5). The white cloud. *New Republic,* 27–28, 30–31.

Bardach, A. L., & Park, B. (1996). The effect of in-group/out-group status on memory for consistent and inconsistent behavior of an individual. *Personality and Social Psychology bulletin, 22,* 169–178.

Bargh, J. A. (1996). Automaticity in social psychology. In E. T. Higgins & A. W. Kruglanski (Eds.), *Social psychology: Handbook of basic principles.* (pp. 93–130). New York: Guilford.

Bargh, J. A. (1997). The automaticity of everyday life. In R. S. Wyer Jr. (Ed.), *Advances in social cognition* (Vol. 10). Mahwah, NJ: Erlbaum.

Bargh, J. A., & Pietromonaco, P. (1982). Automatic information processing and social perception: The influence of trait information presented outside of conscious awareness on impression formation. *Journal of Personality and Social Psychology, 43,* 437–449.

Baron, J. (1997). The illusion of morality as self-interest: A reason to cooperate in social dilemmas. *Psychological Science, 8,* 330–335.

Baron, R. A. (1972a). Aggression as a function of ambient temperature and prior anger arousal. *Journal of Personality and Social Psychology, 21,* 183–189.

Baron, R. A. (1972b). Reducing the influence of an aggressive model: The restraining effects of peer censure. *Journal of Experimental Social Psychology, 8,* 266–275.

Baron, R. A. (1974a). Aggression as a function of victim's pain cues, level of prior anger arousal, and exposure to an aggressive model. *Journal of Personality and Social Psychology, 29,* 117–124.

Baron, R. A. (1974b). The aggression-inhibiting influence of heightened sexual arousal. *Journal of Personality and Social Psychology, 30,* 318–322.

Baron, R. A. (1976). The reduction of human aggression: A field study of the influence of incompatible responses. *Journal of Applied Social Psychology, 6,* 260–674.

Baron, R. A. (1977). *Human aggression.* New York: Plenum.

Baron, R. A. (1979). Aggression, empathy, and race: Effects of victim's pain cues, victim's race, and level of instigation on physical aggression. *Journal of Applied Social Psychology, 9,* 103–114.

Baron, R. A. (1983a). The "sweet smell of success"? The impact of pleasant artificial scents (perfume or cologne) on evaluations of job applicants. *Journal of Applied Psychology, 68,* 709–713.

Baron, R. A. (1983b). The control of human aggression: An optimistic perspective. *Journal of Social and Clinical Psychology, 1,* 97–119.

Baron, R. A. (1986). Self-presentation in job interviews: When there can be "too much of a good thing." *Journal of Applied Social Psychology, 16,* 16–28.

Baron, R. A. (1989a). Applicant strategies during job interviews. In G. R. Ferris & R. W. Eder (Eds.), *The employment interview: Theory, research, and practice* (pp. 204–216). Newbury Park, CA: Sage.

Baron, R. A. (1989b). Personality and organizational conflict: The Type A behavior pattern and self-monitoring. *Organizational Behavior and Human Decision Processes, 44,* 281–297.

Baron, R. A. (1990a). Attributions and organizational conflict. In S. Graha & V. Folkes (Eds.), *Attribution theory: Applications to achievement, mental health, and interpersonal conflict* (pp. 185–204). Hillsdale, NJ: Erlbaum.

Baron, R. A. (1990b). Countering the effects of destructive criticism: The relative efficacy of four potential interventions. *Journal of Applied Psychology, 75,* 235–245.

Baron, R. A. (1993a). Effects of interviewers' moods and applicant qualifications on ratings of job applicants. *Journal of Applied Social Psychology, 23,* 254–271.

Baron, R. A. (1993b). Reducing aggression and conflict: The incompatible response approach, or why people who feel good usually won't be bad. In G. C. Brannigan & M. R. Merrens (Eds.), *The undaunted psychologist* (pp. 203–218). Philadelphia: Temple University Press.

Baron, R. A. (1994). The physical environment of work settings: Effects of task performance, interpersonal relations, and job satisfaction. In M. Staw & L. L. Cummings (Eds.), *Research in organizational behavior* (Vol. 16, pp. 1–46). Greenwich, CT: JAI Press.

Baron, R. A. (1995). *Workplace violence and workplace aggression: Insights and integrations from basic research.* Paper presented at the Meetings of the Academy of Management, Vancouver, British Columbia.

Baron, R. A. (1997a). The sweet smell of helping: Effects of pleasant ambient fragrance on prosocial behavior in shopping malls. *Personality and Social Psychology Bulletin, 23,* 498–503.

Baron, R. A. (1999). Counterfactual thinking and venture formation: The potential effects of thinking about "what might have been". *Journal of Business Venturing,* in press.

Baron, R. A. (1997b). Positive effects of conflict: A cognitive perspective. In C. K. W. deDreu & V. deVliert (Eds.), *Conflict escalation and organization performance.* (pp. 177–191). Thousand Oaks, CA: Sage.

Baron, R. A., & Bell, P. A. (1975). Aggression and heat: Mediating effects of prior provocation and exposure to an aggressive model. *Journal of Personality and Social Psychology, 31,* 825–832.

Baron, R. A., & Bronfen, M. I. (1994). A whiff of reality: Empirical evidence concerning the effects of pleasant fragrances on work-related behavior. *Journal of Applied Social Psychology, 23,* 1179–1203.

Baron, R. A., & Lawton, S. F. (1972). Environmental influences on aggression: The facilitation of modeling effects by high ambient temperatures. *Psychonomic Science, 26,* 80–82.

Baron, R. A., & Markman. (1998). *Social skills and entrepreneurial success: A framework and initial data.* Manuscript submitted for publication.

Baron, R. A., & Neuman, J. H. (1996). Workplace violence and workplace aggression: Evidence on their relative frequency and potential causes. *Aggressive Behavior, 22,* 161–173.

Baron, R. A., & Neuman, J. H. (1998). Workplace aggression—the iceberg beneath the tip of workplace violence: Evidence on its forms, frequency, and potential causes. *Public Administration Quarterly, 21,* 446–464.

Baron, R. A., & Richardson, D. R. (1994) *Human Aggression* (2nd ed.). New York: Plenum.

Baron, R. A., & Thomley, J. (1994). A whiff of reality: Positive affect as a potential mediator of the effects of pleasant fragrances on task performance and helping. *Environment and Behavior, 26,* 766–784.

Baron, R. A., Neuman, J. H., & Geddes, D. (1999). Social and personal determinants of workplace aggression: Evidence for the impact of perceived injustice and the Type A behavior pattern. *Aggressive Behavior, 25.*

Baron, R. A., Rea, M. S., & Daniels, S. G. (1992). Lighting as a source of environmentally-generated positive affect in work settings: Impact on cognitive tasks and interpersonal behaviors. *Motivation and Emotion, 14,* 1–34.

Baron, R. A., Russell, G. W., & Arms, R. L. (1985). Negative ions and behavior: Impact on mood, memory, and aggression among Type A and Type B persons. *Journal of Personality and Social Psychology, 48,* 746–754.

Baron, R. S., Kerr, N. L., & Miller, N. (1992). *Group process, group decision, group action.* Pacific Grove, CA: Brooks/Cole.

Baron, R. S., Moore, D., & Sanders, G. S. (1978). Distraction as a source of drive in social facilitation research. *Journal of Personality and Social Psychology, 36,* 816–824.

Baron, R. S., Vandello, U. A., & Brunsman, B. (1996). The forgotten variable in conformity research: Impact of task importance on social influence. *Journal of Personality and Social Psychology, 71,* 915–927.

Barrett, L. F., & Russell, J. A. (1998). Independence and bipolarity in the structure of current affect. *Journal of Personality and Social Psychology, 74,* 967–984.

Barringer, F. (1993, April 1). 1 in 5 in U.S. have sexually caused viral disease. *New York Times,* pp. A1, B9.

Barry, D. (1998, February 1). A question that drives guys totally crazy. *Miami Herald.*

Bartholomew, K. (1990). Avoidance of intimacy: An attachment perspective. *Journal of Social and Personal Relationships, 7,* 147–178.

Bartholomew, K., & Horowitz, L. M. (1991). Attachment styles among young adults: A test of a four category model. *Journal of Personality and Social Psychology, 61,* 226–244.

Bass, B. I. (1998). *Leadership* (2nd ed.). New York: Free Press.

Batista, S. M., & Berte, R. (1992). Maternal behavior and feminine work: Study with Belgian mothers with infants. *Interamerican Journal of Psychology, 26,* 143–157.

Batson, C. D., & Oleson, K. C. (1991). Current status of the empathy–altruism hypothesis. In M. S. Clark (Ed.), *Prosocial behavior* (pp. 62–85). Newbury Park, CA: Sage.

Batson, C. D., & Weeks, J. L. (1996). Mood effects of unsuccessful helping: Another test of the empathy–altruism hypothesis. *Personality and Social Psychology Bulletin, 22,* 148–157.

Batson, C. D., Early, S., & Salvarani, G. (1997). Perspective taking: Imagining how another feels versus imagining how you would feel. *Personality and Social Psychology Bulletin, 23,* 751–758.

Batson, C. D., Klein, T. R., Highberger, L., & Shaw, L. L. (1995). Immorality from empathy-induced altruism: When compassion and justice conflict. *Journal of Personality and Social Psychology, 68,* 1042–1054.

Batson, C. D., Turk, C. L., Shaw, L. L., & Klein, T. R. (1995). Information function of empathic emotion: Learning that we value the other's welfare. *Journal of Personality and Social Psychology, 68,* 300–313.

Batson, C. D., Duncan, B. D., Ackerman, P., Buckley, T., & Birch, K. (1981). Is empathic emotion a source of altruistic motivation? *Journal of Personality and Social Psychology, 40,* 290–302.

Batson, C. D., O'Quin, K., Fultz, J., Vanderplas, M., & Isen, A. M. (1983). Influence of self-reported distress and empathy on egoistic versus altruistic motivation to help. *Journal of Personality and Social Psychology, 45,* 706–718.

Batson, C. D., Batson, J. G., Todd, R. M., Brummett, B. H., Shaw, L. L., & Aldeguer, C. M. R. (1995). Empathy and the collective good: Caring for one of the others in a social dilemma. *Journal of Personality and Social Psychology, 68,* 619–631.

Batson, C. D., Sager, K., Garst, E., Kang, M., Rubchinsky, K., & Dawson, K. (1997). Is empathy-induced helping due to self–other merger? *Journal of Personality and Social Psychology, 73,* 495–509.

Batson, C. D., Ahmed, N., Yin, J., Bedell, S. J., Johnson, J. W., Templin, C. M., & Whiteside, A. (1999). Two threats to the common good: Self-interested egoism and empathy-induced altruism. *Personality and Social Psychology Bulletin, 25,* 3–16.

Baum, A. (1994). Behavioral, biological, and environmental interactions in disease processes. In S. Blumenthal, K. Matthews, & S. Weiss (Eds.), *New research frontiers in behavioral medicine: Proceedings of the national conference* (p. 62). Washington, DC: NIH Publications.

Baumeister, R. F., Chesner, S. P., Sanders, P. S., & Tice, D. M. (1988). Who's in charge here? Group leaders do lend help in emergencies. *Personality and Social Psychology Bulletin, 14,* 17–22.

Baumeister, R. F., & Leary, M. R. (1995). The need to belong: Desire for interpersonal attachments as a fundamental human motivation. *Psychological Bulletin, 117,* 497–529.

Baumeister, R. F., Wotman, S. R., & Stillwell, A. M. (1993). Unrequited love: On heartbreak, anger, guilt, scriptlessness, and humiliation. *Journal of Personality and Social Psychology, 64,* 377–394

Baxter, L. A. (1990). Dialectical contradictions in relationship development. *Journal of Social and Personal Relationships, 7,* 69–88.

Beall, A. E., & Sternberg, R. J. (1995). The social construction of love. *Journal of Social and Personal Relationships, 12,* 417–438.

Becker, G., & Becker, C. (1994). The maternal behavior inventory: Measuring the behavioral side of mother-to-infant attachment. *Social Behavior and Personality, 22,* 177–194.

Beckwith, J. B. (1994). Terminology and social relevance in psychological research on gender. *Social Behavior and Personality, 22,* 329–336.

Bell, B. (1991). Loneliness and values. *Journal of Social Behavior and Personality, 6,* 771–778.

Bell, B. (1993). Emotional loneliness and the perceived similarity of one's ideas and interests. *Journal of Social Behavior and Personality, 8,* 273–280.

Bell, B. E. (1995). Judgments of the attributes of a student who is talkative versus a student who is quiet in class. *Journal of Social Behavior and Personality, 10,* 827–832.

Bell, B. E., & Loftus, E. F. (1988). Degree of detail of eyewitness testimony and mock juror judgments. *Journal of Applied Social Psychology, 18,* 1171–1192.

Bell, P. A. (1992). In defense of the negative affect escape model of heat and aggression. *Psychological Bulletin, 111,* 342–346.

Bell, P. A., & Baron, R. A. (1976). Aggression and heat: The mediating role of negative affect. *Journal of Applied Social Psychology, 6,* 18–30.

Bell, P. A., Fisher, J. D., Baum, A., & Green, T. E. (1990). *Environmental psychology* (3rd ed.). New York: Holt, Rinehart and Winston.

Bell, R. A. (1991). Gender, friendship network density, and loneliness. *Journal of Social Behavior and Personality, 6,* 45–56.

Bell, S. T., Kuriloff, P. J., & Lottes, I. (1994). Understanding attributions of blame in stranger rape and date rape situations: An examination of gender, race, identification, and students' social perceptions of rape victims. *Journal of Applied Social Psychology, 24,* 1719–1734.

Bellafante, G. (1997, May 5). Bewitching teen heroines. *Time,* 82–84.

Belmore, S. M., & Hubbard, M. L. (1987). The role of advance expectancies in person memory. *Journal of Personality and Social Psychology, 53,* 61–70.

Bem, S. L. (1974). The measurement of psychological androgyny. *Journal of Consulting and Clinical Psychology, 42,* 155–162.

Bem, S. L. (1975). Sex role adaptability: One consequence of psychological androgyny. *Journal of Personality and Social Psychology, 31,* 634–643.

Bem, S. L. (1981). Gender schema theory: A cognitive account of sex typing. *Psychological Review, 88,* 354–364.

Bem, S. L. (1983). Gender schema theory and its implications for child development: Raising gender-schematic children in a gender-schematic society. *Signs: Journal of Women in Culture and Society, 8,* 598–616.

Bem, S. L. (1984). Androgyny and gender-schema theory: A conceptual and empirical integration. *Nebraska Symposium on Motivation: Psychology and Gender, 32,* 179–226.

Bem, S. L. (1995). Dismantling gender polarization and compulsory heterosexuality: Should we turn the volume down or up? *Journal of Sex Research, 32,* 329–334.

Benjamin, E. (1998, January 14). Storm brings out good, bad and greedy. Albany *Times Union,* pp. A1, A6.

Benson, P. L., Karabenick, S. A., & Lerner, R. M. (1976). Pretty pleases: The effects of physical attractiveness, race, and sex on receiving help. *Journal of Experimental Social Psychology, 12,* 409–415.

Berg, J. H., & McQuinn, R. D. (1989). Loneliness and aspects of social support networks. *Journal of Social and Personal Relationships, 6,* 359–372.

Berkowitz, L. (1987). Mood, self-awareness, and willingness to help. *Journal of Personality and Social Psychology, 52,* 721–724.

Berkowitz, L. (1989). Frustration-aggression hypothesis: Examination and reformulation. *Psychological Bulletin, 106,* 59–73.

Berkowitz, L. (1993). *Aggression: Its causes, consequences, and control.* New York: McGraw Hill.

Berman, M., Gladue, B., & Taylor, S. (1993). The effects of hormones, Type A behavior pattern and provocation on aggression in men. *Motivation and Emotion, 17,* 125–138, 182–199.

Bernard, L. C., & Belinsky, D. (1993). Hardiness, stress, and maladjustment: Effects on self-reported retrospective health problems and prospective health center visits. *Journal of Social Behavior and Personality, 8,* 97–110.

Bernath, M. S., & Feshbach, N. D. (1995). Children's trust: Theory, assessment, development, and research directions. *Applied and Preventive Psychology, 4,* 1–19.

Bernieri, F. J., Gillis, J. S., Davis, J. M., & Grahe, J. E. (1996). Dyad rapport and the accuracy of its judgment across situations: A lens model analysis. *Journal of Personality and Social Psychology, 71,* 110–129.

Berry, D. S. (1990). Taking people at face value: Evidence for the kernel of truth hypothesis. *Social Cognition, 8,* 343–361.

Berry, D. S. (1991). Accuracy in social perception: Contributions of facial and vocal information. *Journal of Personality and Social Psychology, 68,* 291–307.

Berry, D. S., & Brownlow, S. (1989). Were the physiognomists right? Personality correlates of facial babyishness. *Personality and Social Psychology Bulletin, 15,* 266–279.

Berry, D. S., & Hansen, J. S. (1996). Positive affect, negative affect, and social interaction. *Journal of Personality and Social Psychology, 71,* 796–809.

Berry, D. S., & Landry, J. C. (1997). Facial maturity and daily social interaction. *Journal of Personality and Social Psychology, 72,* 570–580.

Berry, D. S., & Zebrowitz-McArthur, L. (1988). What's in a face? Facial maturity and the attribution of legal responsibility. *Personality and Social Psychology Bulletin, 14,* 23–33.

Berry, D. S., Pennebaker, J. W., Mueller, J. S., & Hiller, W. D. (1997). Linguistic bases of social perception. *Personality and Social Psychology Bulletin, 23,* 526–537.

Berscheid, E., Dion, K. K., Hatfield (Walster), E., & Walster, G. W. (1971). Physical attractiveness and dating choice: A test of the matching hypothesis. *Journal of Experimental Social Psychology, 7,* 173–189.

Berscheid, E., Snyder, M., & Omoto, A. M. (1989). The Relationship Closeness Inventory: Assessing the closeness of interpersonal relationships. *Journal of Personality and Social Psychology, 57,* 792–807.

Bersoff, D. (1987). Social science data and the Supreme Court: Lockhart as a case in point. *American Psychologist, 42,* 52–58.

Bersoff, D. M. (1999). Why good people sometimes do bad things: Motivated reasoning and unethical behavior. *Personality and Social Bulletin, 25,* 28–39.

Betancourt, B. A., & Miller, N. (1996). Gender differences in aggression as a function of provocation: A meta-analyis. *Psychological Bulletin, 119,* 422–447.

Beyer, S., & Bowden, E. M. (1997). Gender differences in self-perceptions: Convergent evidence from three measures of accuracy and bias. *Personality and Social Psychology Bulletin, 23,* 157–172.

Bickman, L. D. (1975). *Personality constructs of senior women planning to marry or to live independently after college.* Unpublished doctoral dissertation, University of Pennsylvania.

Bienert, H., & Schneider, B. H. (1993). Diagnosis-specific social skills training with peer-nominated aggressive–disruptive and sensitive–isolated preadolescents. *Journal of Applied Developmental Psychology, 26* 182–199.

Bierhoff, H. W., Klein, R., & Kramp, P. (1991). Evidence for the altruistic personality from data on accident research. *Journal of Personality, 59,* 263–280.

Bies, R. J., Shapiro, D. L., & Cummings, L. L. (1988a). Causal accounts and managing organizational conflict: Is it enough to say it's not my fault? *Communication Research, 15,* 381–399.

Bies, R. J., Shapiro, D. L., & Cummings, L. L. (1988b). Voice and justification: Their influence on procedural fairness judgments. *Academy of Management Journal, 31,* 676–685.

Birkimer, J. C., Lucas, M., & Birkimer, S. J. (1991). Health locus of control and status of cardiac rehabilitation graduates. *Journal of Social Behavior and Personality, 6,* 629–640.

Birnbaum, G. E., Orr, I., Mikulincer, M., & Florian, V. (1997). When marriage breaks up—does attachment style contribute to coping and mental health? *Journal of Social and Personal Relationships, 14,* 643–654.

Births to teen girls down, U.S. reports. (1995, September 22). *Washington Post.*

Björkqvist, K., Österman, K., & Hjelt-Bäck, M. (1994). Aggression among university employees. *Aggressive Behavior, 20,* 173–184.

Bjöorkqvist, K., Lagerspetz, K. M., & Kaukiainen, A. (1992). Do girls manipulate and boys fight? Developmental trends in regard to direct and indirect aggression. *Aggressive Behavior, 18,* 117–127.

Black smokers' habit detailed. (1998, April 28). Associated Press.

Blakeslee, S. (1998, August 4). Scientists study role of mother–child bond. *New York Times.*

Blaney, P. H. (1986). Affect and memory: A review. *Psychological Bulletin, 99,* 229–246.

Blanton, H., Buunk, B. P., Gibbons, F. X., & Kuyper, H. (1999). Anything you can do, I can do better than average: A prospective study of social comparison and academic performance. *Journal of Personality and Social Psychology, 76,* 420–430.

Blanton, H., van der Eijnden, R. J. J. M., Buunk, B. P., Gibbons, F. X., Gerrard, M., & Bakker, A. (1999). *Negatively-framed and positively framed prototype in the prediction and prevention of unsafe sex.* Manuscript submitted for publication.

Blascovich, J., Wyer, N. A., Swart, L. A., & Kibler, J. L. (1997). Racism and racial categorization. *Journal of Personality and Social Psychology, 72,* 1364–1372.

Blazer, D. G., Kessler, R. C., McGonagle, K. A., & Swartz, M. S. (1994). The prevalence and distribution of major depression in a national community sample: The National Comorbidity Survey. *American Journal of Psychiatry, 151,* 979–986.

Bober, S., & Grolnick, W. (1995). Motivational factors related to differences in self-schemas. *Motivation and Emotion, 19,* 307–327.

Bobo, L. (1983). Whites' opposition to busing: Symbolic racism or realistic group conflict? *Journal of Personality and Social Psychology, 45,* 1196–1210.

Bodenhausen, G. F. (1993). Emotion, arousal, and stereotypic judgment: A heuristic model of affect and stereotyping. In D. Mackie & D. Hamilton (Eds.), *Affect, cognition, and stereotyping: Intergroup processes in intergroup perception* (pp. 13–37). San Diego, CA: Academic Press.

Bodenmann, G., Kaiser, A., Hahlweg, K., & Fehn-Wolfsdorf, G. (1998). Communication patterns during marital conflict: A cross-cultural replication. *Personal Relationships, 5,* 343–356.

Bodenhausen, G. V., Kramer, G. P., & Susser, G. L. (1994a). Negative affect and social judgment: The differential impact of anger and sadness. *European Journal of Social Psychology, 24,* 45–62.

Bodenhausen, G. V., Kramer, G. P., & Susser, K. (1994b). Happiness and stereotypic thinking in social judgment. *Journal of Personality and Social Psychology, 66,* 621–632.

Boer, F., Westenberg, M., McHale, S. M., Updegraff, K. A., & Stocker, C. M. (1997). The factorial structure of the Sibling Relationship Inventory (SRI) in American and Dutch samples. *Journal of Social and Personal Relationships, 14,* 851–859.

Bogard, M. (1990). Why we need gender to understand human violence. *Journal of Interpersonal Violence, 5,* 132–135.

Bogart, L. M. (1998). The relationship of stereotypes about helpers to help-seeking judgments, preferences, and behaviors. *Personality and Social Psychology Bulletin, 24,* 1264–1275.

Bohren, J. (1993). Six myths of sexual harassment. *Management Review, 18,* 61–63.

Boivin, M., Dodge, K. A., & Coie, J. D. (1995). Individual–group behavioral similarity and peer status in experimental play groups of boys: The social misfit revisited. *Journal of Personality and Social Psychology, 69,* 269–279.

Bolger, N., & Zuckerman, A. (1995). A framework for studying personality in the stress process. *Journal of Personality and Social Psychology, 69,* 890–902.

Bombar, M. L., & Littig, L. W., Jr. (1996). Babytalk as a communication of intimate attachment: An initial study in adult romances and friendships. *Personal Relationships, 3,* 137–158.

Bond, C. F. (1982). Social facilitation: A self-presentational view. *Journal of Personality and Social Psychology, 42,* 1042–1050.

Bond, R., & Smith, P. B. (1996). Culture and conformity: A meta-analysis of studies using Asch's (1952b, 1956) line judgment task. *Psychological Bulletin, 119,* 111–137.

Bookwala, J., Frieze, I. H., & Grote, N. K. (1994). Love, aggression and satisfaction in dating relationships. *Journal of Social and Personal Relationships, 11,* 625–632.

Boon, S. D., & Brussoni, M. J. (1998). Popular images of grandparents: Examining young adults' views of their closest grandparents. *Personal Relationships, 5,* 105–119.

Booth, C. (1998, September 7). The bad Samaritan. *Time,* pp. 59–60.

Booth-Kewley, S., & Vickers, R. R. Jr. (1994). Associations between major domains of personality and health behavior. *Journal of Personality, 62,* 281–298.

Bornstein, R. F. (1995). Interpersonal dependency and physical illness: The mediating roles of stress and social support. *Journal of Social and Clinical Psychology, 14,* 225–243.

Bornstein, R. F., & D'Agostino, P. R. (1992). Stimulus recognition and the mere exposure effect. *Journal of Personality and Social Psychology, 63,* 545–552.

Bossard, J. H. S. (1932). Residential propinquity as a factor in marriage selection. *American Journal of Sociology, 38,* 219–224.

Botha, M. (1990). Television exposure and aggression among adolescents: A follow-up study over 5 years. *Aggressive Behavior, 16,* 361–380.

Bothwell, R. K., & Jalil, M. (1992). The credibility of nervous witnesses. *Journal of Social Behavior and Personality, 7,* 581–586.

Bothwell, R. K., Brigham, J. C., & Malpass, R. S. (1989). Cross-racial identification. *Personality and Social Psychology Bulletin, 15,* 19–25.

Bottoms, B. L., & Goodman, G. S. (1994). Perceptions of children's credibility in sexual assault cases. *Journal of Applied Social Psychology, 24,* 702–732.

Bouchard, T. J., Jr., Arvey, R. D., Keller, L. M., & Segal, N. L. (1992). Genetic influences on job satisfaction: A reply to Cropanzano and Hames. *Journal of Applied Psychology, 77,* 89–93.

Boulton, M. J., & Smith, P. K. (1996). Liking and peer perceptions among Asian and white British children. *Journal of Social and Personal Relationships, 13,* 163–177.

Bourgeois, M. J., Horowitz, I. A., & Lee, L. F. (1993). Effects of technicality and access to trial transcripts on verdicts and information processing in a civil trial. *Personality and Social Psychology Bulletin, 19,* 229–227.

Bower, G. H. (1991). Mood congruity of social judgments. In J. P. Forgas (Ed.), *Emotion and social judgments* (pp. 31–55). Oxford: Pergamon Press.

Bowers, L., Smith, P. K., & Binney, V. (1994). Perceived family relationships of bullies, victims and bully/victims in middle childhood. *Journal of Social and Personal Relationships, 11,* 215–232.

Bowlby, J. (1982). *Attachment and loss: Vol. 1. Attachment* (2nd ed.). New York: Basic Books.

Bowman, L. (1998, December 18). Sweet life longer for candy lovers, research study concludes. Scripps Howard.

Bradbury, T. N., & Fincham, F. D. (1992). Attributions and behavior in marital interaction. *Journal of Personality and Social Psychology, 63,* 613–628.

Branscombe, N. R., & Wann, D. L. (1994). Collective self-esteem consequences of outgroup derogation when a valued social identity is on trial. *European Journal of Social Psychology, 24,* 641–657.

Braver, S. L. (1995). Social contracts and the provision of public goods. In D. Schroeder (Ed.), *Social dilemmas: Perspectives on individuals and groups* (pp. 69–86). Westport, CT: Praeger.

Braza, P., Braza, F., Carreras, M. R., & Munoz, J. M. (1993). Measuring the social ability of preschool children. *Social Behavior and Personality, 21,* 145–158.

Breakwell, G. M., & Fife-Schaw, C. (1992). Sexual activities and preferences in a United Kingdom sample of 16- to 20-year-olds. *Archives of Sexual Behavior, 21,* 271–293.

Breen, T. H. (1996, September 22). The truth about gentle Ben. *New York Times Book Review,* p. 37.

Brehm, J. W. (1966). *A theory of psychological reactance.* New York: Academic Press.

Brennan, K. A., & Bosson, J. K. (1998). Attachment-style differences in attitudes toward and reactions to feedback from romantic partners: An exploration of the relational bases of self-esteem. *Personality and Social Psychology Bulletin, 24,* 699–714.

Brennan, K. A., & Shaver, P. R. (1995). Dimensions of adult attachment, affect regulation, and romantic relationship functioning. *Personality and Social Psychology Bulletin, 21,* 267–283.

Brennan, K. A., Clark, C. L., & Shaver, P. R. (1998). Self-report measurement of adult attachment. In J. A. Simpson & W. S. Rholes (Eds.), *Attachment theory and close relationships* (pp. 47–76). New York: Guilford.

Brewer, B. W. (1993). Self-identity and specific vulnerability to depressed mood. *Journal of Personality, 61,* 343–386.

Brewer, M. B., & Gardner, W. (1996). Who is this "we"? Levels of collective identity and self representations. *Journal of Personality and Social Psychology, 71,* 83–93.

Brewer, M. B., Ho, H., Lee, J., & Miller, M. (1987). Social identity and social distance among Hong Kong schoolchildren. *Personality and Social Psychology Bulletin, 13,* 156–165.

Brickner, M., Harkins, S., & Ostrom, T. (1986). Personal involvement: Thought provoking implications for social loafing. *Journal of Personality and Social Psychology, 51,* 763–769.

Bringle, R. G., & Bagby, G. J. (1992). Self-esteem and perceived quality of romantic and family relationships in young adults. *Journal of Research in Personality, 26,* 340–356.

Bringle, R. G., & Winnick, T. A. (1992, October). *The nature of unrequited love.* Paper presented at the first Asian Conference in Psychology, Singapore.

Brockner, J. (1992). The escalation of commitment to a failing course of action: Toward theoretical progress. *Academy of Management Review, 17,* 39–61.

Brockner, J., Konovsky, M., Cooper-Schneider, R., Folger, R., Martin, C., & Bies, R. J. (1994). Interactive effects of procedural justice and outcome negativity on victims and survivors of job loss. *Academy of Management Journal, 37,* 397–409.

Brockner, J. M., & Wiesenfeld, B. M. (1996). An integrative framework for explaining reactions to decisions: Interactive effects of outcomes and procedures. *Psychological Bulletin, 120,* 189–208.

Brody, G. H., Neubaum, E., & Forehand, R. (1988). Serial marriage: A heuristic analysis of an emerging family form. *Psychological Bulletin, 103,* 211–222.

Brody, J. E. (1995, May 5). Danish study shows wine aiding longevity. *New York Times,* p. A18.

Bromberger, J. T., & Matthews, K. A. (1996). A "feminine" model of vulnerability to depressive symptoms: A longitudinal investigation of middle-aged women. *Journal of Personality and Social Psychology, 70,* 591–598.

Brooks-Gunn, J., & Lewis, M. (1981). Infant social perception: Responses to pictures of parents and strangers. *Developmental Psychology, 17,* 647–649.

Brothers, L. (1990). The neural basis of primate social communication. *Motivation and Emotion, 14,* 81–91.

Brown, C. (1995, September 6). Claverack girls' savior says God made him a hero. Albany *Times Union,* pp. B1, B4.

Brown, J. D. (1991). Staying fit and staying well: Physical fitness as a moderator of life stress. *Journal of Personality and Social Psychology, 60,* 555–561.

Brown, J. D., & Dutton, K. A. (1995). The thrill of victory, the complexity of defeat: Self-esteem and people's emotional reactions to success and failure. *Journal of Personality and Social Psychology, 68,* 712–722.

Brown, J. D., & Rogers, R. J. (1991). Self-serving attributions: The role of physiological arousal. *Personality and Social Psychology Bulletin, 17,* 501–506.

Brown, K. W., & Moskowitz, D. S. (1997). Does unhappiness make you sick? The role of affect and neuroticism in the experience of common physical symptoms. *Journal of Personality and Social Psychology, 72,* 907–917.

Brown, L. M. (1998). Ethnic stigma as a contextual experience: Possible selves perspective. *Personality and Social Psychology Bulletin, 24,* 165–172.

Brown, L. S. (1997). The private practice of subversion: Psychology as *tikkun olam. American Psychologist, 52,* 449–462.

Brown, S. L. (1998). Associations between peer drink driving, peer attitudes toward drink, driving, and personal drink driving. *Journal of Applied Social Psychology, 28,* 423–436.

Brown, S. P. (1996). A meta-analysis and review of organizational research on job involvement. *Psychological Bulletin, 120,* 235–255.

Browne, M. W. (1992, April 14). Biologists tally generosity's rewards. *New York Times,* pp. C1, C8.

Bruch, M. A., Hamer, R. J., & Heimberg, R. G. (1995). Shyness and public self-consciousness: Additive or interactive relation with social interaction? *Journal of Personality, 63,* 47–63.

Bruck, M., & Ceci, S. J. (1997). The suggestibility of young children. *Current Directions in Psychological Science, 6,* 75–79.

Bruck, M., Ceci, S. J., & Hembrooke, H. (1998). Reliability and credibility of young children's reports: From research to policy and practice. *American Psychologist, 53,* 136–151.

Bruder, G. E., Stewart, M. M., Mercier, M. A., Agosti, V., Leite, P., Donovan, S., & Quitkin, F. M. (1997). Outcome of cognitive–behavioral therapy for depression: Relation to hemi-

spheric dominance for verbal processing. *Journal of Abnormal Psychology, 106,* 138–144.

Bruess, C. J. S., & Pearson, J. C. (1993). "Sweet pea" and "pussy cat": An examination of idiom use and marital satisfaction over the life cycle. *Journal of Social and Personal Relationships, 10,* 609–615.

Bryan, J. H., & Test, M. A. (1967). Models and helping: Naturalistic studies in aiding behavior. *Journal of Personality and Social Psychology, 6,* 400–407.

Brylinsky, J. A., & Moore, J. C. (1994). The identification of body build stereotypes in young children. *Journal of Research in Personality, 28,* 170–181.

Buck, R., & Ginsburg, B. (1991). Spontaneous communication and altruism: The communicative gene hypothesis. In M. S. Clark (Ed.), *Prosocial behavior* (pp. 149–175). Newbury Park, CA: Sage.

Budesheim, T. L., & Bonnelle, K. (1998). The use of abstract trait knowledge and behavioral exemplars in causal explanations of behavior. *Personality and Social Psychology Bulletin, 24,* 575–587.

Buehler, R., & Griffin, D. (1994). Change-of-meaning effects in conformity and dissent: Observing construal processes over time. *Journal of Personality and Social Psychology, 67,* 984–996.

Buehler, R., Griffin, D., & MacDonald, H. (1997). The role of motivated reasoning in optimistic time predictions. *Personality and Social Psychology Bulletin, 23,* 238–247.

Buehler, R., Griffin, D., & Ross, M. (1994). Exploring the "planning fallacy": Why people underestimate their task completion times. *Journal of Personality and Social Psychology, 67,* 366–381.

Bumpass, L. (1984). Children and marital disruption: A replication and update. *Demography, 21,* 71–82.

Burger, J. M. (1986). Increasing compliance by improving the deal: The that's-not-all technique. *Journal of Personality and Social Psychology, 51,* 277–283.

Burger, J. M. (1992). *Desire for control: Personality, social, and clinical perspectives.* New York: Plenum.

Burger, J. M. (1995). Individual differences in preference for solitude. *Journal of Research in Personality, 29,* 85–108.

Burger, J. M., & Cooper, H. M. (1979). The desirability of control. *Motivation and Emotion, 3,* 381–393.

Burger, J. M., & Palmer, M. L. (1992). Changes in and generalization of unrealistic optimism following experiences with stressful events: Reactions to the 1989 California earthquake. *Personality and Social Psychology Bulletin, 18,* 39–43.

Burgess, D., & Borgida, E. (1997). Sexual harassment: An experimental test of sex-role spillover theory. *Personality and Social Psychology Bulletin, 23,* 63–75.

Burgoon, J. K., & Hale, J. L. (1988). Nonverbal expectancy violations: Model elaboration and application to immediacy. *Communication Monographs, 55,* 58–79.

Burns-Glover, A. L., & Veith, D. J. (1995). Revisiting gender and teaching evaluations: Sex still makes a difference. *Journal of Social Behavior and Personality, 10,* 69–80.

Burnstein, E. (1983). Persuasion as argument processing. In M. Brandstatter, J. H. Davis, & G. Stocker-Kriechgauer (Eds.), *Group decision processes.* London: Academic Press.

Burnstein, E., Crandall, C., & Kitayama, S. (1994). Some neo-Darwinian rules for altruism: Weighing cues for inclusive fitness as a function of the biological importance of the decision. *Journal of Personality and Social Psychology, 67,* 773–789.

Bushman, B. (1998, February 18). Personal communication.

Bushman, B. J. (1988). The effects of apparel on compliance: A field experiment with a female authority figure. *Personality and Social Psychology Bulletin, 14,* 459–467.

Bushman, B. J. (1998). Effects of television violence on memory for commercial messages. *Journal of Experimental Psychology: Applied, 4,* 1–17.

Bushman, B. J., & Baumeister, R. F. (1998). Threatened egotism, narcissism, self-esteem, and direct and displaced aggression: Does self-love or self-hate lead to violence? *Journal of Personality and Social Psychology, 75,* 219–229.

Bushman, B. J., & Cooper, H. M. (1990). Effects of alcohol on human aggression: An integrative research review. *Psychological Bulletin, 107,* 341–354.

Bushman, B. J., Baumeister, R. F., & Stack, A. D. (1999). Catharsis messages and anger-reducing activities. *Journal of Personality and Social Psychology, 76,* 367–376.

Buss, A. M. (1961). *The psychology of aggression.* New York: Wiley.

Buss, D. M. (1988). Love acts: The evolutionary biology of love. In R. J. Sternberg & M. L. Barnes (Eds.), *The psychology of love* (pp. 100–118). New Haven, CT: Yale University Press.

Buss, D. M. (1989). Conflict between the sexes: Strategic interference and the evocation of anger and upset. *Journal of Personality and Social Psychology, 56,* 735–747.

Buss, D. M. (1990). Evolutionary social psychology: Prospects and pitfalls. *Motivation and Emotion, 14,* 265–286.

Buss, D. M. (1994). The strategies of human mating. *American Scientist, 82,* 238–249.

Buss, D. M. (1995). Evolutionary psychology: A new paradigm for psychological science. *Psychological Inquiry, 6,* 1–30.

Buss, D. M. (1998). *Evolutionary psychology.* Boston: Allyn and Bacon.

Buss, D. M., & Schmitt, D. P. (1993). Sexual strategies theory: An evolutionary perspective on human mating. *Psychological Review, 100,* 204–232.

Buss, D. M., & Shackelford, T. K. (1997). From vigilance to violence: Mate retention tactics in married couples. *Journal of Personality and Social Psychology, 72,* 346–361.

Buss, D. M., Larsen, R. J., Westen, D., & Semmelroth, J. (1992). Sex differences in jealousy: Evolution, physiology, and psychology. *Psychological Science, 3,* 251–255.

Butler, A. C., Hokanson, J. E., & Flynn, H. A. (1994). A comparison of self-esteem lability and low trait self-esteem as vulnerability factors for depression. *Journal of Personality and Social Psychology, 66,* 166–177.

Butler, D., & Geis, F. L. (1990). Nonverbal affect responses to male and female leaders: Implications for leadership evaluations. *Journal of Personality and Social Psychology, 58,* 48–59.

Butler, J. M., & Haigh, G. V. (1954). Changes in the relation between self-concepts and ideal concepts consequent upon client-centered counseling. In C. R. Rogers & R. F. Dymond (Eds.), *Psychotherapy and personality change* (pp. 55–75). Chicago: University of Chicago Press.

Butterfield, F. (1997, November 16). Crime takes a drive. *New York Times.*

Buunk, B. P. (1995). Sex, self-esteem, dependency and extradyadic sexual experience as related to jealousy responses. *Journal of Social and Personal Relationships, 12,* 147–153.

Buunk, B. P., & van der Eijnden, R. J. J. M. (1997). Perceived prevalence, perceived superiority, and relationship satisfaction: Most relationships are good, but ours is the best. *Personality and Social Psychology Bulletin, 23,* 219–228.

Buunk, B. P., & Ybema, J. F. (1997). Social comparison and occupational stress: The identification–contrast model. In B. P. Buunk & F. X. Gibbons (Eds.), *Health, coping, and social comparison* (pp. 359–388). Hillsdale, NJ: Erlbaum.

Buunk, B. P., Doosje, B. J., Jans, L. G. J. M., & Hopstaken, I. E. M. (1993). Perceived reciprocity, social support, and stress at work: The role of exchange and communal orientation. *Journal of Personality and Social Psychology, 65,* 801–811.

Buzwell, S., & Rosenthal, D. (1995). Exploring the sexual world of the unemployed adolescent. *Journal of Community and Applied Social Psychology, 5,* 161–166.

Byrne, B. M., & Shavelson, R. J. (1996). On the structure of social self-concept for pre-, early, and late adolescents: A test of the Shavelson, Hubner, and Stanton (1976) model. *Journal of Personality and Social Psychology, 70,* 599–613.

Byrne, D. (1961a). The influence of propinquity and opportunities for interaction on classroom relationships. *Human Relations, 14,* 63–69.

Byrne, D. (1961b). Interpersonal attraction and attitude similarity. *Journal of Abnormal and Social Psychology, 62,* 713–715.

Byrne, D. (1964). Repression–sensitization as a dimension of personality. *Progress in Experimental Personality Research, 1,* 169–220.

Byrne, D. (1971). *The attraction paradigm.* New York: Academic Press.

Byrne, D. (1991). Perspectives on research classics: This ugly duckling has yet to become a swan. *Contemporary Social Psychology, 15,* 84–85.

Byrne, D. (1992). The transition from controlled laboratory experimentation to less controlled settings: Surprise! Additional variables are operative. *Communication Monographs, 59,* 190–198.

Byrne, D., & Blaylock, B. (1963). Similarity and assumed similarity of attitudes among husbands and wives. *Journal of Abnormal and Social Psychology, 67,* 636–640.

Byrne, D., & Buehler, J. A. (1955). A note on the influence of propinquity upon acquaintanceships. *Journal of Abnormal and Social Psychology, 51,* 147–148.

Byrne, D., & Clore, G. L. (1970). A reinforcement–affect model of evaluative responses. *Personality: An International Journal, 1,* 103–128.

Byrne, D., & Murnen, S. K. (1988). Maintaining loving relationships. In R. J. Sternberg & M. L. Barnes (Eds.), *The psychology of love* (pp. 293–310). New Haven, CT: Yale University Press.

Byrne, D., & Nelson, D. (1965). Attraction as a linear function of proportion of positive reinforcements. *Journal of Personality and Social Psychology, 1,* 659–663.

Byrne, D., & Smeaton, G. (1998). The Feelings Scale: Positive and negative affective responses. In C. M. Davis, W. L. Yarber, R. Bauserman, G. Scheer, & S. L. Davis (Eds.), *Handbook of sexuality-related measures* (pp. 50–52). Thousand Oaks, CA: Sage.

Byrne, D., Kelley, K., & Fisher, W. A. (1993). Unwanted teenage pregnancies: Incidence, interpretation, and intervention. *Applied and Preventive Psychology, 2,* 101–113.

Byrne, D., Gouaux, C., Griffitt, W., Lamberth, J., Murakawa, N., Prasad, M. B., Prasad, A., & Ramirez, M., III. (1971). The ubiquitous relationship: Attitude similarity and attraction: A cross-cultural study. *Human Relations, 24,* 201–207.

Cadenhead, A. C., & Richman, C. L. (1996). The effects of interpersonal trust and group status on prosocial and aggressive behaviors. *Social Behavior and Personality, 24,* 169–184.

Cahoon, D. D., & Edmonds, E. M. (1989). Male-Female estimates of opposite-sex first impressions concerning females' clothing styles. *Bulletin of the Psychonomic Society, 27,* 280–281.

Caldwell, D. F., & Burger, J. M. (1997). Personality and social influence strategies in the workplace. *Personality and Social Psychology Bulletin, 23,* 1003–1012.

Callaci, D. (1993, March 3). The glass is half full. *New York Teacher,* 9–11.

Callan, V. J. (1993). Subordinate manager communication in different sex-dyads: Consequences for job satisfaction. *Journal of Occupational and Organizational Psychology, 66,* 13–27.

Calvert, J. D. (1988). Physical attractiveness: A review and reevaluation of its role in social skill research. *Behavioral Assessment, 10,* 29–42.

Campbell, D. T. (1975). On the conflicts between biological and social evolution and between psychological and moral tradition. *American Psychologist, 30,* 1103–1126.

Campbell, D. T., & Specht, J. C. (1985). Altruism: Biology, culture, and religion. *Journal of Social and Clinical Psychology, 3,* 33–42.

Campbell, J. D., Chew, B., & Scratchley, L. S. (1991). Cognitive and emotional reactions to daily events: The effects of self-esteem and self-complexity. *Journal of Personality, 59,* 473–505.

Campbell, J. D., Trapnell, P. D., Heine, S. J., Katz, I. M., Lavallee, L. F., & Lehman, D. R. (1996). Self-concept clarity: Measurement, personality correlates, and cultural boundaries. *Journal of Personality and Social Psychology, 70,* 141–156.

Canary, D. J., Cupach, W. R., & Messman, S. J. (1995). *Relationship conflict: Conflict in parent–child, friendship, and romantic relationships.* Thousand Oaks, CA: Sage.

Canin, E. (1991). *Blue river.* New York: Houghton Mifflin.

Cann, A., Calhoun, L. G., & Banks, J. S. (1995). On the role of humor appreciation in interpersonal attraction: It's no joking matter. *Humor: International Journal of Humor Research.*

Cappella, J. N., & Palmer, M. T. (1990). Attitude similarity, relational history, and attraction: The mediating effects of kinesic and vocal behaviors. *Communication Monographs, 57,* 161–183.

Caprara, G. V., Barbaranelli, C., Pastorelli, C., & Perugini, M. (1994). Individual differences in the study of human aggression. *Aggressive Behavior, 20,* 291–303.

Carey, M. P., Morrison-Beedy, D., & Johnson, B. T. (1997). The HIV-Knowledge Questionnaire: Development and evaluation of a reliable, valid, and practical self-administered questionnaire. *AIDS and Behavior, 1,* 61–74.

Carli, L. L., Ganley, R., & Pierce-Otay, A. (1991). Similarity and satisfaction in roommate relationships. *Personality and Social Psychology Bulletin, 17,* 419–426.

Carnelley, K. B., Pietromonaco, P. R., & Jaffe, K. (1996). Attachment, caregiving, and relationship functioning in couples: Effects of self and partner. *Personal Relationships, 3,* 257–278.

Carpenter, L. M. (1988). From girls into women: Scripts for sexuality and romance in *Seventeen* magazine, 1974–1994. *Journal of Sex Research, 35,* 158–168.

Carroll, J. M., & Russell, H. A. (1996). Do facial expressions signal specific emotions? Judging emotion from the face in context. *Journal of Personality and Social Psychology, 70,* 205–218.

Carroll, L., Hoenigmann-Stovall, N., King, A., Wienhold, J., & Whitehead, G. I., III. (1998). *Journal of Social and Clinical Psychology, 17,* 38–49.

Carter, D. B., & McCloskey, L. A. (1984). Peers and the maintenance of sex-typed behavior: The development of children's conceptions of cross-gender behavior in their peers. *Social Cognition, 2,* 294–314.

Carver, C. S., & Glass, D. C. (1978). Coronary-prone behavior pattern and interpersonal aggression. *Journal of Personality and Social Psychology, 376,* 361–366.

Carver, C. S., Kus, L. A., & Scheier, M. F. (1994). Effects of good versus bad mood and optimistic versus pessimistic outlook on social acceptance versus rejection. *Journal of Social and Clinical Psychology, 13,* 138–151.

Carver, C. S., Reynolds, S. L., & Scheier, M. F. (1994). The possible selves of optimists and pessimists. *Journal of Research in Personality, 28,* 133–141.

Cash, T. F. (1995). Developmental teasing about physical appearance: Retrospective descriptions and relationships with body image. *Social Behavior and Personality, 23,* 123–130.

Cash, T. F., & Derlega, V. J. (1978). The matching hypothesis: Physical attractiveness among same-sex friends. *Personality and Social Psychology Bulletin, 4,* 240–243.

Cash, T. F., & Duncan, N. C. (1984). Physical attractiveness stereotyping among black American college students. *Journal of Social Psychology, 122,* 71–77.

Cash, T. F., & Trimer, C. A. (1984). Sexism and beautyism in women's evaluation of peer performance. *Sex Roles, 10,* 87–98.

Caspi, A., & Herbener, E. S. (1990). Continuity and change: Assortative marriage and the consistency of personality in adulthood. *Journal of Personality and Social Psychology, 58,* 250–258.

Caspi, A., Herbener, E. S., & Ozer, D. J. (1992). Shared experiences and the similarity of personalities: A longitudinal study of married couples. *Journal of Personality and Social Psychology, 62,* 281–291.

Caspi, A., Begg, D., Dickson, N., Harrington, H. L., Langley, J., Moffitt, T. E., & Silva, P. A. (1997). Personality differences predict health-risk behaviors in young adulthood: Evidence from a longitudinal study. *Journal of Personality and Social Psychology, 73,* 1052–1063.

Castellow, W. A., Wuensch, K. L., & Moore, C. H. (1990). Effects of physical attractiveness of the plaintiff and defendant in sexual harassment judgments. *Journal of Social Behavior and Personality, 5,* 547–562.

Catalano, R., Novaco, R., & McConnell, W. (1997). A model of the net effect of job loss on violence. *Journal of Personality and Social Psychology, 72,* 1440–1447.

Cavoukian, A., & Doob, A. N. (1980). The effect of a judge's charge and subsequent recharge on judgments of guilt. *Basic and Applied Social Psychology, 1,* 103–114.

Cervone, D. (1997). Social–cognitive mechanisms and personality coherence: Self-knowledge, situational beliefs, and cross-situational coherence in perceived self-efficacy. *Psychological Science, 8,* 43–50.

Chacko, T. I. (1982). Women and equal employment opportunity: Some unintended effects. *Journal of Applied Psychology, 67,* 119–123.

Chaiken, S., Giner-Sorolla, R., & Chen, S. (1996). Beyond accuracy: Defense and impression motives in heuristic and systematic processing. In P. M. Gollwitzer & J. A. Bargh (Eds.),

The psychology action: Linking motivation and cognition to behavior (pp. 553–578). New York: Guilford.

Chaiken, S., Liberman, A., & Eagly, A. H. (1989). Heuristic and systematic processing within and beyond persuasion context. In J. S. Uleman & J. A. Bargh (Eds.), *Unintended thought* (pp. 212–252). New York: Guilford.

Chan, C.-J., & Margolin, G. (1994). The relationship between dual-earner couples' daily work mood and home affect. *Journal of Social and Personal Relationships, 11,* 573–586.

Chang, E. C. (1998). Dispositional optimism and secondary appraisal of a stressor: Controlling for confounding influences and relations to coping and psychological and physical adjustment. *Journal of Personality and Social Psychology, 74,* 1109–1120.

Chapman, B. (1992). *The Byrne–Nelson formula revisited: The additional impact of number of dissimilar attitudes on attraction.* Unpublished masters thesis, University at Albany, State University of New York.

Chapman, H. A., Hobfoll, S. E., & Ritter, C. (1997). Partners' stress under-estimations lead to women's distress: A study of pregnant inner-city women. *Journal of Personality and Social Psychology, 73,* 418–425.

Chappell, K. D., & Davis, K. E. (1998). Attachment, partner choice, and perception of romantic partners: An experimental test of the attachment-security hypothesis. *Personal Relationships, 5,* 327–342.

Chatterjee, J., & McCarrey, M. (1991). Sex-role attitudes, values, and instrumental-expressive traits of women trainees in traditional vs. non-traditional programmes. *Applied Psychology: An International Review, 40,* 282–297.

Chen, S., Schechter, D., & Chaiken, S. (1996). Getting at the truth or getting along: Accuracy- versus impression-motivated heuristic and systematic processing. *Journal of Personality and Social Psychology, 71,* 262–275.

Cheney, D. L., & Seyfarth, R. M. (1992). Précis of how monkeys see the world. *Behavioral and Brain Sciences, 15,* 135–182.

Cherek, D. R., Schnapp, W., Gerard Moeller, F., & Dougherty, D. M. (1996). Laboratory measures of aggressive responding in male parolees with violent and nonviolent histories. *Aggressive Behavior 22,* 37–36.

Chermack, S. T., Berman, M., & Taylor, S. P. (1997). Effects of provocation on emotions and aggression in males. *Aggressive Behavior, 23,* 1–10.

Cheuk, W. H., & Rosen, S. (1992). Helper reactions: When help is rejected by friends or strangers. *Journal of Social Behavior and Personality, 7,* 445–458.

Cheung, C.-k., Lee, J.-j., & Chan, C.-m. (1994). Explicating filial piety in relation to family cohesion. *Journal of Social Behavior and Personality, 9,* 565–580.

Cheverton, H. M., & Byrne, D. (1998, February). *Development and validation of the Primary Choice Clothing Questionnaire.* Presented at the meeting of the Eastern Psychological Association, Boston.

Chidester, T. R. (1986). Problems in the study of interracial aggression: Pseudo-interracial dyad paradigm. *Journal of Personality and Social Psychology, 50,* 74–79.

Children's Defense Fund (1992). *The state of America's children, 1992.* Washington, DC: Author.

Choi, I., & Nisbett, R. E. (1998). Situational salience and cultural differences in the correspondence bias and actor-observer bias. *Personality and Social Psychology Bulletin, 24,* 949–960.

Christenfeld, N. (1998, March 27). Paper presented at the meeting of the Society of Behavioral Medicine, New Orleans.

Christensen, P. N., & Kashy, D. A. (1998). Perceptions of and by lonely people in initial social interaction. *Personality and Social Psychology Bulletin, 24,* 322–329.

Christopher, F. S., & Cate, R. M. (1985). Premarital sexual pathways and relationship development. *Journal of Social and Personal Relationships, 2,* 271–288.

Christy, C. A., & Voigt, H. (1994). Bystander responses to public episodes of child abuse. *Journal of Applied Social Psychology, 24,* 824–847.

Christy, P. R., Gelfand, D. M., & Hartmann, D. P. (1971). Effects of competition-induced frustration on two classes of modeled behavior. *Developmental Psychology, 5,* 104–111.

Chronicle of Higher Education. (1996). Changing demographics in the U.S. March 18, pp. A34–A44.

Cialdini, R. B. (1994). Interpersonal influence. In S. Shavitt & T. C. Brock (Eds.), *Persuasion* (pp. 195–218). Boston: Allyn & Bacon.

Cialdini, R. B., & Petty, R. (1979). Anticipatory opinion effects. In B. Petty, T. Ostrom, & T. Brock (Eds.), *Cognitive responses in persuasion.* Hillsdale, NJ: Erlbaum.

Cialdini, R. B., Baumann, D. J., & Kenrick, D. T. (1981). Insights from sadness: A three step model of the development of altruism as hedonism. *Developmental Review, 1,* 207–223.

Cialdini, R. B., Cacioppo, J. T., Bassett, R., & Miller J. A. (1978). A low-ball procedure for producing compliance: Commitment then cost. *Journal of Personality and Social Psychology, 36,* 463–476.

Cialdini, R. B., Brown, S. L., Lewis, B. P., Luce, C., & Neuberg, S. L. (1997). Reinterpreting the empathy–altruism relationship: When one into one equals oneness. *Journal of Personality and Social Psychology, 73,* 481–494.

Cialdini, R. B., Kallgren, C. A., & Reno, R. R. (1991). A focus theory of normative conduct. *Advances in Experimental Social Psychology, 24,* 201–234.

Cialdini, R. B., Kenrick, D. T., & Baumann, D. J. (1982). Effects of mood on prosocial behavior in children and adults. In N. Eisenberg-Berg (Ed.), *Development of prosocial behavior.* New York: Academic Press.

Cialdini, R. B., Schaller, M., Houlainham, D., Arps, K., Fultz, J., & Beaman, A. L. (1987). Empathy-based helping: Is it selflessly or selfishly motivated? *Journal of Personality and Social Psychology, 52,* 749–758.

Cialdini, R. B., Vincent, J. E., Lewis, S. K., Catalan, J., Wheeler, D., & Darby, B. L. (1975). Reciprocal concessions procedure for inducing compliance: The door-in-the-face technique. *Journal of Personality and Social Psychology, 31,* 206–215.

Cialdini, R. B., Wosinska, W., Dabul, A. J., Whetstone-Dion, R., & Heszen, I. (1998). When social role salience leads to social role rejection: Modest self-presentation among women and men in two cultures. *Personality and Social Psychology Bulletin, 24,* 473–481.

Clark, L. F. (1993). Stress and the cognitive–conversational benefits of social interaction. *Journal of Social and Clinical Psychology, 12,* 25–55.

Clark, L. F., & Collins, J. E. II. (1993). Remembering old flames: How the past affects assessments of the present. *Personality and Social Psychology Bulletin, 19,* 399–408.

Clark, M. S., & Grote, N. K. (1998). Why aren't indices of relationship costs always negatively related to indices of relationship quality? *Personality and Social Psychology Review, 2,* 2–17.

Clark, M. S., Ouellette, R., Powel, M. C., & Milberg, S. (1987). Recipient's mood, relationship type, and helping. *Journal of Personality and Social Psychology, 53,* 94–103.

Clark, S. L., & Stephens, M. A. P. (1996). Stroke patients' well-being as a function of caregiving spouses' helpful and unhelpful actions. *Personal Relationships, 3,* 171–184.

Clarke, M. S. (1991). *Prosocial behavior.* Newbury Park, CA: Sage.

Clary, E. G., & Orenstein, L. (1991). The amount and effectiveness of help: The relationship of motives and abilities in helping behavior. *Personality and Social Psychology Bulletin, 17,* 58–64.

Clary, E. G., Snyder, M., Ridge, R. D., Copeland, J., Stukas, A. A., Haugen, J., & Miene, P. (1998). Understanding and assessing the motivations of volunteers: A functional approach. *Journal of Personality and Social Psychology, 74,* 1516–1530.

Clement, U., Schmidt, G., & Kruse, M. (1984). Changes in sex differences in sexual behavior: A replication of a study on West German students (1966–1981). *Archives of Sexual Behavior, 13,* 99–120.

Clinton and AIDS. (1994, December 26). *The New Republic,* 7.

Clore, G. L., Schwarz, N., & Conway, M. (1993). Affective causes and consequences of social information processing. In R. S. Wyer & T. K. Srull (Eds.), *Handbook of social cognition* (2nd ed.). Hilldsale, NJ: Erlbaum.

Cohen, D. (1998). Culture, social organization, and patterns of violence. *Journal of Personality and Social Psychology, 75,* 408–419.

Cohen, D., & Nisbett, R. E. (1994). Self-protection and the culture of honor: Explaining southern violence. *Personality and Social Psychology Bulletin, 20,* 551–567.

Cohen, D., & Nisbett, R. E. (1997). Field experiments examining the culture of honor: The role of institutions in perpetuating norms about violence. *Personality and Social Psychology Bulletin, 23,* 1188–1199.

Cohen, D., Nisbett, R. E., Bowdle, B. F., & Schwarz, N. (1996). Insult, aggression, and the Southern culture of honor: An "experimental ethnography." *Journal of Personality and Social Psychology, 70,* 945–960.

Cohen, S. (1996). Psychological stress, immunity, and upper respiratory infections. *Current Directions in Psychological Science, 5,* 86–90.

Cohen, S., Tyrrell, D. A. J., & Smith, A. P. (1993). Negative life events, perceived stress, negative affect, and susceptibility to the common cold. *Journal of Personality and Social Psychology, 64,* 131–140.

Cohen, S., Nisbett, R. E., Bowdle, B. F., & Schwarz, N. (1996). Insult, aggression, and the Southern culture of honor: An "experimental ethnography." *Journal of Personality and Social Psychology, 70,* 945–960.

Cohen, S., Kaplan, J. R., Cunnick, J. E., Manuck, S. B., & Rabin, B. S. (1992). Chronic social stress, affiliation, and cellular immune response in non-human primates. *Psychological Science, 3,* 301–304.

Cohn, E. G., & Rotton, J. (1997). Assault as a function of time and temperature: A moderator-variable time-series analysis. *Journal of Personality and Social Psychology, 72,* 1322–1334.

Coie, J. D., & Cillessen, H. N. (1993). Peer rejection: Origins and effects on children's development. *Current Directions in Psychological Science, 2,* 89–92.

Cole, T., & Bradac, J. J. (1996). A lay theory of relational satisfaction with best friends. *Journal of Social and Personal Relationships, 13,* 57–83.

Coleman, B. C. (1998, February 23). Female doctors face high harassment rate. Associated Press.

Coles, R. (1997). *The moral intelligence of children.* New York: Random House.

Collins, M. A., & Zebrowitz, L. A. (1995). The contributions of appearance to occupational outcomes in civilian and military settings. *Journal of Applied Social Psychology, 25,* 129–163.

Collins, N. L. (1996). Working models of attachment: Implications for explanation, emotion, and behavior. *Journal of Personality and Social Psychology, 71,* 810–832.

Collins, N. L., Dunkel-Schetter, C., Lobel, M., & Scrimshaw, S. C. M. (1993). Social support in pregnancy: Psychosocial correlates of birth outcomes and postpartum depression. *Journal of Personality and Social Psychology, 65,* 1243–1258.

Colvin, C. R., Block, J., & Funder, D. C. (1995). Overly positive self-evaluations and personality: Negative implications for mental health. *Journal of Personality and Social Psychology, 68,* 1152–1162.

Compas, B. E., Banez, G. A., Malcarne, V., & Worsham, N. (1991). Perceived control and coping with stress: A developmental perspective. *Journal of Social Issues, 47*(4), 23–34.

Computer survey reveals teenage males flirt with greater dangers. (1998, May 8). Associated Press.

Condon, J. W., & Crano, W. D. (1988). Inferred evaluation and the relation between attitude similarity and interpersonal attraction. *Journal of Personality and Social Psychology, 54,* 789–797.

Conger, J. A. (1991). Inspiring others: The language of leadership. *Academy of Management Executive, 5*(1), 31–45.

Connolly, J. A., & Johnson, A. M. (1996). Adolescents' romantic relationships and the structure and quality of their close interpersonal ties. *Personal Relationships, 3,* 185–195.

Constantian, C. (1981). *Solitude, attitudes, beliefs, and behavior in regard to spending time alone.* Unpublished doctoral dissertation, Harvard University.

Contrada, R. J. (1989). Type A behavior, personality hardiness, and cardiovascular responses to stress. *Journal of Personality and Social Psychology, 57,* 895–903.

Conway, M., & Ross, M. (1984). Getting what you want by revising what you had. *Journal of Personality and Social Psychology, 47,* 738–748.

Conway, M., Giannopoulos, C., Csank, P., & Mendelson, M. (1993). Dysphoria and specificity in self-focused attention. *Personality and Social Psychology Bulletin, 19,* 265–268.

Cook, S. W., & Pelfrey, M. (1985). Reactions to being helped in cooperating interracial groups: A context effect. *Journal of Personality and Social Psychology, 49,* 1231–1245.

Cooke, P. (1992). Noises out: What it's doing to you. *New York, 25*(4), 28–33.

Coontz, S. (1992). *The way we never were: American families and the nostalgia trap.* New York: Basic Books.

Cooper, J., & Scher, S. J. (1994). Actions and attitudes: The role of responsibility and aversive consequences in persuasion. In T. Brock & S. Shavitt (Eds.), *Persuasion* (pp. 95–111). San Francisco: Freeman.

Cooper, J., Fazio, R. H., & Rhodewalt, F. (1978). Dissonance and humor: Evidence for the undifferentiated nature of dissonance arousal. *Journal of Personality and Social Psychology, 36,* 280–285.

Cooper, J., Hall, J., & Huff, C. (1990). Situational stress as a consequence of sex-stereotyped software. *Personality and Social Psychology Bulletin, 16,* 419–429.

Cooper, M. L., Shaver, P. R., & Collins, N. L. (1998). Attachment styles, emotion regulation, and adjustment in adolescence. *Journal of Personality and Social Psychology, 74,* 1380–1397.

Cooper, M. L., Frone, M. R., Russell, M., & Mudar, P. (1995). Drinking to regulate positive and negative emotions: A motivational model of alcohol use. *Journal of Personality and Social Psychology, 69,* 990–1005.

Copeland, C. L., Driskell, J. E., & Salas, E. (1995). Gender and reactions to dominance. *Journal of Social Behavior and Personality, 10,* 53–68.

Costa, P. T., Jr., & McCrae, R. R. (1992). *Professional manual for the Revised NEO Personality Inventory and NEO Five-Factor Inventory.* Odessa, FL: Psychological Assessment Resources.

Cota, A. A., Evans, C. R., Dion, K. L., Kilik, L., & Longman, R. S. (1995). The structure of group cohesion. *Personality and Social Psychology Bulletin, 21,* 572–580.

Cottrell, N. B., Wack, K. L., Sekerak, G. J., & Rittle, R. (1968). Social facilitation of dominant responses by the presence of an audience and the mere presence of others. *Journal of Personality and Social Psychology, 9,* 245–250.

Courneya, K. S., & McAuley, E. (1993). Efficacy, attributional, and affective responses of older adults following an acute bout of exercise. *Journal of Social Behavior and Personality, 8,* 729–742.

Cowan, G., & Curtis, S. R. (1994). Predictors of rape occurrence and victim blame in the William Kennedy Smith case. *Journal of Applied Social Psychology, 24,* 12–20.

Cox, M., & Tanford, S. (1989). Effects of evidence and instructions in civil trials: An experimental investigation of rules of admissibility. *Social Behavior, 4,* 31–55.

Cozzarelli, C., Sumer, N., & Major, B. (1998). Mental models of attachment and coping with abortion. *Journal of Personality and Social Psychology, 74,* 453–467.

Craig, J.-A., Koestner, R., & Zuroff, D. C. (1994). Implicit and self-attributed intimacy motivation. *Journal of Social and Personal Relationships, 11,* 491–507.

Cramer, R. E., McMaster, M. R., Bartell, P. A., & Dragma, M. (1988). Subject competence and minimization of the bystander effect. *Journal of Applied Social Psychology, 18,* 1133–1148.

Crandall, C. S. (1988). Social contagion of binge eating. *Journal of Personality and Social Psychology, 55,* 588–598.

Crandall, C. S. (1994). Prejudice against fat people: Ideology and self-interest. *Journal of Personality and Social Psychology, 66,* 882–894.

Crandall, C. S. (1995). Do parents discriminate against their heavyweight daughters? *Personality and Social Psychology Bulletin, 21,* 724–735.

Crandall, C. S., & Martinez, R. (1996). Culture, ideology, and anti-fat attitudes. *Personality and Social Psychology Bulletin, 22,* 1165–1176.

Crano, W. D. (1995). Attitude strength and vested interest. In R. E. Petty & J. A. Krosnick (Eds.), *Attitude strength: Antecedents and consequences* (Vol. 4, pp. 131–157). Hillsdale, NJ: Erlbaum.

Crano, W. D. (1997). Vested interest, symbolic politics, and attitude–behavior consistency. *Journal of Personality and Social Psychology, 72,* 485–491.

Crano, W. D., & Prislin, R. (1995). Components of vested interest and attitude–behavior consistency. *Basic and Applied Social Psychology, 17,* 1–21.

Crawford, M. T., & Skowronski, J. J. (1998). When motivated thought leads to heightened bias: High need for cognition can enhance the impact of stereotypes on memory. *Personality and Social Psychology Bulletin, 24,* 1075–1088.

Crealia, R., & Tesser, A. (1996). Attitude heritability and attitude reinforcement: A replication. *Personality and Individual Differences, 21,* 803–808.

Crocker, J. (1993). Memory for information about others: Effects of self-esteem and performance feedback. *Journal of Research in Personality, 27,* 35–48.

Crocker, J., & Major, B. (1993). *When bad things happen to bad people: The perceived justifiability of negative outcomes based on stigma.* Manuscript submitted for publication.

Crocker, J., Cornwell, B., & Major, B. (1993). The stigma of overweight: Affective consequences of attributional ambiguity. *Journal of Personality and Social Psychology, 64,* 60–70.

Croizet, J. C., & Claire, T. (1998). Extending the concept of stereotype threat to social class: The intellectual underperformance of students from low socioeconomic backgrounds. *Personality and Social Psychology Bulletin, 24,* 588–594.

Cropanzano, R. (Ed.). (1993). *Justice in the workplace* (pp. 79–103). Hillsdale, NJ: Erlbaum.

Cropanzano, R., & James, K. (1990). Some methodological considerations for the behavioral–genetic analysis of work attitudes. *Journal of Applied Psychology, 71,* 433–439.

Crumm, D. (1998, December 11). Keeping the faith may keep mind, body going. Knight Ridder.

Crusco, A. H., & Wetzel, C. G. (1984). The Midas touch: The effects of interpersonal touch on restaurant tipping. *Personality and Social Psychology Bulletin, 10,* 512–517.

Crutchfield, R. A. (1955). Conformity and character. *American Psychologist, 10,* 191–198.

Csikszentmihalyi, M. (1993). Relax? Relax and do what? *New York Times,* p. A25.

Culbertson, F. M. (1997). Depression and gender: An international review. *American Psychologist, 52,* 25–31.

Cunningham, J. D., & Antill, J. K. (1994). Cohabitation and marriage: Retrospective and predictive comparisons. *Journal of Social and Personal Relationships, 11,* 77–93.

Cunningham, M. R. (1979). Weather, mood, and helping behavior: Quasi-experiments with the sunshine Samaritan. *Journal of Personality and Social Psychology, 37,* 1947–1956.

Cunningham, M. R. (1986). Measuring the physical in physical attractiveness: Quasi-experiments on the sociobiology of female facial beauty. *Journal of Personality and Social Psychology, 50,* 925–935.

Cunningham, M. R. (1988). Does happiness mean friendliness? Induced mood and heterosexual self-disclosure. *Personality and Social Psychology Bulletin, 14,* 283–297.

Cunningham, M. R. (1989). Reactions to heterosexual opening gambits: Female selectivity and male responsiveness. *Personality and Social Psychology Bulletin, 15,* 27–41.

Cunningham, M. R., Roberts, A. R., Wu, C.-H., Barbee, A. P., & Druen, P. B. (1995). "Their ideas of beauty are, on the whole, the same as ours": Consistency and variability in the cross-cultural perception of female physical attractiveness. *Journal of Personality and Social Psychology, 68,* 261–279.

Cunningham, M. R., Shaffer, D. R., Barbee, A. P., Wolff, P. L., & Kelley, D. J. (1990). Separate processes in the relation of elation and depression to helping: Social versus personal concerns. *Journal of Experimental Social Psychology, 26,* 13–33.

Cutler, B. L., Maran, G., & Narby, D. J. (1992). Jury selection in insanity defense cases. *Journal of Research in Personality, 26,* 165–182.

Cutler, B. L., Penrod, S. D., & Martens, T. K. (1987). Improving the reliability of eyewitness identification: Putting content into context. *Journal of Applied Psychology, 72,* 629–637.

Cutrona, C. E., Cole, V., Colangelo, N., Assouline, S. G., & Russell, D. W. (1994). Perceived parental social support and academic achievement: An attachment theory perspective. *Journal of Personality and Social Psychology, 66,* 369–378.

da Gloria, J., Pahlavan, F., Duda, D., & Bonnet, P. (1994). Evidence for a motor mechniasm of pain-induced aggression instigation in humans. *Aggressive Behavior, 20,* 1–7.

Dabbs, J. M., Jr. (1992). Testosterone measurements in social and clinical psychology. *Journal of Social and Clinical Psychology, 11,* 302–321.

Dabbs, J. M., Jr. (1993). Salivary testosterone measurements in behavioral studies. In D. Malamud & L. A. Tabak (Eds.), *Saliva as a diagnostic fluid* (pp. 177–183). New York: New York Academy of Sciences.

Dabbs, J. M., Alford, E. C., & Fielden, J. A. (1998). Trial lawyers and testosterone: Blue-collar talent in a white-collar world. *Journal of Applied Social Psychology, 28,* 84–94.

Damasio, A. R. (1994). *Descartes' error: Emotion, reason and the human brain.* New York: Putnam.

Dana, E. R., Lalwani, N., & Duval, S. (1997). Objective self-awareness and focus of attention following awareness of self-standard discrepancies: Changing self or changing standards of correctness. *Journal of Social and Clinical Psychology, 16,* 359–380.

Dane, F. C. (1992). Applying social psychology in the courtroom: Understanding stereotypes in jury decision making. *Contemporary Social Psychology, 16,* 33–36.

Darden, C. (1997, February 17). Justice is in the color of the beholder. *Time,* 38–39.

Darley, J. M. (1991). Altruism and prosocial behavior research: Reflections and prospects. In M. S. Clark (Ed.), *Prosocial behavior* (pp. 312–327). Newbury Park, CA: Sage.

Darley, J. M. (1993). Research on morality: Possible approaches, actual approaches. *Psychological Science, 4,* 353–357.

Darley, J. M. (1995). Constructive and destructive obedience: A taxonomy of principal-agent relationships. *Journal of Social Issues, 125,* 125–154.

Darley, J. M., & Batson, C. D. (1973). From Jerusalem to Jericho: A study of situational dispositional variables in helping behavior. *Journal of Personality and Social Psychology, 27,* 100–108.

Darley, J. M., & Latané, B. (1968). Bystander intervention in emergencies: Diffusion of responsibility. *Journal of Personality and Social Psychology, 8,* 377–383.

Darwin, C. (1871). The descent of man. London: J. Murray.

Daubman, K. A. (1993). *The self-threat of receiving help: A comparison of the threat-to-self-esteem model and the theat-to-interpersonal-power model.* Unpublished manuscript, Gettysburg College, Gettysburg, PA.

Daubman, K. A. (1995). Help which implies dependence: Effects on self-evaluations, motivation, and performance. *Journal of Social Behavior and Personality, 10,* 677–692.

Davie, M. R., & Reeves, R. J. (1939). Propinquity of residence before marriage. *American Journal of Sociology, 44,* 510–517.

Davies, M. F. (1996). Self-consciousness and the complexity of private and public aspects of identity. *Social Behavior and Personality, 24,* 113–118.

Davila, J., Burge, D., & Hammen, C. (1997). Why does attachment style change? *Journal of Personality and Social Psychology, 73,* 826–838.

Davila, J., Bradbury, T. N., & Fincham, F. (1998). Negative affectivity as a mediator of the association between adult attachment and marital satisfaction. *Personal Relationships, 5,* 467–484.

Davis, C., Brewer, H., & Weinstein, M. (1993). A study of appearance anxiety in young men. *Social Behavior and Personality, 21,* 63–74.

Davis, C. G., Lehman, D. R., Wortman, C. B., Silver, R. C., & Thompson, S. C. (1995). The undoing of traumatic life events. *Personality and Social Psychology Bulletin, 21,* 109–124.

Davis, J. H. (1989). Psychology and the law: The last 15 years. *Journal of Applied Social Psychology, 19,* 119–230.

Davis, M. H., Luce, C., & Kraus, S. J. (1994). The heritability of characteristics associated with dispositional empathy. *Journal of Personality, 62,* 369–391.

Davis, M. H., Morris, M. M., & Kraus, L. A. (1998). Relationship-specific and global perceptions of social support: Associations with well-being and attachment. *Journal of Personality and Social Psychology, 74,* 468–481.

Davis, S. F., Miller, K. M., Johnson, D., McAuley, K., & Dinges, D. (1992). The relationship between optimism–pessimism, loneliness, and death anxiety. *Bulletin of the Psychonomic Society, 30,* 135–136.

Day, J. D., Borkowski, J. G., Punzo, D., & Howsepian, B. (1994). Enhancing possible selves in Mexican American students. *Motivation and Emotion, 18,* 79–103.

DeDreu, C. K. W., & McCusker, C. (1997). Gain–loss frames and cooperation in two-person social dilemmas: A transformational analysis. *Journal of Personality and Social Psychology, 72,* 1093–1106.

DeDreu, C. K. W., & Van Lange, P. A. M. (1995). Impact of social value orientation on negotiator cognition and behavior. *Personality and Social Psychology Bulletin, 21,* 1178–1188.

De La Ronde, C., & Swann, W. B., Jr. (1998). Partner verification: Restoring shattered images of our intimates. *Journal of Personality and Social Psychology, 75,* 374–382.

De Vries, H., Backbier, E., Kok, G., & Dijkstra, M. (1995). The impact of social influences in the context of attitude, self-efficacy, intention, and previous behavior as predictors of smoking onset. *Journal of Applied Social Psychology, 25,* 237–257.

de Waal, F. (1996). *Good natured: The origins of right and wrong in humans and other animals.* Cambridge, MA: Harvard University Press.

de Weerth, C., & Kalma, A. P. (1993). Female aggression as a response to sexual jealousy: A sex role reversal? *Aggressive Behavior, 19,* 265–279.

DeBono, K. G., & Krim, S. (1997). Compliments and perceptions of product quality: An individual difference perspective. *Journal of Applied Social Psychology, 27,* 1359–1367.

DeBono, K. G., & Packer, M. (1991). The effects of advertising appeal on perceptions of product quality. *Personality and Social Psychology Bulletin, 17,* 194–200.

DeBono, K. G., & Snyder, M. (1995). Acting on one's attitudes: The role of a history of choosing situations. *Personality and Social Psychology Bulletin, 21,* 629–636.

DeJong, W., & Musilli, L. (1982). External pressure to comply: Handicapped versus nonhandicapped requesters and the foot-in-the-door phenomenon. *Personality and Social Psychology Bulletin, 8,* 522–527.

DeLamater, J. (1981). The social control of sexuality. *Annual Review of Sociology, 7,* 263–290.

DeMare, C. (1998, May 28). Traffic Safety Division jobs a ticket to romance. Albany *Times Union,* p. B1.

den Ouden, M. D., & Russell, G. W. (1997). Sympathy and altruism in response to disasters: A Dutch and Canadian comparison. *Social Behavior and Personality, 25,* 241–248.

DePaulo, B. M. (1992). Nonverbal behavior and self-presentation. *Psychological Bulletin, 111,* 203–243.

DePaulo, B. M., & Bell, K. L. (1996). Truth and investment: Lies are told to those who care. *Journal of Personality and Social Psychology, 71,* 703–716.

DePaulo, B. M., & Fisher, J. D. (1980). The costs of asking for help. *Basic and Applied Social Psychology, 1,* 23–35.

DePaulo, B. M., & Kashy, D. A. (1998). Everyday lies in close and casual relationships. *Journal of Personality and Social Psychology, 74,* 63–79.

DePaulo, B. M., Brown, P. L., Ishii, S., & Fisher, J. D. (1981). Help that works: The effects of aid on subsequent task performance. *Journal of Personality and Social Psychology, 41,* 478–487.

DePaulo, B. M., Dull, W. R., Greenberg, J. M., & Swaim, G. W. (1989). Are shy people reluctant to ask for help? *Journal of Personality and Social Psychology, 56,* 834–844.

DePaulo, B. M., Kashy, D. A., Kirkendol., S. E., Wyer, M. M., & Epstein, J. A. (1996). Lying in everyday life. *Journal of Personality and Social Psychology, 70,* 979–995.

Dean-Church, L., & Gilroy, F. D. (1993). Relation of sex-role orientation to life satisfaction in a healthy elderly sample. *Journal of Social Behavior and Personality, 8,* 133–140.

Deaux, K. (1993a). Reconstructing social identity. *Personality and Social Psychology Bulletin, 19,* 4–12.

Deaux, K. (1993b). Commentary: Sorry, wrong number—A reply to Gentile's call. *Psychological Science, 4,* 125–126.

Deaux, K., & Hanna, R. (1984). Courtship in the personals column: The influence of gender and sexual orientation. *Sex Roles, 11,* 363–375.

Deaux, K., Reid, A., Mizrahi, K., & Ethier, K. A. (1995). Parameters of social identity. *Journal of Personality and Social Psychology, 68,* 280–291.

Denes-Raj, V., & Epstein, S. (1994). Conflict between intuitive and rational processing: When people behave against their better judgment. *Personality and Social Psychology Bulletin, 66,* 819–829.

Dengerink, H. A., Schnedler, R. W., & Covey, M. K. (1978). Role of avoidance in aggressive responses to attack and no attack. *Journal of Personality and Social Psychology, 36,* 1044–1053.

Desmarais, S., & Curtis, J. (1997). Gender and perceived pay entitlement: Testing for effects of experience with income. *Journal of Personality and Social Psychology, 72,* 141–150.

Deutsch, M., & Krauss, R. M. (1960). The effect of threat upon interpersonal bargaining. *Journal of Abnormal and Social Psychology, 61,* 181–189.

Deutsch, F. M., & Lamberti, D. M. (1986). Does social approval increase helping? *Personality and Social Psychology Bulletin, 12,* 149–157.

Deutsch, F. M., Zalenski, C. M., & Clark, M. E. (1986). Is there a double standard of aging? *Journal of Applied Social Psychology, 16,* 771–785.

Deutsch, M., & Gerard, H. B. (1955). A study of normative and informational social influences upon individual judgment. *Journal of Abnormal and Social Psychology, 51,* 629–636.

Dexter, H. R., Cutler, B. L., & Moran, G. (1992). A test of voir dire as a remedy for the prejudicial effects of pretrial publicity. *Journal of Applied Social Psychology, 22,* 819–832.

Diamond, J. (1993). What are men good for? *Natural History, 102*(5), 26–29.

Diehl, M., Elnick, A. B., Bourbeau, L. S., & Labouvie-Vief, G. (1998). Adult attachment styles: Their relations to family context and personality. *Journal of Personality and Social Psychology, 74,* 1656–1669.

Diekmann, K. A., Samuels, S. M., Ross, L., & Bazerman, M. H. (1997). Self-interest and fairness in problems of response allocation: Allocators versus recipients. *Journal of Personality and Social Psychology, 72,* 1061–1074.

Diener, E., Wolsic, B., & Fujita, F. (1995). Physical attractiveness and subjective well-being. *Journal of Personality and Social Psychology, 69,* 120–129.

Dijkstra, P., & Buunk, B. P. (1998). Jealousy as a function of rival characteristics: An evolutionary perspective. *Personality and Social Psychology Bulletin, 24,* 1158–1166.

Dineen, T. (1998). Sacred cows and straw men. *American Psychologist, 53,* 487–488.

Dion, K. L., & Dion, K. K. (1987). Belief in a just world and physical attractiveness stereotyping. *Journal of Personality and Social Psychology, 52,* 775–780.

Dion, K. K., & Dion, K. L. (1991). Psychological individualism and romantic love. *Journal of Social Behavior and Personality, 6,* 17–33.

Dion, K. K., & Dion, K. L. (1993). Individualistic and collectivistic perspectives on gender and the cultural context of love and intimacy. *Journal of Social Issues, 49*(3), 53–69.

Dion, K. K., Berscheid, E., & Hatfield (Walster), E. (1972). What is beautiful is good. *Journal of Personality and Social Psychology, 24,* 285–290.

Dion, K. L., Dion, K. K., & Keelan, J. P. (1990). Appearance anxiety as a dimension of social-evaluative anxiety: Exploring the ugly duckling syndrome. *Contemporary Social Psychology, 14,* 220–224.

Dion, K. K., Pak, A. W.-P., & Dion, K. I. (1990). Stereotyping physical attractiveness: A sociocultural perspective. *Journal of Cross Cultural Psychology, 21,* 158–179.

Dixon, T. M., & Baumeister, R. F. (1991). Escaping the self: The moderating effect of self-complexity. *Personality and Social Psychology Bulletin, 17,* 363–368.

Dodge, K. A., & Coie, J. D. (1987). Social-information-processing factors in reactive and proactive aggression in children's peer groups. *Journal of Personality and Social Psychology, 53,* 1146–1158.

Dodge, K.A., Pettit, G. S., McClaskey, C. L., & Brown, M. M. (1986). Social competence in children. *Monographs of the Society for Research in Child Development, 51*(2), 1–85.

Dodge, K. A., Price, J. M., Bachorowski, J. A., & Newman, J. P. (1990). Hostile attributional biases in severely aggressive adolescents. *Journal of Abnormal Psychology, 99,* 385–392.

Dodgson, P. G., & Wood, J. V. (1998). Self-esteem and the cognitive accessibility of strengths and weaknesses after failure. *Journal of Personality and Social Psychology, 75,* 178–197.

Doherty, K., Weigold, M. F., & Schlenker, B. R. (1990). Self-serving interpretations of motives. *Personality and Social Psychology Bulletin, 16,* 485–495.

Dollard, J., Doob, L., Miller, N., Mowerer, O. H., & Sears, R. R. (1939). *Frustration and aggression.* New Haven, CT: Yale University Press.

Donnerstein, E., & Donnerstein, M. (1976). Research in the control of interracial aggression. In R. G. Geen & E. C. O'Neal (Eds.), *Perspectives on aggression.* New York: Academic Press.

Dorian, B. J., Keystone, E., Garfinkel, P. E., & Brown, J. M. (1982). Aberrations in lymphocyte subpopulations and function during psychological stress. *Clinical and Experimental Immunology, 50,* 132–138.

Dovidio, J. F., & Gaertner, S. L. (1993). Stereotype and evaluative intergroup bias. In D. M. Mackie & D. L. Hamilton (Eds.), *Affect, cognition, and stereotyping: Interactive processes in group perception.* Orlando, FL: Academic Press.

Dovidio, J. F., & Morris, W. N. (1975). Effects of stress and commonality of fate on helping behavior. *Journal of Personality and Social Psychology, 31,* 145–149.

Dovidio, J. F., Brigham, J., Johnson, B. & Garerner, S. (1996). Stereotyping, prejudice, and discrimination: Another look. In N. Macrae, C. Stangor, & M. Hwestone (Eds.), *Stereotypes and stereotyping* (pp. 1276–1319). New York: Guilford.

Dovidio, J. F., Evans, N., & Tyler, R. B. (1986). Racial stereotypes: The contents of their cognitive representations. *Journal of Experimental Social Psychology, 22,* 22–37.

Dovidio, J. F., Gaertner, S. L., Isen, A. M., & Lowrance, R. (1995). Group representations and intergroup bias: Positive affect, similarity, and group size. *Personality and Social Psychology Bulletin, 21,* 856–865.

Downey, G., & Feldman, S. I. (1996). Implications of rejection sensitivity for intimate relationships. *Journal of Personality and Social Psychology, 70,* 1327–1343.

Downey, J. L., & Damhave, K. W. (1991). The effects of place, type of comment, and effort expended on the perception of flirtation. *Journal of Social Behavior and Personality, 6,* 35–43.

Downs, A. C., & Lyons, P. M. (1991). Natural observations of the links between attractiveness and initial legal judgments. *Personality and Social Psychology Bulletin, 17,* 541–547.

Drachman, D., DeCarufel, A., & Insko, C. A. (1978). The extra credit effect in interpersonal attraction. *Journal of Experimental Social Psychology, 14,* 458–465.

Drigotas, S. M., & Rusbult, C. E. (1992). Should I stay or should I go? A dependence model of breakups. *Journal of Personality and Social Psychology, 62,* 62–87.

Drigotas, S. M., Whitney, G. A., & Rusbult, C. E. (1995). On the peculiarities of loyalty: A diary study of responses to dissatisfaction in everyday life. *Personality and Social Psychology Bulletin, 21,* 596–609.

Driscoll, R., Davis, K. E., & Lipetz, M. E. (1972). Parental interference and romantic love: The Romeo and Juliet effect. *Journal of Personality and Social Psychology, 24,* 1–10.

Drivers indifferent to victim on road. (1998, April 22). *Washington Post.*

Drory, A., & Romm, T. (1990). The definition of organizational politics: A review. *Human Relations, 43,* 1133–1154.

Drout, C. E., & Gaertner, S. L. (1994). Gender differences in reactions to female victims. *Social Behavior and Personality, 22,* 267–278.

DuBreuil, S. C., Garry, M., & Loftus, E. F. (1998). Tales from the crib. In S. J. Lynn & K. M. McConkey (Eds.), *Truth in memory.* New York: Guilford.

Duck, J. M., Terry, D. J., & Hogg, M. A. (1998). Perceptions of a media campaign: The role of social identity and the changing intergroup context. *Personality and Social Psychology Bulletin, 24,* 3–16.

Duck, S., & Barnes, M. K. (1992). Disagreeing about agreement: Reconciling differences about similarity. *Communication Monographs, 59,* 199–208.

Duck, S., Pond, K., & Leatham, G. (1994). Loneliness and the evaluation of relational events. *Journal of Social and Personal Relationships, 11,* 253–276.

Duggan, E. S., & Brennan, K. A. (1994). Social avoidance and its relation to Bartholomew's adult attachment typology. *Journal of Social and Personal Relationships, 11,* 147–153.

Duncan, L. E., Peterson, B. E., & Winter, D. G. (1997). Authoritarianism and gender roles: Toward a psychological analysis of hegemonic relationships. *Personality and Social Psychology Bulletin, 23,* 41–49.

Dunn, J. (1992). Siblings and development. *Current Directions in Psychological Science, 1,* 6–11.

Dunne, M. P., Martin, N. G., Statham, D. J., Slutske, W. S., Dinwiddie, S. H., Bucholz, K. K., Madden, P. A. F., & Heath, A. C. (1997). Genetic and environmental contributions to variance in age at first sexual intercourse. *Psychological Science, 8,* 211–216.

Dunning, D. (1995). Trait importance and modifiability as factors influencing self-assessment and self-enhancement motives. *Personality and Social Psychology Bulletin, 21,* 1297–1306.

Dunning, D., & Sherman, D. A. (1997). Stereotypes and tacit inference. *Journal of Personality and Social Psychology, 73,* 459–471.

Dunning, D., & Stern, L. B. (1994). Distinguishing accurate from inaccurate eyewitness identification via inquiries about decision processes. *Journal of Personality and Social Psychology, 67,* 818–835.

Duran, R. L., & Prusank, D. T. (1997). Relational themes in men's and women's popular nonfiction magazine articles. *Journal of Social and Personal Relationships, 14,* 165–189.

Dutton, D. G., & Aron, A. P. (1974). Some evidence for heightened sexual attraction under conditions of high anxiety. *Journal of Personality and Social Psychology, 30,* 510–517.

Dutton, D. G., & Lake, R. A. (1973). Threat of own prejudice and reverse discrimination in interracial situations. *Journal of Personality and Social Psychology, 28,* 94–100.

Dutton, K. A., & Brown, J. D. (1997). Global self-esteem and specific self-views as determinants of people's reactions to success and failure. *Journal of Personality and Social Psychology, 73,* 139–148.

Dykema, J., Bergbower, K., & Peterson, C. (1995). Pessimistic explanatory style, stress, and illness. *Journal of Social and Clinical Psychology, 14,* 357–371.

Eagly, A. H. (1995). The science and politics of comparing women and men. *American Psychologist, 50,* 145–158.

Eagly, A. H., & Chaiken, S. (1998). Attitude structure and function. In G. Lindsey, S. T., Fiske, & D. T. Gilbert (Eds.), *Handbook of social psychology* (4th ed.). New York: Oxford University Press and McGraw-Hill.

Eagly, A. H., & Steffen, V. J. (1986). Gender and aggressive behavior: A meta-analytic review of the social psychological literature. *Psychological Bulletin, 100,* 309–330.

Eagly, A. H., Makhijani, M. G., & Klonsky, B. G. (1992). Gender and the evaluation of leaders: A meta-analysis. *Psychological Bulletin, 111,* 3–22.

Eagly, A. H., Wood, W., & Chaiken, S. (1996). Principles of persuasion. In E. T. Higgins & A. W. Kruglanski (Eds.), *Social psychology: Handbook of basic principles* (pp. 702–742). New York: Guilford.

Earley, P. C. (1993). East meets West meets Mideast: Further explorations of collectivistic and individualistic work groups. *Academy of Management Journal, 36,* 319–348.

Easterbrook, G. (1999, January 4 and 11). America the O.K. *The New Republic,* pp. 19–25.

Edwards, K., & Bryan, T. S. (1997). Judgmental biases produced by instructions to disregard: The (paradoxical) case of emotional information. *Personality and Social Psychology Bulletin, 23,* 849–864.

Edwards, K., Heindel, W., & Louis-Dreyfus, E. (1996). *Directed forgetting of emotional and non-emotional words: Implications for implicit and explicit memory processes.* Manuscript submitted for publication.

Edwards, T. M. (1998, July 13). The opposite of sex. *Time,* 39.

Egbert, J. M. Jr., Moore, C. H., Wuensch, K. L., & Castellow, W. A. (1992). The effect of litigant social desirability on judgments regarding a sexual harassment case. *Journal of Social Behavior and Personality, 7,* 569–579.

Ehrhardt, A. A., Yingling, S., & Warne, P. A. (1991). Sexual behavior in the era of AIDS: What has changed in the United States? *Annual Review of Sex Research, 2,* 25–47.

Eisenman, R. (1985). Marijuana use and attraction: Support for Byrne's similarity-attraction concept. *Perceptual and Motor Skills, 61,* 582.

Eisenstadt, D., & Leipe, M. R. (1994). The self-comparison process and self-discrepant feedback: Consequences of learning you are what you thought you were not. *Journal of Personality and Social Psychology, 67,* 611–626.

Ekman, P., & Friesen, W. V. (1975). *Unmasking the face.* Englewood Cliffs, NJ: Prentice-Hall.

Ekman, P., & Heider, K. (1988). The universality of a contempt expression: A replication. *Motivation and Emotion, 12,* 303–308.

Elkin, R., & Leippe, M. (1986). Physiological arousal, dissonance, and attitude change: Evidence for a dissonance–arousal link and "don't remind me" effect. *Journal of Personality and Social Psychology, 51,* 55–65.

Ellemers, N., Wilke, H., & van Knippenberg, A. (1993). Effects of the legitimacy of low group or individual status on individual and collective status-enhancement strategies. *Journal of Personality and Social Psychology, 64,* 766–778.

Elliot, A. J., & Devine, P. G. (1994). On the motivational nature of cognitive dissonance. Dissonance as psychological discomfort. *Journal of Personality and Social Psychology, 67,* 382–394.

Elliot, A. J., & Sheldon, K. M. (1998). Avoidance personal goals and the personality-illness relationship. *Journal of Personality and Social Psychology, 75,* 1282–1299.

Ellison, C. G. (1991). An eye for an eye? A note on the Southern subculture of violence thesis. *Social Forces, 69,* 1223–1239.

Ellsworth, P. C., & Carlsmith, J. M. (1973). Eye contact and gaze aversion in aggressive encounter. *Journal of Personality and Social Psychology, 33,* 117–122.

Emery, R. E. (1989). Family violence. *American Psychologist, 434,* 321–328.

Emmons, R. A., & Colby, P. M. (1995). Emotional conflict and well-being: Relation to perceived availability, daily utilization, and observer reports of social support. *Journal of Personality and Social Psychology, 68,* 947–959.

Enright, D. J., & Rawlinson, D. (1993). *Friendship.* Oxford, England: Oxford University Press.

Epley, N., & Huff, C. (1998). Suspicion, affective response, and educational benefit as a result of deception in psychology research. *Personality and Social Psychology Bulletin, 24,* 759–768.

Epstein S. (in press). An integration of the cognitive and psychodynamic unconscious. *American Psychologist.*

Erber, R. (1991). Affective and semantic priming: Effects of mood on category accessibility and inference. *Journal of Experimental Social Psychology, 27,* 480–498.

Esses, V. M. (1989). Mood as a moderator of acceptance of interpersonal feedback. *Journal of Personality and Social Psychology, 57,* 769–781.

Estrada, C. A., Isen, A. M., & Young, M. J. (1995). Positive affect improves creative problem solving and influences reported source of practice satisfaction in physicians. *Motivation and Emotion, 18,* 285–300.

Ethier, K. A., & Deaux, K. (1994). Negotiating social identity when contexts change: Maintaining identification and responding to threat. *Journal of Personality and Social Psychology, 67,* 243–251.

Evans, G. W., Bullinger, M., & Hygge, S. (1998). Chronic noise exposure and physiological response: A prospective study of children living under environmental stress. *Psychological Science, 9,* 75–77.

Evans, G. W., Lepore, S. J., & Schroeder, A. (1996). The role of interior design elements in human responses to crowding. *Journal of Personality and Social Psychology, 70,* 41–46.

Exline, R. (1962). Need affiliation and initial communication behavior in problem-solving groups characterized by low interpersonal visibility. *Psychological Reports, 10,* 79–89.

Fabes, R. A., & Eisenberg, N. (1997). Regulatory control and adults' stress-related responses to daily life events. *Journal of Personality and Social Psychology, 73,* 1107–1117.

Fabrigar, L. R., & Krosnick, J. A. (1995). Attitude importance and the false consensus effect. *Personality and Social Psychology Bulletin, 21,* 468–479.

Fagot, B. I., Gauvain, M., & Kavanagh, K. (1996). Infant attachment and mother–child problem-solving: A replication. *Journal of Social and Personal Relationships, 13,* 295–302.

Fajardo, D. M. (1985). Author race, essay quality, and reverse discrimination. *Journal of Applied Social Psychology, 15,* 255–268.

Fan, C., & Mak, A. S. (1998). Measuring social self-efficacy in a culturally diverse student population. *Social Behavior and Personality, 26,* 131–144.

Farnsworth, C. H. (1995, June 4). Canada puts different spin on sensational murder trial. *Albany Times Union,* pp. E-8.

Fazio, R. H. (1989). On the power and functionality of attitudes: The role of attitude accessibility. In A. R. Pratkanis, S. J. Breckler, & A. G. Greenwald (Eds.), *Attitude structure and function* (pp. 153–179). Hillsdale, NJ: Erlbaum.

Fazio, R. H., & Powell, M. C. (1997). On the value of knowing one's likes and dislikes: Attitude accessibility, stress, and health in college. *Psychological Science, 8,* 430–436.

Fazio, R. H., & Roskos-Ewoldsen, D. R. (1994). Acting as we feel: When and how attitudes guide behavior. In S. Shavitt & T. C. Brock (Eds.), *Persuasion* (pp. 71–93). Boston: Allyn and Bacon.

Feather, N. T. (1996). Reactions to penalties for an offense in relation to authoritarianism, values, perceived responsibility, perceived seriousness, and deservingness. *Journal of Personality and Social Psychology, 71,* 571–587.

Fein, S., & Spencer, S. J. (1997). Prejudice as self-image maintenance: Affirming the self through derogating others. *Journal of Personality and Social Psychology, 73,* 31–44.

Fein, S., McCloskey, A. L., & Tomlinson, T. M. (1997). Can the jury disregard that information? The use of suspicion to reduce the prejudicial effects of pretrial publicity and inadmissible testimony. *Personality and Social Psychology Bulletin, 23,* 1215–1226.

Feingold, A. (1990). Gender differences in effects of physical attractiveness on romantic attraction: A comparison across five research paradigms. *Journal of Personality and Social Psychology, 59,* 981–993.

Feingold, A. (1992a). Gender differences in mate selection preferences: A test of the parental investment model. *Psychological Bulletin, 112,* 125–139.

Feingold, A. (1992b). Good-looking people are not what we think. *Psychological Bulletin, 111,* 304–341.

Feingold, A. (1994). Gender differences in personality: A meta-analysis. *Psychological Bulletin, 116,* 412–456.

Feingold, A., & Mazzella, R. (1998). Gender differences in body image are increasing. *Psychological Science, 9,* 190–195.

Feldman, S. S., & Nash, S. C. (1984). The transition from expectancy to parenthood: Impact of the firstborn child on men and women. *Sex Roles, 11,* 61–78.

Felmlee, D. H. (1995). Fatal attractions: Affection and disaffection in intimate relationships. *Journal of Social and Personal Relationships, 12,* 295–311.

Felmlee, D. H. (1998). "Be careful what you wish for . . . ": A quantitative and qualitative investigation of "fatal attractions." *Personal Relationships, 5,* 235–253.

Fenigstein, A., & Abrams, D. (1993). Self-attention and the egocentric assumption of shared perspectives. *Journal of Experimental Social Psychology, 29,* 287–303.

Feshbach, S. (1984). The catharsis hypothesis, aggressive drive, and the reduction of aggression. *Aggressive Behavior, 10,* 91–101.

Festinger, L. (1950). Informal social communication. *Psychological Review, 57,* 271–282.

Festinger, L. (1954). A theory of social comparison processes. *Human Relations, 7,* 117–140.

Festinger, L. (1957). *A theory of cognitive dissonance.* Evanston, IL: Row, Peterson.

Festinger, L., & Carlsmith, J. M. (1959). Cognitive consequences of forced compliance. *Journal of Abnormal and Social Psychology, 58,* 203–210.

Festinger, L., Schachter, S., & Back, K. (1950). *Social pressures in informal groups: A study of a housing community.* New York: Harper.

Fichten, C. S., & Amsel, R. (1986). Trait attributions about college students with a physical disability: Circumplex analyses and methodological issues. *Journal of Applied Social Psychology, 16,* 410–427.

Fincham, F. D., & Bradbury, T. N. (1992). Assessing attributions in marriage: The relationship attribution measure. *Journal of Personality and Social Psychology, 62,* 457–468.

Fincham, F. D., & Bradbury, T. N. (1993). Marital satisfaction, depression, and attributions: A longitudinal analysis. *Journal of Personality and Social Psychology, 64,* 442–452.

Finn, J. (1986). The relationship between sex role attitudes and attitudes supporting marital violence. *Sex Roles, 14,* 235–244.

Fischer, G. J. (1986). College student attitudes toward forcible date rape: I. Cognitive predictors. *Archives of Sexual Behavior, 15,* 457–466.

Fisher, A. B. (1992, September 21). When will women get to the top? *Fortune,* pp. 44–56.

Fisher, H. (1992). *Anatomy of love.* New York: Norton.

Fisher, J. D., Nadler, A., & Whitcher-Alagna, S. (1982). Recipient reactions to aid. *Psychological Bulletin, 91,* 27–54.

Fisher, W. A., Byrne, D., & White, L. A. (1983) Emotional barriers to contraception. In D. Byrne & W. A. Fisher (Eds.), *Adolescents, sex, and contraception* (pp. 207–239). Hillsdale, NJ: Erlbaum.

Fiske, A. P. (1991). The cultural relativity of selfish individualism: Anthropological evidence that humans are inherently sociable. In M. S. Clark (Ed.), *Prosocial behavior* (pp. 176–214), Newbury Park, CA: Sage.

Fiske, S. T. (1993). Social cognition and social perception. In L. W. Porter & M. R. Rosenzweig (Eds.), *Annual Review of Psychology, 44,* 155–194.

Fiske, S. T., & Neuberg, S. L. (1990). A continuum model of impression formation, from category-based to individuating processes: Influence of information and motivation on attention and interpretation. In M. P. Zanna (Ed.), *Advances in experimental social psychology* (Vol. 23). New York: Academic Press.

Fiske, S. T., & Taylor, S. E. (1991). *Social cognition.* New York: McGraw-Hill.

Fitzgerald, J. (1996, September 11). A hero leaps from bridge into breach. Albany *Times Union,* p. B2.

Fitzgerald, L. L. (1993). Sexual harassment: Violence against women in the workplace. *American Psychologist, 48,* 1070–1076.

Flannery, D. J., Montemayor, R., Eberly, M., & Torquati, J. (1993). Unraveling the ties that bind: Affective expression and perceived conflict in parent–adolescent interactions. *Journal of Social and Interpersonal Relationships, 10,* 495–509.

Floyd, K. (1996). Brotherly love I: The experience of closeness in the fraternal dyad. *Personal Relationships, 3,* 369–385.

Foderaro, L. W. (1988, February 4). The fragrant house: An expanding market for every mood. *New York Times,* pp. C1, C10.

Folger, R., & Baron, R. A. (1996). Violence and hostility at work: A model of reactions to perceived injustice. In C. Van den Bos & E. Q. Bulato (Eds.), *Workplace violence* (pp. 51–86). Washington, DC: American Psychological Association.

Folger, R., & Baron, R. A. (1996). Violence and hostility at work: A model of reactions to perceived injustice. In G. R. VandenBos and E. Q. Bulato (Eds.), *Violence on the job: Identifying risks and developing solutions* (pp. 51–85). Washington, DC: American Psychological Association.

Folwell, A. L., Chung, L. C., Nussbaum, J. F., Bethes, L. S., & Grant, J. A. (1997). Differential accounts of closeness in older adult sibling relationships. *Journal of Social and Personal Relationships, 14,* 843–849.

Forgas, J. P. (1995a). Mood and judgment: The affect infusion model (AIM). *Psychological Bulletin, 117,* 39–66.

Forgas, J. P. (1995b). Strange couples: Mood effects on judgments and memory about prototypical and atypical targets. *Personality and Social Psychology Bulletin, 21,* 747–765.

Forgas, J. P. (1998a). Asking nicely? The effects of mood on responding to more or less polite requests. *Personality and Social Psychology Bulletin, 24,* 173–185.

Forgas, J. P. (1998b). On feeling good and getting your way: Mood effects on negotiator cognition and bargaining strategies. *Journal of Personality and Social Psychology, 74,* 565–577.

Forgas, J. P. (1998c). On being happy and mistaken: Mood effects of the fundamental attribution error. *Journal of Personality and Social Psychology, 75,* 318–331.

Forgas, J. P., & Fiedler, K. (1996). Us and them: Mood effects on intergroup discrimination. *Journal of Personality and Social Psychology, 70,* 28–40.

Forge, K. L., & Phemister, S. (1987). The effect of prosocial cartoons on preschool children. *Child Study Journal, 17,* 83–88.

Foster, C. A., Witcher, B. S., Campbell, W. K., & Green, J. D. (1998). Arousal and attraction: Evidence for automatic and controlled processes. *Journal of Personality and Social Psychology, 74,* 86–101.

Frable, D. E. S. (1993). Dimensions of marginality: Distinctions among those who are different. *Personality and Social Psychology Bulletin, 19,* 370–380.

Fraley, R. C., & Davis, K. E. (1997). Attachment formation and transfer in young adults' close friendships and romantic relationships. *Personal Relationships, 4,* 131–144.

Fraley, R. C., & Shaver, P. R. (1998). Airport separations: A naturalistic study of adult attachment dynamics in separating couples. *Journal of Personality and Social Psychology, 75,* 1198–1212.

Frank, R. A. (1996). Tainted therapy and mistaken memory: Avoiding malpractice and preserving evidence with possible adult victims of childhood sexual abuse. *Applied & Preventive Psychology, 5,* 135–164.

Frankel, A., & Prentice-Dunn, S. (1990). Loneliness and the processing of self-relevant information. *Journal of Social and Clinical Psychology, 9,* 303–315.

Frazier, P. A., Byer, A. L., Fischer, A. R., Wright, D. M., & DeBord, K. A. (1996). Adult attachment style and partner choice: Correlational and experimental findings. *Personal Relationships, 3,* 117–136.

Fredrickson, B. L. (1995). Socioemotional behavior at the end of college life. *Journal of Social and Personal Relationships, 12,* 261–276.

Freeberg, A. L., & Stein, C. H. (1996). Felt obligation towards parents in Mexican–American and Anglo–American young adults. *Journal of Social and Personal Relationships, 13,* 457–471.

Freedman, J. L., & Fraser, S. C. (1966). Compliance without pressure: The foot-in-the-door technique. *Journal of Personality and Social Psychology, 4,* 195–202.

Freudenheim, M. (1992, October 14). Software helps patients make crucial choices. *New York Times,* p. D6.

Fricko, M. A. M., & Beehr, T. A. (1992). A longitudinal investigation of interest congruence and gender concentration as predictors of job satisfaction. *Personnel Psychology, 45,* 99–117.

Fried, C. B., & Aronson, E. (1995). Hypocrisy, misattribution, and dissonance reduction. *Personality and Social Psychology Bulletin, 21,* 925–933.

Friedman, H. S., Hawley, P. H., & Tucker, J. S. (1994). Personality, health, and longevity. *Current Directions in Psychological Science, 3,* 37–41.

Friedman, H. S., Riggio, R. E., & Casella, D. F. (1988). Nonverbal skill, personal charisma, and initial attraction. *Personality and Social Psychology Bulletin, 14,* 203–211.

Friedman, H. S., Tucker, J. S., Schwartz, J. E., Martin, L. R., Tomlinson-Keasey, C., Wingard, D. L., & Criqui, M. H. (1995a). Childhood conscientiousness and longevity: Health behaviors and cause of death. *Journal of Personality and Social Psychology, 68,* 696–703.

Friedman, H. S., Tucker, J. S., Schwartz, J. E., Tomlinson-Keasey, C., Martin, L. R., Wingard, D. L., & Criqui, M. H. (1995b). Psychosocial and behavioral predictors of longevity: The aging and death of the "Termites." *American Psychologist, 50,* 69–78.

Froming, W. J., Nasby, W., & McManus, J. (1998). Prosocial self-schemas, self-awareness, and children's prosocial behavior. *Journal of Personality and Social Psychology, 75,* 766–777.

Fry, D. P. (1998). Anthropological perspectives on aggression: Sex differences and cultural variation. *Aggressive Behavior, 24,* 81–95.

Fujino, D. C. (1997). The rates, patterns, and reasons for forming heterosexual interracial dating relationships among Asian Americans. *Journal of Social and Personal Relationships, 14,* 809–828.

Fultz, J., Shaller, M., & Cialdini, R. B. (1988). Empathy, sadness, and distress: Three related but distant vicarious affective responses to another's suffering. *Personality and Social Psychology Bulletin, 14,* 312–325.

Furnham, A., & Rawles, R. (1995). Sex differences in the estimation of intelligence. *Journal of Social Behavior and Personality, 10,* 741–748.

Furr, R. M., & Funder, D. C. (1998). A multimodal analysis of personal negativity. *Journal of Personality and Social Psychology, 74,* 1580–1591.

Gabriel, M. T., Critelli, J. W., & Ee, J. S. (1994). Narcissistic illusions in self-evaluations of intelligence and attractiveness. *Journal of Personality, 62,* 143–155.

Gaertner, S. L., Mann, J., Murrell, A., & Dovidio, J. F. (1989). Reducing intergroup bias: The benefits of recategorization. *Journal of Personality and Social Psychology, 57,* 239–249.

Gaertner, S. L., Dovidio, J. F., Anastasio, P. A., Bachman, B. A., & Rust, M. C. (1993a). The common ingroup identity model: Recategorization and the reduction of intergroup bias. In W. Stroebe & H. Hewstone (Eds.), *European Review of Social Psychology, 4,* 1–26.

Gaertner, S. L., Mann, J. A., Dovidio, J. F., Murrell, A. J., & Pomare, M. (1990). How does cooperation reduce intergroup bias? *Journal of Personality and Social Psychology, 59,* 692–704.

Gaertner, S. L., Rust, M. C., Dovidio, J. F., Bachman, B. A., & Anastasio, P. A. (1993b). The contact hypothesis: The role of a common ingroup identity on reducing intergroup bias. *Small Groups Research, 25*(2), 224–249.

Gaines, S. O. Jr. (1994). Exchange of respect-denying behaviors among male–female friendships. *Journal of Social and Personal Relationships, 11,* 5–24.

Galambos, N. L. (1992). Parent–adolescent relations. *Current Directions in Psychological Science, 1,* 146–149.

Gamble, W. C., & Dalla, R. L. (1997). Young children's perceptions of their social worlds in single and two-parent, Euro– and Mexican–American families. *Journal of Social and Personal Relationships, 14,* 357–372.

Gangestad, S., & Snyder, M. (1985). On the nature of self-monitoring: An examination of latent causal structure. In P. Shaver (Ed.), *Review of Personality and Social Psychology* (Vol. 6, pp. 65–85). Beverly Hills, CA: Sage.

Gangestad, S. W., & Simpson, J. A. (1993). Development of a scale measuring genetic variation related to expressive control. *Journal of Personality, 61,* 133–158.

Gantner, A. B., & Taylor, S. P. (1992). Human physical aggression as a function of alcohol and threat of harm. *Aggressive Behavior, 18,* 29–36.

Garcia, L. T. (1982). Sex role orientation and stereotypes about male–female sexuality. *Sex Roles, 8,* 863–876.

Gardner, R. M., & Tockerman, Y. R. (1994). A computer–TV methodology for investigating the influence of somatotype on perceived personality traits. *Journal of Social Behavior and Personality, 9,* 555–563.

Geen, R., & Donnerstein, E. (Eds.). (1998). *Human aggression: Theories, research and implications for policy.* Pacific Grove, CA: Brooks/Cole.

Geen, R. G. (1998). Some effects of observing violence upon the behavior of the observer. In B. A. Maher (Ed.), *Progress in experimental personality research* (Vol. 8). New York: Academic Press.

Geen, R. G. (1989). Alternative conceptions of social facilitation. In P. B. Paulus (Ed.), *Psychology of group influence* (2nd ed., pp. 10037). New York: Academic Press.

Geen, R. G. (1991a). *Human aggression.* Pacific Grove, CA: Brooks/Cole.

Geen, R. G. (1991b). Behavioral and physiological reactions to observed violence: Effects of prior exposure to aggressive stimuli. *Journal of Personality and Social Psychology, 40,* 868–875.

Geller, P. A., & Hobfoll, S. E. (1994). Gender differences in job stress, tedium and social support in the workplace. *Journal of Social and Personal Relationships, 11,* 555–572.

Gentile, D. A. (1993). Just what are sex and gender, anyway? A call for a new terminological standard. *Psychological Science, 4,* 120–122.

George, J. M. (1990). Personality, affect, and behavior in groups. *Journal of Applied Psychology, 75,* 107–116.

George, J. M. (1995). Leader positive mood and group performance: The case of customer service. *Journal of Applied Social Psychology, 25,* 778–794.

George, M. S., Ketter, T. A., Parekh-Priti, I., Horwitz, B., et al. (1995). Brain activity during transient sadness and happiness in healthy women. *American Journal of Psychiatry, 152,* 341–351.

Gerard, H. B., Wilhelmy, R. A., & Conolley, E. S. (1968). Conformity and group size. *Journal of Personality and Social Psychology, 8,* 79–82.

Gerhart, B. (1987). How important are dispositional factors as determinants of job satisfaction? Implications for job design and other personnel programs. *Journal of Personality and Social Psychology, 72,* 366–377.

Gerlsma, C., Buunk, B. P., & Mutsaers, W. C. M. (1996). Correlates of self-reported adult attachment styles in a Dutch sample of married men and women. *Journal of Social and Personal Relationships, 13,* 313–320.

Gerrard, M., & Luus, C. A. E. (1995). Judgments of vulnerability to pregnancy: The role of risk factors and individual differences. *Personality and Social Psychology Bulletin, 21,* 160–171.

Gervey, B. M., Chiu, C.-y., Hong, Y.-y., & Dweck, C. S. (1999). Differential use of person information in decisions about guilt versus innocence: The role of implicit theories. *Personality and Social Psychology Bulletin, 25,* 17–27.

Gibbons, F. X., & Gerrard, M. (1995). Predicting young adults' health risk behavior. *Journal of Personality and Social Psychology, 69,* 505–517.

Gibbons, F. X., Eggleston, T. J., & Benthin, A. C. (1997). Cognitive reactions to smoking relapse: The reciprocal relation between dissonance and self-esteem. *Journal of Personality and Social Psychology, 72,* 184–195.

Gibbons, F. X., Gerrard, M., & McCoy, S. B. (1995). Prototype perception predicts (lack of) pregnancy prevention. *Personality and Social Psychology Bulletin, 21,* 85–93.

Gibbons, F. X., Gerrard, M., Blanton, H., & Russell, D. W. (1998). Reasoned action and social reaction: Willingness and intention as independent predictors of health risk. *Journal of Personality and Social Psychology, 74,* 1164–1180.

Gifford, R. (1994). A lens-mapping framework for understanding the encoding and decoding of interpersonal dispositions in nonverbal behavior. *Journal of Personality and Social Psychology, 66,* 398–412.

Gigone, D., & Hastie, R. (1993). The common knowledge effect: Information sharing and group judgment. *Journal of Personality and Social Psychology, 65,* 959–974.

Gigone, D., & Hastie, R. (1997). The impact of information on small group choice. *Journal of Personality and Social Psychology, 72,* 132–140.

Gilbert, D. T., & Malone, P. S. (1995). The correspondence bias. *Psychological Bulletin, 117,* 21–38.

Gilbert, D. T., & Silvera, D. H. (1996). Overhelping. *Journal of Personality and Social Psychology, 70,* 678–690.

Gilbert, D. T., Tafarodi, R. W., & Malone, P. S. (1993). You can't not believe everything you read. *Journal of Personality and Social Psychology, 65,* 221–233.

Gilbert, L. A. (1993). *Two careers/one family.* Newbury Park, CA: Sage.

Gillen, B. (1981). Physical attractiveness: A determinant of two types of goodness. *Personality and Social Psychology Bulletin, 7,* 277–281.

Gilovich, T., & Medvec, V. H. (1994). The temporal pattern to the experience of regret. *Journal of Personality and Social Psychology, 67,* 357–365.

Giner-Sorolla, R., & Chaiken, S. (1994). The causes of hostile media effects. *Journal of Experimental Social Psychology, 30,* 165–180.

Giner-Sorolla, R., & Chaiken, S. (1997). Selective use of heuristic and systematic processing under defense motivation. *Personality and Social Psychology Bulletin, 23,* 84–97.

Gladue, B. A., & Delaney, H. J. (1990). Gender differences in perception of attractiveness of men and women in bars. *Personality and Social Psychology Bulletin, 16,* 378–391.

Gladwell, M. (1996, June 3). The tipping point. *New Yorker,* 32–38.

Glaser, J., & Salovey, P. (1998). Affect in electoral politics. *Personality and Social Psychology Review, 2,* 156–172.

Glass Ceiling Commission. (1995). *Good for business: Making full use of the nation's human capital.* Washington, DC: Glass Ceiling Commission.

Glass, D. C. (1977). *Behavior patterns, stress, and coronary disease.* Hillsdale, NJ: Erlbaum.

Glass, D. C. (1989). Psychology and health: Obstacles and opportunities. *Journal of Applied Social Psychology, 19,* 1145–1163.

Gleicher, F., Boninger, D., Strathman, A., Armor, D., Hetts, J., & Ahn, M. (1995). With an eye toward the future: Impact of counterfactual thinking on affect, attitudes, and behavior. In N. J. Roses & J. M. Olson (Eds.), *What might have been: the social psychology of counterfactual thinking.* (pp. 283–304). Mahwah, NJ: Erlbaum.

Glenn, N. D., & Weaver, C. N. (1988). The changing relationship of marital status to reported happiness. *Journal of Marriage and the Family, 50,* 317–324.

Glick, P. C. (1983). Seventh-year itch. *Medical Aspects of Human Sexuality, 17*(5), 103.

Goethals, G. R., & Zanna, M. P. (1979). The role of social comparison in choice shifts. *Journal of Personality and Social Psychology, 37,* 1469–1476.

Gold, J. A., Ryckman, R. M., & Mosley, N. R. (1984). Romantic mood induction and attraction to a dissimilar other: Is love blind? *Personality and Social Psychology Bulletin, 10,* 358–368.

Goldsmith, D. J., & Dun, S. A. (1997). Sex differences and similarities in the communication of social support. *Journal of Social and Personal Relationships, 14,* 317–337.

Goldstein, A. G., Chance, J. E., & Schneller, G. R. (1989). Frequency of eyewitness identification in criminal cases: A survey of prosecutors. *Bulletin of the Psychonomic Society, 27,* 71–74.

Goldstein, M. D., & Strube, M. J. (1994). Independence revisited: The relation between positive and negative affect in a naturalistic setting. *Personality and Social Psychology Bulletin, 20,* 57–64.

Goleman, D. (1994b, May 11). Seeking out small pleasures keeps immune system strong. *New York Times,* p. C11.

Goodman, E. (1998, May 8). Set a new standard for chick flicks. Albany *Times Union,* p. A13.

Goodwin, R., & Findlay, C. (1997). "We were just fated together" . . . Chinese love and the concept of *yuan* in England and Hong Kong. *Personal Relationships, 4,* 85–92.

Gordon, R. A. (1996). Impact of ingratiation in judgments and evaluations: A meta-analytic investigation. *Journal of Personality and Social Psychology, 71,* 54–70.

Gould, D., & Weiss, M. (1981). Effect of model similarity and model self-talk on self-efficacy in muscular endurance. *Journal of Sport Psychology, 3,* 17–29

Graham, S., & Folkes, V. (Eds.). (1990). *Attribution theory: Applications to achievement, mental health, and interpersonal conflict.* Hillsdale, NJ: Erlbaum.

Graham, S., Weiner, B., & Zucker, G. S. (1997). An attributional analysis of punishment goals and public reactions to O. J. Simpson. *Personality and Social Psychology Bulletin, 23,* 331–346.

Graziano, W. G., & Bryant, W. H. M. (1998). Self-monitoring and the self-attribution of positive emotions. *Journal of Personality and Social Psychology, 74,* 250–261.

Graziano, W. G., Jensen-Campbell, L. A., & Hair, E. C. (1996). Perceiving interpersonal conflict and reacting to it: The case for agreeableness. *Journal of Personality and Social Psychology, 70,* 820–835.

Green, L. R., Richardson, D. R., & Lago, T. (1996). How do friendship, indirect, and direct aggression relate? *Aggressive Behavior, 22,* 81–86.

Greenbaum, P., & Rosenfield, H. W. (1978). Patterns of avoidance in responses to interpersonal staring and proximity: Effects of bystanders on drivers at a traffic intersection. *Journal of Personality and Social Psychology, 36,* 575–587.

Greenberg, J. (1996). *The quest for justice: Essays and experiments.* Thousand Oaks, CA: Sage Publications.

Greenberg, J. (1989). Cognitive re-evaluation of outcomes in response to underpayment inequity. *Academy of Management Journal, 32* 174–184.

Greenberg, J. (1990). Employee theft as a reaction to underpayment inequity: The hidden cost of pay cuts. *Journal of Applied Psychology, 75,* 561–568.

Greenberg, J. (1993a). The social side of fairness: Interpersonal and informational classes of organizational justice. In R. Cropanzano (Ed.), *Justice in the workplace* (pp. 79–103). Hillsdale, NJ: Erlbaum.

Greenberg, J. (1993b). Stealing in the name of justice: Informational and interpersonal moderators of theft reactions to underpayment inequity. *Organizational Behavior and Human Decision Processes, 54,* 81–103.

Greenberg, J., & Alge, B. J. (1999). Aggressive reactions to workplace injustice. In R. W. Griffin, A. O'Leary-Kelly, & J. Collins (Eds.), *Dysfunctional behavior in organizations: Vol. 1. Violent behaviors in organizations.* Greenwich, CT: JAI Press.

Greenberg, J., & Alge, B. J. (1997). Aggressive reactions to workplace injustice. In R. W. Griffin, A. O'Leary-Kelly, & J. Collins (Eds.), *Dysfunctional behavior in organizations: Vol. 1. Violent behaviors in organizations.* Greenwich, CT: JAI Press.

Greenberg, J., & Alge, B. J. (in press). Aggressive reactions to workplace injustice. In R. W. Griffin, A. O'Leary-Kelly, & J. Collins (Eds.), *Dysfunctional behavior in organizations: Vol. 1. Violent behaviors in organizations.* Greenwich, CT: JAI Press.

Greenberg, J., & Baron, R. A. (1995). *Behavior in organizations* (5th ed.). Englewood Cliffs, NJ: Prentice-Hall.

Greenberg, J., & Baron, R. A. (1997). *Behavior in organizations* (6th ed.). Upper Saddle River, NJ: Prentice-Hall.

Greenberg, J., & Scott, K. S. (1996). Why do workers bite the hands that feed them? Employee theft as social exchange process. In B. M. Staw & L. L. Cummings (Eds.), *Research in organizational behavior* (Vol. 18, pp. 111–156). Greenwich, CT: JAI Press.

Greenberg, J., Pyszczynski, T., & Solomon, S. (1982). The self-serving attributional bias: Beyond self-presentation. *Journal of Experimental Social Psychology, 18,* 56–67.

Greenberg, J., Pyszczynski, T., Solomon, S., Pinel, E., Simon, L., & Jordan, K. (1993). Effects of self-esteem on vulnerability-denying defensive distortions: Further evidence of an anxiety-buffering function of self-esteem. *Journal of Experimental Social Psychology, 29,* 229–251.

Greenberg, J., Solomon, S., Pyszczynski, ·T., Rosenblatt, A., Burling, J., Lyon, D., Simon, L., & Pinel, E. (1992). Why do people need self-esteem? Converging evidence that self-esteem serves an anxiety-buffering function. *Journal of Personality and Social Psychology, 63,* 913–922.

Greenberg, M. A., & Stone, A. A. (1992). Emotional disclosure about traumas and its relation to health: Effects of previous disclosure and trauma severity. *Journal of Personality and Social Psychology, 63,* 75–84.

Greenberg, M. A., Wortman, C. B., & Stone, A. A. (1996). Emotional expression and physical health: Revising traumatic memories or fostering self-regulation? *Journal of Personality and Social Psychology, 71,* 588–602.

Greenwald, J. (1998, November 23). Herbal healing. *Time,* pp. 58–67.

Greer, A. E., & Buss, D. M. (1994). Tactics for promoting sexual encounters. *Journal of Sex Research, 31,* 185–201.

Grieve, N. (1980). Beyond sexual stereotypes. Androgyny: A model or an ideal? In N. Grieve & P. Grimshaw (Eds.), *Australian women: Feminist perspectives* (pp. 247–257). Melbourne, Australia: Oxford University Press.

Griffin, D. W., & Bartholomew, K. (1994a). The metaphysics of measurement: The case of adult attachment. In K. Bartholomew & D. Perlman (Eds.), *Advances in personal relationships: Vol. 5. Attachment processes in adulthood* (pp. 17–52). London: Jessica Kingsley.

Griffin, D., & Bartholomew, K. (1994b). Models of the self and other: Fundamental dimensions underlying measures of adult attachment. *Journal of Personality and Social Psychology, 67,* 430–445.

Griffin, D. W., & Buehler, R. (1993). Role of construal process in conformity and dissent. *Journal of Personality and Social Psychology, 65,* 657–669.

Griffin, K. W., & Rabkin, J. G. (1998). Perceived control over illness, realistic acceptance, and psychological adjustment in people with AIDS. *Journal of Social and Clinical Psychology, 17,* 407–424.

Groff, D. B., Baron, R. S., & Moore, D. L. (1983). Distraction, attentional conflict, and drivelike behavior. *Journal of Experimental Social Psychology, 19,* 359–380.

Grossman, M., & Wood, W. (1993). Sex differences in intensity of emotional experience: A social role interpretation. *Journal of Personality and Social Psychology, 65,* 1010–1022.

Grote, N. K., Frieze, I. H., & Stone, C. A. (1996). Children, traditionalism in the division of family work, and marital satisfaction: "What's love got to do with it?" *Personal Relationships, 3,* 211–228.

Grusec, J. E. (1991). The socialization of altruism. In M. S. Clark (Ed.), *Prosocial behavior* (pp. 9–33). Newbury Park, CA: Sage.

Guagnano, G. A. (1995). Locus of control, altruism and agentic disposition. *Population and Environment, 17,* 63–77.

Gudjonsson, G. H. (1993). Confession evidence, psychological vulnerability and expert testimony. *Journal of Community and Applied Social Psychology, 3,* 117–129.

Gudjonsson, G. H., & Clark, N. K. (1986). Suggestibility in police interrogation: A social psychological model. *Social Behavior, 1,* 83–104.

Guerrero, L. K. (1998). Attachment-style differences in the experience and expression of romantic jealousy. *Personal Relationships, 5,* 273–291.

Gully, K. J., & Dengerink, H. A. (1983). The dyadic interaction of persons with violent and nonviolent histories. *Aggressive Behavior, 9,* 13–20.

Gump, B. B., & Kulik, J. A. (1997). Stress, affiliation, and emotional contagion. *Journal of Personality and Social Psychology, 72,* 305–319.

Gunter, B. G., & Gunter, N. C. (1991). Inequities in household labor: Sex role orientation and the need for cleanliness and responsibility as predictors. *Journal of Social Behavior and Personality, 6,* 559–572.

Gustafson, R. (1990). Wine and male physical aggression. *Journal of Drug Issues, 20,* 75–86.

Gutek, B. A. (1985). *Sex and the workplace.* San Francisco: Jossey-Bass.

Hackel, L. S., & Ruble, D. N. (1992). Changes in the marital relationship after the first baby is born: Predicting the impact of expectancy disconfirmation. *Journal of Personality and Social Psychology, 62,* 944–957.

Hagborg, W. J. (1993). Gender differences on Harter's Self-Perception Profile for Adolescents. *Journal of Social Behavior and Personality, 8,* 141–148.

Halford, W. K., & Sanders, M. R. (1990). The relationship of cognition and behavior during marital interaction. *Journal of Social and Clinical Psychology, 9,* 489–510.

Hamburger, M. E., Hogben, M., McGowan, S., & Dawson, L. J. (1996). The Hypergender Ideology Scale: Measurement and initial validation. *Journal of Research in Personality, 30,* 157–178.

Hamilton, D. L., & Sherman, S. J. (1989). Illusory correlations: Implications for stereotype theory and research. In D. Bar-Tal, C. F. Graumann, A. W. Kruglanski, & W. Stroebe (Eds.), *Stereotyping and prejudice: Changing conceptions* (pp. 59–82). New York: Springer-Verlag.

Hamilton, G. V. (1978). Obedience and responsibility: A jury simulation. *Journal of Personality and Social Psychology, 36,* 126–146.

Hamilton, M. M. (1995). Incorporation of astrology-based personality information into long-term self-concept. *Journal of Social Behavior and Personality, 10,* 707–718.

Hamilton, V. L., & Sanders, J. (1995). Crimes of obedience and conformity in the workplace: Surveys of Americans, Russians, and Japanese. *Journal of Social Issues, 51,* 67–88.

Harasty, A. S. (1997). The interpersonal nature of social stereotypes: Differential discussion patterns about in-groups and out-groups. *Personality and Social Psychology Bulletin, 23,* 270–284.

Harber, K. D. (1998). Feedback to minorities: Evidence of a positive bias. *Journal of Personality and Social Psychology, 74,* 623–628.

Harkins, S., & Szymanski, K. (1989). Social loafing and group evaluation. *Journal of Personality and Social Psychology, 56,* 934–941.

Harris, J. A., Rushton, J. P., Hampson, E., & Jackson, D. N. (1996). Salivary testosterone and self-report aggressive and pro-social personality characteristics in men and women. *Aggressive Behavior, 22,* 321–331.

Harris, L. R., & Weiss, D. J. (1995). Judgments of consent in simulated rape cases. *Journal of Social Behavior and Personality, 10,* 79–90.

Harris, M. B. (1993). How provoking! What makes men and women angry? *Journal of Applied Social Psychology, 23,* 199–211.

Harris, M. B. (1994). Gender of subject and target as mediators of aggression. *Journal of Applied Social Psychology, 24,* 453–471.

Harris, M. B. (1996). Aggressive experiences and aggressiveness: Relationship to gender, ethnicity, and age. *Journal of Applied Social Psychology, 26,* 843–870.

Harris, M. B., (1992). Sex, race, and experiences of aggression. *Aggressive Behavior, 18,* 201–217.

Harris, M. B., Harris, R. J., & Bochner, S. (1982). Fat, four-eyed, and female: Stereotypes of obesity, glasses, and gender. *Journal of Applied Social Psychology, 12,* 503–516.

Harris, M. J., Milch, R., Corbitt, E. M., Hoover, D. W., Brady, M. (1992). Self-fulfilling effects of stigmatizing information on children's social interaction. *Journal of Personality and Social Psychology, 63,* 41–50.

Harrison, A. A., & Saeed, L. (1977). Let's make a deal: An analysis of revelations and stipulations in lonely hearts advertisements. *Journal of Personality and Social Psychology, 35,* 257–264.

Hart, A. J. (1995). Naturally occurring expectation effects. *Journal of Personality and Social Psychology, 68,* 109–115.

Harvey, J. H., & Omarzu, J. (1997). Minding the close relationship. *Personality and Social Psychology Review, 1,* 224–240.

Harvey, J. H., Stein, S. K., Olsen, N., Roberts, R. J., Lutgendorf, S. K., & Ho, J. A. (1995). Narratives of loss and recovery from a natural disaster. *Journal of Social Behavior and Personality, 10,* 313–330.

Hasart, J. K., & Hutchinson, K. L. (1993). The effects of eyeglasses on perceptions of interpersonal attraction. *Journal of Social Behavior and Personality, 8,* 521–528.

Haslam, N. (1994). Mental representation of social relationships: Dimensions, laws, or categories? *Journal of Personality and Social Psychology, 67,* 575–584.

Hastie, R. (Ed.). (1993). *Inside the juror: The psychology of juror decision making.* Cambridge, England: Cambridge University Press.

Hatchett, L., Friend, R., Symister, P., & Wadhwa, N. (1997). Interpersonal expectations, social support, and adjustment to chronic illness. *Journal of Personality and Social Psychology, 73,* 560–573.

Hatfield, E. (1988). Passionate and companionate love. In R. J. Sternberg & M. I. Barnes (Eds.), *The psychology of love* (pp. 191–217). New Haven, CT: Yale University Press.

Hatfield, E., & Rapson, R. L. (1992). Similarity and attraction in close relationships. *Communication Monographs, 59,* 209–212.

Hatfield, E., & Rapson, R. L. (1993b). Historical and cross-cultural perspectives on passionate love and sexual desire. *Annual Review of Sex Research, 4,* 67–97.

Hatfield, E., & Sprecher, S. (1986a). *Mirror, mirror . . . :* The importance of looks in everyday life. Albany, NY: S.U.N.Y. Press.

Hatfield, E., & Sprecher, S. (1986b). Measuring passionate love in intimate relations. *Journal of Adolescence, 9,* 383–410.

Hatfield, E., & Walster, G. W. (1981). *A new look at love.* Reading, MA: Addison-Wesley.

Hatfield, E., Sprecher, S., Pillemer, J. T., Greenberger, D., & Wexler, P. (1989). Gender differences in what is desired in the sexual relationship. *Journal of Psychology and Human Sexuality, 1,* 39–52.

Hayden, S. R., Jackson, T. T., & Guydish, J. N. (1984). Helping behavior of females: Effects of stress and commonality of fate. *Journal of Psychology, 117,* 233–237.

Hazan, C., & Shaver, P. R. (1990). Love and work: An attachment-theoretical perspective. *Journal of Personality and Social Psychology, 59,* 270–280.

Hebl, M. R., & Heatherton, T. E. (1998). The stigma of obesity in women: The difference is black and white. *Personality and Social Psychology Bulletin, 24,* 417–426.

Hecht, M. A., & LaFrance, M. (1998). License or obligation to smile: The effect of power and sex on amount and type of smiling. *Personality and Social Psychology Bulletin, 24,* 1332–1342.

Hedges, M. (1996, October 13). Violent crime drops, to every 18 seconds. Scripps Howard.

Heider, F. (1958). *The psychology of interpersonal relations.* New York: Wiley.

Heilman, M. E. (1995). Sex stereotypes and their effects in the workplace: What we know and what we don't know. *Journal of Social Behavior and Personality, 10,* 3–26.

Heilman, M. E., Block, C. J., & Lucas, J. A. (1992). Presumed incompetent? Stigmatization and affirmative action efforts. *Journal of Applied Psychology, 77,* 536–544.

Heilman, M. E., Martell, R. F., & Simon, M. C. (1988) The vagaries of sex bias: Conditions regulating the undervaluation, equivalation, and overvaluation of female job applicants. *Organizational Behavior and Human Decision Processes, 41,* 98–110.

Heinberg, L. J., & Thompson, J. K. (1992). Social comparison: Gender, target importance ratings, and relation to body image disturbance. *Journal of Social Behavior and Personality, 7,* 335–344.

Heinberg, L. J., & Thompson, J. K. (1995). Body image and televised images of thinness and attractiveness: A controlled laboratory investigation. *Journal of Social and Clinical Psychology, 14,* 325–338.

Heine, S. J., & Lehman, D. R. (1997a). Culture, dissonance, and self-affirmation. *Personality and Social Psychology Bulletin, 23,* 389–400.

Heine, S. J., & Lehman, D. R. (1997b). The cultural construction of self-enhancement: An examination of group-serving bias. *Journal of Personality and Social Psychology, 72,* 1268–1283.

Helman, D., & Bookspan, P. (1992, February 8). In Big Bird's world, females are secondary. *Albany Times Union,* E–2.

Henderson-King, D. H., & Veroff, J. (1994). Sexual satisfaction and marital well-being in the first years of marriage. *Journal of Social and Personal Relationships, 11,* 509–534.

Henderson-King, E., Henderson-King, D., Zhermer, N., Posokhova, S., & Chiker, V. (1997). In-group favoritism and perceived similarity: A look at Russians' perceptions in the post-Soviet era. *Personality and Social Psychology Bulletin, 23,* 1013–1021.

Hendrick, C., & Hendrick, S. S. (1986). A theory and method of love. *Journal of Personality and Social Psychology, 50,* 392–402.

Hendrick, C., Hendrick, S. S., Foote, F. H., & Slapion-Foote, M. J. (1984). Do men and women love differently? *Journal of Social and Personal Relationships, 1,* 177–195.

Hendrick, S. S., & Hendrick, C. (1987). Love and sex attitudes and religious beliefs. *Journal of Social and Clinical Psychology, 5,* 391–398.

Hendrick, S. S., Hendrick, C., & Adler, N. L. (1988). Romantic relationships: Love, satisfaction, and staying together. *Journal of Personality and Social Psychology, 54,* 980–988.

Henry, W. A. III. (1991). The journalist and the murder. *Time, 138*(15), 86.

Hensley, W. E. (1996). The effect of a ludus love style on sexual experience. *Social Behavior and Personality, 24,* 205–212.

Hepworth, J. T., & West, S. G. (1988). Lynchings and the economy: A time-series reanalysis of Hovland and Sears (1940). *Journal of Personality and Social Psychology, 55,* 239–247.

Herbert, J. D. (1995). An overview of the current status of social phobia. *Applied and Preventive Psychology, 4,* 39–51.

Hershberger, S. L., Lichtenstein, P., & Knox, S. S. (1994). Genetic and environmental influences on perceptions of organizational climate. *Journal of Applied Psychology, 79,* 24–33.

Hetherington, E. M., Bridges, M., & Insabella, G. M. (1998). What matters? What does not? Five perspectives on the association between marital transitions and children's adjustment. *American Psychologist, 53,* 167–184.

Hewstone, M., Bond, M. H., & Wan, K. C. (1983). Social factors and social attributions: The explanation of intergroup differences in Hong Kong. *Social Cognition, 2,* 142–157.

Higgins, E. T. (1990). Personality, social psychology, and person–situation relations: Standards and knowledge activation as a common language. In L. A. Pervin (Ed.), *Handbook of personality: Theory and research* (pp. 301–338). New York: Guilford.

Higgins, E. T. (1996). Emotional experiences: The pains and pleasures of distinct regulatory systems. In D. Kavanaugh, B. Zimmerberg, & S. Fein (Eds.), *Emotion: Interdisciplinary perspectives* (pp. 203–241). Mahwah, NJ: Erlbaum.

Higgins, E. T., & Bargh, J. A. (1987). Social cognition and social perception. *Annual Review of Psychology, 38,* 369–425.

Higgins, E. T., & King, G. (1981). Accessibility of social constructs: Information processing consequences of individual and contextual variability. In N. Cantor & J. Kihlstrom (Eds.), *Personality, cognition, and social interaction* (pp. 69–121). Hillsdale, NJ: Erlbaum.

Higgins, E. T., Rohles, W. S., & Jones, C. R. (1977). Category accessibility and impression formation. *Journal of Experimental Social Psychology, 13,* 141–154.

Hill, C. A. (1987). Affiliation motivation: People who need people but in different ways. *Journal of Personality and Social Psychology, 52,* 1008–1018.

Hill, C. A., Blakemore, J. E. O., & Drumm, P. (1997). Mutual and unrequited love in adolescence and young adulthood. *Personal Relationships, 4,* 15–23.

Hilton, J. L., Klein, J. G., & von Hippel, W. (1991). Attention allocation and impression formation. *Personality and Social Psychology Bulletin, 17,* 548–559.

Hinkley, K., & Andersen, S. M. (1996). The working self-concept in transference: Significant-other activation and self change. *Journal of Personality and Social Psychology, 71,* 1279–1295.

Hinsz, V. B. (1995). Goal setting by groups performing an additive task: A comparison with individual goal setting. *Journal of Applied Social Psychology, 25,* 965–990.

Hixon, J. G., & Swann, W. B., Jr. (1993). When does introspection bear fruit? Self-reflection, self-insight, and interpersonal choices. *Journal of Personality and Social Psychology, 64,* 35–43.

Hogben, M., Byrne, D., & Hamburger, M. E. (1999). *Legitimized aggression and sexual coercion: Individual differences in cultural spillover.* Manuscript submitted for publication.

Hogg, M. A., & Hains, S. C. (1996). Intergroup relations and group solidarity: Effects of group identification and social beliefs on depersonalized attraction. *Journal of Personality and Social Psychology, 70,* 25–309.

Hogg, M. A., Cooper-Shaw, L., & Holzworth, D. W. (1993). Group prototypicality and depersonalized attraction in small interactive groups. *Personality and Social Psychology Bulletin, 19,* 452–465.

Holahan, C. J., Moos, R. H., Holahan, C. K., & Brennan, P. L. (1997). Social context, coping strategies, and depressive symptoms: An expanded model with cardiac patients. *Journal of Personality and Social Psychology, 72,* 918–928.

Holtgraves, T., & Grayer, A. R. (1994). I am not a crook: Effects of denials on perceptions of a defendant's guilt, personality, and motives. *Journal of Applied Social Psychology, 24,* 2132–2150.

Hope, D. A., Holt, C. S., & Heimberg, R. G. (1995). Social phobia. In T. R. Giles (Ed.), *Handbook of effective psychotherapy* (pp. 227–251). New York: Plenum.

House R. J. (1977). A theory of charismatic leadership. In J. G. Hunt & L. L. Larson (Eds.), *Leadership: The cutting edge* (pp. 189–207). Carbondale, IL: Southern Illinois University Press.

House, R. J., & Howell, J. M. (1992). Personality and charismatic leadership. *Leadership Quarterly, 3,* 81–108.

House, R. J., & Podsakoff, P. M. (1994). Leadership effectiveness: Past perspectives and future directions for research. In J. Greenberg (Ed.), *Organizational behavior: The state of the science* (pp. 45–82). Hillsdale, NJ: Erlbaum.

House, R. J., Spangler, W. D., & Woycke, J. (1991). Personality and charisma in the U.S. presidency: A psychological theory of leader effectiveness. *Administrative Science Quarterly, 36,* 364–396.

Hovland, C. I., & Sears, R. R. (1940). Minor studies in aggression: VI. Correlation of lynchings with economic indices. *Journal of Psychology, 9,* 301–310.

Hovland, C. I., & Weiss, W. (1951). The influence of source credibility on communication effectiveness. *Public Opinion Quarterly, 15,* 635–650.

Hovland, C. I., Janis, I. L., & Kelley, H. H. (1953). Communication and persuasion: Psychological studies of opinion change. New Haven, CT: Yale University Press.

Howell, J. M., & Frost, P. J. (1989). A laboratory study of charismatic leadership. *Organizational Behavior and Human Decision Processes, 43,* 243–269.

Howells, G. N. (1993). Self-monitoring and personality: Would the real high self-monitor please stand up? *Journal of Social Behavior and Personality, 8,* 59–72.

Hoyle, R. H., & Sowards, B. A. (1993). Self-monitoring and the regulation of social experience: A control-process model. *Journal of Social and Clinical Psychology, 12,* 280–306.

Huang, I.-C. (1998). Self-esteem, reaction to uncertainty, and physician practice variation: A study of resident physicians. *Social Behavior and Personality, 26,* 181–194.

Huang, K., & Uba, L. (1992). Premarital sexual behavior among Chinese college students in the United States. *Archives of Sexual Behavior, 21,* 227–240.

Huesmann, L. R., & Eron, L. D. (1984). Cognitive processes and the persistence of aggressive behavior. *Aggressive Behavior, 10,* 243–251.

Huesmann, L. R., & Eron, L. D. (1986). *Television and the aggressive child: A cross-national comparison.* Hillsdale, NJ: Erlbaum.

Hughes, C. F., Uhlmann, C., & Pennebaker, J. W. (1994). The body's response to processing emotional trauma: Linking verbal text with autonomic activity. *Journal of Personality, 62,* 565–585.

Hull, J. D. (1995, January 30). The state of the union. *Time,* 52–57, 60.

Hummert, M. L., Crockett, W. H., & Kemper, S. (1990). Processing mechanisms underlying use of the balance scheme. *Journal of Personality and Social Psychology, 58,* 5–21.

Humphreys, L. G. (1998). A little noticed consequence of the repressed memory epidemic. *American Psychologist, 53,* 485–486.

Humphriss, N. (1989, November 20). Letters. *Time,* 12.

Huo, Y. J., Smith, H. J., Tyler, T. R., & Lind, E. A. (1996). Superordinate identification subgroup identification and justice concerns: Is separation the problem, is assimilation the answer? *Psychological Science, 7,* 40–45.

Hur, Y.-M., McGue, M., & Iacono, W. G. (1998). The structure of self-concept in female preadolescent twins: A behavioral genetic approach. *Journal of Personality and Social Psychology, 74,* 1069–1077.

Hurewitz, M. (1998, March 26). Young man finds honesty has its rewards. Albany *Times Union,* pp. B1, B7.

Hyde, J. S., & Plant, E. A. (1995). Magnitude of psychological gender differences: Another side to the story. *American Psychologist, 50,* 159–161.

Ickes, W., Reidhead, S., & Patterson, M. (1986). Machiavellianism and self-monitoring: As different as "me" and "you." *Social Cognition, 4,* 58–74.

Insel, T. R., & Carter, C. S. (1995, August). The monogamous brain. *Natural History,* 12–14.

Insko, C. A. (1985). Balance theory, the Jordan paradigm, and the West tetrahedron. In L. Berkowitz (Ed.), *Advances in experimental social psychology.* New York: Academic Press.

Ito, T. A., & Cacioppo, J. T. (1999). The psychopysiology of utility appraisals. In D. Kahneman, E. Diener, & N. Schwartz (Eds.), *Understanding quality of life: Scientific perspectives on enjoyment and suffering.* New York: Russell Sage Foundation.

Ito, T. A., Larsen, J. T., Smith, N. K., & Cacioppo, J. T. (1998). Negative information weighs more heavily on the brain: The negativity bias in evaluative categorizations. *Journal of Personality and Social Psychology, 75,* 887–900.

Isen, A. M. (1984). Toward understanding the role of affect in cognition. In S. R. Wyer & T. K. Srull (Eds.), *Handbook of social cognition* (Vol. 3, pp. 179–236). Hillsdale, NJ: Erlbaum.

Isen, A. M., & Baron, R. A. (1991). Affect and organizational behavior. In B. M. Staw & L. L. Cummings (Eds.), *Research in organizational behavior* (Vol. 15, pp. 1–53).

Isen, A. M., & Levin, P. A. (1972). Effect of feeling good on helping: Cookies and kindness. *Journal of Personality and Social Psychology, 21,* 384–388.

Istvan, J., Griffitt, W., & Weidner, G. (1983). Sexual arousal and the polarization of perceived sexual attractiveness. *Basic and Applied Social Psychology, 4,* 307–318.

Izard, C. (1991). *The psychology of emotions.* New York: Plenum.

Jackson, L. A., Gardner, P., & Sullivan, L. (1992). Explaining gender differences in self-pay expectations: Social comparison standards and perceptions of fair pay. *Journal of Applied Psychology, 77,* 651–663.

Jackson, L. M., & Esses, V. M. (1997). Of scripture and ascription: The relation between religious fundamentalism and intergroup helping. *Personality and Social Psychology Bulletin, 23,* 893–906.

Jackson, R. L. (1996, September 18). Violent crime down sharply, survey says. *Los Angeles Times.*

Jaffe, Y., Malamuth, N., Feingold, J., & Feshbach, S. (1974). Sexual arousal and behavioral aggression. *Journal of Personality and Social Psychology, 30,* 759–764.

James, W. (1890). *The principles of psychology.* New York: Holt.

Janis, I. L. (1982). *Victims of groupthink* (2nd ed.). Boston: Houghton Mifflin.

Janoff-Bulman, R., & Wade, M. B. (1996). The dilemma of self-advocacy for women: Another case of blaming the victim? *Journal of Social and Clinical Psychology, 15,* 143–152.

Jeffries, V. (1993). Virtue and attraction: Validation of a measure of love. *Journal of Social and Personal Relationships, 10,* 99–117.

Jemmott, J. B. III, & Magloire, K. (1988). Academic stress, social support, and secretory immunoglobulin. *Journal of Personality and Social Psychology, 55,* 803–810.

Jenkins, S. R. (1997). Coping and social support among emergency dispatchers: Hurricane Andrew. *Journal of Social Behavior and Personality, 12,* 201–216.

Jensen-Campbell, L. A., West, S. G., & Graziano, W. G. (1995). Dominance, prosocial orientation, and female preferences: Do nice guys really finish last? *Journal of Personality and Social Psychology, 68,* 427–440.

Jessor, R., Turbin, M. S., & Costa, F. M. (1998). Protective factors in adolescent health behavior. *Journal of Personality and Social Psychology, 75,* 788–800.

Jex, S. M., Cvetanovski, J., & Allen, S. J. (1994). Self-esteem as a moderator of the impact of unemployment. *Journal of Social Behavior and Personality, 9,* 69–80.

Jockin, V., McGue, M., & Lykken, D. T. (1996). Personality and divorce: A genetic analysis. *Journal of Personality and Social Psychology, 71,* 288–299.

Johns, G., & Jia Lin Xie (1998). Perceptions of absence from work: People's Republic of China versus Canada. *Journal of Applied Psychology, 83,* 515–530.

Johnson, A. B., & Byrne, D. (1996, March). *Effects of proximity in familiarity and preferences for places of work.* Paper presented at the meeting of the Eastern Psychological Association, Philadelphia.

Johnson, B. T. (1994). Effects of outcome-relevant involvement and prior information on persuasion. *Journal of Experimental Social Psychology, 30,* 556–579.

Johnson, C., & Mullen, B. (1994). Evidence for the accessibility of paired distinctiveness in the distinctiveness-based illusory correlation in stereotyping. *Personality and Social Psychology Bulletin, 20,* 65–70.

Johnson, D. F., & Pittenger, J. B. (1984). Attribution, the attractiveness stereotype, and the elderly. *Developmental Psychology, 20,* 1168–1172.

Johnson, J. C., Poteat, G. M., & Ironsmith, M. (1991). Structural vs. marginal effects: A note on the importance of structure in determining sociometric status. *Journal of Social Behavior and Personality, 6,* 489–508.

Johnson, K. A., Johnson, J. E., & Petzel, T. P. (1992). Social anxiety, depression, and distorted cognitions in college students. *Journal of Social and Clinical Psychology, 11,* 181–195.

Johnson, M. K., & Sherman, S. J. (1990). Constructing and reconstructing the past and the future in the present. In E. T. Higgins & R. M. Sorrentino (Eds.), *Handbook of motivation and social cognition: Foundations of social behavior* (pp. 482–526). New York: Guilford.

Johnston, C., & Short, K. H. (1993). Depressive symptoms and perceptions of child behavior. *Journal of Social and Clinical Psychology, 12,* 164–181.

Johnston, J.-A. (1998, June 10). Women's pay edges closer to men's, but only slightly. Albany *Times Union,* pp. E1, E4.

Johnston, V. S., & Franklin, M. (1993). Is beauty in the eye of the beholder? *Ethology and Sociobiology, 14,* 183–199.

Johnston, V. S., & Oliver-Rodriguez, J. C. (1997). Facial beauty and the late positive component of event-related potentials. *Journal of Sex Research, 34,* 188–198.

Johnstone, B., Frame, C. L., & Bouman, D. (1992). Physical attractiveness and athletic and academic ability in controversial–aggressive and rejected–aggressive children. *Journal of Social and Clinical Psychology, 11,* 71–79.

Joiner, T. E., Jr. (1994). The interplay of similarity and self-verification in relationship formation. *Social Behavior and Personality, 22,* 195–200.

Joiner, T. E., Jr., & Schmidt, N. B. (1995). Dimensions of perfectionism, life stress, and depressed and anxious symptoms: Prospective support for diathesis–stress but not specific vulnerability among male undergraduates. *Journal of Social and Clinical Psychology, 14,* 165–183.

Jones, E. E. (1964). *Ingratiation: A social psychology analysis.* New York: Appleton-Century-Crofts.

Jones, E. E. (1979). The rocky road from acts to dispositions. *American Psychologist, 34,* 107–117.

Jones, E. E., & Davis, K. E. (1965). From acts to disposition: The attribution process in person perception. In L. Berkowitz (Ed.), *Advances in experimental social psychology* (Vol. 2, pp. 219–266). New York: Academic Press.

Jones, E. E., & McGillis, D. (1976). Corresponding inferences and attribution cube: A comparative reappraisal. In J. H. Harr, W. J. Ickes, & R. F. Kidd (Eds.), *New directions in attribution research* (Vol. 1). Morristown, NJ: Erlbaum.

Jones, E. E., & Nisbett, R. E. (1971). *The actor and the observer: Divergent perceptions of the causes of behavior.* Morristown, NJ: General Learning Press.

Jones, J. H. (1997, August 25 and September 1). Dr. Yes. *New Yorker,* 98–110, 112–113.

Jones, M. (1993). Influence of self-monitoring on dating motivations. *Journal of Research in Personality, 27,* 197–206.

Jones, W. H., Carpenter, B. N., & Quintana, D. (1985). Personality and interpersonal predictors of loneliness in two cultures. *Journal of Personality and Social Psychology, 48,* 1503–1511.

Judd, C. M., Ryan, C. S., & Parke, B. (1991). Accuracy in the judgment of in-group and out-group variability. *Journal of Personality and Social Psychology, 61,* 366–379.

Judge, T. A. (1993). Does affective disposition moderate the relationships between job satisfaction and voluntary turnover? *Journal of Applied Psychology, 78,* 395–401.

Jury rigging laid bare. (1997, June). *Harper's Magazine,* 21, 24.

Jussim, L. (1991). Interpersonal expectations and social reality: A reflection–construction model and reinterpretation of evidence. *Psychological Review, 98,* 54–73.

Kagan, J. (1964). Acquisition and significance of sex-typing and sex-role identity. *Review of Child Development Research, 1.*

Kalichman, S. C., Sarwer, D. B., Johnson, J. R., Ali, S. A., Early, J., & Tuten, J. T. (1993). Sexually coercive behavior and love styles: A replication and extension. *Journal of Psychology & Human Sexuality, 6,* 93–106.

Kalick, S. M., Zebrowitz, L. A., Langlois, J. H., & Johnson, R. M. (1998). Does human facial attractiveness honestly advertise health? Longitudinal data on an evolutionary question. *Psychological Science, 9,* 8–13.

Kameda, T., & Sugimori, S. (1993). Psychological entrapment in group decision making: An assigned decision rule and a groupthink phenomenon. *Journal of Personality and Social Psychology, 65,* 282–292.

Kandel, D. B. (1978). Similarity in real-life adolescent friendship pairs. *Journal of Personality and Social Psychology, 36,* 306–312.

Kanekar, S., Kolswalla, M. B., & Nazareth, T. (1988). Occupational prestige as a function of occupant's gender. *Journal of Applied Social Psychology, 19,* 681–688.

Kaniasty, K., & Norris, F. H. (1995). Mobilization and deterioration of social support following natural disasters. *Current Directions in Psychological Science, 4,* 94–98.

Kaplan, M. F. (1981). State dispositions in social judgment. *Bulletin of the Psychonomic Society, 18,* 27–29.

Kaplan, M. F. (1989). Task, situational and perceived determinants of influence processes in group decision making. In E. Lawler & B. Markovsky (Eds.), *Advances in group processes* (Vol. 6, pp. 87–1050). Greenwich, CT: JAI.

Karau, S. J., & Williams, K. D. (1993). Social loafing: A meta-analytic review and theoretical integration. *Journal of Personality and Social Psychology, 65,* 681–706.

Karoly, P. (1993). Mechanisms of self-regulation: A systems view. *Annual Review of Psychology, 44,* 23–52.

Karraker, K. H., & Stern, M. (1990). Infant physical attractiveness and facial expression: Effects on adult perceptions. *Basic and Applied Social Psychology, 11,* 371–385.

Kassin, S. M. (1997). The psychology of confession evidence. *American Psychologist, 52,* 221–233.

Kassin, S. M., & Kiechel, K. L. (1996). The social psychology of false confessions: Compliance, internalization, and confabulation. *Psychological Science, 7,* 125–128.

Kassin, S. M., & McNall, K. (1991). Police interrogations and confessions: Communicating promises and threats by pragmatic implication. *Law and Human Behavior, 15,* 233–251.

Kassin, S. M., & Sommers, S. R. (1997). Inadmissible testimony, instructions to disregard, and the jury: Substantive versus procedural considerations. *Personality and Social Psychology Bulletin, 23,* 1046–1054.

Kawakami, K., Dion, K. L., & Dovidio, J. F. (1998). Racial prejudice and stereotype activation. *Personality and Social Psychology Bulletin, 24,* 407–416.

Keelan, J. P. R., Dion, K. L., & Dion, K. K. (1994). Attachment style and heterosexual relationships among young adults: A short-term panel study. *Journal of Social and Personal Relationships, 11,* 201–214.

Keinan, G. (1994). Effects of stress and tolerance of ambiguity on magical thinking. *Journal of Personality and Social Psychology, 67,* 48–55.

Keller, L. M., Bouchard, T. J., Jr., Arvey, R. D., Segal, N. L., & Dawis, R. V. (1992). Work values: Genetic and environmental influences. *Journal of Applied Psychology, 77,* 79–88.

Keller, R. T. (1997). Job involvement and organizational commitment as longitudinal predictors of job performance: A study of scientists and engineers. *Journal of Applied Psychology, 82,* 539–545.

Kellerman, J., Lewis, J., & Laird, J. D. (1989). Looking and loving: The effects of mutual gaze on feelings of romantic love. *Journal of Research in Personality, 23,* 145–161.

Kelley, H. H. (1972). Attribution in social interaction. In E. E. Jones et al. (Eds.), *Attribution: Perceiving the causes of behavior.* Morristown, NJ: General Learning Press.

Kelley, H. H., & Michela, J. L. (1980). Attribution theory and research. *Annual Review of Psychology, 31,* 57–501.

Kelly, A. E., & Kahn, J. H. (1994). Effects of suppression of personal intrusive thoughts. *Journal of Personality and Social Psychology, 66,* 998–1026.

Kelly, A. E., & Nauta, M. M. (1997). Reactance and thought suppression. *Personality and Social Psychology Bulletin, 23,* 1123–1132.

Kelly, J. R., Jackson, J. W., & Hutson-Comeaux, S. L. (1997). The effects of time pressure and task differences on influence modes and accuracy in decision-making groups. *Personality and Social Psychology Bulletin, 23,* 10–22.

Kelman, H. C. (1967). Human use of human subjects: The problem of deception in social psychological experiments. *Psychological Bulletin, 67,* 1–11.

Keltner, D., & Robinson, R. J. (1997). Defending the status quo: Power and bias in social conflict. *Personality and Social Psychology Bulletin, 23,* 1066–1077.

Keltner, D., Young, R. C., Heerey, E. A., Oemig, C., & Monarch, N. D. (1998). Teasing in hierarchical and intimate relations. *Journal of Personality and Social Psychology, 75,* 1231–1247.

Kendzierski, D., & Whitaker, D. J. (1997). The role of self-schema in linking intentions with behavior. *Personality and Social Psychology Bulletin, 23,* 139–147.

Kenealy, P., Gleeson, K., Frude, N., & Shaw, W. (1991). The importance of the individual in the 'causal' relationship between attractiveness and self-esteem. *Journal of Community and Applied Social Psychology, 1,* 45–56.

Kenney, D. A., & Kashy, D. A. (1994). Enhanced co-orientation in the perception of friends: A social relations analysis. *Journal of Personality and Social Psychology, 67,* 1024–1033.

Kenney, D. A., Albright, L., Malloy, T. E., & Kashy, D. A. (1994). Consensus in interpersonal perception: Acquaintance and the big five. *Journal of Personality and Social Psychology, 116,* 245–258.

Kenrick, D. T., & Gutierres, S. E. (1980). Contrast effects and judgments of physical attractiveness: When beauty becomes a social problem. *Journal of Personality and Social Psychology, 38,* 131–140.

Kenrick, D. T., Groth, G. E., Trost, M. R., & Sadalla, E. K. (1993). Integrating evolutionary and social exchange perspectives on relationships: Effects of gender, self-appraisal, and involvement level on mate selection criteria. *Journal of Personality and Social Psychology, 64,* 951–969.

Kenrick, D. T., Keefe, R. C., Bryan, A., Barr, A., & Brown, S. (1995). Age preferences and mate choice among homosexuals and heterosexuals: A case for modular psychological mechanisms. *Journal of Personality and Social Psychology, 69,* 1166–1172.

Kenrick, D. T., Montello, D. R., Gutierres, S. E., & Trost, M. R. (1993). Effects of physical attractiveness on affect and perceptual judgments: When social comparison overrides social reinforcement. *Personality and Social Psychology Bulletin, 19,* 195–199.

Kenrick, D. T., Neuberg, S. L., Zierk, K. L., & Krones, J. M. (1994). Evolution and social cognition: Contrast effects as a function of sex, dominance, and physical attractiveness. *Personality and Social Psychology Bulletin, 20,* 210–217.

Kent, R. L., & Moss, S. E. (1994). Effects of sex and gender role on leader emergence. *Academy of Management Journal, 37,* 1335–1346.

Kernis, M. H., Whisenhunt, C. R., Waschull, S. B., Greenier, K. D., Berry, A. J., Herlocker, C. E., & Anderson, C. A. (1998). Multiple facets of self-esteem and their relations to depressive symptoms. *Personality and Social Psychology Bulletin, 24,* 657–668.

Kerns, K. A. (1994). A longitudinal examination of links between mother–child attachment and children's friendships in early childhood. *Journal of Social and Personal Relationships, 11,* 379–381.

Kerns, K. A., & Barth, J. M. (1995). Attachment and play: Convergence across components of parent–child relationships and their relations to peer competence. *Journal of Social and Personal Relationships, 12,* 243–260.

Kerr, N. L., & Kaufman-Gilliland, C. M. (1994). Communication, commitment, and cooperation in social dilemmas. *Journal of Personality and Social Psychology, 66,* 513–529.

Kerr, N. L., Garst, J., Lewandowski, D. A., & Harris, S. E. (1997). That still, small voice: Commitment to cooperate as an internalized versus a social norm. *Personality and Social Psychology Bulletin, 23,* 1300–1311.

Kessler, R. C., Kendler, K. S., Heath, A., Neale, M. C., & Eaves, L. J. (1992). Social support, depressed mood, and adjustment to stress: A genetic epidemiologic investigation. *Journal of Personality and Social Psychology, 62,* 257–272.

Kiecolt-Glaser, J. K., Page, G. G., Marucha, P. T., MacCallum, R. C., & Glaser, R. (1998). Psychological influences on surgical recovery: Perspectives from psychoneuroimmunology. *American Psychologist, 53,* 1209–1218.

Kilduff, M., & Day, D. V. (1994). Do chameleons get ahead? The effects of self-monitoring on managerial careers. *Academy of Management Journal, 37,* 1047–1060.

Kilham, W., & Mann, L. (1974). Level of destructive obedience as a function of transmitter and executant roles in the Milgram obedience paradigm. *Journal of Personality and Social Psychology, 29,* 696–702.

Killeya, L. A., & Johnson, B. T. (1998). Experimental induction of biased systematic processing: The directed through technique. *Personality and Social Psychology Bulletin, 24,* 17–33.

King, L. A., King, D. W., Fairbank, J. A., Keane, T. M., & Adams, G. A. (1998). Resilience-recovery factors in post-traumatic stress disorder among female and male Vietnam veterans: Hardiness, postwar social support, and additional stressful life events. *Journal of Personality and Social Psychology, 74,* 420–434.

Kinsey, A. C., Pomeroy, W., & Martin, C. (1948). *Sexual behavior in the human male.* Philadelphia: W. B. Saunders.

Kinsey, A. C., Pomeroy, W., Martin, C., & Gebhard, P. (1953). *Sexual behavior in the human female.* Philadelphia: W. B. Saunders.

Kirkpatrick, L. A. (1998). God as substitute attachment figure: A longitudinal study of adult attachment style and religious change in college students. *Personality and Social Psychology Bulletin, 24,* 961–973.

Kirkpatrick, L. A. (in press). Attachment and religious representations and behavior. In J. Cassidy & P. R. Shaver (Eds.), *Handbook of attachment theory and research.* New York: Guilford.

Kirkpatrick, L. A., & Epstein, S. (1992). Cognitive–experiential self theory and subjective probability: Further evidence for two conceptual systems. *Journal of Personality and Social Psychology, 63,* 534–544.

Kirkpatrick, S. A., & Locke, E. A. (1991). Leadership: Do traits matter? *Academy of Management Executive, 5*(2), 48–60.

Kirn, W. (1997, August 18). The ties that bind. *Time,* 48–50.

Kitano, H. H. L., Fujino, D. C., & Takahashi, J. S. (1998). Interracial marriage: Where are the Asian Americans and where are they going? In N. Zane & L. Lee (Eds.), *Handbook of Asian American psychology.* Newbury Park, CA: Sage.

Kitayama, S., & Karasawa, M. (1997). Implicit self-esteem in Japan: Name letters and birthday numbers. *Personality and Social Psychology Bulletin, 23,* 736–742.

Kitayama, S., Markus, H. R., Matsumoto, H., & Norasakkunkit, V. (1997). Individual and collective processes in the construction of the self: Self-enhancement in the United States and self-criticism in Japan. *Journal of Personality and Social Psychology, 72,* 1245–1267.

Klagsbrun, F. (1992). *Mixed feelings: Love, hate, rivalry, and reconciliation among brothers and sisters.* New York: Bantam.

Klar, Y., & Giladi, E. E. (1997). No one in my group can be below the group's average: A robust positivity bias in favor of anonymous peers. *Journal of Personality and Social Psychology, 73,* 885–905.

Klein, S. B., & Loftus, J. (1988). The nature of self-referent encoding: The contributions of elaborative and organizational processes. *Journal of Personality and Social Psychology, 55,* 5–11.

Klein, S. B., & Loftus, J. (1993). Behavioral experience and trait judgments about the self. *Personality and Social Psychology Bulletin, 16,* 740–745.

Klein, S. B., Loftus, J., & Burton, H. A. (1989). Two self-reference effects: The importance of distinguishing between self-descriptiveness judgments and autobiographical retrieval in self-referent encoding. *Journal of Personality and Social Psychology, 56,* 853–865.

Klein, S. B., Loftus, J., & Plog, A. E. (1992). Trait judgments about the self: Evidence from the encoding specificity paradigm. *Personality and Social Psychology Bulletin, 18,* 730–735.

Klein, S. B., Loftus, J., Trafton, J. G., & Fuhrman, R. W. (1992). Use of exemplars and abstractions in trait judgments: A model of trait knowledge about the self and others. *Journal of Personality and Social Psychology, 63,* 739–753.

Kleinke, C. L. (1986). Gaze and eye contact: A research review. *Psychological Bulletin, 100,* 78–100.

Kleinke, C. L., & Dean, G. O. (1990). Evaluation of men and women receiving positive and negative responses with various acquaintance strategies. *Journal of Social Behavior and Personality, 5,* 369–377.

Kleinke, C. L., Meeker, F. B., & Staneski, R. A. (1986). Preference for opening lines: Comparing ratings by men and women. *Sex Roles, 15,* 585–600.

Kline, S. L., Stafford, L., & Miklosovic, J. D. (1996). Women's surnames: Decisions, interpretations and associations with relational qualities. *Journal of Social and Personal Relationships, 13,* 593–617.

Kling, K. C., Ryff, C. D., & Essex, M. J. (1997). Adaptive changes in the self-concept during a life transition. *Personality and Social Psychology Bulletin, 23,* 981–990.

Klohnen, E. C., & Bera, S. (1998). Behavioral and experiential patterns of avoidantly and securely attached women across adulthood: A 31-year longitudinal perspective. *Journal of Personality and Social Psychology, 74,* 211–223.

Klohnen, E. C., & Mendelsohn, G. A. (1998). Partner selection for personality characteristics: A couple-centered approach. *Personality and Social Psychology Bulletin, 24,* 268–278.

Klotz, M. L., & Alicke, M. D. (1993). Complaining in close relationships. *Manuscript under review.*

Knee, C. R. (1998). Implicit theories of relationships: Assessment and prediction of romantic relationship initiation, coping, and longevity. *Journal of Personality and Social Psychology, 74,* 360–370.

Knight, G. P., & Dubro, A. (1984). Cooperative, competitive, and individualistic social values: An individualized regression and clustering approach. *Journal of Personality and Social Psychology, 46,* 98–105.

Knight, G. P., Johnson, L. G., Carlo, G., & Eisenberg, N. (1994). A multiplicative model of the dispositional antecedents of a prosocial behavior: Predicting more of the people more of the time. *Journal of Personality and Social Psychology, 66,* 178–183.

Koch, W. (1996, March 10). Marriage, divorce rates indicate Americans are hopelessly in love. Albany *Times Union,* p. A11.

Koch, W. (1998, January 11). State Department lags in promoting women. Albany *Times Union.*

Koehler, J. J. (1993). The base rate fallacy myth. *Psychology, 4.*

Koestner, R., Bernieri, F., & Zuckerman, M. (1992). Self-regulation and consistency between attitudes, traits, and behaviors. *Personality and Social Psychology Bulletin, 18,* 52–59.

Kohl, W. L., Steers, R., & Terborg, Jr. (1995). The effects of transformational leadership on teacher attitudes and student performance in Singapore. *Journal of Organizational Behavior, 73,* 695–702.

Kohlberg, L. (1966). A cognitive-developmental analysis of children's sex-role concepts and attitudes. In E. E. Maccoby (Ed.), *The development of sex differences.* Stanford, CA: Stanford University Press.

Komorita, M., & Parks, G. (1994). Interpersonal relations: Mixed-motive interaction. *Annual Review of Psychology, 46,* 183–207.

Konovsky, M. A., & Pugh, S. D. (1994). Citizenship behavior and social exchange. *Academy of Management Journal, 37,* 656–669.

Korte, C. (1980). Urban–nonurban differences in social behavior and social psychological models of urban impact. *Journal of Social Issues, 36,* 29–51.

Korte, C. (1981). Constraints on helping in an urban environment. In J. P. Rushton & R. M. Sorrentino (Eds.), *Altruism and helping behavior.* Hillsdale, NJ: Erlbaum.

Koss, M. P., & Harvey, M. R. (1991). *The rape victim: Clinical and community interventions* (2nd ed.). Newbury Park, CA: Sage.

Koss, M. P., Dinero, T. E., Seibel, C. A., & Cox, S. L. (1988). Stranger and acquaintance rape: Are there differences in the victim's experience? *Psychology of Women Quarterly, 12,* 1–24.

Kowalski, R. M. (1993). Interpreting behaviors in mixed-gender encounters: Effects of social anxiety and gender. *Journal of Social and Clinical Psychology, 12,* 239–247.

Kramer, J. P., Zebrowitz, L. A., San Giovanni, J. P., & Sherak, B. (1995). Infants' preferences for attractiveness and babyfaceness. In G. G. Bardy, R. J., Bootsman, & Y. Guiard (Eds.), *Studies in perception and action III* (pp. 389–392). Hillsdale, NJ: Erlbaum.

Kramer, L., & Baron, L. A. (1995). Intergenerational linkages: How experiences with siblings relate to the parenting of siblings. *Journal of Social and Personal Relationships, 12,* 67–87.

Kraus, S. J. (1995). Attitudes and the prediction of behavior: A meta-analysis of the empirical literature. *Personality and Social Psychology Bulletin, 21,* 58–75.

Krosnick, J. A. (1988). The role of attitude importance in social evaluation: A study of political preferences, presidential candidate evaluations, and voting behavior. *Journal of Personality and Social Psychology, 55,* 196–210.

Krosnick, J. A. (1989). Attitude importance and attitude accessibility. *Personality and Social Psychology Bulletin, 15,* 297–308.

Krosnick, J. A., Betz, A. L., Jussim, L. J., & Lynn, A. R. (1992). Subliminal conditioning of attitudes. *Personality and Social Psychology Bulletin, 18,* 152–162.

Krosnick, J. A., Boninger, D. S., Chuang, Y. C., Berent, M. K., & Carnot, C. G. (1993). Attitude strength: One construct or many related constructs? *Journal of Personality and Social Psychology, 65,* 1132–1151.

Krueger, J., & Clement, R. W. (1994). The truly false consensus effect: An ineradicable and egocentric bias in social perception. *Journal of Personality and Social Psychology, 67,* 596–610.

Krull, D. S., & Dill, J. C. (1998). Do smiles elicit more inferences than do frowns? The effect of emotional valence on the production of spontaneous inferences. *Personality and Social Psychology Bulletin, 24,* 289–300.

Krupat, E. (1975). *Psychology is social.* Glenview, IL: Scott Foresman.

Krupat, E., & Guild, W. (1980). Defining the city: The use of objective and subjective measures of community description. *Journal of Social Issues, 36,* 9–28.

Kubany, E. S., Bauer, G. B., Muraoka, M. Y., Richard, D. C., & Read, P. (1995). Impact of labeled anger and blame in intimate relationships. *Journal of Social and Clinical Psychology, 14,* 53–60.

Kuhn, D., Weinstock, M., & Flaton, R. (1994). How well do jurors reason? Competence dimensions of individual variation in a juror reasoning task. *Psychological Science, 5,* 289–296.

Kuiper, N. A., & Martin, R. A. (1998). Laughter and stress in daily life: Relation to positive and negative affect. *Motivation and Emotion, 22,* 133–153.

Kulik, J. A., Mahler, H. I. M., & Earnest, A. (1994). Social comparison and affiliation under threat: Going beyond the affiliate-choice paradigm. *Journal of Personality and Social Psychology, 66,* 301–309.

Kulik, J. A., Mahler, H. I. M., & Moore, P. J. (1996). Social comparison and affiliation under threat: Effects on recovery from major surgery. *Journal of Personality and Social Psychology, 71,* 967–979.

Kunda, Z., & Oleson, K. C. (1995). Maintaining stereotypes in the face of disconfirmation: Constructing grounds for subtyping deviants. *Journal of Personality and Social Psychology, 68,* 565–579.

Kunda, Z., & Sherman-Williams, B. (1993). Stereotypes and the construal of individuating information. *Personality and Social Psychology Bulletin, 19,* 90–99.

Kunda, Z., Fong, G. T., Sanitioso, R., & Reber, E. (1993). Directional questions direct self-conceptions. *Journal of Experimental Social Psychology, 29,* 63–86.

Kupersmidt, J. B., DeRosier, M. E., & Patterson, C. P. (1995). Similarity as the basis for children's friendships: The roles of sociometric status, aggressive and withdrawn behavior, academic achievement and demographic characteristics. *Journal of Social and Personal Relationships, 12,* 439–452.

Kurdek, L. A. (1993). The allocation of household labor in gay, lesbian, and heterosexual married couples. *Journal of Social Issues, 49(3),* 127–139.

Kurdek, L. A. (1996). The deterioration of relationship quality for gay and lesbian cohabiting couples: A five-year prospective longitudinal study. *Personal Relationships, 3,* 417–442.

Kurdek, L. A. (1997). Adjustment to relationship dissolution in gay, lesbian, and heterosexual partners. *Personal Relationships, 4,* 145–161.

Kwan, L. K. (1998). *Attitudes and attraction: A new view on how to diagnose the moderating effects of personality.* Unpublished master's thesis, National University of Singapore.

Kwan, V. S. Y., Bond, M. H., & Singelis, T. M. (1997). Pancultural explanations for life satisfaction: Adding relationship harmony to self-esteem. *Journal of Personality and Social Psychology, 73,* 1038–1051.

Kwon, Y.-H. (1994). Feeling toward one's clothing and self-perception of emotion, sociability, and work competency. *Journal of Social Behavior and Personality, 9,* 129–139.

LaFrance, M., & Hecht, M. A. (1995). Why smiles generate leniency. *Personality and Social Psychology Bulletin, 21,* 207–214.

LaPiere, R. T. (1934). Attitude and actions. *Social Forces, 13,* 230–237.

LaPrelle, J., Hoyle, R. H., Insko, C. A., & Bernthal, P. (1990). Interpersonal attraction and descriptions of the traits of others: Ideal similarity, self similarity, and liking. *Journal of Research in Personality, 24,* 216–240.

Lacayo, R. (1997, July 21). Teen crime. *Time,* 26–29.

Lachman, M. E., & Weaver, S. L. (1998). The sense of control as a moderator of social class differences in health and well-being. *Journal of Personality and Social Psychology, 74,* 763–773.

Lafferty, E. (1997, February 17). The inside story of how O. J. lost. *Time,* 29–36.

Lai, J. C. L., Hamid, N. P., & Chow, P. (1996). Gender difference in hassles and symptom reporting among Hong Kong adolescents. *Journal of Social Behavior and Personality, 11,* 149–164.

Lamb, M. E. (1998). Assessments of children's credibility in forensic contexts. *Current Directions in Psychological Science, 7,* 43–46.

Lambert, A. J. (1995). Stereotypes and social judgment: The consequences of group variability. *Journal of Personality and Social Psychology, 68,* 388–403.

Lamm, H. & Myers, D. G. (1978). Group-induced polarization of attitudes and behavior. In L. Berkowitz (Ed.), *Advances in experimental social psychology.* New York: Academic Press.

Lamm, H., & Wiesmann, U. (1997). Subjective attributes of attraction: How people characterize their liking, their love, and their being in love. *Personal Relationships, 4,* 271–284.

Lamm, H., Wiesmann, U., & Keller, K. (1998). Subjective determinants of attraction: Self-perceived causes of the rise and decline of liking, love, and being in love. *Personal Relationships, 5,* 91–104.

Lancaster, L., Royal, K. E., & Whiteside, H. D. (1995). Attitude similarity and evaluation of a women's athletic team. *Journal of Social Behavior and Personality, 10,* 885–890.

Lander, M. (1992, June 8). Corporate women. *Business Week, 74,* 76–78.

Langer, E. J. (1989). *Mindfulness.* Reading, MA: Addison–Wesley.

Langlois, J. H., & Roggman, L. A. (1990). Attractive faces are only average. *Psychological Science, 1,* 115–121.

Langlois, J. H., Ritter, J. M., Roggman, L. A., & Vaughn, L. S. (1991). Facial diversity and infant preferences for attractive faces. *Developmental Psychology, 27,* 79–84.

Langlois, J. H., Roggman, L. A., & Musselman, L. (1994). What is average and what is not average about attractive faces? *Psychological Science, 5,* 214–220.

Langlois, J. H., Roggman, L. A., & Rieser-Danner, L. A. (1990). Differential social responses to attractive and unattractive faces. *Developmental Psychology, 26,* 153–159.

Langston, C. A. (1994). Capitalizing on and coping with daily-life events: Expressive responses to positive events. *Journal of Personality and Social Psychology, 67,* 1112–1125.

Langston, C. A., & Cantor, N. (1989). Social anxiety and social constraint: When making friends is hard. *Journal of Personality and Social Psychology, 56,* 649–661.

Lansing, J. B., & Heyns, R. W. (1959). Need affiliation and frequency of four types of communication. *Journal of Abnormal and Social Psychology, 58,* 365–372.

Lapham, L. H. (1996, September). Back to school. *Harper's Magazine,* 10–11.

Larson, D. G., & Chastain, R. L. (1990). Self-concealment: Conceptualization, measurement, and health implications. *Journal of Social and Clinical Psychology, 9,* 439–455.

Larson, J. H., & Bell, N. J. (1988). Need for privacy and its effects upon interpersonal attraction and interaction. *Journal of Social and Clinical Psychology, 6,* 1–10.

Larson, J. R., Jr., Foster-Fishman, P. G., & Franz, T. M. (1998). Leadership style and the discussion of shared and unshared information in decision-making groups. *Personality and Social Psychology Bulletin, 24,* 482–495.

Larson, J. R. Jr., Christensen, C., Franz, T. M., & Abbott, A. S. (1998). Diagnosing groups: The pooling, management, and impact of shared and unshared case information in team-based medical decision making. *Journal of Personality and Social Psychology, 75,* 93–108.

Larson, R. W., Richards, M. H., & Perry-Jenkins, M. (1994). Divergent worlds: The daily emotional experience of mothers and fathers in the domestic and public spheres. *Journal of Personality and Social Psychology, 67,* 1034–1046.

Latané, B. (1981). The psychology of social impacts. *American Psychologist, 36,* 343–356.

Latané, B., Williams, K., & Harkins, S. (1979). Many hands make light the work: The causes and consequences of social loafing. *Journal of Personality and Social Psychology, 37,* 822–832.

Latané, B., & Dabbs, J. M., Jr. (1975). Sex, group size, and helping in three cities. *Sociometry, 38,* 180–194.

Latané, B., & Darley, J. M. (1968). Group inhibition of bystander intervention in emergencies. *Journal of Personality and Social Psychology, 10,* 215–221.

Latané, B., & Darley, J. M. (1970). *The unresponsive bystander: Why doesn't he help?* New York: Appleton-Century-Crofts.

Latané, B., & L'Herrou, T. (1996). Spatial clustering in the conformity game: Dynamic social impact in electronic groups. *Journal of Personality and Social Psychology, 70,* 1218–1230.

Latest figures: U.S. death rate is lower. (1994, December 16). Associated Press.

Latty-Mann, H., & Davis, K. E. (1996). Attachment theory and partner choice: Preference and actuality. *Journal of Social and Personal Relationships, 13,* 5–23.

Lau, S. (1989). Sex role orientation and domains of self esteem. *Sex Roles, 21,* 415–422.

Lau, S., & Gruen, G. E. (1992). The social stigma of loneliness: Effect of target person's and perceiver's sex. *Personality and Social Psychology Bulletin, 18,* 182–189.

Lauer, J., & Lauer, R. (1985, June). Marriages made to last. *Psychology Today,* 22–26.

Laumann, E. O., Gagnon, J. H., Michael, R. T., & Michaels, S. (1994). *The social organization of sexuality: Sexual practices in the United States.* Chicago: University of Chicago Press.

Laurenceau, J.-P., Barrett, L. F., & Pietromonaco, P. R. (1998). Intimacy as an interpersonal process: The importance of self-disclosure, partner disclosure, and perceived partner responsiveness in interpersonal exchanges. *Journal of Personality and Social Psychology, 74,* 1238–1251.

Lavine, H., Thomsen, C. J., & Gonzales, M. H. (1997). The development of interattitudinal consistency: The shared-consequences model. *Journal of Personality and Social Psychology, 72,* 735–749.

Lazarus, R. S. (1966). *Psychological stress and the coping process.* New York: McGraw-Hill.

Lazarus, R. S. (1993). From psychological stress to the emotions: A history of changing outlooks. *Annual Review of Psychology, 44,* 1–21.

Leary, M. R., Schreindorfer, L. S., & Haupt, A. L. (1995). The role of low self-esteem in emotional and behavioral problems: Why is low self-esteem dysfunctional? *Journal of Social and Clinical Psychology, 14,* 297–314.

Leary, M. R., Tambor, E. S., Terdal, S. K., & Downs, D. L. (1995). Self-esteem as an interpersonal monitor: The sociometer hypothesis. *Journal of Personality and Social Psychology, 68,* 518–530.

Leary, M. R., Spinger, C., Negel, L., Ansell, E., & Evans, K. (1998). The causes, phenomenology, and consequences of hurt feelings. *Journal of Personality and Social Psychology, 74,* 1225–1237.

Leary, W. E. (1988, November 19). Novel methods unlock witnesses' memories. *New York Times,* pp. C1, C15.

Lee, S. M., & Yamanaka, K. (1990). Patterns of Asian American intermarriage and marital assimilation. *Journal of Comparative Family Studies, 21,* 287–305.

Lee, Y. T. (1995). A comparison of politics and personality in China and the U.S.: Testing a "kernel of truth" hypothesis. *Journal of Contemporary China, 9,* 56–68.

Lee, Y. T., & Ottati, V. (1993). Determinants of ingroup and out-group perceptions of heterogeneity: An investigation of Sino-American differences. *Journal of Cross-Cultural Psychology, 25,* 146–158.

Lee, Y. T., & Seligman, M. E. P. (1997). Are Americans more optimistic than the Chinese? *Personality and Social Psychology Bulletin, 23,* 32–40.

Lefcourt, H. M., Davidson, K., Shepherd, R., Phillips, M., Prkachin, K., & Mills, D. (1995). Perspective-taking humor: Accounting for stress moderation. *Journal of Social and Clinical Psychology, 14,* 373–391.

Lehman, T. C., Daubman, K. A., Guarna, J., Jordan, J., & Cirafesi, C. (1995, April). *Gender differences in the motivational consequences of receiving help.* Paper presented at the meeting of the Eastern Psychological Association, Boston.

Leippe, M. R., & Romanczyk, A. (1987). Children on the witness stand: A communication/persuasion analysis of jurors' reactions to child witnesses. In S. J. Ceci, M. P. Toglia, & D. F. Ross (Eds.), *Children's eyewitness memory* (pp. 155–177). New York: Springer-Verlag.

Lennox, R. D., & Wolfe, R. N. (1984). Revision of the self-monitoring scale. *Journal of Personality and Social Psychology, 46,* 1349–1364.

Leonard, M. (1998, February 15). Making a mark on the culture. Boston *Sunday Globe,* pp. C1, C2, C11, C12.

Lepore, L., & Brown, R. (1997). Category and stereotype activation: Is prejudice inevitable? *Journal of Personality and Social Psychology, 72,* 275–287.

Lepore, S. J. (1997). Expressive writing moderates the relation between intrusive thoughts and depressive symptoms. *Journal of Personality and Social Psychology, 73,* 1030–1037.

Lerner, Ma. J. (1980). *The belief in a just world: A fundamental delusion.* New York: Plenum Press.

Levenson, R. W., Carstensen, L. L., & Gottman, J. M. (1994). The influence of age and gender on affect, physiology, and their interrelations: A study of long-term marriages. *Journal of Personality and Social Psychology, 67,* 56–68.

Leventhal, G. S., & Anderson, D. (1970). Self-interest and the maintenance of equity. *Journal of Personality and Social Psychology, 15,* 57–62.

Leventhal, G. S., Karuza, J., & Fry, W. R. (1980). Beyond fairness: A theory of allocation preferences. In G. Mikula (Ed.), *Justice and social interaction* (pp. 167–218). New York: Springer-Verlag.

Leventhal, H., Singer, R., & Jones, S. (1965). The effects of fear and specificity of recommendation upon attitudes and behavior. *Journal of Personality and Social Psychology, 2,* 20–29.

Levine, R. V., Martinez, T. S., Brase, G., & Sorenson, K. (1994). Helping in 36 U.S. cities. *Journal of Personality and Social Psychology, 67,* 69–82.

Levy, K. N., Blatt, S. J., & Shaver, P. R. (1998). Attachment styles and parental representations. *Journal of Personality and Social Psychology, 74,* 407–419.

Lewin, K., Lippitt, R., & White, R. K. (1939). Patterns of aggressive behavior in experimentally created "social climates." *Journal of Social Psychology, 10,* 271–299.

Lewis, M. (1992). Will the real self or selves please stand up? *Psychological Inquiry, 3,* 123–124.

Lewis, M. (1998). *Altering fate: Why the past does not predict the future.* New York: Guilford.

Liberman, A., & Chaiken, S. (1992). Defensive processing of personally relevant health messages. *Personality and Social Psychology Bulletin, 18,* 669–679.

Liden, R. C., & Mitchell, T. R. (1988). Ingratiatory behaviors in organizational settings. *Academy of Management Review, 13,* 572–587.

Lieberman, J. D., & Greenberg, J. (1999). Cognitive-experiential self-theory and displaced aggression. *Journal of Personality and Social Psychology,* in press.

Lind, E. A. (1994). Procedural justice and culture: Evidence for ubiquitous process concerns. *Zeitschrift fur Rechtssoziologie, 15,* 24–36.

Lind, M. (1995, October 23). Jury dismissed. *The New Republic,* 12–14.

Linden, E. (1992a). Chimpanzees with a difference: Bonobos. *National Geographic, 18*(3), 46–53.

Linden, E. (1992b). Rio's legacy. *Time, 139*(25), 44–45.

Lindsay, D. S. (1993). Eyewitness suggestibility. *Current Directions in Psychological Science, 2,* 86–89.

Lindsay, D. S. (1998). Recovered memories and social justice. *American Psychologist, 53,* 486–487.

Lindsey, E. W., Mize, J., & Pettit, G. S. (1997). Mutuality in parent–child play: Consequences for children's peer competence. *Journal of Social and Personal Relationships, 14,* 523–538.

Linville, P. W., & Fischer, G. W. (1993). Exemplar and abstraction models of perceived group variability and stereotypicality. *Social Cognition, 11,* 92–125.

Linville, P. W., Fischer, G. W., & Salovey, P. (1989). Perceived distributions of the characteristics of in-group and outgroup members: Empirical evidence and a computer simulation. *Journal of Personality and Social Psychology, 57,* 165–188.

Linz, D., & Penrod, S. (1992). Exploring the first and sixth amendments: Pretrial publicity and jury decision making. In D. K. Kagehiro & W. S. Laufer (Eds.), *Handbook of psychology and law.* New York: Springer-Verlag.

Lippa, R., & Donaldson, S. I. (1990). Self-monitoring and idiographic measures of behavioral variability across interpersonal relationships. *Journal of Personality, 58,* 465–479.

Living memorial. (1992, October 26). *Time,* 21.

Lobel, T. E. (1994). Sex typing and the social perception of gender stereotypic and nonstereotypic behavior: The uniqueness of feminine males. *Journal of Personality and Social Psychology, 66,* 379–385.

Locke, E. A. (1991). *The essence of leadership.* New York: Lexington Books.

Locke, M. (1995, May 25). Love better with age, study says. *Albany Times Union,* p. C-5.

Loftus, E. F. (1992a). *Witness for the defense.* New York: St. Martin's Press.

Loftus, E. F. (1992b). When a lie becomes memory's truth: Memory distortion after exposure to misinformation. *Current Directions in Psychological Science, 1,* 121–123.

Loftus, E. F. (1997). Memory for a past that never was. *Current Directions in Psychological Science, 6,* 60–65.

Loftus, E. F. (1998). The private practice of misleading direction. *American Psychologist, 53,* 484–485.

Loftus, E. F., & Pickrell, J. E. (1995). The formation of false memories. *Psychiatric Annals, 25,* 720–725.

Loftus, E. F., Coan, J. A., & Pickrell, J. E. (1996). Manufacturing false memories using bits of reality. In L. Reder (Ed.), *Implicit memory and metacognition* (pp. 195–220). Mahwah, NJ: Erlbaum.

Logsdon, M. C., Birkimer, J. C., & Barbee, A. P. (1997). Social support providers for postpartum women. *Journal of Social Behavior and Personality, 12,* 89–102.

Lopez, F. G. (1997). Student–professor relationship styles, childhood attachment bonds and current academic orientations. *Journal of Social and Personal Relationships, 14,* 271–282.

Lopez, F. G., Gover, M. R., Leskela, J., Sauer, E. M., Schirmer, L., & Wyssmann, J. (1997). Attachment styles, shame, guilt, and collaborative problem-solving orientations. *Personal Relationships, 4,* 187–199.

Lord, C. G., Ross, L., & Lepper, M. R. (1979). Biased assimilation and attitude polarization: The effects of prior theories on subsequently considered evidence. *Journal of Personality and Social Psychology, 37,* 2098–2109.

Lorenz, K. (1966). *On aggression.* New York: Harcourt, Brace, & World.

Lorenz, K. (1974). *Civilized man's eight deadly sins.* New York: Harcourt, Brace, Jovanovich.

Losch, M., & Cacioppo, J. (1990). Cognitive dissonance may enhance sympathetic tonis, but attitudes are changed to reduce negative affect rather than arousal. *Journal of Experimental Social Psychology, 26,* 289–304.

Lox, C. L., & Rudolph, D. L. (1994). The Subjective Exercise Experiences Scale (SEES): Factorial validity and effects of acute exercise. *Journal of Social Behavior and Personality, 9,* 837–844.

Lundberg, J. K., & Sheehan, E. P. (1994). The effects of glasses and weight on perceptions of attractiveness and intelligence. *Journal of Social Behavior and Personality, 9,* 753–760.

Lundgren, S. R., & Prislin, R. (1998). Motivated cognitive processing and attitude change. *Personality and Social Psychology Bulletin, 24,* 715–726.

Lurie, A. (Ed.) (1993). *The Oxford book of modern fairy tales.* Oxford, England: Oxford University Press.

Luus, C. A., & Wells, G. L. (1994). The malleability of eyewitness confidence: Co-witness and perseverance effects. *Journal of Applied Psychology, 79,* 714–723.

Luus, C. A. E., Wells, G. L., & Turtle, J. W. (1995). Child eyewitnesses: Seeing is believing. *Journal of Applied Psychology, 80,* 317–326.

Lydon, J. E., Jamieson, D. W., & Holmes, J. G. (1997). The meaning of social interactions in the transition from acquaintanceship to friendship. *Journal of Personality and Social Psychology, 73,* 536–548.

Lyness, K. S., & Thompson, D. E. (1997). Above the glass ceiling? A comparison of matched samples of female and male executives. *Journal of Applied Psychology, 82,* 359–375.

Lynn, M., & Mynier, K. (1993). Effects of server posture on restaurant tipping. *Journal of Applied Social Psychology, 23,* 678–685.

Lyubomirsky, S., & Nolen-Hoeksema, S. (1995). Effects of self-focused rumination on negative thinking and interpersonal problem solving. *Journal of Personality and Social Psychology, 69,* 176–190.

Maas, A., & Clark, R. D. III (1984). Hidden impact of minorities: Fifteen years of minority influence research. *Psychological Bulletin, 95,* 233–243.

Macaulay, J. (1970). A shill for charity. In J. Macaulay & L. Berkowitz (Eds.), *Altruism and helping behavior* (pp. 43–59). New York: Academic Press.

MacCoun, R. J., & Kerr, N. L. (1988). Asymmetric influence in mock jury deliberation: Jurors' bias for leniency. *Journal of Personality and Social Psychology, 54,* 21–33.

MacDonald, T. K., Zanna, M. P., & Fong, G. T. (1996). Why common sense goes out the window: Effects of alcohol on intentions to use condoms. *Personality and Social Psychology Bulletin, 8,* 763–775.

Mack, D., & Rainey, D. (1990). Female applicants' grooming and personnel selection. *Journal of Social Behavior and Personality, 5,* 399–407.

Mackie, D. M., & Worth, L. T. (1989). Processing deficits and the mediation of positive affect in persuasion. *Journal of Personality and Social Psychology, 57,* 27–40.

Mackie, D. M., Allison, S. T., Worth, L. T., & Asuncion, A. G. (1992). The impact of outcome biases on counterstereotypic inferences about groups. *Personality and Social Psychology Bulletin, 18,* 44–51.

Macrae, C. N. (1992). A tale of two curries: Counterfactual thinking and accident-related judgments. *Personality and Social Psychology Bulletin, 18,* 84–87.

Macrae, C. N., & Milne, A. B. (1992). A curry for your thoughts: Empathic effects on counterfactual thinking. *Personality and Social Psychology Bulletin, 18,* 625–630.

Macrae, C. N., Bodenhausen, G. V., & Milne, A. B. (1998). Saying no to unwanted thoughts: Self-focus and the regulation of mental life. *Journal of Personality and Social Psychology, 74,* 578–589.

Macrae, C. N., Milne, A. B., & Bodenhausen, G. V. (1994). Stereotypes as energy-saving devices: A peek inside the cognitive toolbox. *Journal of Personality and Social Psychology, 66,* 37–47.

Macrae, C. N., Shepherd, J. W., & Milne, A. B. (1992). The effects of source credibility on the dilution of stereotype-based judgments. *Personality and Social Psychology Bulletin, 18,* 765–775.

Macrae, C. N., Bodenhausen, G. V., Milne, A. B., & Ford, R. (1997). On the regulation of recollection: The intentional forgetting of sterotypical memories. *Journal of Personality and Social Psychology, 72,* 709–719.

Macrae, C. N., Bodenhausen, G. V., Milne, A. B., & Jetten, J. (1994). Out of mind but back in sight: Stereotypes on the rebound. *Journal of Personality and Social Psychology, 67,* 808–817.

Madon, S., Jussim, L., Keiper, S., Eccles, J., Smith, A., & Palumbo, P. (1998). The accuracy and power of sex, social class, and ethnic stereotypes: A naturalistic study in person perception. *Personality and Social Psychology Bulletin, 24,* 1304–1318.

Maheswaran, D., & Chaiken, S. (1991). Promoting systematic processing in low-motivation settings: Effect of incongruent information on processing and judgment. *Journal of Personality and Social Psychology, 61,* 13–25.

Maio, G. R., Esses, V. M., & Bell, D. W. (1994). The formation of attitudes toward new immigrant groups. *Journal of Applied Social Psychology, 24,* 1762–1776.

Maisonneuve, J., Palmade, G., & Fourment, C. (1952). Selective choices and propinquity. *Sociometry, 15,* 135–140.

Major, B. (1989). Gender differences in comparisons and entitlement: Implications for comparable worth. *Journal of Social Issues, 45,* 99–115.

Major, B. (1993). Gender, entitlement, and the distribution of family labor. *Journal of Social Issues, 49*(3), 141–159.

Major, B., & Adams, J. B. (1983). Roles of gender, interpersonal orientation, and self-presentation in distributive justice behavior. *Journal of Personality and Social Psychology, 45,* 598–608.

Major, B., & Deaux, K. (1982). Individual differences in justice behavior. In J. Greenberg & R. L. Cohen (Eds.), *Equity and justice in social behavior.* New York: Academic Press.

Major, B., & Konar, E. (1984). An investigation of sex differences in pay expectations and their possible causes. *Academy of Management Journal, 27,* 777–792.

Major, B., Carnevale, P. J. D., & Deaux, K. (1981). A different perspective on androgyny: Evaluations of masculine and feminine personality characteristics. *Journal of Personality and Social Psychology, 41,* 988–1001.

Major, B., Sciacchitano, A. M., & Crocker, J. (1993). In-group versus out-group comparisons and self-esteem. *Personality and Social Psychology Bulletin, 19,* 711–721.

Major, B., Richards, C., Cooper, M. L., Cozzarelli, C., & Zubek, J. (1998). Personal resilience, cognitive appraisals, and coping: An integrative model of adjustment to abortion. *Journal of Personality and Social Psychology, 74,* 735–752.

Malamuth, N. M., & Brown, L. M. (1994). Sexually aggressive men's perceptions of women's communications: Testing three explanations. *Journal of Personality and Social Psychology, 67,* 699–712.

Malle, B. F., & Knobe, J. (1997). Which behaviors do people explain? A basic actor–observer asymmetry. *Journal of Personality and Social Psychology, 72,* 288–304.

Mallick, S. K., & McCandless, B. R. (1966). A study of catharsis of aggression. *Journal of Personality and Social Psychology, 4,* 591–596.

Manke, B., & Plomin, R. (1997). Adolescent familial inter actions: A genetic extension of the social relations model. *Journal of Social and Personal Relationships, 14,* 505–522.

Marazziti, D., Rotondo, A., Presta, S., Pancioloi-Guadagnucci, M. L., Palego, L., & Conti, L. (1993). Role of serotonin in human aggressive behavior. *Aggressive Behavior, 19,* 347–353.

Margalit, M., & Eysenck, S. (1990). Prediction of coherence in adolescence: Gender differences in social skills, personality, and family climate. *Journal of Research in Personality, 24,* 510–521.

Margolin, G., John, R. S., & O'Brien, M. (1989). Sequential affective patterns as a function of marital conflict style. *Journal of Social and Clinical Psychology, 8,* 45–61.

Markman, H. J. (1981). Prediction of marital distress: A 5-year follow-up. *Journal of Consulting and Clinical Psychology, 49,* 760–762.

Markus, H., & Nurius, P. (1986). Possible selves. *American Psychologist, 41,* 954–969.

Marsh, H. W. (1995). A Jamesian model of self-investment and self-esteem: Comment on Pelham (1995). *Journal of Personality and Social Psychology, 69,* 1151–1160.

Marsh, K. L., Hart-O'Rourke, D. M., & Julka, D. L. (1997). The persuasive effects of verbal and nonverbal information in a context of value relevance. *Personality and Social Psychology Bulletin, 23,* 563–579.

Marshall, N. L., & Barnett, R. C. (1993). Variations in job strain across nursing and social work specialties. *Journal of Community and Applied Social Psychology, 3,* 261–271.

Martin, C. L. (1987). A ratio measure of sex stereotyping. *Journal of Personality and Social Psychology, 52,* 489–499.

Martin, C. L., & Parker, S. (1995). Folk theories about sex and race differences. *Personality and Social Psychology Bulletin, 21,* 45–57.

Martin, R. (1997). "Girls don't talk about garages!": Perceptions of conversation in same- and cross-sex friendships. *Personal Relationships, 4,* 115–130.

Martz, J. M., Verette, J., Arriaga, X. B., Slovik, L. F., Cox, C. L., & Rusbult, C. E. (1998). Positive illusion in close relationships. *Personal Relationships, 5,* 159–181.

Maslach, C., Santee, R. T., & Wade, C. (1987). Individuation, gender role, and dissent: Personality mediators of situational forces. *Journal of Personality and Social Psychology, 53,* 1088–1094.

Mastekaasa, A. (1995). Age variation in the suicide rates and self-reported subjective well-being of married and never married persons. *Journal of Community and Applied Social Psychology, 5,* 21–39.

Mathis, D. (1998, June 17). Report on girls' lives offers mixed assessment. Gannett News Service.

Matthews, S. H. (1986). *Friendship through the life course.* Newbury Park, CA: Sage.

Maugh, T. H., II. (1998, February 21). To keep marriage going, try giving in to your wife. *Los Angeles Times.*

May, J. L., & Hamilton, P. A. (1980). Effects of musically evoked affect on women's interpersonal attraction and perceptual judgments of physical attractiveness of men. *Motivation and Emotion, 4,* 217–228.

Mayer, J. D., & Hanson, E. (1995). Mood-congruent judgment over time. *Personality and Social Psychology Bulletin, 21,* 237–244.

Mayer, J. D., & Salovey, P. (1995). Emotional intelligence and the construction and regulation of feelings. *Applied & Preventive Psychology, 4,* 197–208.

Mazzella, R., & Feingold, A. (1994). The effects of physical attractiveness, race, socioeconomic status, and gender of defendants and victims on judgments of mock jurors: A meta-analysis. *Journal of Applied Social Psychology, 24,* 1315–1344.

McAdams, D. P. (1979). *Validation of a thematic coding system for the intimacy motive.* Unpublished doctoral dissertation, Harvard University.

McAdams, D. P., Diamond, A., Aubin, E. de S., & Mansfield, E. (1997). Stories of commitment: The psychosocial construction of generative lives. *Journal of Personality and Social Psychology, 72,* 678–694.

McArthur, L. Z., & Eisen, S. V. (1976). Achievements of male and female storybook characters as determinants of achievement behavior by boys and girls. *Journal of Personality and Social Psychology, 33,* 467–473.

McCabe, M. P. (1987). Desired and experienced levels of premarital affection and sexual intercourse during dating. *Journal of Sex Research, 23,* 23–33.

McCall, M. (1997). Physical attractiveness and access to alcohol: What is beautiful does not get carded. *Journal of Applied Social Psychology, 23,* 453–562.

McCall, M. E., & Struthers, N. J. (1994). Sex, sex-role orientation and self-esteem as predictors of coping style. *Journal of Social Behavior and Personality, 9,* 801–810.

McCauley, C., Coleman, G., & DeFusco, P. (1977). Commuters' eye contact with strangers in city and suburban train stations: Evidence of short-term adaptation to interpersonal overload in the city. *Environmental Psychology and Nonverbal Behavior, 2,* 215–225.

McClure, J. (1998). Discounting causes of behavior: Are two reasons better than one? *Journal of Personality and Social Psychology, 74,* 7–20.

McConnell, A. R., & Fazio, R. H. (1996). Women as men and people: Effects of gender-marked language. *Personality and Social Psychology Bulletin, 22,* 1004–1013.

McConnell, A. R., Leibold, J. M., & Sherman, S. J. (1997). Within-target illusory correlations and the formation of context-dependent attitudes. *Journal of Personality and Social Psychology, 73,* 675–686.

McConnell, A. R., Sherman, S. J., & Hamilton, D. L. (1994). Illusory correlation in the perception of groups: An extension of the distinctiveness-based account. *Journal of Personality and Social Psychology, 67,* 414–429.

McCullough, M. E., Worthington, E. L., Jr., & Rachal, K. C. (1997). Interpersonal forgiving in close relationships. *Journal of Personality and Social Psychology, 73,* 321–336.

McDonald, H. E., & Hirt, E. R. (1997). When expectancy meets desire: Motivational effects in reconstructive memory. *Journal of Personality and Social Psychology, 72,* 5–23.

McDonald, K. A. (1995, March 3). Correlations add new detail to sex study. *The Chronicle of Higher Education,* p. A8.

McFarland, C., & Buehler, R. (1995). Collective self-esteem as a moderator of the frog-pond effect in reactions to performance feedback. *Journal of Personality and Social Psychology, 68,* 1055–1070.

McGaughey, K. J., & Stiles, W. B. (1983). Courtroom interrogation of rape victims: Verbal response mode use by attorneys and witnesses during direct examination vs. cross-examination. *Journal of Applied Social Psychology, 13,* 78–87.

McGonagle, K. A., Kessler, R. C., & Schilling, E. A. (1992). The frequency and determinants of marital disagreements in a community sample. *Journal of Social and Personal Relationships, 9,* 507–524.

McGowan, S., Daniels, L. K., & Byrne, D. (1999a). *Self-esteem and interpersonal trust: Evidence consistent with Bartholomew's conceptualization of attachment.* Manuscript submitted for publication.

McGowan, S., Daniels, L. K., & Byrne, D. (1999b). *The Albany Measure of Attachment Style: A multi-item measure of Bartholomew's four-factor model.* Manuscript submitted for publication.

McGuire, S., McHale, S. M., & Updegraff, K. A. (1996). Children's perceptions of the sibling relationship in middle childhood: Connections within and between family relationships. *Personal Relationships, 3,* 229–239.

McGuire, W. J., & McGuire, C. V. (1996). Enhancing self-esteem by directed-thinking tasks: Cognitive and affective positivity asymmetries. *Journal of Personality and Social Psychology, 70,* 1117–1125.

McKelvie, S. J. (1993a). Perceived cuteness, activity level, and gender in schematic babyfaces. *Journal of Social Behavior and Personality, 8,* 297–310.

McKelvie, S. J. (1993b). Stereotyping in perception of attractiveness, age, and gender in schematic faces. *Social Behavior and Personality, 21,* 121–128.

McKenna, K. Y. A., & Bargh, J. A. (1998). Coming out in the age of the internet: Identity "demarginalization" through virtual group participation. *Journal of Personality and Social Psychology, 75,* 681–694.

McKillip, J., & Reidel, S. L. (1983). External validity of matching on physical attractiveness for same and opposite sex couples. *Journal of Applied Social Psychology, 13,* 328–337.

McMullen, M. N., Markman, K. D., & Gavanski, I. (1995). Living in neither the best nor the worst of all possible worlds: Antecedents and consequences of upward and downward counterfactual thinking. In N. J. Roese & J. M. Olson (Eds.), *What might have been: The social psychology of counterfactual thinking* (pp. 133–167). Mahwah, NJ: Erlbaum.

McNulty, S. E., & Swann, W. B., Jr. (1994). Identity negotiation in roommate relationships: The self as architect and consequence of social reality. *Journal of Personality and Social Psychology, 67,* 1012–1023.

McWhirter, B. T. (1997). A pilot study of loneliness in ethnic minority college students. *Social Behavior and Personality, 25,* 295–304.

Mealey, L. (1997). Bulking up: The roles of sex and sexual orientation on attempts to manipulate physical attractiveness. *Journal of Sex Research, 34,* 223–228.

Medvec, V. H., Madey, S. F., & Gilovich, T. (1995). When less is more: Counterfactual thinking and satisfaction among Olympic athletes. *Journal of Personality and Social Psychology, 69,* 603–610.

Medvec, V. H., & Savitsky, K. (1997). When doing better means feeling worse: The effects of categorical cutoff points on counterfactual thinking and satisfaction. *Journal of Personality and Social Psychology, 72,* 1284–1296.

Mehrabian, A., & Piercy, M. (1993a). Positive or negative connotations of unconventionally or conventionally spelled names. *Journal of Social Psychology, 133,* 445–451.

Mehrabian, A., & Piercy, M. (1993b). Affective and personality characteristics inferred from length of first names. *Personality and Social Psychology Bulletin, 19,* 755–758.

Meindl, J. R., & Lerner, M. J. (1985). Exacerbation of extreme responses to an outgroup. *Journal of Personality and Social Psychology, 47,* 71–84.

Melamed, S., Ben-Avi, I., Luz, J., & Green, M. S. (1995). Objective and subjective work monotony: Effects on job satisfaction, psychological distress, and absenteeism in blue-collar workers. *Journal of Applied Psychology, 80,* 29–42.

Meleshko, K. G. A., & Alden, L. E. (1993). Anxiety and self-disclosure: Toward a motivational model. *Journal of Personality and Social Psychology, 64,* 1000–1009.

Mellers, B. A., Richards, V., & Birnbaum, M. H. (1992). Distributional theories of impression formation. *Organizational Behavior and Human Decision Processes, 51,* 313–343.

Menesini, E. (1997). Behavioural correlates of friendship status among Italian schoolchildren. *Journal of Social and Personal Relationships, 14,* 109–121.

Merrill, D. M. (1996). Conflict and cooperation among adult siblings during the transition to the role of filial caregiver. *Journal of Social and Personal Relationships, 13,* 399–413.

Mesquita, B., Frijda, N. H., & Scherer, K. R. (1997). Culture and emotions. In J. E. Berry, P. B. Dasen, & T. S. Saraswathi (Eds.), *Handbook of cross-cultural psychology: Vol. 2. Basic processes and developmental psychology.* (pp. 255–297). Boston: Allyn and Bacon.

Meyers, S. A., & Berscheid, E. (1997). The language of love: The difference a preposition makes. *Personality and Social Psychology Bulletin, 23,* 347–362.

Miceli, M. P., & Lane, M. C. (1991). Antecedents of pay satisfaction: A review and extension. In K. Rowland & O. R. Ferris (Eds.), *Research in personnel and human resources management* (Vol. 9, pp. 235–309). Greenwich, CT: JAI Press.

Michael, R. T., Gagnon, J. H., Laumann, E. O., & Kolata, G. (1994). *Sex in America: A definitive survey.* Boston: Little, Brown.

Mickelson, K. D., Kessler, R. C., & Shaver, P. R. (1997). Adult attachment in a nationally representative sample. *Journal of Personality and Social Psychology, 73,* 1092–1106.

Middlekauff, R. (1996). *Benjamin Franklin and his enemies.* Berkeley: University of California Press.

Middlestadt, S. E., Fishbein, M., Albarracin, D., Francis, C., Eustace, M. A., Helquist, M., & Schneider, A. (1995). Evaluating the impact of a national AIDS prevention radio campaign in St. Vincent and the Grenadines. *Journal of Applied Social Psychology, 25,* 21–34.

Middleton, W., Harris, P., & Surman, M. (1996). Give 'em enough rope: Perception of health and safety risks in bungee jumpers. *Journal of Social and Clinical Psychology, 15,* 68–79.

Mihalko, S. L., McAuley, E., & Bane, S. M. (1996). Self-efficacy and affective responses to acute exercise in middle-aged adults. *Journal of Social Behavior and Personality, 11,* 375–385.

Mikulincer, M. (1995). Attachment style and the mental representation of the self. *Journal of Personality and Social Psychology, 69,* 1203–1215.

Mikulincer, M. (1997). Adult attachment style and information processing: Individual differences in curiosity and cognitive closure. *Journal of Personality and Social Psychology, 72,* 1217–1230.

Mikulincer, M. (1998a). Adult attachment style and individual differences in functional versus dysfunctional experiences of anger. *Journal of Personality and Social Psychology, 74,* 513–524.

Mikulincer, M. (1998b). Attachment working models and the sense of trust: An exploration of interaction goals and affect regulation. *Journal of Personality and Social Psychology, 74,* 1209–1224.

Mikulincer, M., & Florian, V. (1995). Appraisal of and coping with a real-life stressful situation: The contribution of attachment styles. *Personality and Social Psychology Bulletin, 21,* 406–414.

Mikulincer, M., Orbach, I., & Iavnieli, D. (1998). Adult attachment style and affect regulation: Strategic variations in subjective self-other similarity. *Journal of Personality and Social Psychology, 75,* 436–448.

Miles, S. M., & Carey, G. (1997). Genetic and environmental architecture of human aggression. *Journal of Personality and Social Psychology, 72,* 207–217.

Milgram, S. (1963). Behavior study of obedience. *Journal of Abnormal and Social Psychology, 67,* 371–378.

Milgram, S. (1965a). Liberating effects of group pressure. *Journal of Personality and Social Psychology, 1,* 127–134.

Milgram, S. (1965b) Some conditions of obedience and disobedience to authority. *Human Relations, 18,* 57–76.

Milgram, S. (1970). The experience of living in cities. *Science, 167,* 1461–1468.

Milgram, S. (1974). *Obedience to authority.* New York: Harper.

Millar, M. G. (1997). The effects of emotion on breast self-examination: Another look at the health belief model. *Social Behavior and Personality, 25,* 223–232.

Miller, A. C. (1998, December 28). Violent crime down 7%. *Los Angeles Times.*

Miller, A. G., McHoskey, J. W., Bane, C. M., & Dowd, T. G. (1993). The attitude polarization phenomenon: Role of response measure, attitude extremity, and behavioral consequences of reported attitude change. *Journal of Personality and Social Psychology, 64,* 516–574.

Miller, C. T., Rothblum, E. D., Barbour, L., Brand, P. A., & Felicio, D. (1990). Social interactions of obese and nonobese women. *Journal of Personality, 58,* 365–380.

Miller, C. T., Rothblum, E. D., Brand, P. A., & Felicio, D. M. (1995). Do obese women have poorer social relationships than nonobese women? Reports by self, friends, and coworkers. *Journal of Personality, 63,* 65–85.

Miller, C. T., Rothblum, E. D., Felicio, D., & Brand, P. (1995). Compensating for stigma: Obese and non-obese women's reactions to being visible. *Personality and Social Psychology Bulletin, 21,* 1093–1106.

Miller, D. T., & Ratner, R. K. (1996). The power of the myth of self-interest. In L. Montada & M. Lerner (Eds.), *Current societal concerns about justice.* New York: Plenum.

Miller, D. T., & Ross, M. (1975). Self-serving biases in attribution of causality: Fact or fiction? *Psychological Bulletin, 82,* 313–325.

Miller, D. T., & McFarland, C. (1986). Counterfactual thinking and victim compensation: A test of norm theory. *Personality and Social Psychology Bulletin, 12,* 513–519.

Miller, J. G. (1984). Culture and development of everyday social explanation. *Journal of Personality and Social Psychology, 46,* 961–978.

Miller, M. L., & Thayer, J. F. (1989). On the existence of discrete classes in personality: Is self-monitoring the correct joint to carve? *Journal of Personality and Social Psychology, 57,* 143–155.

Miller, N., Maruayama, G., Beaber, R. J., & Valone, K. (1976). Speed of speech and persuasion. *Journal of Personality and Social Psychology, 34,* 615–624.

Miller, P. A., & Jansen-op-de-Haar, M. A. (1997). Emotional, cognitive, behavioral, and temperament characteristics of high empathy children. *Motivation and Emotion, 21,* 109–125.

Miller, R. S. (1991). On decorum in close relationships: Why aren't we polite to those we love? *Contemporary Social Psychology, 15,* 63–65.

Minard, R. D. (1952). Race relations in the Pocahontas Coal Field. *Journal of Social Issues, 8,* 29–44.

Mischel, W. (1967). A social learning view of sex differences in behavior. In E. E. Maccoby (Ed.), *The development of sex differences* (pp. 56–81). London: Tavistock.

Misconceptions about why people obey laws and accept judicial decisions. (1997, April). *APS Observer,* 12–13, 46.

Mixon, K. D., Foley, L. A. K., & Orne, K. (1995). The influence of racial similarity on the O. J. Simpson trial. *Journal of Social Behavior and Personality, 10,* 481–490.

Monsour, M. (1992). Meanings of intimacy in cross- and same-sex friendships. *Journal of Social and Personal Relationships, 9,* 277–295.

Monsour, M., Betty, S., & Kurzweil, N. (1993). Levels of perspectives and the perception of intimacy in cross-sex friendships: A balance theory explanation of shared perceptual reality. *Journal of Social and Personal Relationships, 10,* 529–550.

Montepare, J. M., & Zebrowitz-McArthur, L. (1988). Impressions of people created by age-related qualities of their gaits. *Journal of Personality and Social Psychology, 55,* 547–556.

Montgomery, L. (1996, May 6). Crime takes a beating in 1995. Knight-Ridder.

Moore, C. H., Wuensch, K. L., Hedges, R. M., & Castellow, W. A. (1994). The effects of physical attractiveness and social desirability on judgments regarding a sexual harassment case. *Journal of Social Behavior and Personality, 9,* 715–730.

Moore, D. (1995). Gender role attitudes and division of labor: Sex or occupation-type differences? (An Israeli example). *Journal of Social Behavior and Personality, 10,* 215–234.

Moore, J. S., Graziano, W. G., & Miller, M. G. (1987). Physical attractiveness, sex role orientation, and the evaluation of adults and children. *Personality and Social Psychology Bulletin, 13,* 95–102.

Moore, T. (1993, August 16). Millions of volunteers counter image of a selfish society. *Albany Times Union,* p. A-2.

Moran, G., & Comfort, J. C. (1986). Neither "tentative" nor "fragmentary": Verdict preference of impaneled felony jurors as a function of attitude toward capital punishment. *Journal of Applied Psychology, 71,* 146–155.

Moran, G. (1993, February 23). Personal communication.

Moran, G., & Cutler, B. L. (1991). The prejudicial impact of pretrial publicity. *Journal of Applied Social Psychology, 21,* 345–367.

More Americans living out of wedlock. (1998, July 27). Associated Press.

More delay marriage, live alone. (1996, March 13). *Los Angeles Times.*

Moreland, R. L. (1987). The formation of small groups. In C. Hendrick (Ed.), *Review of Personality and Social Psychology* (Vol. 8, pp. 80–110). Newbury Park, CA: Sage.

Moreland, R. L., & Beach, S. R. (1992). Exposure effects in the classroom: The development of affinity among students. *Journal of Experimental Social Psychology, 28,* 255–276.

Moreland, R. L., & Zajonc, R. B. (1982). Exposure effects in person perception: Familiarity, similarity, and attraction. *Journal of Experimental Social Psychology, 18,* 395–415.

Morey, N., & Gerber, G. L. (1995). Two types of competitiveness: Their impact on the perceived interpersonal attractiveness of women and men. *Journal of Applied Social Psychology, 25,* 210–222.

Morgan, D., Carder, P., & Neal, M. (1997). Are some relationships more useful than others? The value of similar others in the networks of recent widows. *Journal of Social and Personal Relationships, 14,* 745–759.

Morgan, H. J., & Janoff-Bulman, R. (1994). Positive and negative self-complexity: Patterns of adjustment following traumatic versus non-traumatic life experiences. *Journal of Social and Clinical Psychology, 13,* 63–85.

Morokoff, P. J., Quina, K., Harlow, L. L., Whitmire, L., Grimley, D. M., Gibson, P. R., & Burkholder, G. J. (1997). Sexual Assertiveness Scale (SAS) for women: Development and validation. *Journal of Personality and Social Psychology, 73,* 790–804.

Morris, K. J. (1985). *Discriminating depression and social anxiety: Self-efficacy analysis.* Unpublished master's thesis, Texas Tech University, Lubbock.

Morris, M. W., & Larrick, R. P. (1995). When one cause casts doubt on another: A normative analysis of discounting in causal attribution. *Psychological Review, 102,* 331–335.

Morris, M. W., & Pang, K. (1994). Culture and cause: American and Chinese attributions for social and physical events. *Journal of Personality and Social Psychology, 67,* 949–971.

Morrison, A. M. (1992). *The new leaders: Guidelines on leadership diversity.* San Francisco: Jossey-Bass.

Morrison, E. W. (1994). Role definitions and organizational citizenship behavior: The importance of employees' perspective. *Academy of Management Journal, 37,* 1543–1567.

Morrison, E. W., & Bies, R. J. (1991). Impression management in the feedback-seeking process: A literature review and research agenda. *Academy of Management Review, 16,* 322–341.

Morrison, H. W. (1954). *The validity and behavioral manifestations of female need for affiliation.* Unpublished master's thesis, Wesleyan University.

Morrow, G. D., Clark, E. M., & Brock, K. F. (1995). Individual and partner love styles: Implications for the quality of romantic involvements. *Journal of Social and Personal Relationships, 12,* 363–387.

Moscovici, S. (1985). Social influence and conformity. In G. Lindzey & E. Aronson (Eds.), *Handbook of social psychology* (3rd ed.). New York: Random House.

Mosher, D. L. (1991). Macho men, machismo, and sexuality. *Annual Review of Sex Research, 2,* 199–247.

Mosher, D. L., & Anderson, R. D. (1986). Macho personality, sexual aggression, and reactions to guided imagery of realistic rape. *Journal of Research in Personality, 20,* 77–94.

Mosher, D. L., & Sirkin, M. (1984). Measuring a macho personality constellation. *Journal of Research in Personality, 18,* 150–163.

Mosher, D. L., & Tomkins, S. S. (1988). Scripting the macho man: Hypermasculine socialization and enculturation. *Journal of Sex Research, 15,* 60–84.

Moskowitz, D. S. (1990). Convergence of self-reports and independent observers: Dominance and friendliness. *Journal of Personality and Social Psychology, 58,* 1096–1106.

Moskowitz, D. S. (1993). Dominance and friendliness: On the interaction of gender and situation. *Journal of Personality, 61,* 387–409.

Moston, S., & Stephenson, G. M. (1993). The changing face of police interrogation. *Journal of Community and Applied Social Psychology, 3,* 101–115.

Muczyk, J. P., & Reimann, B. C. (1987). The case for directive leadership. *Academy of Management Review, 12,* 637–647.

Mugny, G. (1975). Negotiations, image of the other and the process of minority influence. *European Journal of Social Psychology, 5,* 209–229.

Mullan, E., & Markland, D. (1997). Variations in self-determination across the stages of change for exercise in adults. *Motivation and Emotion, 21,* 349–362.

Munro, G. D., & Ditto, P. H. (1997). Biased assimilation, attitude polarization, and affect in reactions to stereotype-relevant scientific information. *Personality and Social Psychology Bulletin, 23,* 636–653.

Munsterberg, H. (1907). *On the witness stand: Essays in psychology and crime.* New York: McClure.

Murnen, S., K., Perot, A., & Byrne, D. (1989). Coping with unwanted sexual activity: Normative responses, situational determinants, and individual differences. *Journal of Sex Research, 26,* 85–106.

Murnen, S. K., & Byrne, D. (1991). Hyperfemininity: Measurement and initial validation of the construct. *Journal of Sex Research, 28,* 479–489.

Murnighan, K. (Ed.). (1993). *Handbook of social psychology in organizations.* Englewood Cliffs, N.J.

Murphy, S. T., Monahan, J. L., & Miller, L. C. (1998). Inference under the influence: The impact of alcohol and inhibition conflict on women's sexual decision making. *Personality and Social Psychology Bulletin, 24,* 517–528.

Murphy, S. T., Monahan, J. L., & Zajonc, R. B. (1995). Additivity of nonconscious affect: Combined effects of priming and exposure. *Journal of Personality and Social Psychology, 69,* 589–602.

Murray, H. A. (1938). *Explorations in personality.* New York: Oxford University Press.

Murray, S. L., & Holmes, J. G. (1997). A leap of faith? Positive illusions in romantic relationships. *Personality and Social Psychology Bulletin, 23,* 586–604.

Murray, S. L., Holmes, J. G., & Griffin, D. W. (1996). The benefits of positive illusions: Idealization and the construction of satisfaction in close relationships. *Journal of Personality and Social Psychology, 70,* 79–98.

Murrell, A. J., & Jones, J. M. (1993). Perceived control and victim derogation: Is the world still just? *Journal of Social Behavior and Personality, 8,* 545–554.

Myers, D. G., & Diener, E. (1995). Who is happy? *Psychological Science, 6,* 10–19.

Nadkarni, D. V., Lundgren, D., & Burlew, A. K. (1991). Gender differences in self-depriving behavior as a reaction to extreme inequity. *Journal of Social Behavior and Personality, 6,* 105–117.

Nadler, A. (1991). Help-seeking behavior: Psychological costs and instrumental benefits. In M. S. Clark (Ed.), *Prosocial behavior* (pp. 290–311). Newbury Park, CA: Sage.

Nadler, A. (1993, March). Personal communication.

Nadler, A., Fisher, J. D., & Itzhak, S. B. (1983). With a little help from my friend: Effect of a single or multiple acts of aid as a function of donor and task characteristics. *Journal of Personality and Social Psychology, 44,* 310–321.

Narby, D. J., Cutler, B. L., & Moran, G. (1993). A meta-analysis of the association between authoritarianism and jurors' perceptions of defendant culpability. *Journal of Applied Psychology, 78,* 34–42.

Nardi, P. M., & Sherrod, D. (1994). Friendship in the lives of gay men and lesbians. *Journal of Social and Personal Relationships, 11,* 185–199.

National Institute for Occupational Safety and Health, Center for Disease Control and Prevention. "Homicide in the workplace." Document #705003, December 5, 1993.

Nemeth, C. J. (1995). Dissent as driving cognition, attitudes, and judgments. *Social Cognition, 13,* 273–291.

Neto, F. (1992). Loneliness among Portuguese adolescents. *Social Behavior and Personality, 20,* 15–22.

Neuberg, S. L. (1989). The goal of forming accurate impressions during social interaction: attenuating the impact of negative expectancies. *Journal of Personality and Social Psychology, 56,* 374–386.

Neuberg, S. L., Smith, D. M., Hoffman, J. C., & Russell, F. J. (1994). When we observe stigmatized and "normal" individuals interacting: Stigma by association. *Personality and Social Psychology Bulletin, 20,* 196–209.

Neuman, J. H., & Baron, R. A. (1998). Workplace violence and workplace aggression: Evidence concerning specific forms, potential causes, and preferred targets. *Journal of Management, 24,* 391–420.

Neuman, J. H., & Baron, R. A. (1997). Aggression in the workplace. In Giacalone, R. A., & Greenberg, J. (Eds.), *Anti-social behavior in organizations.* Thousand Oaks, CA: Sage.

New AIDS cases down 7% in U.S. (1996, April 19). Associated Press.

Newcomb, T. M. (1956). The prediction of interpersonal attraction. *Psychological Review, 60,* 393–404.

Newcomb, T. M. (1961). *The acquaintance process.* New York: Holt, Rinehart and Winston.

Newton, T. L., Kiecolt-Glaser, J. K., Glaser, R., & Malarkey, W. B. (1995). Conflict and withdrawal during marital interaction: The roles of hostility and defensiveness. *Personality and Social Psychology Bulletin, 21,* 512–524.

Nezlek, J. B., Kowalski, R. M., Leary, M. R., Blevins, T., & Holgate, S. (1997). Personality moderators to reactions to interpersonal rejection: Depression and trait self-esteem. *Personality and Social Psychology Bulletin, 23,* 1235–1244.

Nida, S. A., & Koon, J. (1983). They get better looking at closing time around here, too. *Psychological Reports, 52,* 657–658.

Niebuhr, G. (1998, June 10). Baptists amend beliefs on family. *New York Times.*

Niedenthal, P. M., & Beike, D. R. (1997). Interrelated and isolated self-concepts. *Personality and Social Psychology Review, 1,* 106–128.

Niedenthal, P. M., Setterlund, M. B., & Wherry, M. B. (1992). Possible self-complexity and affective reactions to goal-relevant evaluation. *Journal of Personality and Social Psychology, 63,* 5–16.

Nietzel, M. T., Hasemann, D., & McCarthy, D. M. (1998). Psychology and capital litigation: Research contributions to courtroom consultation. *Applied & Preventive Psychology, 7,* 121–134.

Nisbett, R. E. (1990). Evolutionary psychology, biology, and cultural evolution. *Motivation and Emotion, 14,* 255–264.

Nix, G., Watson, C., Pyszczynski, T., & Greenberg, J. (1995). Reducing depressive affect through external focus of attention. *Journal of Social and Clinical Psychology, 14,* 36–52.

Number of sexually active teens levels off, survey says. (1995, February 24). *Albany Times Union,* A-5.

Number of young U.S. killers triples over past decade. (1996, March 8). *Albany Times Union,* A-4.

O'Brien, M., & Bahadur, M. A. (1998). Marital aggression, mother's problem-solving behavior with children, and children's emotional and behavioral problems. *Journal of Social and Clinical Psychology, 17,* 249–272.

O'Brien, M., & Chin, C. (1998). The relationship between children's reported exposures to inter-parental conflict and memory biases in the recognition of aggressive and constructive conflict words. *Personality and Social Psychology Bulletin, 24,* 647–656.

O'Connell, P. D. (1988). Pretrial publicity, change of venue, public opinion polls—A theory of procedural justice. *University of Detroit Law Review, 65,* 169–197.

O'Connor, K., & Carnevale, P. J. (1997). A nasty but effective negotiation strategy: Misrepresentation of a common-value issue. *Personality and Social Psychology Bulletin, 23,* 504–515.

O'Connor, S. C., & Rosenblood, L. K. (1996). Affiliation motivation in everyday experience: A theoretical comparison. *Journal of Personality and Social Psychology, 70,* 513–522.

O'Grady, K. E. (1989). Physical attractiveness, need for approval, social self-esteem, and maladjustment. *Journal of Social and Clinical Psycholgy, 8,* 62–69.

O'Leary, S. G. (1995). Parental discipline mistakes. *Current Directions in Psychological Science, 4,* 11–13.

O'Sullivan, C. S., & Durso, F. T. (1984). Effects of schema-incongruent information on memory for stereotypical attributes. *Journal of Personality and Social Psychology, 47,* 55–70.

O'Sullivan, L. F., & Allgeier, E. R. (1994). Disassembling a stereotype: Gender differences in the use of token resistance. *Journal of Applied Social Psychology, 24,* 1035–1055.

O'Sullivan, L. F., & Byers, E. S. (1992). College students' incorporation of initiator and restrictor roles in sexual dating interactions. *Journal of Sex Research, 29,* 435–446.

O. J., Sam Sheppard alike in eyes of press, Bailey says. (1998, April 19). Albany *Times Union,* p. A2.

Oggins, J., Veroff, J., & Leber, D. (1993). Perceptions of marital interaction among black and white newlyweds. *Journal of Personality and Social Psychology, 65,* 494–511.

Ohbuchi, K., & Kambara, T. (1985). Attacker's intent and awareness of outcome, impression management, and retaliation. *Journal of Experimental Social Psychology, 21,* 321–330.

Ohbuchi, K., Chiba, S., & Fikushima, O. (1994). *Mitigation of interpersonal conflict: Politeness and time pressure.* Unpublished manuscript, Tohoku University.

Ohbuchi, K., Kameda, M., & Agarie, N. (1989). Apology as aggression control: Its role in mediating appraisal of and response to harm. *Journal of Personality and Social Psychology, 56,* 219–227.

Ohlott, P. J., Ruderman, M. N., & McCauley, C. D. (1994). Gender differences in managers' developmental job experiences. *Academy of Management Journal, 37,* 46–67.

Oliner, S. P., & Oliner, P. M. (1988). *The altruistic personality: Rescuers of Jews in Nazi Europe.* New York: Free Press.

Oliver, J. M., Reed, K. S., & Smith, B. W. (1998). Patterns of psychological problems in university undergraduates: Factor structure of symptoms of anxiety and depression, physical symptoms, alcohol use, and eating problems. *Social Behavior and Personality, 26,* 211–232.

Oliver, M. B., & Hyde, J. S. (1993). Gender differences in sexuality: A meta-analysis. *Psychological Bulletin, 114,* 29–51.

Olmstead, R. E., Guy, S. M., O'Malley, P. M., & Bentler, P. M. (1991). Longitudinal assessment of the relationship between self-esteem, fatalism, loneliness, and substance use. *Journal of Social Behavior and Personality, 6,* 749–770.

Omoto, A. M., & Snyder, M. (1995). Sustained helping without obligation: Motivation, longevity of service, and perceived attitude change among AIDS volunteers. *Journal of Personality and Social Psychology, 68,* 671–686.

O'Neil, J. (1998, December 8). That sly 'don't-come-hither' stare. *New York Times,* p. F7.

Organ, D. W. (1997). Organizational citizenship behavior: It's construct clean-up time. *Human Performance, 10,* 85–98.

Orive, R. (1988). Social projective and social comparison of opinions. *Journal of Personality and Social Psychology, 54,* 953–964.

Orpen, C. (1996). The effects of ingratiation and self promotion tactics on employee career success. *Social Behavior and Personality, 24,* 213–214.

Osborne, J. W. (1995). Academics, self-esteem, and race: A look at the underlying assumptions of the disidentification hypothesis. *Personality and Social Psychology Bulletin, 21,* 449–455.

Osterman, K., Bjorkqvist, K., Lagerspetz, K. M. J., Kaukianainen, A., Hucsmann, L. W., & Fraczek, A. (1994). Peer and self-estimated aggression and victimization in 8-year-old children from five ethnic groups. *Aggressive Behavior, 20,* 411–428.

Osterman, K., Bjorkqvist, K., Lagerspetz, K. M. J., Kaukiainen, A., Landua, S. F., Fraczek, A., & Caprara, G. V. (1998). Cross-cultural evidence of female indirect aggression. *Aggressive Behavior, 24,* 1–8.

Ostrow, R. J. (1995, November 19). As crime fears rise, actual crime falls. *Los Angeles Times.*

Ottati, V., Terkildsen, N., & Hubbard, C. (1997). Happy faces elicit heuristic processing in a televised impression formation task: A cognitive tuning account. *Personality and Social Psychology Bulletin, 23,* 1144–1156.

Ottati, V. C., & Isbell, L. M. (1996). Effects of mood during exposure to target information on subsequently reported judgments. An on-line model of misattribution and correction. *Journal of Personality and Social Psychology, 71,* 39–53.

Oyserman, D., Gant, L., & Ager, J. (1995). A socially contextualized model of African American identity: Possible selves and school persistence. *Journal of Personality and Social Psychology, 69,* 1216–1232.

Page, D., & Gropp, T. (1995, April). *Pretrial publicity: Attitudinal and cognitive mediators.* Paper presented at the meeting of the Eastern Psychological Association, Boston.

Page, N. R., & Wiseman, R. L. (1993). Supervisory behavior and worker satisfaction in the United States, Mexico, and Spain. *Journal of Business Communication, 30,* 161–180.

Page, R. M. (1991). Loneliness as a risk factor in adolescent hopelessness. *Journal of Research in Personality, 25,* 189–195.

Paik, H., & Comstock, G. (1994). The effects of television violence on antisocial behavior: A meta-analysis. *Communication Research, 21,* 516–546.

Pan, S. (1993). China: Acceptability and effect of three kinds of sexual publication. *Archives of Sexual Behavior, 22,* 59–71.

Parks, M. R., & Floyd, K. (1996). Meanings for closeness and intimacy in friendship. *Journal of Social and Personal Relationships, 13,* 85–107.

Pataki, S. P., Shapiro, C., & Clark, M. S. (1994). Children's acquisition of appropriate norms for friendships and acquaintances. *Journal of Social and Personal Relationships, 11,* 427–442.

Paterson, R. J., & Neufeld, R. W. J. (1995). What are my options? Influences of choice availability on stress and the perception of control. *Journal of Research in Personality, 29,* 145–167.

Patrick, C. J., Bradley, M. M., & Lang, P. J. (1993). Emotion in the criminal psychopath: Startle reflex modulation. *Journal of Abnormal Psychology, 102,* 83–92.

Paul, L., Foss, M. A., & Galloway, J. (1993). Sexual jealousy in young women and men: Aggressive responsiveness to partner and rival. *Aggressive Behavior, 19,* 401–420.

Paulhus, D. L., Bruce, M. N., & Trapnell, P. D. (1995). Effects of self-presentation strategies on personality profiles and their structure. *Personality and Social Psychology Bulletin, 21,* 100–108.

Paulus, P. B. (Ed.). (1989). *Psychology of group influence* (2nd ed.). Hillsdale, NJ: Erlbaum.

Pearse, J. (1995). Police interviewing: The identification of vulnerabilities. *Journal of Community and Applied Social Psychology, 5,* 147–159.

Pearson, K., & Lee, A. (1903). On the laws of inheritance in man: I. Inheritance of physical characters. *Biometrika, 2,* 357–462.

Pedersen, D. M. (1994). Privacy preferences and classroom seat selection. *Social Behavior and Personality, 22,* 393–398.

Pelham, B. W. (1995a). Self-investment and self-esteem: Evidence for a Jamesian model of self-worth. *Journal of Personality and Social Psychology, 69,* 1141–1150.

Pelham, B. W. (1995b). Further evidence for a Jamesian model of self-worth: Reply to Marsh (1995). *Journal of Personality and Social Psychology, 69,* 1161–1165.

Pelham, B. W., & Wachsmuth, J. O. (1995). The waxing and waning of the social self: Assimilation and contrast in social comparison. *Journal of Personality and Social Psychology, 69,* 825–838.

Pennebaker, J. W. (1997). Writing about emotional experiences as a therapeutic process. *Psychological Science, 8,* 162–166.

Pennebaker, J. W., Dyer, M. A., Caulkins, R. S., Litowicz, D. L., Ackerman, P. L., & Anderson, D. B. (1979). Don't the girls all get prettier at closing time: A country and western application to psychology. *Personality and Social Psychology Bulletin, 5,* 122–125.

Penner, L. A., & Finkelstein, M. A. (1998). Dispositional and structural determinants of volunteerism. *Journal of Personality and Social Psychology, 74,* 525–537.

Pentony, J. F. (1995). The effect of negative campaigning on voting, semantic differential, and thought listing. *Journal of Social Behavior and Personality, 10,* 631–644.

Peplau, L. A., & Perlman, D. (1982). Perspective on loneliness. In L. A. Peplau & D. Perlman (Eds.), *Loneliness: A sourcebook of current theory, research, and therapy.* New York: Wiley.

Perdue, C. W., & Gurtman, M. B. (1990). Evidence for the automaticity of ageism. *Journal of Experimental Social Psychology, 26,* 199–216.

Perrett, D. I., May, K. A., & Yoshikawa, S. (1994). Facial shape and judgements of female attractiveness. *Nature, 368,* 239–242.

Perrine, R. M. (1993). On being supportive: The emotional consequences of listening to another's distress. *Journal of Social and Personal Relationships, 10,* 371–384.

Pessin, J. (1933). The comparative effects of social and mechanical stimulation on memorizing. *American Journal of Psychology, 45,* 263–270.

Peterson, C., Seligman, M. E. P., Yurko, K. H., Martin, L. R., & Friedman, H. S. (1998). Catastrophizing and untimely death. *Psychological Science, 9,* 127–130.

Peterson, L., & Brown, D. (1994). Integrating child injury and abuse–neglect research: Common histories, etiologies, and solutions. *Psychological Bulletin, 116,* 293–315.

Peterson, R. S. (1997). A directive leadership style in group decision making can be both a virtue and vice: Evidence from elite and experimental groups. *Journal of Personality and Social Psychology, 72,* 1107–1121.

Petkova, K. G., Ajzen, I., & Driver, B. L. (1995). Salience of anti-abortion beliefs and commitment to an attitudinal position: On the strength, structure, and predictive validity of anti-abortion attitudes. *Journal of Applied Social Psychology, 25,* 463–483.

Petrie, K. J., Booth, R. J., & Pennebaker, J. W. (1998). The immunological effects of thought suppression. *Journal of Personality and Social Psychology, 75,* 1264–1272.

Pettigrew, T. F. (1969). Racially separate or together? *Journal of Social Issues, 24,* 43–69.

Pettigrew, T. F. (1981). Extending the stereotype concept. In D. L. Hamilton (Ed.), *Cognitive processes in stereotyping and intergroup behavior* (pp. 303–331). Hillsdale, NJ: Erlbaum.

Pettigrew, T. F. (1997). Generalized intergroup contact effects on prejudice. *Personality and Social Psychology Bulletin, 23,* 173–185.

Petty, R. E., & Cacioppo, J. T. (1986). The elaboration likelihood model of persuasion. In L. Berkowitz (Ed.), *Advances in experimental social psychology,* (Vol. 19, pp. 123–205). New York: Academic Press.

Petty, R. E., & Cacioppo, J.T. (1990). Involvement and persuasion: Tradition versus integration. *Psychological Bulletin, 107,* 367–374.

Petty, R. E., & Wegener, D. T. (1998). Matching versus mismatching attitude functions: Implications for scrutiny of persuasive messages. *Personality and Social Psychology Bulletin, 24,* 227–240.

Petty, R. E., Cacioppo, J. T., Strathman, A. J., & Priester, J. R. (1994). To think or not to think: Exploring two routes to persuasion. In S. Shavitt & T. C. Brock (Eds.), *Persuasion* (pp. 113–147). Boston: Allyn and Bacon.

Petty, R. J., & Krosnick, J. A. (Eds.). (1995). *Attitude strength: Antecedents and consequences* (Vol. 4). Hillsdale, NJ: Erlbaum.

Pezdek, K., Finger, K., & Hodge, D. (1997). Planting false childhood memories: The role of event plausibility. *Psychological Science, 8,* 437–441.

Phelps, E. J. (1981). *The maid of the North.* New York: Holt, Rinehart, & Winston.

Pierce, C. A. (1992). *The effects of physical attractiveness and height on dating choice: A meta-analysis.* Unpublished masters thesis, University at Albany, State University of New York, Albany, NY.

Pierce, C. A. (1996). Body height and romantic attraction: A meta-analytic test of the male-taller norm. *Social Behavior and Personality, 24,* 143–150.

Pierce, C. A., & Aguinis, H. (1997). Bridging the gap between romantic relationships and sexual harassment in organizations. *Journal of Organizational Behavior, 18,* 197–200.

Pierce, C. A., Aguinis, H., & Adams, S. K. R. (1999). *Dissolved workplace romances: Effects of romance type, participants' romance motives, and rater characteristics on judgments and responses to a sexual harassment accusation.* Manuscript submitted for publication.

Pierce, C. A., Byrne, D., & Aguinis, H. (1996). Attraction in organizations: A model of workplace romance. *Journal of Organizational Behavior, 17,* 5–32.

Pietromonaco, P. R., & Barrett, L. F. (1997). Working models of attachment and daily social interactions. *Journal of Personality and Social Psychology, 73,* 1409–1423.

Pihl, R. O., Lau, M. L., & Assaad, J. M. (1997). Aggressive disposition, alcohol, and aggression. *Aggressive Behavior, 23,* 11–18.

Piliavin, J. A., & Unger, R. K. (1985). *The helpful but helpless female: Myth or reality?* In V. E. O'Leary, R. K. Unger, & B. S. Wallston (Eds.), *Women, gender, and social psychology* (pp. 149–189). Hillsdale, NJ: Erlbaum.

Pillai, R., Sittes-Doe, S., Grewal, D., & Meindl, J. R. (1997). Winning charisma and losing the presidential election. *Journal of Applied Social Psychology, 27,* 1716–1726.

Pines, A. (1997). Fatal attractions or wise unconscious choices: The relationship between causes for entering and breaking intimate relationships. *Personal Relationship Issues, 4,* 1–6.

Pinker, S. (1998). *How the mind works.* New York: Norton.

Pion, G. M., Mednick, M., Astin, H. S., Hall, C. C. I., Kenkel, M. B., Keita, G. P., Kohout, J. L., & Kelleher, J. C. (1996). The shifting gender composition of psychology: Trends and implications for the discipline. *American Psychologist, 51,* 509–528.

Pittman, T. S. (1993). Control motivation and attitude change. In G. Weary, F. Gleicher, & K. L. Marsh (Eds.), *Control motivation and social cognition* (pp. 157–175). New York: Springer-Verlag.

Planalp, S., & Benson, A. (1992). Friends' and acquaintances' conversations: I. Perceived differences. *Journal of Social and Personal Relationships, 9,* 483–506.

Platz, S. G., & Hosch, H. M. (1988). Cross-racial/ethnic eyewitness identification: A field study. *Journal of Applied Social Psychology, 18,* 972–984.

Pleck, J. H., Sonenstein, F. L., & Ku, L. C. (1993). Masculinity ideology: Its impact on adolescent males' heterosexual relationships. *Journal of Social Issues, 49*(3), 11–29.

Plesser-Storr, D. (1995). *Self-presentation by men to attractive and unattractive women: Tactics of ingratiation, blasting, and basking.* Unpublished doctoral dissertation, University at Albany, State University of New York, Albany.

Pliner, P., Chaiken, S., & Flett, G. L. (1990). Gender differences in concern with body weight and physical appearance over the life span. *Personality and Social Psychology Bulletin, 16,* 263–273.

Podsakoff, P. M., & MacKenzie, S. B. (1994). Organizational citizenship behaviors and sales unit effectiveness. *Journal of Marketing Research, 31,* 351–363.

Podsakoff, P. M., Ahearne, M., & MacKenzie, S. B. (1997). Organizational citizenship behavior and the quantity and quality of work group performance. *Journal of Applied Psychology, 82,* 262–270.

Pollock, C. L., Smith, S. D., Knowles, E. S., & Bruce, H. J. (1998). Mindfulness limits compliance with the that's-not-all technique. *Personality and Social Psychology Bulletin, 24,* 1153–1157.

Pomazal, R. J., & Clore, G. L. (1973). Helping on the highway: The effects of dependency and sex. *Journal of Applied Social Psychology, 3,* 150–164.

Pomerantz, E. M., Chaioken, S., & Tordesilla, S. (1995). Attitude strength and resistance processes. *Journal of Personality and Social Psychology, 69,* 408–419.

Pool, G. J., Wood, W., & Leck, K. (1998). The self-esteem motive in social influence: Agreement with valued majorities and disagreement with derogated minorities. *Journal of Personality and Social Psychology, 75,* 967–975.

Poole, D. A., & Lindsay, D. S. (1998). Assessing the accuracy of young children's reports: Lessons from the investigation of child sexual abuse. *Applied & Preventive Psychology, 7,* 1–26.

Pooley, E. (1997, May 19). Too good to be true? *Time,* 28–33.

Pope, K. S. (1996). Memory, abuse, and science: Questioning claims about the false memory syndrome epidemic. *American Psychologist, 51,* 957–974.

Poulson, R. L., Braithwaite, R. L., Brondino, M. J., & Wuehsch, K. L. (1997). Mock jurors' insanity defense verdict selections: The role of evidence, attitudes, and verdict options. *Journal of Social Behavior and Personality, 12,* 743–758.

Poulson, R. L., Wuensch, K. L., Brown, M. B., & Braithwaite, R. L. (1997). Mock jurors' evaluations of insanity defense verdict selection: The role of death penalty attitudes. *Journal of Social Behavior and Personality, 12,* 1065–1078.

Powell, G. N., & Butterfield, D. A. (1994). Investigating the "glass ceiling" phenomenon: An empirical study of actual promotions to top management. *Academy of Management Journal, 37,* 68–86.

Prager, K. J., & Bailey, J. M. (1985). Androgyny, ego development, and psychosocial crisis. *Sex Roles, 13,* 525–536.

Pratto, F., Stallworth, L. M., Sidanius, J., & Siers, B. (1997). The gender gap in occupational role attainment: A social dominance approach. *Journal of Personality and Social Psychology, 72,* 37–53.

Pruitt, D. G., & Carnevale, P. J. (1993). *Negotiation in social conflict.* Pacific Grove, CA: Brooks/Cole.

Przybyla, D. P. J. (1985). *The facilitating effect of exposure to erotica on male prosocial behavior.* Unpublished doctoral dissertation, University at Albany, State University of New York.

Ptacek, J. T., & Dodge, K. L. (1995). Coping strategies and relationship satisfaction in couples. *Personality and Social Psychology Bulletin, 21,* 76–84.

Pullium, R. M. (1993). Reactions to AIDS patients as a function of attributions about controllability and promiscuity. *Social Behavior and Personality, 21,* 297–302.

Quigley, B. M., Johnson, A. B., & Byrne, D. (1995, June). *Mock jury sentencing decisions: A meta-analysis of the attractiveness–leniency effect.* Paper presented at the meeting of the American Psychological Society, New York.

Radecki-Bush, C., Farrell, A. D., & Bush, J. P. (1993). Predicting jealous responses: The influence of adult attachment and depression on threat appraisal. *Journal of Social and Personal Relationships, 10,* 569–588.

Rall, M. L., Peskoff, F. S., & Byrne, J. J. (1994). The effects of information-giving behavior and gender on the perceptions of physicians: An experimental analysis. *Social Behavior and Personality, 22,* 1–16.

Ramirez, J., Bryant, J., & Zillmann, D. (1983). Effects of erotica on retaliatory behavior as a function of level of prior provocation. *Journal of Personality and Social Psychology, 43,* 971–978.

Randall, D. M., Fedor, D. P., & Longenecker, C. O. (1990). The behavioral expression of organizational commitment. *Journal of Vocational Behavior, 36,* 210–224.

Raty, H., & Snellman, L. (1992). Does gender make any difference? Common-sense conceptions of intelligence. *Social Behavior and Personality, 20,* 23–34.

Raudenbush, B., & Zellner, D. A. (1997). Nobody's satisfied: Effects of abnormal eating behaviors and actual and perceived weight status on body image satisfaction in males and females. *Journal of Social and Clinical Psychology, 16,* 95–110.

Raviv, A. (1993). Radio psychology: A comparison of listeners and non-listeners. *Journal of Community and Applied Social Psychology, 3,* 197–211.

Ray, G. E., Cohen, R., Secrist, M. E., & Duncan, M. K. (1997). Relating aggressive victimization behaviors to children's sociometric status and friendships. *Journal of Social and Personal Relationships, 14,* 95–108.

Read, S. J., & Miller, L. C. (1998). *Connectionist and PDP models of social reasoning and social behavior.* Mahwah, NJ: Erlbaum.

Reed, D., & Weinberg, M. S. (1984). Premarital coitus: Developing and establishing sexual scripts. *Social Psychology Quarterly, 47,* 129–138.

Reed, M. B., & Aspinwall, L. G. (1998). Self-affirmation reduces biases processing of health-risk information. *Motivation and Emotion, 22,* 99–132.

Regan, P. C. (1998). Of lust and love: Beliefs about the role of sexual desire in romantic relationships. *Personal Relationships, 5,* 139–157.

Regan, P. C., Snyder, M., & Kassin, S. M. (1995). Unrealistic optimism: Self-enhancement or person positivity? *Personality and Social Psychology Bulletin, 21,* 1073–1082.

Reis, T. J., Gerrard, M., & Gibbons, F. X. (1993). Social comparison and the pill: Reactions to upward and downward comparison of contraceptive behavior. *Personality and Social Psychology Bulletin, 19,* 13–20.

Reisman, J. M. (1984). Friendliness and its correlates. *Journal of Social and Clinical Psychology, 2,* 143–155.

Reiss, A. J., & Roth, J. A. (Eds.). (1993). *Understanding and preventing violence.* Washington, DC: National Academy Press.

Reno, R. R., Cialdini, R. B, & Kalgren, C. A (1993). The transsituational influence of social norms. *Journal of Personality and Social Psychology, 64,* 104–112.

Rensberger, B. (1993, November 9). Certain chemistry between vole pairs. *Albany Times Union,* pp. C-1, C-3.

Rentsch, J. R., & Heffner, T. S. (1994). Assessing self-concept: Analysis of Gordon's coding scheme using "Who am I?" responses. *Journal of Social Behavior and Personality, 9,* 283–300.

Revicki, D. A., Whitley, T. W., Gallery, M. E., & Allison, E. J. Jr. (1993). Impact of work environment characteristics on work-related stress and depression in emergency medicine residents: A longitudinal study. *Journal of Community & Applied Social Psychology, 3,* 273–284.

Rhodes, G., & Tremewan, T. (1996). Averageness, exaggeration, and facial attractiveness. *Psychological Science, 7,* 105–110.

Rhodewalt, F., & Davison, J., Jr. (1983). Reactance and the coronary-prone behavior pattern: The role of self-attribution in response to reduced behavioral freedom. *Journal of Personality and Social Psychology, 44,* 220–228.

Rhodewalt, F. R., Madrian, J. C., & Cheney, S. (1998). Narcissism, self-knowledge organization, and emotional reactivity: The effect of daily experience on self-esteem and affect. *Personality and Social Psychology Bulletin, 24,* 75–87.

Richardson, D. R., Hammock, G. S., Smith, S. M., Gardner, W., & Signo, M. (1994). Empathy as a cognitive inhibitor of interpersonal aggression. *Aggressive Behavior, 20,* 275–289.

Ridley, M., & Dawkins, R. (1981). The natural selection of altruism. In J. P. Rushton & R. M. Sorrentino (Eds.), *Altruism and helping behavior.* Hillsdale, NJ: Erlbaum.

Riess, M., & Schlenker, B. R. (1977). Attitude change and responsibility avoidance as modes of dilemma resolution in forced-compliance situations. *Journal of Personality and Social Psychology, 35,* 21–30.

Rind, B. (1996). Effect of beliefs about weather conditions on tipping. *Journal of Applied Social Psychology, 26,* 137–147.

Rind, B., & Bordia, P. (1996). Effect on restaurant tipping of male and female servers drawing a happy, smiling face on the backs of customers' checks. *Journal of Applied Social Psychology, 26,* 218–225.

Riskind, J. H., & Maddux, J. E. (1993). Loomingness, helplessness, and fearfulness: An integration of harm-looming and self-efficacy models of fear. *Journal of Social and Clinical Psychology, 12,* 73–89.

Robarchek, C. A., & Robarchek, C. J. (1997). Waging peace: The psychological and sociocultural dynamics of positive peace. In A. W. Wolfe, & H. Yang (Eds.), *Anthropological contributions to conflict resolution* (pp. 64–80). Athens, GA: University of Georgia Press.

Robberson, N. R., & Rogers, R. W. (1988). Beyond fear appeals: Negative and positive persuasive appeals to health and self-esteem. *Journal of Applied Social Psychology, 18,* 277–287.

Robbins, T. L., & DeNisi, A. S. (1994). A closer look at interpersonal affect as a distinct influence on cognitive processing in performance evaluations. *Journal of Applied Psychology, 79,* 341–353.

Roberts, B. W., & Donahue, E. M. (1994). One personality, multiple selves: Integrating personality and social roles. *Journal of Personality, 62,* 199–218.

Robins, R. W., Spranca, M. D., & Mendelsohn, G. A. (1996). The actor–observer effect revisited: Effects of individual differences and repeated social interactions on actor and observer attribution. *Journal of Personality and Social Psychology, 71,* 375–389.

Robinson, L. A., Berman, J. S., & Neimeyer, R. A. (1990). Psychotherapy for the treatment of depression: A comprehensive review of controlled outcome research. *Psychological Bulletin, 108,* 30–49.

Robinson, R., Keltner, D., Ward, A., & Ross, L. (1995). Actual versus assumed differences in construal: "Naïve realism" in intergroup perception and conflict. *Journal of Personality and Social Psychology, 68,* 404–417.

Rochat, F., & Modigliani, A. (1995). The ordinary quality of resistance: From Milgram's laboratory to the village of Le Chambon. *Journal of Social Issues, 5,* 195–210.

Rodgers, J. L., Billy, J. O. B., & Udry, J. R. (1984). A model of friendship similarity in mildly deviant behaviors. *Journal of Applied Social Psychology, 14,* 413–425.

Rodin, J., & Salovey, P. (1989). Health psychology. *Annual Review of Psychology, 40,* 533–579.

Rodin, M., & Price, J. (1995). Overcoming stigma: Credit for self-improvement or discredit for needing to improve? *Personality and Social Psychology Bulletin, 21,* 172–181.

Roese, N. J. (1997). Counterfactual thinking. *Psychological Bulletin, 121,* 133–148.

Rogers, C. R. (1951). *Client-centered therapy.* Boston: Houghton Mifflin.

Rogers, C. R., & Dymond, R. F. (Eds.). (1954). *Psychotherapy and personality change.* Boston: Houghton Mifflin.

Rogers, M., Miller, N., Mayer, F. S., & Duvall, S. (1982). Personal responsibility and salience of the request for help: Determinants of the relations between negative affect and helping behavior. *Journal of Personality and Social Psychology, 43,* 956–970.

Rogers, R. W. (1980). *Subjects' reactions to experimental deception.* Unpublished manuscript, University of Alabama, Tuscaloosa.

Rogers, R. W., & Ketcher, C. M. (1979). Effects of anonymity and arousal on aggression. *Journal of Psychology, 102,* 13–19.

Rokach, A. (1998). The relation of cultural background to the causes of loneliness. *Journal of Social and Clinical Psychology, 17,* 75–88.

Rosen, K. H., & Stith, S. M. (1995). Women terminating abusive dating relationships: A qualitative study. *Journal of Social and Personal Relationships, 12,* 155–160.

Rosenbaum, M. E. (1986). The repulsion hypothesis: On the nondevelopment of relationships. *Journal of Personality and Social Psychology, 51,* 1156–1166.

Rosenbaum, M. E., & Levin, I. P. (1969). Impression formation as a function of source credibility and the polarity of information. *Journal of Personality and Social Psychology, 12,* 34–37.

Rosenberg, E. L., & Ekman, P. (1995). Conceptual and methodological issues in the judgment of facial expressions of emotion. *Motivation and Emotion, 19,* 111–138.

Rosenfield, D., Greenberg, J., Folger, R., & Borys, R. (1982). Effect of an encounter with a black panhandler on subsequent helping for blacks: Tokenism or conforming to a negative stereotype? *Personality and Social Psychology Bulletin, 8,* 664–671.

Rosenhan, D. L., Salovey, P., & Hargis, K. (1981). The joys of helping: Focus of attention mediates the impact of positive affect on altruism. *Journal of Personality and Social Psychology, 40,* 899–905.

Rosenthal, A. M. (1964). *Thirty-eight witnesses.* New York: McGraw-Hill.

Rosenthal, D. A., & Shepherd, H. (1993). A six-month follow-up of adolescents' sexual risk-taking, HIV/AIDS knowledge, and attitudes to condoms. *Journal of Community and Applied Social Psychology, 3,* 53–65.

Rosenthal, E. (1992, August 18). Troubled marriage? Sibling relations may be at fault. *New York Times,* pp. C1, C9.

Rosenthal, R., & Jacobson, L. (1968). *Pygmalion in the classroom: Teacher expectation and student intellectual development.* New York: Holt, Rinehart, & Winston.

Rosenzweig, J. M., & Daley, D. M. (1989). Dyadic adjustment/sexual satisfaction in women and men as a function of psychological sex role self-perception. *Journal of Sex and Marital Therapy, 15,* 42–56.

Rosin, H. (1995, June 5). The homecoming. *New Republic,* 21–23, 26.

Ross, L., & Ward, A. (1995). Naïve realism in everyday life: Implications for social conflict and misunderstandings. In T. Brown, E. Reed, & E. Turiel (Eds.), *Values and knowledge* (pp. 103–135). Hillsdale, NJ: Erlbaum.

Ross, L., Lepper, M. R., & Hubbard, M. (1975). Perseverance in self-perception and social perception: Biased attributional processes in the debriefing paradigm. *Journal of Personality and Social Psychology, 32,* 880–892.

Rotenberg, K. J. (1994). Loneliness and interpersonal trust. *Journal of Social and Clinical Psychology, 13,* 152–173.

Rotenberg, K. J. (1997). Loneliness and the perception of the exchange of disclosures. *Journal of Social and Clinical Psychology, 16,* 259–276.

Rotenberg, K. J., & Kmill, J. (1992). Perception of lonely and non-lonely persons as a function of individual differences in loneliness. *Journal of Social and Personal Relationships, 9,* 325–330.

Rotenberg, K. J., & Korol, S. (1995). The role of loneliness and gender in individuals' love styles. *Journal of Social Behavior and Personality, 10,* 537–546.

Roth, D. L., Wiebe, D. J., Fillingim, R. B., & Shay, K. A. (1989). Life events, fitness, hardiness, and health: A simultaneous analysis of proposed stress-resistance effects. *Journal of Personality and Social Psychology, 57,* 136–142.

Rothgerber, H. (1997). External intergroup threat as an antecedent to perceptions of in-group and out-group homogeneity. *Journal of Personality and Social Psychology, 73,* 1206–1212.

Rothman, A. J., & Hardin, C. D. (1997). Differential use of the availability heuristic in social judgment. *Personality and Social Psychology Bulletin, 23,* 123–138.

Rothman, A. J., Salovey, P., Antone, C., Keough, K., & Martin, C. D. (1993). The influence of message framing on intentions to perform health behaviors. *Journal of Experimental Social Psychology, 29,* 408–433.

Rotton, J., & Kelley, I. W. (1985). Much ado about the full moon: A meta-analysis of lunar-lunacy research. *Psychological Bulletin, 97,* 286–306.

Rowatt, W. C., Cunningham, M. R., & Druen, P. B. (1998). Deception to get a date. *Personality and Social Psychology Bulletin, 24,* 1228–1242.

Rowe, P. M. (1996, September). On the neurobiological basis of affiliation. *APS Observer,* 17–18.

Roy, M. P., Steptoe, A., & Kirschbaum, C. (1998). Life events and social support as moderators of individual differences in cardiovascular and cortisol reactivity. *Journal of Personality and Social Psychology, 75,* 1273–1281.

Rozin, P., & Nemeroff, C. (1990). The laws of sympathetic magic: A psychological analysis of similarity and contagion. In W. Stigler, R. A. Shweder, & G. Herdt (Eds.), *Cultural psychology: Essays in comparative human development* (pp. 205–232). Cambridge, England: Cambridge University Press.

Rozin, P., Markwith, M., & Nemeroff, C. (1992). Magical contagion beliefs and fear of AIDS. *Journal of Applied Social Psychology, 22,* 1081–1092.

Rozin, P., Millman, L., & Nemeroff, C. (1986). Operation of the laws of sympathetic magic in disgust and other domains. *Journal of Personality and Social Psychology, 50,* 703–712.

Rubin, J. Z. (1985). Deceiving ourselves about deception: Comment on Smith and Richardson's "Amelioration of deception and harm in psychological research." *Journal of Personality and Social Psychology, 48,* 252–253.

Rubin, M., & Hewstone, M. (1998). Social identity theory's self-esteem hypothesis: A review and some suggestions for clarification. *Personality and Social Psychology Review, 2,* 40–62.

Rudman, L. A. (1998). Self-promotion as a risk factor for women: The costs and benefits of counterstereotypical impression management. *Journal of Personality and Social Psychology, 74,* 629–645.

Rudolph, D. L., & Kim, J. G. (1996). Mood responses to recreational sport and exercise in a Korean sample. *Journal of Social Behavior and Personality, 11,* 841–849.

Rusbult, C. E. (1983). A longitudinal test of the investment model: The development (and deterioration) of satisfaction and commitment in heterosexual involvements. *Journal of Personality and Social Psychology, 45,* 101–117.

Rusbult, C. E., & Martz, J. M. (1995). Remaining in an abusive relationship: An investment model analysis of nonvoluntary dependence. *Personality and Social Psychology Bulletin, 21,* 558–571.

Rusbult, C. E., Martz, J. M., & Agnew, C. R. (1998). The Investment Model Scale: Measuring commitment level, satisfaction level, quality of alternatives, and investment size. *Personal Relationships, 5,* 467–484.

Rusbult, C. E., & Zembrodt, I. M. (1983). Responses to dissatisfaction in romantic involvements: A multidimensional scaling analysis. *Journal of Experimental Social Psychology, 19,* 274–293.

Rusbult, C. E., Morrow, G. D., & Johnson, D. J. (1990). Self-esteem and problem-solving behavior in close relationships. *British Journal of Social Psychology,*

Ruscher, J. B., & Hammer, E. D. (1994). Revising disrupted impressions through conversation. *Journal of Personality and Social Psychology, 66,* 530–541.

Rushton, J. P. (1989a). Genetic similarity in male friendships. *Ethology and Sociobiology, 10,* 361–373.

Rushton, J. P. (1989b). Genetic similarity, human altruism, and group selection. *Behavioral and Brain Sciences, 12,* 503–559.

Rushton, J. P. (1990). Sir Francis Galton, epigenetic rules, genetic similarity theory, and human life-history analysis. *Journal of Personality, 58,* 117–140.

Rushton, J. P., Russell, R. J. H., & Wells, P. A. (1984). Genetic similarity theory: Beyond kin selection. *Behavior Genetics, 14,* 179–193.

Russell, A., & Searcy, E. (1997). The contribution of affective reactions and relationship qualities to adolescents' reported responses to parents. *Journal of Social and Personal Relationships, 14,* 539–548.

Russell, D., Peplau, L. A., & Cutrona, C. E. (1980). The revised UCLA Loneliness Scale: Concurrent and discriminant validity evidence. *Journal of Personality and Social Psychology, 39,* 472–480.

Russell, G. W., & Baenninger, R. (1997). Murder most foul: Predictors of an affirmative response to an outrageous question. *Aggressive Behavior, 22,* 175–181.

Russell, G. W., & Mentzel, R. K. (1990). Sympathy and altruism in response to disasters. *Journal of Social Psychology, 130,* 309–317.

Russell, J. A. (1994). Is there universal recognition of emotion from facial expressions? A review of cross-cultural studies. *Psychological Bulletin, 115,* 102–141.

Rutkowski, G. K., Gruder, C. L., & Romer, D. (1983). Group cohesiveness, social norms, and bystander intervention. *Journal of Personality and Social Psychology, 44,* 542–552.

Ryan, R. H., & Geiselman, R. E. (1991). Effects of biased information on the relationship between eyewitness confidence and accuracy. *Bulletin of the Psychonomic Society, 29,* 7–9.

Ryckman, R. M., Butler, J. C., Thornton, B., & Lindner, M. A. (1997). Assessment of physique subtype stereotypes. *Genetic, Social, and General Psychology Monographs, 123,* 101–128.

Ryckman, R. M., Robbins, M. A., Kaczor, L. M., & Gold, J. A. (1989). Male and female raters' stereotyping of male and female physiques. *Personality and Social Psychology Bulletin, 15,* 244–251.

Sadalla, E. K., Kenrick, D. T., & Vershure, B. (1987). Dominance and heterosexual attraction. *Journal of Personality and Social Psychology, 52,* 730–738.

Sadalla, E. K., Sheets, V., & McCreath, H. (1990). The cognition of urban tempo. *Environment and Behavior, 22,* 230–254.

Sadker, M., & Sadker, D. (1994). *Failing at fairness: How America's schools cheat girls.* New York: Charles Scribners Sons.

Safir, M. P., Peres, Y., Lichtenstein, M., Hoch, Z., & Shepher, J. (1982). Psychological androgyny and sexual adequacy. *Journal of Sex and Marital Therapy, 8,* 228–240.

Sally, D. (1998). Conversation and cooperation in social dilemmas: A meta-analysis of experiments from 1958–1992. *Rationality and Society.*

Salmela-Aro, K., & Nurmi, J.-E. (1996). Uncertainty and confidence in interpersonal projects: Consequences for social relationships and well-being. *Journal of Social and Personal Relationships, 13,* 109–122.

Salovey, P. (1992). Mood-induced self-focused attention. *Journal of Personality and Social Psychology, 62,* 699–707.

Salovey, P., Mayer, J. D., & Rosenhan, D. L. (1991). Mood and helping: Mood as a motivator of helping and helping as a regulator of mood. In M. S. Clark (Ed.), *Prosocial behavior* (pp. 215–237). Newbury Park, CA: Sage.

Saltus, R. (1995, November 20). Rare mutant gene may help in probing origins of cancer. *The Boston Globe,* Health/Science, pp. 33, 37.

Sample, E. B., Jr., Li, L., & Moore, D. (1997). Alcohol use, ethnicity, and disability: A comparison of African–American and Caucasian groups. *Social Behavior and Personality, 25,* 265–276.

Sanders, G. S. (1983). An attentional process model of social facilitation. In A. Hare, H. Blumberg, V. Kent, & M. Davies (Eds.), *Small groups.* London: Wiley.

Sanna, L. J. (1997). Self-efficacy and counterfactual thinking: Up a creek with and without a paddle. *Personality and Social Psychology Bulletin, 23,* 654–666.

Sanna, L. J., & Pusecker, P. A. (1994). Self-efficacy, valence of self-evaluation, and performance. *Personality and Social Psychology Bulletin, 20,* 82–92.

Sarason, I. G., Sarason, B. R., & Pierce, G. R. (1994). Social support: Global and relationship-based levels of analysis. *Journal of Social and Personal Relationships, 11,* 295–312.

Sattler, D. N., Adams, M. G., & Watts, B. (1995). Effects of personal experience on judgments about natural disasters. *Journal of Social Behavior and Personality, 10,* 891–898.

Schachter, D. L., & Kihlstrom, J. F. (1989). Functional amnesia. In F. Boller & J. Grafman (Eds.), *Handbook of neuropsychology* (Vol. 3, pp. 209–230). New York: Elsevier.

Schachter, S. (1959). *The psychology of affiliation.* Stanford, CA: Stanford University Press.

Schachter, S. (1964). The interaction of cognitive and physiological determinants of emotional state. In L. Berkowitz (Ed.), *Advances in experimental social psychology* (Vol. 1, pp. 48–81). New York: Academic Press.

Schaefer, J. A., & Moos, R. H. (1993). Relationship, task and system stressors in the health care workplace. *Journal of Community and Applied Social Psychology, 3,* 285–298.

Scher, A., & Mayseless, O. (1994). Mothers' attachment with spouse and parenting in the first year. *Journal of Social and Interpersonal Relationships, 11,* 601–609.

Scher, S. J. (1997). Measuring the consequences of injustice. *Personality and Social Psychology Bulletin, 23,* 482–497.

Scherer, K. R. (1997). The role of culture in emotion-antecedent appraisal. *Journal of Personality and Social Psychology, 73,* 902–922.

Scherer, K. R., & Walbott, H. G. (1994). Evidence for universality and cultural variation of differential emotion response patterning. *Journal of Personality and Social Psychology, 66,* 310–328.

Schleifer, S. J., Keller, S. E., Camerino, M., Thornton, J. C., & Stein, M. (1983). Suppression of lymphocyte function following bereavement. *Journal of the American Medical Association, 250,* 374–377.

Schlenker, B. R., Britt, T., Pennington, J., Murphy, R., & Doherty, K. (1994). The triangle model of responsibility. *Psychological Bulletin, 101,* 632–653.

Schmitt, D. P., & Buss, D. M. (1996). Strategic self-promotion and competitor derogation: Sex and context effects on the perceived effectiveness of mate attraction tactics. *Journal of Personality and Social Psychology, 70,* 1185–1204.

Schneider, B. H. (1991). A comparison of skill-building and desensitization strategies for intervention with aggressive children. *Aggressive Behavior, 17,* 301–311.

Schneider, B. H., Wiener, J., & Murphy, K. (1994). Children's friendships: The giant step beyond peer acceptance. *Journal of Social and Personal Relationships, 11,* 323–340.

Schneider, F. W., & Mockus, Z. (1974). Failure to find a rural–urban difference in incidence of altruistic behavior. *Psychological Reports, 35,* 294.

Schneider, K. (1991, August 13). Ranges of animals and plants head north. *New York Times,* pp. C1, C9.

Schneider, M. E., Major, B., Luhtanen, R., & Crocker, J. (1996). Social stigma and the potential costs of assumptive help. *Personality and Social Psychology Bulletin, 22,* 201–209.

Schooler, J. W., & Engstler-Schooler, T. Y. (1990). Verbal overshadowing of visual memories: Some things are better left unsaid. *Cognitive Psychology, 22,* 36–71.

Schooler, J. W., & Loftus, E. F. (1986). Individual differences and experimentation: Complementary approaches to interrogative suggestibility. *Social Behavior, 1,* 105–112.

Schreurs, K. M. G., & Buunk, B. P. (1995). Intimacy, autonomy, and relationship satisfaction in Dutch lesbian couples and heterosexual couples. *Journal of Psychology & Human Sexuality, 7,* 41–57.

Schuster, E., & Elderton, E. M. (1906). The inheritance of psychical characters. *Biometrika, 5,* 460–469.

Schutte, J. W., & Hosch, H. M. (1997). Gender differences in sexual assault verdicts: A meta-analysis. *Journal of Social Behavior and Personality, 12,* 759–772.

Schwartz, A. E. (1994, December 20). Americans on line seldom fond of disagreement. *Albany Times Union,* p. A-11.

Schwarz, N., Bless, H., Bohner, G. (1991a). Mood and persuasion: Affective states influence the processing of persuasive communications. In M. P. Zanna (Ed.), *Advances in experimental social psychology* (Vol. 24, pp. 161–199). San Diego, CA: Academic Press.

Schwarz, N., Bless, H., Strack, F., Klumpp, G., Rittenauer-Schatka, G., & Simons, A. (1991b). Ease of retrieval as information: Another look at the availability heuristic. *Journal of Personality and Social Psychology, 61,* 195–202.

Schwarzer, R. (1994). Optimism, vulnerability, and self-beliefs as health-related cognitions: A systematic overview. *Psychology and Health, 9,* 161–180.

Schwarzer, R., Jerusalem, M., & Hahn, A. (1994). Unemployment, social support and health complaints: A longitudinal study of stress in East German refugees. *Journal of Community and Applied Social Psychology, 4,* 31–45.

Schwarzwald, J., Amir, Y., & Crain, R. L. (1992). Long-term effects of school desegregation experiences on interpersonal relations in the Israeli defense forces. *Personality and Social Psychology Bulletin, 18,* 357–368.

Scott, K. P., & Feldman-Summers, S. (1979). Children's reactions to textbook stories in which females are portrayed in traditionally male roles. *Journal of Educational Psychology, 71,* 396–402.

Scruton, B. A. (1998, January 13). Thief abuses good deed. *Albany Times Union,* p. B1.

Seal, D. W. (1997). Inter-partner concordance of self-reported sexual behavior among college dating couples. *Journal of Sex Research, 34,* 39–55.

Searcy, E., & Eisenberg, N. (1992). Defensiveness in response to aid from a sibling. *Journal of Personality and Social Psychology, 62,* 422–433.

Sears, D. O. (1988). Symbolic racism. In P. A. Katz & D. A. Taylor (Eds.), *Eliminating racism: Profiles in controversy* (pp. 53–84). New York: Plenum.

Sears, D. O. (1997). The impact of self-interest on attitudes—a symbolic political perspective on differences between survey and experimental findings: Comment on Crano (1997). *Journal of Personality and Social Psychology, 72,* 492–496.

Sears, D. O., Hensler, C. P., & Speer, L. K. (1979). Whites' opposition to "busing": Self-interest or symbolic politics? *American Political Science Review, 73,* 369–384.

Sedikides, C. (1992). Attentional effects on mood are moderated by chronic self-conception valence. *Personality and Social Psychology Bulletin, 18,* 580–584.

Sedikides, C. (1993). Assessment, enhancement, and verification determinants of the self-evaluation process. *Journal of Personality and Social Psychology, 65,* 317–338.

Sedikides, C. (1995). Central and peripheral self-conceptions are differentially influenced by mood: Test of the differential sensitivity hypothesis. *Journal of Personality and Social Psychology, 69,* 759–777.

Sedikides, C., & Skowronski, J. J. (1997). The symbolic self in evolutionary context. *Personality and Social Psychology Review, 1,* 80–102.

Segal, L. (1996, Fall). My grandfather's walking stick, or the pink lie. *Social Research.*

Segal, M. M. (1974). Alphabet and attraction: An unobtrusive measure of the effect of propinquity in a field setting. *Journal of Personality and Social Psychology, 30,* 654–657.

Segerstrom, S. C., Taylor, S. E., Kemeny, M. E., & Fahey, J. L. (1998). Optimism is associated with mood, coping, and immune change in response to stress. *Journal of Personality and Social Psychology, 74,* 1646–1655.

Segrin, C., & Kinney, T. (1995). Social skills deficits among the socially anxious: Rejection from others and loneliness. *Motivation and Emotion, 19,* 1–24.

Selye, H. (1956). *The stress of life.* New York: McGraw-Hill.

Seta, C. E., Hayes, N. S., & Seta, J. J. (1994). Mood, memory, and vigilance: The influence of distraction on recall and impression formation. *Personality and Social Psychology Bulletin, 20,* 170–177.

Shackelford, T. K., & Buss, D. M. (1997). Cues to infidelity. *Personality and Social Psychology Bulletin, 23,* 1034–1045.

Shaffer, D. R., & Bazzini, D. G. (1997). What do you look for in a prospective date? Reexamining the preferences of men and women who differ in self-monitoring propensities. *Personality and Social Psychology Bulletin, 23,* 605–616.

Shanab, M. E., & Yahya, K. A. (1977). A behavioral study of obedience in children. *Journal of Personality and Social Psychology, 35,* 530–536.

Shapiro, J. P., Baumeister, R. F., & Kessler, J. W. (1991). A three-component model of children's teasing: Aggression, humor, and ambiguity. *Journal of Social and Clinical Psychology, 10,* 459–472.

Sharf, J., & Wolf, P. P. (1998). University of Michigan's affirmative action case: A good bet for the Supreme Court. *The Industrial Organizational Psychologist, 35,* 85–88.

Sharp, M. J., & Getz, J. G. (1996). Substance use as impression management. *Personality and Social Psychology Bulletin, 22,* 60–67.

Sharpe, D., Adair, J. G., & Roese, N. J. (1992). Twenty years of deception research: A decline in subjects' trust? *Personality and Social Psychology Bulletin, 18,* 585–590.

Sharpsteen, D. J. (1995). The effects of relationship and self-esteem threats on the likelihood of romantic jealousy. *Journal of Social and Personal Relationships, 12,* 89–101.

Sharpsteen, D. J., & Kirkpatrick, L. A. (1997). Romantic jealousy and adult romantic attachment. *Journal of Personality and Social Psychology, 72,* 627–640.

Shaver, J. (1993, August 9). America's legal immigrants: Who they are and where they go. *Newsweek,* pp. 20–21.

Shaver, P. R., & Brennan, K. A. (1992). Attachment styles and the "big five" personality traits: Their connections with each other and with romantic relationship outcomes. *Personality and Social Psychology Bulletin, 18,* 536–545.

Shaver, P. R., & Hazan, C. (1994). Attachment. In A. L. Weber & J. H. Harvey (Eds.), *Perspectives on close relationships* (pp. 110–130). Boston: Allyn & Bacon.

Shaver, P. R., Morgan, H. J., & Wu, S. (1996). Is love a "basic" emotion? *Personal Relationships, 3,* 81–96.

Shaver, P. R., Papalia, D., Clark, C. L., Koski, L. R., Tidwell, M. C., & Nalbone, D. (1996). Androgyny and attachment security: Two related models of optimal personality. *Personality and Social Psychology Bulletin, 22,* 582–597.

Shavitt, S. (1989). Operationalizing functional theories of attitudes. In A. R. Pratkanis, S. J. Breckler, & A. G. Greenwald (Eds.), *Attitude structure and function* (pp. 311–377). Hillsdale, NJ: Erlbaum.

Shaw, J. I., & Skolnick, P. (1995). Effects of prohibitive and informative judicial instructions on jury decision-making. *Social Behavior and Personality, 23,* 319–326.

Shaw, J. I., Borough, H. W., & Fink, M. I. (1994). Perceived sexual orientation and helping behavior by males and females: The wrong number technique. *Journal of Psychology and Human Sexuality, 6,* 73–81.

Shaw, L. L., Batson, C. D., & Todd, R. M. (1994). Empathy avoidance: Forestalling feeling for another in order to escape the motivational consequences. *Journal of Personality and Social Psychology, 67,* 879–887.

Shaywitz, B. A., Shaywitz, S. E., Pugh, K. R., Constable, R. T., Skudlarski, P., Fulbright, R. K., Bronen, R. A., Fletcher, J. M., Shankweiler, D. P., Katz, L., & Gore, J. C. (1995). Sex differences in the functional organization of the brain for language. *Nature, 373*(6515) 607–609.

Shechtman, Z. (1993). Group psychotherapy for the enhancement of intimate friendship and self-esteem among troubled elementary-school children. *Journal of Social and Personal Relationships, 10,* 483–494.

Sheeran, P., & Abraham, C. (1994). Unemployment and self-conception: A symbolic interactionist analysis. *Journal of Community & Applied Social Psychology, 4,* 115–129.

Sheldon, W. H., Stevens, S. S., & Tucker, W. B. (1940). *The varieties of human physique.* New York: Harper.

Shepperd, J. A., Ouellette, J. A., & Fernandez, J. K. (1996). Abandoning unrealistic optimistic performance estimates and the temporal proximity of self-relevant feedback. *Journal of Personality and Social Psychology, 70,* 844–855.

Sherif, M., Harvey, D. J., White, B. J., Hood, W. R, & Sherif, C. W. (1961). *The Robbers' cave experiment.* Norman, OK: Institute of Group Relations.

Sherman, J. W., & Klein, S. B. (1994). Development and representation of personality impressions. *Journal of Personality and Social Psychology, 67,* 972–983.

Sherman, M. D., & Thelen, M. H. (1996). Fear of intimacy scale: Validation and extension with adolescents. *Journal of Social and Personal Relationships, 13,* 507–521.

Sherman, S. R. (1994). Changes in age identity: Self-perceptions in middle and late life. *Journal of Aging Studies, 8,* 397–412.

Sherman, S. S. (1980). On the self-erasing nature of errors of prediction. *Journal of Personality and Social Psychology, 16,* 388–403.

Shestowsky, D., Wegener, D. T., & Fabrigar, L. R. (1998). Need for cognition and interpersonal influence: Individual differences in impact on dyadic decisions. *Journal of Personality and Social Psychology, 74,* 1317–1328.

Shigetomi, C. C., Hartmann, D. P., & Gelfand, D. M. (1981). Sex differences in children's altruistic behavior and reputations for helpfulness. *Developmental Psychology, 17,* 434–437.

Shinn, M., Morch, H., Robinson, P. E., & Neuner, R. A. (1993). Individual, group, and agency strategies for coping with job stressors in residential child care programs. *Journal of Community and Applied Social Psychology, 3,* 313–324.

Shively, C. A. (1998, March/April). Social stress and disease susceptibility in female monkeys. *Psychological Science Agenda,* 6–7.

Shotland, R. I., & Strau, M. K. (1976). Bystander response to an assault: When a man attacks a woman. *Journal of Personality and Social Psychology, 34,* 990–999.

Shotland, R. L., & Goodstein, L. (1983). Just because she doesn't want to doesn't mean its rape: An experimentally causal model of the perception of rape in a dating situation. *Social Psychology Quarterly, 46,* 220–232.

Showers, C. (1992a). Compartmentalization of positive and negative self-knowledge: Keeping bad apples out of the bunch. *Journal of Personality and Social Psychology, 62,* 1036–1049.

Showers, C. (1992b). Evaluative integrative thinking about characteristics of the self. *Personality and Social Psychology Bulletin, 18,* 719–729.

Showers, C. J., & Kling, K. C. (1996). Organization of self-knowledge: Implications for recovery from sad mood. *Journal of Personality and Social Psychology, 70,* 578–590.

Showers, C. J., & Ryff, C. D. (1996). Self-differentiation and well-being in a life transition. *Personality and Social Psychology Bulletin, 22,* 448–460.

Shulman, S., Elicker, J., & Sroufe, L. A. (1994). Stages of friendship growth in preadolescence as related to attachment history. *Journal of Social and Personal Relationships, 11,* 341–361.

Sigall, H. (1997). Ethical considerations in social psychological research: Is the bogus pipeline a special case? *Journal of Applied Social Psychology, 27,* 574–581.

Sigelman, C. K., Thomas, D. B., Sigelman, L., & Robich, F. D. (1986). Gender, physical attractiveness, and electability: An experimental investigation of voter biases. *Journal of Applied Social Psychology, 16,* 229–248.

Sillars, A. L., Folwell, A. L., Hill, K. C., Maki, B. K., Hurst, A. P., & Casano, R. A. (1994). *Journal of Social and Personal Relationships, 11,* 611–617.

Silverstein, R. (1994). Chronic identity diffusion in traumatized combat veterans. *Social Behavior and Personality, 22,* 69–80.

Sim, D. L. H., & Morris, M. W. (1998). Representativeness and counterfactual thinking: The principle that antecedent and outcome correspond in magnitude. *Personality and Social Psychology Bulletin, 24,* 595–609.

Simmel, G. (1950). The metropolis and mental life. In K. H. Wolff (Ed.), *The sociology of Georg Simmel.* New York: Free Press.

Simon, L., Greenberg, J., & Brehm, J. (1995). Trivialization: The forgotten mode of dissonance reduction. *Journal of Personality and Social Psychology, 68,* 247–260.

Simpson, J. A. (1987). The dissolution of romantic relationships: Factors involved in relationship stability and emotional stress. *Journal of Personality and Social Psychology, 53,* 683–692.

Simpson, J. A., & Gangestad, S. W. (1991). Individual differences in sociosexuality: Evidence for convergent and discriminant validity. *Journal of Personality and Social Psychology, 60,* 870–883.

Simpson, J. A., & Gangestad, S. W. (1992). Sociosexuality and romantic partner choice. *Journal of Personality, 60,* 31–51.

Simpson, J. A., Ickes, W., & Blackstone, T. (1995). When the head protects the heart: Empathic accuracy in dating relationships. *Journal of Personality and Social Psychology, 69,* 629–641.

Singh, D. (1993). Adaptive significance of female physical attractiveness: Role of waist-to-hip ratio. *Journal of Personality and Social Psychology, 65,* 293–307.

Singh, D. (1995). Female judgment of male attractiveness and desirability for relationships: Role of waist-to-hip ratio and financial status. *Journal of Personality and Social Psychology, 69,* 1089–1101.

Singh, R., & Tan, L. S. C. (1992). Attitudes and attraction: A test of the similarity–attraction and dissimilarity–repulsion hypotheses. *British Journal of Social Psychology, 31,* 227–238.

Singh, R., Choo, W. M., & Poh, L. L. (1998). In-group bias and fair-mindedness as strategies of self-presentation in inter group perception. *Personality and Social Psychology Bulletin, 24,* 147–162.

Sivacek, J., & Crano, W. D. (1982). Vested interest as a moderator of attitude-behavior consistency. *Journal of Personality and Social Psychology, 43,* 210–221.

Skarlicki, D. P., & Folger, R. (1997). Retaliation in the workplace: The roles of distributive, procedural, and interactional justice. *Journal of Applied Psychology, 821,* 434–443.

Skowronski, J. J., & Carlston, D. E. (1989). Negativity and extremity biases in impression formation: A review of explanations. *Psychological Bulletin, 105,* 131–142.

Sleek, S. (1998, February). Is psychologists' testimony going unheard? *APA Monitor, 1,* 34.

Smeaton, G. (1998). *STD risk in the eye of the beholder: The effects of physical attractiveness, body piercing, and social perceptions on judgments of STD risk.* Unpublished manuscript, University of Wisconsin–Stout.

Smeaton, G., & Byrne, D. (1987). The effects of R-rated violence and erotica, individual differences, and victim characteristics on acquaintance rape proclivity. *Journal of Research in Personality, 21,* 171–184.

Smeaton, G., Byrne, D., & Murnen, S. K. (1989). The repulsion hypothesis revisited: Similarity irrelevance or dissimilarity bias? *Journal of Personality and Social Psychology, 56,* 54–59.

Smith, A. J. (1957). Similarity of values and its relation to acceptance and the projection of similarity. *Journal of Psychology, 43,* 251–260.

Smith, B. W. (1996). Coping as a predictor of outcomes following the 1993 Midwest flood. *Journal of Social Behavior and Personality, 11,* 225–239.

Smith, C. M., Tindale, R. S., & Dugoni, B. L. (1996). Minority and majority influence in freely interacting groups: Qualitative versus quantitative differences. *British Journal of Social Psychology, 35,* 137–149.

Smith, D. E., Gier, J. A., & Willis, F. N. (1982). Interpersonal touch and compliance with a marketing request. *Basic and Applied Social Psychology, 3,* 35–38.

Smith, E. R., & Henry, S. (1996). An in-group becomes part of the self: Response time evidence. *Personality and Social Psychology Bulletin, 22,* 635–642.

Smith, E. R., & Zarate, M. A. (1992). Exemplar-based model of social judgment. *Psychological Review, 99,* 3–21.

Smith, E. R., Byrne, D., & Fielding, P. J. (1995). Interpersonal attraction as a function of extreme gender role adherence. *Personal Relationships, 2,* 161–172.

Smith, E. R., Byrne, D., Becker, M. A., & Przybyla, D. P. J. (1993). Sexual attitudes of males and females as predictors of interpersonal attraction and marital compatibility. *Journal of Applied Social Psychology, 23,* 1011–1034.

Smith, K. D., Keating, J. P., & Stotland, E. (1989). Altruism reconsidered: The effect of denying feedback on a victim's status to empathetic witnesses. *Journal of Personality and Social Psychology, 57,* 641–650.

Smith, P. B., & Bond, M. H. (1993). *Social psychology across cultures.* Boston: Allyn & Bacon.

Smith, R. E., Smoll, F. L., & Ptacek, J. T. (1990). Conjunctive moderator variables in vulnerability and resiliency research: Life stress, social support and coping skills, and adolescent sport injuries. *Journal of Personality and Social Psychology, 58,* 360–370.

Smith, S. S., & Richardson, D. (1985). On deceiving ourselves about deception: Reply to Rubin. *Journal of Personality and Social Psychology, 48,* 254–255.

Smith, T. W., & Pope, M. K. (1990). Cynical hostility as a health risk: Current status and future directions. *Journal of Social Behavior and Personality, 5,* 77–88.

Smith, V. I., & Ellsworth, P. C. (1987). The social psychology of eyewitness accuracy: Misleading questions and communicator expertise. *Journal of Applied Psychology, 72,* 294–300.

Sneddon, I., & Kremer, J. (1992). Sexual behavior and attitudes of university students in Northern Ireland. *Archives of Sexual Behavior, 21,* 295–312.

Snell, W. E., Jr. (1998). The Relationship Awareness Scale: Measuring relational-consciousness, relational-monitoring, and relational-anxiety. *Contemporary Social Psychology, 18,* 23–49.

Sniffen, M. J. (1991, September 30). Blacks make up 40% of death row. *Albany Times Union,* p. A-3.

Snyder, C. R., & Fromkin, H. L. (1979). *Uniqueness: The human pursuit of difference.* New York: Plenum.

Snyder, M. (1974). Self-monitoring of expressive behavior. *Journal of Personality and Social Psychology, 30,* 526–537.

Snyder, M., & Ickes, W. (1985). Personality and social behavior. In G. Lindzey & E. Aronson (Eds.), *Handbook of social psychology* (3rd ed.) (Vol. 2, pp. 883–947). New York: Random House.

Snyder, M., & Omoto, A. M. (1992a). Volunteerism and society's response to the HIV epidemic. *Current Directions in Psychological Science, 1,* 113–116.

Snyder, M., & Omoto, A. M. (1992b). Who helps and why? The psychology of AIDS volunteerism. In S. Spacapan & S.

Oscamp (Eds.), *Helping and being helped: Naturalistic studies* (pp. 213–239). Newbury Park, CA: Sage.

Snyder, M., & Simpson, J. A. (1984). Self-monitoring and dating relationships. *Journal of Personality and Social Psychology, 47*, 1281–1291.

Snyder, M., Gangestad, S., & Simpson, J. A. (1983). Choosing friends as activity partners: The role of self-monitoring. *Journal of Personality and Social Psychology, 45*, 1061–1072.

Snyder, M., Grether, J., & Keller, K. (1974). Staring and compliance: A field experiment on hitchhiking. *Journal of Applied Social Psychology, 4*, 165–170.

Sorenson, K. A., Russell, S. M., Harkness, D. J., & Harvey, J. H. (1993). Account-making, confiding, and coping with the ending of a close relationship. *Journal of Social Behavior and Personality, 8*, 73–86.

Spencer, S. J., Fein, S., Wolfe, C. T., Fong, C., & Dunn, M. A. (1998). Automatic activation of stereotypes: The role of self-image threat. *Personality and Social Psychology Bulletin, 24*, 1139–1152.

Sprafkin, J. N., Liebert, R. M., & Poulous, R. W. (1975). Effects of a prosocial televised example on children's helping. *Journal of Personality and Social Psychology, 48*, 35–46.

Sprecher, S., & Duck, S. (1994). Sweet talk: The importance of perceived communication for romantic and friendship attraction experienced during a get-acquainted date. *Personality and Social Psychology Bulletin, 20*, 391–400.

Stalling, R. B. (1992). Mood and pain: The influence of positive and negative affect on reported body aches. *Journal of Social Behavior and Personality, 7*, 323–334.

Stangor, C., & Ruble, D. N. (1989). Strength of expectancies and memory for social information: What we remember depends on how much we know. *Journal of Experimental Social Psychology, 25*, 18–35.

Staples, S. L. (1996). Human response to environmental noise: Psychological research and public policy. *American Psychologist, 51*, 143–150.

Stasser, G. (1992). Pooling of unshared information during group discussion. In S. Worchel, W. Wood, & J. H. Simpson (Eds.), *Group process and productivity* (pp. 48–67). Newbury Park, CA: Sage.

Stasser, G., & Hinkle, S. (1994). Research in progress, Miami University, Oxford, Ohio.

Stasser, G., & Stewart, D. (1992). Discovery of hidden profiles by decision-making groups: Solving a problem versus making a judgment. *Journal of Personality and Social Psychology, 63*, 426–434.

Stasser, G., Taylor, L. A., & Hanna, C. (1989). Information sampling in structured and unstructured discussions of three- and six-person groups. *Journal of Personality and Social Psychology, 57*, 67–78.

Steel, R. P., & Rentsch, J. R. (1997). The dispositional model of job attitudes revisited: Findings of a 10-year study. *Journal of Applied Psychology, 82*, 873–879.

Steele, C. M. (1988). The psychology of self-affirmation: Sustaining the integrity of the self. In L. Berkowitz (Ed.), *Advances in experimental social psychology* (pp. 261–302). Hillsdale, NJ: Erlbaum.

Steele, C. M. (1992, April). Race and the schooling of Black Americans. *The Atlantic Monthly, 269*(4), 68–78.

Steele, C. M. (1997). A threat in the air: How stereotypes shape the intellectual identities and performance of women and African-Americans. *American Psychologist, 52*, 613–629.

Steele, C. M., & Josephs, R. A. (1990). Alcohol myopia: Its prized and dangerous effects. *American Psychologist, 45*, 921–933.

Steele, C. M., & Lui, T. J. (1983). Dissonance processes as self-affirmation. *Journal of Personality and Social Psychology, 45*, 5–19.

Steele, C. M., Critchlow, B., & Liu, T. J. (1985). Alcohol and social behavior: The helpful drunkard. *Journal of Personality and Social Psychology, 48*, 35–46.

Steele, C. M., Southwick, L., & Critchlow, B. (1981). Dissonance and alcohol: Drinking your troubles away. *Journal of Personality and Social Psychology, 41*, 831–846.

Steele, C. M., Spencer, S. J., & Lynch, M. (1993). Self-image resilience and dissonance: The role of affirmational resources. *Journal of Personality and Social Psychology, 64*, 885–896.

Stein, R. I., & Nemeroff, C. J. (1995). Moral overtones of food: Judgments of others based on what they eat. *Personality and Social Psychology Bulletin, 21*, 480–490.

Steinhauer, J. (1995, April 10). Big benefits in marriage, studies say. *New York Times*, p. A10.

Stephan, W. G. (1985). Intergroup relations. In G. Lindzey & E. Aronson (Eds.), *Handbook of social psychology* (Vol. 3, pp. 599–658). New York: Addison-Wesley.

Sternberg, R. J. (1986). A triangular theory of love. *Psychological Review, 93*, 119–135.

Sternberg, R. J. (1988a). *The triangle of love*. New York: Basic Books.

Sternberg, R. J. (1988b). Triangulating love. In R. J. Sternberg & M. J. Barnes (Eds.), *The psychology of love* (pp. 119–138). New Haven, CT: Yale University Press.

Sternberg, R. J. (1996). Love stories. *Personal Relationships, 3*, 59–79.

Sternberg, R. J., & Hojjat, M. (Eds.). (1997). *Satisfaction in close relationships*. New York: Guilford.

Stevens, C. K., & Kristof, A. L. (1995). Making the right impression: A field study of applicant impression management during job interviews. *Journal of Applied Psychology, 80*, 587–606.

Stewart, R. B., Verbrugge, K. M., & Beilfuss, M. C. (1998). Sibling relationships in early adulthood: A typology. *Personal Relationships, 5*, 59–74.

Stice, E., Shaw, H., & Nemeroff, C. (1998). Dual pathway model of bulimia nervosa: Longitudinal support for dietary restraint and affect-regulation mechanisms. *Journal of Social and Clinical Psychology, 17*, 129–149.

Stiles, W. B., Walz, N. C., Schroeder, M. A. B., Williams, L. L., & Ickes, W. (1996). Attractiveness and disclosure in initial encounters of mixed-sex dyads. *Journal of Social and Personal Relationships, 13*, 303–312.

Stocker, C. M., & McHale, S. M. (1992). The nature and family correlates of preadolescents' perceptions of their sibling relationships. *Journal of Social and Personal Relationships, 9*, 179–195.

Stone, A. A., Cox, D., Valdimarsdottir, H., Jandorf, L., & Neale, J. M. (1987). Evidence that secretory IgA antibody is associated with daily mood. *Journal of Personality and Social Psychology, 52*, 988–993.

Stone, A. A., Neale, J. M., Cox, D. S., Napoli, A., Valdimarsdottir, H., & Kennedy-Moore, E. (1994). Daily events are associated with a secretory immune response to an oral antigen in men. *Health Psychology, 13*, 440–446.

Stone, J., Wiegand, A. W., Cooper, J., & Aronson, E. (1997). When exemplification fails: Hypocrisy and the motives for self-integrity. *Journal of Personality and Social Psychology, 72*, 54–65.

Stone, J., Aronson, E., Crain, A. L., Winslow, M. P., & Fried, C. B. (1994). Inducing hypocrisy as a means of encouraging young adults to use condoms. *Personality and Social Psychology Bulletin, 20*, 116–128.

Stoppard, J. M., & Gruchy, C. D. G. (1993). Gender, context, and expression of positive emotion. *Personality and Social Psychology Bulletin, 19*, 143–150.

Story, A. L. (1998). Self-esteem and memory for favorable and unfavorable personality feedback. *Personality and Social Psychology Bulletin, 24*, 51–64.

Stotland, E. (1969). Exploratory investigations of empathy. *Advances in Experimental Social Psychology, 4*, 271–313.

Stradling, S. G., Crowe, G., & Tuohy, A. P. (1993). Changes in self-concept during occupational socialization of new recruits to the police. *Journal of Community & Applied Social Psychology, 3*, 131–147.

Strauman, T. J., Lemieux, A. M., & Coe, C. L. (1993). Self-discrepancy and natural killer cell activity: Immunological consequences of negative self-evaluation. *Journal of Personality and Social Psychology, 64*, 1042–1052.

Stroessner, S. J., Hamilton, D. L., & Mackie, D. M. (1992). Affect and stereotyping: the effect of induced mood on distinctiveness-based illusory correlations. *Journal of Personality and Social Psychology, 62*, 564–576.

Stroh, L. K., Brett, J. M., & Rilly, A. H. (1992). All the right stuff: A comparison of female and male managers' career progression. *Journal of Applied Psychology, 77*, 251–260.

Strube, M., Turner, C. W., Cerro, D., Stevens, J., & Hinchey, F. (1984). Interpersonal aggression and the Type A coronary-prone behavior pattern: A theoretical distinction and practical implications. *Journal of Personality and Social Psychology, 47*, 839–847.

Strube, M. J. (1989). Evidence for the Type in Type A behavior: A taxonometric analysis. *Journal of Personality and Social Psychology, 56*, 972–987.

Subich, L. M., Cooper, E. A., Barrett, G. V., & Arthur, W. (1986). Occupational perceptions of males and females as a function of sex ratios, salary, and availability. *Journal of Vocational Behavior, 28*, 123–134.

Sugarman, D. B., & Hotaling, G. T. (1989). Dating violence: Prevalence, context, and risk markers. In M. A. Pirog-Good & J. E. Stets (Eds.), *Violence in dating relationships*. New York: Praeger.

Suls, J., & Fletcher, B. (1985). The relative efficacy of avoidant and non-avoidant coping strategies: A meta-analysis. *Health Psychology, 4*, 249–288.

Suls, J., & Rosnow, J. (1988). Concerns about artifacts in behavioral research. In M. Morawski (Ed.), *The rise of experimentation in American psychology* (pp. 163–187). New Haven, CT: Yale University Press.

Suls, J., & Wan, C. K. (1989). The effects of sensory and procedural information on coping with stressful medical procedures and pain: A meta-analysis. *Journal of Consulting and Clinical Psychology, 57*, 372–379.

Summers, R. J. (1991). The influence of affirmative action on perceptions of a beneficiary's qualifications. *Journal of Applied Social Psychology, 21*, 1265–1276.

Sunnafrank, M. (1992). On debunking the attitude similarity myth. *Communication Monographs, 59*, 165–179.

Swann, W. B., Jr. (1997). The trouble with change: Self-verification and allegiance to the self. *Psychological Science, 8*, 177–180.

Swann, W. B., Jr., & Gill, M. J. (1997). Confidence and accuracy in person perception: Do we know what we think we know about our relationship partners? *Journal of Personality and Social Psychology, 73*, 747–757.

Swann, W. B. Jr., De La Ronde, C., & Hixon, J. G. (1994). Authenticity and positivity strivings in marriage and courtship. *Journal of Personality and Social Psychology, 66*, 857–869.

Swann, W. B. Jr., Stein-Serossi, A., & Giesler, R. B. (1992). Why people self-verify. *Journal of Personality and Social Psychology, 62*, 392–401.

Swann, W. B. Jr., Griffin, J. J. Jr., Predmore, S. C., & Gaines, B. (1987). Cognitive–affective crossfire: When self-consistency meets self-enhancement. *Journal of Personality and Social Psychology, 52*, 881–889.

Swap, W. C. (1977). Interpersonal attraction and repeated exposure to rewarders and punishers. *Personality and Social Psychology Bulletin, 3*, 248–251.

Swim, J. K. (1994). Perceived versus meta-analytic effect sizes: An assessment of the accuracy of gender stereotypes. *Journal of Personality and Social Psychology, 66*, 21–36.

Swim, J. K., Aikin, K. J., Hall, W. S., & Hunter, B. A. (1995). Sexism and racism: Old-fashioned and modern prejudices. *Journal of Personality and Social Psychology, 68*, 199–214.

Tafarodi, R. W. (1998). Paradoxical self-esteem and selectivity in the processing of social information. *Journal of Personality and Social Psychology, 74*, 1181–1196.

Tafarodi, R. W., & Vu, C. (1997). Two-dimensional self-esteem and reactions to success and failure. *Personality and Social Psychology Bulletin, 23*, 626–635.

Tajfel, H. (1982). *Social identity and intergroup relations*. Cambridge, England: Cambridge University Press.

Tajfel, H., & Turner, J. C. (1986). The social identity theory of intergroup behavior. In S. Worchel & W. Austin (Eds.), *Psychology of intergroup relations*. Chicago: Nelson-Hall.

Takata, T., & Hashimoto, H. (1973). Effects of insufficient justification upon the arousal of cognitive dissonance: Timing of justification and evaluation of task. *Japanese Journal of Experimental Social Psychology, 13*, 77–85.

Tan, D. T. Y., & Singh, R. (1995). Attitudes and attraction: A developmental study of the similarity–attraction and dissimilarity–repulsion hypotheses. *Personality and Social Psychology Bulletin, 21* 975–986.

Tannen, D. (1994). *Talking from 9 to 5*. New York: William Morrow.

Tannen, D. (1995, January 9–15). And rarely the twain shall meet. *Washington Post National Weekly Edition* 25.

Tassinary, L. G., & Hansen, K. A. (1998). A critical test of the waist-to-hip ratio hypothesis of female physical attractiveness. *Psychological Science, 9*, 150–155.

Taylor, K. M., & Shepperd, J. A. (1998). Bracing for the worst: Severity, testing, and feedback timing as moderators of the optimistic bias. *Personality and Social Psychology Bulletin, 24*, 915–926.

Taylor, M. S., Locke, E. A., Lee, C., & Gist, M. E. (1984). Type A behavior and faculty research productivity: What are the mechanisms? *Organizational Behavior and Human Performance, 34*, 402–418.

Taylor, S. E., & Brown, J. D. (1988). Illusion and well-being: A social psychological perspective on mental health. *Psychological Bulletin, 103*, 193–210.

Taylor, S. E., Buunk, B. P., & Aspinwall, L. G. (1990). Social comparison, stress, and coping. *Personality and Social Psychology Bulletin, 16*, 74–89.

Taylor, S. E., Neter, E., & Wayment, H. A. (1995). Self-evaluation processes. *Personality and Social Psychology Bulletin, 21,* 1278–1287.

Taylor, S. E., Pham, L. B., Rivkin, I. D., & Armor, D. A. (1998). Harnessing the imagination: Mental stimulation, self-regulation, and coping. *American Psychologist, 53,* 429–439.

Taylor, S. E., Helgeson, V. S., Reed, G. M., & Skokan, L. A. (1991). Self-generated feelings of control and adjustment to physical illness. *Journal of Social Issues, 47,* 91–109.

Taylor, S. P. (1967). Aggressive behavior and physiological arousal as a function of provocation and the tendency to inhibit aggression. *Journal of Personality, 35,* 297–310.

Tedeschi, J. T., & Norman, N. M. (1985). A social psychological interpretation of displaced aggression. *Advances in Group Processes, 2,* 29–56.

Teens top elderly as victims of crime. (1995, June 1). Albany *Times Union,* p. A13.

Terman, L. M., & Buttenwieser, P. (1935a). Personality factors in marital compatibility: I. *Journal of Social Psychology, 6,* 143–171.

Terman, L. M., & Buttenwieser, P. (1935b). Personality factors in marital compatibility: II. *Journal of Social Psychology, 6,* 267–289.

Terry, R. L., & Krantz, J. H. (1993). Dimensions of trait attributions associated with eyeglasses, men's facial hair, and women's hair length. *Journal of Applied Social Psychology, 23,* 1757–1769.

Tesser, A. (1993). On the importance of heritability in psychological research: The case of attitudes. *Psychological Review, 100,* 129–142.

Tesser, A., & Martin, L. (1996). The psychology of evaluation. In E. T. Higgins & A. W. Kruglanski (Eds.), *Social psychology: Handbook of basic principles* (pp. 400–423). New York: Guilford Press.

Tesser, A., Martin, L. L., & Cornell, D. P. (1996). On the substitutability of the self-protecting mechanisms. In P. Gollwitzer & J. Bargh (Eds.), *The psychology of action* (pp. 48–68). New York: Guilford.

Tetlock, P. E., Peterson, R. S., McGuire, C., Change, S., & Feld, P. (1992). Assessing political group dynamics: A test of the groupthink model. *Journal of Personality and Social Psychology, 63,* 403–425.

Tett, R. P., & Meyer, J. P. (1993). Job satisfaction, organizational commitment, turnover intention, and turnover: Path analyses based on meta-analytic findings. *Personnel Psychology, 46,* 259–293.

The global epidemic. (1998, December 1). *Boston Globe.*

Thompson, C. (1998, February 21). Associated Press.

Thompson, D. (1992). The danger in doomsaying. *Time, 139*(10), 61.

Thompson, J. M., Whiffen, V. E., & Blain, M. D. (1995). Depressive symptoms, sex and perceptions of intimate relationships. *Journal of Social and Personal Relationships, 12,* 49–66.

Thompson, L. (1998). *The mind and heart of the negotiator.* Upper Saddle River, NJ: Prentice-Hall.

Thompson, L., & Hastie, R. (1990). Social perception in negotiation. *Organizational Behavior and Human Decision Processes, 47,* 98–123.

Thompson, S. C., Nanni, C., & Levine, A. (1994). Primary versus secondary and central versus consequence-related control in HIV-positive men. *Journal of Personality and Social Psychology, 67,* 540–547.

Thompson, S. C., Sobolew-Shubin, A., Galbraith, M. E., Schwankovsky, L., & Cruzen, D. (1993). Maintaining perceptions of control: Finding perceived control in low-control circumstances. *Journal of Personality and Social Psychology, 64,* 293–304.

Thompson, W. C., Cowan, C. L., & Rosenhan, D. L. (1980). Focus of attention mediates the impact of negative affect on altruism. *Journal of Personality and Social Psychology, 38,* 291–300.

Thornton, B. (1992). Repression and its mediating influence on the defensive attribution of responsibility. *Journal of Research in Personality, 26,* 44–57.

Thornton, B., & Maurice, J. (1998). Physique contrast effects: Adverse impact of idealized body images for women. *Sex Roles, 37,* 433–439.

Thornton, B., & Moore, S. (1993). Physical attractiveness contrast effects: Implications for self-esteem and evaluations of the social self. *Personality and Social Psychology Bulletin, 19,* 474–480.

Thornton, B., Leo, R., & Alberg, K. (1991). Gender role typing, the superwoman ideal, and the potential for eating disorders. *Sex Roles, 25,* 469–484.

Tice, D. M., & Baumeister, R. F. (1997). Longitudinal study of procrastination, performance, stress, and health: The costs and benefits of dawdling. *Psychological Science, 8,* 454–458.

Tice, D. M., Butler, J. L., Muraven, M. B., & Stillwell, A. M. (1995). When modesty prevails: Differential favorability of self-presentation to friends and strangers. *Journal of Personality and Social Psychology, 69,* 1120–1138.

Tidwell, M.-C. O., Reis, H. T., & Shaver, P. R. (1996). Attachment, attractiveness, and social interaction: A diary study. *Journal of Personality and Social Psychology, 71,* 729–745.

Timmers, M., Fischer, A. H., & Manstead, A. S. R. (1998). Gender differences in motives for regulating emotions. *Personality and Social Psychology Bulletin, 24,* 974–985.

Tjosvold, D. (1993). *Learning to manage conflict: Getting people to work together productively.* New York: Lexington.

Tjosvold, D., & De Dreu, C. (1997). Managing conflict in Dutch organizations: A test of the relevance of Deutsch's cooperation theory. *Journal of Applied Social Psychology, 27,* 2213–2227.

Toch, H. (1985). *Violent men* (rev. ed.). Cambridge, MA: Schenkman.

Toi, M., & Batson, C. D. (1982). More evidence that empathy is a source of altruistic motivation. *Journal of Personality and Social Psychology, 43,* 281–292.

Tomaka, J., & Blascovich, J. (1994). Effects of justice beliefs on cognitive appraisal of and subjective, physiological, and behavioral responses to potential stress. *Journal of Personality and Social Psychology, 67,* 732–740.

Tomes, N. (1998). *The gospel of germs: Men, women, and the microbe in American life.* Cambridge, MA: Harvard University Press.

Toobin, J. (1995a, January 9). True grit. *The New Yorker.* 28–35.

Toobin, J. (1995b, July 17). Putting it in black and white. *New Yorker,* 31–34.

Tooley, V., Brigham, J. C., Maass, A., & Bothwell, R. K. (1987). Facial recognition: Weapon effect and attentional focus. *Journal of Applied Social Psychology, 17,* 845–859.

Townsend, J. M. (1995). Sex without emotional involvement: An evolutionary interpretation of sex differences. *Archives of Sexual Behavior, 24,* 173–206.

Traub, J. (1996, November 4). The criminals of tomorrow. *New Yorker, 50,* 52–56, 58, 60, 65.

Triandis, H. C. (1990). Cross-cultural studies of individualism and collectivism. In J. J. Berman (Ed.), *Nebraska symposium on motivation, 1989* (pp. 41–133). Lincoln: University of Nebraska Press.

Trinke, S. J., & Bartholomew, K. (1997). Hierarchies of attachment relationships in young adulthood. *Journal of Social and Personal Relationships, 14,* 603–625.

Trobst, K. K., Collins, R. L., & Embree, J. M. (1994). The role of emotion in social support provision: Gender, empathy, and expressions of distress. *Journal of Social and Personal Relationships, 11,* 45–62.

Tucker, J. S., Friedman, H. S., Schwartz, J. E., Criqui, M. H., Tomlinson-Keasey, C., Wingard, D. L., & Martin, L. R. (1997). Parental divorce: Effects on individual behavior and longevity. *Journal of Personality and Social Psychology, 73,* 381–391.

Tucker, P., & Aron, A. (1993). Passionate love and marital satisfaction at key transition points in the family life cycle. *Journal of Social and Clinical Psychology, 12,* 135–147.

Tuckman, B. W., & Sexton, T. L. (1990). The relation between self-beliefs and self-regulated performance. *Journal of Social Behavior and Personality, 5,* 465–472.

Turner, M. E., Pratkanis, A. R., & Hardaway, T. J. (1991). Sex differences in reaction to preferential selection: Towards a model of preferential selection as help. *Journal of Social Behavior and Personality, 6,* 797–814.

Tversky, A., & Kahneman, D. (1973). Availability: A heuristic for judging frequency and probability. *Cognitive Psychology, 5,* 207–232.

Tversky, A., & Kahneman, D. (1982). Judgment under uncertainty: Heuristics and biases. In D. Kahneman, P. Slovic, & A. Tversky (Eds.), *Judgment under uncertainty* (pp. 3–20). New York: Cambridge University Press.

Twenge, J. M., & Manis, M. M. (1998). First-name desirability and adjustment: Self-satisfaction, others' ratings, and family background. *Journal of Applied Social Psychology, 24,* 41–51.

Tykocinski, O. E., & Pittman, T. S. (1998). The consequences of doing nothing: Inaction inertia as avoidance of anticipated counterfactual regret. *Journal of Personality and Social Psychology, 73,* 607–616.

Tykocinski, O. E., Pittman, T. S., & Tuttle, E. E. (1995). Inaction inertia: Foregoing future benefits as a result of an initial failure to act. *Journal of Personality and Social Psychology, 68,* 793–803.

Tyler, T. R., & Lind, E. A. (1992). A relational model of authority in groups. In M. Zanna (Ed.), *Advances in experimental social psychology* (Vol. 27, 115–191). New York: Academic Press.

Tyler, T. R., & Smith, H. J. (1997). Social justice and social movements. In D. Gilbert, S. T. Firks, & G. Lindzey (Eds.), *Handbook of social psychology* (Vol. 2, 2nd edition, pp. 595–629. New York: McGraw-Hill.

Tyler, T. R., Boeckmann, R. J., Smith, H. J., & Huo, Y. J. (1997). *Social justice in a diverse society.* Boulder, CO: Westview.

Tyler, T. R., Lind, E. A., Ohbuchi, K. I., Sugawara, I., & Huo, Y. J. (1998). Conflict with outsiders: Disputing within and across cultural boundaries. *Personality and Social Psychology Bulletin, 24,* 137–146.

Type A's lack cholesterol aid, study says. (1992, November 18). *Albany Times Union,* p. A-5.

U.S. Department of Justice. (1994). *Criminal victimization in the United States, 1992.* Washington, DC: Office of Justice Programs, Bureau of Justice Statistics.

U.S. Dept. of Labor. (1991). *A report on the glass ceiling initiative.* Washington, D.C.: U.S. Department of Labor.

U.S. Department of Labor. (1992). *Employment and earnings* (Vol. 39, No. 5: Table A-22). Washington, DC: U.S. Department of Labor.

Uchino, B. N., Kiecolt-Glaser, J. K., & Cacioppo, J. T. (1992). Age-related changes in cardiovascular response as a function of a chronic stressor and social support. *Journal of Personality and Social Psychology, 63,* 839–846.

Uchino, B. N., Cacioppo, J. T., Marlarkey, W., & Glaser, R. (1995). Individual differences in cardiac sympathetic control predict endocrine and immune responses to acute psychological stress. *Journal of Personality and Social Psychology, 69,* 736–743.

Udry, J. R. (1980). Changes in the frequency of marital intercourse from panel data. *Archives of Sexual Behavior, 9,* 319–325.

Ullman, C. (1987). From sincerity to authenticity: Adolescents' view of the "true self." *Journal of Personality, 55,* 583–595.

Unger, R. K. (1994). Alternative conceptions of sex (and sex differences). In M. Haug, R. Whalen, C. Aron, & K. L. Olsen (Eds.), *The development of sex differences and similarities in behavior.* Dordrecht, The Netherlands: Kluwer Academic.

Unger, R. K., & Crawford, M. (1993). Commentary: Sex and gender—The troubled relationship between terms and concepts. *Psychological Science, 4,* 122–124.

Ungerer, J. A., Dolby, R., Waters, B., Barnett, B., Kelk, N., & Lewin, V. (1990). The early development of empathy: Self-regulation and individual differences in the first year. *Motivation and Emotion, 14,* 93–106.

Urbanski, L. (1992, May 21). Study uncovers traits people seek in friends. *The Evangelist,* 4.

Valliant, P. M., & Loring, J. E. (1998). Leadership style and personality of mock jurors and the effect on sentencing decisions. *Social Behavior and Personality, 26,* 421–424.

Vallone, R., Ross, L., & Lepper, M. (1985). Social status, cognitive alternatives, and intergroup relations. In H. Tajfel (Ed.), *Differentiation between social groups* (pp. 201–226). London: Academic Press.

Van Buren, A. (1996, February 1). 10 simple rules help keep marriage happy. Albany *Times Union,* p. C2.

Van Dyne, L., & LePine, J. A. (1998). Helping and voice extra-role behaviors: Evidence of construct and predictive validity. *Academy of Management Journal, 41,* 108–119.

Van Goozen, S., Frijda, N., & de Poll, N. V. (1994). Anger and aggression in women: Influence of sports choice and testosterone administration. *Aggressive Behavior, 20,* 213–222.

Van Hook, E., & Higgins, E. T. (1988). Self-related problems beyond the self-concept: Motivational consequences of discrepant self-guides. *Journal of Personality and Social Psychology, 55,* 625–633.

Van Horn, K. R., Arnone, A., Nesbitt, K., Desilets, L., Sears, T., Giffin, M., & Brudi, R. (1997). Physical distance and interpersonal characteristics in college students' romantic relationships. *Personal Relationships, 4,* 25–34.

Van Lange, P. A. M., & Kuhlman, M. D. (1994). Social value orientation and impressions of partner's honesty and intelligence: A test of the might versus morality effect. *Journal of Personality and Social Psychology, 67,* 126–141.

Van Lange, P. A. M., & Rusbult, C. E. (1995). My relationship is better than—and not as bad as—yours is: The perception

Wills, T. A., & DePaulo, B. M. (1991). Interpersonal analysis of the help-seeking process. In C. R. Snyder & D. R. Forsyth (Eds.), *Handbook of social and clinical psychology* (pp. 357–375). Elmsford, NY: Pergamon.

Wilson, D. W. (1981). Is helping a laughing matter? *Psychology, 18,* 6–9.

Wilson, J. P., & Petruska, R. (1984). Motivation, model attributes, and prosocial behavior. *Journal of Personality and Social Psychology, 46,* 458–468.

Wilson, M., Daly, M. & Daniele, A. (1995). Familicide: The killing of spouse and children. *Aggressive Behavior, 21,* 275–291.

Wilson, M., Daly, M., Gordon, S., & Pratt, A. (1996). Sex differences in valuations of the environment. *Population and Environment, 18,* 143–159.

Wilson, T. D. (1990). Self-persuasion via self-reflection. In M. Olson & M. P. Zanna (Eds.), *Self-inference processes: The Ontario Symposium* (Vol. 6, pp. 43–67). Hillsdale, NJ: Erlbaum.

Wilson, T. D., & Brekke, N. (1994). Mental contamination and mental correction: Unwanted influences on judgments and evaluations. *Psychological Bulletin, 116,* 117–142.

Wilson, T. D., & Kraft, D. (1993). Why do I love thee?: Effects of repeated introspections about a dating relationship on attitudes toward the relationship. *Personality and Social Psychology Bulletin, 19,* 409–418.

Wilson, T. D., & Schooler, J. (1991). Thinking too much: Introspection can reduce the quality of preferences and decisions. *Journal of Personality and Social Psychology, 60,* 181–192.

Winett, R. A. (1998). Developing more effective health-behavior programs: Analyzing the epidemiological and biological bases for activity and exercise programs. *Applied & Preventive Psychology, 7,* 209–224.

Winkel, F. W. (1998). Fear of crime and criminal victimization: Testing a theory of psychological incapacitation of the 'stressor' based on downward comparison processes. *British Journal of Criminology, 38,* 473–484.

Winquist, J. R., & Larson, J. R., Jr. (1998). Information pooling: When it impacts group decision making. *Journal of Personality and Social Psychology, 74,* 317–377.

Winstead, B. A., Derlega, V. J., Montgomery, M. J., & Pilkington, C. (1995). The quality of friendships at work and job satisfaction. *Journal of Social and Personal Relationships, 12,* 199–215.

Witte, E., & Davis, J. H. (Eds.). (1996). *Understanding group behavior: Consensual action by small groups.* Hillsdale, NJ: Erlbaum.

Wolf, N. (1992). Father figures. *New Republic, 207*(15), 22, 24–25.

Wolf, S., & Bugaj, A. M. (1990). The social impact of courtroom witnesses. *Social Behaviour, 5,* 1–13.

Wolfe, B. M., & Baron, R. A. (1971). Laboratory aggression related to aggression in naturalistic social situation: Effects of an aggressive model on the behavior of college student and prisoner observers. *Psychonomic Science, 24,* 193–194.

Wolfe, T. (1940). *The web and the rock.* Garden City, NJ: Sundial Press.

Wood, J. V. (1996). What is social comparison and how should we study it? *Personality and Social Psychology Bulletin, 22,* 520–537.

Wood, W. (1982). Retrieval of attitude-relevant information from memory: Effects on susceptibility to persuasion on intrinsic motivation. *Journal of Personality and Social Psychology, 42,* 798–810.

Wood, W., Christensen, P. N., Hebl, M. R., & Rothgerber, H. (1997). Conformity to sex-typed norms, affect, and the self-concept. *Journal of Personality and Social Psychology, 73,* 523–535.

Wood, W., Pool, G. J., Leck, K., & Purvis, D. (1996). Self-definition, defensive processing, and influence: The normative impact of majority and minority groups. *Journal of Personality and Social Psychology, 71,* 1181–1193.

Wood, W., Wong, F. Y., & Cachere, J. G. (1991). Effects of media violence on viewers' aggression in unconstrained social interaction. *Psychological Bulletin, 109,* 371–383.

Workers unite. (1994, July/August). *Men's Health,* 42.

Wright, P. H. (1984). Self-referent motivation and the intrinsic quality of friendship. *Journal of Social and Personal Relationships, 1,* 115–130.

Wright, R. (1994, November 28). Feminists, meet Mr. Darwin. *The New Republic, 34,* 36–37, 40, 42, 44–46.

Wright, R. (1995, March 13). The biology of violence. *The New Yorker,* 68–77.

Wright, S. C., Aron, A., McLaughlin-Volpe, T., & Ropp, S. A. (1997). The extended contact effect: Knowledge of cross-group friendships and prejudice. *Journal of Personality and Social Psychology, 73,* 73–90.

Wuensch, K. L., Castellow, W. A., & Moore, C. H. (1991). Effects of defendant attractiveness and type of crime on juridic judgment. *Journal of Social Behavior and Personality, 6,* 713–724.

Wyer, R. S., Jr., Budesheim, T. L., Lambert, A. J., & Swan, S. (1994). Person memory judgment: Pragmatic influences on impressions formed in a social context. *Journal of Personality and Social Psychology, 66,* 254–267.

Wyer, R. S. Jr., & Srull, T. K. (Eds.). (1994). *Handbook of social cognition* (2nd ed.) (Vol. 1). Hillsdale, NJ: Erlbaum.

Wyer, R. S., Jr., & Srull, T. K. (Eds.)., (1999). *Handbook of social cognition* (3rd edition). Mahwah, NJ: Erlbaum.

Yates, S. (1992). Lay attributions about distress after a natural disaster. *Personality and Social Psychology Bulletin, 18,* 217–222.

Yik, M. S. M., Bond, M. H., & Paulhus, D. L. (1998). Do Chinese self-enhance or self-efface? It's a matter of domain. *Personality and Social Psychology Bulletin, 24,* 399–406.

Yoshida, T. (1977). Effects of cognitive dissonance on task evaluation and task performance. *Japanese Journal of Psychology, 48,* 216–223.

Youille, J. C., & Cutshall, J. L. (1986). A case study of eyewitness memory of a crime. *Journal of Applied Psychology, 71,* 291–301.

Yovetich, N. A., & Rusbult, C. E. (1994). Accommodative behavior in close relationships: Exploring transformation of motivation. *Journal of Experimental Social Psychology, 30,* 138–164.

Yu, W. (1996, May 12). Many husbands fail to share housework. Albany *Times Union,* pp. A1, A7.

Yukl, G. (1989). *Leadership in organizations* (2nd ed.). Englewood Cliffs, NJ: Prentice-Hall.

Yukl, G. (1994). *Leadership in organizations* (3rd ed.). Englewood Cliffs, NJ: Prentice-Hall.

Yukl, G., & Falbe, C. M. (1991). Importance of different power sources in downward and lateral relations. *Journal of Applied Psychology, 76,* 416–423.

Yukl, G., & Tracey, J. B. (1992). Consequences of influence tactics used with subordinates, peers, and the boss. *Journal of Applied Psychology, 77,* 525–535.

Zaccaro, S. J., Foti, R. J., & Kenny, D. A. (1991). Self-monitoring and trait-based variance in leadership: An investigation of leader flexibility across multiple group situations. *Journal of Applied Psychology, 76,* 308–315.

Zachariah, R. (1996). Predictors of psychological well-being of women during pregnancy: Replication and extension. *Journal of Social Behavior and Personality, 11,* 127–140.

Zajonc, R. B. (1968). Attitudinal effects of mere exposure [monograph]. *Journal of Personality and Social Psychology, 9,* 1–27.

Zajonc, R. B., & McIntosh, D. N. (1992). Emotions research: Some promising questions and some questionable promises. *Psychological Science, 3,* 70–74.

Zebrowitz, L. A., Collins, M. A., & Dutta, R. (1998). The relationship between appearance and personality across the life span. *Personality and Social Psychology Bulletin, 24,* 736–749.

Zajonc, R. B., & Sales, S. M. (1966). Social facilitation of dominant and subordinate responses. *Journal of Experimental Social Psychology, 2,* 160–168.

Zajonc, R. B., Adelmann, P. K., Murphy, S. T., & Niedenthal, P. M. (1987). Convergence in the physical appearance of spouses. *Motivation and Emotion, 11,* 335–346.

Zajonc, R. B., Heingartner, A., & Herman, E. M. (1969). Social enhancement and impairment of performance in the cockroach. *Journal of Personality and Social Psychology, 13,* 83–92.

Zammichieli, M. E., Gilroy, F. D., & Sherman, M. F. (1988). Relation between sex-role orientation and marital satisfaction. *Personality and Social Psychology Bulletin, 14,* 747–754.

Zanna, M. P., & Aziza, C. (1976). On the interaction of repression–sensitization and attention in resolving cognitive dissonance. *Journal of Personality and Social Psychology, 44,* 577–593.

Zanna, M. P., & Olson, J. M. (1994). The psychology of prejudice. *The Ontario Symposium* (Vol. 7). Hillsdale, NJ: Erlbaum.

Zdaniuk, B., & Levine, J. M. (1996). Anticipated interaction and thought generation: The role of faction size. *British Journal of Social Psychology, 35,* 201–218.

Zebrowitz, L. A. (1997). *Reading faces.* Boulder, CO: Westview Press.

Zebrowitz, L. A., & Collins, M. A. (1997). Accurate social perception at zero acquaintance: The affordances of a Gibsonian approach. *Personality and Social Psychology Review, 1,* 204–223.

Zebrowitz, L. A., Collins, M. A., & Dutta, R. (1998). The relationship between appearance and personality across the life span. *Personality and Social Psychology Bulletin, 24,* 736–749.

Zebrowitz, L. A., Montepare, J. M., & Lee, H. K. (1993). They don't all look alike: Differentiating same versus other race individuals. *Journal of Personality and Social Psychology, 65,* 85–101.

Zeitz, G. (1990). Age and work satisfaction in a government agency: A situational perspective. *Human Relations, 43,* 419–438.

Ziller, R. C. (1990). *Photographing the self: Methods for observing personal orientations.* Newbury Park, CA: Sage.

Zillmann, D. (1979). *Hostility and aggression.* Hillsdale, NJ: Erlbaum.

Zillmann, D. (1983). Transfer of excitation in emotional behavior. In J. T. Cacioppo & R. E. Petty (Eds.), *Social psychophysiology: A sourcebook* (pp. 215–240). New York: Guilford Press.

Zillmann, D. (1984). *Connections between sex and aggression.* Hillsdale, NJ: Erlbaum.

Zillmann, D. (1988). Cognition–excitation interdependencies in aggressive behavior. *Aggressive Behavior, 14,* 51–64.

Zillmann, D. (1993). Mental control of angry aggression. In D. M. Wegner & J. W. Pennebaker (Eds.), *Handbook of mental control.* Englewood Cliffs, NJ: Prentice-Hall.

Zillmann, D. (1994). Cognition–excitation interdependencies in the escalation of anger and angry aggression. In M. Potegal & J. F. Knutson (Eds.), *The dynamics of aggression.* Hillsdale, NJ: Erlbaum.

Zillmann, D., Baron, R. A., & Tamborini, R. (1981). The social costs of smoking: Effects of tobacco smoke on hostile behavior. *Journal of Applied Social Psychology, 11,* 548–561.

Zillmann, D., Rockwell, S., Schweitzer, K., & Sundar, S. S. (1993). Does humor facilitate coping with physical discomfort? *Motivation and Emotion, 17,* 1–21.

Zimbardo, P. G. (1977). *Shyness: What it is and what you can do about it.* Reading, MA: Addison-Wesley.

Zoglin, R. (1993). The shock of the blue. *Time, 142*(17), 71–72.

Zuber, J. A., Crott, H. W., & Werner, J. (1992). Choice shift and group polarization: An analysis of the status of arguments and social decision schemes. *Journal of Personality and Social Psychology, 62,* 50–61.

Zuckerman, M., Miyake, K., & Elkin, C. S. (1995). Effects of attractiveness and maturity of face and voice on interpersonal impressions. *Journal of Research in Personality, 29,* 253–272.

Zusne, L., & Jones, W. H. (1989). *Anomalistic psychology: A study of magical thinking* (2nd ed.). Hillsdale, NJ: Erlbaum.

Glossary

actor–observer effect • The tendency to attribute our own behavior mainly to situational causes but the behavior of others mainly to internal (dispositional) causes.

additive tasks • Tasks for which the group product is the sum or combination of the efforts of individual members.

affect • Our current feelings and moods.

affect infusion model • A theory explaining the mechanisms through which affect influences social thought and social judgments.

affect-centered model of attraction • A conceptual framework in which attraction is assumed to be based on positive and negative emotions. These emotions can be aroused directly by another person, simply associated with that person, and/or mediated by cognitive processes.

aggression • Behavior directed toward the goal of harming another living being who is motivated to avoid such treatment.

aggression machine • Apparatus used to measure physical aggression under safe laboratory conditions.

altruism • An unselfish concern for the welfare of others.

androgynous • Characterized by possessing both traditional masculine characteristics and traditional feminine ones.

apologies • Admissions of wrongdoing that include requests for forgiveness.

appearance anxiety • Apprehension or worry about whether one's physical appearance is adequate and about the way one's appearance is evaluated by other people.

attachment style • Degree of security in interpersonal relationships; develops in infancy and appears to affect interpersonal behavior throughout life.

attitude polarization • The tendency to evaluate mixed evidence or information in such a way that it strengthens our initial views and makes them more extreme.

attitude similarity • The extent to which two individuals share the same attitudes about a range of topics; in practice, often includes similarity of beliefs, values, and interests.

attitude-to-behavior process model • A model of how attitudes guide behavior that emphasizes the influence of both attitudes and stored knowledge of what is appropriate in a given situation on an individual's definition of the present situation. This definition, in turn, influences overt behavior.

attitudes • Evaluations of various aspects of the social world.

attribution • The process through which we seek to identify the causes of others' behavior and so gain knowledge of their stable traits and dispositions.

augmenting principle • The tendency to attach greater importance to a potential cause of behavior if the behavior occurs despite the presence of other, inhibitory causes.

availability heuristic • A mental shortcut that suggests that the easier it is to bring something to mind, the more frequent or important it is.

balance theory • Theory that specifies the relationships among (1) an individual's liking for another person, (2) his or her attitude about a give topic, and (3) the other person's perceived attitude about the same topic.

bargaining • A negotiating process in which opposing sides exchange offers, counteroffers, and concessions, either directly or though representatives.

Bem Sex-Role Inventory (BSRI) • Bem's measure of the extent to which an individual's self-description is characterized by traditional masculine characteristics, traditional feminine characteristics, both (androgyny) or neither (undifferentiated).

biased assimilation • The tendency to evaluate information that disconfirms our existing views as less convincing or reliable than information that confirms these views.

blank-lineup control • A procedure in which a witness is shown a police lineup that does not include a suspect; this helps police to determine the accuracy of the witness and to emphasize the importance of being cautious in making a positive identification.

body language • Cues provided by the position, posture, and movement of others' bodies or body parts.

bystander effect • The fact that the likelihood of a prosocial response to an emergency is affected by the number of bystanders who are present: as the number of bystanders increases, the probability that any one bystander will help decreases and the amount of time that passes before help occurs increases.

catastrophizing • Interpreting negative life events in pessimistic, global terms. People (especially men) who consistently explain bad events as catastrophes are found to have a shortened life span.

catharsis hypothesis • The view that opportunities to express anger and hostility in relatively safe ways will reduce a person's likelihood of engaging in more harmful forms of aggression.

central route (to persuasion) • Attitude change resulting from systematic processing of information presented in persuasive messages.

charismatic leaders • Leaders who exert exceptionally powerful effects on large numbers of followers or on entire societies; also known as transformational leaders.

child maltreatment • Actions that harm children either physically or psychologically.

classical conditioning • A basic form of learning in which one stimulus, initially neutral, acquires the capacity to evoke reactions through repeated pairing with another stimulus. In a sense, one stimulus becomes a signal for the presentation or occurrence of the other.

close friendship • A relationship in which two people spend a great deal of time together, interact in a variety of situations, exclude others from the relationship, and provide emotional support to each other.

cognitive dissonance • An unpleasant internal state that results when individuals notice inconsistency between two or more of their attitudes or between their attitudes and their behavior.

cognitive tuning model • A theory suggesting that positive affective states, such as those induced by seeing another person smile, inform us that the current situation is safe and doesn't require careful attention or processing of information. In contrast, negative affective states, such as those induced by seeing another person frown, signal us that the situation is potentially dangerous and that careful processing is required.

cognitive–experiential self-theory • A theory suggesting that our efforts to understand the world around us involve two distinct modes of thought: intuitive thought and deliberate, rational thought.

cohesiveness • With respect to conformity, the degree of attraction felt by an individual toward an influencing group. With respect to groups, all the forces that cause members to remain in the group, including factors such as attraction and desire for status.

collective effort model • An explanation of social loafing suggesting that perceived links between individuals' effort and their outcomes are weaker when they work together with others in a group; this, in turn, produces tendencies toward social loafing.

common in-group identity model • Theory suggesting that to the extent that individuals in different groups view themselves as members of a single social entity, positive contacts between them will increase and intergroup bias will be reduced.

companionate love • Love that is based on friendship, mutual attraction, common interests, mutual respect, and concern for each other's happiness and welfare.

complaining • Expressing discontent, dissatisfaction, resentment, or regret; may be used as a means of exerting social influence on others.

compliance • A form of social influence involving direct requests from one person to another.

confirmation bias • The tendency to notice and remember mainly information that lends support to our views.

conflict • A process in which individuals or groups perceive that others have taken or will soon take actions incompatible with their own interests.

conformity • A type of social influence in which individuals change their attitudes or behavior in order to adhere to existing social norms.

consensual validation • The perceived validation of one's views that is provided when someone else expresses identical views.

consensus • The extent to which other persons react to some stimulus or event in the same manner as the person under consideration.

consistency • The extent to which an individual responds to a given stimulus or situation in the same way on different occasions (i.e., across time).

contact hypothesis • The view that increased contact between members of various social groups can be effective in reducing prejudice between them; seems to be valid only when contact takes place under certain favorable conditions.

cooperation • Behavior in which group members work together to attain shared goals.

coping • Responding to stress in a way that reduces the threat and its effects; includes what a person does, feels, or thinks in order to master, tolerate, or decrease the negative effects of a stressful situation.

correlational method • A method of research in which a scientist systematically observes two or more variables to determine whether changes in one are accompanied by changes in the other.

correspondence bias (fundamental attribution error) • The tendency to explain others' actions as stemming from dispositions even in the presence of clear situational causes.

correspondent inference (theory of) • A theory describing how we use others' behavior as a basis for inferring their stable dispositions.

counterfactual thinking • The tendency to imagine outcomes in a situation other than those that actually occurred—to think about "What might have been."

cultures of honor • Cultures in which strong social norms condone violence as a means of answering an affront to one's honor.

deadline technique • A technique for increasing compliance in which target persons are told that they have only limited time to take advantage of some offer or to obtain some item.

debriefing • Procedures at the conclusion of a research session in which participants are given full information about the nature of the research and the hypothesis or hypotheses under investigation.

deception • A technique whereby researchers withhold information about the purposes or procedures of a study from persons participating in it.

decision making • The process of combining and integrating available information in order to choose one out of several possible courses of action.

decision/commitment • In Sternberg's triangular model of love, the cognitive elements involved in the decision that one loves someone and the commitment to maintain that relationship.

dependent variable • The variable that is measured in an experiment.

descriptive norms • Norms that simply indicate what most people do in a given situation.

diffusion of responsibility • Decreased tendency of any individual bystander in an emergency to assume personal responsibility for providing help as the result of the presence of multiple bystanders. The greater the number of bystanders, the less the individual's sense of responsibility to act.

discounting principle • The tendency to attach less importance to one potential cause of some behavior when other potential causes are also present.

discrimination • Negative behaviors directed toward members of social groups who are the object of prejudice.

disease-prone personality • Personality characterized by negative emotional reactions to stress, ineffective coping strategies, and unhealthy behavior patterns; often associated with illness and a shortened life span.

dismissing attachment style • In Bartholomew's model, a style characterized by high self-esteem and low interpersonal trust; usually described as a conflicted and somewhat insecure style in which the individual feels that he or she "deserves" a close relationship but mistrusts potential partners and is thus likely to reject the other person in order to avoid being the one who is rejected.

distinctiveness • The extent to which an individual responds in a different manner to different stimuli or events.

distraction–conflict theory • A theory suggesting that social facilitation stems from the conflict produced when individuals attempt to pay attention simultaneously to other persons and to the task being performed.

distributive justice • The division of available rewards among group members according to what each has contributed to the group (or to any social relationship).

door-in-the-face technique • A procedure for gaining compliance in which requesters begin with a large request and then, when this is refused, retreat to a smaller one (the one they actually desired all along).

drive theories (of aggression) • Theories suggesting that aggression stems from external conditions that arouse the motive to harm or injure others; the most famous of these is the frustration–aggression hypothesis.

drive theory of social facilitation • A theory suggesting that the mere presence of others is arousing and thus increases the tendency to perform dominant responses.

egoism • An exclusive concern with one's own personal needs and welfare rather than with the needs and welfare of others.

elaboration likelihood model (of persuasion) • A theory suggesting that persuasion can occur in either of two distinct ways, which differ in the amount of cognitive effort or elaboration they require.

empathic joy hypothesis • The proposal that prosocial behavior is motivated by the positive emotion a helper anticipates experiencing as a result of having a beneficial impact on the life of someone in need.

empathy • A complex affective and cognitive response to another's emotional distress; includes being able to feel the other person's distress, feeling sympathetic and attempting to solve the problem, and taking the other's perspective. One can be empathetic toward fictional characters as well as toward real-life victims.

empathy–altruism hypothesis • The proposal that prosocial behavior is motivated solely by the desire to help someone in need.

estrogen • The female "sex hormone."

evaluation apprehension • Concern over being evaluated by others. Such concern can increase arousal and so contribute to social facilitation.

evolutionary social psychology • An area of research that seeks to investigate the potential role of genetic factors in various aspects of social behavior.

excitation transfer theory • A theory suggesting that arousal produced in one situation can persist and intensify emotional reactions occurring in later situations.

experimentation (experimental method) • A method of research in which an experimenter systematically changes one or more factors (the independent variables) to determine whether such variations affect one or more other factors (dependent variables).

experimenter effects • Unintended effects on participants' behavior produced by researchers.

extended contact hypothesis • A view suggesting that simply knowing that members of one's own group have formed close friendships with members of an out-group can reduce prejudice against this group.

external validity • The extent to which findings of an experiment can be generalized to real-life social situations and perhaps to persons different from those who participated in the research.

familicide • Instances in which an individual kills his or her spouse and one or more of his or her children.

fearful–avoidant attachment style • In Bartholomew's model, a style characterized by low self-esteem and also low interpersonal trust; usually described as an insecure and quite maladaptive style of attachment.

fixed-sum error • The tendency for bargainers to assume that each side places the same importance or priority as the other on every issue.

foot-in-the-door technique • A procedure for gaining compliance in which requesters begin with a small request and then, when this is granted, escalate to a larger one (the one they actually desired all along).

forensic psychology • Psychological research and theory that deals with the effects of cognitive, affective, and behavioral factors on legal proceedings and the law.

forewarning • Advance knowledge that one is about to become the target of an attempt at persuasion; often increases resistance to the persuasion that follows.

frustration–aggression hypothesis • The suggestion that frustration is a very powerful determinant of aggression.

gender • The attributes, behaviors, personality characteristics, and expectancies associated with a person's biological sex in a given culture. Gender differences can be based on biology, learning, or a combination of the two.

gender consistency • The concept that gender is a basic, enduring attribute of each individual. A grasp of gender consistency usually develops between the ages of four and seven.

gender identity • That part of the self-concept involving a person's identification as a male or a female. Consciousness of gender identity usually develops at about the age of two.

gender stereotypes • Stereotypes concerning the traits supposedly possessed by females and males, which distinguish the two genders from each other.

gender-role identification • The extent to which an individual identifies with the gender stereotypes of his or her culture.

general affective aggression model • A modern theory of aggression suggesting that aggression is triggered by a wide range of input variables; these influence arousal, affective stages, and cognitions.

generativity • An adult's concern for and commitment to the well-being of future generations.

genetic determinism model • The proposal that prosocial behavior is driven by genetic attributes that evolved because they enhanced reproductive success and thus the probability that individuals would be able to transmit their genes to subsequent generations.

glass ceiling • Barriers based on attitudinal or organizational bias that prevent qualified females from advancing to top-level positions.

great person theory • A view of leadership suggesting that great leaders possess certain traits that set them apart from most human beings, traits that are possessed by all such leaders no matter when or where they lived.

group • Two or more persons who interact with one another, share common goals, are somehow interdependent, and recognize that they belong to a group.

group polarization • The tendency of group members, as a result of group discussion, to shift toward more extreme positions than those they initially held.

groupthink • The tendency of the members of highly cohesive groups to assume that their decision can't be wrong, that all members must support the group's decision strongly, and that information contrary to it should be ignored.

health psychology • The study of the effects of psychological factors in the origins, prevention, and treatment of physical illness.

heuristic processing • Processing of information in a persuasive message that involves the use of simple rules of thumb or mental shortcuts.

heuristics • Simple rules for making complex decisions or drawing inferences in a rapid and seemingly effortless manner.

hostile aggression • Aggression in which the prime objective is to harm the victim, as opposed to aggression whose prime objective is some other purpose.

hostile attributional bias • The tendency to perceive hostile intentions or motives in others' actions when these actions are ambiguous.

hyperfemininity • An extreme gender-role identification with an exaggerated version of the traditional female role; includes the belief that relationships with men are of central importance in one's life, that attractiveness and sexuality should be used to get a man and keep him, and that it is reasonable to sometimes say *no* but mean *yes*.

hypermasculinity • An extreme gender-role identification with an exaggerated version of the traditional male role; includes callous sexual attitudes toward women, the belief that violence is manly, and the enjoyment of danger as a source of excitement.

hypocrisy • Publicly advocating some attitude or behavior and then acting in a way that is inconsistent with this espoused attitude or behavior.

hypothesis • An as yet unverified prediction based on a theory.

illusion of out-group homogeneity • The tendency to perceive members of outgroups as more similar to one another (less variable) than the members of one's own in-group.

illusory correlations • Perceived associations between variables that are stronger than actually exist; occur when each variable is distinctive so that the the co-occurrence of the variables is readily entered into and retrieved from memory.

impression formation • The process through which we form impressions of others.

impression management (self-presentation) • Efforts by individuals to produce favorable first impressions on others.

in-group • The social group to which an individual perceives herself or himself as belonging ("us").

in-group differentiation • The tendency to perceive members of one's own group as showing much larger differences from one another (as being more heterogeneous) than those of other groups.

incompatibility error • The tendency for both sides in a negotiation to assume that their interests are entirely incompatible.

incompatible response technique • A technique for reducing aggression in which individuals are exposed to events or stimuli that cause them to experience affective states incompatible with anger or aggression.

independent variable • The variable that a researcher systematically alters in an experiment.

individuation • The need to be distinguishable from others in some respects.

induced compliance • Situations in which individuals are somehow induced to say or do things inconsistent with their true attitudes; also known as *forced compliance*.

industrial/organizational psychologists • Psychologists who study all aspects of behavior in work settings.

inferential statistics • A special form of mathematics that allows us to evaluate the likelihood that a given pattern of research results occurred by chance alone.

information overload • Instances in which our ability to process information is exceeded.

informational social influence • Social influence based on individuals' desire to be correct—to possess accurate perceptions of the social world.

informed consent • A procedure in which research participants are provided with as much information as possible about a research project before deciding whether to participate in it.

ingratiation • A technique for gaining compliance in which requesters first induce target persons to like them, then attempt to change their behavior in some desired manner.

injunctive norms • Norms specifying what ought to be done—what is approved or disapproved behavior in a given situation.

instinct theories • Views suggesting that aggression stems from innate tendencies that are universal among members of a given species.

instrumental aggression • Aggression in which the primary objective is not harm to the victim but attainment of some other goal, such as access to valued resources.

instrumental conditioning • Basic form of learning in which responses that lead to positive outcomes or that

permit avoidance of negative outcomes are strengthened; also known as *operant conditioning*.

interdependence • The characteristic common to all close relationships—an interpersonal association in which two people influence each other's lives and engage in many joint activities.

interpersonal attraction • One person's evaluation of someone else along a dimension that ranges from strong liking to strong dislike.

interpersonal justice • Considerateness and courtesy shown to group members by those responsible for distributing available rewards; an important factor in perceived fairness.

interpersonal trust • A dimension involving one's belief that other people are trustworthy, dependable, and reliable or that they are untrustworthy, undependable, and unreliable.

intimacy • In Sternberg's triangular model of love, the closeness felt by two partners—the extent to which they are bonded.

job satisfaction • Attitudes concerning one's job or work.

leader • The group member who exerts the greatest influence within the group.

leadership • The process through which one member of a group (its leader) influences other group members toward attainment of shared group goals.

leading questions • Questions designed to elicit specific answers.

legal authoritarianism • A general tendency to assume the worst about a person accused of a crime and to favor a verdict of guilty.

leniency bias • A general tendency to make favorable assumptions about a person accused of a crime and to favor a verdict of not guilty.

less-leads-to-more effect • The fact that offering individuals small rewards for engaging in counterattitudinal behavior often produces more dissonance, and so more attitude change, than offering them larger rewards.

loneliness • The unhappy emotional and cognitive state that results from desiring close relationships but being unable to attain them.

love • A combination of emotions, cognitions, and behaviors that can be involved in intimate relationships.

lowball procedure • A technique for gaining compliance in which an offer or deal is changed (made less attractive) after the target person has accepted it.

magical thinking • Thinking involving assumptions that don't hold up to rational scrutiny—for example, the notion that things that resemble one another share fundamental properties.

matching hypothesis • The proposal that individuals are attracted to one another as friends, romantic partners, or spouses on the basis of similar attributes—physical attractiveness; age; race; personality characteristics; or social assets such as wealth, education, or power.

mental contamination • A process in which our judgments, emotions, or behaviors are influenced by mental processing that is unconscious and uncontrollable.

meta-analysis • A statistical technique for combining data from independent studies in order to determine whether specific variables (or interactions between variables) have significant effects across these studies.

mood congruence effects • Our tendency to store or remember positive information when in a positive mood and negative information when in a negative mood.

mood-dependent memory • The fact that what we remember while in a given mood may be determined in part by what we learned when previously in that mood.

multicultural perspective • A focus on understanding the cultural and ethnic factors that influence social behavior.

need for affiliation • Tendency to establish interpersonal relationships.

negative-state relief model • The proposal that prosocial behavior is motivated by the bystander's desire to reduce his or her own uncomfortable negative emotions.

noncommon effects • Effects produced by a particular cause that could not be produced by any other apparent cause.

nonverbal communication • Communication between individuals that does not involve the content of spoken language, but relies instead on an unspoken language of facial expressions, eye contact, and body language.

normative social influence • Social influence based on individuals' desire to be liked or accepted by other persons.

norms • Rules within a group indicating how its members should or should not behave.

obedience • A form of social influence in which one person simply orders one or more others to perform some action(s).

objective self-awareness • An organism's capacity to be the object of its own attention, to be aware of its own state of mind, and to know that it knows and remember that it remembers.

observational learning • Basic form of learning in which individuals acquire new forms of behavior or thought through observing others.

organizational citizenship behavior (OCB) • Prosocial behavior occurring within an organization that may or may not be rewarded by the organization.

out-group • Any group other than the one to which individuals perceive themselves as belonging.

passion • In Sternberg's triangular model of love, the sexual motives and sexual excitement associated with a couple's relationship.

passionate love • An intense and often unrealistic emotional response to another person. The person experiencing this emotion usually interprets it as "true love," whereas those who simply observe it are likely to use the term "infatuation."

peripheral route (to persuasion) • Attitude change that occurs in response to persuasion cues—information concerning the expertise or status of would-be persuaders.

perseverance effect • The tendency for beliefs and schemas to remain unchanged even in the face of contradictory information.

persuasion • Efforts to change others' attitudes through the use of various kinds of messages.

physical attractiveness • The combination of facial and bodily characteristics that are evaluated as beautiful or handsome at the most attractive extreme of the dimension and unattractive at the other extreme of the dimension.

planning fallacy • The tendency to make optimistic predictions concerning how long a given task will take for completion; also known as the optimistic bias.

playing hard to get • A technique that can be used for increasing compliance by suggesting that a person, object, or outcome is scarce and hard to obtain.

pluralistic ignorance • The tendency of bystanders in an emergency to rely on what other bystanders do and say even though no one is sure about what is happening or what to do about it; very often, all of the bystanders hold back and behave as if there is no problem, and all use this "information" to justify their failure to act.

possible selves • Mental representations of what we might become, or should become, in the future.

prejudice • Negative attitudes toward the members of specific social groups.

preoccupied attachment style • In Bartholomew's model, a style characterized by low self-esteem and high interpersonal trust; usually described as a conflicted and somewhat insecure style in which the individual strongly desires a close relationship but feels that he or she is unworthy of the partner and thus vulnerable to being rejected.

priming • Increased availability of information in memory or consciousness resulting from exposure to specific stimuli or events.

procedural justice • The fairness of the procedures used to allocate available rewards among group members.

proportion of similar attitudes • The number of topics on which two individuals hold the same views divided by the total number of topics on which they compare their views; can be expressed as a percentage (or ratio).

prosocial behavior • Helpful actions that benefit others but have no obvious benefits for the person who carries out the action and sometimes even involve risk for the one who helps.

prototype/willingness model • A theory suggesting that attitudes influence behavior through their impact on behavioral intentions and behavioral willingness (willingness to engage in specific actions).

provocation • Actions by others that tend to trigger aggression in the recipient, often because they are perceived as stemming from malicious intent.

proximity • In attraction research, the closeness between two individuals' residences, classroom seats, work areas, and so on. The closer the physical distance, the greater the probability of the individuals' coming into regular contact and thus experiencing repeated exposure.

punishment • Delivery of aversive consequences to individuals in order to decrease some behavior.

random assignment of participants to experimental conditions • The requirement that participants in research experiments have an equal chance of being exposed to each level of the independent variable; a basic requirement for conducting valid experiments.

reactance • Negative reaction to threats to one's personal freedom; often increases resistance to persuasion.

realistic conflict theory • The view that prejudice sometimes stems from direct competition between social groups over scarce and valued resources.

recategorization • Shifts in the boundary between an individual's in-group ("us") and some out-group ("them"), causing persons formerly viewed as out-group members now to be viewed as belonging to the in-group.

reciprocity • A basic rule of social life suggesting that individuals tend to treat others as these persons have treated them.

regulatory control • Successful coping by means of processes that enable one to exert control over what one thinks, how one feels, and where one directs his or her attention.

repeated exposure • Frequent contact with a stimulus. According to Zajonc's theory, repeated exposure to any mildly negative, neutral, or positive stimulus results in an increasingly positive evaluation of that stimulus.

representativeness heuristic • A strategy for making judgments based on the extent to which current stimuli or events resemble other stimuli or categories.

repressed memory • A form of psychogenic amnesia: forgetting the details of a traumatic event as a way of protecting oneself from having to deal with the anxiety and fear associated with that event.

repulsion hypothesis • Rosenbaum's provocative but inaccurate proposal that attraction is not enhanced by similar attitudes but only decreased by dissimilar attitudes.

reverse discrimination • The tendency to evaluate or treat persons belonging to groups that are the object of prejudice more favorably than members of the dominant group.

roles • Sets of behaviors that individuals occupying specific positions within a group are expected to perform.

schemas • Mental frameworks centering around a specific theme that help us to organize social information.

secure attachment style • In Bartholomew's model, a style characterized by high self-esteem and also high interpersonal trust; usually described as the ideal and most successful attachment style.

selective avoidance • Tendency to direct attention away from information that challenges existing attitudes; increases resistance to persuasion.

self-concept • One's self-identity, a schema consisting of an organized collection of beliefs and feelings about oneself.

self-efficacy • A person's evaluation of his or her ability or competency to perform a task, reach a goal, or overcome an obstacle.

self-esteem • The self-evaluation made by each individual; one's attitude toward oneself along a positive–negative dimension.

self-focusing • The act of directing attention inward toward oneself as opposed to outward toward one's surroundings.

self-fulfilling prophecies • Predictions that, in a sense, make themselves come true.

self-healing personality • Personality characterized by effective coping with stress; self-healing individuals are balanced, energetic, responsive to others, and positive about life.

self-monitoring • Regulation of one's behavior on the basis of the external situation and reactions of others (high self-monitoring) or on the basis of internal factors such as beliefs, attitudes, and values (low self-monitoring).

self-reference effect • The fact that cognitive processing of information relevant to the self is more efficient than the processing of other types of information.

self-serving bias • The tendency to attribute one's own positive outcomes to internal causes (e.g., one's own traits or characteristics) but negative outcomes or events to external causes (e.g., chance, task difficulty).

sex • Maleness or femaleness as determined by genetic factors present at conception that result in anatomical and physiological differences.

sex typing • Comprehension of the stereotypes associated with being a male or a female in one's culture.

sex-role spillover theory • A theory suggesting that females working in nontraditional jobs will be seen as "role deviates" and so as more appropriate targets for sexual harassment.

sexism • Prejudice based on gender.

sexual harassment • Unwelcome sexual advances, requests for sexual favors, and other verbal or physical conduct of a sexual nature.

sexual self-schema • Cognitive representations of the sexual aspects of oneself.

social categorization • The tendency to divide the social world into two separate categories: one's in-group ("us") and various out-groups ("them").

social cognition • The manner in which we interpret, analyze, remember, and use information about the social world.

social comparison • The process through which we compare ourselves to others in order to determine whether our view of social reality is or is not correct.

social comparison theory • Festinger's very influential theory dealing with our tendency to evaluate our opinions and abilities by comparing them with the opinions and abilities of others, including our preference for making such comparisons with those who are relatively similar to ourselves.

social decision schemes • Rules relating the initial distribution of group members' views to final group decisions.

social dilemmas • Situations in which each person can increase his or her individual gains by acting in a certain way, but if all (or most) persons act that same way, the outcomes experienced by all are reduced.

social facilitation • Effects upon performance resulting from the presence of others.

social identity • A person's definition of who he or she is, including personal attributes (self-concept) and attributes shared with others such as gender and race.

social influence • Efforts by one or more individuals to change the attitudes, beliefs, perceptions, or behaviors of one or more others.

social learning • The process through which we acquire new information, forms of behavior, or attitudes from other persons.

social loafing • Reductions in motivation and effort when people work collectively in a group compared to when they work individually or as independent coactors.

social norms • Rules indicating how individuals are expected to behave in specific situations.

social perception • The process through which we seek to know and understand other persons.

social phobia • A debilitating anxiety disorder in which an individual perceives interpersonal situations as frightening and thus avoids them in order to guard against embarrassment and humiliation.

social psychology • The scientific field that seeks to understand the nature and causes of individual behavior and thought in social situations.

social self • A collective identity that includes interpersonal relationships plus aspects of identity derived from membership in larger, less personal groups based on race, ethnicity, and culture.

social support • The physical and psychological comfort provided by a person's friends and family members.

sociosexuality • A dispositional characteristic that ranges from an unrestricted orientation (willingness to engage in casual sexual interactions) to a restricted orientation (willingness to engage in sex only with emotional closeness and commitment).

staring • A form of eye contact in which one person continues to gaze steadily at another regardless of what the recipient does.

status • Social standing or rank within a group.

stereotypes • Beliefs to the effect that all members of specific social groups share certain traits or characteristics. Stereotypes are cognitive frameworks that strongly influence the processing of incoming social information.

stereotype threat • The threat perceived by persons who are the target of stereotypes, that they will be evaluated in terms of these stereotypes.

stigma • A personal characteristic that at least some other individuals perceive negatively.

stress • Any physical or psychological event perceived as being able to cause harm or emotional distress.

subjective self-awareness • The ability of an organism to differentiate itself, however crudely, from its physical and social environment.

subliminal conditioning • Classical conditioning that occurs through exposure to stimuli that are below individuals' threshhold of conscious awareness.

superordinate goals • Goals that both sides to a conflict seek and that tie their interests together rather than driving them apart.

survey method • A method of research in which a large number of persons answer questions about their attitudes or behavior.

symbolic self-awareness • An organism's ability to form an abstract concept of self through language; this ability enables the organism to communicate, form relationships, set goals, evaluate outcomes, develop self-related attitudes, and defend itself against threatening communications.

systematic observation • A method of research in which behavior is systematically observed and recorded.

systematic processing • Processing of information in a persuasive message that involves careful consideration of message content and ideas.

testosterone • The male "sex hormone."

"that's-not-all" technique • A technique for gaining compliance in which a requester offers target persons additional benefits before they have decided whether to comply with or reject specific requests.

theories • Frameworks constructed by scientists in any field in an effort to explain why certain events or processes occur as they do.

theory of planned behavior • A theory of how attitudes guide behavior suggesting that individuals consider the implications of their actions before deciding to perform various behaviors. An earlier version was known as the *theory of reasoned action*.

thought suppression • Efforts to prevent certain thoughts from entering consciousness.

tokenism • The performance of trivial or small-scale positive actions for people who are the targets of prejudice. Prejudiced groups often use tokenistic behaviors as an excuse for refusing more meaningful beneficial actions.

triangular model of love • Sternberg's conceptualization of love relationships as encompassing three basic components: intimacy, passion, and decision/commitment.

trivialization • A technique for reducing dissonance by mentally minimalizing the importance of attitudes or behavior that are inconsistent with each other.

type A behavior pattern • A pattern consisting primarily of high levels of competitiveness, time urgency, and hostility.

type B behavior pattern • A pattern consisting of the absence of characteristics associated with the Type A behavior pattern.

ultimate attribution error • The tendency to make more favorable and flattering attributions about members of one's own group than about members of other groups.

voir dire • A French term ("to see and to speak") used in law to mean the examination of prospective jurors to determine their competence to serve; both the judge and the opposing attorneys may dismiss prospective jurors for specific reasons or, within limits, for no stated reason.

workplace aggression • All forms of behavior through which individuals seek to harm others in their workplace.

Name Index

Abdalla, I. A., 191
Abraham, C., 168
Abraham, L. M., 124, 561
Abrams, D., 177
Abramson, J., 537
Ackerman, P., 430
Ackerman, P. L., 282
Adair, J. G., 31
Adams, G. A., 549
Adams, J. B., 199
Adams, J. S., 348, 507, 508
Adams, M. G., 418
Adams, N. E., 183, 184
Adams, R. G., 305
Addison, J., 236
Adlemann, P. K., 213
Adler, N. L., 332
Adler, R., 549
Adler, S. J., 542
Affleck, G., 341
Agarie, N., 109, 471
Ager, J., 167
Agosti, V., 62
Aguinis, H., 326, 327
Ahearne, M., 565
Aikin, K. J., 214, 215
Ainsworth, M. D.S., 306
Ajzen, I., 128, 129
Alagna F. J., 45
Albany Times Union, 261, 338, 530, 555
Alberg, K., 191
Albright, L., 72
Aldeguer, C. M.R., 430
Alden, 322
Alden, L., 182
Alford, E. C., 17, 18, 199
Alge, B. J., 15, 449, 466, 510
Ali, S. A., 332
Alicke, M. D., 91, 378
Allen, J., 330
Allen, S. J., 173

Allen, T. D., 565
Allgeier, E. R., 331, 336
Alliger, G. M., 292, 483
Allison, E. J. Jr., 549
Allison, S. T., 238, 239
Allport, F. H., 119, 486, 487
Allyn, J., 135
Altman, L. K., 338
Alvaro, 372
Amato, P. R., 404, 414
Ambady, N., 72
Ambuel, B., 337
Amir, Y., 234
Amirkham, J., 471
Amirkhan, J. H., 552
Amsel, R., 286
Anastasio, P. A., 237
Andersen, S. M., 169
Anderson, B. L., 163
Anderson, C. A., 11, 22, 24, 39, 320, 443, 444, 447, 451, 459, 460
Anderson, D., 199
Anderson, D. B., 282
Anderson, K. B., 443, 459
Anderson, N. H., 66
Anderson, P. B., 199
Anderson, R. D., 192
Anderson, S. M., 276
Anderson, V. L., 417
Angier, N., 282
Ansell, E., 173
Anthony, T., 232
Antill, J. K., 339
Antone, C., 547
Archer, J., 197, 432
Archibald, F. S., 320
Argyle, M., 43
Armor, D. A., 177
Arms, R. L., 454
Arnone, A., 330
Aron, A., 222, 235, 236, 328, 330, 331, 333, 341

Aron, A. P., 331
Aron, E. N., 328, 330, 331
Aronoff, J., 43
Aronson, E., 144, 145, 149, 150, 151, 234
Arps, K., 431
Arriaga, X. B., 328, 345
Arrigo, J. M., 535
Arthur, W., 193
Arvey, R. D., 124, 561
Asch, S., 65, 358, 359, 361, 365
Asendorph, J. B., 321
Ashmore, R. D., 280
Aspinwall, L. G., 177, 548
Assaad, J. M., 462
Assouline, S. G., 319
Astin, H. S., 195
Asuncion, A. G., 238, 239
Aube, J., 185, 240
Aubin, E., 423
Averill, J. R., 330
Aymmami, R., 199
Azar, B., 330, 345, 415, 417
Aziza, C., 145
Azjen, 131
Azjen, I, 131

Bachman, B. A., 237
Bachorowski, J. A., 455
Bachrach, R. S.
Back, K., 262, 484
Bader, J. L., 199
Baenninger, R., 473
Bagby, G. J., 316
Bahadur, M. A., 343
Bailey, J. M., 191, 325
Bailey, R. C., 286
Bakker, A., 275, 338
Bandura, A., 182, 183, 184, 455, 555
Bane, C. M., 142
Bane, S. M., 553
Banks, J. S., 293

Barbaranelli, C., 470
Barbee, A. P., 280, 285, 556, 557
Barbour, L., 285
Bardach, A. L., 8, 338
Bargh, J. A., 89, 132, 162, 228, 481, 482
Barnes, M. K., 291
Barnett, R. C., 549
Baron, J., 11, 428
Baron, L. A., 311
Baron, R. A., 15, 20, 24, 39, 63, 98, 105, 109, 266, 323, 359, 365, 366, 379, 380, 414, 447, 449, 451, 452, 454, 458, 459, 461, 463, 465, 466, 467, 471, 472, 473, 489, 495, 500, 501, 509, 555, 559, 560
Baron, R. S., 489
Barr, A., 277
Barrett, G. V., 193
Barrett, L. F., 263, 312, 318
Barringer, F., 337
Barry, D., 205
Bartell, P. A., 405
Bartholomew, K., 316, 317, 318, 320
Bass, D. M., 566
Batista, S. M., 342
Bator, R. J., 331
Batson, C. D., 401, 402, 416, 430
Batson, J. G., 430
Bauer, G. B., 347
Baum, A., 276, 549, 550
Bauman, D. J., 414, 431
Baumeister, R. F., 165, 177, 263, 330, 404, 456, 470
Baxter, L. A., 344
Bazerman, M. H., 509
Bazzini, D. G., 325
Beaber, R. J., 136
Beach, 345
Beach, S. R., 259
Beall, A. E., 329
Beaman, A. L., 374
Becker, C., 307, 308
Becker, G., 307, 308
Becker, M. A., 339
Beckwith, J. B., 185
Beehr, T. A., 561
Begg, D., 548
Beike, D. R., 163
Beilfuss, M. C., 312
Belinsky, D., 555
Bell, B., 320, 322
Bell, B. E., 286, 533
Bell, D. W., 123
Bell, K. L., 296
Bell, N. J., 262
Bell, P. A., 27, 459, 460
Bell, R. A., 320

Bell, S. T., 63, 409
Bellafante, G., 197
Belmore, S. M., 93
Bem, S. L., 188, 190
Benjamin, E., 272
Benson, A., 315
Benthin, A. C., 149
Bentler, P. M., 173
Berent, M. K., 129
Berg, J., 319
Berg, J. H., 320
Bergbower, K., 555
Berkowitz, L., 414, 443, 448, 451
Berman, M., 62, 199, 450, 454
Bermank, M., 449
Bernard, L. C., 555
Bernath, M. S., 313
Bernieri, F., 179
Bernieri, F. J., 286
Bernthal, P., 292
Berry, A. J., 175
Berry, D. S., 71, 72, 263, 266, 286
Berscheid, E., 278, 292, 305, 330
Bersoff, D., 401
Bersoff, D. M., 543
Berte, R., 342
Bethes, L. S., 312
Bettencourt, B. A., 17, 240, 456
Betty, S., 291
Betz, A. L., 122, 265
Beyer, S., 193, 242
Bierhoff, H. W., 418
Biernert, H., 472
Bies, R. J., 69, 510
Bindr, R., 202
Binney, V., 317
Birch, K., 430
Birkimer, J. C., 552, 556
Birkimer, S. J., 552
Birnbaum, G. E., 66, 348
Bjorkquist, K., 7
Bjorkqvist, K., 456, 457
Blackstone, T., 327
Blain, M. D., 346
Blakemore, J. E.O., 330
Blakeslee, S., 319
Blaney, P. H., 106
Blanton, H., 132, 133, 145, 275, 338
Blascovich, J., 211, 554
Blatt, S. J., 316, 317
Blaylock, B., 344
Blazer, D. G., 62
Blehar, M. C., 306
Bless, H., 87
Blevins, T., 171
Blieszner, R., 305
Block, C. J., 216
Block, D., 450

Block, J., 173
Bnez, G. A., 553, 554
Bober, S., 168
Bobo, L., 219
Bochner, S., 285
Bodenhausen, G. F., 212, 214, 235
Bodenhausen, G. V., 46, 177, 212, 214, 227
Bodenmann, G., 348
Boeckmann, R. J., 526
Boer, F., 310
Bogard, M., 456
Bohren, J., 245, 246
Boivin, M., 313
Bolger, N., 552
Bombar, M. L., 328
Bond, C. F., 489
Bond, M. H., 11, 16, 165, 171, 224
Bond, R., 358, 359, 361, 366, 367
Boninger, D. S., 129
Bonnelle, K., 67
Bonnet, P., 449
Bookspan, P., 196
Bookwala, J., 332
Boon, S. D., 305
Booth, C., 396
Booth, R. J., 556
Booth-Kewley, S., 555
Boothroyd, P., 330
Bordia, P., 378
Borgida, E., 193, 246
Borkkowski, J. G., 168
Bornstein, R. F., 260, 555
Borough, H. W., 406, 407
Borys, R., 216
Bossard, J. H.S., 262
Bosson, J. K., 319
Botha, M., 451
Bothwell, R. K., 232, 533
Bottoms, B. L., 534
Bouchard, T. J. Jr., 124, 561
Boulton, M. J., 293
Bouman, D., 279
Bourbeau, L. S., 316
Bourgeois, M. J., 543
Bowden, E. M., 193, 242
Bowdle, B. F., 458, 550
Bower, G. H., 106, 109
Bowers, L., 317
Bowlby, J., 306
Bowman, L., 545
Bradac, J. J., 312
Bradbury, T. N., 347
Bradley, M. M., 443
Braithwaite, R. L., 543
Brand, P., 285Ä286
Brand, P. A., 285
Branscombe, N. R., 234

Brase, G., 404
Braun, J. C., 378
Braver, 499
Braza, F., 320
Braza, P., 320
Brazell, B., 199
Breakwell, G. M., 335
Breen, T. H., 256, 257
Brehm, J., 144
Brehm, J. W., 140
Brekke, N., 107
Brennan, K. A., 317, 318, 319, 325, 335
Brennan, P. L., 557
Brett, J. M., 241
Brewer, B. W., 165, 167, 237
Brewer, H., 201
Brickner, M., 493
Bridgeman, D. L., 234
Bridges, M., 343
Bringham, J. C., 533
Bringhamn J. C., 232
Bringle, R. G., 316, 330
Britt, T., 54
Brock, K. F., 332
Brockner, J. M., 508, 509, 510
Brody, J. E., 546
Bromberger, J. T., 192
Bronfen, M. I., 555
Brooks-Gunn, J., 258
Brothers, L., 415
Brouillard, M. F., 182
Brown, C., 419
Brown, D., 463, 464
Brown, J. D., 59, 60, 171, 173, 553
Brown, J. M., 549
Brown, K. W., 549
Brown, L. M., 63, 210
Brown, L. S., 535
Brown, M. D., 543
Brown, M. M., 455
Brown, P. L., 426
Brown, R., 229
Brown, S., 277
Brown, S. L., 9, 361, 460
Brown, S. P., 560
Brown, T. J., 425
Browne, M. W., 433
Brownlow, S., 286
Bruce, M. N., 70
Bruck, M., 534
Bruder, G. E., 62
Brudi, R., 330
Bruess, C. J.S., 348
Brummett, B. H., 430
Brunsman, B., 359, 365, 366
Brusch, M. A., 322
Brussoni, M. J., 305

Bryan, A., 277
Bryan, J. H., 411
Bryan, T. S., 107, 108, 539
Bryant, J., 452, 453
Bryant, W. H.M., 181
Bryden, M. P., 240
Bryne, D., 291
Buchler, J. A., 254
Bucholz, K. K., 335
Buck, R., 433
Buckley, T., 430
Budesheim, T. L., 64, 66, 67
Buehler, R., 94, 95, 172, 359, 364, 365, 366
Bugaj, A. M., 533
Bullinger, M., 549
Bumpass, L., 343
Burge, D., 319
Burger, J. M., 38, 182, 320, 367, 375, 380, 381
Burgess, D., 193, 246
Burgoon, J. K., 139
Burlew, A. K., 199
Burling, J., 173
Burne, D., 192, 286
Burns-Glover, A. L., 194
Burnstein, E., 433, 514
Burton, H. A., 160, 177
Bush, J. P., 346
Bushman, B. J., 11, 22, 24, 42, 385, 451, 456, 459, 460, 462, 470
Buss, A. M., 445
Buss, D. M., 12, 13, 17, 125, 331, 335, 344, 346, 484
Butler, A. C., 175
Butler, D., 242
Butler, J. L., 312
Butler, J. M., 175
Buttenwieser, P., 340, 341
Butterfield, D. A., 243
Butterfield, F., 530
Buunk, B. O., 548
Buunk, B. P., 275, 307, 320, 325, 328, 338, 346, 546
Buzwell, S., 338
Bye, A. L., 325, 342
Byers, E. S., 335
Byrne, B. M., 164
Byrne, D., 68, 192, 254, 258, 261, 263, 271, 289, 290, 293, 296, 316, 317, 318, 326, 327, 337, 339, 344, 347, 409, 542, 558
Byrne, S., 265

Cachere, J. G., 451
Cacioppo, J., 146
Cacioppo, J. T., 119, 136, 137, 139, 291, 550, 556

Cadenhead, A. C., 418
Cahoon, D. D., 286
Caldwell, D. F., 38, 380
Calhoun, L. G., 293
Callaci, D., 194
Callan, V. J., 560
Calvert, J. D., 278
Camerino, M., 549
Campbell, D. T., 408, 428
Campbell, J. D., 163, 552
Canary, D. J., 305
Canin, E., 312
Cann, A., 293
Cantor, N., 322
Cappella, J. N., 290
Caprara, G. V., 470
Carder, P., 555
Carey, G., 53
Carey, M. P., 149
Carli, L. L., 292
Carlo, G., 418
Carlsmith, J. M., 42, 148
Carlston, D. E., 531
Carnelley, K. B., 346
Carnevale, P. J., 496, 502, 503, 504
Carnevale, P. J.D., 191
Carnot, C. G., 129
Carpenter, B. N., 320
Carpenter, L. M., 188
Carreras, M. R., 320
Carroll, J M., 41
Carroll, L., 286
Carstensen, L. L., 348
Carter, C. S., 331
Carter, D. B., 188
Carver, C. S., 169, 322, 454
Casano, 344
Casella, D. F., 286
Cash, T. F., 280, 292
Caspi, A., 332, 339, 548
Castellow, W. A., 542, 543
Catalan, J., 374
Catalano, R., 449
Cate, R. M., 335
Cavoukian, A., 538
Ceci, S. J., 534
Cerro, D., 455
Cervone, D., 182
Chacko, T. I., 216
Chaiken, S., 14, 38, 118, 119, 135, 136, 138, 143, 200, 547
Chan, C.-J., 347
Chan, C.-M, 309
Chance, J. E., 533
Chang, E. C., 555
Change, S., 516
Chapman, B., 291
Chapman, H. A., 549

Chappell, K. D., 319
Chastain, R. L., 556
Chatterjee, J., 191
Chen, S., 138
Cheney. S., 175
Cherek, D. R., 447
Chermak, 449, 450
Cheuk, W. H., 432
Cheung, C.-K., 309
Cheverton, H. M., 286
Chew, B., 552
Chiba, 506
Chidester, T. R., 217
Chiker, V., 225, 226
Chiu, C.-y., 543
Choi, I., 17, 58
Choo, W. M., 224
Chow, P., 549
Christenfeld, N., 551
Christensen, P. N., 191, 321
Christopher, F. S., 335
Christy, C. A.., 406
Christy, P. R., 452
Chuang, Y. C., 129
Chung, L. C., 312
Cialdini, R. B., 9, 141, 149, 361, 362,
    373, 374, 378, 414, 431, 460
Cillessen, H. N., 313
Cioffi, D., 182
Claire, T., 229
Clark, C. L., 316, 318
Clark, E. M., & Brock, K. F., 332
Clark, L. F., 330, 556
Clark, M. E., 201
Clark, M. S., 313, 344, 345, 406
Clark, N. K., 528
Clark, R. D. III, 359
Clark, S. L., 557
Clary, E. G., 415, 422
Claude, S. D., 505
Clement, R. W., 291
Clement, U., 335
Clore, G. L., 106, 109, 265, 424
Coan, J. A., 535
Coe, C. L., 173
Cohen, D., 363, 364, 458
Cohen, N., 549
Cohen, R., 320
Cohen, S., 550, 555
Cohn, E. G., 11, 22, 27, 460, 461
Coie, J. D., 313, 455
Colangelo, N., 319
Colby, P. M., 556
Cole, T., 312
Cole, V., 319
Coleman, B. C., 193
Coleman, G., 404
Coles, R., 412

Collins, J. E. II, 330
Collins, M. A., 60, 72, 73, 276
Collins, N. L., 315, 318, 556
Collins, R. L., 417
Colvin, C. R., 173
Comfort, J. C., 543
Compas, B. E., 549, 553, 554
Comstock, G., 451
Congdon, J. W., 294
Conger, J. A., 517, 572
Connolly, J. A., 324
Conolley, E. S., 361
Conti, L., 442
Contrada, R. J., 552
Conway, M., 83, 106, 109, 177
Cook, S. W., 426
Cooke, P., 404
Coontz, S., 335
Cooper, C., 232
Cooper, E. A., 193
Cooper, H. M., 381, 462
Cooper, J., 145, 148, 150, 151, 197
Cooper, M. L., 315, 555, 557
Cooper-Shaw, L., 292
Copeland, C. L., 193
Copeland, J., 422
Cornell, D. P., 145
Cornwell, B., 200, 201
Costa, F. M., 553
Costa, P. T. Jr., 381, 484
Cottrell, N. B., 489
Courneya, K. S., 182
Covey, M. K., 449
Cowan, C. L., 414
Cowan, G., 63
Cox, C. L., 328
Cox, D., 549
Cox, D. S., 150
Cox, M., 538
Cox, S. L., 63
Cozzarelli, C., 557
Craig, J.-A., 185, 270
Crain, A. L., 150, 151
Crain, R. L., 234
Cramer, R. E., 405
Crandall, C., 433
Crandall, C. S., 202, 285, 360
Crano, W. D., 118, 129, 130, 294,
    372
Crawford, M., 185
Crawford, M. Y., 228
Crealia, R., 124
Criqui, M. H., 343
Critchlow, B., 145, 146, 403
Critelli, J. W., 280
Crocker, J., 172, 173, 200, 201
Crockett, W. H., 291
Croizet, J. C., 229

Cropanzano, R., 500, 507, 560
Crott, H. W., 515
Crowe, G., 169
Crumm, D., 556
Crusco, A. H., 45
Crutchfield, R. A., 359
Cruzen, D., 558
Csank, P., 177
Csikszentmihalyi, M., 555
Culbertson, F. M., 192
Cummings, L. L., 510
Cunnick, J. E., 555
Cunningham, J. D., 339
Cunningham, M. R., 68, 264, 266,
    280, 328, 413, 414, 557
Cupach, W. R., 305
Curtis, J., 194
Curtis, S. R., 63
Cutler, B. L., 531, 532, 537, 543
Cutrona, C. E., 319, 320
Cutshall, J. L., 535
Cvetannovski, J., 173
Cyranowski, J. M., 163

D'Agostino, P. R., 260
D'Alessandro, J. D., 191
da Gloria, J., 449
Dabbs, J. M., 17, 18, 199
Dabbs, J. M. Jr., 199
Dabul, A. J., 195
Daley, D. M., 191
Dalla, R. L., 556
Daly, M., 199, 464
Damasio, A. R., 160
Damheve, K. W., 263
Dana, E. R., 177
Dane, F. C., 540
Daniele, A., 464
Daniels, L. K., 316, 317, 318
Daniels, S. G., 266
Darby, B. L., 374
Darden, C., 540
Darley, J. M., 385, 397, 398, 399,
    400, 401, 402, 403
Darwin, C., 177
Daubman, K. A., 367, 427
Davidson, K., 555
Davie, M. R., 262
Davies, M. F., 163, 322
Davila, J., 319, 347
Davis, C., 201
Davis, C. G., 555
Davis, J. H., 481, 525
Davis, J. M., 286
Davis, K. E., 50Ä51, 316, 319, 331
Davis, M. H., 417, 556
Davison, 140
Dawis, R. V., 124, 561

Dawkins, R., 432
Dawson, K., 418, 430
Dawson, L. J., 192
Day, D. V., 69
Day, J. D., 168
De La Ronde, C., 327, 452
de Poll, N. V., 442
de Waal, F., 433
de Weerth, C., 454
Dean, G. O., 264
Dean-Church, L., 191
Deaux, K., 159, 185, 191, 199, 240, 277
DeBono, K. G., 128, 180, 373
DeBord, K. A., 325, 342
DeCarufel, A., 294
DeDreu, C., 500
DeDreu, C. K.W., 497, 498, 500
DeFusco, P., 404
DeJong, W., 374
DeLamater, J., 337
Delaney, J. J., 283
DeMare, C., 325
den Ouden, M. D., 418
Denes-Raj, V., 90
DeNeve, K. M., 460
Dengerink, H. A., 447, 449
DePaulo, B. M., 40, 71, 296, 312, 425, 426, 557
Derlega, V. J., 292, 557
DeRosier, M. E., 313
Desilets, L., 330
Desmarais, S., 194
Deuser, W. E., 460
Deutsch, F. M., 418, 498
Deutsch, M., 201, 358, 364
Devine, P. G., 145, 146
Devlin, M. J., 200
Dexter, H. R., 532
Diamond, A., 423
Diamond, J., 198
Dickson, N., 548
Diehl, M., 316
Diekmann, K. A., 509
Diener, D., 551
Diener, E., 279
Dietz, J., 466
Dijkstra, P., 346
Dill, J. C., 40, 46, 286, 320
Dimitri, S., 331
Dineen, T., 535
Dinero, T. E., 63
Dink, K. L., 229, 230
Dinwiddie, S. H., 335
Dion, K. K., 278, 280, 309, 325, 332, 393
Dion, K. L., 278, 280, 309, 325, 332
Ditto, P. H., 118, 135, 142, 143

Dixon, T. M., 177
Dobbs, J. M. Jr., 423
Dodge, K. A., 313, 455
Dodge, K. L., 346
Dodgson, P. G., 173
Doherty, K., 54, 428
Dollard, J., 221, 443, 445, 448, 470
Donahue, E. M., 169
Donaldson, S. I., 179
Donnerstein, E., 440, 472
Donnerstein, M., 472
Donovan, S., 62
Doob, A. N., 538
Doob, L., 221, 443, 445, 448, 470
Doosje, B. J., 548
Dorian, B. J., 549
Dougherty, D. M., 447
Dovidio, J. F., 132, 227, 229, 230, 234, 237, 263, 406
Dowd, T. G., 142
Downey, G., 346
Downey, J. L., 263
Downs, A. C., 542
Downs, D. L., 180Ä181
Drachman, D., 294
Dragma, M., 405
Drigotas, S. M., 349
Driscoll, R., 331
Driskell, J. E., 193
Driver, B. L., 129
Drout, C. E., 409
Druen, P. B., 68, 280, 328
Drumm, P., 330
DuBreuil, S. C., 535
Dubro, A., 497
Duck, J. M., 143
Duck, S., 276, 291, 322
Duda, D., 449
Dugoni, B. L., 370
Dull, W. R., 425
Dun, S. A., 557
Duncan, B. D., 430
Duncan, L. E., 191
Duncan, M. K., 320
Duncan, N. C., 280
Dunkel-Schetter, C., 556
Dunn, J., 310
Dunn, M. A., 228
Dunne, M. P., 335
Dunning, D., 166, 277, 537
Duran, R. L., 329
Durso, F. T., 227
Dutta, R., 72, 279
Dutton, D. G., 216, 331
Dutton, K. A., 171
Duval, S., 177
Duvall, S., 414
Dweck, C. S., 543

Dyer, M. A., 282
Dykema, J., 555
Dymond, R. F., 174

Eagly, A. H., 14, 119, 135, 136, 198, 242
Early, J., 332
Early, P. C., 491
Early, S., 416
Easterbrook, G., 530, 545
Eaves, L. J., 551
Eberly, M., 308
Ebert, R., 40
Edmonds, E. M., 286
Edwards, K., 107, 108, 539
Edwards, T. M., 338
Ee, J. S., 280
Egbert, J. M. Jr., 542
Eggleston, T. J., 149
Ehrhardt, A. A., 338
Eich, E., 106
Eisen, S. V., 195
Eisenberg, N., 418, 426, 554
Eisenmann, R., 292
Eisenstadt, D., 171
Ekman, P., 11, 41, 42
Elicker, 314
Elicker, J. & Sroufe, L. A., 313
Elkin, C. S., 286
Ellemers, N., 159
Elliott, A. J., 145, 146, 555
Ellison, C. G., 363
Ellsworth, P. C., 42, 538
Elnick, A. B., 316
Embree, J. M., 417
Emery, R. E., 463
Emmons, R. A., 556
Engstler-Schooler, T. Y., 96
Enright, D. J., 312
Epley, N., 30, 31
Epstein, J. A., 40
Epstein, S., 90
Erber, R., 109, 263
Eron, L. D., 451
Esses, V. M., 123, 172, 408
Essex, M. J., 168
Estrada, C. A., 107
Ethier, K. A., 159
Eustace, M. A., 338
Evans, G. W., 549
Evans, K., 173
Evans, N., 227
Evans, S., 187
Eysenck, S., 199

Fabes, R. A., 554
Fabrigar, L. R., 291, 382
Fagot, B. I., 319

Fairbank, J. A., 549
Fairclough, B., 202
Fajardo, D. M., 217
Falbe, C. M., 382
Fan, C., 183
Farnsworth, C. H., 532
Farrell, A. D., 346
Fazio, R. H., 118, 128, 130, 131, 145, 188, 555
Feather, N. T., 543
Fedor, D. P., 564
Fehn-Wolfsdorf, G., 348
Fein, S., 213, 228, 234, 532
Feingold, A., 17, 200, 276, 278, 524
Feingold, J., 453
Feldman, S. I., 346
Feldman, S. S., 342
Feldman-Summers, S., 197
Felicio, D., 285Ä286
Felmlee, D. H., 344
Fenigstein, A., 177
Fernandez, J. K., 96
Ferris, G. R., 69
Feshbach, N. D., 313
Feshbach, S., 443, 453, 470
Festinger, 135
Festinger, L., 123, 135, 144, 148, 262, 274, 292, 443, 470, 484
Fichten, C. S., 286
Field, P., 516
Fielden, J. A., 17, 18, 199
Fielder, K., 14, 110
Fielding, P. J., 192, 293
Fife-Schaw, C., 335
Fillingim, R. B., 553
Fincham, F. D., 347
Finchman, F., 347
Findlay, C., 332
Finger, K., 535
Fink, M. I., 406, 407
Finklestein, M. A., 423
Finn, J., 191
Fischer, A. R., 325, 342
Fischer, G. J., 63
Fischer, G. W., 213, 224, 232
Fischman, J., 348
Fishbein, M., 128, 131, 338
Fisher, A. B., 239, 241
Fisher, H.
Fisher, J. D., 45, 426, 427
Fisher, W. A., 337
Fiske, S. T., 83, 93, 176, 211, 433
Fitzgerald, J., 396
Fitzgerald, L. L., 245
Flannery, D. J., 308
Flaton, R., 543
Fletcher, B., 558
Flett, G. L., 200

Florian, V., 348, 556
Floyd, K., 311, 312
Flynn, H. A., 175
Foderaro, L. W., 414
Foley, L. A.K., 541
Folger, R., 15, 216, 449, 466, 509
Folkes, V., 50, 62
Folkes, V. S., 471
Folwell, A. L., 312, 344
Fong, C., 228
Fong, G. T., 177, 547
Foote, F. H., 332
Ford, R., 227
Forgas, J. P., 10, 14, 95, 105, 106, 107, 109, 110, 292, 379, 380, 413
Foss, M. A., 13, 454
Foster-Fishman, P. G., 512, 517
Foti, R. J., 566
Fourment, C., 260
Fraczek, A., 457
Fraible, D. E.S., 266
Fraley, R. C., 306, 316
Frame, C. L., 279
Francis, C., 338
Frank, R. A., 535
Frankel, A., 322
Franklin, M., 276
Franz, 512, 517
Fraser, S. C., 374
Frazier, P. A., 325, 342
Fredrickson, B. L., 201, 202, 315
Freeberg, A. L., 309
Freedman, J. L., 374
Freidman, H. S., 286, 343
Fricko, M. A.M., 561
Friday, C., 450
Fried, C., 145, 149
Fried, C. B., 150, 151
Friedman, H. S., 343, 550, 551
Friesen, W. V., 41
Frieze, I. H., 332, 342
Frijda, N., 442
Frijda, N. H., & Scherer, K. P., 112
Froming, W. J., 418
Fromkin, H. L., 367
Frone, M. R., 555
Frost, P. J., 571
Frude, N., 278
Fry, D. P., 442
Fry, W. R., 509
Fuhrman, R. W., 67
Fujino, D. C., 293
Fujita, F., 279
Fukushima, 506
Fultz, J., 431
Funder, D. C., 173, 321
Furnham, A., 193
Furr, R. M., 321

Gabriel, M. T., 280
Gaertner, S. L., 132, 229, 234, 237, 263, 409
Gagnon, J. H., 334, 335, 341
Gaines, S., O. Jr., 305, 349
Galambos, N. L., 308
Galbraith, M. E., 558
Gallery, M. E., 549
Galloway, J., 13, 454
Gallup, 160
Gamble, W. C., 556
Gangestad, S., 179
Gangestad, S. W., 181, 334
Ganley, R., 292
Gant, L., 167
Gantner, 462
Garcia, L. T., 191
Gardner, P., 241
Gardner, R. M., 284
Gardner, W., 165, 473
Garfinkel, P. E., 549
Garry, M., 535
Garst, E., 418, 430
Garst, J., 498
Gauvain, M., 319
Gavanski, I., 99
Gebhard, P., 334, 335
Geddes, D., 466
Geen, R., 440
Geen, R. G., 451, 470
Geffner, R., 234
Geis, F. L., 242
Geislman, R. E., 534
Gelfand, D. M., 423, 452
Geller, P. A., 347
Gentile, D. A., 185
George, J. M., 125, 263
Gerard, H. B., 358, 361, 364
Gerber, G. L., 286
Gerhart, B., 562
Gerlsma, C., 307
Gerrard Moeller, F., 447
Gerrard, M., 133, 172, 275, 337, 338
Gervey, B. M., 543
Getz, J. G., 68
Giannopoulous, C., 177
Gibbons, F. X., 132, 133, 149, 172, 275, 338
Gibson, P. R., 183, 199
Gier, J. A., 45
Giesler, R. B., 294
Giffin, M., 330
Gifford, R., 72
Gigone, D., 512, 516, 517
Giladi, E. E., 41
Gilbert, D. T., 56, 57, 58, 426, 531
Gilbert, L. A., 342
Gill, M. J., 11, 60, 64, 72, 328

Gillen, B., 278
Gillis, J. S., 286
Gilovich, 98
Gilovich, T., 98
Gilroy, F. D., 191
Giner-Sorolla, R., 38, 118, 138, 143
Ginsburg, B., 433
Gist, M. E., 182
Gladue, B., 199, 454
Gladue, B. A., 283
Gladwell, M., 531
Glaser, J., 268
Glaser, R., 346, 550
Glass Ceiling Commission, 242, 243
Glass, D. C., 454, 544
Glasser, R., 549
Gleeson, K., 278
Gleicher, 98
Glenn, N. D., 342
Glick, P. C., 343
Glor, J. E., 378
Goethals, G. R., 515
Gold, D. B., 102, 107
Gold, J. A., 167, 296
Goldnick, W., 168
Goldsmith, D. J., 557
Goldstein, A. G., 533
Goldstein, M. D., 263
Goleman, D., 540, 555
Gonzales, M. H., 135
Goodman, G. S., 534
Goodstein, M. K., 63
Goodwin, R., 332
Gordon, J., 450
Gordon, R. A., 294, 295, 373, 378
Gordon, S., 199
Gottman, J. M., 348
Gouau, C., 290
Gould, D., 182
Gover, M. R., 316, 318
Grabski, S. V., 241
Graham, S., 50, 54, 55, 62, 541
Grahe, J. E., 286
Grant, J. A., 312
Grayer, A. R., 542
Graziano, W. G., 181, 278, 345
Green, 457
Green, L. R., 456
Greenbaum, P., 42
Greenberg, J., 15, 60, 144, 173, 177, 216, 425, 445, 449, 466, 471, 508, 509, 510, 511, 559
Greenberg, M. A., 556
Greenberger, D., 336
Greenier, K. D., 175
Greenwald, J., 545
Greer, A. E., 331
Grether, J., 424

Grewal, D., 517
Grieve, N., 186
Griffin, D., 94, 95, 316, 317, 318, 359, 364, 365, 366
Griffin, D. W., 328
Griffin, K. W., 558
Griffitt, W., 290, 331
Grimley, D. M., 183, 199
Groff, D. B., 489
Groom, R. W., 11, 22, 24, 459, 460
Gropp, T., 541
Grossman, M., 202
Grote, N. K., 332, 342, 344, 345
Gruchy, C. D.G., 195
Gruen, G. E., 320
Grunder, C. L., 403
Grusec, J. E., 415
Guagnano, G. A., 423
Gudjonsson, G. H., 527, 528
Guerrero, L. K., 347
Guild, W., 404
Gulley, M. R., 557
Gully, K. J., 447
Gunter, B. G., 192
Gunter, N. C., 192
Gurtman, M. B., 286
Gustafson, 426
Gutek, B. A., 245
Gutierres, S. E., 282
Guy, S. M., 173
Guydish, J. N., 406

Haar, 418
Hackel, L. S., 314Ä342
Hagborg, W. J., 200
Hahlweg, K., 348
Hahn, A., 290, 549
Haigh, G. V., 175
Hains, S. C., 484
Hair, E. C., 345
Hale, J. L., 139
Halford, W. K., 347, 367
Hall, 334
Hall, C. C.I., 195
Hall, J., 197
Hall, W. S., 214, 215
Hamburger, M. E., 192
Hamid, N. P., 549
Hamilton, D. L., 230, 231
Hamilton, G. V., 386
Hamilton, M. M., 160
Hamilton, P. A., 265
Hammen, C., 319
Hammer, E. D., 66
Hammock, G. S., 473
Hampson, E., 443
Hanna, 513
Hanna, R., 277

Hansen, J. S., 263, 266
Hansen, K. A., 13, 276
Hanson, E., 106
Harasty, A. S., 224
Harber, K. D., 217, 218
Hardaway, T. J., 192
Hardin, C. D., 87, 88
Hardy, A. B., 184
Hargis, K., 414
Harkin, S., 491
Harkins, S., 491, 493
Harkness, D. J., 348
Harlow, L. L., 183, 199
Harner, R. J., 322
Harrington, H. L., 548
Harris, J. A., 443
Harris, L. R., 542, 543
Harris, M. B., 285, 456
Harris, P., 548
Harris, R. J., 234, 285
Harris, S. E., 498
Harrison, A. A., 277
Hart, A. J., 139, 539
Hartmann, D. P., 119, 423, 452
Harvey, J. H., 343, 348, 556
Harvey, M. R., 63
Hasart, J. K., 286
Hasemann, D., 525
Hashimoto, H., 151
Haslam, N., 305
Hastie, R., 504, 512, 516, 517, 539
Hatfield (Walster), E., 278, 292
Hatfield, E., 276, 289, 305, 329, 330, 331, 332, 336
Haugen, J., 422
Haupt, A. L., 173
Hawley, P. H., 551
Hayden, S. R., 406
Hayes, N. S., 105
Hazan, C., 318, 319
Heath, A., 551
Heath, A. C., 335
Heatherson, T. E., 11, 202
Hebl, M. R., 11, 191, 202
Hecht, M. A., 268, 542
Hedges, M., 530
Hedges, R. M., 542
Heerey, E. A., 322
Heffner, T. S., 160, 161
Heider, F., 50
Heilman, M. E., 193, 216, 243
Heimberg, R. G., 322, 323
Heinberg, L. J., 200, 282
Heindel, W., 107
Heine, S. J., 151, 152, 163, 165
Heingartner, A., 489
Helgeson, V. S., 452
Helman, D., 196

Helquist, M., 338
Helquist, M., &, 338
Hembrooke, H., 534
Henderson-King, D., 225, 226
Henderson-King, D. H., 225, 226, 347
Hendrick, C., 332
Hendrick, S. S., 332
Henkemeyer, L., 341
Henry, S., 165
Henry, W. A. III, 529
Hensler, C. P., 129
Hensley, W. E., 332
Hepworth, J. T., 221
Herbener, E. S., 332, 339
Herbert, J. D., 322
Herlocker, C. E., 175
Herman, E. M., 489
Hershberger, S. L., 124
Heszen, I., 195
Hetherington, E. M., 343
Hewstone, M., 67, 224
Higgins, E. T., 89, 160, 162, 167, 213, 341
Higgins, P, 341, 549
Highberger, L., 430
Hill, A., 325
Hill, C. A., 271, 330
Hill, K. C., 344
Hiller, W. D., 71, 72
Hilton, J. L., 93
Hinchey, F., 455
Hiner, S. L., 549
Hinkley, K., 169
Hirt, E. R., 105
Hixon, J. G., 177, 327
Hjelt-Back, M., 456, 457
Ho, H., 237
Ho, J. A., 556
Hobfoll, S. E., 347, 549
Hodge, D., 535
Hoenigmann-Stovall, N., 286
Hoffman, J. C., 266
Hogben, M., 192
Hogg, M. A., 143, 292, 484
Hojjat, M., 305
Hokanson, J. E., 175
Holahan, C. J., 557
Holgate, S., 171
Holmes, J. G., 312, 328
Holt, C. S., 323
Holtgraves, T., 542
Holzworth, D. W., 292
Hong, Y.-Y., 543
Hope, D. A., 323
Hopstaken, I. E.M., 548
Horowitz, B., 171
Horowitz, I. A., 543

Horowitz, L. M., 316, 318
Horwitz, B., 263
Hosch, H. M., 534, 542
Hotaling, G. T., 328
Houlainban, D., 431
House, R. J., 566, 570, 571, 572
Hovland, C. I., 135, 220, 221, 222
Howell, J. M., 570, 571
Howells, G. N., 180
Howsepian, B., 168
Hoyle, R. H., 179, 292
Hoyt, D. R., 325
Huang, I.-C., 182, 183
Huang, K., 334
Hubbard, C., 46, 47
Hubbard, M. L., 93
Hudy, 559
Huelson, 342
Huesmann, L. R., 451
Huff, C., 30, 31, 197
Hughes, C. F., 556
Hull, J. D., 529
Hummert, M. L., 291
Humphreys, L. G., 535
Humphriss, N., 271
Hunter, B. A., 214, 215
Huo, Y. J., 506, 526
Hur, Y.-M., 159
Hurewitz, M., 396
Hurst, A. P., 344
Hutchinson, K. L., 286
Hutson-Comeaux, S. L., 513, 514
Hyde, J. S., 17, 198
Hygge, S., 549
Hyman, L. M., 43

Iacono, W. G., 159
Iavnieli, D., 347
Ickes, W., 128, 179, 180, 279, 327
Insabella, G. M., 343
Insel, T. R., 331
Insko, C. A., 292, 294
Ironsmith, M., 320
Isbell, L. M., 268, 269
Isen, A. M., 105, 107, 132, 229, 263, 331, 413, 414
Ishii, S., 426
Istvan, J., 331, 552
Ito, T. A., 119, 212, 291
Itzhak, S. B., 426
Izard, 40

Jackson, D. N., 443
Jackson, J. W., 513, 514
Jackson, L. A., 241
Jackson, L. M., 408
Jackson, R. L., 529
Jackson, T. T., 406

Jaffe, K., 346
Jaffe, Y., 453
Jalil, M., 533
James, K., 560
James, W., 169
Jamieson, D. W., 312
Jandorf, L., 549
Janis, I. L., 516
Janoff-Bulman, R., 167, 194
Jans, L. G.J. M., 548
Jeffries, V., 308
Jemmott, J. B. III, 549
Jenkins, S. R., 556
Jensen-Campbell, L. A., 286, 345
Jerusalem, M., 290, 549
Jessor, R., 553
Jex, S. M., 173
Jia Lin Xie, 559
Jockin, V., 346
John, R. S., 347
Johns, G., 559
Johnson, A. B., 258, 542
Johnson, A. M., 324
Johnson, B. T., 11, 14, 138, 141, 149
Johnson, C., 230
Johnson, D. F., 279
Johnson, J. C., 320
Johnson, J. E., 322
Johnson, J. R., 332
Johnson, K. A., 322
Johnson, L. G., 418
Johnson, M. K., 94
Johnston, C., 264
Johnston, J.-A., 194
Johnston, V. S., 276, 280
Johnstone, B., 279
Joiner, T. E. Jr., 552
Jones, C. R., 89
Jones, E. E., 50Ä51, 57, 59, 334
Jones, J. H., 373
Jones, J. M., 409
Jones, M., 180
Jones, S., 136
Jones, W. H., 101, 320, 348
Josephs, R. A., 547
Judd, C. M., 211Ä212, 224, 226
Judge, T. A., 562
Julka, 139
Jussim, L., 213, 234
Jussim, L. J., 122, 265

Kacmar, K. M., 70
Kaczor, L. M., 167
Kagan, J., 189
Kahn, J. H., 103
Kahneman, 86, 87
Kaiser, A., 348
Kalichman, S. C., 332

Kalick, S. M., 277
Kallgren, C. A., 361, 362
Kalma, A. P., 454
Kambara, T., 449
Kameda, M., 109, 471
Kameda, T., 516
Kandel, D. B., 292
Kanekar, S., 239
Kang, M., 418, 430
Kaniasty, K., 556
Kaplan, J. R., 555
Kaplan, M. F., 265, 513
Karasawa, 166
Karau, S. J., 491, 492, 493
Karoly, P., 554
Karraker, K. H., 187, 279
Karuza, J., 509
Kashy, D. A., 40, 72, 312, 321
Kassin, S. M., 165, 528, 529, 538
Katz, I. M., 163
Kaufman-Gilliland, C. M., 497, 498, 499
Kaukiainen, A.L, 457
Kaukiainen, A. L., 7, 457
Kavanagh, K., 319
Kawakami, K., 229, 230
Keane, T. M., 549
Keating, J. P., 431
Keefe, R. C., 277
Keelan, J. P., 280
Keelan, J. P.R., 325
Kelnan, G., 101
Keita, G. P., 195
Keller, K., 330, 424
Keller, L. M., 124, 561
Kellcr, R. T., 563
Keller, S. E., 549
Kellerman, J., 330
Kelley, D. J., 414
Kelley, H. H., 52, 53
Kelley, I. W., 11
Kelley, K., 337
Kelly, A. E., 103
Kelly, J. R., 513, 514
Kelman, H. C., 30
Keltner, D., 322, 500, 501
Kemper, S., 291
Kendler, K. S., 551
Kendzierski, D., 161
Kenealy, P., 278
Kenkel, M. B., 195
Kennedy-Moore, E., 150
Kenney, D. A., 72, 312
Kenny, D. A., 566
Kenrick, D. T., 277, 282, 286, 414, 431
Kent, R. L., 242
Keough, K., 547

Kernis, M. H., 175
Kerns, K. A., 313
Kerr, N. L., 495, 497, 498, 499, 543
Kessler, J. W., 263
Kessler, R. C., 62, 316, 344, 503, 551
Ketcher, C. M., 452
Ketter, T. A., 263
Keystone, E., 549
Kibler, J. L., 211
Kiechel, K. L., 528
Kiecolt-Glaser, J. K., 346, 549, 556
Kihlstrom, J. F., 106
Kilbourne, 197
Kilduff, M., 69
Kilham, W., 385, 386
Killeya, L. A., 11, 14, 138
Kim, J. G., 553
Kim, P. Y., 325
King, A., 286
King, D. W., 549
King, L. A., 549
King, M. C., 238
Kinney, T., 322
Kinsey, A. C., 334, 335
Kirkendol, S. E., 40
Kirkpatrick, L. A., 90, 319, 346
Kirn, W., 343
Kitano, H. H.L., 293
Kitayama, S., 165, 166, 433
Klagsbrun, F., 311
Klar, Y., 41
Klein, J. G., 93
Klein, R., 418
Klein, S. B., 64, 66, 67, 160, 162, 163, 177, 430
Klein, T. R., 430
Kleinke, C. L., 42, 263, 264, 331
Kline, S. L., 344
Kling, K. C., 168, 177
Klohen, E. C., 319
Klohnen, E. C., 328
Klonsky, B. G., 242
Klotz, M. L., 378
Klumpp, G., 87
Knee, C. R., 328
Knight, G. P., 418, 497
Knobe, J., 59
Knox, S. S., 124
Koch, W., 193, 350
Koehler, J. J., 86
Koestner, R., 179, 185, 240, 270
Kohl, W. L., 570
Kohlberg, L., 189
Kohout, J. L., 195
Kojetin, B. A., 124
Kolata, G., 334, 335, 341
Kolsawala, M. B., 239
Komorita, M., 495

Konovsky, M. A., 564
Koon, J., 282
Korol, S., 332
Korte, C., 404
Koski, L. R., 316
Koss, M. P., 63
Kowalski, R. M., 171, 322
Kraft, D., 331
Kramer, G. P., 46, 212
Kramer, J. P., 71
Kramer, L., 311
Kramp, P., 418
Krantz, J. H., 68
Kraus, 498
Kraus, L. A., 556
Kraus, S. J., 129, 417
Kremer, J., 335
Krim, 373
Kristof, A. L., 68
Krones, J. M., 277
Krosnick, J. A., 122, 129, 130, 141, 165, 291
Krueger, J., 291
Krull, D. S., 40, 46, 286
Krupat, E., 397, 404
Kruse, M., 335
Ku, L. C., 191
Kubany, E. S., 347
Kuhlman, M. D., 497
Kuhn, D., 543
Kuiper, N. A., 555
Kulik, J. A., 272, 273
Kunda, Z., 177, 227, 234
Kupersmidt, J. B., 313
Kurdek, L. A., 342, 348
Kuriloff, P. J., 63, 409
Kurzweil, N., 291
Kus, L. A., 322
Kwan, L. K., 290
Kwan, V. S.Y., 171
Kwon, P., 549
Kwon, Y.-H., 173

L'Herrou, T., 360
Laboouvie-Vief, G., 316
Lacayo, R., 530
Lachman, M. E., 558
LaFrance, M., 268, 542
Lagerspetz, K. M., 457
Lago, 457
Lai, J. C.L., 549
Laird, J. D., 330
Lake, M. A., 187
Lake, R. A., 216
Lalwani, N., 177
Lamb, M. E., 534
Lambert, A. J., 64, 66, 224
Lamberth, J., 290

Lamberti, D. M., 418
Lamm, H., 329, 330, 514
Lancaser, L., 293
Lander, M., 241, 242
Landry, J. C., 286
Landua, S. F., 457
Lane, J. D., 331
Lane, M. C., 560
Lang, P. J., 443
Langley, J., 548
Langlois, J. H., 279, 280, 281
Langston, C. A., 322, 551
Lapham, L. H., 295
LaPiere, R. T., 126Ä127
LaPrelle, J., 292
Largo, E., 91
Larrick, R. P., 56
Larsen, J. T., 119, 291
Larsen, R. J., 346
Larson, D. G., 556
Larson, J. H., 262
Larson, J. R. Jr., 512, 517
Larson, R. W., 347
Latane, B., 360, 397, 398, 399, 400, 403, 491, 493
Latty-Mann, H., 319
Lau, M. L., 462
Lau, S., 192, 320
Lauer, J., 348
Lauer, R., 348
Laumann, E. O., 334, 335, 341
Laurenceau, J.-P., 312
Lavallee, L. F., 163
Lavine, H., 135
Lawton, S. F., 24, 458
Lazarus, R. S., 548
Learner, S. M., 483
Leary, M. R., 165, 171, 173, 180Ä181
Leary, W. E., 330
Leatham, G., 322
Leber, D., 344
Leck, K., 364, 370
Lee, A., 339
Lee, C., 182
Lee, H. K., 71, 73
Lee, J., 237
Lee, J.-J., 309
Lee, L. F., 543
Lee, Y. T., 60, 61, 232
Lefcourt, H. M., 555
Lehman, D. R., 151, 152, 163, 165, 555
Leibold, J. M., 231
Leite, P., 62
Lemieux, A. M., 173
Lennox, R. D., 381
Leo, R., 191

Leonard, M., 360
LePine, J. A., 563, 564
Lepore, L., 229
Lepore, S. J., 556
Leppe, 171
Lepper, M., 143
Lepper, M. R., 142
Lerner, 224
Lerner, Ma.J., 63
Leskela, J., 316, 318
Levenson, R. W., 348
Leventhal, G. S., 199, 509
Leventhal, H., 136
Levin, I. P., 66
Levin, P. A., 413
Levine, A., 558
Levine, J. M., 370, 371
Levine, R. V., 404
Levy, K. N., 316, 317
Lewandowski, D. A., 498
Lewin, K., 568, 569
Lewis, B. P., 9, 460
Lewis, G. J., 404
Lewis, J., 330
Lewis, M., 160, 258, 319
Lewis, S. K., 374
Li, L., 555
Liberman, A., 136, 547
Lichtenstein, M., Z., 191
Lichtenstein, P., 124
Liden, R. C., 68, 69, 373
Lieberman, J. D., 445, 471, 472
Liebert, R. M., 411
Lieppe, 534
Lind, E. A., 506, 510
Lind, M., 542
Lindsay, D. S., 533, 535
Lindsey, E. W., 305
Link, B. G., 228
Linsenmeier, J. A.W., 325
Linville, P. W., 213, 224, 232
Linz, D., 531
Lipetz, M. E., 331
Lippa, R., 179
Lippit, R., 568, 569
Litowicz, D. L., 282
Littig, L. W. Jr., 328
Liu, T. J., 144, 403
Lobel, M., 556
Lobel, T. E., 188
Locke, E. A., 182, 566
Locke, M., 348
Loftus, E. F., 528, 533, 535
Loftus, J., 66, 67, 160, 162, 163, 177
Logsdon, M. C., 556
Longenecker, C. O., 564
Longo, L. C., 280
Lopez, F. G., 316, 318, 319

Lord, C. G., 142
Lorenz, K., 441
Losch, M., 146
Lottes, I., 63, 409
Lottes, I. L., 335
Louis-Dreyfus, E., 107
Lowery, 40
Lowrance, R., 132, 229, 263
Lox, C. L., 553
Lucas, J. A., 216
Lucas, M., 552
Luce, C., 9, 417, 460
Luks, ., 432
Lundberg, J. K., 285, 286
Lundgren, D., 199
Lundgren, S. R., 138
Lurie, A., 196
Lutgendorf, S. K., 556
Luus, C. A., 534
Luus, C. A.E., 337, 533, 536
Lydon, J. E., 312
Lykken, D. T., 124, 346
Lynch, M., 145, 152, 213
Lyness, K. S., 243
Lynn, A. R., 122, 265
Lynn, M., 43, 44
Lyon, D., 173
Lyons, P. M., 542
Lyubomirsky, S., 177

Maas, A., 359, 533
Macaulay, J., 410
MacCoun, R. J., 543
MacCullen, R. C., 549
MacDonald, H., 94, 95
MacDonald, T. K., 547
Mack, D., 286
MacKenzie, S. B., 564, 565
Mackie, D. M., 46, 106, 231, 238, 239
Macrae, C. N., 98, 177, 214, 227, 228, 402
Madden, P. A.F., 335
Maddux, J. E., 184
Madey, 98
Madon, S., 72
Madrian, J. C., 175
Magee, J., 378
Maglooire, K., 549
Maheswaran, D., 136
Mahler, H. I.M., 272, 273
Maio, G. R., 123
Maisonneuve, J., 260
Major, B., 173, 191, 192, 199, 200, 201, 241, 557
Mak, A. S., 183
Makhiijani, M. G., 242
Maki, B., 344

Malamuth, N. M., 63
Malarkey, W. B., 346
Malcarne, V., 553, 554
Mallamuth, N., 453
Malle, B. F., 59, 171
Mallick, S. K., 470
Malloy, T. E., 72
Malone, P. S., 56, 57, 58, 531
Malpass, R. S., 232
Manis, 11
Manke, B., 311
Mann, J., 237
Mann, J. A., 237
Mann, L., 385, 386
Mansfield, E., 423
Manuck, S. B., 555
Maran, G., 543
Marazziti, D., 442
Margalit, M., 199
Margolin, G., 347
Markland, D., 553
Markman, 323
Markman, H. J., 339
Markman, K. D., 99
Markus, H., 167
Markus, H. R., 165, 166
Markwith, M., 101
Marlarkey, W., 550
Marsh, 139
Marsh, H. W., 171
Marshall, N. L., 549
Marston, 333
Martens, T. K., 537
Martin, C., 334, 335
Martin, C. D., 547
Martin, C. L., 190, 198, 215
Martin, H. J., 175
Martin, L., 12, 118
Martin, L. L., 145
Martin, L. R., 343, 550
Martin, N. G., 335
Martin, R., 315
Martin, R. A., 555
Martinez, R., 285
Martinez, T. S., 404
Martz, J. M., 328, 348
Maruayama, G., 136
Marucha, P. T., 549
Marx, R., 320
Maslach, C., 367
Mastekaasa, A., 342
Mathis, D., 200
Matsumoto, H., 165, 166
Matthews, K. A., 192
Matthews, S. H., 305
Maugh, T. H. II, 345
Maurice, J., 282
May, J. L., 265

May, K. A., 281
Mayer, F. S., 414
Mayer, J. D., 106, 413, 554, 556
Mayseless, O., 316
Mazzella, R., 200, 524
McAdams, D. P., 271, 423
McArthur, L. Z., 195
McAuley, E., 182, 553
McCabe, M. P., 335
McCall, M. E., 10, 191
McCallum, D. M., 549
McCandless, B. R., 470
McCarrey, M., 191
McCarthy, D. M., 525
McCauley, C., 404
McCauley, C. D., 243
McClaskey, C. L., 455
McClintock, 498
McCloskey, A. L., 532
McCloskey, L. A., 188
McClure, J., 56
McConnell, A. R., 188, 230, 231
Mcconnell, W., 449
McCoy, S. B., 133
McCrae, R. R., 381, 484
McCreath, H., 404
McCullough, M. E., 345
McCusker, C., 497, 498, 500
McDonald, H. E., 105
McDonald, K. A., 335
McFarland, C., 172
McGaughey, K. J., 538
McGillis, D., 50
McGonagle, K. A., 62, 344
McGowan, S., 192
McGowans, S., 316, 317, 318
McGue, M., 159, 346
McGuire, C., 516
McGuire, C. V., 173
McGuire, S., 311
McGuire, W. J., 173
McHale, S. M., 310, 311
McHoskey, J. W., 142
McKelvie, S. J., 280, 286
McKenna, K. Y.A., 481, 482
McKillip, J., 292
McKnight, J. D., 552
McLaughlin-Volpe, T., 222, 235, 236
McLean Parks, J., 466
McManus, J., 418
McMaster, M. R., 405
McMullen, M. N., 99
McNall, K., 528
McNultry, 169
McQuinn, R. D., 320
McWhirter, 173
Mealey, 277
Mednick, M., 195

Medvec, V. H., 98, 99
Meeker, F. B., 263
Mehrabin, 287
Meindl, 224
Meindle, J. R., 517
Meine, P., 422
Melamed, 560
Meleshko, 322
Melinat, E., 331
Mellers, 66
Mendelsohn, G. A., 58, 328
Mendelson, M., 177
Mendolia, 345
Menesini, E., 418
Mentzel, R. K., 418
Mercier, M. A., 62
Merrill, D. M., 309
Mesquita, B., 112
Messman, S. J., 305
Meyer, J. P., 562
Meyers, S. A., 330
Miceli, M. P., 560
Michael, R. T., 334, 335, 341
Michaels, S., 335, 341
Michela, J. L., 52
Michkelson, K. D., 316
Middlekauff, R., 256
Middlestadt, S. E., 338
Middleton, W., 548
Mihalko, S. L., 553
Miklosovic, J. D., 344
Mikulincer, M., 316, 317, 319, 347, 348, 556
Milberg, S., 406
Miles, S. M., 53
Milgram, S., 382, 384, 404
Millar, M. G., 547
Miller, A. G., 142
Miller, C. T., 285Ä286
Miller, D. T., 59, 526
Miller, J. G., 58
Miller, L. C., 50, 337
Miller, M., 237
Miller, M. G., 278, 418
Miller, N., 17, 136, 212, 221, 240, 414, 443, 445, 448, 456, 470, 495
Miller, R. S., 320, 347
Millman, L., 266
Mills, D., 555
Milne, A. B., 177, 214, 227, 228, 402
Mischel, W., 198
Mitchell, T. R., 373
Mixon, K. D., 541
Miyake, K., 286
Mize, J., 305
Mizrahi, K., 159
Mockus, Z., 403
Modigliani, A., 387

Moffitt, T. E., 548
Monahan, J. L., 226, 267, 337
Monarch, N. D., 322
Monepare, J. M., 71, 73
Monsour, M., 291, 315
Montello, D. R., 282
Montemayor, R., 308
Montepare, J. M., 286
Montgomery, L., 530
Montgomery, M. J., 315
Moore, C. H., 542, 543
Moore, D., 192, 489, 555
Moore, D. L., 489
Moore, J. S., 278
Moore, P. J., 272, 273
Moore, S., 282, 283
Moore, T., 421
Moos, R. H., 549, 557
Moran, G., 531, 543
Morch, H., 556
Moreland, R. L., 258, 259, 481
Morey, N., 286
Morgan, D., 555
Morgan, G., 532
Morgan, H. J., 167, 328
Morokoff, P. J., 183, 199
Morris, K. J., 182
Morris, M. M., 556
Morris, M. W., 56, 58, 99Ä100
Morris, W. N., 406
Morrison, E. W., 69, 243
Morrison. H. W., 564
Morrisson-Beedy, D., 149
Morrow, G. D., 332
Moscovici, S., 370
Mosher, D. L., 192
Moskowitz, D. S., 72, 549
Mosley, N. R., 296
Moss, S. E., 242
Moston, S., 527
Mowerer, O. H., 221, 443, 445, 448, 470
Muczyk, J. P., 175, 569
Mudar, P., 555
Mueller, J. S., 71, 72
Mugny, G., 370
Mullan, E., 553
Mullen, B., 230, 232
Munnoz, J. M., 320
Munro, G. D., 118, 135, 142, 143
Munsterberg, H., 533, 535
Murakawa, N., 290
Muraoka, M. Y., 347
Muraven, M. B., 312
Murnen, S. K., 192, 291, 347
Murnigham, K., 559
Murphy, K., 313
Murphy, R., 54

Murphy, S. T., 213, 266, 267, 337
Murray, H. A., 270
Murray, S. L., 328
Murrell, A., 237
Murrell, A. J., 237, 409
Musilli, L., 374
Musselman, L., 281
Mustari, L., 491, 493
Mutsaers, W. C.M., 307
Myers, D. G., 514, 551
Mynier, K., 43, 44

Nadkarni, D. V., 199
Nadler, A., 426, 427
Nalbone, D., 316
Nanni, C., 558
Napoli, A., 150
Narby, D. J., 543
Nardi, P. M., 305
Nash, S. C., 342
Nashby, W., 418
National Insititute for Occupational
    Safety and Health, 465
Nauta, M. M., 103
Nazaareth, T., 239
Neal, M., 555
Neale, J. M., 150, 549
Neale, M. C., 551
Negel, L., 173
Neimeyer, 62
Nelson, D., 290
Nemeroff, C., 101, 200, 266
Nemeroff, C. J., 287
Nemeth, C. J., 370
Nesbitt, K., 330
Nesbitt, R. E., 59
Neter, E., 170
Neuberg, S. L., 9, 93, 211, 238, 266, 277, 460
Neufeld, R. W.J., 558
Neuman, J. H., 463, 465, 466, 467
Neuner, R. A., 556
New Republic, 338
Newcomb, T. M., 289, 291
Newman, J. P., 455
Newton, T. L., 346
Nezlek, J. B., 171
Nida, S. A., 282
Niebuhr, G., 195
Niedenthal, P. M., 163, 167, 213
Nisbett, R. E., 17, 58, 363, 364, 458, 500
Nitzel, M. T., 525
Nix, G., 177
Nolen-Hoeksema, S., 177
Noll, S. M., 201, 202
Norasakkunkit, V., 165, 166
Norcliffe, H., 185

Norris, F. H., 556
Novaco, R., 449
Nurius, P., 167
Nurmi, J.-E., 322
Nussbaumn J. F., 312

O'Brien, M., 343, 347
O'Connell, P. D., 532
O'Connor, K., 503
O'Connor, S. C., 270
O'Grady, K. E., 279
O'Leary, S. G., 307
O'Malley, P. M., 173
O'Neil, J., 264
O'Rourke, 139
O'Sullivan, C. S., 227
O'Sullivan, L. F., 335, 336
Oemig, C., 322
Oettingen, 60
Oggins, J., 344
Ohbuchi, K., 109, 449, 471, 506
Ohlott, P. J., 243
Oleson, K. C., 227, 234, 430
Oliner, P. M., 419
Oliner, S. P., 419
Oliver, J. M., 549
Oliver, M. B., 17
Oliver-Rodriguez, J. C., 280
Olmstead, R. E., 173
Olsen, N., 556
Olson, J. M.
Omarzu, J., 343
Omoto, A. M., 305, 422
Orbach, I., 347
Orenstein, L., 415
Organ, D. W., 563
Orive, R., 291
Orne, K., 541
Orpen, C., 295
Orr, I., 348
Osborne, J. W., 171
Osterman, K., 7, 456, 457
Ostrom, T., 493
Ostrow, R. J., 529
Ottati, V., 46, 47, 232
Ottati, V. C., 268, 269
Ouellette, J. A., 96
Ouellette, R., 406
Oyserman, D., 167
Ozer, D. J., 339

Packer, M., 180
Page, D., 541
Page, G. G., 549
Page, N. R., 560
Page, R. M., 322
Pahlavan, F., 449
Paik, H., 451

Palego, L., 442
Palmade, G., 260
Palmer, M. L., 182
Palmer, M. T., 290
Pan, S., 334
Pancioloi-Guadagnucci, M. L., 442
Pang, K., 58
Papalia, D., 316
Parekh-Priti, I., 263
Paris, M., 328
Park, B., 8
Parke, B., 211Ä212, 224, 226
Parker, S., 198, 215
Parks, G., 495
Parks, M. R., 312
Pastorelli, C., 470
Pataki, S. P., 313
Paterson, R. J., 558
Patrick, C. J., 443
Patterson, C. P., 313
Patterson, M., 180
Paul, B. Y., 212
Paul, L., 13, 454
Paulhus, 165
Paulhus, D. L., 70
Paulhus, P. B., 482
Pearse, J., 528
Pearson, J. C., 348
Pearson, K., 339
Pederson, D. M., 263
Pelfrey, M., 426
Pelham, B. W., 171, 173
Pennebaker, J. W., 71, 72, 282, 556
Penner, L. A., 423
Pennington, J., 54
Penrod, S., 531
Penrod, S. D., 537
Pentice-Dunn, S., 322
Pentony, J. F., 268
Peplau, L. A., 320
Perdue, C. W., 286
Peres, Y., 191
Perlaman, D., 320
Perot, A., 192
Perrett, D. I., 281
Perrine, R. M., 556
Perry-Jenkins, M., 347
Perugini, M., 470
Peskoff, 558
Pessin, J., 487
Peterson, C., 550, 555
Peterson, L., 463, 464
Peterson, R. S., 516, 567, 569, 570, 571
Petkova, K. G., 129
Petrie, K. J., 556
Petruska, R., 402
Pettigrew, T. F., 222, 234, 235

Pettit, G. S., 305, 455
Petty, R., 141
Petty, R. E., 136, 137, 139
Petty, R. J., 130
Petzel, T. P., 322
Pezdek, K., 535
Pham, L. B., 177
Phelps, E. J., 197
Phillips, M., 555
Pickrell, J. E., 535
Pierce, C. A., 279, 286, 326, 327
Pierce, G. R., 555
Pierce-Otay, A., 292
Piercy, 287
Pietromonaco, P., 89
Pietromonaco, P. R., 312, 318, 346
Pihl, R. O., 462
Piliavin, J. A., 423
Pilkington, C., 315
Pillai, R., 517
Pillemer, J. T., 336
Pinker, S., 432
Pion, G. M., 195
Pittenger, J. B., 279
Pittman, T. S., 49, 99
Planalp, S., 315
Plant, E. A., 198
Platz, S. G., 534
Pleck, J. H., 191
Plesser-Storr, D., 154
Plog, A. E., 66
Plomin, R., 311
Podsakoff, P. M., 564, 565, 566
Poh, L. L., 224
Pomare, M., 237
Pomazal, R. J., 424
Pomeranz, 142
Pomeroy, W., 335
Pond, K., 322
Pool, G. J., 364, 370
Poole, D. A., 535
Pooley, F., 531
Pope, K. S., 535
Pope, M. K., 552
Porter, 334
Posokhova, S., 225, 226
Poteat, G. M., 320
Poulos, R. W., 411
Poulson, R. L., 543
Powel, M. C., 406
Powell, G. N., 243
Powell, M. C., 555
Prager, K. J., 191
Prasad, A., 290
Prasad, M. B., 290
Pratkanis, A. R., 192
Pratt, A., 199

Pratto, F., 195
Presta, S., 442
Price, J., 266
Price, J. M., 455
Priester, J. R., 136
Prin, K. S., 320
Prislin, R., 129
Prkachin, K., 555
Pruitt, D. G., 496, 502, 503, 504
Prusank, D. T., 329
Przybyla, D. P.J., 339, 425
Ptacek, J. T., 346, 556
Pugh, S. D., 564
Pullium, R. M., 422
Punzo, D., 168
Purvis, D., 370
Pusecker, P. A., 182
Pyszcynnski, T., 60, 173, 177

Quigley, B. M., 542
Quina, K., 183, 199
Quinn, D. M., 201, 202
Quintana, D., 320
Quitkin, F. M., 62

Rabin, B. S., 555
Rabkin, J. G., 558
Rachal, K. C., 345
Radecki-Bush, C., 346
Rainey, D., 286
Rammirez, J., 452, 453
Randall, D. M., 564
Rapson, R. L., 289, 305, 329
Ratner, R. K., 327, 526
Raty, H., 190
Raudenbush, B., 201
Raviv, A., 426
Rawles, R., 193
Rawlinson, D., 312
Ray, G. E., 320
Rea, M. S., 266
Read, P., 347
Read, S. J., 50
Reber, E., 177
Reed, D., 342
Reed, G. M., 452
Reed, K. S., 549
Reed, M. B.
Reeves, R. J., 262
Regan, P. C., 165, 330
Reichers, 559
Reid, A., 159
Reidel, S. L., 292
Reidhead, S., 180
Reimann, B. C., 569
Reis, H. T., 317
Reisman, J. M., 322
Reiss, A. J., 450

Reno, R. R., 361, 362
Rensberger, B., 331
Rentsch, J. R., 160, 161, 561, 562
Revicki, D. A., 549
Reynolds, S. L., 169
Rhodes, G., 282
Rhodewalt, F., 145
Rhodewalt, F. R., 175
Richard, D. C., 347
Richards, C., 66, 557
Richards, M. H., 347
Richardson, D., 31, 457
Richardson, D. R., 63, 447, 449, 456, 473
Richman, C. L., 418
Ridge, R. D., 422
Ridley, M., 432
Rieser-Danner, L. A., 279
Riess, M., 148
Riger, A. L., 320
Riggio, R. E., 286
Riley, A. H., 241
Rind, B., 378, 379
Risinger, R. T., 552
Riskind, J. H., 184
Rittenauer-Schatka, G., 87
Ritter, C., 549
Ritter, J. M., 280
Rittle, R., 489
Rivkin, I. D., 177
Robarchek, C. A., 442
Robarchek, C. J., 442
Robberson, N. R., 136
Robbins, M. A., 167
Roberts, A. R., 280, 342
Roberts, B. W., 169
Roberts, R. J., 556
Roberts, T.-A., 201, 202
Robich, F. D., 280
Robins, R. W., 58
Robinson, 62
Robinson, P. E., 556
Robinson, R., 500
Robinson, R. J., 501
Robinson, S. L., 466
Rochart, F., 387
Rockwell, S., 558
Rodin, J., 544
Rodin, M., 266
Roese, N. J., 31, 98
Rogers, C. R., 174
Rogers, M., 414
Rogers, R. J., 59, 60
Rogers, R. W., 31, 136, 452
Roggman, L. A., 279, 280, 281
Rohdewalt, 140
Roholes, W. S., 89
Roll, 558

Romanczyk, 534
Romer, D., 403
Romis, 131
Ropp, S. A., 222, 235, 236
Rosen, K. H., 328
Rosen, S., 432
Rosenbaum, M. E., 66, 290
Rosenberg, E. L., 11, 42
Rosenblatt, A., 173
Rosenblood, L. K., 270
Rosenfield, D., 216
Rosenfield, H. W., 42
Rosenhan, D. L., 413, 414
Rosenthal, A. M., 312, 397
Rosenthal, D., 338
Rosenthal, D. A., 338
Rosenthal, R., 72, 85
Rosenzweig, J. M., 191
Rosin, H., 338
Roskos-Ewoldsen, D. R., 118, 128, 130, 131
Rosnow, J., 30
Ross, D., 451
Ross, L., 84, 142, 143, 500, 509
Ross, L. D., 59
Ross, M., 59, 83, 94
Ross, S., 451
Rotenberg, K. J., 320, 322
Roth, D. L., 553
Roth, J. A., 450
Rothblum, E. D., 285Ä286
Rothenberg, K. J., 332
Rothgerber, H., 191, 232
Rothman, A. J., 87, 88, 547
Rotondo, A., 442
Rotton, J., 11, 22, 27, 460, 461
Rowatt, W. C., 68, 328
Rowe, P. M., 270
Royal, K. E., 293
Rozin, P., 40, 101, 266
Rubchinsky, K., 418, 430
Rubenstein, T. S., 312
Rubin, J. Z., 31
Rubin, M., 67
Ruble, D. N., 83, 314Ä342
Ruderman, M. N., 243
Rudman, L. A., 195
Rudolph, D. L., 553
Rusbult, C. E., 328, 345, 348, 349
Ruscher, J. B., 66
Rush, M. C., 565
Rushbult, C. E., 349
Rushton, J. P., 292, 432, 443
Russell, A., 308
Russell, D., 320
Russell, D. W., 132, 133, 319
Russell, F. J., 266
Russell, G. W., 418, 454, 473

Russell, H. A., 41
Russell, J. A., 41, 263, 337
Russell, M., 555
Russell, R. J.H., 432
Russell, S. M., 348
Rust, M. C., 237
Rutkowski, G. K., 403
Ryan, C. S., 211Ä212, 224, 226
Ryan, R. H., 534
Ryckman, R. M., 167, 296
Ryff, C. D., 168

Sadalla, E. K., 286, 404
Sadker, D., 85
Sadker, M., 85
Saeed, L., 277
Safir, M. P., 191
Sager, K., 418, 430
Salas, E., 193
Sales, S. M., 488
Salmela-Aro, K., 322
Salovey, P., 177, 213, 232, 268, 413, 414, 544, 547, 555
Salvarani, G., 416
Sam, O. J., 540
Sample, E. B. Jr., 555
Samuels, S. M., 509
San Giovannni, J. P., 71
Sanders, G. S., 489
Sanders, M. R., 347, 367
Sanitioso, R., 177
Sanna, L. J., 98, 182
Santee, R. T., 367
Sarason, B. R., 555
Sarason, I. G., 555
Sarwer, D. B., 332
Sattler, D. N., 418
Sauer, E. M., 316, 318
Savitsky, 98, 99
Schachter, D. L., 106
Schachter, J. A., 549
Schachter, S., 108, 262, 272, 284, 331
Schaller, M., 431
Schectner, C., 138
Scheier, M. F., 169, 322
Scher, A., 316
Scher, S. J., 148, 507
Scherer, K. R., 17, 111, 112
Schilling, E. A., 344
Schirmer, L., 316, 318
Schleifer, S. J., 549
Schlenker, B. R., 54, 148, 428
Schmidt, D. P., 331, 336
Schmidt, G., 335
Schmidt, N. B., 552
Schmitt, D. P., 335
Schnapp, W., 447
Schneider, B. H., 313, 472

Schneider, F. W., 403
Schnelder, R. W., 449
Schneller, G. R., 533
Schooler, J., 97
Schooler, J. W., 96, 528
Schreindorfer, L. S., 173
Schreurs, K. M.G., 325
Schroeder, M. A.B., 279
Schulman, 314
Schulz, R., 421
Schuster, E., 289, 339
Schutte, J. W., 542
Schwankovsky, L., 558
Schwartz, J. E., 343
Schwartz, N., 87, 106, 109, 458, 550
Schwarzer, R., 290, 549
Schwarzwald, J., 234
Schweitzer, K., 558
Sciacchitano, A. M., 173
Scott, K. P., 197
Scott, K. S., 511
Scratchley, L. S., 552
Scrimshaw, S. C.M., 556
Scruton, B. A., 396
Seal, D. W., 326
Searcy, E., 308, 426
Sears, D. O., 129, 215
Sears, R. R., 220, 221, 222, 443, 445, 448, 470
Sears, T., 330
Secrist, M. E., 320
Sederhold, H., 378
Sedikides, C., 110, 160, 163, 170, 177, 320, 380
Segal, M. M., 261
Segal, N. L., 124, 561
Segrin, C., 322
Seibel, C. A., 63
Sekerak, G. J., 489
Seligman, 60
Seligman, M. E.P., 60, 61, 550
Selye, H., 548
Semmelroth, J., 346
Seta, C. E., 105
Seta, J. J., 105
Setterlund, M. B., 167
Sexton, T. L., 182
Shackelford, T. K., 12, 13, 344
Shaffer, D. R., 325, 414
Shaller, M., 431
Shanab, M. E., 385
Shapiro, C., 313
Shapiro, D. L., 510
Shapiro, J. P., 263
Sharf, J., 218
Sharp, M. J., 68
Sharpe, D., 31
Sharpsteen, D. J., 346

Shavelson, R. J., 164
Shaver, F. M., 335
Shaver, J., 123
Shaver, P. R., 306, 315, 316, 317, 318, 319, 325, 328, 335
Shavitt, S., 138
Shaw, H., 200
Shaw, J. I., 406, 407, 430, 538
Shaw, L. L., 430
Shaw, W., 278
Shay, K. A., 553
Shaywitz, B. A., 202
Shaywitz, S. E., 202
Shechtman, Z., 175
Sheehan, E. P., 285, 286
Sheeran, P., 168
Sheets, V., 404
Sheldon, K. M., 555
Sheldon, W. H., 283
Shepard, H., 338
Shepher, I., 191
Shepherd, R., 555
Shepperd, J. A., 96
Sherak, B., 71
Sherif, M., 219, 505
Sherman, D., 227
Sherman, J. W., 64, 67
Sherman, M. D., 320
Sherman, M. F., 191
Sherman, S. J., 94, 230, 231
Sherman, S. R., 159
Sherman, S. S., 387
Sherman-Williams, B., 177, 227
Sherrod, D., 305
Shestowsky, D., 382
Shigctomi, C. C., 423
Shinn, M., 556
Shively, C. A., 549
Short, K. H., 264
Shotland, R. I., 63, 405
Showers, C., 178
Showers, C. J., 177
Shulman, S., 313
Sidanius, J., 195
Siegel, R., 378
Siers, B., 195
Sigall, H., 30
Sigelman, C. K., 280
Sigelman, L., 280
Signo, M., 473
Sillars, A. L., 344
Silva, P. A., 548
Silvera, D. H., 426
Silverstein, R., 169
Sim, D. L.H., 99Ä100
Simmel, G., 404
Simon, L., 144
Simon, L., 173

Simons, A., 87
Simpson, J. A., 180, 181, 327, 334, 348
Singelis, T. M., 171
Singer, R., 136
Singh, D., 276
Singh, R., 224, 291
Sirkin, M., 192
Sittes-Doe, S., 517
Sivacek, 129
Skarlicki, D. P., 466
Skohan, L. A., 452
Skolnick, P., 538
Skowronski, J. J., 160, 228, 531
Slapion-Foote, M. J., 332
Sleek, S., 525
Sloboda, 465
Slovik, L. F., 328
Slutske, W. S., 335
Smeaton, G., 192, 263, 291
Smith, A. J., 289
Smith, B. W., 549, 555
Smith, C. M., 370
Smith, D. E., 45
Smith, D. M., 266
Smith, E. R., 66, 165, 192, 193, 339
Smith, H. J., 506, 507, 526
Smith, K. D., 431
Smith, N. K., 119, 291
Smith, P. B., 11, 16, 358, 359, 361, 366, 367
Smith, P. K., 293, 317
Smith, R. E., 556
Smith, S. M., 473
Smith, S. S., 31
Smith, T. W., 552
Smith, V. I., 538
Smoll, F. L., 556
Sneddon, I., 335
Snell, W. E. Jr., 327
Snellman, L., 190
Sniffen, M. J., 540
Snyder, C. R., 367
Snyder, M., 128, 165, 179, 280, 305, 422, 424
Sobolew-Shubin, A., 558
Solomon, M. R., 280
Solomon, S., 60, 173
Sommers, S. R., 538
Sonenstein, F. L., 191
Sorenson, K., 404
Sorenson, K. A., 348
Southwick, L., 145, 146
Sowards, B. A., 179
Spafkin, J. M., 411
Spangler, W. D., 572
Specht, J. C., 428
Speer, L. K., 129

Spencer, S. J., 145, 152, 213, 228, 234
Spranca, M. D., 58
Sprecher, S., 276, 330, 336
Springer, C., 173
Srull, T. K., 80, 83, 211
Stack, A. D., 470
Stafford, L., 344
Stalling, R. B., 558
Stallworth, L. M., 195
Staneski, R. A., 263
Stangor, C., 83
Staples, S. L., 549
Statham, D. J., 335
Stech, 498
Steel, R. P., 561, 562
Steele, C. M., 144, 145, 146, 152,
    172, 213, 229, 403, 547
Steers, R., 570
Steffen, V. J., 198
Stein, C. H., 309
Stein, M., 549
Stein, R. I., 287
Stein, S. K., 556
Stein-Serossi, A., 294
Steinhauer, J., 342
Stepehens, M. A.P., 557
Stephan, W. G., 224
Stephenson, G. M., 527
Sterberg, R. J., 329
Stern, L. B., 537
Stern, M., 279
Sternberg, R. J., 305, 331, 332
Stevens, C. K., 68
Stevens, J., 455
Stevens, S. S., 283
Stewart, 517
Stewart, M. M., 62
Stewart, R. B., 312
Stice, E., 200
Stiles, W. B., 279, 538
Stillwell, A. M., 312, 330, 404
Stith, S. M., 328
Stocker, C. M., 310, 311
Stone, A. A., 150, 549, 556
Stone, C. A., 342
Stone, J., 149, 150, 151
Stoppard, J. M., 195
Story, A. L., 173
Stotland, E., 416, 431
Strack, F., 87
Stradling, S. G., 169
Strasser, G., 513, 517
Strathman, A. J., 136
Strau, M. K., 405
Strauman, T. J., 173
Stroessner, 106
Stroessner, S. J., 231
Stroh, L. K., 241

Stroufe, 314
Strube, M., 455
Strube, M. J., 263
Struthers, N. J., 10, 191
Stukas, A. A., 422
Subich, L. M., 193
Sugarman, D. B., 328
Sugimori, S., 516
Sullivan, L., 241
Suls, J., 30, 483, 558
Sumer, N., 557
Summers, R. J., 216
Sundar, S. S., 558
Sunnafrank, M., 290
Surman, M., 548
Susser, G. L., 46
Susser, K., 212
Swaim, G. W., 425
Swan, S., 64, 66
Swann, 169
Swann, W. B. Jr., 11, 60, 64, 72, 170,
    177, 294, 327, 328, 452
Swap, W. C., 260
Swart, L. A., 211
Swartz, M. S., 62
Swickert, R. J., 552
Swim, J. K., 214, 215
Szymanski, K., 491

Tafarodi, R. W., 173, 531
Tajfel, H., 224, 225
Takahashi, J. S., 293
Takata, T., 151
Tambor, E. S., 180Ä181
Tamborini, R., 461
Tan, L. S.C., 291
Tanford, S., 538
Tannen, D., 195
Tassinary, L. G., 13, 276
Taylor, 462, 513
Taylor, C. B., 182
Taylor, M. S., 182
Taylor, S., 199, 449, 454
Taylor, S. E., 170, 171, 173, 176, 177,
    452, 548
Taylor, S. P., 446, 447
Taylor. S., 450
Tellegen, A., 124
Tennan, H., 341, 549
Terborg Jr., 570
Terdal, S. K., 180Ä181
Terkildsen, N., 46, 47
Terman, L. M., 340, 341
Terry, D. J., 143
Terry, R. L., 68
Tesser, 345
Tesser, A., 12, 118, 124, 125, 145
Test, M. A., 411

Tetlock, P. E., 516
Tett, R. P., 562
Thelen, M. H., 320
Thomas, D. B., 280
Thompsen, C. J., 135
Thompson, C.
Thompson, D., 545
Thompson, D. E., 243
Thompson, J. K., 200, 282
Thompson, J. M., 346
Thompson, L., 406, 503, 504
Thompson, S. C., 558
Thompson, W. C., 414
Thornton, B., 191, 282, 283, 409,
    410
Thornton, J. C., 549
Tice, D. M., 312, 552
Tidwell, M.-C. O., 317
Tidwell, M. C., 316
Tierney, W. M., 549
Tindale, R. S., 370
Tjosvold, D., 495, 500, 505
Toch, H., 472
Tockerman, Y. R., 284
Todd, R. M., 430
Toi, M., 430
Tomaka, J., 554
Tomes, N., 544
Tomkins, S. S., 192
Tomlinson, T. M., 532
Tomlinson-Keasey, C., 343
Toobin, J., 540, 541
Tooley, V., 533
Torquati, J., 308
Townsend, J. M., 337
Tracey, J. B., 380
Trafton, J. G., 67
Trapnell, P. D., 70, 163
Traub, J., 530
Tremewan, T., 282
Triandis, H. C., 58
Trinke, S. J., 318
Triplett, N., 487
Trobst, K. K., 417
Trost, M. R., 282
Tucker, J. S., 343, 551
Tucker, P., 341
Tucker, W. B., 283
Tuckman, B. W., 182
Tuohy, A. P., 169
Turbin, M. S., 553
Turk, C. L., 430
Turner, C. W., 455
Turner, J. C., 224
Turner, M. E., 192
Turtle, J. W., 534
Tuten, J. T., 332
Tuttle, E. E., 99

Tversky, 86, 87
Twenge, 11
Twenge, J. M., 201, 202
Tykockinski, O. E., 99
Tyler, R. B., 227
Tyler, T. R., 506, 507, 526

U.S. Department of Justice, 230
U.S. Department of Labor, 242
Uba, L., 334
Uchino, B. N., 550, 556
Udry, J. R., 341
Uhlmann, C., 556
Ullman, 177
Unger, R. K., 185, 240, 423
Updegraff, K. A., 310, 311
Urbanski, L., 312
Urrows, S., 341, 549

Valdimarsdottir, H., 150, 549
Vallone, R., 143
Vallone, R. D., 331
Valone, K., 136
Van Buren, A.
Van den Bos, K., 510
van der Eijnden, R. J.J. M., 275, 328, 338
Van Dyne, L., 563, 564
Van Goozen, S., 442
Van Hook, E., 160
Van Horn, K. R., 330
van Knippenberg, A., 159, 370
Van Lange, P. A.M., 328, 497, 500
Van Overwalle, F., 49, 56
Van Vianen, A. E.M., 241
Van yne, L., LePine, J. A.
Vanbeselaere, N., 224
Vandello, U. A., 359, 365, 366
Vanman, E. J., 212
Vaughn, L. S., 280
Veith, D. J., 194
Verbrugge, K. M., 312
Verette, J., 328
Verette, J. A., 471
Vermunt, R., 510
Veroff, J., 344, 347
Vershure, B., 286
Vickers, R. R. Jr., 555
Vietor, N. A., 286
Vincent, J. E., 374
Vinokur, A., 515
Vobejda, B., 338, 343
Vogel, D. A., 187
Voigt, H., 406
Volpe, T., 222, 235, 236
von Hippel, W., 93
Vonk, R., 70, 294, 370

Vorauer, J. D., 327, 505
Voyer, D., 240
Voyer, S., 240
Vu, C., 173

Wachsmuth, J. O., 173
Wack, K. L., 489
Wade, C., 367
Wade, M. B., 194
Wagner, B. M., 549
Walbott, H. G., 111
Walker, S., 456
Wall, 306
Waller, N. G., 124
Walmsley, D. J., 404
Walsh, T., 200
Walster, G. W., 292, 331
Walter, 135
Walz, N. C., 279
Wan, C. K., 483, 558
Wan, K. C., 224
Wann, D. L., 234
Wanous, 559
Ward, A., 84, 500
Wardle, J., 202
Warne, P. A., 338
Waschull, S. B., 175
Washington Post, 338, 396
Waters, H. F., 450
Watson, C., 177
Watts, B., 418
Watts, D. L., 293
Wayment, H. A., 170, 171
Wayne, S. J., 68, 69, 70, 73
Weaver, C. N., 342
Weaver, S. L., 558
Weeks, J. L., 430
Wegener, D. T., 139, 382
Wegner, D. M., 102, 107, 331
Weidner, G., 331, 552
Weigold, M. F., 428
Weinberg, M. S., 335, 342
Weinberger, M., 549
Weiner, B., 53, 54, 55, 408, 471, 541
Weinstein, M., 201
Weinstock, M., 543
Weis, D. L., 337
Weismann, U., 330
Weiss, 242
Weiss, D. J., 542, 543
Weiss, M., 182
Weiss, W., 135
Weldon, E., 491, 493
Wells, G. L., 533, 534, 536
Wells, P. A.(Walls), 432
Werner, J., 515
Wesbay, L., 333
West, S. G., 221, 286, 425

Westcombe, A., 202
Westen, D., 346
Westenberg, M., 310
Wetzel, C. G., 45
Wexler, P., 336
Whaley, A. L., 228
Whaley, K. L., 312
Wheeler, D., 374
Wherry, M. B., 167
Whetstone-Dion, R., 195
Whiffen, V. E., 346
Whisenhunt, C. R., 175
Whisman, M. A., 549
Whitaker, D. J., 161
Whitbeck, L. B., 325
Whitcher S. J., 45
Whitcher-Alagna, S., 427
White, J. E., 219, 293
White, R. K., 568, 569
Whitehead, G. I. III, 286
Whiteside, H. D., 293
Whitley, B. E. Jr., 333
Whitley, T. W., 549
Whitmire, L., 183, 199
Whitney, G. A., 349
Wicker, A. W., 125
Wiebe, D. J., 549, 553
Wiederman, M. W., 331
Wiegand, A. W., 150, 151
Wiener, J., 313
Wiener, Y., 175
Wienhold, J., 286
Wiesenfeld, B. M., 508, 509, 510
Wilder, D. A., 235
Wilhelmy, R. A., 361
Wilke, H., 159
Wilke, H. A.M., 510
Willemsen, T. M., 241
Williams, 491
Williams, D. E., 191
Williams, G. P., 331
Williams, K. D., 491, 492, 493
Williams, K. D..l, 491, 493
Williams, K. J., 292, 483
Williams, L. L., 279
Williamson K., 491
Williamson, G. M., 421
Williamson, T. M., 526, 527
Willis, F. N., 45
Wills, T. A., 557
Wilson, D. W., 413
Wilson, J. P., 402
Wilson, M., 199, 464
Wilson, T. D., 96, 97, 107, 331
Windschitl, P. D., 533
Wingard, D., 343
Winnick, T. A., 330
Winquist, J. R., 517

Winslow, M. P., 150, 151
Winstead, B. A., 315, 557
Wiseman, H., 320
Wiseman, R. L., 560
Witte, E., 481
Woike, B. A., 43
Wolf, N., 195
Wolf, P. P., 218
Wolf, S., 533
Wolfe, B. M., 447
Wolfe, C. T., 228
Wolfe, R.N, 381
Wolfe, T., 403
Wolff, P. L., 414
Wolsic, B., 279
Wong, F. Y., 451
Wood, J. V., 173
Wood, W., 135, 141, 191, 202, 364, 370, 451
Woody, 242
Worsham, N., 553, 554
Worth, L. T., 238, 239
Worth, T. L., 46
Worthington, E. L., Jr., 345
Wortman, C. B., 555, 556
Wosinska, W., 195
Wotman, S. R., 330, 404
Woycke, J., 572
Wright, D. M., 325, 342

Wright, P. H., 270
Wright, R., 173, 198
Wright, S. C., 222, 235, 236
Wu, C.-H., 280
Wu, S., 328
Wuensch, K. L., 542, 543
Wyer, M. M.W., 40
Wyer, N. A., 211
Wyer, R. S. Jr., 64, 66, 80, 83, 211
Wyssmann, J., 316, 318

Yabya, K. A., 385
Yankeelov, P. A., 557
Yates, S., 426
Ybema, J. F., 275
Yingling, S., 338
Yoshida, T., 151
Yoshikawa, S., 281
Youille, J. C., 535
Young, M. J., 107
Young, R. C., 322
Yovetich, N. A., 345
Yu, W., 342
Yukl, G., 380, 382, 558, 566
Yurko, K. H., 550

Zaccaro, S. J., 566
Zachariah, R., 556

Zajonc, R. B., 213, 258, 266, 267, 488, 489
Zalenski, C. M., 201
Zammichieli, M. E., 191
Zanakos, S., 102
Zanna, M. P., 145, 515, 547
Zarate, M. A., 66
Zdanick, B., 370, 371
Zebrowitz, L. A., 38, 60, 71, 72, 73, 276, 286
Zebrowitz-McArthur, L., 286
Zeitz, G., 5, 61
Zellner, D. A., 201
Zembrodt, I. M., 348, 349
Zhermer, N., 225, 226
Zierk, K. L., 277
Ziller, R. C., 160
Zillman, D., 109, 443, 452, 453, 461, 470, 472, 558
Zillmann, D., 452, 453
Zimbardo, P. G., 42
Zoglin, R., 288
Zubek, 557
Zuber, J. A., 515
Zucker, G. S., 54, 55, 541
Zuckerman, A., 552
Zuckerman, M., 179, 286
Zuroff, D. C., 270
Zusne, L., 101

Subject Index

Abortion, 337
Abstractions, mental, 66–67
Academia, gender discrimination in, 194–195
Accuracy
  motivation, 138
  in scientific methods, 7, 7*f*
Acquaintances, 254–255
  becoming. *See* Affiliation
  close, 270
  in countering prejudice, 234–237, 236*f*
  moving toward friendships, 288–297, 290*f*, 294*f*–296*f*
  superficial, 270
Actions, *vs.* attitudes, 126–127, 127*f*
Actor-observer effect, 59, 61, 75
Additive tasks, 491
Adolescence, parent-offspring relationship and, 308, 309*f*
Adult relationships, attachment style and, 316–319, 317*f*
Adversarial approach, 526
Advertising
  image *vs.* quality in, 180, 181*f*
  nontraditional gender roles in, 197, 198*f*
Affect
  associated effect of, 263
  definition of, 81, 105, 114, 263
  influence
    on cognition, 105–108, 105*f*, 107*f*, 108*f*, 109–110
    of cognition on, 108–109
  intensity of, 263
  interpersonal attraction and, 257
  multiple sources of, 266–267
  negative, effect on cognition, 106
  nonconscious, 267
  positive
    childhood friends and, 313
    cognitive effects, 106
    creating, in coping with stress, 555
    definition of, 298
Affect-centered model of attraction, 296–297, 296*f*
Affect infusion model (AIM), 109–110, 110*f*, 379
Affective state
  attraction and, 255, 263–269, 264*f*, 265*f*, 267*f*, 269*f*
  direct effects of, 263–264, 264*f*, 265*f*

  in general affective aggression model, 444
  indirect effects of, 264–266, 265*f*
  manipulation, vulnerability to, 267–268, 267*f*, 269*f*
  role of, 114
  sexual arousal and, 453
Affiliation
  beneficial effects of, 273, 273*f*
  encouraging, 298–299
  motivation, 255
  need for
    definition of, 270
    individual differences in, 270–271, 271*t*
    situational determinants of, 271–273, 273*f*
  reciprocal positive evaluations and, 294–296, 295*f*
Affirmative action programs
  in reducing prejudice, 239
  reverse discrimination and, 217–218, 219*f*
African Americans
  discrimination of, 215
  reverse discrimination of, 217–218, 218*f*, 219*f*
African-Americans
  as defendants, 540–542, 541*f*
Agape (selfless love), 332, 332*t*
Age, physical appearance and, 286
Aggression
  causes of, 475
  childhood, 548
  child maltreatment and, 463–465, 464*f*
  covert *vs.* overt, 466
  culture and, 473
  definition of, 440
  direct, 456
  displaced, 221
  forms of, 442
  frustration and, 221–222, 222*f*
  gender differences in, 456–457, 473
  hostile, 455
  human, study technique for, 446–447, 447*f*
  human cost of, 441*f*
  indirect, 456, 466
  instrumental, 455
  personal factors in, 454–458, 475

Aggression *(continued)*
  prevention/control of, 468–474, 469*f*, 471*f*
  situational factors in, 475
    alcohol, 461–463, 461*f*, 462*f*
    temperature, 458–460, 459*f*, 461*f*
  social factors in, 447–454, 448*f*, 450*f*, 453*f*, 475
  theoretical perspectives
    drive theories, 443
    instinct theories, 441–443, 442*f*
    modern theories, 443–445, 444*f*
  in workplace, 449, 465–468, 465*f*, 467*f*
Aggression machine, 446–447, 447*f*, 454
Agreeableness, interpersonal conflict and, 345
AIDS patients
  helping, volunteering for, 422, 422*t*
  mortality rates, 338
AIM (affect infusion model), 109–110, 110*f*, 379
Albany Measure of Attachment Style (AMAS), 318
Albright, Madeleine, gender discrimination in workplace,
    193–194, 194*f*
Alcohol
  aggression and, 461–463, 461*f*, 462*f*
  stress relief and, 555
Alcohol myopia, 547
Allport, Floyd H., 486*f*
Altruism, 414–415, 564
Altruistic personality
  characteristics of, 424*f*
  definition of, 418–419, 428
  volunteerism and, 423
AMAS (Albany Measure of Attachment Style), 318
Androgyny (androgynous)
  definition of, 189–190, 203
  secure attachment style and, 316
  vs. gender-typed behavior, 191–192
Apologies, 470–472, 471*f*, 474
Appearance
  anxiety, 280
  comparing with others, 205
  men's awareness of, 205
  realism and, 204
  women and, 201–202
Appraisals, in general affective aggression model, 444
Arousal
  cognitive dissonance and, 146
  in general affective aggression model, 444
  heightened, aggression and, 452, 453*f*
  other persons as source of, 488–489, 488*f*
  sexual, aggression and, 452–454
Asch, Solomon, 358, 358*f*
Aschematics, 164
Asian Americans, interracial dating among, 293–294, 294*f*
Asian culture, correspondence bias and, 58–59
Assimilation effect, 171
Attachment style
  adult behavior and, 318–319
  childhood friends and, 313, 314*f*
  effect on adult relationships, 316–319, 317*f*

interpersonal relationships and, 306–307, 307*f*, 315,
    323
  jealousy and, 346–347
Attention, 83
Attitude. *See also specific attitudes*
  accessibility of, 129
  in attraction, 255–257, 256*f*, 257*f*
  changing, 119, 120*f*. *See also* Persuasion
    dissonance and, 146–149, 147*f*–149*f*
    resistance to, 140–143, 142*f*, 153–154
  definition of, 118–120, 133
  dissimilar, influence on attraction, 291–292
  formation, 120
    classical conditioning and, 121–122, 121*f*
    genetic factors in, 124–125, 124*f*
    social comparison and, 123
    social learning and, 120–121
  functions, 138–139
  importance of, 129
  influence on behavior, 125–134, 126*f*, 127*f*, 130*f*, 132*f*
    gap between, 133–134, 134*f*
    immediate reactions, 131–132
    reasoned thought and, 131
    riskiness and, 132–133, 132*f*
    situational constraints and, 127–128
    vested interest and, 129–130, 130*f*
  intensity of, 129
  knowledge of, 129
  negative, prejudice and, 212–213, 212*f*
  origin of, 128
  polarization, 141–143, 142*f*
  positive, prejudice and, 212–213, 212*f*
  as schemas, 211
  similar. *See* Attitude similarity
  specificity, 130
  strength of, 129–130, 130*f*
  vs. actions, 126–127, 127*f*
Attitude similarity
  definition of, 288
  as determinant of attraction, 289, 290*f*
  influence on attraction, 291–292
  proportion of similar attitudes, 289–290
  repulsion hypothesis and, 290–291
Attitude-to-behavior process model, 131–132
Attorneys
  testosterone levels of, 18, 18*f*
  trial outcome and, 537–538, 537*f*, 544
  use of nonverbal cues to influence jury, 47–49, 48*f*
Attraction
  affect-centered model of, 296–297, 296*f*
  attitude similarity and, 289, 290*f*
  attitudes in, 255–257, 256*f*, 257*f*
  encouraging, 298–299
  matching hypothesis and, 292–293
  physical attractiveness and, 275–276
  prosocial behavior and, 406–407
  repeated unplanned contacts and, 257–263, 258*f*, 259*f*,
    261*f*

Attribute-driven processing, 238
Attribution
definition of, 38, 49–50, 49f, 57
depression and, 62–63, 62f, 64
error sources, 57–61, 61f
faulty, in conflict development, 500
minimizing effect of, 75
rape and, 63, 64
theories
applications of, 62–64, 62f, 64
augmenting principle, 56–57
discounting principle, 55–56, 56f
Kelley's, 51–55, 53f
noncommon effects, 50–51
ultimate error in, 224
of victim responsibility, 407–410, 408f, 410f
Attributional bias, hostile, 455–456
Audience presence, performance and, 485–490,
485f–488f, 490f
Authority, compliance and, 373
Authority figures
destructive obedience and, 385, 386f
resisting influence of, 387
Autocratic leadership style, 568–569
Automatic priming, 89
Availability heuristic
bases for, 86–87, 88f
definition of, 8–9
priming and, 88–89
Avoidant coping, 555

"Baby-faced" persons, 71
Baby talk, in romantic relationship, 328, 329t
Balance theory, 291–292
Bargaining, 502–505, 504f, 507
Base rates, 86
Behavior. See also specific types of behavior
adult, attachment and, 318–319
gender-role, 191–193
influence
on attitudes, 144–152, 145f, 147f–149f, 151f, 152f
of attitudes on, 125–134, 126f, 127f, 130f, 132f
monitoring, on basis of internal vs. external factors,
179–181, 180f, 181f
negative vs. positive, 70
of others, social behavior/thought and, 10–11, 10f
sexual, changes in, 334–336, 335f
slimy vs. nonslimy, 70, 70f
type A, 454–455, 457, 501, 552
type B, 454–455, 457, 501, 552
Behavioral intentions, 131
Behavioral willingness, 132
Belief in a just world, 63, 419
Bem Sex-Role Inventory (BSRI), 190–191, 190t
Bias
control, by judge during trial, 538–540, 539f
leniency, 543
self-serving. See Self-serving bias

Biased assimilation, 138, 141–143, 142f
Biological factors
in aggression, 441–443, 442f
in empathy, 416, 416f
potential role of, 17–18, 18f
social behavior/thought and, 12–13, 12f
Blacks. See African Americans
Blank-lineup control, 536–537, 536t
Body image, women and, 201, 201f
Body language
in courtroom, 47–49, 48f
as nonverbal communication, 42–44, 44f
Body position, in nonverbal communication, 43, 44f
Body weight
importance of, 204–205
perceived physical attractiveness and, 282–286, 284f,
285t
women and, 201
Books
children's, gender roles in, 196, 196f
nontraditional gender roles in, 197
Boredom, in marriage, 347
Bridging tactic, 505t
Broadening the pie tactic, 505t
BSRI (Bem Sex-Role Inventory), 190–191, 190t
Businesslike style, of police interrogation, 527, 527f
Buss, Arnold, 446–447, 446f
Bystander
effect, 398, 399f
responsive, suggestions for, 435–436

Capital punishment, 468, 543
Caregiver-based variables, in child maltreatment, 463–464
Catastrophizing, 551
Categorical processing, 163
Category-driven processing, 238
Catharsis hypothesis, 470, 471f, 474
Causal attributions
dimensions of, 53–54, 55f
Kelley's theory of, 51–53, 53f
Causation, correlation and, 21–22, 22f, 33–34
CEM (collective effort model), 491–492, 494
Central route (systematic processing), 136, 515
Central traits, 65–66
CEST (cognitive-experiential self-theory), 90
Charismatic leaders, 570–573, 572f
Child-based variables, in child maltreatment, 464
Childhood, development of loneliness in, 320–321, 322f
Childhood friends, 312–315, 313f, 314f
Child maltreatment, 463–465, 464f, 468
Children's stories, gender roles in, 196, 196f
Civic virtue, 564
Classical conditioning, attitude formation and, 121–122,
121f
Classroom seating assignments, attraction and, 260–262,
261f
Client-centered therapy, 174
Clinical trials, 358

Close friendship. *See* Friendship, close
Clothing, physical appearance and, 286
Cognition
    aggression and, 452
    deficits, overcoming in dealing with aggression, 472
    definition of, 105
    in general affective aggression model, 444
    influence
        on affect, 108–109, 112
        of affect on, 105–108, 105*f*, 107*f*, 108*f*
    need for, stereotypical information and, 228
    social. *See* Social cognition
    in social behavior/thought, 11
Cognitive clarity, 272
Cognitive dissonance, 152
    attitude change and, 146–149, 147*f*–149*f*
    for beneficial behavior change, 149–150, 149*f*, 151*f*
    cultural factors in, 151–152, 152*f*
    definition of, 144
    job satisfaction and, 560
    less-leads-to-more effect and, 147–149, 148*f*
    nature of, 145–146
    reducing, 144–145
        direct approaches, 144
        indirect approaches, 144–145, 145*f*
Cognitive-experiential self-theory (CEST), 90
Cognitive therapy
    for aggression, 470–472
    for loneliness, 322–323
Cognitive tuning model, 46, 49
Cohabitation, 338–339
Cohesiveness
    conformity and, 360
    definition of, 360, 366, 484
    groupthink and, 516
Cold stare, 42
Collective effort model (CEM), 491–492, 494
Collective groupings, 165
Collective identity, 165
Collectivism, *vs.* individualism, 165–166, 166*f*
Collectivistic cultures, 58, 491
Collusive style, of police interrogation, 527, 527*f*
Commissions, 503
Commitment, compliance and, 373
Commitment stories, generativity and, 423
Common in-group identity model, 237, 238*f*
Common-value issues, 503
Communal behavior, 344
Communication, faulty, in conflict development, 500
Compartmentalized self-organization, 177–178
Compassionate love, 332, 332*t*, 334
Competitive orientation, cooperation and, 497
Complaining, 378, 382, 389
Compliance
    definition of, 357
    false confessions and, 529
    gaining, tactics for, 377, 382, 388–389
        commitment/consistency based, 373–374
        complaining, 378

friendship/liking based, 373
        ingratiation based, 378–380, 380*f*
        reciprocity based, 374–376, 375*f*
        scarcity based, 376–377, 377*f*
    principles of, 372–373
Compliance professionals, 372
Concurrence seeking, 516
Conditioning
    classical, 121–122, 121*f*
    instrumental, 122
    subliminal, 122
Confabulation, 529
Confessions
    false, eliciting from innocent persons, 528–529, 530*f*
    vs. evidence in police interrogation, 527, 527*f*
Confidence, of females, 242
Confirmation bias, 8
Conflict
    across ethnic and cultural boundaries, 506–507
    causes of, 500–502, 502*f*
    definition of, 494, 507
    elements in, 499–500
    resolution, in marriage, 344–345, 347–348
    resolution techniques, 502–507, 504*f*, 505*t*
Conformity
    bases of, 364–367, 366*f*
    cohesiveness and, 360
    culture and, 367–368, 368*f*
    definition of, 360, 372
    factors affecting, 360–363, 362*f*, 363*f*
    group size and, 360–361
    justifying, 365–366
    measuring, 365, 366*f*
    minority influence and, 369–372, 371*f*
    social norms and, 357–358, 357*f*
Conformity and, 356–357
Confounding, of variables, 25–26, 25*f*
Confrontation, *vs.* cooperation in police interrogation, 527, 527*f*
Conscientiousness, 564
Consensual validation, 292, 297
Consensus, 53
Consistency
    compliance and, 373
    definition of, 53
Construals, 14
Consummate love, 352
Contact hypothesis, 234–235
Contagion, law of, 101
Contrast effect, 282–283, 283*f*
Control, 548
Controllable causes, attribution and, 53–54
Cooperation
    definition of, 494, 499
    factors influencing, 496–499, 498*f*
    failure of, 494, 495*f*
    nature of, 495–496, 496*f*
    vs. confrontation in police interrogation, 527, 527*f*

Coping
   definition of, 548
   with stress, 552–553
      creating positive affect, 555
      during illness/medical treatment, 557–558, 557f
      increased physical fitness and, 553
      social support for, 555–557
      strategies for, 553–554, 554f
Copycat crimes, 451
Core self, 169
Correlational method
   causation and, 21–22, 22f, 33–34
   definition of, 20
Correspondence bias, 57–58, 61, 75
Correspondent inference, 57
Correspondent inference theory, 50, 51f
Co-schematics, 164
Cost cutting tactic, 505t
Counseling style, of police interrogation, 527, 527f
Counterarguments, 141
Counterfactual thinking
   definition of, 97, 113
   impact of, 81
   inaction inertia and, 99
   positive and negative effects of, 98–100, 100f
   stress and, 555
   upward, 98–99
Courtesy, 564
Creativity
   affect and, 112
   mood and, 106–107
Crime
   of passion, 453–454
   perceptions, media effects on, 529–531
   wrongdoer, media coverage effect on guilt/innocence
      perceptions, 531–532, 532f
Cross-racial facial identification, 232
Cues, nonverbal, 39
Culture
   aggressive intentions and, 473
   appraisal of emotions and, 111–112, 111f
   cognitive dissonance and, 151–152, 152f
   conformity and, 367–368, 368f
   cross-cultural conflicts, 506–507
   differences
      in familial obligations, 309–310, 310f
      in self-serving bias, 60–61, 61f
   of honor, 362–363, 363f
   social behavior/thought and, 11

Darley, John, 397, 398f
Date rape, 63
Dating
   behavior, 327–328, 327f
   interracial, among Asian Americans, 293–294, 294f
   physical abuse and, 328
Deadline technique, 376–377, 377f
Death, early predictors of, 551
Death penalty, 468, 543

Death wish (thanatos), 441
Debriefing, 31, 31f, 32
Deception, 30–32, 31f
Decision/commitment, in triangular model of love, 333,
   333f
Decision making
   definition of, 512
   process of, 512–514
   social behavior/thought and, 14
Defendant
   appearance of, 542
   characteristics, influence on verdict, 540–542, 541f
   gender, status and behavior of, 542
   race of, 540–542, 541f
Defense mechanisms, victim blame and, 409–410, 410f
Defensive motivation, 138
Democratic leadership style, 568–569
Dependent variable, 23
Depersonalized attraction, 484
Depression, attribution and, 62–63, 62f, 64
Descriptive norms, 361–362, 362f
Desensitization
   definition of, 184
   effects, 451
Destructive criticism, in conflict development, 500
Destructive obedience, authority figures and,
   385, 386f
Diffusion of responsibility, 397–398, 491
Directive-permissive leaders, 569
Discounting principle, 55–56, 56f, 57
Discrimination
   blatant, 214, 215f
   definition of, 214, 218
   against females, 239, 241–244, 243f
   reverse, 217–218, 218f, 219f
   subtle, 214–216, 216f, 241–244, 243f
   vs. prejudice, 210, 211
Disease-prone personality, 551, 552t
Dismissing attachment style, 317f, 318
Disobedient models, 387
Displaced aggression, 472
Dispositional causes (internal)
   attribution and, 52, 53
   overestimating role of, 57–58
Dissonance. See Cognitive dissonance
Dissonance theory, 144
Distinctiveness, 53
Distinctiveness-based interpretation, of illusory
      correlations, 230–231
Distraction-conflict theory, 489–490, 490f
Distributive justice, 508–509, 508f, 512
Divorce, 342–343
Dominant responses, 488
Dominant style, of police interrogation, 527, 527f
Door-in-the-face technique, 374–375, 389
Dorian Gray effect, 72
Double-blind procedure, 26
Dress codes, vs. personal freedom, 368–369, 369f
Drive, leaders and, 566

Drive theories
  of aggression, 443, 444
  of social facilitation, 488–489, 488*f*, 490
Drug use, stress relief and, 555

Eating preferences, interpersonal judgments and, 287
Economic conditions, racial violence and, 221–222, 222*f*
Ectomorphs, 283, 284
Education, possible selves and, 167–168
Egocentrism, low, altruistic personality and, 419
Egoism, 415
Ego-threat, aggression and, 456
Elaboration likelihood model (ELM), 136–137
Elaborative processing, 162–163
ELM (elaboration likelihood model), 136–137
Emergency
  event, noticing, 401
  interpretation of, 401–403
  response, 395–398, 396*f*–398*f*, 412
    bystander effect and, 398, 399*f*
    decision process for, 398, 400*f*, 401–406, 402*f*, 405*f*
    diffusion of responsibility and, 397–398
    final decision, 405–406
    knowledge for, 404–405, 405*f*
    pluralistic ignorance and, 403
    time pressure and, 401, 402*f*
Emergent group norms, 516
Emotional arousal, love and, 351
Emotional clarity, 272
Emotional infidelity, 13
Emotional state, of bystander, helping and, 413–414, 413*f*
Emotions
  appraisal of, culture and, 111–112, 111*f*
  negative, effect on prosocial behavior, 414, 415*f*
  positive
    effects of, 263
    prosocial behavior and, 413–414, 413*f*, 415*f*
Empathetic joy hypothesis, 429*f*, 431–432, 432*f*, 433
Empathy
  affective component, 415, 416
  altruistic personality and, 419
  avoidance, 431
  biological factors in, 416, 416*f*
  cognitive component, 415
  definition of, 415, 428
  development of, 416–418
  individual differences in, 417, 417*f*
Empathy-altruism hypothesis, 429*f*, 430–431, 433
Encoding, 83
Endogenous opioids, 182
Endomorphs, 283, 284
Entrepreneurs, counterfactual thinking and, 98
Environment, social behavior/thought and, 11
Eros. *See* Passionate love
Estrogen, 199–200
Ethnic cleansing, 210, 211*f*
Ethnic diversity, multicultural perspective and, 15–17, 16*f*, 18
Ethnic groups, conflicts between, 506–507

Ethnicity, self-perceptions and, 202
Evaluation apprehension, 489
Event schema, 82
Evidence, *vs.* confession in police interrogation, 527, 527*f*
Evolutionary social psychology, 12–13
Excitation transfer theory, 452, 453*f*
Executives, female, glass ceiling and, 242–244, 244*f*
Exemplars, 66
Exercise, stress and, 553
Expectancies, gender and, 193
Expectancy-valence theory, 491–492
Experimentation (experimental method)
  definition of, 23, 27
  nature of, 23–24, 24*f*
  requirements for, 24–26, 25*f*
Experimenter effects, 26
Explanation, 23
Explicit motivation, 270
Extended contact hypothesis, 235–236, 236*f*, 237
External causes, attribution and, 52
External validity, 26
Eye contact, 42
Eyewitness. *See* Witness

Facial expression
  influence of, 39–40, 45, 49
  interpreting, 41–42, 41*f*
  range of, 41, 41*f*
  social thought and, 45–47, 47*f*
Failure, in collectivist *vs.* individualistic cultures, 165–166, 166*f*
Fairness
  judgments of, 507–508
  perceived, in groups, 507–512, 508*f*, 509*f*, 511*f*
Falling in love, 330–331
False consensus effect, 291
Familicide, 464–465, 468
Fantasy, in perspective taking, 416
Fearful-avoidant attachment style
  marital satisfaction and, 346
  nature of, 317, 317*f*, 318–319
Feelings
  negative, attraction and, 263–264, 264*f*
  positive. *See* Positive feelings
  of self-efficacy, 183–185, 184*f*
  sympathetic, 416
Females. *See* Women
Fertility, physical attractiveness and, 277
Festinger, Leon, 274, 274*f*
Fighting instinct, 441, 442*f*
First-shift rule, 513
Fitness, stress and, 553
Fixed-sum error, 504–505
Flattery, 68–69, 294–295, 373
Foot-in-the-door technique, 374, 389
Forced compliance, 146–147, 147*f*
Forensic psychology
  definition of, 525
  pretrial, 526–533, 526*f*, 527*f*, 530*f*, 531*f*

Forewarning, 141, 143
Framing, charismatic leaders and, 572
Franklin, Benjamin, 256–257, 257f
Freud, Sigmund, 441
Friendship
    childhood, 312–315, 313f, 314f
    close
        in childhood, 313–314, 314f
        definition of, 312, 315
        development in adolescence/adulthood, 315
        vs. romantic relationship, 325–328, 326f, 327f
    compliance and, 373
    formation
        attitude similarity and, 289, 290f
        encouraging, 298–299
        matching hypothesis and, 292–293
        reciprocal positive evaluations and, 294–296, 295f
    intergroup, in countering prejudice, 234–237, 236f, 249
Friendship love (storge), 332, 332t
Frustration, aggression and, 222f, 2211–222
Frustration-aggression hypothesis, 443, 448–449, 448f, 454
Fundamental attribution error, 57

GAAM (general affective aggression model), 443–445, 444f
Game-playing love (ludus), 332, 332t
Gazing, 42
Gender
    consistency, 186–187
    definition of, 185, 203
    differences, 17
        in aggression, 456–457
        in aggressive intentions, 473
        in empathy, 417
        origin of, 185–186, 186f
        in receiving help, 423–425, 425f
        in self-perception, 199, 200–202
        sex differences and, 197–199
        in sociosexuality, 335–336, 336f
    discrimination
        in academia, 194–195
        in workplace, 193–194, 194f
    stereotypes, 190–191, 190t
    toys and, 186, 187f
Gender identity
    basis of, 187–188, 189f
    definition of, 186, 203
    development of, 186–187, 187f
Gender-role behavior, 191–193
Gender-role identification, 190–191, 190t, 203
Gender roles
    definition of, 203
    effects on behavior, 192–193
    traditional, 195–197, 196f, 203
Gender schema theory, 188
Gender stereotypes
    encouraging signs of progress beyond, 197, 198f
    types of, 240–241, 240f

General affective aggression model (GAAM), 443–445, 444f
Generativity, 423
Genetic determinism model, 429f, 432–433
Genetic factors
    in attitude formation, 124–125, 124f
    in job satisfaction, 561
Genital herpes, 338
Georgians, Russian reactions to, 225–226, 225f
Gestalt psychologists, 65
Gestalt psychology, 65
Gestures, in nonverbal communication, 43–44, 44f
Glass ceiling, 242–244, 244f
God, response to, attachment style and, 319
Gratz, Jennifer, 217–218
Great person theory, 566, 567f, 573
Group polarization, 514–515, 515f, 517
Groups. See Social groups
Group size, conformity and, 360–361
Groupthink, 516, 517

Harm avoidance, 548
Hate, prejudicial. See Prejudice
Health, physical attractiveness and, 277
Health information
    accepting, rejecting and acting on, 547–548
    using, 545–546, 546f
Health psychology
    definition of, 544
    processing health-related information, 544–548, 545f, 546f
Health-related attitudes
    gap with overt behavior, 133–134, 134f
    hypocrisy and, 149–150, 149f, 151f
Health-related behavior, hypocrisy and, 149–150, 149f, 151f
Health-related information, processing, 544–548, 545f, 546f
Helper's high, 432
Help (helping)
    asking for, 425–426
    as function of bystander's emotional state, 413–414, 413f
    receiving
        gender and, 423–425, 425f
        reactions to, 426–427, 427t
    situational factors in, 406–412, 407f, 408f, 410f, 411f
Heroism, 420, 421f
Heterosexuals, partner preferences, 277–278, 278f
Heuristic cue, in affect infusion model, 109
Heuristic information processing, 14, 46
Heuristic processing, 136, 137f, 140
Heuristics
    availability, 86–87, 88f
    definition of, 80, 86
    representativeness, 86, 89
Hidden profile, 517
Hispanic-American families, attitudes/interactions of, 309–310, 310f

HIV infection, 338
Homosexuals
    preference for younger male partners, 277
    prosocial behavior and, 406–407, 407f
Hopelessness, suicide and, 322
Hostile aggression, 455
Hostile attributional bias, 455–456, 457
Hostility, expressions, in workplace, 466
Hoveland, Carl, 221, 221f
Hyperfemininity, 192
Hypermasculinity, 192
Hypocrisy, 149–150, 149f, 151f, 152
Hypothesis, 21, 28

Identification, gender-role, 190–191, 190t
Illness
    coping with stress of, 557–558, 557f
    stress and, 548–551, 550f
Illusion of out-group homogeneity, 231–232
Illusory correlations, 230–231, 232
Implicit motivation, 270
Impression
    first, 64, 64f
    formation
        accuracy of, 71–74, 73f
        central and peripheral traits in, 65–66
        cognitive approach, 66–68, 67f
        definition of, 38
    management
        charismatic leaders and, 572
        definition of, 38–39, 68, 71
        factors in, 68–71, 69f, 70f
        pitfalls, 70, 70f
        uncontrollable factors in, 70–71
    mood and, 107–108, 108f
    motivation, 138
Inaction inertia, 99
Incompatibility error, 504
Incompatible response technique, 472–473
Independent variable, 23, 25, 25f
Individual differences, in aggression development, 444
Individualism, vs. collectivism, 165–166, 166f
Individualistic cultures, 58
Individualistic orientation, cooperation and, 497
Individuation, 367–368, 368f
Induced compliance, 146–147, 147f, 152
Industrial/organizational psychologists, 559
Infantcide, 457–458
Infants, response to attractive vs. unattractive adults,
    279–280, 279f
Inferences, social behavior/thought and, 11
Inferential prisons, stereotypes as, 227–228, 228f
Inferential statistics, 27, 29
Information
    affective association and, 268, 269f
    amount, availability heuristic and, 87
    confirmation bias and, 8
    emotion-provoking, inability to ignore, 107–108, 108f

health-related, processing of, 544–548, 545f, 546f
inconsistent
    dealing with, 93–94
    encoding, 83
overload, 80, 86, 89
processing
    heuristic, 14, 46
    mood and, 106, 107
    rational vs. intuitive, 90–92, 91f, 92f
    systematic, 14, 46
sharing with groups, difficulties with, 516–517
Informational social influence, 365, 366f, 367, 513–514
Informed consent, 31, 32
Ingratiation
    definition of, 373, 389
    in gaining compliance, 378–380, 380f
In-group
    becoming out-group, 225–226, 225f
    definition of, 223–224
    differentiation, 232
Injunctive norms, 361–362f
Injustice, reactions to, 510–512, 511f
Input variables, in general affective aggression model,
    443–444, 444f, 447–454, 448f, 450f, 453f
Inquisitorial approach, 526
Insecure-ambivalent attachment style, 306–307, 307f,
    317f, 318
Insecure-avoidant attachment style, 306–307, 307f
Insight, self-focusing and, 177
Instinct theories, 441–443, 442f, 445
Instrumental aggression, 455
Instrumental conditioning, 122
Instrumentality, 492
Integrative agreements, 504, 505t
Intellective task, 513
Intent, evil, perceiving in others, 455–456
Intentions, behavioral, 131
Interdependence
    definition of, 305, 315
    of groups, 481
Internal causes (dispositional)
    attribution and, 52, 53
    overestimating role of, 57–58
Internalization, 529
Internal locus of control, altruistic personality and, 419
Interpersonal attraction, 255–257, 256f, 257f, 269
Interpersonal behavior
    gender differences in, 198–199, 200t
    self-efficacy and, 182–183
Interpersonal justice, 509–510, 512
Interpersonal relationships, 304–305
    among siblings, 310–312, 311f
    social self and, 165
Interpersonal trust, 306, 418
Interracial dating, among Asian Americans,
    293–294, 294f
Intimacy, in triangular model of love, 333, 333f
Intuitive processing, 90–92, 91f, 92f

Japan, success *vs.* failure in, 165–166, 166*f*
Jealousy
    attachment style and, 346–347
    sexual, 454
Jews, stereotypes of, 213
Job satisfaction
    definition of, 559–560, 573
    factors affecting, 560–562, 560*f*
    job involvement and, 561–562, 562*f*
    task performance and, 562–563, 563*f*
Judge, role in trial outcome, 538–540, 539*f*
Judgments
    affect infusion model and, 109–110, 110*f*
    availability heuristic and, 8–9
    based on physical attractiveness, 276–280,
        278*f*, 279*f*
    of fairness, 507–508, 510
    interpersonal
        eating preferences and, 287
        stereotypes and, 278–279
    juror, 575–576
    making by resemblance, 86
Jurors
    characteristics of, 540–542, 541*f*, 542–544
    judgments of, 575–576
Jury
    controlling bias for, 538–540, 539*f*
    incompetence, 542–543
Justice
    distributive, 508–509, 508*f*, 512
    interpersonal, 509–510, 512
    procedural, 509, 512

Kelley's theory of causal attribution, 57
Knowledge function, 138

Laissez-faire leadership style, 568–569
LaPiere, Richard T., 126–127, 126*f*, 127*f*
Latané, Bibb, 397, 398
Law of contagion, 101
Law of similarity, 101
Lawyers
    testosterone levels of, 18, 18*f*
    trial outcome and, 537–538, 537*f*, 544
    use of nonverbal cues to influence jury, 47–49, 48*f*
Leader
    charismatic or transformational, 570–573, 572*f*
    definition of, 566
    directiveness, 569–570, 571*f*, 573
    traits/situations and, 566
Leadership
    definition of, 566
    motivation, 566
    styles, 567–570
Leading questions, 538
Learning
    based on association, 121–122, 121*f*
    observational, 122–123, 123*f*

Legal aspects, of reverse discrimination, 217–218
Legal authoritarianism, 543
Legal system, social psychology applications. *See* Forensic
        psychology
Leniency bias, 543
Less-leads-to-more effect
    cognitive dissonance and, 147–149, 148*f*
    definition of, 152
Lewin, Kurt, 15, 62, 568, 568*f*
Liking
    compliance and, 373
    mutual, 294–296, 295*f*
    prosocial behavior and, 406–407
Line judgment task, 358–359, 359*f*
Lineups, 536–537, 536*t*
Logical love (pragma), 332, 332*t*
Logrolling tactic, 505*t*
Loneliness
    cognitive therapy for, 322–323
    consequences of, 320
    definition of, 320
    development of, 320–323, 321*f*
    social skills training for, 323
Lorenz, Konrad, 441
Love
    compassionate, 332, 332*t*, 334
    definition of, 328–329
    emotional arousal and, 351
    falling in, 330–331
    forms of, 331–334, 332*t*, 333*f*
    logical or pragma, 332, 332*t*
    marriage and, 341
    passionate, 329–330, 331, 332*t*, 341
    possessive, 332, 332*t*
    reason for, 331
    selfless or agape, 332, 332*t*
    unrequited, 330
Love object, appropriate, 331
Love style, 352
Lowball procedure, 374
Loyalty, marital, 349, 349*f*
Ludus (game-playing love), 332, 332*t*

Magical thinking, 100–101, 104
Majorities, influence on minorities, 369–372, 371*f*
Majority-wins rule, 513
Male
    role, in date rape, 63
    stereotypes of, 240–241, 240*f*
Mania (possessive love), 332, 332*t*
Marital dissatisfaction, 350
Marital relationship
    failure, 348–350, 349*f*
    problems
        costs/benefits and, 344–345, 345*f*
        dissimilarities and, 347
        divorce and, 342–343
        solutions and, 343–348, 343*f*, 348*f*

Marital satisfaction
    attachment style and, 346
    nature of, 340–341, 341t
Marriage, 350
    boredom in, 347
    conflict resolution in, 344–345, 347–348
    happiness in, 342, 346
    interracial, 294f
    love and, 341
    name change in, 343–344
    parenthood and, 341–342
    sexual satisfaction in, 347
    similarity and, 339–340, 341t
    success, husband-wife similarity and, 340, 341t
Mass media, prejudice development and, 222–223,
        223f
Matching hypothesis, 292–293
Mate preference, 12–13, 12f
Media
    coverage, effects on guilt/innocence of wrongdoer,
        531–532, 532f
    effects on crime perceptions, 529–531
    violence, exposure to, 449–452, 450f
Medical student syndrome, 88
Medical treatment, coping with stress of, 557–558, 557f
Memory/memories
    mood and, 106, 107f
    mood-dependent, 106, 107f
    repressed, 534–535
    social behavior/thought and, 11, 14
    storing information about self in, 177–179, 178f
Mental contamination, 107
Mesomorphs, 283, 284
Meta-analysis, 27–28, 29
Minor, testimony by, 534, 534f
Minorities, influence on majorities, 369–372, 371f
Misleading postevent information, 533
Modern racism, 215, 216f
Moldavians, Russian reactions to, 225–226, 225f
Monitoring process, thought suppression and, 102
Mood
    effects, 9
    in gaining compliance, 378–380, 380f
    good, putting others in, 389
Mood congruence effects, 106, 107f, 112
Mood-dependent memory, 106, 107f, 112
The Moral Intelligence of Children (Coles), 412
Moral values, prosocial behavior and, 428
Mother, murder of newborn infant by, 457–458
Mother-infant interaction, 307–308, 308t
Motivation
    accuracy, 138
    affiliation, 255
    defensive, 138
    explicit, 270
    gender and, 193
    implicit, 270
    leadership, 566
    in planning fallacy, 94–95, 95f

self-concept and, 167
    for volunteering, 421–423, 422t
Movement, in nonverbal communication, 42–44, 44f
Movies, nontraditional gender roles in, 197
Multicultural perspective, adoption of, 15–17, 16f, 18
Murder, of newborn infant by mother, 457–458

Naïve realism, in conflict development, 500–501
Name change, in marriage, 343–344
Narcissism, aggression and, 456
Naturalistic observation, 19–20, 19f
Natural selection, 12
Need for affiliation
    definition of, 270
    individual differences in, 270–271, 271t, 288
    situational determinants of, 271–273, 273f
Need for approval, 418
Need for cognition, social influence tactics and, 382
Negative-affect escape model, 459
Negative attitude change, 140–141
Negative frame, cooperation and, 497–499, 498f
Negatively framed health message, 548
Negative outcomes
    attribution of, 62, 62f
    loneliness and, 322
    planning fallacy and, 96
Negative-state relief model, 429f, 431, 433
Neglect, child, 463
Nonaggressive models, exposure to, 472
Noncommon effects, 50–51, 57
Nondirective therapy, 174
Nonspecific compensation tactic, 505t
Nonverbal behaviors, toward female leaders, 242
Nonverbal communication (cues)
    channels
        body language, 42–44
        eye contact, 42
        facial expression, 39–42, 41f, 45
        touching, 44–45
    in courtroom, 47–49, 48f
    definition of, 38, 40, 45
    persuasion and, 139–140, 139f
Normative social influence, 364, 367, 513–514
Norms, 484

Obedience
    definition of, 357, 382, 387
    destructive, 387
        authority figures and, 385, 386f
        consequences of, 383, 383f
        experiments on, 383–385, 384f
        resistance of, 386–387
        social psychological basis for, 385–386, 386f
Obesity, prejudice against, 285–286, 285t
Objective self-awareness, 160
Objectivity, in scientific methods, 7, 7f
Observable characteristics, 255, 270
Observational learning, 122–123, 123f
Obstructionism, 466

OCB. *See* Organizational citizenship behavior
Omissions, 503
One-sided approach, 135
Open-mindedness, in scientific methods, 7, 7f
Operating process, thought suppression and, 102
Optimism
    social cognition and, 104
    unrealistic, 548
Optimistic bias, 94–96, 95f
Organizational behavior, 559
Organizational citizenship behavior (OCB)
    causes/effects of, 564–565, 565f
    definition of, 559, 573
    forms of, 563–564
Organizational commitment, 560, 564
Orientations, toward bargaining, 503–504
Other-enhancement, 68–69, 71
Outcome directiveness, 570
Out-group
    definition of, 224
    homogeneity, illusion of, 231–232
    making judgments and, 87
    perceived similarity to, 225–226, 225f
Overestimation, illusory correlations and, 230–231
Overload, work, 560

Parent-child relationship
    attachment style and, 306–307, 307f
    importance of, 307–309, 308t
    nature of, 305–306
Parenthood, marriage and, 341–342
Parents
    elderly, cultural differences in obligations to, 309–310, 310f
    relationship with children. *See* Parent-child relationship
    role in countering prejudice, 233–234, 233f
Passion, in triangular model of love, 333, 333f
Passionate love (eros)
    marital satisfaction and, 341
    nature of, 329–330, 331, 332t, 334
Perceived behavioral control, 131
Perceived control, 558
Perceived unfairness, workplace aggression and, 466–468, 467f
Perceptions, social comparison and, 274–275, 275f
Perceptual salience, 58
Performance
    maximizing, 518–519
    self-efficacy and, 182, 183
Peripheral route (heuristic processing), 136, 137f
Peripheral traits, 65–66
Perseverance effect, 84
Personal factors, in job satisfaction, 560–561
Personal freedom, *vs.* dress codes, 368–369, 369f
Personality, dimensions, tactics of social influence and, 381–382, 381t
Personal negativity, loneliness and, 321–322
Personal orientation, in cooperation, 497–499, 498f
Personal self, 165

Person schema, 82
Perspective taking, 416
Persuasion
    attitude functions and, 138–139
    cognitive approach, 136–138, 137f
    definition of, 134–135
    early approach, 135–136, 135f
    nonverbal cues and, 139–140, 139f
    resistance to, 140–143, 142f, 153–154
Pessimism
    attribution of, 62, 62f
    loneliness and, 322
    planning fallacy and, 96
Physical abuse
    of children, 463. *See also* Child maltreatment
    dating and, 328
Physical appearance
    age and, 286
    behavioral differences and, 286–287
    clothing and, 286
    as observable characteristic, 299
    of others, social behavior/thought and, 10–11, 10f
Physical attractiveness
    components of, 280–282, 281f
    definition of, 275–276
    eating preferences and, 287
    facial features and, 280–282, 281f
    fertility and, 277
    health and, 277
    infant responses to, 279–280, 279f
    judgments based on, 276–280, 278f, 279f, 288
    of mate, gender differences in, 277
    negative attributes of, 280
    perceived
        physique and body weight influence on, 282–286, 284f, 285t
        situational influences on, 282–283, 283f
    personal attributions based on first names and, 287, 287t
Physical fitness, stress and, 553
Physical proximity, 255
Physique, influence perceived physical attractiveness, 282–286, 284f, 285t
Planned behavior, theory of, 131
Planning fallacy
    motivation in, 94–95, 95f
    nature of, 81, 94–96, 95f, 113
Playing hard to get, 376, 389
Pluralistic ignorance, 403
Police interrogations
    eliciting false confessions from innocent persons, 528–529, 530f
    procedural effects, 526–528, 527f
Politics, positive affective and, 267–268, 267f, 269f
Positive examples, power of, 410–412, 411f
Positive feelings, 263
    arousal of, attraction and, 263–264, 264f
    physical attractiveness and, 276
    prosocial behavior and, 413–414, 413f, 415f

Positively framed health message, 547–548
Positive outcomes, attribution of, 62, 62f
Positive regard, seeking, 174
Possessive love (mania), 332, 332t
Possible selves, 167–168
Posture
  in nonverbal communication, 42–44
  threatening, 43
Pragma (logical love), 332, 332t
Preadolescence, attachment and friendship formation in, 313–314, 314f
Preattribution, 472
Predictions, from correlational method, 21
Pregnancy, unwanted, 337
Prejudice
  countering, 233–239, 233f, 236f, 238f
    cognitive interventions for, 238–239
    direct intergroup contact and, 234–237, 236f
    recategorization and, 237
  definition of, 211
  development, stereotypes and, 229–230, 230f
  emotional reactions to, 212–213, 212f
  evil face of, 210, 211f
  gender-based. See Sexism
  against obesity, 285–286, 285t
  origins of, 219, 226
    direct intergroup conflict, 219–222, 221f, 222f
    illusory correlations, 230–231
    in-group differentiation, 231–232
    out-group homogeneity, 231–232
    social categorization, 223–226, 225f
    social learning, 222–223, 223f
    stereotypes, 226–230, 228f, 230f
  persistence of, 213–214, 214f
  reducing, techniques for, 249
  as schema, 211–212
  stereotypes and, 229–230, 230f, 232
  vs. discrimination, 210, 211
Premarital sex
  effect on later marriage, 338–339
  gender differences in, 335–336, 336f
  sexually transmissible diseases and, 337–338
Preoccupied attachment style, 317f, 318
Pressure tactics, 380
Primacy effect, 66
Priming
  in affect infusion model, 109, 110, 379
  definition of, 88–89
Procedural justice, 509, 512
Process directiveness, 570
Pro-choice advocates, 337
Pro-life advocates, 337
Proportion of similar attitudes, 289–290, 297
Prosocial behavior
  definition of, 428
  in emergency response, 395–398, 396f–398f, 412
  empathy and, 415–418, 417f

explaining, 428–429, 429f
  empathetic joy hypothesis, 429f, 431–432, 432f, 433
  empathy-altruism hypothesis, 429f, 430–431, 433
  genetic determinism model, 429f, 432–433
  negative-state relief model, 429f, 431, 433
forms of, 394–395, 396f
geographic differences in, 403–404
heroism, 420, 421f
models for, 410–412, 411f
personal characteristics and, 418
personality factors in, 418–420
responding, dispositional differences in, 414–420, 416f, 417f
situational factors in, 406–412, 407f, 408f, 410f, 411f
in work settings, 563–565, 565f
Prototype, 548
Prototype/willingness model, 132–133, 132f
Provocation, aggression and, 449, 450f, 454
Proximity
  attraction and, 262–263
  childhood friends and, 313
  classroom seating assignments and, 260–262, 261f
  definition of, 258, 269
  factors, 298
Psychological androgyny, 188–190
Psychology field, women in, 195
Psychoneuroimmunology, 549
Public conformity, vs. private acceptance, 359
Punishment
  definition of, 474
  as deterrent for violence, 468–470, 469f
  role of attributions in, 54, 55

Questions, leading, 538

Race, role in trial outcome, 540–542, 541f
Racial violence, economics of, 221–222, 222f
Racism, modern, 215, 216f
Random assignment of participants to experimental conditions, 24–25
Rape, attribution and, 63, 64
Reactance
  definition of, 140–141, 143
  thought suppression and, 103, 103f
Realistic conflict theory, 219–220
Reasoned action, theory of, 131
Reasoning, social behavior/thought and, 14
Rebound effect, thought suppression and, 102, 104
Recategorization, 237, 239, 249
Reciprocity
  compliance and, 373, 374–376, 375f
  nature of, 496–497, 499
Regret, counterfactual thinking and, 98
Regulatory control, 553–554
Relational model, 506
Repeated exposure
  attraction and, 258–260, 259f
  proximity and, 269

Representativeness heuristic, 86, 89
Repressed memory, 534–535, 544
Repression, 409
Reproductive success, love and, 331
Repulsion hypothesis, 290–291
Requests, mood and, 378–380, 380f
Responsibility
  assuming, in emergency situation, 404
  victim, attributions of, 407–410, 408f, 410f
Restraint, contagion of, 472
Retrieval, 83
Reverse discrimination, 217–218, 218f, 219f
Rivalry, sibling, 310–311, 311f, 315
Road rage, staring, 42, 43f
"Robber's Cave" experiment, 220, 235–236, 236f
Rogers, Carl, self-theory and, 174–175, 174f, 175f
Role
  conflict, 483
  definition of, 483
  deviates, 246
  gender. See Gender roles
  schema, 82
Romantic destiny, belief in, 328
Romantic love, 17
Romantic relationship
  baby talk in, 328, 329t
  definition of, 334
  illusions in, 328
  physical intimacy and, 323–325, 324f
  sexuality in, 334–339, 335f–337f
  vs. close friendships, 325–328, 326f, 327f
Rosenthal, Robert, self-fulfilling prophecies and, 84–85, 84f
Russians, reactions to Ukrainians, Moldavians and Georgians, 225–226, 225f

Safe sex attitudes, hypocrisy and, 149–150, 151f
Safety devices, adoption of, 91–92, 92f
Salience, perceptual, 58
Sampling, survey method and, 20
Scarcity, compliance and, 373, 376–377, 377f
Schemas
  attitudes as, 118
  definition of, 80, 81, 82f, 85
  impact on social cognition, 83–85, 84f
  self-confirming, 84–85, 84f, 113
  with strong emotional content, 109
  types of, 82–83
Science, social psychology and, 6–9, 6f, 7f
Sears, Robert, 221, 221f
Secretory immunoglobulin A, 549–550
Secure attachment style
  adult relationships and, 316–317, 317f
  interpersonal trust and, 306–307, 307f
  marital satisfaction and, 346
  mother-infant interaction and, 308t
  social support and, 556
Selective avoidance, 141

Self-affirmation, 145
Self-assessment, 170
Self-awareness
  objective, 160
  subjective, 160
  symbolic, 160
Self-concept
  central vs. peripheral, 163
  changing, 168–169, 168f
  clarity, 163
  content of, 160, 161f
  cultural influences on, 165–166, 166f
  definition of, 160
  general, 169, 170f
  interrelatedness of, 163
  possible selves and, 167–168
  role-specific, 169, 170f
  social, 164–165, 164f
  social identity and, 158, 159, 176
  structure, 163–165
  working, 167
Self-confirming schemas, 113
Self-defeating pattern of attributions, 62, 62f
Self-efficacy
  increased feelings of, 183–185, 184f
  interpersonal behavior and, 182–183
  performance as function of, 182, 183
Self-enhancement, 68, 69f, 71, 170
Self-esteem
  changes, 173
  definition of, 169–170, 176
  function, 138
  high vs. low, 173
  learning, 306–307
  paradoxical, 173
  persistence of prejudice and, 213–214, 214f
  social comparison and, 171–173, 172f
  unrealistically positive, 173
  variable, 175
Self-evaluation, 170–171
Self-expression, 138
Self-focusing
  affective aspects of, 176–177
  cognitive aspects of, 176–177
  definition of, 176
  vs. external world focus, 176–179, 178f, 185
Self-fulfilling prophecy, 84–85, 84f
Self-healing personality, 551, 552t
Self-ideal discrepancy, 174, 175f
Self-identity function, 138
Selfless love (agape), 332, 332t
Self-monitoring
  differences in, 180–181, 181f
  internal vs. external factors, 179–180, 180f, 185
Self-objectification, 201–202
Self-organization
  compartmentalized, 177–178
  evaluatively integrated, 178–179

Self-perception
    change, 174
    ethnicity and, 202
    of females, 242
    gender differences in, 199, 200–202
    negative, dealing with, 204–205
Self-presentation. *See* Impression, management
Self-reference effect, 161–163, 162*f*, 176
Self-regulation, 177
Self-schemas
    cognitive effects of, 161–163, 162*f*
    importance of, 82–83
Self-serving bias
    cultural differences in, 60–61, 61*f*
    definition of, 59–60, 75
    in perceived fairness, 508–509, 509*f*
Self-theory, 174–175, 175*f*
Self-verification, 170
Sensitization, 409
Serotonin
    aggression and, 442
    self-esteem and, 173
Sex
    definition of, 185, 203
    differences, 186*f*
        gender differences and, 197–199
        gender identity and, 187–188, 189*f*
    marital, 341
    premarital. *See* Premarital sex
Sexism, 210, 239
Sex-role spillover theory, 245–246
Sex typing, 188
Sexual abuse, of children, 463. *See also* Child
        maltreatment
Sexual arousal, aggression and, 452–454
Sexual attitudes/behavior, changes in, 334–336, 335*f*
Sexual attraction, falling in love and, 330
Sexual harassment
    definition of, 244
    lecture as, 247
    nature of, 244–245, 245*f*
    reduction of, 245, 246*t*
Sexual infidelity, 13
Sexuality
    in romantic relationships, 334–339, 335*f*–337*f*
    romantic relationships and, 328
Sexual jealousy, 13, 454
Sexually transmissible diseases (STDs), 337–338
Sexual revolution
    changes from, 334, 335*f*
    negative consequences of, 336–338, 337*f*
Sexual satisfaction, in marriage, 347
Sexual self-schema, 163–164
Sexual violence. *See* Rape
Sibling
    relationships, 310–312, 311*f*, 315
    rivalry, 310–311, 311*f*
Significance, statistical, 27, 29

Similarity
    law of, 101
    marriage and, 339–340, 341*t*
    to self, empathy and, 417–418
Single persons, happiness and, 342
Situational causes (external), 59
Situational constraints, attitudes/behavior and, 127–128,
        133
Situational factors
    in aggression, 458–463, 459*f*, 461*f*, 462*f*
    in prosocial behavior, 406–412, 407*f*, 408*f*, 410*f*,
        411*f*
Situational influences, on perceived physical attractiveness,
        282–283, 283*f*
Situation influences, on affiliation, 298–299
Skepticism, in scientific methods, 7, 7*f*
Slime effect, 70, 70*f*, 294
Smoking, stress relief and, 555
Social behavior
    actions/characteristics of others and, 10–11, 10*f*
    causes, social psychology and, 10–13, 10*f*, 12*f*
    cognitive processes and, 11
Social categorization, in prejudice development, 223–226,
        225*f*
Social cognition (social thought)
    actions/characteristics of others and, 10–11, 10*f*
    causes, social psychology and, 10–13, 10*f*, 12*f*
    cognitive processes and, 11
    components. *See* Schemas
    definition of, 80
    error sources, 85, 89–104, 113–114
        counterfactual thinking, 97–100, 100*f*
        magical thinking, 100–101
        planning fallacy, 94–96, 95*f*
        rational *vs.* intuitive processing, 90–92, 91*f*, 92*f*
        thinking too much, 96–97
        thought suppression, 101–103, 102*f*
    facial expressions and, 45–47, 47*f*
    impact of schemas on, 83–85, 84*f*
    impression formation and, 66
    influence of affect on, 105–108, 105*f*, 107*f*, 108*f*
    mental shortcuts in. *See* Heuristics
    mood effects and, 9
    optimism and, 104
    in prejudice development, 226
        illusion of out-group homogeneity, 231–232
        illusory correlations, 230–231
        in-group differentiation, 232
        stereotypes and, 229–230, 230*f*
Social comparison
    attitude formation and, 123
    self-esteem and, 171–173, 172*f*
Social comparison theory, 274–275, 274*f*, 275*f*
Social decision schemes, 513
Social desirability, 51, 51*f*
Social dilemmas, 495–496, 496*f*, 499
Social diversity, multicultural perspective and, 15–17, 16*f*,
        18

Social facilitation
    arousal and, 518–519
    basis for, 486–487, 487f
    definition of, 487, 490
    drive theory of, 488–489, 488f
Social groups
    cohesiveness of, 484
    conflict in. See Conflict
    cooperation in. See Cooperation
    decision making, 512–518
        definition of, 512
        information sharing and, 516–517
        nature of, 514–515, 515f
        potential dangers of, 516–517
        process for, 512–514
    definition of, 480–481, 481f
    direct competition between, 219–220
    effects on individual performance, 484–485
        in presence of others, 485–490, 485f–488f, 490f
    formation of, 482, 482f
    influence from, 480
    informational influences, 513–514
    information sharing, difficulties with, 516–517
    normative influences, 513–514
    norms, 484
    perceived fairness in, 507–512, 508f, 509f, 511f
    roles, 483
    status and, 483, 483f
    virtual, 481
Social identity
    components of, 159–160
        gender. See Gender
        self-concept. See Self-concept
        self-esteem. See Self-esteem
        self-focusing, 176–179, 178f
    definition of, 159
    groups and, 482
Social impact theory, 491
Social influence
    definition of, 356, 356f, 360
    individual differences in, 380–382, 381f
    informational, 365, 366f, 367
    normative, 364, 367
Social judgments, making, 80, 81f
Social knowledge, application of, 15
Social learning
    definition of, 120–121
    of prejudice, 222–223, 223f
Social loafing
    collective effort model and, 491–492, 494
    definition of, 490–491
    minimizing, 518–519
    reducing, 492–494, 493f
Social models, positive, power of, 410–412, 411f
Social norms
    collision of, 368–369, 369f
    conformity and, 357–358, 357f
    definition of, 131, 222, 360

persistence of, 362–363, 363f
    types of, 361–362, 362f, 366
Social perception
    accuracy of, 71–74, 73f
    definition of, 38, 39f, 45
Social phobia, 322
Social pressure, 358–359, 359f
Social psychology
    applications, 524–525
        to health-related behavior. See Health psychology
        to legal system. See Forensic psychology
        for workplace, 559–573, 560f, 562f, 563f, 565f, 567f
    causes of social behavior/thought, 10–13, 10f, 12f
    cognitive perspective, 14–15, 15f
    common sense and, 7–8
    definition of, 6, 13
    exporting, 15
    individual behavior and, 9
    research methods
        correlation, 20–23, 22f
        deception, 30–32, 31f
        experimentation, 23–27, 24f, 25f
        interpretation of results, 27–28
        systematic observation, 19–20, 19f
    scientific nature of, 6–9, 6f, 7f
    scope of, 4–5, 4f, 5t
    theory and, 28–29, 29f
Social responsibility, altruistic personality and, 419
Social self, 165–166, 176
Social selves, 169
Social situations, plans/intentions, mood and, 106, 107f
Social skills training
    for loneliness, 323
    in preventing/controlling aggression, 472
Social support, 555–557
Social thought. See Social cognition
Social validation, compliance and, 373
Sociocultural variables, in child maltreatment, 463
Sociology, nature of, 9
Sociosexuality, 334–335
Somatotype, 283–284, 284f
Sportsmanship, 564
Staring, 42, 43f
Statistics, inferential, 27, 29
Status, 483, 483f
STDs (sexually transmissible diseases), 337–338
Stereotypes
    behavioral, 286–287
    definition of, 213, 226, 232
    gender, 240–241, 240f
    interpersonal judgments and, 278–279
    physique, 284
    prejudice and, 229–230, 230f, 232
    processing of social information and, 226–228
    undermining, 249
Stereotype threat, 228–229
Sternberg's triangular model of love, 332–333, 333f, 334
Stigma, 266

Storge (friendship love), 332, 332t
Stress
    coping with, 552–553
        creating positive affect, 555
        during illness/medical treatment, 557–558, 557f
        increased physical fitness and, 553
        social support for, 555–557
        strategies for, 553–554, 554f
    definition of, 548
    effects, individual differences in, 551–552, 552t
    illness consequences of, 548–551, 550f
Subjective norms, 131
Subjective self-awareness, 160
Subliminal conditioning, 122
Subtraction rule, 55–56, 56f
Success, in collectivist vs. individualistic cultures, 165–166, 166f
Suicide, hopelessness and, 322
Superordinate goals, 220, 505–506, 507
Survey method, 20, 22
Symbolic self-awareness, 160
Sympathetic feelings, 416
Systematic information processing, 14, 46
Systematic observation, 19–20, 19f, 22
Systematic processing
    definition of, 136, 140
    minority influence and, 370–372, 371f

Tacit inferences, 227
Tactics
    bargaining, 502–505, 504f
    for gaining compliance. See Compliance, gaining, tactics for
    pressure, 380
    of social influence, 381–382, 381t
Teasing behavior, loneliness and, 322
Television, in modeling prosocial behavior, 410–412, 411f
Temperature, aggression and, 458–460, 459f, 461f
Terman, Lewis M., 340
Testimony, of witness. See Witness, testimony of
Testosterone
    aggression and, 443
    gender differences in, 199
    levels, of trial lawyers, 18, 18f
Thanatos (death wish), 441
"That's-not-all" technique, 375–376, 375f
Theories, 28–29, 29f
Theory of planned behavior, 131
Thought suppression
    difficulty with, 101–103, 102f, 104, 113
    reactance and, 103, 103f
Time pressure
    emergency response and, 401, 402f
    group decision making and, 513
Tokenism, 215–216, 218
Tolerance, teaching, 234, 249
Touching, as nonverbal communication, 44–45

Toys, gender and, 186, 187f
Traditionalism, 548
Transformational (charismatic) leaders, 570–573, 572f
Transparency overestimation, 505
Trial outcome
    attorney's role in, 537–538, 537f
    defendant characteristics and, 540–542, 541f
    judge's role in, 538–540, 539f
Triangular model of love, 332–333, 333f
Trivialization, 144
Truth-wins rule, 513
Twin studies, on attitude formation, 124
Two-career families, 343
Two-component model, 453
Two-factor theory of emotion, 108–109, 331
Two-sided approach, 135
Type A behavior, 454–455, 457, 501, 552
Type B behavior, 454–455, 457, 501, 552

UCLA Loneliness Scale, 320
Ukrainians, Russian reactions to, 225–226, 225f
Ultimate attribution error, 224
Uncontrollable causes, attribution and, 54, 55f
Underload, work, 560
Unfairness, perceived, reactions to, 510–512, 511f
United States, success vs. failure in, 165–166, 166f
Upward counterfactual thinking, 98–99
Urbanism, appraisal of emotion and, 111–112, 111f
Us-versus-them effect, 223–226, 225f

Variables
    child-based, in child maltreatment, 464
    confounding of, 25–26, 25f
    in correlational method, 21
    dependent, 23
    independent, 23
Velvet glove, 382
Verdict. See Trial outcome
Vested interest, 129–130, 130f
Victim
    innocent, blaming in rape, 63, 64
    responsibility, attributions of, 407–410, 408f, 410f
Violence. See also Aggression
    within families, 464–465
    media, exposure to, 449–452, 450f
    perceptions, media effects on, 529–531
Virtual groups, 481
Vitamin C, 546–547, 546f
Voir dire, 537–538
Volunteering, motivations for, 421–423, 422t
Volunteerism, 428

Weighted average, 66
Western culture, correspondence bias and, 58
Willingness, behavioral, 132
Win-lose situations, 504
Win-win situations, 504
Within-subjects study design, 486

Witness
  compliant/obedient responding, 528
  testimony of
    children and, 534, 534f
    improving accuracy of, 535–537, 536t
    recovering forgotten memories of past events,
      534–535
    when witness is mistaken, 533–534, 534f
Women
  body image and, 201, 201f
  body weight and, 201
  confidence of, 242
  discrimination against, sexual harassment, 244–247,
    245f, 246t
  executives, glass ceiling and, 242–244, 244f
  expectations of, 241
  leaders, negative reactions to, 242
  in psychology field, 195
  role, in date rape, 63
  self-perceptions, 242
  stereotypes of, 240–241, 240f
  waist-to-hip ratio, male response to, 276–277
Working models of attachment style, 306, 316–318, 317f
Workplace
  aggression in, 449, 466
  gender discrimination in, 193–194, 194f
  gender roles in, 192–193
  glass ceiling and, 242–244, 244f
  reduction of sexual harassment in, 245, 246t
  romantic relationships in, 325–327, 326f
  social psychology applications, 559–573, 560f, 562f,
    563f, 565f, 567f
  stressors in, 548–549
  violence in, 465–468, 465f, 467f

PHOTO CREDITS

Chapter 1
Page 4 left, Zigy Kaluzny/Tony Stone Images; 4 right, Cyberimage/Tony Stone Images; 6, Robert A. Baron; 7, Bonnie Kamin; 12 left, Grant LeDuc/Stock, Boston; 12 right, Esbin-Anderson/Image Works; 15, Robert A. Baron; 18 left, Bob Daemmrich/Stock, Boston; 18 right, John Neubauer, PhotoEdit; 19 left, Catherine Karnow/Woodfin Camp & Associates; 19 right, Bob Daemmrich/Stock, Boston; 31, Robert A. Baron; 33, Bill Horsman/Stock, Boston; 34, Bob Daemmrich/Stock, Boston

Chapter 2
Page 41 top left, Fabian Falcon/Stock, Boston; 41 top right Benito/Gamma Liaison, 41 bottom, Robert A. Baron; 43, Tom Wurl/Stock, Boston; 44 bottom, all Robert A. Baron; 48, PhotoDisc, Inc.; 51, Robert A. Baron; 55, Reed Saxon/AP/Wide World; 69, Stacy Walsh Rosenstock/Impact Visuals; 75, Bonnie Kamin

Chapter 3
Page 82, Timothy Shonnard/Tony Stone Images; 84 left, courtesy of Harvard University; 84 right, Corbis/Bettmann; 91, Brad Bower/Stock, Boston; 92, Peter Menzel/Stock, Boston; 93, Robert A. Baron; 111 left, Bachmann/Stock, Boston; 111 right, Stuart Cohen/Image Works; 113 top, Lawrence Migdale/Stock, Boston; 113 middle, Peter Cade/Tony Stone Images; 113 bottom, Bonnie Kamin

Chapter 4
Page 119 left, Kathy Willens/AP/Wide World; 119 right, Laurie Evans/Tony Stone Images; 123, Jeffrey Dunn/Stock, Boston; 124, Stuart Cohen/Image Works; 126, Archives of the History of Psychology; 135, Jack Loleth/Stock, Boston; 145, Michael L. Abramson/Woodfin Camp & Associates; 147, Leslie Sponseller/Tony Stone Images; 149 left, Christopher Brown/Stock, Boston; 149 right, Robert A. Baron; 152 left, Fujifotos/Image Works; 152 right, Michael Dwyer/Stock, Boston; 153, Bonnie Kamin; 145, A. Ramey/Stock, Boston

Chapter 5
Page 162, United Artists/Shooting Star/© All rights reserved; 168, Steve Starr/Saba/Stock, Boston; 170, all photos Bonnie Kamin; 180, John Gillis/AP/Wide World; 186, Philip Jon Bailey/Stock, Boston; 194, Pablo Martinez Monsivais/AP/Wide World; 196, Shooting Star/© All rights reserved; 198, Courtesy of Spiegel; 201, Donn Byrne; 204, Bachmann/Stock, Boston; 205, Andre Perlstein/Tony Stone Images

Chapter 6
Page 211, David Longstreath/AP/Wide World; 215, Corbis-Bettmann; 216, Impact Visuals; 218, Kevin Horan/Stock, Boston; 221 top, Archives of the History of Psychology; 221 bottom, Stanford News Service; 223, Myles Aronowitz/Shooting Star; 225, Charles Steiner/Image Works; 233, Adam Tanner/Image Works; 238, B. Daemmrich/Image Works; 224, Robert Burke, Tony Stone Images; 245 left, Craig Fujii/AP/Wide World; 245 right, Adil Bradlow/AP/Wide World; 249 top, J. Sohm/Image Works; 249 bottom, Walter Hodges/Tony Stone Images

Chapter 7
Page 257, Corbis-Bettmann; 258, Robert Daemmrich/Tony Stone Images; 267, Najian Feanny/Stock, Boston; 274, Archives of the History of Psychology; 278, Barry Yee/Tony Stone Images; 294, Alon Reininger/Stock, Boston; 298 top, Kevin Horan/Stock, Boston; 298 bottom, F. Hoffmann/Image Works; 299 top, Matthew Borkoski/Stock, Boston; 299 bottom, Bob Daemmrich/Stock, Boston